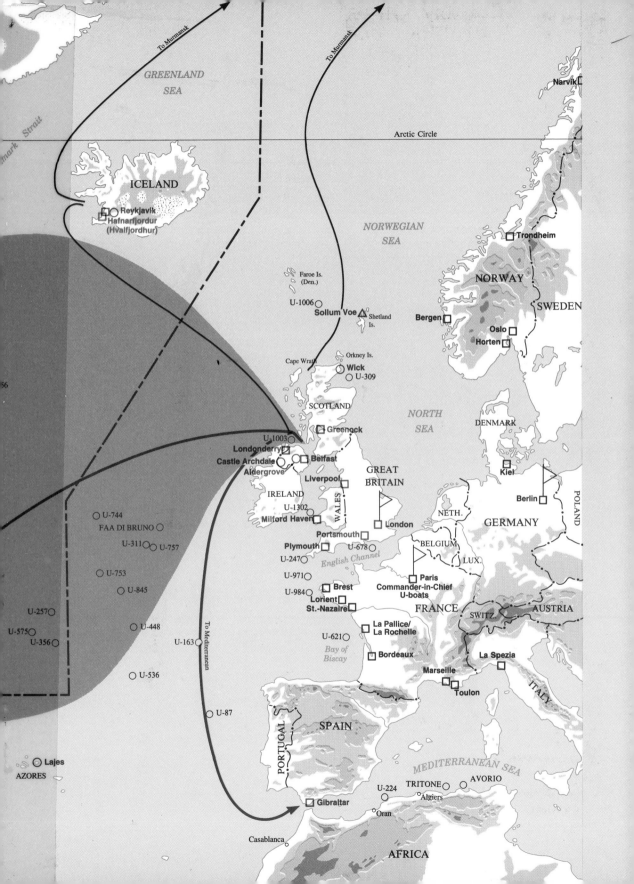

No Higher Purpose

The Official Operational

History of the Royal

Canadian Navy in the

Second World War,

1939-1943

Volume II, Part 1

NO HIGHER PURPOSE

The Official Operational History of the Royal Canadian Navy
in the Second World War, 1939-1943

Volume II, Part 1

W.A.B. Douglas, Roger Sarty, Michael Whitby

Robert H. Caldwell, William Johnston, William G.P. Rawling

Vanwell Publishing Limited
St. Catharines, Ontario

Published by Vanwell Publishing and the Department of National Defence in cooperation with the Department of Public Works and Government Services.

Catalogue Number: D2-132/2002-2-1E (Part 1)
                    D2-132/2002-2-2E (Part 2)

Vanwell Publishing acknowledges the financial support of the Government of Canada through the Book Publishing Industry Development Program for our publishing activities.

Design: Linda Moroz-Irvine
Cover Photograph: Courtesy DND, DHH

Vanwell Publishing Limited
1 Northrup Crescent
P.O. Box 2131
St. Catharines, Ontario L2R 7S2
sales@vanwell.com
phone 800.661.6136
fax 905.937.1760

Distributed in the United States by Naval Institute Press
291 Wood Road, Annapolis, Maryland 21402-5034

Printed in Canada

National Library of Canada Cataloguing in Publication Data

Douglas, W.A.B. (William Alexander Binny), 1929-
    No higher purpose / W.A.B. Douglas, Roger Sarty, Michael Whitby ; with Robert H. Caldwell, William Johnston, William G.P. Rawling. — 1st ed.

(The official history of the Royal Canadian Navy in the Second World War, 1939-1943 ; v. 2, pt.1)
Issued also in French under title: Rien de plus noble.
ISBN 1-55125-061-6 (v. 2, pt. 1)

    1. Canada. Royal Canadian Navy—History—World War, 1939-1945. 2. World War, 1939-1945—Naval operations, Canadian. I. Sarty, Roger Flynn, 1952- II. Whitby, Michael J. (Michael Jeffrey), 1954- III. Title. IV. Series: Official history of the Royal Canadian Navy v. 2, pt. 1.

D779.C2D68 2002   940.54'5971   C2002-902819-1

Contents

Maps and Diagrams vii

Glossary and Abbreviations ix

Introduction xvii

SECTION 1: EVOLVING A ROLE

Chapter 1   Planning, Mobilization and War, September 1939 to May 1940 27

Chapter 2   Responding to the New Challenge, May to December 1940 91

Chapter 3   The RCN and the Anglo-American Alliance, January to July 1941 151

Chapter 4   Implementing Anglo-American Convoy Agreements I, July to October 1941 . . 207

Chapter 5   Implementing the Convoy Agreements II, October to December 1941 263

SECTION 2: CRISIS AND RESPONSE

Chapter 6   The Pacific Coast and Alaska, December 1941 to July 1943 331

Chapter 7   *Paukenschlag* and the Caribbean, January 1942 to August 1942 373

Chapter 8   The Battle of the St Lawrence, February 1942 to December 1943 429

Chapter 9   North Atlantic Convoy Operations I, July to September 1942 477

Chapter 10 North Atlantic Convoy Operations II, October to December 1942 531

Chapter 11 The Creation of Canadian North-West Atlantic Command 579

APPENDICES

App I   Royal Canadian Navy Personnel Casualties - 1939-1945 631

App II   Senior Appointments within the Royal Canadian Navy,
            September 1939 to April 1943 641

App III   Canadian Navy Warship Losses, September 1939 to April 1943 644

App IV   Axis Submarine Losses to Canadian Forces,
            September 1939 to April 1943 645

App V   German Officer Ranks and RCN/RN Equivalents 646

Index of Ships 647

Index 653

Maps and Diagrams

Principal Theatres of Royal Canadian Navy Operations, 1939–1945 . . . . end plate

Royal Canadian Navy Pacific Operations, 1941–1945 . . . . end plate

Convoy SC 3, 14–15 September 1940 . . . . 96A

Convoy SC 11, 21–24 November 1940 . . . . 128A

Convoy SL 73, 20 May 1941 . . . . 160A

Convoys HX 133 and OB 336, 23–28 June 1941 201

Convoy SC 42, 9–11 September 1941 238

Convoy SC 48, 5–18 October 1941 274

Convoy SC 48, 15–18 October 1941 . . . . 288A

Convoy SC 52, 29 October to 4 November 1941 289

Royal Canadian Navy Pacific Operations, British Columbia and Alaska, 1941–1945 336

U–Boat Patrol Areas, January 1942 . . . . 360A

Ships Sunk by German U-Boats, January–February 1942 . . . . 392A

Caribbean Theatre, Principal Convoy Routes 409

Ships Sunk by German U-Boats, March–June 1942 . . . . .424A

Merchant Vessels and RCN Ships Sunk or Damaged by German U-Boats, 1942–1944 . . . . 424B

Royal Canadian Navy Operations in the Gulf of St. Lawrence, 1942–1945 . . . . 456A

German Naval Grid 488A

Convoy ON 115, 26 July to 4 August 1942 493

Convoy ON 127, 5–14 September 1942 517

Convoy SC 107, 24 October to 10 November 1942 545

Convoy ONS 154, 19–29 December 1942 567

RCN Operations in the Mediterranean, 1942–1945 599

Colour Plates

War Art 321-328

Glossary and Abbreviations

A/S	Anti-submarine
A/Cdr	Acting Commander
A	time zone GMT minus one hour (Z-1)
AA	anti-aircraft
AB	Able Seaman
ACC	The Atlantic Convoy Conference held in Washington, DC in March 1943 to resolve command relations in the Battle of the Atlantic
ACNS	Assistant Chief of Naval Staff
Acting	Prefix used to denote a higher rank temporarily being held
Adm	Admiral, Admiralty
ADM	Acting Deputy Minister
Admiralty	Royal Navy headquarters in London
ADOP	Admiralty Director of Plans
ADT	Atlantic Daylight Time
AFHQ	Air Force Headquarters, Ottawa
AH	Aruba to Halifax convoys
AHS	Admiralty Historical Section
AMC	Armed Merchant Cruiser
AOC	Air Officer Commanding
APD	Admiralty Planning Department
app	appendix
Asdic	Underwater sound-ranging apparatus for determining the range and bearing of a submerged submarine. Now known as Sonar
ASW	Anti-Submarine Warfare
AT	US to UK troop convoys
ATC	Air Training Command
AVM	Air Vice Marshal
AW	Aruba to Curaçao convoys
AWI	America and West Indies Squadron
AWI WD	America and West Indies War Diary
B	British

B-Dienst	*Beobachtungsdienst*, the German navy radio monitoring and cryptographic service
BAD	British Admiralty Delegation (Washington, DC)
BATM	British Admiralty Technical Mission
BdU	*Befehlshaber der Unterseeboote* or Commander of the German U-boat service
BHC	British High Commisioner
BHX	Bermuda section of HX convoys
"Bold"	German code name for a device released by a submerged U-boat to decoy allied sonar
BHC	British High Commissioner
BRO	British Routeing Officer
BS	Corner Brook to Sydney convoys
Bull	Bulletin
BW	Sydney to St John's convoys
BX	Boston to Halifax convoys
C-in-C	Commander-in-Chief
CAM	Catapult Aircraft Merchant ships
Capt	Captain
CAS	Chief of the Air Staff
CCCS	Commodore/Captain Commanding Canadian Ships
CCNF	Commodore Commanding Newfoundland Force
Cdr	Commander
Cd'A	Chargé d'Affaires
CESF	Commander, Eastern Sea Frontier
CET	Central European Time
CG	Consul General
CGS	Chief of the General Staff
CHOP	Acronym for Change of Operational Control, a time or position when command or operational authority changed

chs	chapters
CID	(British) Committee on Imperial Defence
CINCLANT	C-in-C US Atlantic Fleet
CL	St John's-Sydney-Halifax convoys
Cmdre	Commodore
CNA	Canadian Northwest Atlantic Command
CNO	Chief of Naval Operations (USN)
CNS	Chief of Naval Staff
COAC	Commanding Officer Atlantic Coast
Coastal Forces	Light craft used in coastal operations, such as Motor Torpedo Boats and Motor Gun Boats
COMINCH	C-in-C United States Navy
CONNAV	US Navy Department's convoy routing authority
COPC	Commanding Officer Pacific Coast
CPO	Chief Petty Officer
CS	Cruiser Squadron
CSC	chiefs of staff committee
CT	UK to Canada troop convoys
CTF	Commander Task Force
CVE	Escort or auxiliary aircraft carrier
CWC	Cabinet War Committee
CWCM	Cabinet War Committee Minutes
DASW	Director Anti-Submarine Division
DCER	*Documents on Canadian External Relations*
DCNS	Deputy Chief of Naval Staff
DDSD(Y)	Deputy Director of the Signals Division in charge of 'Y' or interception services
Deck Log	Record of ship's movements, events, and weather
Degauss	A measure taken to counter magnetic mines, which involved passing a current through an electric cable encircling a ship's hull
DEMS	Defensively Equipped Merchant Ships. The term was applied to the ships, the weapons, the naval or army personnel operating the equipment and the naval staff coordinating the organization
DF	Direction Finding
DHH	Directorate of History and Heritage, National Defence Headquarters
Div	Division
DM	Deputy Minister
DND	Department of National Defence
DNE	Director of Naval Engineering
DNI	Director Naval Intelligence
DNI&P	Director of Naval Intelligence and Plans
DNOT	Director of Naval Operations and Training
DNP	Director of Naval Personnel
DNR	Director of Naval Reserves
DNS	Department of the Naval Service
DO	Dominions Office (United Kingdom)
DOC	Director of Censorship
DOD	Director Operations Division
DOP	Director of Plans
Drafting	The process of assigning personnel to ships
DSC	Distinguished Service Cross
DSD	Director of Signals Division
DSec	Dominions Secretary
DTD	Director of the Trade Division
E-Boats	Allied term for German MTBs
E-in-C	Engineer-in-Chief
EAC	Eastern Air Command
Echo Sounding	Means of measuring water depth using the principles of ASDIC. The product is a continuous trace which can display the contour of the sea bottom beneath a vessel
EG	Escort Group. Escorts groups were also designated 'C' for Canadian, as in C 1, 'B' for British and 'A' for American

"Enigma"	The German cypher machine adopted by the *Kriegsmarine* in 1926. The output, when decyphered, was known by the Allies as "Ultra"
EOMP	Eastern Ocean Meeting Point. The position where a UK-based escort group transferred responsibility to an Iceland-based group
ERA	Engine Room Artificer
ESF	Eastern Sea Frontier
FH	Saint John's to Halifax convoys
First Lieutenant	Officer in the rank of Lieutenant, serving as second-in-command or executive officer of a warship. Also sometimes referred to as Number One or Jimmy-the-One
Flag Rank	Officers of the rank of Admiral of the Fleet, Admiral, Vice-Admiral, and Rear-Admiral
FO	Foreign Office
Fo'c'sle	The forecastle or foremost weather deck of a ship
FOIC	Flight Officer in Charge
FONF	Flag Officer Newfoundland
GMT	Greenwich Mean Time
Gyro Compass	An electrically driven compass which points to True North and not, like a magnetic compass, to Magnetic North
HA	Halifax to Aruba convoys
HA	High Angle, to describe naval guns that could elevate high enough to be used as AA weapons
HC	High Commission
Hedgehog	A multi-barrel anti-submarine mortar, firing a large number of contact-fused projectiles
HF	Halifax to Saint John's convoys
HF/DF	High Frequency Direction Finding. Commonly referred to as "Huff Duff"
HG	Gibralter to UK convoys
HHX	Halifax section of ships joining HX convoys originating in New York
HJ	Halifax to St John's convoys
HLDF	Halifax Local Defence Force
HMCS	His Majesty's Canadian Ship
HMS	His Majesty's Ship
HO	Hostilities Only
HofC	House of Commons
HOMP	Halifax Ocean Meeting Point. A location and timing off Halifax where shipping met or detached from HX convoys
HON	Halifax section joining ON convoys destined for New York
hp	horse power
HQ	headquarters
HT	Halifax to Trinidad convoys
HX	Fast convoys from Halifax and later New York to the UK
HXA	English Channel section of HX convoys
HXF	Halifax to UK fast convoys
ICOMP	Iceland Ocean Meeting Point. The position where ships sailing to or from Iceland left or met a convoy
IJN	Imperial Japanese Navy
JH	St John's to Halifax convoys
JSC	Joint Staff Committee
JSC	Joint Services Committee
KMF	UK to Mediterranean fast convoys
KMS	UK to Mediterranean slow convoys
Kriegsmarine	The German naval service
KTB	*Kriegstagebuch* (German war diary)
LC	Sydney to St John's convoys
LCA	Landing Craft Assault, a small landing craft used for assaults on enemy beaches
LCdr	Lieutenant-Commander
LCI	Landing Craft Infantry
LN	St Lawrence to Labrador convoys
Lower Deck	A term used to refer to the ratings of a ship

LS	Leading Seaman
LSI	Landing Ship Infantry. Large vessels used to carry infantry to assault area. There were two types; some carried LCIs on davits, and some were designed to be grounded on the beach and disembark infantry through bow doors or down side ramps
Lt	Lieutenant
MAC	Merchant Aircraft Carrier
"Major Hoople"	Anti-submarine search tactic. When attack was expected from surfaced U-boats at night, escorts illuminated designated positions in the hopes of thwarting the attack or catching the attacker unawares. Later refined and disseminated through WACIs as Operation "Pineapple"
MF/DF	Medium-Frequency Direction Finding
MASR	*Monthly Anti-Submarine Report* (Admiralty)
memo	memorandum
Merchant Navy	A collective term for a nation's shipping that embraces merchant ships of all varieties from passenger liners to cargo and tanker ships through to small coasters. The term does not include fishing vessels.
Mess deck	Living accommodation in a warship
Metox	Radar detection equipment issued to U-boats in 1942. The German term for the equipment was *Funkmess-Beobachtungsger‰t*, abbreviated FuMB
MF/DF	Medium Frequency Direction Finding
MG	Manuscript Group
MGB	Motor Gun Boat
Mid	Midshipman
MKF	Mediterranean to UK fast convoys
MKS	Mediterranean to UK slow convoys
MOD	Minister/Ministry of Defence, England

MOEF	Mid-Ocean Escort Force
MOMP	Mid-Ocean Meeting Point
MOP	Minutes of Proceedings
MTB	Motor Torpedo Boat
MWT	Ministry of War Transport
NA	Canada to UK troop convoys
NAC	National Archives of Canada
NAEF	North Atlantic Escort Force
Nautical Mile	Unit of horizontal measurement 1852 metres in length (about 6076 feet). This is the approximate value of a sea mile, which is the length of one minute of arc. During the Second World War a nautical mile referred to a British Standard Nautical Mile, which was 1853.18 metres (about 6080 feet), and which is now an obsolete measurement
Naval Council	Decision-making body created in 1940, and replaced with the Naval Board in 1942
Naval Staff	The naval coordinative staff in NSHQ responsible for policy, plans, and the day-to- day running of the navy, which answered to the Naval Council and later the Naval Board
Naval Board	The senior decision-making staff in NSHQ presided over by the Minister for the Naval Service of Canada. The Naval Board replaced the Naval Council in 1942 and by 1944 it consisted of the Deputy Minister, CNS, Chief of Naval Personnel, Chief of Naval Equipment and Supply, Chief of Naval Engineering and Construction, Chief Staff Officer Reserves, and the Secretary to the Naval Board.
NB	Naval Board
NC	Naval Council
NCM	Naval Council Minutes
NCS	Naval Control of Shipping

NCSO	Naval Control of Shipping Officer
nd	no date
ND	Naval District
NDHQ	National Defence Headquarters
NEF	Newfoundland Escort Force
NGO	Naval General Order
NJ	Newfoundland coast to St John's convoys
NL	Labrador to St Lawrence convoys
NMCJS	Naval Member Canadian Joint Staff
no	number
NOIC	Naval Officer in Charge
NPRC	National Personnel Records Centre (Ottawa)
NRC	National Research Council of Canada
ns	no signature
NS	Naval Staff
NSec	Naval Secretary
NSHQ	Naval Service Headquarters
NSM	Naval Staff Minutes
NSS	Naval Staff Secretary
NStaff	Naval Staff
NWR	*Naval Weekly Report*
OA	Liverpool/Methil to North Atlantic convoys
OB	North Atlantic convoy originating from Liverpool
"Observant"	Antisubmarine search tactic. Escorts used the last estimated position of a submerged U-boat as a datum point from which they conducted square searches with asdic along the estimated course of the submarine to a distance of one mile. The search could be expanded or concentrated depending upon number of escorts involved
ODC	Overseas Defence Committee
OG	UK to Gibralter convoys
OIC	Operational Intelligence Centre
OKM	German naval high command
ON	UK to North America convoys
ONS	UK to North America slow convoys
ORB	Operations Record Book
OS	Ordinary Seaman. The rank of the lowest trained rating before advancement to Able Seaman
OT	Aruba to Trinidad convoys
P	Atlantic Standard Time
Paravane	The "float" portion of minesweeping equipment designed to cut mine cables
PC	Privy Council
PC	Patrol Craft
per	personnel
PJBD	Permanent Joint Board on Defence
Plot	Record of movement of vessel made either manually or mechanically which allows a current reckoning of ship's position
PM	prime minister
pr	press release
PRO	Public Record Office (United Kingdom)
QS	Québec to Sydney convoys
R/T	Radio Telephony
Rudeltaktik	Group or Wolfpack U-boat tactics
RA 3 BS	Rear-Admiral Commanding 3rd Battle Squadron
RAdm	Rear-Admiral
RAF	Royal Air Force
"Raspberry"	Anti-submarine search tactic. After an attack by an unseen U-boat at night, escorts moved to pre-arranged positions to fire starshell in hope of revealing the attacker
RASS	Report Anti-Submarine School
RCAF	Royal Canadian Air Force
RCN	Royal Canadian Navy. The permanent force component of the Canadian Naval Service
RCNR	Royal Canadian Naval Reserve

RCNVR	Royal Canadian Naval Volunteer Reserve
RDF	Radio Direction Finding, the British/Canadian term for radar
rep	report
RG	Record Group
RMC	Royal Military College
RN	Royal Navy
ROP	Report of Proceedings. A report describing a ship's activities and any other items of interest not covered by a separate report
S-boote	German term for E-boats or MTBs, also *Schnellboote*
SB	Sydney to Corner Brook convoys
SC	Sydney, Halifax, and New York to UK slow convoys
SC	slow convoy
Schnellboote	German term for E-boats or MTBs, also *S-boote*
Schnorchel	A hinged mast fitted to a submarine, embodying an air intake and diesel exhaust, permitting use of diesels and battery-charging at periscope depth
Sec	Secretary
SH	Sydney to Halifax convoys
SHX	Sydney section joining HX convoys
SKL	*Seekriegsleitung*, the German naval staff
SLt	Sub-Lieutenant
SNO	Senior Naval Officer
"Snowflake"	Illumination rocket primarily used by merchant ships
SO	Senior Officer or Staff Officer
SO (A/S)	Staff Officer, Anti-submarine
SOE	Senior Officer Escort (commanding escort group)
SO (I)	Staff Officer (Intelligence)
SO(O)	Staff Officer, Operations
Sonar	USN term for asdic
SPENAVO	United States Special Naval Observer

SQ	Sydney to Québec convoys
SRC	Service Record Card
SS	Secretary of State
SSC	Feeder convoys from Sydney to SC convoys
SSEA	Secretary of State for External Affairs
Stone Frigate	Naval slang for a naval shore establishment commissioned as one of HMC Ships, e.g., HMCS *Stadacona*
Support Group	An escort group used to support convoys under, or threatened by, attack
TA	UK to USA troopships
TAG	Trinidad-Aruba-Guantanamo convoys
TAW	Trinidad-Aruba-Key West convoys
TBS	Talk between ships
TC	Canada to UK troop convoys
TE	Torch Eastbound Convoys, Gibralter to North Africa
TEF	Tanker Escort Force
TF	Task Force
tg	telegram
TG	Task Group
TH	Trinidad to Halifax convoys
TM	Trinidad to Mediterranean convoys
TO	Trinidad to Aruba convoys
Torch	Allied invasion of North Africa in November, 1942
Triangle Run	Colloquial term used for WLEF (later WEF) convoy escort operations after 1942. The "triangle" was usually between Halifax, WESTOMP, and New York City
U-Bootwaffe	The German submarine arm
Ultra	Allied codeword for Enigma decrypts
USAAF	United States Army Air Force
USN	United States Navy
USSEA	Under-Secretary of State for External Affairs
v	volume

V/S	Visual Signalling		WEF	Western Escort Force
VAdm	Vice-Admiral		WESTOMP	Western Ocean Meeting Point, sometimes referred to as WOMP
VCNS	Vice-Chief of Naval Staff			
VHF	Very High Frequency		WLEF	Western Local Escort Force
VLR	Very Long Range. The designation for maritime patrol aircraft with a range of 600 miles and the ability to then remain over a convoy for four hours		Work-up	A training phase to achieve all-round effectiveness, especially after commissioning or a long refit
WA	Western Approaches		WRCNS	Women's Royal Canadian Naval Service
WA WD	Western Approaches War Diary		WRNS	Women's Royal Naval Service
WAC	Western Approaches Command		WS	Wabana, Newfoundland to Sydney convoys
WACIs	Western Approaches Convoy Instructions			
Wardroom	Officers' mess in a warship or naval shore establishment		WSB	War Supply Board
			XB	Halifax to Boston convoys
WAT	Key West-Aruba-Trinidad convoys		Y	The interception of signals including direction finding
WATU	Western Approaches Tactical Unit		Z	Greenwich Mean Time (GMT)
WD	War Diary			

Introduction and Acknowledgments

THIS BOOK, AND THE SERIES IT INAUGURATES, builds upon the first official history of the Naval Service of Canada. Completed in the late 1940s and published in 1952, that history was somewhat truncated as a result of deep reductions in the budget for the Department of National Defence following the Second World War. Told that he must complete his work by 1948, Dr. Gilbert N. Tucker, a professor of Canadian history who, early in the war, had taken up the newly created position of naval historian, was entirely satisfied with the materials his team had been able to assemble for two of the volumes. These dealt with "the origins" of the Canadian navy to the outbreak of the Second World War and with "Activities on Shore" during that conflict, touching on such topics as shipbuilding, the development of bases, and personnel policy. Tucker believed, however, that the planned third volume, on operations from 1939 to 1945, should not be produced until his team could examine the records of enemy naval forces as well as the classified records of intelligence about the enemy that had been the basis for Allied and Canadian operations. These would not be available for some time. Not wanting the war at sea to go unnoticed, however, in 1950 the department published *Far Distant Ships*. Written by Joseph Schull, a public affairs officer and a popular writer well known to Canadians, this book was based primarily on the running accounts of operations that had been put together by historical officers on Tucker's staff from interviews with ships' personnel as they returned to harbour and any preliminary reports that might be available.

In the 1950s and early 1960s a small naval historical section continued to assemble research files and prepare specialized studies, but it did not have the resources or mandate to revisit the volumes completed in the 1940s. When this section combined with the historical staffs of the army and air force in 1965, the priority for the integrated Directorate of History was an official history of the air force. Research on maritime air operations for this project, and new scholarship in Canada, Germany, Britain and the United States that drew on the German and Allied intelligence sources that Tucker had wished to use, underscored the need for a fresh examination of the navy's wartime story. Accordingly, the Department of National Defence approved the preparation of a single new volume of naval official history that would focus on Second World War operations as well as summarize new findings concerning the development of Canadian maritime forces from the time of Confederation.

In 1986-7 a newly organized team at the Directorate set about the tasks of building knowledge of Canadian naval archives, locating relevant British, American and German sources, and distilling international scholarship since the 1940s that suggested lines of inquiry for understanding the Canadian experience. So much was found that in 1990 the department authorized the production of two additional volumes. One would treat more fully the story prior to 1939, and the other would deal with the period from the end of the Second World War until 1968 when, with the unification of the three Canadian services, the Royal Canadian Navy ceased to exist.

This new impetus led to a restructuring of the entire official naval history project. The Second World War operational history, which had been intended as the final volume to Tucker's series, will now stand as Volume II in the revised Official History of The Royal Canadian Navy. And, indeed, in order to present the full value of the research, Volume II has been divided into two parts. The first, *No Higher Purpose*, largely covers the period from the outbreak of war in September 1939 to the creation of Canadian Northwest Atlantic Command in April 1943. The second, *A Blue Water Navy*, will continue the story to V-J day. Some crossover could not be avoided, however, so that the account of the RCN's role in Operation JUBILEE, the raid on Dieppe, is in Part 2. Likewise, various appendices that cover subjects such as training, morale and discipline, the Canadian merchant marine and the Women's Royal Canadian Naval service, whose activities and contributions were not limited by our chronological divide, will be found in Part II. Also, like previous Canadian official histories, this work does not study the hundreds of young Canadians, volunteer and regular, who served in the ships of the Royal Navy. That said, the reader must understand that wherever British ships operated throughout the Second World War, Canadian sailors served—and many died—and that those Canadians are an integral part of our naval heritage.

One of the benefits of the endeavour to sustain a major project is that many people have participated. First and foremost, the Directorate of History and Heritage acknowledges the support that successive ministers, Chiefs of the Defence Staff, deputy ministers, Admirals commanding Maritime Command, Chiefs of the Maritime Staff and other leaders of the department and the armed forces have given the project. Within the directorate itself, Dr Serge Bernier, Director, History and Heritage, has consistently given full support to the project, including the assignment of precious resources at critical times. Dr Norman Hillmer, past senior historian at the Directorate of History and Dr Steve Harris, current chief historian, Directorate of History and Heritage, supervised the organization of the team and set the scholarly standards that have guided the project throughout.

The great bulk of the research was conducted by the members of the naval history team. They have served for varying periods of time and under varying terms of employment, but all devoted an extraordinary effort to the project. Members of the core team included Colonel (ret'd) Catherine E. Allan (signals intelligence), Dr Shawn Cafferky (operations in the Mediterranean, naval aviation, policy), Mr William Constable (cartographer), Mr Robert C. Fisher (Battle of the Atlantic and Caribbean, 1942), Dr William R. Glover (training), Mr Donald E. Graves (combined operations, naval aviation, coastal forces, policy), Lieutenant (N) Richard Mayne (policy), Ms Gabrielle Nishiguchi (illustrations), and Professor Jane Samson (policy). Dr Isabel Campbell, Mr Owen A. Cooke and Ms Donna Porter, archivists at the Directorate of History and its successor, the Directorate of History and Heritage, efficiently organized the large quantities of documentation acquired for the project, while librarians Jean Durocher, Réal Laurin and Madeleine Lafleur-Lemire left no stone unturned in their search for secondary sources. David Wiens and Commodore (ret'd) Jan Drent carried out research in German sources and translated, and in the latter case analyzed, German-language material used in this history.

We were also fortunate to have research reports or other contributions from Mr John Bell, Ms Pamela Brunt, Dr Lisa Dillon, Dr Richard Gimblett, Mr Tony Griffin, Mr Bob Gurney, Ms Marilyn Gurney, Professor Michael Hennessy, Professor Keith Jeffrey, Commander Norm Jolin and the ship's company of HMCS *Montréal*, Mr Doug Knight, Warrant Officer Mike Lever, Lieutenant-Commander (ret'd) Malcolm Llewelyn-Jones RN, Dr Wilf Lund, Ms Ann Martin, Dr Kenneth S. Mackenzie, Mr Fred McEvoy, Commander (ret'd) Fraser McKee, Major Michael R. McNorgan, Mr David O'Keefe, Mr David Perkins, Mr Jody Perrun, Dr Bernard Ransom, Mr Vincent Rigby, Ms Andrea Schlect, Mr Warren Sinclair, Mr Sean Stack, Mr Dan Tiffin, Dr Nicholas Tracy, Ms Sylvie Tremblay and Commander (ret'd) Michael Young. Lieutenant-Commander Doug McLean and Professors Michael L. Hadley, Robert Love, Marc Milner, Theodore Wilson and David Zimmerman graciously shared their expertise with the team. The French language edition has been brought forward by Josette Pelletier, head of the translation services bureau within the department, and reviewed by Dr Jean-Pierre Gagnon and Dr Jean Martin. These volumes are a co-production with Vanwell Publishing Ltd., and we would wish to thank Mr David Fortin and Ms Christiane Séquin of Canada Communication for their assistance in facilitating the co-publishing agreement. Lastly, Canadian naval veterans, too many to mention, displayed encouragement and patience with this project and also contributed by giving interviews, responding to questions or by coming forth with papers and photographs. The Naval Officer's Association of Canada has also provided steadfast support.

The bulk of the navy's archives are held by the National Archives of Canada. For swift, enthusiastic and imaginative help in finding materials among very large collections that were only partially organized, we are grateful to Mr Tim Dubé, Mr Paul Marsden, Ms Barbara Wilson and Mr Glenn Wright. Ms Laura Brandon and Margot Weiss of the Canadian War Museum made available the war art featured in both volumes. The late Mr David Brown and his staff at the Naval Historical Branch, Ministry of Defence, in London, and, at the Naval Historical Center in Washington, Dr Dean Allard, the former director, and Dr William S. Dudley, the present director, and their staff gave exceptional help in the discussion of historical issues, and in the location of documents. The efficiency of the staff at the Public Record Office in Kew, the National Archives and Records Administration in Washington and the National Security Agency at Fort Meade enabled team members to examine a very broad range of British, US and German naval records that illuminate and provide context for the Canadian story. In Germany, Dr Jürgen Rohwer collaborated in research in German sources.

In acknowledging the assistance of so many people, and the constant encouragement by their colleagues at the old Directorate of History and the current Directorate of History and Heritage, the authors wish to emphasize that they alone are responsible for any errors or omissions. Moreover, they wish to make it clear that they have been given full access to relevant official documents in possession of the Department of National Defence, but that the inferences drawn and opinions expressed are theirs, and the department is in no way responsible for their reading or presentation of the facts as stated.

Evolving a Role

Rear-Admiral P.W. Nelles, Chief of the Naval Staff, by the acclaimed portraitist Youssef Karsh. Taken on 6 September 1939, four days before Canada entered the Second World War. (NAC, PA 206626)

Top: Prime Minister W.L. Mackenzie King inspects sailors on HMCS *Assiniboine* in the autumn of 1940. The ship's captain, Commander C.R.H. Taylor is to his right, Chief Petty Officer C. Rhodes stands proudly at left, while Lieutenant M.G. Stirling is in the background with the telescope. (NAC, PA 104223)

Bottom: Rear-Admiral H.E Reid, RCN as Flag Officer Newfoundland in January 1943. The poster at left warns that "Convoys have been seen 36 miles away by their smoke." (NAC, PA 204357)

Captain E.S. Brand, RCN, Director of the Trade Division for much of the war. The poster emphasizes "The Life-line is firm thanks to the Merchant Navy." (NAC, PA 204258)

Senior staff at NSHQ in June 1940. Front row, left to right, Captain L.W. Murray, RCN, Rear-Admiral P.W. Nelles, Engineer-Captain A.D.M. Curry, RCN, Pay-Captain J.C. Cossette, RCN. Second row, Mr. V. Barbes, Commander (E) A.C.M. Davy, RCN, Captain E.S. Brand, Captain C.R.H. Taylor, Commander F.L. Houghton, Commander D.W. Farmer, RN. Back row, Major E. Lisle. (DND, WRN-176)

CHAPTER ONE

Planning, Mobilization and War
September 1939 - May 1940

DURING THE CONFLICTS OF THE TWENTIETH CENTURY Canada played an important role, sometimes an irreplaceable one, contributing manpower and providing North American supplies to the European theatre of war. Especially in the Second World War, when the Royal Navy was spread thin, Britain had a desperate need for sea-borne supplies, and Germany tried with equal desperation to cut them off. Japan forced the United States to divert the bulk of its naval power to the Pacific Ocean, and when the Allies then faced the immense challenge of mounting amphibious assaults on occupied Europe they needed an enormous transfusion of naval strength, in the form of both personnel and warships. The Royal Canadian Navy, consequently called upon to participate in practically every phase of the war at sea, expanded faster, to a larger size, and engaged in a wider range of naval operations, than possibly could have been foreseen when the war broke out.

This essential contribution to victory also fundamentally transformed Canada's navy. In 1939 the RCN was a small coastal defence force with "blue water" aspirations.[1] Modelled on the RN, it formed part of an Imperial navy, a worldwide network of British naval communications, intelligence, and trade defence. RCN officers and a significant proportion of ratings, like their opposite numbers in the other navies of the Commonwealth, were products of RN training ships and establishments. Political, financial, and materiel constraints limited the RCN's horizons, with the exception of annual exercises in the Caribbean, to the waters adjacent to the Atlantic and Pacific coasts of Canada. Yet, by the end of the Second World War, the RCN, largest of the Commonwealth navies next to the RN, had a record of service in the North Atlantic, the waters of northwest Europe, the Arctic, the Mediterranean, and the Pacific. In short, the Royal Canadian Navy had achieved the status of a blue water navy, and the tens of thousands of Canadians who served in the RCN during the Second World War formed a national constituency that had never before existed. This is their story.

To fully appreciate the transformation that the Canadian navy underwent during the war at sea and to comprehend the severity of the challenges it faced in that struggle, it is necessary to understand

---

1. "Blue water" theory, which came out of nineteenth-century debates on the function of navies, argued that the frontier of a naval power was the coast line of her foe, or as VAdm Philip Colomb, RN, expressed it, "Nothing can be done in the way of territorial attack with a disputed command of the sea," cited in Donald M. Schurman *The Education of a Navy: The Development of British Naval Strategic Thought, 1867-1914* (London 1965), 46; see also Arthur Marder, *The Anatomy of British Sea Power: A History of British Naval Policy in the Pre-Dreadnought Era 1810-1905* (London 1964), 70-71 n8

the RCN as it was in September 1939, and how it came to be that way. First and foremost, the Canadian navy that went to war was an extremely modest one. In September 1939 the RCN comprised just ten modern warships and had a strength of 309 officers and 2,967 ratings, of whom only 129 officers and 1,456 ratings were professionals of the permanent force. Ashore, the RCN had two major bases—at Halifax, Nova Scotia, and Esquimalt, British Columbia—and there was a string of Naval Reserve Divisions across the country where reservists honed their skills in the evenings and on weekends. On the Pacific, another reserve force, the Fishermen's Reserve, patrolled the craggy, inlet-studded coast of British Columbia. At Naval Service Headquarters in Ottawa, a small naval staff, headed by Rear-Admiral Percy W. Nelles, RCN, Chief of the Naval Staff (CNS) from 1934, provided policy direction and leadership. In its short history since 1910 the RCN had been charged with protecting Canadian sovereignty and defending commercial shipping in the focal points off the Atlantic and Pacific coasts.[2] Before that, Canadians had been content to rely on the security provided by the Royal Navy. Early initiatives in the years after the Boer War to establish a dominion naval service were given impetus by Germany's massive naval expansion before the First World War. But after the dreadnought crisis of 1909, the challenge to British naval mastery also polarized opinion about the nature and purpose of any Canadian force. Prime Minister Sir Wilfrid Laurier's compromise, the Naval Service Act of 1910, was to create a Canadian navy intended primarily for Canadian waters. When Conservative Party leader Robert Borden won the election of 1911, he wanted to repeal the Naval Service Act and organize a rather smaller navy more closely integrated with the RN. In 1912 the British asked for an emergency contribution of $35 million—a prodigious sum—for battleship construction; Borden introduced a Naval Aid Bill, but in doing so created such an intense political backlash that he was forced to stay the course that Laurier had set.

At the outbreak of the First World War the Royal Canadian Navy consisted of just the obsolete cruisers HMCS *Niobe* and HMCS *Rainbow*. RN cruisers based at Halifax protected the vast North Atlantic shipping traffic upon which the Allied war effort would become increasingly dependent, and the RCN cruisers, as Laurier's legislation allowed, operated as part of the newly arrived British squadrons. The only operations by Canadian ships under Canadian control were local patrols in harbour approaches carried out by minor vessels taken up from civilian departments. Neither Ottawa, nor the Admiralty in London, saw any need to change this situation. Borden did not want to stir up the still politically contentious naval question, and he was happy to comply with British advice that Canada's war effort should focus on the provision of troops for the great battles on the Western Front. British leaders, moreover, promised that if enemy warships did operate in Canadian waters, they would immediately despatch additional forces to deal with the threat. That proved illusory.

---

2.   This overview of the RCN's history to 1939 is based largely on R. Sarty, *Canada and the Battle of the Atlantic* (Montréal 1998), 21-36; the monograph was produced under the auspices of the Directorate of History and Heritage and intended as a preliminary sketch of elements of the research done for the RCN official history. Other important contributions to the RCN's pre–Second World War history include G.N. Tucker, *The Naval Service of Canada: Its Official History* I (Ottawa 1952); M. Hadley and R. Sarty, *Tin-Pots and Pirate Ships: Canadian Naval Forces and German Sea Raiders, 1880-1918* (Montréal and Kingston 1991); M. Milner, *Canada's Navy: The First Century* (Toronto 1999); R. Gimblett, "Reassessing the Dreadnought Crisis of 1909 and the Origins of the Royal Canadian Navy," *The Northern Mariner* 4/1 (1994), 35-53; R. McKillop, "Staying on the Sleigh: Commodore Walter Hose and a Permanent Naval Policy for Canada," *Maritime Warfare Bulletin*, special historical ed (Halifax 1991); M. McLeod, "The Royal Canadian Navy, 1918-39," *The Mariner's Mirror* 56/2 (1970), 169-86; and M. Whitby, "In Defence of Home Waters: Doctrine and Training in the Canadian Navy During the 1930s," *The Mariner's Mirror* 77/2 (1991), 167-77.

When long-range U-boats launched attacks in Canadian waters late in the war, the British were in no position to fulfil their promise. The RN cruisers on station at Halifax were designed to counter the traditional threat of enemy surface forces, and their size and lack of manoeuvrability made them vulnerable to submarines. At the other end of the spectrum, the minor vessels the RCN used on patrol duties lacked the capability required to counter the powerful "U-cruisers" deployed to North American waters. The most effective antisubmarine ships had proved to be destroyers, or torpedo-boat destroyers as they were often classified—fast, manoeuvrable, multipurpose warships with the weaponry to defeat submarines. The RN, however, needed all its destroyers to counter the main submarine offensive in European waters. The United States had joined the war against Germany in April 1917, but the bulk of its destroyer force was similarly deployed on the other side of the Atlantic.

Canada was on its own. The navy's east coast flotilla had to expand immediately from a mere dozen vessels to more than a hundred and, despite the immensity of the challenge, Canadian industry and the RCN managed to build and get that fleet to sea within a few short months. At the same time, following the British solution to mounting shipping losses, a nascent convoy system was established. Halifax and Sydney, with support from Saint John, Québec, and Montréal, became the principal ports for the assembly and despatch of merchant vessels carrying supplies to Britain. Such traffic was most vulnerable in coastal approaches, where vessels could be most readily detected by U-boats. To prevent this, the hastily produced RCN flotilla fulfilled three main operational roles: screening merchantmen as they left port and formed into large trans-Atlantic convoys, escorting smaller groups of merchant ships between Canadian ports, and maintaining a general watch along the coast. They did better than could have been expected at these tasks, given the haste with which the ships had been built and the crews recruited. During the war and after, however, it was their failures—including only one unsatisfactory engagement with a U-boat, where the patrol vessel concerned had sought assistance instead of engaging the enemy, enabling the submarine to escape unscathed—that had been spectacularly obvious. Success, measured in ocean-going merchant ships not attacked or sunk, was exceedingly subtle. The RCN remained a coastal defence force between the wars, and in 1935, the Chief of the Naval Staff described the navy's planned wartime responsibilities as "the protection of trade to and from Canadian ports, and ... communications in our coastal areas."[3] Nothing had changed since before the First World War.

As with the other Canadian services between the wars, the Royal Canadian Navy had few resources to fulfil its role. The vessels of the east coast antisubmarine fleet were hurriedly paid off after the armistice—along with the short-lived Royal Canadian Naval Air Service, established in September 1918—but the RCN's future had still looked fairly bright at the outset of the 1920s. Admiral of the Fleet Earl Jellicoe, late First Sea Lord and Commander of the Grand Fleet, visited Canada in 1919 as part of a tour of Empire naval organizations and advised that a minimally adequate naval coastal defence force would cost no less that $5 million a year. After much internal squabbling, the Conservative government in Ottawa cut that figure by half. Britain had, however, provided the light cruiser *Aurora*, the destroyers *Patriot* and *Patrician*, and two submarines free of charge from its surplus wartime fleet. This gave the RCN something of a balanced fleet until, soon

---

3.   Nelles memo, "The Naval Defence Policy of Canada," 9 Nov. 1935, NAC, RG 24, 3840, NSS1017-10-18. NAC citations are
       given in the order: record group, volume, file.

after winning the federal election in December 1921, Mackenzie King's Liberal government further slashed the navy's budget to $1.5 million.

The professional head of the navy who confronted this crisis was Commodore Walter Hose, a tough-minded, politically skilled officer. British by birth, Hose had transferred from the Royal Navy to the RCN in 1912 because he felt stifled by the structured routines of a big well-established service. He wanted to make a difference, and his experience during the First World War as the front-line commander of the impoverished Canadian sea forces gave him a grasp of what was truly essential. With reluctance, he gave up *Aurora* and the submarines, keeping just the two destroyers, and in 1923 reorganized Canada's navy as a reserve force built around the Royal Canadian Naval Reserve and the Royal Canadian Naval Volunteer Reserve. The RCNR, with a strength of some 200, was for "officers and men who have followed a seafaring life."[4] They received a course of naval training every year or two at Halifax or Esquimalt. The RCNVR, for those without professional maritime experience, comprised units located predominantly at inland cities, which, although far from the sea, were at the concentration of population and thus more likely to help the navy become part of the nation's psyche. These volunteers, who quickly numbered almost a thousand, attended training sessions at local drill halls one or two nights per week, and in the summer went to Halifax or Esquimalt for training at sea. Although both the RCNR and RCNVR were modelled on their British counterparts, there was an important difference: the British reserves provided a modest augmentation to the large professional service, but the situation in Canada in 1923 was the reverse. The small permanent force, now limited to 400, existed largely to train the reserves.

In spite of this fundamental shift in naval organization, Hose did not abandon the dream of a seagoing force nor the professional interests of the permanent force. The budget cut left him with only the two destroyers *Patriot* and *Patrician*, one of which went to each coast, together with a couple of the trawler-type antisubmarine and minesweeping vessels built in the emergency program of 1917–18. According to mainstream naval thought of the time, destroyers did not provide much basis for a fleet; the British suggested that Canada might obtain slower and less-heavily armed but more spacious and cheaper general-purpose patrol vessels—sloops—as a stepping stone to the day when the government might see its way clear to acquire cruisers.[5] But Hose stood firmly by destroyers, seeking six as the nucleus of the fleet. It was just such a force that the British had recommended, and had been unable to provide, to counter the U-boat offensive off Nova Scotia in 1918. As Hose knew from that experience and his understanding of naval warfare, destroyers were the smallest true fighting ships that could give the RCN independent striking power against a variety of threats, including submarines and surface commerce raiders. He also understood that the service was fated to operate on a shoestring and appreciated the depth of the political resistance to cruisers. Not only were they expensive, but these big, long-ranged, blue water warships also raised the spectre of distant entanglements in the military affairs of Empire that were anathema to Mackenzie King's Liberals. On the other hand, the idea of a destroyer force committed directly to the defence of Canadian waters to uphold Canadian interests meshed well with the

---

4.   G.J. Desbarats to USSEA, 30 Dec. 1922. NAC, RG 24, 5597, NS 26-2-3

5.   HMS *Clematis* was a typical RN sloop of the period. Commissioned in 1915, she was 250 feet in length, displaced 1,200 tons and had a top speed of about 16 knots. She was armed with two 4-inch and four 3-pdr guns. See *Jane's Fighting Ships 1925* (London 1925), 82-5.

Liberals' nationalist foreign policy. Hose's vision set Canada's burgeoning navalism on a steady course. In subsequent years Canadian naval planning concentrated on forces that could support national goals. In time a modest balanced fleet became achievable. Although technological advances have had a fundamental influence on force structure, ships that can trace their lineage back to the destroyers of the 1920s have always been an integral component of the Royal Canadian Navy.

Scarce resources limited the size of the destroyer fleet until the late 1930s. In the late 1920s, *Patriot and Patrician* were replaced by two similar RN destroyers that had been completed shortly after the end of the First World War and had been in reserve ever since. Commissioned as *Champlain* and *Vancouver*—they remain the only major Canadian warships named for individuals—their low speed, obsolete equipment, and unreliability made them barely adequate for training.[6] At the same time, the King government ordered the construction in Britain—it would have cost significantly more to build them in Canada—of two of the modern Acasta or A class destroyers then coming into service with the RN: *Skeena* and *Saguenay* were commissioned in 1931. They were impressive. At 1,330 tons standard displacement, they were nearly a third larger, had more than double the weight of armament, were faster, and had greater endurance than the First World War types. The first major warships built specifically for the RCN, *Skeena* and *Saguenay* were fitted with systems that made them more suitable for Canadian conditions, including additional strengthening against floating ice, a large margin of stability to counterbalance possible accumulation of ice topside, and crew amenities such as ice-cupboards, shower-baths, steam heating, and a more efficient ventilation system.[7] They each had a complement of 150, which resulted in a near doubling of the strength of the RCN to 700 regular personnel.

The Liberals were out of office from 1930 to 1935, the worst years of the Great Depression, but their return to power occurred against a backdrop of an accelerating disintegration of stability in Europe. With Japan's increasing bellicosity in Asia, war in both the Pacific as well as the Atlantic now seemed a possibility. Mackenzie King, in the face of strained finances and widespread isolationist sentiment, launched a limited rearmament program that concentrated on the defence of Canada; he would not in any way commit the country to, or make preparations for, the despatch of an army overseas, as had been done at such terrible cost in the First World War. The rearmament program gave priority to the Royal Canadian Air Force and the Royal Canadian Navy, the services most concerned with home defence. Encouraged by the program, the British Admiralty made available from its active fleet a half flotilla of four modern Crusader class destroyers at a fraction of the cost of new construction. The government seized the opportunity and the vessels came into the RCN as *St Laurent* and *Fraser* in 1937 and *Ottawa* and *Restigouche* in 1938. Although not 'Canadianized' like *Skeena* and *Saguenay*, they were slightly larger and faster and had greater endurance. Another important improvement was that they were fitted with asdic (which has become known as sonar), the revolutionary submarine detection device. Modest as the strength of the RCN was, on a ship-to-ship basis its six River class destroyers compared favourably with the destroyers of other navies.

---

6.   The ships were the ex-HMS *Torbay* and *Toreador*. They had been designed for close-quarters action in the North Sea and English Channel, and although they had a design speed of 36 knots, they could barely achieve 30 by the time they joined the RCN. See E.J. March, *British Destroyers, 1893-1960* (London 1966), 215-23.

7.   Tucker, *Naval Service of Canada* I, 336

The navy's two main shore establishments were the dockyards at Esquimalt and Halifax. Although splendidly situated strategically and both fine harbours, in terms of appearance and capacity, as Gilbert Tucker (Canada's first official naval historian) pointed out, at the outbreak of war both bases remained little changed from when the navy had taken them over from the British in 1910.[8] Esquimalt was in better shape and featured a large graving dock; in terms of barracks, training schools, docking facilities, machine shops, supply shops, and jetties—in other words, the basic infrastructure required to support naval operations—both bases were in a poor position to support a navy much larger than the one that existed in the summer of 1939.

The situation was far better in terms of the infrastructure to gather the raw material required for signals intelligence. Throughout the First World War, the RN had taken a keen interest in direction finding as a new and powerful dimension to naval intelligence; simply put, any ship or aircraft that transmitted a radio signal could have its presence and position compromised.[9] Because radio communications were linked to the control of shipping, the Canadian government placed all the radio telegraph stations in the dominion on a war footing in 1914, and gave the Department of Naval Service responsibility for expanding the potential of radio, telegraphy, and direction finding.[10] By war's end, there were four D/F stations on the east coast: at Saint John, New Brunswick, Cape Race, Newfoundland, and Chebucto Head and Canso, Nova Scotia. In 1922 these stations, transferred back to the Department of Marine and Fisheries—and later to the Department of Transport—became aids to marine navigation. This service expanded, and by 1936 the four original D/F stations had been supplemented by nine more, seven of which were in the Maritimes.[11] These were all eventually incorporated into the RN's global control of shipping organization (of which more will be said later in this chapter). The upshot was that in 1939 the RN and the Department of Transport were more or less ready to commence signals intelligence operations based on D/F data gathered in the western Atlantic from Canadian stations.

The Royal Canadian Navy was run from Naval Service Headquarters, where a small naval staff crowded into the Robinson Building at 72 Queen Street, Ottawa. Commander Eric Brand, a Royal Navy officer serving as the RCN's Director of Naval Intelligence and Plans, painted a vivid picture of the modest scale of both the Canadian naval staff and its office spaces on the eve of the Second World War:

> On the ground floor on the west side was a delicatessen. The first and second, or second and third floors, I can't remember, were something to do with Agriculture. I think it was records of sheep or pigs ... Then we had two floors which would be the third and fourth, I think, and the fifth floor was the Radio Licenses Branch ... It was an extremely inconvenient rabbit warren as offices. I had an enormous office which had plant pots and things all over it. Beautiful ferns growing there ... As far as Intelligence is concerned, I had a SO Intelligence, Lieutenant-Commander [F.R.W.R.] Gow ... and quite shortly before I arrived ... Commander Lane ... had persuaded somebody to give him a Staff Officer Plans [Lt-Cdr F.L. Houghton] ... There was a wonderful old lady who had been all through the First War, Miss Evans, who ... ran the office and watered the ferns. She had, I think, one typist with her.

8.   Ibid, II, 107, 221

9.   A. Hezlet, *The Electron and Sea Power* (New York 1975), 177-8

10. DNS, *Annual Report for 1915* (Ottawa 1916), 125

11. See S. Babaian, *Radio Communication in Canada: An Historical and Technological Survey* (Ottawa 1989), 37

In a little cubby hole just along was Mr Edsel, civil servant, who had two underlings [to collate tracking information on the large Axis merchant ships] ... Then I had Mr Elder Fraser who was the Naval Distributing Authority who ran all the Confidential Books and distributed them and he was assisted by an ex-WT Petty Officer Mr Barnes ... That was about all from the Intelligence angle. CNS [RAdm R. W. Nelles] had a secretary, Miss Lyon. Paymaster Commander [M.J.R.O. Cossette] was the Naval Secretary and he was assisted by a civil servant, Joe LeBlanc ... [Captain L.W. Murray was director of Naval Operations and Training] Commander [C.R.H] Taylor was [Director of] Naval Personnel and he was assisted by ... a retired Paymaster Captain, RN, Gerald Youle, who had, at one time been the Naval Secretary here, and was living in Ottawa and was brought back by the RCN ... early in 1939 to help with Personnel. Then on the Engineering side there was Engineer Commander [A.D.M] Curry, who was Director of [Naval] Engineering [and had two assistants]. Then to finish up there was a Mr Lyle who was Chief of Naval Stores and Alan Coulter was Deputy Naval Stores ... That, I think, makes up what I often describe as "eleven men over a grocer's shop."[12]

Quite apart from their small number and lack of office space, the officers on the naval staff, as well as most permanent force officers in the service, suffered a lack of administrative training and planning experience. Certainly, some schooling and experience in those areas was received in deployments with the RN, but the Royal Canadian Navy itself was simply too small, too poor, and its slim officer cadre too overburdened to implement any detailed staff processes or build up a strong staff tradition. Upon taking over as Director of Intelligence in August 1939, Commander Brand, fresh from an RN staff position, recalls telling the Staff Officer (Plans), Lieutenant-Commander F.L. Houghton "that we must get on with some plans and fast as there is a war coming soon." He received the reply, "That's all very well but we have no money here for that sort of thing."[13]

Money was a factor in all matters concerning the interwar RCN, but it does not fully explain the lack of a staff tradition. Perhaps the most significant contributory factor was that permanent force officers considered service afloat to be more essential—not to mention more enjoyable—than staff time for their professional development, and their ambitions and aspirations therefore lay at sea. The story of the Canadian naval officer declaring, "I learned everything I needed to know as a naval officer on the bridge of the ship" is likely apocryphal, but rings true nonetheless. Typically, the career goal of an RCN officer was not to achieve a position on the naval staff, but to attain command of a destroyer and then of one of the two destroyer divisions. There were no RCN big-ship commands. Command at sea was what mattered.

What staff training there was came at British institutions. Promising officers at the rank of commander and lieutenant-commander attended the RN Staff Course at Greenwich. Although it was seen as a useful step to high command, the staff course was not necessarily much sought after, and even in the RN it was not considered to be an essential element of officer development. Not all flag officers were graduates, and even then its focus towards preparing officers for operational staff jobs afloat and not planning ashore, only reinforced Canadian attitudes towards the primacy of sea service. Four senior RCN officers also attended the Imperial Defence College during the inter-

---

12. Brand interview, 22 Feb. 1967, DHH, 81/145 pt 7, Brand papers, 6-7

13. Brand Journal, DHH, 81/145 v 13, 179

war period where they were schooled in the strategic thinking required for the higher ranks of the services.[14] But it was British thinking that reflected British attitudes towards centralized imperial defence, attitudes that the historian D.M. Schurman has described as "strategically sound for an Empire ... [but] politically antiquated for a Commonwealth."[15]

The relationship between the Royal Canadian Navy and the RN, especially at the senior officer level, is important to understand. The prewar RCN has been well described as a subsystem or home port division of the British navy.[16] Its ships were British; it wore RN pattern uniforms; personnel training above new entry training was conducted in Britain by RN instructors; its doctrine and tactics came from RN manuals and were refined in exercises with British fleet units; it followed RN customs; and, with no real fighting tradition of its own, the RCN proudly embraced those of the RN, with occasions like Trafalgar Day marked by enthusiastic celebrations in the ships and shore establishments of the Canadian navy. That such a close connection existed could only be expected given the strong political, social, and cultural bonds between the still relatively young dominion and a Britain still generally accepted as the mother country. And learning at the feet of what was still widely considered the world's finest navy could be no bad thing. Even with these close ties, however, a distinction should be borne in mind. Although the RCN closely followed the RN, it would be going too far to describe the senior leadership and officer corps of the RCN as British thinking or of being willing to subvert Canadian national objectives to British ones. While perhaps culturally and professionally "British" in appearance, we have seen that officers like Commodore Hose sought Canadian responsibilities that were in step with the views of the government of the day and reflected the progressive Canadian nationalism at play in the country. The RCN had its share of both anglophiles and anglophobes, but, as would be confirmed throughout the war, "Britishness"—an interest and belief in British institutions, ideals, and conventions that made up the RCN officer type—did not necessarily entail sacrificing Canadian interests and conditions.

There was, moreover, in the Canadian navy, a distinct way of getting things done: what can perhaps be described as the Canadian naval way of war. As Joseph Schull explained in *The Far Distant Ships*, as the war got under way permanent force officers were "faced with responsibilities which might well have daunted them, had the pattern of future events been unrolled at that time":

> The one obvious and specific qualification which all shared at the moment was that they were available. Another, which was to become apparent as time went on, was the ability to improvise under stress. They had, perhaps, a certain breadth of outlook where naval affairs were concerned because their experience had been deliberately varied. It might also be that "exigencies of service" had given them some peculiar advantages for the present task [of directing a war at sea]. Canadian naval officers were forced to cultivate a certain resourcefulness and ingenuity because they always had to make do with less than was required.[17]

---

14.   The officers were G.C. Jones (1930), L.W. Nelles (1933), V.G. Brodeur (1936), and L.W. Murray (1938).

15.   Schurman, *Education of a Navy*, 129

16.   See W.A.B. Douglas, "Conflict and Innovation in the RCN, 1939-1945," in G. Jordan (ed), *Naval Warfare in the Twentieth Century* (London 1977) and W.R. Glover, "Officer Training and the Quest for Operational Efficiency in the RCN, 1939-1945," PhD dissertation, University of London, 1998.

17.   J. Schull, *The Far Distant Ships: An Official Account of Canadian Naval Operations in World War II* (Ottawa 1950), 3

This "can-do" mentality, which drove much of the RCN decision making and operational art during the Second World War, has been—both for good and for bad—at the heart of the Canadian naval ethos ever since.

In its main ambition, which was the requisition of capable ships, the professional RCN had succeeded during the 1930s with the arrival of modern destroyers, even if there were not many of them. There is, of course, more to sea power than ships, and a brief analysis of the exercises and sea training that the RCN carried out in the late 1930s allows an evaluation of the RCN's general operational effectiveness and demonstrates where its priorities lay.[18] Canadian naval planners thought that in the event of war in Europe or the Far East, the British and American navies would contain the main enemy fleets. Surface raiders, operating independently or in pairs, and submarines would be the main threat to shipping in Canadian coastal waters.[19] As will be seen, both the RCN and the RN were overconfident about their ability to detect and destroy submarines, and the RCN focused instead on countering surface raiders.

The general idea behind some of the exercises that the RCN carried out, either in Canadian waters or in the Carribean with the cruisers of the RN's America and West Indies Squadron, was to show the RCN what it could expect to confront in war. During the segment of a program carried out in August 1932, for example, the cruiser HMS *Norfolk* represented a "hostile commerce raider which has been destroying shipping off Halifax for twenty-four hours, and is now proceeding to the southwestward with the probable intention of similar operations in the Fundy trade route." In July 1939, in its final exercises before the outbreak of war, the West Coast Division practised a series of evolutions against surface raiders:

> Single destroyers attacking single cruiser, unobserved, in moderate visibility.
>
> A sub-division of destroyers attacking a single cruiser in moderate visibility.
>
> A sub-division of destroyers attacking two cruisers which are being shadowed and reported.
>
> A division of destroyers attacking a cruiser where speed has been reduced by Torpedo Bombers.[20]

A destroyer's most powerful weapon was the torpedo, and scenarios like these depended upon ships obtaining a favourable position from which to launch a spread of torpedoes against surface targets. Destroyers attacked in tight, closely controlled formations in order to concentrate the mass of their torpedoes or gunfire; success, therefore, largely depended upon precision of manouevre and skilled, high-speed ship handling. The value of training designed to produce these results is borne out by a 1937 Admiralty report that considered "service in command of, or in, destroyers, even when not in company with a fleet, is the finest form of training that can be given to officers and men."[21]

---

18. See Whitby, "In Defence of Home Waters."

19. Nelles memoir, "Naval Defence Policy of Canada," and CNS memo "The Objective of the Canadian Naval Service," 17 Jan. 1939, 1-2, DHH, NHS Naval Policy 1650-1 v 1

20. From exercise operational orders in NAC, RG 24, 4012-4014

21. Adm, Naval app to "Review of Imperial Defence by the Chiefs of Staff Sub-Committee of the Committee of Imperial Defence," 24 Mar. 1937, 14, PRO, CAB 21/700

Off to war. (NAC, PA 204286)

Good sea training was the thing, then, but how well did the RCN perform? Specific commentaries are scarce, and those that survive provide mixed reviews. In 1933 the Commander-in-Chief, America and West Indies Squadron evaluated the destroyers *Saguenay* and *Champlain* in five categories. The Canadians' ship handling was good, and the admiral was satisfied with their signalling efficiency and appearance, but he was critical of their gunnery and torpedo performance. In 1934 station-keeping, signalling, and tactical knowledge were considered the primary weaknesses, but by the next year all of these were much improved. Four years later, in the final exercise program before the war, the RCN West Coast Division performed well in a night attack, scoring hits with three of four torpedoes, but a day attack went awry when one destroyer missed an executive signal and ended up separated from the rest of the force. Overall, the ships were deemed to have performed capably.[22] Perhaps the most useful evaluation during this period came from Commander R.I Agnew, RCN, after a series of exercises in the Caribbean in 1935 involving his ships and a RN flotilla:

> I do not consider that the general standard of the 5th Destroyer Flotilla [RN] was very high, except as regards visual signalling, which was noticeably more rapid than any that I had ever before observed. As a result of this they were "quick off the mark." The release of flotillas to the attack was noticeably quick and well understood. The Canadian Division did not approach this standard. In actual attacks, except from smoke from obsolete ships and an almost continual "lag" of "Vancouver," I consider that the Canadian Division were as good by day and better in night attacks than the 5th Destroyer Flotilla. In low speed manoeuvres, there was nothing to choose between them. In general drills, both at sea, and in harbour, again there was nothing to choose between them, in time. In technique I consider that the RN Ships were superior and that ours were more enthusiastic.[23]

The measurement of operational efficiency is often subjective and depends largely upon the eye of the beholder; nevertheless that Agnew thought his ships held their own was important. The interwar RN was still recognized as the world's finest navy and it says something of the effective-ness of the Royal Canadian Navy that it thought it could come close to matching the performance of one of the RN's destroyer flotillas. That impression, and the fact that it could train alongside a navy of such skill and professionalism, bolstered confidence throughout the RCN and gave the service a measure of pride. Rear-Admiral L.W. Murray, RCN, later recalled, "It was great fun getting on board the [RN] Fleet flag ship and being able to show them that in spite of their longer histo-ry, our people could keep up the game and be just as smart as theirs."[24]

The RCN's emphasis on surface warfare at the expense of antisubmarine operations during the interwar years faithfully followed the priorities of its mentor, the Royal Navy. "Secondary" areas such as antisubmarine warfare received little attention and were career backwaters. There was, moreover, a sanguine belief that asdic, a form of detection that uses sound waves to locate sub-

---

22. C-in-C AWI to CNS, 29 July 1933, DHH, NHS RCN/Adm Liaison 1700-193/96. Capt G.C. Jones, "Full Calibre Firings—27 Mar. 1939," 23 Apr. 1939, and Capt G.CS. Jones, "Torpedo Practices—July 1939," 8 Aug. 1939, and DNOT memo, 21 Aug. 1939. NAC, RG 24, 4012, NSC1057-61-11

23. Cdr R.I. Agnew, "Some Remarks on Training during Winter Cruise 1935," 22 Apr. 1935, 1-2, DHH, 81/520 HMCS *Saguenay* I (ROPs 1932-40) 8000

24. RAdm L.W. Murray, "Recollections of His Naval Career," May 1970, 26, DHH, Murray Biog file

merged submarines, had solved the problem of finding and destroying them. In 1937 Chief of Naval Staff, Commodore Nelles predicted, "If international law is complied with, Submarine attack should not prove serious. If unrestricted warfare is again resorted to, the means of combatting Submarines are considered to have so advanced that by employing a system of convoy and utilizing Air Forces, losses of Submarines would be very heavy and might compel the enemy to give up this form of attack."[25] Events on the North Atlantic in May 1943 would ultimately prove Nelles correct. Nevertheless, at no point in the 1930s was the RCN in a position to force an enemy to abandon dedicated submarine warfare.

The RCN did not possess asdic-equipped destroyers until it acquired *St Laurent* and *Fraser* in February 1937. Even then, because the navy had no submarines, there were no realistic targets to practise against. Only two RCN officers had received specialist training in that field, and that had been back in the late 1920s. Moreover, shore-based facilities to train asdic ratings were not established until just after the war broke out. Vice-Admiral R.P. Welland, one of the "converted" who qualified as an antisubmarine specialist during the war recalls:

> Only a few officers knew all about Asdic and even after I qualified in 1940, petty officers and sailors were not told all about it, and weren't allowed access to the books [as a security measure]. Only specialist anti-submarine officers knew all about the machine. Consequently, captains of ships didn't understand what the instrument was capable of doing, and didn't know how to use the damned thing. So a lot of gung-ho guys in destroyers felt the world revolved around guns and torpedoes, when actually the most important instrument on board was the Asdic. None of them had ever been trained on it—none![26]

Interwar ASW training can best be characterized as rudimentary, as a 1937 exercise report demonstrates: "Two Depth Charge exercises were carried out on passage," *Saguenay*'s commanding officer reported. "The 'target' was a U-shaped wake made by *Saguenay* altering course 180 degrees at 25 knots. *St Laurent* located wake with her asdic, and acting as directing ship, directed *Saguenay* to the attack, afterwards attacking herself. Dummy charges were dropped and dummies fired by throwers from both ships. Two runs were carried out."[27] Although the directing tactics foreshadowed those used effectively during the war, such exercises could only emphasize manoeuvring to a point at which to launch depth charges rather than the detection of a mobile submerged object. They were, therefore, essentially depth charge drills from which asdic operators would gain little benefit, for although an echo would be detected, it would be stationary and bear little resemblance to that of an actual submarine. Ships needed to practice against the real thing, and although the matter was raised before the war, it was not until the war was well under way that a submarine became available for training in Canada.[28] Thus, the navy destined for a bitter war against German U-boats on the North Atlantic was singularly unprepared for that type of warfare.

25.   Cmdre P.W. Nelles, "The Defence of Trade," 12 Feb. 1937, NAC, MG 27, III B5 v 37

26.   Quoted in Ottawa Branch NOIC, *Salty Dips* VI: *Ready Aye Ready* (Ottawa 1999), 153

27.   *Saguenay* ROP, 2 Sep. 1937. Unless specified otherwise, e.g., by USS or HMS etc, ships mentioned in footnotes are assumed to be HMCS.

28.   An Admiralty report to the 1937 Imperial Conference suggested that RN submarines "pay periodic visits" to the dominions for ASW training. Adm, Naval app, "Review of Imperial Defence"

Rear-Admiral G.C. Jones, RCN, Commanding Officer Atlantic Coast, takes the salute at a graduating parade at HMCS *Kings* in September 1942. Commander A.M. Hope, RCN is to the left
while Lieutenant C.P. Nixon, RCN is on the right. (NAC, PA 204606)

The Royal Canadian Navy that went to war in September 1939 was modest in all but its aspirations. For much of the twenty-nine years of its existence, it had struggled to survive, let alone thrive, in the face of limited support. The result was a service with limitations. Canadian naval professionals, like their counterparts in other countries and other services, had no illusions about the nature of war. Yet war was what they had trained for, and war offered the opportunity to establish a reputation for the RCN. They were determined in this war to build, for the first time, a firm foundation for the future of the navy as a Canadian institution; to expand its function beyond that of a coastal defence force to a blue water navy. The sailors ultimately succeeded, thanks mainly to their courage, skill, and tenacity in their war at sea. But the campaign was long and difficult, and when one considers where the RCN stood in September 1939, it seems incredible that not only would it prove the value of a navy to Canada, but also it would make an essential contribution to the final Allied victory in the Second World War.

The uncertain time immediately before and after the beginning of hostilities in 1939 was one of both special danger and opportunity in the struggle for seagoing trade, so vital to the survival of Britain and her Empire. Prepositioned enemy raiders might inflict grievous damage if port and shipping defence measures were delayed. At the same time prompt, concerted action by the members of the Empire could result in the capture or destruction of valuable enemy merchant vessels as they attempted to run for friendly or neutral ports, or alternatively, to mount armament and operate as armed merchant cruisers. Neutral vessels carrying cargoes of war materiel consigned to the enemy had also to be intercepted.

There was, of course, an inherent conflict in the need for instant and uniform action under Admiralty direction, on the one hand, and aspirations by the dominions for autonomy, on the other. In the early 1920s the creation of dominion naval intelligence areas had provided a solution to this problem. The key link was the appointment of experienced British officers as the directors of naval intelligence in the dominion services, who, however, were responsible to the respective dominion governments. Another, more formal if more limited, guarantee of Canadian cooperation was the 1909 agreement under which the British government had turned control of the Imperial dockyards at Halifax and Esquimalt over to the dominion government in exchange for permanent access by Royal Navy warships to those ports. Even while rejecting the Admiralty's recommendations for Canadian acquisition of warships and asserting Canada's right not to participate in Britain's wars, Canadian governments of the interwar period sanctioned additional measures for cooperation that fleshed out these basic arrangements. The RCN assumed responsibility for the wartime control of shipping at Canadian ports, including organization of trade convoys. The RN stored guns and reserves of ammunition at Halifax and Esquimalt to provide for the "defensive equipment of merchant ships" and to outfit four armed merchant cruisers at Esquimalt. Canada undertook to mount this armament on the outbreak of war and to supply half of the personnel needed to man the armed merchant cruisers, as well as gunnery ratings for the defensively equipped merchant ships. In return, the Admiralty allowed that on mobilization the RCN could employ any of the Royal Naval Reserve and retired RN officers resident in Canada.[29]

---

29.   Adm, "North America and West Indies [AWI] Station Co-ordination of Imperial and Dominion Navies in Time of War," 19 June 1930, Conference paper E (30), 5; "British Commonwealth of Nations—Naval Policy 1930," DHH, 77/352 folder 2; Nelles to DM, 7 Mar. 1934, DHH, NHS 1700-193/96; Hadley and Sarty, *Tin-Pots and Pirate Ships*, 55

As early as 1926 Under-Secretary of State for External Affairs O.D. Skelton, the principal architect of Canada's campaign for a distinct voice in foreign policy, worried that these "more or less hypothetical" commitments might compromise the dominion's ability to choose not to participate in a British war. "I do not know," he brooded, "how many hypotheses it takes ... to make an established fact."[30] The government did make some of the further-reaching agreements, such as one for the transfer of headquarters for the America and West Indies Station from Bermuda to Esquimalt in the event of a Pacific war, contingent on "a state of hostilities being declared in Canada." There was renewed concern, however, at External Affairs when in the mid-1930s the Admiralty endeavoured to complete the arrangements for Canadian cooperation.[31] The new commitments were minor, but they had a cumulative effect: "If the Canadian Parliament decided not to participate in a war in which Great Britain was involved," observed one official, "the plans of the British Admiralty might be quite badly upset ... There is danger of the Canadian parliament's freedom of action being compromised beforehand as that of the British Parliament was in 1914 through the strong moral claim acquired by France on British assistance [through joint plans made by the French and British admiralties]."[32]

In the event, the King government did not interfere in specific measures for naval cooperation and, moreover, ignored demands from the opposition benches in Parliament for denunciation of the Halifax and Esquimalt agreements.[33] Still, Imperial naval authorities could scarcely disregard the prime minister's repeated declarations during the foreign policy and defence debates of the late 1930s that Canada was bound by no military commitments. He insisted that Parliament would decide, at the moment of crisis, whether or not the dominion would go to war. In November 1937, Sir Francis Floud, the British High Commissioner in Ottawa, sounded the warning: "There is a grave possibility of an interval occurring between the date on which the United Kingdom ... become[s] fully involved and the date on which this applies to Canada."[34] Canadian Chief of Naval Staff, Commodore Percy Nelles had recently refused a request from the Commander-in-Chief, America and West Indies, that the Canadian staff should, during the precautionary stage, send notifications to certain retired and reserve British officers in Canada who were designated for war service with the RN. Most of these officers were allocated to the consular offices in the United States which, although administered by the commander-in-chief, reported through Naval Service Headquarters. "A very awkward situation might arise," suggested Floud, "in the event of an interval occurring between the date when the United Kingdom instituted the precautionary stage and the date on which the corresponding action might be taken by the Canadian Government, were in this interval the Canadian defence authorities discovered to be acting on our behalf." Such a revelation would be invaluable ammunition for the large number of Canadian neutralists who could be expected to press "non-participation with any means available."[35]

---

30.   Skelton to Desbarats, 4 Aug. 1926, DHH NHS 1700-193/96

31.   NStaff, "Memo for the PM: Esquimalt as Base for North America and West Indies Squadron in War," 25 Jan.1929, NAC, RG 25 D-1, 755, 236

32.   "Canadian Defence Commitments," nd, NAC, RG 25 D-1, 755, 239

33.   Escott Reid, "An Anglo-Canadian Military Alliance?" *Canadian Forum* 17/197 (1937), 84-5; F.H. Underhill, "To Protect Our Neutrality," *Canadian Forum* 17/205 (1938), 376; HofC, *Debates*, 25 Mar. 1938, 1729, 24 May 1938, 3213, 1 July 1938, 4527

34.   Floud to Batterbee, 23 Nov. 1937, PRO, ADM 1/9488

35.   Ibid

Nelles's action signalled a still larger danger. The Canadian intelligence area might not be able to take its place in the worldwide Admiralty organization during the critical period immediately preceding and following the outbreak of war, causing a gap in the Imperial trade defence system whose basis was close control over merchant shipping through "reporting officers" at virtually every port where British vessels plied. In Canada, collectors of customs were designated for this service, under the administration of the intelligence staffs at Halifax and Esquimalt. In peacetime, RCN intelligence officers from the two dockyards visited each collector annually, ensured that they were provided with a complete set of Admiralty manuals, and ran exercises in code and cypher communication.[36] In wartime, reporting officers were to send daily telegrams detailing shipping movements, code named Vesca telegrams, directly to the Admiralty, with copies to the relevant intelligence area headquarters. Only with this information could senior naval authorities assess the threat posed by an enemy raider in a particular area and organize countermeasures. If there was danger of attack, instructions to remain in port, follow an evasive route, or proceed to a convoy assembly port were issued to ships through the reporting officers.[37] Aside from these fundamental services, the Admiralty depended upon the RCN for broadcast of wireless instructions and information to merchant shipping, the examination of neutral vessels for contraband cargo, and the organization of convoys in the event they became necessary.

These issues weighed heavily on Commander H.A.C. Lane, the RN officer then serving as Director of Naval Intelligence and Plans in Ottawa, when he travelled to Bermuda in the autumn of 1937 for a conference on trade defence at the headquarters of the Commander-in-Chief, AWI, Vice-Admiral Sir Sidney Meyrick. The purpose of the meeting was to brief Admiral Sir Eldon Manisty, RN, an expert on the control of shipping in the First World War, whom the Admiralty had brought out of retirement to perfect arrangements on conditions in the western hemisphere in the event of a future conflict. Lane evidently unburdened himself, and there was general agreement about the potential seriousness of the Canadian situation. Floud concluded that the High Commission in Ottawa should be prepared, for a brief period at least, to assume the role of a shadow naval intelligence headquarters, much as British embassies in neutral countries had done during the First World War.[38]

A minute by Captain T.S.V. Phillips, Director of Plans at the Admiralty, proved to be the blueprint for action on the part of the Imperial authorities. It is worth quoting at length:

> The appointment of United Kingdom High Commissioners to the Dominions is a comparatively recent feature of Empire organisation. In some ways they resemble Ambassadors to foreign countries, but it is considered that it would be a grave error to extend their functions in any way which would lead to a lessening of the system of direct negotiation between the Mother Country and the Dominions ...
>
> Whilst the possibility of Canadian neutrality in the event of Great Britain becoming involved in war has long been recognised, it is considered that we are fully justified in basing our plans and policy on the more probable eventuality that the Dominions will co-operate with the Mother Country in war time. Even should one of

36. E.g., annual report of DIO/SO(I), Halifax, 1924-39, NAC, RG 24, 8200, NSS 1920-152/1 pt 1

37. APD, "Protection of Shipping at Sea," Feb. 1939, CB 01764(39), 54-61, 71, PRO, ADM 199/3

38. Floud to Batterbee, 23 Nov. 1937

the Dominions, say Canada, abstain from a formal declaration of war, it is felt that we should be able to rely upon her putting at our disposal the facilities of her ports and the assistance of her intelligence organisations which have been built up and utilised in peace time. If we raise these points too much in peace time we are more likely to meet with a rebuff than if we leave them to the day. Canada might be loath to guarantee in peace time what she would do in war time, even if not at war herself.[39]

Senior Dominions Office and Admiralty officials particularly endorsed the wisdom of not giving Canada any hint of British concerns. The planning assumption continued to be that Canada would enter a war simultaneously with the United Kingdom, no record of alternative plans would appear in Admiralty publications, "and certainly not in documents accessible to the Canadian Authorities, since it is considered of the first importance that the Dominion should remain unaware that we have ever envisaged the possibility of Canada not entering a war simultaneously with the United Kingdom."[40] The most delicate issue was the most important one: continued unfettered cooperation between the Admiralty and the Ottawa intelligence area. The King government ruled in the spring of 1937 that liaison letters between the British and Canadian air and military staffs must be personally vetted by the Minister of National Defence and then despatched through the Department of External Affairs. This useful line of communication now became cumbersome and slow, and British officials were deeply worried that perceived isolationists at External Affairs might meddle in the much more voluminous traffic between the Canadian and British directors of naval intelligence.[41] In that event, as the British DNI succinctly put it, "a satisfactory intelligence system between this country and Canada would ... cease to function."[42] If they tried to build up a shadow intelligence headquarters, in say Bermuda or Newfoundland, the Canadians would undoubtedly find out, and this might trigger precisely the reaction that was feared. RN planners rejected out of hand the obvious solution of moving the British officer serving in Ottawa as DNI&P to the High Commission, should Canada delay her entry into the war. That would be an unacceptable affront: the officer was, after all, an employee of the Canadian government.[43] In the end, the commander-in-chief at Bermuda was instructed to earmark a suitable retired RN officer living in the AWI area who could be quickly and "quietly" transported to the High Commission.[44] Worst case scenarios, such as arranging for sympathetic shipping companies to carry out reporting officer functions should Canada observe rigid neutrality, were fully discussed within the Admiralty, but only on a theoretical basis. The Admiralty was scrupulous in avoiding preparations through the High Commission or the America and West Indies Station.[45] It was some comfort that the Canadian prime minister gave such warm support to British appeasement, and the dominion government made no difficulty about RCN participation in the RN's increasingly comprehensive preparations for trade

39.   DOP min, 5 Jan. 1938, PRO, ADM 1/9488

40.   Barnes to Batterbee, 11 Feb. 1938, PRO, ADM 1/9488

41.   Ibid, 22 Nov. 1937; J. Eayrs, *In Defence of Canada: Appeasement and Rearmament* (Toronto 1965), 83-4; C.P. Stacey, *Arms, Men and Governments: The War Policies of Canada, 1939-1945* (Ottawa 1970), 72-6

42.   Troup min, 12 Jan. 1938, PRO, ADM 1/9488

43.   Ibid; Barnes to Batterbee, 11 Feb. 1938

44.   Adm to C-in-C AWI, 26 Apr. 1938, PRO, ADM 1/9488

45.   Cdr Eric Brand, RN, who replaced Lane in 1939, did in fact keep the BHC fully informed about RCN plans. Brand interview, 3

defence. Nevertheless, Mackenzie King's continued declarations of no commitments were as maddeningly ambiguous, and the apparent strength of isolationist sentiment in Canada as potentially dangerous, as ever.[46]

The most important development in trade defence was the Admiralty's decision in the spring of 1938 to make arrangements for the immediate sailing of merchant ships in convoys on the outbreak of war with Germany. It is important to emphasize that, after the experience of 1917–18, the Admiralty had never doubted that convoy was the best defence against an unrestricted submarine assault against shipping. However, because of a misplaced confidence in the ability of offensive hunting groups of warships to track down and destroy submarines, and a suspicion, despite contrary evidence from the First World War, that delays in sailing inherent in convoy substantially reduced the carrying power of the merchant marine, senior British naval authorities still regarded the system as an exclusively defensive measure of last resort. Policy until early 1938 was that convoy should only be adopted when the enemy had clearly begun to "sink on sight." There was, moreover, good reason to expect that Germany might not do so in view of the disastrous result of the unrestricted U-boat campaign of 1917, which had quickly brought the United States into the war on the Allied side. Even if convoy had to be implemented, the Admiralty was, at that point, willing to accept a six-week delay that seemed to be necessary to assemble escorts and expand naval control service staffs at convoy ports.[47]

It was not fresh insights into the value of convoy that induced a change in policy, but the climate of political and public opinion. "There are many indications at the present time that the nation as a whole is 'convoy minded,'" observed the key Plans Division paper:

> This may be seen from questions in the House of Commons and from letters in the press. Furthermore, the contacts between Plans Division and the Shipping Interests leave no doubt that shipowners are not only keen advocates of convoy but assume, as a matter of course, that it will be instituted early in war.
>
> It is probably reasonable to say that the nation has been brought up to realise that the institution of the convoy system in 1917 saved it from starvation and defeat which is largely true; but it has probably also been instilled with the idea that the introduction of convoy was effected in spite of Admiralty opposition, which is largely untrue. Hence general public probably feel that the institution of convoy will in future be met by opposition on the part of the Admiralty.
>
> Indeed it seems probable that our entry into a German war would be accompanied by a general agitation for the immediate institution of convoy, regardless of whether this was necessary on account of losses, or not. For instance, the sinking of s.s. ENDYMION off the coast of Spain on 31st January 1938 [during the Spanish Civil War] was immediately followed by notification of a question in Parliament regarding the institution of convoy, and by letters in the press to the same effect.

---

46. E.g., Floud to Harding, 21 June 1938, PRO, ADM 1/9488

47. CID paper 1368-B, Nov. 1937, "Protection of Trade," PRO, ADM 199/2365; APD, "Extracts from CB 01957 ("The Protection of Shipping at Sea") of Sep. 1936," PRO, ADM 199/2365; APD, "Convoy at the Outset of a War with Germany," 19 Feb. 1938, PRO, ADM 1/9501. For a useful survey of the convoy system, see A. Hague, *The Allied Convoy System, 1939-1945: Its Organization, Defence and Operation* (St Catharines 2000).

Any attempt that the Admiralty might make in war to avoid going into convoy, however good the reasons might be, would merely be regarded as short-sighted and pig-headed obstruction, which would increase public agitation for the institution of convoy and weaken public faith in the Admiralty.[48] The Admiralty instructions of May 1938 to the station commanders-in-chief to revise their mobilization arrangements so that convoy could be immediately implemented frankly admitted the reason for the change: "Whilst fully realizing that the flow of shipping suffers to a certain extent by the imposition of a convoy system, My Lords are convinced that such a system would give confidence to the Merchant Navy and to the nation as a whole of incalculable value."[49]

A new edition of the Trade Defence Manual explained more precisely when the Admiralty believed convoy should be introduced. Because delays in sailing caused by convoy did not reduce merchant ship carrying power nearly so much as generally thought, it was "mistaken" to believe that the measure should be introduced only after shipping losses had actually begun to soar. "It follows," concluded the manual, "that it should be our policy to institute convoy in any area or on any route as soon as there is reason to believe that attacks will be made … in that area or route in sufficient strength to cause serious losses comparable to the loss of carrying power to be anticipated."[50] Privately, the Plans Division at the Admiralty admitted that the "decision on this score requires a nice balancing of advantages [of increased security in convoy] and disadvantages [of lost carrying power] and is one which will have to be taken by the Government of the day with a due regard for the effect on public opinion."[51]

The Admiralty despatched a copy of the May 1938 convoy directive to NSHQ in July, after an official pointed out that Halifax was earmarked as a principal assembly port.[52] Lane drew up a detailed assessment of the naval control of shipping staffs that would be needed to organize transatlantic convoys. Halifax was to have a "Class I" staff of nineteen officers and ratings, Sydney an only slightly smaller Class II staff of fifteen personnel, and smaller staffs were needed at Saint John, Québec City, and Montréal. The required officers could be found among the retired RN and RNR officers resident in Canada; most of the ratings, however, would have to be RCNVR as the RCN's complement "barely cover[s] the requirements of RCN. Ships now in commission or expected to be commissioned in the near future."[53]

In the wake of the Munich crisis in the autumn of 1938, the Admiralty pressed RN mobilization arrangements towards completion, and the RCN coordinated its more modest efforts with

---

48. APD, "Convoy at the Outset of War"

49. Adm to Cs-in-C, 26 May 1938, PRO, ADM 1/9501; C.B. Behrens, *Merchant Shipping and the Demands of War* (London, 1955)

50. APD, " Protection of Shipping at Sea"

51. APD, "Convoy at the Outset of War"

52. Information copies had been automatically sent to New Zealand and Australia, even though there was no intention of preparing for the early convoy of Pacific shipping; possibly the failure to include Canada (and South Africa) in the initial distribution reflected sensitivity about the autonomist stances of those governments. ADOP, min, 8 July 1938, PRO, ADM 1/9501; copy sent to Canada in NAC, RG 24, 3971, NSS 1048-48-1 pt 4

53. NCS staffs, it must be noted, were on mobilization to be established to carry out reporting officer functions at all major ports, not only possible convoy ports, where there was a large volume of British shipping. Lane to CNS, 5 Aug. 1938, NAC, RG 24, 3971, NSS 1048-48-1 pt 4; Tucker, *Naval Service of Canada* II, 355-6

those of the AWI Station.[54] The main focus was on the various services that were to be organized from the reserves, which included, in addition to naval control of shipping, the extensive measures required for port defence, including crews for auxiliary minesweeping and antisubmarine vessels. Shortages of personnel quickly became apparent. Compared with the requirement for 684 reserve officers, for example, only 327, including retired British and Canadian officers resident in Canada, were actually available.[55] Accordingly, in January 1939 the government lifted the ceiling on the strength of the RCNR to 170 officers and 500 ratings (as compared with an actual strength of fifty-eight officers and 192 ratings) and that of the RCNVR to 300 officers and 3,000 ratings (as compared with an actual strength of 108 officers and 1,195 ratings).[56] In March 1939, Rear-Admiral Nelles—he had been promoted in August 1938—reported to the Commander-in-Chief, AWI, that the Royal Canadian Navy would be able to provide all services at Canadian ports as laid down in the agreements with the Admiralty, but it would be hard pressed to provide certain seagoing personnel, such as crews for the four British armed merchant cruisers that were to be fitted out in Canada.[57]

Mobilization presented parallel difficulties; however, there were better defined precedents to follow there. Realizing that national mobilization for a modern war would have to be swift and comprehensive, the British Committee of Imperial Defence had developed departmental War Books and a government-wide War Book for interdepartmental cooperation prior to 1914. These documents laid down step-by-step procedures, complete with draft telegrams, orders-in-council and the like that would be necessary to mobilize the armed forces, protect important civil and military establishments against sabotage or espionage, impose censorship on civil communications, requisition civil property needed by the military, and generally control every aspect of national activity that might bear on security against hostile actions or the military effort. The Canadian services had prepared their own War Books prior to 1914 and had assisted other departments in completing a general War Book just in time for mobilization. Difficulties arose during the 1920s and 1930s when NSHQ periodically revised its departmental War Book in accordance with advice from the Admiralty and the CID, but the Canadian government did nothing about interdepartmental arrangements. One reason was that the increasingly specific and comprehensive measures recommended by the British during the 1930s required the creation of Cabinet subcommittees for planning that would have virtually replicated the CID. Such a step, External Affairs officials advised in 1937, would not only fly in the face of more informal Canadian tradition and practice, but it would also leave the government open to charges of having become entangled in Imperial defence commitments. The departments of National Defence and External Affairs reached a compromise early in 1938. Interdepartmental planning committees were established that reported to the Minister of National Defence and not to Cabinet. Thanks largely to the energetic efforts of Colonel M.A. Pope, the militia staff officer who coordi-

---

54.   Adm to Cs-in-C, 24 Nov. 1938; VAdm Sidney Meyrick, C-in-C AWI to Sec Adm, 31 Jan. 1939, NAC, RG 24, 3852, NSS 1018-6-2 pt 2

55.   Gow to DNI&P, 28 Oct. 1938, DNI&P to DNR, 28 Oct. 1938, NAC, RG 24, 3852, NSS 1018-6-8

56.   CNS to DM, 20 Dec. 1938, PC 167/26 Jan. 1939, NAC, RG 24, 3852, NSS 1018-6-8

57.   CNS to C-in-C AWI, 24 Mar. 1939, NAC, RG 24, 3852, NSS 1018-6-2 pt 2

nated the work of the committees, a "provisional" but essentially complete War Book was submitted to the government in July 1939.[58]

When Commander-in-Chief, AWI, Meyrick visited Ottawa at the end of June 1939, the British and Canadian naval staffs were able to review their preparations together.[59] Liaison conferences had been held at roughly two-year intervals since at least 1929, but this time the Admiralty had particularly asked the commander-in-chief to sound out the Canadian government. Prime Minister Mackenzie King was present at two luncheons held in the admiral's honour, and according to the latter privately promised that "I could rely on Canadian help in case of war."[60] In fact, nine months before, at the time of the Munich crisis, King had informed his Cabinet colleagues that there was no question of Canada standing aside if Britain went to war with the dictators. His often-repeated promise "Parliament will decide" applied only to "the nature and extent of our Participation."[61] Still, in deference to the policy of no commitments, Nelles declined to keep a copy of the America and West Indies war plan, even though all references in it to Canadian forces carried the tactful notation "if and when available."[62]

Canadian participation in a test of the AWI intelligence organization was one of the subjects discussed during the Ottawa meeting. Since 1934, at the Admiralty's request, NSHQ had been tracking the movements of large Japanese merchant vessels suitable for conversion into raiders. German ships of this class had been added at the time of the Munich crisis and then similar Italian vessels in early 1939. Now, in the third week of July 1939, the Ottawa centre, in conjunction with the Jamaica intelligence centre, updated this information using only sources that would be available in wartime, and transmitted daily reports to the commander-in-chief in accordance with the latest Admiralty procedures.[63] Midway through the exercise Commander E.S. Brand, RN, relieved Commander Lane, who had completed his tour as DNI&P. Nearing mandatory retirement, Brand had lobbied for the Ottawa appointment as a final posting—both he and his wife wanted to "see North America." When the time neared to go out to Ottawa, it was abundantly clear that the position would be anything but a quiet sinecure, and before departing the new DNI&P spent three weeks at the Admiralty learning about the latest developments in trade defence and other matters.[64]

58. "Interdepartmental Conference, MOP, 12 Jan. 1914," NAC, RG 24, 3848, NSS 1018-1-1, NSec IDC to DM and DNS, 15 Feb. 1913, with encl "DNS: Action in an Emergency," NAC, RG 24, 3852, NSS 1019-1-2 pt 1. See R.F. Sarty, "Silent Sentry: A Military and Political History of Canadian Coast Defence 1860-1945," PhD dissertation, University of Toronto, 1982, 255-6, 521; Stacey, *Arms, Men and Governments*, 69-70; M.A. Pope, *Soldiers and Politicians: The Memoirs of Lt-Gen Maurice A. Pope* (Toronto 1962), 127-9; DNI&P to CNS, 9 Oct. 1928, NAC, RG 24, reel C-8271, HQC 1393; War Book, DHH, 75/194

59. Interview with RAdm L.W. Murray, 30, Murray Biog file

60. Ns, nd, research note, "Liaison by Visit and Correspondence," which cites Adm file M-00715/39, DHH, NHS 1700-193/96. King mentions the luncheons in his diary (28, 29 June 1939) but does not record his conversations with Adm Meyrick, other than to describe them as "pleasant." Mackenzie King diary, DHH, 83/530

61. Mackenzie King diary, 28 Sep. 1938

62. "Liaison by Visit and Correspondence"

63. C-in-C AWI to 8th CS, signal 1605/16 June 1939, C-in-C AWI to CNS, 3 July 1939, CNS to C-in-C AWI, 31 July 1939, NAC, RG 24, reel C-5848, NSS 1023-1-6

64. Brand interview, 4-5; NSHQ, "Outline History of Trade Division NSHQ Ottawa, 1939-1945," 5, DHH, 81/520/8280 v 1, 8280 B pt 2

In Ottawa, Brand busied himself with the task of making defence schemes, which laid down the local organization and allocated specific personnel for all naval functions, for each of the east coast ports. NSHQ had drafted a very brief outline plan for the east coast as part of the tri-service Plan for the Defence of Canada that the Joint Staff Committee completed in June 1938, and a few details had been added at the time of the Munich crisis. Three operating areas were to be established, each with a base: the Bay of Fundy and its approaches, including the waters off southern Nova Scotia (Saint John), the approaches to mainland Nova Scotia (Halifax), and the approaches to Cape Breton and the Cabot Strait (Sydney). The naval officer in charge of each base was to control patrols in his area by auxiliary craft, with the officer in charge of the Halifax dockyard exercising overall command on the coast, including operations by the destroyers, which were to be concentrated as a striking force.[65]

Preliminary discussions about the east coast war organization and port defence schemes were still under way between the Halifax dockyard staff and headquarters when Brand arrived. Fortunately, he had during his last posting in the United Kingdom been engaged in updating port defence schemes at Rosyth with an eye to early mobilization. While in Halifax on 18–19 August to consult with the Commander-in-Chief, AWI, Brand worked on sketch interim schemes with Commander H.E. Reid, RCN, the commander-in-charge of the dockyard, and his staff. The assignment of retired officers to Naval Control Service appointments already in progress provided a good foundation: the senior NCS officer at each port was simply "double-hatted" as the naval officer in charge, with authority to carry out all required services. Utilizing the detailed surveys done since 1936 on the full defences proposed for the ports, the sketch schemes laid down measures that could be improvised.[66] In the case of Halifax, Brand settled a dispute between headquarters, which had urged economy in the allocation of personnel, and Reid, who wanted to build up full staffs as quickly as possible on mobilization to ensure that he could effectively exercise his overall command on the coast, in favour of Reid.[67]

On 14 August 1939, two weeks before the outbreak of war, NSHQ began receiving and despatching an enormous volume of cypher and code signals as part of an Admiralty test of the Empire's naval radio communications system. During the fourth week of August, after Hitler concluded his non-aggression pact with the Soviet Union on the twenty-third, which freed him to increase pressure on Poland, the Admiralty continued the exercise, and began to issue the messages—most of them single code words that referred to measures laid down in the War Books—which brought the precautionary stage into effect. The first of these arrived on 22 August, when the Admiralty advised that it was placing officers designated for the naval control service on twelve hours' notice. NSHQ followed suit that same evening, after Captain L.W. Murray, RCN, Director of

65. JSC, "JSC Plan for the Defence of Canada," 27 June 1938, NAC, RG 24, 2696, HQS 5199-F pt 1; JSC, "JSC Emergency Plan for the Defence of the Eastern Coast of Canada," 16 Sep. 1938, NAC, RG 24, 2700, HQS 5199-O pt 1; "Action in an Emergency," 16 Sep. 1938, NAC, RG 24, 11129, "COAC Secret and Personal"

66. Reid to Oland, 31 Aug. 1939 (sketch scheme for Saint John), NAC, RG 24, 11124 , 501-5-1; Reid to Goolden, 29 Aug. 1939 (sketch scheme for Sydney), ibid, 501-6-1; Brand, "Annual Report of DNI Ottawa, for Year 1939," 1-3, Brand papers

67. Brand overstates his own role, but the essentials are confirmed by the correspondence of June-Aug. 1939 on the east coast organization, esp. complete reversal by HQ on the need for economy in the Halifax organization. Significantly, this appeared in the letter written immediately after Brand's return from Halifax. Brand interview, 12-14; Murray to CNS, 9 June 1939, and NSec to C-in-C Halifax, 22 Aug. 1939, NAC, RG 24, 3832, NSS 1017-10-1 pt 2

Naval Operations and Training, and the second most senior officer at NSHQ, and Brand—Admiral Nelles was hurrying back to Ottawa from leave in Colorado—visited the Minister of National Defence at his rooms in the Hotel Chateau Laurier to obtain approval.[68] Next day the Prime Minister issued a press release on his own initiative that declared the government's readiness to meet any emergency and promised that Parliament would immediately be recalled if war broke out.[69]

When Cabinet met on 24 August, King was relieved to find agreement that Canada should participate if Britain went to war. The one thorny issue was whether an army expeditionary force should be sent to Europe; there was no controversy about the navy.[70] Skelton, in a paper advocating a "limited liability" war effort that Cabinet approved, suggested extending aid to Newfoundland and the West Indies: "In view of the possibility of German raids, this would be of definite value to Britain. It would appeal to Canadians as being an important worthwhile objective, and it is an effort in which we would have the goodwill and possibly eventually the cooperation of the United States."[71] King specifically noted his colleagues' support for full cooperation with the Commander-in-Chief, America and West Indies.[72]

The Royal Navy was already going to war stations. The cruiser HMS *Berwick*, flying the flag of the commander-in-chief, was in the Gulf of Maine, having made a scheduled visit to Bar Harbor, Maine, after leaving Halifax on 21 August. A second cruiser, HMS *York*, was coming from Bermuda to join her. The intention was to base these ships at Halifax for the protection of shipping on the main north Atlantic route, but, ever sensitive to the niceties of Canada's status, Admiral Meyrick forbade either cruiser to enter port until authorization came from Ottawa. The remaining ships on the AWI Station—two cruisers and two sloops—were assigned to the Caribbean where Kingston, Jamaica, was the principal operating base, with the sloops having the special task of protecting the vital oil trade. The cruisers were to operate in pairs, so that they might have a reasonable chance against the 11-inch guns of a German pocket battleship; the Admiralty warned that two of these formidable raiders were at large in the Atlantic.[73] Regarding his request to base *York* and *Berwick* at Halifax, "The High Commissioner, Ottawa," Meyrick recorded, evidently with some relief, "informed me he had received a letter from Minister of National Defence stating that the Canadian Government 'had no objection whatsoever to use of Halifax by HM Ships and that they were willing and anxious to extend every possible co-operation.'"[74]

That same night, the government authorized the militia to adopt the precautionary stage, which entailed the mobilization of about 10,000 non-permanent troops for port defence on both coasts and the guarding of certain inland "vulnerable points." When despatching the precautionary stage

---

68. AWI WD, 22 Aug. 1939, PRO, ADM 199/367; Murray interview, 30-1; Brand interview, 14-16; Nelles, "Report of Naval Activities from 21 Aug. to 10 Oct. 1939," NAC, MG 26 J1, 275, 233068-70

69. H.B. Neatby, *William Lyon Mackenzie King* III: *1932-1939: The Prism of Unity* (Toronto 1976), 316

70. Mackenzie King diary, 24 Aug. 1939

71. Skelton, "Canadian War Policy," 24 Aug. 39, NAC, RG 25 D-1, 780, 388 pt 2, extracts printed in Stacey, *Arms, Men and Governments*, 9

72. Mackenzie King diary, 25 Aug. 1939, includes further notes on the Cabinet of 24 Aug.

73. AWI WD, 21 Aug–3 Sep. 1939

74. Ibid, 24 Aug. 1939. The date is incorrect: see Skelton to King, 25 Aug. 1939, King to Skelton, 28 Aug. 1939, NAC, MG 26 J4, 396, 56, C278843, C278845.

telegrams to the militia coastal district commanders on the evening of 25 August, the general staff in Ottawa simultaneously sent an advisory message that "Navy and Air Force are not as yet adopting Precautionary Stage."[75] Unfortunately, the available documentation provides no precise answer as to what this meant. Certainly, it was true that neither the naval nor the air force reserves were mobilized, and the reasons are clear. After the chiefs of staff had originally recommended implementation of the precautionary stage on 25 August, King had responded that nothing should be done that might require the summoning of Parliament before war had actually broken out. Consultation with the Department of Justice confirmed that section 63 of the Militia Act allowed the minister to call-up non-permanent units without the sanction of Parliament, and it was under this section that Cabinet authorized the partial mobilization. By contrast, the Naval Service Act required Parliament to meet within fifteen days of the reserves being called out, and the auxiliary air force could be mobilized only by invoking the War Measures Act.[76]

In fact, there was no need to call-up naval reserves for the precautionary stage, as Nelles explained when the chiefs of staff met with the minister on 25 August.[77] Policy was to place members of the reserves on active service only as and when they were actually needed; otherwise the limited accommodation and training facilities at the dockyards would be overwhelmed.[78] The requirement for large numbers of personnel would not arise until auxiliary ships were taken up, and that was a war stage measure. In the meantime, the regular force, the retired officers who had already been warned and a handful of specialist reserve personnel, most of them signallers, were sufficient. The air force was in a similar situation, as its only equipped operational squadrons were permanent force units, and these were able, under the minister's authority, to begin to move to the coasts on 26 August.

The navy's primary responsibility for coast defence during the precautionary stage was the vital task of providing port war signal stations and examination services, which constituted the "trip wires" for the coast artillery. Located on an advanced headland of a defended port, the port war signal station identified incoming warships, and then informed the defences whether the vessel was friendly or hostile. Merchant ships were dealt with by the examination service, whose operational component was a small steamer stationed at the harbour entrance that ordered all vessels to stop. If the vessels did not stop or behaved suspiciously, the examination steamer could instantly call for fire from a nearby coastal fort. Dockyard personnel brought the port war signal stations and examination services at Halifax and Esquimalt into operation on 26 August. This was a familiar routine, and the navy and the coast artillery had periodically carried it out during peacetime exercises.[79]

75.   CGS to district officers commanding MD 5, 6, 7, 11, tg GS 50, 25 Aug. 1939, NAC, RG 24, 2647, HQS 3498 pt 13

76.   C.P. Stacey, *Six Years of War: The Army in Canada, Britain and the Pacific* (Ottawa 1955), 40-2, CSC, min of 64th mtg, 25 Aug. 1939, NAC, RG 24, 2685, HQS 5199 pt 5; Naval Service Act 1910, c 43, s 1, para 21

77.   CSC, min of 64th mtg

78.   Nsec, "Employment of RCNVR Personnel in Emergency," 26 Sep. 1938, original in NS 1019-1-5, which appears no longer to exist, copy in DHH, NHS 1700-905

79.   For a personal account of the establishment of the Port War Signal Station at Halifax, see Gow, *Alongside, The Navy, 1910-1950: An Intimate Account* (Ottawa 1999). The author's husband, A/Cdr F.R. Gow, RCN, oversaw the Halifax station at the outset of the war.

In short, although the reserves were not mobilized, both the RCAF and the RCN carried out precautionary stage measures, and this suggests that the militia staff's advisory telegram referred to rules of engagement. The latter, which were closely based on instructions adopted by the British forces at the time of the Munich crisis, had been promulgated to coastal commanders in February 1939. Prior to the declaration of the precautionary stage, forces were only to engage those of a potential enemy if the latter undertook in an unmistakably "hostile act," such as discharging weapons "with hostile intent" or laying mines within Canadian territorial waters. On the declaration of the precautionary stage, however, the forces were also permitted to engage foreign warships or merchant ships that ignored a warning from the port war signal station or the examination service at a defended port.[80] Although the issue is not discussed in any surviving document, that the "adopt Precautionary Stage Germany" signal was not despatched to the air force and naval coastal commanders suggests that the government or senior officers wished to limit action against a German vessel that failed to respond to warnings. Fire from fixed coast guns in the near approaches of a harbour was unambiguously defensive; action by aircraft and warships outside of territorial limits was not.[81]

At least as important as the partial mobilization of the port defences was the passage of an order-in-council that brought Canadian-registered merchant shipping under naval control on 26 August, one day after Admiralty control over British shipping came into force. During the next two days, the retired officers designated for naval control and port defence duties began to move to their stations while the Naval Distributing Authority at NSHQ travelled by aircraft to issue Confidential Books to the British consular offices in the United States.[82]

In the case of the Halifax command, Nelles rushed through Commander Reid's promotion to captain so that Reid would have no difficulty exerting his authority over the senior retired officers coming out to the east coast. Nelles, who praised Reid's "rapid appreciation of the present situation and his improvisation of the essential services with the small staff available to him," had no doubts that Reid should retain the Halifax command.[83] Short, heavy set, and athletic, "Rastus" Reid had entered the Royal Naval College of Canada in 1912 and was remembered for his lack of pretension and down to earth approach to life and duty.[84] Reid had commanded both Canadian and British destroyers before the war; he was an ardent nationalist, and senior officers remarked on his devotion to the RCN.[85] By all accounts affable and gracious, he had sometimes failed to impress while undergoing training with the RN and was known occasionally to unveil rigid opinions and cling to them obstinately.[86]

80. JSC to minister, 31 Dec. 1938, "General Instructions Regarding the Action to Be Taken by the Canadian Defence Forces Prior to a Declaration of War," NAC, RG 24, 2685 HQS 5199 pt 4. See also, CID, ODC, 6 Sep. 1938, "General Instructions Regarding the Action to Be Taken ...," NAC, RG 25 G-1, 1881, 829

81. Tucker, *Naval Service of Canada* II, app 2, 525

82. Nelles diary, 25-31 Aug. 1939, Nelles Biog file, folder A; Nelles to minister, 27 Aug. 39, original in NSC 1015-4-4 pt 1, which file appears no longer to exist, copy in NHS notes in DHH, 81/520/1440-127; Trade Division History, 5-6; *Canada Gazette*, 16 Sep. 1939, 777-8, lists the retired officers who were called up in late August with the dates and their appointments.

83. Nelles to DM, 28 Aug. 1939, H.E. Reid Biog file

84. RAdm 2nd BS (RN), conf rep, 19 Aug. 1932, Cmdre Walter Hose, conf rep, 31 Dec. 1933, NPRC, file O-61610

85. Hose, conf rep, 31 Dec. 1933, Capt V.G. Brodeur, conf rep, 31 Oct. 1937, NPRC, file O-061610

86. Brodeur, ibid

Shortly after his promotion on 30 August, Reid received the new title Commanding Officer Atlantic Coast.[87] Reid himself had suggested Senior Canadian Naval Officer, East Coast of Canada, which Captain L.W. Murray at NSHQ had rejected as inelegant and parochial:

> It is not anticipated that the senior officers of any RN forces which may operate from Canadian bases in time of war will in any way interfere with the local defence measures, which will be in Canadian hands. We do not think it necessary therefore to continue the use of the word "Canadian" in this connection and all reference to this title in multiple address groups in Admiralty cyphers and codes was removed on the instigation of NSHQ only two months ago.

When, with an expansion of the organization on the west coast in 1938, Esquimalt had become a captain's command, the title had been changed to Commanding Officer, Coast of British Columbia. It was this precedent that inspired Murray to suggest Commanding Officer Atlantic Coast.[88] The formulation had a ring to it, and the title of the Esquimalt command was changed again to Commanding Officer Pacific Coast.

On 28 August Nelles had advised the minister that the time had come to move destroyers round from the Pacific coast. All four asdic-equipped ships were based at Esquimalt. On the east coast only *Skeena* was available for operations; her sister-ship *Saguenay* was undergoing a refit that included the installation of asdic. After receiving the concurrence of the Admiralty, which advised that the Foreign Office believed there was no imminent threat from Japan, on 31 August Nelles ordered *St Laurent* and *Fraser* to Halifax "'with all convenient despatch'(approximately 25 knots)."[89] Although the ships were then with *Ottawa* and *Restigouche* on a public relations visit to Vancouver's Pacific Exhibition, they were under way within three hours. *Fraser* reached Halifax on the evening of 14 September, fourteen days and thirty-five minutes after leaving Vancouver. *St Laurent* arrived four hours later, having been separated from the senior ship for three days after misreading a signalled change of course.[90]

Two scant hours after the destroyers departed Vancouver, German forces crossed the Polish border. As the news reached Ottawa on the night of 31 August to 1 September, King called an early morning Cabinet meeting where he took decisive action. In short order, the government summoned Parliament for 7 September, invoked the War Measures Act—a state of "apprehended condition of war" was declared to have existed since 25 August to provide blanket authority for the precautionary measures that had already been taken—placed the regular components of the armed forces on active service, and authorized the call-up of the reserves for active service. King was most anxious to anticipate British action to show that Canada had responded to the outbreak of war on her own initiative and not merely followed London's lead as a dutiful colony.[91]

As planned, the initial call-ups from the naval reserves on 1 to 3 September were on a modest scale. All RCNR ratings—something fewer than 200—and 400 RCNVR ratings were ordered to

---

87. Reid's service record card shows that he received the title with effect from 2 Sep. 1939. NPRC, file O-61610

88. Murray to CNS, 9 June 1939

89. Nelles to minister, 31 Aug. 1939, DHH, NHS NSS 1057-1-1 pt 1

90. Cdr (D) *Fraser* ROP, 29 Sep. 1939, CO *Fraser* to CO *St Laurent*, 21 Sep. 39, CO *St Laurent* to CO *Fraser*, 24 Sep. 1939. NAC, RG 24, 11075, 45-2-1

91. Mackenzie King diary, 1 Sep. 1939

Halifax and Esquimalt, but many of the latter were already at the bases where they had been undergoing routine summer training.[92] The *Canadian Navy List* shows that, in addition, 108 RCNR and RCNVR officers were placed on active service.[93] Included in the latter were the commanding officers of the RCNVR divisions who, in accordance with prewar plans, ran the units as recruiting and training centres. Members of the divisions continued with their civil employment and trained in the evenings and on weekends; as they were called up for active service on the coasts or at NSHQ, the division was again recruited up to full strength. Most divisions had long lists of eager applicants awaiting a chance for entry.[94]

On 1 September the RCN began to take up ships in the civil government departments that had been earmarked for auxiliary patrol and other services. Requisitioning of civilian craft did not begin until 4 September, the government having delayed the requisition order and enjoined the navy to proceed by "amicable negotiations" with owners.[95] This was a source of increasing annoyance and worry for the CNS. On 25 August the Admiralty had advised the dominions to start fitting out auxiliary vessels because the RN, itself short of minesweeping and antisubmarine craft, could spare none.[96] At the end of August Nelles had complained at a Chiefs of Staff Committee meeting about his shortage of patrol vessels and the government's unwillingness to hurry the requisition order.[97]

It was only on the morning of 1 September, when the government placed the forces on active service, that NSHQ finally despatched a warning signal to the destroyers and coastal commanders: "Ship warheads and be in all respects ready for action. Do not start an engagement until ordered from NSHQ but be prepared to defend yourselves in case of attack."[98] This was evidently Admiral Nelles's interpretation of the precautionary stage rules of engagement, for at this same time air force headquarters despatched the precautionary stage signal to the air commands.[99] On the receipt of these messages, destroyers and air squadrons abandoned peacetime routine and began reconnaissance patrols.[100] In effect, naval and air operational units had been placed at the precautionary stage level of readiness a full week after the same posture had been ordered for the coast fortresses.

On 3 September, when Britain went to war with Germany, the Chief of the General Staff asked Minister of National Defence Ian Mackenzie to authorize the despatch of the "war telegram" to the coastal commanders. That would free them to deal with German forces as if Canada had already

---

92. Nelles, "Report of Naval Activities"; Tucker, *Naval Service of Canada* II, 7

93. *Canadian Navy List*, 15 Oct. 1939, 26-32, 38-9

94. NSec, "Employment of RCNVR Personnel"; "Summary of War Effort—Naval, 1 Jan.–31 Dec. 1939," 18 Jan. 1940, 4-5, copy in DHH, NSM; Tucker, *Naval Service of Canada* II, 6

95. Nelles diary, 1 Sep. 1939; Nelles, "Report of Naval Activities"

96. Tucker's notes in Adm file LD 0287/39, DHH NHS 1700-193/96; Skelton to King, 25 Aug. 1939, C278842

97. CSC, min 66th mtg, 31 Aug. 1939, pt 6

98. NSHQ to Capt (D), *Skeena*, *Fraser*, C Halifax, C Esquimalt, (R) C-in-C AWI, and Adm, 1152/1 Sep. 1939, notes in NSS 1037-1-3 in DHH, NHS 1650 (Operations General) pt 2

99. CAS to Officers Commanding WAC, EAC, ATC, and RCAF Station Ottawa, tg 18-1/9, NAC, RG 24, 2696, HQS 5199-F pt 2

100. Capt (D) *Ottawa* ROP, 11 Sep. 1939, DHH, NHS NSS 1057-1-1 pt 1; EAC, ORB, 1-3 Sep. 1939, DHH; 5 Squadron RCAF ORB, 1-3 Sep. 1939, DHH

gone to war. "For most effective military defence," Major-General T.V. Anderson urged, "it is high-ly desirable that Coast Defence commanders should no longer be tied down."[101] Mackenzie, after consulting Cabinet, approved a modified form of the war telegram that reflected the government's emphasis on exclusively defensive action for the immediate and direct protection of Canada: "To take all necessary defence measures which would be required in a state of war. (Emphasize secret nature of these instructions)."[102] This went immediately to the militia and air commanders on the coasts, but action in the case of the navy is less clear.[103] Although Nelles recorded in his diary that he was advised of the new rules of engagement by Colonel Pope of the general staff, the admittedly incomplete naval records suggest that he did not inform the commands. Earlier that day, howev-er, on warning the commanders that war had broken out between Britain and Germany, Nelles had reiterated the rules of engagement promulgated on 1 September—"COs ships informed to be in every way prepared to defend themselves but not to start anything" was how he put it in his diary.[104] Similarly, AFHQ reminded the air commands of the precautionary stage rules of engage-ment.[105] It may be that senior naval and air officers interpreted the government's emphasis on defensive action in its revision of the "war stage" telegram as effectively restricting mobile units to the precautionary stage rules of engagement. Canada was not formally at war until 10 September 1939 when, Parliament having met and endorsed the government's recommendation of "immediate participation," King George VI approved the Canadian proclamation of war. NSHQ informed subordinate commands, warships, the Admiralty and the Commander-in-Chief, AWI, at 1300, Ottawa time, with the coded signal "Grapnel Germany repetition Grapnel Germany."[106]

When this signal went out, the retired and reserve officers designated for naval control service and port defence duties had been at work for up to eleven days. As the NOIC and NCSO at Saint John, Commander J.E.W. Oland, RCN (ret'd), reported, the change was a jolt for some of the old hands: "Having been ashore engaged in civilian pursuits for periods varying from four to nineteen years, [they were] striving to transform their minds overnight from a civilian mentality back into Service channels."[107] Immediately on arriving, the NCSOs had relieved customs officials of control of shipping duties. On the east coast, small patrol boats of the RCMP Marine Section, still manned by their police crews, brought examination services into force at Sydney and Québec on 6 September and at Saint John on the 19th.[108] On the Pacific coast at Vancouver, a small private yacht carried out the examination service from 6 September. The venerable coal-burning Battle class trawler *Armentières*, originally built for the RCN in 1917–18 and subsequently turned over to the Department of Marine and Fisheries, returned to the navy for the examination service at Yorke

---

101. CGS to minister, 3 Sep. 1939, NAC, RG 24, 2685, HQS 5199 pt 6

102. Pope to CSC, 1220/3 Sep. 1939, ibid. See also, Mackenzie King diary, 3 Sep. 1939.

103. CGS to district officers commanding MD 5, 6, 7, 11, tg GS 148, 1250/3 Sep. 1939, pt 14

104. NSHQ to Capt (D) *Skeena*, *Fraser*, 3 Sep. 1939; Nelles diary, 3 Sep. 1939

105. CAS to AOCs EAC, WAC, ATC, tg 28-3/9, 3 Sep. 1939, NAC, RG 24, 2700, HQS 5199-P

106. NSHQ to COAC, COPC, *Fraser*, *St Laurent*, Adm, C-in-C AWI, SO(I) Kingston, 1300/10 Sep. 1939, notes from NSS 1037-1-3, DHH, NHS 1650 (Operations General) pt 2

107. Port of Saint John, NB, ROP, 1 Sep.–29 Feb. 1940, DHH, NHS NSS 1000-5-11 pt 1

108. Ns, nd, "Resume of Naval Control Organization Port of Québec, 1939-1945," DHH, 81/520/1440-127; NOIC Sydney to COAC, "Report of NOIC," 8 Sep.1939, NAC, RG 24, 11063, 36-1-8 pt 1; Saint John ROP, 1 Sep.

Island, off Esquimalt. At Prince Rupert, remote from areas where German operations were likely, an examination service was not established until the end of October.[109]

One of the few surviving contemporary accounts of conditions at the outbreak of war comes from Captain Massey Goolden, RN (retd), the NOIC and NCSO at Sydney. On arriving on 4 September, he discovered that the port defences consisted of one 4.7-inch gun on shore, five RCAF seaplanes "at present without bombs," and two RCMP patrol boats that were too lightly constructed for prolonged examination service duties. Spurred on by a fortunately unfounded U-boat report, Goolden had improvised "depth charges"—blasting powder in metal drums—rigged for the RCMP launches and arranged exercises with the air force. The unarmed sea planes would swoop down to force the U-boat to submerge, while the launches went out to unload their dubious weapons. Base facilities comprised a section of the Department of Public Works wharf.[110]

COAC, Captain Reid could only urge Goolden to make the best of what he had; Halifax had priority for all that was available and that was little enough.[111] Equipment was on hand for two more Battle class trawlers from Marine and Fisheries, *Arras* and *Arleux*, and these vessels joined the two modern minesweepers *Fundy* and *Gaspé* in making daily sweeps in the Halifax harbour approaches. Three of the larger RCMP vessels, *Fleur de Lis, Laurier*, and *French* were pressed into antisubmarine patrol service, but at only 200 to 300 tons displacement and ten to twelve knots speed these were modest craft. The navy took up an additional thirty-nine vessels for the Atlantic coast from civil departments and private owners during the autumn of 1939. Most of them, however, were harbour craft, capable at best of relieving the smaller, interim examination service vessels. Only five of the vessels were at all suited for minesweeping and antisubmarine duties. These included the hydrographic survey ships *Acadia* and *Cartier*, both veterans of the RCN's First World War antisubmarine flotilla, and three commercial trawlers, two of which had served in the RN's auxiliary patrol of 1914–18.[112] Fewer auxiliary vessels were deployed on the less-vulnerable west coast. In addition to the recently built Fundy class minesweepers *Nootka* and *Comox* at Esquimalt, the only substantial patrol craft were the RCMP vessel *Macdonald* and the large private yacht *Sans Peur*, whose conversion was not complete until the end of 1939. Patrols along much of the British Columbia coast were left to fifteen fishing craft chartered for full-time service with the Fishermens' Reserve. (See Chapter 6.)

A critical issue that the Canadian declaration of war did not settle was the relationship between the Royal Canadian Navy and the RN. The Commander-in-Chief, America and West Indies, wanted the Canadian destroyers to reinforce his small squadron that was already stretched thin. On learning that *St Laurent* and *Fraser* were coming round from Esquimalt, Admiral Meyrick asked the High Commission in Ottawa if he might retain the two ships for the Caribbean force.[113] On 6 September,

---

109. NOIC Vancouver ROP, Sep. 1939–11 Feb. 1940, 15 Apr. 1940, COPC to NSec, 16 Dec. 1939, DHH, NHS NSS 1000-5-10 pt 1

110. NOIC Sydney to COAC, 8 Sep. 1939, NAC, RG 24, 11063, 36-1-8 pt 1

111. COAC to NOIC Sydney, 12 Sep. 1939, ibid

112. Nelles to minister, "Review of the Naval Requirements of Canada and the Existing Situation, 29 Sep., 1939," DHH, NHS 1650-1 (Policy) pt 1; NWR 1-16, for weeks ending 25 Sep. 1939–4 Jan. 1940, DHH, NHS NSS 1000-5-7, pt 1; "Summary of Naval War Effort, 1 Jan.–31 Mar. 1940"2, DHH, NHS NSS 1000-5-8. *Acadia* is on exhibit at the Maritime Museum of the Atlantic in Halifax.

113. AWI WD, 31 Aug. 1939

in response to the Canadian government's request for advice as to what military assistance it could render, the British authorities urged that the RCN destroyers be placed at Admiralty disposal, and that *Ottawa* and *Restigouche* be brought to the Atlantic.[114] As soon as Meyrick learned that Canada was officially at war, he tried again, asking NSHQ directly if *St Laurent* and *Fraser*, then approaching Jamaica, could be assigned to that station, and if either *Ottawa* or *Restigouche* could also be brought to Jamaica. Nelles balked at the last proposal.[115] Already in late August Nelles had explained to the minister that he did not want to reduce the force available on the west coast to fewer than two destroyers, because no British warships were in the northeast Pacific, and German merchant ships were at large that might readily be converted to raiders; no doubt he recalled the panic in British Columbia about inadequate naval defence in 1914.[116] Certainly Ian Mackenzie, who represented the province, needed no reminding. Nelles wanted to help out in the Caribbean, but because Canadian government policy tied his hands, he did not respond to Meyrick's request for *St Laurent* and *Fraser* before both ships had already been rushed through to Halifax.[117]

The Naval Service Act provided for placing RCN warships at the Admiralty's disposal, that is, under British operational control, but when preparing orders-in-council for mobilization of the forces on 1 September, Prime Minister King had refused to endorse the one that reflected this provision. Under his leadership, Cabinet was determined to avoid any appearance of having committed Canada to action in distant theatres, and King, who had been present in Laurier's Cabinet when the Naval Service Act was drafted, also believed that the intention of the "at disposal" provision had never been to give the Admiralty blanket authority over the entire Canadian fleet.[118] On 11 September Cabinet again declined to pass the required order-in-council and referred the matter to Nelles, asking, "Could not instructions to co-operate (with the RN) suffice?" Nelles was exasperated.[119] Yes, he responded, but only if cooperation was so far-reaching as to effectively place the destroyers under British command. It was "most desirable," he continued, "that we have one Officer and Staff only directing naval operations at sea on the America and West Indies Station and the most suitable person is the Commander-in-Chief of the Station:"

> To have more than one person and staff directing operations will cause confusion, delays, and will not produce the efficient effort necessary.
>
> If co-operation means that the Commander-in-Chief, America and West Indies will direct operations of HM and HMC Ships on the America and West Indies Station as was done in the last war with great success, then it achieves my object and will be eminently suitable.[120]

The latter paragraph was history through rose-coloured glasses—things never worked that smoothly during the First World War—but, as is clear from the concluding part of the memoran-

114. BHC to Skelton, 6 Sep. 1939, NAC, RG 24, 3842, NSS 1017-10-23 pt 1

115. AWI WD, 10 Sep. 1939

116. See Tucker, *Naval Service of Canada* I, 262-78.

117. Nelles to minister, 31 Aug. 1939

118. Nelles diary, 1 Sep. 1939; Mackenzie King diary, 1 Sep. 1939

119. Nelles diary, 11 Sep. 1939

120. Nelles to minister, 12 Sep. 1939, NAC, RG 24, 3842, NSS 1017-10-23 pt 1

dum, Nelles's overriding concern was with the German surface raider threat and the RCN's inability to meet the danger without substantial British assistance. The edge in his tone is understandable. Having refused to acquire cruisers or heavily gunned Tribal class destroyers in peacetime, the government was now apparently attempting to deny the dependence upon the RN that was the inevitable result:

> The case in point is that four destroyers cannot defend our East Coast and focal areas. The Commander-in-Chief has therefore stationed two eight-inch cruisers to add to our efforts. Great submarine activities are presently reported in the Caribbean [sic] which is a direct threat to the oil fuel supplies of Great Britain and Canada. The *Fraser* and *St Laurent*—ideally suited to hunt submarines—are now in the Caribbean with orders to proceed to Halifax where no immediate submarine threat has been felt to date.
>
> Failing the *Fraser* and *St Laurent* hunting the submarines in Caribbean waters the Commander-in-Chief will probably deem it necessary to remove his cruisers to West Indian waters to ensure supply of oil fuel.
>
> In this event the defence forces on our East Coast will gain two destroyers and lose two eight inch cruisers.[121]

King had no intention of reneging on the government's promise of full support for the America and West Indies station. He was, rather, concerned purely with constitutional form. On 14 September Cabinet passed an order-in-council that directed the RCN destroyers to "co-operate to the fullest extent with Royal Naval Forces," and within a week, *Saguenay*, having completed refit and the installation of asdic, was on her way to Jamaica under the commander-in-chief's orders.[122] The reports of U-boat activities in the Caribbean proved to be false, but this in no way altered the usefulness of the destroyer in these waters.

It was events in European waters, however, that defined what would be the RCN's principal role in the Second World War. By the commencement of hostilities with Britain on 3 September 1939, eighteen U-boats, virtually the *Kriegsmarine*'s entire strength in seagoing submarines, had taken up station in the Atlantic, most of them off the western coast of the British Isles. *U30*, under the command of Kapitänleutnant F.-J. Lemp, opened the battle for the sea lanes that same day by sinking without warning the unarmed, unescorted passenger liner *Athenia* northwest of Ireland. This was the only attack during the first weeks of the war that clearly violated international law; Lemp had, in fact, disobeyed orders. Nevertheless, Winston Churchill, who had re-entered the British government as First Lord of the Admiralty on 3 September, declared that unrestricted U-boat warfare had begun and ordered the convoy of merchant shipping in home waters and the Atlantic.[123] A signal from the Admiralty on 8 September brought convoy into force in the western ocean. From that date the naval control and reporting officers at Canadian and all but the most southerly Atlantic ports in the United States routed ships bound for the United Kingdom to Halifax.[124]

---

121. Ibid

122. Nelles diary, 15 Sep. 1939; NSHQ to C-in-C AWI, 15 Sep. 1939, C-in-C AWI to NSHQ, 16 Sep. 1939, NSHQ to C-in-C AWI, 18 Sep. 1939, NAC, RG 24, 6796, NSS 8375-4; AWI WD, 15-20 Sep. 1939

123. M. Gilbert, *Finest Hour: Winston S. Churchill, 1939-41* (London 1983), 5-6, 9, 12; *MOD, The U-Boat War in the Atlantic* I: *1939-1941* (London 1989), 7, 41-2. This study of U-boat strategy, operations and policy was prepared after the war by Fregattenkapitän Günter Hessler, a son-in-law of Dönitz, at the request of the Admiralty.

124. Adm to CNS and C-in-C AWI, 8 Sep. 1939, NAC, RG 24, 3971, NS 1048048-1 pt 4

Bedford Basin chock full of merchant ships waiting to sail in convoy. (NAC, PA 196590)

A convoy conference in Halifax in March 1941. Captain R.H. Oland, RCN stands at centre issuing instructions to the masters of merchant ships. The convoy Commodore is seated immediately to his left. (NAC, PA 105297)

The Sydney dockyard in July 1940 with two minesweeping trawlers alongside. (NAC, PA 206678)

Four corvettes alongside in Sydney in November 1941. K 141 is HMCS *Summerside*, while *Drumheller* is inboard with a SW1C antenna visible on her foremast. (NAC, PA 205169)

The first Halifax convoy, HX 1—the same designator that had been used in 1917–18 and which stood for "Homeward from Halifax"—sailed during the early afternoon of 16 September. The eighteen merchant ships were slow to take up their cruising positions in short columns on a broad three-and-a-half mile front as they emerged single-file from harbour, but then did well keeping station. The cruisers *York* and *Berwick* patrolled the flanks ranging up to five miles ahead of the convoy, while *St Laurent* and *Saguenay* provided close-in antisubmarine protection, each destroyer generally a mile or two ahead of the lead merchant ships on the wing columns. One or two Supermarine Stranraer flying boats from RCAF Station Dartmouth provided daylight air escort during the first twenty-four hours—about 200 miles—of passage. During the evening of 18 September, when about 400 miles out of harbour and at the limits of the approach routes to the coast where German submarines and surface raiders could most readily locate shipping, the cruisers and destroyers parted company and turned for port.[125] A heavy warship was supposed to stay with the merchant ships for protection against surface raiders, but such was the shortage of capital ships and cruisers in the RN that early HX convoys lost their remaining escorts at mid-passage.[126] The Admiralty had accepted that risk because there was much greater danger of submarine attack in the western approaches to the United Kingdom, where U-boats were sinking as many as four independently sailed merchant ships a day. When it closed its destination, HX 1 met its escort southwest of Ireland in the morning of 29 September—the time and position had been set before the convoy had sailed and despatched to the naval control service staff at Halifax. Indeed, the tight schedule of the under-strength and overworked antisubmarine escort forces based at British ports dictated the schedules of the whole convoy system.

The HX series, meant to be for ships capable of steaming at not less than nine knots and not more than fifteen knots, continued to sail from Halifax every six days. A second "fast" series, for ships of fifteen knots or more, began with the sailing of HXF 1 on 19 September; it was also on a six-day cycle. The speed of these ships made them relatively safe from U-boat attack, and they were to sail independently once they had been fitted with guns—the dockyards at Halifax and Esquimalt were already fitting merchant ships with the armament that the Admiralty had stockpiled for this purpose. Escorts, such as there were, sailed with each convoy. *Fraser* alone led the eight ships of HXF 1 through the Halifax approaches. *Saguenay* and *Skeena*, already at sea, encountered the convoy and joined the escort for a few hours on the evening of 19 September.[127]

The burden of this burgeoning activity on the Naval Control Service Officer at Halifax was a heavy one. His was the responsibility for ensuring that merchant ships assigned to a convoy were properly fuelled, victualled, equipped, and organized to sail in time to meet the crucial rendezvous with the RN escort in the western approaches to Great Britain. He received instructions from the Admiralty about the route of the convoy, and the time and position of the rendezvous with the escort in British waters. He and his staff assigned sailing positions within the convoy on the basis of each ship's speed and destination, plotted the individual courses each ship should follow in case it became separated from the convoy, and was then responsible for briefing the merchant captains.

---

125. "Convoy HX 1 from Halifax ...," in Convoy Sailing Lists, DHH, NHS NSHQ Convoy Files; CO HMS *Berwick* to COAC, 22 Sep. 1939 (ROP HX 1), DHH, NHS NSS 8280-HX 1 mfm; ORB, 5 Squadron RCAF, 16-17 Sep. 1939

126. Adm to C-in-C AWI, 7 Sep. 1939, C-in-C AWI to CNS, 7 Sep. 1939, NAC, RG 24, 3971, NS 1048-48-1 pt 4

127. Adm to CNS, C-in-C AWI, 8 Sep. 1939, NAC, RG 24, 3971, NS 1048-48-1 pt 4; "Convoy HXF 1, from Halifax 1400/19 Sep.," Halifax Convoy Sailing Lists, DHH, 77/553 v 2; CO *Fraser* ROP HFX-1, 21 Sep. 1939

When the convoy departed, the NCSO then had to despatch a signal to the Admiralty that confirmed the sailing time and listed each ship that had actually sailed.[128]

The naval control service at Halifax worked smoothly from the start, so much so that when two British officers arrived in mid-September to assist, there was nothing for them to do.[129] Much of the credit is due to Commander Richard Oland, a retired RCN officer who had taken up the appointment of NCSO on 29 August. Oland had entered the Royal Naval College of Canada in 1913, and like most young RCN officers, spent much of the First World War and the decade following with the Royal Navy. He left the RCN in 1930 to take up a career in business. After the Munich crisis he asked to be earmarked for war service and was allocated to the NCS Halifax. Oland's varied naval experience—he had served in British warships ranging from submarines to battleships—and experience in business ideally suited him for the task.[130] Captain Reid, a man not normally generous with praise, sent a glowing commendation to NSHQ:

> I cannot speak too highly of [Oland's] efforts which have produced a most efficient organization. The rapid growth of Halifax as a Convoy port is well known, yet he has so administered his Department that it has at all times functioned in an orderly and impressive manner. The main contact with the National Harbours Board and shipping firms in Halifax has been maintained through the Naval Control Service Officer, who has shown great tact and cheerfulness which is largely responsible for the present friendly relations between the Royal Canadian Navy and these organizations.[131]

A senior British officer who worked closely with Oland reported to the Admiralty in equally glowing terms, and like Reid recommended him for special recognition.[132] Oland was subsequently awarded the Order of the British Empire. Unhappily, he suffered a fatal heart attack in September 1941 at the age of forty-four, but the organization he had created at Halifax operated efficiently throughout the war.

The increased scale and tempo of activities at Halifax in September 1939 proved to be only a prelude to still larger developments. On the last day of the month, the German pocket battleship *Admiral Graf Spee* stopped, boarded, and sank the steamer *Clement* off northwestern Brazil, but not before the merchant vessel transmitted a distress signal. This was the first evidence to reach the Admiralty that powerful German raiders were actually at large in the Atlantic; hoping that France and Britain might agree to peace following the fall of Poland, Hitler had not authorized the warships to begin operations until 26 September. Firm intelligence about the presence of a second pocket battleship, *Deutschland*, on the North Atlantic was not available until 20 October, when reports from crews whose ships had been recently stopped or sunk to the east of Newfoundland began to reach London.[133]

---

128. APD, "Protection of Shipping at Sea," 72. For a memoir of a NCSO, see F.B. Watt, *In All Respects Ready: The Merchant Navy and the Battle of the Atlantic, 1940-1945* (Scarborough 1985)

129. Brand to DNI, Adm, 25 Sep. 1939, NAC, RG 24, 3841, NSS 1017-10-22 pt 1

130. Personnel file of Richard Hibbert Oland, NPRC, file O-56280

131. Reid to NSec, 8 Dec. 1939, NPRC, file O-56280 pt 2

132. Notes in report of RAdm L.E. Holland, 23 Dec. 1939, DHH, 81/520 HMS *Seaborn* 8000

133. AHS, *The Defeat of the Enemy Attack on Shipping, 1939-1945: A Study of Policy and Operations* 1A (London 1957), 216; S.W. Roskill, *The War at Sea, 1939-1945* I (London 1954), 70; F.H. Hinsley, *British Intelligence in the Second World War* I (London 1979), 105. See also, E. Grove (ed), *The Defeat of the Enemy Attack on Shipping, 1939-1945: A Revised Edition of the Naval Staff History* (Aldershot 1997).

To strengthen the defence of trade in the face of this threat, the Admiralty concentrated shipping into fewer, larger convoys, escorted across the entire breadth of the North Atlantic by major warships. By originating in Halifax, all transatlantic convoys to the United Kingdom could follow the great circle route, the shortest distance across the North Atlantic, and the precious few heavy warships available could be used to best effect in a shuttle back and forth across the ocean. Under Admiralty instructions of 7 October, convoys ceased to assemble at Jamaica and all ships from southern ports were routed to Halifax. Masters were to follow the United States coast, close to the limits of territorial waters, on the correct assumption that Hitler would not want to disturb the neutral Americans by allowing raider operations close to their shores. The additional ships created problems in convoy organization, so in February 1940 HXF convoys ceased to sail and HX convoys, open to all ships of nine to 14.9 knots, began a new convoy cycle sailing every three to five days.[134]

The ocean escort force that reached Halifax on 16 October included the two battleships of the 3rd Battle Squadron, HMS *Resolution* and HMS *Revenge*, and two E class cruisers.[135] *Emerald* sailed on 17 October with HX 5, *Revenge* with HXF 6 on 24 October, and *Resolution* with HX 6 on 25 October.[136] It took about three weeks to complete the cycle of sailing, returning, and being ready for the next crossing, so more escorts were in urgent demand. Accordingly, four armed merchant cruisers arrived in November, among them HMS *Letitia*, which had fitted out at Canadian Vickers at Montréal in accordance with the prewar agreements.[137] Late in November, the powerful modern German battlecruisers *Scharnhorst* and *Gneisenau* revealed their presence in the Denmark Strait by sinking the armed merchant cruiser HMS *Rawalpindi*. Because German raiders, despite British air and naval patrols covering the exits from the North Sea, could break out onto the Halifax convoy route under the cover of long winter nights and foul weather, the battleships *Malaya* and *Royal Sovereign* joined the Halifax escort force until April 1940.[138] Still, the shortage of warships was so severe that the Admiralty had taken the further and unusual step of employing large submarines as surface escorts. Seven of these vessels, three British and four French, arrived at Halifax in late November with the intention that two should reinforce convoys escorted only by a cruiser or armed merchant cruiser, and one if the escort was a battleship.[139] Winter conditions on the North Atlantic, however, proved too severe for surfaced submarines. Each made one crossing in December, but not until the weather improved in March–April 1940 did four French submarines return to Halifax for escort duty.[140]

---

134. Opening HXF convoys to ships of 12 knots and over meant that HFX-6 sailed on 24 Oct. with six vessels and HX 6 sailed the next day with 53. Reducing the HXF speed requirement to 11 knots helped but did not correct the imbalance. RA 3 BS to COAC, 29 Nov. 1939, DHH, NHS NSS 8280-HX 6; NCSO Halifax Sailing Lists, DHH, 77/553, pt 2-3; Adm to COAC, 28 Oct. 1939, COAC to Adm, 29 Oct. 1939, Adm to CNS and COAC, 7 Oct. 1939, NAC, RG 24, 3971, NS 1048-48-1 pt 4; Adm to NSHQ, 12 Feb. 1940, PRO, ADM 1/10356

135. AWI WD, 16 Oct. 1939

136. NCSO Halifax records, DHH, 77/553 pt 2. A third battleship, HMS *Warspite*, joined in November, but during her first escort with HX 9 late in the month, she was diverted to search for the battle cruisers. AHS, *Home Waters and the Atlantic* I, 29

137. Adm to RA 3 BS, 20 Nov. 1939, PRO, ADM 1/10356; NCSO Halifax records, DHH, 77/553 pt 2; Nelles diary, 2, 8 Sep. 1939; Adm to NSHQ, 25 Oct. 1939, NAC, RG 24, 11105, 53-1-4; Tucker, *Naval Service of Canada* II, 10

138. AWI WD, 3 Dec. 1939, and RA 3 BS WD, Jan.–Apr. 1940, PRO, ADM 199/367 pt 1&2; AHS, *Home Waters and the Atlantic* I, 39-49

139. Adm to RA 3 BS, 20 Nov. 1939; Tucker, *Naval Service of Canada* II, 109

140. AWI WD, 19 Dec 1939; NCSO Halifax records, DHH, 77/553 pts 2-3; NWR 14 Mar.–9 May 1940

The large convoys and major warships now regularly sailing from Halifax, vulnerable as they were to submarine attack, fortunately encountered no U-boats.[141] Through all of October and much of November there were only two RCN destroyers, *St Laurent* and *Fraser*, available for operations at Halifax, *Skeena* having entered dry dock for refit and the installation of asdic. The two destroyers were at sea almost constantly, making the 400-mile run out the approaches with each convoy and screening major British warships entering and leaving port. There was no question of getting *Saguenay* back from the Caribbean without a relief. Aside from the increased threat from the Kriegsmarine's surface warships, strengthened patrols were needed off neutral ports in the Caribbean to ensure that German merchant vessels that had taken refuge there did not break out to supply the raiders. Canada had purchased the destroyer HMS *Kempenfelt* under the last peacetime estimates, but although, for the sake of good relations with Canada, the British government had not cancelled the sale, as they had in the case of warship sales to other countries, they did ask to retain the ship until auxiliary antisubmarine vessels were taken up.[142] Repairs necessitated by *Kempenfelt*'s involvement in a collision then delayed her commissioning as HMCS *Assiniboine* until 19 October. After work-ups in British waters, she arrived at Halifax on 17 November. Since she had been rushed into service without the usual fitting of a steam heating system essential for winter operations in Canadian waters, she changed places with *Saguenay* in the Caribbean.[143] The two remaining RCN destroyers, *Restigouche* and *Ottawa*, were not able to join from the west coast until 7 December. At the time of the convoy reorganization in early October the Admiralty had offered to send a cruiser to Esquimalt so that the destroyers could be transferred to the Atlantic, but it was six weeks before the cruiser could make her way from Britain, and the destroyers needed that time to complete essential refits. Departing from Esquimalt on 15 November, they had to steam at economical speed to make the long passage from Esquimalt to the Cocos Islands west of Central America, where they refuelled from the cruiser HMAS *Perth* before transiting the Panama Canal.[144]

––––––––––

The buildup of the large British ocean escort force in the western Atlantic placed Rear-Admiral L.E. Holland, RN, commander of the 3rd Battle Squadron, in Halifax. Holland's three R class battleships operated independently, making it difficult for him to administer his force while shuttling

141. In February 1940, Adm Raeder, C-in-C of the German Navy, recommended sending two U-boats to operate in the harbour approaches, only to have Hitler reject the proposal "in view of the psychological effect on the USA." British intelligence, aware that U-boats might strike suddenly without any prior warning, had no way of knowing that Hitler's caution towards the US extended to a ban on operations in Canadian waters. It would be many months before the equipment, organization, and techniques needed to track German submarines through interception of their radio traffic were developed enough to produce useful results. Adm, *Fuehrer Conferences on Naval Affairs, 1939-1945*, 23 Feb. 1940; P. Beesly, *Very Special Intelligence* (New York 1981), ch 2; AHS, *Home Waters and the Atlantic* I, 49-50

142. M Branch min, 5 Sep. 1939, DOP min, 6 Sep. 1939, Adm to DO, 8 Sep. 1939, PRO, ADM 1/10208. At the outbreak of war, the RN had taken over the contracts of 6 H class and two I class destroyers building in British yards for Brazil and Turkey respectively. M.J. Whitley, *Destroyers of World War II* (Annapolis 1988), 112-13; AWI WD, Oct.–Nov 1939; "*Skeena* History," 12 Dec. 1956, 8, DHH, HMCS *Skeena* I 8000

143. *Saguenay* reached Halifax on 23 Nov. and *Assiniboine* arrived at Kingston, Jamaica, on 8 Dec. "*Assiniboine* History," 16 Nov. 1961, 3-6, DHH, HMCS *Assiniboine* 8000; "*Saguenay* History," 31 Oct. 1956, DHH, HMCS *Saguenay* I 8000

144. American neutrality laws stipulated that warships of belligerent nations refuelling in US ports could only take on enough fuel to return to the nearest belligerent port, i.e., Esquimalt. This had not applied to *Fraser* and *St Laurent*, which sailed before Canada was at war. *Ottawa* ROP, 15 Dec. 1939, NAC, RG 24, 4012, NSC 1057-61-3 pt 1

back and forth across the ocean, and he therefore moved his flag ashore on 24 October 1939. NSHQ had evidently been satisfied with the Admiralty's assurance that "Rear-Admiral's duties would be strictly limited to administration and organization of [ocean] escort force ... and would in no way interfere with present responsibility of RCN authorities regarding organization of convoys themselves or command of the base."[145] Within less than three weeks, Nelles appealed directly to the First Sea Lord, Admiral Sir Dudley Pound, to withdraw Rear-Admiral Holland from Halifax. Captain Reid, Nelles explained, would be promoted Commodore on 1 January 1940, and he should then become the sole operating authority on the Canadian seaboard. Reid already assigned RCN destroyers and arranged for air cover from Eastern Air Command in accordance with the wishes of the Commander-in-Chief, AWI. There was no reason why he could not also interpret and transmit Admiral Holland's instructions for British ocean escorts:

> It is believed that considerable overlapping takes place in the work of Rear-Admiral 3rd Battle Squadron and Commanding Officer Atlantic Coast particularly since the administration of the port and Dockyard facilities is a Canadian affair and Rear-Admiral 3rd Battle Squadron must ask COAC to arrange berths, refuelling, provisioning etc. for HM Ships. By First January the staff of COAC will be augmented to such an extent that he will be able to undertake any duties now carried out by RA Third BS and it will be unnecessary for that officer to remain after that date ... The inherent difficulty of the present arrangement whereby a senior officer of the RCN is placed in a position of inferior authority in his own port is caused by the fact that of necessity, the equivalent ranks and responsibilities in the RCN have been scaled to meet our resources.[146]

The last sentence tends to confirm Admiral Holland's view that the whole question had been raised by Reid, who he claimed was furious about being outranked by a British officer ashore.[147] But there was more at issue than injured pride. Reid was determined that the senior Canadian officer at Halifax should control operations at sea as well as services at ports, which was why—in June 1939—he had urged the creation of a large staff on the outbreak of war.[148] Despite initial reluctance at NSHQ because of the shortage of qualified officers, from the first days of mobilization the organization rapidly expanded along the lines that Reid had recommended. In September he received a personal secretariat of two officers and was also relieved of direct responsibility for technical services in the dockyard by the appointment of a senior commander as Naval Superintendent.[149]

At the end of the year, a second senior commander—the Commander-in-Charge, Halifax—who had his own staff officer and secretariat, relieved Reid of immediate responsibility for the mushrooming shore establishments and the port defence and auxiliary craft organizations. Only the essential operational staffs—operations, intelligence, signals, antisubmarine, and the Naval Control Service—reported directly to Reid. All this freed him to focus on operational matters.[150]

---

145. NSHQ to COAC and RA 3 BS, 23 Nov. 1939, quoting Adm signal 1700/15 Oct. 1939, DHH, HMS *Seaborn* 8000

146. CNS to First Sea Lord, 13 Nov. 1939, DHH, HMS *Seaborn* 8000

147. "Report of RAdm L.E. Holland, 23 Dec. 1939"

148. Reid to NSec, 1 June 1939, NAC, RG 24, 3832, NSS 1017-10-1 pt 2

149. *Canadian Navy List*, 15 Oct. 1939, 35-6, 39-40

150. Ibid, 15 Mar. 1940, 41-3

It also increased the size of the staff at Halifax from four officers before the war to fifty-nine in October 1939.[151] By March 1940 it had grown to 102, compared with only thirty-eight officers at NSHQ and fifty-five under the COPC at Esquimalt.[152] That notwithstanding, the First Sea Lord pointedly reminded Nelles when he responded to the Canadian signal of 13 November, that no RCN officer had ever commanded a force of anything like the size of Admiral Holland's squadron. Pound proposed that if Holland was such a thorn in the side of the Halifax organization, he would simply shift his flag to *Resolution* and run the force from the battleship.[153]

Nelles and Norman Rogers, now the Minister of National Defence, were able to work out a compromise when they visited Halifax at the end of November. Holland explained that he had done everything possible to show that he was a guest at Halifax, and not the senior naval authority; he had not flown his flag at the offices that had been found for him at EAC headquarters and, when consultation was necessary, he invariably went to see Reid in the dockyard rather than summoning the Canadian officer. The sole difficulty for Reid was Holland's presence on shore. Nelles and Rogers, therefore, arranged for the transfer of a large yacht, which had been previously requisitioned by the RCN, for use by the Rear-Admiral 3rd Battle Squadron.[154] Commissioned as HMS *Seaborn* on 1 January 1940, she was permanently tied alongside at the dockyard. Although now "afloat," the British admiral still had the advantages, such as superior communications and close contact with refit, fuelling, and other support facilities, of a headquarters on shore.[155]

Having made his bid of 13 November for Canadian control of the British force, Nelles had evidently accepted Pound's rebuff. By the end of 1942, however, Nelles's earlier unreserved praise of Reid's abilities had been coloured by profound doubts about the latter's "anti-RN attitude which seems to give him a strange inferiority complex."[156] That assessment may have originated in the November 1939 affair, but nonetheless provides a revealing insight into Nelles's view of the limits to which RCN autonomy might be pushed. Like critics of thoroughgoing Canadian nationalism from the nineteenth century to the present day, Nelles was arguing that the true colonials were those who lacked the self-confidence to work closely for mutual benefit with Canada's great power friends.

In fairness to Reid, it should be noted that the relationship between the British and Canadian staffs at Halifax was an inherently difficult one, even after the Rear-Admiral 3rd Battle Squadron moved on board *Seaborn*. The Commander-in-Chief, America and West Indies, admitted as much in a 1941 report on Holland's successor in the ocean escort command, Rear-Admiral S.S. Bonham-Carter, RN (Reid, too, had long since departed from Halifax):

> He [Bonham-Carter] has done very good work under very difficult conditions; so have his staff, although some of the latter have not been too tactful vis-a-vis Canadians. Their view is, I think, that it is very hard to be tactful continuously for months at a

151. Ibid, 1 Apr. 1939, 21; and 15 Oct. 1939, 35-6, 39-40

152. Ibid, 15 Mar. 1940, 40-5, 51-3

153. Adm to CNS, 18 Nov. 1939, DHH, HMS *Seaborn* 8000

154. "Report of RAdm L.E. Holland, 23 Dec. 1939"

155. "Brief History of *Venture*," 13, DHH, NHS HMS *Seaborn*; RN Ship Movement Cards, DHH; B. Warlow, *Shore Establishments of the Royal Navy: Being a List of Static Ships and Establishments of the Royal Navy* (Lodge Hill 1992), 118

156. Nelles, conf rep, Dec. 1942, NPRC, file O-61610

stretch when they see that experienced advice is not truly acceptable. Whilst making allowances for Canadian touchiness, I do think the whole Canadian Navy has done well. I have had nothing but help from Nelles.[157]

The Conservative press was not so sympathetic. Word of the situation at Halifax had spread quickly, and the government felt compelled to respond at length in the House of Commons to the Toronto *Globe and Mail*'s mockery of the RCN's "ridiculous pomposity"—a reflection of the prime minister's own hypersensitivity about sovereignty—towards the RN officer who actually bore the major responsibility for protecting ocean convoys.[158]

The dispute ashore did not affect the intimate cooperation between the RCN destroyers at Halifax and the British ocean escorts. The 400-mile run through the Halifax approaches with each convoy that had begun in September continued through the early spring of 1940. After the expansion of the Canadian force to six ships in early December, three destroyers escorted the HX convoys, and two the smaller HXF series. In addition, a division of two destroyers provided local escort to units of the ocean escort force as they returned from overseas after each convoy cycle, and to other British and French cruisers and capital ships that visited the port. This monotonous routine was interrupted only by the occasional U-boat search in response to false reports, and the lavish escort arrangements that were laid on for periodic troop convoys that transported Canadian soldiers and airmen to the United Kingdom.[159] The first of these, designated TC 1, sailed from Halifax on 10 December 1939, and included five passenger liners with 7,400 men of the 1st Canadian Infantry Division. *Ottawa*, *Fraser*, *Restigouche*, and *St Laurent* provided the local escort. The aircraft carrier HMS *Furious*, the battlecruiser HMS *Repulse*—these two ships had been carrying out surface-raider patrols from Halifax during the preceding month—the battleship HMS *Resolution* and the cruiser HMS *Emerald* formed the ocean escort.[160]

Despite the threat from surface raiders, the most fearsome foe during the winter of 1939–40 turned out to be a wicked North Atlantic winter. In November seas breaking across the forward decks of the destroyers were so heavy, reported Commander Creery of *Fraser*, that their forward gun shield was "very liable to become 'dished' so badly that the gun cannot be worked." During the following month, as temperatures dropped, spray formed ice so quickly that despite the best efforts to remove it the forward guns of the destroyers could not be kept ready for action.[161] The official language of Reports of Proceedings do not convey the real danger of operating under these conditions, but some incidents stand out. On the night of 2/3 March 1940, while escorting HX 24, with winds of over fifty knots (or about 100 kilometres an hour), *Saguenay* was "pooped"—a dangerous occurrence when heavy following seas rush over the vulnerable after decks—no fewer

---

157. RAdm Kennedy-Purvis to First Sea Lord, 25 Aug. 1941, PRO, ADM 205/7

158. DND, pr 210, 5 Mar. 1940, DHH, HMS *Seaborn* 8000; HofC, *Debates*, 15 May 1941, 3063-4, clipping from *Globe and Mail*, 15 May 1941, both in NAC, MG 26 J4, 396, C278923-4

159. See the monthly ROPs for the RCN Halifax Force, Jan.–Apr. 1940, DHH, NHS, NSS 1000-5-12.

160. "*Ottawa* History," 8, DHH, 81/520 HMCS *Ottawa* I 8000 v 2; AWI WD, 10 Dec. 1939; C.P. Stacey, *The Canadian Army, 1939-1945: An Official Historical Summary* (Ottawa 1948), 6

161. HMC Destroyers–Halifax Force, ROP, 9 Dec 1939, Halifax Force, ROP, 5 Jan 1940, DHH, NHS NSS 1057-1-1 pt 1. The forward turrets on Canadian and British warships were designated A and B, while those at the stern were X and Y. Under severe icing conditions, a turret—usually B—was frequently traversed so as to keep ready for action.

than five times, and *Skeena* barely maintained control. On this occasion, as on many others, the returning Canadian destroyers performed a valuable service by seeking out stragglers (merchant ships that had fallen behind convoys and thus become extremely vulnerable to attack) and giving them sailing directions for regaining contact with the convoy.[162] In January the destroyer HMS *Hereward* was caught by a storm while on passage from Bermuda. She limped into Halifax leaking heavily from badly strained plates, one of the mess compartments flooded, the foremast snapped off, and her upper decks a tangle of damaged boats and equipment.[163] Rear-Admiral Bonham-Carter, who had replaced Admiral Holland in January 1940, confessed to the Admiralty that he had been completely unprepared for the severe weather; even the battleships required constant dockyard attention.[164]

While the destroyers pounded relentlessly back and forth through the Halifax approaches, the staffs ashore struggled to improve the fleet's antisubmarine capability. The Admiralty had warned of the potential gravity of the U-boat menace only months before the outbreak of war; the Canadian service had taken action, including the purchase of asdic sets for *Saguenay* and *Skeena*, but there was too little time and money for anything like adequate preparation. In September 1939 there were, at most, only eight ratings who had qualified as Submarine Detectors, and a handful on course in the United Kingdom. Only two officers, one for each coast, had taken the year-long antisubmarine specialist's course, both of them in the 1920s.[165] One of them, Lieutenant-Commander A.R. Pressey, who was appointed Director of Anti-Submarine and Anti-Submarine Defences on the staff of COAC, had been attending an antisubmarine net refresher course in England when war broke out; he stayed for another month to hone his rusty knowledge of asdic.[166] When Pressey returned to Halifax at the beginning of November, responsible for both antisubmarine equipment afloat and fixed harbour defences, he was inundated. The most urgent requirement, "aside from setting up a training program," was for a maintenance organization for the defect-prone asdics in the destroyers—the shortage of spare parts to make good damage inflicted by heavy seas on the hull installations, together with "the ravages of the enthusiastic amateur" repairmen on the ships, compounded their problems. An effective maintenance staff was desperately needed at the dockyard. Civilian technicians with the necessary basic skills hurriedly entered into the RCNVR and given a brief period of training, provided the solution.[167]

Antisubmarine training was rudimentary. Before the war all such training had been conducted in the United Kingdom and the Canadian navy only received its first antisubmarine attack teacher in the last weeks of peace. With its few qualified antisubmarine ratings required at sea, and its two specialist officers occupying appointments ashore, the RCN needed help in setting up its own train-

---

162. *Saguenay* ROP, 6 Mar. 1940, CO *Skeena* to CO *Saguenay*, DHH, NHS Sydney file 48-2-2 pt 2

163. RA 3 BS WD, 27 Jan. 1940

164. RA 3 BS to Adm, 13 Feb. 1940, ibid

165. A.R. Pressey, "History of Anti-Submarine Measures on the Canadian Atlantic Coast," June, 1940, DHH, 81/520/1000-973 pt 2

166. Service Record Card, A.R. Pressey, NPRC, file O-60170 pt 1

167. After *Manchester Regiment*, the merchant ship bringing stores of replacement parts from England, was lost in a collision with another vessel off Nova Scotia in early December, these technicians proved adept at improvisation. Pressey, "History of Anti-Submarine Measures." This account states that the shipment of spares was lost in the "*Manchester Guardian,*" but the circumstances described and the date suggest it was actually *Manchester Regiment*. See NWR 7 Dec. 1939.

ing establishment. The RN responded to NSHQ's request for instructors at the outbreak of war by sending out Lieutenant J.W. White and Petty Officer D.L. Cheesman with *Assiniboine* in November 1939.[168] They ran courses on board ships, and White supervised installation of the antisubmarine attack teacher equipment in the Anti-submarine School then under construction in the dockyard. Weekly sessions for destroyer teams in the trainer, and courses for officers and ratings slated for new construction ships, began in February 1940.[169] Two auxiliary vessels, HMCS *French* and *Acadia*, both fitted with the type 123 trawler asdics purchased before the war, offered sea training of a sort, but they had neither the draft nor the speed necessary to make this realistic.[170] British and French submarines, when they were in port, offered limited opportunities for destroyers to track real submarines, but they were no substitute for the permanent training submarine so desperately needed.[171]

More advanced training, especially important for the type 124 destroyer asdic, could only be obtained in the United Kingdom. The first group of twenty ratings for the Higher Submarine Detector course went to England in November 1939 and returned in April 1940, when a second batch of twelve ratings went overseas.[172] The first Canadian officer to take the long antisubmarine specialist course in wartime appears not to have qualified until June 1941. As the RCN's needs expanded, NSHQ resisted repeated requests for White's return, and he did not leave Halifax until March 1942.[173] He died only nine months later when HMS *Firedrake*, the destroyer in which he was first lieutenant, was torpedoed in the battle for convoy ONS 153. (See Chapter Ten) Commander Pressey's warm tribute left little doubt that White was the father of antisubmarine training in the RCN: "He had been loaned to the RCN in the early days of the war to take charge of a virtually non-existent A/S school, and the present school through which the majority of RCN asdic officers and ratings have passed stands today a monument to his skill, patience and industry." But no matter what White's accomplishments, the RCN was to suffer for not having an antisubmarine training establishment up and running when war broke out.[174]

———————

While her sister destroyers fought the stormy North Atlantic, *Assiniboine* (Commander E.R. Mainguy, RCN) was kept in southern climes. During the winter of 1939–40 the destroyer was on detached service with the America and West Indies squadron in the Caribbean, conducting constant patrols from Florida to the Venezuelan coast.[175] The work was largely uneventful, but during the night of 7 to 8 March, while on patrol in the Mona Passage between Puerto Rico and the Dominican

168. NSHQ to Adm 1629/16 Sep. 1939, NAC, RG 24, 3841, NSS 1017-10-22 pt 1

169. Service Record Card, James William White, RN, NPRC, file O-77490; Pressey, "History of Anti-Submarine Measures"; monthly RASS, Mar.–May 40, DHH, NHS NSS 1000-5-13 pt 2

170. Pressey, "History of Anti-Submarine Measures"; monthly RASS, Mar.–May 1940

171. Halifax Force, ROP, 9 Dec 1939, Halifax Force, ROP, 5 Jan 1940, DHH, NHS NSS 1057-1-1 pt 1; Capt (D) *Assiniboine* to NSec, 6 May 40, DHH, NHS, NSS 1000-5-12

172. RASS, Apr. 1940

173. COAC to *Stadacona*, 20 June 1942, James William White personnel file, NPRC, O-77490

174. Pressey to CNP, 24 Feb. 1943, NS 114-1-31 v 2, copy in DHH, NHS 1700-905 v 1

175. "*Assiniboine* History," 16 Nov. 1961, 6-11

Republic, the most convenient passage to the Atlantic, *Assiniboine* joined the cruiser HMS *Dunedin*, which had four hours earlier intercepted the large German freighter steamer *Hannover* outbound from Aruba.[176] The German crew had wrecked the steering gear and set their ship on fire. An onshore wind threatened to carry the steamer into neutral Dominican waters, but the Canadian destroyer immediately took the ship under tow, while *Dunedin* pumped sea water onto the flames. Later in the morning, *Dunedin* took over the tow, and *Assiniboine* put a party on board *Hannover* to assist the British sailors in suppressing the flames. After four difficult days, the two warships brought the listing hulk into Kingston, Jamaica. It was a fine piece of seamanship, and *Dunedin*'s captain credited the Canadian destroyer's prompt and professional assistance for the operation's success.[177] This adventure was the last in these waters for *Assiniboine*, who returned to Halifax for refit on 31 March, when *Fraser* took her place with the America and West Indies squadron.[178]

The Royal Canadian Navy had slipped more or less effortlessly into the administration of trade defence because Canadian naval personnel, instructed in British naval doctrine and linked with the RN's worldwide intelligence and communications network, had been training and exercising with the RN since the end of the First World War. Control of shipping procedures from that war were still fresh in the minds of certain senior RCN officers, and the Canadian government had been willing to cooperate in the maintenance and development of a shadow organization since 1918.[179] But expanding the navy, and undertaking the naval shipbuilding program that expansion required was a different matter altogether. The Canadian armaments industry of 1914–18 had quickly melted away and in any case had never manufactured sophisticated equipment. Except for submarines built by Vickers of Montréal for the Royal Navy, the small coastal escorts produced during the First World War had all been slightly modified civilian types.[180] Energetic efforts by industry and the naval staff to create a naval shipbuilding capacity in the interwar years had been frustrated by limited defence budgets and the reluctance of governments to support programs that might represent a tangible, material commitment to Great Britain, and create home-grown "merchants of death." *Skeena* and *Saguenay*, for example, the first truly modern destroyers acquired by the RCN in 1931, had been built by a British shipyard. When war broke out, as Chief of Naval Staff, Admiral Nelles had repeatedly warned his political masters, neither the overburdened Admiralty nor the British shipbuilding industry—itself suffering from the effects of naval disarmament in the 1920s and economic depression in the 1930s—were in any position to supply assistance or even full information to Canada.

The weakness of technical liaison between NSHQ and the Admiralty, and the effects of the Canadian government's caution, were strikingly demonstrated by the unusual way in which the

---

176. AWI WD, 29 Feb. 1940. At daybreak on 5 Mar., *Assiniboine*, who had to scramble to cover two widely separated anchorages at Curaçao, was able to give warning that the steamers *Seattle* and *Mimi Horn* had slipped out during the night but could not find them in a subsequent search. They escaped from the Caribbean, only to be lost when they arrived in European waters, "*Assiniboine* History," 8-9; AWI WD, 5 Mar. 1940; AHS, *Home Waters and the Atlantic* I, 15

177. "*Assiniboine* History," 9-11; DND, pr 290, 9 May 1940, DHH, 81/520 *Assiniboine* I 8000. *Hannover* would be converted to become HMS *Audacity*, the first escort aircraft carrier.

178. "*Assiniboine* History," 11; "*Fraser* History," 15-16, DHH, 81/520 HMCS *Fraser* 8000

179. RAdm L.W. Murray interview, Murray biog file

180. D. Perkins, *Canada's Submariners, 1914-1923* (Erin 1989), 59-87

naval staff learned of vitally important developments in British naval shipbuilding in September 1939. Early in August, in the wake of failures by individual firms to win British armaments contracts or to arrange concurrent British and Canadian orders, the Canadian Manufacturers' Association sent a large delegation to the United Kingdom to meet with the supply departments of the British services and study the latest designs and production methods for items that might be manufactured in Canada. This was the kind of private initiative Mackenzie King had always been willing to sanction because it allowed his government to keep at arm's length from the controversial issue of Imperial war production in Canada. Thus, the prime minister allowed A.G.L. McNaughton, president of the National Research Council and former Chief of the General Staff, one of his officials, and Colonel N.O. Carr of the army's ordnance department to accompany the delegation, and provided support through the Canadian High Commission in London.[181] Once in London, McNaughton used his close ties with senior British officers and officials to gain the delegation extraordinary access to information and facilities.

The Admiralty agreed that, as in the First World War, Canadian industry should concentrate on the smaller types of warships that could be produced without assistance from the United Kingdom. The only engines that could be readily built in Canada were reciprocating steam engines and small diesels—steam turbines, needed to power the larger and faster classes of warships, had never been manufactured in Canada—so the Admiralty supplied the delegation with basic drawings and specifications for the latest types of minesweepers and patrol craft, no prototypes of which had yet been completed in British yards.[182] Notable among the designs shown to the delegation was a new minesweeper, later known as the Bangor class, which at sixteen knots and 672 tons displacement was considerably faster and more versatile than the RCN's twelve-knot, 460-ton Fundy class.[183] The delegation also received two drawings and a good deal of information about the "whale hunting" antisubmarine vessel. During the First World War, William Reed of Smith's Dock Company had adapted his whaling vessel design for antisubmarine work. Faster, more manoeuvrable, and with a shallower draft than standard trawlers, these vessels were better suited for chasing submarines, whose movements and capabilities, after all, resembled those of whales in some important respects. When, in the spring of 1939, the Admiralty again sought a design for an antisubmarine vessel that could be quickly and cheaply built in yards without experience in the exacting specifications of naval construction, Reed successfully promoted Smith's latest whale catcher. This was the genesis of the 950-ton, 205-foot-long, sixteen-knot warship that would become famous as the Flower class corvette.[184] On 13 September, about a week after McNaughton returned to Canada, one of his officials turned the warship drawings over to Engineer Commander A.D.M. Curry, Director of Naval Engineering. This was the first detailed information about the new British designs to reach

---

181. "Report from CMA Delegation to UK," 5 Sep. 1939, NAC, MG 26 J4, reel C4288, C154961; Mackenzie King diary, 28 June 1939; Stacey, *Six Years of War*, 25

182. "Report from CMA Delegation to UK," 5 Sep. 1939, app 2, ibid, C154983-4; "CMA Mission to the United Kingdom . Final Report Shipbuilding Committee," 1 Sep. 1939, DHH, NHS 8200 (1939-45) pt 1

183. P. Elliott, *Allied Escorts Ships of World War II* II: *A Complete Survey* (London, 1977), 346; R. Barrie and K. Macpherson, *The Ships of Canada's Naval Forces, 1910-2002* (St Catharines 2002)

184. Tucker, *Naval Service of Canada* II, 30-1; Reed to Kerr, 31 Aug. 1944, "Report on Interviews with Mr William Reed, OBE, 17 and 18 Aug., 1944," DHH, NHS 8200 (General) pt 1. See also, K. MacPherson and M. Milner, *Corvettes of the Royal Canadian Navy, 1939-1945* (St Catharines 1993), 9-23, and J. MacKay and J. Harland, *The Flower Class Corvette* Agassiz (St Catharines 1993)

the naval staff. It had a profound impact on plans then being formulated for the Canadian ship-building program.[185]

Nelles's initial recommendation of 6 September, when the government requested estimates for sustaining a war effort until the end of January 1940, was that the program he had been pressing since January 1939 should be carried out. Two Tribal class destroyers and four antisubmarine/minesweeping vessels of the British Improved Halcyon class should be laid down. Eighteen Fundy class minesweepers rather than the twelve proposed in January should be built immediately, rather than over a period of years. "Here's hopeing [sic]," Nelles wrote in his diary.[186] How the naval staff set about implementing these proposals cannot be documented, but on the same date, in a response to the Canadian government's offer of military assistance, the Admiralty provided useful ammunition. Their Lordships stated that eight minesweeping and antisubmarine vessels must be available at Sydney, that a further six were needed at St John's, Newfoundland, and others for service in the West Indies. The British also asked about the "possibility of [Canada] building vessels, escort 'Black Swan' type, small Mine sweepers and Anti-Submarine trawlers for RN."[187] On 17 September, when Cabinet required long-term proposals from the three services, the naval staff added a large shipbuilding program to be initiated as soon as Parliament met to approve the new estimates in January 1940. This included two Tribal destroyers, thirty-six small antisubmarine ships, probably of the trawler type, ten minesweepers, and thirty-two motor torpe-do boats rather than the sixteen recommended in January 1939.[188]

Naval planners made the prescient argument that, as in 1918, Canada might face a U-boat cam-paign off the coasts of eastern Canada and in the Gulf of St Lawrence with little assistance from Allied navies. "To cover the large areas involved ... at least eight groups of five A/S vessels each will be required and this programme ... is designed to provide the forty A/S craft required." MTBs were for inshore naval reconnaissance in the Gulf and on the coast of British Columbia, "and to provide a ready means of immediate attack on probable enemy submarine bases in the various inlets on the North Shore of the Gulf of St Lawrence or Newfoundland."[189] By spring, when experience suggested German submarines were likely to attempt operations in the western Atlantic, there needed to be a trade defence system as extensive as the one in place at the end of the First World War. It would probably be necessary to run feeder convoys from Québec City to Sydney and Halifax.[190] Moreover, given the few RCN destroyers available and Britain's shortage of cruisers, there would be a need for escorts to deter surface raiders for convoys. The powerful Tribals were a long-term solution, but an

185. McNaughton, memos, 3 and 9 Sep. 1939, file "CMA Mission," NAC, MG 30 E133 v 241; Nelles diary, 7 Sep. 1939; Gill to McNaughton, 13 Sep. 1939, file "CMA Mission to UK" pt 1, NAC, RG 77, 57; Curry to CNS, 24 Jan. 1940, NAC, RG 24, 5607, NS 29-25-1 pt 2

186. Nelles diary, 4-6 Sep. 1939

187. BHC to USSEA, 6 Sep. 1939, *DCER* VI, 1303-5

188. "Participation by RCN Instructed to Work in Closest Co-operation with HM Forces," app A to CSC to minister, 17 Sep. 1939, NAC, RG 24, 2685, HQS 5199; ns, nd [but filed with RCAF and Militia draft estimates of 5-6 Sep. 1939], "Naval Service War Estimates to January 31st 1940...," NAC, MG 27 III B5 v 39, file D-94. For the acquisition of MTBs, see Donald E. Graves, "'Hell Boats' of the RCN: The Canadian Navy and the Motor Torpedo Boat, 1936-1941," *The Northern Mariner* 2/3 (1992), 31-45.

189. "Participation by RCN Instructed to Work in Closest Cooperation"

190. Nelles to minister, "Review of Naval Requirements"; Brand to Godfrey, 25 Sep. 1939, NAC, RG 24, 3841, NSS 1017-10-22 pt 1

immediate start could be made on converting the three Prince ships into armed merchant cruisers. Besides this, Canada could meet some of the Admiralty's requests by laying down two Black Swan class sloops early in 1940. Looking further ahead, it would be necessary, early in 1941, to lay down two more Tribals (and two a year thereafter, as Nelles had urged in January 1939), ten minesweepers, and sixteen MTBs.[191] With these recommendations came a steep price tag—the navy would need a total of $63 million for the period to 1 September 1940, of which more than half would be allocated to shipbuilding—and the warning that a good deal of assistance from the United Kingdom would be essential, especially in building the sophisticated Tribals and Black Swans. As it turned out, neither the full estimates nor substantial British help were forthcoming.[192]

The armed forces programs presented on 17 September had been drafted under the direction of a Cabinet subcommittee of senior ministers, formed because of Ian Mackenzie's ineffectiveness in Cabinet.[193] Minister of Finance J. L. Ralston was in the chair, a fact that foreshadowed the overriding influence financial considerations would have in shaping Canada's war effort during its initial stages. On 19 September Minister of Labour Norman M. Rogers was promoted to the National Defence portfolio, and Mackenzie took over the junior portfolio of Pensions and National Health. The subcommittee had reported to Cabinet the day before, 18 September, with the revelation that the combined programs of the three services for the first year of the war would cost some $500 million—the RCAF's estimates came to $136 million and those of the army to $328 million. This, Ralston's officials pointed out, amounted to nearly a third of the total income that might be expected by all levels of government in the country, even with substantial increases in taxation rates. Runaway expenditure on that scale might damage the nation's financial credit. On this basis, the chiefs of staff were instructed to make do with a total of $314 million, including the unexpended portion of the estimates originally voted for fiscal year 1939–40. The army's share was $188 million, the air force's $86 million, and the navy's $40 million.[194]

The process of cutting back the estimates bore more than a passing resemblance to similar prewar exercises. In late August King had been horrified at the Chiefs of Staff Committee's advice that a full army corps of two divisions should be sent overseas: this flew in the face of the government's repeated declarations that its policy was primarily for the direct defence of Canada and its commitment not to introduce conscription for overseas service. Thus, the chiefs spent a good deal of time during the next three weeks persuading Cabinet that the vast bulk of their recommendations was indeed essential for local Canadian defence; as Nelles laconically recorded in his diary, the ministers wanted to know "what to tell Parliament."[195]

The navy and air force programs were the ones most exclusively concerned with home defence, so the army sustained the brunt of the cuts. Only one division would be sent overseas, and one, rather than two, would be maintained in Canada. There was a striking absence of discussion about

---

191. CSC to minister, 17 Sep. 1939, NAC, RG 24, 2685, HQS 5199 pt 6

192. Ibid identifies Ralston as the chairman.

193. Although Ian Mackenzie was a member, the subcommittee's very existence had been his swan song. He had proved "really pathetic helpless," said the PM, in presenting the services' proposals in Cabinet. Mackenzie King diary, 15 Sep. 1939

194. Mackenzie King diary, 18 Sep. 1939; Maclachlan and DesRosiers to minister, 18 Sep. 1939, file 52, NAC, MG 26 J4, 395, C278350-2; Ralston to Rogers, 21 Sep. 1939, DHH, NHS 8200 (1939-45) pt 3; Stacey, *Arms, Men and Governments*, 14

195. Nelles diary, 5 Sep. 1939

the naval proposals. Nelles's insistence that his program provided the bare minimum needed for the defence of the coasts and shipping in adjacent areas, and his criticism of the government's pre-war naval policy as having put financial constraints ahead of strategic realities, was apparently accepted without demur. King's only comment in his record of the crucial meetings of 18 September on trimming estimates was the observation that the government had met "most of the demands of the Chiefs of Naval Service." His use of the plural may indicate that he was also refer-ring to the Admiralty's requests of 6 September.[196] Although shipbuilding estimates had been cut by more than half to about $15 million, King was not guilty of overstatement. Nelles told Cabinet on 19 September that $40 million was sufficient, and privately he was delighted to have received that much. "Inwardly think" he admitted in his diary, "that [the construction program possible with $15 million] is all our shipyards can cope with in next 12 months."[197]

When accepting the reduced estimates, Nelles unveiled a greatly revised version of his ship-building proposals featuring the British designs his staff had received a week before from McNaughton. The two Tribals and the conversion of the Prince ships remained, but in place of the four Bramble class antisubmarine escorts, thirty-six smaller antisubmarine vessels and twenty-eight Fundy class minesweepers, he recommended twenty "whale catchers"—soon to be known as corvettes—and twelve Bangor class minesweepers. He dropped MTBs for the time being.[198] The navy liked the new Bangors and whale catchers because they were not only simple designs, whose manufacture was within the capacity of Canada's technically unsophisticated shipbuilding indus-try, but they were also more capable ships and better sea-keepers than the modest, single-purpose Fundy class and the small antisubmarine vessels of the original program. Designed as an anti-submarine escort, the whale catcher could also carry a full minesweeping outfit. Bangor minesweepers could also make efficient antisubmarine escorts and coastal defence vessels.[199]

The large sophisticated Tribal class destroyers could only be built in Canada as a last resort under wartime conditions, so Cabinet authorized Nelles to suggest a "barter" arrangement. Canada would produce a sufficient number of Black Swan sloops for the Admiralty to free up facilities in Britain for the construction of Tribals for the Royal Canadian Navy—even then, a great deal of British help would still be needed, for the Black Swans were only somewhat less complex than the big modern destroyers.[200] On 20 September, however, the Admiralty replied, in answer to the naval staff's request to build Tribals on the Canadian account: "Regret that it is impracticable ... as we are now building to full capacity."[201] Canada had to concentrate on what it could produce inde-

---

196. Mackenzie King diary, 18 Sep. 1939

197. Nelles diary, 18-21 Sep. 1939

198. Ibid, 19 Sep. 1939

199. These types possessed most of the virtues that had originally attracted the naval staff to the more expensive and difficult to produce Bramble class escorts. See Brand to Godfrey, 25 Sep. 1939; Nelles to minister, "Review of Naval Requirements," 8; Tucker, *Naval Service of Canada* II, 32-3

200. "No armament, munitions, asdics, etc. available in Canada. Canadian shipbuilding resources can cope with Whale Catchers and below. Black Swans and, if necessary, destroyers, can be produced in Canada if the assistance of Admiralty Naval Constructors and Overseeing Staff is made available. Production of machinery other than steam reciprocating type at pres-ent doubtful." CNS to First Sea Lord, 22 Sep. 1939, Adm to CNS, 30 Sep. 1939, in "History of Barter Arrangements with Admiralty," 4 Mar. 1940, DHH, NHS 8200 (1939-45) pt 1

201. CNS to Adm, 16 Sept 1939, Adm to CNS, 20 Sep. 1939, in "History of Barter Arrangements"

pendently, and the Admiralty was especially anxious for corvettes, asking the Canadian government at the end of October to place orders for ten on British account even if a barter arrangement was not in the cards. Such was the pressure on British yards that no amount of Canadian construction of minor warships on the RN's behalf would make it possible to open slips for additional Tribals. Furthermore, the Admiralty's earlier suggestion that Black Swans might be built in Canada had been made in ignorance of Canadian conditions. No weapons or associated equipment could be supplied for Canadian-built sloops or destroyers, and the loan of constructors and overseers was "almost certainly impracticable." Although the Admiralty promised to supply guns and antisubmarine outfits for the RCN's own corvette and Bangor program, Their Lordships "desired to stress how important it is for Canada to obtain as much equipment, ammunition—and particularly depth charges—as possible, by full exploitation of her local resources amongst which the United States may be included."[202]

As the First Sea Lord already knew, Nelles was determined to have Tribals.[203] His reasons had at least as much to do with the RCN's past and its postwar future as with fighting the war. Fully two-thirds of a ten-page briefing on ship requirements prepared for Rogers shortly after he assumed the defence portfolio dealt with the Tribals, but only a few lines mentioned the current conflict. Rather, it repeated at length the original argument of January 1939 that a force of eighteen destroyers was the barest minimum that could afford Canada reasonable security even in peacetime. Indeed, Nelles now confessed, the January 1939 program had seriously understated Canada's needs. The naval staff had been too zealous in its effort to accommodate the government's financial concerns. To prove the point, he reproduced a study that had been prepared in 1935 by Captain L.W. Murray, then Commander-in-Charge at Halifax. Murray had concluded that at least twenty destroyers were needed on the east coast alone to ensure that the necessary strength, two destroyers, could at all times be concentrated against an armed merchant cruiser or submarine raider in the Gulf of St Lawrence and in the Halifax and Sydney approaches. At least half that strength again was needed for the Pacific coast. With the addition of eight-inch cruisers and then capital ships to the scales of attack in 1937–8, even the thirty-destroyer force became palpably inadequate. Cruisers were needed. So the January recommendations, "highly coloured by the knowledge that money could not be obtained to provide the complete answer," and that the time available to expand the small navy then in existence would only permit completion of the program then proposed, were now outdated. The Tribal destroyer program, in other words, was the very incarnation of the Canadian governments' penchant for modest armed forces, and it continued to be relevant both for wartime development and as the basis for the postwar navy:

> This programme is not designed to cope with hostilities against any particular country ... it is a purely defensive one. All these forces are required to combat a scale of attack in which the main force to be met consisted of an Armed Merchant Cruiser, or

---

202. The quotes are from the commitment to supply armament for the RCN minesweepers and antisubmarine vessels in Adm to NSHQ, 14 Oct. 1939, Godfrey to Brand, 16 Oct 1939, NAC, RG 24, 3841, NSS 1017-10-22 pt 1; on Adm order for 10 corvettes, Nelles diary 26 Oct. 1939

203. On 25 Sep., Brand informed his opposite number at the Admiralty that "CNS has already explained to the 1st Sea Lord his reasons for being very anxious to build Tribals which will be the best form of 'permanent' men of war for Canada to own in the long run." Brand to Godfrey, 25 Sep. 1939. For a detailed study of the Tribal acquisition, see M. Whitby, "Instruments of Security: The RCN's Procurement of the Tribal-class Destroyers, 1938-1943," *The Northern Mariner* 2/3 (1992), 1-15

a submarine, either of which are within the powers of any European or Asiatic country to produce, in spite of the protection afforded generally by the ships of the British Navy, or even of the United States Navy if allied to us. No ships of the programme will be available to add to the offensive effort of the Empire and our allies. It is therefore put forward as the absolute minimum of basic naval defence to be maintained by Canada in time of peace, regardless of the state of international politics, and any building which we may accomplish towards this standard during the war, will be of equal advantage when the war is over.[204]

Nelles had already suggested to Cabinet, albeit in equally obscure prose, that the procurement of Tribals must be tied to the provision of fully efficient Canadian crews. For that reason he was content to hold to the schedule of two ships per year originally put forward in January; it would take that length of time to train the necessary personnel without expanding training facilities.[205]

Among friends Nelles was more direct. He told Admiral Sir Frederick Dreyer, RN, who while serving as a commodore in HX convoys visited Ottawa in January 1940 to discuss the shortage of RCN escorts on the east coast, that besides wanting to win the war he planned, before the war was over, to have a number of Tribals, fully manned by Canadians, which "could not be wiped off the slate by whatever Canadian Government is then in power, as might be the case if only worn out Canadian Destroyers existed." A witness of previous retrenchment in the RCN—Nelles had been Flag Lieutenant to the CNS when the Canadian government imposed its ruthless cuts after the First World War—he rejected Dreyer's suggestion that the RN could at the end of the war simply give the RCN suitable warships surplus to British needs.[206]

Admiral Pound's discouraging responses of late September and early October had not entirely shut the door on the Canadian Tribal program. He had allowed that "Consideration will be given at a later stage to question of supplying Canada from existing [British] orders which have been placed." Nelles seized on this at the end of October to revive the barter proposal. In exchange for destroyers off British orders, Canada would lay down additional corvettes for the Admiralty. The cost estimates available in Ottawa suggested that five corvettes would be a fair swap for each Tribal. This time Pound agreed in principle. The First Sea Lord apparently saw an opportunity in Canada's willingness to undertake large-scale corvette production—the RN urgently needed the ships—and in the fact that Nelles's destroyer program looked to the future development of the Royal Canadian Navy, not to the early provision of additional forces in Canadian home waters. "Intermediate" destroyers of the RN's emergency program—O and P class destroyers equivalent in terms of size, performance, and armament to the RCN's River class destroyers—could, Pound proposed, be earmarked for the RCN. These ships were already building and would be complete in the spring of 1941. For the present, they would remain under British control in European waters, but

---

204. Nelles to minister, "Review of Naval Requirements"

205. CSC to minister, 17 Sep. 1939, app A, 3

206. As flag lieutenant to the head of the Naval Service, Nelles had witnessed his chief's desperate but unsuccessful efforts to acquire modern warships for the RCN until the last day of the war, and to the unhappy sequel: the government's ability to dispose of the motley fleet of minor antisubmarine craft and their "hostilities only" crews, and in 1922 to pay off three of five "gift" warships and the borrowed RN personnel who manned them, without a murmur of public protest. Dreyer to Sec Adm, 31 Jan. 1940, PRO, ADM 1/10608; Tucker, *Naval Service of Canada* I, 327-8; Eayrs, *In Defence of Canada*, 168-76; Hadley and Sarty, *Tin-Pots and Pirate Ships*, 291-303; Whitby, "Instruments of Security"

would be fully turned over the RCN no later than the end of the war and sooner if the strategic situation allowed. In the meantime, they could effectively become Canadian ships through manning by RCN crews at whatever rate NSHQ found convenient. In this way, the RCN could lend valuable assistance to the RN in meeting the immediate wartime crisis, while also gaining the ships and seasoned personnel needed to put the postwar service on a strong footing[207].

Nelles hesitated only because the Intermediate-type destroyer was offered. On 20 December he informed Pound that the RCN must have Tribals or their equivalent; the full armament of eight 4.7-inch guns was essential to meet the standard he had set in January 1939 that Canada's fleet must be able to counter armed merchant cruisers "singlehandedly," without assistance from allies. Obviously, cruisers were really needed, he explained, but because of the political and other constraints already known to Pound, the most powerful destroyers would have to be procured instead. Pound agreed to consider laying down two Tribals for Canada as part of the Admiralty's 1940 program.[208]

Nelles was already engaged in a bureaucratic struggle to expand the Canadian building program both for the RCN and the barter arrangement with the RN. When, in October, the government's senior financial officials began to consider estimates for the period after September 1940, he argued consistently and often against having "to adjust our building program to fit the money available, instead of to fit the strategical situation."[209] Another twenty corvettes for a total of forty, and sixteen Bangors for a total of twenty-eight, together with the entire group of thirty-two motor torpedo boats, were the absolute minimum needed for adequate protection of the east coast. They could probably be completed by the end of March 1941; thereafter ten corvettes, ten minesweepers and sixteen motor torpedo boats a year would be needed as replacements. The total estimated cost to early 1943, including the $15 million set aside in the estimates provided in September 1939 and the funds for eight Tribals, came to $111,860,000.[210] Ruling that an additional ten per cent had to be set aside as a "General Reserve," the Minister of Finance shaved nearly $7 million from funds available to the navy.[211] Nelles had to absorb the loss by cutting the shipbuilding allotment from $15 million to $10 million—"an absurd ... hopelessly inadequate" figure—but since much of the construction could not be completed until after 1 September 1940 there was no cause for panic.[212] Early in November, however, when the Department of Finance ruled that full funding had to be available for all projects initiated before September 1940, regardless of their completion dates, Nelles balked.[213] "That fright-

---

207. Adm to CNS, 20 Sep. 1939, CNS to First Sea Lord, 25 Oct 1939, Adm to CNS, 6 Nov. 1939, Adm to NSHQ, 15 Nov. 39, all in "History of Barter Arrangements"; Tucker, *Naval Service of Canada* II, 34

208. CNS to Adm 20 Dec. 1939, Adm to CNS, 1 Jan. 1940, in "History of Barter Arrangements." In terms of size and strength, the only viable alternative to the Tribals that the RN could offer were the L and M class destroyers then under construction. They were roughly the displacement of Tribals, had six 4.7-inch guns in new enclosed high-angle turrets, and eight as opposed to four torpedo tubes. They reflected the latest thinking in British destroyer design, but it does not appear that the RCN sought them as an alternative, or that the RN offered them. See E.J. March, *British Destroyers, 1892-1953* (London 1966), and Whitley, *Destroyers of World War II*.

209. Nelles to minister, "Review of Naval Requirements," 8

210. Nelles to ADM (Navy and Air), 12 Oct. 1939, NAC, RG 24, 3841, NSS 1017-10-22 pt 1; same to same, 30 Oct. 1939, NAC, RG 24, 2826, HQC 8215 pt 1

211. ADM (Militia) and ADM (Navy and Air) to CNS, CGS, and CAS, 20 Oct. 1939, DHH, NHS 8200 (1939-45) pt 3

212. Nelles to ADM (Navy and Air), 23 Oct. 1939, DHH, NHS 8200 (1939-45) pt 1

213. ADM (Militia) and ADM (Navy and Air) to CNS, CGS and CAS, 8 Nov. 1939, NAC, RG 24, 3841, NSS 1017-10-22 pt 1

ens me ... takes the wind completely out of my sails," he exploded.[214] Although he could carry on with the twenty corvettes he would have to slash the Bangor order from twelve to a single vessel and postpone the Tribal and Prince ship projects. To let the accountants run the war effort to this extent "is simply not facing our problem and is analogous to the ostrich burying its head in the sand."[215]

Rogers, convinced by evidence that Nelles produced of naval requirements in 1917–18, supported his Chief of Naval Staff.[216] On 28 November he informed the Minister of Finance that funds available for the 1939 shipbuilding program would have to be increased from $10 million to $25,650,000, the full estimated cost of the first two Tribals, the conversions of three Prince-type Canadian National liners to armed merchant cruisers, the twenty corvettes, and the twelve Bangors. Ralston claimed that there had been a "misapprehension" about his directives, but continued to declare his preference on grounds of "Parliamentary procedure and ... control over expenditure" for restricting the numbers of ships ordered in any given year to the number that could be paid for with the money that had actually been voted. He did allow, however, that there was a case for placing larger orders if that would result, through economies of scale, in savings in expenditure.[217]

Narrowly focused as it was, Ralston's comment struck at a central problem, which derived from the difficulties of technical liaison with the Admiralty. The naval staff's building program largely rested on educated guesses because the detailed drawings and specifications for the corvettes and minesweepers began to arrive only in mid-November.[218] Without this information it was impossible to make accurate assessments of the Canadian industry's capacity or the costs of production.[219] The Defence Purchasing Board, asked to establish contact with shipbuilders so that the program could be put on a sounder footing, replied that there was no point until full specifications were available.[220] For its part, an already overburdened Admiralty was hard-pressed to supply copies of the literally hundreds of drawings required. These were recent designs, and all they could do in most instances was pass the Canadian requests on to the private firms that had developed them. The firms were, of course, already under pressure organizing their own production and reproducing drawings for other British yards. Canadian firms, moreover, required a great deal of additional information because the designs had been intended only for production in Britain where practices and standards were often different—and in the case of shipbuilding, more

---

214. Nelles to DM, 14 and 16 Nov. 1939, NAC, RG 24, 3841, NSS 1017-10-22 pt 1

215. Ibid

216. "At the end of the last war, we had some 125 small craft based on Halifax and Sydney. The smaller number of craft now envisaged will look after Halifax and possibly the secondary convoy port of Sydney, which will be required next year. Until adequate naval protection is provided and depending on the action of the enemy, the defence of shipping in the St Lawrence simply cannot be coped with, a situation I feel certain the Government would not wish to countenance. Such a situation might easily result in all overseas trade from the East Coast of Canada being routed by rail through Halifax, a most uneconomical procedure." Nelles to DM, 16 Nov. 1939; also see same to same, 17 Nov. 1939, ibid.

217. Rogers to Ralston, 28 Nov. 1939, Ralston to Rogers, 5 Dec. 1939, NAC, RG 24, 2826, HQC 8215 pt 1

218. Curry to CNS, 24 Jan. 1940, NAC, RG 24, 5607, NS 29-25-1 pt 2

219. Nelles to DM, 16 Nov. 1939

220. Machlachlan to Vaughn, 27 Sep. 1939, Vaughn to Machlachlan, 30 Sep. 1939, NAC, RG 24, 5607 NS 29-24-1 pt 1

developed—than those in Canada.[221] Only on 9 December was the naval staff able to complete specifications that were necessary for shipyards to tender for corvette contracts.[222]

By this time, the Defence Purchasing Board, which had lacked the authority and resources to administer wartime expansion of production, had been reorganized and expanded as the War Supply Board.[223] With the specifications for tenders on the corvettes, the War Supply Board also received a request from the naval staff that the board investigate industry's ability to meet requirements for the full program proposed for the period down to 1943.[224] From these researches and the tenders for the corvettes, which were received from industry early in January 1940, the board concluded that economical production and the necessary expansion of building capacity could be achieved only with the government's commitment to a two-year program. In that case, thirty vessels—either minesweepers or corvettes or some of each type—could be built by the end of 1940, and another sixty could be completed by the end of the following year. On 7 February 1940 Cabinet approved, apparently without discussion, the two-year, ninety-ship program at an estimated total cost of $49,250,000 down to 31 March 1942. Ralston, evidently satisfied that economies of scale would be achieved, had joined Rogers and Howe in sponsoring the report to council.[225] The decisive support, however, undoubtedly came from the prime minister.

King's role in the development of the defence program after August 1939 was in many respects as ambivalent as it had been during prewar rearmament. It was he who imposed rigid financial ceilings and insisted upon close Cabinet control. Yet, for reasons that combined domestic political considerations and genuine concern about Canadian and Commonwealth security, he often pressed for more energetic action.[226] As it happened, the shipbuilding proposal reached Cabinet only four days after King had called a snap election for March in response to a resolution from the Ontario legislature that denounced the half-heartedness of the federal war effort. There was no doubt about the central issue of the election campaign, and on 29 January King lectured Cabinet on "the necessity of Canada getting under way with the manufacture of further arms, rifles, etc. and munitions for our own armies." Germany and the Soviet Union might soon control the Scandinavian countries and,

---

221. The frustrations that developed are well reflected in the response of a senior RN officer in Canada when asked by NSHQ to have the Admiralty expedite the shipment of drawings: "I have requested these and been rudely rebuffed. I have been informed Controller [at Adm] is collecting all the information and will forward it in due course, so don't depend on me. I would like you to shake up the Home [i.e., Adm] Departments if you can." Eng RAdm H.A. Sheridan, RN, to LCdr F.S.A. Heward, RN, for DNE, NSHQ, 16 Feb. 1940, NAC, RG 24, 5608, NS 29-25-1 pt 3

222. Curry to CNS, 24 Jan. 1940

223. The DPB, when created in July 1939 as a direct result of the political controversy over contracts placed with a Toronto firm for the manufacture of Bren machine-guns, had had the very different purpose of regulating private industry profits and protecting the government from charges of patronage. New legislation passed under the War Measures Act cloaked the WSB with wide powers and allowed simplified procurement procedures. A further important change was the transfer of the board in mid-November from the responsibility of the Minister of Finance to that of C.D. Howe, the energetic and aggressive Minister of Transport whom Ralston and King agreed was the "best man" to get things moving. J. de N. Kennedy, *History of the Department of Munitions and Supply: Canada in the Second World War* I: *Production Branches and Crown Companies* (Ottawa 1950), 4-5; J. W. Pickersgill, *The Mackenzie King Record* I: *1939-1944* (Toronto 1960), 27; Robert Bothwell and William Kilbourn, *C.D. Howe: A Biography* (Toronto 1979), 121-4

224. ADM (Navy and Air), memo, 7 Dec. 1939, NAC, RG 24, 3841, NSS 1017-10-22 pt 1

225. PC 438/7 Feb. 1940

226. E.g., Stacey, *Arms, Men and Governments*, 485-6

we might find ourselves where own coasts might be attacked on the Atlantic, and I thought quite possibly, before the year was out, on the Pacific, and our own position such that we could not get munitions from Britain ... the last thing the people would forgive would be any shortage at a time of need. I have also stressed the necessity of shipbuilding time and again, but have met with opposition on that score. That we cannot do more, etc. While I have been the one that has been pressing these matters strongly, and unable to make headway because of the arguments and colleagues, I am the one whom our opponents are blaming as holding my colleagues back and responsible for not having done more.[227]

King appreciated that Canada's own modest requirements could not sustain economical production of many items, and that requisite complementary British orders were not forthcoming because of the United Kingdom's need to conserve dollars and the ability of her own industry largely to meet supply needs in the peculiarly peaceful circumstances of the "Phoney War." The prime minister seems also to have realized that naval shipbuilding, because of the nature of production and the RCN's substantial requirements, was one area in which Canada could embark on her own program.[228] References in his diary to the danger of attack in Canadian waters leave little doubt that the outbreak and course of the war had sharpened King's long-standing concern about the vulnerability of the coasts.[229] When in December 1939 Rear-Admiral Holland visited Ottawa, King was clearly delighted to hear that "Canada had been wise in the purchases she had made. She had got the right kind of ships (destroyers) for the purpose of our coasts, and got the best value for her money ... [and] that Halifax, for a British station, was the most important from his point of view, in the world today. That, for example, he would say that the command of that station was much more important than the command of the Mediterranean."[230] The navy, in short, almost perfectly embodied the principles on which King endeavoured to build the war effort: substantial support for Britain but not at the expense of local Canadian defence, and a priority for industrial production over the "indiscriminate recruitment" of manpower for military service.[231] This, together with the modest scope of the naval program as compared with those of the militia and air force, probably accounts for the success of Nelles's appeals to Cabinet.

Still, in terms of scheduling, the ninety-ship program fell short of the naval staff's requirements. Nelles had hoped the first thirty-two Bangors and corvettes would be delivered during the spring and summer of 1940, when the easing of weather on the north Atlantic and the heavy traffic through the St Lawrence after the ice cleared in April and May might well bring the first submarine attacks in Canadian waters; he had expected that most of the minimum force of sixty-eight Bangors and corvettes were to be available by the spring of 1941.[232] When in January to February 1940 the War Supply Board placed contracts for sixty-four corvettes under the two-year program,

227. Mackenzie King diary, 29 Jan. 1940

228. CWCM, 8 Dec. 1939, NAC, MG 26 J4 423, C302580-5; Mackenzie King diary, 8 Dec. 1939

229. Mackenzie King diary, 6 Sep., 4 Oct. 1939

230. Ibid, 15 Dec. 1939

231. SSEA to BHC, tg 331, 20 Sep. 39, NAC, MG 26 J4 395, C278361-4; draft dated 19 Sep. and amended in Mackenzie King's own hand is in ibid, C278357-8

232. C.G. Power to C.D. Howe, 7 Feb. 1940, NAC, RG 24, 2826, HQC 8215 pt 1

it was already becoming clear that the schedule was slipping.[233] Few ships would be available during the 1940 navigation season (in the event, none were), and even in 1941 there would be fewer ships than the minimum required for basic protection on the east coast.[234] The situation would be graver still if the "corvettes for Tribals" barter scheme came into effect and ten corvettes per year had to be diverted to Britain, as the contracts placed for the sixty-four corvettes included the ten that the Admiralty had ordered in October 1939. These ten had always been regarded as entirely distinct from the corvettes for Tribals barter scheme, but in mid-February 1940 this changed as the strain on Canada's meagre shipbuilding resources became apparent. If the barter arrangement came to fruition, Nelles informed the Admiralty, Canada would assume the cost of the ten vessels in exchange for the first two Tribals; if and when Britain laid down additional Tribals for the RCN, Canada would lay down additional corvettes for the RN.[235] The new arrangement left the remaining fifty-four corvettes for the RCN no matter what became of the barter proposal.

The War Supply Board took up the Bangor minesweeper program only after building capacity had been allocated for the corvettes. Nelles had urged that contracts be placed for both the twenty-eight vessels of the minimum force and the first replacement batch of ten, but tenders received at the end of February 1940 had such unsatisfactory price and delivery dates that the board only placed contracts for fourteen. Additional canvassing turned up a builder for another four.[236] It was by ordering some diesel-powered Bangors early in March 1940 that the naval staff was able to complete the program. Production of these engines at Dominion Engineering got under way in July 1940. Contracts for ten hulls—enough to make up the minimum force of twenty-eight Bangors—were placed in late August.[237]

233. This total seems to have reflected the WSB's judgment, on the basis of tenders received and investigations of the industry, of the number of vessels shipyards could produce on schedule and at a reasonable cost. Tucker, *Naval Service of Canada* II, 37-8

234. The first 29, most of them laid down by May 1940, were not due for delivery until the end of the year. To meet the RN's pressing need, this included the 10 on order for the Admiralty, leaving 19 for the RCN. Another 16 were expected early in 1941, and the remaining 19 at the end of that year, so the full "minimum" force of 40 corvettes for Canadian waters would not be available until the 1942 shipping season. Even this, warned the E-in-C, might be optimistic. Nelles to DM and ADM (Navy and Air), 2 Feb. 1940, NAC, RG 24, 5607, NS 29-25-1 pt 2; Curry to DNP, 13 Apr. 1940, NAC, RG 24, 3841, NSS 1017-10-22 pt 1; Burgess and Macpherson, *Ships of Canada's Naval Forces*, 212-13

235. CNS to Adm, 16 Feb. 1940, in "History of Barter Arrangements," 4

236. Nelles to ADM (Navy and Air), 16 Feb. 1940, DHH, NHS 8200 (1939-45) pt 1

237. Nelles to DM, 22 Feb. 1940, PC 842/ 28 Feb. 1940, NAC, RG 24, 5607, NS 29-24-1 pt 1. There is some evidence that one difficulty was a shortage of capacity for the construction of additional steam engines. It may have been as well that the naval staff wished to broaden building capacity, for Canadian industry had some experience in manufacturing diesels, although none as large as the twin 1,000 hp engines needed for the Bangors. In any event, the invitation to tender for unengined hulls, on the one hand, and diesels, on the other, evoked an enthusiastic response. Carswell to NSec, 27 Mar. 1940, Davy to E-in-C, 5 May 1940, NAC, RG 24, 5609, NS 29-28 pt 1; Vancouver Iron Works to NSec, 23 Mar. 1940, Carswell to Shields, 25 Apr. 1940, Carswell to Sheridan, 25 Apr. 1940, NAC, RG 24, 5607, NS 29-24-1 pt 2; Tucker, *Naval Service of Canada* II, 43. Of all the diesels offered, only the sturdy Swiss Sulzer did not require major redesign of the hull, the crowding in of additional machinery, or the possibility of maintenance and operating difficulties with more sophisticated and less rugged equipment. The naval staff decided to run the risk of delay through domestic production of the Sulzer by Dominion Engineering of Montréal, which had never built the type, rather than purchase an American-built version whose high price would add nearly 10 percent to the cost of each warship (the estimate for the initial Bangor with Dominion engines was $557,250, as compared with $606,250 for one with American engines). Curry to Nelles, 7 May 1940, NSec to Carswell, 8 May 1940, NAC, RG 24, v 5609, NS 29-28-1 pt 1; Carswell to Howe, 5 Aug. 1940, NAC, RG 24, 3841, NSS 1017-10-22 pt 1; PC 4048/21 Aug. 1940, Curry to minister NS, 27 Sep. 1940, NAC, RG 24, 5609, NS 29-29-1 pt 1

As delays in the beginning of construction dragged on during the winter of 1939–40, the naval staff became increasingly alarmed about the coming spring and summer, when "it would be reasonable to expect never less than two submarines on this side," quite possibly equipped with mines as well as torpedoes.[238] The Gulf of St Lawrence, with its constricted shipping routes and broad expanses of shallow, mineable waters, was a special concern. There were only twelve patrol vessels available on the east coast, even when reinforced by the minesweepers *Comox* and *Nootka*, transferred from Esquimalt in April. Commodore Reid stated the need for at least twenty-four corvettes and four motor torpedo boats to cover Halifax, Sydney, and the gulf.[239] Admiral Dreyer, who praised the efficiency with which the RCN employed its few vessels, was nevertheless alarmed at the vulnerability of merchant ships to submarine attack as they slowly formed-up into convoys off Halifax, and he argued for an even larger force of twenty-four destroyers and ninety-two minesweeping and antisubmarine vessels. At least a sixth of all British imports, he reminded the Admiralty, came in the HX convoys.[240] The Admiralty replied that the RN's "limited antisubmarine Forces" were already fully engaged with the enemy in European waters. Nothing could be done until U-boats actually began to move to the western Atlantic.[241]

When faced with a shortfall of patrol vessels, the navy, as it had in the First World War, turned to the owners of large private yachts for sale in the United States. In December 1939 Commander J.W.R. Roy, RCN, Director of the Operations Division at NSHQ, travelled incognito to New York and Boston to identify suitable craft. To circumvent new American neutrality laws, yachtsmen, who generously agreed to enlist in the venture, travelled to the United States, purchased fourteen vessels and, from March to May 1940, brought them back to Canada where they were requisitioned. Eleven were allotted to the east coast and three, from the western United States, to British Columbia. On commissioning into the RCN they were given animal names, ranging from the benign *Reindeer* to the ferocious *Grizzly*.[242]

Four armed yachts began operations at Halifax and Sydney during the summer of 1940. The need for more extensive refits than had been anticipated and the press of work at shipyards delayed completion of the remaining vessels until the fall and, in some cases, early winter. Each was fitted with type 123 asdic—deliveries of sets ordered from Britain at the outbreak of war began in the summer of 1940—depth charges, and a 6-pounder, 12-pounder or 4-inch gun. At ten to twelve knots, most of the vessels were, at best, only marginally faster than the existing patrol craft, and some, proving unequal to the rigours of the open ocean, could only be employed in the immediate sheltered approaches of ports. However, seven of the vessels routinely carried out arduous

238. Director, PD, to Sec, CSC, 14 Mar. 1940, NAC, RG 24, 2722, HQS 5199-V

239. COAC to NSec, 22 Feb. 1940, NAC, RG 24, 11123, 501-2-1 pt 2; same to same, 7 Mar. 1940, NAC, RG 24, 6788, NSS 8280-166/16 pt 1; Burgess and MacPherson, *Ships of Canada's Naval Forces*, 26

240. Dreyer to Nelles, 27 Jan. 1940, Dreyer to Sec Adm, 31 Jan. 1940 and 12 Feb. 1940, PRO, ADM 1/10608

241. Adm to Dreyer, 2 May 1940, ibid

242. Copies of the most important naval service documents are in DHH, 81/520 Armed Yachts 8000, and several of these have been reproduced in F. McKee, *The Armed Yachts of Canada* (Erin 1983). See also, Tucker, *Naval Service of Canada* II, 24-6, H. L. Keenleyside, *Memoirs of Hugh L. Keenleyside II: On the Bridge of Time* (Toronto 1982), 22-30.

The passenger steamer *North Star* alongside during her conversion to the auxiliary cruiser *Prince Henry*, 11 August 1940. (NAC, PA 204670)

Top: Many corvettes were built in small Great Lakes shipyards. This is HMCS *Napanee* on the ways at Kingston Shipbuilding Co. Ltd., Kingston, Ontario. (NAC, PA 204281)

Bottom: RCN Flower class corvettes and a Bangor minesweeper, left, fitting out at Davie Shipbuilding and Repairing, Co. Ltd, Lauzon, Québec, June 1941. (NAC, PA 105423)

escort and patrol duty off the Atlantic coast during the years that ships were most desperately needed—more desperately than anyone had imagined in the winter of 1939–40.[243]

No less important than acquisitions of warships, as the RCN knew from its experience in 1917–18, was the provision of sufficient, adequately trained manpower for crews and shore establishments. Nelles's early expansion scheme of 17 September 1939 had estimated personnel requirements at a modest total active service strength of 5,472 officers and ratings by 31 March 1940 and 7,000 a year later.[244] At the end of October 1939, when the expansion program had been more clearly defined, he held to the first figure, but warned that 8,770 personnel would be required by 31 March 1941 and 14,385 by 31 March 1943.[245] Detailed estimates in early January 1940, based on the assumption that twelve yachts would be obtained in the United States, and that the three Prince ships, twenty corvettes, and twelve Bangors would be completed within the next fifteen months, raised the requirement for 31 March 1941 to 9,438 officers and ratings.[246] The expanded corvette program approved by the government in the following month and other new commitments including certain additional auxiliary vessels, lifted the target for 31 March 1941 still higher, to 11,450 personnel.[247]

Actual strength on active service as of 2 May 1940 was 6,528 officers and ratings, as compared with 2,673 on 22 September 1939. Table 1.1, which breaks down the totals for the two dates into the numbers of personnel from the permanent force, reserves, and volunteer reserves, gives some idea of how expansion was carried out during the first eight months of the war.

Table 1.1   Personnel Expansion, September 1939 to May 1940

Date	22.9.39	2.5.40	22.9.39	2.5.40	22.9.39	2.5.40
	Officers	Officers	Ratings	Ratings	Total	Total
RCN	191	215	1799	1,996	1,910	2,211
RCNR	74	287	71	1,103	145	1,990
RCNVR	132	437	406	2,490	538	2,927

Modest growth in the permanent force reflected the fact that "training in the RCN [was] being carried on as far as possible in the normal manner," and facilities for this full program were limited. As in peacetime, officer cadets, midshipmen, sublieutenants, and lieutenants received most of their training with the Royal Navy. Thus, at the end of April 1940 no fewer than forty-nine officers in these ranks, nearly a quarter of the total strength of the permanent officer corps, were serving in British ships and establishments. As already noted in the case of antisubmarine detection,

---

243. McKee, *Armed Yachts*, chs. 6-8, and Macpherson and Burgess, *Ships of Canada's Naval Forces*, 136-9, 219. There are some discrepancies in these brief accounts of armed yacht operations on the Atlantic coast that have been resolved by consulting the monthly Auxiliary Vessels reports filed with COAC WD, DHH, NHS NSS 1000-5-13 pt 3-4

244. CSC to minister, 17 Sep. 1939, app A

245. CNS to ADM (Navy and Air), 30 Oct. 1939

246. DNP to DCNS, 4 Jan. 1940, NAC, RG 24, 5586, NS 1-24-1 pt 3

247. Power to Treasury Board, 10 May 1940, Navy Estimates Book for 1940-1, DHH, 75/456

increased numbers of ratings also went to the United Kingdom to receive higher qualifications in the various trades that would be needed to man the expanded fleet.[248] The most striking statistic came from the RCNR, which experienced a nearly ten-fold expansion, largely because the crews of the civil government and private ships that were taken up volunteered en masse. A total of 875 personnel, including nearly 200 from the RCMP Marine Section, joined up. This enthusiastic response, as Admiral Nelles remarked, solved the problem of manning the auxiliary flotilla.[249] In addition, NSHQ continued to give first priority and every encouragement to the entry of qualified merchant seamen and officers.

Not revealed in these figures is the pivotal role played by what Nelles called the "hidden reserve." This included not only retired officers who had been earmarked for mobilization duties, but the still larger numbers of retired British and Canadian personnel who came forward at the outbreak of war. It was these experienced men who made possible the rapid expansion of shore establishments and ports services that were the navy's most fundamental commitment and the foundation for its seagoing operations.[250] Little is known of the ratings, but information about officers that can be gleaned from the *Canadian Navy List* gives some sense of the scale of the contribution. Of the some 372 officers serving in shore establishments at the end of April 1940, more than a third were old hands who had received temporary, wartime commissions (approximately fifty-two of 114 RCN officers, thirty-two of seventy-six RCNR and sixty of 182 RCNVR). At headquarters, the proportion was higher: nineteen of the forty-seven officers at NSHQ, twenty-four of the fifty-one officers on the COAC's immediate staff, and twenty of forty-one on the COPC staff.[251]

The chief limitation on more rapid expansion through additional call-ups from the RCNVR divisions was the meagre accommodation and training facilities available at Halifax and Esquimalt, adequate only for the service's modest peacetime requirements. By the end of April 1940 over 500 personnel were undergoing training at each establishment. In addition to basic new entry and seamanship training for recent recruits, the torpedo, gunnery, and signal schools, and the engine room branches at the two bases were continuing with long courses for permanent force ratings and shortened courses for RCNR and RCNVR officers and ratings.[252] In January 1940 Commander C.R.H. Taylor, Director of Naval Personnel, complained,

> Halifax and Esquimalt Barracks are overcrowded. There are over 900 ratings at Halifax Barracks which include crews under training for ships to be commissioned to early summer [this number also included all ratings serving at the various Halifax shore establishments]. Twenty-five percent of these are on lodging [off base] ... due

---

248. "Summary War Effort—Naval,"18 Jan. 1940; *Canadian Navy List*, 30 Apr. 1940, 22-3

249. CNS to Sec PM, 10 Oct. 1939, NAC MG 26J1, reel C-3747, 233068-70; COAC to NSec, 12 Sep. 1939, NAC, RG 24, 11063, 31-1-2; Nelles to minister, "Review of Naval Requirements"

250. Nelles to minister, "Review of Naval Requirements"

251. *Canadian Navy List*, 30 Apr. 1940, 42-59

252. In Esquimalt, 538 personnel were under training. The figures for Halifax, extracted from detailed reports by each school, suggest that 507 personnel were actually under training at the end of April 1940, and a further 29 officers had just completed their courses. The Halifax schools did not report in a consistent format, the reports are ambiguous on a number of points, and it is possible that some of the smaller training sections did not report. Halifax Training Reports for Apr. 1940, forwarded by CO *Stadacona* to COAC, 13 May 1940, DHH, NHS NSS 1000-4-13 pt 1; Esquimalt Training Reports for Apr. 1940, forwarded by CO *Naden* to COPC, 7 May 1940, DHH, NHS NSS 1000-5-10 pt 1

to lack of accommodation. The remaining ratings are accommodated in improvised accommodation in Rink, Gymnasium or any other building that can be made available. Instructors are taxed to the limit.[253]

By April the situation was worse. Expansion of the Halifax shore establishments and the training program had increased the number of ratings to 1394, but only 556 could be accommodated in barracks. Although the first blocks of temporary buildings were expected to be completed within a month, they would hold only an additional 400 ratings.[254] One rating, who identified himself only as "an RCNVR," complained to the minister in stark, if unschooled terms:

> The RCNVR barracks are a breeding ground for disease and is unfit for any human. There is approximately sixty-five reservists sleeping there, and there is only one toilet and three wash basins. The odor [sic] from the one toilet is so vile that it is only used in emergency. A great deal of the time there is no water so the one and only toilet and three wash basins are of no use anyway. It is to [sic] cold to sleep there nights, although cardboard has been put up at the broken windows. With the furness [sic] not being used there is no hot water. Seventy-five percent of the fellows have severe colds and the flue [sic].
>
> The food is good, but there isn't enough of it icredable [sic] as it seems. There is no reason for a shortage of food.
>
> There is a shortage of clothes, but we are left standing on the field for divisions while someone is sent to look for an "officer who didn't show up." A good many of these fellows are unfit to be on parade even if they had an overcoat.[255]

Officers at Halifax were, in fact, pleased at how well discipline and morale held up, while the administrative and supply systems adjusted to the demands of mobilization.[256]

The strain on the training organization led the Director of Naval Personnel to restate strongly the priority for qualified merchant officers who could be readied for service with short courses in only the essential military subjects.[257] By the end of May, however, Commander H.F. Pullen in charge of the Gunnery School at Halifax, was forced to conclude by the high rate of failure and weak leadership qualities among RCNR candidates that "the supply of Officer personnel from the Merchant Service has been exhausted." By contrast, Pullen praised the members of the RCNVR Supplementary Reserve, who, having received eight weeks basic instruction at HMCS *Stone Frigate* in Kingston, were completing their training on the coasts.[258]

If impoverished in training resources, the navy was embarrassed by the flood of applications for entry into the RCNVR from men whose only qualification, if any, was yachting experience. As early as 6 September 1939 the Admiralty had asked for all reserve personnel Canada might spare, and Nelles readily agreed that any beyond the 4,500 he then estimated would be needed by 31

253. DNP to DCNS, 29 Jan. 1940 (placed before 2nd naval staff mtg. of the same date), DHH, NSM

254. LCdr K.F. Adams, "Report of Activities in the Executive Branch during March 1940," 13 Apr. 1940, DHH, NHS NSS 1000-5-13 pt 1

255. "An RCNVR" to the minister, 20 Oct. 1939, NS 114-2-1, which appears no longer to exist, copy in DHH, NHS 1700-905

256. Adams, "Report of Activities in the Executive Branch"

257. DNP to DCNS, 29 Jan. 1940

258. Gunnery Officer Atlantic Coast, 1 June 1940, DHH, NHS NSS 1000-5-13 pt 1

March 1941 should be sent.[259] He pressed the point in early November, urging the minister that the many yachtsmen volunteering for service and not needed for the RCN in the foreseeable future should be sent to the United Kingdom for training and experience with the RN; they might then be brought back when the expansion of the Canadian fleet was at a more advanced stage. "This question is not being brought up entirely in an altruistic frame of mind," he noted:

> though such a contribution from Canada would be one of which the country could be proud, but it is also forced upon us by the fact that the Army and Air Force are rapidly approaching the state where they will be sending people Overseas and unless something is done to offer action at an early date with the tacit promise of further action for the remainder, it is very much feared that these people ... will be lost to the other Services who could promise quicker action.[260]

The Admiralty rejected Nelles's initial proposal that up to a hundred untrained RCNVR officers be sent to the RN "for at least a year probably longer," but was willing to take fifty so long as they stayed for the duration of the war.[261] This Nelles willingly accepted on the grounds of service prestige that he had alluded to in his original proposal. "I am ... prepared," he explained to the minister, "to release these 50 young men from home service to serve in the more interesting appointments overseas and represent Canada at the scene of active operations."[262] Selection of the fifty officers began at the end of February. Members of the Supplementary Reserve who had not yet been called up were eligible, as were experienced yachtsmen who had volunteered for service. Members of the nine "Royal" yacht squadrons across the country received preference.[263] Meanwhile, selection of a second batch of twenty direct entry RCNVR officers had begun in response to the Admiralty's request for personnel with education in electronics and engineering for radar and asdic duties.[264] The two groups, totalling seventy junior officers, reached the United Kingdom by the end of April 1940.[265]

The despatch of these personnel more than faintly recalled the raising of the Royal Naval Canadian Volunteer Reserve Overseas Division during the First World War. There was little doubt that because the RCN was fully extended in meeting commitments in home waters, the overseas effort would necessarily be a limited one. Indeed, during the first eight months of the Second World War, the RCN found itself thrust back to the Atlantic campaign of 1917–18. The early introduction of convoy not only threw an enormous operational burden onto the Canadian service, but in its very success—only five of 3,500 ships sailed in convoy in 1939 were lost to U-boats as compared with the sinking of ninety ships that were proceeding independently—raised the concern that submarines would again come to Canadian waters in pursuit of easier targets, and that the RN would again be able to render little assistance.[266]

---

259. Campbell to Skelton, 6 Sep. 1939, NAC, RG 24, 3842, NSS 1017-10-23 pt 1; CSC to minister, 17 Sep. 1939, app A

260. Nelles to minister, 2 Nov. 1939, NS 101-1-6 pt 1, copy in DHH, NHS 1700-193/96

261. NSHQ to Adm, 20 Dec. 1939, Adm to NSHQ, 30 Dec. 1939, NS 101-1-6, copy in DHH, NHS 1700-193/96

262. Nelles to minister, 29 Jan. 1940, NS 101-1-6, copy in DHH, NHS 1700-193/96

263. NSec to COAC, COPC et al, 20 Feb. 1940, NS 101-1-6, copy in DHH, NHS 1700-193/96

264. Ns, nd, NHS research note, "RCNVR (Special Branch) Personnel on Loan to RN (Based on Canada House File A/50/39)," DHH, HS 4425-150

265. *Canadian Navy List*, 30 Apr. 1940, 23-4

266. Grove, *Defeat of the Enemy Attack*, 302

There the similarities came to an end. The Canadian navy that went to war in 1939 had been fortunate in senior officers who had persuaded governments not to abandon entirely the maritime defence of the country between the wars. The RCN, with its modest fleet of six modern destroyers manned by professional ships' companies, was infinitely better prepared for war than it had been in the First World War. This was the force the senior officers of 1917–18 had desperately wanted and failed to get; on the outbreak of war in 1939 the naval staff's advocacy of the destroyer in the 1920s and 1930s was immediately vindicated.

Prime Minister Mackenzie King may have indulged in studied ambiguity, during the period 1937 to 1939, as to whether Canada would go to war at Britain's side, but never did he prevent joint naval preparations, and at the moment of crisis he allowed the Royal Canadian Navy to implement all essential measures in concert with the RN. The result was that the service functioned effectively as a component of the British America and West Indies Station, but at the same time was able, through the existence of a capable organization, to ensure national control over operations at Canadian ports. These two elements—intimate cooperation with the Imperial fleet and the safeguarding of Canadian sovereignty—were crucial to both naval leaders and their political masters.

The events of 1939–40 laid the foundation for Canadian naval planning during the Second World War. Remembering the antisubmarine campaign of 1917–18 and its sad aftermath, and having apparently found, in 1939, the key to gaining government support for their policies, the members of the naval staff had planted the seed for a postwar navy, what later came to be known as "the continuing RCN." Senior officers anticipated that, as in 1918, an antisubmarine and port defence service would undoubtedly fall victim to peacetime budget cuts. What would endure, they believed, would be a professional balanced surface warfare fleet. By early 1940, thanks to the prime minister's influence, the government had fully supported both the acquisition of British-built Tribals and the construction in Canada of small warships to the very limit of the industry's capacity. Both of these ambitious programs rested on the politically appealing requirement of home defence. In this light, the depredations of the U-boats and German surface raiders during the fall and winter of 1939 provided the ultimate proof for the RCN case that the navy was a national necessity, and not an Imperial extravagance. Despite delays, the shipbuilding program was now apparently off to a strong start. Large numbers of retired naval personnel and merchant seamen who volunteered for service had provided a margin for the orderly recruitment and training of new permanent force and reserve personnel. In the early spring of 1940 it looked as though the way was open for both the rapid expansion of an antisubmarine fleet and the more gradual development of the permanent, professional one. In view of Nelles's anxiousness for the RCN to be represented overseas by a small number of servicemen who he hoped would find dramatic and glamorous employment with the Royal Navy, it does not seem that the staff in 1939–40 actually intended the fleet to venture far beyond North American waters. It was a preconception that would not long survive the unexpected demands of war.

CHAPTER TWO

Responding to the New Challenge
May to December 1940

THE OPENING OF THE MAIN GERMAN OFFENSIVE in the west on 10 May 1940, with the invasion of the Netherlands and Belgium, greatly increased the danger of a German attempt, by subversion or other means, to disable oil facilities in the Dutch West Indies. *Fraser*, on station since 31 March, immediately returned to Kingston, Jamaica, embarked 273 troops from the British garrison, and landed them on 12 May at Curaçao to assist the Dutch authorities. In company with the destroyer, and also carrying troops, was the cruiser HMS *Caradoc*, released earlier by Nelles from British Columbia waters in view of the greater potential dangers in the Caribbean.[1] Canada offered two additional destroyers, but the Dutch naval presence in the West Indies made that unnecessary. RCN destroyers, suggested the Commander-in-Chief, America and West Indies, would be more useful intercepting Italian ships off the US coast if—as seemed likely—Mussolini brought Italy into the war.[2] There were in fact Italian trawlers on the Grand Banks, but when *St Laurent* and then *Restigouche* each made a two-day patrol in the area, during the week of 15 May, they found that reports of their number and sinister intentions were greatly exaggerated. There were only two Italian craft, neither of them behaving suspiciously. Nevertheless, Prime Minister King seized this occasion to announce in the House of Commons Canada's increasing commitment to the defence of Newfoundland.[3] It was a dubious claim in May 1940, but the successful German offensive sweeping across northwest Europe would cause upheavals that transformed the entire context of Canadian, Newfoundland, and North American security.

---

1. During one six-day period *Fraser* intercepted and identified no fewer than 80 vessels. "*Fraser* History," 16-19; AWI WD, 9-11 and 15 April, and 10-12 May 1940, PRO, ADM 199/367

2. SSEA to HC in Great Britain, tg 517, 10 May 1940, D.R. Murray (ed), *Documents in Canadian External Relations, 1939-1941*, pt 1, 7 (Ottawa 1974), 765. See also 816-18; CNS Ottawa to C-in-C AWI, 10 May 1940, NAC, RG 24, 6796, NSS 8375-4; C-in-C AWI to CNS, 1 May 1940, Nelles to milsec, 11 May 1940, NAC, RG 24, 6796, NSS 8374.

3. This was stretching the point. When Newfoundland revived the question of military assistance with Britain, and Britain could spare no forces, the Crown colony had perforce to look to Canada. The Canadian Army was installing coast guns to protect the iron mines at Bell Island in Conception Bay, and the RCAF was preparing to despatch aircraft to patrol the Strait of Belle Isle. But as the Newfoundlanders rightly observed, these measures were designed for the protection of Canadian territory and interests and left virtually uncovered such vulnerable and important island centres as St John's. Paul Bridle (ed), *Documents on Relations between Canada and Newfoundland* I, *1935-1949, Defence, Civil Aviation and Economic Affairs* (Ottawa 1974) 70-6; NSM, 13 May 1940, DHH; COAC to NSec, DND(NS), "ROP—Halifax Force, 1-31 May, 1940," 11 June 1940, NSS 1000-5-12; DHH, 81/520 HMCS Restigouche I 8000,"*Restigouche* History," 14

On 23 May, as the Germans threatened French and Belgian ports on the English Channel, Vincent Massey, the Canadian High Commissioner in London, telegraphed a British request for the despatch of all available RCN destroyers to European waters:

> Urgency due to possibility in near future of sea-borne invasion of United Kingdom ... Largely by means of destroyers that such invasion would be opposed and sea-borne trade in home waters maintained. Recent developments and the attitude of Italy have left the United Kingdom sadly lacking in available destroyers in home waters for these tasks. Furthermore, submarines in the near future certain to be very active against shipping but more especially in waters adjacent to the United Kingdom than in wider oceans. To this extent likelihood of submarine attack off Canadian shores has diminished.[4]

At a hurriedly called Cabinet War Committee meeting later that day, Rear-Admiral Nelles reported that of the RCN's seven destroyers, four were available for immediate duty overseas—of the other three, one was in the West Indies, while two were in Halifax dockyard under repair. Although it meant that the east coast would be without destroyer protection until the two in Halifax emerged from repairs in about a week's time, "in view of the extreme urgency of the situation," the War Cabinet agreed that the four available ships "should be made available at the earliest possible moment."[5] Mackenzie King, who was of two minds about committing the destroyers, was deeply moved the next day when he learned that his nephew, Lieutenant-Commander Horatio Nelson Lay, commanding officer of *Restigouche*, was the senior officer of the three ships that were sailing from Halifax. "He is the one chosen to take the Canadian navy into action in defence of the British Isles. One wonders if Canadian destroyers will come back. We may find our own coasts left bare in giving our last possible aid to the Mother country. That, however, to my mind, is right. We owe to her such freedom as we have. It is right we should strike with her the last blow for the preservation of freedom."[6]

Pressing as never before were the central issues that had dominated Canadian defence policy since at least the late 1920s: the implications of British weakness for Canadian security, and for the relationship of Canada and the Empire to the United States. When in late April King had visited Roosevelt at the president's retreat in Warm Springs, Georgia, Roosevelt had not masked his alarm at the Allied defeats in Norway, and warned of increased danger of attack on the North American seaboard. "I could see," King wrote, "he was quite concerned about the inadequacy of the defence of Canada both on the Atlantic and the Pacific. That our inadequacy of defence presented a real danger to the United States. I admitted that we had done very little comparatively speaking, and that in the circumstances we were doing the best we could."[7]

A month later, on 23 May, Hugh Keenleyside of the Department of External Affairs returned from Washington with a personal message for King from Roosevelt about the danger of Britain's defeat.

---

4.   HC in Great Britain to SSEA, tg 673, 23 May 1940, *DCER* pt 7, 845-6

5.   CWCM, 23 May 1940. In fact, the Canadian coast was not stripped of Canadian warships. *Fraser*, the destroyer on duty in the West Indies proceeded overseas, and the C-in-C AWI did not demand a replacement for service in southern waters, leaving three destroyers at Halifax. In addition, the C-in-C allocated the cruiser HMS *Caradoc* to northern waters under the control of COAC. AWI WD, 19, 24, 25 May 1940, DHH, PRO, ADM 199/367; Burgess and MacPherson, *Ships of Canada's Naval Forces*, 38

6.   Mackenzie King diary, 24 May and 4 June 1940

7.   Ibid, 24 April 1940

The Commanding Officers of the three destroyers rushed overseas in May 1940. From left, Lieutenant-Commanders H.G. DeWolf, H.N. Lay and J.C.H. Hibbard. (DND, N-33)

Capital ships of the Royal Navy were sometimes called upon to provide heavy cover to mercantile and troop convoys in case of an attack by German surface raiders. This is the battle cruiser HMS *Repulse* passing through the Halifax boom in August 1941. (DND, REA 393-14)

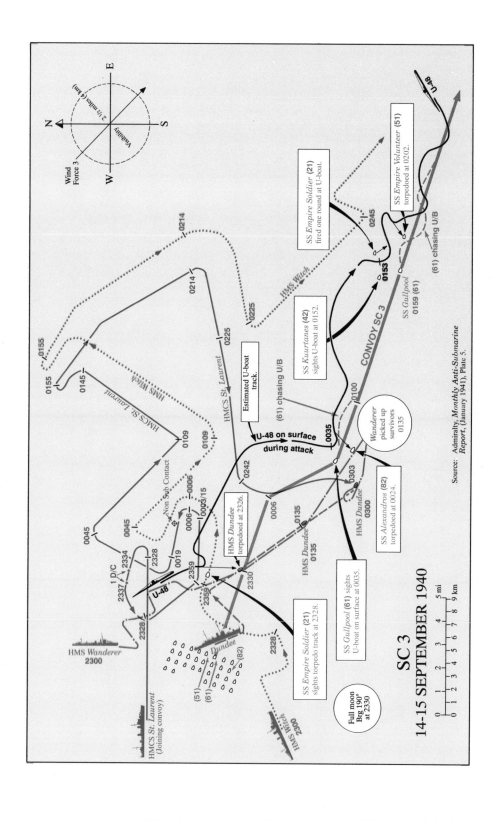

SC 3
14-15 SEPTEMBER 1940

Wind Force 3

Visibility 2½ miles (4 km)

SS Empire Soldier (21) fired one round at U-boat.

SS Empire Volunteer (51) torpedoed at 0202.

(61) chasing U/B

SS Kuurtanes (42) sights U-boat at 0152.

CONVOY SC 3

SS Gullpool (61) 0159

HMS Witch

Estimated U-boat track.

(61) chasing U/B

Wanderer picked up survivors 0135

U-48 on surface during attack

SS Alexandros (82) torpedoed at 0024.

HMS Dundee 0300

HMS Dundee 0135

HMS Dundee torpedoed at 2326.

HMCS St. Laurent

HMS Witch

SS Gullpool (61) sights U-boat on surface at 0035.

SS Empire Soldier (21) sights torpedo track at 2328.

Full moon Brg 190° at 2330

Non Sub Contact

1 D/C

U-48

HMS Wanderer 2300

HMCS St. Laurent (Joining convoy)

Dundee

HMS Witch 2300

Source: Admiralty, Monthly Anti-Submarine Report, (January 1941), Plate 5.

0 1 2 3 4 5 mi
0 1 2 3 4 5 6 7 8 9 km

Fraser arrived from Bermuda on 3 June, and Commander W.B. Creery, her captain, became senior officer of the Canadian force.[19] The ships went into dockyard hands at Plymouth to have their anti-aircraft armament strengthened—in view of destroyer losses from air attack in the Channel and off Norway, a 3-inch high-angle anti-aircraft gun replaced the after set of torpedo tubes and a pair of multibarrelled .5-inch machine guns replaced the two ineffective 2-pounder pom-poms— and the crews went to refresher courses ashore, just as Operation Dynamo, the evacuation of more than 338,000 British and French troops from Dunkirk was coming to an end.[20] Further south, the 51st (Highland) Division was falling back towards Le Havre at the mouth of the Seine; under Operation Cycle, a flotilla of warships and transports sailed for that port on the night of 9–10 June to take them off.[21] *St Laurent* and *Restigouche*, with scarcely a chance to try out their new weapons, sailed with them.

At Le Havre, all was confusion. The city was under heavy air attack—flames could be seen thirty miles out to sea—and the naval flotilla withdrew to the English coast during daylight to avoid German air strikes. The next night, the C-in-C Portsmouth, Admiral Sir William James, in charge of evacuations from northern ports, crossed to France himself in an MTB and learned that the 51st Division had been able to reach only the resort town of St Valery-en-Caux, a notch in the formidable coastal cliffs about forty miles northeast of Le Havre. He got word to the evacuation flotilla, again hovering off Le Havre, during the early hours of 11 June, and the ships arrived off St Valery about first light.[22] Destroyers could not safely enter the tiny harbour, so Lieutenant D.W. Piers and a signalman went ashore from *Restigouche* in her motor cutter. Piers found the 51st Division's naval liaison officer on the waterfront but could persuade neither the RN party nor the division staff to begin evacuation because their French area headquarters had given no order, and the British were prepared to fight on.[23] Meanwhile, *St Laurent*, under the command of Lieutenant-Commander H.G. DeWolf, RCN went three miles east along the coast, and brought off a detachment of forty-one French troops.

When *St Laurent*, having recovered her boats, turned back to St Valery, enemy shells began to splash near a transport in the vicinity. One of *St Laurent*'s officers, Lieutenant C.P. Nixon, RCN recalled the sense of unreality: "We were such innocent lambs for the slaughter that we saw these splashes near the ship and it took a while to dawn [on] us that they were German shells— 'My God they're firing at us. What a mean thing to do.'"[24] DeWolf manoeuvred to draw the fire

19.   Summary of *Fraser*'s ROP, 18 July 1940, DHH, 81/520 Fraser 8000 pt 1

20.   "Wanderings of the 'Restigouche,'" 5-6; "*Restigouche* History," 17; "*Fraser* History," 21. Several Canadians took part in Dynamo and related operations. Cdr J.C. Coulston, a Canadian in the RN, who sadly drowned as the operation came to an end, received special commendation for his service on the beaches; Midshipman Bob Timbrell, RCN, taken off courses to command HMS *Llanthony*, a small vessel in the evacuation, won the DSC. Sub-Lt Jack Pickford, also taken off courses, was mentioned in despatches for leading demolition parties to destroy as much as possible in Brest before the Germans arrived. Churchill Archive, Ramsay Papers. RMSY 6/6; DHH, Pickford biog file

21.   Roskill, *The War At Sea* I, 231

22.   HS, *Home Waters and the Atlantic* II, 120-1; "*St Laurent* History," 12-13, DHH, 81/520 St Laurent 8000; "*Restigouche* History," 17-19

23.   The naval liaison officer put Piers in touch with Division HQ by telephone. "Wanderings of the 'Restigouche,'" 2-3; Piers interview, 7 Jan. 1982, DHH, Piers biog file

24.   Nixon interview, 3 Feb. 1987, 29, DHH, C.P. Nixon biog file

away from the vulnerable merchant ship and opened up with his own main guns. The Canadians were unable to see the German position, which was back from the edge of the cliff, but nevertheless blazed away at the height of land.[25] "We felt better," DeWolf remembered, "once our guns were going."[26] It was the RCN's first exchange of fire with the enemy during the Second World War.

At St Valery, Lieutenant Piers's mission experienced further frustration. When casting off, the boat's crew discovered that the propellor had been damaged: "my God the boat would hardly move ... there we were, with a propeller shaft making a hell of a noise, going about half a knot."[27] As the boat finally struggled out of harbour, *Restigouche* came to the rescue. At 0745, just as the destroyer was hoisting in the motor cutter, a battery of German field artillery placed salvos within a hundred yards of the ship. As the boat was coming up to the davits, Lay ordered full speed and steamed towards the splash of each successive salvo to throw off corrections by the enemy gunners. *Restigouche*'s 4.7-inch guns, together with those of *St Laurent* and the British destroyer *Saladin* further offshore, blasted the cliff-top where the enemy was apparently hidden. The language of *Restigouche*'s Report of Proceedings was professional—"no direct hits were received, and only a few splinters came aboard which did no damage"[28]—but both Lay and Piers vividly recalled the terror of the "shrapnel whizzing through the rigging." "We were extremely lucky," wrote Lay; "I was bloody glad to get back on board," recalled Piers.[29]

The ships returned to Plymouth at best speed about an hour later, and for the next ten days the four RCN destroyers joined large British escort forces to bring in an Australian and then a Canadian troop convoy. These were long missions. The escorts joined hundreds of miles out to sea, and took the convoys into northern UK ports, to avoid the concentration of enemy aircraft and submarines in the vicinity of the Channel.[30] During the brief layover at Greenock, a motor boat carrying A.V. Alexander, First Lord of the Admiralty, came alongside *St Laurent*. DeWolf, still in seagoing rig, said "Welcome on board sir." Alexander replied, "No my boy, I've come to welcome you. I bring you a message from the Prime Minister." DeWolf called over the other captains, whose ships were alongside, and Alexander told them that the prime minister had asked him "to tell you gentlemen, that you have come at a time when destroyers are worth their weight in gold." It was, observed DeWolf in later years, "inspired leadership."[31]

St Laurent and *Skeena* remained in the Western Approaches for antisubmarine duty while *Fraser* and *Restigouche* headed for the southernmost corner of the French Atlantic coast to participate in the last phase of the general evacuation from ports south of the Seine. This had begun on 15 June, when it had become clear that organized French resistance could collapse within days. *Fraser* arrived at St Jean de Luz, a small port near the Spanish border, late on the 21st, the

---

25. "*St Laurent* History," 3; "*Restigouche* History," 15

26. DeWolf interview, 39

27. Piers recalls that the boat laboured for an hour, and the incomplete records suggest it may have been that long; certainly it seemed an eternity for he could hear gunfire not far offshore. Piers interview, 64

28. Both quotes are from a passage from the ROP (no longer extant) reproduced in "*Restigouche* History," 20

29. Piers interview, 65, 60; "Wanderings of the 'Restigouche,'" 9

30. "*Fraser* History," 21

31. DeWolf interview, 42

day the French government accepted Hitler's terms for an armistice. Next morning she ran north about seventy-five miles to the vicinity of Arachon, under orders from Vice-Admiral A.T.B. Curteis, commanding the 2nd Cruiser Squadron and senior officer in the evacuation area, to bring out Sir Ronald Campbell, the British ambassador to France. As the destroyer neared her destination she was hailed by a small sardine boat that was struggling in the ocean swell and driving rain. On board were Campbell, Lieutenant-Colonel Georges P. Vanier, the Canadian minister to France, the South African minister, and other officials, who had escaped Arachon shortly before the Germans arrived. Returning to St Jean de Luz, *Fraser* transferred the diplomatic party to the cruiser HMS *Galatea*, which departed for England, while Admiral Curteis shifted his flag to the cruiser HMS *Calcutta*. *Restigouche* had made a slow passage from Plymouth escorting the transport *Arandora Star*, and did not arrive until the late afternoon of 23 June.[32]

Both destroyers maintained an antisubmarine patrol off the port and their boats assisted in ferrying evacuees to steamers. The warships put into the congested harbour on the morning of 25 June to re-embark the evacuation parties; *Restigouche* also took off thirty-five civilians and Polish troops, including two generals. *Fraser*, meanwhile, remained to screen the crowded steamers as they took on their last passengers. At mid-day a detachment of French troops deployed a field gun on a hill commanding the port, began to train on the anchorage but did not fire. This the naval officers took to be a warning from French authorities that they intended to enforce the terms of the armistice with Germany that had come into effect at noon. The evacuation ended and the steamers slowly made their way out of port, to be escorted towards England by other British warships in the area.[33]

Calcutta and the two Canadian destroyers proceeded up the French coast, apparently to intercept a damaged French merchant vessel that without assistance would have had to make for an occupied port. Shortly after nightfall on 25 June, when the force was off the mouth of the Gironde River, about 150 miles north of St Jean de Luz, disaster struck.[34] The destroyers had been sweeping ahead of the cruiser when *Calcutta* ordered them to take up station in line astern as the cruiser's CO, Captain D.M. Lees, RN saw no need in that pre-radar era for the destroyers to continue the difficult task of keeping station on the bows of his ship on a moonless night under blackout conditions.[35] *Fraser* was about one-and-a-half miles off the cruiser's starboard bow and Commander Creery, who was on the bridge, directed the officer of the watch to turn to port, in order to swing in towards the cruiser and pass down her starboard side without crossing her bows. As was his habit in encouraging the junior officers, he allowed the officer of the watch to execute the manoeuvre. The officer ordered a turn to port, but only under slight helm that gave a wide turning circle increasing the possibility of *Fraser* crossing *Calcutta*'s bow. Creery did not realize this, and because of the imperfect visibility in the gathering darkness saw no danger; however, he ordered an increase in speed to twenty knots to hurry the manoeuvre.

---

32. "*Fraser* History," 21-2; "*Restigouche* History," 16; and "*St Laurent* History," 15

33. "*Fraser* History," 23-4; "*Restigouche* History," 17

34. WAC WD, entries for 1130, 1750, and 2006, 25 June 1940; AHS, "The War at Sea: Preliminary Narrative I—September 1939 to December 1940" (London 1943), 91

35. "Walrus," "The Loss of HMCS *Fraser*," *The Naval Review* 47/2 (1959), 174. Writers in this journal often use pen names; in this case the author was an officer on the staff of RAdm Curteis and was in *Calcutta* at the time of the collision.

Within a minute, as the destroyer accelerated and the distance to *Calcutta* began to close rapidly, Creery saw that the margin of error was exceedingly narrow. He instantly took control of the ship, ordering in quick succession increased and then full port helm, to tighten the turn inside the cruiser's starboard side. Tragically, Lees had misinterpreted *Fraser*'s wide turn as meaning she would cross his bows to pass down his port side and, at about the time Creery had tightened his turn, altered to starboard. Unwittingly the two ships had come directly onto a collision course.[36] When, seconds later, Creery heard the blast on *Calcutta*'s siren that signalled her turn to starboard, he went hard to starboard to check his swing into the cruiser's path, but immediately realized it was futile: the ships were closing at the rate of thirty-four knots. He therefore went hard to port and full speed astern on both engines to prevent a head-on collision. An instant later—just three minutes after *Calcutta* had ordered the change in formation—the cruiser's bow sliced half way through *Fraser*'s starboard side, inflicting mortal damage.[37]

Engine room personnel in *Fraser* had no idea what had happened when the lights went out, until Stoker Tom Kennington, sent up to investigate, saw the destroyer's bow "which had torn aft to the daymen's mess, then the stoker's mess, then the mess of the engine room artificers, and then broken *Fraser*'s keel. The forward boiler room was flooded and the tanks suctions came whack-a-mess and everything died."[38] *Calcutta* lowered one of her whalers, ordered *Restigouche* to pick up survivors, and continued on her way. Lay, unaware that *Fraser* had been rammed, found the after part of the ship floating, but saw no sign of the bow and bridge superstructure. He took off fifty-nine men when he brought *Restigouche* alongside what was left of the destroyer, and lowered a boat which, with *Calcutta*'s whaler, rescued another eleven officers and ninety-six men who had abandoned the fore part of the ship. Personnel on board the still floating hulk passed over medical supplies to the ship's doctor, who was tending the injured survivors in *Restigouche*. The most extraordinary aspect of this episode was that *Fraser*'s bridge superstructure, all that was left of the forward part of the ship, came to rest on *Calcutta*'s fo'c'sle, allowing Creery, the first lieutenant, the officer of the watch, and three hands of the bridge staff to simply jump on to the cruiser's upper deck. *Calcutta*, festooned with the tangled remains of *Fraser*'s bridge, was an unforgettable sight as she entered Plymouth harbour.[39]

Boards of Inquiry are routinely called to investigate the circumstances surrounding the loss of a warship, and in this case it blamed the incident on an error of judgment by Commander Creery. That was certainly true, but it is worth relating the impression of an officer on Rear-Admiral Curteis's staff who thought that fatigue was a factor: "Under such circumstances [the operations to evacuate forces from France] destroyers spent little time in harbour, no more than the few hours needed to refuel. Night after night at sea bore heavily on their captains and, to a lesser extent, on their officers of the watch. They were very tired men. Human nature is always fallible, but the

---

36. "Walrus" says Lees reacted by first ordering "Stop Engines" and then "Emergency full astern." Walrus, "Loss of HMCS *Fraser*," 174

37. "*Fraser* History," 25-7; "Loss of HMCS *Fraser*," DHH, 81/520 Fraser I 8000 II

38. Cited in Hal Lawrence, *Tales of the North Atlantic*, (Toronto 1985), 177-8. According to one account, those who came from below to congregate on *Fraser*'s stern initially thought the bow they could clearly see was the remains of a U-boat that had been rammed by the destroyer. P. Whinney, "The Fall of France: A Shrimp's Eye View," unpublished ms, 109, DHH, 88/144

39. Ibid; H.N. Lay, *Memoirs of a Mariner* (Ottawa 1982), 110-13

judgment of a man whose brain is clouded by lack of sleep is specially fallible."[40] Nonetheless, it was a tragic loss, not only because it had resulted from a mistake in judgment rather than enemy action, but because the small Canadian navy could ill afford the loss of a destroyer and the forty-seven men (nineteen RN sailors taking passage in *Fraser* after being evacuated also died) who lost their lives.[41]

The RCN had begun to pay the price of Admiralty.[42] Operations in British home waters would soon add to it. Admiral Karl Dönitz, *Befehlshaber der Unterseeboote (BdU)* or flag officer U-boats, had deployed submarines in the Western Approaches to the United Kingdom as boats completed refit in the wake of the Norwegian campaign. During June, a dozen or more boats on patrol sank fifty-eight merchant ships, the highest total for any month since the outbreak of war. Antisubmarine doctrine was in flux. The concept of convoy as an effective countermeasure to submarine attack received lip service, but there was a widespread feeling that destroyers, which were in critically short supply, were wasted in convoy escort.[43] The very immunity of even weakly escorted convoys had to some extent reinforced the prejudice that convoys were a purely defensive measure.[44] Even after the loss of the aircraft carrier HMS *Courageous* to the U-boat she was hunting in October 1939, the C-in-C Western Approaches, Admiral Sir M.E. Dunbar-Nasmith, as well as the Admiralty's Director of Anti-Submarine Warfare, held to the need for offensive schemes and, as corvettes became available to replace destroyers in escort groups, the expansion of hunting forces.[45] It was this role that *Skeena* and *St Laurent* took up in late June while *Fraser* and *Restigouche* were on the coast of France. The theory was that the warships would respond to reports of U-boats with a determined hunt. In practice, the reports usually came from merchant ships that had been attacked: the destroyers arrived on the scene some hours after the fact, made an unproductive search of the vast area where the submarine might now be located—the limited range of asdic meant that very large numbers of warships were in fact needed to saturate the area of probable location—and gained experience in rescuing merchant seamen, a task that Canadian warships were to carry out with depressing and increasing regularity.

The largest rescue took place from the liner *Arandora Star* on 2 July. *U 47*, the same boat that had audaciously penetrated Scapa Flow and sunk the battleship *Royal Oak* in October 1939 under Korvettenkapitän Günther Prien, had torpedoed the liner northwest of Ireland, only a few hours out of Liverpool. On board were 1,299 German and Italian internees and German prisoners of war, together with a crew and military guard of 374. *St Laurent* was eighty-four miles away screening

---

40. "Walrus," "Loss of HMCS *Fraser*," 175

41. "Loss of HMCS *Fraser* (River Class Destroyer)," DHH, 81/520 HMCS *Fraser* I

42. "If blood be the price of Admiralty / Lord God we ha' paid in full." Rudyard Kipling, "The Song of the Dead"

43. FO to The Marquess of Lothian (Washington), tg 1148, 17 June 1940, PRO, ADM 116/4656. On 15 June, only sixty-eight of the 133 destroyers in British home waters were available, largely because of the heavy operational strain they had been under since the outset of the Norwegian campaign.

44. On 20 March 1940, the DOP protested that effective protection of convoys was "the most satisfactory method of combatting the *unrestricted* U-boat menace," and on 21 March, the DTD pointed out that the safe arrival and departure of sufficient ships to meet the requirements of the ministries of Supply and Food took priority over the sinking of submarines. PRO, ADM 1/10468

45. DASW, "Review of Methods of Dealing with the U-boat menace," Feb. 1940, PRO, ADM1/10468; C-in-C WA to Adm, 5 Aug. 1940, PRO, ADM 199/2078

the battleship HMS *Nelson* when ordered to the scene about four-and-a-half hours after the *Arandora Star* had gone down. Advancing at full speed, the destroyer arrived at 1325. A Coastal Command Sunderland flying boat that had been circling the survivors and dropping food and first aid equipment in waterproof packs, homed the Canadian warship and guided her to clusters of men. "On reaching the position, ten lifeboats, all fairly well filled, formed a group, while the area to Windward (Westward) for two or three miles was littered with rafts and small wreckage, to which were clinging many survivors, singly and in small groups."[46] DeWolf manoeuvred slowly among what another officer described as "an absolute floating island of survivors," ordering all boats away to pick up individuals.[47] The destroyer rescued groups of three or four from rafts and heavy wreckage, "painfully slow work ... in many cases it was necessary to have a man over the side to pass a line around them and hoist them bodily inboard. Some were very heavy."[48] *St Laurent* lingered, at great risk in an area where a U-boat was known to be present, for over two-and-a-half hours until every survivor—a total of 857—had been recovered. They were landed at Albert Harbour in the Clyde early on the morning of 4 July.[49]

By July 1940 German aircraft and submarines posed an unacceptable threat to ocean convoys arriving and departing in the southwest approaches to the United Kingdom. Ocean shipping was therefore routed northward around Ireland; HX 55, the first of the Halifax convoys to take the northern route, rendezvoused with her antisubmarine escort to the west of Ireland on 15 July.[50] The northern route gave direct access to west coast ports, but the virtual closure of the English Channel forced sections of incoming convoys bound for the east coast north around Scotland to Rosyth, where they joined local convoys running inside the east coast defensive minefields. These were being expanded as rapidly as possible to afford further protection against U-boats. Similarly, outbound ships from the east coast ran north and joined their ocean escort at Rosyth. With the shift to the north, the area where Western Approaches escorts broke off from outbound convoys and met incoming convoys was moved further west, from 12° to 15°West at 50°North to 17°West at about 56°North, approximately 300 miles from northern Ireland or about two days steaming at the convoys' actual rate of advance of slightly more than eight knots.[51] Outbound convoys of transatlantic ships—the OA series from east coast British ports, and OB from the west coast—continued to disperse after the Western Approaches antisubmarine escort departed. All this necessitated a shift in escort bases, and within six days of the changeover, the RCN destroyers were working out of Rosyth.

The Canadian destroyers, now fully committed to convoy escort, observed a normal routine of five days out, north about Scotland, to 17°W, where they parted company with the outbound convoy,

46. FOIC Greenock to Adm, 4 July 1940, DHH, 81/520 St Laurent I 8000 (1937-43)

47. Capt C.P. Nixon cited in NOIC Ottawa, *Salty Dips* VI (Ottawa 1999), 97

48. Ibid

49. "The *Arandora Star* Rescue," *Crowsnest* 10/9 (1958), 8-9. The Italian internees sent word to NSHQ of their "profound gratitude"to *St Laurent*'s crew "for all they did in their endeavour to save the shipwrecked and for the kind attentions which were afterwards accorded." The government of the Federal Republic of Germany recognized the "brave and unselfish" efforts of the first *St Laurent* in 1957, when the new destroyer *St Laurent II* visited Kiel.

50. *U 61* and *U 57* each sank a ship from this convoy the next day. Rohwer, *Axis Submarine Successes*, 23

51. Adm to WA, 28 June 1940, Adm to COAC, NCSOs Bermuda and Freetown, FOIC NAS, 28 June 1940, "Convoy General," 1 June to 15 July 1940, DHH, NHS convoy signals cabinet; NCSO (Halifax) Convoy Records, Convoys HX 52-60, DHH 77/553 pt 3; AHS, *Atlantic and Home Waters* II, 190; Adm, *MASR*, July and Aug. 1940, 26-7; Rohwer, *Axis Submarine Successes*, 23-5

picked up an inbound one and brought it into port. Seldom working together—the escort for each convoy was usually only two destroyers, at least one of which would be RN—they then had a three-day layover and repeated the cycle. Dönitz had anticipated the northward movement of shipping and U-boats were patrolling the region, but not in great numbers. Boats deployed in the all-out effort in June had to replenish and the number on station fell to five or less. Indeed, the total number of operational U-boats had fallen from thirty-nine in September 1939 to twenty-seven a year later, and new boats would not be ready to replace losses until early 1941. Nevertheless, those on patrol in July 1940 sank thirty-nine ships.[52] By August, the availability of bases on the French Atlantic coast—naval detachments had arrived on the heels of the army to prepare facilities—compensated for the reduced numbers of operational U-boats. These new bases would prove an enormous strategic asset. Brest, Lorient and St Nazaire were 450 miles closer to the British northwestern approaches than German bases, and the broad approaches to the Bay of Biscay were not as vulnerable as the North Sea to British minelaying or air and submarine patrols. What was more, the well-equipped French ports did not suffer from the overcrowding that often delayed refits at the German bases. In the estimate of one authority, the use of the Biscay ports shortened the transit time to patrol areas by a week, thereby increasing a boat's time in the operational zone by twenty-five percent.[53]

The first antisubmarine action in which a Canadian warship actually confronted a U-boat took place on 4 August. *St Laurent*, now under the command of Lieutenant-Commander H.S. Rayner, RCN, and HMS *Sandwich*, rendezvoused with convoy HX 60 at daybreak in the vicinity of 17°W. During the night, about three hours earlier, *U 52* had torpedoed two of the merchant ships. The submarine was still shadowing the convoy, and at 0820 local time, about three-and-a-half hours after the destroyers had joined, she torpedoed SS *Geraldine Mary* on the starboard flank of the convoy in a submerged attack. *St Laurent* was screening about 1800 yards off the leading ship in the starboard column and closed on the *Geraldine Mary* as she fell out of line. While the convoy made an emergency 90-degree turn, *Sandwich*, who had been on the port side, began an asdic search and gained a contact, which *St Laurent* picked up immediately after.

Sandwich and *St Laurent* persisted in the hunt for three hours, each firing four full patterns of six charges and *Sandwich* another of four.[54] One of the shortcomings of asdic was that its sound waves projected at a fixed angle of about 45 degrees downward, so that as the warship closed on a contact, it disappeared under the cone of sound, requiring the hunter to fire its depth charges by guesswork assisted by a stop watch. The presence of the two destroyers enabled them to employ the standard tactics to overcome this deficiency. One ship held the contact while directing the second where and when to drop its depth charges, but the ships had great difficulty in maintaining contact as the extreme motion of the destroyer hulls caused by the heavy swell that was running seriously interfered with asdic transmission and reception. After the ninth attack there were no

52. Rohwer, *Axis Submarine Successes*, 22-4 shows 39 ships sunk in July in British waters, one of which was a destroyer, and a prize taken on 12 July by *U 99*, which must also have been in this region, and another ship sunk by *U 30* somewhere off Spain.

53. MOD, *The U-boat War in the Atlantic* I (London 1989), 48, and diagrams 3 and 9

54. The standard six-charge pattern was laid by dropping a charge from each of the two stern chutes, firing one from a thrower on each side, and then dropping a second pair from the stern. The pressure fuze on each charge was set to a different depth, in this case between 100 and 600 feet. The object was to catch the boat in a box of charges, one or more of which would with luck be within the lethal range of approximately twenty feet.

promising returns, so *Sandwich*, which had only two patterns of depth charges left, terminated the hunt and rejoined the convoy. *St Laurent* joined later after sinking the hulk of the *Geraldine Mary*.[55] *U 52* escaped, but because of heavy damage inflicted by the destroyers had to make for port, only eight days after she had sailed from Lorient on the French Biscay coast, and remained under repair for four months.[56]

As the Canadian destroyers settled into an escort routine in British waters, a worldwide shipping crisis was placing unexpected demands on the convoy system. The amount of shipping under British control had actually increased significantly, from about 18.7 million deadweight tons prior to the spring of 1940 to over 21 million thereafter, with the availability of merchant ships that had been abroad as their countries were overrun by the German offensive in the west.[57] Nevertheless, this windfall was not equal to the need to ship materiel by the longer routes necessitated by enemy victories. The proportion of British imports from suppliers in Europe and Western North Africa plummeted from twenty percent during the first eight months of 1940 to fours percent the following year, while the proportion from North America—more distant but now the handiest source of most commodities—shot up from thirty-six to fifty-four percent. Moreover, once Italy entered the war in June 1940, merchant ships bound for ports east of Suez had to avoid the Mediterranean and steam around the Cape of Good Hope, lengthening the run to Suez from 3,000 to 13,000 miles, and to Bombay from 6,000 to 11,000 miles. Britain had to supply these and other distant areas to sustain vital civilian needs as well as large military forces. Shipping capacity inevitably fell when ships had to sail in convoy, as was now necessary for a larger proportion of the merchant fleet, so efficiency in the worldwide control of convoys had to increase.[58]

In North America, vessels from south of Chesapeake Bay and the summer traffic from the St Lawrence River began to assemble at Bermuda and Sydney, Cape Breton, respectively, to sail in groups that rendezvoused directly with the main convoy at sea rather than backtracking to join at Halifax. The first HX convoy to link up with a Bermuda section, after Canadian naval control of shipping officers had gone to Bermuda to organize a staff there, was HX 41, whose main body sailed from Halifax on 6 May.[59] The RCN had also been making contingency plans for convoy

---

55.   WA WD, 4 Aug. 1940, PRO, ADM 199/372; HX 60, DHH 77/553 pt 3; CO HMS *Sandwich* to Sec to the Adm, 8 Aug. 1940, CO *St Laurent* to CO HMS *Sandwich*, 6 Aug. 1940, PRO, ADM 199/127

56.   *BdU*, *Kriegstagebuch* (KTB), 27 July, 5 Aug. 1940; C. Blair, *Hitler's U-boat War* I: *The Hunters*, 1939-1942 (New York 1996), 178

57.   Behrens, *Merchant Shipping*, 69, 91-103

58.   Ibid, 108-10, esp 109n1

59.   RCN planners at first balked at this because vile weather conditions in the northwest Atlantic would make the junctions dangerous, and the meagre forces available could not adequately protect the subsidiary groups. The Admiralty won the Canadians over by explaining that the link ups would take place beyond the Grand Banks fog belt, and that the most pressing defence requirements would be met so long as the sections were fully consolidated by the time the convoy reached the rendezvous with its antisubmarine escort in the Western Approaches to the UK. "Homeward—North Atlantic Convoys Summary to June 1940," nd, PRO, ADM 199/2078; NSec to COAC, 4 Jan. 1940, NAC, RG 24, 11079, file 48-1-11 pt 2; COAC to NSec, 18 Jan. 1940, NSec to COAC, 13 Mar. 1940, Nelles to Burrough, 5 Apr. 1940, NAC, RG 24, 11079, file 48-1-11 pt 2; Oland to Morey, 13 March1940, Morey to Oland, 20 April 1940, PRO, ADM 199/2078; NSHQ, "Outline History of Trade Division," 14

assembly at Sydney. The first Sydney section assembled and sailed on 31 July, under the local escort of HMCS *Ottawa*, to join HX 62.[60]

Increased shipping capacity achieved by this convoy reorganization provided only a partial solution to the crisis. Because North American supply was the key to survival, the entire system rested on the safe passage of increasingly slow and cumbersome convoys in the North Atlantic, menaced by a growing submarine presence and the occasional foray by surface raiders. Demands on deep sea vessels were insatiable. Slow, sometimes barely seaworthy ships had to brave the dangers of the sea and the violence of the enemy in all weathers and in all seasons. On 29 July, NSHQ received urgent appeals for instructions from British naval control of shipping authorities in New York and New Orleans, following rumours that convoys for slow ships were being organized. Masters of neutral vessels too slow for the nine to fifteen-knot HX series were refusing to sail unless they received a guarantee of convoy protection. They more than anybody knew that slow, independently sailed vessels were the most vulnerable to attack.[61] NSHQ, as much in the dark about a slow convoy series as the shipping officials, immediately queried the Admiralty. They replied on 30 July that as many as a hundred additional slow ships per month were expected to load at North American ports to move bulk items no longer available from the usual sources in Europe. The Admiralty proposed to organize a convoy for vessels of seven and a half to nine knots that would depart Sydney for the Clyde every eight days, which was to be designated the SC series. The expectation was that stockpiles could be built up that would allow the termination of the series in October, before the onset of winter weather increased the difficulty of sailing these slow vessels on the punishing North Atlantic. The only warships available as escorts were two sloops withdrawn from the West Indies, one of which was to sail with each convoy.[62]

Despite the short notice, SC 1 sailed on 15 August.[63] The Admiralty's instruction that no more than thirty ships should be included in each SC convoy immediately proved unrealistic. There were forty ships in SC 1, fifty-three in SC 2, and forty-seven in SC 3. The idea of terminating them in October soon went by the wayside as well. The SC convoys became a safety valve for overburdened HX convoys, which during the spring and summer of 1940 often swelled to sixty ships and more. The SC series, moreover, absorbed marginal ships that, despite the ardent claims of masters desperate to escape the fate of independents, proved incapable of maintaining the nine-knot minimum and slowed the passage of fast convoys.[64]

Dönitz, who had fully expected that the British would respond to rising losses by gathering an increasing proportion of vulnerable independents into convoy, initiated a new and intense phase of the U-boat offensive as the SC convoys began to sail. As a junior submarine commander at the

---

60. Slow deliveries of components from the United States needed to complete the antisubmarine net held up sailings until late July. *NWR*, no. 40, 20 June 1940, no 46, 1 Aug. 1940, DHH, NHS NSS 1000-5-7 pt 1; NSHQ to COAC, 1629/11 July 1940, "Convoy General," 1 June to 15 July 1940

61. Consul General, New Orleans to NSHQ, 29 July 1940, Consul General, New York to NSHQ, 29 July 1940, NSHQ to HM Consul General, New Orleans, 29 July 1940, Consul General, New Orleans to NSHQ, 30 July 1940, "Convoy General," 16 July to 30 Sept. 1940

62. NSHQ to Adm, 30 July 1940, Adm to NSHQ, 30 July 1940, "Convoy General," 16 July to 30 Sep. 1940; AHS, *Home Waters and the Atlantic* II, 191; VCNS to PM, 19 Aug. 1940, PRO, ADM 199/2078

63. COAC to NSHQ, 30 July 1940 and 1 Aug. 1940, "Convoy General," 16 July to 30 Sept. 1940; SC 1, DHH 77/553 III

64. Adm, *MASR*, Sep.-Oct.1940, 22

end of the First World War, Dönitz had witnessed the inability of individual U-boats to counter an expanded convoy system. He advocated a greater concentration of boats at the vital point, that is to say the convoy itself. From prewar exercises it was clear that close centralized command from a headquarters ashore—possible with the improvements in wireless communication—could, if fed with adequate intelligence, direct boats to move in support of the submarine with the most promising contact. That boat, the shadower, would track the convoy at visibility distance, trimmed hull-down on the surface so that it could not be sighted by enemy vessels, and would periodically transmit homing signals to assist other boats in closing. Once a group of boats was in contact, they would swarm the convoy, divide the escorts and throw them off balance, then strike repeatedly, rather than making the single or few attacks possible when only one submarine was up against an organized defence.

To succeed at what the Germans called *Rudeltaktik* and the allies "wolf-pack" tactics, Dönitz needed a substantial density of boats on each of the possible convoy routes. At sea, the largest convoys are visible at only slightly longer ranges than a single ship, and location by a few widely deployed boats, whose lookouts could search only to restricted ranges from the low conning towers, was a matter of chance, even if the convoy did not follow evasive courses. Moreover, visibility on the North Atlantic was frequently poor.[65] Submarines, therefore, had to patrol close enough to each other so that a convoy could not slip unseen between any two boats in an extended patrol line across the estimated convoy track. If U-boats could cover a line more than a hundred miles in length they could deal with any deviation from expected convoy courses, or even evasive steering designed to bring the convoy around the concentration. Depth of deployment, achieved through staggered, or "checkerboard" patrol areas, which, in effect, forced the convoy to pass through two or more lines of boats, was also important to allow for the arrival of the merchant ships on an unexpected course, poor visibility or a slack lookout in one particular boat. In theory, such a formation of numerous boats within mutually supporting distance of each other automatically helped to solve the second phase of the Dönitz's tactical problem: rapid reinforcement of the submarine that sighted and shadowed the convoy.[66] Full development of *Rudeltaktik* demanded at least a hundred boats in operational areas, which meant a total strength of some 300, given that a third of the boats would be returning from or heading to their patrol area while another third would be refitting and replenishing in port.

Dönitz had always attempted to concentrate boats against convoys, but his possession of only a tenth of the number he wanted greatly limited the results of these efforts. Access to the Biscay ports increased the strength of the force he could sustain in the northwest approaches, but the transfer of RAF Coastal Command aircraft to the area was already driving the boats out of waters close to the coast. It was here, where the density of shipping funnelling into port approaches had all but removed the difficulty in locating targets, that the submariners had had a field day since the end of May. Now the regular appearance of aircraft forced the boats to submerge, and with their low underwater speed they were unable to pursue ships.

---

65. In the "air gap" southeast of Greenland where many of the major convoy battles were fought visibility is less than five nautical miles between 20 and 30 percent of the time. Data derived from Office of Climatology, US Department of Commerce, *Climatological and Oceanographic Atlas for Mariners* I: *North Atlantic Ocean* (Washington 1959)

66. MOD, *U-boat War* I, 64-6

In theory, the withdrawal of the submarines seaward, where shipping was more widely dispersed and difficult to locate, should have greatly hindered their operations. In late August, however, the German naval signals intelligence organization, B-Dienst, which had penetrated the British convoy cypher, delivered an unusually large number of timely signals.[67] They provided the precise position and time at which convoys were to rendezvous with their Western Approaches escorts, positions that U-boats working from French bases had the range and endurance to watch even before the escorts for inward-bound convoys had joined, and after those for outbound ones had left. Because Coastal Command aircraft could not yet make sustained searches that far west there was little interference from the air, and because escorts were so few in number, convoys had to be routed on adjacent tracks through a narrow funnel into the northwest approaches, so that escort groups bringing out an overseas convoy could readily pick up a homeward bound one for the return trip.[68]

U-boat commanders did not take long to appreciate this situation during the last two weeks of August, and although bad weather prevented the desired centralized coordination by the few available boats, single submarines attacked five convoys and three boats combined to strike at a sixth. They sank twenty-one ships, bringing the total for August to fifty-six, only two less than in June. Most alarming was the fact that in spite of the shift to the north, and despite strengthened defences, more than thirty of these losses had been in convoy or among stragglers, compared with fourteen in June. Moreover, when *U 37* attacked SC 1 in the mid-North Atlantic, southwest of Iceland on the night of 24/25 August, sinking the sloop HMS *Penzance* and a merchant ship, it was a sign that U-boats could operate far to the west of previous areas, and the Admiralty warned NSHQ that a transatlantic offensive might be under way.[69]

In the first three weeks of September, U-boats attacked six convoys sinking seventeen merchant vessels and one RN sloop. The boldness and initiative of experienced U-boat commanders was the chief ingredient of their success. They attacked on the surface at night, when the looming bulk of surface ships stood out clearly but the small conning tower of a submarine was virtually invisible. The U-boats were therefore free to exploit their high surface speed of eighteen knots to gain a good approach position, close to point-blank torpedo ranges of 1,000 metres or less, and withdraw at speed to a course parallel to the convoy to reload for another strike. There was not much risk of effective countermeasures, because lookouts on board escorts sometimes even had difficulty determining if a ship had been hit, let alone which one or the direction from which the attack had come. Thus, these attacks were really night surface actions, which the Allies had failed to anticipate, even though the tactic had been employed by some U-boats at the end of the First World War. The surface attacks almost entirely neutralized asdic in the active mode, although it retained a limited

---

67. Normally only a small proportion of traffic could be broken, much of it too late to be of operational use, not least because there was often no submarine within reach of a particular convoy. For further discussion see, among others, W.J.R.Gardner, *Decoding History: The Battle of the Atlantic and Ultra* (Annapolis 1999), D. Syrett, *The Defeat of the German U-boats: The Battle of the Atlantic* (Columbia 1994), Ralph Erskine, "Afterword" in P. Beesly, *Very Special Intelligence* (3rd ed, London 2000), and J. Rohwer and W.A.B. Douglas, "Canada and the Wolf Packs, September 1943," in W.A.B. Douglas (ed), *The RCN in Transition* (Vancouver 1988), 126-43

68. Adm, *MASR*, Nov. 1940, 9

69. *BdU*, KTB, 16-30 Aug. 1940; Rohwer, *Axis Submarine Successes*, 26-7; Syrett, *Defeat of the German U-boats*, 148; CNS to sec to the PM, 26 Aug. 1940, NAC, MG 26 J4, 396, file 56, C278991; *MASR*, July-Aug. 1940, 7; *Defeat of Enemy Attack on Shipping*, 1B, table 13. It was not until 1943 that the RN admitted that the convoy cypher had been broken.

capacity to detect surfaced submarines when used passively as a listening device.[70] Reluctantly, Western Approaches Command had to abandon the hunting force concept "until such time as sufficient forces are available for every convoy to have enough escorts to ensure the destruction and detection of any U-boat attacking it."[71]

The Canadian destroyers, following these developments, shifted base westward from the east coast of Scotland to work from Greenock, on the Clyde, and from Liverpool, solely for the escort of convoys through the northwest approaches. The time was approaching when they would have to go into refit, which Admiral Nelles insisted be done in Canada, and to ensure their services were lost for the least amount of time he promised that the whole of the refit periods would be absorbed by early rotations from the meagre forces left in Canadian waters. So when *Restigouche* sailed for refit at the end of August she escorted two outbound convoys to 20°W, then proceeded independently for Halifax as *Ottawa* screened a troopship convoy eastward all the way from Halifax, arriving on 4 September.[72] Nelles's policy achieved two objectives. Personnel had the opportunity to take leave in Canada and, more importantly in the eyes of the CNS, he could raise the prestige of the service and improve its professional competence by concentrating the RCN's most effective forces in the active war zone off the UK. Although this entailed risks—only two operational destroyers were left on the east coast of Canada—it nonetheless paid dividends, as personnel based overseas could take courses not available in Canada, part of an effort to qualify some of the many additional seamen needed for warships building in Canada. So that advantage could be taken of training opportunities in the United Kingdom, the destroyers all carried extra personnel.[73]

The loss of *Fraser* had temporarily reduced the RCN's overseas commitment, and to ensure this would not become a permanent reduction Nelles went to the Cabinet War Committee with two options tailored to appeal to nationalist sentiment. Canada could either place *Fraser*'s survivors "unreservedly at the disposal of the Royal Navy" or, as he recommended, purchase a replacement destroyer for the RCN. Cabinet approved the purchase, which proved to have mutual benefit for the two navies.[74] The Admiralty offered HMS *Diana*, a D class destroyer, virtually identical to the three C class already in the RCN and thus easy to take into the RCN. The sale would bring a small but welcome infusion of dollars to the United Kingdom at a time when British currency reserves were pouring into the purchase of North American supplies and, because the ship would be used to

---

70. MOD, *U-boat War* I, 66-7. For a description of night-surface tactics derived from British experience, Adm, *MASR*, Sep.-Oct. 1940, 7-8; *BdU*, KTB, 1-12 Sep. 1940

71. Adm Dunbar-Nasmith went on to say, "Once this condition is satisfied surplus forces will be employed as striking forces," but his views were evidently not shared by key Admiralty personnel. Adm T.V.S. Phillips had advised PM Churchill in mid-August that "if the submarine is to do harm he must come to the convoy and that is consequently the place to put your hunters." C-in-C WA to Adm 5 and 26 Aug. 1940, and VCNS to PM, 19 Aug. 1940, PRO, ADM 199/2078

72. Adm to C-in-C WA, 31 Aug. 1940, NAC, RG 24, 6796, NSS 8375-4; *Restigouche* ROP for 25 Aug. to 5 Sep. 1940, 5 Sep. 1940, DHH, 81/520 Restigouche I 8000 pt 1; Adm to CNS, 2 Aug. 1940, CNS to Adm, 3 Aug. 1940, NAC, RG 24, 6796, NSS 8375-4; "*Restigouche* History," 37; "*Ottawa* History," 10

73. In July LCdr Lay had recommended sending a pool of 128 officers and men as spares, to which NSHQ eventually responded by establishing HMCS *Dominion*, the RCN manning depot in Plymouth, England. CNS to Adm, 3 Aug. 1940, NAC, RG 24, 6796, NSS 8375-4; *Restigouche* ROP for 25 Aug. to 5 Sept. 1940; CO RCN Barracks Halifax to NSec, 6 Aug. 1940, NAC, RG 24, 5632, NS 30-26-2

74. "After some discussion in which emphasis was given to the importance of retaining the remainder of the 'Fraser's' crew intact as Canadian personnel under Canadian command," CWCM, 4 July 1940

bring up the Canadian overseas presence to four destroyers, the Royal Navy would not only suffer no loss of strength, but would be relieved of the responsibility for the cost and manning of the vessel.[75] Beyond this, and of considerable long term significance for the RCN, the Admiralty reckoned the sale "will go some way towards ensuring that Canada's interest in maintaining a navy in the post war years does not wane."[76]

Diana commissioned in Canadian service on 6 September as HMCS *Margaree*, under the command of Commander J.W.R. Roy, RCN, a French-Canadian officer who was formerly Director of Operations at NSHQ.[77] The timing of the transfer was not auspicious. The destroyer went into London's Albert Docks for refit during the most intense phase of the German blitz on the British capital. She survived the heavy bombing attacks on the docklands, but it was a near miracle that she did so.[78] Lieutenant W.M. Landymore, RCN, who was standing by the ship with the damage control party as the bulk of the ship's company had been sent to Devonport barracks at Plymouth for their safety, recalls the bomb that could have killed her:

> One night we were sitting in the wardroom ... and we were on the dockside of the wardroom on the settee and suddenly we could feel something coming. Now, how does that happen? We both, just suddenly, froze and the next minute the bang happened. Now we couldn't hear it. But there must have been some kind of sense, air pressure or something that got to us because both of us stopped dead. We knew it was a bomb and it landed on the jetty, right above our heads. By actual measurement, just over ten feet from our heads. It put in a crater about eight feet across [in the jetty]. But the ship, fortunately at that time, was just flush [i.e., the water level in the dock was low enough that the whole of the destroyer's hull, which would otherwise have suffered severe damage, was masked by the jetty wall]. There were a few splinter holes and dents in places but really no damage to the ship. Wasn't that lucky? Very lucky![79]

In the meantime, Canadian destroyers were discovering the futility of the RN's countermeasures against U-boats running on the surface at night. *St Laurent* was joining SC 3 from astern at about 2300 on 14 September, and two other destroyers, HMS *Wanderer* and *Witch*, were sweeping ahead on each bow of the convoy, with the ocean escort sloop HMS *Dundee* between them,

---

75. Adm to CNS, 13 July 1940, min by DOD(H), 6 July 1940, DPS, 7 July 1940, Military Branch, 8 July 1940, PRO, ADM 116/4410

76. The terms of purchase, which cost £195,407, were modelled by the British Treasury on those for *Assiniboine* (ex-HMS *Kempenfelt*). That ship was purchased when Britain had been reluctant to part with a destroyer on the eve of war in 1939, and the cost was about £30,000 more than was paid for the C class destroyers purchased in 1937-8, even though the Admiralty urged no "suggestion of niggardliness concerning the price." Min by Military Branch, 8 July 1940; Phillips, PAS (S) Adm to Sec, Treasury, 26 July 1940, reproduced in notes on Admiralty file M 013066, and Notes on Canada House file A 168/40, "Admiralty File M.013066 ... Purchase of HMS *Diana*," nd, DHH, NHS, 81-520 Margaree I 8000

77. During the negotiations for *Diana*, Nelles learned that there was a second D class destroyer in British home waters, HMS *Delight*. He immediately inquired about the prospects of purchasing her, but on 29 July, she was sunk during a bombing raid off Dover. CNS to Adm, 25 July 1940, Adm to CNS, 1 Aug. 1940, PRO, ADM 116/4410

78. NSHQ cabled the Canadian High Commission about the "embarrassing" danger of *Margaree* suffering the same fate as her sister *Delight* before ever seeing the open sea as a Canadian ship, and the High Commission asked Admiralty about the possibility of replacing *Margaree* with another destroyer in condition at least to be moved to a safer port in the UK. Notes on Canada House file A 168/40, appended to notes on "Purchase of HMS Diana"; NCM, 19 Sep. 1940, NAC, RG 24, 4044, NSS 1078-3-4 pt 1

79. Interview with W.M. Landymore, 7 Apr. 1986, 42-3, DHH, Landymore biog file

when *U 48*, commanded by Kapitänleutnant Wolfgang Lüth, slipped between the latter warship and her charges, clearly silhouetted by a full moon, about 260 miles west-northwest of Ireland. (See map at page 120.) At 2324 and 2326, the U-boat fired single torpedoes, one of which missed a merchant ship, while the other blew the stern off *Dundee*. *Wanderer* stood by the crippled sloop, and despatched *Witch* and *St Laurent* on a three-hour hunt. Assuming that the U-boat had withdrawn at speed into the darkness on the port side of the convoy, the destroyers searched in that direction to a distance of twelve miles, but *U 48* simply remained on the surface ahead of the convoy, and fatally damaged two more merchant ships in two subsequent attacks over the next three hours.[80] The convoy commodore's ship twice sighted the U-boat moving fast on the surface and gave chase but *Wanderer*, nearest to the scene, did not learn of the second attack until almost an hour after it had taken place, when she sighted a flare four miles distant, closed and discovered the survivors of the sunken merchant vessel at about 0135 on 15 September. *Witch* closed the convoy at 0245, after the third attack, and *St Laurent* back-tracked, under *Wanderer*'s orders to help her with *Dundee*.[81]

Ottawa and *Skeena*, with the destroyer HMS *Arrow*, were scheduled to join SC 3 on the afternoon of 15 September, after parting company with a fast outbound convoy. Closer than expected to the eastbound convoy, possibly because a gale in the northwest approaches on 13 September had slowed their outward passage, they responded to *Wanderer*'s broadcast about the initial attack on SC 3 and arrived on the scene at 0330. Commander Mainguy, CO of *Ottawa* and now the senior officer present, set about regrouping the scattered merchant ships and bringing them back onto course. *Skeena* joined the screen, while *Arrow* relieved *Wanderer* standing by the sloop's hulk until *St Laurent* took it in tow. Mainguy, as much in the dark as the other destroyer captains, had taken up a position in the van of the convoy and unwittingly brought the night's action to an end at 0420. In the words of the U-boat commander, "the 'sweeper' [escort] stationed ahead of the convoy suddenly turns towards us at high speed. She must have heard us or sighted our wake in the bright moonlight. I dived as evading on the surface was no longer possible."[82] *Ottawa*, in fact, had not seen anything; the manoeuvres appear to have been the result of Mainguy's efforts to reorganize the convoy.

At mid-day on 15 September, despite *St Laurent*'s efforts, *Dundee*'s shattered hull sank.[83] No other ships were lost from the convoy, *U 48*'s attempts to regain contact being defeated by the appearance of aircraft later in the morning. One merchantman that had straggled, however, was picked off by another U-boat after sunrise. The destroyer HMS *Amazon* responded to her distress signal, rescued the survivors and, joined by *Arrow* and *St Laurent* later in the day, made an unsuc-

---

80. During this same period, at 0141 on the morning of 15 Sep., *Lotos*, which had sailed with SC 3 but become separated from the convoy, was, according to Rohwer, sunk by *U 99* some 8 degrees to the northwest (Square AM 1751 on the U-boat grid, as compared with AM 1998, the position of *U 48*'s attacks). Rohwer, *Axis Submarine Successes*, 28; NCS sailing list for SC 3, in DHH 77/553 pt 3, confirms that *Lotos* sailed with the convoy and was later reported lost by the Admiralty.

81. WAC WD, 15 Sep. 1940; Rohwer, *Axis Submarine Successes*, 28; Adm, *MASR*, Jan.1941, 13-15, in which the Admiralty staff's analysis of the submarine's movements is confirmed in almost every particular by the *U 48* KTB, 14-15 Sep. 1940. U-boat war diaries cited in this history are held in DHH, 83/665. Most have been translated into English.

82. *U 48*, KTB, 15 Sep. 1940

83. WAC WD, 15 Sep. 1940; CO *Ottawa* to C-in-C WAC, Ottawa ROP for 3-17 Sep. 1940, 19 Sep. 1940, DHH, 81/520 Ottawa I 8000 pt 2

cessful hunt for the second killer.[84] German propaganda broadcasts crowed about losses inflicted on SC 3 and announced the award of the Iron Cross to *U 48*'s captain.

The new German tactics soon produced even more important results. On 20 September, Korvettenkapitän Gunter Prien in *U 47* encountered the eastbound HX 72 at about 24°West, more than two days out from the rendezvous with its antisubmarine escort. With Prien's accurate position reports and favourable weather conditions, *BdU* could for the first time concentrate boats at the scene. Five of them, including *U 48*, from as far as 380 miles away, began arriving in the early hours on 21 September and soon sank four of the merchant vessels; the first escorts did not reach the convoy until the afternoon. These five warships—a destroyer, a sloop, and three corvettes—were unable to deter the submarines, which sank another seven merchantmen during the night of 21–22 September, bringing the convoy's losses to more than 25 percent of the forty-one merchant vessels that had been in company.[85]

"Actions during the last few days," wrote Dönitz with enormous satisfaction, "have shown that the principles established in peace time for use of radio in sight of the enemy and the training of U-boats for attacks on convoys were correct."[86] He immediately drove the point home with another successful group operation. On 24 September, *U 29* found and began to shadow the outbound convoy OB 217, about to part company with its escort group, under the command of *Ottawa*. By noon on 25 September, at about 20°W and as ships in the convoy began dispersing to follow independent courses, *U 43* and *U 31* joined the shadower. DF intercept stations ashore had picked up *U 29*'s shadowing reports, and Western Approaches ordered *Ottawa*, just as she sighted her next charge, HX 73, to return to OB 217's track, following the convoy as long as fuel would allow. This standard tactic for catching a shadowing submarine proved ineffective on this occasion. *Ottawa* was no more than six hours behind the convoy and if the boats had waited for nightfall before launching their attacks she would have been in position to deal with them. This time, the three boats attacked immediately. Remaining submerged, *U 43* sank SS *Sulairia* and about five miles away, *U 29* torpedoed SS *Eurymedon*. Mainguy responded immediately to the distress signals, increased speed to thirty knots, reached *Eurymedon* at 1600 and spent nearly an hour recovering some sixty survivors from boats. Not until 1800, when the destroyer was again moving along the mean track of the dispersed convoy, did Mainguy learn to his chagrin from one of the merchantman's officers—he had not been able to persuade the merchantman's captain and chief officer to leave the hulk—that a U-boat had surfaced near *Eurymedon* as recently as forty-five minutes before *Ottawa*'s arrival. As he confessed in his Report of Proceedings, if he had thought immediately to hail the survivors for this kind of intelligence, the U-boat might still have been close enough that a hunt would have been successful. Any further chance of locating and attacking a U-boat disappeared on the night of 25–26 September when Western Approaches ordered *Ottawa* to end her search to the west and return to the scene of the attack. As the destroyer found and res-

---

84. Rohwer, *Axis Submarine Successes*, 28; WAC WD, 15 Sep. 1940

85. *BdU*, KTB, 20-2 Sept 1940; Rohwer, *Axis Submarine Successes*, 29-30; Blair, *Hitler's U-boat War*, 194; MOD, *U-boat War* I, 50, diagram 9; WAC WD, 21 Sep. 40, 164, 167; D. O'Brien, *HX 72: The First Convoy to Die: The Wolfpack Attack that Woke Up the Admiralty* (Halifax 1999). There are slight discrepancies in these sources.

86. *BdU*, KTB, 22 Sep. 1940

Top: Naval Board meeting in the winter of 1941/1942. Angus L. Macdonald presides with Vice-Admiral P.W. Nelles, Rear-Admiral H.E. Reid and Captain H.T.W. Grant to his right. To his left is Engineer Rear-Admiral Stephens. (DND, NP-260)

Right: Captain E.R. Mainguy, RCN in September 1942 when Captain D Newfoundland. He is in The Crowsnest, which he established as a seagoing officers club to give some respite to the officers of the Newfoundland Escort Force. He also opened a recreational camp for ratings outside St John's. (NAC, PA 204634)

Keeping ships running under difficult conditions often posed a challenge. Here, Warrant Engineer S.A. Clarke, RCNR examines a worn engine part in HMCS *Pictou*, March 1942. The breakdown occurred at sea and had to be repaired by the crew onboard ship. (NAC, PA 204599)

cued the survivors from *Sulairia*'s boats, *U 32* and *U 37* sank three more of the ships dispersed on 24 September.[87]

U-boats continued sinking ships sailing independently in British home waters on an almost daily basis until, in the second week of October, as a period of unfavourable operating conditions came to an end, and as boats came back to the area from replenishing, they began to find convoys again. From 17 to19 October, benefiting from the discovery of a northward diversion of routes made in response to the September battles, seven boats ravaged SC 7, destroying twenty-two of the thirty-four ships in the convoy. Then, on the night of 19–20 October, five boats, including some from the SC 7 action, sank twelve of forty-nine vessels in HX 79.[88] Unlike HX 72, these were defended convoys, benefiting from reinforcements as well as escorts released from anti-invasion duties. Initially, SC 7 had the protection of only the single sloop that had brought the convoy out from Sydney, reinforced during the battle by two additional sloops and two corvettes, but HX 79 had an escort of two destroyers, four corvettes, three trawlers and a minesweeper. As with SC 3, the escorts groped in the dark, and often left merchantmen without a screen as they rescued crews of sinking ships or hunted promising contacts.[89]

British authorities addressed the situation calmly and logically. A weekly conference of some thirty representatives from the naval and air force headquarters divisions and commands responsible for the defence of shipping, who began meeting on 1 October, developed a blueprint by the end of November that would guide development of the war against the U-boats over the next two and a half-years.[90]

Recognition of critical shortcomings was the first step. Foremost among these were inadequate training at the ship and group level, poor coordination, and the absence of night search equipment and tactics. The many reservists, both officers and ratings, who manned recently commissioned corvettes—a substantial part of the escort for SC 7 and HX 79—lacked basic skills. Ship exercises, especially against "tame," "clockwork mouse" submarines and group training of ships were badly needed, but impossible to ensure until the tempo of operations fell off. There was no alternative to continuing the expansion of training centres, increasing output and attempting to leaven green crews with experienced personnel—a very scarce commodity. However, ten permanently organized escort groups formed in this period were expected to underpin the development of teamwork, under the leadership of Senior Officers capable of the quick appreciation needed for successful action against U-boats by night. For the moment, there would still have to be "scratch" assignments of warships to escort missions, but there would no longer be the fatal weakness of preceding months, when ships at different ports were thrown together at the last minute, and the commanders only consulted by signal as the convoy got under way.[91]

---

87. *Eurymedon* had suffered heavy casualties from hits by two torpedoes but remained afloat. Her captain and chief engineer, who had refused to leave the ship when *Ottawa* rescued the survivors, were among fifty-five in the boats from *Sulairia*, which only lost one man. *Ottawa* ROP 22-8 Sep. 1940; WAC WD, 24-6 Sep.1940; Rohwer, *Axis Submarine Successes*, 30; BdU, KTB, 24 Sep. 1940

88. Rohwer, *Axis Submarine Successes*, 32-4

89. Adm, *MASR*, Nov. 1940, 20-5, and Sep.-Oct. 1940, plate 5: "Distribution of A/S Vessels, Sep. 16th 1940" and plate 6: "Distribution of A/S Vessels, Oct. 11th 1940"; AHS, *Home Waters* II, 230-4; MOD, *U-boat War* I, 52; AHS, *Defeat of Enemy Attack on Shipping, 1939-1945: A Study in Policy and Operations* (London 1957), IA, 65-6

90. Min 66th mtg Adm Conference, 12 Nov. 1940, PRO, ADM 199/2078, ff 1005-6

91. Min 4th and 6th mtgs Adm Conference, 22 Oct. and 12 Nov. 1940; Adm, *MASR*, Nov. 1940, 7

Solutions to technological problems were easier, except that the German penetration of the convoy cypher escaped notice. Had that been remedied, Dönitz would have been deprived of his most useful asset. Other measures, however, did improve the situation for convoy escorts. All of them were to receive radio telephone sets, whose high-frequency signals were not vulnerable to enemy direction-finding. This was better than short-range signal lamps flickering morse code. Radar was also becoming available. Before the war, the RN had focused on antiaircraft and gunnery control sets for major warships. When in 1939 the need for surface scanning radar became apparent, the navy had belatedly turned to the RAF, where compact air-to-surface-vessel (ASV) sets were being fitted in Coastal Command aircraft. ASV trials suggested that the sets could be installed in destroyers, and thus inspired the naval adaptation that came to be known as type 286. As the general installation program for both Coastal Command and the RN began in the fall of 1940, air squadrons and destroyers in the northwest approaches received priority. By mid-November, seven escort destroyers had been fitted, including *Ottawa*. Type 286, however, had severe limitations and teething problems. Expectations raised by trials in calm conditions that it could detect surfaced submarines at ranges of three and a half to four miles were unrealistic. Operating on a wavelength of approximately 1.5 metres, type 286 lacked the discrimination to detect dependably such a small, low-profile target in a seaway. In warships, the antenna was relatively close to the ocean surface, which threw back confusing returns. Rough seas completely masked the U-boat echo. Moreover, the antennas fitted in warships, until improved designs could be developed and manufactured in 1941, also had serious weaknesses. They could not be rotated and could scan only in a forward arc, meaning that the whole ship had to be turned towards the contact to get an accurate bearing. The antennas also threw off strong emissions to the sides and rear that often picked up the returns of ships in company in the convoy. Finally, the simple "A-scan" cathode ray tube in the receiving console merely registered a contact as a "blip" on a single range scale, making it difficult to distinguish the back and side returns from one forward of the ship. [92]

The Germans themselves opened up another means of electronic detection. Under *Rudeltaktik*, Dönitz depended on long-range signalling from submarines to concentrate his boats against convoys, and British high frequency direction finding (HF/DF) stations ashore intercepted the transmissions of shadowing U-boats. Possibly this is why on 12 September convoy routing was centralized in the Admiralty Trade Division, whose plot of merchant shipping allowed comprehensive application of submarine information from the Operational Intelligence Centre (OIC). [93] British intelligence, although still unable to decrypt enemy signals, had identified the "E-bar" character in morse code with which the U-boats preceded their convoy sighting reports. This, with DF bearings and the merchant shipping plot, revealed to the Trade Division which convoy had been located. It may have been the interception of such an E-bar signal that had brought Western Approaches to divert *Ottawa* from HX 73 on 25 September to OB 217. In that case, as we have seen, the Canadian destroyer received the warning too late.

---

92. Min 3rd and 6th mtgs Adm Conference, 15 Oct. and 12 Nov. 1940, ff 856, 1002; Adm, *MASR*, Jan. 1941, 9; D. Howse, *Radar at Sea: The Royal Navy in World War* II (Annapolis 1993), 58, 79; F.A. Kingsley (ed), *The Development of Radar Equipments for the Royal Navy, 1935-45* (Houndmills 1995), 169-72

93. "Considerable evasive routing is now practised in view of U/B [U-boat] and A/C [aircraft] enemy reconnaissance." "Halifax Convoys—September 1940," ns, nd, PRO, ADM 199/2078, 666

Officers at the Admiralty defence of shipping conference considered that this kind of delay occurred too often. The naval liaison officer to Coastal Command cited two recent convoys, SC 6 and HX 77, which had suffered losses of three and seven ships respectively.[94] DFs available some hours before these attacks had strongly suggested the presence of shadowers, but warning signals had reached the convoy late in the first instance and not at all in the second. On other occasions, aircraft in the vicinity of a DF fix did not receive the information until they were near their limit of endurance or had departed the area. Representatives from the Admiralty's antisubmarine and signals divisions explained that, with the few DF stations available, bearings were usually inaccurate and therefore required careful sifting and analysis at the OIC. One obvious solution to the problem of inaccuracy would have been the erection of stations along the west coast of Ireland, but that was impossible because of Ireland's (Eire's) neutrality. Tests at alternative sites in Iceland and the Faeroes had yielded disappointing results, because of problems associated with high latitudes, but engineers from the BBC, Marconi, and other agencies were at work on the problem.[95] The RCN, as we shall see, also had an important contribution to make in completing the North Atlantic system of DF stations.

Air Chief Marshal Sir Frederick Bowhill, AOC Coastal Command, suggested that escorts should monitor high-frequency, short-range transmissions by German reconnaissance aircraft. As the Director of the Signals Division noted, this posed serious technical difficulties. Bowhill's proposal, moreover, exaggerated the importance of German maritime patrol aircraft—they rather than German signals intelligence were given the credit for playing the key role in locating convoy and homing U-boats. Nevertheless, his idea was the germ of what would later become a major Allied counter-measure, the detection of shadowing U-boats by ship-borne HF/DF equipment.[96]

Canadian destroyers played no part in the convoy battles of October, 1940. On 14 October *Skeena* stood by the armed merchant cruiser HMS *Cheshire*, which had been torpedoed northwest of Ireland, embarked 220 of the crew, and screened her for three days as tugs brought her into Belfast. *Ottawa* was diverted from a convoy to assist one torpedoed vessel and search for survivors from another. *Margaree*, finally out of dock, prepared to go to Halifax and complete her refit to Canadian standards. *Saguenay* departed Halifax on 16 October to replace *Margaree*, which sailed from Londonderry with OL 8, a fast convoy of five ships on 20 October.[97]

Margaree's convoy was about 400 miles west of Ireland on the night of 21 October when rain closed down visibility. The destroyer was running 2000 to 3000 yards ahead of the merchant ships, so the first lieutenant, standing the first watch (2000 to midnight), reduced speed slightly, to allow *Margaree* gradually to fall back on the main body so as to remain at visibility distance. When he left the bridge at midnight, he carefully explained the situation to his relief. At 0100 brief blinding squalls began to blow and when one of these lifted at 0125 a watch keeper on the bridge of the large transport *Port Fairy* sighted the destroyer close off the starboard bow: inexplicably, none of the look-

---

94. Cdr D.V. Peyton-Ward, RN, an ex-submariner and keen analyst of the antisubmarine war, author of the postwar study "The RAF in Maritime War," DHH, 79/599

95. Min 3rd Adm Conference, 15 Oct. 1940, ff 856-8, Min 4th Adm Conference, 22 Oct. 1940, f 862

96. Min 3rd Adm Conference, ff 856-7. On the exaggerated view of the success of German air reconnaissance, see also min 2nd Adm Conference, 8 Oct. 1940, f 853, and min 6th Adm Conference, 12 Nov. 1940, f 1006; Adm, *MASR*, Nov. 1940, 7

97. WAC WD, 14-17 Oct. 1940; *Saguenay* ROP, 24 Oct. 1940 (ROP 1932-40); "*Margaree* History," 4-5

outs aboard the destroyer sighted the merchantman. Four minutes later *Margaree* suddenly turned hard to port, right across *Port Fairy*'s bow. Horrified, the chief officer of the merchantman ordered full port rudder and reversed his engines, signalling his action with three blasts on the ship's horn. This may have been the first inkling that the destroyer had of her danger, for she suddenly took evasive action. It was too late. *Port Fairy*'s towering bows ripped through the destroyer's bridge, severing the forward part of the warship. So great was the force of the collision that the plates of the destroyer's forward section were peeled off the frames, and the structure sank almost immediately. This was the tragedy; most of the crew had been sleeping in the forward messdecks, while the captain was in his sea cabin beneath the bridge. Consequently, 140 men went down with the severed bows, including Commander Roy. There were only thirty-six survivors: off-duty officers whose cabins were in the wardroom flat aft, engine room personnel, and the quarter-deck watch.[98]

One of the fortunate was Lieutenant William Landymore, who like many in *Margaree*, had already endured the uncannily similar destruction of *Fraser*. Landymore, who had been in his cabin, "didn't even take time to put on a pair of sea-boots. I ran up the deck in my great big socks and I could see the bridge had been smashed all to hell... The ladder up to the break of the fo'c's'le was still in place and there was another ladder on the back of the bridge... So, I scaled those as fast as I could to see if there was anybody alive. It had been knocked off as straight as a die, there wasn't anything—just a piece of the bulkhead."[99] The force of the impact brought the after section of the destroyer alongside *Port Fairy*, where willing hands helped thirty survivors scramble up from the wreck as the hulls ground up and down against each other. Two others fell between the ships to be crushed to death. Three officers, including the First Lieutenant, P.F.X. Russell, senior among the survivors, and a rating had remained aboard the destroyer, to ensure that the depth charges were set to "safe" so they would not detonate and damage *Port Fairy* as the stern sank. This little group then made off on a Carley float that *Port Fairy* managed to recover only after the raft had been swept about in the seas for an hour. The destroyer, however, remained afloat, even after twenty-six rounds from the merchantman's 4-inch gun were fired into her. After daybreak on 22 October an RCN party took a boat back over to the *Margaree* to attempt to scuttle her, but did not dare board because fires were evidently burning in the vicinity of the after magazine. She then began to settle after hits by a further ten rounds from *Port Fairy*'s gun.

The Board of Inquiry convened to determine the cause of *Margaree*'s loss could come to no firm conclusion because none of the bridge watch had survived. The fatal turn across *Port Fairy*'s bows may have been the result of an equipment malfunction, faulty transmission or execution of a rudder order, or an error on the part of the officer who gave it. Lieutenant Russell subsequently suggested an alternative explanation, which like the others could be neither proved nor disproved by the skimpy evidence. *Margaree* had been falling back between *Port Fairy* and the *Staffordshire*, which was about 1200 yards on *Port Fairy*'s starboard beam. It was possible, given the rapidly changing and poor visibility, that lookouts on the destroyer's bridge sighted *Staffordshire* and the officer of the watch swung to port to get clear of her, failing to see *Port Fairy* on the opposite beam.[100]

---

98. "Loss of HMCS *Margaree*," nd, DHH, 81/520 Margaree I 8000; "*Margaree* History," 5-8

99. Lawrence interview with RAdm W. Landymore, DHH, Landymore biog file

100. In conversation with Lt J. George, RCNVR, an historical officer, in Sep. 1944. Narrative A, 15, DHH, 84/123

In any event, the merchant ship bore no share of the blame; indeed, the one heartening aspect of the accident was *Port Fairy*'s unstinting and skilful rescue work.

Although nobody realized it at the time, the navy's fortunes turned two weeks after the loss of *Margaree* when *Ottawa*, in company with HMS *Harvester*, attacked and destroyed the Italian submarine *Faa di Bruno*.[101] This, the first submarine kill ever made by a ship of the Canadian navy, came about in a strange fashion and did not gain recognition for more than forty years. *Ottawa*, *Saguenay,* and *Skeena*, working under the new group organisation instituted by the Admiralty, had sailed on 2 November as part of a heavy screen for WS 4, a fast troop convoy bound for the Middle East. On 4 November, *Saguenay*, *Skeena*, and a British destroyer detached to pick up the inbound HX 83. *Ottawa* and *Harvester* broke off to rendezvous with SC 9, about a day's run north. About halfway there, on the evening of 4 November, they received orders from Western Approaches to backtrack in support of the Gibraltar-bound OG 45, off the southwestern approaches. Although there were only four German boats left on station after those taking part in the intense October operations had withdrawn to replenish, a submarine, probably the Italian *Malaspina*, was known to be shadowing.[102]

The submarine had in fact been sighted by the ships in the convoy, which the Commodore had scattered in an attempt to throw off the expected attack. *Ottawa* found one of the ships, which reported the situation, early on 5 November. Commander Mainguy, the senior officer, decided to proceed to southward, hoping to keep the two destroyers somewhere near the independent courses being steered by the merchantmen.[103] He had just received new orders from Western Approaches to join another outbound convoy when the armed merchant cruiser HMS *Salopian* broadcast that she was engaging a submarine on the surface thirty miles to the southeast. *Ottawa* and *Harvester* sped to this position, using it as a datum point to search along the estimated southward track of OG 45 until the afternoon of 5 November. By that time nothing had turned up and fuel was running too low to risk further hunting to the south or west. The destroyers therefore turned to the northeast, in the general direction of home, to assist two merchant ships, *Melrose Abbey* and *Gartbratten*, formerly of OG 45, which had been damaged in a collision after the convoy had scattered.

After daybreak on 6 November, the destroyers, searching around the last reported position of the merchant ships, received a message that *Melrose Abbey* was being chased by a submarine ninety miles to the northeast. To conserve fuel, the warships proceeded at only twenty-four knots, but their luck held. At mid-day, *Melrose Abbey* signalled that she was being fired on by a surfaced submarine at a position only thirty miles away. The destroyers altered course to assist, increased to their full speed of thirty-four knots, and at 1335 sighted the merchant vessel still under attack from

---

101. Originally the U-boat assessment committee at the Admiralty assessed *Ottawa* and *Harvester*'s result as "probably damaged," and gave credit to HMS *Havelock*. But a review of evidence in 1982 by the MOD, taking into account the research of Italian official historians who suggested *Havelock* had damaged, not sunk, the *Marconi* on 8 Nov., concluded that *Ottawa* and *Harvester* had indeed sunk the *Faa di Bruno* on 6 Nov. Coppock to Corsetti, 15 Dec. 1982, DHH; AHS, *Defeat of the Enemy Attack on Shipping*, app C, amendments to app 2 (iv): "Italian U-boats Destroyed," liv

102. Italian submarines had begun to operate in the Atlantic under *BdU*'s direction in Aug. By 1 Nov, six were on station west of 15°, beyond most air and sea patrols. *BdU*, KTB, 27 Oct. and 1-3 Nov. 1940; MOD, *U-boat War* I, 60-1

103. Mainguy complained that the commodore had not sent any word of the decision to scatter, leaving the destroyers little alternative but to meander southward in this fashion. *Ottawa* ROP, 13 Nov. 1940

the surfaced submarine. Four minutes later, when the range was about five-and-a-half miles, *Ottawa*, in the van, opened fire with her forward guns and *Harvester* joined in.

The submarine dived at 1341 when the range was still four-and-a-half miles. The Canadian destroyer maintained full speed for another two miles, slowed to hunting speed of sixteen knots and with *Harvester* began an asdic search. For five-and-a half hours there were only "doubtful echoes" until *Harvester*'s captain, Commander M. Thornton, RN realised the boat was probably stealing away to the northwest. As the destroyers took up position at the furthest distance the submarine might have moved in that direction, *Ottawa* gained a solid contact. A patient set-piece attack ensued, each ship in turn holding the contact and directing the other on its depth charge run. Over a period of nearly six hours *Ottawa* dropped four patterns, for a total of twenty-one depth charges, while *Harvester*, fitted with a second pair of depth charge throwers so she could fire a more powerful ten-charge pattern, dropped fifty-two depth charges in five attacks. After a final attack by *Ottawa* at 0046, 7 November, the asdic returns "disappeared with grinding squeaks."[104] A systematic sweep around the position continued until the forenoon and revealed a large patch of oil. The destroyers persisted in the search until 1500 on 7 November, to ensure that the boat, if only damaged, did not surface. Finally, depleted fuel and a gale warning forced them to make for home. *Harvester*'s bunkers were so low that she could not complete the run to Greenock and had to put into Londonderry.

Mainguy submitted a self-effacing report of the action. He blamed himself for opening fire too soon, which cost him the advantage of surprise. That he failed to make asdic contact on his first approach was because the destroyer had not reduced speed soon enough, and overshot the boat. "Perhaps I was over-keen... 'Ottawa' has never exercised with one of our submarines, although I had three 90 minutes exercises at Portland a year ago, two of them in an A/S trawler. However, I do not wish to make excuses. 'Harvester' [Commander Thornton] naturally feels very upset about the whole operation. I should like to emphasize that as far as I know he made no mistakes, and he was most helpful and restrained."[105]

Notwithstanding this report, C-in-C Western Approaches commended both ships, particularly their commanding officers, asdic and depth charge crews, for what he considered the certain destruction of the submarine. The assessment committee in the Admiralty, exercising their customary and necessary rigour, did not accept this judgment, but even though it was not until forty years later that proper credit could be given on the basis of research in Italian records, the experience was useful. It demonstrated the urgent need for more adequate antisubmarine training resources in Canada, not least because the pressure of operations in British waters allowed no opportunity for the destroyers that had gone overseas to avail themselves of RN facilities. On reading Mainguy's report, Admiral Nelles minuted that the RCN's long-standing requirement for a training submarine at Halifax had become urgent.[106]

Ottawa and *Harvester*'s attack gave Western Approaches command its third kill in eight days, and *Harvester* her second.[107] Three days later, *U 31* was sunk in another systematic hunt, this time

---

104. Notes from C-in-C WAC, 23 Nov. 1940, DHH, 81/520 Ottawa I 8000 pt 1

105. *Ottawa* ROP, 13 Nov. 1940

106. Murray to NSec, 7 Jan. 1941, and CNS min to DM and MNS, 15 Jan. 1941, DHH, 81/520 Ottawa I 8000 pt 2

107. On 30 Oct., in circumstances remarkably like the destruction of *Faa di Bruno*, *U 32* had been destroyed by HMS *Highlander* and *Harvester*. Adm, *MASR*, Nov. 1940, 36-9

by HMS *Antelope*.[108] Since Western Approaches escorts had failed to destroy a single submarine since early July, this run of four successes showed that the strengthening of the escort forces was having a positive effect. The successes, moreover, had accounted for the only two boats available to search for shipping in the waters to the east of 15°West where the convoy routes converged towards the North Channel. The inexperienced Italian submarines further west were having such difficulty making accurate sighting reports and shadowing that Dönitz was taking no account of them. For some days, therefore, U-boat Command was nearly blind. And when the replenished German boats took up station towards the middle of the month, to begin passing useful information, heavy weather made it impossible to organize attacks on convoys.[109] During the first three weeks of November, only twelve merchant ships were lost in the Western Approaches. Towards the end of the month, however, when U-boats were again able to strike, it became clear that the tactical problem of defence against night surface attacks had by no means been solved. SC 11 lost six ships over an eight-hour period on 23 November, and another ship thirteen hours later, all to one U-boat, and OB 244 lost eight ships to two U-boats from 21 to 23 November.[110] (See map at page 120.) Canadian destroyers were involved in the battle for SC 11, which illustrates well the problems then still facing escorts.

Ottawa, St Laurent, Saguenay, and *Skeena* had sailed as part of a large escort for the fast troop convoy WS 4B on 18 November. Thanks to its speed and rising seas, that convoy escaped attack by the six U-boats in contact. On 20 November Western Approaches ordered the four destroyers to join SC 11 and three of them made the rendezvous on the morning of 22 November after *St Laurent* had been sent off to search for survivors of the SS *Cree*, an independent torpedoed on 21 November.[111] Sea conditions were extremely difficult, with steep swells in which the narrow-hulled destroyers could neither keep station without losing steerage way nor make the customary dusk sweep, while squalls closed visibility to half a mile or less. By nightfall on 22 November, *U 100* (Kapitänleutnant Joachim Schepke), one of the boats drawn from a patrol well to the northwest, had sighted and begun to shadow SC 11.[112]

The ocean escort, the sloop HMS *Enchantress* (Commander A.K. Scott-Moncrieff, RN), was senior ship in the van of the convoy, and the destroyers were stationed on the flanks.[113] After dark, about 2300 local time, when the convoy made a hard turn in an effort to throw off the

---

108. Adm, *MASR*, Dec. 1940, 18-20

109. *BdU*, KTB, 30 Oct. to 6 Nov. 1940

110. Rohwer, *Axis Submarine Successes*, 35-6

111. On passage to join SC 11, Mainguy had diverted all four destroyers to investigate a vague submarine report from Western Approaches, then sent *St Laurent* off to search vainly for survivors of the SS *Cree*, sunk by *U 123*, the sighting of which Western Approaches had failed to explain was the source of the vague submarine report. *Ottawa* ROP, 25 Nov. 1940; *BdU*, KTB, 19 Nov. 1940; WAC WD, 21-2 Nov. 1940

112. Western Approaches reported the convoy had been sighted by aircraft, but there is no record of this in the *BdU*, KTB. Schepke, who had sunk three ships in the battle for HX 79, appears to have happened on SC 11 by accident, and was able to bring in *U 93*, which had no luck. Mainguy thought he was to blame for not detecting the boat responsible for sinking *Cree*, but that boat was in fact elsewhere, sinking six ships in OB 244. Blair, *Hitler's U-boat War*, 208; *BdU*, KTB, 19-22 Nov. 1940; WAC WD, 21-2 Nov. 1940; *Ottawa* ROP, 18-25 Nov. 1940

113. The following account is based on *Enchantress* ROP, 25 Nov. 1940, esp "Enclosure 'A' ... 'Torpedo attacks by enemy submarines on Convoy SC.11 on Saturday, Nov. 23, 1940,'" PRO, ADM 199/59, and *Ottawa* ROP, 18-25 Nov. 1940, with additional details from *BdU*, KTB, 22-3 Nov. 1940; WAC WD, 23 and 25 Nov. 1940

suspected shadower, ships dropped out of formation astern and many showed navigation lights to avoid collision in the grim weather. About an hour after the turn, Schepke torpedoed the first of the ships that had fallen farthest behind. Over the next hour he torpedoed two more. Although the stricken vessels fired rocket flares, now standard procedure to help overcome the visibility and communications problems of night actions, the escorts saw and heard nothing until 0314, when *U 100* closed again and torpedoed a ship on the port quarter of the convoy.[114] While *Enchantress* worked her way back through the convoy towards the victim, a second ship, *Salonica*, sighted the surfaced submarine and fired a flare. As *Enchantress* altered course towards *Salonica*, the latter was hit by a torpedo at about 0335. Although the sloop had been firing starshell and was only 1400 yards from the position of the attack, she could neither see the submarine nor make asdic contact in the wild seas. Scott-Moncrieff ordered *Skeena* to assist in the search around the torpedoed ships. The Canadian warship had been stationed on the port flank of the convoy and should have been nearby, but when she did not appear, Scott-Moncrieff requested that she fire starshell. Only when it burst in the distance did it become evident that *Skeena* had fallen some four miles behind the main body of the convoy, leaving the port side of the convoy undefended. It took an hour for her to beat back to her proper position. She then assisted *Enchantress* in rescuing survivors.

Scott-Moncrieff had meanwhile ordered *Ottawa* and *Saguenay* to stay with the convoy. *Ottawa*, steaming back and forth at the minimum speed needed to maintain steerage way off the leading ships on the starboard side, managed to position herself in the van. But nothing was heard from *Saguenay*, who should have been on the starboard quarter. In fact, she had lost contact with the convoy altogether and was hove to fighting the seas. While *Ottawa*—now the sole escort—was struggling at the head of the convoy, *U 100* again closed on the port quarter. At 0702, just before first light, Schepke torpedoed a merchant ship, evidently the *Leise Maersk*. The bridge watch in *Ottawa* saw a flash and heard an explosion, but could not discern where in the convoy it had occurred. Assuming, correctly, that the boat had come in down-moon on the port side, *Ottawa* searched that flank and then swept to the rear of the convoy to the position where the hit would have taken place, but it could find no trace of wreckage, survivors, or *U 100*.

After daybreak on 23 November, *Enchantress* and then *Skeena* rejoined. *St Laurent*, having abandoned the search for *Cree*'s survivors, was attempting to rendezvous but not having much luck. *Saguenay* never did succeed in rejoining. The gale was still blowing hard, and in one particularly sickening roll *St Laurent* lost two men overboard, only one of whom she managed to rescue.[115] Two Coastal Command aircraft, however, were able to reach the convoy and provide daylight support. That was the form of defence best able to suppress shadowing submarines. It speaks

---

114. NHS extracts from NS 1030-10-37 pt 1, in DHH, 81/520/8280, box 9, SC 11; Rohwer, *Axis Submarine Successes*, 36, indicates that it was the SS *Cotmarsum* [sic, listed as *Ootmarsum* on Naval Staff (Trade Division), Admiralty, *British and Foreign Merchant Vessels Lost or Damaged by Enemy Action during Second World War* (BR 1337) (1 Oct. 1945), 142,] that was hit at 0414 Central European Time (or 0314 British Summer Time, which the escorts were keeping). However, *Enchantress*'s ROP shows that it was *Bruse* that was hit at 0314 BST. Her fore part remained afloat and *Skeena* stood by the wreck until after daylight on the 23rd; see below. Rohwer claims that *Bruse* was hit at 0117 CET (0017 BST). Thus, it would seem that it was actually *Ootmarsum* that was hit in the earlier attack. As these records show, there was much confusion surrounding the reports of U-boat attacks by merchantmen.

115. "*St Laurent* History," 19

volumes for Schepke's tenacity, and for the vulnerability of the slow SC convoys to pursuit, that he nevertheless remained in contact.

At nightfall on the same day, after the convoy had executed an evasive turn, *U 100* torpedoed another merchant ship. Sea and visibility conditions were nearly as dreadful as they had been the night before and it was extremely difficult for the escorts to assess the situation. Concluding from the shreds of information available that the boat had come in on the down-moon port quarter as before, *Enchantress* and *Skeena* searched that vicinity, with assistance from *St Laurent,* who was finally joining from astern, and, for a brief period, from HMS *Westcott*, an escort that was in the vicinity but had not been able to join the convoy because of mechanical defects that necessitated her early return to port. Only *Ottawa*, whose asdic had broken down, swept the starboard flank. It later emerged that the victim had been the grain ship *Bussum* on the starboard, not the port, quarter. The ship had not gone down immediately and *Ottawa* was able to rescue the entire crew. This was the last U-boat attack, but the ordeal of the ill-fated convoy was not yet over. During the morning of 24 November, as SC 11 entered the North Channel, the escorts heard explosions from a deep antisubmarine minefield nearby and briefly hoped that their tormentor had finally overreached his boldness. It was not to be. Instead, one of the merchant ships had somehow triggered the deep charges and was now sinking. That, finally, marked the end of the struggle. Commander Scott-Moncrieff's assessment of SC 11's ordeal was to the point: the heavy weather had disorganized the efforts of the too-few escorts to cover the convoy's flanks, but had not prevented the enemy from taking advantage of the open lines of approach.

Soon after the battle for SC 11 the RCN suffered its first casualties from enemy action. On the night of 30 November/1 December, *Saguenay* was escorting the homeward bound HG 47 with HMS *Highlander* and *Rochester*. In rain and darkness *Saguenay*, stationed astern of the convoy, lost contact. She had been among the first of the Western Approaches escorts to be fitted with radar, but the early sets had serious limitations, because back and side echoes often obscured contacts. After the rain cleared and visibility improved during the early hours of 1 December, and as the destroyer was regaining her proper station just before 0400, she altered course to investigate a brilliant flare. Seconds later, a torpedo virtually demolished the bows of the destroyer as far back as "A" gun, a length of some thirty feet. The commanding officer, Commander G.R. Miles, RCN, who was on the bridge, took control from the officer of the watch, Lieutenant R.B. Warwick, RCNVR. The latter kept a sharp lookout, sighted the low profile of the Italian submarine *Argo* at a distance of about 800 yards a couple of minutes later, and leapt from the bridge down to "B" gun. He directed two rounds that straddled but did not hit the enemy boat as it dived.[116]

The torpedo explosion had blasted Lieutenant (E) H.H. Wright, RCNVR, the engineer officer, out of his bunk aft. He checked to make sure the ship was still under power and then rushed to the forward messdecks, which were immediately above and aft of the explosion. Pushing past the stunned men coming out, he pulled clear one of the very few ratings to have escaped from the lower messdeck, the one nearest the explosion. Wright, in his own words, "then went down over

116. This account is based on NOIC Barrow to C-in-C WA, "Report and Minutes of a Board of Inquiry Held into the Action Damage Sustained by HMCS *Saguenay* on 1 Dec., 1940," 20 Dec. 1940, and Miles, "ROP of HMCS *Saguenay,* 30 Nov. to 5 Dec., 1940," 6 Dec. 1940, NAC, RG 24, 6790, NSS 8340-353/26; DNC Department, Adm, Bath, "HMCS *Saguenay*: Torpedo Damage. 1-12-40," DHH, 81/520 Saguenay I 8000 pt 1

the wreckage to try and pull another man out, when there was quite a flash from the paint shop, and the man I was trying to get out caught fire and fell back, and I saw that there was not much chance of getting anybody else out until we had the fire under control." Wright ordered the forward magazines flooded and then went aft to urge on the men who were bringing up the fire hoses. Just as the hoses were about to come into action, they had to be pulled back to close the forward watertight doors, a standard precaution Miles had ordered to ensure that the hull did not flood. Wright hurried up to the bridge, reported that the ship was not in danger of sinking, and received permission to reopen the doors. Nine minutes had passed since the torpedo hit. The forward doors were promptly opened, but the fire party was driven back by smoke so quickly that the hoses got tangled and had to be cut so that the compartment could be resealed. Although the party re-rigged the hoses on the upper deck, the flames licking up from below continued to gather intensity.[117] At 0450 Miles, forced by the threat of fire to abandon the bridge and shift control to the emergency steering position on the searchlight platform aft, ordered preparations to abandon ship should the submarine home on the now clearly visible flames and make a second attack. *Saguenay* was still making way, although even with Miles's manoeuvres to run with the wind and seas, engine revolutions that would normally have delivered nine knots were pushing the crippled vessel at no more than four.

Saguenay had managed to make a signal at 0404.[118] *Highlander* had closed, made sure the Canadian ship was not sinking, then hurried back to screen the convoy against *Saguenay*'s attacker. At 0700 *Highlander* returned and found the stricken destroyer "still floating comfortably although she was burning fiercely forward; the fire however seemed to be under control." At midday, Miles transferred five officers and eighty-five men—all those not strictly needed to nurse the shattered hull to port—to *Highlander* by whaler.[119] Lieutenant L.C. Audette, RCNVR, was one of the last to go. After he climbed from the boat onto *Highlander*'s deck he had his first experience of shock arising from sudden relief from strain:

> When I finally got both feet on *Highlander*'s deck and was about to step over the guardrail ... I merely stood there ... incapable of anything except rather silly laughter, it was a very disconcerting situation. A British sailor, observing this curious apparition, nudged one of his mates and pointed at me. His mate, obviously much brighter than he, made a wild leap at me, grasped me firmly under my armpits and hauled me unceremoniously over the guardrail. I became even more embarrassed when I discovered that I could neither stand nor walk. As a result, I was ignominiously carried down to *Highlander*'s wardroom. There, the First Lieutenant naturally took me for one of the wounded and wanted to call the doctor. I explained that there was nothing wrong with me that a noggin of Cognac would not correct.[120]

By early afternoon, it was finally possible to reopen the forward watertight doors and beat down the flames directly. Wright was then able to have timber shoring erected to support the for-

---

117. Evidence of Lt (E) H.H. Wright, RCNVR, "Board of Inquiry," 20 Dec. 1940, NAC, RG 24, 6790, NSS 8340-353/26

118. WAC WD, 1 Dec. 1940

119. *Highlander* ROP, 7 Dec. 1940, NAC, RG 24, 6790, NSS 8340-353/26

120. L.C. Audette, "Naval Recollections," unpublished ms, 18-19, DHH, 80/256, f 9

ward bulkheads, now exposed to the open sea. One officer in *Saguenay* recalled that Wright "was a mining engineer and he practically rebuilt the biggest gold-mine in the world down there!"[121] The weather stayed calm and the first of two tugs reached the stricken ship late on the morning of 2 December. Soon after, a section of the destroyer's mangled bows fell away, increasing her freeboard and reducing the drag so she could make six knots while pumping out flooded compartments without rapidly exhausting her fuel. Miles released one tug and did not have to accept a tow from the second until the afternoon of 4 December, when the ships were through the North Channel into the Irish Sea. After riding out a gale under the shelter of the Isle of Man, the tug *Schelde* towed *Saguenay* into Barrow-in-Furness on 5 December.

Investigation of the incident revealed that the destroyer had been proceeding at only twelve knots at the time of attack, making her a relatively easy target, but the Board of Inquiry accepted Miles's explanation that he had needed to conserve fuel. Commander W.A. Dallmeyer, RN of *Highlander* noted that in accordance with Western Approaches instructions, *Saguenay* had been running her asdic passively. This provided scarcely any chance of picking up sounds from a surfaced submarine stopped or moving slowly, as *Argo* evidently had been. Active asdic, Dallmeyer suggested, might well have been able to detect a surfaced boat that was as close in as *Saguenay*'s attacker.[122] The accuracy of the attack suggested that the boat had been surfaced for some minutes before firing and the board regretted that the lookouts had not sighted it in time. They also suggested that the fire-fighting gear should have been better prepared. According to standing orders, moreover, no men should have been sleeping in the lower forward messdecks, where most of the casualties occurred. The board, however, was satisfied with Miles's explanation that there was no other space available, a result, no doubt, of NSHQ's policy of augmenting the destroyer crews for training purposes. Losses, in any event, had been relatively light—twenty-one killed or missing and eighteen injured—considering the extent of damage to the ship. The timing of the attack, just before the change of watch at 0400 when men had been coming up from the messes, had been fortunate.

These were minor criticisms of a crew that had been in the midst of an exhausting long-range mission. The Board of Inquiry, its members impressed by their visit to the shattered, fire-scarred hull, concluded "that the steaming of this ship safely back to harbour, in the condition in which we saw her, represents a very considerable feat of seamanship and endurance, and it is one that reflects great credit on her Captain, Officers and Ship's company."[123] The C-in-C Western Approaches, moreover, commended the crew for quickly engaging the submarine despite the severe damage sustained by the ship: "opening fire may well have saved the convoy by forcing the U-boat to dive and lose contact."[124] For saving *Saguenay*, Commander Miles was made an Officer of the Order of the British Empire (OBE).[125] Dönitz, for his part, observed that *Argo* was "the first Italian boat to complete a really satisfactory patrol in the area W[est] of the North Channel."[126] Dönitz knew, however, no doubt

---

121. NOAC, "And All Our Joints Were Limber," *Salty Dips* II (Ottawa 1985), 156

122. RCN, Narrative A, 23-4

123. Board of Inquiry, 20 Dec. 1940

124. Quoted in Narrative A, 24

125. Ibid, 23

126. Significantly, she was one of the few Italian submarines designed like the German boats with a low profile and modest-sized hull for stealthy operations. *BdU*, KTB, 13 Dec. 1940

N.º 4
7-12-40

PAINT BURNT
OFF BY FIRE.

Top: *Saguenay* in Barrow-in-Furness after being torpedoed by the Italian submarine *Argo* on 1 December 1940. Twenty-one sailors were killed or declared missing. (NAC, PA 114155)

Bottom: Wives, sweet-hearts and family members welcome *Skeena* home to Halifax in March 1941. She had been overseas since the previous May. Note the type 286 RDF antenna atop her foremast. (NAC, PA 105177)

Never forget. The memorial service for the loss of HMCS *Fraser* in Ottawa, 8 July 1940. (NAC, PA 204665)

from the extensive radio traffic generated by the rescue operations for *Saguenay*, that the destroyer had survived, although with serious damage.[127]

As *Saguenay* struggled to survive, *St Laurent* became involved in one of the worst convoy disasters of the period, when seven German U-boats mauled HX 90. The destroyer had been escorting the armed merchant cruiser HMS *Forfar* in the northwest approaches, as the former liner steamed to join SC 14, which had sailed from Cape Breton without an escort.[128] Shortly before midnight on 2 December, after parting company with *Forfar*, *St Laurent* received instructions to go to the aid of an unknown ship torpedoed about six hours fast steaming to the west. This was in fact the *Appalachee*, sailing in HX 90, the victim of Kapitänleutnant Ernst Mengersen in *U 101*, one of the most successful U-boat commanders of the war, who had intercepted and begun to shadow the convoy before its escort group arrived.[129] At 0335z (Greenwich Mean Time), 2 December, the destroyer caught up with *Forfar* on a parallel course and, because the armed merchant cruiser appeared to have opened fire, Lieutenant Rayner, *St Laurent*'s CO, assumed his ship had been mistaken for a surfaced submarine and flashed his recognition lights.

Forfar's crew probably did indeed initially mistake *St Laurent* for a surfaced submarine, for the good reason that minutes before the destroyer's arrival they had sighted the shadow of *U 99*. The submarine, commanded by another "ace," Korvettenkapitän Otto Kretschmer, had been coming to join the attack on HX 90 when it encountered the armed merchant cruiser. Kretschmer saw a destroyer arrive, almost certainly *St Laurent*, and fired a "snap" torpedo attack at the armed merchant cruiser as he crash dived to avoid detection; the gunfire Rayner heard may have been the detonation of the torpedo or defensive shooting from *Forfar*. Although *Forfar* was damaged by this torpedo, it was not in danger of sinking. Unaware of these events, and having received no response to the recognition signal, *St Laurent* made off to the northwest where a signal rocket had appeared.[130] It almost certainly came from HX 90 where *U 101*, now supported by other boats, was striking again but Rayner still had no idea he was approaching a convoy under attack.[131]

It was at about 0400z that *St Laurent* finally came on the beleaguered and defenceless convoy.[132] Rayner dropped single depth charges and fired starshell as deterrent measures. At 0500 he sighted two boatloads of survivors from the tanker *Conch*. He recovered them quickly. "Herbert

127. This, according to a rather unreliable Italian account, was a blow to *Argo*, which had recovered some of the destroyer's papers and was sure she had gone down. Admiral Aldo Cocchia, *Submarines Attacking*, 46-9, translated extract in DHH, 81/520 *Saguenay*

128. AHS, *Home Waters* II, 229; *St Laurent* deck log, 30 Nov. 1940, NAC, RG 24, 7928

129. Cdr V.P. Alleyne, RCN [Convoy Commodore], "Report on Convoy H.X. 90," forwarded by COAC to NSec, 8 Jan. 1941, DHH, NHS file 48-2-2 pt 5. The covering letter by Cmdre G.C. Jones, RCN, is worth quoting: "The report is forwarded not only for its interest, but to draw attention tho the fact that Commander Alleyne is the only Canadian Officer serving as Commodore of Convoy. This duty he has carried out since the beginning of hostilities. He was actually Commodore of HX no. 1."

130. *St Laurent* log, 2 Dec. 1940; *U 99*, KTB, 2 Dec. 1940; NHS, "Notes on the Activities of HMCS *St Laurent* during the period 30 Nov. to 6 Dec., 1940," 7 Nov. 1958, DHH, 81/520 St Laurent I 8000 (1937-43)

131. The other U-boat commanders included Kapitänleutnant Salman in *U 52*, Kapitänleutnant Schreiber in *U 95*, Fregettenkapitän Lüth in *U 43* and Prien in *U 47*, a formidable group. Blair, *Hitler's U-boat War*, 210-12; Rohwer, *Axis Submarine Successes*, 37-8

132. The following account is based on Adm, *MASR*, Jan. 1941, 15-22; WAC WD, 1-4 Dec.1940; *St Laurent* log, 1-4 Dec. 1940; NHS, "Notes on the Activities of HMCS *St Laurent*"; AHS, *Battle Summary No. 51. Convoy and Anti-Submarine Warfare Reports*, 1-6, copy from PRO, ADM 234/370; Cdr V.P. Alleyne, RCN [Convoy Commodore], Report on Convoy HX 90

Rayner, as usual," recalled Lieutenant C.P. Nixon, "was very calm under duress ... the captain [of *Conch*] came aboard ... and I thought that maybe he could tell us about what was going on in the tactical situation. So I took him up to the bridge and I shouted out to Rayner 'Captain, sir, I have the captain of this shipload of survivors ... maybe he can tell you something.' Rayner turned round and put his hand out to shake hands with this man as if he was receiving guests at a cocktail party."[133] Western Approaches now radioed orders for the destroyer to go to the assistance of *Forfar*, which had finally been sunk by four additional torpedoes from *U 99*. At 0832, while searching for the armed merchant cruiser, *St Laurent* sighted a U-boat on the surface, very likely *U 95*, ninety minutes before that boat launched a torpedo into the abandoned hulk of *Conch*.[134] Rayner held fire as he closed the range to give his guns a better chance of hitting, but the submarine crash dived. The destroyer made asdic contact and, assisted by the destroyer HMS *Viscount*, which joined at 0930Z, hunted for over four hours. The destroyers dropped a total of eighty-one depth charges. After the last pattern, the asdic contact disappeared.[135] They had not destroyed the submarine but *St Laurent* and *Viscount*'s determined action brought Admiral Dönitz's frustrated summation of the reports he received during the late morning and afternoon of 2 December: "Contact was nevertheless lost for day. Apparently there was strong A/S and escort forces with the enemy."[136]

In the meantime, the merchant vessel *Dunsley* from HX 90 had come across *Forfar*'s survivors, begun rescue work, and called for help. *Viscount* broke off from the hunt for *U 95* at 1245z while *St Laurent* conducted a final search before responding to *Viscount*'s call for more help about forty-five minutes later. Nixon recalled:

> First, we thought [the survivors in the water] were negroes ... We had some Chinese survivors and we thought now we're going to get some negroes. These poor fellows were all British and they were covered in oil. I remember they always talk about British understatement and on this occasion there was a masterpiece. There were about four survivors sitting on a small square raft, not much larger than a card table ... and one of them turned out to be the purser, a man of fifty or so. He was exhausted. They would have been dead if we hadn't found them in an hour or two because it was terribly cold. So we helped scrub the oil off them and gave them a couple of shots of rum and he made an observation 'You know, there's no comfort on one of those rafts.'[137]

Having completed the rescue of *Forfar*'s survivors, *St Laurent* escorted *Loch Ranza*, a merchant vessel that had been badly damaged in the U-boat attacks of the night before. The crippled ship could creep along at no more than a few knots, while *St Laurent* circled to provide protection. It was a harrowing four-day journey back to port, a good part of it in gale conditions. When *St Laurent* reached the Clyde late on 6 December, she had been continuously engaged in the most demanding and stressful operations for a solid 152 hours.[138] HX 90's ordeal, however, had continued. On the

---

133. Nixon interview, 35

134. The submarine's KTB describes these events with timings that match *St Laurent*'s report; *U 95*, KTB, 2 Dec. 1940

135. "Extract from ROP—HMCS *St Laurent*," 0928 to 1431 2 Dec. 1940, NAC, RG 24, 1075, 45-7-1 pt 1; Adm, *MASR*, Jan., 1941, 18

136. Ibid; *U 101*, KTB, 2 Dec. 1940; *BdU*, KTB, 2 Dec. 1940

137. Nixon interview, 35

138. NHS, "Notes on the Activities of HMCS *St Laurent*"

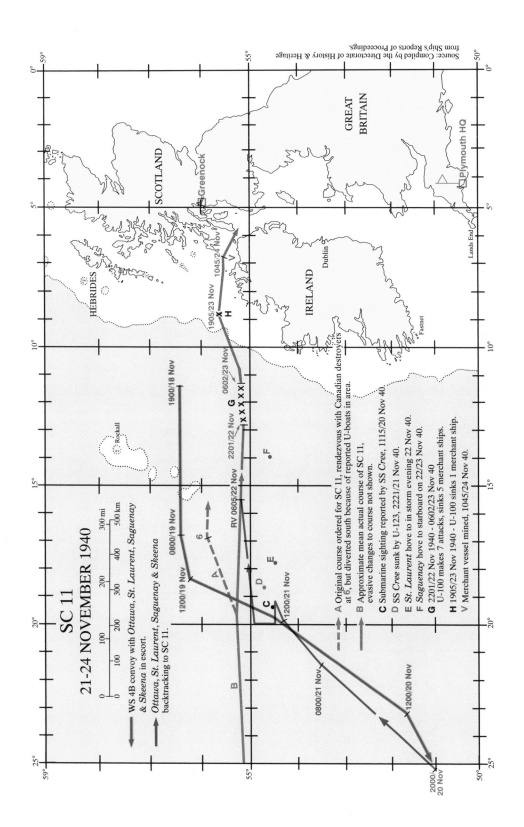

SC 11
21-24 NOVEMBER 1940

→ WS 4B convoy with *Ottawa, St. Laurent, Saguenay*
& *Skeena* in escort.

→ *Ottawa, St. Laurent, Saguenay* & *Skeena*
backtracking to SC 11.

A Original course ordered for SC 11, rendezvous with Canadian destroyers
at 6, but diverted south because of reported U-boats in area.
B Approximate mean actual course of SC 11,
evasive changes to course not shown.
C Submarine sighting reported by SS *Cree*, 1115/20 Nov 40.
D SS *Cree* sunk by U-123, 2221/21 Nov 40.
E *St. Laurent* hove to in storm evening 22 Nov 40.
F *Saguenay* hove to to starboard on 22/23 Nov 40.
G 2201/22 Nov 1940 - 0602/23 Nov 40
U-100 makes 7 attacks, sinks 5 merchant ships.
H 1905/23 Nov 1940 - U-100 sinks 1 merchant ship.
V Merchant vessel mined, 1045/24 Nov 40.

Source: Compiled by the Directorate of History & Heritage
from Ship's Reports of Proceedings.

late afternoon of 2 December, when the demands of rescue work had reduced the screen to the sloop HMS *Folkestone* and the corvette HMS *Gentian*, *U 94* sank two more merchant ships. That same evening another merchant ship fell victim to a long-range German aircraft. Of the thirty vessels in the original convoy, ten had been lost and one severely damaged, and the valuable armed merchant cruiser *Forfar* had been sunk nearby, all in a span of about thirty-four hours.[139]

Even with the small number of U-boats at sea the Germans had once again concentrated their entire effort, eleven ocean-going submarines in the convoy focal area about 400 miles or so to the west of Ireland, where escort was still infrequent and weak. Senior British officers drew the conclusion that the enemy had a more highly developed search system than was in fact the case, including two elements that the Germans never achieved: effective coordination of *Luftwaffe* reconnaissance flights with submarine patrols and effective surface search radars for U-boats. "This combination," concluded a staff study written in the wake of the HX 90 battle, "is destroying our shipping at a rate of nearly 3½ million tons a year, as compared with a replacement rate of 1 million, increasing to 1¼ million tons a year." That negated the increased tonnage acquired by capture or requisition from allies, undermined plans for amphibious operations, and interrupted the flow of supplies from North America, "an essential part of our strategic plan for winning the war." Inevitably, rationing in the United Kingdom would become more severe. Even more alarming was the risk of weakening morale in the Merchant Navy, "in view of the apparent inability of the Royal Navy to protect them effectively against the renewed submarine cum air menace ... Any such weakening of morale might result in a general paralysis of our war effort, for which reason the North Western Approaches assume an importance transcending even the effect of night bombing of the United Kingdom."[140] The British consequently rushed into effect measures that had already been discussed but for the more distant future when more resources became available.[141]

On 20 December the Admiralty announced that henceforward convoy routes would be much more widely dispersed, as far as 63° 30' North—the parallel just south of Iceland—as far as possible from enemy air and submarine bases. Escort groups were now to accompany convoys for roughly three rather than two days from northern United Kingdom ports. To ease this increased burden on the escort force, the convoy cycles would open, in the case of the Canadian series from two HX and one SC convoy every eight days to the same number over a cycle of ten days.[142] At the same time, the Admiralty hastened development of a refuelling base at Iceland so that shorter-ranged destroyers could top up after leaving an outbound convoy and before joining an incoming one. Coastal Command also endeavoured to further develop its northern bases, including facilities in Iceland, to provide fuller support to the north and west.[143]

---

139. The figures extracted from Adm, *MASR*, Jan. 1941, 16-19, agree with Rohwer, *Axis Submarine Successes*, 37-8

140. DOP to ACNS, 19 Dec. 1940, forwarding "Appreciation of the A/S War in the Atlantic," PRO, ADM 116/4324

141. "Ninth Meeting Held at the Trade Division Conference Room, Admiralty to consider A/S Measures for Better Protection of Convoys, 3 Jan. 1941," PRO, ADM 199/2079

142. Adm, *MASR*, Nov. 1940, 16; Dec. 1940, 6,11; the original messages are Admiralty to Address Information Group 47, 20 Dec. 1940 and [Admiralty] to C-in-C WA, 20 Dec. 1940, PRO, ADM 116/4324

143. "Ninth Meeting," and "Thirteenth Meeting ... 11 Mar. 1941," both PRO, ADM, 199/2079. The minutes of the latter meeting report that "escort vessels were already using Iceland as a base, for refuelling and effecting minor repairs," which would mean the escorts began using Iceland in early March at the latest, and probably sometime in February. J. Terraine, *Business in Great Waters* (London 1989), 338, presumably following *Defeat of the Enemy Attack on Shipping*, 31 states that this did not happen until April 1941.

One reason the Admiralty was able to extend and improve antisubmarine protection to convoys earlier than anticipated was the availability of the "forty to fifty" US destroyers that Churchill had originally requested and Roosevelt refused to give in May 1940. From a low point of only some thirty ocean-going escorts in late June 1940, the strength of Western Approaches Command had grown to nearly 100 by late December as a result of the completion of the first emergency war program escorts, repair of ships damaged in the Norwegian and French campaigns, and the easing of the invasion threat. The US destroyers increased that strength by over 40 percent, to 137 escorts.[144]

Canada played a prominent part in the intense and complex diplomacy that persuaded Roosevelt to release the destroyers, a pivotal role in arrangements for their speedy transfer to British control, and accepted responsibility for manning and operating six of these vessels for which the RN lacked crews. What is more, Canada made a firm commitment that a large portion of the corvettes building for the RCN would be made available for service in British waters starting in the spring 1941, expanded the industrial effort needed to make good on this promise, and thereby provided a critical margin to the Admiralty in its plans to sustain and further improve defences for convoys. (Admiralty planners hoped to double the number of ocean escorts during 1941 to 289; their projections were that some fifty-eight of these—one in five—would be RCN ships, a figure that the RCN bettered, as will be seen in Chapters 4 and 5.)[145] In these important undertakings, Canada fulfilled its new responsibility as Britain's largest ally, but was able to do so because the King government forged a new and close defence relationship with the United States.

After the first RCN destroyers were deployed across the Atlantic in May 1940, Mackenzie King sent word to Churchill of Roosevelt's genuine efforts to support Britain in the face of isolationist sentiment. On 5 June Churchill replied that "We must be careful not to let Americans view too complacently prospect of a British collapse, out of which they would get the British Fleet and guardianship of the British Empire, minus Great Britain."[146] King immediately sent his envoy, Hugh Keenleyside, back to the president, warning that Churchill did not bluff when he said his government might be replaced by one that would bargain the fleet away as part of a peace settlement. At the same time, he endorsed Churchill's faith in the United Kingdom's undiminished fighting spirit and urged American assistance for Britain.[147]

With Italy's entry into the war and the fall of France, King and his military and political advisors, determined not to run to the United States for protection in the face of increased concerns for Canadian security, sought means of bringing Britain and the United States more closely together. Immediately at issue were the British possessions in the Western Hemisphere, right on the doorstep of the United States: Newfoundland, Bermuda and the British West Indies. The immi-

---

144. DOP to ACNS, 19 Dec. 1940, forwarding "Appreciation of the A/S War." See esp table showing the existing escort force and projections for its expansion.

145. Ibid. The Admiralty projection for 289 escorts by Dec. 1941 included thirty-eight RCN corvettes, to which must be added ten corvettes built in Canada for the Admiralty that the RCN manned, and ten RCN River and ex-US destroyers.

146. DSec to SSEA, tg, 5 June 1940, *DCER* pt 8, 88

147. A possible change in government was a matter of constitutional fact. Memo by PM, 6 June, 1940, *DCER* vol 8, 89-93

nence of a British collapse raised alarm in the US press and government that Axis forces might gain access to the islands unless American forces occupied them and turned them into a first line of defence for the United States. Churchill wanted to bargain over US access to the islands: the Americans could base forces there only if they provided substantial military assistance to Britain, not just the destroyers but also further-reaching commitments. He was, in fact, determined to secure the United States's entry into the war by whatever means possible. Without a deal that brought the United States a considerable way towards participation, Churchill feared, the additional protection afforded by the island defence line would encourage the Americans more than ever to lock themselves up in their own hemisphere. Lord Lothian, the British ambassador in Washington, urged nearly the opposite. A magnanimous offer of military base sites with no strings attached, he argued, would win sympathy and support, but bargaining over such a sensitive issue as the security of the American seacoast would produce nothing but ill will.[148]

King, who warned the British government that Churchill's strident demands for US belligerency "were actually prejudicing the President's ability to go as far in the way of effective cooperation as might otherwise be possible," believed Lothian was right.[149] When, in April, Britain had requested a Canadian military force to occupy the Danish possession of Greenland following the German occupation of Denmark, King had met Roosevelt's objections to the measure by agreeing that their two countries could cooperate by sending supplies and arms to the inhabitants. Roosevelt allowed that if German forces were detected in the Greenland area, an American aircraft carrier "would bomb them to hell."[150] Similar cooperation in the defence of British islands on the American littoral would inevitably, King informed the British government, draw the Americans into the Commonwealth war effort.[151]

In Ottawa during the last two weeks of June, planning for the defence of Canada in view of France's collapse and the peril to England highlighted the importance of joint preparations with the United States, not least on the Atlantic islands. The Chiefs of Staff recommended approaching Newfoundland to base Canadian land forces at Gander and the adjacent seaplane facility at Botwood; the PM instructed the chiefs to review Atlantic defences and report on facilities needed to base the British fleet at Canadian ports; and he took up the chiefs' recommendation for Canadian–American staff talks for "cooperation in event of trans-ocean attack on North America." Jay Pierrepont Moffat, the newly appointed American ambassador in Ottawa, was receptive but cautious in the extreme.[152] Roosevelt, however, instructed Moffat to see what precisely the

---

148. D. Reynolds, *The Creation of the Anglo-American Alliance*, 117-18; Stetson Conn and Byron Fairchild, *The Framework of Hemisphere Defense* (Washington 1960), 46-8; Leutze, *Bargaining for Supremacy*, 78-9; Charge d'Affaires in United States to USSEA, 24 May 1940, Mem from USSEA to PM, 1 June 40, *DCER* pt 8, 72-3, 84-7

149. SSEA to DSec, tg, 17 June 1940, *DCER* pt 8, 98-9

150. Quote from Keenleyside [memo of conversation with Roosevelt, 26 May 1940], *DCER* pt 8, 70-1. See also, 78, 81, 83. On Greenland, see Mackenzie King diary, 23-4 April 1940; *DCER* pt 8, 947-1022; Stacey, *Arms, Men and Governments*, 367-9; on US Coast Guard operations in Greenland, Patrick Abbazia, *Mr Roosevelt's Navy: The Private War of the U.S. Atlantic Fleet, 1939-1942* (Annapolis 1975), 86-8.

151. King diary, 25 Apr. 1940

152. "The President had already spoken to him about steps of the kind being taken," but the armed forces were ill prepared, Germany might utilize its already considerable influence in Brazil to gain a military lodgement there, and political constraints on the president were severe. "It would create suspicion in Washington, were he to turn up for the day, after he had been in Canada." CWCM, 14 June 1940; King diary, 14 June 1940

Canadians wanted to talk about, and King arranged for the American minister to meet J.L. Ralston and Minister of National Defence for Air C.G. Power on 29 June.[153]

Guided by service briefings, Ralston and Power noted that the need of the Axis powers to consolidate their victories in Europe, and the harsh Atlantic winter, would delay any major attack on North America until the spring of 1941 at the earliest. By that time, completion of the RCN's first lot of corvettes and Bangors would provide defence against submarines.[154] Because nearly all RCN destroyers were committed to the Eastern Atlantic, however, defence against surface raiders would have to depend on the RN and USN. Should the RN retreat to North American waters or substantial USN forces move into the Atlantic, both would have to rely on large American ports for major support, in view of the limited facilities in Canada.[155] The most urgent need was for the United States to help Canada push the North American perimeter outward to Newfoundland, Greenland, and Iceland—at which Moffat protested that Iceland was in the American view part of Europe—and the Canadians suggested that the time had come for the USN to concentrate more on the Atlantic than the Pacific.[156]

Staff conversations took place under a cloak of secrecy in Washington on 11–12 July. Brigadier K. Stuart, Deputy Chief of the General Staff, Air Commodore A.A.L. Cuffe, Air Member, Air Staff, and Captain L.W. Murray, Deputy Chief of the Naval Staff, met with Brigadier General G.V. Strong, Assistant Chief of Staff, US Army, Commander F.P. Sherman, Chief Aviation Officer, Bureau of Naval Operations, and Captain H.W. Hill, Director of Plans, USN. The Canadians made it clear that they urgently needed equipment, especially for land and air forces, and asked what base facilities the US forces would need in Canada and Newfoundland. Because of their own unpreparedness the Americans only wanted to despatch forces in case of an actual attack. The Canadians pointed out that this might be too late, but they were careful to say, having correctly sensed that their counterparts thought England was as good as defeated and that sending any more supplies across the Atlantic was futile, that no material assistance should be provided to Canada at the expense of Britain.[157]

---

153. Power was the new Minister of National Defence for Air. Ralston, the Finance Minister, would be assuming the defence portfolio, responsible for both the army and navy, because Norman Rogers had died in an air crash on 10 June. Stacey, *Arms, Men and Governments*, 332-3

154. The Chiefs of Staff prepared an appreciation arguing that if Great Britain lost control of the North Atlantic, the security of Canada and the United States would be at immediate risk. This was not to be unduly stressed, merely put forward as a possibility not to be ignored. CSC to minister, "The General Defence of the East Coast of the North American Continent against German-Italian Aggression," 28 June 1940, NAC, RG 24, 2700, HQS 5199-0 pt 1

155. Defences and facilities at Halifax and Sydney had to be improved, antisubmarine nets, coast artillery batteries, and fleet support services were needed at Gaspé and Shelburne. Gaspé was a large, readily defensible harbour capable of accommodating major warships. Shelburne, too shallow for ships larger than cruisers, was defensible and, as in the First World War, well located for cooperation with the United States if raiders attempted to strike at the heavy shipping traffic off southern Nova Scotia. It would also complement the increasingly overburdened facilities at Halifax. NSec to COAC, 12 Aug. 1940. NAC, RG 24, 3810, NS 1010-11-1 pt 2

156. Power, "Notes," 28 June 1940 and "Memo of conversation with the American Minister, Mr Moffat, June 29th 1940," 30 June 1940, Queen's University Archives, Power papers, box 69, file D-2018. In the case of Newfoundland, a reconnaissance of the coast by HMS *Caradoc* (operating, it will be recalled, under Canadian control), and consultations with the C-in-C AWI, showed that St John's, although the harbour was small, was the only year-round port with communications to the interior. It was selected as the primary defended base. The large northern harbour of Botwood, which, like Gaspé, was closed by ice in the winter, would become a summer base. *Documents on Relations between Canada and Newfoundland* I, 126-33, 160-1

157. The Canadians were pleased that Adm Stark, chief of naval operations, and Gen Marshall, chief of staff, US Army, attended the first session: Memo by the DCGS, nd, *DCER* pt 8, 156-61. The Canadian army's seasoned staff officers dominated strategic planning in Ottawa, and Murray recollected that "Our best talker was General Stuart." Douglas interview with Murray, 37, DHH, Murray biog file

The naval discussions, which mainly concerned base facilities, became quite positive after news arrived of the British attacks on the French fleet at Mers-el-Kebir to ensure that the warships did not fall under German control. After this dramatic demonstration of Britain's undiminished fighting spirit, recalled Murray, "we became fast friends in the idea of keeping the war on the other side of the Atlantic." The US fleet probably had enough repair and supply vessels to sustain itself in Canada and Newfoundland but was short of dry dock capacity.[158] If the British fleet arrived, Canadian yards therefore would have to undertake the refit and repair of many ships.[159] The sailors quickly got down to the specifics of command arrangements. "[It] is the expectation of the United States Navy," reported Murray, "that if they come to Canadian waters, local defence and A/S patrol connected with local defence will be carried out as now by the R.C.N. and under R.C.N. authority. They will, of course, expect to command their own fleet and I went so far as to inform them that in all probability H.M.C. Ships then operating on the east coast would be attached to the larger command of the U.S. Navy for operational purposes, though still being administered by the R.C.N."[160]

Meanwhile in Ottawa, the prime minister had recruited Angus L. Macdonald, premier of Nova Scotia, to serve as Minister of National Defence for Naval Services. This was a gap that badly needed filling. The events bringing the navy into direct support of Britain in European waters had greatly increased the administrative burden for Colonel J.L. Ralston, formally appointed Minister of National Defence on 5 July. Previous increases of responsibility for home defence had already brought J.S. Duncan, of Massey-Harris, as a third "associate acting deputy minister" responsible for the air force, leaving Lieutenant-Colonel K.S. Maclachlan free to concentrate on the navy as its deputy minister. Finding a naval minister had been complicated by King's refusal to create a national government of all parties, and Macdonald was not King's first choice, although he had strong support from Ralston and Power.[161]

Macdonald was a scholar. He had a doctorate of laws from Harvard University and had taught at Dalhousie University. He had succeeded in politics, and he considered his reformist liberalism to be rooted in the traditions of Sir Wilfrid Laurier. If these could be taken as similarities to the prime minister, his origins and background—one of fourteen children brought up in both Gaelic and English on a farm in Cape Breton, he had served as a platoon commander on the Western Front and been severely wounded four days before the armistice in 1918—placed him on quite a different plane.[162] Enormously popular in Nova Scotia, he was used to commanding authority in Halifax, and did not adjust easily to the cut and thrust of Ottawa.[163] Certainly, he soon came to resent King's

---

158. Murray interview, 37

159. Murray wondered if a squadron based in the vicinity of Boston might intervene to enforce the neutrality zone should German raiders approach Canada. The Americans pointed out that the US fleet had not intervened when British forces had pursued an enemy ship inside US territorial waters at the time of the *Graf Spec* incident. That worked in favour of the Empire. More could not be expected. Memo by the DCNS, *DCER* pt 8, 166

160. Ibid

161. J.S. Duncan, who did not wish to run for Parliament, was the first choice. King had tried to persuade Macdonald to come to Ottawa as the "Maritime spokesman" in 1935, and succeeded in 1940 only by recalling Macdonald's promise to do anything he could to help the war effort. H. Blair Neatby, *William Lyon Mackenzie King* III: *1932-1939: The Prism of Unity* (Toronto 1976), 130; HoC, *Debates*, 8 July 1940, 1398, 1402; Stacey, *Arms, Men and Governments*, 122; J.W. Pickersgill, *Mackenzie King Record* I (Toronto 1960), 94, 96, 100; King diary, 28 June 1940

162. J. Hawkins, *The Life and Times of Angus L.* (Windsor 1969), 42-53

163. J. Murray Beck, *Politics of Nova Scotia* II: *Murray-Buchanan, 1896-1988* (Tantallon 1988), 138-40, 153-85; *Speeches of Angus L. Macdonald* (Toronto 1960), 1-17; John Hawkins, *Angus L.*, 223-6

convoluted methods and the tight rein he kept on his ministers, and did not mask his bitterness at the manner in which the prime minister left the question of a seat in the House of Commons to hang fire for some weeks, then offered him no choice but to stand in Norman Rogers's old riding of Kingston, Ontario, an area where the strong "Orange" element might embarrass the Catholic Macdonald. In the event, the minister won the seat by acclamation, but the incident was early evidence of the mistrust between the two men that flared into open confrontation towards the end of the war.[164]

The situation in the North Atlantic was troubling. Intelligence from the Admiralty indicated that German raiders had broken out into the open ocean, and on 1 August the C-in-C America and West Indies, down to four cruisers as ships went into refit, asked for the return of *Caradoc* from the RCN's operational control. King "reluctantly agreed," grumbling that he had already consented to sending Canadian destroyers overseas, and he fretted about the delay of delivery by the British of long range gun mountings to defend Halifax.[165] There was, however, encouraging news on 3 August that the US cabinet was considering a formula that might break the impasse over further American aid to Britain. The fifty old USN destroyers that Britain desperately wanted should be traded for base sites on the Atlantic islands and an assurance that the British fleet would fight on if Britain were defeated. With these terms the president could demonstrate to isolationists that the whole arrangement was strengthening hemispheric defence, and thereby at least appear to meet the requirements of the neutrality laws. Although a pale show of the commitment Churchill wanted, this was progress. It reflected a growing belief in Washington that Britain might survive, and the influence of the pro-intervention Republicans Henry L. Stimson and Frank Knox, whom Roosevelt had appointed as secretaries of war and the navy.[166]

An option that the American administration was considering, in the event the neutrality laws prevented a direct transfer of the destroyers to Great Britain, was to turn them over to Canada, nominally for hemisphere defence, but without any restriction that would prevent Canada from then turning them over to Britain. Here King saw an opportunity to ensure that Canada's own capacity for self-defence was not neglected, and he quickly dispatched Captain Murray to Washington to ask Admiral Stark informally if Canada could purchase four destroyers outright to strengthen coverage of the denuded east coast. Stark's advice, to go directly to the president since this was a political question, won immediate favour in the Cabinet War Committee.[167] If the trans-

---

164. Hawkins, *Angus L.*, 222-3. King, taken aback by Macdonald's toughness in negotiations about the seat, reflected: "He gave me the impression of being a little more ambitious as to his future, and certain as to its promise, than I had thought he really felt." King diary, 3 Aug. 1940

165. As pointed out to the British in June, "Our own Canadian coasts have become increasingly vulnerable as a consequence of our having parted with aircraft and destroyers to assist the United Kingdom in the present emergency." SSEA to DSec, tg, 17 June 1940, *DCER* pt 8, 98-9; C-in-C AWI to NSHQ, 1 Aug. 1940, C-in-C AWI to Adm, 4 Aug. 1940, NAC, RG 24, 11,101, 50-5-1; AHS, *Home Waters* II, 202-3, 218-9; King diary, 2 Aug. 1940

166. Minister in US to SSEA, 3 Aug. 1940, *DCER* pt 8, 112-3; Reynolds, *Creation of the Anglo-American Alliance*, 124-7

167. Pound had already unofficially sounded out Nelles about manning some of the destroyers, and Nelles had replied (in phrases that suggest he had consulted his political masters), the RCN could man up to four because of the shortage of qualified personnel in the RCN. Stark, who had no objection, was in some anguish over the legal requirement to sign a declaration that the destroyers were surplus to US requirements, thus suggested consulting the president. 1st Sea Lord to CNS, 13 June 1940, NAC, RG 24, 11056, 30-1-5 pt 1; CNS to 1st Sea Lord, 14 June 1940, ibid; Murray to Nelles, 7 Aug. 1940, DHH, 81/520 Destroyers (Town) 8000 General; CWCM, 7 Aug. 1940; *DCER* pt 8, 112-3, Doc. 71, 114, Doc. 74, 117-18, King to Canadian Minister in Washington, tg 162, 12 Aug. 1940

fer of as many as fifty destroyers to Britain came to fruition, Macdonald informed his colleagues, he believed that Canada had a good claim to four of them, and he expected that it would also be possible to bring the RCN River class destroyers home from British waters.[168]

Roosevelt, as he pressed forward with the idea of a swap of destroyers for bases, passed word that he was disappointed not to have stronger encouragement from Ottawa.[169] King immediately instructed Loring Christie, the Canadian minister in Washington, to convey Canada's full support, and remind the president that King had consistently given that support, while sending Canada's own destroyers to help Britain: "We of course continue to regard the English Channel as the first line of defence for ourselves and other democratic peoples." King also seized the opportunity to raise again Canada's particular needs. "In appropriate measure, however, we consider it desirable to discuss cooperation in the second line of defence of North America and in particular the desirability of obtaining a small number of destroyers or equivalent vessels for service on the Canadian coasts."[170]

Events now moved quickly. On 15 August, the day Christie delivered King's message to Roosevelt, Churchill provisionally accepted the president's offer to transfer fifty destroyers in exchange for ninety-nine year base site leases in seven British possessions, including Newfoundland, and a reiteration of his public statement of 4 June that the British fleet would not be surrendered or scuttled.[171] Roosevelt responded to Christie's warning about the defencelessness of the Canadian coast by suggesting further staff talks and, the next day, invited the Canadian prime minister to meet at Ogdensburg, New York.[172]

At the Ogdensburg meeting, on 17–18 August, the president and the prime minister quickly agreed to the creation of the Canada–United States Permanent Joint Board on Defence. The board would include representatives from each of the armed services of the two countries, together with senior civilian officials, who would study common defence problems and make recommendations to each of the governments which, as a safeguard to sovereignty especially important for Canada, retained full authority for approval and implementation. True to the intentions of the two leaders, the board remains to this day the umbrella agency for Canada–US military cooperation.[173]

Detailed arrangements for the physical transfer of the fifty USN destroyers were getting under way at the same time as the historic Ogdensburg meeting. On 17 August Admiral Pound wired Nelles to ask if RN personnel could take over the ships at Halifax, and if facilities could be made available so that the ships could "shake down" to give their "half-baked"—the Admiralty's

---

168. CWCM, 13 Aug. 1940

169. Christie had reported that friends of the president were suggesting Roosevelt was disappointed at not receiving stronger word from Canada in favour of the deal. Minister in the US to SSEA, 10 Aug. 1940, *DCER* pt 8, 115

170. SSEA to Minister in US, 12 Aug. 1940, *DCER* pt 8, 117-18

171. Roosevelt to Churchill, 13 Aug.1940, Churchill to Roosevelt, 15 Aug. 1940, W.F. Kimball, *Forces in War: Roosevelt, Churchill and the Second World War* (New York, 1997) 58-61

172. *DCER* pt 8, 125-9

173. Stacey *Arms, Men and Governments*, 337-42; W.A.B. Douglas, "Democratic Spirit and Purpose," in J. Sokolsky and J. Jockel (eds), *Fifty Years of Canada-US Defense Cooperation: The Road from Ogdensburg* (Lewiston 1992), 31-58

phrase—new British crews some experience before crossing the Atlantic.[174] Previously, Nelles had agreed that the RCN might be able to provide crews for four of the destroyers, but Pound now suggested that the Canadians should, like the British, scrape the bottom of the barrel to man more ships. On 18 August Nelles agreed to the arrangements at Halifax, and offered to provide crews for six destroyers.[175] This encouraging response prompted the Admiralty to put out feelers to the British High Commissioner in Ottawa to see if Canada could be pushed further, to commit all six of the destroyers, or even better four of them as well as two more of the modern River class destroyers, to England, leaving just two of the old American destroyers in Canadian waters. On 28 August, Gerald Campbell told the Admiralty to back off.[176]

The prime minister was in a foul mood, and more than ever worried about the vulnerability of the east coast. His cheerful report to Churchill about the progress of the negotiations for the destroyers, and of the new Canada–United States defence pact had yielded a bitter blast from the British prime minister on 22 August. Where King, who like Lord Lothian had a keen appreciation of the domestic opposition Roosevelt faced, saw progress in drawing the United States into the Allied cause, Churchill saw in the same events the American withdrawal into hemispheric defence that he had always feared. The severity of the terms that Roosevelt proposed for the destroyer-bases deal—ninety-nine year leases to substantial tracts of land in seven British possessions as straight payment for fifty old destroyers and some aircraft and other equipment—so obviously favoured the United States that Churchill, anticipating censure in Britain, had come round to Lord Lothian's (and King's) earlier view that it would be wiser to offer the bases as a gift to symbolize the association of the United States with the Allied cause. "It would be better to do without the destroyers sorely as we need them than to get drawn into a haggling match between the experts as to what we ought to give in return for munitions," he thundered at King. As for the Canada–US defence agreement, "Here again there may be two opinions ... Supposing Mr Hitler cannot invade us and his Air Force begins to blench under the strain all these transactions will be judged in a mood different to that prevailing while the issue still hangs in the balance."[177] This suggestion that Canada was cutting and running for American protection particularly stung King, and he took it as a vindication when on 26 August the warning arrived from the Admiralty that the U-boat attack on SC 1 west of Iceland might be the beginning of a push into Canadian waters.[178] "It disclosed so completely the wisdom of the establishment of the Permanent Joint Board," King recorded, that he read it to the American members whom he was greeting, then called in the Canadian members and read it again.[179]

---

174. The Admiralty was counting on refitting delays for time to address the manning problem, and anticipating that damage to other British ships necessitating long periods in dockyard would make their key personnel available. "C.L.," 'American Destroyers,'" 14 Aug. 1940, min by Harcourt, 19 Sept. 1940, Tait, 20 Sept. 1940, Edward, 21 Sept. 1940, PRO, ADM 116/4410

175. First Sea Lord to CNS, 17 Aug. 1940, CNS to First Sea Lord, 18 Aug. 1940, NAC, RG 24, 11056, file 30-1-15 pt 1

176. [Dominions Office] toBHC, tg 1874, 28 Aug. 1940, BHC to [Dominions Office], tg 1948, PRO, ADM 116/4410 pt 1

177. PM of Great Britain to PM, 22 Aug. 1940, *DCER* pt 8, 142. See also Stacey, *Arms, Men and Governments*, 341; Reynolds, *Creation of the Anglo-American Alliance*, 128-30.

178. Nelles to Sec to the PM, 26 Aug. 1940, NAC, MG 26J4, 396, f 56, C278991

179. King diary, 26 Aug. 1940

Part of the reason for King's anger may well have been the fact that, although Canada was offering substantial assistance to the Royal Navy in manning the ex-USN destroyers, he had all but abandoned his efforts to have the ships assigned to Canadian waters. During the Ogdensburg talks King had asked Roosevelt about the possibility of Canada taking over "four or five" of the destroyers for employment at Halifax. Roosevelt responded, in light of the good progress of the destroyers for bases arrangements, that Canada should now pursue this project through the Admiralty. The president, whose service as an assistant secretary of the navy during the First World War gave him a firmer grasp of naval strategy than King or any other member of the Canadian Cabinet, strongly recommended that Canada should also take the advice of the Admiralty as to whether these ships should be deployed at Halifax or elsewhere. King had readily agreed, and dutifully reported to Churchill that the ships would be sent where the Admiralty thought they were most needed.[180]

The Canadian naval staff, which had never supported the government's desire to strengthen home defences at the expense of the commitment in British waters, firmed up arrangements to have the Canadian-manned ex-USN destroyers reinforce Western Approaches Command. On 1 September Admiral Nelles undertook the education of Macdonald, the new navy minister. Nelles explained that, because the transfer arrangements would give the Admiralty full control of the destroyers, it was not in Britain's interest to allow the ones manned by Canada to be commissioned as RCN ships, especially if the government intended to hold them back in Canadian waters. He also explained that the Admiralty was right. The critical struggle in the Western Approaches, and the absence of any actual threat in the Western Atlantic, meant there was no strategic case for bringing back any of the River class or for retaining the ex-USN ships at Halifax. In a gesture to the government's alarm about east coast defence, Nelles suggested that two of the destroyers should be kept in Canadian waters. The government, however, should offer to deploy the remaining four overseas in exchange for the Admiralty's agreement that all six vessels should be commissioned into the RCN. Macdonald, the government, and the Admiralty quickly approved these arrangements.[181]

On 2 September the British and US governments signed the agreements for the transfer of the destroyers and for the acquisition by the United States of base sites in the British possessions. Newfoundland and Bermuda were to be regarded as gifts, as Churchill wanted, and the Caribbean sites as payment for fifty First World War–vintage American destroyers, which the RN would call the "Town" class.[182] Just four days later, the first eight destroyers arrived at Halifax, only hours after more than a thousand British naval personnel arrived in the troop ship *The Duchess of Richmond*. They moved into improvised accommodation—300 triple-decker bunks in the Grand Stadium of the Halifax exhibition grounds—had two days' familiarization with their USN counterparts, then took over the ships on 9 September after a simple ceremony "appropriate under the circumstances for a neutral nation." The Americans marched off to waiting railway cars on a nearby siding, while

180. SSEA to DSec, 18 Aug. 1940, *DCER* pt 8, 137; N.H. Hooker, *The Moffat Papers: Selections from the Diplomatic Journals of Jay Pierrepont Moffat, 1919-1943* (Cambridge 1956), 329

181. CNA to minister, 1 Sep. 1940, DHH, 81/520 Destroyers "Towns" 8000 General; CWCM, 5 Sep. 1940; First Sea Lord to CNS, 1039/11 Sep. 1940, copy in DHH, 81/520 Destroyers Town Class 8000 A-Z

182. Reynolds, *Creation of the Anglo-American Alliance*, 130-1

Top: Canadian crews take over USN destroyers transferred under the destroyers for bases deal. (DND, H-255)

Bottom: The White Ensign is hoisted as *St Croix*, *St Francis* and *Columbia* are commissioned into the RCN at Halifax on 24 September 1940. (NAC, PA 104283)

Shipyard workers drive in wedges preparatory to the launch of HMCS *Moose Jaw* at Collingwood Shipyards Ltd, Collingwood, Ontario. (NAC, PA 204282)

some 960 British sailors, who had been formed up clear of the pier, moved on board, commissioned the ships into the RN and began ten days of work-ups, helped by rear parties of key USN personnel. On 18 September, the next eight destroyers entered port and their British crews arrived on 20 September, the same day that the six destroyers allocated to the RCN arrived. The Canadians commissioned their ships on 24 September: USS *Mackenzie, Haraden, Thatcher, Williams, McCook,* and *Bancroft* became HMCS *Annapolis, Columbia, Niagara, St Clair, St Croix,* and *St Francis,* respectively.[183]

At a stroke, the RCN had doubled its destroyer strength. The old American ships were much less capable than the River class, however, and the crew requirements for the additional ships had severe repercussions on the rapidly expanding navy. The decision to accede to the First Sea Lord's request to man all six destroyers came only weeks after Canada, in response to another request from the Admiralty for help in managing British manpower shortages, had committed 540 officers and ratings to supply crews for the ten corvettes building to Admiralty account in Canada. Although the commitment was only supposed to be for a few months until the Admiralty believed it could find personnel to take over the ships from the Canadians, it coincided with demands on the RCN to provide crews for large numbers of converted civilian ships—projects that were in several cases supposed to have been completed some months earlier but had been delayed—and for new construction vessels. In mid-August COAC staff estimated that crew requirements for the coming four months on the east coast alone would include two armed merchant cruisers, eight armed yachts, the first batch of thirteen corvettes building on Canadian account, and eighteen auxiliary vessels. There were still further demands for personnel for new bases and other shore facilities. Accelerated intakes of recruits had increased the strength of the service from 6,528 officers and ratings in early May to 10,752 in early September, but over three-quarters of the new personnel were members of the RCNVR. By early September, for the first time, more than half of the entire active service force was RCNVR. These new people had little or no previous marine experience, and the delays in completion of the conversion of the yachts and other civilian vessels had greatly reduced the opportunity for recent recruits to receive a full program of sea training and to gain experience in seagoing appointments. The unexpected requirement to provide crews for the ten Admiralty corvettes had deepened an existing shortage of experienced officers, and the new demand to provide some 840 personnel for the American destroyers could be met only by extracting seasoned personnel from their appointments and hurrying others to sea before they were fully qualified.[184]

The British requests had, in other words, transformed the manning situation from "comfortable" to "strained," and the navy was in danger of mortgaging its future to the point of bankruptcy. The naval staff was acutely aware of the danger, and anxious not to prejudice the long-term "blue water" aspirations that Nelles and his planners were preparing to put before

---

183. Named after rivers—all but one on the US-Canadian border—they were nevertheless called "Town" class, following the RN example, so as not to be confused with the British-built River class in the RCN. D. Freeman, *Canadian Warship Names* (St Catharines 2001); Reid to CO *Stadacona,* 14 and 23 Sep. 1940, NAC, RG 24, 11,126, 501-11-12; North Atlantic Escort Force WD, Sep. 1940, PRO, ADM 199/367; CO HMS *Seaborn* II to Sec of Adm, 16 Sep. 1940, PRO, ADM 199/624

184. DNP, "Agenda for Conference on Manning and Training Commitments Held at Naval Service Headquarters, August 28 and 29, 1940," nd, NAC, RG 24, 4045, NSS 1078-3-5; COAC to NSec, 16 Aug. 1940, DNP to CNS, 23 Aug. 1940, NAC, RG 24, 5586, NS 1-24-1 pt 3; NWR, nos. 33 (2 May 1940) and 51 (5 Sep. 1940)

Cabinet.[185] It was a significant challenge, one that would require the most delicate balancing of requirements, and perhaps a deeper understanding of the purposes and needs of a blue water navy than the members of the naval staff could hope to have acquired in their limited experience.

Captain C.R.H. Taylor, Director of Naval Personnel, remembering the chaotic expansion of 1917–18, "when the dregs of conscription which were not required for the army were entered in the Navy and were rat[ed] Leading Seamen and Petty Officers," called together senior training officers from both coasts to frame manning and training policy. They decided to take qualified personnel from the River class destroyers whenever they came in for refit to build up what training facilities they could in Canada; to form a manning pool of spare destroyer men in Britain that could benefit from opportunities for training with the RN; and provide for quicker promotion on the lower deck. NSHQ retained control over advancement of ratings through master rosters that listed all leading seamen and above by seniority in order to avoid a repetition of the wholesale promotions that had taken place on the east coast in 1917–18.[186] Because engine-room personnel were in particularly short supply, Taylor's staff organized a recruiting drive among Great Lakes seamen, to join after the end of the 1940 navigation season.[187] Qualified officers were even scarcer. The Town class destroyers, having arrived in one batch instead of at intervals, as recommended by COAC, had taken all the merchant navy officers joining the RCNR, together with experienced RCNVR officers, whom he had counted on to begin reducing the backlog of 163 seagoing appointments that needed to be filled.[188] The training officers arrived at the consensus that "it had become essential to have an Officer's Training Establishment *at once*." Modelled on HMCS *Stone Frigate* in Kingston, Ontario, an officer training program began in September with ninety-two RCNVR and nineteen RCNR officers, the latter excused the three weeks of sea training.[189] According to a training report, the VR's had difficulty grasping the material but they proved much less hidebound, and better able to absorb new information, than the merchant officers, who showed surprisingly wide gaps in basic knowledge of seamanship and navigation.[190]

---

185. Cdr F.L. Houghton, Director of Plans and Signals at NSHQ, later commented, "My many ROP, written when I was commanding one or other of four ships, had unfortunately led the Chief of the Naval Staff to believe that I possessed some small ability to sling words together, and as Director of Plans I was constantly being required to prepare 'briefs' on an endless variety of matters." As secretary of the Naval Council he found that the army dominated strategic planning in Ottawa, but it is clear that he and others were developing a strategy to exert influence on Angus L. Macdonald in the emphasis on overseas employment of RCN ships in the autumn of 1940. RAdm F.L. Houghton, "A Sailor's Life for Me, 1913-1951," nd, 141, DHH, Houghton biog file; Bidwell to CNS and DCNS, 15 Aug, 1940, DHH, NHS 8280 pt 2; CWCM, 1 Oct 1940; W.A.B. Douglas, "Conflict and Innovation in the Royal Canadian Navy, 1939-1945," 210-32

186. Taylor, "Agenda for Conference on Manning and Training"; "Memo of Conference on Manning ... Aug. 30, 1940," ns, nd, NAC, RG 24, 4045, NSS 1078-3-5; NSec to COs RCN Barracks, Halifax and Esquimalt, 4 Sep. 1940, NAC, RG 24, 4045, NSS 1078-3-5; Naval General Order 1052, 12 Oct. 1940

187. Naval General Order 1062, 26 Oct. 1940

188. Reid to Commander in Charge, Halifax, CO *Stadacona*, et al, "Officer Personnel—Atlantic Coast Command," 20 July 1940, NAC, RG 24, 11657, DH 3-2-1; Reid to NSec, 16 Aug. 1940, NAC, RG 24, 5586, NS 1-24-1 pt 3

189. See app, "Training, Discipline and Morale in the RCN, 1939-45" in Vol II pt 2

190. Webber, Monthly Report—Officers' Training, 5 Oct. and 8 Nov., NSS 1000-5-13 pt 3

On 16 September Taylor left Ottawa to take command of *Assiniboine* and temporarily became Commander, Halifax Force.[191] He was therefore responsible for ordering the Town class work-ups. These "entirely unknown, foreign, elderly and somewhat decrepit" ships, only two of which were commanded by officers fully up to date in current naval practice—Lieutenant-Commander H.F. Pullen, RCN in *St Francis* and Lieutenant M.A. Medland, RCN in *St Croix*—did not lend themselves to the kind of work-up needed to produce an efficient fighting team.[192] With no training staff ashore, no training aids, no standardized routine—commanding officers were given complete freedom to employ their own training methods—and no final inspection by a senior officer, the most that could be achieved as they began working-up out of Shelburne, Nova Scotia on 1 October, was familiarization with the ships' layouts, cleaning and painting where necessary, and a beginning in seamanship training for sailors who in an earlier age would have been called "landsmen."[193]

The demands of accelerated expansion would raise difficulties of nightmarish proportions in training and manning, and also shipbuilding and equipment supply, in 1941, 1942, and 1943, but in the summer of 1940 opportunities seemed to outweigh the challenges. In the case of shipbuilding and equipment supply, the Admiralty, after months of meagre British orders in Canada, began to cooperate in developing production, one notable step being the creation of the British Admiralty Technical Mission (BATM) in Ottawa at the end of July 1940.[194] Already, in early April 1940, the Canadian government had endeavoured to put military procurement on a firmer basis by replacing the War Supply Board with a new ministry, the Department of Munitions and Supply, which had virtually unlimited power to purchase or organize the manufacture of materiel, sell or otherwise dispose of it, and to regulate the economy to secure the necessary production and distribution. The minister was C.D. Howe, who as minister of transport since that department's establishment in 1937, had demonstrated formidable skills in dealing with the private sector and cutting through the impediments of vested interests and overlapping authority within the government.[195] For the navy, accelerated Canadian industrial development created an opportunity for achieving long cherished dreams of building major warships in Canada, thereby raising the profile of the navy's wartime role and laying the foundation for a substantial professional postwar fleet. Nelles and his staff exploited this opportunity with considerable success during the summer and fall of 1940.

North American industry was unexplored territory for most Englishmen. The BATM, formed to supplement essential naval requirements from Canadian and American sources, thus had to find

---

191. This was part of a shuffle in appointments. Jones relieved Reid as COAC on 28 Sep. and Reid moved to NSHQ as DCNS. *Canadian Navy List*, 15 Sep. 1940 and 15 Oct. 1940

192. VAdm Sir Guy Sayer, cited in Glover, "Officer Training and the Quest for Operational Efficiency"

193. Ibid, 110-17

194. The British Purchasing Mission now operated from New York, but at the end of July eleven senior British technical officers, under VAdm Albert Evans, arrived to establish the BATM. RAdm H.A. Sheridan's naval section of the supply mission joined the new group, and he became deputy head. "History of the British Admiralty Technical Mission," 30 Apr. 1946, 1-2, 42, DHH, 82/29

195. "An Act to Amend the Department of Munitions and Supply Act, 1940 (4 George VI, Chap. 31)," extracts printed in C.P. Stacey (ed), *Historical Documents of Canada* V (Toronto 1972, 643; R. Bothwell and W. Kilbourn, *C.D. Howe* (Toronto 1979), 123-35

out what industrial capacity Canada and the United States had, see if educational orders needed to be placed so that work could be done for the UK in an emergency, and whether material of North American design could be used in the meantime.[196] What the technical officers found in Canada was "appalling" ignorance in what before the war had been "a moribund industry." Among the yards building corvettes for the RN—Canadian Vickers in Montréal, Marine Industries in Sorel, and Davie Shipbuilding and Repair Company in Québec—only the older Vickers employees who had served in England at Barrow-in-Furness knew anything about warship equipment. The Canadian offices of Lloyds and the British Corporation had very little idea of Admiralty standards and had to be shown how to conduct inspections, an important point since "The U.K. drawings from which the ships were built, and particularly the machine drawings, were sometimes incorrect, often insufficiently detailed and had not been properly checked and amended in [the] Admiralty before issue."[197] With one or two exceptions none of the firms employed electrical engineers or had formed properly organized electrical departments.[198]

These difficulties aside, the shipbuilding branch of the old War Supply Board, responsible for contracts and management of production, was now in place at the Department of Munitions and Supply, and there was some expertise and administrative capacity at NSHQ. Commander (E) A.C.M. Davy, RCN, who in September 1939 had been preparing to join *Assiniboine* as engineering officer, had been summoned to Ottawa to supervise conversion of requisitioned non-naval vessels. Such was his competence and the shortage of technical officers that, to his chagrin, he did not escape from Ottawa for the rest of the war.[199] The BATM overcame fears that it would "run" the RCN by setting up an informal pooling of overseer personnel, a rationalisation of services according to the particular strengths and needs of the RCN and the British mission, and a full sharing of information.[200]

Differences in North American and British industrial practices hindered the shipbuilding program but they created still more challenging obstacles in the production of armament and precision equipment. Mass production did not allow for the Admiralty system of close oversight of all work by expert tradesmen and the introduction "on the shop floor" of modifications that were often not thoroughly documented. This meant that the BATM seldom placed orders in the United States for equipment to be built to Admiralty specifications, but instead purchased "stand alone" items of American pattern already in production. The underdevelopment of Canadian industry thus actually offered a slight advantage of openness to organization to suit British needs. One example among many successes, and one of particular significance, was the production of asdic, which had run into a bottleneck in Britain, and was at risk from enemy air attack there. In response to Admiral Nelles' proposals of May 1940, emphasizing priority for asdic, Mr A.E.H. Pew, a pioneer in the field, brought over eight tons of equipment in July 1940, and NSHQ established the antisubmarine equipment divi-

---

196. BATM History, DHH, 82/29, 2

197. Ibid, 42-3

198. After finding one local man who had received training in British yards who could be relied on to provide quality control, the BATM brought over three Admiralty overseers. Ibid, 107-8, 111-12

199. He had entered the service in 1917, and stood second in his qualifying course at the Royal Naval Engineering College at Keyham in 1929. Davy, NPRC personnel file O-18580

200. Quote from BATM History, 39. See also 44.

sion to manage production for both Canadian and British orders. The National Research Council in Ottawa, which provided the large quartz discs that converted current into high-frequency directional sound, also trained additional technicians and provided a workshop to produce the remaining components of the equipment. The Admiralty and the RCN each ordered a hundred sets: type 123 for corvettes, type 128 for destroyers, and type 134 for motor launches. The first set, completed in July 1941, was four months behind schedule, but it set the scene for a solid production system that allowed the naval staff to make a commitment to Canadian sets for all the RCN's future needs.[201]

During late June and early July 1940, when C.D. Howe and his officials consulted with the services to determine which items might practically be produced in Canada, Nelles essentially repeated what he had said in1938 and 1939. It was "absolutely necessary" to build Tribal class destroyers, and in so doing organize a shipyard on each coast capable of high-end naval construction.[202] A great deal of British assistance in the form of expert personnel would be required. That the Admiralty could not provide such help did not discourage optimism among the planners, but there were some doubts.[203] Commander Davy despatched a cautionary note to his superiors in mid-July. He "assumed" that "it has been established, in collaboration with the Admiralty, that building vessels of this type is the most suitable employment for certain Canadian Shipyards." Seeing that both the RCN and Canadian industry were bereft of qualified overseer, supervisory, and technical staff, the project could be realized only through the most intimate collaboration between the RCN and Canadian industry on the one hand, and the Admiralty and British firms with expertise in destroyer construction on the other.[204]

As this discussion was taking place, Howe wrote to Macdonald asking for additional orders for escort vessels, because early launchings of the first hulls was opening building slips and would soon leave workers idle.[205] The naval staff, which appears to have been taken unaware by this important news, did not miss a beat.[206] The recommendation went out for six additional corvettes and ten more Bangors, which the government authorized on 15 August.[207] In September, citing the large new commitments Canada was assuming for the defence of Newfoundland, the staff decided to place follow-on orders for another ten corvettes and ten Bangors, for grand totals of seventy and

---

201. The RCN increased its order to 165 sets for delivery by the end of the year.

202. "Memo re Mtg held in Room 201, House of Commons ... June 25 1940," DHH, NHS 8200 (1939-45) pt 1, copy from NSS 8200-355, pt 1; ADM (NS) to DM Munitions and Supply, 28 June 1940, "Min of Mtg re Production of Canadian Naval Requirements in Canada," 5 July 1940, ibid; Tucker, *Naval Service of Canada* II, 52

203. NSM, 9 July 1940

204. Director of Shipbuilding to E-in-C, "Factors Involved in Building Destroyers in Canada," 16 July 1940, DHH, 81/520 Destroyers "Tribal" 8000 General

205. Howe to Macdonald, 3 Aug. 1940, NAC, RG 24, 3841, NSS 1017-10-22 pt 1

206. Probably in response to the inquiry, K.S. Maclachlan, ADM for the NS, that same day asked his counterpart at Munitions and Supply to have the shipbuilding industry resurveyed to see if there was scope for further escort construction. Significantly, Eng Capt A.D.M. Curry, RCN, who as E-in-C was the navy's senior technical officer and a member of the naval staff, was taken by surprise. "As far as can be made out," he wrote in answer to requests for advice, the construction program "is rather more than was envisaged for the first two years of the war; but certain of the Shipyards will shortly be in a position to lay down more keels, and it is for consideration whether steps should not be taken to obtain the necessary authority to proceed with further construction." ADM NS to DM M&S, 3 Aug. 1940, NAC, RG 24, 3841, NSS1017-10-22 pt 1;E-in-C to CNS, 7 Aug. 1940, NAC, RG 24, 3841, NSS 1017-10-22 pt 1 (quoted)

207. PC 3942, 15 Aug. 1940, NAC, RG 24, 3841, NSS 1017-10-22 pt 1; NSM, 12 Aug. 1940

forty-eight vessels of these types. The staff expected that all of these vessels would be completed by the end of calendar 1941, meaning that the entire original four-year program, with another ten corvettes into the bargain, would be realized in only twenty-two months.[208]

Such increases in naval construction demanded new plans. On August 15 the Director of the Operations Division, Commander R.E.S. Bidwell, had drawn up a tentative scheme by which every third corvette and every third Bangor would be deployed to British waters. On 26 September he produced another, when the prime minister asked the services to state their requirements for the next fiscal year, arguing that, although the RCN destroyer commitments in British waters should be maintained, all 118 Bangors and corvettes would be needed at home, whatever the outcome of the war in the Eastern Atlantic. On the surface this was an odd document, for it apparently contradicted the staff's consistent arguments for overseas employment. It may have been designed to reassure an anxious government, and thereby secure the long-term overseas deployment of the destroyers, the heart of the Canadian fleet. In any case, the plan did not last beyond the Cabinet War Committee meeting of 1 October, at which Macdonald gained significant support for further commitments in British waters, and for ambitious long-term RCN objectives.[209] The minister's determination, during his first weeks in office, that the navy should focus on coastal defence, had now entirely melted away.

Nelles had received on 26 September an urgent appeal from the First Sea Lord to send over all six Town class destroyers, not just the four that Canada had agreed to provide. By this time it was clear that the attack on SC 1 that had led the Admiralty to warn of a possible U-boat offensive across the Atlantic was in fact the opening of an assault on the convoys as they approached the British Isles, with the initial interceptions taking place outside the zone in which Western Approaches Command could provide cover. Under the circumstances, Macdonald told the committee on 1 October, it was impossible to refuse this request for the additional two Towns. Moreover, there was a requirement for minesweepers in British home waters that only Canada could meet. In July, Nelles had reacted cautiously to the Admiralty's request that the first twelve Bangors to complete in Canada—expected for delivery in 1941—should be earmarked for the Royal Navy. Now, at the meeting of the Cabinet War Committee of 1 October, Macdonald reported that in view of the intensity of the struggle in British waters and the fact that raids on Canada's coast had not materialized, the CNS recommended that the first twelve RCN Bangors go overseas. The committee agreed. At the same time Munitions and Supply was reporting that twelve Bangors ordered by the Admiralty in Canada could be completed in 1941 as well, meaning that the British appeal for Canadian help netted commitments to send twenty-four, not just twelve, Bangors.[210]

---

208. Davy questioned the wisdom of tying up so much capacity for naval construction, given the Allied need for merchant vessels, but the naval staff as a whole held what Davy considered to be the altogether too optimistic view that large warship and cargo vessel programs could both be sustained through expansion of industry. NS mtg, 12 Aug. 1940; K. Mackenzie, "The Canadian Merchant Marine and the Canadian Shipping Board,"13, DHH, 2000/5; NSM, 30 Sep. 1940; Davy to DOD, 30 Sept. 1940, DHH NHS 8280 pt 2; Bidwell, "Proposed Disposition and Employment of RCN New Construction Corvettes," 30 Sep. 1940, DHH, NHS 8280 pt 2

209. Bidwell to CNS and DCNS, 15 Aug. 1940, and Bidwell, "Proposed Disposition and Employment of RCN New Construction Corvettes;" CWCM, 1 Oct. 1940

210. CWCM, 5 Sep. 1940, 1 Oct. 1940; First Sea Lord to CNS, 26 Sep. 1940, NAC, RG 24, 6797, NSS 8375-354; Hankinson to Skelton, 15 July 1940, Skelton to Hankinson, 26 July 1940, Hankinson to Skelton, 24 Sep. 1940, Skelton to Campbell, 9 Oct. 1940, DCER pt 8, 847-51; Maclachlan to Skelton, 24 July 1940, NAC, RG 24, 3841, NSS 1017-10-22 pt 1; DCER pt 7, 849

Moose Jaw in the water, 9 April 1941. (NAC, PA 204283)

The naval minister did not stop there, and embraced the naval staff's vision of a substantial professional navy that would take shape during and after the war. He was particularly drawn by the fact that the staff's scheme for the creation of a task force capable of independent action on each coast and for national self-sufficiency in training and shipbuilding, echoed the principles that Laurier had put before the country three decades before. At the meeting of 26 September he had won approval to form a training school for wartime RCNVR officers that would, when it had produced sufficient graduates for that purpose, be converted to a cadet training establishment for permanent RCN officers. Situated on the west coast near Victoria, HMCS *Royal Roads*, under the command of Captain J.M. Grant, RCN was the natural successor to the Royal Naval College of Canada, which had closed as a result of budget cuts in 1922. Macdonald followed up on 1 October with a plan for building Tribal class destroyers in Canada. Citing political reasons as well as the perilous state of British industry, he maintained that the construction of destroyers "would be favourably received by the public and evoke a greater interest in Canadian naval development." He would bring up the need to build destroyers time and again over the ensuing weeks. [211]

It is of more than passing interest that Macdonald's presentation of the navy's case to the Cabinet War Committee took place after discussion of the army's plan to send the 3rd and 4th Infantry Divisions overseas, together with a wide range of support units to complete a field corps and an armoured brigade as the first installment of a full armoured division. He did not hesitate to play on the prime minister's fears, raising the spectre of conscription for overseas service, wondering if "too much stress might be placed on increased contributions of infantry," and urging a balancing of the effort with "increased emphasis ... in the naval and air spheres." It was after the committee had ruminated about the manpower implications of such a large army that Macdonald made his pitch for the navy, and it was noteworthy that the prime minister echoed his sentiments.[212]

The naval staff seized the moment. By 6 October "Naval Appreciation. Canada's War Effort During 1941" was ready for distribution and by 9 October it was in the hands of the Cabinet War Committee. It allocated thirty-eight corvettes and twenty-four Bangors to British waters, leaving only thirty-two corvettes and twenty-four Bangors for home defence, providing British fortunes did not take a turn for the worse. "It is reasonable to assume," the paper argued, "that [the enemy] will remain in European waters so long as his submarines are able to find sufficient targets over there for their torpedoes." The paper does not appear to have been the subject of discussion in Cabinet, where protracted wrangling over the army and the size of the overall war effort was the principal concern, and approval of the scheme is implicit in the document despatched to the Admiralty in January 1941 as a statement of Canada's intention.[213]

Mackenzie King was a key player in this process. Already sympathetic to the navy, he visited Halifax in mid-October to see some of the American destroyers handed over. "Nothing more significant has taken place in the present war," he concluded. His admiration of the men who put to

---

211. Min of mtg held in Minister's office, 28 Aug.1940, RG 24 (acc 83-84/67), box 529, NSC 1700-121/2(1), cited in W.A. March, "A Canadian Departure: The Evolution of HMCS *Royal Roads*," in M.L. Hadley, R.N. Huebert, and F.W. Crickard, *A Nation's Navy: In Quest of Canadian Naval Identity* (Montréal and Kingston 1996), 297-309; CWCM, 26 Sep. and 1 Oct. 1940

212. CWCM, 1 Oct. 1940

213. CWCM, 3 and 9 Oct. 1940; First Sea Lord to CNS, 13 Jan.1941, NAC, RG 24, 6796, NSS8375-4

sea in these uncomfortable-looking ships and his appreciation of the wartime role being played by Halifax, grew with word of *Margaree*'s loss. Profoundly moved by a memorial service for her at Christ Church on 4 November, he wrote in his diary: "One feels Canada growing into a nation with the navy coming to take the part it is."[214] Three days later, on 7 November, the navy had a very good day at the Cabinet War Committee. Macdonald won approval for early orders in the United Kingdom for a second pair of Tribals, which would sustain the two-a-year program while production in Canada might be organized, received clearance formally to approach the British government for assistance with destroyer construction in Canada and got approval in principle for the new naval college.[215] King lent his full support. He read aloud a telegram from the British government about the devastating effectiveness of the new U-boat pack tactics, and, later in the meeting, alluded to his long-standing conviction that adequate naval forces were an essential safeguard of Canadian sovereignty with respect to the United States: "It was very important for Canada to build up her navy. The new responsibility undertaken by Canada for the joint defence of North America made it all the more necessary to develop the Royal Canadian Navy so that we could bear our share of the burden of naval defence"[216]

Over the next two weeks the naval staff developed firm objectives that amounted to the consolidation of blue water doctrine for the RCN. On 11 November a paper on "Canada's Post War Navy" argued that "the Royal Navy is the hub of British Sea-Power ... and round it are gathered the navies of Australia and Canada, of New Zealand, India and South Africa. We possess indeed an Imperial Navy, and the whole Empire shares in its provision and support." The "paper programs and shattered hopes" of the past thirty or more years, occupying fully a third of this paper, were dismissed as irrelevant to current requirements, not surprisingly in the light of Cabinet support over the previous few weeks, and the need for sustained government support was clearly implied. As in all previous appreciations, from 1909 to the Jellicoe Report of 1920, and subsequent studies by Commodore Hose between the wars, strategic coverage by the British and American fleets would permit Canada to concentrate on offensive operations in territorial waters—including the important new concern of Newfoundland and Labrador— to prevent hit and run raids on ports and focal trade areas, as well as providing assistance in the main theatres of war. A notable item in the recommendations was the staff's willingness, for the first time since the mid-1920s, unambiguously to call for cruisers, two for each coast, which they suggested might be purchased or borrowed from among the latest British 6-inch classes. The remainder of the recommendations, for nine Tribals and a nucleus of minesweeper and antisubmarine groups on each coast, expanded, modernized main bases at Halifax and Esquimalt and secondary bases at Gaspé, Sydney, and Prince Rupert, largely replicated Nelles's report to cabinet of January 1939.[217]

On 19 November Macdonald announced his plans for the postwar navy in Parliament. Without abandoning a reliance on "British ports, British ships, British naval skill and British naval tradi-

---

214. King diary, 19 Oct., 4 Nov. 1940

215. For the staff recommendation see Maclachlan to CNS, 27 Sep. 1940, NAC, RG 24, 3841, NSS1017-10-22 pt 1; Naval Council minutes, 30 Oct. 1940, NAC, RG 24, 4044, NSS 1078-3-4; Nelles to minister, 4 Nov. 1940, DHH, 81/520 Destroyers Tribal 8000 General

216. CWCM, 7 Nov. 1940; King diary, 7 Nov. 1940

217. "Canada's Postwar Navy. Staff Memorandum," 11 Nov. 1940, NAC, RG 24, 3844, NSS1017-10-34 pt 1

tion," he advocated "a navy worthy of our importance in the world of nations, adequate to the needs of the great trading nation which Canada now is, and which she is bound to become in greater measure after the war; a navy sufficient to meet the obligations which rest on us as members of the British commonwealth, and as a country in close association with the United States in the matter of the joint defence of this continent." A Canadian naval college and sophisticated Canadian-built warships would pave the way for "the day, and I think that it will be a proud day for this country, when our Canadian naval effort will be directed by Canadian men, trained in Canada and operating in ships built in this country."[218] It is clear from this speech that he was fully aware of the naval staff's position when the Naval Council met on 22 November. The navy regarded the proposals in the paper of 11 November "as a minimum." Macdonald responded that he "concurred generally in the proposals," and declared "that it was most necessary to lay down an objective towards which we could build."[219] Later that day he took the navy's proposals to the Cabinet War Committee and told his colleagues that "the postwar Canadian navy should consist of two cruisers, eight destroyers, and forty smaller craft on each coast. This would require a personnel of approximately 1,000 officers and 10,000 ratings. The upkeep per annum would be at the neighbourhood of $16,000,000." He won agreement for a navy "of the general nature of that described" with little discussion. This would stand him in good stead later on, when he made specific proposals for the postwar establishment.[220]

It was not until 2 January 1941 that Macdonald brought in these proposals. The reason for this delay is not clear, but it could have been his efforts to reform personnel policy. The clue is to be found in a letter from the Naval Secretary on 27 January stating that "although the transfer of likely, young ratings [to the permanent RCN] is to be encouraged and such transfers will be made as recommendations are received," no officers were to be transferred until after the war, so that talented young men serving overseas, distant from senior Canadian officers who might recommend them, would have a fair chance.[221] Macdonald had been pressing the naval staff to promote men from the lower deck rather than by direct entry, perhaps as a result of his experience on the Western Front in the First World War, perhaps because he took to heart sentiment in Halifax that the officer corps was remote, elitist, and—as frequently charged after the Halifax explosion of 1917—incompetent. It was undoubtedly his influence that led to press releases that made much of the fact that of the hundred probationary officers of the first volunteer reserve course at *Royal Roads*, eighteen were ratings who had been selected for commissions.[222]

Macdonald's proposal in Cabinet on 2 January, which he explained he was presenting then because of the time needed properly to train seamen, was aimed at securing the qualified personnel that would be needed after the war. When J.L. Ilsley (Finance) and C.G. Power (Minister of National Defence for Air) protested that it was too soon for such decisions, which would lead the other services to make similar demands, the Cabinet secretary pointed out to them that they had

---

218. House of Commons, *Debates*, 19 Nov. 1940, 206-7

219. Naval Council minutes, 19 Sep. to 22 Nov. 1940

220. CWCM, 22 Nov. 1940

221. NSec to COAC, COPC et al. 27 Jan. 1941, NAC, RG 24, 5586, NS 1-24-1 pt 4

222. DND Press Liaison Office, Release No. 586, 17 Jan. 1941, DHH, NHS 1900-120/1; Naval Council minutes, 29 Apr. 1941; Hadley and Sarty, *Tin Pots and Pirate Ships*, 204

already made a commitment to the postwar fleet and Macdonald won approval.[223] On 20 January 1941 Macdonald went back to Cabinet with ambitious proposals for the Halifax base. Besides taking over the army's Wellington Barracks, on the hill above the overcrowded dockyard, the navy wanted to develop the site with new schools, barracks, and recreational facilities costing nearly $2.8 million. With accommodation for 2,000 men, that would take care of the postwar navy's needs. In addition, temporary schools and barracks for an additional 2,000 men, at a cost of $383,000, was to meet the present accommodation crisis and further personnel increases now under way. The Finance Minister protested the cost but Mackenzie King stopped him short: "The committee had already agreed on the type of postwar navy which Canada should maintain ... Halifax was destined to remain a vital Empire and continental port. The provision of adequate naval defences continued to be essential. Development on this line was natural to Canada."[224]

It was a remarkable statement. King's support for the navy was whole-hearted. Under the pressure of war, and it must be said the not so subtle manipulation of Macdonald—once again at this meeting he used the army program as a *bête noire* ("it was evident that we did not need a large army now")—King, while never departing from the need to defend Canadian waters, had himself, whether he knew it or not, been uttering blue water doctrine, and he was deeply moved by the service and sacrifice of Canadian seamen.[225] The members of the Cabinet War Committee had little choice but to go along, and they approved most of Macdonald's program. Despite this coup, it was not long before the naval staff was discovering the impossibilities of wartime construction, the difficulties of obtaining designs for and building masonry structures suitably impressive as the home base of the new navy when costs were skyrocketing and qualified architects and contractors were overloaded.[226] In January 1941, however, when many of these tribulations had yet to be encountered, and when the worst problems of naval expansion still lay in the future, there was every reason to believe that the calamitous events of the past eight months had confirmed the soundness of plans for naval development articulated before May 1940. Indeed, the global crisis seemed only to increase the scale of those plans and their chances of realization.

223. CWCM, 2 Jan. 1941

224. Ibid, 20 Jan. 1941

225. King diary, 20 Jan. 1941

226. See for example Naval Council minutes for 24, 31 March, 9, 22, 29 April, 5 May 1941

CHAPTER THREE

The RCN and the Anglo-American Alliance January to July 1941

BRIGHT AS THE NAVY'S FUTURE LOOKED to the Canadian naval establishment in the fall of 1940, decisions made in Ottawa were not always easy to implement in Halifax, nearly a thousand miles away. There was something beyond a geographical gulf between Naval Service Headquarters and the fleet. The naval dockyard and marine firms in Halifax, swamped by the demands of preparing fifty obsolescent RCN and RN Town class destroyers for sea, could do little more than reduce top weight and carry out a few alterations and additions to give these ships a chance of survival in the winter seas of the North Atlantic. Of the first three Canadian four-stackers to sail overseas from Halifax on 30 November—*St Croix*, *St Clair*, and *Niagara*—only the latter two were able to complete the last leg of the passage from St John's, Newfoundland to Scotland's Firth of Clyde. Battered and bruised, nearly having foundered, *St Croix* returned to St John's on 13 December.

St Croix 's miserable experience deserves recounting in detail, as it illuminates both the poor performance of the Towns and the harshness of the northwest Atlantic. The first three days out of St John's, the fragile steering gear often failed and trouble with the fuel uptake lines caused sudden power losses. Early on the fourth day, 7 December, the winds and seas mounted rapidly, all three vessels in company were barely under control, and Captain C.R.H. Taylor, RCN, senior officer of the flotilla who was taking passage in *St Croix*, ordered a turn to the south to try to escape from the centre of the vicious storm. Within hours, as visibility closed down, the ships lost touch. To make matters worse, each had only a single radio transmitter and receiver, and, designed for communication with shore stations, the transmitters could not work on the frequencies at which the receivers operated. In other words, the vessels could not talk directly to one another, but had to make long range broadcasts to shore stations, which in turn would rebroadcast to the other ships.[1]

In the predawn blackness on 8 December, Taylor reported afterwards, the seas were "mountainous (about 60 feet)" and *St Croix* was "practically unmanageable ... Three successive waves swept the ship and removed the forecastle guard rails, stanchons [*sic*] ventilators, voice pipe etc. and buckled in the lower bridge structure and caused numerous leaks from the forecastle deck with

---

1.   Taylor, "ROP—HMCS *St Croix, Niagara, St Clair,* 4-14 Dec. 1940," 14 Dec. 1940, DHH, NHS NSS 1057-1-1

the living accommodation beneath, i.e., Petty Officer Mess, Officer's Cabins and Ward Room which necessitated these compartments being kept bailed out." The ship was rolling more than fifty degrees off the perpendicular, on the very brink of capsizing. Commander H. Kingsley, RCN, the commanding officer, ordered the crew to put on life jackets in case the vessel should suddenly turn turtle. Good seamanship won out. The expedient of stopping the engine on the side of the oncoming seas while maintaining power on the other engine gradually brought her under control, although she could still make no headway.[2]

Taylor broke radio silence to warn the shore authorities of the desperate situation: "It is essential that contact be made [with *Niagara* and *St Clair*] ... there is a grave possibility that these ships may have foundered by falling off in very large steep sea encountered last night. This catastrophe was very narrowly averted by 'HMCS Saint Croix' which is still hove to."[3] It was three long days before *Niagara* and *St Clair* were able to respond to the repeated calls from shore stations. Rear-Admiral 3rd Battle Squadron at Halifax alerted two of his armed merchant cruisers at sea in the vicinity to search for the possibly stricken destroyers. In the event, the other two ships had managed to run ahead of the seas to the eastward and arrived at the Clyde on 11 December.[4] The captains forgave the cranky steering and the fuel line problems: the removal of top weight at the Halifax shipyards had made the old destroyers "very good sea boat[s]."[5]

Having narrowly avoided a maritime catastrophe, Rear-Admiral 3rd Battle Squadron promptly recommended no further attempts at winter crossings by Towns.[6] In Ottawa, the decision was made to keep the four remaining Towns in Halifax and send over instead *Assiniboine* and *Restigouche*, which were just completing refit. This would put all of Canada's most capable ships, the River class destroyers, in British waters, not only replacing *Saguenay* while she was repaired, but increasing the complement of Rivers in British waters to five rather than the normal four. "Can you give us any further help during this lean period[?]," came a renewed appeal from Admiral Pound.[7] On Christmas Eve, Admiral Nelles responded that two Towns, *St Francis* and *Columbia*, would accompany *Assiniboine* and *Restigouche*. Canada was denuding its east coast: "Halifax destroyer force will then be out to a clinch with one only seaworthy Town class speed presently limited to 24 knots."[8] "Am deeply grateful," replied Admiral Pound in a personal message on Christmas Day, "most acceptable Xmas gift."[9]

When the two Rivers and two Towns made their passage, between 15 and 26 January 1941, accompanied by two RN Towns, the old American ships were still baulky. They needed additional dockyard work in Britain, and none of the Canadian Towns were ready for operations until the lat-

2.   Ibid. See also NHS, "*St Clair* History," 23 Jan. 1964, DHH, 81/520 Clair St 8000; NHS, nd, "Notes on the History of HMC Destroyer *Niagara*," DHH, 81/520 Niagara 8000

3.   Capt (D) Can. Destroyer Div to COAC, 8 Dec. 1940, DHH, NHS NSS 1057-1-1, pt 2

4.   Signals, 8-11 Dec. 1940, DHH, NHS NSS 1057-1-1, pt 2

5.   Quoted in NHS, "Notes on the History of ... *Niagara*," 3

6.   RA 3 BS to C-in-C AWI, 10 Dec. 1940, NAC, RG 24, 6797, NSS 8375-354

7.   Adm to CNS, 22 Dec. 1940, NAC, RG 24, 6796, NSS 8375-4

8.   CNS to First Sea Lord, 24 Dec., 1940, NAC, RG 25 G-1, 1994, 1177C pt 1

9.   First Sea Lord to CNS, 25 Dec. 1940, ibid

ter part of March 1941. *Assiniboine* and *Restigouche*, manned by experienced, mostly regular force personnel, went straight into convoy escort operations in the northwest approaches.[10]

Corvettes offered a striking contrast. In spite of the speed with which the basic hulls had been completed, only HMS *Trillium* and *Windflower*, the first two of the ten corvettes built in Canada to Admiralty account, were ready by the end of 1940. There had been delays in the arrival of essential equipment from Britain and the development of alternative Canadian sources was still in its earliest stages. Even *Trillium* and *Windflower* were only partially completed and equipped. Among the missing items were the main 4-inch guns—the crews rigged up dummies with timber on the fo'c'sles in a desperate attempt to deter stalking U-boats. The ships' companies did not join until the corvettes left their builders' hands at Québec late in October 1940. They immediately made the passage to Halifax where they took on additional personnel. Workers from the builders and dockyard corrected the most glaring defects and prepared the ships for sea as best they could. There was no more than a few days for trials and rudimentary exercises before they sailed as additional escorts for convoy HX 94 on 6 December.[11]

The crews for the corvettes were exceedingly raw because the RCN's pool of experienced people had been all but drained by the unexpected need to man the Town class destroyers. Each corvette generally had only one experienced officer, the commanding officer, who was usually a member of the RCNR with long merchant service but limited naval training. Among the petty officers and ratings there were normally only two or three regulars or RCNRs, not necessarily qualified for the key appointments. The rest were RCNVR, many of whom had been in the service for only a few months and scarcely been to sea. As Lieutenant Alan Easton, RCNR later remembered, "it was hard to perform our simple task; hard to keep steam up, avoid the shoals or even to steer a straight course. Had anything warlike occurred there would have been a shambles."[12]

Trillium and *Windflower* weathered the storm in which *St Croix* nearly came to grief. Slow as the corvettes were—their maximum speed was sixteen knots—they had a greater endurance than destroyers and did not have to put into St John's to refuel. Moreover, their broad, short whaling ship hulls rode over the ocean swell and proved to be less vulnerable to heavy seas and wind than the long, sleek hulls of destroyers designed to cut through the water at speed. Lieutenant-Commander R.F. Harris, RCNR, commanding officer of *Trillium*, reported that the storm during the second week of December produced "the highest sea I have seen in the twenty years I have been at sea," but that "Trillium's performance under these conditions was magnificent. I fully expected a sea to poop [broach the ship from astern] at any instant, but the ship lifted every time, and beyond the heavy spray, and the infrequent occasions when she rolled her rail under, the decks were dry. At times she would roll as much as 52 degrees either way, but not in what I considered a dangerous fashion. Indeed, from my experience on this passage, I would greatly prefer to run in heavy weather rather than heave to."[13]

10.   Cmdre Commanding Halifax Force, "ROP—HMCS *Assiniboine*...," 29 Jan. 1941, DHH, NHS NSS 1057-1-1 pt 2

11.   Ships Movement cards for *Trillium* and *Windflower*, DHH; NHS 8000 files for *Trillium* and *Windflower*, DHH, 81/520

12.   Alan Easton, *50 North: An Atlantic Battleground*,(Toronto 1963), 15

13.   The ship's log confirms these remarks: "[1200 8 Dec.] Ship labouring and rolling heavily— spraying fore and aft ... [2400 15 Dec.] Whole gale—with violent squalls—shipping water mid-ships ... [2000 16 Dec.] Fresh Gale with frequent squalls of full gale force. High, dangerous following sea. Vessel rolling and pitching easily, shipping little water and riding gale well." *Trillium* ROP, 23 Dec. 1940, DHH, 81/520 Trillium 8000; *Trillium* log, NAC, RG 24, 7956

Lieutenant J.H.S. MacDonald, RCNR, commanding officer of *Windflower*, was somewhat less effusive. The main engines were, he wrote, "somewhat doubtful." Ever since the acceptance trials bearings had burned out when running at full power, "seeming to indicate faulty alignment of Engine. It has been suggested ... that the Engine be given a thorough overhaul and the Shaft clocked if necessary for alignment."[14] He gave this rendition of his repeated complaints in June 1941, there never having been time or facilities available to undertake this major work. Such defects were the inevitable result of newly expanded shipyards undertaking the construction of a new design on the basis of the often incomplete British drawings, and they troubled many of the corvettes of the 1940 program. As in the case of *Windflower*, the pressure of operations and the inundation of repair facilities often entailed months of delay while the crews nursed their vessels through difficult conditions.

Shipyards on the St Lawrence and Great Lakes had to scramble to get as many as possible of the partially completed corvettes to the Atlantic coast before the winter freeze-up at the end of 1940. Most of the remaining eight corvettes building for the Admiralty and four of the RCN corvettes came out of the St Lawrence in December, when the ice had already begun to form and thicken. They sailed in four groups, the last of which left Québec on 31 December, in the wake of Department of Transport icebreakers clearing a path ahead of them. The report of Lieutenant-Commander F.C. Smith, RCNR, commanding *Chambly*, captures the urgency with which the final arrangements had to be made. On Friday 13 December, "at approximately 1000 Mr. Wardle, Manager of Vickers Marine Dept. informed me HMCS CHAMBLY had to be sailed from Montréal by noon on December 14th, Saturday, as the harbour authorities were closing the port of Montréal for the winter." The ship had no bedding, stores or mess traps, no mooring hawsers, and no crew. Vickers undertook to man the ship as far as Québec, where the ship's company would join. Smith contacted Commander A.C.M. Davy and on his instructions bought bedding. "Commander Stewart, N.O.I.C. at Montréal, already had sent 35 mattresses on board, and I had Mr. James of the Munitions and Supply Board buy blankets, sheets, pillows and pillow cases, also food for Vickers crew to Québec, also food to take the ship to Halifax, and two coils of rope. Vickers supplied most of the mess traps with the exception of a few dishes which had to be bought locally." The ship sailed on the afternoon of 14 December after Davy and Mr Wardle had embarked, and the main engines, telemotor, steering gear, navigation and secondary lights had been found satisfactory. The icebreaker CGS *N.B. McLean* led the way, breaking heavy ice.[15]

The Admiralty corvettes sailed for the United Kingdom as soon as dockyard personnel and parties sent by the shipbuilding companies to Halifax could bring them up to seagoing condition. *Hepatica*, *Arrowhead*, *Eyebright* and *Spikenard* crossed in January, *Snowberry* and *Mayflower* in February, followed by *Bittersweet* and *Fennel*, which left Halifax with HX 113 on 5 March and arrived in Britain on the 21st. All put into British yards for completion, which, because of the strain on the facilities, took eight weeks or more. By this time, the plan of turning over these ships to the RN on arrival had changed. On the eve of *Trillium* and *Windflower*'s departure from Halifax in December, it had become clear that all but a handful of the new RCN corvettes would be icebound

---

14.   Macdonald to CCNF, 22 June 1941, DHH, 81/520 Windflower 8000

15.   LCdr F.C. Smith, RCNR to CO HMC Dockyard, Halifax, 26 Dec. 1940, NAC, RG 24, 5828, NS 8000-331/21

A convoy steams out of Halifax for the United Kingdom in March 1941. (NAC, PA 105235)

The newly completed HMS *Windflower* in Halifax, December 1940. She was built to Admiralty account by Davie Shipyards and later transferred to the RCN. Note that her guns have yet to be fitted. (NAC, NA PA 104467)

in the St Lawrence until the 1941 spring thaw. There was consequently a temporary surplus of manpower in the RCN and too few ships in which to provide urgently needed experience for these mostly newly entered personnel. The Admiralty gladly accepted NSHQ's suggestion that the RCN crews should remain with the ships until the spring of 1941 to gain their sea legs before taking over RCN corvettes.[16] In the event, given the repeated British calls for further help, it could not have come as any surprise when in April 1941 the Admiralty asked that the crews should take over the ships permanently. NSHQ agreed, the Admiralty having accepted the condition that the vessels be commissioned as Canadian ships.[17] Thus, a substantial Canadian corvette force, manned by some 540 RCN personnel, reached British waters some months earlier than provided for in the plan approved by government for 1941.[18]

Expansion of the Canadian force in British waters was the occasion for establishing a well-defined system of national control and support overseas. In July 1940, Lieutenant-Commander Lay had recommended sending a pool of 128 officers and men as spares for the River class destroyers, to which NSHQ responded by establishing HMCS *Dominion*, the RCN manning depot in Plymouth, England on 1 October.[19] Perhaps not inappropriately, given that there were growing worries about the danger of Canadian ships and seamen becoming lost in the vastness of the RN, the premises that housed the depot had been requisitioned from the United Services Orphanage. The initial staff was a small group of paymasters and clerks who travelled up and down the length of England and Scotland to give the destroyers administrative support as they shifted from base to base. The main body of the manning pool did not leave Halifax until the end of November, and even then it was fewer than fifty men, less than half the number originally intended. They were urgently needed. Commander H.G. DeWolf, now serving as Staff Officer (Operations) in Halifax, complained about the practice of shifting key ratings from one of the Rivers serving in British waters to fill vacancies in another. "The ratings who have been serving in U.K. ... should be given a break! ... some ratings will spend the war at sea, others at home!"[20]

Captain Taylor, who as Captain (D) of the Town class flotilla was slated to command *Dominion* and "carry out liaison duties between Canadian ships and personnel in United Kingdom waters, and the Admiralty," finally made a successful passage overseas early in January.[21] By that time Nelles had changed Taylor's terms of reference. Still in command of *Dominion*, he would now report to Commodore L.W. Murray. Following his service in NSHQ earlier in the war, Murray had gone to Halifax as Senior Officer Halifax Force in June 1940 with the rank of Commodore, but that

---

16. NSM, 28 Oct. 1940; HC London to NSHQ, 14 Nov. 1940, NS 30-26-3

17. Adm to NSHQ, 4 Apr. 1941, COAC to NSHQ, 5 Apr. 1941, Adm to NSHQ, 27 Apr. 1941, NAC, RG 24, 6796, NSS 8375-4

18. "Memo of Conference on Manning and Training Held at Naval Service Headquarters, Aug. 30, 1940," nd, N Sec to COs RCN Barracks, Halifax and Esquimalt, 4 Sept. 1940, NAC, RG 24, 4045, NSS 1078-3-5

19. CNS to Adm, 3 Aug. 1940, NAC, RG 24, 6796, NSS 8375-4; CO RCN Barracks Halifax to NSec, 6 Aug. 1940, NAC, RG 24, 5632, NS 30-26-2; NSec Memo, "Canadian Destroyers in England," 27 Sep. 1940, NAC, RG 24, 5632, NS 30-26-2; Philip Chaplin, "The Administration of HMC Destroyers in European Waters before the Commissioning of HMCS *Dominion*—May to Oct. 1940," DHH, NHS 8440-40 "Halifax Escort Force"; NSec Memo, "Canadian Destroyers in England," 27 Sep. 1940, NAC, RG 24, 5632, NS 30-26-2; Tucker, *Naval Service of Canada* II, 450

20. SO(O) Halifax min, nd, on CO RCN Barracks Halifax to NSec, 20 Nov. 1940. N Sec to COAC, 23 Nov. 1940, NAC, RG 24, 11, 114, 58-1-1, v 1-2

21. Tucker, *Naval Service of Canada* II, 448

appointment was to lapse in view of the small number of ships left on the east coast. In effect, Nelles was transferring the top Canadian seagoing command from Halifax to the United Kingdom, which symbolically as well as in fact demonstrated the navy's shift of focus on a long term basis from North American to European waters. Murray's service as Deputy Chief of the Naval Staff (DCNS) had "given him a good insight into our policy and exchange of views with the High Commissioner and Admiralty since the outbreak of hostilities."[22] It also implemented a policy that Murray had himself advocated in September 1940, when it was known the Towns would be going overseas.

Nelles's justification of this appointment to the naval minister confirmed, "the policy recommended by myself and the Naval Staff, and approved by you, of employing our major effective units in the more active war zone," a policy which he and Macdonald had so successfully pursued with the prime minister and cabinet in previous months. In addition to the four destroyers arriving in the United Kingdom late in January, Nelles reminded the minister that the RCN had "manned with Canadian personnel a number of Corvettes which are now employed with the Royal Naval Forces in British waters."

> 4. Amongst other Canadian personnel abroad are R.C.N. Reserve Officers and men serving in the Royal Navy ... We are also committed to send Canadian Corvettes and Minesweepers to England when our dispositions on this side have been filled.
>
> 5. To co-ordinate and draw the threads together of these many divided efforts, it is desirable that a Senior Officer be appointed in command of the combined forces Overseas. His duty would, of necessity, be administrative unless the Admiralty should in due course require his services in an operational capacity. It would also be greatly to our advantage to have some authority to look after the welfare of personnel and transmit to this country a regular and concise account of their proceedings.
>
> 10. I feel that your decision to concentrate our main effort abroad can be speedily and efficiently applied by the establishment of this organisation.

Macdonald's agreement to the appointment was another sign of the government's acceptance that the Canadian navy should be more than a local coastal defence force, that it should have the "blue water" capabilities and mission to operate in distant waters in support of national and alliance needs, even if the RCN overseas remained a fragmented force attached to the RN.[23]

Murray would come to be known as "Commodore Commanding H.M.C. Ships and Establishments in the U.K." (CCCS). It was not only his firsthand knowledge of Canadian political and military policy, but the unusually diverse and successful record of his naval background, and his long and close ties with key figures in the Admiralty, that made him a fortunate choice for the position. A series of appointments afloat and ashore with the Royal Navy between the wars had given Murray familiarity with large-scale naval operations and acquainted him with a number of officers destined for senior positions. While serving in major warships his captains included Dudley Pound, Percy Noble, and G.O. Stephenson, and he discovered after attending a daily staff

---

22. CNS to minister, 7 Jan. 1941, NAC, RG 24, 5632, NS 30-26-2

23. CNS to minister, 7 Jan. 1941, and Macdonald, min, 11 Jan. 1941, NAC, RG 24, 5632, NS 30-26-2

meeting in the Admiralty in 1943, that he had served with or developed close professional contacts with twenty-two of the thirty-five officers present.[24]

The commodores commanding Halifax Force had always worn their pendants in *Assiniboine*, which was fitted with extra accommodation as a flotilla leader. The expectation when Murray crossed the Atlantic in the latter part of January was that he could exercise his new command from the ship, keeping close touch with the other RCN and RCN-manned vessels operating under Western Approaches command, although Admiral Nelles had made it clear that his duty was administrative, "unless in due course the Admiralty require his services in an operational capacity."[25] Immediately on *Assiniboine*'s arrival at the Clyde, however, Murray had to make his way south to London. At that time, the Canadian government was making a forceful and ultimately successful effort to have its special interests in Newfoundland recognized in the Anglo-American negotiations that were then taking place in the British capital concerning the transfer of specific base sites to the United States under the destroyers-for-bases agreement of the previous fall. Murray's work as DCNS had given him firsthand knowledge of the issues and personalities on all sides, and he therefore acted for nearly two months as the naval advisor to the Canadian High Commission.[26] When, in the latter part of March 1941, Murray was finally able to concentrate on his new command, he quickly found that it was impractical for him to operate from *Assiniboine*. Given the increasing complexity and scope of the British organization, the only hope for keeping current with developments affecting the Canadian force was to remain in London, handy to the Admiralty, the sole point where all the threads seemed to come together. Murray made his decision to locate permanently in London in part on the "helpful and very frank" advice of the new C-in-C Western Approaches, Admiral Sir Percy Noble, whom Murray visited in Liverpool.[27] The Canadian officer's seniority was undoubtedly a factor in Noble's thinking. As Murray later recalled, "upon arrival in Greenock, which was the headquarters where our ships were working, I discovered the system was such that I disturbed the ocean much more than the U-boats. My seniority as a Commodore 1st Class wasn't workable at sea, and I had to step ashore and be satisfied with merely the administration of Canadian regulations and requirements."[28] To London it was.[29]

One of the changes that made it difficult to insert a Canadian command presence in Britain was the transfer in February 1941 of the headquarters of Western Approaches command from Plymouth north to Liverpool, closer to the main transatlantic convoy routes in the north west approaches.

---

24. Cdr K. Edwards, *Seven Sailors* (London 1945), 175. See also R. Sarty, "Rear-Admiral L.W. Murray and the Battle of the Atlantic: The Professional Who Led Canada's Citizen Sailors," in B. Horn and S. Harris (eds), *Warrior Chiefs: Perspectives on Senior Canadian Military Leaders* (Toronto 2001), 165-90

25. CNS to minister, 7 Jan. 1941, NAC, RG 24, 5632, NS 30-26-2

26. Stacey, *Arms, Men and Governments*, 357-60; Murray interview, 39; P. Neary, *Newfoundland in the North Atlantic World, 1929-1949* (Kingston and Montréal 1988), 144-9

27. Murray to NSec, 27 Mar. 1941, NAC, RG 24, 5632, NS 30-26-2

28. Murray interview, 39

29. "Connected by a confidential telephone line to the Admiralty Exchange which will allow me to get in touch with Commanding Officers at any port ... and will allow them also to get in touch with me ... in case of trouble, damage, or any situation in which my assistance or advice may be required, it will be possible for me to arrive at the scene of action by over-night train journey in a much simpler manner than if my headquarters were established at any other place in the British Isles ... Finally I shall be close at hand in case the High Commissioner wishes to be kept in touch with any matter concerning Canadian Naval forces." Murray to NSec, 27 Mar. 1941

The Plymouth area now became a separate command, meaning that *Dominion* was isolated administratively as well as geographically from the main area where Canadian ships were operating, although the ships continued to come south for refit in Plymouth's Devonport dockyard.

Murray's report to NSHQ of 27 March 1941 illuminated these difficulties. Only the four River class ships remained in the 10th Escort Group operating from the Clyde. The Towns were, he understood, to be based on Londonderry, and the corvettes were expected to be scattered among various ports in England. Present RN administration, including "the overhaul of A/S installation on return to harbour, supply of victuals, ammunition, etc., and even the arrangement of dry-docking for urgent but trivial repairs from time to time " met operational needs most adequately. He would have had to duplicate the RN system with a staff of specialists, which not only was unavailable, but would have been uneconomical to maintain for so few ships. Maintenance was centrally controlled so that RCN ships could be sent to "other ports such as Plymouth, Rosyth, Tyne or Cardiff for refit, or temporary repairs, in which case they would be out of my direct communication," and he expected that RCN corvettes and minesweepers would, on arrival, be allocated to other commands.[30]

At Halifax, Murray's replacement was Commander W.B. Creery. One of his tasks was to get the first corvettes built for the RCN up and running, a job he delegated to Commander J.D. Prentice, RCN, one of the most formidable characters of the wartime navy. A native of British Columbia, "Chummy" Prentice had entered the RN as an officer cadet in 1912, a few months before his thirteenth birthday. Noted for his zeal and intellect, he left the service in 1934 only because cut-backs during the Great Depression ended the possibility of promotion, and took up a second career in his family's ranching business in British Columbia.[31]

In accordance with the agreements between the British and Canadian services, Prentice, as a Canadian resident, registered for service with the RCN in the event of war. Called out at the end of August 1939, he became executive officer at Sydney, playing a key role in organizing that important base with few experienced personnel and almost no resources, but begged for a sea appointment. NSHQ seems to have recognized his special qualities, selecting him in September 1940 to command one of the new corvettes and also for appointment as senior officer of the first group of RCN corvettes to commission.[32]

Prentice's restless mind was seized by both the possibilities and limitations of the new ships. He forwarded a memorandum to headquarters urging that the magnetic compasses fitted in the ships should be replaced by modern, stabilized, electrically powered gyro-compasses, which gave an unvarying indication of true north and which were not affected by the many sources of magnetic fields in a ship. A magnetic compass was in constant motion in a lively ship like a corvette, and for accurate navigation and steering its readings had to be corrected on different headings. A steady compass was essential for accurate searches and attacks and a definite asset when manoeuvring in close quarters. Prentice also recommended changes in the structure of the bridge that could help even if it were not possible to fit gyro compasses.[33] The response to Prentice's enthusi-

---

30. Ibid

31. Prentice papers include a complete set of his service certificates. DHH, Prentice biog file 32

32. COAC to NSHQ, 13 Sep. 40, NS, NPRC O-60140 pt 1

33. Prentice to NSec, 20 Nov. 1940, Prentice papers

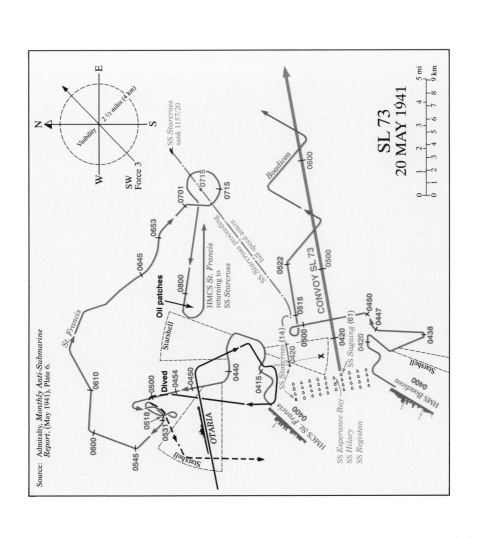

Source: Admiralty, *Monthly Anti-Submarine Report*, (May 1941), Plate 6.

SL 73
20 MAY 1941

astic offer to help with work on the new vessels at the St Lawrence and Great Lakes shipyards shows that his reputation for forthrightness was already well established: "The Director of Shipbuilding will be glad to have his cooperation ... but particularly requests that he will not ask for the ship to be redesigned and that he will not upset the overseer who is of course in charge of the ship. I told Prentice this was a delicate mater [*sic*]!"[34]

After the four RCN corvettes passed through the St Lawrence to Halifax at the end of 1940, much of the next three months was taken up with completion work, while members of the crews took courses. Among them was Prentice who, as might be expected given his vast experience, passed the fourteen-day officers' course at the antisubmarine school with the top marks in his class. When *Chambly*, the last of the vessels to be fully fitted out, completed in late March, Prentice took command, while retaining the appointment Senior Officer Corvettes.

Meanwhile, in December 1940, NSHQ had confirmed the east coast's priority for new construction from British Columbia yards. "Our dispositions on the West Coast will be very light indeed, and there will probably be few, if any, new construction vessels operating there until late next year."[35] The corvettes *Wetaskiwin* and *Agassiz* reached San Diego on passage to the Panama Canal and Halifax on 13 February 1941, but then received orders to return to Esquimalt, where they arrived once more on 19 February.[36] Movement of the Japanese fleet south to Indo-China had aroused alarm in London that the government in Tokyo was preparing to attack British or Dutch territories.[37] The scare passed, but Vincent Massey, the Canadian High Commissioner in the United Kingdom, sent Mackenzie King "Reliable information of a very secret character ... that in official Japanese circles considerable interest is being taken in the position of western coast of Canada. The suggestion that any Japanese offensive against Canada would bring in the United States is discounted on the ground that, under some conditions, it might be well to bring in United States and keep her fleet concentrated round British Columbia. Reference is also made to large number of Japanese settled in British Columbia and on western coast of United States, who are all said to have their duties."[38]

The two corvettes, together with a third, *Alberni*, set out again from Esquimalt on 17 March and reached Halifax on 13 April 1941. Here they became part of Prentice's group, bringing its strength to seven vessels, and joined in a nine-week sea training program that had begun in mid-March. Most days there were exercises in formation steaming and manoeuvres, minesweeping, gunnery, and antisubmarine operations out in the harbour approaches. Generally two to four corvettes participated, while the others took turns providing local escort for convoys as they formed up and made their first few hours of passage. The corvettes also conducted standing patrols outside the harbour.[39]

A submarine had become available full time for training duties at Halifax just as the corvette exercise program got under way in March. The only sure method for educating the ears and

---

34. Thompson, nd [Nov. 1940], teletype printout, Prentice papers

35. Reid to minister, 5 Dec. 1940, NAC, RG 24, 6797, NSS 8375-330

36. NWR, no. 75, 20 Feb. 1941, DHH, NHS NSS 1000-5-7, v 2

37. J.R.M. Butler, *Grand Strategy* II (London 1957), 498-9

38. Massey to King, tg 349, 28 Feb. 1941, *DCER* pt 8, 1370-1

39. *Chambly* deck log, 18 Mar. to 20 May 1941, NAC, RG 24, 7184

instincts of asdic crews to detect a U-boat in the complex environment of the ocean was to have them practice against an actual submarine. Although British and other allied submarines were operating from Halifax as part of the ocean escort force under Rear-Admiral 3rd Battle Squadron, their schedules allowed no more than occasional training duty, which did not at all meet needs. During the fall of 1940 the naval staff began to search for a submarine that could be permanently allocated.[40] Commander E.R. Mainguy's report in November that *Ottawa*'s lack of opportunity to train with a submarine had resulted in the destroyer's great difficulties in making asdic contact during the action against *Faa Di Bruno* stiffened the staff's determination. Ultimately, the Admiralty agreed to provide the Dutch submarine *O-15*, which had passed to British control after the German occupation of the Netherlands.[41] By early 1941, the submarine was badly in need of refit and due to return from the West Indies to Britain for this highly specialized and technically demanding work. The necessary facilities did not exist at Halifax, but the Dutch crew and the dockyard managed to refurbish the boat sufficiently for training duties by mid-March.[42] The submarine then embarked on a heavy schedule to allow practice by classes from the antisubmarine school and corvettes of the Halifax Force. During Prentice's nine-week work-up program, the corvettes had the use of the submarine over a three-week period, and on two occasions when *O-15* was not available, Rear-Admiral 3rd Battle Squadron assigned a submarine from the British flotilla.[43]

Prentice drove the ships and their crews hard. "He is persistent almost beyond endurance at times," reported Creery, "but his interests are towards the benefit of the ships he is responsible for and not towards himself."[44] He was making his mark for what another of his superiors noted with admiration, in 1944, as a "mixture of leadership and slave-driving."[45] Typical of his approach was a memorandum he produced in March on the eve of the sea training program, "Commissioning for Service—Hints to Commanding Officers," a checklist of items that needed to be attended to when sailing. Despite the exhaustive and somewhat nerve-racking attention to detail that he demanded, common sense and humanity were predominant:

> *Quartermasters*—make Quartermasters realize that they are doing a drunken man, whatever his rating, a good turn by reporting him to the Officer of the Day when he comes on board since if he is found drunk on board he has committed a very serious offense.

> *Discipline*—Remember that the Naval Discipline Act places power in the hands of Officers but also protects the men from any unfair treatment. See that every case brought up is thoroughly investigated, that every witness whose evidence may bear upon the case is called and that the case is dealt with as far as possible as it would be in a court of law.[46]

---

40. NSM, 30 Sep. 1940

41. Murray to NSec, 7 Jan. 1941, and following correspondence NSS 8020-476

42. D. Perkins, "Allied Training Submarines Allocated to RCN Use, 1939-46," nd, 3-4, DHH, 2000/5

43. A/S School, "Monthly Reports of Items of Interest (Mar., 1941)," 15 Apr. 1941, DHH, NHS NSS 1000-5-13 pt 5; White to CO *Stadacona*, "Tentative Programme for A/S Exercises," 15 Mar. 1941, NAC, RG 24, 11,543, H-10-7; *Chambly* log, 27 Mar.to 20 May 1941

44. Creery, form 206, 21 Apr. 1941, NS, NPRC O-60140 pt 2

45. Murray, form 450, 20 Apr. 1944, Prentice papers

46. Prentice, 1 Mar. 1941, A.F. Pickard papers, DHH, 80/125 docket 7

The months in Halifax with limited operational commitments gave Prentice the time and resources to concentrate on the problems of antisubmarine warfare. He became a nearly fanatical exponent of the corvette, so much so that he declined a prestigious appointment in command of a destroyer.[47] What particularly excited him about the corvette was its tight turning circle, 200 yards, as compared to 400 yards for a submerged U-boat and as much as 1,000 yards for the unwieldy Town class destroyers. British doctrine was that an antisubmarine vessel should, on making an asdic contact, open the range to 1,200 yards to smooth out the angles of contact registered on the asdic recording equipment, and thereby obtain an accurate estimate of the submarine's speed and bearing. Similarly, the attack run across the path of the submarine should begin at 800 yards to allow the asdic crew time to track evasive manoeuvres by the submarine. Prentice saw that the superior manoeuvrability of the corvette gave it a great advantage in surprising the submarine with an immediate attack that would allow it little or no time for evasion: he trained his crews to estimate a submarine's course from a range of only 400 yards and alter to the attack run at a distance of only 200 yards.[48]

Prentice recognized and dealt with the need not simply to turn a group of individual seamen into an efficient team, but to teach men fresh from civilian life ashore how to cope with conditions in a warship. On the other side of the Atlantic, Commodore G.O. Stephenson, commanding HMS *Western Isles*, the RN's working-up establishment at Tobermory on Scotland's Isle of Mull, did the same. The legendary "Terror of Tobermory" found that he had to "take it for granted that everyone knows nothing about his job and start from rock bottom." He made no attempt "to teach any but the simplest tactics or to carry out any advanced exercises."[49] The first three Canadian-manned corvettes to come out of their completion refits, *Trillium*, *Windflower,* and *Hepatica*, did the ten-day program at Tobermory, which included four days of exercises with a submarine, during the first half of March 1941. The remaining seven Canadian-manned corvettes did not complete refit and work-ups until May and June. The *Western Isles* staff's comments on *Hepatica* and *Windflower* deserve note:

HMCS HEPATICA

The A/S team as a whole is good, but their previous training has been almost entirely theoretical, and the experience of operating under actual sea conditions has been something of a shock to them.

Lieutenant [C.] Copelin [RCNR], the Commanding Officer, is an experienced and sound officer.

HMCS HEPATICA should be a very efficient unit.

HMCS WINDFLOWER

The ship suffers from lack of any A/S officer who has had any A/S experience at sea, but the Captain now has done a short course and Mate Collin, the A/S C.O. [anti-submarine control officer] showed great keenness and made good progress. Both have a fair knowledge of hunting and attacking tactics.

---

47.   Capt (D) Newfoundland, "Extract from Report on Confidential File No. 1012-5-50," [1 Jan. 1942], NS, NPRC O-60140 pt 2

48.   Prentice to Tucker, 15 Jan. 1947, DHH, 81/520/8280-SC 42

49.   CB 04050/44, 14-16, cited in Glover, "Officer Training in the RCN," 115-16

Lieutenant [J.H.S.] Macdonald [RCNR], the Commanding Officer, is a very cool, deliberate and most able officer, determined that his ship shall be ready for anything ... The
ship's company are excellent and very well disciplined.

HMCS WINDFLOWER should be a most valuable unit and will not need to be
spurred on.[50]

Trillium, *Windflower,* and *Hepatica* began operations from the Clyde as part of the 4th Escort
Group as soon as they had completed the work-up. Late in March, the four RCN Town class destroyers also joined that group and began convoy operations.[51]

The Towns had had less opportunity for working-up than the corvettes. After initial repairs on
the Clyde to make good damage from the ocean crossing, all four ships had gone south to
Plymouth—which was then under repeated bombing attack—to complete the alterations necessary
for Atlantic convoy work.[52] The delays in *St Clair*'s completion for sea were typical of the experiences of the old, unwieldy destroyers with their vulnerable propellers, which jutted out awkwardly beyond the hull line:

On the 28th [February], at 0230, while ST. CLAIR was at the jetty outside the "Town"
Class destroyer, HMS SALISBURY, a torpedo lighter came alongside and was swamped.
A tug sent out to remove the craft had to abandon the operation temporarily because
of the weather. Later in the morning, ST. CLAIR, with the aid of tugs, slipped from
SALISBURY and went alongside the jetty. There the loading of torpedoes was com-
pleted in the afternoon.

On 1 March 1941, the destroyer slipped from the jetty and went out to anchor in
the stream. The tug RETORT, which was alongside, reported the loss of its towing
hawser. It was found that it had become fouled in ST. CLAIR's port propeller. Divers
came to clear it and worked until the 6th. Throughout the period the air-raid sirens
continued to sound their warnings.

On the 7th the ship landed her ammunition and went into dry-dock the next day.
While leaving it on the 13th, she struck the entrance of the dock. Plates and frames
on the starboard side were sprung slightly by the impact.

Each day the gun crews closed up as the air raids continued. At 2130 on the 14th,
numerous incendiary bombs landed on the jetty close to the starboard quarter of the
ship, and the duty watch were sent ashore with sand and shovels to extinguish them.

The ship after loading ammunition the previous day, sailed out to Plymouth Sound
on the 18th. While proceeding at 0205 the next morning, she suffered another steering engine breakdown, which was repaired by 0355.[53]

During the weeks of shuttling in and out of dry dock, the destroyers had no more than a few
days for training exercises, although these benefited from the full facilities available at Plymouth.

---

50.   Capt (D) Greenock to C-in-C WA, "The Efficiency of Canadian-Manned Corvettes," 10 June 1941, NAC, RG 24, 11567, D.O-
      30-1

51.   *Trillium* deck log, Mar. 1941, NAC, RG 24, 7956; Adm movement sheets for *Trillium, Windflower, Hepatica, Mayflower,
      Arrowhead, Spikenard, Snowberry, Eyebright*, DHH

52.   Adm movement sheets for *St Clair, Niagara, St Francis, Columbia*, DHH

53.   "*St Clair* History," 15-16

Trillium suffered the first battle casualties to be sustained by the RCN's new warships in a brief, ugly incident during one of their earliest ocean escort missions. The corvette, together with *Windflower* and *Hepatica*, the four Canadian Towns, and several British warships put out from the Clyde on 4 April with the westbound convoy OB 306.[54] On the second day, a German aircraft swooped in and bombed one of the merchant ships. It burst into flames and subsequently sank; the anti-aircraft fire from the escorts and merchant ships had no apparent effect. After reaching Iceland on 9 April, the escort headed south to rendezvous with the United Kingdom–bound HX 117. Late in the morning of 12 April, when the convoy was northwest of the Hebrides:

> HMS Trillium [in the words of her commanding officer] was stationed between the 6th and 7th columns ... abeam of the centre ships of columns, when an enemy aircraft was observed approaching the convoy ... The aircraft ... flew over at an altitude of 200 to 400 feet, dropping a number of bombs [without effect]. My guns' crews being already closed up from a previous warning, the 4-inch, port Hotchkiss MG and the pom-pom were brought to bear and fire opened when the plane was over and between the 5th and 6th columns ... One round was fired from the 4-inch but the results were not observed. The pom-pom fired 21 rounds with unknown effect and then unfortunately jammed. The port Hotchkiss continued to fire until the belt was exhausted and almost certainly scored many hits on the fuselage of the plane without, I regret to say, any apparent result ... During the attack machine gun bullets were flying over and around us and a number of fragments apparently from the AA projectiles of other ships were later picked up on deck.
>
> 2. I regret to confirm that eight of my ratings were wounded ... of whom three subsequently died.
>
> 3. At the beginning of the attack, a number of ratings had taken cover in the protected engine room lobby. The door was left open to admit a straggler when a projectile of undetermined nature struck the bulwark ... and filled the shelter with flying fragments. It was here that all of the casualties occurred with the exception of Able Seaman Donald Robertson ... , who was wounded at his post at the pom-pom gun and subsequently died.[55]

The officer responsible for the pom-pom, Sub-Lieutenant J.B. O'Brien, RCNVR, vividly recalled the scene some fifty years later:

> Suddenly I noticed the gunner on the port side, Donald Robertson, knocked off his seat. But, grabbing his left shoulder, he climbed back on and continued firing...
>
> ...when the Focke-Wulf flew off ... I had a chance to survey the situation. Robertson was now slumped over the gun, badly wounded ... I half-dragged and half carried Robertson to the forward messdeck. It was not a pretty sight ... Shrapnel causes blood to flow pretty freely and the messdeck was awash with blood mixed with sea-water...
>
> Harry Rhoades was our cook, and also doubled as sick berth attendant, having had a first aid course while with Ogilvy's department store in Montréal.

---

54. Capt (D) Greenock to C-in-C WA, 3 Apr. 1941, DHH, 88/1 reel 5, file OB 306

55. Harris to Capt (D) Greenock, "ROP—Air Attack on HX 117, 12 Apr., 1941," 15 Apr. 1941, DHH, 81/520 Trillium 8000

Because there was no doctor on board, *Trillium* closed the destroyer HMS *Boadicea* to collect her medical officer.

> We strapped the unconscious Robertson to the messdeck table ... The doctor took out a book and turned to the chapter on amputations ... The operation began with our cook assisting and I acting as anaesthetist. Every time the doctor took a slice or two, he would turn a page in his book ... As the doctor cut deeper, you could see how the shrapnel had shattered Robertson's shoulder, imbedding pieces of the grey duffel coat two or three inches into his body.
>
> Robertson was fighting for his life, with his chest giving mighty heaves. The operation took about two hours. Unfortunately, Robertson died on the messdeck table almost simultaneously with the final removal of his arm.
>
> The doctor left and went down to the wardroom where I found him later, lying prone on the settee. I told him he had done all he could. He answered that he was fresh out of medical school and this was the first operation he had ever performed. And if it hadn't been for the calming influence of the cook he would have panicked a couple of times.[56]

During their first six weeks of operations, Canadian ships made at least four attacks on asdic contacts, and in another instance joined a hunt already under way. The Town class destroyers took the lead in these operations, and the results were not encouraging. There were equipment failures, errors in settings of depth charges and a tendency to rush ahead with attack after attack, emptying the magazines, when the situation demanded deliberation and care. The Canadian and recently commissioned British ships in the group were too quick to dash off in response to a contact that had not been confirmed and leave gaps in the escort screen; on one occasion they failed to pass full information to the other members of the escort.[57] During the third week of May, therefore, schedules were adjusted so that ships could come in for exercises with a submarine off Moville in the approaches to Londonderry, which was becoming one of Western Approaches main operating bases as new facilities neared completion.[58] In this case, its proximity to the convoy routes would allow escorts to come in for exercise before they joined an outgoing convoy, or after they parted company with an incoming one. The week's schedule was immediately disarranged by continuing defects in the Town class. HMS *Broadway* had had to go into refit, *Niagara* suffered a breakdown that took the ship entirely out of action for the week, while *St Clair* and *Columbia* came in a day late, the latter with one fuel tank out of action. The senior officer, Commander E.C.L. Turner, RN, in *Boadicea*, issued a plea for further work on the ships to increase their reliability.[59]

On completion of the revised exercise program, the group antisubmarine officer submitted a damning report. In *Columbia* and *St Clair*, "The difficulties of the Commanding Officers, both of whom, due to no fault of their own, lack experience, are greatly increased by the lack of support

---

56.   M. Johnston, *Corvettes Canada: Convoy Veterans of WWII Tell Their True Stories* (Toronto 1994), 13-14

57.   Narrative A, 29-30; "Notes on the History of HMC Destroyer *Niagara*," 3-4. For reports on four of the attacks by Canadian ships, see PRO, ADM 199/1127 (26 Mar. 1941) and PRO, ADM 199/1124 (three attacks on 8-9 May 1941). The ADM files do not, however, include the extremely critical commentary cited in the DHH sources, which are drawn from documents that have not yet come to light.

58.   C-in-CWA to FOIC Greenock, NOIC Londonderry, D Greenock, 14 May 41, PRO, ADM 237/49. For development of Londonderry, see on PRO, ADM 116/4386.

59.   HMS *Boadicea*, "ROP—4th Escort Group," 24 May 1941, PRO, ADM, 237/49

from their subordinate officers. This reflects adversely on the ship's company who appear keen, but await a lead which is not always forthcoming." He said much the same thing about the corvettes. Of their RCNR commanding officers he remarked "No one could possibly question either their courage or endurance at sea, and they are fine seamen. Their lack of technical knowledge is their great difficulty, and possibly due to their age, they are very slow to learn." Captain S.K. Bain, RN, who as Captain (D) at Greenock administered the 4th Escort Group, was less quick to criticize the officers and disagreed that *Trillium, Windflower,* and *Hepatica* were inefficient.[60]

The impatience of the 4th Escort Group staff as compared to the attitude of Captain (D) Greenock and Commodore Stephenson was a matter of perspective. The escort group, facing immediate operational tasks, naturally wanted efficient, dependable ships; the more senior officers, grappling with the problems of expansion, knew what could reasonably be expected. As Captain C.R.H. Taylor would point out in July, when these reports reached Canadian authorities in England, the corvettes had been manned with the intention that the RCN crews would turn the vessels over to the RN before the ships became operational, and had thus not undergone the necessary operational training. When commanding HMCS *Niobe*—the new name for the RCN manning depot in the United Kingdom—he had endeavoured to find additional qualified personnel to strengthen the crews but in many cases had been unable to do so. It is hard to disagree with his conclusion that "Great credit should therefore be given to the Commanding Officers of HMCS TRILLIUM, WINDFLOWER and HEPATICA due to the fact that under these condition [*sic*] they worked their ships up to a state of efficiency which the Commodore WESTERN ISLES reported as surpassing many R.N. Corvettes."[61] Indeed, the lesson Captain (D) Greenock took from the troubles in the 4th Escort Group was the need for fuller and more thorough training. "The 10 days working-up programme at Tobermory," he reported, "is not sufficient for newly commissioned ships who have had little or no previous experience, and it is recommended that this be followed by a further 10 days intensive ... exercises."[62]

Taylor was also very familiar with the problems in the Town class destroyers. As he informed Captain (D) Greenock, "It was ... strongly recommended [in the fall of 1940] that the R.C.N. Town Class Destroyers ... should be allowed six months to work-up based on Bermuda in order that [their] 'raw' personnel should gain more experience prior to operating in United Kingdom waters. This could not be approved as Naval Service Headquarters were informed by Admiralty that these ships were urgently required in the United Kingdom."[63] Captain (D) Greenock's complaint on this occasion was that the lack of qualified Engine Room Artificers (ERAs) in *Niagara* was putting an impossible burden on the ship's engineer officer and senior engine room artificer. Of the six ERAs, only two had any experience with the intricacies of marine steam turbine plants and that was slight: one for a period of two months as part of the training program in the British armed merchant cruisers oper-

---

60. Capt (D) at Greenock to C-in-C WA, "The Efficiency of Canadian-Manned Corvettes," 10 June 1941, NAC, RG 24, 6909, NSS 8970-330

61. Reports from Cmdre Stephenson survive for two other RCN corvettes, *Mayflower* and *Snowberry,* and both of these earned favourable comment, *Snowberry* after an inefficient officer had been relieved. CCCS to NSec, 14 July 1941, NAC, RG 24, 6909, NSS 8970-330; Stephenson to DA/SW, "HMS *Snowberry*—Report of Working-up," 26 Apr. 1941, NAC, RG 24 (Acc 83-4/167), 2571, NSS 6100-330 pt 1; same to same, "HMS *Mayflower*—Report of Working-up," 4 June 1941, NS, NPRC O-69740; Stacey, *Arms, Men and Governments,* 310

62. Capt (D) at Greenock to C-in-C WA, "Efficiency of Canadian-Manned Corvettes"

63. Taylor to Capt (D) Greenock, 2 Apr. 1941

ating from Halifax and the other in the turbine yacht *Grilse* when it served in the RCN during the First World War. Among the other ERAs, two had qualifications as stationary and steam engineers but no marine experience.[64] Taylor explained "Canada has a very small sea-faring population and therefore E.R.A.'s (H.O. [Hostilities Only]) with turbine experience are few." In this case, qualified reliefs for *Niagara* could be found only by an exchange of personnel with *Ottawa*.[65]

Ships sent to exercise at Moville in May were not the only ones in the 4th Escort Group to demonstrate the effects of inexperience. On the afternoon of 19 May, shore DF stations picked up transmissions from what intelligence correctly identified as an Italian submarine, some 450 miles west of southern Ireland, close by the route of convoys coming from or going to the South Atlantic. There was time to divert convoy OG 62, escorted by some ten ships of the 4th Escort Group, half of them Canadian; however, the incoming SL 73, protected only by an armed merchant cruiser, was already closing the area, about 120 miles from OG 62. Western Approaches ordered the 4th Escort Group to send support, and the destroyers HMS *Boadicea* and *St Francis* raced ahead, reaching SL 73 in the dark early hours of 20 May.[66] (See map at page 160.) At "about 0415," when *St Francis* was sweeping approximately 3,000 yards off the port quarter of the convoy, the lookout on the after gun platform saw a surfaced submarine not more than 100 feet away, headed in the opposite direction. He frantically tried to inform the bridge over his telephone headset but could get no response. Within minutes, as he was still trying to raise the alarm, the Italian submarine *Otaria* torpedoed the freighter *Starcross* at the end of the port column. *St Francis* responded quickly to the sound of the explosion, and at 0454 made asdic contact, on which she delivered two depth charge attacks. The counter-attack had been hampered, however, by the fact that *Boadicea*, on the other side of the convoy, did not receive the initial torpedoing report because of a malfunction in its radio-telephone equipment. *St Francis*, moreover, made no attempt to alert an RAF Catalina that was flying cover for the convoy. The starshell, fired initially by *St Francis* and then by *Boadicea* in an attempt to illuminate the submarine in case it was attempting to escape on the surface, dissipated in low cloud; worse, the flash of the guns temporarily blinded bridge personnel in both destroyers.[67]

Starcross, meanwhile, had remained afloat and made slow headway, thanks to the courage and determination of the captain, who repeatedly refused to abandon ship so long as there was the faintest hope of salvage. After daybreak, *St Francis* stood by and attempted a tow, but then took off the last of the ship's people as the flooding increased beyond control. The ship, however, did not go down, and because the hulk was a danger to navigation it fell to *St Francis* to sink it. Lieutenant L.C. Audette, the gunnery officer, found the subsequent events both disconcerting and profoundly moving.

> At the outset, the task appeared ... to present no particular problem. It was broad daylight, a relatively calm sea and STARCROSS was not under way. Indeed, it seemed an excellent exercise for my gun's crew. To everyone's confusion, after firing round after round and hit-

---

64. Capt (D) at Greenock to CO *Niobe*, 22 Mar. 1941, 2 Apr. 1941, NAC, RG 24 (acc 83-84/167), 1418, NS 4100-354/15

65. Taylor to Capt (D) Greenock, 2 Apr. 1941

66. HMS *Boadicea*, "ROP—4th Escort Group," 24 May 1941; evidence of A/Cdr E.C.L. Turner, RN, HMS *Boadicea*, "Greenock, 13th June, 1941. Proceedings at Board of Inquiry in Regard to HMCS *St Francis*," 19, ibid; C-in-C WA to *Boadicea*, for *Arrowhead, St Francis, Snowberry, Egret, Esperance Bay*, 19 May 1941, ibid.

67. Adm, *MASR*, May 1941, 13-15. See also Bain to C-in-C WA, 30 May 1941, PRO, ADM 237/49.

ting the target, STARCROSS still floated bravely. It was more than a little mystifying until Burgess, her Captain, pointed out that she was laden with 5,000 tons of peanuts. Finally she upended and sank, whereupon her Captain burst into uncontrollable tears; this was not any uncommon occurrence and reflects only credit upon him.

Those who have never beheld the dread moment of the death of a ship can hardly imagine the enormous drama of such an occasion, doubled of course for those who served in her ... Even for ships of which I was not part of the ship's company, I never witnessed such a spectacle without deep emotion. For those who had been ... part of her ship's company, the spectacle was downright overwhelming and many such men broke into tears on witnessing her demise. Few non-seagoing men will ever understand the strange bond of love for a ship on the part of men who serve in her or even a ship in which they have not served.[68]

The depressing fact was that an enemy submarine had sunk a merchantman minutes after encountering an escort whose sole purpose was to protect that merchantman; the enemy had then escaped. It was a classic case of otherwise small lapses combining under the pressure of extreme circumstances to produce disaster. At 0400 the watch had changed. Although the seaman who took over the ship's internal telephone on the bridge had regularly performed this duty, it was only the second time he had stood a watch at night. He was not certain whether the routine was the same as during the day and therefore had not promptly put on his headset, which is why the report from the after lookout had not been received. At the same time, the oncoming bridge watch had not allowed sufficient time for their eyes to become accustomed to the dark, which was probably why they had not seen the submarine themselves.[69] The errors could not have been more embarrassing for the commanding officer, Lieutenant-Commander H.F. Pullen, RCN, who took great pride in running a tight ship. Captain Bain at Greenock, in his intimate knowledge of the problems of new ships trying to get up to speed in the demanding Western Approaches theatre, was reassuring:

After investigation I admonished [Pullen] and emphasised the gravity of [the failure to take action against the surfaced submarine] ... He had, however, already taken the requisite measures to prevent a recurrence of this deplorable episode, and I decided that further action on my part was unnecessary. I was encouraged in this course by the fact that Lieutenant-Commander Pullen of ST. FRANCIS is a keen, smart young officer and undoubtedly one of the most capable of the Canadian Commanding Officers working in the North Western Approaches.[70]

Bain's approach appalled Western Approaches staff and Admiral Noble fired a "rocket" to Greenock.[71] The Captain (D) had to convene a board of inquiry into the incident, which formally fixed the blame on Pullen as commanding officer for poor supervision but did not uncover anything that had not already been reported on by Bain.[72] He had already issued a warning to ships

---

68.   Audette, "Naval Recollections," 34-5

69.   C-in-C WA min, "*St Francis*—Failure to Attack and Report U/B," 8 June 1941, PRO, ADM 237/49

70.   Capt (D) Greenock to C-in-C WA, 26 June 1941, PRO, ADM 237/49

71.   C-in-C WA min, "*St Francis*—Failure to Attack"

72.   "Proceedings at Board of Inquiry in regard to HMCS *St Francis*"

under his command about *St Francis*'s errors; Western Approaches now issued a general signal that did not name the destroyer but cited the "reprehensible" failure of internal communications and sloppiness about night vision.[73]

As the RCN's new fleet went through its harsh apprenticeship in British waters, the focus of action in the Atlantic was beginning to move towards North America, and the United States was becoming ever more involved. These were developments of profound significance to Canada.

The destroyers for bases agreements in September 1940, as Churchill had so fervently hoped, proved to be a first step towards American participation. Further commitment, however, was slow as President Roosevelt repeatedly adjusted course in the face of isolationist opinion among the American electorate. His victory for an unprecedented third term in the election of November 1940 brought relief in allied capitals and an early measure of unparalleled importance: the president's sponsorship of the "Lend-Lease" bill, which would empower him to transfer war materials to nations fighting the Axis powers. Without the bill, or some similar measure, Britain's war fighting capability would have been gravely threatened, for its reserve of American dollars was nearly exhausted. Congress began to debate the legislation in January 1941 and passed it in March.[74] On 20 April, in a meeting at Roosevelt's estate at Hyde Park, New York, Mackenzie King successfully concluded negotiations in which the US administration agreed to place Canadian firms engaged in defence production on the same basis as American ones in the protected US market. The increased American orders in Canada provided US dollars that allowed the King government to avoid having to apply for lend-lease. It was a sensible, perhaps inevitable, step, given the close integration of Canadian and US industry. American components, priced in US dollars, were essential to most Canadian war production, while at the same time Canada's mobilized industry was able to provide many items to the US government and to American firms as they tooled up for war production.[75]

President Roosevelt was in a tricky situation. He had outflanked isolationist opponents in the 1940 election with his pledge to keep the United States out of the war. Indeed, he successfully presented lend-lease as the means to keep Britain fighting and thereby ensure that the United States did not have to become a belligerent. That, despite Winston Churchill's brave public words, was contrary to Britain's own assessment, which Churchill and the military staffs freely shared with the officers and special envoys Roosevelt had sent to gather information about the military situation. Many American officials were convinced that Britain would not survive, and that aid of the type envisioned in lend-lease would inevitably be lost. The British sought to reassure the Americans but also argued that the enemy could not be defeated without full intervention by the United States. After the 1940 election, the British succeeded in drawing the Americans into secret military staff consultations about combined strategy and effort, if and when the United States became a belligerent. In late January 1941, senior British officers, dressed in civilian clothes and travelling

73. C-in-C WA to Ships in Escorts Groups in WA Command (R) CCNF, 8 July 1941, PRO, ADM 237/49

74. W.F. Kimball, *The Most Unsordid Act: Lend-Lease, 1939-1941* (Baltimore 1969)

75. R. Warren James, *Wartime Economic Co-operation: A Study of Relations between Canada and the United States* (Toronto 1949), 1-42; J.L. Granatstein, *Canada's War: The Politics of the Mackenzie King Government, 1939-1945* (Toronto 1975), 132-45

under the guise of members of the British Purchasing Commission, arrived in Washington for what came to known as the ABC (American–British Conversations) talks.[76]

As with the destroyers-for-bases negotiations, the conversations featured hard, at times acrimonious, bargaining. At issue on the American side was nothing less than leadership of the western alliance. Senior USN officers had become convinced of that when, during the summer and fall of 1940, the British naval staff made detailed recommendations as to where and how the American fleet could most usefully assist the allied cause. American officers were especially alarmed at the Admiralty's urging that the USN should send a battle fleet to Britain's main base in the Far East at Singapore to deter or check Japanese aggression, something which the British fleet, overextended in the Atlantic and Mediterranean, could not hope to achieve. This was a counsel of desperation from the British but it had some precedent. Since the 1920s Britain had accepted that the United States was the predominant western power in the Pacific and the main thrust of the USN's war planning and fleet development was indeed for a conflict with Japan. In the circumstances of late 1940, however, senior US officers believed that the Singapore strategy—or the USN's own Plan Orange for an offensive against Japan across the central Pacific[77]—could only severely diminish American influence on the course of the war. Deployment of a battle fleet in the western Pacific and reinforcement of that fleet if, as American officers thought certain, the Japanese responded to such a provocation by declaring war, would consume most of the existing resources of the navy and any additional strength it could muster in the foreseeable future. The USN would be bogged down in the Pacific, when it was in the Atlantic, where Germany, the principal and most dangerous enemy had to be engaged and where the outcome of the war would be decided.

"Shall we direct our efforts towards an eventual strong offensive in the Atlantic as an ally of the British, and a defensive in the Pacific?" asked Admiral Harold R. Stark, the US Chief of Naval Operations (CNO). It was a rhetorical question that he answered with a resounding affirmative. In a study prepared for the administration in November 1940, he recommended nothing less than completely reorienting the focus of US strategic planning from the Pacific to the Atlantic, the Mediterranean, Europe, and Africa, and it was this recommendation that became the basis for American participation in the secret staff talks with the British.[78] In the extraordinary initiative Stark took in reshaping American policy, he was carrying out the wishes of the president, although the paper trail is still impossible to reconstruct, so cautious was Roosevelt in the face of isolationist opinion.[79]

In December 1940, early steps were already under way to prepare the navy, which was still on a peacetime basis in everything from manning to training and equipment, for early intervention in

---

76. Not "American-British-Canadian," still repeated by some authorities and a misnomer in view of the limited part played by Canada. Leutze, *Bargaining for Supremacy*, 128-215, is a detailed, scholarly account, from which the following paragraphs are largely drawn.

77. For the evolution of Plan Orange, see E.S. Miller, *War Plan Orange: The US Strategy to Defeat Japan, 1897-1945* (Annapolis 1991).

78. Stark, "Memo for the Secretary," 12 Nov. 1940, file 79 pt 4, NARA, RG 313, Entry NHC 76, Comaveu subject file, box 15. This is the famous "Plan Dog" memo. The beat-Germany-first proposal was the fourth among the lettered strategic alternatives Stark presented, and "Dog" was the military communications word symbol for the letter D. See also B.M. Simpson, *Admiral Harold R. Stark: Architect of Victory, 1939-1945* (Columbia, SC 1989), ch 4

79. Leutze, *Bargaining for Supremacy*, 203-5

the Atlantic. In that month, Vice-Admiral Ernest J. King, a hard-driving, uncompromising officer—and a distinct anglophobe—took command of the Patrol Force, as the old Atlantic squadron had been named to reflect its responsibilities for the neutrality watch. His mandate was to prepare his command so that it would be ready to carry out escort of convoys and despatch a strong force of destroyers and patrol aircraft to the United Kingdom the moment the government gave the order—there would be no piecemeal deployment of small groups of warships at the summons of the Admiralty as in 1917 and 1918. On 1 February 1941, the expanding Patrol Force became the Atlantic Fleet, signalling its greatly increased importance, and King was promoted full admiral. Meanwhile, American forces began to arrive in Newfoundland to develop the base sites acquired under the destroyers-for-bases agreement, and at the end of December 1940, the navy began construction of a large base, for the operation of both warships and aircraft, at Argentia.[80] Soon after, an army garrison arrived at St John's and began to assist the Canadian force already defending that port.[81]

If the Canadian government had felt itself caught awkwardly between the United States and Great Britain in the destroyers-for-bases negotiations, it was now increasingly shunted aside as the great powers laid the foundation for a military alliance. Perhaps the most sensitive and difficult issue in arranging for the combined operations of the armed forces of two or more countries is the question of command, which so concerned the United States in relation to cooperation with Great Britain, and which similarly worried Canadian authorities with respect to the Americans.

Existing published accounts of Canada–United States defence relations remark that the Permanent Joint Board on Defence skirted the command question during the first months of its existence, notably in the "Joint Canadian–United States Basic Defence Plan—1940," completed in October of that year. This plan was only a skeleton that laid down the tasks the armed forces of each nation were to undertake in the event that Britain should fall and North America faced a major attack.[82] In December, the Canadian and US navies negotiated the details of command to produce an operational plan that fleshed out the earlier version.[83]

The arrangements in the naval plan closely followed what Captain Murray and his USN-counterparts, Captains Hill and Sherman, had quickly agreed to in the initial Canada–United States staff meeting of July 1940. In the event of a British collapse, the USN would assume responsibility for the offshore defence of the Canadian coasts and Newfoundland, offshore defined as outside thirty miles. Operations off the British Columbia coast would be commanded by the USN's existing North West Sea Frontier headquarters at Seattle, Washington, while operations off Newfoundland and the maritime provinces would come under a new American coastal frontier headquarters that would be established at Halifax. The RCN's Halifax Force, which included the few Canadian destroyers and armed merchant cruisers available for offshore defence, would come under the new American headquarters at Halifax for operational purposes, although not for internal administra-

80. Abbazia, *Mr Roosevelt's Navy*, 133-44; T.B. Buell, *Master of Sea Power: A Biography of Fleet Admiral Ernest J. King* (Boston 1980), 132-3; Neary, *Newfoundland*, 137-43, 153-5

81. Dzuiban, *Military Relations*, 96

82. Stacey, *Arms, Men and Governments*, 349; Dzuiban, *Military Relations*, 87-9

83. "Operational Plan of Royal Canadian Navy to Implement Joint Canadian-United States Basic Defence Plan, 1940," 19 Dec. 1940, NAC, RG 24, 11,127, file Joint Defence Plan 1940

tion and discipline. The operational role of COAC and COPC, and of the subordinate naval officers in charge at the bases on each coast, would be limited to local defence of the approaches to the bases to a distance of thirty miles. COAC would also be responsible for maintaining a patrol in the Strait of Belle Isle and, until adequate US forces became available, for the defence of the waters between Cape Breton and Newfoundland.

The naval plan of December 1940 conceded greater powers to the USN in Canadian home waters than Canada had allowed to the RN, a fact explained by the gravity of the situation—imminent large scale attack in the wake of Britain's collapse—envisioned by the plan. But, beginning at the end of January 1941, in light of the contingency that now seemed increasingly likely—that Britain would survive and the United States would become a belligerent—Canadian officers and officials were determined to negotiate comprehensive arrangements covering all three services that respected Canadian sovereignty and the autonomy of Canadian forces. Under the new appreciation, the threat to North America would only be occasional raids, a task for which Canadian forces were becoming more adequate. There would be no compelling military necessity to allow American commanders sweeping authority over Canadian forces. According to Captain H.E. Reid, now Deputy Chief of the Naval Staff at NSHQ, the Canadian members of the joint board "brought considerable pressure to bear on the US Members" to discuss this scenario but the American officers resisted, "obviously awaiting" the outcome of the ABC talks between the British and US staffs in Washington.[84]

Canada was not a party to the ABC meetings, the result of American concerns about "encirclement" by a large number of British Commonwealth and other Allied delegations.[85] All that could be offered to the dominions was the presence of a "camouflaged" observer, who, the State Department advised, should be a naval officer, "since it is anticipated that 99% of conversations will be on naval matters."[86] The Canadian government sent Commander P.B. German, RCN, who arrived in Washington as the meetings started at the end of January and stayed until their conclusion in late March. He did not attend the sessions but, together with an officer from the Royal Australian Navy, sat daily with the British delegation and regularly reported back to Ottawa.

In the proceedings of the conference there was little that was surprising or controversial so far as Canada was concerned. The main source of acrimony was the British officers' pressure for the USN to send a battle fleet to Singapore, and the Americans' stubborn refusal to advance any large force west of the existing main base at Pearl Harbor in the Hawaiian Islands. Otherwise, there was generally ready agreement. Despite the suspicions of the Admiralty's intentions on the part of senior American officers, the British were ready to concede the US demand for strategic control of theatres of mainly American interest, and of clear national command over US forces allocated to areas of British control. Thus, if and when the US became a belligerent, it would assume responsibility for the Pacific and for the Atlantic west of 30°West. In effect, the USN would take over the RN's America and West Indies station, and the detailed planning included a US heavy ship force at Halifax to relieve the British force there in providing anti-surface raider protection to convoys. For the RCN, the only change would be the replacement of British major warships with American ones; Nelles remarked that it might be necessary to ensure that the USN understood that, as in the

---

84. Reid to [German], 7 Mar. 1941, file 1-AL(s) pt 1. See also "Permanent Joint Board on Defence Memo as to the Command of Joint Operations, 4 Nov. 1940," ibid., and printed in *DCER* pt 8, 184-8

85. Charge d'Affaires in US to SSEA, tg 336, 23 Dec. 1940, *DCER* pt 8, 1193-4

86. Ibid, tg 25, 17 Jan. 1941, *DCER* pt 8, 1198

arrangements between the British and Canadian navies, US commanders could give orders to only those Canadian ships that had specifically been allocated for offshore trade protection and to not otherwise interfere with Canadian forces.[87]

During the conference, there was considerable progress with plans for US destroyers and patrol planes to provide much needed support in the northwest approaches to Britain, still the focal point of the antisubmarine war. Certainly, the British did not quibble about the American determination to keep effective national command over the force, although they took some care to inform the US officers about the organization of escort groups that the RN had found to be most effective and warned about the necessity of both nations endeavouring to build up the escort forces so that a group of twelve warships would be available for each convoy.[88] Meanwhile, the USN had begun to organize an antisubmarine warfare force as part of the Atlantic Fleet that would be available for the mission in British waters if and when the government so ordered. The Northeastern Escort Force, whose name was soon changed to the more neutral Support Force, came into existence on 1 March 1941, under the command of Rear-Admiral Arthur L. Bristol. That same month, a location at Londonderry, adjacent to the existing RN base, was selected for the main US facility, and construction began soon after.[89]

Events at sea gave particular meaning to the ABC talks. The winter storms that created difficulties for U-boats in the Western Approaches to Britain during the winter of 1940–41, also enabled the powerful fast battlecruisers *Gneisenau* and *Scharnhorst* to escape British air and sea patrols and break out into the Atlantic late in January. Their mission was to sink merchant shipping and avoid battle with major enemy warships. The appearance of the fighting tops of British battleships over the horizon prevented them from lingering in any one area but with a speed of thirty-one knots—four more than the most modern British battleships and ten knots or more than the older ships that formed much of the RN's battle squadrons—they were readily able to escape, dashing from the Arctic to the northwest Atlantic, across to the North African coast, and back again. They sank a total of twenty-two merchant vessels, a modest return for such a major operation, but the startling fact was that the raiders were able to range the oceans unscathed for sixty-days, completely disrupting convoy schedules, and then safely return to port despite the best efforts of much of the British fleet.[90]

These forays came uncomfortably close to Canada. The raiders had their greatest success in the northwest Atlantic. They sank five merchantmen about 500 miles off St John's on 22 February, and they either sank or took as prizes sixteen more even closer to Newfoundland on 15–16 March. The victims were sitting ducks, merchantmen that had been dispersed from convoys outward-bound from the United Kingdom after the antisubmarine escort had departed.[91] Mackenzie King reacted

---

87.   German to CNS, tg 30, 1 Mar. 1941, NAC, RG 25, 5695, A-AL(s) pt 1

88.   E.g., "British-United States Staff Conversations. Min ... 5 Feb. 1941,"4-6, file 192, NARA, RG 313, Entry NHC 76, Comnaveu "Subject File," box 27

89.   Abbazia, *Roosevelt's Navy*, 142-4; Roskill, *War at Sea* I, 373-9

90.   AHS, *Home Waters and the Atlantic* II: *9th April 1940–6th December 1941* (London 1961), 275-96

91.   During the second attack, the German raiders narrowly escaped the battleship HMS *Rodney*, which had been escorting an eastbound Halifax convoy nearby. The presence of such a powerful ship on convoy duty was the result of the Admiralty's reinforcement of the North Atlantic route in response to the raiders. For that same reason, HMS *King George V*, the most modern battleship in the fleet, was available at Halifax and came out on the 16th. North Atlantic Escort Force WD, 15-16 Mar. 1941, PRO, ADM 199/409. See also AHS, *Defeat of the Enemy Attack on Shipping*, 121

viscerally when told about the first of the raider attacks off Newfoundland. His worst fears were being realized. "I reminded [the Chiefs of Staff] ... how I had always pressed for not sending everything to Britain but retaining protection here." Nelles, who was able to report that two of the River class destroyers in British waters, *St Laurent* and *Skeena*, were returning to Halifax for refit, had to point out that even if all of the Canadian warships in British waters were brought back, it would not materially improve security against a modern capital ship and, to his credit, King eventually accepted this appreciation.[92]

At the prime minister's direction, the Chiefs of Staff quickly produced a brief about the dangers Canada faced of direct attack.[93] This held firm that Britain's survival was the best defence of Canada. It admitted, however, that "every day increases the chances of "tip-and-run" sea and air raids," that is to say swift attacks by heavy ships' guns and aircraft. The appearance of *Gneisenau* and *Scharnhorst* so close to North America led the chiefs to conclude that Hitler was no longer restrained by fears of bringing the United States into the war. That was only logical on his part, given the increasing American support to the Allies, but it deprived the western Atlantic of what had been its best shield. The chiefs did not ignore the Pacific, where they warned that war could break out with Japan at any time, but stood by a nearly absolute priority for the Atlantic.

The Chiefs of Staff noted the increase in British forces based at Halifax for anti-surface raider escort of convoys but remarked that "these are barely adequate for this essential duty." Additional striking forces of heavy warships and bombers were needed to provide specific coverage of the approaches to Canadian ports and focal areas of shipping offshore, with priority for Newfoundland, "Flanking as it does the trans-Atlantic air and sea-routes to North America, a strongly held Newfoundland, upon which are based adequate Navy, Army and Air forces, represents a powerful deterrent to enemy air and surface action against our coasts and territorial waters." Only the United States, however, could supply the necessary forces. The chiefs urged King to make a personal appeal to President Roosevelt, which he was later to do.

In the meantime, he cabled the substance of the report to Churchill, emphasising the difficult position of his government in having left Canada's coasts open to attack by sending so much overseas. Churchill and his officials responded on 24 March with gratitude for the Canadian help received, an admission there were not enough ships and aircraft to go round, a restatement of the need to concentrate resources where they were most needed and a promise for rapid redisposition in case of an increased threat to Canada. There were assurances about the unlikelihood of a major German warship risking a close approach to the coast and intelligence that no German bomber could reach Newfoundland or Canada while carrying a substantial bomb load. The Canadian chiefs readily endorsed the British messages and passed word to their ministers that the RN's continued assignment of battleships to the Halifax convoys demonstrated its determination to secure the western Atlantic. All of this King accepted.[94] To some extent, King was content to have formally registered his doubts about denuding the Canadian coast for the benefit of Britain. He was at this

---

92. King diary, 22 Feb. 1941. See also CWC minutes, 26 Feb. 1941

93. For this and following two paragraphs, "Chiefs of Staff Committee. Brief Appreciation of the Situation as of 24th February 1941," 25 Feb. 1941, NAC, RG 24, 2687, HQS 5199 pt 9; See also CWC, 26 Feb. 1941.

94. SSEA to DSec, 2 Mar.-10 Apr. 1941, NAC, RG 24, 3832, NSS 1017-10-1 pt 3 (Printed in *DCER*, VII, 939-45); Chiefs of Staff Committee to ministers, 3 Apr. 1941, DHH, 193.009(D2).

time worried about widespread calls in the press to replace the Liberals with a national government to prosecute the war effort more effectively. In that light, King saw the political damage from an attack on Newfoundland or Canadian soil as being as dangerous as the physical damage. He might, however, contain the backlash if he could demonstrate his government had followed the best military advice; the prime minister was always extremely careful to defend his administration by setting down carefully what he called a "record."[95]

The big surface raiders were only part of the problem. While the Canadian messages did the rounds at Whitehall, on 14 March the Admiralty warned Nelles of "indications" that U-boats might soon begin to move into the western Atlantic.[96] The cause of alarm may have been a radio transmission on a U-boat frequency that, according to DF plots, originated from 43° West, about 250 miles off Newfoundland.[97] The British wanted to know what forces the Canadians had to cover the Halifax approaches and what more was needed. Nelles responded that the minimum was nine destroyers and fifteen corvettes. There were three Town class destroyers, although two were still refitting, together with the recently returned *St Laurent* and *Skeena*, which he proposed to keep in Canadian waters when they completed refit. He also wanted to bring back the four remaining River class destroyers still operating from the UK to complete the flotilla. The RCN corvettes already in commission together with the first batch to come down from the St Lawrence with the spring thaw would be sufficient for that class, but he advised the Admiralty he would need the return of the crews that had ferried the Canadian-built RN corvettes to Britain so as to bring the newly built vessels quickly into service.[98]

By the latter part of March, the British were confident that the U-boats were not in fact about to push into the Canadian area, and the Admiralty asked Nelles not to withdraw any ships from the Western Approaches. Soon after, as we have seen, the Admiralty also asked that crews on the corvettes built for the RN should remain with the ships in British waters. Churchill, in his otherwise reassuring message to King about surface raiders, advised that antisubmarine defence in the western Atlantic would be dependent on Canadian resources, but underscored the need for the Admiralty to have the final say in dispositions:

> We are of the opinion that enemy will only adopt less economical use of submarines in western Atlantic for the purpose of making us over-insure ourselves there at the expense of decisive areas in western approaches [to the UK]. Every effort will be made to strike right balance between providing essential anti-submarine force for Canadian coast and maintaining our freedom on this side of the Atlantic.[99]

This carefully crafted paragraph reflected the dilemma that British maritime commands and the government itself confronted as the tempo and intensity of the German anti-shipping offensive picked up in late February and March 1941. One source of encouragement during the winter of

---

95. See, eg., King diary, 22 Feb., 28 Mar. 1941; CWCM, 26 Feb. 1941, esp King's comments recorded in para 12

96. The Admiralty-NSHQ signal traffic referred to in this paragraph is reproduced in CSC to ministers, 3 Apr. 1941, DHH, 193.009(D2).

97. DOP, "Defence of Trade," 28 Mar. 1941, PRO, ADM 199/935

98. CSC to ministers, 3 Apr. 1941

99. DSec to SSEA "for PM from my PM," tg 48, 24 Mar. 1941, NAC, RG 24, 3832, NSS 1017-10-1 pt 3 (printed in *DCER* pt 7, 943-5); Adm to NSHQ, 2254/29 Mar. 1941, DHH, 193.009 (D2)

1940 had been the freedom of the critically important transatlantic convoys from sustained U-boat attack. This was the result partly of weather, and partly of the fact that fewer U-boats—sometimes only four—were on patrol as the German submarine force refitted in the wake of the push in the summer and fall of 1940 and worked-up new boats for service. Of at least equal importance had been the expansion of the British escort force that had allowed much wider diversions in the routing of convoys in the Western Approaches. With more escorts available it was no longer so necessary to keep the convoys within a restricted funnel so that the limited number of escort groups could quickly switch over from an outward bound to an incoming convoy, the cycle that had previously dominated operations. The good result was that U-boats, in the winter of 1940, had little luck finding convoys in the North Atlantic, but shipping losses nevertheless continued to be substantial. In January 1941, during which fewer Allied ships were lost to enemy action than in any month since the spring of 1940, the *Luftwaffe*, surface raiders, and U-boats, which had success mainly against independently sailed merchant ships and those that had straggled from convoys, still destroyed sixty-four merchantmen.

Losses jumped to 100 in February and 139 in March, the latter figure surpassing the 134 destroyed in June 1940, the worst month of the war. Churchill, in a famous passage in his memoirs, recalled his reaction as news arrived of increased losses: "At this time my sole and sure hope of victory depended upon our ability to wage a long and indefinite war until overwhelming air superiority was gained and probably other Great Powers were drawn in on our side. But this mortal danger to our life-lines gnawed my bowels." In a directive of 6 March 1941, Churchill proclaimed "the Battle of the Atlantic." "This," he explained, "like featuring 'the Battle of Britain' nine months earlier, was a signal intended to concentrate all minds and all departments concerned upon the U-boat war."[100]

Amidst the gloom, there were some hopeful developments. The German push put twelve or more U-boats in the operational area between Britain and Iceland. In late February through mid-March, these forces located four transatlantic convoys in time to concentrate three to five submarines against each. Losses were serious, with four to nine ships sunk or severely damaged in each of the actions; they could have been worse had some of the boats not suffered torpedo failures. More importantly for the British, the Germans paid dearly for their successes, losing six U-boats—a quarter of the number available for operations—in the northwest approaches to Britain in just over four weeks between 7 March and 5 April. Among those lost were the three most successful commanders, Prien in *U 47*, Kretschmer in *U 99*, and Schepke in *U 100*. The British victories were in each instance achieved by the tenacious efforts of one or two experienced ships. The presence of such vessels in the right place at the right time, however, was the result of the massive increase of defences in the Western Approaches—by March 1941, there were some 120 seagoing antisubmarine escorts available in the Western Approaches as compared to thirty in July 1940—which allowed strong escorts for most convoys out to 25°West, immediately to the west of Iceland.[101]

---

100. W.S. Churchill, *The Second World War* III: *The Grand Alliance* (London 1950), 122

101. DOP memo, "Defence of Trade," para 53-4, states that there were on 26 Mar., eighty-seven ships "in the N.W. Approaches ... actually available for sea," a figure that he notes corresponded to a total force of approximately 120 allowing for refit and routine maintenance. AHS, *Defeat of the Enemy Attack on Shipping* 1B, plan 55, gives a total of 175 on 1 Apr. for the whole of Western Approaches Command, a figure that presumably includes vessels assigned for local escort.

Top: The four-stacker destroyer HMS *Ripley* escorts a troop ship into British waters in the spring of 1941. (NAC, PA 204334)

Bottom: The ship's company of *Moose Jaw* in St John's, 19 March 1942. (NAC, PA 204274)

The other enemy. The corvette *Moncton* strains against a tumultuous North Atlantic, November 1942. (NAC, PA 204688).

Dönitz's response to his heavy losses was the same as it had been to Britain's initial extension of effective escort in the north western approaches the previous fall: to station U-boats further west to hit convoys before the escorts joined. This succeeded. Between 2 and 5 April, a pack of seven U-boats concentrated against SC 26 beginning at 28° 30' West and sank six of its twenty-two merchant ships before the escort joined.[102]

The British commands had been intentionally conservative in extending escort coverage, awaiting firm evidence that the enemy had shifted a significant part of his strength into a new area. The reason was the imperative to concentrate large numbers of escorts so that the defence would be effective. Otherwise, the wide dispersion of convoy routes that was the best defence would be lost, and it would be impossible to maintain an adequate screen around the perimeter of each convoy. Numbers, moreover, were critical to efficiency. The groping, uncoordinated efforts against German high-speed night attacks on the surface in the fall of 1940 had driven home the need to form permanently organized escort groups with stable composition. Only in this way could the warships, through continual group training and experience, become an effective team whose members would automatically carry out coordinated tactics with the minimum of communication possible in the confused, swift-paced night actions. It was for this reason that British authorities had reacted so strongly to lapses by recently commissioned Canadian and British ships in the newly organized 4th Escort Group, and ordered special training exercises. To spread thin the escort forces prematurely in anticipation of possible German movements would be to guarantee weakness everywhere. This was the source of the British explanation to the Canadians of the need to keep forces concentrated, with deployment under control of the Admiralty, which alone had the full sources of information necessary to gauge when the enemy was moving into new areas in strength.

The movement of the U-boats towards 30° West in mid-ocean at the end of March came as no surprise to the British. What is more, they expected it was only a first step. The Admiralty, no less than the naval staff in Ottawa, remembered 1917–18, when effective convoy defences in European waters had brought the Germans to seek undefended shipping in a search that within months brought them to the coast of Newfoundland and Nova Scotia. "I see no reason why they should not send some [U-boats] to the 'Windy Corner' off Newfoundland," commented Admiral Pound during the SC 26 battle. "The passage there and back would take a long time but if a U-boat could get contact with a convoy and take a dozen ships out it would pay them."[103] Nevertheless, the Admiralty reacted conservatively, extending escort out only to 35° West in mid-April.[104] All authorities acknowledged that this was a half measure, but wanted to delay as long as possible the dissipation of the escort forces. In the words of one Admiralty officer:

> We have chosen our battleground for the summer in the North Western Approaches where, with the help of Iceland, we can bring the maximum possible surface and air escort into play. We should aim to beat the enemy on that battleground. When we have driven him from it so that he is forced to attack elsewhere, then will be the time to change our dispositions.

---

102. Rohwer, *Axis U-boat Successes*, 48

103. First Sea Lord to DOP, 4 Apr. 1941, PRO, ADM 1/11338

104. Adm to RA 3 BS, 15 Apr. 1941, NAC, RG 24, 3972, NSS 1048-48-1, v 6

.... We should pursue the plan of campaign which we have made for this summer, which may be called the Iceland plan, and not be diverted from it until enemy attack compels us to act. Meanwhile, plans should be made to enable a quick redisposition to be effected, and included in these plan [*sic*] the necessary preparations for air and sea bases in Newfoundland.[105]

Admiralty officials anticipated that the arrival of newly-built warships in the coming months—including, notably, the fifty-four corvettes in the Canadian program—would help when the inevitable move to full transatlantic escort took place; they also hoped that Churchill could persuade the Americans to provide additional assistance.[106]

In extending escort out to 35°West, the Admiralty and Western Approaches attempted to preserve the hard-won cohesion of the well-established large groups by moving three of them to Iceland. To keep up with the convoy schedule, groups were divided into two divisions. A division based in the United Kingdom escorted a westbound convoy to the vicinity of Iceland, and broke off there to pick up an inbound convoy; meanwhile, a division from one of the Iceland groups took over the escort of the westbound convoy, carrying on to 35°West before breaking off to rendezvous with an eastbound convoy.[107] Thus, the protection afforded to each convoy was cut nearly in half to "two to three destroyers, three corvettes and two trawlers."[108] These figures, according to an assessment made only weeks before, would considerably increase the threat of losses: "Experience has shown that an escort of at least 12 ships, of which at least 6 should be Destroyers, is required to ensure that a submarine attacking an ocean convoy is located."[109]

The reduced screen for each convoy was only part of the price paid for "telescoping" the escorts through Iceland. Use of the island as a relief base for the escorts, and the renewed necessity to route incoming and outgoing convoys close enough together so that escort divisions could change over from one to the other both near Iceland and at the 35°West limit, made impossible the wide diversions of routes that had provided such effective defence during the winter. Where previously the convoys had been spread across a north-south front of some 800 miles at 20°W, they now could not be distributed across a front of much more than 200 miles, which four or five U-boats at visibility distance from one another could effectively patrol.

This especially was a problem to the west of Iceland, where the convoys would be furthest from reinforcement. In theory, it should have been possible to distribute the routes across a front of some 1500 miles from north to south in this open ocean, but it was essential for them to keep within the narrow zone of the Iceland route where the escorts could operate. To make matters worse, the Iceland route, some 600 miles north of the direct great circle route at the middle latitudes between Newfoundland and the United Kingdom, was a circuitous one that entailed several extra days steaming, and thus allowed still less scope for diverse routes. One way of trimming the

---

105. Min, DOD (Home), 19 Apr. 1941, PRO, ADM 1/11338

106. E.g., "Appreciation of the A/S War in the Atlantic," Dec. 1940, esp para 32, forwarded by DOP, 19 Dec. 1940; also revised version, "Appreciation of the A/S War in the Atlantic," Apr. 1941, forwarded by DOP, 11 Apr. 1941, para 33, 36, PRO, ADM 1/11338

107. Adm, *MASR*, Apr. 1941, 18

108. C-in-C WA to Adm, 6 Apr. 1941, PRO, ADM 1/11338. See also same to same, 3 Apr. 1941 and Adm to C-in-C WA, 4 Apr. 1941, ibid.

109. DOP, "Defence of Trade," 26 Mar. 1941, para. 47

long run between Iceland and Newfoundland's Cape Race was to employ the considerably shorter northern route through the Strait of Belle Isle, between the island of Newfoundland and Labrador, which would reduce steaming time and allow for more evasive routing in the western ocean beyond the Iceland escort zone. From December through most of June, however, the strait is blocked with ice.[110]

The reason for dependence on Iceland as an escort staging base was the relatively limited endurance of destroyers. These were the most effective escorts because they were the only ones with the speed to pursue U-boats on the surface and to return to a convoy in reasonable time after putting down a submarine. But they had been designed primarily to operate against surface ships within a few days' steaming of friendly bases and their fuel capacity had been sacrificed in favour of hitting power, speed, and survivability. Moreover, even the faster HX convoys moved at a rate several knots below the economical speed for destroyers. That, and the necessity for destroyers to take advantage of their speed to sweep out from the convoy or around its perimeter to check contacts or respond to other emergencies, quickly drained their fuel bunkers. The ships could be modified, sacrificing a few knots of speed by replacing one boiler with additional fuel tanks, but completion of the prototype alone would take several months. A design had been made for a true ocean escort—the "twin screw corvette" or frigate—with both the speed and endurance to combat U-boats and easier to build than destroyers, but the first of these could not be completed before the end of the year. Sloops had the endurance required, but lacked speed and had already suffered such heavy weather damage on the North Atlantic that they had had to be withdrawn in the winter months. In any event, there were only a score of them and some were needed for the long runs to Gibraltar and Sierra Leone, where U-boat attacks against hitherto unescorted convoys were creating an additional strain on escort strength even as the Admiralty faced the "further west" problem on the North Atlantic.[111]

That left corvettes, which constituted about half the escort force. They were long-legged and, as we have seen, remarkably seaworthy, although they were notoriously uncomfortable for their crews. "With these small ships," the Admiralty's Director of Anti-Submarine Warfare (DASW) remarked, "it is believed that the fuel would outlast the endurance of the personnel." They were also smaller, slower, and less well-armed than sloops. Still, the best basic long-endurance escort unit that could be organized with available resources would consist primarily of four corvettes. This was a far from satisfactory solution. "It must be accepted," warned DASW, "that 4 corvettes are incapable of protecting a convoy at night and only by good fortune and inept handling of the attacking U-Boat can the corvettes hope to locate the enemy and counter-attack."[112]

West of Iceland, the next suitable base for escort operations lay in Newfoundland. By mid-May, Admiralty staff, who had recognized the potential importance of the island for trade defence since before the war, began actively addressing this need.[113] Reluctant as they were further to stretch the

---

110. C-in-C WA, "Protection of North Atlantic Shipping. Appreciation by Commander-in-Chief, Western Approaches," 16 Apr. 1941, Director of antisubmarine warfare, min, 26 Apr. 1941, PRO, ADM 199/935; "Submarine Attack on Trade in the North Atlantic," para 14, forwarded by DOP, 11 Apr. 1941, PRO, ADM 1/11338

111. "Appreciation of the A/S War in the Atlantic," paras 20, 41

112. DA/SW to ACNS (Foreign), 27 Mar. 1941, PRO, ADM 199/935

113. "A/S Protection of North Atlantic Trade. Minutes of a Meeting held on 14 May, 1941," PRO, ADM 1/11338

limited escort pool and risk weakness everywhere, they had little choice. Policy was to extend anti-submarine escort only when there was no alternative and that moment had arrived. Seven U-boats, ordered west after attacking OB 318 and sinking seven ships in that convoy south of Iceland from 7 to 10 May, formed a "western group" of nine boats 350 miles southeast of Cape Farewell. On 15 May, Dönitz sent them another 240 miles to the southwest, where they formed a line athwart the convoy routes south of Greenland. On 19 May, the same day that *St Francis* was engaged far to the east in the defence of SL 73, boats at the western end of the new patrol line intercepted HX 126. Over the next three days, the pack converged on the convoy and sank nine of its ships, five of them before the escort could join, the most westerly operation yet undertaken by U-boats during the Second World War.[114]

On the night of 19–20 May, just as the attack on HX 126 opened, the Admiralty signalled NSHQ to ask how many of the new RCN corvettes might be available "in event of anti-submarine escort being needed in Newfoundland focal area."[115] To this simple and not very informative inquiry, the Admiralty received an extremely full response the next evening, 21 May, in which the RCN offered to assume responsibility for the whole enterprise. NSHQ was prepared to sail seven of the new corvettes to St John's as early as 23 May and fifteen more corvettes could be sent "within one month." If, in addition, the Canadian destroyers operating in British waters could be redeployed to Newfoundland, then "we should feel confident of being able to carry out antisubmarine convoy escort from Newfoundland Banks to rendezvous with Iceland escort." NSHQ proposed a Canadian commanding officer for the new force, Commander E.R. Mainguy, whose "experience of operations in Western Approaches" would qualify him for the appointment in the rank of captain. The message offered assurance that this national initiative would not interfere with overall British command of escort operations: "It is hoped that Admiralty will assume direction of this force when necessary to coordinate its operations with those of the Iceland escort."[116]

The groundwork for the proposal for an all-Canadian force had already been laid in the false alarm about a westward offensive in March, when the British had intimated that Canada would have to meet the threat with its own resources, and Nelles had replied that it would be necessary to bring the RCN destroyers home from British waters. Even so, the specific knowledge shown in the Canadian message of 21 May that the British intended that the Newfoundland escort should link up with Iceland-based escorts suggests that the CCCS, Commodore Murray, may have communicated with Ottawa. Because of Murray's recent experience in Newfoundland defence issues, the Admiralty was consulting him at about this time.[117] Whatever Murray's role, Macdonald and the naval staff recognized an opportunity to create a substantial Canadian command in the foremost theatre of the maritime war, and seized the moment. In their rapid work, the minister and the staff made sure they had the full support of the government. During the afternoon of 21 May, Macdonald had taken a draft of the long signal to the prime minister. King caught the essence immediately: "The cable was to say that we would be willing to take on this work ourselves with our own destroyers if the British wished to have them returned to Canada." Macdonald confessed

114. MOD, *U-boat War* I, 73, diagram 11; Milner, *North Atlantic Run*, 31; Rohwer, *Axis Submarine Successes*, 51-3

115. Adm to NSHQ, 0016b/20 May 1941, NAC, RG 24, 3892, NSS 1033-6-1 pt 1

116. NSHQ to Adm, 2108z/21 May 1941, NAC, ibid

117. Murray interview, 40

some hesitation about the scheme, in view of the emphasis that he and the naval staff had placed on the commitment of the destroyers overseas: it might be "taken that we wanted to get out of the fight in European waters." King, who just the day before had reacted with his usual alarm about reports of the westward movement of the U-boats, was instantly reassuring. "I said it was obviously the sensible and right thing to do; our people know our own shores and it was the right place for them to take on this obligation." He added, with his characteristic sensitivity to the evolving military relationship with the United States, that sufficient Canadian warships should be available in the western Atlantic to "co-operate with American destroyers and cruisers, if needed."[118]

At the Admiralty, the First Sea Lord understood the linkage between a large Canadian commitment and the appointment of a Canadian officer to command the force. Pound scarcely had any choice, as NSHQ on 24 May dispatched a reminder about the need to consider the Canadian proposal, and pressed Murray to take a strong line, authorizing him to muster the support of the Canadian High Commission if he needed help.[119] Pound was already convinced, but unwilling, as NSHQ had proposed, to have a newly promoted captain assume command at St John's.[120] On 24 May, he wired to Nelles that "In view of the importance of this appointment it would appear desirable that a flag officer should fill it. As Commodore Murray's duties on this side would be so greatly reduced and as he has a very good knowledge of conditions in Western Approaches he would be most suitable and it would give us great confidence if you saw your way to selecting him."[121] Murray later recalled that his presence at the Admiralty to help in making the arrangements was probably what had brought him to the First Sea Lord's attention: "this is what comes of being in the right place at the right time."[122] Murray left London to spend several days at Western Approaches headquarters in Liverpool, before flying westward for further consultations at NSHQ in Ottawa and then continuing on to St John's.[123]

While Murray was in Liverpool, further consideration by the Western Approaches staff greatly increased the scope of the Newfoundland project. The Admiralty's original conception, during the emergency planning of 20–3 May, was to have an "out and back" shuttle by escorts based at St John's, that would meet up with the similar out-and-back shuttle that was already running from Iceland.[124] The meeting point would be at 35°West, mid-way between Iceland and Newfoundland and the limit of the existing Iceland shuttle. Thus, the Newfoundland-based escorts would run four or five days towards Iceland with an eastbound convoy, while, at the same time a group based in Iceland headed towards Newfoundland with a westbound convoy, and at 35°West the groups would exchange convoys and turn back for home; the Iceland-based groups would then, as was already happening with the system put in place in April, do a similar swap with United

---

118. King diary, 21 May 1941. See also 20 May 1941.

119. CNS to First Sea Lord, 2253z/24 May 1941, NAC, RG 24, 3892, NSS 1033-6-1 pt 1; Plans Division, "History of North Atlantic Convoy Escort Organization and Canadian Participation Therein, Sep.1939 to Apr. 1943," 1 May 1943, 7, DHH, NHS 1650-1 Plans. "The Base at St John's Newfoundland must inevitably be under the Canadian authorities. This has been recognised..." Adm (1st Sea Lord personally) to C-in-C AWI, 2004b/25 June 1941, PRO, ADM 116/4387

120. CCCS to CNS, 1633b/25 May 1941, NAC, RG 24, 3892, NSS 1033-6-1 pt 1

121. Adm to CNS, 1520b/24 May 1941, ibid

122. Murray interview, 41; CCCS to CNS Ottawa, 1633b/25 May 1941

123. CCCS to NSHQ, 1012b/28 May 1941, NAC, RG 24, 3892, NSS 1033-6-1 pt 1

124. Mansergh for ACNS (T), memo, 23 May 1941, PRO, ADM 199/935

Kingdom–based groups near Iceland. It was on the basis of this scheme that the Admiralty estimated a force of about thirty-six escorts would be needed at St John's, enough, the planners hoped,
to provide a group of at least three destroyers and three corvettes for each convoy, approximately
three in each direction every eleven days.[125]

Staff officers at the Admiralty and, especially, at Western Approaches, were not keen on the
shuttle system, because the meeting at 35°West and the necessity of coordinating it with yet a second meeting south of Iceland, imposed extreme rigidity. The escort group turnovers at sea could
only be achieved if the convoys were sailed on fixed routes at fixed times that the enemy could all
too readily discover. That aside, such elaborate arrangements were practically guaranteed to fail
given the many unpredictable factors, including weather and mechanical failures in ships, that frequently delayed convoys. So concerned was the Western Approaches staff that they were willing
to forego the support available at Iceland, and run convoys along the shorter, more southerly great
circle route between Atlantic Canada and the United Kingdom. The corvettes and other long-range
escorts had sufficient endurance to make the full Atlantic passage at slow convoy speeds. The critically important destroyers—the mainstay of the defence—could complete the crossing by breaking off part way and proceeding at economical speed; the zones at mid-ocean where destroyers
based in the United Kingdom and in Newfoundland had to break off overlapped, so that it was possible for destroyers from one side to relieve those from other.[126]

Western Approaches, to which the Admiralty gave the task of making the detailed arrangements, worked out a compromise that provided more flexibility on the northern route.[127] The
essence was to concentrate the escort forces at bases in the United Kingdom and at St John's, withdrawing the British groups that had been sent to Iceland in April, and using that island mainly as
a refuelling base to allow the escort forces—especially the destroyers—to provide continuous coverage on the long northern route. There would be only one meeting point, to the southwest of
Iceland, at approximately 25°West. Groups from Newfoundland would bring eastbound convoys
all the way to this meeting point, turn over to a group based in the United Kingdom, proceed to
Iceland to refuel, and then sail once more to the meeting point to pick up a westbound convoy,
whose UK-based escort would in turn refuel at Iceland. The principal advantage was that the two
mid-ocean rendezvous were reduced to one, and that one within reach of support, including air
patrols, from Iceland. The relieving group, moreover, would have topped up with fuel at Iceland,
and gathered the latest available intelligence. This made for much greater flexibility as compared
to the interlocking shuttles. If a convoy was delayed, or had to be diverted to avoid suspected submarine patrol areas, the rendezvous with the relief group could readily be adjusted. Moreover, by
eliminating the escort group shuttle based on Iceland, it would be possible to abandon the northern route in the event of an enemy concentration there, or because of the severe weather that is so
common in the high latitudes, and adopt the southerly great circle route.[128]

---

125. [WAC], "Trans-Atlantic Escort," 21 May 1941, ibid

126. Ibid; Adm to C-in-C WA, C-in-C HF, CNS etc, 1909b/1920b/1939b/23 May 1941, NAC, RG 24, 3892, NSS 1033-6-1 part 1

127. Adm to C's-in-C, NSHQ etc, 2027/23 May 1941, PRO, ADM 199/2080

128. "Min 19th mtg, Adm Conference, 3 June, 1941, to Consider Trade Protection Measures," PRO, ADM 199/2080; C-in-C WA
    to Adm, NSHQ, COAC, etc, 1710b/3 June 1941, NAC, RG 24, 3972, NSS 1048-48-1 pt 6; "Progress Report on RCN Activities
    for Defence Council," no. 22, 7-14 June 1941, DHH, 112.1 (D79)

Murray signalled NSHQ on 31 May with the first word that the new force would include as many as eighty, rather than thirty-six escorts, but that he would nevertheless be in charge.[129] British records indicate that the Admiralty expected that about half of the force would be made up of Canadian warships, rather more than the eight destroyers from British waters, and the twenty new RCN corvettes that the RCN had promised.[130] Already the Admiralty was pressing NSHQ to commit to the Newfoundland force the five destroyers based at Halifax for the defence of Canadian waters, but it would also release for service at St John's the ten Canadian corvettes then operating in the Western Approaches.[131]

On 3 June, the British government sent formal notice of the intention to increase the strength of the new force. This telegram estimated that a total of sixty-three ships—thirty destroyers, twenty-four corvettes, and nine sloops—would be working from the port. These would barely provide the running strength of six or more escorts per convoy that had been the basis of planning and allow no margin for ships undergoing refit. The Admiralty was intending to assign additional ships as they became available, including an "increasing number of R.C.N. corvettes."[132]

Because Murray was still to command—indeed have command over a substantial number of British as well as Canadian ships—Macdonald and the naval staff welcomed the news. Such was the determination of the minister and the staff to place a strong Canadian stamp on the enterprise that they had, on 27 May, obtained the agreement of the government that Canada should undertake and pay for the necessary base facilities at St John's. The effect of the expansion of the escort strength was to double the amount of required berthing space and shore accommodation, and, because of the underdeveloped nature of the port of St John's, at least double the estimated cost to $10 million. Macdonald recommended this greatly increased project to Cabinet on 10 June in nationalistic terms: "the establishment of this force, consisting largely of HMC ships, commanded by a high-ranking Canadian Officer and working from a base developed with Canadian funds, gives the dominion an unprecedented opportunity to shoulder responsibility for fighting half the Battle of the Atlantic, upon the outcome of which so much depends."[133] The prime minister, by contrast, was outraged.

> The report was so obviously ludicrous ignoring altogether the part the US might have to play in the matter and put on us a role we could not possibly assume that I felt almost indignant at the way these obligations were being assumed when not even requested from the British side. We were being let into the whole thing at our own instance. I said quite frankly that I thought some of the Defence people were losing sight altogether of our responsibilities, with expenditures of moneys of the kind, to

129. C-in-C WA to NSHQ, 1707b/31 May 1941

130. Head of Military Branch, min M.09406/41, 15 June 1941, PRO, ADM 116/4387.

131. Adm to C's-in-C, NSHQ Ottawa, etc, 2027/23 May 1941, PRO, ADM 199/2080; Adm to CNS, 1633b/25 May 1941, NSHQ to Adm, 0345z/25 May 1941, NAC, RG 24, 3892, NSS 1033-6-1 pt 1. NSHQ agreed to commit three of the five destroyers; see ch 4.

132. DSec to Governor of Newfoundland and BHC, Ottawa, tg 489, 3 June 1941; Bridle, *Documents on Relations between Canada and Newfoundland* I, 566; [Adm summary] "May 1941," PRO, ADM 199/2080

133. Cited in B. Ransom, "Canada's 'Newfyjohn' Tenancy: The Royal Canadian Navy in St John's, 1941-1945," *Acadiensis* 22 (Spring 1994), 51

undertake naval bases, etc. in a country over which we had no control, which was controlled by the British Government, was going rather too far.[134]

When the issue came to Cabinet War Committee again, on 20 June 1941, King's attitude was unchanged: "The truth is the Department of Naval Affairs wants to claim that it is taking the whole command of the Battle of the Atlantic on this side, which is something I think far beyond its capacity and more than either Great Britain or the US would for a moment admit we should or could possibly do."[135]

Yet, despite these reservations, at the Cabinet War Committee meeting on 24 June, King agreed that in view of the urgency of the strategic situation, the navy should proceed with development of the base, with the questions of title to the lands and sharing of costs being settled later. The prime minister was in fact deeply relieved that Canadian and British escorts were concentrating in the western Atlantic, just as he was profoundly disturbed by the intelligence that arrived through June about the westward progress of U-boats and the first sinkings in the approaches to Newfoundland. The minutes of the Cabinet War Committee record a further element in the decision: "The Prime Minister mentioned that so far as the United States' interest was concerned, Mr. A.A. Berle, Assistant Under-Secretary of State, had remarked to him in conversation recently, that the United States would welcome Canada taking a more direct responsibility for Newfoundland. This was an important consideration."[136] President Roosevelt himself had in fact said much the same thing when King had met him in late April, and the president had explained both the steps he was taking to build up US naval strength in the Atlantic, and the limits domestic politics placed on his ability to allow those forces directly to assist in the protection of trade convoys.[137]

No less delicate than the question of Canadian development of large-scale base facilities in a British dependency was the issue of command of convoy operations west of Iceland. The initial Canadian offer to establish the Newfoundland Escort Force (NEF) had acknowledged—but in guarded terms—that a Canadian commander would have to work under the direction of the Admiralty. It was the only headquarters that had the complete intelligence picture necessary to control transatlantic convoys, and, in Canada's important participation in the convoy system since 1939, NSHQ had acted as an agency of the Admiralty. For heavy warship support to convoys in the western and central Atlantic, which Canada could not provide, the Admiralty exercised its control through the regional British authority, the C-in-C America and West Indies, based in Bermuda. That officer, in the face of the great demands of convoy operations, delegated this responsibility to the Rear-Admiral 3rd Battle Squadron at Halifax, who, as seen in Chapter 1, quickly learned to exercise fine diplomacy with NSHQ and COAC, so that he could coordinate Canadian participation without seeming to interfere in the RCN's administration. The role of the America and West Indies

---

134. King diary, 10 June 1941. See also CWCM, 10 June 1941, which provides a full account of the acrimonious discussion, and the account by Macdonald in his diary entry for 10 June 1941, NSARM, Angus L. Macdonald papers, F 389. Although Macdonald wrote this a year after the event, his memory was detailed and accurate. He dated the division of the cabinet into pro-and anti-conscription factions from this time, believing that his own support for army expansion and Ralston's support for the big base at St John's resulted in King perceiving the development of a party in the Cabinet opposed to him.

135. King diary, 20 June 1941

136. CWCM, 24 June 1941. See also King diary, 3, 5, 11, and 13 June 1941. On the development of the base facilities, see Tucker, *Naval Service of Canada* I, 189-203; Ransom, "Canada's 'Newfyjohn' Tenancy," 45-71.

137. King diary, 20 Apr. 1941

command and the subordinate Rear-Admiral 3rd Battle Squadron in convoy operations was in large measure eclipsed by the paramount need for end-to-end antisubmarine escort, which was primarily the responsibility of Western Approaches command.

The Newfoundland force would essentially be a westward extension of the Western Approaches Command. On 28 May, the Admiralty "authorized" the C-in-C Western Approaches "to communicate directly with officer commanding" in Newfoundland, a diplomatic way of saying that Commodore Murray would administer and deploy his British and Canadian escorts according to the orders of Western Approaches Command.[138] Murray, who was still at the Admiralty at this time and had had several months experience administering Canadian ships under Western Approaches in the eastern Atlantic, understood that the Newfoundland force would be operating as an integral part of the same system, no doubt one reason why Pound had nominated him for the appointment at St John's.

NSHQ, for its part, put limits on the geographical reach of British control. On 6 June the Canadian headquarters announced the creation of a Newfoundland command that would be entirely separate from the Atlantic Coast command. Under the new arrangements, COAC would continue to control all RCN operations for the defence of Canadian waters in the Gulf of St Lawrence, including the west coast of Newfoundland and the approaches to the Cabot Strait along Newfoundland's southwest coast, together with the entire Atlantic coast of Nova Scotia and the Bay of Fundy. The new Newfoundland command included the Atlantic coast of the island and Labrador.[139] The effect of the separation of Newfoundland from the Canadian Atlantic Coast command was to ensure that NSHQ could continue to retain some ocean-capable ships at Halifax for the immediate protection of Canadian waters. "Canada," as Vice-Admiral Kennedy-Purvis, the C-in-C America and West Indies, observed, "is very touchy concerning local Coastal Command."[140]

These nationalist sensitivities, in Pound's view, resulted in unsound strategy. He was loath to perpetuate the situation at Halifax where "we have an organisation without parallel in the Dominions, under which a R.N. Officer [Rear-Admiral 3rd Battle Squadron] is operating and administering on behalf of the Admiralty from ashore certain of H.M. ships, and working alongside a R.C.N. Officer in command of the base and the coast. There must have been much goodwill to have enabled the organisation to work as well as it has done."[141] There was in fact goodwill on both sides. Although Newfoundland fell within the America and West Indies station, Kennedy-Purvis had nevertheless asked for the agreement of NSHQ before he visited St John's early in June 1941, and NSHQ warmly welcomed this opportunity to have his advice.[142] Both Kennedy-Purvis and his subordinate, Rear-Admiral S.S. Bonham-Carter, Rear-Admiral 3rd Battle Squadron, toured the port in order to help organize British support for the new base.[143]

Kennedy-Purvis, who flew to Ottawa to consult Admiral Nelles and Angus L. Macdonald after his Newfoundland trip, doubted that goodwill alone was enough for the Newfoundland arrangements

138. Adm to C-in-C WA, Home Fleet, CNS etc, 2322b/28 May 1941, NAC, RG 24, 3892, NSS 1033-6-1 pt 1

139. NSHQ to COAC, 1941z/6 June 1941, NSHQ to Adm, 2155z/6 June 1941, ibid

140. C-in-C AWI to Adm, 1931q/26 June 1941, PRO, ADM 116/4387

141. Adm to C-in-C AWI, 2004b/25 June 1941, ibid

142. CNS to C-in-C AWI, 1536z/27 May 1941, NSHQ to COAC, 1806z/27 May 1941

143. "WD of the North Atlantic Escort Force—June 1941," PRO, ADM 199/409

to succeed. "Past experience," he informed Pound, "shows that the Canadians will always jump at taking on anything, regardless of whether they have the necessary experience or not."[144] The Canadians admitted they needed help. At their request, the Admiralty appointed Captain C.M.R. Schwerdt, RN to Murray's staff to administer base operations. Schwerdt, who had retired from the service in 1936 to become secretary to the governor of Newfoundland, had returned to duty in 1939 as naval officer in charge of St John's, and, with a tiny staff and almost no other resources, had done a magnificent job in organizing naval control of shipping and other essential services.[145] The other important senior staff position was Captain (D), responsible for the maintenance and efficiency of the escort fleet. Western Approaches provided Captain E.B.K. Stevens, RN, who was carrying out these duties at Liverpool, for a six-month tour of duty at St John's until Murray's nominee, Commander Mainguy, who was shortly due for promotion, became available.[146]

Kennedy-Purvis agreed with Pound that the loan of British specialist officers would not achieve the required unity of effort across the whole transatlantic route. Pound wanted to appoint a senior British officer at Halifax to assume control of both British and Canadian forces in the western Atlantic, including those in Newfoundland; the senior British officer would be seconded to Canadian service and would nominally be under the authority of NSHQ, but would in practical terms function as a subordinate of the C-in-C Western Approaches. Pound and Kennedy-Purvis were keenly aware that the Canadians would be extremely reluctant to accept such an apparent slight to the prestige of the Canadian service, and meddling in its internal administration.[147] Indeed, in mid-July, NSHQ did not act on Pound's suggestion that Murray should take over control of the ocean escorts operation out of Halifax as well as those at St John's, a halfway measure towards centralization.[148] By that time the Admiralty had further developed the proposal to extend the Western Approaches area to Halifax and install a British admiral there to direct all Canadian forces in the western Atlantic, but let it drop shortly thereafter in view of the US Navy's impending assumption of responsibility for convoy operations west of Iceland.[149] Still, the proposal is striking evidence of the Admiralty's profound lack of confidence in the RCN and its capabilities.

The decisions made during the last ten days of May and the first three weeks of June transformed the RCN's part in the Battle of the Atlantic, and increased the pressure on the fleet. Until that time the intention had still been to carry out the option provided for in the plans made in the fall of 1940 to send thirty-two of the seventy corvettes built and building to British waters. These deployments were to take place at a measured pace to allow new ships the same opportunity for work-ups and undemanding local operations that had been afforded to Prentice's initial group of seven

144. C-in-C AWI to Adm, 1041p/15 June 1941, PRO, ADM 116/4387

145. NSHQ to COAC, 1941z/6 June 1941; Tennyson and Sarty, *Guardian of the Gulf* (Toronto 2000), 287

146. CCCS to NSHQ, 1012b/28 May 1941; C-in-C WA to Adm, 1643b/8 June 1941, NAC, RG 24, 11745, CS 341; NSHQ to CCNF, 1922z/20 Jun 41, NPRC O-45990 pt 3

147. Adm to C-in-C AWI, 2004b/25 June 1941, C-in-C AWI to Adm, 1931q/26 June 1941, PRO, ADM 116/4387

148. Adm to NSHQ, 1612b/12 July 1941, Adm to CNS, 1624b/12 July 1941, NAC, RG 24, 3892, NSS 1033-6-1 pt 1; NSHQ to Adm, 1937z/14 July 1941, NAC, RG 24, 11941, "15 Group 11—Organisation"

149. M. Branch, "St John's, Newfoundland: Project Base for Escort Forces," 20 July 1941, PRO, ADM 116/4387

corvettes. The plan was to send all seven of these worked-up corvettes to Sydney in late May, where they would continue training and local operations until they had been reinforced by the first three of the additional corvettes to be worked up among the newly built vessels already arriving at Halifax. Once all ten were ready for operations, five would go to Britain, while five moved to Newfoundland to carry out the purely local defence responsibilities that Canada had undertaken there. As additional groups of five corvettes became ready at Halifax, they in their turn would proceed to Sydney or Newfoundland, allowing the groups at those places to proceed to Britain.[150]

This scheme, with its careful provision for the raw corvette crews to acquire skills and experience before being launched into demanding operations, began to fall apart immediately with the Admiralty's call for help on 20 May. Prentice immediately received orders to prepare all seven of his corvettes to depart directly for Newfoundland on 23 May.[151] Mate A.F. Pickard, RCNR, navigating officer of *Chambly* and one of the handful of experienced sailors scattered among the corvettes, kept a diary that records the passage to Newfoundland and the first arrival of Canadian corvettes at St John's. It was a clear indication that they were engaged in a naval conflict of enormous scope that the passage of these little ships would coincide with the breakout of the German battleship *Bismarck*:

> May 21st 1941
>
> To-night Fran [Pickard's wife] & I had dinner with Commander & Mrs. Prentice. The "Old Man" had a surprise. He told us the 7 ships of our flotilla were off for "parts unknown" on Friday. Eny. Submarines have been reported in 57°N. 42°W.—Some action at last.

> May 22nd 1941
>
> A general rush all round to-day preparing for departure to-morrow. In the morning we swung ship for compass adjustment. The afternoon was spent in a "general panic" all round. Our charts finally arrived at 7.30 pm. Additional ammunition came. A.A. armament (2 Twin Colts .5") were mounted ...

> May 23rd 1941
>
> *IN HMCS. "CHAMBLY"*
>
> We slipped at 0945 (ADST) ... There was a dense fog—everything was wet & rather miserable. We sounded a signal for the other ships to follow us [in line ahead] ...
>
> We proceeded "slow" & kept about a cable off the jetties & piers, visibility being only about a cable and a half. Passing the ferry (to Dartmouth) Pier, we gave a long blast on the siren. Fran said she might be there but I could not see her ...

> May 24th 1941—SATURDAY—
>
> Dense fog all day. D/F Bearings of Sable Island & Cape Ray seemed to indicate we are on our course but a little behind the position we should be in by log ... I do not trust the D/F any too well, as it is not absolutely accurately calibrated ... Only "Orillia" & "Collingwood" indicated Noon positions—"Orillia" about 5 miles south of us, but "Collingwood"'s entirely different. Lord knows what she bases her position on. She seems to think we are about 35 miles south of where we think we are. We shall

150. COAC to NSec, "HMC Corvettes—Disposition,"19 May 1941, NAC, RG 24, 6797, NSS 8375-330

151. NSHQ to Adm, 21 May 1941, NAC, RG 24, 3892, NSS 1033-6-1 v 1

Corvettes of the newly founded Newfoundland Escort Force steaming to St John's in May 1941. (NAC, PA 115350)

Commander J.B. Prentice, RCN on the bridge of HMCS *Chambly* in the summer of 1941. (NAC, PA 204284)

A rating from HMCS *Chambly* carrying food from the galley to his mess deck, summer of 1941. (NAC, PA 204285)

Orillia, lower right, and *Cobalt* going alongside in 'Newfy John' for the first time on 25 May 1941. (NAC, PA 204677)

"see"—although litterally [*sic*], I do not expect to *see* much with this S.E. wind. Fog will persist off Cape Race & up the Coast.

About 6 pm. We received the news that HMS "HOOD"—our biggest battlecruiser had been sunk by the ... 'BISMARCK.' Almost unbelievable news—the 'HOOD' for over 20 years has been symbolic of our Naval power. She was the world's biggest warship.

May 25th 1941

Rounded Cape Race about 20 miles off at 0345 this morning—D/Fs of us by Cape Race put us about 12 Miles south of our E.P. [Estimated Position].

At about 11 AM. D/Fs of St JOHNS Signal Station indicated we should head in & we accordingly A/C [Altered Course] ... Approaching Cape Spear the fog turned to rain & presently we could see the land.

The entrance to St JOHNS Harbour is very narrow—about 2 cables, or 400 yds. The coastline is extremely precipitous with high reddish cliffs rising to about 500 feet on each side of the entrance. The water is very clear, but cold—35°–37°. There are numerous gullies & crevices in the cliffs, into which the sea swells & boils, and there is deep water right up to the land. When the weather is fine & the sun is shining on the cliffs, the effect must be exceedingly striking & beautiful. On a day like to-day with the mist scudding across & obscuring the peaks, there is a brooding, ominous look about these tall precipices as if they waited only upon a signal to pour down the pent up power of frowning centuries upon us in one huge cascade of wrath. Steaming through the entrance you look up & feel very small indeed.

Inside there is a good harbour. A strong smell of fish greets us.[152]

Although the deployment of Prentice's meagre force to St John's was a watershed in Canadian naval history, it was completely overshadowed by the epic hunt of the *Bismarck*. The operation that culminated in the destruction of the powerful raider was almost entirely a British success, but Canada played a slight role. Lieutenant S.E. Paddon, RCNVR, one of the more than 120 Canadians who served as radar officers in British warships, was in HMS *Prince of Wales* when the newly commissioned British battleship met her German adversary, but his radar was unable to contribute to the shadowing effort after his ship was damaged in the engagement that saw *Hood* sunk. When *Bismarck* escaped her shadowers, and her position and intentions were unknown, Eastern Air Command aircraft confirmed that the raider was not in their search areas in the northwest Atlantic. In Ottawa, NSHQ received many of the signals related to the operation—but not, for the most part, as an action addressee—and was able to maintain a reasonably accurate plot based on W/T intercepts and some Admiralty situation reports. But the main Canadian contribution appears to have been direction finding as some weeks after the *Bismarck* action was brought to successful conclusion, the Admiralty sent the following congratulatory signal to NSHQ:

A study of the bearings reported to Admiralty by overseas [D/F] stations during the period of the chase of the Bismark [*sic*] has been made with the following result—

(a) bearings from Hartlen Point [Nova Scotia] and Georgetown [British Guiana] were accurate;

---

152. Pickard diary, 21-5 May 1941, A.F. Pickard papers, DHH 80/125 pt 7

(b) bearings from Bermuda were erratic but it is appreciated that inaccuracy of H/F D/F bearings is largely a matter of local conditions out of human control.

2. The bearings from the above stations were of considerable value in locating the "Bismark."[153]

It is difficult to determine the precise contribution of Hartlen Point, the D/F station outside Dartmouth, to the hunting down of *Bismarck* as those records have gone missing. But the station was assigned to guard U-boat frequencies, and it might be that it reported bearings from U-boats signalling their positions as they gathered to escort *Bismarck* to safety. That said, Hartlen Point was respected as a particularly effective DF station, and its role may have been greater.[154]

The destruction of the German battleship allowed no respite to Prentice's group, who had almost no chance to settle into their new surroundings. On 28 May, German naval Enigma, the machine cypher on which signals were put into code, revealed the current intentions of Dönitz to British intelligence. The British Government Code and Cypher School at Bletchley Park had begun to read German naval Enigma signals consistently in mid-March. By 10 May, it was possible to read enemy signal traffic with a delay of three to seven days, and the capture of coding documents from the weather trawler *München* and *U 110* that month, and from another weather trawler, *Lauenburg*, at the end of June, would lead to an ability to read all traffic for the following months with little delay.[155] On 25 May, *BdU* had ordered six boats to establish a patrol line at 45° West.[156] Thanks to the acquisition of the June settings for Enigma, Bletchley Park was immediately able to follow the reinforcement of this effort, including a message on 2 June that expanded the western group to eleven boats and ordered them to push as far as 50° West, within three hundred miles of St John's.[157]

Prentice's seven corvettes were the only escorts available in the western Atlantic. In response to the Admiralty's request they immediately began long-range ocean escort missions from Newfoundland to the vicinity of Iceland. On 2 June 1941, *Chambly, Orillia,* and *Collingwood* put to sea to join HX 129, while *Alberni, Agassiz,* and *Wetaskiwin* took up the escort of HX 130 on 6 June.[158] Meanwhile, the Admiralty rushed additional escorts from Britain, including most of the Canadian warships that had been operating in the eastern Atlantic and were now allocated to the NEF. Included in the first groups, which sailed at the end of May and reached St John's between 7 and 10 June, were the River class destroyers *Ottawa, Restigouche,* and *Saguenay,* as

153. Adm to NSHQ, 26 June 1941, NAC, RG 24, 3807, S1008-75-44 v 1

154. For the RCN's role, and the role of signals in the pursuit of the *Bismarck* generally, see C.E. Allan, "The Bismarck Operation, May 1941," June 1989. DHH, 2000/5

155. H. Hinsley, *British Intelligence in the Second World War* II (London 1981), 163; D. Kahn, *Seizing the Enigma: The Race to Break the German U-Boat Codes, 1939-1943* (Boston 1991), 161-8; Ralph Erskine, "Afterword," in Beesly, *Very Special Intelligence*, 268

156. ZTP 796, German Naval Section GCCS to ID8G, 0535/28 May 1941, BdU to *U 93, U 43, U 46, U 557, U 66,* and *U 94,* TOO [Time of Origin] 2232/TOI [Time of Intercept] 2054/25 May 1941, PRO, DEFE 3/1 pt 4

157. ZTP 1209 German Naval Section GCCS to ID8G, 2355/30 May 1941 From BdU TOO 2050/22 May 1941, TOI 1936/22 May 1941; ZTP 1385 German Naval Section GCCS to ID8G, 1239/2 June 1941, From BdU, TOO 1032/2 June 1941, TOI 0925/2 June 1941, both PRO, DEFE 3/2 pt 1

158. Adm to NSHQ, 29 May 1941, Adm to NSHQ, 2 June 1941, NOIC St John's to Adm, 3 June 1941, NAC, RG 24, 3892, NSS 1033-6-1 pt 1; Keate, nd, "The Royal Canadian Navy in Newfoundland, 1940-1944," 9-11, DHH, 81/520 Avalon (Base) 8000

well as the Towns *Columbia, Niagara,* and *St Clair.*[159] Even as the additional escorts arrived at St John's, the western group of U-boats was able to locate, at about 40°West, merchantmen that had dispersed at the existing 35°West limit for escort of west-bound merchant ship convoys—some of the destroyers coming out from the United Kingdom supported the outward bound convoys but the limited range of the warships at slow convoy speeds forced them to break off before the dispersal and proceed directly to St John's. From 6 to 10 June, U-boats sank four of the unprotected merchantmen. These losses, and fresh intelligence that the U-boats were pressing still further into the shipping routes south of Cape Race and east of Halifax, caused the Admiralty to reinforce OB 331, OB 332, and OB 334, which sailed from Liverpool between 8 and 11 June, with long-range escorts. These included eight of the ten RCN corvettes that had been operating in British waters. *Assiniboine,* the last Canadian River class destroyer operating in UK waters, also made the crossing as part of the screen for OB 331. The original intention had been that the convoys would disperse seaward of Newfoundland, but although many of the merchant ships bound for ports in the United States and further south did break off at that point, the Admiralty instructed the vessels making for Canadian ports on the now threatened route between Cape Race and Nova Scotia to stay together with a portion of the corvettes right into Halifax. By the time the convoys reached that port between 20 and 23 June, some of the corvettes had been at sea, with benefit of nothing more than a brief refuelling stop at Iceland, for fourteen days.[160]

The Admiralty, meanwhile, was endeavouring to use the destroyers and smaller warships newly arrived at St John's to bolster antisubmarine escort for convoys on the long leg between Newfoundland and the vicinity of Iceland. So acute was the shortage of escorts for this huge new commitment, and so inadequate were the screens of only three or four warships that had thus far been achieved with emergency deployments, that the Admiralty ruled that slow SC and fast HX convoys should combine at sea so that together they should have the benefit of eight or ten escorts. These would depart south of Iceland, turning the combined convoy over to an RN group for the rest of the passage. Meanwhile, the Newfoundland group would refuel in Iceland, and take over a westbound convoy for the passage to Newfoundland.

The new arrangements first came into effect with HX 132 and SC 34, which on 10 June departed from Halifax and Sydney respectively. The main body of the escort, three Canadian and two British destroyers, and a Canadian and a British corvette, left St John's on 14 June, and was to meet the convoys early on 15 June about 200 miles east of St John's. Western Approaches also ordered the destroyer *Restigouche* to reinforce the screen. *Restigouche* was at sea assisting in efforts to rescue the survivors of the merchant vessel *Tressilian,* which had been torpedoed by *U 77* on 13 June, about 330 miles southeast of Cape Race. This attack confirmed evidence from Enigma radio traffic, which Bletchley Park was still reading with only a few hours delay, that BdU, frustrated by the

159. Mainguy to Capt (D) Greenock, 13 June 1941, "ROP—Period 3 to 10 June, 1941," 13 June 1941, DHH, 81/520 Ottawa 8000 pt 3; "*St Clair* History"; "RCN Operations in UK Waters—May 1940 to June 1941," 32, DHH, 84/123

160. Rohwer, *Axis Submarine Successes,* 55-6; OB 333, with a wholly RN escort, was routed well south of the U-boat operating area, coming in on the latitude of 40°N—south of New York—and dispersed well out at sea, 34°W. Files for OB 331, OB 332, OB 333, OB 334 in DHH, 88/1 reel 5

lack of success to the northeast of Newfoundland, was moving the western group of U-boats to a new patrol line well to the south of Cape Race.[161]

It was in response to this intelligence that the Admiralty set the rendezvous for the two convoys and escorts directly to the east of St John's, north of the normal passage south of Cape Race. The convoys were already at sea when this decision was made, one result of which was that HX 132 would lose time by having to divert northward. The staffs at St John's and Halifax, however, failed to broadcast full details about the changed arrangements and also did not pass a message from the battleship HMS *Revenge*, which was providing cover to HX 132, that the convoy would be ten hours late for the rendezvous. Thus, although the Newfoundland escort met SC 34 with no difficulty on 15 June, HX 132 was nowhere in sight. The escorts, including *Restigouche*, pounded the ocean searching for HX 132. The situation was saved only because *Revenge* steamed clear of the convoy and broadcast the information about its delay on a frequency the other escorts could read, enabling *Restigouche* to link up with HX 132 and then bring it together with SC 34, making a total of sixty-eight ships, by late on 16 June.[162]

Commander Lay in *Restigouche* sent a blunt report on the failure of the shore organization to Commodore Murray, who had just arrived in St John's on 13 June. Murray replied that the slips in rebroadcasting signals were "reprehensible" but "not surprising." He explained that his signals staff had had to cope with the suddenly and hugely increased burden with no more than a corporal's guard, assisted by Mainguy and some of his people from *Ottawa* who had come ashore to pitch in. Murray commended the signallers and Mainguy for doing as well as they did. When Murray reached St John's he had "found that the four cypher officers who had arrived only two days before had been working continuously for thirty six hours, trying to keep pace with the volume of cyphering and coding, there being no coding staff to assist. Similarly with no signalmen to run a Signal Distributing Station; no available typists and a shortage of typewriters, the Signal Officer, a Sub-Lieut. R.C.N.V.R., was making a very creditable but vain effort to keep the volume of traffic under control." This compared with what NSHQ had had to handle in September 1939, with no civilian help, no office equipment—not even desks—"only an insecure radio-telephone to supplement the cable which must be sent in code or cypher, and no power of requisition to obtain additional office space." Murray reported, however, that the crisis had already passed. On 14 June, the depot ship HMS *Forth* had arrived, as the Admiralty had promised, and in that ship was an operations and signal staff, together with personnel and equipment for ship repair. The provision of still more cypher staff, presumably from Canada, further alleviated the situation.[163]

As for the failure to collate and analyse the effects of convoy diversions on the time and place of rendezvous, Murray warned NSHQ that there was still a "lack of trained and reliable staff being made available for use as Watch keepers in the operations room of both Halifax and Saint John's." Murray appealed to Ottawa to recognize the extent of the responsibilities the RCN had accepted in the western half of the Atlantic. "The extreme importance of [watchkeeping in the main command

---

161. ZTP 1855 German Naval Section GCCS to ID8G, 2300/5/6/41, From BdU TOO 2115/5 June 1941, PRO, DEFE 3/2 pt 6; ZTP 2524 German Naval Section GCCS to ID8G, 1815/10 June 1941, BdU to *U 111*, TOO 1630/10 June 1941, PRO, DEFE 3/3; ZTP 3201 German Naval Section GCCS to ID8G, 0820/14 June 1941, From *U 111*, TOO 0140/14 June 1941, PRO, DEFE 3/4; ZTP 3240 German Naval Section GCCS to ID8G, 1220/14 June 1941, BdU to *U 111*, TOO 1007/0834/14 June 1941, ibid.

162. *Restigouche* ROP, 20 June 1941; HMS *Revenge* ROP, 25 June 1941, DHH, NHS 48-2-2 pt 5

163. CCNF to NSec, "ROP—HMCS *Restigouche*," 28 June 1941, DHH, NHS 48-2-2 pt 5

operations room], when ships, groups and convoys are being operated from a shore establishment in order to maintain wireless silence," he emphasized, "cannot be too greatly stressed."

> The Senior Officer of the force at sea is already probably contending with fog, rain and high winds and it is essential that information passed to him from the operations room on shore should be as complete and accurate as it can from the latest information available. The difficulty of providing such staffs in our greatly expanded Naval Service is fully realized but with the advent of active operations on this side of the Atlantic it has become one of such outstanding importance that every effort to meet it is most strongly recommended."[164]

This was just the first of such warnings the Commodore Commanding Newfoundland Force (CCNF) would send to Ottawa on a broad range of subjects during the coming months.

Murray was in full agreement about the inadequacy of the "short-legged" Town class for the Newfoundland–Iceland run. *Niagara* and *Columbia* were part of the initial escort for HX 132 / SC 34, and at the slow convoy speeds that were uneconomical for destroyers, could stay with the convoy for only four days, less than half of the nine days required. Refuelling at sea—a difficult evolution with the equipment then in use in the RN and RCN—had not yet been implemented on the North Atlantic, and if the destroyers stayed any longer, they would not have enough fuel remaining to make the long run at economical speed either to Iceland or back to Newfoundland. Effectively, fully half of the destroyers' sea time was wasted in the long passage back to port, while the convoy's protection was correspondingly weakened in dangerous waters. The shortage of escorts, however, especially destroyers, left little choice but to continue with such costly and unproductive missions.

As it was, two of the destroyers with HX 132 / SC 34, *Restigouche* and *Columbia*, both developed defects and had to return to St John's when only two days out from the Newfoundland rendezvous. Because the Admiralty successfully routed the convoy clear of the enemy there were no losses as a result.[165] Still, the incident highlighted what had already been a serious problem in the eastern Atlantic and would quickly become a critical one on the longer Newfoundland-Iceland run. Destroyers, the most valuable antisubmarine convoy escort and also the type in shortest supply, were the most prone to break down, because their high-performance machinery and long narrow hulls were ill-suited to constant pounding in the North Atlantic at the low speeds at which convoys proceeded.

It was a stroke of good fortune that the *Bismarck* operation diverted a large proportion of U-boats then at sea from anti-shipping operations.[166] Thanks to this, as well as the successful diversion of convoys based on Ultra, as Allied intelligence staffs labelled the decryptions of German Enigma signals, and the ubiquitous fog on the Grand Banks, U-boats in the western Atlantic were not sighting convoys. BdU ascribed the failure to possible new convoy routes or to an ability to break through patrol lines in the fog. "If our boats wish to find the nodal points of shipping," noted Dönitz in his war diary for 20 June, "they will have to operate west of 50°W, that is, off the Canadian and American ports of departure. But at present political considerations [the planned invasion of Russia, due to begin on 22 June, also prompted Hitler to forbid attacks on warships in the western Atlantic in case they were American] preclude this."[167] He decided to scatter his boats

---

164. Ibid

165. *Restigouche* ROP, 20 June 1941; HMS *Revenge*, ROP, 25 June 1941

166. MOD, *U-Boat War* I, 73-5; Blair, *Hitler's U-Boat War*, 287-94

167. BdU, KTB, 20 June 1941, cited in MOD, *U-boat War* I, 75; Blair, *Hitler's U-Boat War*, 305

over a wide area, and on 23 June, Kapitänleutnant R. Mützelburg in *U 203* sighted HX 133 about 400 miles south of Cape Farewell while proceeding to his new position. He commenced shadowing and brought in two other boats, *U 79* and *U 371*. Dönitz authorized them to attack early on 24 June.[168] Thus the incomplete and only partly organized NEF entered into battle for the first time. The events that followed revealed the weaknesses of escorts in the western Atlantic that had made British planners so reluctant to attempt the Newfoundland enterprise.

The main body of HX 133 had sailed from Halifax on the morning of 16 June, with *Annapolis* providing the local escort to the rendezvous with the NEF. Another RCN Town, *St Croix,* was bringing a joiner group from Sydney and the armed merchant cruiser HMS *Laconia* accompanied another section from Bermuda. All three groups had a miserable time in heavy fog—*St Croix* only had two brief glimpses of her convoy until 0300 on 20 June—and in executing turns south of Newfoundland the Halifax group suffered collisions that sent three ships back to port.[169] Two ships that collided in the Bermuda group also had to turn back. From Enigma decrypts the Admiralty knew that Dönitz was maintaining the western group of U-boats southeast of Cape Race, and therefore, as with HX 132 / SC 34, routed the HX 133 groups sharply northward to combine about 200 miles northeast of St John's. On 21 June, the Newfoundland escorts assigned for the mid-ocean run shepherded the groups together, organizing the forty-nine vessels into nine columns. The escort included only the destroyer *Ottawa* and the corvettes *Orillia* and *Collingwood*, with *Chambly* joining on 23 June.[170]

U 203 had picked up the convoy on its acoustic equipment, and had sighted the convoy less than an hour later in visibility that was now "moderate" to "very good."[171] Within five hours of the submarine's sighting report, the Admiralty had all the details. Western Approaches broadcast a warning to *Ottawa*, under the guise of an accurate DF bearing on the U-boat's transmission, that a submarine was in contact.[172] After sunset, HX 133 made a "drastic" alteration of course, as Western Approaches ordered, while *Ottawa* made a sweep five miles ahead of the lead ships. The destroyer drove *U 203* off, but not for long.[173]

After dark on 23 June, *Ottawa* swept five miles astern of the convoy in an attempt to put down the submarine in case it had detected the change of course. *Chambly* had meanwhile replaced *Ottawa* ahead of the convoy sweeping back and forth across the line of advance. *Collingwood* and

---

168. Ibid, 309; *U 203*, KTB, 21-3 June 1941; BdU, KTB, 23 June 1941

169. *St Croix* ROP HX 133, nd, 48-2-2 pt 5, NHS, DHH

170. NCSO Halifax, "Convoy HX 133," DHH 77/553 v 4, which notes that by signal 1935B/16 June 1941 the admiral changed the rendezvous off Newfoundland to the northeast. Previously the rendezvous had been planned well to the southeast of Cape Race at 45° 30' N 46° 20' W (CCNF to COAC (R) Adm, 16 June 1941, 8280-HX 133, DHH 89/34 pt 8. ZTP 3240 German Naval Section GCCS to ID8G, 1220/14 June 1941, decrypt of BdU to *U 111*, TOO 1007/14 June 1941, PRO, DEFE 3/4 is an example of the German traffic Bletchley Park was reading concerning the continued deployments southeast of Cape Race. For the organization and movement of the convoy and its escorts see *Ottawa*, "ROP for the period 19 to 28 June 1941. Escorting HX 133 ...," 29 June 1941, NA, RG 24, 11311, 8280-HX 133, and "Analysis of U-boat Operations in Vicinity of Convoys HX 133 and OB 336, 23 to 29 June, 1941," Adm, *MASR*, Aug. 1941, 19-32. These two documents are the main source for the account that follows.

171. *U 203*, KTB, 21-3 June 1941

172. Adm to *Ottawa*, 23 June 1941, 8280-HX 133, DHH 89/34 pt 8. See also Hinsley, *British Intelligence* II, 171. There is a list of all the decrypts the Admiralty had to hand for HX 133 in Naval Section [GCCS], ZIP/ZG/116, "U-Boat Methods of Combined Attack on Convoys. From Feb. 1 to Oct. 31, 1941," 10 Nov. 1941, PRO, ADM 233/1. The decrypts themselves in PRO DEFE 3/21 confirm that all of these were available within a few hours of their transmission.

173. *U 203*, KTB, 23-4 June 1941

Orillia were on either bow of the convoy. *U 203* was ahead of the convoy, and when *Chambly* swept off on one leg, Mützelberg slipped down the centre on the surface, firing a total of four torpedoes at two ships towards the rear of the fourth column. He missed one target but hit and sank the steamer *Soloy*. It all happened in a flash, and the response within the convoy can only be described as confused. Although one merchant ship and the armed merchant cruiser HMS *Wolfe* saw the submarine on the surface as it entered the convoy, it appeared to have dived instantly. Within three minutes, white rockets and red flares appeared from one of the merchant ships that saw the attack on *Soloy,* but these seemed to come from the port side, not the centre of the convoy, and it was to the port side that *Ottawa* dashed, while *Collingwood* swept out from the same side in case the submarine was escaping in that direction. Mützelberg saw *Ottawa* sweeping astern of the convoy, crash-dived after the attack, and got clear away.[174]

Fortunately, *Ottawa* and *Collingwood*'s misdirected sweeps against *U 203* unwittingly drove off Kapitänleutnant H. Driver's *U 371*, moving into position off the port quarter just as *U 203* struck. When Driver again reached position two hours later, he fired so wide of the mark that no one in the convoy saw the torpedo track. By this time, day was breaking on 24 June and he was too low on fuel to shadow the fast convoy. When dropping back, however, *U 371* came across and sank *Vigrid*, which had straggled about 10–15 miles behind HX 133 the day before with engine trouble. Only two of four lifeboats got clear of the doomed ship, and the twenty-one occupants had to endure three weeks on the open ocean before being rescued.[175]

Meanwhile, confusion also dogged another convoy, OB 336, outward bound from the Clyde on a course that would bring it close to HX 133. On 20 June, five corvettes—HMS *Gladiolus* and *Polyanthus*, and HMCS *Wetaskiwin*, *Agassiz,* and *Alberni*—sailed from Iceland to take over the escort from the British group that had come out from the United Kingdom and departed on 22 June. In thick fog, the five corvettes searched in vain for OB 336, which was making better than estimated speed. The convoy sailed on unescorted, while the five corvettes beat the ocean, zigzagging back and forth along the estimated course, trading signals with shore authorities who were trying to determine the position of the convoy without forcing it to broadcast and reveal its position to the enemy. The situation got more confused on 23 June, when Western Approaches ordered OB 336, and also OB 335—which had sailed from Liverpool on the same day, and was on a course parallel to OB 336 about thirty miles away—to divert from their planned route to avoid the U-boat pack now concentrating around HX 133. Unfortunately, the inexperienced signaller on the staff of the convoy commodore of OB 336 could not locate the codes necessary to read the diversion signals and put them to one side.[176]

So far as Western Approaches knew OB 335 and OB 336 had been safely diverted out of danger. Consequently, after the first attack on HX 133 on the morning of 24 June, and with Ultra decrypts to hand showing that additional submarines were in pursuit, the escorts of both westbound convoys received orders to detach and reinforce HX 133's meagre screen.[177] Just as Western

---

174. *U 203*, KTB, 24 June 1941; "HMCS *Chambly*: Record of Movements from Time of Each Initial Attack on Convoy 'HX 133' to End of Search," nd, DHH 80/125, f 7

175. *U 371*, KTB, 24 June 1941

176. OB 335 and OB 336, DHH, 88/1 pt 5

177. C-in-C WA to SS. *Harpagon* for cmdre [of OB 336], 24 June 1941, OB 336; C-in-C WA to [escorts of OB 335 and OB 336], pt 1, 24 June 1941, same to same, pt 2, 24 June 1941, OB 335

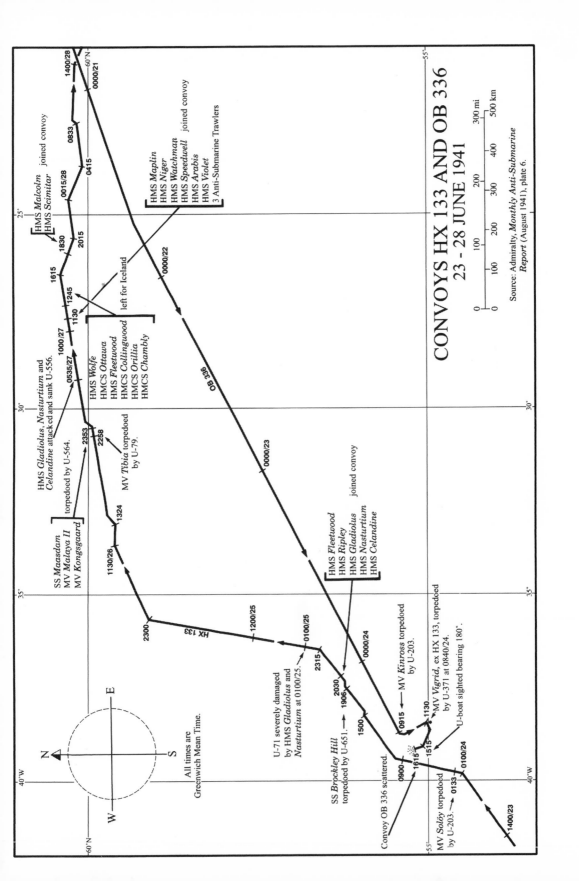

CONVOYS HX 133 AND OB 336
23 - 28 JUNE 1941

Source: Admiralty, *Monthly Anti-Submarine Report* (August 1941), plate 6.

0   100   200   300 mi

0   100   200   300   400   500 km

HMS *Malcolm*   joined convoy
HMS *Scimitar*

HMS *Maplin*
HMS *Niger*
HMS *Watchman*
HMS *Speedwell*   joined convoy
HMS *Arabis*
HMS *Violet*
3 Anti-Submarine Trawlers

1400/28
0000/21
0833
0415
0015/28
1830
2015
1615
1245
1130
1000/27
0535/27
0000/22

left for Iceland

HMS *Wolfe*
HMCS *Ottawa*
HMS *Fleetwood*
HMCS *Collingwood*
HMCS *Orillia*
HMCS *Chambly*

HMS *Gladiolus*, *Nasturtium* and
Celandine attacked and sank U-556.

SS *Maasdam*
MV *Malaya II*   torpedoed by U-564.
MV *Kongsgaard*

MV *Tibia* torpedoed
by U-79.

2353
2258
1324
1130/26
2300

OB 336

0000/23

HMS *Fleetwood*
HMS *Ripley*
HMS *Gladiolus*   joined convoy
HMS *Nasturtium*
HMS *Celandine*

MV *Kinross* torpedoed
by U-203.

U-71 severely damaged
by HMS *Gladiolus* and
Nasturtium at 0100/25.

1200/25
0100/25
2315
2030
1906
1500
0915

MV *Vigrid*, ex HX 133, torpedoed
by U-371 at 0840/24.

U-boat sighted bearing 180°.

HX 133

0000/24

1130
1515

SS *Brockley Hill*
torpedoed by U-651.

Convoy OB 336 scattered.

0900
1615
1515

0100/24
0133

MV *Soløy* torpedoed
by U-203.

1400/23

N
E
W
S

All times are
Greenwich Mean Time.

Approaches was making these signals, *U 203* sighted OB 336, then passing within visibility distance of HX 133. Mützelberg, because he saw no escorts with the new convoy and his boat was suffering technical defects that made him reluctant to risk a run-in with warships, took advantage of the opportunity. He made a submerged attack, sinking the *Chinrest*, shadowed on the surface for another five hours before making a second submerged attack, which was wide of the mark and then headed for home.[178]

It was standard operating procedure for merchant ships, when attacked, to break radio silence and broadcast their position. Lieutenant-Commander G.S. Windeyer, commanding *Wetaskiwin*, the senior officer present among the corvettes assigned to OB 336, heard the appeals for help from this convoy just as he received his orders to join HX 133. Assuming that Western Approaches had not yet intercepted the messages—they revealed that OB 336 was about fifty miles southwest of his position—he disregarded his instructions, took his main body to support the unescorted OB 336, and despatched only HMS *Gladiolus* to HX 133.[179]

At about the same time, during the forenoon of 24 June, there was an odd incident in HX 133, as it drew away from OB 336. *Ottawa*, on receiving a radio report that one of the merchant ships had sighted a surfaced submarine, proceeded to hunt with *Collingwood*. Commander Mainguy then ascertained that none of the ships in HX 133 had in fact made such a report. Now aware that OB 336 was in the vicinity he abandoned the hunt after half an hour. German sources reveal, however, that *U 79*, commanded by Kapitänleutnant W. Kaufmann, had been closing on the surface at the time of the report and dived shortly thereafter to make a submerged attack. Kaufmann had to break off because "Destroyer H-60 [*Ottawa*'s pendant number] keeps altering course towards the boat ... 2 destroyers could now be heard in the listening device. One stops, the other proceeds at listening speed. One destroyer passes continually over the boat. Kept under water [for two-and-a-half hours] by both destroyers." Kaufmann was not able to regain contact with the convoy until late on 26 June. Although he did not realize it at the time, Mainguy's efforts had effectively prevented Kaufman from making further attacks on the convoy, possibly saving a number of merchant vessels from a watery grave.[180] It is thus long after the event that we sometimes learn of the effectiveness of actions then thought to be inconsequential or mistaken.

Two other U-boats, *U 651* and *U 71*, made contact with HX 133 on 24 June. During the afternoon, *U 651* sank *Brickle Hill* at the rear of the third column. Once again, because the escort was so small, the Canadian warships could only make a brief, cursory hunt. An hour later, the reinforcements ordered by Western Approaches arrived; *Gladiolus* from the OB 336 group, and, from OB 335, the destroyers HMS *Fleetwood* and *Ripley*, and the corvettes HMS *Celandine* and *Nasturtium*, for a total of ten escorts. Within hours, the effect of the strengthened screen became apparent. After dark on the night of 25/26 June, *Gladiolus* spotted *U 71* trying to close at speed on the surface and, when it dived, delivered accurate depth-charge attacks with the help of *Nasturtium* that damaged the boat. *U 71* surfaced two hours later and *Gladiolus* scored a hit with her four-inch gun that appeared to destroy the submarine. Although severely damaged, *U 71* made it home.[181]

178. *U 203*, KTB, 24 June 1941

179. *Wetaskiwin* to WA, 24 June 1941, OB 336

180. *U 79*, KTB, 24 June 1941

181. Blair, *Hitler's U-Boat War*, 311

The next night, 26–27 June, was to be the most difficult for the convoy. Just as darkness descended, *U 79* approached submerged from ahead of the convoy and torpedoed *Tibia*, the second ship in the centre column. *Ottawa*, *Ripley*, *Chambly,* and *Collingwood* responded, and although depth charges fired by *Chambly* were wide of the mark, they kept Kaufmann down and effectively put him out of the battle.[182] An hour after this attack, Korvettenkapitän R. Suhren's *U 564*, having gained an ideal attacking position in the path of the convoy, submerged and fired three torpedoes at ships in the van as they passed at short range, scoring hits on *Maasdam*, *Kongsgaard,* and *Malaya II*. The latter, which was carrying liquid TNT, disintegrated; only six of a crew of forty-nine survived. Suhren's account of this catastrophe is particularly vivid:

> I am just about to fire a 4th torpedo at a tanker when a steamer, which must have had an ammunition cargo, blows up entirely. The periscope is now enveloped in a black cloud for a considerable period. Loud breaking noises and boiler explosions, the typical sounds of sinking steamers, can be heard. I run to the south at full speed at periscope depth in order to get clear of the black cloud ... When the boat emerged from the cloud, I saw that the convoy was proceeding in complete confusion.

As Suhren manoeuvred to make a second attack:

> I saw a destroyer [*Ottawa*] closing ... at high speed. I increased to full speed so as to make the destroyer pass astern with the aim of enabling a shot from the stern tube which was ready to fire. I did not fire because the destroyer passed only 100 m[etres]. off the stern. 6 heavy depth charge explosions then shook the boat. Both electric motors stopped and we soon were suspended at 25 m[etres] ... How long it took until the engines again came to life can no longer be established, but at the time it seemed an eternity. It may have been between 2 and 5 minutes.
>
> Our situation could have been quite serious especially because the acoustic operator reported screw noises that were closing. From my position in the control room I also then heard a vessel closing from the port side at roughly 12 knots which then passed over our stern. Not a pleasant moment.

When the electric motors began to run again, *U 564* dove deep to escape the escorts. Suhren was under the impression from the sounds on his acoustic equipment that the escorts continued to hunt above him for some six hours, until 0600z. "From [0500z] onwards we hear in our listening device that acoustic conditions were becoming unfavourable because of the increasing sea state. Up until that time no depth charges [other than the initial pattern] had been dropped. The boat's command team is still puzzled by the reasons why the enemy acted in this way because he obviously could hear us but perhaps only imprecisely."[183]

In fact, the escorts had not regained asdic contact after *Ottawa*'s initial attack, nor had the warships persisted in the search, despite Suhren's different impression, and there was no mystery whatever for Mainguy as to what had gone wrong. He was livid, and gave vent to his frustration at the incomplete equipment and training of the RCN corvettes; corvettes considered among the best-trained in the Canadian escort force. At the time of *U 564*'s attack, *Ottawa*, the three Canadian corvettes, and *Ripley* had been sweeping back to the convoy from astern, continuing the hunt for

---

182. *U 79*, KTB, 26-7 June 1941

183. *U 564*, KTB, 27 June 1941

U 79. Mainguy had ordered a line abreast formation, with a spacing of about a mile between ships. He found the movements of the corvettes were "considerably confused ... and they more or less had to be pushed into place." As he later discovered, none of the ships had been issued with the amendment of the signals book that included the code for the manoeuvre he had ordered. Things got worse as the formation came abeam of *U 564*'s victims and *Ottawa* made the asdic contact that resulted in the effective attack. During the run-in for the attack, *Ottawa* lost the contact: "Unfortunately two corvettes turned into OTTAWA's wake so that they prevented her from 'sweeping astern' efficiently and contact was not regained." Mainguy ordered the corvettes to continue the hunt at the position of his attack, while he swept out further in case the boat had managed to escape at speed. His signal to the corvettes, however, "was incompletely received and they only searched for a few minutes ... It is here emphasised," Mainguy fumed, "that Canadian corvettes are not fitted with R/T [radio-telephone], and their signalmen are very slow and inaccurate at [visual] signalling ... [This] is a great handicap which it is recommended very early steps be taken to remedy." He went on to remark how little initiative had been displayed by the screening vessels: "that they pay too much attention to station keeping and obeying orders in preference to investigating a contact thoroughly. It must be impressed on them that a contact, until proven 'Non Sub,' especially in the open ocean, counteracts all previous orders and they must not leave it even to report to the S.O. what they are doing. In this connection their low powered signalling projectors are another handicap and even when in station on the screen they have to close to pass a signal by day."[184]

Mainguy might have taken some slight satisfaction if he knew how badly he had shaken *U 564*. In the wake of the encounter with *Ottawa*, Suhren brooded:

> Boats on their first war patrols [like *U564*] with a new crew should in general at all costs avoid difficult situations such as, for example, allowing themselves to penetrate the middle of a convoy. This applies in particular to attacks on convoys. Despite the disadvantage of longer firing ranges such boats should fire several torpedoes into a convoy from outside—even if one of two of these torpedoes miss.
>
> The boat should initiate an attack in such a manner that there is sufficient time after firing to calmly get to a sufficient depth whilst under defensive attack by the escorts. Otherwise the result will be a tenacious acoustic pursuit with depth charging with the same result as occurred to my boat, i.e., being restricted in manoeuvrability and in addition making so much noise because of pumping and much movement of the rudders and hydroplanes so that the enemy continuously encounters enhanced acoustic opportunities.

Suhren had had enough, and withdrew; "I considered that trailing the convoy would be pointless and would be an incorrect course of action for our very weary boat."[185]

Within hours of *U 564*'s escape, the different fate of *U 556* at the hands of the British corvettes underscored the shortcomings of the Canadians. That boat had been shadowing the convoy to the north, opposite the southern flank where *U 79* and *U 564* had been engaged. After daybreak on 27 June the mist suddenly cleared and *U 556*, proceeding on the surface, realized it had come in

---

184. *Ottawa*, "ROP for the Period 19 to 28 June, 1941. Escorting HX 133 ....," 29 June 1941, app III, NAC, RG 24, 11311, 8280-HX 133

185. *U 564*, KTB, 27 June 1941

too close, and crash-dived. *Nasturtium* gained an initially weak asdic contact but was relentless. The other British corvettes, *Gladiolus* and *Celandine*, came up in support and the three warships hunted for over five hours, *Nasturtium* homing in the other ships, which could not pick up the contact, to drop pattern after pattern of depth charges. *U 556* finally came to the surface, the crew abandoning ship as the British corvettes poured gunfire into the sinking submarine. The victory was an especially significant one as the commanding officer, Kapitänleutnant Wohlfahrt, was one of the U-boat aces.

Although four ships had been hit during the attacks on 26–27 June, only two had been lost. *U 79*'s victim, *Tibia,* and *Kongsgaard* not only remained afloat but in a feat that struck awe among the escorts, regained the convoy and ultimately made port. As Mainguy said of *Tibia*'s crew: "all on board seemed to be totally unconcerned about their disaster."[186] By this time, the late morning of 27 June, the convoy was south of Iceland, from which had come a group of eleven British escorts under Commander C.D. Howard-Johnston to relieve the mid-ocean group. The Canadian ships, and *Fleetwood*, *Ripley*, and *Gladiolus* shaped course for Iceland; *Celandine* and *Nasturtium* remained to reinforce the escort. The U-boats continued pursuit, but were not able to penetrate the strong screen until 29 June, when *U 651* succeeded in submerging ahead of the convoy and sinking the commodore's ship, *Grayburn*. The ship following, *Anadara*, collided with the submerged boat, causing enough damage that the submarine was forced to the surface, where the crew abandoned ship in the midst of gunfire from the British warships.

In the words of the Admiralty Antisubmarine Warfare Division analysts, "There is little doubt that this sustained attack must have been a great disappointment to the enemy. Five ships were sunk, but only at the cost of at least two U-Boats, one of which was commanded by a U-Boat ace." In addition, as we have seen, a third boat, *U 71*, had been put out of action with heavy damage. Yet, in the words of a recent historian, "The Canadian group ... was criticized—and even ridiculed—for 'losing' five ships of the convoy and accomplishing nothing in return."[187] The Antisubmarine Warfare Division analysis, restrained in tone because it was included in the confidential publication *Monthly Anti-Submarine Report* that was intended to build morale as well as efficiency, was damning nevertheless: "It is clear that the communication difficulties of the Canadian escorts greatly reduced the efficiency of their counter measures against the U-Boats. Once a corvette became detached, she had no idea what the other escorts were doing and was unable to inform 'Ottawa' of her own movements." That was a fair summary of Mainguy's own report, and senior British authorities had to set the rigorous standards by which they judged the performance of ships and men in combat, but as an overall conclusion this judgment scarcely did justice to the achievement of these little warships, pushed to the forefront when only partly trained and seriously underequipped. As the analysts noted, "in nearly every case of a U-Boat making an attack, it subsequently lost contact with the convoy." This was true when the Canadians were holding the line alone and also during the two attacks on the night on 26–27 June, which had come in against sectors of the convoy protected by the Canadian ships. Much of this good result was a tribute to *Ottawa*'s experience and efficiency, but as the U-boat logs make clear, the Canadian corvettes did their part. It is worth remarking too that the U-boats had succeeded in penetrating the screen

---

186. *Ottawa*, "ROP ... 19 to 28 June, 1941"

187. Blair, *Hitler's U-Boat War*, 312-13

on 26–27 June when the escort had been greatly strengthened by experienced British ships, and did so again on 29 June when fully thirteen warships were present. The *Monthly Anti-Submarine Report* also published the criticism by C-in-C Western Approaches that *Gladiolus* had not ensured the destruction of *U 71* by ramming. In this case, the instinct of that corvette's commanding officer was almost certainly right and that of the C-in-C suspect. As future incidents would demonstrate, there was every likelihood that ramming would seriously damage the thin plating of an escort, a particularly serious consideration when the convoy was still 600 miles from port, and when escorts were in such short supply.[188]

In the battle for HX 133, the Allies enjoyed an enormous advantage: Bletchley Park delivered virtually current Ultra for several weeks before and throughout the operation. The Admiralty had therefore been able to build up a clear picture of German deployments and intentions, and was in a position the moment *U 203* contacted HX 133 to divert OB 335 and OB 336 clear, and transfer their escorts to the endangered convoy. Having the upper hand in intelligence not only allowed the Allies to thus concentrate their forces but also largely denied that ability to the enemy. The Germans located HX 133 only by chance after Dönitz, in frustration at the failure to find convoys off Newfoundland with concentrated patrol lines, scattered his submarines at wide intervals across much of the northern ocean. The Germans were unable at any one time to concentrate a sufficient number of submarines around the convoy to make a true pack attack. Access to Enigma had further contributed to this good result by giving the Allies the position of the supply tankers that the Germans had deployed in remote regions of the Atlantic. British cruisers and fleet destroyers had destroyed these vessels in early June, including *Belchen* south of Greenland, which had been refuelling the western group of U-boats. As a result, several submarines could not join in the pursuit of the convoy because of fuel shortages or had to break off contact prematurely. The escorts thus did not face the supreme test of having simultaneously to meet attacks from several directions. More than anything else this is why, in June 1941, serious consequences did not attend the allocation of a small and poorly coordinated Canadian group to the defence of a convoy under the threat of heavy submarine attack.

The shortcomings among the Canadian corvettes escorting HX 133, successful although the outcome of that battle was, did much to strengthen the view in Western Approaches and the Admiralty, already coloured by lapses in the performance of RCN Town class destroyers and corvettes in the eastern Atlantic, that the new Canadian fleet was one of error-prone amateurs. But errors were inevitable given the steep learning process they had to endure; more importantly, error-prone or not, they had become indispensable and because of that more would soon be demanded of them.

---

188. "Analysis of U-boat Operations in Vicinity of Convoys HX 133 and OB 336, 23-29 June, 1941," Adm, *MASR*, Aug. 1941, 23, 32

CHAPTER FOUR

Implementing Anglo-American Convoy Agreements I July to October 1941

WHAT IN THE FIRST PART OF 1941 was a rush to get additional Royal Canadian Navy ships to sea became a race during the latter part of the year. Although the United States Navy joined convoy escort operations in this period, giving substantial relief to the Royal Navy, it was not enough fully to counter expansion of the U-boat fleet. The U-boats, moreover, enjoyed the advantage of being able suddenly to strike into new areas and quickly shift the weight of their attack from one theatre to another. Increasingly, the Royal Canadian Navy found itself filling the breach in the North Atlantic, with diminished support from the great western powers. There was little or no chance to address the many problems of training and equipment in the novice fleet, problems recognized at the time, but with the press of operations there was not much choice but to carry on.

One large difficulty for the Canadians was constant redeployments that kept the Newfoundland Escort Force, and the forces based on Canadian home ports, in a state of flux. In June, as has been seen, to counter U-boat thrusts south of Cape Race, the Admiralty ordered escorts to Halifax to provide coverage west of the NEF rendezvous, which took place just as the RCN was attempting to establish its Newfoundland operation on a firm footing. To solidify these emergency arrangements, long-range sloops and corvettes would run between the Canadian coast and Iceland, and shorter-range destroyers from St John's would provide reinforcements east of Newfoundland. Although the extended run put a serious strain on men in the long-range escorts, it offered the possibility of reducing the very great costs of base development at St John's while allowing the new Canadian ships to work from Halifax, where they could be supported more adequately.

By mid-July everything had changed once again. It was then clear that the U-boats had pulled back from the western Atlantic towards Iceland. With the large number of submarines now at his disposal, Dönitz was able to attack convoys to Gibraltar and West Africa—the latter lacking anti-submarine escort for much of the passage—more or less at will. The Admiralty, therefore, withdrew the four sloops and former US Coast Guard cutters, which had been among the principal long-range escorts of the NEF, cancelled plans to send additional warships of these types to St John's, and diverted the vessels to the West African run. As part of this re-organization, the Admiralty now urged Canada to strip its home ports of escorts and pour everything into Newfoundland.[1]

Canada had virtually done that already. The Admiralty had asked that convoys should begin to use the route north around Newfoundland through the Strait of Belle Isle. This kept shipping well clear of the short great circle route between southern Newfoundland and the U-boat bases in France, saved passage time between Newfoundland and the escort rendezvous near Iceland, and for both reasons, greatly widened the possibilities for evasive routing. The difficulty was that the choke point at the Strait of Belle Isle would have to be regularly patrolled, and for that service the RCN disrupted its plans for home ports in order to despatch six more corvettes to Newfoundland in early July. These, designated the Newfoundland Force, were separate from the NEF, intended as they were to carry out solely local defence.[2]

In June, five recently commissioned corvettes sailed to Sydney to cover the vulnerable SC convoys as far as the rendezvous with the Newfoundland transocean escort groups. Experienced officers and specialist staffs at Sydney took the crews under their wings to help complete their training. Halifax now became essentially a work-up base for newly completed corvettes, not yet ready for even the most basic employment.[3] After mid-July, when the last of the escorts assigned to Halifax to meet the U-boat thrust south of Cape Race redeployed to the Newfoundland–Iceland run, protection of Halifax convoys out to the Newfoundland rendezvous fell to the two least capable of the Town class destroyers:[4] *Annapolis*, which had burned out a boiler shortly after its transfer to the RCN, and *Hamilton*, which had suffered collision damage.[5] Meanwhile, through much of 1941, the armed yachts, originally intended as only a temporary stopgap for extended seaward patrol and escort, continued to be employed in these roles that far exceeded their capabilities.

The Admiralty's plan to compensate for the weakness of shipping defences in the western Atlantic by routing convoys through the Strait of Belle Isle was unsuccessful. The first convoys to attempt the route were HX 138, which sailed from Halifax on 11 July, and SC 37, which cleared Sydney the following day. The convoys proceeded separately through the Cabot Strait, up the west coast of Newfoundland, and were then to combine outside the Strait of Belle Isle, where they would meet their escorts for the run to the Iceland rendezvous. Fog descended as HX 138 turned to enter the Cabot Strait, and as the columns of merchant ships attempted the change of course in blind conditions, four of them suffered collision damage that forced their return to port. As the convoys approached the Strait of Belle Isle on the evening of 14 July, conditions in that pre-radar era

---

1.   Adm to NSHQ, 12 July 1941, "15 Group 11—Organization," NAC, RG 24, 11941

2.   NSec to COAC, 13 June 1941, and COAC to NSec, "Disposition—HMC Corvettes," 30 June 1941, and minutes on this document, NAC, RG 24, 6797, NSS 8375-330.

3.   Ibid. See also Capt (D) Halifax to NSec, "Disposition of Canadian Corvettes," 5 Sep. 1941, also in NAC, RG 24, 6797, NSS 8375-330.

4.   NSHQ to Adm, 14 July 1941, "15 Group 11—Organization"

5.   A latecomer to the RCN, *Hamilton*, after initial transfer to the British in the fall of 1940, had suffered severe damage in a collision in St John's, and underwent repairs until July 1941, when Canada acceded to a request from the manpower-strapped Admiralty that the ship should be commissioned in the RCN. The destroyer suffered yet another collision at Halifax in Sep., just as she had completed work-ups. *Annapolis*, therefore, carried on alone with the HX series until Nov. when *Hamilton* again came out of dockyard. "*Hamilton* History," 3-8, DHH, 81/520 Hamilton 8000

became grim. Commander H. Kingsley, commanding officer of *St Croix,* who together with *Annapolis* was escorting HX 138, described the passage:

> Convoy remained in 9 columns but before dark destroyers took station astern and Convoy speed reduced to 6 knots, and fog began closing down. Large bergs and growlers were now (0135/15) in all directions and at 0230 thick fog shut down. The convoy became disorganized in avoiding icebergs and when fog lifted temporarily about 0330 the rear ship which "St Croix" had been following was now one of the leading ships. Enormous icebergs and innumerable growlers were seen to be in all directions; the ship ahead was going full astern to avoid ramming one and a large tanker was steering 90° to the course, straight for "St Croix," 200 yards off. The convoy was not in recognizable columns but steering various courses and speeds to try and find a way through. A conservative estimate of the largest iceberg's height, judging from the height of the mast of the Commodore's ship, would be 200 feet and they were probably aground in 55 fathoms.[6]

SC 37 hove to in the southern straits through the night, but even so the armed merchant cruiser HMS *Aurania* was forced to return to Halifax after striking an iceberg.[7] The next combined convoy, SC 38 and HX 140, experienced similar conditions of fog and ice in the straits on 24 to 25 July, and at least six ships had to turn back with collision and ice damage.[8] As a result, the Admiralty did not route another convoy through the straits until late August. Further south, although ice had cleared from the route off Cape Race, there was still the omnipresent fog. HX 142 and SC 39, for example, were supposed to link up east of Newfoundland on 4 August, but the two convoys groped along parallel courses, five to twenty miles apart, with the worried escorts vainly trying to find out who was where until they finally succeeded in joining up the two groups on 10 August, only two days out from the rendezvous south of Iceland with the eastern Atlantic escorts.[9]

At the strong recommendation of the Canadian east coast commands, the link-ups at sea had already been somewhat simplified by cancelling the HX joiner groups from Bermuda. These joiners, as COAC staff pointed out, no longer served any purpose, as they had only an antisurface raider escort, and the main threat was now submarines, for which defences could not be provided. The ships were put doubly at risk and suffered delays in the difficult link-ups in the fog-shrouded waters around Newfoundland.[10] The cancellation of the Bermuda series was part of a larger reorganization of the convoy system in July 1941. Many of the ships that assembled at Bermuda after taking on cargo at ports in the southern United States, and further south in the western hemisphere, made their initial passages from the United Kingdom in OB convoys that were routed south, and dispersed southeast of Britain leaving the vessels to cross the ocean independently. That again increased the danger of interception by the enemy. The Admiralty now divided the OB series into two new ones; ON, which followed the northern route to Canadian ports, and in which

---

6.   *St Croix,* "ROP—Convoy HX 138," 18 July 1941, DHH, NHS Sydney files 48-2-2 pt 5

7.   *Matapedia* ROP, 16 July 1941, DHH, 81/520/8280, box 9, "SC 37"; Tennyson and Sarty, *Guardian of the Gulf,* 253-4

8.   "*Columbia* History," 16-17, DHH, 81/520 Columbia 8000

9.   HMS *Churchill* ROP, HX 142-SC 39, 13 Aug. 1941, NAC, RG 24, 11334, 8280-SC 39

10. COAC to NSHQ, 2022z/24 June 1941, NAC, RG 24, 3972, NSS 1048-48-1 (6); Adm to C-in-C AWI, NSHQ, COAC, 0017b/6 July 1941, f. 312, PRO, ADM 199/2080; AHS, *Home Waters* II, 317

all ships bound for the western hemisphere were included; and OS, which, with the cutters and sloops released from the NEF, became a through convoy direct from Britain to Freetown. The ON convoys were alternately slow and fast to correspond with the eastbound HX and SC series.[11]

As the composition of the NEF began to stabilize during the latter part of July, the Admiralty directed that the ships be assigned to twelve permanently organized groups, on the successful model established in the eastern Atlantic. This would allow for the regular cycle of convoys, with the necessary margin for groups to clean their boilers after every three crossings, and for periodic refit, repairs, and special missions.[12] The force at that time had a total of only fifty escorts, twenty destroyers (thirteen RN, seven RCN), and thirty corvettes (eleven RN and nineteen RCN). This was considerably smaller than the strength of sixty-three escorts that British authorities had estimated would be needed, because pressures in the eastern Atlantic had prevented the RN from sending nine promised additional ships, seven destroyers and two corvettes. Even had these ships been available, the total would have been less capable than originally planned by British authorities: thirty destroyers and nine sloops, but only twenty-four corvettes. More than half of the destroyers, moreover, were the breakdown-prone Town class, and, of course, the bulk of the fleet were new, frequently ill-equipped, and poorly trained RCN corvettes. These weaknesses were all the more serious because most of the best destroyers, the Canadian River class and the RN's A-I equivalents, were occupied much of the time in escorting troop convoys. As a result, the groups assigned to the merchant ship convoys, for the most part, included only one Town and three corvettes. With groups so small, and ships so liable to break down in the hard North Atlantic running, the group system did not, in fact, function at all. As Commodore Murray, the Commodore Commanding Newfoundland Force, put it: "Resort has had to be made to various expedients in order to strengthen groups which through defective ships or non-arrival of ships have been below the minimum number considered necessary." Captain Stevens, Captain (D) Newfoundland, was more blunt: "With the Escort Force so much below paper strength it is impossible to avoid frequent changes [of escorts from one group to another] in order to prevent convoys sailing virtually unescorted."[13]

The critical shortage of ships in the NEF, following the Admiralty's decision to pull or hold back some of the most capable escorts for the eastern Atlantic, reflected the operational benefits of timely intelligence, and the ability of the Admiralty's centralized but flexible command organization to act on it quickly. In the battle for HX 133, timely, well-processed intelligence had allowed the Admiralty to concentrate the escorts available in the western Atlantic, woefully inadequate as they were, around that threatened convoy, and thereby fight the U-boats to a standstill. Intelligence had then confirmed that the U-boats' redeployment towards Iceland and the approaches to Britain was complete and helped to reveal the locations of U-boat patrol lines, as Dönitz endeavoured to concentrate his forces for the effective attacks on convoys that had proved difficult to impossible in the distant west. With this information the Admiralty was able to route all transatlantic convoys clear of the enemy through much of the summer of 1941. The Admiralty's confidential *Monthly Anti-Submarine Report* crowed:

---

11.   Adm to C-in-C WA, 0002b/15 June 1941, f 215, PRO, ADM 199/2080; Adm, *MASR*, July 1941, 17

12.   Adm to NSHQ, 12 July 1941, "15 Group 11—Organization"

13.   Adm to C-in-C WA, 3 June 1941; Capt (D) Newfoundland, "Organization of the NEF," 27 July 1941, DHH, NHS 8440-70; CCNF WD, July 1941, DHH, NHS NSS 1000-5-20 pt 1

During July there were, on the average, two dozen or more German U-Boats, and half a dozen or more Italian U-Boats, operating in the Atlantic. A tendency was apparent for an increase rather than a decrease in the numbers on patrol, and it seems reasonable to suppose that, towards the end of the month, the enemy's summer campaign was in full extension. Certainly the effort exerted by the U-Boat Command rose steadily from early May to August and there have been indications that U-Boat crews have been called upon to make extended cruises of as long as five weeks' duration.

Having regard to the intensity of the enemy's effort, remarkably poor results were achieved for the number of merchant ships sunk was only twenty-one [none of these in the western Atlantic] ... the lowest total recorded since May, 1940. The number of ships sunk was less than half the June total, and the losses in tonnage were reduced to one-third of the previous figure.[14]

In August the figures were good again, with only twenty-three ships lost to U-boat attack and none of these in the western Atlantic, even though "the increase in U-Boat construction, begun at the outbreak of war, is now being translated into a steady increase in the numbers of U-Boats operating ... Good management has earned good luck and fortune has smiled on us."[15]

The Americans, moreover, were on the brink of joining in the escort of convoys. This had become an early possibility as a result of Roosevelt's decision at the beginning of June to despatch American troops to garrison Iceland. At that time Germany was poised for a major summer offensive, but where was not clear. What was evident was the Allies' vulnerability in practically every direction, from Britain itself, through the Mediterranean, and to north and western Africa. The latter possibility particularly worried US planners because Axis forces in the western bulge of Africa could extend control into the southern Atlantic and influence sympathetic nations in South America. Roosevelt chose to occupy Iceland to send a strong message to the Axis from a place that he could present politically as a purely defensive move essential to the security of the Western hemisphere. The president won that essential domestic support when he publicly announced the occupation on 7 July, just as the USN disembarked 4,000 Marines on the island.[16]

Meanwhile, the Germans had launched their summer offensive on 22 June 1941, but against the Soviet Union. Admiral Stark urged the president to seize that occasion to declare war and despatch air squadrons and the twenty-seven destroyers with the Support Force to the northwest approaches to Great Britain, as envisaged in the ABC-1 agreement. Stark, it will be remembered, had promoted the agreement because of his conviction the Axis could not be defeated without full American participation in the war, and he had helped to design the agreement to ensure that the United States had full say in the strategy and outcome of the conflict. The president did not agree that the time was right to risk a declaration of war, sensing that he had moved as far as he dared with the troop movement to Iceland. In fact, Senator Burton K. Wheeler, one of the leading isolationists, was already charging that the USN was undertaking escort and demanding a full investigation by the Senate Naval Affairs Committee.[17]

---

14.   Adm, *MASR*, July 1941, 6

15.   Ibid, Aug. 1941, 7, 11

16.   Morison, *Battle of the Atlantic*, 74-9

17.   Simpson, *Admiral Harold R. Stark*, 87-8

The presence of US forces in Iceland that had to be supplied by sea shipments from North America, however, carried its own logic for escort of convoy. Already in mid-June, Admiralty and USN planning staffs in London had raised the idea that the recent movement of the U-boats west and the creation of the Anglo-Canadian NEF suggested a more rational organization of forces in the Atlantic. Would it not make more sense for the Americans to take over the Newfoundland commitment, and allow the Commonwealth navies once more to concentrate their forces in the eastern Atlantic?[18] Churchill, on learning of the proposal, took grave exception: Britain's entire purpose in the ABC-1 negotiations was to press the United States into full participation in the war at the earliest moment.[19] At almost this same time, the C-in-C Atlantic Fleet (CINCLANT), Admiral Ernest King, who loathed the idea of deploying his Support Force into a British-controlled theatre, urged a similar adjustment of the ABC-1 plans. Stark, who like Churchill wanted full US participation although for quite different, nationalistic reasons, flatly rejected King's argument:

> The basing of important U.S. naval forces in the United Kingdom will undoubtedly have a beneficial effect on the morale of the British people, and will intensify the interest of the American people in the outcome of the war. Although submarine activity has been extended to the westward, the area east of 30°West Longitude [between Greenland and Iceland] remains the most vital area of danger to shipping. Shipping in this area will not be adequately protected until escort by surface craft and patrol planes, and by shore based fighters east of 15°West Longitude.[20]

Nevertheless, the administration's caution about too-precipitous involvement in the war made escort of convoys west of Iceland an option that had to be considered. On 3 July 1941 Rear-Admiral R.K. Turner, head of the US Navy War Plans Division, forwarded a draft outline plan (Western Hemisphere Defence, Plan No. 3, short title WPL-50) to the British naval staff in Washington for consultations "in case the Government of the United States decides to escort trans-Atlantic convoys in Western Hemisphere waters [i.e., between the North American coast and the vicinity of Iceland], without a formal declaration of war against the Axis Powers." Turner explained that this was not intended to replace the ABC-1 plan for US forces to operate in British waters: when the US declared war "ABC-1 would immediately take effect." Even so, the draft plan number 3 (WPL-50) would greatly assist the situation east of Iceland, for the Americans proposed to relieve all British antisubmarine escorts committed to the NEF so these vessels could be redeployed.

The Americans would need help. Because the USN had not yet begun to build specialized antisubmarine escorts like corvettes, only destroyers were available for the role, and the fleet's limited numbers of this valuable type could not all be committed to the Iceland run. In 1917–18, as senior officers remembered, the United States had been too generous in its response to British appeals for help in convoy escort, with the result that the American fleet's larger units had been virtually immobilized by the lack of essential antisubmarine screens. Therefore, one of the basic requirements of WPL-50 was that the Canadian escort fleet should remain in the western Atlantic

18. "Conference Held in Captain Everett's Office, Admiralty, at 1200, Friday June 13, 1941," "Admiralty Conferences, 1941," NARA, RG 313, Entry NHC 76, "Subject files," box 1

19. E.g., Cornwall Jones to Coleridge, 7 July 1941, PRO, CAB 122/1582, ff 270-1

20. CINCLANT to CNO, 18 June 1941, file A7-3(1), NARA, RG 313 Red, CINCLANT, 1941, secret, box 154; same to same, 2 July 1941, CNO to CINCLANT, 16 July 1941 (quoted), A14-1 (Jacket no. 2), NARA, RG 313 Red, CINCLANT, 1941, secret, box 108

to share the burden, and for that reason Turner asked the British Admiralty delegation to have Commodore V.G. Brodeur, RCN, the Canadian naval attaché, hand-carry the sensitive documents to Ottawa by aircraft for comment by Naval Service Headquarters.[21]

Turner wanted a speedy response so that the Canadian and British naval representatives in Washington could immediately consult on the details of the plan. In Ottawa, members of all three service staffs, Minister of National Defence Colonel Ralston, Undersecretary of State for External Affairs Norman Robertson, and the naval minister, Angus L. Macdonald, set to work the moment Brodeur delivered the draft plan on the evening of 4 July.[22] Their main reservation was to emphasize that the availability of Canadian forces for employment under American command was "subject ... to agreement and arrangement between the appropriate United States and Canadian Chiefs of Staff." This enunciated the same principle the Royal Canadian Navy had developed with respect to RN commands in the western Atlantic. The American flag officer commanding the western Atlantic ocean escorts could exercise control over only those Canadian forces assigned to him by the Canadian service chiefs on behalf of their government; he was not free to redeploy other RCN ships or interfere in the operation of shore bases.[23] It was a particularly sensitive point at the time. The Canadian staffs were in the last weeks of their prolonged, but ultimately successful, struggle in the Permanent Joint Board of Defence to persuade their American counterparts that, under the Canada–United States Basic Defence Plan No. 2 for the defence of North America, in the event that Britain did not fall and the US joined the war, American commanders should not exercise the broad powers over the Canadian forces provided for in plan 1, which had been drafted in 1940 when Britain's collapse seemed imminent.[24]

The ministers and the military staffs recognized that WPL-50 "would clearly be in the interests of the British Commonwealth and their allies," and instructed Brodeur to "use every endeavour to obtain agreement for the final draft of this Plan." In particular, they gave the attaché some latitude on the important question of the numbers of ships to be assigned. The American draft stated that only "20 destroyers and A/S vessels" would be needed from the Commonwealth navies, considerably fewer than the eight destroyers and twenty corvettes the RCN was already committed to provide for the NEF. Nelles and Macdonald informed Brodeur that the commitment would be scaled back to five destroyers and fifteen corvettes if twenty vessels was indeed the total the USN wanted. But they wondered about the low numbers, knowing as they did about the nagging destroyer shortage. If the Americans had meant "20 destroyers plus a number of A/S vessels," then Canada would increase the number of destroyers to eight. They warned that additional commonwealth destroyers beyond these eight—the Rivers, all of which had long endurance, and the two Towns that had "long legs"—would have to come from the British.[25] On the evening of 6 July Commander P.B. German, carrying the American papers and the draft instructions for Brodeur, flew to Prince Albert, Saskatchewan, where the prime minister was visiting his constituency. King quickly telegraphed Macdonald his "complete accord with colleagues and yourself."[26]

21.   USN, WPD to BAD, 3 July 1941, DHH, 75/191

22.   Macdonald to Mackenzie King, 6 July 1941, NAC, MG 26 J4, reel C-4865, 261007-8

23.   CNS and Naval Minister, "Directive to Canadian Naval Attaché, Washington," 6 July 1941, NAC, RG 24 (Acc 83-4/167), 218, NSS 1400-WPL-50

24.   Stacey, *Arms, Men and Governments*, 349-55

25.   CNS and Naval Minister, "Directive to Canadian Naval Attaché, Washington," 6 July 1941

26.   Mackenzie King to Macdonald, tg, 7 July 1941, NAC, MG 26 J4, reel C-4865, 261009

The British, no less than the Canadians, "at once realized the very great degree of added security which would be given to our trade in Atlantic if [Plan No.3 (WPL-50)] were to be implemented." On 6 July the Admiralty provided Admiral Sir Charles Little, head of the BAD in Washington, with a long, cabled response to Turner's request for early comments. Here the British staff laid bare much of their thinking about the Atlantic battle, and delved into numerous specific issues, including convoy organization and communications, that would have to be resolved if the Commonwealth and US navies were to share the burden effectively.[27] This paper set the agenda for the conference Turner had requested with Little and his staff and Brodeur, which took place in Washington on 8 July; Brodeur's contribution was, for the most part, to give assurances that Canadian port and communications facilities required by the Americans would be available.[28] This important meeting in turn provided the framework for continued consultations in Washington and in London.

These early negotiations did not resolve the ambiguities that the Canadians believed existed concerning the number of RCN ships to be allocated. The Admiralty's 6 July paper for Little agreed with the American draft that escort west of Iceland would require "9 or 10" escort groups, each of ten vessels, "5 to 6 destroyers and 2 to 4 corvettes." The requirement was for roughly a hundred vessels in total, and the Admiralty noted that these were available from Canadian and US sources, so that all RN ships could indeed be withdrawn from the NEF. In calculating the hundred vessels, the Admiralty included, in addition to the fifty-four USN destroyers mentioned in the US draft, forty-six RCN vessels—thirteen destroyers and thirty-three corvettes—or virtually the whole of the Canadian antisubmarine fleet, including ships assigned for the defence of home waters. It seems highly likely that the Canadian staff had similarly worked through the requirement for a hundred vessels apparent in the US plan, and this may well account for their questioning the US statement that only twenty of their escorts would be needed and their warning that some RN ships might have to remain in the Newfoundland Escort Force.

The Admiralty staff, far from alerting the USN to the apparent shortage of ships, argued that the draft American plan piled up too many escorts west of Iceland. Even the release of all RN ships assigned to the NEF:

> will be inadequate to bring both A/S escorts East of 026°West up to standard of escorts West of 026°West and at same time provide escorts for Gibraltar and Freetown [convoys] which are at present inadequately escorted [over] part of their route and not escorted at all during remainder of route. It is quite likely that introduction of Defence Plan No. 3 may, if GERMANS do not wish to bring U.S.A. into the war, result in U-Boats concentrating on North Atlantic convoys East of 026°West and on Gibraltar and Freetown convoys.

The Admiralty suggested that it would be "a great help therefore if US could provide some additional destroyers so as to release some Canadian destroyers and some cutters to release some Canadian corvettes" for employment in the eastern Atlantic.[29]

---

27. Adm to BAD, "Personal for Admiral Little from 1st Sea Lord," 6 July 1941, PRO, ADM 199/2080

28. "US Navy Western Hemisphere Defense Plan No. 3 (WPL-50). Note of a meeting in Admiral Turner's Room ... 8 July, 1941," DHH 75/191. See also BAD, "Notes for a Mtg with Admiral Turner ... 8 July, 1941 ...," nd, ibid, and USN, WPD to Little, 11 July 1941, "Atlantic Area—British Joint Staff Correspondence no. 2," NARA, RG 38, Series VII, "Anglo-American Co-operation," box 116; Adm to BAD, "Personal for Admiral Little from 1st Sea Lord," 6 July 1941

29. Adm to BAD, "Personal for Admiral Little from 1st Sea Lord," 6 July 1941

The 8 July conference, no doubt deferring to Canadian sensibilities that would have been put forward by Brodeur, acknowledged that the "Canadians would retain 3 to 5 destroyers and 10 corvettes under their own control for local defence." They would, however, maintain the five destroyers and fifteen corvettes committed to the NEF "at full strength." Ships undergoing refit or extended repair would be replaced by ships from the local defence forces. The Americans, for their part, announced they were already too thinly stretched to offer any additional destroyers, as the British requested, but they did agree to limit the western ocean escort force to seventy-four vessels, the fifty-four US destroyers, five Canadian destroyers, and fifteen Canadian corvettes. This would allow the British to draw on "3 to 5" Canadian destroyers and five Canadian corvettes for deployment in the eastern Atlantic.[30] Soon after, on 12 July, Little passed a significant revision to Admiral Turner:

> I have now heard that the Admiralty do not propose to ask the Canadian Authorities to employ any Canadian destroyers or corvettes at the present time in the Eastern Atlantic although circumstance may make this desirable later on.
>
> This has been discussed with Commodore Brodeur, RCN, who agrees.
>
> There will therefore be the 8 Canadian destroyers and 20 Canadian corvettes [i.e., the numbers already committed to the NEF] always available for convoy escort in the Western Atlantic ... These numbers will be maintained irrespective of refits.[31]

Admiral Stark reported all this to King as a basis for Atlantic fleet planning. Stark, however, transmuted Little's qualified statement that Canadian ships were not at that moment required in the eastern Atlantic into an ironclad commitment: "All Canadian naval vessels are in the future to be operated in the Western Atlantic, and not sent to the Eastern Atlantic regardless of eventualities."[32] Little's conclusion, moreover, that the RCN would contribute their entire existing ocean escort force of eight destroyers and twenty corvettes, and draw on their home forces to sustain the ocean escort at a full running strength of twenty-eight vessels, appears to have been based either on wishful thinking, or a misunderstanding with Brodeur. It went considerably beyond what Macdonald and Nelles had suggested in their formal response to draft plan 3 (WPL-50), which said that they would be willing to leave the Canadian force of eight destroyers and twenty corvettes in place, but had not mentioned the issue of replacements for ships under refit, which, given the hard conditions on the transatlantic run, was a significant one. Little, moreover, seems to have communicated his optimistic conclusion only to the Americans. They, in turn, although basing their plans on the availability of twenty-eight rather than twenty Canadian ships, failed to revise the draft of a new plan, Western Hemisphere Defence Plan No. 4 (WPL-51), which was just now taking the place of number 3 (WPL-50). Thus, when on 14 July the office of the First Sea Lord distributed a briefing note at the Admiralty on the new US plan number 4, it stated that the Canadians were still committed to provide only five destroyers and fifteen corvettes if the USN took over escort in the western Atlantic.[33]

---

30. "US Navy Western Hemisphere Defense Plan No. 3 (WPL-50)"

31. Little to USN WPD, 12 July 1941, "WPL-51," NARA, RG 38, Plans, Series IX, box 147K

32. CNO to CINCLANT, 17 July 1941, file A16-3, NARA, RG 313, CINCLANT Red, 1941, Secret, box 156

33. Naval Staff memo to Adm, 14 July 1941, PRO, ADM 205/9, f 4

The president had rejected Defence Plan No. 3 (WPL-50) on 10 July 1941. The objection was that the plan would have placed the US Atlantic escorts under Admiralty direction. The consultations earlier in the month among the naval staffs had quickly concluded that the only way the system could work, at least for some months to come, would be for the existing British-Canadian organization to continue assembling and scheduling convoys. Although the United States Department of the Navy would have control over the routing of convoys—and assignment of escorts—west of Iceland, the department would be dependent on "proposals" from the Admiralty based on its highly developed facilities for gathering and analysing U-boat intelligence. This was acceptable to the US naval staff. Indeed, within the navy department, Lieutenant-Commander J.G. Mackinlay, RCNVR, was now working at fever pitch instructing US officers in the British-Canadian convoy organization methods so that the Americans could begin to integrate their shipping and build up the capability to run convoys from their own ports.[34] But from a political perspective the president was unwilling to have US escort forces slotted into the trade defence system of a belligerent nation. The more chauvinistic Plan No. 4 (WPL-51), which appeared on 11 July, included USN escort of only American and Icelandic shipping. Almost immediately, on 12 July, an amendment made provision for Allied shipping to join the US convoys, an effort to provide the same assistance to the British as would have been available in the defunct Plan No. 3 (WPL-50), but under the cover of US operations designed solely for the protection of the Western Hemisphere.[35]

While the US staff grappled with the president's political difficulties in mid-July, the Admiralty, as we have seen, began to pull back sloops and cutters from the NEF to meet the U-boat thrusts against the southward routes in the eastern Atlantic, and urged the Canadians to increase their commitment on the run between Newfoundland and Iceland. Rapid movement of U-boats into weakly defended waters had left the Admiralty no choice. It may be significant that, only days before, Admiral Little in his letter of 12 July, had passed word to the US staff that Britain would not for the time being withdraw Canadian ships from Newfoundland for duty in the eastern Atlantic, a decision that obviously deferred to the US Navy's insistence that it would need all the Canadian help it could get in the western Atlantic. Uninformed as the Admiralty was about how Little's letter had brought the Americans to believe they could count, irrevocably, on having twenty-eight RCN escorts fully ready for operations at all times, the Admiralty itself clearly regarded the western Atlantic as a Canadian commitment. Although, as a matter of form, the Admiralty paid heed to Canadian concerns about the need to maintain home defence forces in Canadian waters, we have seen that, in fact, the British authorities—correctly from a strategic point of view—regarded the whole of the Canadian fleet as an important resource that had to be deployed according to the swiftly changing thrusts of the enemy. Given the global shortage of escorts, the Admiralty could scarcely do otherwise.

In short, the senior navies tacitly agreed that the Canadians should meet all Commonwealth obligations for escort of merchant convoys in the western Atlantic. This same common assumption, however, hid from view the fact that there was already misunderstanding over the crucial details: how many escorts the RCN should provide, and for how long. The USN believed it had

---

34. Correspondence, 16-31 July 1941, "Assistant Naval Attache (General Correspondence) (0-1)," pt 1, NAC, RG 24, 11978

35. Hemisphere Defence plans file, Stark papers, Naval Historical Center (NHC), Washington Navy Yard; chronology in DHH 75/191

access to a running strength of twenty-eight escorts for a considerable time to come; the RN believed the firm commitment was only for twenty escorts, and that although additional ones might well be provided to assist the Americans, the Admiralty had protected its right also to redeploy Canadian escorts in the event that the Atlantic war took another unfavourable turn. Lurking in these weeds was a much larger issue: was the Canadian escort fleet effectively being turned over completely to American strategic direction, or was it a matter of only temporary arrangements that in no way disrupted, as the British saw it, the essential unity of the two royal navies? This gap in understanding had opened between the United States and Great Britain, even with the lavish liaison measures that included a full British staff in Washington and a full American staff in London. Canada, of course, had no such facilities, and the limited access it possessed was under a strain. During the latter part of July, moreover, US proposals that the Canadian escorts should operate as a distinct national force seemed to promise that American needs for help would be finite, and minimally disrupt the existing organization of the Commonwealth navies.

The initiative for continuation of the NEF as a purely Canadian one came from Admiral Stark, possibly arising from his discussions with Admiral King about how they might implement escort. The American officers were not concerned about Canadian nationalism; their interest was to protect the autonomy of their Atlantic Fleet in the event, as Stark expected and wanted, that US escort in the western Atlantic soon provoked war with Germany and triggered the despatch of the main USN escort force to British waters. In a memorandum to King, Stark explained it was thanks to his insistence that the ABC-1 agreement had prevented the distribution of American naval forces among British naval units in British home waters, thus ensuring control of USN forces by USN officers. He suggested, "In order to give all possible support to this position," that when cooperating with the RCN,

> Canadian naval vessels be formed into task forces entirely separate from United States task forces. That is to say, in employing the 8 destroyers and 23 corvettes (including 3 [Free] French corvettes [whom the British had agreed to leave in the Newfoundland Escort force under Canadian command]) of the Canadian Navy, it would appear preferable to form two to four task groups consisting entirely of Canadian vessels, and to form entirely separate task groups consisting of United States naval vessels.[36]

Admiral King, not surprisingly given his visceral opposition to mixed national forces, was entirely receptive. In fact, he seized on the idea to solve serious operational problems he faced in trying to prepare his fleet for escort in the western Atlantic: the very great difficulty in organizing sufficient and regular sailings of American and Icelandic ships to coincide with the British convoy schedule and the impossibility of having more than thirty destroyers ready for what amounted to full-scale war duty within the foreseeable future.[37] King, in a characteristically abbreviated style, set down the solution: "U.S. and *Canada* 'alternate' in providing escort detachments—U.S. about 30 DDs; Canada, about 30 DDs and escort vessels."[38] Thus, instead of supplying only a modest augmentation to a much larger American escort force as originally envisaged, King, who had the responsibility for implementing the arrangements, wanted Canada to carry fully half the burden.

---

36. CNO to CINCLANT, 17 July 1941

37. W. Heinrichs, *Threshold of War: Franklin D. Roosevelt and American entry into World War II* (New York 1988), 113-15

38. CINCLANT memo, 17 July 1941, "WPL-51," NARA, RG 38, "Plans," Series IX, box 147K

In consultations at the BAD, and at a meeting on 22 July 1941 of the British and American staffs over which Stark himself presided, Commodore Brodeur agreed that the RCN should operate its own escort groups. He also agreed that the Canadian groups would take full charge of convoys assigned by the USN flag officer in consultation with Commodore Murray at St John's. The surviving documents do not, however, mention any discussion of the scale of effort that might be expected of Canada; indeed it is not clear how much of an impact King's summary of his thinking had on the US staff, and it seems certain that it was not communicated to the British.[39]

What can be established is that Brodeur was having a rough ride. Although the Canadian was able to pass on analytical descriptions of the new USN plan 4 (WPL-51), based on the British mission's own reports and full information from Stark, his repeated requests to be allowed to show the full plan to the authorities in Ottawa were turned down flat:

> with very strong words by U.S. intimating that information of the previous plan had been talked about by [Canadian] civilians and they were not going to have it again. These statements were not quite as polite as I am telling you. At the same time they pointed out that no department here except the three services knew of all this. Even their State Department and Treasury Board who have tried to get copies have been turned down.

"You remember," Brodeur wrote in this personal letter to Nelles, "that a few weeks ago Wrong, our Minister-Counsellor here, held a meeting in Ottawa where you all agreed that service attachés should have no secrets from their Minister, which of course is absolutely right and since receipt of your official instructions to that effect, I have passed on every possible information I have received about 'Plans' etc. to our Canadian Minister ... I am in a sort of dual capacity here, whereby I am given a lot of information by our friends with very strong request, it is for naval and service members consumption only. Of course in view of my instructions as a Naval Attaché I cannot accept that request though I have not told our US friends that. So I am more or less a sort of spy at present ... The USN do not understand our political setup and simply will not agree with it."[40]

The embarrassing dissemination of information about plan number 3 (WPL-50) did nothing to further Canada's larger campaign for direct representation with the US forces in Washington. On this issue Brodeur could be open with Wrong. On 26 July, just as Canada's role was looming larger in the Anglo-American plans, Brodeur alerted Wrong about his lowly status as a very junior adjunct of the BAD:

> 1. No invitation to attend any important meeting at the Navy Department except the one with the Chief of Naval Operations [presumably the meeting of 22 July] has ever been received direct by the Canadian Attaches; the information of meetings always coming from the British Mission ...

> 4. When the original plan of co-operation between the USA and British Empire was made, copies were sent to the British Mission requesting them to ask the Canadian Naval Attache

39. Op-12B-McC, "Matters to Be Discussed at Conference on July 22, 1941," nd; Little, Moore, Danckwerts, Brodeur, Belben, "Draft Memo: Matters to Be Discussed at Conference on July 22nd, between Admiral Stark and Admiral Little," nd, DHH 75/191; Stark diary, 22 July 1941, NHC, Operational Archives, Stark papers, series II, box 4; Op. 12b B.R., "Agreements between United States, United Kingdom and Canada Concerning Operation of Convoys and Escorts in the Western Atlantic Area in Relation to WPL 51," 22 July 1941, NAC, RG 24 (acc 83-4/167), 218, NSS 1400-WPL-51

40. CNA to CNS, 24 July 1941, NAC, RG 24, 11967, NW 0-170

to fly to Ottawa with this plan. Your Attache had no idea whatever that such a plan was contemplated but others obviously knew it.

Clearly, and this was confirmed by Rear-Admiral V.H. Danckwerts at the BAD in terms that brooked no discussion, USN authorities had not the slightest intention of dealing directly with Canadian authorities. If Canada did not accept the British mission as its representative, said Danckwerts, "Then there will not be any dealing, that's all!" In maintaining close touch with the British-American Delegation, Brodeur found himself being summoned for discussions—"no one from the Mission would think of coming to see the CNA," he grumbled—even on matters that could easily have been dealt with by correspondence.[41] Brodeur was known to be prickly about anything that touched on Canada's autonomous status with respect to Britain, but his reading of the situation was by no means exaggerated. A private letter by the secretary of the British mission in July explained how he and his colleagues dealt with Canadian requests for information:

> They [the Canadian government] put up a tentative suggestion ... through the State Department, which we gather was not at all favourably received, as the Americans not unnaturally preferred to deal with one body representing all-empire military opinion. They came back to us, quick as a flash, and suggested, without telling us of their rebuff, that it would of course be most desirable that they should keep in the closest possible touch with our Mission pending the setting up of their own. To this we could do nothing but agree, so we are now in the curious position of having the Canadian Attachés (all three of them) attending all our official meetings in what might be described as the role of Observers. They see our M.M. Papers, and our Gleam Telegrams: but it has necessitated the setting up of a special series of M.M. *(S)* Papers, having special M.M. *(S)* meetings, and withholding from them the more secret Gleam and Boxes Telegrams.[42]

Western Hemisphere Defence Plan No. 4 (WPL-51) came into force on 26 July, but in a truncated form. Measures brought into effect placed the Atlantic Fleet on an essentially wartime footing, including the darkening of American warships at night— where previously they had been brightly lit to signal their identity to Axis forces. There was also scope within the plan's ambiguous language for USN commanders to open fire on Axis warships, and the plan brought into full effect the organization of the Atlantic Fleet forces for ocean escort. The Roosevelt administration, however, excluded the part of the plan that allowed for the inclusion of Allied merchant ships in US-escorted convoys. This measure, even with the cover of the inclusion of US or Icelandic ships in each convoy, and the autonomous Canadian-escorted convoys, could only be implemented by invoking the British-American Naval Agreement of 22 July 1941, which would constitute a political association between the United States and the belligerent powers.[43]

The president would not allow such a step until he had a larger political understanding with the British.[44] That occasion came at the Riviera Conference, held at Placentia Bay, Newfoundland,

---

41. CNA min, to "the Minister" [of Legation in DC], 26 July 1941, NAC, RG 24, 11962, NMS 4 v 1. This minute enlarged upon the warning Brodeur had given in June that Canadian attachés would only have an equal voice in the British mission with political help, CNA to "the Minister" [of Legation in DC], 18 June 1941, NAC, RG 24, 11962, NMS 4 pt 1

42. "Richard" [Coleridge] to Cornwall-Jones, 28 Aug. 1941, PRO, CAB 122/1582, f 239

43. CINCLANT, "Administrative History of the US Atlantic Fleet in World War II: Commander in Chief, US Atlantic Fleet," 1946, v 1, pt 1, 187

44. Heinrichs, *Threshold of War*, 116

where Churchill and the British chiefs of staff, embarked in the battleship HMS *Prince of Wales*, conferred with Roosevelt and the US Chiefs of Staff, who had come in Admiral King's flagship, the cruiser USS *Augusta* and in the cruiser USS *Tuscaloosa,* on 9 to 12 August 1941. Canadian participation was limited to the corvettes *Chilliwack* and *Trail*, who carried out an endless-chain antisubmarine patrol off Placentia Bay for the duration of the conference, and the destroyers *Assiniboine*, *Restigouche*, and *Saguenay*, which were among the escorts for *Prince of Wales*.[45] The role of the three Canadian destroyers, which as part of the screen of the battleship were under the direction and scrutiny of its captain but had no say in their position, course, or speed, was analogous to the attitude of the conference participants towards Canada. Although Riviera would have an important impact on the RCN's role in the Battle of the Atlantic, no Canadians were invited to attend; they would simply be told where to go and when.

The main work of the conference was the Atlantic Charter on war aims, in which Churchill and Roosevelt agreed on the basic political principles that would guide Anglo-American collaboration. As well, on 11 August they agreed to implementation of the escort part of Plan No. 4 (WPL-51), while their respective naval staffs fine-tuned the details.[46] The evidence that has come to light suggests the discussions focused on a new appendix to the plan, "Detailed Instructions for the Operation of Convoys and Escorts."[47] The paragraph dealing with the Canadian role bore the markings of Admiral King's terse pen:

> b. The Commander in Chief, US Atlantic Fleet, will be responsible for the protection of United States and Iceland flag convoys between North America and Iceland. He will arrange with Canadian naval and air authorities for cooperation by Canadian naval and air forces in this protection, in general conformity with the following:
> 1. Canadian ocean escort groups will escort such of the Iceland flag convoys as cannot be escorted by United States ocean escort groups. Canadian ocean escort groups will not escort United States flag convoys.[48]

This paragraph allowed King exactly the sort of prerogative that he insisted should be left to an operational commander, a prerogative that he would not hesitate to use. As later events would show, the question of precisely what proportion of the convoys the Canadians would escort appears not to have been discussed. Possibly, the staffs agreed that the RCN should be assigned slow convoys, because the corvettes that made up most of the Canadian ocean escort force lacked the speed desirable for fast convoys, but had long endurance suited to the plodding, prolonged crossing of the slow merchant vessels. Certainly, the American naval staff, since the time of the ABC-1 meetings early in the year, had made clear their preference for smaller and faster convoys than the British were running. This, the US officers declared, was a sure measure for beating the U-boats,

---

45. "*Assiniboine* History," 16-18

46. Gilbert, *Finest Hour*, 1160. For Riviera, see esp Theodore Wilson, *The First Summit: Roosevelt and Churchill at Placentia Bay, 1941* (New York 1969).

47. "US Navy Western Hemisphere Defense Plan No. 4. Appendix I: Detailed Instructions for the Operation of Convoys and Escorts," Aug. 1941, "Hemisphere Defense Plans," NHC, Stark papers, Series XIII, box 84, which appears to be the original US draft. Goodenough-Turner correspondence, 11-12 Aug. 1941, "WPL-51," NARA, RG 38, "Plans," Series IX, box 147K concerns amendments discussed at the Riviera Conference.

48. "US Navy Western Hemisphere Defense Plan No. 4. Appendix I,"para 1-201 b, "Hemisphere Defense Plans." See CINCLANT to CNO, 0405/10 Aug. 1941, file 1-31 Aug. 1941, NARA, RG 313, entry NHC 69, Atlantic Fleet Secret messages. This signal contains amendments to the draft appendix, including the wording of the paragraph concerning Canada.

Senior Allied staff onboard HMS *Prince of Wales* at Riviera in August 1941. Left to right, front row, Admiral of the Fleet Sir Dudley Pound, Admiral H.R. Stark, and Admiral E.J. King. Back row, General G.C. Marshall, General H.H. Arnold and Captain F. Sherman. (Imperial War Museum, A 4984)

Winston Churchill comes onboard *Assiniboine* during the period the destroyer escorted *Prince of Wales* for the RIVIERA conference in August 1941. Churchill is walking past the commanding officer, Lieutenant J.S. Stubbs, RCN, because he assumed an officer so junior and so young could not be in command of a destroyer. (NAC, PA 140559)

an apparent statement of the obvious that enormously irritated the British, who had reluctantly organized the overlarge convoys of old slow ships because desperate circumstances allowed no other choice.

The difficulty in attempting to define the respective Canadian and American roles by allocating slow convoys to the RCN, while also meeting the US political desire to have escort groups of the nations operate separately, lay with the existing organization of the convoy system. As already noted, the SC convoys were being combined with HX convoys, so there were no independent SC sailings. Now, the imminent arrival of US escorts offered relief from the unwieldy combined convoys. On 13 August, the day after the last meeting at Placentia Bay, the Admiralty promulgated notice of impending changes in the North Atlantic convoy system. If the British officers mentioned the revision during the conference, it had not been in detail, for on 15 August the BAD passed the new scheme to the Department of the Navy, and promised not to implement it without American approval.[49]

The concentration of shipping in the North Atlantic convoys had made them, as accepted doctrine then would have it, perilously large. In addition to the ships bound for southern ports in the western hemisphere that had previously sailed independently, in June, at Churchill's direction, the Admiralty had begun once more to include the ships of thirteen to fifteen knots that had been sailing independently since March.[50] By the summer of 1941 most HX convoys had more than sixty ships, and some more than seventy. There were usually forty ships in SC convoys, meaning that the combined HX and SC sailings comprised more than a hundred vessels. The size appalled naval officers, subscribing as they did to the "too many eggs in one basket" theory, the fear that this mass of ships would be vulnerable to slaughter. What they did not realize, until in 1942 operations research scientists applied mathematical analysis to convoy tactics, was that a hundred ships with eight escorts were much better protected than two fifty-ship convoys each with four escorts. The tactical problem was to defend the perimeter of the convoy against penetration by submarines; if the hundred-ship convoy had a perimeter of say thirty-six miles, two fifty-ship convoys with the same spacing between ships would have a perimeter of fifty-two miles. In the first case, each escort would have to screen only 4.5 miles of perimeter, a manageable task. In the latter case each escort was responsible for 6.5 miles, a much more challenging proposition. With a total of only four escorts available, moreover, one at most could be detached to chase approaching submarines, whereas with a total of eight, two or three could be sent out to ward off the enemy without virtually denuding the merchant ships of their protective screen.

Better founded were the Admiralty's concerns about the dangers of linking up the HX and SC convoys in the miserable conditions off Newfoundland, and the serious reduction in the carrying power of fully half of the fast ships in the North Atlantic convoys because every second HX convoy could only proceed at the speed of the old, slow vessels in the attached SC convoys. Unsurprisingly, the Americans approved the British scheme to sail more and faster convoys, and

49.   Adm to C-in-C WA, NSHQ, COAC, RA 3 BS, BAD, 1400a/13 Aug. 1941, "Memoranda Re: BJSM Matters," NARA, RG 38, Series VII, Anglo-American Cooperation, box 117; Danckwerts to McDowell, 15 and 17 Aug. 1941, "Atlantic Area ... No. 1," NARA, RG 38, Series VII, Box 116

50.   The attempt to increase the carrying power of the beleaguered merchant fleet by sailing these moderately fast ships as independents to avoid the delays of convoy failed dismally; heavy losses to U-boats confirmed the correctness of the earlier appreciation that only at fifteen knots or better could ships dependably avoid detection and pursuit by submarines.

all authorities accepted the resulting requirement for more frequent and larger slow convoys. Although the Navy Department warned that the USN could not begin escort operations before mid-September, the earliest that American and Icelandic shipping could be organized to sail according to the convoy schedules, the Admiralty pressed ahead with the new scheme.[51] At the end of August the shipping control staff described the rapid implementation of the changes with evident satisfaction:

> Convoy HX 144, which sailed [from Halifax, with 60 ships] on 10th August, was the last 9-knot convoy to be retarded on passage by having, for economy of escort, to keep in company with an SC 7¹/₂-knot convoy [SC 40, from Sydney on 10 August with 46 ships].
>
> Beginning on 29th August with Convoy H.X. 147, the convoy cycle has been changed to every six days for both HX and SC convoys. Minimum speeds are now 10 knots for inclusion in the former and 7¹/₂ knots for the latter.[52]

The effect was to increase the number of sailings from two every eleven days, that is a large HX convoy and still larger combined SC and HX convoy, to four sailings, two HX and two SC, each of a more moderate size, some fifty to sixty merchant ships apiece. The increase in demands on escorts was from three groups each eleven days (one for the HX and two for the combined HX and SC convoy), to four groups.

In theory, this was not a great additional burden. The British informed the Americans that the merchant convoy requirement would be for ten groups instead of "9 to 10." (The NEF, it will be recalled, was organized into twelve groups and, as Murray had confirmed in response to the Admiralty's signal of 13 August, he could, in terms of groups, accommodate the additional sailings.) The difficulty lay in the numbers of escorts. With barely enough ships in the NEF to sail four in each group, Murray had to all but disband the local Newfoundland Force so that its corvettes could stand in for NEF ships with breakdowns or due for refit. SC 41 exemplified the problem. Departing Sydney on 24 August, it was the first slow convoy since the inauguration of the NEF not to be combined with an HX convoy and thereby be screened by a double escort. During the first seven days of the twelve-day run between Newfoundland and Iceland, the sixty-six merchant ships had the protection of only the Town class destroyer *St Croix* and two corvettes. One of the three corvettes originally assigned had repeatedly broken down and returned to Newfoundland; a replacement, the Town HMS *Ramsey*, reached the convoy when it was just four days from the rendezvous with the British eastern Atlantic escort south of Iceland.[53] The double groups that had sailed with the combined convoys had allowed a greater margin for the unexpected; the loss of one or two escorts among a total of eight or nine warships was not nearly so critical as it was, in this case, to a single group of only four warships.

Any hope that the entry of the USN Atlantic Fleet into escort operations would ease the strain on the Canadians disappeared on 19 August, when King passed a copy of WPL-51 to NSHQ

51.   OPNAV to SPENAVO London, 23 Aug. 1941, file 1 pt 6, NARA, RG 313, Entry NHC 76, CONAVEU "Messages," box 1

52.   Adm, *MASR*, Aug. 1941, 18

53.   *St Croix*, "ROP—Escort Group 21—Convoy SC 41," 6 Sep. 1941, NAC, RG 24, 11334, 8280 SC 41; Gale, "Convoy Form D, Mercantile Convoy No. SC 41," 13 Sep. 1941, PRO, ADM 199/56; Escort "Arrivals and Departures" section of CCNF WD, Aug.1941, DHH, NHS NSS 1000-5-20, pt 1, confirms that *Ramsey* came all the way out from St John's to overtake the convoy.

through the US naval attaché in Ottawa Commander L. Lothrop and reminded the Canadians, in an echo of the leak of WPL-50, that the plan was for military eyes only: it should only be shown to the minimum number of senior civilians possible under the dominion's constitutional system. Lothrop also passed on King's pressing query as to what size of force the Canadians were ready to provide and under what conditions.[54] The reply revealed the extent to which Ottawa had been left out of the loop. The Canadians were under the impression that the USN Atlantic Fleet would escort most of the HX and SC convoys, and that the RCN was being called on to escort only those for which Icelandic and US-flagged merchant ships could not be arranged; the total RCN commitment would be only twenty ships, five destroyers, and fifteen corvettes.[55]

King responded that he, in fact, wanted the Canadians to look after all the SC convoys, "initially at least," meaning fully half of all convoys and the most vulnerable ones at that. Moreover, believing that five was "the minimum effective" number of escorts for any convoy—that would be the American standard—King considered "that the twenty escort vessels mentioned in your letter of August 20th are, in his opinion, inadequate. He hopes that you may be able to make available ten additional vessels in order that there may be six escort units of five ships each under the orders of the Royal Canadian Naval Service."[56]

The interchange between Admiral King and NSHQ hit the British delegation in Washington like a bombshell. It suddenly dawned on Admiral Little that the Americans were now building their plans on the verbal commitment Little believed he had obtained from Brodeur in mid-July, which assumed that the RCN would keep a running strength of twenty-eight escorts available in Newfoundland. Little had his staff rush a full explanation and a plea for help to Ottawa. If the Canadians baulked, he intimated, and instead met King's standard, the RN would not be able to withdraw British escorts from Newfoundland for the thinly defended southern routes in the eastern Atlantic, where convoys were now coming under strong attack:

> 2. During our discussions of Plan No. 4 the U.S. Authorities at first asked only for 20 Canadian escorts ... to join with U.S. Destroyers in providing ocean escort in the Western Atlantic ... Commodore Brodeur indicated that the number continuously available for ocean escort duty would be approximately 8 destroyers and 19 corvettes. These numbers were inserted in the later editions of Plan No. 4 and it is possible that the figures of 5 Canadian destroyers and 15 Canadian corvettes given in Captain Reid's letter to Commander Lothrop is the result of an oversight, the figures in the first edition of Plan No. 4 being repeated by mistake.

> 4. Admiral Little would be grateful, therefore ... that the number of 8 Canadian destroyers and 19 Canadian corvettes available for ocean escort duty in the Western Atlantic may be confirmed without delay.[57]

---

54. CINCLANT to ALUSNA, Ottawa, 19 Aug. 1941, file 1-31 Aug. 1941, NARA, RG 313, entry NHC 69, Atlantic Fleet secret messages, box 1; Lothrop to CNS, 19 Aug. 1941, NAC, RG 24, 11129, "Joint Defence Plan"

55. DCNS to Lothrop, 20 Aug. 1941, NAC, RG 24, 11129, "Joint Defence Plan"

56. Lothrop to CNS, 23 Aug. 1941, NAC, RG 24, 11129, "Joint Defence Plan"; CINCLANT to ALUSNA, Ottawa, 23 Aug. 1941, file 1-31 Aug. 1941, NARA, RG 313, entry NHC 69, Atlantic Fleet secret messages, box 1

57. Belben to Mackinlay, 23 Aug. 1941, NAC, RG 24, 11129, "Joint Defence Plan"

Top: Naval recruits marching at HMCS *York*, the naval reserve division in Toronto, February 1942. Note the mock-up of the *King George V* class battleship in the background. (NAC PA 204587)

Bottom: Officers relax in the corvette *Pictou*'s wardroom in March 1942. The commanding officer, Lieutenant Tony Griffin, RCNVR is standing at left. (NAC, PA 204598)

Top: Corvettes and Town class destroyers in the Halifax Dockyard in August 1941. Halifax Shipyards is in the immediate background. (NAC, PA 105509)

Right: HMCS *Lévis* goes down after being torpedoed by *U74* southeast of Greenland on 19 September 1941. (NAC, PA 204290)

These large questions landed in Ottawa at a less than ideal time. The minister, Admiral Nelles, and Captain F.L. Houghton, the Director of Plans, were all absent in the United Kingdom; the Director of the Trade Division Captain Brand was visiting the west coast, and in Washington Commodore Brodeur was on leave. Thus, the BAD's appeal came to Commodore H.E. Reid, the DCNS. Reid explained that Brodeur's reference to eight destroyers and nineteen corvettes had been to the total numbers of RCN ships in the NEF, and not the running strength that could be continuously maintained. In fact, five destroyers and fifteen corvettes, the force often mentioned in the documents the Canadians had seen, was the running strength that could be sustained from the twenty-seven escorts. In the critical matter of destroyers, Reid bluntly declared "we can give nothing more." All eight of the long-legged destroyers, "the only ones really suitable for the Newfoundland–Iceland escort," were already committed to that role. "We estimate that about one-third of the destroyer force will be continuously out of action for refit and repairs—Western Approaches had 50% out of action during last winter—and at the present moment only eight of our thirteen [destroyers] are in operation." Reid pointed out that it was essential to keep some of the short-legged destroyers at Halifax for escort of fast, high-value ships, including visiting capital warships, but neglected to mention that often only a single ship, *Annapolis*, the least effective of the Towns, was available for this duty.

For the moment, Reid agreed to maintain the NEF at its existing strength of twenty-five corvettes, that is, the original nineteen and the six originally assigned for local defence that had been effectively transferred to escort duties. He did, however, say that some of the eight destroyers might later be reassigned for troop convoys. Within the limits of this strength, he allowed, "We are quite prepared to accept the responsibility of providing AS escort for SC convoys." Although he suggested that additional new construction corvettes might at some point be available, he virtually ruled out the possibility for the near future: "We ... are not prepared to augment the above forces with untrained and inefficient units and should this strength be considered insufficient steps should be taken to retain additional RN destroyers of the Newfoundland Escort Force."[58] This was a telling argument, warning the senior powers that they could purchase a larger effort from the RCN only at the expense of continued inefficiency. It is not surprising that Reid made the linkage, for at this very time NSHQ—and Reid in particular—was grappling with the Admiralty's trenchant criticisms of the Canadian Town class destroyers and corvettes. Indeed, Reid's words echoed a strong letter that the Admiralty had sent to Ottawa in July:

> The new corvettes of the Royal Canadian Navy are completing in Canada and are being employed on escort duty in the Atlantic after working up in Canadian waters. It is presumed that the standard of efficiency of these corvettes is found to vary over a wide range, as was likely to be the case with their sister ships at Tobermory [ie, the ten corvettes that had operated in British waters]. My Lords have no doubt you will agree that, at a time when our convoy escort forces are reduced in strength in order to provide A/S escort right across the Atlantic, no reduction in individual efficiency can safely be accepted.[59]

---

58.   DCNS to assistant CNA, Washington, 25 Aug. 1941, NAC, RG 24, 11,505, MS 1550-146/36-1

59.   Adm to CNS, MA/SW 16 July 1941, RG 24, 6909, NSS 8970-330

The Admiralty offered the advice that it resolved similar problems of inefficiency among its own recently commissioned antisubmarine escorts by prolonged work-ups and by replacing inefficient officers and antisubmarine specialists with more promising or better trained personnel. NSHQ could only respond that Canada had no such reserve of trained personnel, and indeed had only recently been able to put the work-up organization at Halifax on a firm basis with officers who had been relieved from sea duty.[60] For the RCN, in other words, such options were a luxury if operational tempo was to be maintained.

A long personal letter from Vice-Admiral Kennedy-Purvis, C-in-C Americas and West Indies, to Admiral Pound in late August confirmed much of what the Canadian naval staff was telling the Admiralty:

> During my recent visit to Halifax and Ottawa I was much impressed with the great improvement in the administration and in the keenness of training since I first came out. The work in Halifax training establishments is well carried out insofar as instructors are available. Their chief trouble is the smallness of their nucleus of trained officers and men as compared with their very great growth in numbers. They are rather inclined to think that the addition of a stripe or so is the equivalent of experience ...
>
> I am not too happy about the efficiency of their A/S escorts at the present moment. Here again they suffer from lack of experience and hurried training. Captains of Armed Merchant Cruisers have told me of the relief they experience when met at the eastern rendezvous by British escort forces with their precision of manoeuvre and obvious knowledge of what they are there for and how to do it.[61]

The staff in Ottawa admitted things could improve, but only with British help. Happily, such help was forthcoming. At the end of August, precisely when the British and Americans were pushing for a bigger Canadian effort, NSHQ gratefully confirmed arrangements with the Admiralty whereby newly commissioned corvettes would receive only basic work-ups at Halifax and proceed to Tobermory in Scotland to complete the program at the much better staffed and equipped RN establishment there. Reid himself was instrumental in setting up this scheme, which in part accounts for his care in warning the British and the Americans that new Canadian corvettes should not be rushed into transatlantic operations.[62]

As Reid wrote, he almost certainly had to hand a recent complaint from Commodore Murray in St John's that suggested NSHQ was already making counterproductive haste in the manning and training of new construction ships.[63] So great was the shortage of trained personnel that *Stadacona* in Halifax could find qualified and specialist ratings only by stripping them out of ships already in service. Murray blasted this practice, complaining that "during a recent visit to Halifax":

> the ship's company of HMCS "Collingwood" was reduced again to the standard of that of a newly commissioned ship by the drafting away, under orders of "Stadacona," of all

---

60. CNS to Adm, 29 Aug. 1941, ibid

61. C-in-C AWI to First Sea Lord, 25 Aug. 1941, PRO, ADM 205/7 pt 2

62. CNS to Adm, 29 Aug. 1941. Reid had initiated arrangements for Canadian corvettes to continue to go through the Tobermory program when he visited the UK in July. See CCCS to NSHQ, 19 July 1941, NAC, RG 24 (acc 83-84/167), 218, NSS 1400-WPL-51

63. DCNS to CCNF, "Most Secret and Personal," 25 Aug. 1941. NAC, RG 24 (acc 83-84/167), 218, NSS 1400-WPL-51, "suggestions that you have recently put forward have to await the return of the C.N.S. and Minister."

three Leading Seamen ... including the two most reliable S.D. [Submarine Detection] ratings.

2. Removals from the crew of HMCS "Niagara" were of a similar nature ...

5. It is desired, for the recreation of the ships' companies, and to reduce the congestion in St. John's Harbour, to send each group in turn to Halifax for one of their boiler cleaning periods.

6. It will be unfortunate if I cannot send H.M.C. Ships to their home port ... in order to prevent those ships' companies, who have been worked up to a state of efficiency suitable for escort in submarine waters, from being put back into such a low state that I hesitate to send them with a convoy.

7. It is pointed out that the ship's companies of H.M.C. Ships, (including our best destroyers), have reached their existing state of efficiency, not through the number of higher non-substantive ratings borne, but almost entirely through having worked together from scratch, through being trained by their own officers whom they learn to appreciate, and by constant work with each other. The resultant efficiency is far above that of any one individual, but it only remains as long as that team is kept together.[64]

The Tobermory scheme, in fact, went some way towards meeting Murray's recommendation that increased collective training of new, inexperienced crews was preferable to parachuting experienced individuals in and out of ships, but at a pace of only three corvettes with intervals of some weeks, it was clearly a long-term solution, not a quick fix to immediate operational demands.

Despite agreeing with Murray's call for improved training of new ships, NSHQ nevertheless (and paradoxically) imposed increased operational challenges on his command with no promise of reinforcement. On 25 August Reid immediately forwarded a copy of his response to the British and Americans to St John's with a personal note that was sympathetic, but brutally frank:

> As the United States are sending two of their Merchant Flag Ships to Halifax on September 10th, it is anticipated they will start escorting H.X. convoys about September 15th. When this commences, it is our task to take over the escort of SC and TC [troopship] convoys with Canadian Forces ... The force that I have enumerated in the attached letter [.i.e, Murray's existing force of eight destroyers and 25 corvettes] is all that we can spare at the moment ... If you consider this force inadequate, attempt will be made to retain some RN destroyers, but we anticipate great difficulty in convincing the Admiralty of the need for them when the main attack is taking pace on the Sierra Leone & Gibraltar convoy route.
>
> If you experience difficulty, and you probably will, in providing escort for TC convoys, we may have to use one or two of COAC's "short legs" to assist. The orders for withdrawal of R.N. Forces will probably be issued before the anticipated date of WPL 51 being put into force, that is about September 15th.
>
> I hope that CNS and Houghton will have some information upon their return [from Britain] this week. We have experienced great difficulty in getting information from Washington as to what their plans are and when they intend to put them in force. As

64. CCNF to NSec, 14 Aug. 1941. NAC, RG 24, 11929, 00-220-3-6

a consequence, up to now, we have not been able to give you much help. However, I think the way is clearer and this may be of some assistance to you.[65]

As it was, however, the situation was not quite so bleak as Reid believed. Nelles did, in fact, receive assurance at the Admiralty that the RN would continue to protect TC convoys "until a later date ... when the Americans had had experience of escorting mercantile convoys."[66] Although welcome, that still left Murray with a daunting task at very short notice.

Both British and American officers in Washington were shocked at how King had barrelled in and decided that the Canadians—a navy of which he knew very little—accept responsibility for all the SC convoys. Rear-Admiral Danckwerts, RN, an officer not noted for his patience with Canada, nevertheless despatched a thinly veiled attack on King to Rear-Admiral Turner: "I am somewhat disturbed at the situation at present existing as between the Commander-in-Chief, Atlantic Fleet, and the Canadian Command ... it seems that there has been so far little direct contact between the two and good deal of misunderstanding, particularly as regards the numbers of escorts available and required." King's demands on the Canadians, he suggested, were doing little "to hasten the full adoption of WPL 51, and the consequent relief of British escorts, which are so badly needed elsewhere."[67]

Admiral Stark was equally surprised at the news of King's methods. "We have been wrestling with this problem in the hope that we would not have to ask the British to augment the Canadian Forces," he reminded the fleet commander. Although "sufficient" escort for the convoys might require British assistance, did King really need it? The Canadians, able to guarantee a running strength of five destroyers and fifteen corvettes, could only really sustain three escort groups, leaving a requirement for eight others to match the Anglo-Canadian organization of eleven groups—ten to maintain the schedule and one spare for necessary reliefs. King had enough destroyers in the Atlantic Fleet to form eight groups of five vessels each, so why was he holding back so many from mercantile escort in units for heavy ship screens and "emergency" forces in a navy not yet at war? And why, Stark wanted to know, was King being so standoffish with the Canadians?

> I cannot help but feel that a personal contact between you and the Canadian Chief of Staff, Admiral Reid [*sic*], would be very helpful. You would get to know each other, talk over the problems involved first-hand. I know that in writing to Admiral Pound I now feel on a very different basis from what I did before our recent meeting [at Placentia Bay] took place. I would be delighted if you would hop up there and see Admiral Reid ... I believe it would be genuinely helpful—all-round.[68]

King responded to Stark's admonitions on 29 August with a stubborn nationalism that, much as he himself was impressed by Admiral Pound when they met at Placentia Bay, was steeped in the traditional American mistrust of the British. "I have *now* 8 escort units of 5 ships each *in sight*," King admitted to Stark, but he did not want to unbalance the organization of the Atlantic Fleet, compromise the proper fitting out and upkeep of ships, and sacrifice the training and necessary rest for their crews by attempting too much too quickly. His flat rejection of Stark's recommenda-

---

65. DCNS to CCNF, "Most Secret and Personal," 25 Aug. 1941

66. "Min of Mtg Held in the Upper War Room, Admiralty ... 13 Aug., 1941," NAC, RG 24, 3842, NSS 1017-10-23

67. Danckwerts to Turner, 26 Aug. 1941, "WPL-51," NARA, RG 38, Series IX, box 147K

68. CNO to CINCLANT, 27 Aug. 1941, E.J. King official papers, DHH 91/431 mfm

tion that he should release for mercantile convoy duty destroyers permanently assigned as screens for heavy ship groups—something the British themselves were doing, as Stark advised King— again suggests that King remembered too well the events of the First World War, when the release of all available destroyers to RN commands for convoy duty had, by paralyzing the heavy ship units of the US fleet, essentially handed operational control of American forces over to the Admiralty. "I think—as usual—that the British are much too intent on managing *our* affairs—and the Canadian." King begged Stark for support in a hard line:

> I hope you will see fit to put all possible pressure on the British and Canadians to pro-
> vide and maintain a *net of 30* escort vessels (6 units of 5 or 5 units of 6), instead of the
> *net of 20* which they *say* only are available ... in a pinch ... we can furnish an occasional
> escort unit for the "slow convoys" but the convoy *must* have in it an Icelandic *or* US flag
> ship. I prefer to keep this probability "up my sleeve"—and hope you will.

King was determined to exercise full US control in the western Atlantic and on the terms that best suited the interests of the USN. Perhaps the clearest indication of his attitude was his refusal to lower himself, as he saw it, by visiting Ottawa:

> Please do not let people worry you about our cooperation with the Canadians ... as I have
> all of that in hand ... I do not think it "becoming" that I should go to the Canadians in
> person, as your letter proposes—but—I will be glad to confer with their *principal* naval
> people, either here [in his flagship, then at Newport, Rhode Island] or in Washington.[69]

King had, in fact, already established direct contact with the Canadians. Captain C.F. Bryant, commanding officer of the battleship USS *Arkansas*, visited Murray in St John's on 26 August, and Captain F.S. Low, of King's personal staff, met Reid in Ottawa on 27 August. Low found a "coop-erative and genuinely friendly attitude" and reported to King that Reid "asked me to express to you his keen appreciation of your having established this initial liaison." The Canadians were "gener-ally very pleased with proposal that they take SC, we HX convoys." They would be able to take on the SC convoys, however, only if the British indeed accepted responsibility for the troop convoys— NSHQ had still not learned of the Admiralty's recent commitment to Nelles in London. But even with that assistance, they could provide units of only four escorts, one destroyer and three corvettes, which the Canadian officers also admitted was inadequate. When Low "invited attention to Commodore Murray's minimum of 6, they concurred (said they would like 12) but pointed out that they had no other ships. They feel that pressure for British DD [destroyers] must come from CNO." This appeal for American help in dealing with the British impressed King. So too did Low's report of his inquiry "as to the status of British DD ... employed [in escorting troop convoys] or ... added to [Canadian] groups for escort purposes." The Canadians replied "that RN ships are always under RN." This state of affairs, Low warned King, "requires clarification and is important."[70]

One wonders if Low—or King—understood the full extent to which Murray operated under the orders of the RN's Western Approaches Command and, in the case of the British escorts, did little more than schedule such ships as Western Approaches assigned to him. Or did they understand perfectly, and anticipate that the British would exert control over any of their ships allocated to

---

69.   CINCLANT to CNO, 29 Aug. 1941, ibid

70.   Low to CINCLANT, "Liaison Visit to Ottawa, Aug. 27, 1941," 28 Aug. 1941, ibid

help the Canadians so as to counterbalance the authority of the US Atlantic Fleet when it assumed control in the western ocean? Whatever his knowledge of the existing Commonwealth organization, King believed that the British were determined to hang on to the strings in the western Atlantic. The one piece of hard evidence King offered Stark of British untrustworthiness came from Low's report:

> Both in Ottawa (direct) and in St John's (implied) I learned that [Canadian] experience has been that the British have not placed—and do not intend to place—RN ships under Canadian naval control ... [if Admiral] Bristol [is to be] in charge of ordinary escort-of -convoy matters ... he has British officers attached to his staff, which I consider "undesirable" so long as he is to cooperate with Canadians, as there seems to be enough "friction" in that quarter now.[71]

The enthusiasm with which King leapt on the evidence of tensions between the Canadians and British, and Reid's appeal for American help in dealing with the Admiralty, is unsurprising in view of the deep suspicions of British intentions that the American admiral harboured. The Canadians, it seemed, supported full US control in the western Atlantic, and this accounts for King's assurance to Stark that he and the Canadians already understood one another.

Yet the tone of Low's report of his visit to Ottawa suggests that the Americans, no less than the British, were somewhat disinclined to treat with full gravity Canadian caution on national and operational grounds in expanding the RCN's ocean escort effort.

> The remaining 7 DD [sic, 5] are not only short legged (and hence, [the Canadians] state unsuitable for trans-Atlantic duty) but they feel under the necessity of having some available for escort of large ships too fast for corvettes to stay with ...
>
> They appear to be alive to the possibility of submarines operating off the approaches to Halifax (and other convoy assembly ports) and emphasize this as a reason that they must maintain a sufficient number of A/S vessels at and off such ports...
>
> While they concede that the 40 corvettes under construction will ultimately add to ocean escort strength they indicate delay in ultimate attainment because:
>
> (1) They are apparently committed to augmenting local defense forces including the West Coast where they now have but one corvette.
>
> (2) They refuse to place a new ship in this service until she is, in fact, ready. They have a 3 or 4 week shaking down period plus about an equal period of training for each new ship at a school in England.

The overall suggestion here—beyond an accurate assessment of the strategy Dönitz would adopt after Pearl Harbor—is that the RCN did, in fact, have additional resources that could be committed to ocean escort, and these passages were very likely the basis for King's appeal to Stark for help in pressing the Canadians as well as the British to maintain a running strength of thirty ocean escorts.

In one matter, Low found Canadian operational insights to be profound and useful. He and other members of King's staff were inclined to accept British advice about the importance of permanently assigning ships to specific escort groups. Rear-Admiral A.L. Bristol, USN, commanding the newly formed Support Force, did not agree because American destroyers were already organ-

---

71. CINCLANT to CNO, 29 Aug. 1941

ized into permanent squadrons of six to nine sister or near-sister destroyers. In view of the fact that the proposed escort groups each would initially contain only five destroyers, and it would be necessary also to mix some from different classes so that each group would have the benefit of the newest and most capable vessels, Bristol thought it wisest to make temporary assignments from the well-established squadron organization. Low put the issue to the Canadians, who "emphasized (almost violently) their belief in the principle of integrity [of the escort groups]; said they and the British practiced it and consider it 'essential'—with regularly designated group commanders. They concede the necessity of minor departures but maintain that the nucleus is always there and that the coordination and indoctrination resulting from this practice is worth all the effort exerted to maintain these groups."[72] What the Canadians do not appear to have explained was that the instability of the NEF's composition and its overcommitment had made it impossible for Murray, as has been seen, to introduce permanent group organization until the latter part of July, and it was not yet effectively functioning because of the shortage of ships.

Admiral King could not believe that with "thirty-three or more destroyers and corvettes" in the NEF, the Canadians could guarantee that only twenty would be available for operations. He thought that the Canadians could provide five escort groups, each with a running strength of five ships.[73] Murray, in fact, was doing better than that. Captain Bryant reported after his visit to Newfoundland that Murray, in anticipation of an early order for the withdrawal of all British ships from the NEF, was already reorganizing the Canadian ships into six groups, each with five or six ships. These would be adequate to meet the SC cycle, although each group would have a running strength of only four or five ships. In this, as in other aspects of cooperative measures to prepare for the USN entry into convoy escort, King and Bryant were impressed by Murray's positive and open attitude. Something of the sense in the US Atlantic Fleet that the Canadians, in contrast to the British, could be trusted can be seen in Bryant's report: "Someone is endeavoring to get us to furnish more escorts probably Admiral Commanding Western Approaches. Do not believe Canadians are in on this. Certainly not CCNF. He is planning to have six groups and thinks you might be able to get along with five. I earnestly request you do not quote him on this."[74]

On 13 September, four days before a USN destroyer group would begin its first mercantile convoy escort, taking over HX 150 from the local Canadian escort, King despatched his instructions to Murray. In view of the United States' neutrality and Canada's status as a combatant, King was uncharacteristically diplomatic. "Dear Sir," he addressed Murray,

> As I do not consider it appropriate, in the current circumstances, to include the forces under your command in my operation plans nor to write to you a formal letter of instructions, I enclose herewith ... the draft of such a letter, which I hope you will find appropriate and useful in effecting the necessary cooperation.
>
> The liaison already effected through Captain Bryant (Arkansas) appears to have been adequate for all immediate needs but I request and urge you to communicate to me such inquiries as may tend to promote effective cooperation.

72. Low to CINCLANT, "Liaison Visit to Ottawa, Aug. 27, 1941"

73. CINCLANT to OPNAV, 8 Sep. 1941, file 1-20 Sep. 1941, messages from CINCLANT, NARA, RG 313, Entry NHC 69, Atlantic Fleet Secret Messages, box 1

74. CO USS *Arkansas* to CINCLANT, 11 Sep. 1941, file 1-20 Sep. 41, NARA, RG 313, Entry NHC 69, file 1-20 Sep. 1941, messages to CINCLANT, box 1

With all good wishes for success in the aims which we have in common—and with cordial personal greetings.[75]

Arrangements for RCN defence of the SC convoys under the direction of the US Atlantic Fleet thus appeared finally to have been put into place. The RCN had undertaken to stretch its resources to meet US needs, but with the tacit agreement that the USN should help in pressing the RN to meet any Canadian shortfall. This was almost all King's work, the product of his direct dealing with the Canadians. As we have seen, he told even his own chief, Admiral Stark, to stand aside when Stark had suggested King might reach more deeply into his own resources to reduce the pressure on the Canadians and allow the RN to withdraw fully from the waters west of Iceland. But even as King concluded the arrangements on his own terms, events at sea demonstrated that the Canadians were already desperately overextended.

It is important at this point to reflect briefly on the repercussions of the almost casual acceptance by NSHQ that the RCN would escort the SC convoys. First, as we have seen, and as we will continue to see, the navy simply did not have the ships—let alone trained ships—to fulfil the commitments it had undertaken. Second, because they made slow headway, usually about five to seven knots, the SC convoys were always the most vulnerable in the North Atlantic convoy system because their passages took longer and they were less able to manoeuvre around U-boat patrol lines. Consequently, as operational research reports would later show, ships in slow convoys stood a 30 percent greater chance of being torpedoed than those in fast convoys.[76] Although the RCN's inexperience and lack of trained, well-equipped ships played a role in what followed, there is no question the navy's reputation suffered as a result of the decisions that left it with the main escort responsibility of the slow SC convoys—those likeliest to be attacked. In the vernacular, the cards were stacked against the RCN by decisions taken at an NSHQ fully cognizant of the risks involved in meeting the wishes of its allies. Unhappily, as it turned out, the RCN held fewer trump cards than anyone could have predicted.

Disasters seldom, if ever, have a single cause. They are the product of many circumstances and events, interwoven, as it seems in retrospect, with a relentless and increasing tightness, much as one carefully stacks wood on paper and kindling, and then lights a match. The records of convoy SC 42, which sailed from Sydney on the morning of 30 August, convey precisely that sense of impending doom, unfavourable turn succeeding unfavourable turn, always at the worst possible moments.[77]

SC 42 was only the second of the slow convoys to sail alone, without the benefit of the double escort provided in the combined SC/HX convoys. Moreover, because it sailed so early in the reorganized cycle, there had not yet been time to balance the numbers of merchant vessels among the

---

75. CINCLANT to CCNF, 13 Sep. 1941, NAC, RG 24, 3974, NSS 1048-48-27

76. Cited in Milner, *North Atlantic Run*, 61

77. The best published accounts of the SC 42 battle are Bernard Edwards, *Attack and Sink!: The Battle for Convoy SC 42* (Corfu 1995), and Douglas and Rohwer, "'The Most Thankless Task' Revisited: Convoys, Escorts, and Radio Intelligence in the Western Atlantic, 1941-43," in J.A. Boutilier (ed), *RCN in Retrospect, 1910-1968*, (Vancouver 1982), 193-207. Unless noted otherwise, the basic reference for this account is the excellent narrative produced by the Admiralty Anti-Submarine Division, "Analysis of U-Boat Attacks on Convoy SC 42, 9-16 Sep. 1941," that was published in Adm, *MASR*, Oct. 1941, 20-35.

HX convoys and the now more numerous SC ones to produce the moderately sized convoys that the new schedules were designed to achieve. As a result, SC 42 was large. Sixty-two merchant ships departed from Sydney, and five more joined from Wabana, the anchorage in Conception Bay near St John's, where ships loaded in Newfoundland assembled. These numbers created an impossibly long perimeter for the standard western-ocean escort group of only four warships to protect.[78]

The senior ship, *Skeena*, was arguably as experienced and professional a destroyer as any then on the North Atlantic run. Lieutenant-Commander J.C. Hibbard, RCN, affectionately known in the fleet as "Jumpin' Jimmy" on account of his excitability on the bridge, had assumed command in April 1940, shortly before *Skeena* crossed to Britain. As in all the Canadian River class destroyers, there was still a large proportion of regulars on board, including some of the RCN's most promising young officers. Of the three corvettes that made up the rest of the escort, *Orillia* and *Alberni* had been among the original seven vessels in Commander Prentice's work-up program at Halifax in the early spring, before they rushed into operations as charter members of the NEF in June. Their captains, Lieutenant W.E.S. Briggs and Lieutenant-Commander G.O. Baugh, were two of the more capable RCNR commanding officers. Still, their ships, although veterans in the Canadian sense of the word, had scarcely three months time on operations and were manned by RCNVR personnel with little previous experience. The third corvette, *Kenogami* (Lieutenant-Commander R. "Cowboy" Jackson, RCNVR), had spent just over six weeks at Halifax fitting-out and working-up, after commissioning on 29 June.[79]

The arrangements for SC 42 seem at first sight to have been a recipe for disaster. In fact, they were built on success. The reorganization of the convoys, essential to increase the carrying power of the merchant fleet's best ships, also ensured that American assistance, only days away and expected to be on a considerably larger scale than proved to be the case, could immediately be deployed to the best effect. No transatlantic convoy, moreover, had come under sustained attack in over two months, the last being HX 133 in late June. That convoy, too, had been lightly escorted, but it had been possible to make a timely reinforcement with escorts from nearby convoys not under direct threat, thanks to decrypts of German radio traffic, in combination with the well-developed system of HF/DF stations that now ringed the North Atlantic.

Despite the fact that the daily settings for Enigma machines had expired at the end of July, Bletchley Park was still in a position to provide useful information. The decryption staff had amassed enough information about German naval signals and encryption procedures to narrow the nearly infinite possible settings to a number that could be tested within days rather than weeks or months.[80] Electrical-mechanical "bombes," whose wiring duplicated that of the Enigma

---

78. It will be recalled that in the spring, when Admiralty officials were faced with the challenge of transocean escort of convoys, they had cited the ineffectiveness of four-ship units, the largest, as they accurately predicted, that could be provided for that duty, as a major reason for not attempting that measure. It will also be recalled that in British waters several slow convoys had suffered heavy losses to very small numbers of U-boats during the autumn of 1940, even though those convoys were smaller than SC 42, and protected by four-ship groups entirely comprised of destroyers and sloops, vessels considerably more effective than the corvettes that made up the bulk of the group that joined SC 42 outside the Strait of Belle Isle on 2 Sep. Mackenzie, "Mercantile Convoy No. 'SC 42,' Convoy Form D," 20 Sep. 1941, PRO, ADM 199/56

79. Macpherson and Burgess, *Ships of Canada's Naval Forces*, 35, 68, 78, 82

80. German navy procedure was to change the rotors in the Enigma machine every two days, selecting three from a total of eight; these three were placed in varying order in the machine. On the second day, the principal change was only the starting setting on each of these same rotors, which remained in the same order. R. Erskine, "Naval Enigma: A Missing Link," *International Journal of Intelligence and Counterintelligence* 3 (1989), 499, and "Naval Enigma: The Breaking of Heimisch and Triton," *Intelligence and National Security* 3 (Jan. 1988), 164-8

machines, rapidly ran settings to select the one that produced a meaningful text. It took Bletchley "about three days to solve the settings for the first of a pair of days of August traffic, and under 24 hours for those of the second day," which gave "an average delay of 50 hours." That was normally good enough to divert convoys clear of danger, given the near instant availability of approximate positions from the direction-finding system when the U-boats themselves signalled, the fact it usually took some days for U-boats to reach newly assigned positions, and the compilation in the Submarine Tracking Room at the Admiralty of a full picture of U-boat deployments based on meticulous analysis of all information from all sources.[81]

There was, of course, risk, but there was the need to accept risk in order to assure continued success. Ironically, the threat to SC 42 developed in part because of the very effectiveness of British defence measures. The Admiralty had routed the convoy to the north, towards Greenland, to take it over the top of a large group of U-boats, *Markgraf*, southwest of Iceland. Not only had these boats, deployed in compact patrol lines, failed to locate any shipping, but maritime patrol aircraft based in Iceland had damaged two of them, enabling surface vessels to destroy another and capture a fourth. On 6 September, therefore, BdU ordered fourteen boats to take up widely scattered patrol areas from midway between Iceland and Greenland down to Cape Farewell and some 400 miles further south, thus covering in a very loose fashion the central and northern routes between Newfoundland and Iceland.[82] By a stroke of bad luck, and it was nothing more, Bletchley Park could not decrypt the orders for this movement west until 8 September, when it became clear, too late, that SC 42 was standing into danger.[83]

Even so, the Admiralty was able to divert most convoys to the south of this large area. One, the slow ON 12, was already west of Iceland and could remain on the northern route in the high latitudes. SC 42, however, had run into an easterly gale on 3 September that raged on until the morning of 7 September. Stiff headwinds and heavy seas reduced its speed to as little as 2.56 knots, so that by 8 September it was approaching Cape Farewell, seventy-two hours behind schedule instead of being, as it should have been, clear to the north of the new U-boat disposition. And the escorts, after the prolonged struggle to maintain their heading and keep contact with the merchant vessels in the teeth of the gale, were too low on fuel for the extra run of several hundred miles necessary for a diversion to the south. Thus committed to the Greenland route, they were heading straight for the northwestern end of the new U-boat deployment. On the evening of 8 September the Admiralty diverted SC 42 straight north towards Cape Farewell hoping that, by hugging the eastern coast of Greenland, it could make an end run around the most westerly of the submarines, and then cut east again over top of the German patrol areas. It so happened that the fast westbound convoy ON 13 was approaching the waters south of Iceland, roughly along the latitude of 58°30" North, with an escort of five destroyers, four corvettes, and two antisubmarine trawlers. (This in contrast to the four escorts with the much larger SC 42 was vivid evidence of the difference in scale of the defences provided in the eastern Atlantic as compared to the western ocean.) British command authorities ordered the destroyers, HMS *Douglas* (SOE), *Leamington*, *Veteran*, *Skate*, and *Saladin* to detach for Iceland and refuel so they would be available as reinforcements. To provide

---

81. Ibid

82. BdU, KTB, 27 Aug.-6 Sep. 1941; Blair, *Hitler's U-Boat War*, 339-48

83. Douglas and Rohwer, "Most Thankless Task,"195-6

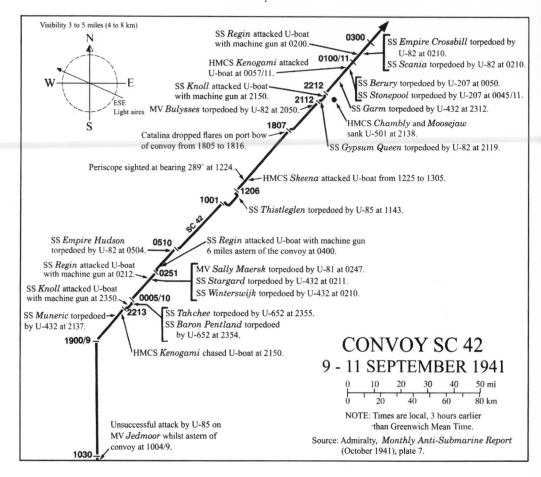

Visibility 3 to 5 miles (4 to 8 km)

N
W —— E
ESE
Light aires
S

SS *Regin* attacked U-boat with machine gun at 0200.

0300

SS *Empire Crossbill* torpedoed by U-82 at 0210.
SS *Scania* torpedoed by U-82 at 0210.

HMCS *Kenogami* attacked U-boat at 0057/11.

0100/11

SS *Knoll* attacked U-boat with machine gun at 2150.

2212

SS *Berury* torpedoed by U-207 at 0050.
SS *Stonepool* torpedoed by U-207 at 0045/11.

2112

SS *Garm* torpedoed by U-432 at 2312.

MV *Bulysses* torpedoed by U-82 at 2050.

1807

HMCS *Chambly* and *Moosejaw* sank U-501 at 2138.

Catalina dropped flares on port bow of convoy from 1805 to 1816.

SS *Gypsum Queen* torpedoed by U-82 at 2119.

Periscope sighted at bearing 289° at 1224.

HMCS *Skeena* attacked U-boat from 1225 to 1305.

1206

1001

SS *Thistleglen* torpedoed by U-85 at 1143.

SC 42

SS *Empire Hudson* torpedoed by U-82 at 0504.

0510

SS *Regin* attacked U-boat with machine gun 6 miles astern of the convoy at 0400.

SS *Regin* attacked U-boat with machine gun at 0212.

0251

MV *Sally Maersk* torpedoed by U-81 at 0247.
SS *Stargard* torpedoed by U-432 at 0211.
SS *Winterswijk* torpedoed by U-432 at 0210.

SS *Knoll* attacked U-boat with machine gun at 2350.

0005/10

SS *Muneric* torpedoed by U-432 at 2137.

2213

SS *Tahchee* torpedoed by U-652 at 2355.
SS *Baron Pentland* torpedoed by U-652 at 2354.

1900/9

HMCS *Kenogami* chased U-boat at 2150.

CONVOY SC 42
9 - 11 SEPTEMBER 1941

0   10   20   30   40   50 mi
0   20   40   60   80 km

NOTE: Times are local, 3 hours earlier than Greenwich Mean Time.

Source: Admiralty, *Monthly Anti-Submarine Report* (October 1941), plate 7.

Unsuccessful attack by U-85 on MV *Jedmoor* whilst astern of convoy at 1004/9.

1030

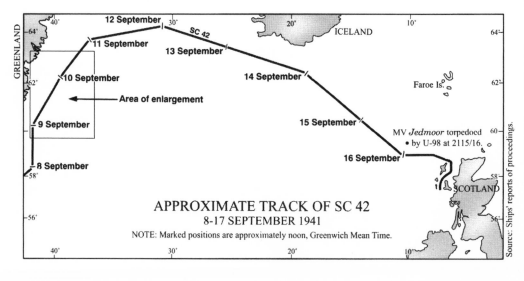

GREENLAND

40°   **12 September**   30°   SC 42   20°   ICELAND   10°   64°
64°   **11 September**
13 September
10 September
←—— **Area of enlargement**   **14 September**   Faroe Is.   62°
62°
9 September   **15 September**
8 September   MV *Jedmoor* torpedoed   60°
58°   by U-98 at 2115/16.   **16 September**
SCOTLAND   58°

56°   56°

40°   30°   20°   10°

APPROXIMATE TRACK OF SC 42
8-17 SEPTEMBER 1941
NOTE: Marked positions are approximately noon, Greenwich Mean Time.

a further reserve, instead of sending a Newfoundland group out from Iceland, to take over the escort of ON 13 for the western part of its voyage, routing authorities in the United Kingdom diverted the convoy southward and dispersed it when the corvettes and trawlers remaining from the Western Approaches escort had to return to port.[84]

A more modest but unconventional reinforcement was also on its way. In August, while commanding *Chambly* and as Senior Officer Corvettes, Commander Prentice had returned from the nearly constant convoy operations undertaken since June to take up local defence duties and to train the most recently commissioned corvettes before they started ocean escort. (The pressure of operations and unexpected breakdowns of ships had again overtaken the scheme. *Chambly* had to sail for a patrol to the Strait of Belle Isle until late in August, and then only one of the newly arrived corvettes, *Moose Jaw*, could be assigned to Prentice's group.[85]) Thus, on 4 September, while struggling to put together an exercise program with the limited facilities available at St John's, Prentice noticed in the Admiralty's daily signal of estimated U-boat positions the initial movement of a large number of U-boats west of Iceland. He persuaded Commodore Murray and Captain Stevens that instead of carrying on with their local training program, *Chambly* and *Moose Jaw* should "top up with fuel tomorrow ... and then sail to work up together on a cruise on convoy routes."[86]

Prentice was seizing the opportunity to realize his ambition of organizing a special submarine hunting group, free of responsibility for escort, and ready to support any threatened convoy by sweeping well ahead to catch U-boats that were moving up on the surface to attacking positions.[87] It was a bold, almost reckless initiative. Although *Moose Jaw* was one of the very few corvettes commanded by a regular force officer, Lieutenant F.E. Grubb, RCN, most of his inexperienced crew, missing several key specialist personnel, "was seasick for the first four days at sea, some of them being quite incapable of carrying out their duties."[88]

As luck would have it, after days of thick weather, when SC 42 passed Cape Farewell and proceeded up the Greenland coast, visibility was excellent, and nothing could persuade ships in the convoy to stop making smoke, which the Convoy Commodore later reported "was [doubtless] visible for at least thirty miles."[89] At about daybreak on 9 September *U 85*, under the command of Oberleutnant-zur-See Greger and westernmost of the *Markgraf* group, sighted "smoke plumes" and, after positioning himself ahead of SC 42, a manoeuvre that took several hours, made a submerged daylight attack, firing four torpedoes from close range into the merchant ships at the rear. One torpedo failed to leave the tube, and the other three missed. Then, shortly after 1000 local

84. *Skeena*, "ROP SC 42," 15 Sep. 1941, "SC 42," DHH 81/520/8280, box 9 (hereafter *Skeena* ROP); "ON 12" and "ON 13," DHH 88/1 mfm, reel 6; Douglas and Rohwer, "Most Thankless Task," 195-7 (this account incorrectly states that ON 12 was diverted south and ON 13 diverted north).

85. CCNF to Adm, 1745z, 1751z, 1759z/10 Aug. 1941, and CCNF to NSHQ, 1324z /11 Aug. 1941, and 1531z/31 Aug. 1941, file C-15, "Group 11—Organisation"; CCNF WD, Aug. 1941

86. Adm to "all concerned," "Estimated U-Boat Disposition," 1430a/3 Sep. 1941 and 1410a/4 Sep. 1941, Capt (D) Newfoundland to CCNF, "Secret Hand Message," 1733z/4 Sep. 1941, CCNF to Capt (D) Newfoundland, "Secret Hand Message," 1856/4 Sep. 1941, staff officer (operations) to *Chambly*, nd, CCNF to *Chambly*, *Moose Jaw*, 1858/4 Sep. 1941, file 7, A.F. Pickard papers, DHH, 80/125

87. *Chambly* ROP, 14 Sep. 1941, NAC, RG 24, 6901, NSS 8910-339/21; Prentice to Tucker, 18 Jan.1947, "SC 42," DHH, 81/520/8280, box 9

88. *Moose Jaw* to Capt (D) Newfoundland, 6 Nov. 1941, NAC, RG 24, 11334, 8280-SC 42

89. The convoy commodore, RAdm W.B. Mackenzie, RNR, quoted in *MASR,* Oct. 1941, 22

time, Greger fired from his stern tube at the transport *Jedmoor*, which was straggling behind the convoy. "Just at this moment," Greger recorded, "the steamer turned towards me. This shot therefore also missed. All of the shots were made using a target speed of 8 knots. However, I later established that the convoy was proceeding at 6 knots. What a dismal start ... It must be because it is our 13th day at sea!"[90]

A sweep by the escorts in response to *Jedmoor*'s report of torpedo tracks and a periscope turned up nothing, but C-in-C Western Approaches, informed by U-boat signals that emanated from the northern route between Iceland and Greenland, sailed reinforcements from Iceland for both SC 42 and ON 12, and Murray ordered *Chambly* and *Moose Jaw* to make for SC 42.[91] It would take Prentice's little group some twenty-four hours, and the ships coming from Iceland over thirty-six hours, to reach SC 42, and since excellent radio transmission conditions ensured that *U 85*'s contact report got through immediately to the other boats of *Markgraf* and BdU, a full-scale attack was well under way long before the arrival of reinforcements. At least three boats, on receiving Greger's sighting report, had already turned to intercept the convoy and thanks to the moderate seas, three of them, *U 81*, *U 432*, and *U 652*, had joined *U 85* by the early hours of darkness that same day.[92]

At 2130, Oberleutnant-zur-See Schultze's *U 432*, remaining submerged because of the bright moonlight, fired four torpedoes and drew first blood. At least two hit *Muneric*, loaded with iron ore at the rear of the port wing column, and the ship sank like a stone with all hands.[93] In the confusion of explosions, emergency rockets, and starshell, the escorts did not at first realize *Muneric* had disappeared. Schultze, hearing the sounds of pursuit—probably *Kenogami* which had already been "very much a nuisance" during his approach—laid low.[94] Greger in *U 85*, closing on the surface ahead of the port wing column, was shaken to see starshell bursting in his direction, probably from *Skeena* crossing the van of the convoy in response to the report of the attack on *Muneric*. Withdrawing in the direction of the Greenland coast, he found himself under pursuit from a "destroyer." It was actually *Kenogami*, which had sighted a submarine fleeing on the surface and given chase. Wanting to remain on the surface and to fire, Greger attempted weaving five degrees to each side of his course but, as he wrote in his log, "The destroyer closes rapidly, gradually turns to follow me. This is a cat and mouse game. I clear everyone off the bridge except myself." When *Kenogami* opened fire at 2158 Greger took his only option, an emergency dive.[95] Somehow,

90. *U 85*, KTB, 9 Sep. 1941. This states that Greger fired the first four, individually aimed shots into the rear of the convoy starting at 0859 local time, then manoeuvred and tracked *Jedmoor* for some time, before firing the single stern shot at 0903 local time, only four minutes after he had begun the initial attack on the rear of the convoy, a clear impossibility. British sources state that *Jedmoor* saw the torpedo track at 1004, local time, which is probably correct, as this would have allowed Greger an hour and four minutes rather than only four minutes for the sequence of events he describes. See Coppock to Douglas, 21 Mar. 1980, "SC 42," W.A.B. Douglas files, DHH.

91. C-in-C WA to [Flag Officer Iceland?], repeated Adm, escorts SC 42, CCNF, 1521a/9 Sep. 1941, DHH 80/125 ordered reinforcements to sail from Iceland for SC 42. "ROP of Senior Officer Escort ON 12," 16 Sep. 1941, "ON 12," DHH 88/1 mfm, reel 6 shows that HMS *Worcestershire*, and *Ramsey*, *Buctouche*, and *Galt* reached ON 12, just west of Iceland, at 0900z/ 10 Sep., thus reinforcing the escort to a total of three destroyers and four corvettes. See also file "ON 13," ibid, *Chambly* ROP, 14 Sep. 1941.

92. Drent, "SC 42 Sequence of U-Boats Incidents," 2 June 1999, DHH, 2000/5

93. All figures for casualties in merchant ships are from *Lloyds' War Losses* I, 288-90.

94. *U 432*, KTB, 10 Sep. 1941; *Skeena* ROP

95. *U 85, KTB*, 10 Sep. 1941

Kenogami had not been supplied with starshell and so could not indicate her position for *Skeena* to join. Nevertheless, *U 85* did not dare to surface for nearly two more hours.[96]

As Greger dove for cover, several merchant ships in the centre of the van reported a U-boat on the surface, probably *U 81*, and opened fire, causing a fourth submarine, *U 652* under Oberleutnant-zur-See Fraatz, to abort its approach.[97] A little less than two hours later, Fraatz pushed right into the convoy from the starboard quarter, selecting a tanker as his target "beyond which there are sufficient other targets for the remaining available bow tubes." For his pains, *U 652* "was fired on with 8.8 cm. shells by the rear-most ship in the right-hand column, range 300 m. Red tracer fire from a 2 cm. machine gun is being directed above the conning tower and the net cutter from my port quarter."[98]

The merchant ships providing this hot reception broke radio silence to report the situation. From *Skeena*'s bridge, Hibbard could see rockets on the starboard quarter of the convoy, and as he received the report he increased to eighteen knots and steamed between columns seven and eight, right down the centre of the convoy, as it executed an emergency turn of 45 degrees to port. "Ships in columns 7 and 8 were steering various courses," stated Hibbard, "and full speed ahead and astern had to be used on the engines to avoid collision." Unable to fire starshell because of its blinding effect, Hibbard switched on his navigation and fighting lights and manouevred precariously as captains shouted sighting reports to him by megaphone. *Skeena* "was between columns 6 and 7 ... when the U-boat was sighted. #74 [SS *Southgate*] called by megaphone that a submarine was on her starboard beam. At about [2354 SS *Tahchee* and SS *Baron Pentland* were hit by torpedoes; these ships were] ... within about 200 yards of HMCS 'Skeena' on the starboard quarter." Unable to ram with merchant ships so close, Hibbard fired starshell and dropped a pattern of charges on the position of the sighting.[99] *U 652* did not see *Skeena*, but was now coming under accurate fire from the merchant ships, and therefore crash-dived the instant it had fired two torpedoes. That Fraatz did not suspect the presence of the destroyer made *Skeena*'s counter attacks all the more unnerving. He counted seven charges and thought they must have been dropped by the merchant ship that had fired on him:

> There were no escorts in the close vicinity. Opened out on courses between 220 and 150. Screw noises are heard in the listening device from two vessels, rapidly turning screws, which station themselves on the port and starboard quarters and the vessel on the port quarter appears to be equipped with an asdic device ...
>
> When I turn around course 180 the screw noises reappear. I suspect the presence of a piece of search gear, in any case I do not understand the small number of well-aimed depth charges.

The aggressiveness of Hibbard and the merchant ship captains may have appeared chaotic and ineffective, but it kept Fraatz under for the next nine hours. Although he then pursued the convoy,

96. Ibid; *Skeena* ROP; *Kenogami*, "ROP, Convoy SC 42," 21 Sep. 1941, PRO, ADM 199/55

97. *U 81* shot four torpedoes at the lead ships in the centre columns at 2203 to 2204, but scored no hits. *U 81*, KTB, 10 Sep. 1941; Rohwer, *Axis Submarine Successes*, 64

98. *U 652*, KTB, 10 Sep. 1941. Times have been converted to local, which was five hours earlier than the Central European Time kept by the U-boats.

99. *Skeena* ROP. He reported that *Winterswijk* was sunk at this time, but the Admiralty's postaction analysis, which included interviews with the merchant personnel as well as the escorts' reports, concluded that it had been hit at 0210/10 Sep. Adm, *MASR*, Oct. 1941. This has been confirmed by Rohwer, *Axis Submarine Successes*, 64.

he did so cautiously, eventually making two attacks that missed their targets, which in both cases appear to have been stragglers behind the main body.[100]

At 0029 on 10 September, *Skeena* ordered *Orillia* to drop astern and rescue the survivors of *U 652*'s successful thrust into the centre of the convoy. *U 432* saw the corvette falling back, and Schultze got through the resulting gap in the screen to work his way up the dark port side. Beginning at 0207, he fired four torpedoes that sank SS *Stargard* in the port wing column and SS *Winterswijk* in the second column. "Powerful explosion," he recorded, "white-coloured explosive cloud, sinking not observed as the sky is now brightly illuminated by starshells, depth charges are being dropped and 2 corvettes [in fact, almost certainly *Skeena* and *Kenogami*] are closing the boat"—the large cloud probably came from *Winterswijk*, which was carrying a cargo of phosphates and lost twenty people from a crew of thirty-three. While *U 432* was making its escape from *Skeena* and *Kenogami*, *U 81* was closing the opposite, starboard, side of the convoy. Between 0228 and 0253, Oberleutnant-zur-See Guggenberger fired five torpedoes, the last of which sank MV *Sally Maersk*, leading the starboard column. Accurate fire from the surrounding merchant ships drove the submarine off and *Skeena*, in response to their radio reports, ordered *Alberni*, the only escort available on the starboard side of the convoy, to make a search.[101]

Kenogami and *Alberni*, under orders from Hibbard not to linger in their searches for the most recent attackers, refused to ignore survivors in the water. Not until about 0500 did they rejoin, *Kenogami* carrying the entire thirty-four man crew of *Sally Maersk*. SS *Regin* had courageously stopped, and then dropped back during *U 652*'s attack, to rescue *Stargard*'s crew. *Orillia*, astern of the convoy since about 0047, was fairly overwhelmed with more than a hundred survivors from *Tahchee*, *Baron Pentland*, and *Winterswijk*. At 0425, *Orillia* located the still-floating hulks of *Tahchee* and *Baron Pentland*. Lieutenant Briggs, an experienced merchant mariner, saw possibilities for saving one or both of the vessels, and obtained permission from Hibbard to delay his return to the convoy.[102]

The escorts had driven off all four submarines originally in contact, but a fifth, *U 82* under Oberleutnant-zur-See Rollmann, had reached the scene during the night. At first deterred by the escorts' sweeps and an emergency turn by the convoy, Rollman was able, with the departure for rescue work of all of the warships save *Skeena*, to make a submerged attack on the port wing. At 0457 he loosed a salvo of two torpedoes that hit SS *Empire Hudson*, a brand-new freighter at the head of the second column equipped with fighter aircraft and catapult launching gear.[103] *Skeena* rushed to the position, and had just "dropped depth charges on a good echo," when the convoy commodore, at the centre of the van, signalled a periscope sighting report.[104] Hibbard had to abandon the hunt to head off what appeared to be a new attack.[105]

---

100. *U 652*, KTB, 10-11 Sep. 1941. *U 652*'s report to BdU on 11 Sep. was that the boat had been "held off" the convoy after its successful attack on the night of 9/10 Sep.," BdU, KTB, 11 Sep. 1941

101. *U 432*, KTB, 10 Sep.1941; *U 81*, KTB, 10 Sep. 1941; *Skeena* ROP. (As noted above, Hibbard believed *Winterswijk* had been sunk in *U 652*'s attack just before midnight, 9 Sep.)

102. *Skeena* ROP; *Kenogami*, "ROP, Convoy SC 42,"; *Orillia*, "ROP... 9 to 15 Sept. 1941," nd, "Orillia," NAC, RG 24, 11305, *Kenogami*, deck log, 10 Sep, 1941, NAC, RG 24, 7428; *Alberni*, deck log, 10 Sep. 1941, NAC, RG 24, 7010

103. These vessels, designated CAM, came into service in mid-1941. Hague, *The Allied Convoy System*, 77-80

104. Both *Skeena* and *U 82* had had very close brushes with disaster near *Empire Hudson*'s hulk. Rollman "fired single shot from Tube II at destroyer ... range 300 m ... 20 sec. later five depth charges explode quite close but much deeper than us. At first I believed that my torpedo has hit [the destroyer] but this was not the case ... the destroyer had pennant number I-59 [*Skeena*'s number] painted on midships ... single mountings, 2 funnels, stern similar to that of 'Flusser' [a US destroyer] and she was possibly flying an American ensign. However, I may be mistaken." *U 82*, KTB, 10 Sep. 1941

105. The U-boat logs suggest that no submarine other than *U 82* was in contact at the time, so this was probably a false sighting.

In the meantime, Briggs in *Orillia* remained with the hulks of *Baron Pentland* and *Tahchee*. *U 82* watched these efforts from periscope depth. Rollman did not attack because he suspected a "U-Boat trap." A plume of smoke from the hulk's funnel as volunteers from the tanker's and *Orillia*'s crews began to raise steam convinced him that the hulk was not what it seemed and might be a heavily armed vessel disguised as an easy target.[106] At about 0940 therefore, with "ice-covered mountains of Greenland" in the "brilliant sunshine" astern, Rollmann set off in pursuit of the "few pale smoke plumes" of the main convoy.[107] *Orillia* and *Tahchee* trailed, ever more distant from the convoy, which was now more vulnerable than ever with only three escorts. Clearly, five or six would have left the convoy in better shape when the U-boats reacted so definitely to the mere suspicion that a warship was near by.

At 1000, Greger in *U 85* was already diving ahead of the van, dodging *Skeena*. Like Rollmann, Greger somehow took the destroyer to be a US ship, "flying the American ensign ... and banners with stars on the bridge and hull." Through his periscope, Greger also saw an aircraft circling overhead, the first of the Iceland-based long-range Catalina flying boats to reach the convoy.[108] The lead merchant ships, meanwhile, sighted *U 85*'s periscope, opened fire, and called *Skeena*, which swept through the area, but could not get an asdic contact. Hibbard dropped depth charges anyway, but they were so wide of the mark that Greger believed the detonations were torpedoes being fired against other parts of the convoy. Nearly two hours later, at 1142, he fired two torpedoes that hit SS *Thistleglen*, at the head of the ninth column, near the starboard wing of the convoy. *Skeena* quickly closed the stopped, stricken ship now drifting astern of the convoy, ordering *Kenogami* and *Alberni* to take up positions abreast of the destroyer for a coordinated sweep astern of the convoy. Shortly after noon they could see merchant vessels ahead of them firing at an object in the water, soon identified as a periscope, that disappeared within sixty seconds. *Skeena* rushed in at twenty-four knots—too fast for asdic to function—and made a snap visual attack near the position of the periscope. Greger had, in fact, just fired two torpedoes into the convoy; both missed, but no one noticed them amidst the gun fire and the depth-charge explosions, and *Skeena*'s attack was far off target.[109] She subsequently made asdic contact, obscured when *Alberni* attacked another, less certain one, but *Skeena* and *Kenogami* then regained the contact with a more deliberate approach. *Kenogami* helped to guide the destroyer on her attack run, and at 1305 *Skeena* dropped a pattern of ten charges that brought a large air bubble, followed by smaller air bubbles and a small oil patch to the surface. None of the warships could now get an echo, and Hibbard concluded after fifteen minutes that the submarine had been destroyed. *U 85* had, in fact, survived, but only just:

---

106. Briggs and the merchant captains had already examined *Baron Pentland*, and found that her engines had been destroyed. One of *Tahchee*'s three boilers was serviceable, which would provide enough power to give her some steerage and thereby allow *Orillia* to manage a tow. The tanker did not gain as much headway as the salvors had hoped, creeping along, not properly under control. Given the enemy menace, Briggs delayed taking up the tow, and patrolled near the hulk, creating the scene that aroused Rollmann's suspicions. *Orillia*, "ROP, 9 to 15 Sep. 1941"

107. *U 82*, KTB, 10 Sep. 1941

108. For air coverage of SC 42, see Adm, *MASRs*, Oct. 1941, 34-5, and Dec. 1941, 42.

109. *U 85*, KTB, 10 Sep. 1941; *Skeena* ROP; *Kenogami* ROP

6 depth charges explode at close range. All manometers except for the main one are knocked out, as are the depth rudder, gyro compass repeats, the magnetic compass, the side rudder, the engine room telegraph and all lighting. The port engine stops. The boat descends, but the dive is arrested at depth 85 [a drop of 25 metres from its previous cruising depth of 60] by trimming using the crew [to gather aft] and running one engine at 3/4 speed.[110]

The escorts, unable to regain contact, perhaps because of this fast plunge, resumed their stations around the convoy.[111]

With the destruction of *Thistleglen*, Hibbard realized he could no longer spare *Orillia*, even in daylight hours. He did not want to reveal to listening U-boats the diminished state of the escort and give away *Orillia*'s position, so rather than making a signal by radio he flashed the recall instructions to one of the Catalinas, asking the aircraft to search out the corvette and pass the message. These instructions never reached *Orillia*, and in a superb feat of seamanship Briggs subsequently jury-rigged a tow to the huge, balky *Tahchee*, bringing the valuable tanker safely to Iceland.[112] This was a wonderful achievement, but because it reduced the already meagre screen by twenty-five percent it imperilled scores of ships for the sake of one. Briggs should have delayed his return no longer than it took to save lives, something an experienced naval officer would have known instinctively. Briggs, not surprisingly after only a few months in command, was still thinking like the merchant mariner and fine seaman that he was.

An hour and three quarters after near destruction, *U 85* surfaced, but was almost immediately forced to crash-dive by a Catalina. When Greger came to the surface half an hour later the aircraft, which had lingered in the vicinity, attacked with depth charges that forced Greger to take his boat down again until after dark, when he crept away on the surface to make such repairs as were possible and head for home.[113] Meanwhile, Guggenberger in *U 81* thought the determined action against *U 85* had been meant for him, even if it seemed to be poorly directed, so he aborted his submerged approach and lay low for nine hours. When he surfaced at 1500, he soon had to crash-dive as a Catalina neared, and with only one torpedo remaining he too decided to turn for home.[114]

The Catalinas held the U-boats at bay through the afternoon and evening of 10 September, but more submarines were gathering for the kill. *U 84*, *U 202*, *U 207*, *U 433*, and *U 501* in addition to *U 82*, *U 432*, and *U 652*, were endeavouring, with fast surface runs, to gain favourable attack positions ahead of SC 42. They had to abandon the effort repeatedly as the appearance of aircraft forced them down, but Rollman in *U 82*, after three crash-dives to avoid aircraft, realized that he would shortly lose any hope of contact, and therefore boldly stayed on the surface. At first on tenterhooks—there were two Catalinas on patrol in the late afternoon and early evening—his confidence grew when he realized the aircrew could not see him in the dimming light. As he closed from ahead, cloud cover frequently blacked out the moon in the vicinity of the convoy, enabling him to

110. *U 85*, *KTB*, 10 Sep. 1941

111. *Skeena*, "Narrative of Attack on U-Boat," 18 Sep. 1941, NAC, RG 24, 11318, 8280-ON 16

112. *Skeena* ROP; *Orillia* ROP

113. *U 85*, KTB, 10 Sep. 1941

114. *U 81*, KTB, 10 Sep. 1941

approach the starboard side, where he would otherwise have been silhouetted by the moonlight shining from that direction. He fired three torpedoes, and at about 2056 hit MV *Bulysses*, leading one of the starboard-most columns:

> the large tanker explodes, a red tongue of flame shoots vertically upwards roughly 300-400 m., changes colour to bright yellow and lights the convoy as if it were daylight. There is the stench of fuel and I can see a tall black smoke cloud in the sky for a long time. The remains of the tanker, a section of ship roughly 30 m. in length, continues burning.[115]

Incredibly, fifty of the fifty-four man crew got away, thanks largely to the Polish freighter *Wisla* which, in the midst of the danger and chaos, immediately stopped to pick up the survivors. It may have been this scene that a boat newly in contact, Kapitänleutnant Ey's *U 433*, witnessed. He prepared to attack the rescuers, but pulled away when a Catalina showing lights swooped close by. *Skeena* searched well ahead of the convoy, assuming that the submarine had retreated into the darker conditions there. But *U 82* had kept close, and at 2112 fired a torpedo that hit SS *Gypsum Queen* at the head of the eighth column, almost precisely at the moment the ship broadcast a submarine sighting report.[116] The countermeasures were not without effect, however, for yet a third submarine, *U 84* under Kapitänleutnant Uphoff, had been closing to attack. After being "driven back by escorts several times" the U-boat fired four torpedoes at 2130—without result—and then quickly withdrew in the face of an apparent pursuit by "a destroyer."[117]

It was at this moment that *Chambly* and *Moose Jaw*, Prentice's reinforcements from Newfoundland, sighted the signal rockets shooting up from the merchant vessels. They were a few miles to the northwest of the convoy, a notable navigational achievement after a six-day run in which the correction on the corvettes' magnetic compasses had proven to be inaccurate and had had to be adjusted in mid-passage. Prentice had hoped he might catch a submarine closing from ahead of the convoy—the U-boats' preferred tactics—and lauded the "exceptionally good navigating of my Navigating Officer, Mate A.F. Pickard, RCNR." *Chambly* got a firm asdic contact, "port beam, range 700 yards," and Prentice decided "in view of the handiness and small turning circle of a corvette" to attack at once. The target, which turned out to be *U 501*, and the corvette were closing rapidly "head-on, on opposite courses," so at 2138 Prentice ordered an "early drop" of a five charge pattern.

> The Port Thrower misfired and the OD [ordinary seaman] at the Port Rails, a relief for a man in hospital who had only been in the ship for a few days, failed to pull his lever when the firing gong went. This omission was instantly corrected by Sub-Lieutenant Chenoweth, RCNVR, an officer who has also just joined the ship and has never been to sea before. The result was that the first and second charges were dropped close together.

---

115. *U 82*, KTB, 10 Sep. 1941

116. Ibid; *U 433*, KTB, 11 Sep. 1941; *Skeena* ROP. *U 433* describes the hit on *Bulysses* in detail, but mentions that in addition to a "small steamer" stopped near the burning hulk there was also a "thin destroyer silhouette." This was *Wisla* and *Alberni*. *Alberni*, deck log, 10 Sep. 1941

117. Probably *Skeena*'s sweep, if Uphoff was indeed in the van of the convoy as he believed. Uphoff claimed he had hit one of the lead steamers, but that was not the case; possibly the explosion and flash of light he witnessed came from the hulks of *Gypsum Queen* or *Bulysses*. *U 84*, KTB, 10-11 Sep. 1941

The first and second charges were heard to explode almost together and several observers counted a further three explosions, the last appearing to be of a different nature and more violent than the remainder.[118]

Prentice believed the first two charges, dropped almost simultaneously because of Chenoweth's quick thinking, were closest to the mark. The submariners below later agreed.[119] While *Chambly* turned to make another depth-charge attack, the damaged U-boat surfaced near *Moose Jaw*. The boat attempted a hasty withdrawal and *Moose Jaw* opened fire, but an overexcited sailor in the 4-inch gun's crew jammed its mechanism. What then took place was not untypical of the close-range combat that could occur in submarine warfare. In the words of *Moose Jaw*'s commanding officer, Lieutenant Grubb:

14. The next few minutes was spent in chase ... At one time four of the submarine's crew made a determined move to the after gun. As our own gun was still jammed, no action could be taken except to increase speed and try to ram before they could fire. This I did, although the chance was small, but, fortunately, someone on the conning tower ordered them back. The .5 inch machine guns were bearing at the time, but when the trigger was pressed, they failed to fire. A subsequent check showed no defects, so I assume that in the excitement the crew failed to cock them.

15. I managed to go alongside the submarine, starboard side to, and called on her to surrender. To my surprise, I saw a man make a magnificent leap from the submarine's deck into our waist [the mid-part of the corvette], and the remainder of her crew move to do likewise. Not being prepared to repel boarders at that moment, I sheered off. The submarine altered across my bows and I rammed her [a glancing blow that, fortunately, did not seriously damage the corvette] ...

16. After the impact she moved across my bows at reduced speed. The gun being cleared by that time I opened fire again. The crew jumped into the sea as soon as the first round went, and I ordered fire to be stopped. I subsequently learned that the shell had passed low enough over the conning tower to knock down the men who were standing thereon ...

18. The man who I had seen jump on board turned out to be the submarine's commanding officer. He was badly shaken and when he was brought to me on the bridge appeared to be worried at the amount of light we were showing in order to pick up survivors.[120]

Chambly put an armed boarding party on the submarine in an attempt to capture it, but the Germans refused even at gunpoint to re-enter *U 501*, now sinking by the stern. Lieutenant E.T. Simmons, RCNVR, *Chambly*'s First Lieutenant, courageously struggled through the hatch into the conning tower, but only in time to see a wall of water surging through the compartments below. The party and the survivors from the German crew had to jump clear for rescue by the corvettes'

---

118. *Chambly* ROP

119. "Two charges exploded near her, one above her, abaft the conning tower, the other close to her stern ... she was driven downwards ... her hydroplanes and all her instruments were put out of action and ... for this reason the tanks were blown and she was brought to the surface." Ibid

120. *Moose Jaw* ROP, 6 Nov. 1941, NAC, RG 24, 11334, 8280-SC 42

boats as the U-boat quickly settled.[121] One of the Canadians did not survive. Stoker W.I. Brown, RCNVR, Prentice later reported, "was known to be a strong swimmer and his life-belt was blown up. He had only a short distance to swim to the boat and was seen to push off from the submarine as she sank. It is thought that in some way he must have been caught up and drawn down with her as a thorough search was made by the boat and later by Chambly herself."[122]

U 501 was the RCN's first confirmed U-boat sinking. As fate would have it, the inexperienced Canadians had come up against an inexperienced submarine, in commission for only four and a-half months, on its first operational mission, and making its first attack on a convoy. The commanding officer, thirty-seven-year-old Kapitänleutnant Hugo Forster, had joined the navy in 1923 but, as the British intelligence officers who interrogated him reported, "had only recently transferred to the U-Boat branch. He had taken a shortened U-Boat course and ... his first and last cruise in command was in 'U 501' ... in the heat of the action, [Forster's] resolution failed him, perhaps because he was rather older than the general run of U-Boat captains."[123] The Admiralty staff judgment that although "Providence certainly took a hand and put the U-Boat in the corvettes' path ... the destruction of a U-Boat can never be a matter of luck alone; it can only be achieved by a well-handled ship with a well-trained crew, who know how to seize their opportunity" closely paraphrased Prentice's own report.[124] Prentice gave full credit to his crew: Pickard's superb navigation had put the corvettes in a tactically sound position, so that the asdic team could quickly and correctly track the submarine's movements during a snap attack from a short approach, when the data was changing rapidly and difficult to interpret. Prentice could have added that it was on the basis of his own astute analysis that he had insisted on the approach from ahead of the convoy, and the snap attack.[125]

Hibbard thought that Chambly and Moose Jaw had caught U 82, but Rollman was on the other side of the convoy, trying to push in between the columns. Fire from the merchant ships forced him into an emergency dive at 2155. Skeena swept the area, firing starshell, but contacted nothing and concluded the submarine was not an immediate threat.[126] By this time escorts and merchant ships had destroyed, damaged, or forced under all the U-boats in close contact during the afternoon and early evening of 10 September. Nonetheless, U 433 was still at hand. U 432, which had made the initial sinking earlier the previous night, was again closing, as was U 202 and probably U 207 as well. At 2246, U 433 fired a single torpedo that missed, and appears not to have exploded or been noticed by anyone in the convoy. Twenty minutes later, Schultze in U 432 fired two torpedoes and after more than three minutes saw an explosion on a distant steamer, probably the hit that sank Garm, which was towards the rear of the second column.[127] Kenogami, responding to an order from Skeena to rescue survivors, headed towards the stricken ship, but received a signal from one of the

---

121. Simmons to Chambly, "Report of Boarding Party,"nd, NAC, RG 24, 6901, NSS 8910-339/21

122. Chambly ROP

123. Adm, MASR, Oct. 1941, 41

124. Ibid, 43

125. Chambly ROP

126. Skeena ROP; U 82, KTB, 11 Sep. 1941

127. Ibid; U 433, KTB, 11 Sep. 1941. Skeena ROP states that she received a report that SS Garm was hit at 2312/10 Sep. Admiralty analysts concluded that she had not been torpedoed until 0230/11 Sep. Adm, MASR, Oct. 1941, 30. U 432's KTB suggests that Hibbard's initial report was the correct one. This is the conclusion in Rohwer, Axis Submarine Successes, 65.

lead merchant ships on the port wing that a surfaced submarine was nearby. Within two minutes, at 2313, the corvette "sighted a submarine on the surface ... the gun could not be brought to bear, however, and three minutes later it dived and we attacked with a 10 depth charge pattern, which fell immediately in its wake. An excellent contact was maintained and at [2337] we carried out a deliberate attack. Three minutes afterwards the contact disappeared entirely."[128] *Kenogami* had found *U 432,* but the pattern was too shallow. Schultze believed there was more science to the convoy's defence than in fact there was. He had noticed the Catalina with its navigation lights on, as had *U 433* two hours earlier, and was convinced the aircraft had somehow located the submarine then homed the corvette on to it.[129] Meanwhile, *U 433* had fired two torpedoes at 2308, just two minutes after Schultze's salvo.[130] Ey was not aware of the presence of *U 432* and did not see the hit on *Garm,* but heard depth-charge attacks, presumably by *Kenogami.* He saw at least one escort put on a burst of speed and steer search courses, assumed he was the target of the hunt and broke off, not attempting another attack run until over an hour later.[131]

The numerous explosions and counter-attacks brought the darkness to life, and the battle scape gave pause to Kapitänleutnant Linder in *U 202.* "Observed explosion," he recorded in his log at 2310: "To port there is a burning ship beyond the horizon. The convoy can be seen clearly. Both aircraft are overhead of it with their lights switched on. The escorts are almost continually firing illuminants, some merchant ships are firing machine-guns. These appear to be 2-cm. (bullets making a white line) and 3.7-cm. twin anti-aircraft guns, occasionally two red lines of light can be seen. In addition, the escorts are passing course or speed instructions using flashing lights, all in all the entire northern horizon is full of activity!" A close approach by an aircraft disrupted Linder's observation and forced him under.[132]

Moose Jaw and *Chambly,* having completed the rescue of *U 501*'s survivors, joined the convoy at 2315. *Skeena*'s starshell in search of *Garm*'s attacker illuminated the corvettes, and they were greeted by streams of tracer from some of the merchant ships before they could identify themselves.[133] They were still taking up station, at 0032, 11 September, *Chambly* on the port bow of the convoy and *Moose Jaw* on the starboard beam, when *Alberni,* also to starboard, signalled that *Stonepool* at the head of the starboard column had been hit. A few minutes later, the ship following in the same column, *Berury,* was also torpedoed. *Skeena* headed towards the starboard flank, firing starshell, and a Catalina dropped parachute flares in the same area.[134] At 0115, *Skeena* ordered *Moose Jaw* to

128. *Kenagami* ROP

129. *U 432,* KTB, 11 Sep. 1941

130. The position of *U 433* relative to the convoy is unclear. One of the torpedoes was a surface runner that failed to detonate, and the second exploded at 2312, the end of its run. Possibly it was this explosion that brought a false radio report that *Bastum,* astern of *Garm* in the second column, had been hit. *U 433,* KTB, 11 Sep. 1941

131. Ibid

132. *U 202,* KTB, 11 Sep. 1941

133. *Chambly* log, 10 Sep. 1941, NAC, RG 24, 7184; *Moose Jaw* ROP; *Skeena* ROP

134. The time given in *Skeena*'s ROP for the message from *Alberni* about the attack on *Stonepool,* 0032/11 Sep., might be a bit early. *Skeena*'s deck log (NAC, RG 24, 7860) records that *Stonepool* was hit at 0034. *Alberni*'s log (NAC, RG 24, 7010) records that an unidentified ship was hit at 0040, and that *Stonepool* was then hit at 0042; other evidence in the log shows that *Alberni* had confused *Stonepool* and *Berury.* *Kenogami*'s log (NAC, RG 24, 7429) records "flash and explosion in convoy" at 0040. In any event, the evidence in the logs, which appears not to have been available to the Admiralty investigators, strongly suggests that the times given in their analysis, 0045 for the hit on *Stonepool* and 0050 for the hit on *Berury,* are a few minutes late. Adm, *MASR,* Oct. 1941, 30. The probable attacker, *U 207,* was destroyed the next day, as will be seen, so no German record is available to clarify the timing.

search for survivors but, at that very moment the corvette came across *Berury*, still afloat. There were boats nearby and many men in the water, a large number of them dead.[135] *Alberni*, the other corvette on the starboard side of the convoy, joined to assist in the rescue and to provide cover for *Moose Jaw*, as did *Kenogami*, which had evidently been pulling up from astern of the convoy after its hunt for *U 432*.[136] Searching the water with the corvette's small boats, pulling in the exhausted survivors, and then hoisting them up the side of the warship was slow work.[137]

While the escorts were making the initial response to *U 207*'s attack, *U 82* and *U 202* were heading towards the van. At 0145 and 0148, *U 202* fired two spreads of two torpedoes each at what appeared to be the two lead ships of a column, but they all missed. Then, between 0205 and 0208, Rollman in *U 82* fired three torpedoes that hit *Scania* and *Empire Crossbill*, the second and third ships in the fourth column, towards the port side of the convoy's centre. *Empire Crossbill*, loaded with steel, plunged to the bottom with forty-nine people on board; the Swedish *Scania*, loaded with Canadian timber for Britain, remained afloat. Hibbard, knowing that with the large number of submarines in contact, an attack on one side of the convoy would likely be quickly followed by a blow on the other, swept the starboard flank, while *Chambly* patrolled ahead and to port. These tactics were correct, for Linder in *U 202* appears to have been on the starboard side: "Suddenly, starshells are fired over me from the horizon on exactly the same bearing as the merchant ship [that he had just attacked]. These are bursting quite far from me but are sufficiently close to make me visible on the bright horizon." Unknown to Hibbard, *Skeena* and *Chambly* were searching without support; he had assigned *Moose Jaw* alone for rescue duties after *U 207*'s attack, and his latest information had been that *Alberni* and *Kenogami* were returning to their stations. When he later discovered that they had been delayed picking up the survivors of *Stonepool* and *Berury*, he was sympathetic to the dilemma faced by the corvette captains, but was dismayed that the defences had been left so thin.[138]

Rollman, running low on fuel, made no attempt to remain in contact after his attack. The hits on the ships had created a large amount of smoke that he used to cover his retreat as he shaped course for home.[139] Still in close pursuit of the convoy were *U 84*, *U 202*, *U 207*, *U 432*, *U 433*, and *U 652*. Between 0246 and 0705, *U 202*, *U 432*, and *U 652* made four attacks, while *U 84* and *U 433*'s attempts were thwarted by aircraft and, as the submarines reported, pursuits by the escorts.[140] All of these attacks appear to have been made against the rear of the convoy, or against ships that had fallen astern, and none seem even to have been noticed by the intended victims, let alone to have triggered countermeasures by the escorts. Indeed, the three corvettes engaged in rescue work, Hibbard's disapproval notwithstanding, had forced the U-boats to keep their distance.

---

135. *Stonepool* had gone down quickly, and only seven among the crew of forty-nine survived; by contrast only one man had been lost in *Berury* as she had slowly settled. *Skeena* ROP

136. *Moose Jaw* ROP; *Kenogami* ROP; *Skeena* ROP. The corvettes may, in fact, have driven off *U 433*, which at the time was pursuing the convoy from astern. *U 433*, KTB, 11 Sep. 1941

137. *Berury*'s captain informed Grubb that he had been unable to remove the confidential books from the bridge of his ship. The seas were too high to board the vessel, so *Moose Jaw* fired sixty-six rounds of 4-inch shell, which set the hulk on fire and caused it to settle further, but still could not overcome the buoyancy of the cargo in the holds. *Moose Jaw* ROP

138. *U 82*, *U 202*, KTBs, 11 Sep. 1941; *Skeena* ROP; *Chambly* ROP

139. *U 82*, KTB, 11 Sep. 1941

140. *U 84*, *U 202*, *U 432*, *U 433*, and *U 652*, KTBs, 11 Sep. 1941

The submarine crews, after nearly forty-eight hours of intense operations, were reaching their limit. Dönitz knew this, and broadcast admonitions during the morning of 11 September, refusing permission for *U 652* to depart for port because it had expended all its torpedoes, and urging all boats "to do everything that the situation permits to make it easier for other U-boats to get at the enemy. No boat can break off pursuit of a convoy merely because of absence of torpedoes. It must push on and keep contact."[141]

Other submarines were coming up to help, but between 0730 and 0815 on the morning of 11 September, the Iceland reinforcement—five British destroyers of which HMS *Douglas* was the senior ship, the corvettes HMS *Gladiolus*, *Wetaskiwin,* and FNFL *Mimosa*, and the antisubmarine trawlers HMS *Buttermere* and *Windermere*—finally arrived.[142] Commander W.E. Banks, RN, in *Douglas* took over as senior officer from *Skeena*. It was now possible to send ships out on sweeps for suspected shadowing U-boats. On the afternoon of 11 September, HMS *Leamington* and *Veteran* responded to an aircraft report, sighted what was almost certainly *U 207* in the distance and made asdic contact after the submarine had dived. A four-hour hunt, joined in by two of the other British destroyers, produced no definite result, but *U 207* was never heard from again. Declared missing by BdU from this date, postwar analysis confirmed it was sunk by the two destroyers first in contact.[143]

During the early hours of 12 September *Skeena* detached for Iceland and had only twenty tons of fuel oil, less than 5 percent of capacity, left on arrival.[144] Late that day the destroyers *St Croix* and *Columbia* joined the screen. As SC 42 neared Iceland on 13 and 14 September, three USN destroyers, *Hughes*, *Russell*, and *Simms*, carried out distant sweeps around the convoy, and responded to aircraft U-boat reports, but as one of the first combat patrols by American warships in direct support of a convoy, they were under instructions not to join the close escort.[145] The U-boats, hampered by fog, had to stay down even when conditions cleared in the face of aggressive sweeps by the strengthened surface escort, and air cover that increased in scale as the convoy approached Iceland. During the morning of 14 September, U-boat Command called off the six submarines still in pursuit.[146] But the ordeal was not quite finished. On the morning of 16 September, when SC 42 was approaching northern Scotland, it was found that Lieutenant Grubb in *Moose Jaw* required hospitalization. Eleven days at sea in gruelling weather and combat conditions had taken a severe toll on the young corvette captain, who bore an especially heavy burden as virtually the only experienced member of the crew. Suffering from acute pain in his chest and stomach and unable to keep down food, he underwent examination by a medical officer from one of the British destroyers, who recommended that he be hospitalised immediately. *Douglas* directed *St Croix* to

---

141. Paraphrase by British intelligence of German signals subsequently decrypted by Bletchley Park, signal timed 0921/11 Sep. 1941 quoted, see also those timed 0503 and 0707/ 11 Sep., Naval Section [Bletchley Park], "ZTP/ZG/116: U-boat methods of combined attack on convoys. From Feb. 1st to Oct. 31st 1941," 10 Nov. 1941, PRO, ADM 223/1

142. *Skeena* ROP

143. *U 207*, KTB [reconstructed by BdU]; Grove, *Defeat of the Enemy Attack on Shipping,* app 2, 252

144. *Skeena* ROP

145. *St Croix*, "ROP—HMCS "St Croix" 11 Sep. to 17 Sep.," 20 Sep. 1941, NAC, RG 24, 11318, 8280-ON-17; OPNAV to CINCLANT, 1520/12 Sep. 1941, senior officer present afloat Iceland to CINCLANT, 1845/12 Sep. 1941, file 1-20 Sep. 1941, NARA, RG 313, Entry NHC 69, Atlantic Fleet secret messages, box 1; Abbazia, *Roosevelt's Navy*, 249

146. BdU, KTB, 13-14 Sep. 1941; *U 432* and *U 433*, KTBs, 12-14 Sep. 1941

Top: Mate A.F. Pickard and CPO W. Spence, Chief ERA, both of HMCS *Chambly*, in late 1942. Pickard navigated *Chambly* successfully to its reinforcement with the beleaguered SC42, while Spence had just received the Distinguished Service Medal for "bravery and enterprise in action with German submarines." (NAC, PA 204345)

Bottom: HMCS *St Laurent*, one of the RCN's work horse destroyers, moored to a buoy in September 1941. (NAC, PA 204336)

Stoker's mess deck in the corvette HMCS *Sherbrooke*, 1941. (NAC, PA 200123)

Top: Relaxation, anywhere, anytime you can get it. These are ratings in HMCS *Saguenay* 30 October 1941. (NAC, PAC 204327)

Bottom: *Saguenay* ratings practising depth charge drill. October 1941. (NAC, PA 204329)

Top: AB Winters manning the secondary steering position in *Saguenay*, October 1941. Note the wind protectors shielding his eyes. (NAC, PA 204335)

Bottom: Ratings Sandy Donaldson and Norm Gasse "dhobbying" – doing their laundry – in *Saguenay*, October 1941. (NAC, PA 204338)

escort the crowded, undermanned, and battered little warship into port.[147] That afternoon, as the two escorts emerged from a rain squall, they sighted Korvettenkapitän Gysae's *U 98*. The boat crash-dived. *St Croix* made asdic contact and delivered four depth-charge attacks, and British destroyers subsequently scoured the area, but *U 98* escaped further detection. After nightfall Gysae attacked and sank MV *Jedmoor*, which had survived *U 85*'s failed initial salvoes on 9 September. Another iron ore carrier, she went down quickly; just six of thirty-seven on board survived.[148]

SC 42 was one of the worst convoy disasters of the war. Fifteen ships sunk and one severely damaged comprised nearly a quarter of those that had sailed. All but one loss took place between *U 85*'s initial contact on the morning of 9 September and the arrival of large-scale reinforcements on the morning of 11 September, a span of forty-four hours during which the tiny RCN escort held the ring alone. Of the approximately 625 people aboard the fifteen ships lost, at least 203—approximately a third—lost their lives in fire, explosions, or drowning in the paralyzing Arctic waters. Over 70,000 tons of cargo—a number that would have been considerably larger had not most vessels in the SC series been so pitifully small and old—went down with the ships. The material lost included 21,286 tons of high-grade iron ore, pig iron, and finished steel, 21,617 tons of wheat and other grains, 9,778 tons of chemicals, 9,300 tons of fuel oil, and over 10,000 tons of lumber—enough material to house and feed thousands of people, fill thousands of bombs and shells, and build several ships.[149]

Circumstances had favoured the U-boats. Moderate seas in the opening stages of the battle helped them close the convoy once it had been sighted at long range in excellent visibility. Clear skies also enabled the U-boats to determine their positions accurately using celestial navigation, so that once the convoy was located the pack closed relentlessly without having to overcome plotting problems. Finally, excellent radio conditions facilitated the receipt of locating and shadowing reports. BdU had alerted the rest of the pack within sixty minutes of the initial sighting report, an impressive time for command and control systems of the time. SC 42 became a perfect target for the many U-boats, amply supplied with fuel and torpedoes, close at hand.

The reaction of Captain Stevens in Newfoundland was typical of comments on both sides of the Atlantic: This was "an appalling tale of disaster," in which it was "impossible to criticise any single action of the Senior Officer, Lieutenant-Commander J.C. Hibbard, RCN ... On the contrary," he continued, "I consider that he handled what must have appeared to be a hopeless situation with energy and initiative throughout, probably thereby averting worse disaster."[150] Commodore Murray praised Hibbard for remaining alert and active during sixty-six hours of unremitting battle, and never losing hope, "which, with the meagre force at his disposal, a lesser man might have done." He had "acquitted himself in a manner of which the Royal Canadian Navy may well be proud."[151] The Admiralty's Anti-Submarine Warfare Division classed the defence of SC 42 as "valiant" and praised the destruction of *U 501* by *Chambly* and *Moose Jaw* as well as the "several promising

---

147. *Moose Jaw* had twenty-nine prisoners and thirty-five merchant seamen from torpedoed ships on board, and her asdic had broken down as a result of damage incurred when the corvette rammed *U 501*.

148. *St Croix* ROP, 20 Sep. 1941; *U 98*, KTB, 16-17 Sep. 1941

149. *Lloyds' War Losses* I, 288-90

150. Capt (D) Newfoundland to CCNF, 1 Oct. 1941, DHH, 81/520/8280-SC 42

151. "The strain of responsibility and command," wrote Murray, "was not in any way made easier by the fact that his group had only recently been formed and that it was *Kenogami*'s first appearance in the NEF." Douglas and Rohwer, "Most Thankless Task," 204

attacks" by *Skeena* and *Kenogami*, and HMS *Veteran* and *Leamington*. As it later proved, they had severely damaged *U 85* and destroyed *U 207*, besides driving back and possibly demoralizing several other boats at critical points in the battle.[152]

Strikingly, in view of the heavy losses, the people who most appreciated the escorts' efforts were the masters of the ships in the convoy, experienced mariners not easily given to praise. When SC 42 reached Loch Ewe on 17 September, they "unanimously and spontaneously" asked the naval control service officer to pass word directly to Admiral Noble, Commander-in-Chief, Western Approaches, of their "appreciation of the work of the escort vessels in endeavouring to protect Convoy SC 42 against the heavy and concentrated attacks made on the Convoy by the enemy."[153] That said, the merchant ship crews themselves and the DEMS personnel who operated the armament of the cargo vessels deserved great credit for aggressiveness and skill. Quick, accurate radio reports of U-boat sightings enabled the escorts to carry out effective countermeasures, and the readiness with which the DEMS crews opened fire on surfaced submarines drove them off on at least two occasions.

The praise might well have been more fully shared with the aircrews of Coastal Command. The appearance of the Catalinas on 10 September largely kept the pack at bay during daylight, and the aircrews' persistence through that night deterred several of the German captains, convincing them that the RAF had developed much more effective means for aerial detection in darkness than actually existed. Even one of the U-boat commanders noted how exhausting the extended air patrols from Iceland must have been, and the close cover the Catalinas provided at night required skill at a time when equipment and techniques for overwater flying in darkness were not well developed.[154]

One of Captain Stevens's comments, when he read Hibbard's report, was that although Hibbard had written it "during the only night in a month which HMCS Skeena spent in harbour," it was exceptionally lucid.[155] The historian is able to add, after comparing it with German war diaries, that Hibbard had a firm grasp of virtually every tactical twist and turn, over scores of square miles of ocean, from the beginning of the battle to the end. At most of the critical points, the Admiralty staff, after sifting a great deal of additional evidence, was able simply to reproduce Hibbard's account in their detailed analysis. The clear, complete picture of events that Hibbard was able to maintain, together with the well-directed pursuit *Skeena* was therefore able to make in response to every significant contact, was the key to the defence. Here, in a nutshell, was why the River class destroyers, and the seasoned, professional seamen who formed a large portion of their crews, had an importance far beyond their limited numbers in the RCN's escort fleet.

As for the corvettes, it must be borne in mind that *Alberni, Orillia,* and *Chambly* had been on full-time operations for barely three months, while *Moose Jaw* and *Kenogami* had no operational experience whatsoever. *Chambly* and *Moose Jaw*'s destruction of *U 501* was testament to Prentice's tactical skill. And as already noted, the despatch of a raw ship like *Moose Jaw* to make her first cruise on the open ocean amidst a known large concentration of U-boats showed boldness, if not desperation, on the part of Prentice, who suggested it, and Murray and Stevens, who authorized

152. Adm, *MASR*, Sep. 1941, 6

153. NCSO Loch Ewe to C-in-C WA, 19 Sep. 1941, DHH 81/520/8280-SC 42

154. *U 82*, KTB, 10 Sep. 1941

155. Capt (D) Newfoundland to CCNF, 1 Oct. 1941

it. Certainly, the mission and its outcome showed how great was the influence within the RCN of its small cadre of experienced professionals like Prentice. It also sheds light on the spirit within the NEF during its early days when the senior officers were willing to allow individuals like Prentice to take extraordinary risks in view of the gravity of the situation at sea. In this case, the gamble paid off with the destruction of *U 501*. Despite a litany of errors on the part of *Moose Jaw*'s green complement, the ships struck at the right place at the right time. No less remarkable was the performance of *Kenogami* throughout the battle. Although this was the corvette's first transatlantic mission, she chased down two U-boats in tricky night actions, and helped guide *Skeena* during the attack that damaged *U 85*.

Prentice's confidential report on the action not only serves as a moving tribute to the men under his command, it also helps explain why some of the corvettes, against all odds, succeeded from the time they entered service:

> The ship's company carried out their duties efficiently and well although six months ago they were completely untrained and in the majority of cases had never been to sea in their lives before. This I attribute to the hard work and efficiency of my First Lieutenant [Lieutenant E.T. Simmons, RCNVR]. This officer has been responsible almost entirely for the working up of the ship since during the training period at Halifax, the whole of my time was taken up with training programmes, etc., of the group of corvettes under my command. I had little or no time to give to my own ship. He has carried out his duties with a zeal and energy and an efficiency which has surprised me in one who has not before been to sea. I could not ask for a better First Lieutenant.[156]

The beleaguered Lieutenant Grubb, with his untried crew, also provided comments on personnel that give an insight into the unsuspected strengths—and weaknesses—among the people hurriedly thrown together to get Canada's corvettes to sea in 1941. In relating the rescue of survivors from *Berury* and *Stonepool* in the early hours of 11 September, Grubb wrote:

> 33. The energy and initiative of Mr Herbert W. Ruddle-Browne, Mate, RCNR (Temporary) was outstanding. It became evident to me in the early stages of the action, that the Executive Officer ... was unequal to the task confronting him, and I therefore sent Mr Browne from the bridge to assist him. It is chiefly due to [Browne's] efforts that so many men were saved and accommodated with a minimum of confusion ...

> 34. Sub-Lieutenant Harold E.T. Lawrence, RCNVR, went away in the boats in general charge, and many of the survivors, in my opinion, owe their lives to his initiative and ability ...

> 37. At 1015 the Chief Engineroom Artificer reported that he had run out of water feed for the boilers, and that it would be necessary to stop for about half an hour. I informed Skeena of this and Wetaskiwin was sent to screen. At 1035 the ship was again under weigh [*sic*]. Enquiry into the matter showed that the Chief E.R.A. had forgotten to distill [sea water to make fresh water for the boilers] during the excitements of the night. It is considered that he should have done so during the previous day at the lat-

---

156. *Chambly* ROP, 14 Sep. 1941

est. This rating has shown himself inefficient throughout the entire cruise, with some signs of improvement lately.

38. Two ratings were found to be drunk on board during the night. [A regular force] Leading Stoker ... was seen to be drunk whilst the ship stopped to rescue the submarine survivors ... [an RCNR] Stoker Petty Officer ... was seen to be drunk whilst the ship was shelling SS "Berury." Neither of these ratings would state where they had obtained the liquor. They were both punished with ninety days detention.[157]

If the corvettes had performed surprisingly well under extremely adverse conditions, their routine operations revealed just how raw they were. Commander Banks, who took over as senior officer of the reinforced escort on 11 September, was scathing in his comments about the lack of communications discipline and the poor station-keeping by the NEF ships, both in his force and Hibbard's original group:

(1) R/T [radio telephone] and P/L [plain language, i.e., unencoded messages] was used without reason, i.e., not in the presence of enemy. (2) R/T and P/L was used indiscreetly, i.e., ships trying to join convoy in fog used P/L "where is convoy," "I think it is about 3' 140°," "join me at port side of convoy," "we are returning to Iceland," etc. (3) Station keeping appalling, i.e, Corvette Moose Jaw actually crossed my bow when supposed to be on A/S screen in daylight in a position 2 miles from Douglas and at night they were all over the place. (4) When the convoy altered course escorts either proceeded on same course or took up new positions slowly.[158]

These problems reflected lack of training and the impossibility, given the pressure of operational schedules that continually became more demanding, to form the NEF ships into stable groups. As Hibbard commented, "The 24th group, having only recently been formed, a far greater volume of signals was necessary than would ordinarily be the case where ships of an escort group know and understand the Senior Officer of the Escort's intentions."[159] Lieutenant Briggs of *Orillia*, in his commentary on the battle, suggested that overreliance on insecure radio telephone, and the failure of ships to manoeuvre quickly and accurately in response to orders flashed by signal light, lay in difficulties in bringing newly recruited signalmen up to speed in this challenging art:

Signalman [*sic*] drafted to corvettes in some cases have never seen a signal projector. Practically *none* have ever *used* one. We find that no doubt a signal man can read a lamp if comfortably installed in a classroom. He can also send—on a [radio] key. Suggest that signalmen in training be given opportunity to use projector and learn how to "train" light. The story is very different when they have to contend with violent motion in a corvette. Have to keep light trained, read and send in blinding rain, hail, snow, spray and also pick it out in a fog. We realize that a signalman is being asked to acquire a great deal of knowledge in a very short time and we think they do very well all things considered, but if possible, would further suggest that signalmen be trained for *hot* work ... In other words concentrate on certain phases and become proficient, rather than have a smattering of knowledge of all aspects of the work. Would

---

157. *Moose Jaw* ROP, 6 Nov. 1941

158. Chief of Staff WA to CCNF, "Conduct of Escorts," 7 Oct. 1941, NAC, RG 24, 11929, 0020-3-6

159. *Skeena* ROP, 15 Sep. 1941

submit it is not too far fetched to suggest that a platform be built in such a manner that it can be mechanically manipulated to represent a heaving, pitching or rolling ship. Signalmen could even be dressed in oilskins and a shower device played on them to represent the misery of rain etc, when pads get wet and eyes are blinded.[160]

Interestingly, Briggs's suggestion about the use of simulation equipment in training establishments, an idea he got from the air force's mechanical simulators, prefigured in some respects the revolutionary Night Attack Teacher Hibbard himself would develop at Halifax in 1942. As it was, Briggs's comments lent convincing weight to Banks's devastating criticisms.

Because this convoy was up against great odds, and so small a "band of brothers" faced those odds with such slender resources, it had the flavour of a heroic saga. When the distinguished Canadian poet E.J. Pratt accepted an invitation to write an epic poem about the navy's wartime achievements, and found that his original subject, the Tribal class destroyer HMCS *Haida*, was already to be the subject of a book, he turned without hesitation to the exploits of *Skeena* and SC 42. The result was *Behind the Log*, perhaps the only narrative poem ever to chronicle a North Atlantic convoy battle. "Apart from a few minor transpositions and enlargements for dramatic effect for which official indulgence is requested," wrote Pratt, "the record follows the incident":[161]

> When ships announced their wounds by rockets, wrote
>
> Their own obituaries in flame that soared
>
> Like some neurotic and untimely sunrise
>
> Exploding tankers turned the sky to canvas,
>
> Soaked it in orange fire, kindled the sea,
>
> Then carpeted their graves with wreaths of soot ...
>
> Only the names remained uncharred ...
>
> Merely heroic memories by morning.[162]

Pratt could hardly have chosen better.

———————————

The mauling of SC 42 convinced Dönitz that the repeated evasion of his carefully placed submarine concentrations in the eastern North Atlantic had been the result of British maritime aircraft locating U-boats. The waters immediately southeast of Greenland thus looked even more promising than earlier in the month when he had despatched the *Markgraf* group to the area, just to get the boats clear of air patrols from Iceland. Moreover, he reflected, these waters were something of a choke point for shipping. Convoys between Newfoundland and Iceland could most conveniently

160. *Orillia* ROP

161. David G. Pitt, *E.J. Pratt: The Master's Years 1927-1964* (Toronto 1987), 334, 338-9; E.J. Pratt, *Behind the Log* (Toronto 1947), xiv

162. Ibid, 27-8

follow the route off the Greenland coast. Late on 16 September, therefore, he ordered nine recently replenished boats to take up positions like those earlier occupied by *Markgraf*. He designated the new group *Brandenburg*.[163]

Bletchley Park, which had recently been stymied by a new BdU method of concealing the location of its U-boats, detected no trace of the new movement into the waters off Cape Farewell.[164] Since *Markgraf*, the only known concentration in the Greenland area, had pursued SC 42 far to the east, the Admiralty had reverted to northern routing. SC 44 sailed from Sydney on 11 September and on 14 September, outside the Strait of Belle Isle, met its ocean escort, the Town HMS *Chesterfield*, and the corvettes HMS *Honeysuckle*, HMCS *Mayflower*, *Lévis,* and *Agassiz*, and the Free French *Alysse*. In the short time since the attack on SC 42, Commodore Murray had been able to increase the escort, but only modestly. The convoy was somewhat smaller than SC 42, but still large, with a total of fifty-six merchant ships.[165]

During the late afternoon of 18 September, Kapitänleutnant Kentrat's *U 74* sighted smoke from SC 44 some 130 miles southeast of Cape Farewell. This was pure chance. The convoy had already passed to the east of the area where U-boat Command had ordered *Brandenburg* to patrol, but Kentrat was still proceeding to his assigned position at the northwestern end of the line, immediately off Cape Farewell. Fortunately for the convoy, conditions for radio transmission were poor, so that neither BdU nor any of the other U-boats in the area received *U 74*'s initial sighting reports. Moreover, Kentrat had difficulty in his first attempts to close the convoy late on 18 and early on 19 September, thinking that the escorts could see him in the illumination of vivid northern lights.[166] The escorts, in fact, suspected nothing. Kentrat was able to slowly work his way around in front of the convoy to the dark, port side and at 0203/19 September fired four torpedoes from his forward tubes at the unusually long range of 3,000 metres, and then, as he turned to escape, a fifth from his stern tube. Kentrat heard four explosions and believed he saw hits on two of the merchant vessels. That was not the case; what he probably saw was a torpedo ripping into *Lévis*, patrolling on the port side of the convoy. The torpedo's warhead demolished the forward forty feet of the hull, nearly up to the 4-inch gun mount. The point of impact was in the stokers' mess, and the blast killed most of the occupants; a total of seventeen men were lost from the crew of sixty-nine. The captain, in his cabin just aft of the explosion, was severely shaken. Seeing the damaged forecastle sloping down into the water he hastily ordered "abandon ship," and then departed in the boats. The first lieutenant was busy on deck getting survivors to abandon ship and it fell to inexperienced junior officers and ratings to carry out the terrifying task of searching the shattered hull. In the words of Sub-Lieutenant Ray Hatrick, who led these efforts, "There was a heavy smoke from the explosion and with my torch I could only see about two or three feet. As a result, I had to grope around. I found several bodies which were obviously dead and I hailed at the top of my voice and

163. BdU, KTB, 16 Sep. 1941; *U 74* and *U 552*, KTB, 17 Sep. 1941

164. Hinsley, *British Intelligence* II, 173; LCdr L.A. Griffiths, RNVR (ed), *Government Code and Cypher School Naval History* XVIII: *The Battle of the Atlantic*, nd, 168-9, Center for Cryptologic History, National Security Agency, Fort Meade, Maryland

165. Robinson, "Mercantile Convoy No. 'SC 44.' Convoy Form D," 30 Sep. 1941, PRO, ADM 199/56; HMS *Chesterfield* to Capt (D) Greenock, "Convoy SC 44," 2 Oct. 1941, PRO, ADM 237/68

166. *U 74*, KTB, 19 Sep. 1941

then I kept silent and listened. I received no reply."[167] Belatedly, Hatrick received recognition in 1946, when he was awarded the Distinguished Service Cross.

Mayflower, stationed off the van of the port wing ahead of *Lévis*, and whose crew, according to *Chesterfield*'s report, saw the torpedo track, was quickly on the scene. *Mayflower* made a depth-charge attack, which Kentrat heard in the distance as he escaped on the surface. After other escorts had joined the search and come up empty-handed, *Mayflower*, which together with *Agassiz* had picked up *Lévis*'s survivors, put a party back on board the stricken corvette. Lieutenant George Stephen, RCNR, *Mayflower*'s commanding officer, was a highly skilled seaman; before the war he had been chief officer in the Hudson Bay Company's supply ship RMS *Nascopie*, which carried out annual voyages into the perilous ice-filled waters of the Canadian Arctic archipelago. Stephen began to tow *Lévis*'s hulk, stern first. That evening, however, some fifteen hours after the attack, *Lévis* took on an increased list and slipped below the surface.[168]

Other U-boats in *Brandenburg* had begun to pick up *U 74*'s signals during the night of 18 to 19 September but were unable to plot interception courses. Because of poor radio propagation BdU did not receive any traffic until late on 20 September, and therefore Dönitz was not in a position to coordinate. At least three U-boats, *U 94*, *U 373,* and *U 562* attempted to pursue the convoy, but failed; a fourth, *U 575*, closed within sighting distance of *U 74* during daylight on 19 September, but lost contact later that day—after the two U-boat commanders had a spirited argument by signal lamp about the most suitable tactics and the radio procedure that should be followed in the prevailing poor atmospheric conditions.[169] For its part, British intelligence had no evidence that the attack on *Lévis* was anything other than a chance encounter by a single U-boat until the afternoon of 19 September, when shore stations intercepted submarine transmissions whose origin, which could only be approximately plotted, were possibly from the vicinity of SC 44. Confirmation came some hours later, with the decryption of the German traffic since 16 September concerning the establishment of *Brandenburg*. By that time SC 44 was under renewed assault.[170]

Because communications difficulties made proper homing procedures by *U 74* impossible, only two boats, *U 552* and *U 69*, joined Kentrat in his attacks during the night of 19 to 20 September. The darkness of that night, clear visibility, and the reduction of the escort to only four vessels as a result of the loss of *Lévis* and the absence of *Mayflower*, which had fallen far back while towing the hulk, favoured the submarines. Between 2113 and 2327 on 19 September they sank four ships, including as one British officer noted, the "Best ships in Convoy." Among the losses were two

---

167. Testimony at the board of inquiry, quoted in Johnston, *Corvettes Canada*, 55. See also F. McKee and R. Darlington, *The Canadian Naval Chronicle* (St Catharines 1996), 37-9.

168. The board of inquiry into the sinking concluded that the loss might have been avoided. The senior officers who were members of the board were shocked to discover that the corvettes had not been supplied with such essential emergency equipment as timbers to shore up bulkheads that, as in the case of *Lévis*, had been weakened and exposed to the ocean by the severe damage to the hull. Neither had the corvette crews been trained in damage control procedures. Future shipbuilding contracts specified that building yards were to provide damage control timber. HMS *Chesterfield* to Capt (D) Greenock, 2 Oct. 1941; *Mayflower* to *Chesterfield*, 0320/19 Sep.1941, *Chesterfield* to Adm, 1605z/19 Sep. 1941, PRO, ADM 237/68; MacRitchie, *"St Laurent* U-Boat Story No. 2,"[stamped "Senior Canadian Naval Officer (London) 5 Apr. 1944 "], *"St Laurent,"* NAC, RG 24, 11754, includes biographical notes on Lt Stephen; Johnston, *Corvettes Canada*, 58; McKee and Darlington, *Canadian Naval Chronicle*, 39

169. *U 74, U 552, U 69*, KTBs, 19 Sep. 1941; BdU, KTB, 20-21 Sep. 1941

170. Adm to *Chesterfield*, 2131a/19 Sep. 1941, PRO, ADM 237/68; CTF 24, "Escort of Convoy and Operations Log," 19-20 Sep. 1941, NARA, RG 313 Red, CTF 24, box 8710

tankers and the *Empire Burton*, a new freighter fitted as a CAM ship.[171] Although none of the escorts made a firm contact, their persistent sweeps persuaded the U-boats to break off before daylight. *U 74* had expended all its torpedoes, was running low on fuel, and as Kentrat recorded: "To be honest I must admit that my ships' company and I were fairly drained after more than thirty hours of shadowing interspersed with attacks and attempted attacks over the course of 2 nights." *U 69* was also short of fuel and turned for home. Only *U 552* continued to pursue the convoy, but, after no success in relocating it, abandoned the chase on 21 September.[172] That same day, reinforcements reached SC 44 in the form of the corvettes HMCS *Arrowhead* and *Eyebright*. They had been detached from HX 149, well ahead of the slow convoy, but the nearest one that was unthreatened and whose escort could safely be reduced in face of the threat to SC 44. As the corvettes approached, they made a search for survivors from the attacks on the night of 19 to 20 September, and came across the prow of one of the victims, jutting thirty feet into the air.[173] Meanwhile, a group of five US destroyers that had sailed from Iceland early on 20 September in response to the reports of the heavy attack that night, patrolled towards the convoy but did not join the escort.[174]

U-boat Command kept *Brandenburg* southeast of Greenland, but the Admiralty had already diverted convoys clear of the area. Replenished submarines outward bound from Europe that would have reinforced *Brandenburg* and allowed a wider ranging effort south of Greenland, had meanwhile been deployed southeast of Ireland to support operations against the Gibraltar convoys, against which the U-boats began to achieve renewed success on 20 September with an attack on OG 74.[175] Thus, the menace on the routes to the south of Britain, which since the spring had forced the Admiralty to accept lightly escorted convoys west of Iceland on the transatlantic run, had become all the more serious just when the attacks on SC 42 and SC 44 demonstrated that the escort groups based in Newfoundland had to be greatly strengthened.

171. *U 74, U 552, U 69*, KTBs, 19-20 Sep. 1941; [Adm staff chronology], "Convoy SC 44," nd, PRO, ADM 199/1709

172. *U 74, U 552*, and *U 69*, KTBs, 20-1 Sep. 1941; BdU, KTB, 29-1 Sep. 1941; *Chesterfield* to Capt (D) Greenock, 2 Oct. 1941

173. *Arrowhead* ROP, NSS 8280-SC 44, DHH mfm 89/34, reel 27; *Chesterfield* to Capt (D) Greenock, 2 Oct. 1941; Adm to *Chesterfield*, 2131A/19 Sep. 1941

174. NOIC Iceland to Escort of SC 44, 1156/21 Sep. 1941, C-in-C WA to *Chesterfield*, 1556a/21 Sep. 1941, PRO, ADM 237/68; Abbazia, *Roosevelt's Navy*, 250

175. BdU, KTB, 22-30 Sep. 1941; MOD, *The U-Boat War in the Atlantic*, I, 83; *MASR* (Sep. 1941), 6, 10-11. For diversion of the eastbound convoys see "Escort of Convoy and Operations Log," 21-3 Sep. 1941, NARA, RG 313 Red, CTF 24, box 8710. The westbound ON 16 had, when in the vicinity of Iceland, already been diverted south before the attack on SC 44 to avoid U-boats known to be in the northern latitudes immediately to the west of Iceland: C-in-C WA to escorts of ON 16, 00129A/19 Sep. 1941, "ON 16," DHH 88/1 mfm, reel 7; the same seems to have true of ON 17, which was following close behind: "H.M.S. *Gladiolus*. ROP," nd, NAC, RG 24, 11318, 8280-ON 17

CHAPTER FIVE

Implementing the Convoy Agreements II
October to December 1941

THE SUDDEN AND HEAVY ATTACKS on the slow convoys, laying bare as they did the inadequacy of the arrangements made by Admiral Ernest King and the Royal Canadian Navy, cracked the whole question of escort allocation wide open. The extent to which Admiral King's initiative had shut down the flow of information is evident in the striking fact that the Admiralty only heard about the RCN accepting responsibility for all the slow SC convoys on 9 September, and then only by chance through a signal from Murray about his reorganization of the Canadian ships of the Newfoundland Escort Force into six groups. So surprised was the Admiralty staff that they asked for specific confirmation from Admiral Nelles that the RCN had indeed made this large commitment.[1] At the same time, word arrived about the attack on SC 42, and the Admiralty, Naval Service Headquarters, and Commodore Murray's staff quickly agreed that the escort groups had immediately to be reinforced to a minimum of two destroyers and six corvettes each.[2] By despatching every British and Canadian ship available at St John's, Murray was able to muster a force of one destroyer and six corvettes for the next convoy due to sail from Sydney, SC 45 on 18 September, and two destroyers with four corvettes for SC 46, departing Sydney on 24 September.[3]

Meanwhile, on 18 September, in a long personal message to Nelles, Admiral Pound expressed his dismay about the arrangements King and NSHQ had made for the slow convoys:

> We had expected when Plan 4 came into force we would be able to withdraw all RN escort ships from Newfoundland and use them to augment escorts in Western Approaches area and also for Sierra Leone convoys which are very thinly escorted at present.
>
> (ii) It came as rather a blow when we heard Canadian forces were to provide escort for all SC convoys with consequential weakening of groups to 6 ships in each as given in CCNF's 1807z/9. In view of relative strength of force allocated we had expected the USA to escort a larger proportion and that the Canadians would have been allocated possibly every other SC convoy.

---

1. Adm to BAD, (R) NSHQ, 1236a/11 Sep. 1941, NSHQ to Adm (R) BAD,1404z/11 Sep. 1941, NSS 1048-48-2, copies in DHH, NHS 8440-70 "NEF"

2. CNS to Adm (personal for First Sea Lord), 1403z/13 Sep. 1941, NSS 1048-48-2, copy in NHS 8440-70 "NEF"

3. FONF WD, Sep. 1941, DHH, NSS 1000-5-20 pt 1

(iii) Would it be practicable for you to reduce destroyers and corvettes at present allocated to local duty and thereby increase those immediately available to CCNF for SC convoys. If possible in sufficient numbers to release all RN ships at present in Nfld Force ...

(iv) I would welcome any help you can give in this way.

(v) We will also have to ask you to assist with TC convoys [troop convoys from Canada to UK] as Western Approaches has been so denuded of long legged destroyers capable of coming straight across. This will of course reduce number of destroyers you can put on to SC convoys but we will have to accept that.[4]

This was all bleak news. The only help Pound could offer was to say that he would, in the circumstances, not expect Canada to uphold its earlier commitment to despatch a substantial portion of its new construction corvettes for service in British waters—this in addition to the Admiralty promise already noted not to make an early call for Canadian help in European waters— but he had at the same time to go back on the earlier British undertaking entirely to relieve the RCN of responsibility for troop convoys.

Murray viewed the difficulties with a seaman's eye. He, like all the operational commanders, disliked the Iceland route. Its long diversion to the north drained the fuel of escorts and reduced the scope, as in the case of SC 42, for evasive routing. Moreover, it subjected the ships to northern storms, a potentially fatal danger to the slow, unmanoeuvrable ships of the eastbound SC and westbound ONS convoys. The route would become virtually untenable in winter weather, and the very long nights would give the wolf packs further advantage. Murray, repeating arguments he had probably heard at Western Approaches in May when he had participated in the initial planning for transocean escort, recommended an early shift of the SC and ONS convoys to a more southerly and shorter great circle route, where with the saving of time—and reduced storm damage—the two slow series could be handled by five, rather than six groups. The corvette component of six per group for five groups could be supplied by a total force of thirty-eight corvettes, which the RCN could provide. To keep two destroyers running in each group would require a total force of thirteen long-leggers, meaning that the RN would have to supply only five for the mercantile convoys, plus another five for the troop convoys. Murray noted that Admiral Bristol, who had recently arrived at Argentia to establish his headquarters, also preferred the southern route, and when Nelles passed Murray's proposal to the British, Admiral Noble chimed in with his endorsement.[5]

The Admiralty, familiar with the case for the southern route Western Approaches had pressed since the spring, rejected them once more for the same reason that on balance the northern route offered better possibilities for defence with the support available from Iceland. That aside, the entire agreement with the Americans hinged on Iceland, the limit to which US naval forces were permitted to operate. Although the SC and ONS series slow convoys were now to be more completely managed by the Canadians than envisaged in the original agreement, these convoys still had to be available for slow US and Iceland-flag ships destined for Iceland, and control of them west of Iceland was now vested in the US Navy Department, not the Admiralty. In fact, the Admiralty had recently advised the Navy Department that there was no advantage in an early move to a more southerly

4.   First Sea Lord to CNS, 2141a/18 Sep. 1941, NSS 1048-48-1 pt 7

5.   CCNF to CNS, 1437z/21 Sep. 1941, NSS 1048-48-1 pt 7; CNS to Adm (personal for First Sea Lord), 1407a/22 Sep. 1941, and C-in-C WA to Adm, repeated NSHQ, 1723a/25 Sep. 1941, both PRO, ADM 199/935

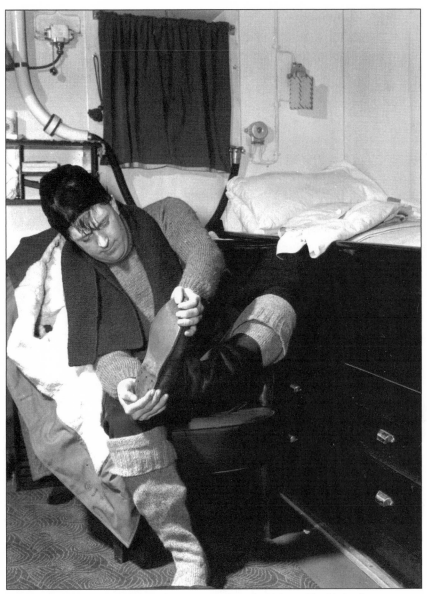

Layers of clothing provided the only protection from the biting cold. This is Lieutenant A.C. Jones, RCNR, commanding officer of *Oakville*, coming off watch. (NAC, PA 204342)

Comics, tea and smoke. Stand easy in the stoker's mess HMCS *Kamsack*, February 1943. (NAC, PA 204360)

route, as that would make it more difficult for British relief escorts staged through Iceland to reach the convoys, and forego air cover from Iceland.[6] The Admiralty staff had no doubt that changes in the northern route would be necessary as the winter set in, but did not recommend taking the initiative in reopening the question. In the words of one officer, "I think all we want to do at present is to keep the scheme running steadily, and this can be done without much change in escorts."[7]

What gave the Admiralty staff this confidence that the northern routing scheme could continue to operate was the news that the Canadians were willing to reinforce the ocean escorts to a strength of thirty-eight corvettes. No one remarked on Nelles's warning that the corvettes could only be supplied by rushing them forward from the Halifax and Sydney forces that were "really used for working-up new corvettes."[8] The ships, in other words, would be incompletely trained and inexperienced, which should have sounded a note of caution given the persistent complaints from British and Canadian operational commanders about the inadequacy of recently commissioned Canadian ships. Although Pound confirmed that the Tobermory work-up program would continue to be available to the Canadians according to schedules that best suited them, we have seen that it would be some months before a significant portion of the new Canadians ships could go through that cycle.[9]

Pound replied to Nelles gratefully accepting the increase of the NEF to thirty-eight corvettes, but he rejected the southern route. He promised to leave seven British corvettes in Newfoundland, giving a total of forty-five, enough to provide six runners for the total of six groups needed for the northern route. He also agreed not to withdraw five British destroyers.[10]

As the details of these arrangements reached Murray, it became clear he would actually receive very little help in the short term. Of the seven British corvettes Western Approaches chose to leave with the NEF, four were undergoing long refits or had recently suffered major breakdowns, and the remaining three were due for refits as soon as shipyard space could be scheduled. And, of the five destroyers allocated by Western Approaches, two were in or scheduled for refits, and a third had recently broken down and would need major repairs in Britain. To ensure the availability of two destroyers in each of the six groups required for the northern route, moreover, there would have to be fifteen long-leggers in the pool, not the thirteen that the Admiralty had deemed sufficient.[11] There was more bad news. As Admiral Pound had warned might happen, Western Approaches needed help with troop convoys. On 23 September, the Admiralty signaled that it could provide only three of the six long-leg destroyers needed to escort a large Canadian Army convoy, TC 14, due to sail from Halifax on 9 October. Murray would have to find the other three destroyers.[12] Nelles warned the Admiralty that four SC convoys in October, beginning with SC 48 due to sail from Sydney early in the month, would have to sail with only one destroyer.[13]

6.   OPNAV to CINCLANT, 1640/18 Sep.1941, rebroadcast of SPENAVO to OPNAV, 0636/14 Sep. 1941, file 1-20 Sep. 1941, NARA, RG 313, Entry NHC 69, file 1-20 Sep. 1941, messages to CINCLANT, box 1

7.   For the Admiralty analysis in this and following paragraph, see Schofield, DTD, 23 Sep. 1941, and "NRM," min, register no. TD 0721/41, 26 Sep. 1941, PRO, ADM 199/935

8.   CNS to Adm (personal for First Sea Lord), 1407a/22 Sep. 1941, PRO, ADM 199/935

9.   First Sea Lord to CNS, 2141a/18 Sep. 1941

10.   First Sea Lord to CNS, 0116A/27 Sep. 1941, NSS 1048-48-1 pt 7

11.   CCNF to CNS, 0116z/29 Sep. 1941, NSS 1048-48-1 pt 7

12.   Adm to CCNF, 1950A/23 Sep. 1941, "TC-14," DHH 88/1 mfm, reel 40

13.   CNS to First Sea Lord, 1437z/30 Sep. 1941, NSS 1048-48-1 pt 7

Limited as the British assistance to the Canadians on the northern route would be, Pound cited this unexpected demand on British resources when he went to the Americans begging for additional help for the RN in the eastern Atlantic. On 15 September Stark passed King the following message:

> Admiral Pound requests that I present the following situation to you most informally to get your personal reaction. If your reaction is favorable he will present it through official channels and if negative he will drop the subject. On account of short cruising radii of British escort vessels it is necessary to refuel at Iceland as long as meeting point is west of 26 degrees west long. Furthermore British escort ships are required to augment Canadian escort forces. The result is that suitable escorts are not and cannot be made available for Sierra Leone and Gibraltar convoys which are suffering severely from lack of adequate escort at present time. Strong escorts have assisted materially in [combatting U-boats]. If meeting point were changed from 26–30 west to about 22 west but always in the already modified western hemisphere defence zone, British would be able to release 3 extra escort groups for Sierra Leone and Gibralter convoys. In Admiralty opinion this would appreciably increase security of these convoys ... Admiral Pound further reiterates that if this is in any way embarrassing to you he wants to drop the subject.[14]

Pound, urgent as was his tone, still understated a difficult situation. Even though August had been a good month in terms of global British losses, the concentration of U-boats on the routes to Gibraltar and points further south had extracted a considerable toll, sinking nineteen merchant vessels and two escort vessels. The worrying aspect about the attacks on SC 42 and SC 44 was that the enemy, while maintaining pressure on the southern routes, was now able to mount simultaneous pack operations in the north as well. During the last week of September the submarines on the Gibraltar route would have substantial successes against two more convoys, sinking sixteen merchant vessels and an escort.[15] The continued menace on the southern routes goes far to explain the British relief at the RCN's readiness to rush additional corvettes to sea on the northern route, and Pound's unwillingness to leave more than a bare minimum of RN ships in the NEF.

Admiral Little, head of the BAD, having just returned to Washington from a visit to the Admiralty, gave Stark fuller information about how narrow the balance was in the Atlantic, how utterly dependent convoy defence was on evasive routing based on wireless intelligence, intelligence that in the future would almost certainly diminish in effectiveness. SC 42 had in fact been an accident waiting to happen:

> 2. During June, July and August import figures for the United Kingdom show a distinct improvement and our shipping losses have been very much reduced, there has been a tendency in the public mind to imagine that in some way we have eliminated the dangers and are on the high road to win the "Battle of the Atlantic." I found the First Sea Lord showed concern on this aspect of the matter and was bringing the facts clearly before Statesmen.
>
> 3. That we have won the "Battle of the Atlantic" is far from being the case, and our comparative immunity has been due to the skilful use made of the information we have

---

14.   OPNAV to CINCLANT, 1710/15 Sep. 1941, file 1-20 Sep. 1941

15.   Adm, *MASR*, Aug. 1941, 6; and Sep. 1941, 6

about the positions of submarines operating. The Germans are doubtless aware that we make much use of D/F bearings for plotting submarines, and sooner or later I feel that they may restrict greatly the use of W/T by submarines so as to prevent us taking advantage of this information. The very recent experiences of Convoy SC 42 show how at any moment we are liable to suffer grievous losses through steering into unsuspected groups of German submarines and with insufficient strength of escort.

4. I enclose a narrative and chartlet showing the movements of convoys HX 144, SC 40 and HX 145 on the 23rd to 29th August, illustrating how greatly the immunity of those particular convoys, all of which arrived without loss or even being attacked, was due to use of information about submarine positions.

5. I think the narrative is also instructive in showing what great diversions have to be made if these great convoys are to be kept free from attack, and how it may even be necessary almost to reverse the course of the convoy at very short notice ...

7. Another point which is brought up by this narrative ... is the steady increase in the number of German submarines operating in the Atlantic at any moment ... the average number of German submarines at sea has increased from something like 20 in April to over 30 at the end of August, though we do destroy some and particularly when a well escorted convoy is attacked. If the numbers operating get large enough, it will be increasingly difficult to dodge the groups of submarines and unless we have sufficient escort forces and really powerful counter-attacking forces with each convoy, shipping losses cannot be reduced.[16]

King agreed to Pound's request that the rendezvous with the British escorts in the eastern Atlantic should be shifted eastward towards 22° West, which in the high latitudes of the northern route could be achieved without a great deal of extra steaming on the part of the Canadian and United States escorts. That, however, was as far as King was willing to go. On 20 September Captain F.L. Houghton, Director of Plans at NSHQ, made a liaison visit to King onboard USS *Augusta* at Newport, Rhode Island:

> Before I [Houghton] had mentioned the possibility that we might, in view of the increased threat, require some assistance in the escorting of SC Convoys, Admiral King took pains to make it clear that he was having considerable difficulty in providing sufficient escorts for HX Convoys. By various means he hoped to provide groups of 6, but this relied entirely upon the RCN and RN, assuming full responsibility for SC's. He was very definite about this, and I gathered that one of his difficulties was the length of time his ships were not running due to refits, and time in Dockyard hands for fitting of new material.[17]

On 3 October Pound responded to the complaints from Canada that Western Approaches Command's allocation of RN ships that were mostly refitting to the Newfoundland command left Murray in a serious bind. Pound admitted this was the case, and confirmed that the Admiralty accepted that the minimum number of two destroyers with each convoy could not always be

16. Little to Stark, 16 Sep. 1941, "Atlantic Area ... No. 1," NARA, RG 28, series VII, box 116

17. Houghton to CNS, 23 Sep. 1941, NAC, RG 24, 3974, NSS 1048-48-27

achieved. "With limited forces at our disposal and balancing threat of attack both in western Atlantic and on southern convoy routes it is regretted no additional ships can be spared." The First Sea Lord also shot back with recriminations of his own: "We are unaware here of circumstances which caused you to agree with Americans that you should provide escort of all SC convoys. It is this heavy commitment which is causing considerable difficulty."[18] Nelles, on 8 October, responded that it had been a manageable commitment with the existing Canadian resources in the NEF at that time when escort groups included only five vessels. The commitment had mushroomed only after the attack on SC 42, when Pound himself had initiated urgent action to expand the groups. Nelles might have reminded Pound that Commodore Reid, in the original correspondence, had carefully explained that the RCN could undertake nothing more than to provide its existing thirty-three–ship force: Canada had already allocated all of its long-legged destroyers, and failures in operations had demonstrated the need for extended work-ups of new construction corvettes.

Most importantly, Nelles assured Pound that the RCN was no longer taking any notice of the limits previously placed on its contribution to the NEF. The RCN had already built up the non-RN corvette component of the force at St John's to the thirty-eight discussed in September: ten corvettes had been withdrawn from the Halifax and Sydney forces to bring up to strength the escorts of SC 46, SC 47, and SC 48. This reinforcement would continue: "I am at present despatching all available corvettes to strengthen the NEF and will use newly commissioned [Bangor] minesweepers to take their places in local defence forces at Halifax etc. I regret that this action may delay the departure of the first Minesweeper flotilla for United Kingdom waters." (It will be recalled that in the autumn of 1940, the Naval Staff had agreed that the first batches of Bangors to complete should be assigned to British waters.) The issue of full and proper work-ups for new construction that had figured so prominently in planning during the summer had now definitely taken a distant second priority. The Canadian staff's intention of assigning the five short-legged Town class destroyers to Halifax had also been put on the back burner, although that did not help much with the shortage of destroyers for ocean escort: *Hamilton*, *Niagara*, and *St Clair* were all in dockyard hands for extended refits or repairs, leaving only *Columbia* available for Murray's command. *Annapolis* continued its solo commitment to fast escort out of Halifax. Houghton, during his visit to King, had already informed the American admiral that the RCN was now committed to an all-out effort, including the assignment of most of the short-leg Towns and all the new corvettes to the NEF.[19] In short, by early October, the crisis on the North Atlantic route had brought the Canadian staff to commit virtually the whole of the forces it had wanted for Canadian home waters to ocean escort, much as both the British and American staffs had counted upon during their negotiations in July and August.

Pound, in his remonstrance of 3 October, had asked Nelles to work for another solution: "Would it be possible for you to approach Americans and endeavour to get them to agree to provide for say 1 SC convoy in 3?" This would allow the RN to withdraw its twelve remaining escorts from Newfoundland. Nelles visited King immediately, and received exactly the same response as Houghton had two weeks earlier: the Atlantic fleet could undertake no further commitments as it was already straining its resources to build up the escort groups for the HX series from five to six escorts each. This much Nelles reported to Pound. King, however, passed on a more detailed record

---

18. First Sea Lord to CNS, 1514a/3 Oct. 1941, NSS 1033-6-1, copy on NHS 8440-70 "NEF"

19. Houghton to CNS, 23 Sep. 1941

of the meeting to Stark. Clearly, the discussions had been more wide-ranging than Nelles had reported. The Canadian, according to the American admiral, evidently unburdened himself no less than Reid had done in August about the RCN's difficulties in dealing with the Admiralty:

> Admiral Nelles ... left this afternoon after a very pleasant and profitable visit and exchange of views.
>
> He is concerned—and rightly so—over the matter of an adequate number of destroyers for the Canadian Escort units. They have 8 Canadian [long-legged] and need 7 more—which is well known to the Admiralty—in order to "net" 2 per Escort unit. So far, the Admiralty has made available only 5—most of those assigned being under "refit" in Britain.
>
> Will you not use your good offices with Admiral Pound to ensure that the Canadians are able to do their part—otherwise, the Canadians are going to come back on us to do what they (British and Canadians) well know they have undertaken to do ...Nelles tells me that Bonham-Carter (now in Halifax [as Flag Officer North Atlantic Escort Squadron]) is to go home shortly and is not to be replaced. Thus, the Canadians and ourselves will have full scope in the Western Atlantic Area.
>
> Nelles confirms my notice that the Admiral Commanding Western Approaches apparently does not yet understand and appreciate that he has nothing to do with the control of Canadian Escort units any more than he has of American units—which is nil. The "interference"—so far—is evidenced by (1) failure to meet an SC convoy at MOMP and ordering the Canadian Escort unit to continue to Londonderry [this was the escort of SC 45] (2) his Iceland representative ... messing into the affairs of Canadian Escort units while in Iceland waters which is our (my) affair.
>
> I write thus in order to see if you cannot straighten these matters out with a view to obviating my having to bring them up officially.[20]

Stark passed King's concerns on to Rear-Admiral R.L. Ghormley, USN, in London. Admiral Pound invited Ghormley to vent these complaints at the Battle of the Atlantic committee, attended by all of the most senior Admiralty officers who had responsibility for the battle. The British VCNS, Vice-Admiral H.R. Moore, explained that the assignment of destroyers midway through refit to the Canadians had been better than the only other alternative, which was to assign destroyers that were due to begin refit. Moore also pointed out that Western Approaches had interfered in the direction of Canadian ships soon after the entry of the United States into operations; the commander-in-chief "now fully understood that Canadian escorts were not in his operational control." This meeting took place in mid-November, some five weeks after King had registered his complaints. In the meantime, the USN had become involved in combat close beside British and Canadian forces. Ghormley's easy acceptance of the British explanations to some extent reflected the fact that the American officers in London had always had a fuller appreciation of the difficulties the British faced than did the authorities in Washington or with C-in-C US Atlantic Fleet (CINCLANT).[21] At the same time, the Americans' firsthand experience of warfare with the U-boats in the

---

20.   King to Stark, 5 Oct. 1941, DHH 91/431 mfm, reel 1

21.   "Battle of the Atlantic Meeting Held 18 Nov. 1941," PRO, ADM 205/23. See "Battle of the Atlantic Committee. 24th Mtg—11 Nov. 1941," ibid concerning the difficulties the Admiralty had in dealing with the Navy Department in Washington, as compared with the close relationship with Admiral Ghormley's staff in London.

North Atlantic had also awakened a sharper awareness in their senior command about the common challenges all three navies now faced.

When SC 48 sailed from Sydney on 5 October, therefore, the strain on British and Canadian escorts in the North Atlantic was extreme. This was the fourth eastbound convoy for which an increased escort had to be found, but as the first of the expanded escort groups, which had sailed with SC 45, was just starting its homeward run with the westbound convoy ON 21, the pool of ships at St John's was nearly exhausted.[22] Beyond that, *Saguenay* and *Assiniboine*, a third of the RCN's force of River class destroyers, the fleet's most capable escorts, were returning from a month-long trip across the ocean and back with the troopship *Pasteur*, and both would have to go into refit immediately. Meanwhile, the British had called for help in completing the escort for the troop convoy TC 14, which would sail from Halifax on 9 October. The RCN committed three River class destroyers, *Restigouche*, *Skeena*, and *Ottawa*. These special assignments, together with the demands for increased escorts for the mercantile convoys, left just *Columbia* for SC 48, a short-ranged destroyer that could remain with the convoy for only part of the crossing towards Iceland.[23]

To help compensate for this weakness, FONF and COAC assigned seven corvettes to SC 48. There were three experienced ships, *Wetaskiwin*, FFS *Mimosa,* and HMS *Gladiolus*, although *Gladiolus* could be assigned only by delaying the refit for which it was due, a tragic turn of events as it would prove.[24] *Columbia* and these corvettes had done several crossings together, so there was cohesion within the group. This was essential as the remaining four corvettes, *Baddeck*, *Camrose*, *Rosthern*, and *Shediac*, were novices on their first Atlantic crossing. *Baddeck* had commissioned in May, but engine defects had kept the ship in dockyard for extended periods of time. The other three had reached Halifax for completion and work-ups only at the end of June or in July, meaning that they had had at best only about six weeks' experience with local escort out of Halifax or Sydney.[25]

Baddeck and *Shediac* provided the initial escort of the fifty-two merchant ships from Sydney, up past the western coast of Newfoundland and through the Strait of Belle Isle.[26] *Baddeck's* commanding officer, Lieutenant Alan Easton, RCNR, was the senior officer of the escort for this part of the trip. He later recalled his nervousness despite a previous career in the merchant navy, and his near continuous Naval Service at sea since 1940:

> Being almost devoid of practical knowledge I hoped no occasion would arise when I would have to display my ignorance before the Commodore.
>
> No one could be blamed for this ignorance. Halifax did not, at that time, undertake to instruct a captain in how he should do any job assigned to him. There were no schools for this precise purpose any more than there were instructors to help him work-up his ship on commissioning into a useful vehicle of war. Those ashore knew very little about convoying; those who did were mostly at sea doing it. It was the escort commander's job to

---

22. LCdr C.D. Soule, "Thurmann's Convoy: The German U-Boat View of the Battle for Convoy SC.48 (as told by a Canadian Submariner)," unpublished research paper, Royal Military College of Canada (Kingston 1999)

23. "*Saguenay* History"; Adm to CCNF, 1950a/23 Sep. 1941, CCNF to Adm, 1255z/24 Sep. 1941, SO(I) Halifax to Adm, 1835z/9 Oct. 1941, TC 14 file, DHH 88/1 mfm, reel 40

24. NSHQ to Adm, 2236z/2 Oct. 1941, PRO, ADM 237/187

25. Ken Macpherson and John Burgess, *Ships of Canada's Naval Forces*, 71, 72, 84, 85; Easton, *50 North*, 11-46

26. Elliott, "Mercantile Convoy No. 'SC 48,' Convoy Form D," 21 Oct. 1941, PRO, ADM 199/56

acquaint his forces with the technique of shepherding the ships; but when he did not
know, as in my case, he could only apply such common sense as he possessed.[27]

Indeed, Easton received a copy of Western Approaches Convoy Instructions, the "bible" of
ocean convoy procedures and tactics, only when SC 48 met the NEF escorts outside the Straits of
Belle Isle, and *Wetaskiwin* passed the publication to *Baddeck* and *Shediac* by line. "I was aware
of the book's existence and had even looked through a copy in Halifax once when the captain of
a British escort had shown it to me. Now I had it! I was all set ... Now I could fight anything! I
had the gen!"[28]

SC 48's initial course was well to the north, towards Greenland, and had been assigned by the
US Navy Department at the end of September on the basis of advice from the Admiralty, who had
no indications of a renewed German effort in these waters. Dönitz was in fact at that very time
planning a new deployment to the waters southeast of Greenland to begin about 10 October when
a wave of boats, fresh from replenishment and refit, would be able to reach that area. Dönitz was
concerned that in the latter part of September deployments of boats to the area off Norway and to
the Mediterranean, and the concentration in the South Atlantic that was producing meagre
returns, had diffused his strength, mostly at the cost of the crucial North Atlantic theatre: "It must
be emphasized repeatedly that the enemy today can no longer be found and successfully attacked
by small numbers of boats."[29]

On 7 and 8 October, as Bletchley Park broke the U-boat cyphers for 5 and 6 October, there was
evidence of this new deployment but precisely where in the north was unclear. The square assigned,
disguised as GB 39, seemed to be AK 39 to the southwest of Iceland and clear of the route assigned
to SC 48. By 9 October, however, the Operational Intelligence Centre at the Admiralty was concerned
about the possibility that the square might actually be AJ 39, southeast of Greenland and right in
SC 48's path. Early on 10 October, on the Admiralty's recommendation, the US Navy Department
directed the convoy to follow a more southerly route. German radio traffic for 9 through 11 October,
which Bletchley Park was able to decode on 12 October, confirmed that the patrol line was being
established southeast of Greenland. Three boats had already been assigned to the northern part of
the line, and now BdU directed four others to extend the line to the south, across SC 48's new
course.[30] The US Navy Department quickly accepted the Admiralty's advice and at mid-day on 12
October ordered the convoy to immediately make a sharp alteration to the southeast.[31]

Heavy seas and poor visibility that had complicated the joining up of SC 48 with the mid-ocean
escort north of Newfoundland had never let up. On the evening of 10 October, *Shediac*, the least
experienced of the escorts, had fallen away from the convoy. The ship, as the commanding officer
explained, was "not provided with a telescope so that flag signals may be read at a distance." The
signal crew had therefore apparently missed the visual signals ordering an evasive alteration of

---

27. Easton, *50 North*, 49

28. Ibid, 56; confirmed by *Wetaskiwin* ROP, 2 Nov. 1941, NAC, RG 24, 11334, 8280-SC 48

29. BdU, KTB, 10 Oct. 1941, 26 and 30 Sep. 1941

30. J. Rohwer, "Special Intelligence und die Geleitzugsteuerung im Herbst 1941," *Marine Rundschau* 11 (Nov. 1978), 711-19,
     translation, "'Special Intelligence' and Convoy Control in the Fall of 1941," 16-24, in DHH, SGR II 224. The decrypted mes-
     sages are in PRO, DEFE 3/32, and have been digested in Tremblay, "North Atlantic Convoy ... SC 48," app 1, DHH, 2000/5

31. *Columbia* ROP; Adm to C-in-C WA, 1958a/12 Oct. 1941, PRO, ADM 237/187

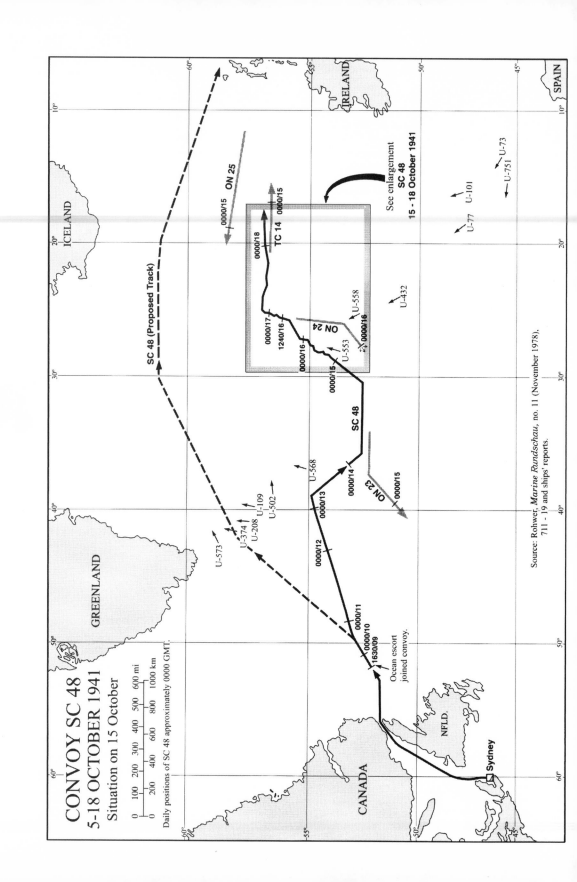

CONVOY SC 48
5-18 OCTOBER 1941
Situation on 15 October

Daily positions of SC 48 approximately 0000 GMT.

0 100 200 300 400 500 600 mi
0   200   400   600   800   1000 km

ICELAND

GREENLAND

CANADA

NFLD.

Sydney

SC 48 (Proposed Track)

SC 48

ON 25
0000/15

0000/15
TC 14   0000/15

0000/18

See enlargement
SC 48
15 - 18 October 1941

0000/17

1240/16

0000/16
U-553

0000/16
U-558

U-432

0000/15

U-568

0000/14

0000/13

ON 23
0000/15

0000/12

0000/11

0000/10

1630/09

Ocean escort
joined convoy.

U-573

U-374   U-109
U-208   U-502

ON 24
0000/16

IRELAND

SPAIN

U-73
U-751

U-101
U-77

Source: Rohwer, *Marine Rundschau*, no. 11 (November 1978),
711 - 19 and ships' reports.

course to take place with the onset of darkness.[32] The next night, *Rosthern* lost the convoy in increasingly heavy weather. Compounding the difficulty was the fact that the ship's compass could not be trusted. Just prior to sailing from Halifax, the dockyard had installed a radio telephone that affected the local magnetic field on the bridge, which meant that a new set of deviation corrections to apply to raw readings from the magnetic compass would have to be worked out. As the commanding officer explained, "No opportunity arose at sea to find the deviation and on joining the convoy courses were set by keeping station, and because of inexperienced wheelsman no accurate estimate of deviation could be obtained. Throughout the whole trip there was too much rolling and unsteady steering for good azimuths."[33] Neither *Rosthern* nor *Shediac* ever managed to find the convoy again as it diverted further and further to the south.

The escort would thus comprise the five remaining corvettes until such time as *Columbia*, with her limited endurance (she sailed from St. John's on the morning of 9 October, one day later, so that she could proceed at economical speed to conserve fuel) linked up with the convoy well out to sea. But as things turned out, what was intended to be the escort's sole destroyer was unable to locate the convoy on 11 October—or any time soon.[34] The changes in SC 48's routing, uncertainty about its rate of advance in the heavy seas, and the impossibility in the overcast conditions of getting a sun or star shot to correct the dead-reckoning navigation, set the destroyer on a frustrating pursuit, sprinting to a succession of interception positions and slowly cruising along search courses at each of them without result.[35]

On 12 October the weather built into a full gale. Several of the merchant ships were so severely battered they had to heave to and drop back from the convoy. So too did another of the novice corvettes, *Camrose,* which fell in with two of the straggling merchantmen, including the commodore's ship. On the morning of 14 October this group came across the westbound ON 23, but although the senior officer was able to give them SC 48's new route, the stragglers did not succeed in making contact during the next day and a half.[36] Of the four corvettes remaining with the convoy, one of them, *Baddeck*, had long since discovered that the extended attention of the dockyard at Halifax had not cured her engine defects and her speed was limited to about twelve knots, too slow to pursue a surfaced U-boat. The frustration and anxiety of the crew was only heightened when, on 14 October, the asdic failed and resisted all attempts at repair. These were cruel blows, as *Wetaskiwin*, acting as senior officer in the absence of *Columbia*, had been impressed by *Baddeck*'s efficiency.[37]

SC 48, therefore, had only three fully effective escorts when fate dealt another blow. Skillfully as the Admiralty and US Navy Department had routed the convoy clear of the U-boat patrol line forming southeast of Greenland, even the best intelligence, such as the Ultra that had made these diversions possible, could not take account of the fast movements of submarines as they took up

---

32. Clayton to CCNF, 30 Oct. 1941, PRO, ADM 199/55

33. *Rosthern* ROP, 22 Oct. 1941, PRO, ADM 237/187

34. Elliott, "Mercantile Convoy No 'SC 48'"; ROP of HMCS *Columbia* from Oct. 9 to Oct. 1941" (Hereafter, *Columbia* ROP), 18 Oct. 1941, PRO, ADM 237/187; *Wetaskiwin* ROP

35. *Columbia* ROP

36. *Camrose* to SOE, Convoy SC 48, 20 Oct. 1941, NSS 8280-SC 48, DHH, 89/34 reel 27; Elliot, "Mercantile Convoy No. 'SC 48'"

37. Easton to Adm Commanding Iceland, "Report of Movements of HMCS *Baddeck* on First Attack," 25 Oct. 1941, PRO, ADM 237/187; Easton, *50 North*, 59-62; *Wetaskiwin* ROP

the positions ordered by BdU. During the dark early hours of 15 October, when the sea had moderated and visibility had improved, *U 553*, commanded by Kapitänleutnant Karl Thurmann, which was heading northwest to join the Greenland patrol line, sighted the convoy just as the moon was setting. The depleted screen caused him little difficulty and, in a period of fifteen minutes just before first light, made five attacks, firing a single torpedo in each. Only at one point did he believe he was being pursued by an escort, but first one and then another soon turned and swept back through the convoy—evidently believing the submarine had passed through—firing starshell and making depth charge attacks, far from *U 553*'s actual position ahead of the starboard outer column. The readiness with which Thurmann could manoeuvre and take aim, and still maintain position close to the head of the columns, showed the special vulnerability of the slow convoys. That said, his five measured attacks destroyed only two vessels, one of moderate size and the second a small merchantman, because in the excitement the torpedo firing team had failed, after the second shot, to cancel the initial settings before applying corrected data.[38]

Easton later recorded the shock that he and his crew in *Baddeck* felt when they were confronted with their first experience of the results of war at sea: "Wreckage was strewn over an area of about half a mile, floating in widely separated patches. It must have been a severe explosion which tore this ship apart. We passed slowly through it. Lumber there was, many small wooden hatch covers, gratings, doors, sides of deck houses ripped in jagged patterns, ladders and cargo—light stuff which would have floated up as the ship sank."[39] The crew sighted a single man in the water, his head and one arm thrust through the centre of a life buoy. He had evidently drowned while struggling to get his body through the ring: "With the movement of the buoy on the little waves the man's legs moved and made it appear as though he were feebly trying to swim."[40]

> For three and a half hours our men applied artificial respiration to the sailor ... and although it had throughout most of this time looked very hopeful—his gums had been warm and his blood had not coagulated—he finally stiffened ...
>
> He had been a man between forty-five and fifty, a fireman I would have thought, who had probably been off watch sleeping in his underwear. He possessed no identification whatever.
>
> It was my intention at this time to report the unhappy incident with a description of the man so that he could be accounted for. I decided against doing so later—I was only obliged really to report survivors—because I felt that the knowledge of his hours of mental anguish and physical suffering and then his near revival would be harder for his family to bear, if he had a family, than it would be for them to assume that he had probably been killed outright or drowned quickly.
>
> Much as I tried to sleep that afternoon I could not. The picture of that forlorn body in the water simulating the power to swim disturbed me too much.[41]

---

38. *U 553*, KTB, 7-15 Oct. 1941. The most detailed reports of this attack from the Allied side are, "Report of Actions by M.V. Silverelm," nd, "Shipping Casualties Section, Trade Division: Report of Interview with the Chief Radio Officer ... SS Tanker 'W.C. Teagle'...," 23 Oct. 1941, and "Questionnaire for Ships in Convoy Attacked by U-Boat," 23 Oct. 1941, [manuscript notes for preceding report], PRO, ADM 199/1709

39. Easton, *50 North*, 65

40. Ibid, 66

41. Ibid, 67

With the attack, *Wetaskiwin* had been able to break radio silence and make a report. *Columbia*, on receiving the actual position of the convoy, discovered it was just two hours' steaming away, and immediately shaped course to intercept. At virtually the same moment *Columbia* sighted the convoy, a lookout also spotted *U 553*, "about 7 or 8 miles from us." The destroyer's commanding officer, Lieutenant-Commander S.W. Davis, RCN, held fire, hoping "we might sneak up close enough to make a certain depth charge attack."[42] Thurmann had indeed been caught unawares:

> A 4-funnel destroyer ... range 6,000 m., is pushing me towards the convoy. I attempt to extract myself to the west and to get around the destroyer to the north ... she is closing, and is staying with me tenaciously.
>
> Dived when range = 2,500 [metres] and subsequently made 90 degree alteration of course to the north, periscope depth. The destroyer is lying stopped ... range = 1,200 m, previously she had dropped two patterns of 3 depth charges in the location where I dived. The destroyer gets under way, stops, gets under way, I continually keep my stern pointed towards her.
>
> Fired from Tube V at the destroyer lying stopped, angle on target bow = 90 [degrees], range = 1,600 [metres], target speed = 7 knots, aiming point forward edge of the bridge on the assumption that she was just getting under way. The torpedo had barely left the tube when she got under way with high speed and moved off to the west steering zigzags. Missed astern. When range = 5,000 m., the destroyer reverses course and returns at high speed, at range 1,000 m., bows right, angle on right bow = 30 [degrees], I turned towards, bow tubes ready to fire, suddenly the destroyers turns to inclination 0. I quickly go to great depth. 3 depth charges in a very tight pattern land between depth = 50 and depth = 60 [metres]. Everything that can be knocked out is. Reaction of the ship's company outstanding. No loud yelling. Quiet clear commands, reports, questions and answers. Settled at depth = 90. Corrected defects.[43]

Columbia had had a very close call, and the ship's survival, like *U 553*'s, reflected the sharpness of the ship's company. The destroyer had taken the rapid evasive action to avoid the torpedo on the strength of a report by a lookout that could not be confirmed; nevertheless the ship had manoeuvred instantly and, as no one onboard appreciated, had perhaps avoided destruction by seconds. Similarly, Thurmann's rapid manoeuvres and his deep dive had thrown *Columbia* off the scent. *Gladiolus* had come out from the convoy to assist but when Davis learned that only two corvettes remained with the merchant ships, he called off the hunt.[44] Hours later, during the evening of 15 October, *U 553* regained contact with the convoy briefly, but was then driven off by what Thurmann described as a forty-five-minute pursuit by one of the escorts. In fact, the escorts were not aware of the submarine's presence, but their sweeps had a good result. *U 553* was unable to regain contact amidst rain squalls and limited visibility for the next seventeen hours.[45]

U 568, under the veteran commanding officer Kapitänleutnant Joachim Preuss, however, had also been in contact with the convoy since the afternoon of 15 October. Preuss, outbound from

---

42. Davis, "Report of Attack on U Boat by HMCS *Columbia* on 15 Oct. 1941," 18 Oct. 1941, ADM 199/1130

43. *U 553*, KTB, 15 Oct. 1941

44. Davis, "Attack on U Boat by HMCS *Columbia*"

45. *U 553*, KTB, 15-16 Oct. 1941

France and like Thurmann assigned to the southern end of the Greenland patrol line, was only some fifty miles from *U 553* when Thurmann made his first attack report. Long after dark, three hours after the escorts had unwittingly driven off *U 553*, *U 568* slipped in to torpedo *Empire Heron*, the last ship in the outboard starboard column, which went down quickly leaving only one survivor. *Columbia*, in the van, raced back firing starshell, as did *Mimosa* and *Gladiolus*, the corvettes in that sector, and in this case it was effective, forcing *U 568* to withdraw.[46] Lieutenant-Commander G. Windeyer RCN, in *Wetaskiwin* remarked with some feeling that "it was very noticeable that *Columbia* did not (as *Wetaskiwin* did not, on the previous night) receive any information. It is strongly urged that, after waiting five minutes for a positive report to be put in, each ship should come up with a negative report. Such reports, as 'Definitely not Port side' would be extremely helpful."[47]

Bletchley Park would be able to decode the first signals about *U 553*'s contact on SC 48 only at mid-day on 16 October, but as the German historian Jürgen Rohwer has observed, this specific information was not necessary. The characteristic pattern of Thurmann's convoy reports and homing signals, their location in the vicinity of SC 48 by shore-based direction finding stations, and the knowledge from the Admiralty's U boat plot—which was reproduced at the US Navy Department—that there were several submarines well-positioned to support Thurmann enabled the shore authorities to take quick action to reinforce SC 48's small escort. Closest to the scene was the fast westbound ON 24, which on the evening of 15 October the US Navy Department ordered to disperse so that its escort, the USN destroyers *Plunkett* (SO), *Livermore*, *Kearny*, *Decatur,* and *Greer*, could go to SC 48. (See map at page 280.) Somewhat further away, TC 14, the Canadian troop convoy, detached the destroyers HMS *Highlander* and *Broadwater*, while ON 25 sent the corvettes HMS *Veronica* and *Abelia*.[48] ON 25 detached a third corvette on the night of 15 to 16 October, HMCS *Pictou*, in response to a submarine report from the independently routed Canadian steamer *Vancouver Island*, from a position well to the south of both ON 25 and SC 48. (*Vancouver Island*, the former German *Weser* that HMCS *Prince Robert* had captured in September 1940 (see Chapter 6), was in fact sunk by *U 558*, one of the boats responding to Thurmann's shadowing reports to the northwest.) As we will see, *Pictou*, after failing to find any survivors, would on the night of 16–17 October while attempting to rejoin ON 25, encounter the embattled SC 48 and reinforce its escort.[49] Finally, the RN's 3rd Escort Group, with five destroyers (HMS *Bulldog*, SOE), a corvette, and three trawlers, which was scheduled to take over from *Columbia*'s group on the morning of 17 October, sailed from Iceland, some 500 miles to the northeast of the convoy, on 15 October, and shore authorities urged the group to make best speed.[50] The battle was a race against time for both sides. Dönitz, in addition to the five submarines already south and west of Iceland—*U 553*, *U 568*, *U 502*, *U 432,* and *U 558*—also assigned four boats just outward bound from France and over 400 miles from the scene, *U 73*, *U 77*, *U 101*, and *U 751*.[51]

46.   *U 568*, KTB, 14-16 Oct. 1941; Davis to C-in-C WA, "Report of Attack on SC 48 on Night of 15 Oct. 1941," 18 Oct. 1941, PRO, ADM 237/187

47.   *Wetaskiwin* ROP

48.   Rohwer, "'Special Intelligence' and Convoy Control"; C-in-C WA to Douglas, 1525a/15 Oct. 1941, ADM 237/187; Hornell, "Mercantile Convoy Form D, ON 24," 23 Oct. 1941, ON 24 file, DHH mfm 88/1 reel 7; C-in-C WA to Forth, 1849a/15 Oct. 1941, TC 14 file, DHH mfm 88/1 reel 40

49.   *U 558*, KTB, 15 Oct. 1941, DHH; "Report of Attack on Submarine by HMCS *Pictou*, 17 Oct. 1941." PRO, ADM 199/1130; "A Naval Officer's War: Episode Three," *Starshell* 7 (Autumn 1999), 9

50.   Rohwer, "'Special Intelligence' and Convoy Control," 22

51.   BdU, KTB, 15 Oct. 1941

During daylight on 16 October the US destroyer group, less *Greer*, which had been held back by defects, joined the convoy. Captain Hewlett Thebaud, USN, as the senior officer present took command of the escort, but seems to have left control of the Canadian group to Lieutenant-Commander Davis in *Columbia*. There were three destroyers, including *Columbia*, in the van of the convoy, a corvette and USN destroyer on each beam, and two corvettes astern. At nightfall *Baddeck*, which appears to have been the only one of the escorts equipped with radar, moved 4,000 yards in front of the convoy, in advance of the destroyers.[52]

All five of the first group of U-boats were in the near vicinity of the convoy by 16 October but were having trouble making firm contact. Long-range air patrols from Iceland were forcing the boats to submerge and one aircraft inflicted minor damage on *U 558*. Similarly, sweeps by the surface escorts around the periphery of the convoy kept the submarines at bay. Furthermore, the heavy seas and overcast skies that had created such difficulties for the convoy, limited U-boats to navigation by dead reckoning, so that as they caught glimpses of the convoy at different times through the day, they were reporting positions that varied significantly. A contact report by *U 568* brought Kapitänleutnant von Rosentiel, commanding officer of *U 502*, who had the convoy in sight, to grumble "As happened on 15 October, we have the convoy in a completely different position."[53] BdU, in an example of Dönitz's centralized system of command and control, transmitted a long signal that mediated between the frustrated skippers in determining which of the positions was most accurate.[54] The tenacious Thurmann, who had managed to get a navigational star shot on the morning of the 16th, proved to be the most accurate and most successful in tracking the convoy, but not without considerable effort: "These are the most wretched conditions for shadowing. Rain squalls last between 3/4 and 5/4 of an hour. They reduce visibility to absolutely 0. We continually have to pursue, turn away, pursue, turn away."[55]

In the early hours of darkness of a rainy, "inky black night," *U 553* edged carefully past the escorts into the forward part of the convoy. With a "slight improvement" of visibility, Thurmann saw a destroyer only 150 metres distant, but he was not detected. Between 2000 and 2007, Thurmann fired four torpedoes, of which the last hit, setting off what the U-boat commander described as an "enormous fiery tanker flame."[56] He then "turned away with maximum helm so as to put freighters between me and the destroyers," which were apparently the escorts at the head of the starboard column and on the starboard side, two US destroyers and the Free French corvette *Mimosa*, according to *Columbia,* which also swept towards the area. "A destroyer whose 2 gun mountings can clearly be seen on the forecastle, range = 400 m., turns towards us. Emergency dive! Passed through depth 35 m, went to depth = 90, outstanding manoeuvre by the Engineering Officer, everything was done with calm speed. 3 depth charges at the diving location but high

52. Thebaud to CNO, "Report of Operations Involving Convoy SC48 and Torpedoing of *Kearny,*" 20 Oct. 1941, file A-14, NARA, RG 313 Red, CTF 24, 1941 Confidential, box 8804; Davis to C-in-C WA, *Columbia* ROP; Easton to Adm Commanding Iceland, "Report of Movements of HMCS *Baddeck* on Night of Oct. 16 and 17," 25 Oct. 1941, PRO, ADM 237/187

53. *U 502*, KTB, 16 Oct. 1941

54. ZTPG 12366, from BdU, 1505/16 Oct. 1941 (decrypted 2345/18 Oct. 1941), PRO, DEFE 3/32

55. *U 553*, KTB, 16 Oct. 1941

56. Davis to C-in-C WA, "Report of Attack on SC 48 on the Night of 16/17 Oct. 1941," 18 Oct. 1941, PRO, ADM 199/1130; HMS *Highlander* to Capt (D) Liverpool, 10 Nov. 1941, and attached signal log, 17-18 Oct. 1941, PRO, ADM 237/187; Windeyer, "Narrative Covering Night of 16-17 Oct. 1941—while Escorting SC 48," 30 Oct. 1941, NAC, RG 24, 11334, 8280-SC 48

above us ... the destroyer obviously still had to get around the freighter, there is no asdic pursuit. Went back up to the surface 20 min. later, but by that time I was positioned somewhat further out to the south of the convoy."[57] *U 558* and *U 432*, also to the south of the convoy, both witnessed "starshells and explosions covering the entire northern horizon," and these beacons resolved the navigation problems. *U 558* penetrated the starboard quarter making four torpedo attacks between 2128 and 2214 that first sank the tanker *W.C. Teagle* and then the steamers *Erriken* and *Rym*, both of which had stopped to pick up *Teagle*'s survivors.[58]

At about the time of *U 558*'s attacks, the two groups of reinforcing escorts that had been detached from other convoys the previous day were joining SC 48. Like the U-boats, they had been slowed in their passage by the heavy seas, and like the U-boats they homed on the explosions of the attacks. HMS *Highlander* and *Broadwater*, from TC 14, reached the perimeter of the convoy at 2130, and about ninety minutes behind were three corvettes, HMS *Veronica* and *Abelia* from ON 25, in company with HMCS *Camrose*. The latter had intercepted a signal from SC 48 about the attack earlier in the day, and had therefore parted company with the stragglers she was escorting and made best speed to come to the assistance of the beleaguered convoy, happening upon the British corvettes on passage.[59]

Highlander was just pushing up the port side of the convoy when the first torpedoes from *U 558* struck home. The destroyer reversed course firing starshell and her commanding officer, Commander S. Boucher, RN was disturbed to see no other escorts—from his vantage point, he could not see that the attacks were in fact taking place in nearly the opposite corner of the convoy. Assuming control of the Anglo-Canadian group, Boucher called for all escorts that might have become detached to rejoin. Soon, he was able to make contact with *Plunkett* and *Columbia*, and join them in the van. Still, he found the "situation was very vague and most unsatisfactory, as it appeared to me that none of the corvettes were with the convoy."[60]

Wetaskiwin had dropped back from her position on the port beam of the convoy, under the same mistaken impression as *Highlander* that the submarine was striking on that side, and began rescuing survivors seen in the water. Perhaps, she was one of the two escorts whose presence persuaded Kapitänleutnant Krech of *U 558* to slip away after the shot at *Rym*. Possibly, he also saw the reinforcements arriving, for starshell was illuminating *Broadwater* taking on survivors and, somewhat later at 2310, when a US destroyer flashed on its searchlight, *Camrose* came into view. *Veronica* and *Abelia* were also in the vicinity picking up survivors. At 2355 *Broadwater*, having finished picking up seven crewmen from *Teagle*, departed to join the screen on *Highlander*'s instructions, and directed *Wetaskiwin* and *Veronica* to carry on the rescue work. *Wetaskiwin* tried and failed to get a message to *Camrose* to take over this duty so that she could also return to her position in the screen.[61]

---

57. *U 553*, KTB, 17 Oct. 1941; Davis, "Attack on SC 48"

58. *U 558* and *U 432*, KTB, 17 Oct. 1941; "Convoy SC 48. 9-19 Oct. 1941," nd, and attached merchant ship survivor's questionnaires, ADM 199/1709

59. HMS *Highlander* to Capt (D) Liverpool, 10 Nov. 1941; HMS *Veronica* to Capt (D) Londonderry, 19 Oct. 1941, ADM 237/187; *Camrose*, to senior naval officer, Convoy SC 48, 20 Oct. 1941, NSS 8280-SC 48, DHH 89/34 mfm reel 27

60. HMS *Highlander* to Capt (D) Liverpool, 10 Nov. 1941; *Highlander* signal log, 17 Oct. 1941, PRO, ADM 237/187; Davis, "Attack on SC 48"

61. Windeyer, "Narrative Covering Night of 16-17 Oct. 1941"; *Highlander* signal log, 17 Oct. 1941; HMS *Veronica* to Capt (D) Londonderry, 19 Oct. 1941; commanding officer, HMS *Abelia*, nd, PRO, ADM 237/187

Certainly, the convoy needed additional protection. *U 432*, homing on the "cloud of belching smoke" from *Teagle*, and taking advantage of the distraction created by *U 558*'s attack, ran ahead of the convoy and steamed fully surfaced down the centre columns. Between 2343 and midnight, the U-boat fired four torpedoes that sank one freighter and also hit the larger oil tanker *Barfonn*. Incredibly, the submarine "stopped in the vicinity of the tanker which was still dawdling along slowly and re-loaded Tube II on the surface with considerable difficulty because of the heavy sea state."[62]

Preuss's *U 568* was at this moment closing on the port side of the convoy. The submarine had been held back by the escorts carrying out rescue work, and by the sweeps and starshell of the other escorts whom he feared had picked him up with their sound detection equipment. Finally, at 0015, just fifteen minutes after *U 432*'s last shot, Preuss "Fired salvo of 4 torpedoes at a destroyer which repeatedly blocked my way ... One hit after 1 min. 50 sec. running time. The destroyer breaks in two amidships and sinks rapidly. She appears to be of the [British] A or B class. 2 funnels." He had, in fact, torpedoed USS *Kearny*, the first American ship to be so attacked in the Atlantic war. Although ripped open from the keel to the upper deck in the forward boiler room, just aft of the bridge, the destroyer survived and was shortly under way, albeit at a crawl.

Preuss was meanwhile pursuing the convoy on a "parallel course" off to port, evading several corvettes. At 0140, approximately an hour and twenty minutes after the attack on *Kearny*, he sighted a corvette closing off his bow:

> I turn away and increase to full speed. The corvette follows at a distance of 800 m in my wake and cannot be shaken off. When it suddenly starts raining I decide to decrease speed and to turn away as my wake is shining very brightly. However, this does not help, the corvette closes in to 400 m., now and again drops depth charge and fires with her forward mounting (6 rounds).
>
> 0602 [0202 local time] I fired the stern torpedo when the corvette is again positioned precisely in my wake ... Missed.
>
> 0615 [0215] Emergency dive because I am unable to escape on the surface ...
>
> The corvette returns and drops a further 5 depth charges which are fairly well placed over the boat.[63]

U 568's attacker was *Pictou*. Lieutenant A.G.S. Griffin, RCNVR, the corvette's commanding officer, takes up the story:

> Broken water was sighted 20 degrees off the port bow at almost identically the same moment as strong Hydrophone effect and A/S contact was obtained at a range of 500 yards. We hauled around to bear directly on the target ... Speed was increased to 16 knots ... A counter attack was carried out and a pattern of six charges laid down according to the reading on the track. At the time the pattern was fired, the ship was not up to speed, consequently the Asdic went out of commission ...
>
> The submarine's wash was now plainly visible dead ahead and our speed was increased to 180 rpm. and finally to the maximum as it was seen that she was outstripping us ... Fire was opened with our four inch gun ... no hits ...

---

62. *U 432*, KTB, 17 Oct. 1941

63. *U 568*, KTB, 17 Oct. 1941

At this point we were following directly in the submarine's wake, and she fired one torpedo which was seen to pass parallel to us down the port side at a distance of fifteen feet. We immediately hauled out of the wake and followed parallel to it ... Fire was kept up continually and at intervals depth charges were dropped from the rails to confuse him, and cause him to make wild changes in course which had the effect of reducing his speed ...

We were gradually closing the range now, and word was passed "stand by to ram" ... The submarine made a wide turn to starboard and for the first time was plainly visible. We altered in his direction in an attempt to ram him ... He put his helm hard to port and we followed suit being inside his turning circle. We were now heading towards his port beam ...

Submarine crash dived ... at a distance of 100 to 200 yards, and a full pattern of ten depth charges ... was dropped squarely over him. After detonation of the charges had taken place, a muffled explosion ... was heard by all, and a tremendous dome-shaped bubble of air which rose to a height of approximately fifteen feet was seen.[64]

The asdic being still out of commission, this pattern, which Preuss described as "fairly well placed," had been dropped by estimate. Preuss noted with relief that as *Pictou* searched there was no sound of asdic. *Wetaskiwin, Highlander*, two other corvettes, and a US destroyer responded to *Pictou*'s call for assistance but none of the ships made firm contact. At about 0300, when most of the searchers had returned to the convoy, *U 568* withdrew and lost contact with SC 48.[65]

While these events unfolded on the port side of the convoy, *U 432*, after boldly reloading torpedo tubes on the surface in the shadow of *Barfann*, fired a coup de grace into the tanker at 0040, and then withdrew to follow the convoy from astern. To starboard, *U 553*, which had returned after the earlier attacks of that night, encountered opposition:

A destroyer of the starboard defences fires starshells which explode directly above us ... Painful! We have to move off to the south. The after escort of the leading group joins with the ship that fired at us previously to create a veritable fireworks of starshells directed at us, it is as if we are on a serving platter, an awful feeling. However, because no dangerous shell splashes can be seen in the vicinity I do not dive. As long as these chaps busy themselves with us, our comrade [*U 432*], who just knocked off the two merchant ships, will be free to operate undisturbed.[66]

Thurmann's plan did not work out. At approximately 0130, a destroyer, probably *Broadwater*, in an action much like *Pictou*'s, picked up hydrophone effect from *U 432*, began a surface pursuit and then made a snap depth charge attack as the submarine crash-dived. Damaged by this attack, the boat surfaced two hours later only to come under attack again —possibly by a US destroyer— and fled the scene. At about the same time, *U 553* encountered a destroyer, almost certainly American from Thurmann's description, fired and missed with the last two torpedoes, and withdrew under pursuit by the warship. Meanwhile, *U 558*, approaching for another attack just at the

64. Griffin, "Attack on Submarine by HMCS *Pictou*"

65. *U 568*, KTB, 17 Oct. 1941; *Highlander* signal log, 17 Oct. 1941

66. *U 553*, KTB, 17 Oct. 1941

moment *Barfann* exploded, had dropped off to avoid being illuminated and, in the face of destroyer sweeps, never regained position.[67]

Shortly before daybreak on 17 October, the four destroyers of the RN's 3rd Escort Group, *Bulldog* (SOE), *Amazon*, *Georgetown,* and *Richmond* joined. At mid-day the US destroyers, *Columbia,* and, with her undependable engines, *Baddeck* departed, as had the visiting *Pictou*. *Columbia* had so stretched her limited fuel supply that the tanks ran dry when the ship was still eight miles out of Reykjavik; the ship had to drop anchor and await help. The original corvettes of the escort, FFS *Mimosa*, HMS *Gladiolus*, HMCS *Wetaskiwin,* and *Camrose,* which like HMS *Veronica* and *Abelia* had dropped astern during the night rescuing survivors and pursuing contacts, would normally have departed as well to refuel in Iceland before picking up a westbound convoy, but *Highlander* directed them to remain as reinforcements.[68] As the vessels reported by radio and rejoined after daylight on 17 October, there was no sign of *Gladiolus,* nor was any trace of the ship or her people ever found.[69] None of the U-boat logs record an attack on anything that might have been a corvette during the night of 16–17 October, but Jürgen Rohwer, a leading authority on submarine attack records, has concluded that one of the several torpedoes fired by *U 558* and *U 432* that ran past their intended targets in the midst of a *mêlée* of explosions probably sank the corvette.[70]

A particularly welcome reinforcement for the escorts as dawn broke on 17 October was renewed air cover. "Emerging from the wreck-strewn sea," recalled Easton,

> I suddenly became aware of another searcher, one which I had never expected to see. Coming directly towards us was a flying boat, no more than two hundred feet above the water, travelling very slowly. It seemed as strange a sight and as unnatural as if an albatross had come up from its native haunts in the Southern Ocean and suddenly appeared over a northern sea.
>
> As she drew nearer, a light flashed on and off, a signal was being passed. She was one of those slow giants, a Catalina. She circled around us, leaning over laboriously yet gracefully as she turned, sometimes showing her broad belly, until she had received our message. Then, straightening out, she flew off to the west. It was the first time I had ever seen an aircraft so far out at sea, six hundred miles from Ireland.[71]

The aircraft forced the U-boats to submerge repeatedly so that they could not pursue the convoy closely.[72] In addition, the British corvette *Veronica*, which had lingered longer than the other corvettes in the vicinity of the night action to search for survivors, intercepted a submarine on the surface, almost certainly *U 751* as she was rejoining the convoy during the afternoon of 17 October. The boat crash-dived and *Veronica* dropped thirty-four depth charges in five attacks over the next hour. None were close to the mark, however, they kept down not only *U 751* but also

67. *U 558*, *U 553*, and *U 432*, KTB, 17 Oct. 1941; Astwood to Capt (D) Londonderry, "Report of Attack on U-Boat by HMS *Broadwater* on 17 Oct. 1941," 22 Oct. 1941, PRO, ADM 237/187; Thebaud to CNO, "Report of Operations Involving Convoy SC48 and Torpedoing of *Kearny*," 20 Oct. 1941, file A-14, NARA, RG 313 Red, CTF 24, 1941 Confidential, box 8804

68. HMS *Highlander* to Capt (D) Liverpool, 10 Nov. 1941; *Columbia* ROP

69. ACIC to C-in-C WA, 1646/21 Oct. 1941, PRO, ADM 237/187

70. Rohwer, *Axis Submarine Successes*, 69

71. Easton, *50 North*, 87

72. Drent, "Summary of Battle around SC 48 as Reported by U-Boat KTBs," 29 Dec. 1999, DHH

U 502, who had been forced under by an aircraft sweep in the area before *Veronica* had arrived on the scene. "This fellow apparently wants to unload his entire cargo on us," wearily commented von Rosentiel of *U 502*.[73]

This action and the air sweeps prevented most of the submarines, which now included the four reinforcing boats that had come up from the French coast, from making contact as they searched at speed through the night of 17-18 October. However, *U 101* found *Broadwater* when the destroyer dropped behind the convoy and fired a spread of four torpedoes that demolished the forward part of the vessel with heavy loss of life during the dark early hours of 18 October. Kapitänleutnant Ernst Mengersen, the experienced commanding officer of the submarine, regretted that he had fired all his forward torpedoes and could therefore not also attack the other warships that came to rescue the survivors. The hulk remained afloat through the night, while trawlers of the 3rd Escort Group took off survivors.[74] None of the submarines was able to regain contact with SC 48, and Dönitz called off the pursuit, but the convoy's ordeal was not over.[75] A full gale on 19 October scattered the remaining ships and caused serious damage to at least two of the merchantmen and one of the escorting destroyers.[76]

With nine merchant ships and two escorts sunk, and a USN fleet destroyer badly damaged, SC 48 was a disaster on a scale approaching that of SC 42. But unlike the earlier battle, SC 48's escort had been reinforced massively and in good time. Captain Thebaud commented with some feeling on the apparently insuperable difficulties of protecting slow convoys, "It is submitted that a convoy proceeding at a speed of 7 knots and shadowed by submarines is doomed to the acceptance of very severe losses unless escorted by an impracticably large number of screening vessels." Thebaud was particularly frustrated at the invisibility of the attackers, despite good asdic and visibility conditions. "It is hard to avoid the conclusion that the torpedoes were fired from positions well outside of the screening ships and well beyond the effective range of their listening gear."[77] In other words, the slowness of the movement of the ships, and their large numbers in a relatively compact mass had enabled the submarines to fire virtually unaimed shots from very long range and still hit targets. Of course, this was not at all the case. The American ships had experienced at first hand the difficulties without effective radar of detecting surfaced submarines within a few hundred yards of the escorts themselves. Even the U-boat commanders, as we have seen, had on several occasions been certain they had overplayed their hand, and were surprised at not being detected. As Thurmann concluded, "you will never be seen on the surface at night, even at very short ranges, provided that you remain silent and cold-blooded."[78]

Part of the answer, as British authorities fully realized, was centimetric radar, which SC 48's escorts lacked. That made escort cohesion all the more important, but this was also notable by its absence. Inevitably, the reinforcements were a patchwork of ships from many groups. The

---

73. *U 502* and *U 751*, KTB, 17 Oct. 1941; HMS *Veronica* to Capt (D) Londonderry, 19 Oct. 1941, PRO, ADM 37/187

74. *U 101*, *KTB*, 18 Oct. 1941; *Highlander* to Capt (D) Liverpool, 10 Nov. 1941; CO HM Trawler *Cape Warwick* to Capt (D) Greenock, "Rescue of Survivors from HMS *Broadwater*," 22 Oct. 1941, ADM 237/187

75. BdU, KTB, 19 Oct. 1941

76. Elliot, "Mercantile Convoy No 'SC 48,'"; SO 3rd Escort Group to C-in-C WA, 0925/20 Oct. 1941, PRO, ADM 237/187

77. Thebaud to CNO, "Operations Involving Convoy SC 48 and Torpedoing of *Kearny*."

78. *U 553*, KTB, "Lessons Learned"

Americans, moreover, had begun convoy operations scarcely four weeks before. Although the agreements between the USN and RN had laid down that the senior officer present, whatever his nationality, should assume overall command, detailed coordination presented an enormous challenge, especially given the inexperience of the Americans and many of the Canadian ships. Commander Boucher of *Highlander* was especially critical of the lack of communications discipline among the Canadian corvettes and the American destroyers. The problem among the Canadian ships, however, had arisen only after dawn on 17 October: "the [RCN] corvettes seemed to consider that once daylight had come there was no further reason to maintain R/T silence, failing to appreciate that enemy reports from detached ships, of which there were several, are of the greatest importance." Commodore Murray, for the sins of the corvettes, was criticized by the C-in-C Western Approaches, Admiral Noble, about the "incredible state of R/T indiscipline."[79] Much more serious had been chatter among the US ships who at critical points in the action on the night of 16 to 17 October had overwhelmed Canadian and British escorts with their constant message traffic sent at high power.[80]

The real answer to defence of a convoy known to be under pursuit by U-boats, suggested Commander A.J. Baker-Cresswell, RN, senior officer of the 3rd Escort Group, was to have a special group of ships fitted with HF/DF equipment and short-wave radar ready to close the scene and hunt submarines as they attempted to shadow. Senior authorities could only minute that as much as could be done was being done, and Baker-Cresswell himself acknowledged that the hunting group could only function properly if the convoy had "enough escorts ... to form a good close screen," the central problem of antisubmarine defence in the autumn of 1941.[81] Thebaud, who would have been much less well versed in the potential of radar and shipborne HF/DF thought a similar result could be produced by aggressive use of aircraft to put down shadowers. This, of course, had largely been achieved on 17 October, at the time of the US group's departure, when the convoy moved within range of continuous shore-based air cover. As for the problem of the limited range of shore-based aviation, Thebaud asked "might not carrier based planes be used operating from a carrier in the North Atlantic herself screened by destroyers and regulating her position to coordinate with the known movements of slow convoys?"[82] The British were working on such a solution, but with the shortage of resources were focusing on the route to Gibraltar, where there was a heavier threat than on the central North Atlantic.

The Admiralty never completed an analysis of the SC 48 battle, presumably because the night actions were so confused and the records inconclusive. The U-boat records now available confirm the importance of defence in depth, the effectiveness of the air cover on 17 October, and of even the limited air support possible on 16 October. Equally important, all four attacks by Commonwealth surface escorts in which the presence of a submarine can be confirmed were achieved by ships that were just joining the convoy, or trailing behind it, who surprised submarines attempting to contact or withdraw from the convoy at speed on the surface. German records also confirm that the convoy had the misfortune to encounter a large pack of recently

---

79.   C-in-C WA to Capt (D) Liverpool, "ROP of Third Escort Group with convoy SC 48 ...," 4 Dec. 1941, PRO, ADM 237/187

80.   HMS *Highlander* to Capt (D) Liverpool, 10 Nov. 1941, PRO, ADM 237/187

81.   Baker-Cresswell to Capt (D) Greenock, "Escort for Convoy SC 48," 21 Oct. 1941, PRO, ADM 237/187

82.   Thebaud to CNO, "Operations involving Convoy SC 48 and Torpedoing of *Kearny*"

replenished boats, most commanded by experienced and aggressive officers. The miserable weather conditions that forced the least experienced corvettes to lose contact and caused many of the merchantmen to straggle would have almost certainly prevented most of the U-boats ever gaining contact had it not been for the superb seamanship and relentless tenacity of a single German commander, Thurmann.

The SC 48 battle certainly highlighted the shortcomings of the Canadian escorts. Equally, that fully half of the initial escort included ships that had not yet completed basic work-ups and completion refits—in contravention of policies and standards the RCN had recently adopted as a result of the best British advice—underscores the desperate shortage of warships among the Allied forces. Yet, it is also striking that Canadian escorts made two of the four attacks by Commonwealth ships that are known to have deterred the U-boats. *Pictou*'s achievement was particularly noteworthy, for the ship had commissioned only at the end of April and had lost two commanding officers, the first proving unequal to the strain and the second receiving a transfer to a shore appointment after a fortnight in command. Such was the shortage of qualified commanding officers that Lieutenant Griffin, the executive officer, had then taken command, only five weeks before the SC 48 operation. Griffin, although he had done a year of his university education at the Royal Military College at the beginning of the 1930s, had joined the RCNVR at the outbreak of war and been commissioned only in July 1940.[83] *Columbia*'s textbook attack on *U 553* that put that grimly determined U-boat off the trail was also a vindication of sorts. The commanding officer, Lieutenant-Commander S.W. Davis, had served with the RN from 1910 to 1926, and came out with the RCN on the outbreak of war, serving initially as a staff officer at headquarters where he impressed Commodore Murray, who may well have influenced the decision to give him command of *Columbia* when that destroyer was transferred from the USN in the autumn of 1940. Although Davis did not impress Commodore G.C. Jones's staff at Halifax—"A tired old man" was how Jones described him (Davis was forty-four in 1941)—Murray stood by him, and would later fight successfully for his promotion.[84]

The German deployment south of Greenland that resulted in the attack on SC 48 marked the beginning of a fresh push into the western part of the North Atlantic. Dönitz had long been eager to repeat the springtime thrust against convoys as they departed from the vicinity of Newfoundland, an effort that he believed would produce better results with the increased number of U-boats that had become available, and in weather conditions that could only have improved from the ice packs and nearly constant fog of May and June. Hitler's injunction against provocation of the United States during the early stages of the land offensive into Russia had been a major impediment to a renewed campaign in the west, but on 19 October the Naval Staff gave Dönitz the permission he wanted. He immediately ordered the four submarines that had formed the northern end of the Greenland patrol line and not become involved in the SC 48 battle to advance to within 100 miles of the Strait of Belle Isle. These boats now became known as Group *Mordbrenner*. Behind them were two other groups, with a total of sixteen submarines. Group *Schlagetod*, consisting mainly of newly deployed boats, was to patrol about halfway between Newfoundland and Greenland to intercept convoys following the north route from Cape Race. Group *Reissewolf*, which for the most part includ-

83. A. Griffin, "A Naval Officer's War: Episode One," *Starshell* 7 (Spring 1999), 10-12; Ken Macpherson and John Burgess *Ships of Canada's Naval Forces*, 198

84. COAC min, 21 Apr. 1942 on Capt (D) Halifax, Form 206, 18 Apr. 1942, NSC, NPRC O-18540

ed participants in the SC 48 battle that still had torpedoes and sufficient fuel, was to deploy to the immediate east and south of *Schlagetod*, about a third of the way between Newfoundland and Iceland, to catch convoys that took the southern, great circle route towards Iceland.[85]

Soon after the *Mordbrenner* boats began to arrive off the Straits of Belle Isle on 20 October, British intelligence was able to pass warnings to the Canadian and US forces in Newfoundland. Canadian and American aircraft began a heavy schedule of patrols on 24 October that soon forced under three of the four submarines but thereafter weather forced a curtailment of air operations.[86] Aircraft was all the submariners saw, for no shipping was passing through the strait. The last convoy to go north around Newfoundland had been SC 48 ten days earlier. Since then convoys had gone south of Cape Race, possibly because SC 46, on navigating the straits at the end of September, had suffered heavy losses to collisions and groundings in a sudden fog, a warning of the arrival of difficult autumn conditions.[87]

Meanwhile, the submarines crossing the ocean to reinforce the distant patrols on the routes from Cape Race had been delayed while pursuing contacts on convoys in the eastern Atlantic. The resulting radio traffic enabled British intelligence to divert most convoys clear of the danger areas.[88] The focus of the German chase became ON 28, a fast westbound convoy that *U 74* located on 27 October southwest of Iceland. The speed of the convoy and heavy weather made it exceedingly difficult for the submarines to keep contact, and they exposed themselves to sightings and counterattacks by the US destroyers. Although the escorts did not sink any of the U-boats, they limited the convoy's losses to only one tanker.

Although British intelligence knew the convoy was being pursued, they were aware of only the one or two U-boats that from time to time reported contact. In fact, U-boat Command was attempting a concentration to catch ON 28 as it approached Cape Race, an area that the Allies were unaware was threatened. On 28 to 29 October Dönitz, correctly concluding that there was no traffic in the Strait of Belle Isle, ordered the four *Mordbrenner* boats to positions in an arc covering the Avalon peninsula from fifty miles off St John's down to fifty miles south of Cape Race. Then on 31 October, in view of ON 28's success in outrunning its pursuers, Dönitz ordered the *Mordbrenner* group southeast of Cape Race across the convoy's presumed course. Several of the *Reissewolf* group of boats, on the Cape Race–Iceland route, were running low on fuel as a result of the pursuit of ON 28. Reinforcements were arriving for this group, which BdU renamed *Strosstrupp*. Both this group and *Schlagetod*, to the northwest on the route to Greenland, were closing to within 300 to 400 miles of Newfoundland. Dönitz despatched one of the *Schlagetod* submarines, *U 123*, to take up the close watch on the Strait of Belle Isle. Thus, by 1 November there was a total of sixteen submarines west of 42° West, five of them south of Cape Race.[89]

It was not until the early hours of 31 October that Bletchley Park was able to decrypt the settings for German signals sent during the preceding three days. The cryptographers could not solve

85. BdU, KTB, 19 Oct. 1941

86. DeMarbois to DNI, "Narrative of Submarines off Newfoundland," 9 May 1942, NAC, RG 24, 6901, NSS 8910-166/25 pt 1; M. Hadley, *U-boats against Canada* (Kingston 1985), 25; W.A.B. Douglas, *Creation of a National Air Force* (Toronto 1986), 481-4

87. FONF WD, Oct. 1941; *Ottawa* ROP, SC 46, 6 Oct. 1941, "SC 46," DHH 88/1mfm, reel 31

88. Kahn, *Seizing the Enigma*, 191-4; files for ON 24 through ON 29, NARA, RG 313 Red, CTF 24, box 8703

89. BdU, KTB, 27 Oct. to 1 Nov. 1941

the disguised letter designations for the main German map grid squares, but there was evidently enough information in the undisguised numeric designations of the subsquares and contextual data to indicate the deployment of *Mordbrenner* to the vicinity of Cape Race.[90] The eastbound SC 52, which had departed Sydney on 29 October, was at that very time approaching Cape Race, and the US Navy Department immediately diverted the convoy to the south, well clear of the cape, just as the local escort of two RCN corvettes, turned over to the first element of the NEF mid-ocean group, the Canadian corvettes *Windflower* and *Buctouche*, the British corvette *Nasturtium*, and the Free French corvette *Aconit*.[91] During the day on 31 October, Bletchley Park was able to read Enigma within a very few hours, including signals directing the *Mordbrenner* boats further south to try to catch ON 28.[92] This placed them across SC 52's new course; as well, there were indications that the boats following ON 28 from the east were still in contact.[93] Therefore, during the early evening of 31 October, the Navy Department reversed the course of the convoy, due north to run seaward of the Avalon Peninsula, through waters which, according to Ultra, the U-boats should already have vacated in pursuit of ON 28 far to the south.

Unknown to Allied intelligence, *U 374* had not moved south but lingered off St John's, where, early on 31 October, it had sunk the independently routed merchant ship *King Malcolm*. The vessel went down almost instantly, without being able to transmit a signal, and without any survivors. During the late morning of 1 November, about sixty miles off St John's, it was *U 374* that located SC 52 on its new northbound course. BdU ordered the boat not to attack but to shadow, while most of the *Schlagetod* group, some 300 miles to the northeast, and *U 123*, which was approaching the Strait of Belle Isle, closed for a mass attack. Dönitz hoped in this way to concentrate ten or more submarines, which he designated *Raubritter*.[94] Allied intelligence was unaware of the new threat. Bletchley Park was unable to solve the Enigma settings for 1 November and the days following until 4 November, and *U 374*'s contact reports appear not to have been DF'd. In fact, the Admiralty confirmed a new route for SC 52 on the morning of 1 November that took the convoy almost due north nearly to the Arctic circle and backtracking towards the northern tip of Labrador, with the intention of keeping it clear of the *Schlagetod* boats, some of which Allied intelligence had located and believed were still hovering out at sea on the route between Cape Race and Greenland.[95]

The remainder of the escort for SC 52, the British destroyers *Broadway* (Lieutenant-Commander T. Taylor, RN, SOE) and *Burwell*, and the Canadian corvettes *Galt* and *Cobalt* joined on 1 November. Just as the last of the additional escorts were arriving that night, *Aconit* made a U-boat sighting report and attacked. Other escorts joined her to sweep for the contact, but when there were no early

90. ZTPG 14269, BdU to *Mordbrenner*, TOO 1001/1046/29 Oct. 1941, NS to IG8G, 0055/31 Oct. 1941, PRO, DEFE 3/34, ZTPG 14359; BdU to *Mordbrenner*, TOO 2012/28 Oct. 1941, NS to ID8G, 0625/31 Oct. 1941, PRO, DEFE 3/34

91. *Battleford* to NOIC Sydney, "Report on Convoy Duty with ... SC 52," 1 Nov. 1941, "SC 52," DHH 81/520/8280, box 9; White, "Convoy Form D, Mercantile Convoy 'SC 52,'" 5 Nov. 1941; Adm to C-in-C WA, 1355A/31 Oct. 1941, repeated OPNAV to escorts SC 52, 0721/31 Aug. 1941, PRO, ADM 237/188

92. ZTPG 14428, TOO 2123/31 Oct. 1941, NS to ID8G, 1137/31 Oct. 1941, ZTPG 14550, TOO 1214/31 Oct. 1941, NS to ID8G, 1629/31 Oct. 1941, PRO, DEFE 3/34

93. Adm to OPNAV, 1504a/31 Oct. 1941, NSS 8280 "ON 28," DHH 89/34 mfm, reel 17

94. BdU, KTB, 1 Nov. 1941

95. Adm to C-in-C WA, 1120A and 1252A/1 Nov. 1941, PRO, ADM 237/188; "Escort of Convoy SC 52," 1 Nov. 1941, NARA, RG 313 Red, CTF 24, box 8710

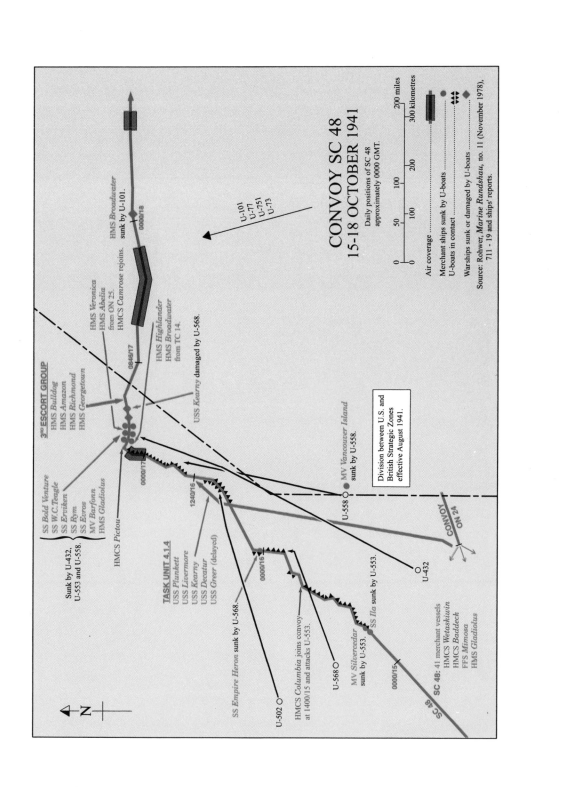

CONVOY SC 48
15-18 OCTOBER 1941

3RD ESCORT GROUP
HMS Bulldog
HMS Amazon
HMS Richmond
HMS Georgetown

SS Bold Venture
SS W.C.Teagle
SS Erviken
SS Rym
SS Evros
MV Barfonn
HMS Gladiolus

Sunk by U-432,
U-553 and U-558.

HMCS Pictou

HMS Veronica
HMS Abelia
from ON 25.
HMCS Camrose rejoins.

HMS Broadwater
sunk by U-101.

0000/18

0046/17

HMS Highlander
HMS Broadwater
from TC 14.

USS Kearny damaged by U-568.

0000/17

1240/16

TASK UNIT 4.1.4
USS Plunkett
USS Livermore
USS Kearny
USS Decatur
USS Greer (delayed)

SS Empire Heron sunk by U-568.

U-502

HMCS Columbia joins convoy
at 1400/15 and attacks U-553.

U-568

MV Silvercedar
sunk by U-553.

0000/16

SS Ila sunk by U-553.

0000/15

SC 48: 41 merchant vessels
HMCS Wetaskiwin
HMCS Baddeck
FFS Mimosa
HMS Gladiolus

SC 48

U-432

MV Vancouver Island
sunk by U-558.

U-558

Division between U.S. and
British Strategic Zones
effective August 1941.

CONVOY
ON 24

U-101
U-77
U-751
U-73

Daily positions of SC 48
approximately 0000 GMT.

Air coverage

Merchant ships sunk by U-boats

U-boats in contact

Warships sunk or damaged by U-boats

Source: Rohwer, *Marine Rundshau*, no. 11 (November 1978),
711 - 19 and ships' reports.

0   50   100   200 miles
0   100   200   300 kilometres

N

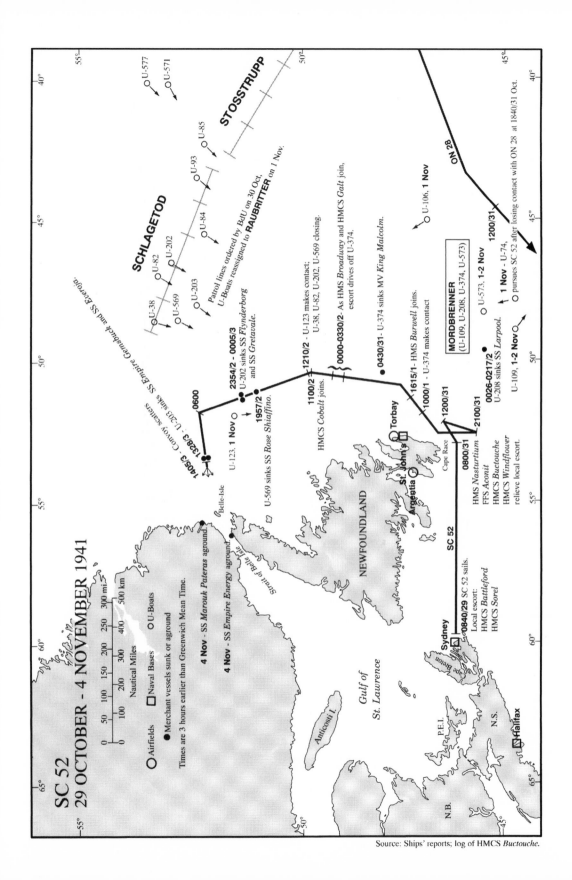

SC 52
29 OCTOBER - 4 NOVEMBER 1941

Nautical Miles

0   50   100 150 200 250 300 mi.

0   100 200 300 400 500 km

○ Airfields □ Naval Bases

● U-Boats

● Merchant vessels sunk or aground

4 Nov - SS Marouk Pateras aground.

4 Nov - SS Empire Energy aground.

Times are 3 hours earlier than Greenwich Mean Time.

STOSSTRUPP

U-577 U-571

U-85

U-93

SCHLAGETOD

U-84

U-202

U-82

U-203

U-38

U-569

Patrol lines ordered by BdU on 30 Oct. U-Boats reassigned to **RAUBRITTER** on 1 Nov.

1405/3 - Convoy scatters

1328/3 - U-203 sinks SS Gretavale and SS Empire Gemsbuck and SS Everton.

0600

2354/2 - 0005/3 - U-202 sinks SS Flynderborg and SS Gretavale.

1957/2

U-569 sinks SS Rose Shiaffino.

U-123, **1 Nov** ○

1210/2 - U-123 makes contact; U-38, U-82, U-202, U-569 closing.

1100/2 - HMCS Cobalt joins.

0000-0330/2 - As HMS Broadway and HMCS Galt join, escort drives off U-374.

0430/31 - U-374 sinks MV King Malcolm.

1615/1 - HMS Burwell joins.

1000/1 - U-374 makes contact

MORDBRENNER (U-109, U-208, U-374, U-573)

U-573, **1-2 Nov** ○

0026-0217/2 U-208 sinks SS Larpool.

U-109, **1-2 Nov** ○

1 Nov - U-74 ○

○ U-106. **1 Nov**

1200/31

ON 28

○ pursues SC 52 after losing contact with ON 28 at 1840/31 Oct.

1200/31

2100/31

0800/31

Cape Race

Torbay

St. John's

Argentia

HMS Nasturtium
FFS Aconit
HMCS Buctouche
HMCS Windflower
relieve local escort.

SC 52

0840/29 SC 52 sails.

Local escort:
HMCS Battleford
HMCS Sorel

Belle-Isle

Strait of Belle Isle

NEWFOUNDLAND

Sydney

Cape Breton I.

Anticosti I.

Gulf of St. Lawrence

P.E.I.

N.S.

Halifax

N.B.

Source: Ships' reports; log of HMCS Buctouche.

results Taylor called it off, for reasons that indicated the full extent to which intelligence had failed to appreciate the threat to the convoy: "As ... submarine disposition [intelligence report] did not suggest the possibility of [a U-boat] in this area, I decided object seen was probably a whale ... Subsequent events seem to show my view of situation was wrong."[96] *Aconit*'s attack had indeed driven off *U 374* but at mid-day on 2 November, *U 123*, coming from the north, sighted the convoy about 200 miles seaward and somewhat to the south of the Strait of Belle Isle. By nightfall, four other boats were in contact or nearby.[97]

U 569 was the first to close to attack, coming across the van and then trying to penetrate the starboard side in the early hours of darkness on the evening of 2 November. Twice the boat was forced back by an escort, probably HMS *Nasturtium*. Purposeful as the corvette's manoeuvres seemed to the submarine, the British crew had made only a fleeting and uncertain sighting that on investigation yielded an unpromising asdic contact. Finally, on the third attempt, the submarine fired a long range salvo of four torpedoes at the mass of steamers 4,000 metres away and heard two detonations.[98] Some of the escorts and merchant vessels also heard the explosions but believed they were depth charge attacks, *Broadway* having ordered the warships immediately to attack any contact and report only if investigation yielded evidence of a U-boat. *U 569* made a fourth approach, only to find an escort closing and hastily fired two torpedoes that missed.[99]

U 123, still acting as the main shadower and observing from a distance, was convinced, like *U 569*, that the escorts knew the convoy was under attack. From the time of the depth charge and torpedo explosions resulting from *U 569*'s third and fourth approaches, according to *U 123*, "shadowing became difficult because the escorts had been drawn to the front of the convoy in order to drive off boats that were penetrating into the convoy from ahead. Everywhere our boats could be seen prowling around. These came into sight as soon as they came over the horizon because of the good visibility with the result that on approaching one another we often turned away from each other. Then the destroyers made thrusts out from the convoy and attempted to drive the boats away."[100]

The escorts remained ignorant of the gathering pack. It was just before midnight 2 November, that *U 202* finally revealed its presence, sinking the two lead freighters on the port wing of the convoy, the 2,022-ton SS *Flynderborg* and the 4,586-ton SS *Gretavale*.[101] Because of the strength of the screen and the brightness of the night, the U boat had made a submerged attack. The response came quickly: "2 depth charges, which were well aimed; the boat is driven deeper in a remarkable manner. One light bulb is knocked out, otherwise everything is in order ... Now the attackers start

---

96. HMS *Broadway*, "ROP for Convoy SC 52 and ON 29," "ON 29" file, DHH mfm 88/1, reel 7. Cobalt returned to St John's at mid-day on 1 Nov. and then rejoined the convoy late the next morning.

97. BdU, KTB, 1-2 Nov. 1941; *U 123*, KTB, 2 Nov. 1941

98. These may well have marked the death of *Rose Schiaffino*, a 4,200-ton steamer carrying iron ore from Wabana. Her disappearance was not noticed until the convoy reached port nearly a week later, and it seems likely that *U 569*'s torpedoes had sent the heavily laden ship to the bottom so quickly that she left no trace. Rohwer, *Axis Submarine Successes*, 71; *Lloyd's War Losses* II, 1301

99. *U 569*, KTB, 2-3 Nov. 1941; HMS *Nasturtium* to Capt (D) Newfoundland, "Report of Movements after Attacks on SC 52," 5 Nov. 1941, PRO, ADM237/188; HMS *Broadway*, "Report of Attacks on SC 52 to Accompany Letter of Proceedings," DHH, 88/1 mfm, reel 7, ON 29

100. *U 123*, KTB, 3 Nov. 1941

101. "Local time" here is taken as three hours earlier than GMT, and five hours earlier than Central European Time, which gives a reasonable reconciliation of the various time zones reported by the escorts.

their old familiar game: one stops, other proceeds at listening speed. Then they change roles. This lasts for a fairly long time, both the destroyer and the escort remain in my vicinity." In fact, both destroyers of the escort were engaged in the hunt and although they did not make asdic contact, succeeded in keeping *U 202* down long enough that it could not regain the convoy. While hunting, Taylor "ordered *Windflower* to pick up survivors of both ships—which he did with commendable skill."[102]

Like *U 202*, *U 123* and *U 203* had been given pause by the brightness of the moon and the activity of the escorts. As a low fog developed at about 0300 on 3 November, they closed on the surface and *U 123* fired two torpedoes that missed but alerted the escorts; *Broadway* picked up hydrophone effect from the torpedoes on her asdic. The low visibility, aggressive searches being conducted by the escorts, and the collision-threatening movements of the merchant ships in the fog caused the submarines to lose contact.[103]

News of *U 202*'s successful attacks was already bringing the Admiralty to the conclusion that it would be suicide for the slow convoy to continue across the Atlantic. The heavy losses of SC 42 and SC 48, which the submarines had not found until they were well out into the North Atlantic, must have greatly influenced the decision: what chance would SC 52 have when the U-boats had begun to concentrate at the very beginning of its fourteen-day voyage? Hazy as the intelligence picture had become, it was still clear that there were many boats in the western part of the ocean available to reinforce the pack and the submarines' recent tenacious pursuit of ON 28 across the entire breadth of the North Atlantic left no doubt about Dönitz's intentions. The routing staff at the US Navy Department agreed with the Admiralty's pessimism, and in the forenoon of 3 November ordered SC 52 to swing into the Strait of Belle Isle by the "shortest route" and return through the Gulf of St Lawrence to Sydney.[104] It was the only convoy of the war to be turned back by the threat of submarine attack alone.

Air cover for convoys south of the Strait of Belle Isle was the responsibility of the US Naval Air Station at Argentia. Aircraft despatched in the very good flying conditions on 1 and 2 November had failed to make contact, apparently because of the convoy's many radical diversions. The inevitable time lag between despatch of the diversion signal, and its receipt and execution by the convoy, created considerable uncertainty as to its actual position. Now, on the morning of 3 November, the station prepared to fly off several aircraft, but was defeated by the heavy fog.[105]

Of the U-boats, only *U 203* under Kapitänleutnant Mützelburg managed to keep contact with the convoy in the fog. In the early afternoon of 3 November, when the convoy was about seventy miles due east of the Strait of Belle Isle, Mützelburg stealthily penetrated the convoy in low visibility and made a blind submerged attack, using sound bearings to aim a spread of four torpedoes that sank two ships, the 5,626-ton *Empire Gemsbuck* and the 4,830-ton *Everoja*, on the starboard quarter of the convoy. While HMCS *Buctouche* and HMS *Nasturtium* rescued the crews, *Broadway*

---

102. *U 202*, KTB, 3 Nov. 1941; HMS *Broadway*, "Report of Attacks on SC 52 to Accompany Letter of Proceedings"

103. *U 123* and *U 203*, KTB, 3 Nov. 1941; HMS *Broadway*, "Report of Attacks on SC 52 to Accompany Letter of Proceedings"

104. Adm to C-in-C WA, 1726A/3 Nov. 1941, reporting OPNAV's concurrence at 1215a (1315 GMT), PRO, ADM 237/188; HMS *Broadway*, "ROP for Convoy SC 52 and ON 29" states that *Broadway* passed OPNAV's instruction to return through the Strait of Belle Isle to the convoy commodore for execution at 1150/3 Nov. local time.

105. "Escort of Convoy SC 52," 3-4 Nov. 1941, NARA, RG 313 Red, CTF 24, box 8710. The entry for 3 Nov. contains the air operations reports for 1-2 Nov. as well as for the early part of 3 Nov.

and *Burwell* led the counterattack. Lieutenant-Commander Taylor and the convoy commodore quickly agreed that in the fog there was no hope of organizing a coordinated defence of the convoy perimeter, and therefore ordered the merchant ships to scatter, making their own way through the Strait of Belle Isle. The escorts remained, scouring the vicinity of the attack, and managed to keep *U 203* under for six hours.[106]

The ordeal was not over. While entering the Strait of Belle Isle on 4 November, two of the ships ran aground and became total losses.[107] Captain S.N. White, RNR, the commodore of SC 52, was incensed by the entire experience. "I beg to report that I have just returned to Sydney, C.B., after a cruise round Newfoundland lasting a week, starting with 35 ships and returning with 28." To White, who was aware only of the early intelligence that had placed a U-boat concentration off the Strait of Belle Isle and not of the late breaking intelligence about the movement of these boats to the south, the diversion of the convoy northwards late on 31 October seemed madness, and the chance sighting by a boat that had been late to comply with the orders to move south, the result of incompetence:

> On returning here I find all my doubts and lack of confidence confirmed. Neither Sydney, Halifax nor C-in-C WA had any knowledge of our movements beyond belated information that we were returning!! When I asked "Who is this OPNAV," I am told "Washington"!!!
>
> With all due respect I would suggest that, if this is so, I do not feel that SC 52 was given a fair chance.[108]

When White returned to Britain later in the month, he was still angry, and complained again to Western Approaches:

> If, as seems the case, the foci of enemy attacks on our convoys are becoming concentrated in the western portions of the Atlantic, it may be that one reason for this is to avoid the greater efficiency of the British escort groups.
>
> Without wishing in any way to disparage our Canadian or American friends; I would submit that it is only logical that, as they have had nothing like the opportunity of actual contact with enemy submarines, they cannot be expected to have reached the same degree of mutual understanding and team work that exists in the British escort groups.
>
> Is there no possibility of greater exchange of personnel or of vessels or the transferring of some of the more experienced of our escort group commanders to work on the Canadian side and give them the benefit of their experience.
>
> Frankly, at present, however zealous the Canadian escort personnel may be, I do not feel that they have quite the degree of efficiency required to deal effectively with the type of attack experienced by SC 52.[109]

White voiced the frustration felt by many British convoy commodores and escort commanders, and there was much that was true in what he said and useful in what he recommended. He could

---

106. *U 203*, KTB, 3 Nov. 1941; HMS *Broadway*, "Report of Attacks on SC 52 to Accompany Letter of Proceedings"; MacKay, "Report of Attack on Submarine 3 Nov. 1941," 25 Mar. 1942, ibid; HMS *Nasturtium* to Capt (D) Newfoundland, 5 Nov. 1941, PRO, ADM 237/188

107. CCNF WD, Nov. 1941, DHH, NHS NSS 1000-5-20 pt 1; Simpson, "A History of Naval Control Service at Sydney, NS," nd, DHH, 81/520/1440-127

108. White to C-in-C WA, "Report of Convoy SC 52, 6 Nov. 1941, PRO, ADM 237/188

109. White to C-in-C WA, 28 Nov. 1941, PRO, ADM 237/188

not have known, however, that the diversions of which he complained, and the decision to send the convoy back to Sydney, came from the Admiralty. The escort, moreover, was a strong one, whose core was indeed experienced British, Free French, and Canadian warships, and the U-boat records leave no doubt that they did exceptionally well under difficult circumstances, limiting a considerable pack of U-boats to a few shots, most in haste and at long range; the fact that these attacks nevertheless destroyed four merchantmen was a measure of what sitting ducks these slow-moving vessels were. Although SC 52 was the only convoy of the war to be turned back, and faced the threat of attack nearly within sight of friendly territory, this reflected the vulnerability of the slow convoys given the numbers of escorts and the type of equipment available in 1941. Certainly the decision to turn back was the right one. The pack was lying in wait across the convoy's seaward route the moment it slipped into the Strait of Belle Isle. Most of SC 52's ships soon sailed from Sydney in SC 54 on 10 November and reached Britain without casualties. SC 52 could have been nearly wiped out; as it was, the ships lost barely two weeks of time.

White's sharp criticism of Canadian escorts, although they could be challenged with respect to SC 52, echoed what senior Canadian officers themselves were saying about the state of the fleet. On 15 October—paradoxically just hours after SC 48 came under attack—Murray had signalled Ottawa to sharpen his earlier warnings about the overcommitment of his forces. "It has only been possible to maintain a standard of eight ships in each group by overworking these ships which are able to continue at sea to such a serious extent that more frequent and more serious breakdowns may be expected in material and personnel of these ships in the near future unless the strain is considerably reduced." Even with the new corvettes coming forward from Halifax and Sydney, he had been able to keep the groups more or less up to strength only by pulling three corvettes out of each group due for rest and training at St John's and hurrying them back out to sea with another group. "It is believed that at least 12 ships instead of 10 are required to maintain an 8 ship group, making a requirement of 72 ships in all instead of 60. As there is no prospect of an increase in number of long legged destroyers it is strongly urged that corvettes strength of NEF be increased to 59, that is, an increase of 10 above present strength."[110] NSHQ responded by informing Murray of the new policy to assign all corvettes to the NEF, which would give him a total of sixty Canadian vessels of this type by year's end, an increase of twenty-one over the existing strength. This would provide a margin to relieve the corvettes provided by Western Approaches, seven Royal Navy and three Free French.[111]

Meanwhile, Captain (D) at St John's sent Murray a bleak assessment of conditions in the force:

> Recently corvettes have escorted convoys Eastbound for sixteen days and then after between four and eighteen hours in harbour have returned with Westbound convoys, this voyage lasting between fourteen and sixteen days. This is quite unacceptable.

> 3. There seems to be a strong tendency to estimate the endurance of these small ships principally on their fuel carrying capacity. This is not only fallacious, but positively dangerous.

> The factor which will ultimately control their ability usefully to keep the sea, is that of the endurance of personnel, particularly that of Commanding Officers.

110. CCNF to NSHQ, 2002z/15 Oct. 1941, NAC, RG 24, 11941, file C-15, "Group 11—Organisation ..."

111. NSHQ to CCNF, 2046z/16 Oct. 1941, NSHQ to COAC, 1715z/18 Oct. 1941, NAC, RG 24, 11941, file C-15, "Group 11—Organisation ..."

Scraping ice off *Saguenay*'s quarterdeck in St. John's harbour. (NAC, 200114)

Top: Grub's up in *Mayflower*. Left to right, Sub-Lieutenant J.A. Pape, CPO J. Cosser, and seamen G. Wilson and E. Audet. (NAC, PAC 204340)

Bottom: Icing and cold were constant shipmates in the North Atlantic winter. (NAC, PA 204685)

It is essential to remember in this connection that for the most part commanding Officers have not one other officer on whom they can completely rely; furthermore many of these ships are grossly under manned, which imposes extra duty on men who are already suffering most arduous conditions ...

6. Unless very urgent steps can be taken ...I must report that grave danger exists of breakdowns in health, morale and discipline.

Murray forwarded Captain Stevens's note to headquarters. He recommended it as an accurate statement of the existing state of affairs, but was more optimistic about the future. Stevens's greatest fear was that winter weather damage would reduce the force to as little as 50 percent running strength, Western Approaches Command's experience in the winter of 1940, in which case the Newfoundland force would collapse if it continued to try to meet the existing schedules. Murray believed Western Approaches' large percentage of ships under repair had been mainly the result of the early difficulties with the newly arrived Town class destroyers. He hoped to keep two-thirds of the force's ships running, in which case the reinforcements promised by headquarters would give an adequate margin.

Relief also came from another quarter. Admiral King had agreed to share the burden of the slow westbound convoys to allow some breathing room to the Canadians. The Americans, starting in early November, would escort every second slow westbound ON convoy, allowing the Canadians to take every second fast ON convoy, and thereby save three days or more sea time to assure periodic extended layovers at St John's or Halifax for rest, training, and repairs. These more regular layovers would help to bring the crews of the escorts up to strength, as part of the manning problem was the inability of new personnel to reach their ships as a result of the escorts' short, unpredictable stays in port and the absence of accommodation at St John's for a manning pool.

Within two weeks these glimmers of optimism were gone. The extended combat and bad weather during the last part of October, climaxed by the return of SC 52, highlighted the fleet's myriad problems, many of them of long standing. On 5 November Stevens passed to Murray with his strong endorsement an alarming report from Commander Prentice, who had seen his training efforts disintegrate in the face of escalating operational demands even while the arrival of newly commissioned ships made training more imperative. His remarks were more scathing than the most trenchant criticisms by British officers:

It is honestly believed that unless immediate steps are taken to improve the material and the training of the ships of the Newfoundland Escort Force, it will shortly become impossible to run convoys in the face of the enemy's present attacks upon these convoys west of 30°west.

The majority of the RCN corvettes ... have been given so little chance of becoming efficient that they are almost more of a liability than an asset to an escort group.

The Commanding Officers have apparently been given no instruction in convoy work and little chance to train their Officers ... most of whom are without sea experience of any sort. The result is that ships are seldom in station in low visibility and are continuously losing their convoys even on moonlight nights. In many cases ships cease zig-zagging for fear of collision under conditions of weather and visibility which make it imperative that they should continue to do this for the sake of their own safety alone.

As serious as the lack of training was the continued failure to achieve stability in the organization of escort groups, much as this was recognized as essential for effective convoy defence. "It has been impossible to keep any escort group together for more than one convoy. In most cases it has been impossible to hold a meeting of Commanding Officers before sailing. This has prevented the development of even the most rudimentary form of cohesive action ... To put the situation colloquially," Prentice concluded, "it is as though we were attempting to play against a professional hockey team with a collection of individuals who had not even learned to skate."[112]

Prentice placed a good part of the blame for the failure of ships to make more progress on the continued removal by the manning authorities at Halifax of experienced personnel from Newfoundland ships to provide for new construction. The practice greatly set back the efficient ships, but did little to help new construction escorts whose raw crews could only become an effective team if they collectively underwent work-up training of the kind Prentice himself had established at Halifax in the spring. Murray had already in August condemned the stripping of personnel from his ships and strongly urged collective training of crews. He now forwarded Prentice's report to headquarters with a blistering endorsement, citing the case of *Orillia*, which, although unfit for service, he had just been obliged to sail as part of the escort for SC 53. *Orillia* was a veteran of the NEF, but postings while the ship was at Halifax, and an injury to the executive officer, for whom no qualified replacement was available, had left the commanding officer, Lieutenant Briggs, as the only experienced officer in the ship. He would have no choice but "to spend on the bridge as much of every 24 hours as his constitution will stand."

> This, coupled with the necessity of acting as Executive Officer of the ship, A/S Control Officer, Gunnery Officer and cypher staff, is more than the best constitution can be expected to support over a period of 28 days, with only a short break of a few hours in harbour in the middle.
>
> ... we are asking a lot of the morale of an inexperienced crew, to expect them to be happy, and remain fighting fit and aggressive, in a ship in which they know their safety from marine accident alone, and not from any action of the enemy, depends upon the ability of the Captain to remain awake.
>
> It should also be remembered that this fortitude is being expected from men who have seen gasoline tankers disintegrate in five seconds, less than half a mile away from them, and who have also been through the harrowing experience of seeing men with little lights on their shoulders bobbing up and down in the water and shouting for help ...
>
> Only the desperate operational situation which exists off our coast at the present time persuaded me to allow "Orillia" [to] proceed ... She is quite unfitted to meet the enemy, and in no other Service would a unit be placed in the firing line before the officers had mastered the use of their weapon. She has been allowed to proceed, however, because her presence will fill a gap in the A/S screen visible to the enemy, and her

---

112. Prentice to Capt (D), Newfoundland, 4 Nov. 1941, NAC, RG 24, 11929, 00-220-3-6

113. CCNF to NSec, NSHQ, "Relief of Trained Officers and Men from HMC Ships of the NEF," 6 Nov. 1941, NAC, RG 24, 11929, 00-220-3-6

presence may result in saving the lives of many merchant seamen, in which case the sacrifice of the health of one Commanding Officer would be justified.[113]

Events at sea were at this very time confirming both the shortcomings of Canadian ships and the impossibility of maintaining existing schedules in the worsening autumn weather. SC 53, which sailed from Sydney on 4 November, soon encountered heavy fog. By the time the Newfoundland escort, HMS *Burnham* and seven RCN corvettes, was due to join on 6 November, the convoy had broken into two groups, not all the merchant vessels having received a diversion to keep them clear of the U-boats known to have concentrated northeast of Newfoundland to catch SC 52. Further diversions, and the departure of the Sydney local escorts from the main body of the convoy despite the failure of the Newfoundland escort to join, set *Burnham*'s group on a week-long chase through the fog. The corvettes repeatedly lost contact with *Burnham,* whose commanding officer bitterly commented "As was represented before sailing the training and experience of the officers of most of these ships left much to be desired." A further difficulty was that not all of the corvettes had yet been fitted with radio telephone, and some were missing other radio equipment, so that the communications staff in the British destroyer had to keep constant watch on four frequencies to keep some semblance of order in the group. As *Burnham*'s commanding officer concluded, "ships not fitted with R/T in *addition* to their normal W/T set cannot be considered fit for convoy duties."[114]

Meanwhile, on 8 November, a group that initially included two British and three Canadian corvettes—*Collingwood* joined-up later—under *St Laurent* sailed from Iceland into a full gale to link up with the slow westbound ON 33. The escorts were soon separated in the heavy weather. *St Laurent* and HMCS *Snowberry* reached the convoy on the morning of 10 November; the other escorts joined over the next thirty hours, except for HMS *Polyanthus*, which was unable to make contact until 15 November. *St Laurent*, which had had her topmast carried away by a huge wave shortly after leaving Iceland, continued to suffer damage and had to struggle to keep control at the slow convoy speed. On 13 November the destroyer parted company and made for Halifax at economical speed for repairs. The convoy was at a virtual standstill for the next week as the gale continued to blow. More than twenty merchant ships lost contact, and, one by one, as the escorts became dangerously low on fuel, they had to run for St John's. When the weather moderated, briefly as it turned out, on the evening of 20 November, "we had fifteen merchants scattered over about 40 square miles with [HMS] Primrose and Snowberry as the only escorts present and began to make progress." These corvettes had to depart to fuel on 21 November, and the few merchant ships remaining of the main body did not reach the dispersal point south of Newfoundland until 23 November.[115] Meanwhile, two of the merchantmen had, during the struggle east of Newfoundland, run out of fuel. Both ships were ultimately saved, after a struggle of two weeks or more, by the extraordinary efforts of civilian rescue tugs.[116] Farley Mowat's account of one of these operations, by the Canadian tug *Foundation Franklin*, gives some sense of the extreme conditions.

---

114. HMS *Burnham*, "Convoy Proceedings, SC 53," 13 Nov. 1941, "SC 53," DHH, 88/1 mfm, reel 31; Submarine estimate in "Escort of Convoy and Operations WD," 7 Nov. 1941, NARA, RG 313 Red, CTF 24, box 8710, shows intelligence about U-boat concentration northeast of Newfoundland.

115. *St Laurent* ROP, ON 33, 18 Nov. 1941, HMS *Primrose*, "ROP, ON 33," nd; Cochrane, "Convoy Form D, ONS 33," 25 Nov. 1941, ON 33, DHH, 88/1 mfm, reel 7

116. CCNF WD, Dec. 1941, DHH, NHS NSS 1000-5-20 pt 1

As the little ship ran her easting down [out of Halifax], the storm worsened. By the third day it had become so wild that [Harry] Brushett [the master] was forced to heave-to. The anemometer mounted on the wheelhouse registered a wind speed of eighty-eight miles an hour, and then gave up and simply blew away. *Franklin* staggered under the weight of the seas, then rolled herself free and came up to face the next assault.

When she eventually raised the *West Neris*, the storm was still so intense that four hours were required to make the connection between the ships, and another three hours were needed to swing the unwieldy Irishman on course for St. John's

Then the slogging match began ...

The gale was still from the west, and *Franklin* was driving straight into its eye. The antagonists were face to face ... Snow, mingling with the spume, froze on *Franklin*'s upper-works, but could not last upon her decks, for it was pounded off by the hammer of the seas.[117]

The bad weather may have helped save ON 33 from a worse fate. When the *Raubritter* group did not locate any shipping in the waters near Newfoundland after the SC 52 action, Dönitz had redeployed the submarines off Greenland's Cape Farewell, the scene of several earlier successes. No shipping turned up there, and on 11 November Dönitz ordered the group southward after intelligence disclosed the position of ON 33's mid-ocean meeting point, southwest of Iceland. It was a long shot, as Dönitz admitted, for he did not know what course the convoy was following, but on the 14th *U 106* reported a destroyer, possibly the damaged *St Laurent*, making for Halifax. Dönitz, reasoning that ON 33 was nearby, used the destroyer's track to issue fresh orders for the hunt to the west of 35° West. The next day, he had to order the *Raubritter* group, whose boats were now low on fuel, to the eastern Atlantic for operations on their homeward track. That, however, was not the end of the thrust towards Newfoundland. On 13 November, Dönitz had directed five other submarines, fresh from rest and replenishment, to move from the central ocean to Cape Race; he later assigned a sixth submarine and designated the new group *Steuben*.[118] Bletchley Park was able to decrypt German traffic within a matter of hours on 14 and 15 November, and this was probably why on 16 November the Admiralty and US Navy Department diverted ON 33 further south on a track that would take it clear of Cape Race.[119] To the north was the fast ON 34, under USN escort, which, despite the better speed and manoeuvrability of the ships, was suffering fully as much in the gale. The US Navy Department had already diverted this convoy further to the north, clear of *Raubritter*'s southern thrust, and now directed it to come in to the north of Cape Race, and then, when close to land fall, cut sharply south, ahead of the new group of submarines.[120]

Dönitz intended that the *Steuben* group should operate very aggressively. He had been impressed by *U 374*'s reconnaissance off St John's in which the boat had sunk one steamer and

---

117. Farley Mowat, *The Grey Seas Under* (Toronto 1958), 232-3

118. BdU, KTB, 12-17 Nov. 1941

119. BdU to Group *Raubritter*, TOO 1816/14 Nov. 1941, Naval Section BP to ID8G, 0345/15 Nov. 1941, ZTPG 16942; "ON 33," NARA, RG 313 Red, CTF 24, box 8706. This is for the renewed hunt to the west based on the sighting of a destroyer at BD 1425, approximately 49-50° N, 36-40° W. *Columbia*'s ROP for SC 54 cites "the U-Boats reported in Commander in Chief Naval Operations (US)'s 0026/16 [Nov. 1941] as moving towards Cape Race." Davis to Capt (D) Newfoundland, "ROP of HMCS *Columbia* for period Nov. 10, 1941, to Nov. 22, 1941," nd, "SC 54," DHH, 88/1 mfm, reel 31

120. "ON 34," NARA, RG 313 Red, CTF 24, box 8706; Abbazia, *Roosevelt's Navy*, 316

located SC 52. The submarine's report left no doubt that the area was a promising one for future operations: "Close inshore, conditions are still as in peace-time. Lights are showing. No patrolling. Probably no barrages. Good conditions for surface and underwater patrolling. Steamships and patrol vessels proceed in and out singly."[121] Dönitz ordered two of the *Steuben* boats to make surprise attacks on the night of 25 to 26 November, one at the entrance to St John's and the other against the anchorage in the vicinity of the iron ore loading pier at Bell Island in Conception Bay. The remaining four submarines were to await these opening actions and then sweep in to the shores of the Avalon Peninsula. U-boat headquarters broadcast these orders early on 21 November. It took Bletchley Park some seventy-two hours to decrypt the high-level cypher.[122] As soon as the decrypt was in, the Admiralty despatched a warning to the US Navy Department, NSHQ, and the RCN's east coast commands under the cover of direction finding bearings on the U-boat's transmissions: "East coast Newfoundland. Attack on shipping at St. John's Nfld and at Wabana anchorage is anticipated in very near future. Recommend all possible anti-submarine precautions be taken without delay. Any preparations should be carried out with greatest secrecy."[123] The RCAF's 1 Group and Commander Task Force 4 (CTF 4) arranged for special air coverage of the St John's approaches, while RCN corvettes began "special patrols" that continued until the end of the month.[124] Another defence measure appears already to have been in effect. As soon as U-boats were reported in Newfoundland waters in late October, Murray had strongly recommended that the practice of assembling ships that loaded in Newfoundland in Conception Bay to sail as joiners of the SC convoys should cease. He noted the lack of defences in Conception Bay, and the fact that when the SC convoys had to be re-routed because of the presence of U-boats in the Newfoundland area, it became impossible for the "WSC" groups to make the junction, as had just happened in the case of SC 52. Because St John's, the only defended port, was too crowded for the assembly of merchantmen, he suggested that the ships should be sailed for Sydney or Halifax, which seems to have been done almost immediately.[125]

Dönitz in fact had been forced to cancel the preliminary attacks on St John's and Wabana because the boats did not have the charts necessary to navigate at night in shallow waters so close to shore. Then, on 23 November, when none of the *Steuben* submarines was much closer than Flemish Cap, some 300 miles from St John's, Dönitz directed the whole group to move immediately to the waters off Gibraltar. The German High Command had ordered an all out submarine effort in the Mediterranean area against the ships that were supplying the British Crusader offensive in North Africa. "U-boat warfare in the Atlantic," the log of Dönitz's headquarters recorded, "has practically ceased."[126] The St John's approaches and the waters close round the Avalon Peninsula, however, had not slipped from the sights of the U-boat command. One of the significant outcomes

---

121. *U 374* to BdU, "Offizier S," TOO 1612/3 Nov. 1941, Naval Section BP to ID8G, 2100/22 Nov. 1941, ZTPG 18286, PRO, DEFE 3/69

122. BdU to Group *Steuben*, "Offizier N," TOO 0155/21 Nov. 1941, Naval Section, BP to ID8G, 2313/23 Nov. 1941, ZTPG 18381, [continuation of signal], TOO 0313/0356/21 Nov. 1941, Naval Section BP to ID8G, 0322/24 Nov. 1941, PRO, DEFE 3/69

123. Adm to COAC, NSHQ, CCNF, NOIC St John's, OPNAV, 0155Z/24 Nov. 1941, DHH, 181.002(D173)

124. Douglas, *Creation of National Air Force*, 484; CCNF WD, Nov. 1941, DHH, NHS NSS 1000-5-20 pt 1

125. CCNF to NSHQ, 1509z/1 Nov. 1941, PRO, ADM 199/2081. The records for SCs 53 through 58 contain no reference to WSC joiners.

126. BdU, KTB, 21-3 Nov. 1941, 22 Nov. entry quoted.

of the reconnaissance of October and November 1941, and the successful attack on SC 52, was that they identified targets for the German offensive of 1942, which would open within a matter of weeks, with a group much like *Steuben* pushing close round the Avalon Peninsula.

It was not the enemy, but the ferocious weather that brought Murray, on 22 November, to advise headquarters that his force could not continue with the existing organization and schedule. He wanted to reorganize from six escort groups to eight, accepting that only six rather than eight escorts would normally be available for operations in each group. In a halfway variant of his earlier plea for routing of the slow convoys on the shorter and less stormy great circle run, he asked that discretion be given to escort commanders of SC convoys to continue on to northern UK ports for their refuelling and turnaround. Evasive routing placed the Mid-Ocean Meeting Point, where the Newfoundland groups passed off to the UK groups, as much as four hundred miles south of Iceland, a distance that the escorts had to navigate in the face of the strong autumn and winter winds.[127]

Murray noted that Admiral Bristol, CTF 4 at Argentia, had recently changed the US escort organization from seven to eight groups, each of these able to run only five warships. The American decision to run more and smaller groups was, as Murray suggested, their response to the punishing conditions in the North Atlantic. When, on 10 October, Atlantic Fleet had delegated control of escort operations to CTF 4, King, in his official instructions, underscored the need to increase the running strength of the escort groups to six destroyers.[128] Privately, however, he admitted to Bristol that it might not be possible: "While I am very anxious to expand our own escort units to six vessels I do not yet see my way clear to do so, especially when I consider the winter gales to come, breakdowns, overhauls, and availabilities to receive important material installations."[129]

Bristol soon produced a study of the problem that led to the establishment of the extra group. The existing strength of his command included forty-four escorts, forty-two destroyers, and two Coast Guard cutters; reinforcements promised for the near future included eight destroyers. With the eight additional ships he could assure six runners in each of the seven groups, but he recommended against it. His calculations revealed the full extent to which the USN emphasized ship maintenance and proper rest and training of crews. The paucity of support facilities in Newfoundland, and the exposure of its waters to enemy attack had from the beginning brought the Atlantic Fleet to schedule groups to return to Boston after every round trip between Argentia and Iceland, even though the run from Argentia to Boston and back consumed four to five days in each cycle. With the seven groups, each cycle could be no more than forty-two days, which left only five to eight days in Boston. Bristol's list of benefits from the extra time in port that would be possible with eight groups nicely encompassed the areas where the RCN was scrimping:

1. ... adequate time for maintenance and repairs to storm damage;

2. ... navy yard overhaul for those ships that really need it;

3. ... recreation time for artificers...

127. NSHQ to Adm, 2049/24 Nov. 1941, DHH, NHS 8440-70 NEF; Staff officer (operations) to Adm commanding in Iceland, 25 Oct. 1941, Adm docket MO19041/41, extract in ibid mentions the 400-mile run from MOMP to Iceland for the SC escorts.

128. King to Bristol, 10 Oct. 1941, file A14-1 (Aug.-Oct.), NARA, RG 80, Secret 1940-1, box 232

129. King to Bristol, 8 Oct. 1941, DHH, E.J. King papers

5. ... reserves to piece out groups depleted by damage, overhauls, or special demands;

6. ... reservoir for hunting groups or for strategic strengthening of dispositions at Cast [Iceland] and Roger [Argentia]; and,

7. ... more extensive time for repairs to damaged ships without disturbing composition of units.[130]

The British and the Americans were aware of how hard pressed the Canadians were. In late October the senior US officer at Iceland had warned Bristol that, "Having only six units, [the Canadians'] cycle is 36 days with convoy intervals of 6 days. This gives them 10 to 14 days at home. The pinch comes at this end where they have a maximum of 2 days which is often reduced to 36 hours or less and they are feeling the strain. The voyage out has often taken them 11 days. They arrive here tired out and the DDs just barely making it ... With winter coming on their problem will be more difficult. They are going to have break downs and ships running out of oil at sea."[131] A senior officer at the Admiralty, on seeing Murray's appeal of late November to be permitted to create two additional escort groups, set out statistics that proved the NEF was being stretched beyond all reasonable limits:

> Under the present organization the ratios of sea to harbour time of the NF [Newfoundland] and WA [Western Approaches] escort groups employed with SC-ON convoys are as follows:
>
> NF At sea 24 days. In harbour 12 days.
> WA " " 11 " " " 13 "
>
> It is clear that the NF escorts are therefore being worked twice as hard as those in WA. In addition the longer voyages carried out by NF escorts impose a greater strain on personnel and material.[132]

During the latter part of December as the British and Americans came to agreement on southern routing to ease the battering of the escort forces and merchant vessels, one of the first steps was to give the RCN permission to reduce the number of ships in each group as Murray had asked.[133] In preparing for the new routing arrangements, Bristol mentioned to King, not for the first time, his particular worry about the Canadians, "who are having a very difficult time of it ... Just why they are having so much trouble in keeping an adequate number of ships running is difficult to understand unless one appreciates that their maintenance ideas plus maintenance facilities leave much to be desired."[134]

Bristol was, in fact, understating the problem. The Canadian fleet lacked adequate technical sup-

---

130. Bristol to King, 24 Oct. 1941, file A16-3 Warfare Operations, NARA, RG 313 Red, CTF 24, 1941-2 Secret, box 8829. Note that the account of this study in CINCLANT, "Administrative History of the US Atlantic Fleet in World War II, v II: Commander Task Force Twenty-Four," 1946, 91-2, DHH mfm 79/16, misinterprets the conclusion as being to reinforce the existing seven groups.

131. Deyo to Bristol, 23 Oct. 1941, quoted in CINCLANT, "Administrative History of US Atlantic Fleet" II

132. DTD, min, 26 Nov. 1941, Adm docket M019041/41, extracts in NHS 8440-70 NEF

133. Adm to NSHQ, repeated C-in-C WA, COAC, CCNF, 2210A/15 Dec.1941, E.J. King papers, reel 1; FONF ROP, Dec. 1941, DHH NSS 1000-5-20, pt 1

134. Bristol to CINCLANT, 20 Dec. 1940, E.J. King papers, reel 1. See also same to same, 8 Nov. 41, serial 00136, NARA, RG 313 Red, CINCLANT 1941 Secret, box 154, A14-1 Jacket no. 2.

port at all levels. The missing elements included everything from essential engineering knowledge on the part of shipboard personnel to the capacity of government and industry to deliver major items of equipment and improvements in ship design. These difficulties were most serious for the corvettes, and not surprisingly so. The vessels had been designed as coastal defence vessels and had been rushed into the highly specialized and demanding mid-ocean escort role, in most cases before the crews had been trained and the vessels fully equipped even for less exigent coastal waters duty.

Complaints from experienced British, Canadian, and American officers about the performance of the RCN corvettes reflected technical as much as training problems. It is impossible completely to separate the two. The inability of the corvettes on many occasions to keep proper station, manoeuvre promptly and accurately on instructions from the senior officer, or maintain contact with a convoy in heavy seas or conditions of poor visibility resulted from both the shortage of experienced signals personnel, who had to be of top quality to master the great challenges of convoy work in the North Atlantic, and the lack of equipment, including full radio outfits, high-power signal lights, and even good binoculars. Furthermore, the ships' magnetic compasses were less dependable and accurate than gyro compasses.

The Canadian corvettes, moreover, had already begun to fall behind their British counterparts in structural features that were critical to performance on the open ocean. In the autumn of 1940 the Admiralty had started to introduce important improvements in response to the experience of the first British corvettes committed to long-range escort duty. The increase in the armament, number of personnel, equipment, and provisions carried for long-distance missions had made the vessels very crowded and wet ships. The extra weight brought the bows down lower in the water, resulting in the seas more frequently breaking over the short forecastle, plunging into the well deck forward of the bridge, smashing equipment, endangering personnel, and drenching accommodation spaces below decks. Among the new features approved by the Admiralty for new construction ships, and for modification of existing ships as they underwent refit, was an increased flare of the bows so that they would more readily deflect the seas, and extension of the forecastle well back, past the bridge to mid-ships—fully half the length of the hull. The lengthened forecastle helped keep the ship drier and also provided much needed accommodation space.[135] NSHQ did not receive the plans for the modifications until April 1941, when it was too late to revise the design of any of the vessels of the original sixty-four-ship program that were still under construction, or of the first six additional ships that had been ordered in the autumn of 1940. The only vessels that could be built to the new standard were the final ten authorized in the autumn of 1940, which were just being laid down in the spring of 1941.[136]

There was little progress with upgrading the existing corvette fleet. In September 1941 Captain (D) at Halifax recommended that the vessels in service should, in addition to some hundreds of minor improvements, be refitted with the extended forecastle, and with gyro compasses. Headquarters replied that it had not yet approved the extension of the forecastle in RCN ships, a

135. Adm to NSHQ, signal in four parts, 0856, 0915, 0955, 1010/31 Jan. 1941, transcript in DHH 8000 "Flower Class Corvettes (A-Z)"; A.W. Watson, "Corvettes and Frigates," in R. Baker, *Selected Papers on British Warship Design in World War II from the Transactions of the Royal Institution of Naval Architects* (Annapolis 1983), 86, 118, 123-4

136. Naval Council, 29 Apr.1941. See also Tucker, *Naval Service of Canada* II, 61.

137. Capt (D) Halifax to Superintendent HMC Dockyard Halifax, "Standard List of Alterations and Additions for Corvettes," 15 Sep. 1941, NAC, RG 24, 11065, 41-1-1 pt 1

major modification that entailed reconstruction of the whole forward part of the vessel, and that there were no supplies of gyro compasses available.[137]

The seven corvettes that crossed to the United Kingdom from October to December 1941 for work-ups at Tobermory suffered such shortcomings that all required substantial work in British shipyards before they were in condition to make training worthwhile.[138] The state of these vessels was not fully representative of the fleet. Most of them were ships that had been rushed into the NEF to achieve the emergency expansion of the escort groups in the wake of the SC 42 disaster, and Murray's staff scheduled them for early work-ups at Tobermory especially so they could have "completion refits" in British yards. In some instances the dangerous autumn storms on the passage to Iceland had uncovered serious builders' defects, and it was safer for them to continue on to the United Kingdom than to attempt the passage home. Nevertheless, British authorities were surprised at how much basic work in the ships had not been completed (in most cases, it seems, because fixtures were not available in Canada) and that few if any "additions and alterations" approved by the Admiralty in light of operational experience had been undertaken in Canadian dockyards. The Admiralty complained to NSHQ that Canada was making unreasonable demands on the overstretched British yards, noting the example of HMCS *Barrie*, which "was in hand for 2 months at Messrs Harland & Wolff, Belfast," a length of time required by most of the seven Canadian corvettes. Work laid out in the original specifications and not completed by the builders in *Barrie* included twenty-four items, among them the fitting of two ventilation fans, many of the voice pipes and electric buzzers, and bells for communications between the bridge, fighting positions, and engine room, night fighting equipment for the main gun, and a compass for the steering compartment. Although there were no time and resources to extend the forecastle, Harland and Wolff did rebuild and enlarge the bridge according to the latest British standards and made thirty other more minor "additions and alterations" to the original design, including fittings in the mess decks to accommodate the increased numbers of crewmen, water-tight lockers for the fighting equipment, and additional voice pipes and electric buzzers for communication within the ship.[139]

While warmly acknowledging "the great work which has been done by the Canadian Shipyard[s] in building these Corvettes," the Admiralty begged that more be done to keep up with alteration and additions in Canadian yards. The Admiralty also asked that information about the precise state of the ships—and NSHQ's priorities for completion work and "alterations and additions"—should be forwarded before the vessels arrived in Britain.[140] There had been no such notice about the first seven corvettes, and as a result dockyard personnel had had to analyse the state of the ships, and then scramble to find space and other resources to undertake the work. The sort of information the Admiralty wanted, however, was not readily available among the harassed engineering staffs at St John's, Halifax, or in Ottawa. Certainly Captain Agnew, CCCS in the United Kingdom, was no better informed than the Admiralty.[141] Nor were the few Canadian engineering

---

138. These corvettes were *Moose Jaw*, *Chicoutimi*, *Sherbrooke*, *Barrie*, *Brandon*, *Rosthern*, and *Morden*. FONF WD, Oct. 1941; NAC, RG 24, 1745, CS 384-1, CS 384-2, CS 384-3

139. "HMCS *Barrie*. List of items not completed in Canada," "HMCS *Barrie*. Alterations and Additions Carried out by Messrs. Harland & Wolff, Limited Belfast. 5 Oct. 1941 to 5 Dec. 1941," enclosed with Adm to NSec, 22 Jan. 1942, NAC, RG 24,11,745, CS 384-1

140. Adm to NSec, 22 Jan.1942

141. CCCS to Sec of Adm, 6 Nov. 1941, NAC, RG 24, 11745, CS 384-1

officers under Agnew's command in any position to gather full information. So deficient were the Canadian ships, and so lacking the guidance from any Canadian authority, that the British yards did as much as they could largely on the basis of whatever guidance the local British naval authorities and the CCCS staff could provide. In March 1942 Lieutenant-Commander (E) G.L. Simpson, an engineer officer on the staff of CCCS, complained of the "great discrepancy in the work which is carried out in different Corvettes."

> In the case of HMCS "Sorel" the forecastle has been extended while in other Corvettes this item is not considered essential. In HMCS "Barrie" an RDF [radar] set, type 271, was installed ... but this has not been installed in any other Canadian Corvette. It seems that the items completed vary according to the yard at which the ship refits.
>
> It is evident that Canadian Authorities will expect that when a Canadian Corvette finishes a completion Refit it will be ready to operate efficiently on convoy duties. As an instance HMCS "Morden" will be presumed to be an efficient ship for convoy duties whereas this is not the case in view of the lack of R/T [radio telephone], RDF, 20 Inch Searchlight ... and Standard Compass.
>
> It is suggested that better results could be obtained from these Completion Refits if there was a closer liaison [sic] between the Canadian Authorities, Captain "D" [presumably of Western Approaches], the Admiralty and the contractors.

Simpson warned that the engineering staff of CCCS should not be doing any of the liaison about approvals of items for refit: the proper function of the engineering officers was to be present on the ships to supervise the work. This was essential as the corvettes carried no engineer officer, only chief engine room artificers who did not have the experience or rank properly to oversee refits.[142]

Simpson's memorandum, aside from revealing a chaotic situation, also suggested backwardness on the part of NSHQ. The installation of the latest British type 271 radar in *Barrie*, and the fitting of extended forecastles in *Sorel* and *Drumheller* in early 1942, were local British initiatives that were contrary to Canadian policy. Certainly NSHQ's slowness in adopting, and pressing for, these important changes reflected the weakness in liaison between Canadian and British authorities, but it was also the result of strains of Canadian and British resources that forced hard choices in Ottawa that, often as not, had to be made in the absence of full information.

Radar is a case in point. The Canadian Naval Staff learned only in February 1941, and then only after specifically asking the Admiralty for a statement of policy, that the RN was equipping its corvettes with radar. The Canadian staff immediately decided similarly to outfit RCN corvettes and, in accordance with practice since the summer of 1940, arranged for production in Canada. This was an unavoidable decision given the long-standing difficulties in obtaining material from British sources. The British and Canadian governments were already cooperating in organizing production of army and air force radar in Canada, through a new Crown corporation, Research Enterprises Limited, in Leaside, a suburb of Toronto. Among the sets scheduled for early manufacture was ASV, the RAF equipment on which the Admiralty had based its compact 1.5-metre type 286 for service in escort vessels. With the ASV sets available in the country, the National Research Council of Canada was able quickly to design and build the prototypes for its own naval version

---

142. Engineer Officer, *Niobe* to CCCS, 10 Mar. 1942, NAC, RG 24, 11745, CS 384-3

of the equipment, the set that was to become known as SW1C (surface warning One Canadian), and its later variants, SW2C and SW3C. The prototype performed well in sea trials conducted aboard *Chambly* in May 1941, and the Naval Staff approved production, but supply bottlenecks, and problems at Research Enterprises, whose facilities were still under construction, delayed the beginning of significant deliveries from August, when they had originally been expected, until the end of 1941. By that time fifteen corvettes, just under a quarter of the RCN's vessels of that type, had been fitted with the new Canadian equipment, which approximated type 286, and incorporated a light-weight rotating antenna, the major improvement that the British had introduced for the type 286 in the late spring and summer of 1941.[143]

By any normal method of accounting this would have been a splendid effort, but 1941 was anything but a normal year. A revolution in naval radar technology was under way in Great Britain with the leap to short-wave technology. It stretched British scientific and industrial resources to the limit and took place with such speed that there was little chance for communication of results, especially to an institution like the RCN that was woefully short of scientific expertise, and had scarcely begun to develop the organization needed to assemble and analyze highly technical information.

In February 1941 the Admiralty had taken the risk of ordering immediate production of the type 271 short-wave radar before sea-trials of the prototype had taken place.[144] Thus, even as upgrading of the original type 286 sets with rotatable antennas got under way in the British fleet in mid-1941, type 271 sets that would supersede the 1.5-metre equipment were beginning to be rushed from the factories to the dockyards.[145] By early January 1942 a total of seventy-eight British escorts had already been fitted with type 271, at the very time the RCN had just begun to fit its vessels with the now obsolescent 1.5-metre sets.[146]

According to David Zimmerman, the Canadian Naval Staff did not become fully aware of the potential of short-wave technology for the detection of surfaced submarines until the summer of 1941. NRC scientists were already working on short-wave fire control radar for anti-aircraft artillery as part of the cooperative efforts begun with the British in late 1940. The scientists responded to a call from the Naval Staff for more effective naval radar by borrowing an experimental set that American scientists had built on the basis of information shared by the British. Trials with the American set at Halifax in July and August showed that it was "more than twice as effective as SW1C." NRC, with encouragement from the navy, immediately began development of a naval short-wave set, "RX/C." The scientists worked, however, without the full information and examples of British equipment that had been available for the SW1C. The Naval Staff had requested a type 271 set from the Admiralty, which readily agreed to provide one, but an inexperienced RCN liaison officer in London failed to realize that he—not the Admiralty—had to make arrangements for shipment, and the set did not reach Canada until January 1942. By that time RX/C development was too far along for major changes. The further extensive work required to prepare it for operational use

143. D. Zimmerman, *The Great Naval Battle of Ottawa: How Admirals, Scientists, and Politicians Impeded the Development of High Technology in Canada's Wartime Navy* (Toronto 1989), 39-47

144. Howse, *Radar at Sea*, 83-4

145. "Min 18th Mtg ... 20th May 1941 ... To Consider Trade Protection Measures," PRO, ADM 199/2080

146. "Battle of the Atlantic Committee 28th Mtg—13 Jan.1942," PRO, ADM 205/23

147. Zimmerman, *Great Naval Battle of Ottawa*, 72-6, 73

had been allowed to slip behind other pressing priorities, moreover, primarily because the Naval Staff now expected that supplies of a USN short-wave radar that promised to be at least the equal of type 271 and was certainly well in advance of the experimental RX/C, would soon be available to meet the RCN's needs. These hopes for ready supply from the US would, in fact, soon fade because of the great demands of the American forces for radar and radio equipment that resulted from the United States' entry into the war following the Japanese attack on Pearl Harbor.[147]

The materiel problems of the Canadian fleet were compounded in 1941 by a major expansion and restructuring of the Canadian shipbuilding effort whose unintended results included upheaval in the warship construction program.[148] That upheaval, rather paradoxically, grew out of the very success of the 1939-40 corvette building program in its initial stages. As noted in Chapter 2, by the autumn of 1940 the launching of corvette hulls well ahead of schedule brought Munitions and Supply to look for work to fill empty slips, enabling the navy to place further orders for Bangors and corvettes. This meant that the full four-year navy program projected in 1939-40 would be completed within two years; even with the navy's follow on orders, most hulls would be launched by the spring of 1941, opening up a great deal of shipyard capacity. The Naval Staff foresaw no requirement for continued mass production of emergency-type minesweepers and escorts as the rapid progress of the expanded 1939-40 program promised to meet all apparent requirements for North American waters with a generous margin for deployment to Britain. The main interest of the Naval Staff was rather in developing one or two first class shipyards capable of building Tribal fleet destroyers, with a view to equipping the Canadian service, during the war and after, with true fighting ships in contrast to modest, utilitarian, auxiliary craft like the corvettes and Bangors.

Some members of the Canadian cabinet and senior officials, including, as we have seen, members of the engineering staff at NSHQ, believed that the follow on to the accelerated corvette and Bangor program should be merchant ships. Britain was facing an imports crisis as a result of the longer hauls for supplies following the collapse of western Europe, and the heavy losses of merchant vessels to the German U-boat and air offensive in the eastern Atlantic. Perhaps this was where Canada's technically unsophisticated shipbuilding industry could make the greatest contribution; merchant vessels posed many fewer difficulties than even the simplest warship. In October 1940 a British mission under the prominent shipbuilder R.C. Thompson arrived in New York to investigate merchant ship construction in North America. In Canada, Munitions and Supply responded enthusiastically to the British mission, and through the winter of 1940-1 negotiated contracts for the production of twenty-six vessels by the end of 1942.[149]

The North American contracts were for merchant ships of the "North Sands" type, named for the British shipyard that had developed the design expressly for efficient mass production.[150] They were about 440 feet in length overall and 9,300 deadweight tons. Vessels of this size could not be

148. The following account of the shipbuilding program in 1941 draws on the following excellent studies: Tucker, *Naval Service of Canada* II, 54-70; Kenneth S. Mackenzie, "The Shipyard of the Freedom of the Seas," nd, DHH; Kenneth S. Mackenzie, "Naval vs Merchant Shipbuilding #2," Feb.1993, DHH; William Rawling, "Forging Neptune's Trident: Manufacturing Ships and Equipment for the Wartime RCN," Apr. 1998, DHH; Michael A. Hennessy, "The Rise and Fall of a Canadian Maritime Policy, 1939-1965: A Study of Industry, Navalism and the State" (PhD dissertation, University of New Brunswick, 1995), 35-76

149. Merchant Shipbuilding Mission to Admiralty for Sir Amos Ayre, 2 July 1941, PRO, ADM 116/5469, is a good digest of the initial British contracts in Canada and the US.

150. S.C. Heal, *A Great Fleet of Ships: The Canadian Forts & Parks* (St Catharines 1999), 25-44

constructed at the Great Lakes yards because they were too long for the St Lawrence canals, which gave access to the ocean. Munitions and Supply made plans to place the orders with Davie Shipbuilding at Lauzon, Québec, Vickers at Montréal, and Burrard Dry Dock Company at Vancouver, the three ocean shipyards most capable of undertaking the construction of large ships. The smaller yards were adequate for the corvettes and other minor vessels that then comprised the whole of the navy program, and in November 1940 the Naval Staff therefore agreed to the diversion of the three big yards to merchant ship construction, with the sole proviso that it should not interfere with plans to build destroyers in Canada. The Naval Staff attached that condition because the cargo ship program would leave only one first class ocean facility with the capability to undertake the destroyer project, Halifax Shipyards, which was already crowded with repair work.[151]

D.B. Carswell, director general of the naval shipbuilding branch at Munitions and Supply, immediately gave his assurance that the repair commitments would not interfere with destroyer construction at Halifax.[152] He evidently believed that a large building project would complement other efforts to improve the situation at Halifax by providing stable employment, thereby overcoming the tendency of workers to depart for better jobs in the inland provinces during the summer months when shipping traffic and demands for repairs fell off with the opening of the St Lawrence route and the improvement in the weather.[153] Even the best resources in the country would not be sufficient for the Tribals, however, as these warships were so far advanced over any other vessels that had been built in Canada. That was why the engineering staff at NSHQ had always insisted that substantial British assistance—teams of expert personnel and the supply of key components—would be essential to the success of the project. The Admiralty, with Churchill's support, flatly refused the Canadian government's requests. All the British authorities were willing to do was to put the Canadians in touch with private firms that carried out destroyer construction for the RN. These firms ultimately provided a small number of highly qualified personnel.[154]

While the Naval Staff and Macdonald, the minister, continued to promote the Tribal class destroyer program as essential for Canadian interests, it was becoming clear that Britain's most immediate need was for very large numbers of merchant ships. The North American building contracts negotiated in late 1940 and early 1941 were scarcely a drop in the bucket in terms of replacements for the mounting losses to enemy action.[155] News of the depth of the British shipping crisis coincided, in February and March 1941, with the efforts of the Canadian Department of Munitions and Supply to firm up plans for the ongoing shipbuilding program. Initially, Munitions and Supply

---

151. Director of Shipbuilding , DM&S to DM Naval Service, 13 Nov. 1940, CNS to DM Naval Service, 14 Nov. 1940, NAC, RG 24, 5602, NS 29-1-31 pt 1

152. DM Naval Service to Director of Shipbuilding, 19 Nov. 1940, ibid

153. E.g., Chairman, Wartime Requirements Board to DM Naval Service, 6 Mar. 1941, NAC, RG 24, 5632, NS 30-31-2. This reports on investigations of labour shortages that took place during the winter of 1940-1 and discusses the use of shipbuilding projects at Halifax to stabilize the labour pool. The report discourages a project as complex as destroyer construction, but the phrasing makes it clear that such a project at Halifax had been under consideration for some time.

154. Tucker, *Naval Service of Canada* II, 55-8; Whitby, "Instruments of Security: The RCN's Procurement of the Tribal Class Destroyers," 5-6; Canmilitry to Defensor (Howe to Macdonald), tg 1359, 30 Dec. 1940, NAC, MG 27 IIIB2, v 42, file S-25 pt 2; Minister M&S to Minister Naval Service, 28 June 1941, NSARM, Macdonald papers, F-1222/19, copy in DHH 80/218 folder 21

155. "Memo for Lord Halifax," nd, copy forwarded by Keenleyside to Jarrett, 1 Feb.1941, PRO, ADM 1/11620; K. Smith, *Conflict over Convoys:Anglo-American Logistics Diplomacy in the Second World War* (Cambridge 1996), 34-7, 64-70

proposed building a smaller type of ocean-going merchant vessel, the 4,700-deadweight ton "Gray" design. It was too long for the St Lawrence canals and would have to be built at some of the smaller slips in the coastal yards. The Naval Staff encouraged a more ambitious merchant ship program than this. They doubted that the Grays had the required capacity or speed, and suggested that the 9,300-ton vessels already ordered by Britain were the type that was really needed. Having no reason to believe that the accelerated corvette and Bangor program did not fully meet all the RCN's anticipated requirements, the staff made no call for additional escorts and minesweepers, but warned that the yards devoted to this work might well be required for British orders for these classes of warships.[156]

This advice came to the Defence Requirements Board, which C.D. Howe, minister of Munitions and Supply, had established in response to criticism from the Department of Finance that priorities had not been clearly established for defence manufacturing. H.R. Macmillan, an aggressive and brilliant timber magnate from British Columbia, was chairman of the board. He had recently embarrassed the government, and challenged Howe's leadership of Munitions and Supply, by talking to the press about what the board had found about the shortcomings of the defence industrial effort.[157] Macmillan, in surveying the whole of the marine industries across the country, however, became convinced that with strategic government assistance Canada could efficiently produce large numbers of ocean-going merchant vessels. Howe had resisted a large-scale merchant ship building program because the government's attempt to do the same thing during the latter part of the First World War had produced few ships too late and at enormous cost.[158] The gravity of the British crisis and Macmillan's views[159] persuaded the minister to change his mind. As he informed the House of Commons in March, "We are going all-out on [merchant] ships. We are going to build as many ships as we can build by reasonably sound economic methods."[160] In April Howe appointed Macmillan to head a new Crown corporation, Wartime Merchant Shipping Limited. Macmillan immediately called together the executives of firms that had the capacity to build large merchant ships, asked them how greatly they could expand without compromising effective management, promised the necessary government financial backing—which the Cabinet had yet to approve—and told them to get to work.[161] By early September Macmillan had negotiated contracts for the construction of 124 merchant ships, most for completion by the end of March 1943, through expansion of the three firms that were undertaking the British contracts and at eight other yards.[162] The program was a success from the beginning. Vickers delivered *Fort Ville Marie*, the first ship from the British contracts, in

---

156. Director General of Shipbuilding, Munitions, and Supply to Minister M&S, 20 Feb. 1941, DM Naval Service to Sec, WRB, 27 Feb. 1941, NAC, RG 24, 4044, NS 1078-3-4 pt 1

157. Bothwell and Kilbourn, *C.D. Howe*, 140-1, 144-9

158. E.g., HofC, *Debates*, 10 Mar. 1941, 1392-3

159. CWCM, 5 Mar. 1941

160. HofC, *Debates*, 11 Mar. 1941, 1451

161. Macmillan to Minister M&S, 7, 21, 25 Apr. 1941, UBC Archives, H.R. Macmillan papers, box 100, file 16; Macmillan to DM M&S, 24 Apr. 1941, ibid, file 17

162. "Wartime Merchant Shipping Limited—Orders in Council," nd, NAC, RG 58, v 252, file 1941-45, pt 15

163. Heal, *Great Fleet of Ships*, 227-308. Heal gives a total of 402 vessels; Kennedy, *Munitions and Supply* I, 505, which is less specific about the types included, gives a total of 410.

164. Heal, *Great Fleet of Ships*, 48-9, 62-4

December 1941, and by the end of 1942 Canadian yards completed ninety vessels, eighty for operation by the British government and ten for Canadian service under the administration of a new
crown corporation, the Park Steamship Company. Canadian merchant ship production reached a
total of over 400 vessels by the end of the war,[163] of which 183 operated under Park Steamships and
185 operated under the British Ministry of War Transport. Most of the remainder were built as support ships for the Royal Navy late in the war.[164]

The swift inauguration of the merchant ship program in 1941, with the immediate commitment
of over $210 million to cover costs during the first two years, reflected the realization that Britain's
resources were exhausted and that Canada had no choice but to take extraordinary initiative for
the common cause. That realization had struck home largely as a result of Britain's appeals to the
US for help under the lend-lease program. Lend-lease, moreover, held out the promise of American
financial assistance that would directly benefit Canada. Britain's shortage of dollar reserves had
always been the main impediment for large British orders in Canada, and Canada's own shortage
of US dollars had set boundaries on its industrial expansion. At the same time, it was necessary
to define industrial sectors in which the country had a strong capacity, lest the emerging Anglo-
American economic alliance should leave it in the position of merely supplying raw materials.
During the negotiations that resulted in the opening of the US market to Canadian defence production under the Hyde Park Agreement of April 1941, Howe promoted shipbuilding as a key sector in which Canada had the proven ability to produce well beyond domestic needs.[165] Ultimately
the United States would pay for ninety of the Canadian-built merchant vessels transferred to
British control in 1942-3.[166]

The most immediate prospect for earning US dollars in 1941, however, lay in the construction
of naval vessels for Britain, which the American government was willing fully to fund. Howe
declared that there was capacity to make an early start on about fifty escorts and minesweepers,
and the Admiralty promptly began discussions on this basis. The priority British needs were for
two new types of warships, the "twin-screw corvette" (later known as the frigate) and the Algerine
class minesweeper, essentially larger versions of the corvettes and Bangors that had proved too
small for extended open-ocean missions.[167]

The Admiralty had originally sent word of the development of the frigate to NSHQ in December
1940, but the first sketch plans did not arrive until late April 1941, when the staff also learned of
the Algerine type. The implications for the Canadian shipbuilding program were great, for aside
from the requirement to build the Algerines and frigates on Admiralty contracts, the RCN also needed these improved types for its own use.[168]

Production would pose difficulties already well known from the corvette and Bangor programs.

165. Financial attaché, Legation in US, "Memo of mtg with Morgenthau, Apr. 18, 1941," *DCER* pt 8, 321-3; Minister M&S to
      PM, "Regarding Statement of Policy Formulated by the President and the PM on Apr. 20, 1941 ...," 25 Apr. 1941, ibid, 333;
      Hennessy, "Rise and Fall of a Canadian Maritime Policy," 56, 59-60

166. Behrens, *Merchant Shipping*, 384 mentions eighty-nine vessels, but Heal, *Great Fleet of Ships*, 63, lists ninety.

167. Financial attaché, Legation in US, "Memo of mtg with Morgenthau,"321-3; Taylor to Purvis, 18 June 1941, NS 29-25-1 pt
      22, copy on DHH, NHS, 8200 "Construction—Ships, 1939-45," pt 3; Superintendent of shipbuilding to engineer-in-chief,
      4 May 1941, NS 29-25-1 pt 20, copy on DHH, NHS 8200 (1939-45) pt 1; *British Warship Design*, 86, 92-3, 98-9, 112, 114,
      119-20

168. [NHS], "1942-1943 Shipbuilding Programme: Frigates (River Class)," nd, DHH, NHS 8200 "Construction of Ships 1939-45"
      pt 2; [NHS], "1942-1943 Shipbuilding Programme: Algerine Escorts," nd, DHH, NHS 8000 "Minesweepers 'Algerine' Class"

Six-inch guns in Halifax Dockyard awaiting installation in HMCS *Prince Henry*. At right is one of the RCN's four Fundy class minesweepers. (NAC, PA 104153)

The rudimentary, fragile SW1C radar antenna on the foremast of HMCS *Drumheller*, November 1941. (NAC, PA 105513)

Direction finding of U-boat transmissions was of critical importance in the Battle of the Atlantic. These are the Adcock antennae of the Department of Transport DF station at Hartlen Point, Nova Scotia. Despite its modest appearance, Hartlen Point was acknowledged to be one of the most accurate stations in the Atlantic network. (NAC PA 105719)

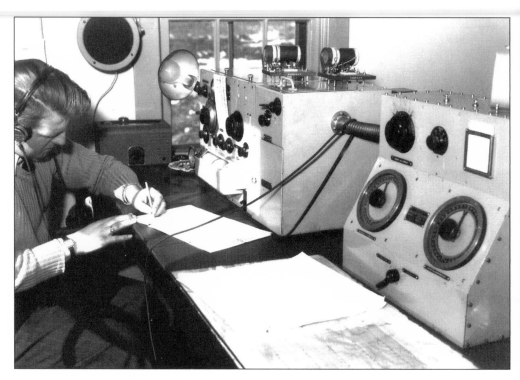

Department of Transport employee, Mr P. Ritcey, operating a Marconi set and radiogoniometer at the DF monitoring station at Hartlen Point. (NAC, PA 105724)

The full drawings needed by North American firms could not be provided until after the first vessels were completed, but in the summer of 1941 the prototype Algerines and frigates were still in the builders' hands. There was a further problem with the frigates, as they were 301 feet in length, too big to fit thorough the St Lawrence canals; they would therefore have to be built in the same coastal yards that were already being filled by the merchant ship orders. Although suited to speedy construction by British firms, moreover, the frigate was a major challenge for Canada's much less experienced builders. With a displacement of over 1,300 tons, nearly half again bigger than the corvette, twin engines, increased armament and equipment, the frigate was comparable in many ways to a modern sloop or escort destroyer, and a major step forward for Canadian industry.

The Naval Staff soon decided to order ten frigates for the RCN.[169] At the same time the BATM in Ottawa established that ten frigates could be built on British account in the Canadian coastal yards without unduly interfering with the merchant ship or RCN programs. In addition, the Admiralty placed orders for fifteen Algerines, fifteen long-forecastle, single-screw corvettes, and sixteen 164-foot antisubmarine trawlers, all of which could be built in Great Lakes yards.[170]

The energetic and optimistic Macmillan was willing to do everything possible to accommodate the naval program. Colonel Maclachlan, deputy minister for the Naval Service, and engineering officers at NSHQ were impressed by Macmillan's approach. During the spring of 1941 it was becoming clear that fitting out of the corvettes and Bangors of the 1939 and 1940 programs was considerably more difficult and time consuming than launching the basic hulls. The Director General of Shipbuilding branch at Munitions and Supply had left the procurement of the "boilers, engines, generators, pumps, valves, piping, electrical equipment and many other small items" to the shipbuilding firms, but most of these did not have the required expertise, especially in a seller's market of desperately short supply. Macmillan had in a few weeks grasped the problem, and built a strong procurement organization in Wartime Shipping Limited to work directly with manufacturers for centralized supply of the hundreds of fittings needed for the merchant ship program. Maclachlan thought this was a convincing model of how the job should be done, and warned that Munitions and Supply had no choice but to do something similar for the naval program. In June 1941 Munitions and Supply adopted what appeared to be the readiest solution, and turned over to Wartime Shipping Limited a large portion of the new naval program.[171]

The new arrangements were not a success. Within weeks, the engineering staff at NSHQ and the BATM received reports that Macmillan's procurement officers were approving equipment that did not meet stringent naval standards. Wartime Shipping Limited, moreover, encountered nothing but frustration in attempting to arrange contracts for the construction of the frigates. Contracting for a new

---

169. NSM, 25 Apr. 1941; E-in-C to CNS, 2 Feb. 1942, NAC, RG 24, 5604, NS 29-1-31 pt 2

170. Min of "Conference re Building 10 Twin-Screw Corvettes," 3 July 1941, NS 29-44-1 pt 1, copy on DHH, NHS 8000 "Frigates (River Class)"; Head of Mission, BATM to DG Shipbuilding, M&S, 29 July 1941, NAC, RG 24, 5613, NS 29-44-1 pt 1; Taylor to Evans, BATM, 18 Aug. 1941, enclosing President, Wartime Shipping Ltd to Taylor, 18 June 1941, NS 29-25-1 pt 22, copies on DHH, NHS 8200 "Construction—Ships 1939-45," pt 3

171. DM Naval Service, "Memo of 'Phone Conversation with Mr. H.R. Macmillan, 5-6-41," NAC, RG 24, 5602, NS 29-1-31 pt 2; DM M&S to directors-general and heads of branches, "Shipbuilding," 20 June 1941, ibid, pt 3; President, Wartime Shipping Ltd to Minister M&S, 16 May 1941, UBC Archives, Macmillan papers, box 100, file 16; President, Wartime Merchant Shipping Ltd to DM M&S, 11 and 14 June 1941, ibid, file 17

172. NAC, RG 24, 3844, NSS 1017-10-38, contains full correspondence.

173. DG Shipbuilding to Minister M&S, 13 Mar. 1942, NAC, RG 28, 77, file 1-1-166

and complicated type of warship on the basis of specifications and drawings that were not yet complete was a quite different challenge than establishing prices and schedules for the well-known standard merchant vessels. In September Wartime Shipping Limited withdrew from warship production, which once again became wholly the responsibility of the shipbuilding branch of Munitions and Supply.[172] Desmond A. Clarke, the new director general, expanded the small staff in part to implement centralized purchasing of components on the model of Wartime Shipping Limited.[173]

The pressures on Clarke's organization were enormous. The Bangors ordered in 1940 were still behind schedule, as was the small ship program, including notably Fairmile motor launches for which contracts that had been placed with wooden boat builders on the Great Lakes and on both coasts. As well, the RCN program was expanding. In October the Navy informed Munitions and Supply that it would be increasing its orders for frigates from ten to thirty, and also placing orders for ten Algerine minesweepers.[174] Macdonald bluntly declared to the Cabinet War Committee that the naval program should, in fact, have precedence over the merchant ship program: "There was no doubt of the urgent need of providing as many escort vessels as could be built. Unless adequate escorts were provided, it was useless to build merchant vessels."[175]

By October and November the plans and specifications that Munitions and Supply had said were necessary to conclude contracts for the frigates were finally available, but the efforts of Clarke's organization to claim berths where merchant ships were about to be laid down aroused Macmillan's ire.[176] The compromise reached in early January 1942 was to concentrate the frigates in three yards that would be entirely turned over for naval work, Vickers yard at Montréal, whose speed in producing its first run of merchant ships would soon clear its berths, the Morton yard at Québec City that had not yet begun merchant ship construction, and the small but experienced Yarrows facility at Victoria, Esquimalt. Clarke regarded this as a defeat. He reported to the navy, which had pressed for deliveries of the Admiralty's ten frigates and the RCN's first ten by early 1943, that these ships could not likely be delivered until the end of 1943, and that the remaining RCN frigates would not be available until the end of 1944, with deliveries very likely trickling over into 1945.[177]

Early in January 1942 Captain G.L. Stephens, the engineer-in-chief at NSHQ, decided that in the rush to mass produce merchant ships, Munitions and Supply had lost the flexibility necessary for naval construction that Canadian industry had demonstrated in the corvette programs. Those orders had been placed "with far less information available than was available for the Twin Screw Corvettes, yet these ships were successfully constructed and commissioned."[178] This was a fair statement. After start-up delays in 1940 the program had generally proceeded according to sched-

---

174. E-in-C to CNS, 2 Feb. 1942, NAC, RG 24, 5604, NS 29-1-31 pt 12; NCM, 8 and 28 Oct., 3 and 17 Nov. 1941

175. CWCM, 19 Nov. 1941

176. President, Wartime Merchant Shipping Ltd to DM M&S, 26 Nov. 1941, UBC Archives, Macmillan papers, box 100, file 17

177. DG Shipbuilding to Sec, DND, Naval Service, 6 Jan. 1942, Technical Advisor to DG Shipbuilding to Sec, DND, Naval Service, 7 Jan. 1942, forwarding "Department of Munitions and Supply ... Naval Construction Programme 1942-1943-1944," tables I through IV, E-in-C to CNS, 10 Jan. 1942, NAC, RG 24, 5604, NS 29-1-31 pt 12. See also E-in-C to CNS, 30 Dec. 1941, NAC, RG 24, 3841, NSS 1017-10-22 pt 1.

178. E-in-C to DM Naval Service, 19 Feb. 1942, NS 29-44-1 pt 3, copy on DHH, NHS 8000 "Frigates (River Class)"

179. "Shipbuilding Situation," NCM, 5 May 1941, NAC, RG 24, v 4044, NSS 1078-3-4 pt 1; NHS [table showing contract and completion dates of corvettes], nd, DHH, NHS 8000 "Flower Class Corvettes (A-Z)"; Macpherson and Burgess, *Ships of Canada's Naval Forces*, 212-14

ule and even made up time, with some sixty-nine vessels commissioning by the end of December 1941.[179] Although these ships suffered from compromises in the fitting of components that did not fully meet specifications, suffered from serious builders' defects, and lacked the latest improvements introduced by the Admiralty, it was fortunate for the Allied cause that Canadian authorities had not delayed production to address these shortcomings. These were the vessels that filled the gap in the British and US escort forces in the autumn of 1941, thus allowing the development of the convoy system across the whole breadth of the North Atlantic and on the routes to the Mediterranean and Africa; it was this extension of the convoy system that first and foremost contained the U-boat offensive.

The other main warship contracts let in 1940 and 1941 for forty-eight Bangor minesweepers and thirty-six Fairmile motor launches were about six months late because of delays in the deliveries of components and problems with the original design of the Bangor that resulted in changes both by the Admiralty and by Canadian authorities. The vessels began to commission in the latter part of 1941, with deliveries continuing into the spring and summer of 1942; the difficulties with production of diesel engines held up the last three Bangors of this type until the autumn of 1942.[180] Still, the bulk of the Fairmiles and Bangors were available—even if just barely—when they were most needed to counter the German thrust close to Canada's coasts and in the near approaches of the main ports.

Frigate production, in the end, considerably improved on the pessimistic forecasts of early 1942. The builders delivered the ten vessels for the Admiralty contract and sixteen for the RCN in 1943, and all but two of the forty ordered in 1941 commissioned by the end of June 1944. In the meantime, during the autumn of 1943 deliveries began of additional frigates ordered by the RCN in 1942, and most of the thirty-three vessels of this program commissioned by the summer of 1944.[181] This was a creditable performance that provided the RCN with capable ships in the numbers needed for the large-scale offensive operations during the last two years of the war. Nevertheless, the RCN did not receive its first frigates until the summer of 1943, meaning that corvettes—most of them the unimproved vessels of the original programs—had to continue to hold the line against the wolf packs at mid-ocean all through the German offensive of 1942 to early 1943.

Despite the unparalleled new demands that the war at sea made on Canadian industry in 1941 the Naval Staff and Macdonald held firm on the need to continue the Tribal class destroyer building program at Halifax Shipyards. By April 1941 evidence of the meagre assistance available from Britain, and the conclusion of the Naval Staff and shipbuilding experts that there would be no advantage in acquiring US types, convinced Howe, the prime minister, and certain senior naval engineers that resources could be used more efficiently by building less-complex vessels in Canada. Nelles and Macdonald rejected these arguments. The CNS was concerned at delays in the building of the four Tribals Canada had already ordered in Britain, especially in light of the fact that the pre-

180. "Shipbuilding Situation," NCM, 5 May 1941; NHS [table showing contract and completion dates of Bangor minesweepers], nd, DHH, NHS 8000 "Minesweepers: 'Bangor Class'"; Macpherson and Burgess, *Ships of Canada's Naval Forces*, 217-18, 195-7; DG Shipbuilding to E-in-C, 30 Jan. 1941, NAC, RG 24, 5602, NS 29-1-31 pt 2; Superintendent of Shipbuilding to E-in-C, 4 May 1941, NS 29-25-1 pt 20, copy in DHH, NHS 8200 (1939-45) pt 1; Tucker, *Naval Service of Canada* II, 51, 61; Smith, "12 Fairmile Type Motor Vessels Required for RCN," 15 July 1942, NAC, RG 28, 77, file 1-1-166

181. Tucker, *Naval Service of Canada* II, 69; Macpherson and Burgess, *Ships of Canada's Naval Forces*, 210-11

war River class destroyers, which were the only full-fledged, general purpose warships in the Canadian fleet, would reach the limits of their useful lifespan in 1943-4 because of the punishing effects of constant war service in the North Atlantic. The CNS was determined to set in stone the government's commitment, and to ensure the existence of the manufacturing capacity, to replace these ships with ships that were at least as capable. The Tribal, as he reminded his political masters, was the ship that the Naval Staff had long since identified as the one that best met long-term Canadian needs.[182] The Cabinet War Committee approved laying down of two Tribals at Halifax on 21 May 1941, the meeting at which the government first learned of the German U-boat thrust towards Newfoundland and of the Admiralty's intention to base an escort force at St John's. Macdonald remarked in his plea for the destroyer program that this news underscored Canada's need for more independent naval capabilities.[183] Howe, for his part, was willing in the end to support the destroyer program because of the continued expectation that the project would provide employment to ensure the retention of skilled workmen in the Halifax area needed to meet unpredictable peaks in demand for ship repairs. For that reason the destroyer project remained under Carswell, even though at this time he gave up his other responsibilities for shipbuilding. The Tribal program encountered all the difficulties that the engineers had predicted, and the first two were not laid down at Halifax until May 1942. By that time the government had already approved the construction of a third and fourth Tribal at Halifax.[184]

Nelles and Macdonald's advocacy for destroyer construction won through despite reservations from the prime minister. The key was that the growing intensity of the Battle of the Atlantic, and its approach close to Canada's shores, had strengthened the government's commitment to a blue water navy even in this case where the RCN's long-term goals had little relationship to the demands of the immediate crisis. Mackenzie King's willingness to let the navy have what it wanted reflected, in part at least, his continued fears that an overemphasis on the deployment of forces overseas would lead to conscription and the disruption of national unity. He repeatedly responded to Ralston's demands for the commitment of large numbers of additional troops by declaring that the army's program had to be balanced against the fully equal importance of the navy and the air force.

There were some who believed that the multiplication of Canada's maritime effort in 1941 assured Canadian unity and prosperity much more broadly than in the matter of military manpower policy. In mid-December 1941, shortly after the United States' entry into the war, officers on the staff of Rear-Admiral G.C. Jones in Halifax, produced a paper entitled "Subjects requiring further study in relation to future size and composition of the Royal Canadian Navy."[185] The authors—Captain W.B. Creery, Commander H.G. DeWolf, Lieutenant D. Harvey, and F. Alport, the senior civil engineer responsible for expansion of the base facilities—argued that the Anglo-US alliance was

---

182. CNS to Minister, 4 Nov. 1940, CNS to DM Naval Service, 12 and 28 Apr. 1941, Minister Naval Services to Gov-Gen in Council, 30 Apr. 1941, NSS 8200-355 pt 1, copies on DHH, NHS 8000 "Destroyers 'Tribals' General"

183. CWCM, 21 May 1941. See also CWCM, 6 May 1941; Macdonald to Howe, 30 April 1941, NSARM, Macdonald papers, file F/1222/10

184. Mackenzie, "Carswell," 7-8; Kennedy, *Munitions and Supply* II, 202; Tucker, *Naval Service of Canada* II, 60

185. NAC, RG 24, 3844, NS 1017-10-34 cited in Douglas, "Conflict and Innovation in the RCN," 210-32

186. The study group referred to, but did not quote, the Atlantic Charter, which Churchill and Roosevelt drafted at the Argentia Conference. It is reproduced in DSec to BHC, 13 Aug. 1941, *DCER* pt 7, 238-9

in essence the combination of the leading maritime powers for the creation of a new world order based on increased maritime trade, the freedom of "all men to traverse the high seas and oceans without hindrance" that Churchill and Roosevelt had proclaimed as a common goal at the Argentia Conference in August 1941.[186] Canada, by encouraging through every means the coming together of Britain and the United States since 1939, had fulfilled its unique history and geographical situation as the link between the two great powers. The vastly increased commitment of both the Canadian navy and industry to the war at sea in 1941 was not only the logical outcome, but the path to the future. In 1918 the Allies had demobilized too completely and rapidly, with a resulting postwar economic slump that, in the case of Canada, had contributed to the rise of radical politics, regional disparity, and severe tensions within confederation. Now, in 1941, maritime industry had become a unifying national economic effort.

The authors of the so-called Halifax Paper were especially excited about the merchant shipbuilding program, especially the many ships being built solely on Canadian account for operation by the Canadian government, and the great expansion of ship repair and servicing facilities. It was nothing less than the revival of a Canadian merchant marine, the preeminent basis of maritime strength: "It is a noticeable result of the present emergency that the public has ... appraised the close association between the merchant marine and the navy. The concept of 'Convoy' is the clearest expression of the condition that one service is ancillary to the other. The value of the sea-borne commerce of a nation is a measure of its dependence on the freedom of the seas and so of its need for naval forces." That linkage was the key to the postwar world. The Allied powers would not disarm so completely as they had mistakenly done in 1918, and maritime trade would be the principle means by which the world's shattered economies would be rebuilt. Canada would have a leading role, both naval and in trade, to assist Britain especially in rebuilding its depleted strength. The continuation in peacetime of the closer relationship between Britain and Canada that had developed in the war would, moreover, help counterbalance the potentially dominating influence of the United States. "It is emphasized," the Halifax group's paper concluded:

> that the future political unity of the Dominion will depend on industrial integration, overseas markets and maritime ability. For the sake of her internal economy, for the benefit of her national prestige and for the fulfilment of her responsibilities toward Imperial Defence, a Canadian Merchant Marine and a Canadian Navy are essential. For the maintenance of her autonomy, to link Hemisphere Defence with Imperial Defence ... the formulation of a Canadian Naval Policy is imperative. For the benefit of "morale" and stability, the early promulgation of such a Policy is an urgent necessity.[187]

Given the heavy responsibilities of two of the authors for the readiness of the fleet—Creery was Captain (D) at Halifax while DeWolf was double-hatted as Staff Officer (Operations) and Chief Staff Officer to Admiral Jones—the last sentence may well have referred to the strain on seagoing personnel and the ship servicing staffs ashore created by the push to hurry corvettes into commission and onto the North Atlantic run during the autumn of 1941.

---

187. Harvey to COAC, 19 Dec. 1941, enclosing "Subjects Requiring Further Study in Relation to Future Size and Composition of the RCN," NAC, RG 24, 1,129, "Canadian Naval Policy"

188. DOP, "Memo on Post-War Planning," 17 Nov. 1941, NAC, RG 24, 3844, NSS 1017-10-34 pt 1

An aerial view of Halifax Shipyards Ltd showing *Ottawa* in the floating dry dock and work just under way on the first two Tribal class destroyers. (NAC, PA 204595)

Officers at headquarters shared the concern about long-term, and especially postwar planning. In November Captain F.L. Houghton had revisited his postwar fleet paper of the year before and remarked that the Canadian maritime effort had so expanded in 1941 that issues had become much more complex. Postwar policy would have to be studied as part of a broad, government-wide initiative.[188] Thereafter the file petered out. Only in May 1942 did Commodore Reid, then VCNS, comment on Houghton's appeal, and then to say, "I agree that it is a big problem which should be kept in mind and the Planning organization formed the moment signs of peace are in evidence."[189] There were precious few signs of peace just now for either the Pacific or Atlantic commands of the navy. The best intentions voiced by senior staff at the end of 1941 to ease off on the hectic pace of expansion, to allow better maintenance of ships and more training and rest for crews, had instantly gone by the board when at the beginning of 1942 the enemy closed within sight of the shores of the Maritime provinces, and seemed ready to strike at least as heavily in British Columbia's waters.

189. VCNS to DOP, 12 May 1942, NAC, RG 24, 3844, NSS 1017-10-34 pt 1

Passing, by Harold Beament (CWM 10055)

Quarterdeck of HMCS Drumheller, by T.C. Wood (CWM 10601)

Opposite: *Fog*, by D.C. MacKay (CWM 10413)

Light Thunderstorm Over Convoy, by Harold Beament (CWM 10048)

Poster (CWM 19750599-013)

Poster (CWM AN 19720114-012)

Interior of Boiler Shop, by Alma Mary Duncan (CWM 14346)

Opposite: *Asdic Hut, Corvette, HMCS* Drumheller, by T.C. Wood (CWM 10542)

HMCS St Croix *and U-Boat in North Atlantic*, by Ronald Charles Weyman (CWM 1025275)

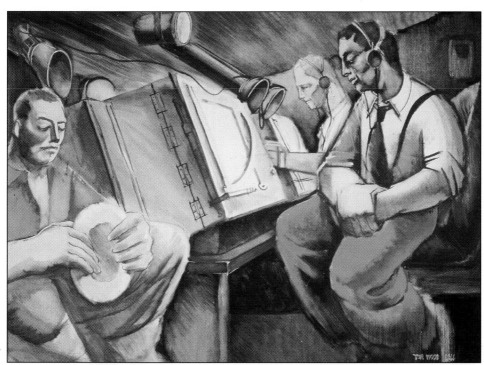

Drowning Sailor, by Jack Nichols (CWM 10505)

Crisis and Response

The Pacific Coast and Alaska
December 1941 to July 1943

CANADIAN WARSHIPS, indispensable to the Allies in the North Atlantic, filled a more modest requirement on the west coast of Canada. The need to provide maritime defences in the region had a long history, however. In the mid-nineteenth century Tsarist Russia, having completed its expansion eastward into Siberia and southward into Central Asia, seemed poised to make moves into the Pacific, and often sent ships there. Later Japan emerged as a world power, defeating China in 1894–95 and Russia in 1904–05, eventually proving a serious competitor to other colonial powers, notably the United States. In fact, in 1935 General A.G.L. McNaughton, then Chief of the General Staff, had warned that the most pressing danger on the west coast was a war between the United States and Japan, in which case Canada would be forced to defend its neutrality.[1] That potential danger was soon overtaken by events, and the direction in which Canadian policy subsequently evolved, exemplified by secret talks with representatives of the American services from 18 to 20 January 1938, was towards joint defence.[2] Later, in 1940–41, the Permanent Joint Board on Defence prepared the Joint Canadian–United States Basic Defence Plans, Numbers 1 and 2, to coordinate, respectively, the defence of North America and operations following US entry into the war.[3] In the event, when war with Japan broke out in December 1941, no serious threat to shipping developed, and the Canadian Chiefs of Staff never believed there was much likelihood of a Japanese invasion. So the west coast remained a backwater for the Royal Canadian Navy from November 1939, when the last two destroyers on the west coast sailed for Halifax, until the summer of 1943, when the campaign to drive Japanese forces from the Aleutians took place.[4] The enemy nevertheless seemed uncomfortably close for those who lived in British Columbia, and those charged with its defence.[5]

It was not just the immediate defence of the Canadian west coast that occupied RCN warships in the Pacific. The reader will recall that in 1940 three former Canadian National passenger ships, *Prince Henry, Prince David,* and *Prince Robert*, had been purchased by the RCN for conversion to armed merchant cruisers (AMCs). As *Prince Robert*'s conversion was nearing completion at the end of July 1940, her future employment became a matter of some discussion between Naval Service

1. "The Co-ordination of Canadian Defence," 28 Sep. 1935, DHH, 74/256, v 1, pt 10

2. Stacey, *Arms, Men and Governments*, 97

3. Ibid, 349

4. CSC, Appreciation, 10 Dec. 1941, DHH, CWCM

5. Stacey, *Arms, Men and Governments*, 133-4, 388; Douglas, *Creation of a National Air Force*, 400-6

Headquarters and the C-in-C America and West Indies. Although the RCN had initially wanted to retain the merchant cruiser in British Columbian waters, the C-in-C AWI proposed that the vessel be used to make "periodical surprise visits" to the west coast of South America to discourage enemy shipping movement and intercept enemy merchant ships as they left the sanctuary of neutral ports. That argument found a receptive audience at NSHQ. "It is greatly in our interests in Canada to have the White Ensign shown in Central and South American waters," Rear-Admiral Nelles wrote the deputy minister in early September 1940, "as, in case any of these [enemy] vessels are able to arm themselves, or even able to act as auxiliaries to armed raiders which may have broken out from Germany, they would immediately become a menace to our British Columbia coasting trade and, of course, to our trade route from British Columbia to the Panama Canal."[6]

The interception of German merchant vessels had taken on greater importance in July 1940 when the Admiralty received the first reports that German armed merchant raiders were at large in the central Atlantic. The German raiders were converted merchant ships "of seven or eight thousand tons, armed with six to eight modern 5.9-inch guns in addition to torpedo tubes and, in most cases, one or two aircraft. They were fuelled and provisioned to enable them to make long cruises and were furnished with numerous and skilful aids to disguise"[7] such as false bulwarks, deck houses, and cargoes to conceal their main armament. Operating on the shipping lanes of the South Atlantic, Indian, and Pacific Oceans, the disguised raiders often depended on resupply from those German tankers and cargo ships that had taken refuge in neutral ports at the outbreak of war. Amidst reports of "signs of restlessness amongst the German ships" sheltering in various ports along the Mexican and South American coast, NSHQ and the C-in-C AWI reached an agreement in mid-July 1940 that *Prince Robert* would be used to reinforce the blockading RN ships off the Mexican coast once its conversion was completed.[8]

Of particular concern was the German ship *Weser*, a 9,000-ton freighter that had sailed from Costa Rica to Manzanillo, Mexico, in mid-July. Although the vessel was reported to be short of fuel—and stocks in the Mexican port low—rumours persisted that *Weser* would soon attempt a breakout to join up with one of the German surface raiders. It was with some urgency, therefore, that work on *Prince Robert*, which had been officially commissioned into the RCN on 31 July under the command of Commander C.T. Beard continued through the end of August. Fortunately, by the time NSHQ issued the ship's instructions for its South American patrol on 7 September, the German freighter was still showing no immediate signs of putting to sea. Such was the haste with which *Prince Robert* was made ready for active service that the ship's scheduled departure date of 11 September was spent embarking ammunition, fuel, and stores, while a brief gunnery shoot that same afternoon substituted for a proper shakedown cruise. It was not until the early hours of 12 September, therefore, that the Canadian armed merchant cruiser departed for Mexican waters in, according to Commander Beard, "a very unready state."[9]

The voyage south proved uneventful and *Prince Robert* reached its patrol area off Manzanillo on 18 September to find *Weser* still in harbour. Lacking a reporting agent in the Mexican port,

---

6.   CNS to DM, 7 Sep. 1940, quoted in "HMCS Prince Robert from Commissioning to Reconversion," nd, DHH, 81/520 Prince Robert 8000

7.   Roskill, *War at Sea* I, 277

8.   CNS to DM, 7 Sept. 1940, quoted in "HMCS Prince Robert From Commissioning to Reconversion"

9.   *Prince Robert* ROP, 3 Oct. 1940, quoted in ibid

Beard had to keep the harbour entrance under constant surveillance to detect the German freighter's departure without, he hoped, revealing his presence to the enemy. For the next week, the Canadian warship lurked just beyond the horizon from Manzanillo during daylight while moving inshore at night. As the *Prince Robert* took up its patrol position off the harbour mouth after dark on 25 September, a ship was spotted clearing the breakwater. "The suspicious ship proceeded on a course directly out to seaward," Beard reported, "which permitted me to place *Prince Robert* between the harbour entrance and the ship. Course was then altered outwards for a few minutes to get a silhouette, as the moon was about to rise and visibility was increasing. I was not anxious to use my searchlight as this would have given away to any enemy ship in the harbour that the harbour entrance was being watched, had the ship I was shadowing been acting as a decoy." The Canadians still had to stalk their quarry until it reached international waters beyond the three-mile limit:

> The ship was identified as the Weser when a position off her port quarter had been arrived at and search light was then switched on. Weser was hailed and told to stop, which she did immediately, shouting back some remarks in Spanish, as the Master told me later that he thought that we were a Mexican patrol vessel. A cutter was manned and lowered containing Lieutenant-Commander G.B. Hope and a special armed boarding party, which had been prepared for this eventuality. Weser showed no resistance and no attempt to escape was made ... Only one round was fired, and this star shell well above the Weser. She was, however, warned that all guns were bearing on her and that I would not hesitate to open fire if she gave me cause. These messages were shouted across by megaphone.[10]

Taken by surprise, the German crew proved cooperative and the boarding party was able to secure the ship with little difficulty. A skeleton crew was retained to operate the ship under RCN guard with the remainder, including the master, being transferred to *Prince Robert* and the two vessels made an uneventful return voyage to Esquimalt. Although the *Weser* had reportedly been destined for a rendezvous with the German raider *Orion*, only "a quantity of oil" that was found on board would have served the needs of an auxiliary cruiser while the ship's main cargo of coke and peatmoss would have been entirely useless. The capture was of considerable public relations value to the RCN, while the vessel itself was soon put into allied service as the *Vancouver Island*, making several transatlantic crossings before being torpedoed and sunk in October 1941.[11] *Prince Robert*, meanwhile, returned to keep watch on the numerous other enemy merchant vessels that were still sheltering in Mexican and South American ports. In early February 1941, she was replaced on patrol by a British cruiser and diverted to escort Australian troop convoys across the Pacific for the next seven, uneventful months.

The RCN's two other armed merchant cruisers, *Prince Henry* and *Prince David*, had commissioned in December 1940 at Montréal and Halifax respectively. After working up at Bermuda, *Prince Henry*, under the command of Commander R.I. Agnew, RCN, was ordered to join the British cruiser *Diomede* on patrol off the west coast of South America. After passing through the Panama Canal on 26 February 1941 and making her appointed rendezvous with *Diomede*, the Canadian

---

10. Ibid

11. "HMCS Prince Robert From Commissioning to Reconversion"

warship commenced a three-week period of patrolling in Pacific waters.[12] On 19 March *Prince Henry* was directed to the port of Callao, Peru, to keep an eye on four German merchantmen located there. Five days later the Canadian warship entered the harbour of Bahia del Callao and dropped anchor "about two cables to leeward of the line of four German ships *Muenchen*, *Hermonthis*, *Leipzig*, and *Monserrate*."[13] Agnew learned from British intelligence officers ashore,

> that transfer of oil fuel in harbour from ship to ship was quite possible and probable and that therefore all four ships probably had ample fuel supply for a break-away, that all four ships were "wired" for immediate firing and demolition; that owing to fouling it was probable that maximum speed of ships would be nine knots. My own observation did not confirm this opinion concerning speed. All ships had been careened at anchor, scrubbed and water-lines painted. I was of the opinion that all four ships would probably obtain 11 knots speed in a break-away.
>
> I formed the opinion that at least two ships and probably all four would come out. That they would leave as soon as possible after dark and that they would proceed at maximum speed on diverging courses ... with a view to being across the trade route and spread by daylight.[14]

After the Canadian officers made the social rounds of the port to gather what other information they could about the enemy vessels, *Prince Henry* again put to sea, cruising in a wide arc beyond the horizon "with instructions that if possible any ships sighted were to be avoided before they had an opportunity of sighting *Prince Henry*."[15] The ruse proved successful when, at 1915 on 31 March, the Canadians received a signal from British officers in Lima that the *Hermonthis* and *Muenchen* had asked for permission to sail that night. Twenty minutes later, a second signal reported that both vessels had, in fact, left Callao. *Prince Henry* was at that time some seventy miles south of the port but quickly raised steam to work up to eighteen knots. At 2130 the shore lights were sighted and the Canadian warship commenced a curved search pattern to the north that allowed "for a speed of advance of the enemy of eleven knots." For the next nine hours the *Prince Henry* searched anxiously for the enemy merchantmen. Finally, at 0622 on 1 April, one-half hour after dawn, "a ship was sighted hull down bearing 260 degrees distant about fifteen miles." The vessel immediately began making course alterations as the *Prince Henry* continued to close until, at 0629, "the stranger had been identified as one of the German ships from Callao and the boarding party was now called away."

> At 0645 the International Signal to "Stop instantly or I will open fire" was made by 10" signalling projector and repeated continuously for fifteen minutes. At 0700, at a range of about 12,000 yards, one practice round was fired to miss ahead. It was not seen to pitch but at 0701 a small cloud of cordite coloured smoke burst from the after end of the superstructure. In a minute or two a low train of dense black smoke ran aft and forward from the superstructure for the full length of the ship and flames from the superstructure were

---

12.   Commander R.I. Agnew to C-in-C, AWI, "Letter of Proceedings, Period Thursday 12 Dec., 1940 to 28 Feb., 1941," 28 Feb. 1941, DHH, 81/520 Prince Henry 8000 ROP

13.   Agnew to C-in-C, AWI, "Letter of Proceedings, Period Sunday 23 Mar. to Monday 31 Mar., 1941," 2 Apr. 1941, ibid

14.   Ibid

15.   Agnew to C-in-C, AWI, "Letter of Proceedings, Period Sunday 23 Mar. to Monday 31 Mar., 1941

observed. By 0703 the ship was covered by a dense black pall of smoke with vivid fire in the superstructure and on all the hatch covers. The first [German life] boat was observed to be down at this time and three boats were seen by 0715. At 0730 *Prince Henry* passed about two cables to windward and identified the ship as the *Muenchen*. I then formed the opinion that the fire was too far advanced to permit entry below and that the salvage would therefore be a long and probably impossible job.[16]

Prince Henry left the German vessel and her sailors and proceeded south to search for the *Hermonthis*. After a five-hour search, the Canadian warship sighted a second merchant ship at 1225. The vessel immediately turned away from the Canadians and was observed to be on fire with her boats swung out. As *Prince Henry* closed the German merchantman, her crew began abandoning ship, but the Canadians ordered them to return to their vessel in the company of a Canadian boarding party. By 1400 a portion of the German crew and the boarding party were on board *Hermonthis* where a quick examination found the fire forward to be out of control. On his third attempt Agnew managed to lay the *Prince Henry* alongside, and by 1540 hoses had been rigged in an effort to salvage the ship as a prize. Despite the valiant efforts of the boarding party, who fought the fires for over an hour, it became clear that the *Hermonthis* could not be saved. The Canadian warship, meanwhile, had been taking a "severe" pounding as the two ships repeatedly banged together in the wind and swell. In their efforts, the Canadians "had lost ten hoses, half our manilla lines and half our fenders. Not less than eight lines of hose or more than twelve had been kept playing from 1540 until [1700] but no more spare hoses were available. The fire was out of control forward in cotton and oil soaked wood dunnage [and] ... the insulation of the refrigerator space burst into flame as soon as *Prince Henry* shoved off at 1711. It was then realized that the ship would be a total loss."[17] After rounding up the remaining German crew—by then fifteen miles off under sail for the Peruvian coast—*Prince Henry* sank the merchant ship by gunfire. The Canadian warship then turned north to the estimated position of the *Muenchen* but could find no trace of either the ship or her crew. The mystery was solved at noon on 2 April when *Prince Henry* closed the cruiser *Almirante Grau* and were informed by the Peruvians that they had sunk the *Muenchen* by gunfire and picked up her crew.[18]

Prince Henry continued her patrol for another three weeks before returning to Esquimalt with her prisoners. She continued to patrol and exercise in western Canadian waters for the remainder of the summer months until ordered back to Bermuda in early September 1941 where the C-in-C AWI planned to use her in tandem with *Prince David* as a surface raider hunting team in the Carribean. The latter's scheduled refit at Halifax later that same month delayed those plans, however, while *Prince Henry*'s assignment to St John's in mid-November to act as a depot ship for the Newfoundland Escort Force postponed them indefinitely. The departure of a British accommodation vessel from St John's had created an urgent need for space to lodge naval personnel in Newfoundland and NSHQ could find no alternative to deploying an operational warship for that purpose. Despite the transfer of three-fifths of her crew, however, the Prince ship was too small to meet the burgeoning accommodation needs of the RCN's expanding naval base.[19]

---

16.   Agnew to C-in-C, AWI, "Letter of Proceedings, Period Monday 31 Mar. to Tuesday, 2 Apr., 1941"

17.   Ibid

18.   Ibid; Schull, *Far Distant Ships*, 64

19.   "HMCS Prince Robert from Commissioning to Reconversion"

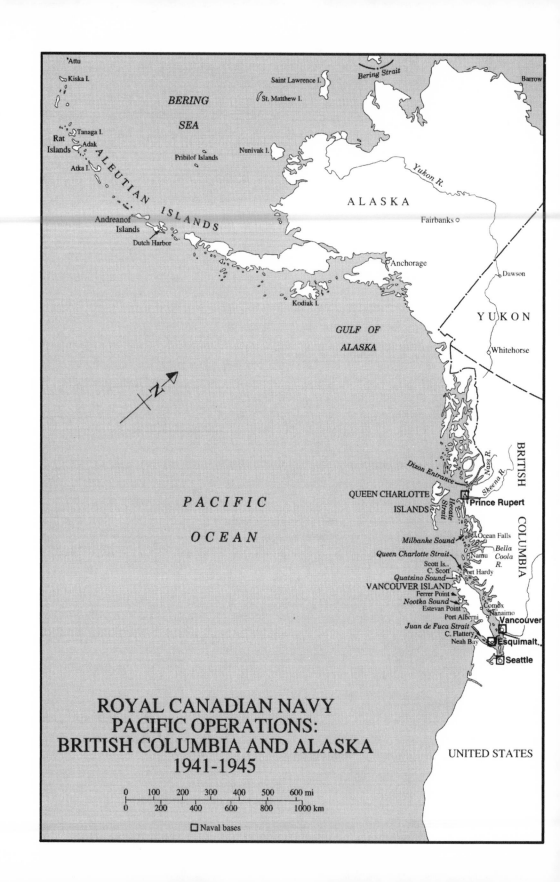

'Attu

Kiska I.

BERING

SEA

Saint Lawrence I.

St. Matthew I.

Bering Strait

Barrow

Tanaga I.

Rat
Islands

Adak

Atka I.

ALEUTIAN ISLANDS

Andreanof
Islands

Dutch Harbor

Pribilof Islands

Nunivak I.

Yukon R.

ALASKA

Fairbanks ○

Kodiak I.

Anchorage

GULF OF

ALASKA

Dawson

YUKON

Whitehorse

N

PACIFIC

OCEAN

Dixon Entrance

Nass R.

Skeena R.

BRITISH

QUEEN CHARLOTTE

ISLANDS

Hecate Strait

Prince Rupert

Ocean Falls

Milbanke Sound

Bella
Coola
R.

Queen Charlotte Strait

Namu

COLUMBIA

Scott Is.

C. Scott

Quatsino Sound

Port Hardy

VANCOUVER ISLAND

Ferrer Point

Comox

Nootka Sound

Estevan Point

Port Alberni

Nanaimo

Vancouver

Juan de Fuca Strait

C. Flattery

Neah Bay

Esquimalt

Seattle

ROYAL CANADIAN NAVY
PACIFIC OPERATIONS:
BRITISH COLUMBIA AND ALASKA
1941-1945

UNITED STATES

| 0 | 100 | 200 | 300 | 400 | 500 | 600 mi |
| 0 | 200 | 400 | 600 | 800 | 1000 km |

□ Naval bases

In the latter months of 1941 *Prince Robert*, the only RCN merchant cruiser remaining in the Pacific, found herself on the periphery of great events. In November, following a two-month refit at Esquimalt, she escorted the troopship *Awatea* carrying "C-Force," the Canadian Army's ill- fated, two-battalion brigade for the defence of Hong Kong, to the Far East. With the troopship already "crowded and uncomfortable," 109 members of the Royal Rifles of Canada made a more comfort-able passage on board the former CN cruise ship. The most notable part of the return passage was the fact that *Prince Robert* entered Honolulu on 3 December and sailed the next day, only three days before the Japanese navy's surprise attack began the Pacific war.[20] On 7 December the Canadian ship received the signal that Canada was at war with Japan, and that same signal report-ed a distress call from the US Army transport *Cynthia Olson*, only 150 miles from *Prince Robert*'s position. She closed at best speed and searched for three hours, but the Japanese submarine *I 26* had sunk the transport with all hands. It was as uncompromising an announcement of hostilities as the sinking of the *Athenia* in 1939, if less overwhelming than Nagumo's attack on the USN's Pacific Fleet, and from that moment until the Japanese attack on the Aleutian Islands the next sum-mer, RCN operations in the Pacific concentrated on the defence of Canada's west coast.[21]

The seaward defence of British Columbia posed a considerable challenge as its rugged coastline extends more than 5,550 miles, including the offshore islands. Complete surveillance was out of the question, even with the assistance of the RCAF, given the limited naval strength available to the Commanding Officer Pacific Coast, Commodore W.J.R. Beech, RCN. Beech, a quiet unassuming professional who had served in RN submarines during the First World War, had a small force at his disposal, including just three corvettes, five Bangor class minesweepers, four armed yachts, and an old coal-fuelled Battle class trawler, based variously at Esquimalt, Vancouver, or Prince Rupert. *Prince Robert* was only days out of Esquimalt on its return from the Far East, and over the ensuing months *Prince David* and *Prince Henry* arrived to reinforce his fleet.[22] An auxiliary force, the Fishermen's Naval Reserve, volunteers who carried out inshore patrols in their fishing vessels, had come into being in 1938. The principal role of this force was to curb possible espionage and sabotage by Japanese-Canadian fishermen whose intimate knowledge of the coast could have been helpful to hostile Japanese forces. "Should the Canadian Government desire to intern enemy aliens on the coast," one civilian employee at the Department of National Defence had commented, "the [proposed] Fishermen's Reserve would be admirably suited to effect this purpose, while the larger RCN ships are not well adapted for this work." He went on to suggest that "A press despatch of this kind would reassure the fishermen in regard to the nature of the obligations they would assume by joining the Fishermen's Naval Reserve and would have an excellent effect on recruiting. It would be welcomed by the press and would be of great interest to the general public and particularly

---

20.   Ibid; Stacey, *Six Years of War* I, 448

21.   *Prince Robert* ROP, 10 Dec. 1941; A.R. Moore, *A Careless Word ... A Needless Sinking* (Kings Point 1984), 67. There were reports after the war that *Prince Robert* actually made contact with the Japanese force sailing to attack Pearl Harbor, but her track was well away from Admiral Nagumo's force. See *The Crowsnest* 6/7 (1954), 13-16, and *Globe and Mail*, 14 July 1954

22.   COPC WD, DHH, NSS 5000-5-10, v 6; *Prince Robert*, *Prince David*, *Prince Henry*, Ship Movement Cards, DHH

pleasing to the people of British Columbia as a demonstration that the government is taking whatever steps are possible to offset the Japanese menace in the event of war."[23]

The Fishermen's Reserve was a hybrid creation, a navy within a navy.[24] Conditions of service, regulations, and dress were all different from the RCN, RCNR, and RCNVR. Its members could not be transferred to general service or other theatres of war, nor could they be used in industrial disputes; enlistment was limited to white men—neither Japanese nor aboriginal fishermen were eligible—who made their living by fishing. Usually, a complete crew joined up with its own boat, which was chartered by the navy at a monthly rate—the 57-foot *San Tomas*, for example, cost $390 a month—and, in peacetime, a crew would receive one month's training when the fishing season was closed. The officer responsible for recruiting the first fishermen, Lieutenant-Commander C.D. Donald, RCN had thought that the reservists would want to wear civilian clothes, but was surprised to learn that they wanted uniforms so they would be identified with the navy. A unique dress evolved; officers wore a seaman's jersey and bell-bottoms with an officer's hat, and seamen wore uncollared jerseys with bell-bottoms. Often, however, the fishermen resorted to their more familiar civilian working rig of Cowichan sweaters, trousers, and gumboots; as a result they informally became known as "the gumboot navy."[25]

Fishermen have their own way of doing things. Gilbert Tucker, the navy's first official historian, called it "a sturdy individuality."[26] Many did not think that naval duty was sufficient reason to stop them from practising their livelihood. Some of the vessels had retained their fishing gear and would stop to fish in the midst of patrol duties, one veteran exclaiming: "the dickens with the war."[27] Stills were not uncommon on board vessels and those less enterprising could find liquor at the many fishing hamlets or canneries visited during patrols. It must be said, however, that they did not allow this to interfere with their patrol duties. They took their responsibilities seriously, and were bred to the sea. One officer who worked with them commented on their outstanding seamanship, and their superb knowledge of west coast waters was a priceless asset. The twenty-nine Fishermen's Reserve boats in commission at the outbreak of the Pacific war varied in size, speed, and age, but because they had to pass navy inspection they were all good sea boats. Once accepted, they were painted, fitted with a radio, and provided with an armament of rifles or a Lewis gun, and some of the larger craft received minesweeping gear. With the exception of one vessel, the *Ehkoli*, however, it was not until 1942 that any received asdic or depth charges. Although slow, lightly armed, and often poorly equipped, they were well-suited for the task of poking into inlets and patrolling inshore waters.[28]

---

23. Tucker, *Naval Service of Canada* I, 15, 363-4; II, 269. PO G.F.A. Hughes, RCNVR, "The West Coast Fishermen's Reserve, RCNR (FR), 1939-1940," 1, DHH, 77/557; Carol Popp, *The Gumboot Navy* (Lantzville 1988), 63; Whitby, "The Quiet Coast: Canadian Naval Operations in Defence of British Columbia, 1941-42," in Haydon and Griffiths, *Canada's Naval Pacific Presence: Purposeful or Peripheral* (Halifax 1999), 61-81

24. Capt (D) Esquimalt to COPC, Nov.1942, DHH, NHS 1700-902

25. Canada, *Royal Canadian Navy Reserve Regulations* II: *Fishermen's Reserve (West Coast)*, (Ottawa 1939); Tucker, *Naval Service of Canada* I, 364-5; Hughes, "West Coast FR"; Tucker interview with SLt J. Sherlock, RCNVR, 29 Jan. 45, DHH, NHS 1700-902

26. Tucker, *Naval Service of Canada* I, 364

27. Popp, *Gumboot Navy*, 90

28. Hughes, "West Coast FR"; Various Esquimalt Monthly Reports, DHH, NHS 1000-5-10, v 6

The most significant act of the Fishermen's Reserve once the Pacific war erupted was to participate in the seizure of fishing boats belonging to Canadians of Japanese ancestry in British Columbia, an operation that began on 8 December 1941, the day after Canada declared war. The RCN and Cabinet had what they thought were logical reasons for appropriating the vessels—the intention was, first, to deprive Japanese-Canadian fishermen of the capacity to provide intelligence to the enemy or possibly even help the enemy effect landings on the coast and, second, to acquire badly needed vessels to augment meagre patrol forces—but it also proved to be the first step in a policy that would lead to the forcible evacuation of over 22,000 Japanese-Canadians from west coast areas. The RCN, like the other armed services and the RCMP, played only a secondary role in the decision to remove these people; Commodore Beech recommended only those living in the Queen Charlotte Islands should be relocated, but his views reflected how members of the armed forces stationed in British Columbia came to identify with local attitudes towards this immigrant community.[29] Certain Canadian naval officers had regarded fishermen of Japanese ancestry with suspicion for some years and in the late 1930s took seriously rumours that Japanese naval officers were posing as fishermen. In particular, the naval intelligence officer at Esquimalt, Lieutenant-Commander F.R. Gow, RCN reported to NSHQ the local myth that it was likely that many Canadian-born *Nisei* were returning to their homeland for military training.[30] Gow confided his personal belief to a retired RN officer that Japanese-Canadians on the coast were not only organized "to some extent," but that there could be no "doubt whatsoever that a very great proportion of them are Naval or Military Reserves. Many of the young Canadian-born Japanese when they are of age go back to Japan for two years military training ... I think one good thing is that the White people are beginning to open their eyes and are beginning to realize the danger with which they are rubbing shoulders, daily." Ironically, he admitted that because Japanese-Canadians were "for all intents and purposes, very good citizens," he admitted there was very little excuse for searching their fishing boats.[31]

In September 1941 Beech echoed similar concerns, even after the RCMP failed to find anyone in the Japanese community with naval or military experience.[32]

> Some 32,000 Japanese of one type or another live in British Columbia, practically all of them within the coastal areas. Most of the Japanese settlements in coastal areas have been located either by accident or by design in strategic positions.
>
> Many of the Japanese communities, if not the majority of them, are culturally, socially and ethnically Japanese. Retention of contact with Japan is maintained by a large majority of Japanese, native born or otherwise, through the Japanese Consul.

---

29. Beech acted strictly within the limits of his authority, unlike AVMarshal L.F. Stevenson, Air Officer Commanding Western Air Command, who in Jan. 1942 bypassed the JSC and wrote directly to Air Force Hq to recommend removal of all axis aliens from the coast. I.A. Mackenzie to W.L. Mackenzie King, 10 Jan. 42, Enclosure I, NAC, Mackenzie King Papers, MG 26, J1, v 328; Roy, Granatstein, Iino, and Takamura, *Mutual Hostages: Canadians and Japanese during the Second World War* (Toronto 1990), 77-84; Douglas, *Creation of a National Air Force*, 408

30. NSO, Esquimalt to DNIP, 9 Feb.1938, NAC, NSS1023-18-2, mf C5853; Roy et al, *Mutual Hostages*, 46; J.L. Granatstein and G.A. Johnson, "The Evacuation of the Japanese-Canadians, 1942: A Realist Critique of the Received Version," in N. Hillmer, B. Kordan, and L. Luciuk (eds), *On Guard for Thee* (Ottawa 1988), 113-14

31. Lt-Cdr F.R. Gow, RCN, to Adm R. Nugent, RN (Ret'd), nd, but 1938, NAC, RG 24, 11879, E5-05-28

32. For one example, see "E," Vancouver Island Section to OC "E" Div, 4 June 1941, NAC, RG 18, 3564, C11-19-2-24

> In early life, Japanese children go to the Public Schools, but later in the day they
> go on to Japanese Schools where Japanese Masters instill Japanese concepts and ide-
> ologies. There can be little doubt that the actual standards of loyalty of at least some
> of these Japanese is questionable.
>
> While there must of necessity be some doubt in the matter, it is thought fully possible
> that as great a degree of danger can arise from the Canadian/Japanese as from the
> Japanese Citizens themselves and some suspicion is warranted regarding particularly the
> younger generations of the Canadian born Japanese for the reasons mentioned above.
>
> The question of ultimate loyalty to Canada and the Democratic Institutions as
> opposed to that to the Makado [*sic*] and the ancient Japanese culture is one that
> remains to be decided. Nevertheless in view of the vast amount of damage possible of
> accomplishment by small groups of determined saboteurs it is felt that chances should
> not be taken.[33]

Beech reported that organized Japanese espionage had been going on in the United States for
years, a statement based on good evidence, as it happened. After breaking the Japanese diplomatic code during the summer of 1940, US intelligence decrypted information, which they passed on
to the British, that Japanese diplomats, including at the consulate in Vancouver, had been instructed to gather intelligence with the help of "second generation" and "resident nationals." Beech had
no evidence that fishermen in British Columbia were gathering intelligence, but his point—and the
point made by all the service chiefs on the west coast—was that they had the potential to do a
great deal of damage. In January 1942 Commander J. McCulloch, RCN, in charge of auxiliary vessels in Esquimalt, explained to the official naval historian Gilbert Tucker that "what was mainly
feared was that many Jap-manned boats might be used to meet Jap transports out at sea and land
Jap soldiers," it being calculated that a fishing vessel could transport about ten armed men.[34]
Moreover, in June 1941 Beech had informed the army and air force of his intention to seize
"approximately 20 Japanese fish packers," which, along with vessels already in commission and
those building as part of the 1941 program, would boost his patrol force to sixty-five vessels.[35]

The legality of such a seizure was questionable. In February 1941 the naval minister had
informed the Under Secretary of State for External Affairs that "in the event of hostilities breaking
out with Japan, it is proposed to immediately seize all Japanese fishing vessels." Those with owners of Japanese origin who held Canadian naturalization papers "would also be sent into defended ports for thorough investigation." Without indicating support for either of these measures,
Norman Robertson replied that both were legal under international law.[36] When, however, Beech
had revealed in May details of the plan to collect "Japanese and Japanese owned boats on the West
Coast," Hugh Keenleyside of External Affairs rejected the notion. Writing to Commander P.B.
German, then in the Naval Intelligence Division at NSHQ, he pointed out that the owners of the

---

33.   COPC to NSec, 12 Sep. 1941, NAC, RG 24, 2769, HQS 6615-6, v 4

34.   Naval Historian's interview with Commander J. McCulloch, "Seizure of Jap. Fishing Boats, BC, Dec. 41," 7 Jan. 1942, DHH,
      81/520/1440-7, v 9

35.   JSC-Pacific Coast Min, 17 June 1941, DHH, 322.009 (D 53)

36.   Angus L. Macdonald to Norman A. Robertson, 20 Feb. 1941; Robertson to Macdonald, 21 Feb. 1941, NAC, RG 25, 2859,
      1698-C-40

vessels were British subjects and Canadian nationals. "If this is Beech's plan it is, of course, wholly impossible. I would suggest that the matter should be cleared up by definite instructions to the Officer Commanding on the Pacific Coast that the proposals outlined in his memorandum under reference are applicable only to vessels owned and operated by Japanese *nationals*."[37]

Although the government's attitude was to change with the attack on Pearl Harbor, it originally had no plans for the wholesale relocation of even Japanese nationals, and was rightly concerned that measures against Japanese and Japanese-Canadians in British Columbia be uniform and consistent.[38] Beech's intention to round up all vessels operated by fishermen of Japanese ancestry was clearly out of step and had to be altered to fit in with government policy. NSHQ therefore passed Keenleyside's objections on to Beech who revised his plan.[39] Rather than seizing Japanese boats, he now called for "the rapid examination of all fishing and other craft in British Columbia harbours and waters." In fact, the plan remained exactly the same, with the adjective "Japanese" excised, Beech then arguing that "the operation outlined is not directed against any particular race, but in the event of War (declared or undeclared) with Japan, persons of Japanese origin should naturally receive more immediate attention than those not of enemy origin."[40] When this plan came to the attention of Norman Robertson in November, he expressed his satisfaction, noting that it seemed "thoroughly sound."[41]

Unaware that their fate was being discussed in such terms, Japanese-Canadian fisherfolk still realized that their position would be precarious in case of war with Japan, and sought to prove their loyalty. As the RCMP Officer commanding E Division informed his commissioner, a certain Mr Noguchi, "who spoke for the fishermen, particularly those at Steveston, stated that in the event of war with Japan he presumed the Japanese fishing fleet might be tied up by the authorities and stated that he believed most of the Japanese fishermen, of whom almost all are either Canadian born or naturalised British subjects, would wish to voluntarily offer their boats to the authorities for what use they might be in the protection of this coast."[42] The offer availed them nothing, because the manner in which the Pacific war broke out brought the government around to Beech's view. Near-simultaneous attacks all around the Pacific rim demonstrated the scope and reach of Japanese forces, and losses at Pearl Harbor seemed, in the first instance, to have tilted the strategic balance in their favour. Although discounting the threat of invasion, Canada's chiefs of staff nonetheless concluded: "It is possible that Japan may endeavour to exploit her preliminary successes by attempting to harass the West Coast of North America, either by sea-borne air attack, bombardment, or a combination of both."[43] Beech, perhaps in the belief that Pearl Harbor had silenced any defenders the fishermen of Japanese ancestry may have had, felt free to implement his original

---

37. H. Keenleyside to Cdr P.B. German, 14 Aug. 1941, ibid

38. For government policy, see N.A. Robertson memo, "Summary of Action to Be Taken by the Canadian Government on the Commencement of War between Canada and Japan," 7 Nov. 1941, NAC, RG 25, 2859, 1698-A-40

39. H. Keenleyside, memo for file, 21 Oct. 41; Capt E.S. Brand to H. Keenleyside, 31 Oct. 41, ibid

40. COPC Memo, "Examination of All Vessels in the Event of Hostilities Directly Affecting BC Coast," 11 Sep. 1941, NAC, RG 24, 11867, DE10-7-1

41. For Norman Robertson's handling of the Japanese-Canadian question, see J.L. Granatstein, *A Man of Influence: Norman A. Robertson and Canadian Statecraft, 1929-68* (Toronto 1980), 157-67

42. OC E Div to Commissioner, 3 Dec. 1941, NAC, RG 18, 3564, C11-19-2-24

43. Appreciation, 10 Dec. 1941, RG 2, 7C, v 6

round-up plan. On 8 December the armed yacht *Wolf* and the Fishermen's Reserve vessels *Moolock* and *Talapus* sailed from Esquimalt to gather up fishing boats in the Vancouver area. The next day, the FR craft *BC Lady* and *Ehkoli* were sent into the Gulf Islands and up the eastern shore of Vancouver Island, while the corvette *Quesnel* and the FR vessels *Marauder* and *Van Isle* headed to Bamfield to scour the west coast of the island. At Prince Rupert, three FR vessels, *Macdonald*, *Signal*, and *Queen Bee*, checked the area around the port and south to the Skeena River, *Leelos* and *Takla* were sent north into the Nass River area, and the armed yacht *Cougar* was despatched to the Queen Charlottes. To facilitate this work, naval officers were flown into isolated hamlets and canneries to conduct preliminary inspections.[44]

Although the vessels operating out of Esquimalt had begun sending fishing boats to central locations from the start, there was some confusion at Prince Rupert. Before leaving port for the Skeena River area on 11 December, Coxswain J.K. Juerson, commanding the FR vessel *Signal*, received strict orders from the NOIC, Commander A. Reed, RCNR, "*Not* to let any Japanese craft or other alien craft out of the river."[45] Upon arrival on the Skeena, Juerson anchored in mid-stream opposite the Inverness Cannery, in a position that would block any vessels attempting to head out to sea. On 13 December, however, the FR vessel *Macdonald*, with Lieutenant-Commander F. Wissler, RCNR—presumably one of the special officers charged with the task of implementing the September 1941 plan—arrived with new orders; Juerson was now instructed to round up all Japanese-Canadian boats and convoy them to Prince Rupert. Similarly, *Takla* was sent into the Nass River area on 9 December, the skipper, Coxswain C. Parkwold, initially checking the identity of Japanese-Canadians—one fisherman, Sasuke Nakagawa, had served in the Canadian Expeditionary Force during the Great War—but on 15 December the harbour craft *PML 8* arrived with orders to tow all Japanese-Canadian fishing boats to Prince Rupert, and to put those that had been beached for winter out of action. Parkwold complied, towing two craft to the port, but he left two others behind because the locals would otherwise have no means of transportation in case of emergency.[46]

After being forced to turn back once because of rough weather, the armed yacht *Cougar* crossed Hecate Strait on 11 December. At first the commanding officer, Chief Skipper G.F. Cassidy, visited the various hamlets or canneries, checking identification of any Japanese-Canadians and confiscating their firearms. Orders then changed. On 14 December *Cougar* had to retrace part of her route and took on board, under guard, five Japanese-Canadians whom Cassidy had been willing to let go about their business three days earlier—one watchman, according to Cassidy, "was very relieved to see the Japanese being taken away." With others the skipper was more compassionate. On two occasions, he left behind Japanese-Canadians who had been in the country a long time, one since 1898, on condition that their employers agree to keep an eye on them. After another stormy crossing of Hecate Strait, *Cougar* returned to Prince Rupert on 19 December.[47]

In Ottawa, Cabinet dealt further blows to Japanese-Canadian fishermen. On 16 December the government passed an order-in-council banning any "person of the Japanese race" from operating "any vessel within waters adjacent to the West coast of Canada" without permission from the

---

44. *Wolf* ROP, Dec. 1941; *Cougar* ROP, Dec. 1941, DHH, NHS NSS 1000-5-10, v 6

45. *Signal*, Report on Special Duty Trip, Skeena River, 14 Dec. 1941, ibid

46. *Takla* ROP, 17 Dec. 1941, ibid

47. *Cougar* ROP

HMCS *Prince Robert* with her prize the German merchant ship *Weser* in September 1940.
(DND, PMR 86-414)

Prince David on a west coast patrol. Note how her hull has been camouflaged to resemble a destroyer or cruiser. (DND, RCAF AY 144A)

The Fishermen's Reserve
vessel *Barkley Sound* in
late 1942. (DND, E 4501)

Confiscated Japanese-Canadian fish packets at Bamfield, British Columbia, December 1941. (DND, PMR 72-223)

RCMP. Penalty was seizure of the vessel, and the order was made retroactive to 8 December 1941, the day the first boat was taken for inspection.[48] Since no Japanese-Canadian was going to receive permission to operate his craft, in practical terms the order-in-council meant that all vessels operated by fishermen of Japanese ancestry would be impounded, with Steveston, at the mouth of the Fraser River and home to many Japanese-Canadians, selected as the concentration site. Fishermen, believing they would get their boats back, gave full cooperation and did not even submit claims when some were damaged during the transfers.[49]

Fishing vessels arrived at Steveston from all over British Columbia, but the task of getting them there from the Prince Rupert area posed by far the greatest challenge. In mid-December the FR vessels *Macdonald, Leelos,* and *Kuitan*, and the navy tug *Stanpoint*, departed Prince Rupert for a long voyage of over 500 miles in rough December seas. According to Masao Nakagawa and Isamu Kayama, who were running one of the fishing boats, "We left the morning of December 16th at 8:30 with the two seiners, the *Leelos* and the *Kuitan,* towing the gillnetters in two long lines, the boats stretching for about three-quarters of a mile," although some of them, according to RCN reports, began banging into one another.[50] "On the 18th we began to have trouble. At the mouth of Millbanke Sound we ran into heavy seas and twice the *Stanpoint* line broke and three hours were spent by the corvette [sic] crew repairing the damage. Six boats drifted loose and the sea became so rough that anchoring in a channel became necessary. The *Leelos* proceeded to Bella Bella to obtain gasoline for the 20 boats with engines in running order,"[51] so it would no longer have to tow them. Leaving Bella Bella, the weather did not improve.

> It was a terrible experience. We did not have suitable clothing. Our small boats were not ready for a long trip in the middle of winter. We were always cold and wet. We huddled close to our cabins, braced against the waves that hit our bows and sprayed our unprotected bodies. With sleepy and tired men at the wheel, the boats ran out of line and began hitting each other in the dark. Only a few had lanterns in use. The rough sea lifted the boats and brought them down with a terrible thud that shook our bones and now and then the propellor spun helplessly in mid air. Near Namu, a fisherman from North Pacific Cannery, having closed his cabin too tight to ward off the cold was overcome by gas fumes. The boat was observed running in circles. Another boat took her in tow. The sea became rougher. Many were seasick and it was anchorage for us in an inlet for the rest of the night.[52]

They arrived in Steveston on 28 December. The stricken boat belonged to the veteran of the CEF's 10th Battalion, Sasuke Nakagawa.

The sailors of the Fishermen's Reserve who had been thought so suitable for this task carried it out with mixed emotions. As one related years later, "It was a thing that had to be done. It was a shame because 95 per cent of the Japanese in [Prince] Rupert were all good Canadians. They had been here for many, many years. I had many on the boat with me during the years. But it had to

---

48.   Order-in-Council PC 9761, 16 Dec. 1941, DHH, 81/520/1440-7, v 9

49.   Roy et al, *Mutual Hostages*, 76-7

50.   Roy Ito, *Stories of My People* (Hamilton 1994), 223

51.   Ibid, 223-4

52.   Ibid, 224-5

be done because you couldn't take a chance,"[53] although the confiscations could be heart-rending nonetheless. "I felt sorry for the Japanese," another sailor recalled. "A lot of them I knew personally and those fellows hadn't ever seen Japan. Some were veterans from World War I. They wore their tunics when they brought their boats in, and all their badges. They had tears in their eyes. It was pretty sad. There is no fair way in wartime."[54]

Japanese-Canadian fishermen were the victims of group identification. It is ironic that while their knowledge of coastal waters made them excellent candidates for the naval reserves, their ethnicity and cultural background placed them—in the eyes of other British Columbians—in the ranks of the enemy.[55] For this, the navy was obliged to engage in the labour-intensive task of inspecting, rounding up, and transporting over a thousand fishing boats to Steveston. No doubt the patrol vessels and personnel could have been better used elsewhere—at least two senior officers, the NOIC Prince Rupert and the Commanding Officer of *Naden* barracks, complained to Commodore Beech about the drain on their resources[56]—but even decades later, and with the benefit of hindsight, the issue is difficult to resolve. One could argue that, strictly from the point of view of security, in the climate of hysteria that pervaded the province, Japanese-Canadians would have been viewed with deep suspicion had they been allowed to continue fishing, and the requirement to constantly stop and check their vessels would have absorbed far more effort. On the other hand, strictly from the operational point of view, rounding up Japanese-Canadian fishing boats distracted naval vessels from other tasks, robbed the armed services of potentially useful reservists (and interpreters for the campaign in the Pacific), and perpetuated regional feelings of insecurity by seeming to confirm their validity. If there is a moral to this sad story, perhaps it is that armed forces and governments should focus on the enemy that has actually proven hostile rather than one whose existence is no more than hypothetical.

While the distasteful work of impounding the fishing vessels went on, nine Japanese fleet submarines were closing the west coast of North America. By mid-December they had taken up patrol positions from San Diego to the approaches to Juan de Fuca Strait. Fortunately for west coast shipping and the resource-strapped forces of Pacific Coast Command, the Japanese, in contrast to the *Paukenschlag* and *Zeithen* U-boats that caused such devastation and consternation along the eastern seaboard of North America at this time (see Chapter 7), adhered to a doctrine that restricted them for the most part to fleet reconnaissance.[57] They attacked few ships. "Thank the Lord," wrote Admiral Ernest King, USN, "they did not understand or learn much about managing U-boats from

---

53. Popp, *Gumboot Navy*, 65

54. Ibid, 67

55. For the same reason, the RCN would be deprived of Japanese-speaking interpreters when they were needed for operations with the British Pacific Fleet.

56. NOIC Prince Rupert to COPC, "Japanese Fishing Boats," 5 Jan. 1942, NAC, RG 24, 11867, DE10-7-1; CO RCN Barracks memo, "Strategic Employment of Ratings," 23 Apr. 1942, NAC, RG 24, 11767, PC 014-21-17, v 1

57. For Japanese submarine doctrine and operations, see C. Boyd and A. Yoshida, *The Japanese Submarine Force and World War II* (Annapolis 1996); C.G. Reynolds, "Submarine Attacks on the Pacific Coast, 1942," *Pacific Historical Review* 33/2 (1964); and Whitby, "Quiet Coast," 61-81

the Nazis."[58] What King did not appreciate was that Japan's resources were far more limited than those of the United States, forcing a more focused approach to war. Having adopted a doctrine of closing with and destroying the enemy in a decisive fleet battle, a doctrine proven against China in 1894–95 and Russia in 1904–05, the Imperial Japanese Navy, lacked the resources also to prepare for a long war by such means as a large fleet of submarines for commerce raiding. Furthermore, with its focus on a decisive naval engagement, the navy designed its submarines to operate with surface units or in a reconnaissance role. The paramount requirement was to gather and report intelligence, necessitating a boat's survival and precluding the kind of aggressive merchant-ship hunting practised by the German U-boat arm.[59]

Canada and the United States were not, however, aware of their good fortune, and prepared to defend against attacks on shipping, the main burden of which was to be taken up by the USN. Under ABC-22, the Canadian-American hemispheric defence plan, Canada's air and naval forces were responsible for defending the seaward approaches to Esquimalt-Victoria, Vancouver, and Prince Rupert, controlling shipping in Canadian waters and patrolling the inshore waters of British Columbia. The RCN was also called on to help defend Alaska by assisting in the movement, by sea, of American forces to the northern state. For its part, the USN was given responsibility for offshore surface and air patrols in the approaches off southeastern Alaska, British Columbia, and the American northwest, protection of shipping in the Gulf of Alaska, and control of shipping in all areas they patrolled.[60] Under this system, the RCN could thus focus on the practicable, if tedious, task of coastal patrol and by 9 December the Canadians could commit between five to seven warships to that duty.[61]

The naval defence of British Columbia, with this modest fleet, was a simple affair. Working out of Esquimalt, Prince Rupert, and Vancouver, ships simply patrolled choke points—the Strait of Juan de Fuca, the Gordon Channel off the entrance to Queen Charlotte Strait, and the Hecate Strait—and the bays and inlets along the coast of the province and the west coast of Vancouver Island. *Prince Robert* and, when they joined later, *Prince Henry* and *Prince David*, conducted offshore patrols about 150 miles to sea. RCAF aircraft patrols and radar coverage complemented the naval patrols and helped fill the inevitable gaps in naval surveillance. The most important naval coverage was out of Esquimalt, across Juan de Fuca Strait, at the eastern end between Race Rocks and Ediz Hook, or further up between Sheringham Point and Low Point. The few corvettes available usually worked the more important Sheringham–Low Point line, steaming back and forth on "endless chain" patrols between the Canadian and American shores, using asdic in the daylight hours, but housing the asdic dome at night or in periods of low visibility to help avoid damage from the

---

58. Since the cryptologists had yet to break the Japanese naval code, there was no warning equivalent to that provided by Enigma when submarines were approaching. For King's remark, see Thomas B. Buell, *Master of Seapower: A Biography of Fleet Admiral Ernest J. King*, (Boston 1980), 299

59. For more detail on the issue, see David C. Evans and Mark R. Peattie, *Kaigun: Strategy, Tactics, and Technology in the Imperial Japanese Navy, 1887-1941* (Annapolis 1997); H.P. Wilmot, *Empires in the Balance: Japanese and Allied Pacific Strategies to April 1942* (Annapolis 1982), S.E. Peltz, *The Race to Pearl Harbor* (Cambridge 1974); Arthur Marder, *Old Friends, New Enemies: The Royal Navy and the Imperial Japanese Navy—Strategic Illusions* (New York 1981); and Gordon Prange, *At Dawn We Slept: The Untold Story of Pearl Harbor* (New York 1981).

60. "Operational Plan of RCN to Implement Joint Canadian–United States Basic Defence Plan, 1940 (Short Title: Joint Plan 1940)," 17 Dec. 1940, NAC, RG 24, 11764, PC010-9-1, v 1

61. COPC WD, Dec. 1941

numerous submerged and semi-submerged logs that lurk in the waters off Canada's west coast. This operating procedure was also believed to reduce the chance of warships being detected by a submarine, because in this passive listening mode, whereby the vessel stopped fifteen minutes in every hour to carry out a hydrophone sweep, the vessel was not emitting underwater sound signals. The US Coast Guard carried out similar patrols out of Neah Bay, and when important traffic such as a major warship passed through the Strait, both Canadian and American ships carried out antisubmarine sweeps up and down its length.[62]

The operations begun by the corvettes *Dawson* and *Edmundston*, in December 1941, illustrate the nature of patrol work in the strait. When Pearl Harbor came under attack on 7 December 1941, *Dawson* was on a visit to Nanaimo. Obeying the immediate sailing orders for Esquimalt, she refuelled on arrival and sailed early next morning to begin the Race Rocks–Ediz Hook patrol. Shortly after noon, *Edmundston*, which *Dawson* joined in Esquimalt, reported a "well-defined echo off Ediz Hook." *Edmundston* carried out a deliberate attack with two depth charges, and as the echo persisted without movement concluded correctly that it was "non-sub"— *Dawson* confirmed it was a submerged log. The two ships continued the patrol in the manner described above, asdic by day, hydrophone by night, for the next two days. On 11 December the US Coast Guard Station at Ediz Hook flashed a visual signal that a submarine had been sighted to the east. The corvettes investigated and found nothing. The Bangor minesweeper *Chignecto* relieved *Dawson* that night, the ships investigated another false contact reported by the Coast Guard on 13 December and yet another, in Sooke Inlet, from a US Coast Guard patrol aircraft on 14 December. On 15 December *Edmundston*'s asdic became unserviceable, and Lieutenant R.D. Barrett, RCNR followed Commodore Beech's instructions to revert to hydrophone listening until the armed yacht *Sans Peur* relieved *Dawson* and *Edmundston* on 17 December.[63]

Barrett's report of this nine-day patrol noted that in many cases contact gained through hydrophone turned out to be US patrol vessels. "Risk of collision is considerable when a darkened ship searches for another by hydrophone on a dark rainy or hazy night. After a number of such encounters, there is an increasing tendency to ignore hydrophone effect at night, unless accompanied by an echo."[64] He proposed either closer cooperation with the US Coast Guard or independent patrols, presumably in different areas. There had also been problems with communications. Cypher messages with large address groups were "unduly bulky," resulting in some of them being corrupted during receipt, and because officers and coders were new to deciphering there was undue delay in getting the messages to the bridge.[65] With experience, however, it would be possible to iron out most of these teething problems. The first antisubmarine sweep along the length of the Strait of Juan de Fuca, from 15 to 17 December, seemed to be successful. A joint task force (*Dawson* and *Sans Peur*, the destroyers USS *Gilmer* and *Morris*, and patrol vessels USCGS *Onandaga* and *Eagle*) carried out "vigorous anti-submarine operations." They only turned up one non-sub contact, but

---

62. Patrol routines are derived from individual ships' ROPs found in various volumes of the war diary, Pacific Command, DHH, NSS1000-5-10. See also Whitby, "Quiet Coast," 66-7

63. USN, Office of Naval History, *Administrative History of the 13th Naval District and North-west Sea Frontier* I, 283 Naval Historical Center, Washington; *Edmundston* ROP, 17 Dec. 1941; *Dawson* ROP, 12 Dec. 1941; COPC to Commandant 13th Naval District, 12 Dec. 1941, NAC, RG 24, 11780, COPC 8910-1 v 1

64. *Edmundston* ROP

65. Ibid

they were able to conclude that no submarines were operating in the area.[66] Sweeps later in the month by Canadian vessels operating singly or in pairs, which produced no definite contacts, reinforced this conclusion.[67]

Pacific Coast Command's second priority was the Western Patrol, the main duty of Bangor minesweepers then being commissioned in British Columbia. They would normally head up the west coast of Vancouver Island, about five miles offshore, but going in closer to inspect the entrances of the larger inlets or sounds. Once past the Scott Islands they patrolled in the vicinity of Gordon Channel off the entrance to Queen Charlotte Strait.[68] This was an important focal point for trade, and although the command did not implement a convoy system, it did provide an escort for individual merchant ships or USN transports transiting the area. After remaining on station from two to four days, the Bangors retraced their steps to Esquimalt, unless weather was poor, in which case they used the less exposed inside passage between Vancouver Island and the mainland. Here again, they searched with asdic by day and hydrophone by night. On a typical patrol in late December, *Chignecto*, starting out on Christmas Eve, was supposed to spend the first night alongside at Bamfield, but her commanding officer, Lieutenant L.F. McQuarrie, RCNR received orders to search for a suspicious fishing smack. At midnight she went to action stations on sighting a group of vessels anchored off Barclay Sound and singled out a two-masted ship which, in something of an anti-climax, proved to be the *Arctic* out of Ketchican. The "white crew" were found to be "bona fide fishermen" and *Chignecto* continued her patrol up the west coast. On Christmas Day, having twice been challenged by friendly aircraft, she entered Quatsino Sound to spend the night, possibly because of poor weather. Weighing anchor next morning and rounding Cape Scott, *Chignecto* relieved her sister-ship *Outarde* off Pine Island, at the western entrance to Queen Charlotte Strait, and patrolled between there and Clarke Point for the next two days, most of the time carrying out an antisubmarine sweep but also escorting three merchant ships entering and four ships exiting Queen Charlotte Strait.[69] Apart from examining a fishing boat, investigating an asdic contact that proved to be a rock, and hitting a number of deadheads, the work was uneventful. On 28 December *Quatsino* took over, and *Chignecto* began to make her way back to port. After checking the entrances to Quatsino Sound and Nootka Sound, and responding to a challenge from a corvette off Sheringham Point, she conducted an antisubmarine sweep through the Esquimalt approaches before securing alongside during the forenoon of 30 December.[70]

No submarines were encountered on these patrols but there were some false contacts. During the first week of January *Outarde* depth charged a non-sub echo and pursued a false periscope, and an RCAF patrol aircraft led *Quatsino* onto a contact that also proved to be non-sub. Perhaps because the patrols were much simpler than those conducted in the Juan de Fuca Strait, and perhaps because they were not operating alongside American forces, COs did not forward any com-

---

66. From the limited evidence available it would seem that, unless the USN used the same procedures, the "task force" adopted RCN antisubmarine tactics. On 16 Dec. Adm Freeman signalled to COPC: "Deeply appreciate your cooperation in our anti-submarine and listening patrol." NAC, RG 24, 11840, 8100-10, v 1; *Administrative History of 13th Naval District* I, 283; *Givenchy* ROP, 26 Jan. 1942

67. See, e.g., *Chignecto* ROP, 31 Dec. 1941

68. Gordon Channel is referred to in this account, according to common usage, as Queen Charlotte Strait, of which it is a part.

69. *Chignecto* ROP

70. Ibid

plaints or suggestions in their patrol reports. Indeed, the only critical comments came from a minute written by the Staff Officer (Antisubmarine), Lieutenant R.P. Welland, RCN, who noted that the minesweepers were taking up station too close to vessels being escorted across Queen Charlotte Strait, which prevented them from providing an effective screen.[71]

The Fishermen's Reserve, busy rounding up Japanese fishing vessels and providing escort for other fishing vessels, did not take part in these operations until the end of December 1941. When FR vessels did begin regular patrols, their methods tended to leave naval authorities nonplussed. On 29 December, off Clayoquot Sound, the *Talapus* sighted "a Large Vessel ... heading in an easterly direction at about 20 knots. She was without lights and when called with flashing lamp she failed to answer. From her silhouette she could be taken for either a very large Freighter or an Aircraft Carrier, being long, flat and high, with bridge amidships." The captain, who simply "continued inshore and secured alongside Tofino" waited another two hours before reporting this to Commander McCulloch, who as commanding officer auxiliary vessels in Esquimalt was responsible for defensive measures in this area. McCulloch forwarded the report to COPC without comment (knowing the seamen of the Fishermen's Reserve, he likely read between the lines that they had eliminated the possibility that the vessel they had sighted posed any danger), but when the report found its way to Ottawa it provoked a visceral reaction. "This rather—indeed very—casual report *could* have been a Jap Aircraft Carrier taking up her position for an air attack on Bremerton," wrote the alarmed Director of Plans, Captain F.L. Houghton, underlining the comment in red.[72]

Armed merchant cruisers gave Pacific Coast Command an appearance of more substance. *Prince Robert*, after returning from Hong Kong and completing some repairs, began offshore patrols on 17 December. This was a USN responsibility, but Commodore Beech could do little else with vessels of such size. Too cumbersome for inshore patrols, a Prince ship might have intercepted and reported a Japanese task force, and had it done so it would no doubt have gone down fighting, as the armed merchant cruiser HMS *Jervis Bay* had done when she engaged the German pocket battleship *Scheer* in the North Atlantic on 5 November 1940. Unlike the armed merchant cruisers in the Atlantic, however, the likelihood of such an encounter was slim in the extreme. The AMCs could, fortunately, provide reassurance to British Columbians that the navy was serving their interests without having to pay the price of Admiralty—in 1914, HMCS *Rainbow* had performed the same function, although with much more chance of meeting the enemy. On the first, very brief, patrol *Prince Robert* passed through the Strait of Juan de Fuca under cover of darkness in case submarines were about; a precaution that remained in force throughout the Prince ships' service on the west coast. Immediately after clearing the boom defence at Esquimalt, Commander Hart streamed paravanes, in case the enemy had laid mines, which they had not, and increased speed to twenty knots as a further precaution against torpedo attack. During the night rough seas damaged the fo'c'sle deck and forced a reduction in speed to fifteen knots; and when the paravanes were recovered in the morning they were found badly damaged, probably from striking logs. Zigzagging "most of the time" while steaming north, the ship headed for the Dixon Entrance into Prince Rupert, streaming paravanes for the final approach. On 20 December the ship landed depth charge throwers and ammunition for the

---

71. *Quatsino* ROP, 10 Jan. and 19 Jan. 1942; *Outarde* ROP, 17 Jan. 1942; *Bellechasse* ROP, 15 Jan. 1942; COPC to *Givenchy*, 19 May 1942, NAC, RG 24, 11840, 8100-10, v 1

72. *Talapus* ROP, 31 Dec. 1942; DOP min, 11 Feb. 1942; *Givenchy* min, 3 Jan. 1942, DHH, NHS NSS1000-5-10, v 6

Prince Rupert escort force and sailed the following morning for the RCAF base at Ocean Falls. En route Hart was to investigate a suspicious fishing vessel sighted by aircraft in the vicinity of the Scott Islands, at the northwestern tip of Vancouver Island, but because of darkness and bad weather he received permission to delay the search until after calling at Ocean Falls. In the event, *Prince Robert* returned to Esquimalt on Christmas Eve after the visit to Ocean Falls, where Hart had gone ashore to confer with local authorities about the "Japanese situation." It had not been a particularly productive week for such a large fuel consumption.[73]

On 30 December *Prince David*, under Commander V.S. Godfrey, RCN arrived in Esquimalt after a long passage from Halifax. Such was the perceived urgency of the situation in the Pacific that she had departed from the east coast immediately after emerging from refit and as a result the ship came alongside without having completed the usual trials.[74] On 7 January she sailed for her first west coast operation, patrolling 150 miles offshore and returning a week later without having seen a single ship.[75] Between them, *Prince Robert* and *Prince David* would complete twenty-four such patrols. *Prince Henry*, which arrived much later, carried out only one. All were similarly uneventful, but not without their difficulties. The greatest danger lay in the night passage through the Juan de Fuca Strait, where ships were blacked out and navigational aids, coastal lights, and radio beacons were switched off. "The danger of collision with the other ships during the dark hours," reported Commander Godfrey, "is more acute than the risk of attack of enemy submarines during daylight hours."[76] Commodore Beech was unmoved, and the mandatory night-time passages continued. Ships and aircraft encountered were often slow to display recognition signals or flashed the wrong ones. Russian vessels (still neutrals in the Pacific war) on passage between Vladivostok and the United States were the chief offenders, and it was frequently necessary to stop them to confirm their identity.[77]

Throughout the Prince ships' employment in this role, the requirements for maintenance and refits meant that two ships were not enough to maintain a constant presence in offshore waters. Over a period of 251 days, before they were deployed elsewhere, the two AMCs in the command were only on actual patrol for 147. In March 1942 one of the ships was on station for twenty-eight days, but over the entire period the offshore station was only manned for 60 percent of the time. In December 1941 and in June 1942, the two periods of Japanese submarine activity, there was a ship on station for six of twenty-four days (25 percent) and twenty-one of thirty days (70 percent) respectively. In February 1942 Hart, in an attempt to overcome such problems, worked out a schedule of operations that would ensure one of two Prince ships was always on patrol. He conceived a twenty-day cycle that saw each of them spending thirteen days at sea, four at base, and three conducting training at anchor. But with only two ships available, routine maintenance requirements made it all but impossible to ensure that such a schedule could be managed. A staff officer at COPC's headquarters minuted that Hart's plan was "quite nice in theory" but was "willing to bet that it might work *just once* and then the entire schedule would be out of whack because of 'repairs to boilers' or some other such contingency."[78]

---

73. *Prince Robert* ROP, 10 Jan. 1942

74. *Prince David* ROP, 5 Jan. 1942

75. *Prince David* Sailing Orders, 7 Jan. 1942, DHH, NSC8705-412/1

76. *Prince David* ROP, 3 June 1942

77. COPC min sheet, 5 July 1942; *Prince David* ROP, 2 July 1942

78. Cdr F.G. Hart to COPC, 23 Feb. 1942; SO(O) min, 10 Mar. 1942, DHH, 81/520 Prince Robert 8000 v 1

COPC evidently shared this opinion, and for the time being the Prince ships' patrol schedule continued on an ad hoc basis. In Ottawa, the Director of Plans noted that "while these patrols … achieve the object of ships being in the best position to intercept a sea or possibly sea-borne air attack on the coast, I feel that in view of the weakness of our sea defence force too much consideration cannot be given to ensure that such forces are employed to the best advantage." Houghton may have been interested in the subject because he was to take over command of *Prince Robert* in June. Nevertheless, after a lengthy discussion on the current situation and possible Japanese intentions, he could offer no solutions beyond suggesting that the RCN and RCAF coordinate their patrols, and that better protection might be offered if two Prince ships operated in company.[79] In June *Prince David* and *Prince Robert* did, in fact, carry out a patrol together, meeting during the day to conduct officer of the watch manoeuvres, inclination, station-keeping, and signalling exercises, but parting company at night. Both COs reported that the manoeuvres were beneficial, but *Prince Robert*'s captain was especially pleased. After two years of operating in relative isolation, Hart was delighted to have company, and in his report of proceedings he noted the "exercises were of the greatest value in giving Reserve Officers experience in the handling of the ship. Opportunity for this has never been available before as HMCS 'Prince Robert' has been operating entirely on her own during the two (2) years in commission."[80] In early August all three Prince ships were finally operational at the same time, but before a comprehensive patrol schedule could be implemented they were ordered north to support the Aleutians campaign. The one important and consistent contribution by the Prince ships in this period lay in training. AMCs were excellent platforms for educating seamen with the space and orderly routine of a large ship's company to give systematic instruction. Service in the ships was typically of short duration, but officers and ratings went on to other ships with a very good grounding in the various branches of seamanship.[81]

The RCN's west coast resources, not surprisingly, increased in the months following Pearl Harbor. Naval vessels built in British Columbia shipyards had previously gone to the Atlantic, but those commissioning after 7 December remained on the west coast, at least for a time. During the first five months of 1942 four corvettes (*Dundas*, *New Westminster*, *Timmins,* and *Vancouver*), eight Bangors (*Bayfield*, *Canso*, *Caraquet*, *Guysborough*, *Ingonish*, *Lockeport*, *Courtenay,* and *Kelowna*), and six Fairmile B motor launches (*Q 066* through *Q 071*) joined Commodore Beech's force. As the new corvettes and minesweepers became operational, they gradually lessened the need to rely on obsolete or unsuitable craft such as the armed yachts *Cougar*, *Wolf,* and *Sans Peur*, allowing these to be used for local patrols, and later as training vessels. The increase in strength also allowed Beech to send modern ships to Prince Rupert, four Bangors being transferred there by the end of April 1942. When the Fairmiles were ready in May they took over most local duties in Juan de Fuca Strait, releasing corvettes and minesweepers for more appropriate responsibilities such as the long west coast patrol.[82]

---

79. DOP memo, "Operation of Auxiliary Cruisers—West Coast," 13 Apr. 1942, DHH, NHS Operations-Pacific 1650-239/5

80. *Prince Robert* ROP, 15 June 1942; COPC to *Prince David*, Sailing Orders, 2 June 1942, DHH, NSC8705-412/1; *Prince David* ROP, 16 June 1942

81. *Prince David* ROP, 30 Mar. 1942

82. COPC WD

In June 1942 Canada's west coast naval defences received their only real test in the face of the enemy. As part of the preparatory moves for their operations against Midway and the Aleutians, the Japanese Combined Fleet deployed over twenty submarines on reconnaissance missions, including six which were to survey American bases in the Aleutians. After that mission, two large *Junsen* Type B fleet submarines *I 25* and *I 26*, veterans of the December operations off the American coast, were ordered "to guard the entrance to the port of Seattle during the period of the invasion."[83] Their voyage south from the Aleutians was without incident—although *I 26* missed an opportunity to bring the Pacific war home to Canadians when it sighted, but did not attack, "two vessels which looked like large cruisers," almost certainly *Prince Robert* and *Prince David* who were on patrol off the Queen Charlottes at the time—and the I-boats arrived off the approaches to Juan de Fuca Strait towards the end of the first week of June. There does not seem to have been any advanced warning of their arrival. Although the minutes of the Cabinet War Committee make it clear that the Americans had shared intelligence with the Canadian government about the Midway and Aleutian operations, it does not appear that there was any forewarning of *I 25* and *I 26*'s missions.[84]

Under orders not to enter Juan de Fuca, *I 26* took up a patrol position about thirty miles southwest of Cape Flattery, and on the afternoon of 7 June the boat sighted the *Coast Trader*, a 3,300-ton US Army transport outbound from Port Angeles for San Francisco with a cargo of rolled newsprint.[85] *I 26*'s captain, Commander Yokata, fired only one torpedo, which struck the starboard side, opening Number 4 hold to the seas, and the merchantman began to settle by the stern. Upon receiving news of the attack, the Americans requested RCN assistance. After alerting his forces that enemy ships might be operating in the area, Commodore Beech despatched *Edmundston* and *Sans Peur* to the scene and asked the RCAF for help in the search. At 0530 on 9 June, just before a patrol aircraft signalled *Edmundston* that it had located survivors, the corvette sighted a flare from the civilian vessel *Virginia I*, which was effecting a rescue, and closed the scene. The Canadian ship found *Coast Trader*'s remaining crew "numb and cramped from 39 hours crowded together on the rafts, but seemed otherwise unhurt [although one sailor had succumbed to exposure]. One pint of rum was issued from stock and this, together with hot coffee and subsequently breakfast, lunch and some sleep, appeared to restore them practically to normal."[86] *Edmundston* put into Port Angeles early in the afternoon, and after landing the survivors rejoined the Sheringham Point–Pillar Point antisubmarine patrol.

After this the two Japanese submarines, intent on reconnaissance, allowed numerous ships to pass without attacking them.[87] That changed on 19 June when *Fort Camosun*, a Canadian-built

83. These boats displaced 2,589 tons (surfaced) and had a length of 356 feet 6 inches, making them about the same size as a Second World War Fleet destroyer. They were armed with a 5.5-inch deck gun and seventeen 21-inch torpedoes. On some patrols they carried a float plane, but on this operation *I 25* and *I 26* took extra fuel instead. Boyd and Yoshida, *Japanese Submarine Force*; G.W. Prange, *Miracle at Midway* (New York 1982), 31, 157

84. CWCM, May-June 1942

85. Japanese Monograph no. 110, "Submarine Operations in Second Phase Operations, Part I, Apr.-Aug. 1942," 21-3, DHH, 81/107; Reynolds, "Submarine Attacks on the Pacific Coast," 190; Prange, *Midway*, 31, 157; and F.C Aitkens ms, "Abridged ROP, Japanese Submarine Attacks on Estevan Point, BC, and Fort Stevens, Oregon," 4, DHH, 87/164

86. Moore, *Careless Word*, 60-1; *Edmundston* ROP, 10 June 1942; COPC, "Signals Re. Torpedoing of SS *Coast Trader*," NAC, RG 24, 11764, PC.05-11-5; Air Cmdre L.F. Stevenson to Sec National Defence for Air, NAC, RG 24, 11764, PC.05-11-5; Webber, *Silent Siege*, 38-9

87. Japanese Monograph no. 110, 2, 23. The heavy flow of shipping is evident from the COPC WD.

freighter bound for England from Vancouver on her maiden voyage with a cargo of lumber, was torpedoed by *I 25* approximately seventy miles south-southwest of Cape Flattery. She immediately settled by the bow, taking on a heavy list to port. After transmitting two distress signals, *Fort Camosun*'s master, Captain T.F. Eggleston, ordered his crew to boat stations at 2300, and to abandon ship thirty minutes later. When a muster was taken in the boats, two crew members were discovered to be missing; returning to the ship, Eggleston found them sound asleep in their hammocks! After hustling the two startled sailors aboard the waiting life boat, Eggleston cast off and stood by the ship.[88] They escaped just in time, as *I 25* hove into view to finish off the freighter with her 5.5-inch deck gun. But after scoring only a single hit, the submarine withdrew and *Fort Camosun* stubbornly remained afloat.[89]

Edmundston, on the Sheringham Point–Pillar Point patrol, and *Quesnel*, returning from escorting a tanker to Alaska, were ordered to the scene.[90] An American patrol aircraft gave *Quesnel* an updated position of the torpedoed ship, and she sighted *Fort Camosun* at 0812. The corvette quickly obtained an asdic contact and carried out depth charge attacks on what *Edmundston* later correctly classified as a non-sub echo.[91] The freighter appeared to be in little danger of sinking, so Lieutenant Barrett in *Edmundston* took her in tow, but despite good seamanship the freighter proved unmanageable.[92] Releasing the tow, the corvette's crew attempted to lighten *Fort Camosun* by pumping the ship out and taking off some gear. At this point the instincts of sailors—both naval and civilian—came into play. "Removing everything of value, both personal and ship's, that could be found," the naval ratings, according to the freighter's chief officer, began liberating the spirit locker, and Barrett was forced to instruct his men "that we were going to save the entire ship and not bits of it." When asked for assistance, members of the freighter's crew remaining on *Quesnel* responded "that the ship had been abandoned and they were not going to help," and those few who subsequently returned "were only interested in saving their own gear, and when obliged to work, slunk away at the first opportunity."[93] *Fort Camosun*'s master later accused *Edmundston*'s crew of looting, although a court of inquiry found that any losses were the result of enemy action and the efforts to save the ship. In correspondence with Commander McCulloch, Eggleston regretted that the charges had been made and emphasized that Lieutenant Barrett had done everything

---

88. "Report Furnished by Captain Eggleston SS Fort Camosun," undated, NAC, RG 24, 11845, COPC 8852-F96. All timings within this report are based on the ship's clock, which was one hour and fifteen minutes behind PWT.

89. Why the submarine did not despatch the ship with a second torpedo is a matter of speculation, although it may have been that Japanese submarine captains were under orders to expend only one torpedo at such targets. Ibid; COPC, "A Report of the Movements of SS *Fort Camosun* on Her Action with Enemy Submarine and the Subsequent Salvage Operations," NAC, RG 24, 11919, HQ13-1-110-2; Webber, *Silent Siege*, 40-1

90. According to Beech, *Quesnel* carried out this duty because 13th ND was "temporarily short of A/S escort vessels." COPC to NSHQ, 1841z 11 June 1942, NAC, RG 24, 6808, NS S8700-331/82; McCullough to COPC, "Salvage of SS Fort Camuson," 22 July 1942, NAC, RG 24, 11845, COPC 8852-F96

91. The US Coast Guard cutter *Invincible* offered to take *Fort Camosun*'s crew aboard, but they chose to remain on the Canadian ship. *Quesnel* ROP, 20 June 1942; *Quesnel*, "Attack on Suspected Submarine," 24 June 1942, NAC, RG 24, 11780, COPC 8910-1 v 2; *Edmundston*, "Report on A/S Patrol, 19 to 25 June, 1942," 25 June 1942, NAC, RG 24, 11845, COPC 8852-F96

92. The COs of the Canadian ships, both RCNR officers, may have seen the opportunity to collect some salvage money. *Quesnel* to COPC, 20 June 1942; *Vancouver* to COPC, 20 July 1942, NAC, RG 24, 8845, COPC 8852-F96

93. *Edmundston*, "Report on A/S Patrol," 25 June 1942; McCulloch to COPC, "Salvage of SS *Fort Camosun*"

possible, even suggesting that it was thanks to the young officer's efforts that the merchantman reached Esquimalt safely.[94]

On 20 June 1942, as the struggle to save *Fort Camosun* was under way, *I 26* launched the first direct attack against Canadian soil since the Fenian raids of the 1860s and 1870s. After sinking the *Coast Trader*, Commander Yokata had lain low and, although undoubtedly presented with opportunities to attack shipping, it was two weeks before he chose to strike again. Upon leaving their patrol areas Japanese submarines routinely shelled shore installations; indeed, they became so predictable in this regard that later in the war American naval intelligence officers took such bombardments as firm indications to normalize their shipping movements.[95] Thus, early on 20 June *I 26* cruised slowly up the west coast of Vancouver Island at periscope depth studying the approaches to the "compass station" at Estevan Point—actually a magnificent 125-foot lighthouse—and the nearby fishing hamlet, Hesquiat Harbour. Noting that Estevan was undefended, Yokata plotted a location from which to shell the station and then proceeded on a wide sweep to the east, coming to a position approximately 400 yards off Hesquiat; there he also found people going about their normal chores with no defences in sight. With all apparently peaceful, Yokata decided to surface. At approximately 1800, Mrs Thomas Dick was on the beach near Hesquiat Harbour when she saw "something come up out of the water. It came up just like a whale only it didnt [*sic*] make splashes. It came up near the buoy and slowly went down again. It stayed up for nearly five minutes. I was very excited. It had a long top on it something like a ship. I ran to get my son but when we looked again it was gone."[96] Later that same evening, a crew member in the American fishing vessel *Sea Breeze*, spotted the submarine on the surface four miles west of Estevan Point. After approaching to within 400 feet, it submerged, only to reappear astern thirty minutes later.[97] Neither of these witnesses raised the alarm.

Sometime after 2200, *I 26* surfaced about two miles off the Estevan Point lighthouse and opened fire with its 5.5-inch deck gun. After the war Yokota recalled: "It was evening when I shelled the area with about 17 shots. Because of the dark, our gun-crew had difficulty in making the shots effective. At first the shells were way too short—not reaching the shore." In his attempt to bring the war to North America, Yokota thus found himself in the embarrassing position of being unable to hit the broadside of a continent, but he soon put things right. "I remember very vividly my yelling at them, 'Raise the gun! Raise the gun!' to shoot at higher angle. Then the shells went too far over the little community toward the hilly area. Even out at sea we could hear the pigs [in a farmyard near the operating crew's quarters] squealing as shells exploded."[98] While Yokota directed the shelling from *I 26*, the lightkeeper at Estevan Point had a much closer view. R.M. Lally had just finished lighting the powerful lantern atop the majestic lighthouse when he sighted a strange

---

94. "Findings of Board of Inquiry into Allegations That the Ship's Company of HMCS *Edmundston* Removed Both Ship's and Personal Gear from SS *Fort Camosun*," nd, NAC, RG 24, 11845, COPC 8852-F96; Capt T.F. Eggleston to Cdr J. McCulloch, 26 June 1942, ibid. *Fort Camosun* was repaired, but had the misfortune of again being torpedoed, this time by a Japanese submarine off East Africa in Dec.1943, but was again repaired. S.C. Heal, *A Great Fleet of Ships* (St Catharines 1999), 244.

95. Boyd and Yokata, *Japanese Submarine Force*, 65

96. Statement from Mrs Thomas Dick to Skipper J.T Detweiler, 22 June 1942, NAC, RG 24, 11845, 8910-20 v 1

97. USN Combat Intelligence Filter Center, Astoria Oregon to Operations Office, 13th Naval District, "Submarine-Reported Sighting Of," 3 Aug. 1942, NAC, RG 24, 11845, 8910-20, v 1

98. Quoted in Webber, *Silent Siege*, 100

vessel zigzagging towards the point from the southwest. Any doubts about the stranger's identity were shattered when it opened fire and, as the second salvo crashed into the surf, Lally hurried down the long spiral stairs of the lighthouse to warn his wife to take cover. He then made the long climb back to douse the light, and, as a Great War veteran might do, observed the remaining fall of shot as the submarine attempted to get the range. Fortunately, *I 26*'s gun crew never did, and shells fell harmlessly in front of the tower or exploded in the bush behind. Lally later claimed that two ships were firing but, like other reports that an aircraft was flying overhead during the bombardment, this proved without foundation.[99]

I 26 also broke up a card game. Edward T. Redford, in charge of the Estevan wireless station, was playing bridge with another operator, and their wives, "when the first shell exploded on the beach about 150 yards from our house." When Redford saw the submarine, he sent his guests to safety and broadcast "the general call of CQ along with the information that we were being shelled by an enemy submarine and that we were shutting down and going off the air temporarily."[100] COPC in turn broadcast a warning message, and within half an hour *Sans Peur* and *Timmins*, on antisubmarine patrol in Juan de Fuca Strait, and *Lockeport*, off Cape Beale returning from a west coast patrol, received orders to respond. The Fishermen's Reserve vessels *Moolock* at Ucluelet and *San Tomas* in the Tofino area, on hearing COPC's message also steamed towards Estevan on their own initiative. Another FR vessel, the newly commissioned *Merry Chase,* was in Refuge Cove, approximately thirteen miles from the lighthouse, and when the watch reported five explosions to westward, the commanding officer, Coxswain D.W. Peck, immediately contacted Estevan Point "to ascertain if they had heard anything." Unable to raise an answer, Peck mustered his hands to action stations and ordered his wireless telegraph operator "to keep a continuous watch throughout the night, in anticipation of a signal." Receiving no instructions, he remained anchored until next morning.[101] As it was, only the RCAF managed to get forces into the area that night, but the one Supermarine Stranraer patrol aircraft that responded to the alarm was not equipped with radar and detected no sign of the enemy.[102]

Lockeport under Lieutenant D. Trail, RCNR arrived five and a half hours after the attack, followed shortly afterwards by *Moolock*. Unable to raise the lighthouse by signal lamp, Trail sent the smaller vessel into Hesquiat Harbour to investigate while he conducted an antisubmarine search offshore. *Sans Peur*, commanded by Lieutenant-Commander T. MacDuff, RCNR, arrived next morning in company with *Timmins,* but was also unable to get a response from the lighthouse. Being the senior officer present, MacDuff ordered the corvette to investigate a patch of smoke on the horizon, which turned out to be *Lockeport*, while he took his ship into Hesquiat Harbour.[103] Finding that *Moolock*'s

99.   DOT, Lighthouse Emergency WD, Estevan Point, 22 June 1942; R.M. Lally statement to Skipper J.T. Detweiler, 22 June 1942; Detweiler to COPC, *San Tomas*, "Re: Hostile Engagement at Estevan Lighthouse," 22 June 1942, DHH, NSS 1000-5-10, v 10; F.C. Aitkens ms, "Abridged ROP Japanese Submarine Attacks on Estevan Point, BC, and Fort Stevens, Oregon," 1-2

100. Quoted in Webber, *Silent Siege*, 100

101. It is doubtful whether COPC would have expected this tiny 58-foot fishing vessel to engage an enemy warship, and even if *I 26* were still in the area by the time the vessel arrived the submarine, in view of the tactics being followed by Japanese submarines at the time, would probably have submerged and left the scene. *Merry Chase* ROP, 1 July 1942, NAC, RG 24, 11845, 8910-20 v 1

102. Douglas, *Creation of a National Air Force*, 420

103. *Sans Peur* ROP, 20 June 1942; *Moolock* ROP, 21 June 1942; *Lockeport* ROP, 21 June 1942, DHH, NHS NSS 1000-5-10, v 10

CO, Coxswain J. Fiander, had already gone ashore to investigate, he left harbour to patrol towards Estevan Point, while *Timmins* and *Lockeport* swept further westward. Not surprisingly, none of the ships found any sign of the submarine. When Fiander rejoined his vessel, he closed *Sans Peur* to inform MacDuff that he had witness statements and shell fragments on board and was heading to Port Alberni with some of the women and children from the station.[104] Commodore Beech recalled the searching vessels when it was clear that the enemy was no longer there.[105] *I 26* had, in fact, begun her long return passage to Japan by way of the Aleutians. The day after Yokata left his calling card at Estevan Point, *I 25* closed the Oregon coast near Astoria, lobbed a few ineffective parting shots in the direction of Fort Stevens, and then also headed for home.[106]

From a Japanese standpoint, *I 25* and *I 26* had accomplished their reconnaissance mission, but little else. They carried out four attacks, sinking one merchant ship, damaging another, and bombarding two shore installations with scant result. By their final act before leaving the scene, the Japanese were clearly attempting to cause alarm, and in this respect they met with some success. The attacks brought the war home to the west coast and garnered attention in the press. In the larger objective of compelling Canada to unbalance its forces by concentrating additional ships for patrols along the coast of British Columbia, however, the Japanese failed. As will be seen, the RCN did precisely the opposite.

From a Canadian naval standpoint, although the almost complete lack of offensive action by the enemy limited the value of the test, COPC's patrol system nevertheless passed muster. Commodore Beech could not cover everything with his limited resources, and he concentrated his most effective patrol vessels, corvettes and Bangors, on the major focal points of trade: Juan de Fuca and Queen Charlotte straits. If either of the two submarines had chosen to operate aggressively in either area, they would have faced effective opposition, at least in terms of numbers of ships. As it was, they remained outside the area of specific Canadian responsibility until *I 26* shelled Estevan Point. At that time, twelve patrol vessels were covering the coast of Vancouver Island from Nootka Sound to Esquimalt, while six more were deployed between Scott Channel and Millbanke Sound. The only area left unguarded was between Nootka and Quatsino sounds. These dispositions would have been about the same at any time and left the area only open to pinprick attacks like *I 26*'s.[107] If that was all the enemy could accomplish, then the navy can be said to have done its job.

––––––––––––––

In June 1942 the tide began to turn in the Pacific, with the crippling reverse for the Japanese in the Battle of Midway when the USN had sunk four invaluable fleet carriers and rebuffed the planned Japanese invasion of Midway. Subsequently, the strategic situation on the west coast underwent a significant change. In a subsidiary operation to the main attack on Midway, the Japanese had suc-

---

104. *Sans Peur* ROP

105. On passage to Esquimalt, COPC had *Sans Peur* return to Estevan to follow up a submarine sighting that proved to be false, ibid; COPC to AOC WAC, 22 June 43, NAC, RG 24, 11845, 8910-20, v 1

106. COPC to *Dundas, Dawson, New Westminister,* and *Canso,* 21 June 1942, NAC, RG 24, 11845, 8910-20 v 1; Japanese Monograph no. 10, 23; Reynolds, "Submarine Attacks on the Pacific Coast," 191; Webber, *Silent Siege,* 139-41

107. Ships positions derived from various ROPs in COPC WD for June 1942

Top: The corvette *Edmundston* and a Fishermen's Reserve vessel struggle to tow the torpedoed SS *Fort Camosun* to Esquimalt in June 1942. (DND, E-3086)

Bottom: The corvette *Dawson* alongside her sister-ship *Vancouver* at Dutch Harbor, Alaska, probably in August 1943. (US National Archives, 80-G-72700)

cessfully occupied the islands of Kiska and Attu in the Aleutians chain. Rather than "leaving the Japs to freeze in their own juice on Kiska and Attu," and because the presence of the enemy in the Aleutians was a severe irritant to both the Canadian and American populations on the Pacific coast, the US Joint Chiefs began plans in June 1942 to recover the islands.[108] At a 24 June joint planning meeting of American and Canadian commanders in San Francisco, Lieutenant General J.L. DeWitt of the Western Defence Command informed the Canadians of tentative plans to recapture Kiska in August or September 1942. Queried on possible Canadian naval assistance, Commodore Beech responded that although his resources were limited, "we might be able to help to a certain extent in providing A/S escorts for troop convoys."[109] Claiming "the necessity for absolute secrecy," Beech did not see fit to report these discussions to his superiors until early July, when Admiral Nelles visited the west coast on an inspection tour. At that time, the CNS agreed that the three Prince ships, now fitted with asdic, "might be used for this purpose." On that tentative basis the matter rested until bursting forth weeks later.[110]

On 15 August, when Beech learned that the US intended to occupy Tanaga Island, 150 miles east of Japanese-held Kiska, he offered RCN assistance "within our limited capacity." The Americans accepted immediately. The next day they asked how many escort and antisubmarine vessels Beech could spare, and dropped the bombshell that they were needed in Kodiak on 20 August, just four days hence. The short notice undoubtedly startled Beech, but he reacted quickly. Within three hours he offered the USN the three Prince ships and two corvettes, and he ordered those vessels to begin preparations for sea. Early on 17 August the Americans queried if two additional corvettes were available, but Beech replied they could not be spared. Later that day, *Prince David* and *Prince Henry* and the corvettes *Dawson* and *Vancouver* put to sea, and *Prince Robert* was diverted from its west coast patrol.[111]

Even before the ships hurried north, questions about their suitability arose in Ottawa. Three and half hours after promising the vessels to the USN on 16 August, Beech had signalled Nelles that he had offered the ships, also reminding him that they had discussed the matter previously.[112] The CNS was in Halifax so the message went to the VCNS, Commodore H.E Reid, then in the midst of a Naval Board meeting chaired by the minister. As soon as the session adjourned, Reid contacted Nelles, who recalled "that some discussions had taken place on the West Coast on broad lines regarding assistance being rendered by the RCN to the United States forces in Alaska at any time they might be required, and mention was made of a possible early operation taking place." Nelles then instructed Reid to obtain the minister's approval before sending Beech a response.[113]

The memoranda to file written by all concerned with the decision indicate that the minister was disturbed by the news. He observed not only that the notice was unacceptably short, but, evidently

---

108. Stacey, *Six Years of War*, 496

109. COPC memo to CNS, 20 Aug. 1942, NAC, RG 24, 11763, PC01-51-2, v 1

110. Ibid

111. Adm Freeman's signal originated at 1943z and Beech's response was sent at 2204z. Beech later informed NSHQ that the short notice provided by the Americans was a result of the destroyers assigned to escort duty in Alaska being re-allocated to fleet duties at the last minute. CNWSF to COPC, 16 Aug. 1942, COPC memo to CNS, 20 Aug. 1942, and COPC to CNWSF, 17 Aug. 1942, ibid; COPC to NSHQ, "Operations with US Forces in Alaska," 26 Aug. 1942, NAC, RG 24, 8149, 1650-3

112. COPC to CNS, 17 Aug. 1942

113. Cmde H.E. Reid, memo to file, 17 Aug. 1942, NAC, RG 24, 8149, 1650-3

not consulting or having been consulted by the CNS, that armed merchant cruisers like the Prince ships were unsuitable for this type of operation. Macdonald instructed Reid to contact Beech forthwith to see if corvettes could be substituted for the auxiliary cruisers. Upon learning that it was too late and the ships had already sailed, an exasperated naval minister directed Beech to inform the Americans of the poor fighting abilities of the Prince ships, later reiterating in his own memo to file that he was "in agreement with the general principle of our assisting the American Navy on the West Coast or elsewhere, and my only doubt in the matter is as to the suitability of the three cruisers for the task."[114] The Cabinet War Committee discussed the matter on 26 August, Macdonald expressing concern that the Americans had not fully informed the Canadians of what the ships were to be used for: "This was not as it should be, for if we were to be asked to provide Canadian forces to support American operations, we had the right to full information upon which the government could base an independent judgment." The prime minister, in his only recorded comment on the issue, emphasized that service chiefs had to understand that their ministers and the war committee had final responsibility in such matters, and had to "be put in possession of all the facts in order to enable them to arrive at decisions."[115] Under ABC-22, COPC did have the authority to offer forces, and Beech had kept the CNS informed, but Nelles may not have realized before this that the Prince ships, as will be seen in a later chapter, were being considered for conversion to Landing Ships (Infantry) for European operations, and should not have been committed to a long campaign in the Pacific.

Leaving controversy swirling in their wake, the Canadian ships, designated Force D, made their way to the Aleutians, arriving at Kodiak on the morning of 20 August.[116] They formed part of Task Force 8, under the command of Rear-Admiral R.A. Theobald, USN, whose orders from Admiral Nimitz, the USN's C-in-C Pacific Fleet, were to isolate Japanese-occupied Kiska and Attu and destroy their usefulness to the enemy.[117] This force comprised two heavy cruisers and three light cruisers, a destroyer striking force, six old S-class submarines, and a number of auxiliary vessels besides the RCN's small contribution. Theobald could also rely on a weak but slowly expanding air component, mostly under army control, which included RCAF elements.[118] Although disappointed at the composition of Force D, Theobald—who like Macdonald would have preferred corvettes to the AMCs—did not waste any time integrating the new arrivals into his command.[119]

For the most part the auxiliary cruisers and corvettes operated separately. The Prince ships were kept away from the battle area and used primarily to escort convoys on the 600-mile run between Kodiak and Dutch Harbour. Although the convoy cycle was frequently upset by foul weather, they usually completed a return trip every seven days, followed by a four-day maintenance period in Kodiak, although occasionally such routine was interrupted to escort tankers.[120] Regardless of

---

114. Angus L. Macdonald, memo to file, 18 Aug. 1942, ibid

115. CWCM, 26 Aug. 1942

116. *Prince David* ROP, 22 Aug. 1942; *Dawson* ROP, 26 Sep. 1942

117. He was, in other words, to keep the islands "pounded down until forces could be spared to recover them." S.E. Morison, *History of United States Naval Operations in World War II* VII: *Aleutians, Gilberts and Marshalls* (Boston 1951), 4

118. Morison, *Aleutians, Gilberts and Marshalls* 4; B. Garfield, *The Thousand Mile War* (Garden City 1969), 122; Douglas, *Creation of a National Air Force*, 413-17; E.B. Potter, *Nimitz* (Annapolis 1976), 81-91, 107, 245-6

119. *Prince David* ROP, 22 Aug. 1942; *Vancouver* ROP, 4 Oct. 1942

120. *Prince Robert* ROP, 2 Sep. 1942

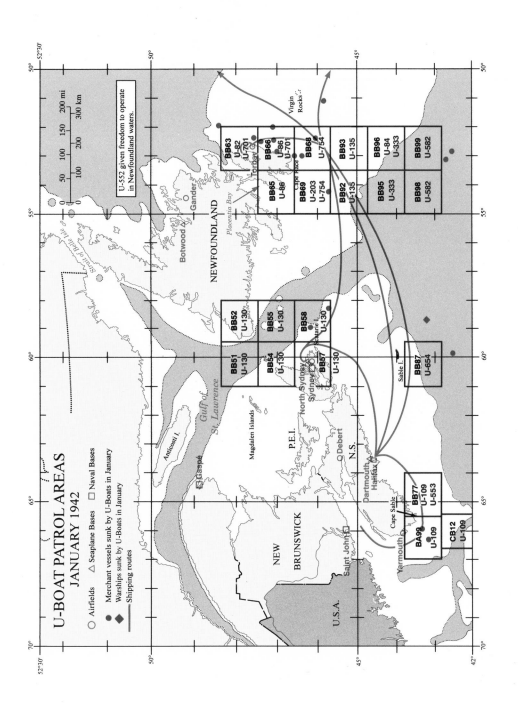

U-BOAT PATROL AREAS
JANUARY 1942

○ Airfields   △ Seaplane Bases   □ Naval Bases

Merchant vessels sunk by U-Boats in January
● ◆
Warships sunk by U-Boats in January
—— Shipping routes

U-552 given freedom to operate in Newfoundland waters.

0   50   100   150   200 mi
0   100   200   300 km

U.S.A.

NEW BRUNSWICK

Saint John

Gulf of St. Lawrence

Anticosti I.

Gaspé

Magdalen Islands

P.E.I.

North Sydney
Sydney

Debert

N.S.

Dartmouth
Halifax

Cape Sable

Yarmouth

Sable I.

NEWFOUNDLAND

Botwood

Gander

Placentia Bay

Torbay

Cape Race

Scatarie I.

Strait of Belle Isle

Virgin Rocks

BB51 U-130
BB52 U-130
BB54 U-130
BB55 U-130
BB57 U-130
BB58 U-130

BB87 U-654

BB63 U-82 U-701
BB65 U-86
BB66 U-86
BB68 U-754
BB69 U-203 U-754
BB92 U-135
BB93 U-135
BB95 U-333
BB96 U-84 U-333
BB98 U-582
BB99 U-582

BB77 U-109 U-553
BA99 U-109
CB12 U-109

assignment, the Prince ships normally sailed individually, sometimes assisted by USN destroyers or patrol vessels. The corvettes operated to the west of Dutch Harbor, where Japanese submarines were more likely to strike, although within two weeks of their arrival *Dawson* and *Vancouver* were involved in an unopposed landing on Adak, the island ultimately chosen to be the advanced base in the western Aleutians in preference to Tanaga because of its superior harbour. After screening the assault force the corvettes spent the rest of their Aleutian deployment escorting convoys transporting the men and materials required to transform the island into a major base, and carrying out anti-submarine patrols off the anchorage where transports unloaded their cargoes.[121] It was exceptionally demanding work. *Vancouver* did not shut down her main engines for two weeks once operations began, and the only real break the corvettes received was a five-day period for boiler cleaning.[122]

The worst enemy was the climate. The moist warm air over the tropical Japan Current meets the cold dry Siberian air mass in the vicinity of the Aleutians to create some of the worst maritime weather in the world. An ever-present dense fog blankets the region, while Arctic storms and strong winds known locally as "williwaws" make these waters "perhaps the only place on earth where high winds and thick fog attacked simultaneously—round-the-clock Aleutian gales sometimes reached 140 miles an hour, yet most of the islands had no more than eight or ten clear days in a year. There was no calm or dry season."[123] Radar on board the Canadian ships (SW1C or SW2C) was rudimentary, but without radar and echo sounders, navigation would have been almost impossible.[124] Schull, in his account of Canadian naval operations, was not exaggerating when he claimed that "men who had had, or were later to have, experience of the worst weather provided by the Atlantic still give evil precedence to their days in the North Pacific."[125] Merchant vessels forced to endure these awful conditions were even more ill-equipped to withstand such battering. Most of them were barely able to exceed six or seven knots, and when beset by heavy gales convoys frequently had to scatter, ships finding shelter as best they could. The problem was especially acute on eastward passages, when merchantmen were travelling light.[126] The Prince ships, which despite their extensive conversions still had high freeboard and a large superstructure, also suffered badly. Never easily manoeuvrable, they routinely rolled between thirty and forty degrees, and when forced to match the slow speed of convoys, it was not unusual for them to have to increase revolutions on the leeward shaft to maintain a steady course.[127] The corvettes had difficulty maintaining speed and often had to seek shelter along the coast, although weather sometimes worked to their advantage when it forced tankers, usually faster than their escorts, to reduce speed.[128] Conditions did not improve much in harbour because the holding ground in many anchorages was poor. On one occasion, in Chernofski Harbor, *Vancouver* had her starboard anchor and 450 feet of chain paid out yet still continued to drag through the volcanic silt that comprised the shelter's bottom.

121. Garfield, *Thousand Mile War*, 131, 141

122. *Vancouver* ROPs, 4 Oct. and 5 Nov. 1942

123. Garfield, *Thousand Mile War*, 57

124. *Prince Robert* to COPC, 2 Sep. 1942, NAC, RG 24, 11763, PC01-51-2, v 1; *Prince David* ROP, 8 Sep. 1942

125. Schull, *Far Distant Ships*, 123

126. *Prince David* ROP, 19 Oct. 1942, 5 Nov. 1942; *Prince Henry* ROP, 10 Oct. 1942

127. *Prince Robert* ROP, 31 Oct. 1942

128. DHH interview with RAdm A.H.G. Storrs, 29, DHH, Biog S

Remarkably, the Canadians were witnesses to few accidents caused by weather. In one convoy escorted by *Prince Robert*, a USN patrol boat collided with a merchantman and sank.[129] In another, one of the AMCs was forced to stand by the transport *Satartia* when that ship ran aground in heavy fog and had to be floated free before the Prince ship could escort the merchant ship safely to Kodiak.[130]

Japanese submarines—five boats were based on Kiska—met with sufficient success to keep escorts on their toes. On 29 August *RO 61* stole into the anchorage at Atka Island's Nazan Bay and torpedoed the seaplane tender USS *Casco*, which suffered five killed and twenty wounded, but was beached and returned to service. The next day a patrol plane depth charged *RO 61*, opening seams in its hull that allowed fuel to escape; the destroyer USS *Reid* then followed the trail, blasted the submarine to the surface with depth charges, and sank it with gunfire.[131] The Canadians, however, had no confirmed submarine contacts. On 12 September, while escorting a convoy with USS *Reid*, *Dawson* and *Vancouver* attacked a possible submarine picked up by the American destroyer on the starboard quarter of the convoy. *Reid* ordered the corvettes to rejoin the screen, by now almost over the horizon, when they had not regained contact by 1830. On the way back, however, *Vancouver* saw *Dawson* dropping a depth charge pattern and turned to join the hunt. At 2100, *Vancouver* gained a contact at a range of 500 yards and two minutes later fired a five-charge pattern, but two of the weapons failed to leave the rails. According to Lieutenant P.F.M. DeFreitas, RCNR, the ship's captain, contact was regained at 2136 and definitely classified as a submarine. They fired another pattern but lost the scent before finally rejoining the convoy.[132]

The RCN's allies provided as much or more excitement as the enemy. USN signalling procedures were casual and their gunners quick on the draw. On the night of 22 August *Prince Robert*, escorting her first convoy, encountered unidentified ships belonging to another convoy about which the routing officer at Kodiak had failed to inform the Canadian ship. After sounding action stations, Captain Houghton ordered his convoy to alter course, and had his signalman flash the challenge. There was no response, and tensions mounted until an American destroyer in company with *Prince Robert* closed the unknown ships and identified them as friendly. On another occasion, *Prince David* was escorting two merchant ships to Dutch Harbour when thick fog suddenly rolled in and, as a precaution, Captain Godfrey streamed a fog buoy. One of the merchantmen, SS *Elias Howe*, immediately gave an emergency signal of six blasts on her whistle and opened fire on the marker, thinking it was a periscope. Godfrey's diplomatic comment was that the merchant ship's crew "showed a fine degree of alertness." In another incident, *Prince David* encountered a destroyer which, when requested to identify itself, improperly flashed "US Navy." Fortunately, the Canadians were able to recognize the old four-stacker before the incident escalated into something more serious.[133]

Logistics in Alaska bordered on the nightmarish. There were few amenities, even in port, to relieve the exhausting grind of convoy duty, and only *Prince David* had arrived fully provisioned.

---

129. *Prince Robert* ROP, 6 Oct. 1942

130. *Prince David* came into contact with an underwater obstacle when fog closed down in Kodiak harbour on 30 Sep., but was not seriously damaged. *Prince David* ROP, 16 Oct. 1942

131. Japanese Monograph no.110, 25; Garfield, *Thousand Mile War*, 135-6; Morison, *Aleutians, Gilberts and Marshalls*, 13

132. *Vancouver* ROP, 4 Oct. 1942

133. *Prince Robert* ROP, 2 Sep. 1942; *Prince David* ROP, 8 Sep. 1942, 16 Oct. 1942

Other ships, which did not have the opportunity to return to port when diverted from other tasks, were short of critical items, most pressing of which was depth charge equipment.[134] After making an attack on a "good contact," Captain Houghton of *Prince Robert* informed Esquimalt that he had only enough carriers and cartridges to launch two more full patterns. *Prince Henry* also needed items of depth charge equipment, while both ships required asdic and radar spares.[135] The difficulties resolved themselves, however, when the Canadian squadron departed from the Aleutians as suddenly as it had arrived. On 27 October Theobald summoned Captain Godfrey to inform him that his units were "in all probability returning to Canada within the next few days." The five ships gathered in Woman's Bay, and after a farewell speech in which Theobald referred to the Canadians as "comrades of the mists," they departed on 30 October.[136]

The Alaskan campaign would grow in scale in 1943, but it remained a distinctly secondary concern in Allied strategy.[137] Developments in the European war, in fact, had a greater impact on Pacific Coast Command. On 14 September 1942 five corvettes sailed for the east coast as replacements for some of the seventeen corvettes allocated to Operation Torch (see Chapter 10, below). This left the command with only two corvettes, the three Prince ships, thirteen Bangor minesweepers, and six Fairmiles, besides the Fishermen's Reserve vessels.

The needs of the European theatre would also shape a new initiative begun locally on the west coast, to create amphibious warfare training establishments. In March 1942 Commander J.M. Grant, RCN, commanding officer of HMCS *Royal Roads*, the revived naval college situated near Esquimalt, had suggested to COPC that amphibious forces should be organized to counter any enemy attempt to grab a brief foothold at a vulnerable point along the coast. Commodore Beech agreed, and he took the suggestion to the Joint Services Committee—Pacific Coast.[138] The army and air force members of the committee expressed doubts about feasibility, suggesting that US forces would have to be involved if there was to be any chance of success, and, even with their cooperation, an enemy party would likely be screened by naval forces strong enough to secure at least temporary superiority over the thin resources the Allies could bring to bear.[139] Nevertheless, the JSC agreed to test the concept of responding to Japanese landings on the west coast. The result was the largest amphibious exercise carried out in wartime Canada. On 27 May, two days after a dry run without troops, five corvettes, seven Fishermen's Reserve vessels, and several scows embarked the 1st Battalion of the Dufferin and Haldimand Rifles, with ancillary troops, and transported them to the landing site at Ucluelet Inlet.[140] The corvettes moved as close inshore as possible, ships' whalers and other small

134. *Prince David* to COPC, 3 Sep. 1942, NAC, RG 24, 11763, PC01-51-2, v 2

135. *Prince Robert* to COPC, 2 Sep. 1942; *Prince Henry* to COPC, 6 Sep. 1942; COPC to CNWSF, 25 Aug. 1942, ibid

136. *Prince David* ROP, 5 Nov. 1942

137. Stacey, *Six Years of War*, 496

138. For the origins, development, and function of the Joint Services Committees, see Stacey, *Arms, Men and Governments*, 130-4

139. JSC-Pacific Coast, min 19 Dec. 1941 mtg. DHH, 193.009(D3); JSC-Pacific Coast min 24 Mar. 1942, DHH, 193.009 (D6); Tucker, *Naval Service of Canada* II, 86

140. Originally slated for Hardy Bay at the northern tip of Vancouver Island, the scheme was moved to Ucluelet Inlet to minimize its intrusion upon routine naval and air patrols. JSC-Pacific Coast, min 10 Apr. 1942, DHH, 193.009 (D7)

boats served as landing craft, and the corvettes peppered the shoreline with their 4-inch guns—a bomber attack in support of the landing had to be scrubbed on account of unfavourable weather. Major-General R.O. Alexander, Chairman of the JSC, reported that the exercise had brought out many valuable lessons, of which the most important was that the army and RCN still had much to learn about combined operations, even on a battalion scale.[141]

As will be explained in Part 2 of this history, the RCN had already committed fifty officers and 300 ratings to the RN's Combined Operations organization. Although the Japanese landings in the Aleutians served as justification, it was perhaps the nation's commitments overseas and the intervention of General A.G.L. McNaughton during a visit to Canada in March 1942 that led to eventual RCN support for a combined operations training facility in British Columbia. As a result of McNaughton's efforts, a hundred wooden landing craft or "powered lighters" would be built for training purposes, of which eighty-seven were destined for the west coast. The army agreed to provide the vessels with spare parts and to administer, accommodate, and feed all base personnel. The navy took responsibility for manning and maintaining the craft as well as training their crews. For the latter task, the RCN proposed to build a facility at William's Head, just south of Esquimalt, while an assault course was to be set up at a location where both the army and navy already had permanent facilities. Esquimalt was originally proposed for this site but the Courtenay-Comox area was ultimately chosen. Finally, operational bases that would serve as jump-off points to counter any possible enemy landings were to be established at Port Alberni, Nanaimo, Comox, and Prince Rupert, each under army command with a naval officer on staff.[142]

Training at William's Head began almost immediately, the Director of Naval Personnel having authorized Beech to recruit a new batch of Fishermen's Reserve personnel for the landing craft to avoid transferring sailors from other tasks.[143] On 20 July the inaugural sixty-day course began with fifty men receiving instruction in a wide range of skills:

> you had to learn everything. When you went in you had to take motor mechanics, seamanship, navigation, first aid, then all the commando training. You had to know every type of gun and how to assemble them. It didn't matter whether you were a motor mechanic or a signalman, you had to take about eighteen words a minute on a key, semaphore. The idea was if a man got knocked off, another man should be able to take his place. Some of the courses were scramble nets, tunnels, close combat. We had a good army man give us the close combat ... how to kill a man fast and so on.[144]

Most graduates of this course shifted to the army's Combined Operations Training Centre at Courtenay, where, beginning in October, they operated landing craft used to train such specialist personnel as RCNVR officers selected as flotilla leaders and beach masters. Other graduates of the Williams Head course manned vessels situated at the operational centres located along the coast, and the navy also established a basic maintenance facility at a small shipyard in Nanaimo. The

---

141. HQ Pacific Command, "Report on Combined Operations Exercise," 6 June 1942, DHH, 181.003 (D2432); HQ Pacific Command, "Combined Operations for Retaking Points Occupied by the Enemy," 10 June 1942, DHH, 193.009 (D8)

142. Staff Officer (Combined Operations) memo, "Canadian Participation in Combined Operations," 28 Aug. 1943, DHH, 81/520/1250, v 4; NBM, 22 June 1942; DHH, NSM, 1 Apr. 1943, app A, "Combined Operations Training in Canada"; Lt-Cdr W. Brooke, "Canadian Naval Participation in Combined Operations," 28 Aug. 1943, app I, 2, DHH, 81/520/1250, v 4

143. NBM, 8 July 1942; NSM, 1 Apr. 1943

144. Anonymous source quoted in Popp, *Gumboot Navy*, 112

Captains F.L. Houghton and V.S. Godfrey, commanding officers of *Prince Robert* and *Prince David*, with a silver plate the Canadian ships donated for an inter-ship basketball competition at Kodiak, Alaska. (DND, E-36171)

navy's participation in combined operations largely rested on this basis through the rest of the winter of 1942. Change came in early 1943, when the army decided that since Japan was definitely on the defensive, that the operational bases set up as jump-off points in case of enemy landings were no longer required.[145] This reduced the navy's role on the west coast to manning boats at the Courtenay training base and indoctrinating its own landing craft personnel. This presented difficulties. By April the goal of preparing crews for the eighty-seven vessels that would be operated on the west coast had not been met, so NSHQ authorized COPC to make up the shortfall with Fishermen's Reserve personnel. Because their terms of service restricted them to local waters, however, they had to volunteer for the RCNVR before they could be sent overseas and, when Commander G.S. Windeyer, the newly appointed Staff Officer, Assault Landing Craft, asked for volunteers, only sixty-four of 230 were willing to make the jump.[146] This setback further delayed the program, numbers eventually being made up from General Service personnel.[147] In June 1943 the landing craft training centre at Williams Head closed down. Personnel went instead to the Combined Operations School at Courtenay, where most sailors had to sleep under canvas until October, when the navy opened its own establishment at Comox. The latter was commissioned as HMCS *Givenchy III* under Commander Windeyer. As will be seen, however, the quality of instruction did not meet the standards required overseas (See Volume II, Part 2).[148] In July 1943, Lieutenant W.C. Gardner, RCNVR, an officer who had served at William's Head and Courtenay throughout the previous year, voiced his worries to Lieutenant W.S. Brooke, RCNVR, the Staff Officer (Combined Operations) at the naval mission in London, that there were no experienced naval officers on staff at the training centres.[149]

Brooke, who became the RCN's leading proponent of combined operations, was concerned that inexperience of this kind along with poor course content would cause training in Canada to fall completely out of step with the current operational art. He first saw to it that Lieutenant A.B. Love, RCNVR, an officer well versed in such matters, was transferred to the west coast from the United Kingdom, and despatched pamphlets, reports on major amphibious exercises, and an up-to-date training syllabus to COPC for use at Comox and Courtenay.[150] Beginning that summer, naval personnel on the latter's instructional staff went to the United States Marine Corps Amphibious Training Center at San Diego, where they were exposed to recent developments from the service that was arguably the most advanced in the field among all the Allied forces.[151]

Improvements to the training system came at a propitious time. In September (as will be seen in the next volume of this history) the RCN agreed to man three LCI(L) flotillas, two by personnel

---

145. Tucker, *Naval Service of Canada* II, 232

146. COPC WD, July 1943, DHH, NSS 1000-5-10, v 24. This provides an interesting parallel with the attempts in 1944 to persuade NRMA personnel in the army to volunteer for general service overseas. Stacey, *Arms, Men and Governments*, 481-3

147. COPC WD, July 1944, DHH, NSC 1926-102/2, v 1

148. Ratings who entered the RN's training cycle after completing instruction in Canada had only two weeks deducted from their ten-week course in the UK. SCNO(L) WD, June 1943, DHH, NSS 1000-5-35, v 1

149. COPC WD, July 1943. Windeyer had no combined operations background. He had commanded escorts on the North Atlantic until transferred to the west coast after his harrowing experience with ONS 154 (see Chapter 10). Lt W.C. Gardner to Lt W. Brooke, 5 July 1943, NAC, RG 24, 11719, 33-5-6

150. Brooke to SCNO(L), 20 July 1943, NAC, RG 24, 11719, 33-5-6; SecNB to COPC, 3 July 43, NAC, RG 24, 11765, NS 012-39-12

151. It is not certain whose idea this was, but there can be little question that what they learned would be of great value.

trained in Canada. Commander Windeyer had to supply approximately twenty-four officers and 204 ratings for the flotillas, and, to his credit, he was able to meet the commitment.[152]

In the meantime, Pacific Coast Command continued to contribute to operations in the Alaskan theatre. On 1 February 1943 the new Commandant of the Northwest Sea Frontier, Vice-Admiral F.J. Fletcher, USN, asked Commodore Beech if he could again spare escorts for the Aleutian campaign, since weather damage had taken a toll on his existing force. The Americans would accept either auxiliary cruisers or corvettes and intimated that the vessels would be returned as soon as their own had been repaired in six to eight weeks.[153] This time Beech was careful to first inform NSHQ of the request, telling Admiral Nelles that he preferred to send the Prince ships, since all but two corvettes had sailed for the east coast to replace the Torch vessels.[154] But by then the Naval Board had decided to convert two of the Prince ships into Landing Ships (Infantry) for amphibious operations in European waters, and Nelles asserted in no uncertain terms that the AMCs were not to go. "Two corvettes are to be lent for a period of six to eight weeks," Nelles informed Beech, "as it is considered they could be more usefully employed in the Alaskan sector.[155] Later that day Beech dutifully informed Fletcher that only *Dawson* and *Vancouver* were available.[156]

The corvettes' second Aleutian deployment was much the same as the first, consisting of interminable convoy duty, foul weather, with scarce and unappealing shore time. They received a warm appreciation for their work from Vice-Admiral Fletcher of a kind that would have been welcomed by their frequently maligned compatriots of the Mid-Ocean Escort Force:

> During this period of slightly over three months the two vessels carried out sixteen escort missions in company. This included mostly convoys between Adak and Dutch Harbor. Vancouver carried out a total of ten separate missions. Five of these were routine escorts between Adak and Dutch Harbor and the others were special rendezvous and escorts.
>
> Dawson carried out a total of nine separate missions, five being routine escorts between Adak and Dutch Harbor and the others being rendezvous and assisting in the screening of Task Force Fifty-one vessels.
>
> There were two noteworthy factors in their performances. First; neither ship ever missed a rendezvous, an exceptional performance compared with the record of our escort vessels in this area. Second; both vessels were ready for any service at any time and were on a number of occasions called for unexpected duty on short notice or no notice at all. Throughout their duty was performed with smartness, efficiency, and effectiveness. I wish to express my appreciation for the services rendered by the two Commanding Officers, Lieutenant Commander Storrs, and Lieutenant DeFreitas, and

---

152. SecNB mmo, "Combined Operations," 14 Sep. 43, NAC, RG 24, 11702, N-012-1-1; Windeyer, min sheet, 14 Sep. 1943, NAC, RG 24, 11765, NS 012-39-12; COPC WD, Dec. 1943

153. CNWSF to COPC, 1 Feb. 43, NAC, RG 24, 11763, PC.01-51-2, v 3

154. COPC to NSHQ, 3 Feb. 43, ibid

155. NSHQ to COPC, 10 Feb. 43, ibid

156. COPC to CNWSF, 10 Feb. 43, ibid

to compliment them on the obviously high state of training and efficiency of their commands.[157]

The RCN's third and final Alaskan deployment was in support of the landings on Kiska in August 1943, when Canadian ships escorted the only convoy assembled by Pacific Coast Command during the Second World War.[158] In March 1943 the US Joint Chiefs of Staff had approved an attack on Attu, which initiated "a thoroughly nasty little campaign, in which the Japanese fought to be killed and the Americans obliged them."[159] At the Trident Conference of May 1943 the Allies agreed that the Japanese should be ejected from the Aleutians and approved an attack on Kiska. In Ottawa, the Cabinet War Committee promptly, although with much discussion, approved the participation of a Canadian brigade group.[160] On 13 July four US Army transports carrying almost 5,000 Canadian troops headed through the Strait of Georgia to Discovery Island, where they met an escort consisting of the destroyer USS *Hatfield* (SO), the corvette *Dawson*, and the Bangors *Chignecto* and *Outarde*. After heading out through Juan de Fuca Strait and steaming due west for a day the convoy, designated David, rendezvoused with two USN ships, the gunboat USS *Charleston,* and the minesweeper USS *Oracle*, which had come south from the Aleutians to relieve the Canadian minesweepers.[161] The convoy then proceeded north to Adak. Western Air Command was supposed to provide air cover throughout the passage, but dismal weather kept aircraft grounded and conditions were no better at sea.[162] *Dawson* remained with David to its destination— allowing some of the crew to pocket extra change. With a legendary maverick Lieutenant-Commander T.P. "Two Gun" Ryan, RCNR now in command, sailors, against all regulations, were given the option of either drinking or saving their daily tot of rum. The more enterprising among them hoarded their issue on the seven-day voyage and sold it to thirsty Americans at Adak for as much as a dollar an ounce. With her sailors well financed for a good run ashore, *Dawson* headed back to Esquimalt after escorting a merchant ship from Adak to Dutch Harbor.[163]

The impact of operations in the Aleutians was not limited to the ships and sailors of the RCN: modern war requires a substantial logistical tail, and for US and allied forces in the north Pacific that included Prince Rupert. One does not have to seek far to understand why. Located nearly 500 miles north of Vancouver on Kaien Island, Prince Rupert was the western terminus of the CNR, the most northerly transcontinental railway in North America. It is close to Alaska, approximately fifty miles away, and closer to Japan than any other port on the west coast of the United States or the southern coast of British Columbia. Moreover, it has a good harbour that could accommodate any class of Second World War warship and was protected by Digby Island from seaward observation.[164] Until the

---

157. VAdm F.J. Fletcher, USN, to COPC, quoted in COPC to Capt (D) Esquimalt, 11 June 1943, ibid

158. Tucker, *Naval Service of Canada* II, 215

159. Stacey, *Six Years of War*, 496

160. Ibid, 497-8; Stacy, *Arms, Men and Government*, 391

161. CNWSF to COPC, 131545Z/7/43, COPC to Capt (D) Esquimalt, 082300z Aug. 1943; *Outarde* to Capt (D) Esquimalt, 141000z July 1943, NAC, RG 24, 11763, PC.01-51-2, v 4; COPC WD, July 43

162. CWAC to CNWSF, 162155z July 1943. An experienced officer in *Dawson* recalls never being so seasick. One can only imagine the level of suffering in the army transports, W.A. Edge, "HMCS *Dawson* and the Aleutian Campaign, 1942-43," 3, DHH, 88/58

163. Edge, "*Dawson* and the Aleutian Campaign"; COPC WD, July 43

164. Tucker, *Naval Service of Canada* II, 233-4

outbreak of war with Japan, Prince Rupert had a low priority for naval operations, although certain minimum activities were undertaken. Patrols were carried out "southwards from Prince Rupert to a line 240 degrees from the mainland through Day Point, Price Island. Patrol also includes waters surrounding Queen Charlotte Islands." The naval complement at Prince Rupert totalled three examination vessels, two patrol vessels, and five Fisheries Reserve craft. Air patrols covering an area 200 miles to sea from Prince Rupert were the responsibility of Western Air Command.[165]

Prince Rupert's situation changed dramatically in the wake of the attack on Pearl Harbor. In the words of an assessment by the Joint Services Committee, Pacific Coast dated 1 January 1942: "The isolated position of Prince Rupert makes it particularly vulnerable to attack by enemy raiding parties. The main value of Prince Rupert is in its use as a railhead and naval convoy concentration port for US Forces in Alaska, and its dockyard and oil storage. Its value as a naval convoy concentration port would increase with a serious threat to Alaska."[166] The Americans officially opened a sub-port at Prince Rupert on 5 April 1942; it eventually encompassed extensive port facilities at Prince Rupert itself, an ammunition dump at Watson Island, twelve miles away, and a staging area at Port Edward, three miles distant.

Local defence was a Canadian responsibility.[167] The land forces available—coast artillery fortifications and two infantry battalions in Prince Rupert, an infantry company at Port Edward, and a brigade group at Terrace—were adequate, the Joint Services Committee believed, to repel "any probable enemy attack."[168] As for the RCN's contribution to the port's defences, in February 1942 the NOIC was informed that Prince Rupert would be reinforced by three Bangors as well as Fisheries Reserve minesweepers and patrol vessels.[169] Plans for expanding the naval base were approved, with a need for increased accommodation particularly pressing, but the extensive building program being carried on by the Americans used up the entire available labour supply.[170] The US presence had another effect; namely, the need to provide for some means of coordination between the forces of the two countries in Prince Rupert. In June 1942 a joint Canadian–US Services Committee was formed at the port "for co-ordination of mutual problems." The committee comprised on the Canadian side the Officer Commanding, Prince Rupert Defences, the NOIC, and the senior RCAF officer; on the American side, the Commanding Officer, Sub-Port of Embarkation, United States Army, and an officer to be designated by the Commander, Northwest Sea Frontier. The committee was chaired by the most senior officer present.[171]

One question with the potential to cause friction arose in the spring of 1943, when Captain E.S. Brand, Director of Trade Division at NSHQ, concluded while carrying out an inspection on the west coast, that a Naval Control Service was necessary at Prince Rupert. With US port operations at their peak he noted that ships were not being routed and proper Vesca signals were not being employed. Fearing that the Americans would appoint their own port director, a Naval Control Service Officer,

---

165. JSC-Pacific Coast, min 17 June 1941, NAC, RG 24, 2688, HQS 5199-1

166. JSC-Pacific Coast, Appreciation of the Situation as at 1 Jan. 1942, DHH, 193.009 (D3)

167. Tucker, *Naval Service of Canada* II, 238

168. JSC-Pacific Coast, Appreciation of the Situation as at 1 Apr. 1942, DHH, 193.009 (D6)

169. Staff Officer, A/S to COPC, 19 May 1942, COPC to SecNB, 26 May 1942, NAC, RG 24, 11802, PC 16-1-17

170. NSM, 1 Oct. 1942

171. Sec JSC-Pacific Coast to Officer Commanding, Prince Rupert Defences, 17 June 1942, DHH, 322.019 (D23)

Lieutenant F.N. Eddy, RCNR, was set up in Prince Rupert on 23 June 1943. Despite some unusual problems—the office cat had kittens on top of some files—he quickly established a proper organization.[172] Tact was called for in informing the American army that the control of its shipping, including boarding and inspection of vessels, would be handled by the Canadian NCSO. "The danger of vessels proceeding without proper routeing instructions and with obsolete or uncorrected books was stressed, and also the fact that Prince Rupert was still a Canadian Port and as such, the control of vessels was a Royal Canadian Naval commitment."[173] The Americans provided full cooperation and a system of signalling coastal traffic was worked out; as well a working relationship was forged with the US Coast Guard at Ketchican, Alaska. Local reporting officers were appointed at outports along the coast, providing full information on cargo loaded and unloaded in their facilities.

The need for such cooperation was shortlived. In the summer of 1943 the Japanese abandoned the Aleutians, and the Pacific war moved westward. American activities peaked in July 1943, but then began to decline rapidly, so that by the summer of 1944 the United States had reduced the strength of its establishment at Prince Rupert and put non-essential installations on standby.[174] Canadian reductions followed suit, although the commanders on the Pacific Coast did not always agree with how higher authority assessed their needs. When the RCAF closed down Prince Rupert as an operating base early in 1944, COPC sought additional ships in order to make extended surface patrols. The reply from NSHQ was to the point: RCAF plans had been approved by the CSC and the "number of escort and patrol vessels allocated to your command is adequate for anticipated scale of attack which is continually under review at Headquarters."[175]

A more relaxed attitude following the recapture of the Aleutians was evident among others guarding Canada's west coast as well. "With the unopposed capture of Kiska by the combined US-Canadian forces," recorded the COPC war diarist in August 1943, "the last foothold of the Japanese on the North American continent has disappeared. There has been a noticeable lessening of tension on the Canadian Pacific Seaboard which has been reflected in the press and it is generally appreciated that our Naval, Air and Military forces must now think more in terms of 'offense' rather than 'defence.'"[176] Although no doubt encouraged by the reduction in tensions, the new COPC, Commodore V.G. Brodeur, RCN, must have wondered what he was to go on the offensive with. In June 1942 Pacific Command had comprised thirty-one war vessels, including three auxiliary cruisers, seven corvettes, and thirteen Bangors, but a year later, with no change in responsibilities, only sixteen seagoing ships were available, of which eight were Bangors and none were auxiliary cruisers.[177] True, there had been no Japanese naval activity off the Pacific coast since October 1942, when a float plane launched from *I 25* had unsuccessfully attempted to ignite Oregon's forests, but there had been several "flaps." In November there were reports of two

172. Lt-Cdr F.N. Eddy, "History of the Naval Control Service, Prince Rupert, BC," 9 Jan. 1946, DHH, 81/520/1440-127

173. Ibid

174. Tucker, *Naval Service of Canada* II, 241; Joseph Bykofsky and Harold Larson, *The Transportation Corps: Operations Overseas* (Washington 1957), 43

175. COPC to NSHQ, 1 Mar. 1944, NSHQ to COPC, 2 Mar. 1944, NAC, RG 24, 11772, COPC 1400-7

176. COPC WD, Aug. 43

177. Tucker, *Naval Service of Canada* II, 229, 241

Japanese aircraft carriers 600 miles off Vancouver Island, and in March 1943, when a Japanese task force was said to be approaching, forces along the west coast were put on alert.[178] These proved to be false alarms.

Therefore, what had been a backwater at the outbreak of the Pacific war was even more so after the Japanese abandoned their Aleutian garrisons. In effect, the resources allocated to Pacific Coast Command, similar to those in Western Air Command and the army's Pacific Command, served for the most part a prophylactic role, ensuring that the defence of Canada's west coast, however minor the operations which the Japanese might see fit to mount, and however modest the RCN commitment, were not entirely dependent on the United States. Possibly the action of most significance had been the rounding up of Japanese-Canadian fishing boats, not because there was any evidence that their owners had the slightest intention of cooperating with Japanese forces, but because that action had consequences that took decades to resolve. To put it another way, west coast naval operations were aimed at an external enemy whose priorities lay elsewhere and an internal enemy whose existence was not proved.

178. HQ Pacific Command to COPC, 1020z/18 Nov. 1942; COPC to "All FR Vessels at Sea," 0450z/30 Mar. 1943; AOC WAC to COPC, 0215/31 Mar. 1943, all NAC, RG 24, 11764, PC05-11-7

Christmas at sea. *Skeena*'s wardroom and a mess deck in *Saguenay* celebrate the festive season. *Skeena*'s captain, Lieutenant-Commander J.C Hibbard, sits beside the tree. (NAC, PA 204586 and PA 200124)

Paukenschlag and the Caribbean
January 1942 to August 1942

BEYOND THRUSTING CANADA into a global conflict, Japan's devastating attack on Pearl Harbor transformed the Battle of the Atlantic. Hitler had barred his U-boats from attacking shipping in the western Atlantic in the summer of 1941 so as not to provoke the United States into an open declaration of war while the fate of the Russian campaign remained undecided.[1] But after Japan's bold attacks across the Pacific, Germany formally declared war on the United States on 11 December 1941,[2] clearing the way for U-boat operations in Canadian and American coastal waters at the same time that Allied attention became distracted by the Japanese threat. The first wave of five U-boats sent to North American waters was designated Operation *Paukenschlag*, but the name—meaning "crash of the kettle drum" or "roll of drums"— has become synonymous with the inshore campaign as a whole, which lasted through the summer of 1942.

Paukenschlag was not the first U-boat offensive to reach across the North Atlantic. A quarter of a century earlier a previous generation of German submariners had attacked off the Canadian coastline and the tiny Royal Canadian Navy had reacted with a system of ad hoc escort arrangements that protected shipping off North American coasts. In 1942, however, the challenge was stiffer, as in a little-known corollary to the main *Paukenschlag* offensive, Dönitz sent successive waves of U-boats into Canadian waters throughout the first half of the year. The defence against this attack strained RCN resources to the limit, but, as it had been twenty-five years before, the response was effective. To fully understand the impact of the German offensive in the western Atlantic it is necessary to look beyond Canadian waters. *Paukenschlag*, and the other operations associated with it, must be viewed in a wider global context as the offensive intensified the escort shortage that underlay the problems encountered in 1941 and led to important decisions that affected the Battle of the

---

1.   MOD, *U-boat War in the Atlantic* I, 86-7

2.   Gerhard Weinburg, "22 June 1941, The German View," *War in History* 3/2 April 1966, 225- 33, shows that after defeating western European rivals Hitler expected an easy victory over the backward eastern power, after which he would challenge the US for whose strength he had little respect. The decision to attack the USSR was taken by summer 1940, and Hitler would have preferred to carry out the attack in the autumn of 1940. Even after launching the offensive on the eastern front, he gave priority to preparing for war against the US, and was building a blue water fleet for this purpose. Thus, he reserved steel for shipbuilding and not for tanks. Even in the last months of the war this emphasis prevailed. Dönitz, moreover, repeatedly convinced Hitler to subordinate strategy on the eastern front to the requirements of the submarine campaign. Japan's blue water fleet could counter US naval strength, and thus when Japan attacked the US Hitler declared war, as he had always said he would. Weinberg cites H.D. Grier, "Hitler's Balkan Strategy," PhD dissertation, University of North Carolina, 1991.

Atlantic. Moreover, many historians who have studied this still contentious campaign overlook the fact that it was a common battle, involving the navies of Canada, Great Britain, and the United States. All were involved, and all had a stake in its outcome.[3]

In late autumn 1941 the Battle of the Atlantic had nearly ground to a halt. During the second half of that year the exchange ratio between sinkings and the number of U-boats at sea fell dramatically. This was because, on the Allied side, evasive routing of convoys around known U-boat dispositions improved because of decrypts of German radio traffic, the convoy system extended to include more ships and destinations, and the effectiveness and numerical strength of both aircraft and escorts increased, partially as a result of largely covert assistance by the United States Navy. The German strategic decision to divert submarines from the North Atlantic was an additional factor of great significance.[4] After the attacks on SC 48 and SC 52 in November the *U-bootewaffe* sank only a handful of merchant ships as Axis attention focused squarely on the Mediterranean theatre.[5] With the North Atlantic stripped of U-boats for the Mediterranean and the area off Gibraltar, BdU was unable to take immediate advantage of the sudden entry of the United States into the war.[6]

Since the downturn in the Battle of the Atlantic, Dönitz had been pressing for restrictions on U-boat attacks in the western Atlantic to be lifted. Indeed, the day before the attack on Pearl Harbor, the *Seekriegsleitung* (SKL), or German naval staff, renewed "its demand for permission to wage war within the entire Pan-American Safety Zone," arguing that if:

> the basic policy of avoiding any incidents with the US is to be followed, the war against merchant shipping no longer offers any prospects of success. If American ships are able to bring supplies to Britain, even though only as far as Iceland or some intermediate port, without running any risk of submarine attack, chances of a successful war against merchant shipping diminish in the same proportion in which American tonnage replaces that of the enemy. The fact remains that the only course with some prospect of forcing Britain to make peace is at present an attack on her supply lines and destruction of tonnage in her service. Therefore the Naval Staff considers the present instructions no longer tenable under which the United States, which is in fact an active participant in the war, receives more considerate treatment than a country which is actually neutral.[7]

The SKL had expressed the classic German dilemma: Britain could not be forced to the peace table without unrestricted submarine warfare, but that, in turn, risked pulling the United States into the conflict as a declared combatant.

The dramatic events of December 1941 resolved this dilemma, sweeping away all political objections to the projection of the U-boat war to North America. Hitler directed that "All orders limiting the use of weapons in the defined blockade areas (Atlantic Ocean, Mediterranean Sea, Black Sea, Arctic Ocean) are rescinded," and that "the so-called Pan-American Safety Zone is no longer

3. Milner emphasized this point in "Squaring Some of the Corners: The RCN and the Pattern of the Atlantic War," in T.J. Runyan and J.M. Copes (eds), *To Die Gallantly: The Battle of the Atlantic* (Boulder 1994), 128-9.

4. Gardner, *Decoding History*, 169, and Werner Rahn, "Die Seekriegführung im Atlantik und Küstenbereich," in *Der Deutsche Reich und der Zweite Weltkrieg* VI (Stuttgart 1990), 335

5. Rohwer, *Axis Submarine Successes*, 71-3. German U-boats sank only fourteen merchant ships in the North Atlantic between 1 Nov. and 31 Dec.1941.

6. BdU, KTB, 2 Jan. 1942; and Dönitz, *Memoirs*, 197

7. SKL, KTB, 6 Dec. 1941, DHH, SGR II/261

to be respected."[8] Dönitz had prepared a plan to greet the entry of the United States into the war and reacted quickly to the changed circumstances in the western Atlantic:

> The whole area of the American coasts will become open for operations by U-boats, an area in which the assembly of ships takes place in single traffic at the few points of departure of Atlantic convoys. There is an opportunity here, therefore, of intercepting enemy merchant ships under conditions which have ceased almost completely for some time. Further, there will hardly be any question of an efficient patrol in the American coastal area, at least of a patrol used to U-boats. Attempts must be made to utilize as quickly as possible these advantages, which will disappear very shortly, and to achieve a "spectacular success" on the American coast.[9]

The Nova Scotian ports of Sydney and Halifax were at the top of BdU's list of "the main points of attack for such U-boat operations," because of their proximity to the U-boat bases in western France (2,200 to 2,400 miles) and their importance as transatlantic convoy assembly ports. The list also included Bermuda, New York, Galveston, Aruba, and Trinidad, all at greater distances (3,000 to 4,600 miles) from the Biscay bases. German estimates suggested that the endurance of medium type VII U-boats enabled them to operate as far west as Nova Scotia, but that more distant operations required the use of large type IX submarines. Dönitz requested the release of twelve type IXs for employment in the western hemisphere, including those already stationed off Gibraltar, arguing that the large submarines were not suitable for operations in the Mediterranean Sea or against the heavily escorted UK–Gibraltar convoys.[10] The SKL relented, but released only six large submarines for *Paukenschlag* to be taken from those currently in harbour or outbound from Germany; the release of the six already on station off Gibraltar was "out of the question."[11]

The need to ease inexperienced U-boat officers into the rigours of the Battle of the Atlantic was also a factor in Dönitz's planning, particularly since his most seasoned submarines had been transferred to the Mediterranean. The defeat of Group *Seeräuber* in mid-December at the hands of the large and powerful EG 36—comprising four destroyers, seven corvettes, two sloops, and the first escort carrier, HMS *Audacity*—in operations against HG 76 resulted in the loss of five U-boats for the sinking of three merchant ships, a destroyer, and the escort carrier; an unacceptable rate of exchange for the Germans.[12] Dönitz complained that "new boats with inexperienced Commanding Officers" were "not at all a match for these convoys and for the defence forces West of Gibraltar. Therefore, I shall send in no further boats from home waters for operations against HG or OG convoys or in the Gibraltar area amongst the numbers of boats ordered by the Naval War Staff." Instead, he proposed to use a group of new "medium-sized boats with young and inexperienced Commanding Officers coming out from home waters" to operate "in the Western Atlantic, probably off the Newfoundland Bank" after refuelling at the French bases. This portended a sizable invasion

---

8.   SKL, KTB, 9 Dec. 1941

9.   BdU, KTB, 9 Dec. 1941. Dönitz had first discussed plans for a surprise attack in American waters at Hitler's headquarters in autumn 1941 and had asked for advance warning of a declaration of war on the US in order to have his U-boats in place.

10. BdU, KTB, 9 Dec. 1941; and MOD, *U-boat War* II, 2-3

11. SKL, KTB, 10 Dec. 1941

12. Terraine, *Business in Great Waters*, 396-9

Escorts and weather played a major role in frustrating U-boat operations in the Canadian coastal zone during the winter of 1941/1942. Above are typical seas of that winter as experienced by *Saguenay* (NAC, PA 200128), while, opposite, the ice-covered corvette *Lunenburg* lies alongside in Halifax in January 1942. (NAC, PA 105681)

of Canadian waters that was clearly meant to complement *Paukenschlag* and make up for the shortfall of the six large type IX boats.[13]

The nature of the shipping that Dönitz expected his boats to encounter off the coast of North America dictated the overall strategy of the offensive and the tactics he utilized:

> Their object must be to intercept vessels proceeding independently and to make use of the enemy's inexperience and the fact that they are not used to operations by U-boats. For this purpose operations must not and cannot be too massed, rather the boats should spread to such an extent that good prospects of success are ensured at one point; they may not, however, spread out to such an extent that the one boat may achieve good success but that, considered as a whole, the area is spoiled for operations in a wide radius without chances of success having been exhausted. Since there are only 6 boats available, *all* places mentioned cannot be patrolled in any case. If the first operations by these boats are made only in the North, i.e., from Halifax to New York, there is a prospect that in the area in the South, i.e., Aruba-Trinidad the conditions will remain unaltered and will promise success at a later date. On the other hand, if operations were carried out in the South the northern area, which lies closer to the German departure bases, would certainly also be spoiled. The decision must, therefore, be made in favour of operations in the northern area, where 3 boats can be sent in, both off Halifax and New York. It is only regrettable that there are *not* sufficient boats available to strike a truly "spectacular blow."

In this fashion, Canada's "East Coast Port," as Halifax was commonly referred to in the Canadian press, became the deliberate target of enemy attack.[14]

Even as the *Paukenschlag* boats approached their patrol positions, Dönitz had to fend off two attempts to divert them to other theatres. In late December Gruppe Nord "requested permanent disposition of 3 U-boats for protection of the Norwegian coast," while the senior Kriegsmarine officer in Italy requested an increased allocation of U-boats to the Mediterranean.[15] In response, Dönitz argued "that the U-boat is the *only* weapon with which we can conduct naval warfare against England *on the offensive*. If one considers the battle against Britain as decisive for the outcome of the war, then the U-boats must be given *no* tasks which divert them from the main theatres of this battle. The war in the Atlantic has been suspended for weeks now—the first objective must be to resume it with new forces as soon and thoroughly as possible."[16] He emphasized the heavy losses suffered by U-boats passing through the Straits of Gibraltar and since Axis fortunes in the Mediterranean had improved, it was no longer necessary "to send submarines through the Strait of Gibraltar at any price." He finally won the point, and apart from three boats to make good recent losses, the naval staff envisioned no further reinforcements for the Mediterranean.[17]

The resolution of these disputes allowed U-Boat Command to concentrate on taking the war to the western Atlantic. Five *Paukenschlag* boats had already been sailed for North American waters in two subgroups starting on 18 December. A sixth type IX boat was unable to depart, which left

---

13. BdU, KTB, 19 Dec. 1941. These three "follow-up" U-boats for *Paukenschlag* were *U 107*, *U108*, and *U 67*.

14. BdU, KTB, 10 Dec. 1941

15. Ibid, 29 Dec. 1941 and 4 Jan. 1942

16. Ibid, 29 Dec. 1941

17. SKL, KTB, 9-10 Jan. 1942; BdU, KTB, 30 Dec. 1941

only two boats, *U 109* and *U 130*, for Nova Scotian waters instead of the intended three.[18] BdU deployed *U 130* off Sydney and in the Cabot Strait, and directed *U 109* to a large hunting ground stretching between Halifax and Cape Sable, which had been formed by combining her attack area with the one intended for the sixth U-boat. The three boats destined for American waters received attack areas off Cape Cod (*U 125*), New York (*U 123*), and Cape Hatteras (*U 66*), but transit to these stations by the great circle route would take them through Canadian waters.[19] In addition, the plan to send a group of medium type VII U-boats to the Newfoundland area to complement *Paukenschlag* had gone ahead in modified form.

Once restrictions on releasing further boats for the Western Atlantic had been lifted, seven type VII submarines sailed as Group *Ziethen*. Five more boats joined this formation over the next few days; three came from the *Seydlitz* group operating off the Azores and the others were either already on passage to that area or were sailed directly from their bases.[20] The twelve submarines began arriving off Newfoundland on January 9, assigned to patrol areas where U-boat Command antici-pated that traffic would be found.[21] The North Atlantic shipping tracks off Newfoundland passed within 200 nautical miles south of the island. Moreover, westbound convoys were being dispersed south of Placentia Bay (at about 55° West), from whence they made for their North American desti-nations independently.[22] U-boat Command expected "the greatest traffic and least defence of enemy ships" south of Newfoundland.[23] *Ziethen* boats went to five patrol areas in a 200-mile north–south column that straddled the ocean shipping routes south of Cape Race, while *U 654* was to patrol an area south of Sable Island on the shortest track for transatlantic traffic to and from New York and Boston. Others went to allocated areas off the Avalon Peninsula to intercept traffic in and out of St John's. BdU ordered *U 553* to proceed towards an area off Cape Sable on the southwestern shore of Nova Scotia, and the most experienced commanding officer, Korvettenkapitän Erich Topp in *U 552*, had freedom to select his own area east and south of the Avalon Peninsula.[24] Although less known than *Paukenschlag*, the deployment of Group *Ziethen* to Canadian coastal waters allowed Dönitz to deploy a much larger force than had originally been requested from the naval staff. The inclusion of the twelve medium-range type VII boats meant that the main weight of the initial attack—four-teen of seventeen submarines—fell in Canadian, not American, waters.[25]

---

18. Ibid

19. BdU, KTB, 9 Jan. 1942. BdU's signal of 9 Jan. assigned attack areas IV and V to *U 109* while each of the other four *Paukenschlag* U-boats received a single attack area: I, II, III, and VI. Cited in M. Gannon, *Operation Drumbeat* (New York 1990), 198.

20. BdU, KTB, 2 Jan. 1942; MOD, *U-Boat War* II, 4; and J. Rohwer and G. Hümmelchen, *Chronology of the War At Sea, 1939-1945* (London 1972-4), 115

21. German intelligence about convoy routes and dispersals was sketchy as B-Dienst, the radio intercept organization, was only occasionally breaking Allied convoy traffic. Information provided by Dr Jurgen Rohwer in letter dated 31 Jan. 2000.

22. Blair, *Hitler's U-Boat War*, 353

23. BdU, KTB, 11 Jan. 1942

24. KTBs for *U 84*, *U 86*, *U 87*, *U 135*, *U 203*, *U 333*, *U 502*, *U 503*, *U 582*, *U 654*, *U 701* and *U 754*, Jan. 1942. These boats spent an average of fourteen days off Newfoundland and Nova Scotia.

25. Two of the fourteen boats in the Canadian area subsequently shifted south. Even as these seventeen U-boats moved towards their patrol areas at economical speed, U-boat Command planned more distant incursions in the western hemi-sphere. Five type IXC boats, with 25 percent longer range than the type IXBs, would depart in mid-January for a surprise attack in the Aruba–Trinidad area "during the new moon period in February before anti-submarine activities are organ-ised to any great extent." BdU, KTB, 8 Jan. 1942

The first boat to reach the Canadian zone was the large type IX *U 125*, deployed as part of the *Paukenschlag* group, which crossed 40° West on 28 December, reached quadrant CC-21, 240 miles south of Cape Race on the last day of 1941, and waited there for two weeks until the other boats arrived. Dönitz had ordered the boats to maintain radio silence and not to attack shipping in order to preserve the element of surprise; they had freedom to attack only if they found a target of 10,000 tons or more. When all of the boats had reached their stations, they would strike together at a time ordered by BdU. The second boat on station, *U 123*, passed 40°West a few days after *U 125*, and settled down to wait in quadrant CC-20 for the order to attack. By 9 January 1942 the five *Paukenschlag* and twelve *Ziethen* U-boats were either approaching or lying off North America, poised to strike. (See maps at page 380.) Dönitz set the opening of the campaign for 13 January.[26]

Despite Dönitz's efforts, surprise was already lost. Although information was vague in the weeks leading up to *Paukenschlag*, on the very eve of its outbreak *Ultra* intelligence provided the RN's Operational Intelligence Centre with an accurate picture of German intentions. On 12 January Commander Rodger Winn, RNVR, head of the Submarine Tracking Room at the Admiralty, reported that the U-boat "situation is now somewhat clearer and the most striking feature is a heavy concentration off the North American seaboard from New York to Cape Race. Two groups have so far been formed. One, of six U-boats, is already in position off Cape Race and St John's, and a second, of five U-boats, is apparently approaching the American coast between New York and Portland. It is known that these 5 U-boats will reach their attacking areas by 13th January." Winn also observed that another ten westbound boats, five of which had already reached 30°West, were probably headed for the same areas. The Admiralty shared this information with Naval Service Headquarters, but events intervened before any dispositions could be made.[27]

On the night of 11/12 January Kapitänleutnant Reinhard Hardegen in *U 123* sounded the first beat of the drum roll. While on passage to his designated patrol area off New York, he encountered the 9,076-ton British passenger freighter SS *Cyclops* 125 miles southeast of Cape Sable.[28] Despite Dönitz's prohibition against attacking targets of less than 10,000 tons he attacked, and the ship went down quickly after two torpedoes struck home. Communicators ashore heard the merchant ship's distress call, and a Catalina flying boat and two minesweepers patrolling off Halifax, *Red Deer* and *Burlington*, were sent to the scene. *Burlington* arrived too late to assist in the rescue work, but carried out an antisubmarine sweep that came up empty. Hardegen had already left to take up his station off New York.[29]

Faced with a palpable threat, Rear-Admirals G.C. Jones and L.W. Murray, Commanding Officer Atlantic Coast and Flag Officer Newfoundland respectively, moved quickly to convoy shipping. First, they made efforts to reinforce the local escorts of eastbound SC and HX convoys between Halifax and

26. BdU, KTB, 28 Dec. 1941 to 9 Jan. 1942; Operation order cited in Gannon, *Operation Drumbeat*, 199

27. OIC, U-boat Situation Report, 12 Jan.1942, PRO, ADM 223/15. See also, D. Syrett (ed.), *The Battle of the Atlantic and Signals Intelligence* (Aldershot, Hants and Brookfiled, VT 1998), 1-5, and Blair, *Hitler's U-Boat War*, 441-2, 454

28. American sources usually describe the position of the sinking as 300 miles due east of Cape Cod, but it was only 125 miles southeast of Cape Sable, or 160 miles south of Halifax. Gannon, *Operation Drumbeat*, 205-13; Rohwer, *Axis Submarine Successes*, 73

29. Although only two of the 181 passengers and crew on board the *Cyclops* had been killed by the explosions, the survivors had to suffer through a frigid night in five lifeboats and eighteen rafts, and many of them succumbed to the icy waters. *Red Deer* did not come upon the frozen castaways until early afternoon. In the end, the minesweeper rescued eighty-nine of the 179 who had survived the initial attack. SS *Cyclops*, Particulars of Attacks on Merchant Vessels by Enemy Submarines, 11 Jan. 1942, and Naval Messages, all in NAC, RG 24, 4023, NSC 1062-13-10 (6); Hadley, *U-boats against Canada*, 60-2

the West Ocean Meeting Point now that enemy submarines threatened their route along the coast. In addition to the escort groups provided by the Halifax Escort Force, usually a Town class destroyer and one or two corvettes, the Halifax Local Defence Force supplied two or three minesweepers or corvettes to round out the protection to five or six warships.[30] Local escort, however, was not provided for westbound ocean convoys. Rather than dispersing these convoys south of Newfoundland at about 55° West, the Admiralty ordered, with USN concurrence, that ocean escorts stay with the ON and ONS convoys to the limits of their endurance. "Unfortunately," the Admiralty account of these events later recorded, "a period of very bad weather coincided with the new danger, and convoys ON 51 to 56 inclusive were all scattered before arrival at the prearranged dispersal point." This increased the number of unprotected merchant ships in the western Atlantic.[31]

Coastal shipping presented another problem altogether. The number of escorts required to establish a comprehensive convoy network between St John's, Sydney, Halifax, Saint John, and Boston simply did not exist. Nevertheless, "by the middle of January" the RCN's senior commanders on the east coast believed it "imperative that coastal shipping should be escorted." Jones and Murray started sailing informal convoys between St John's and Halifax on 16 January—navigation out of Sydney had closed for the winter on 9 January after SC 64 cleared so that this port was not included in the winter coastal convoys—just four days after the sinking of SS *Cyclops*.[32] The RCN scraped the bottom of the barrel in the search for escort vessels. The now familiar use of inexperienced escorts was deemed preferable to sending shipping unprotected through submarine-infested waters off Newfoundland and Nova Scotia. Whenever possible, ships proceeding from Newfoundland to Halifax for refit, boiler cleaning, or other reasons did the job.[33] Dockyard authorities juggled completion dates for work being done on ships so that they could augment others. In addition, "newly-commissioned corvettes not ready for escorting or patrolling until completion of alterations and completing short refit were pressed into service."[34] Fortunately, the 1939–40 program for Bangor class minesweepers was now beginning to bear fruit, and by January seventeen of these versatile warships were operational in Halifax and Newfoundland.

The first ad hoc coastal convoy sailed on 16 January when the Bangor HMCS *Thunder* left St John's with two merchant ships. By the end of the month, eighteen more such convoys, ranging in size from one to nine ships, usually protected by one, but occasionally two escorts, had sailed to or from Newfoundland.[35] Only one came under attack, but an abnormal number of stragglers coming into St John's—seven with weather damage from SC 63 alone after that eastbound convoy had dispersed in a heavy storm on 13 January—added to the burden because they then had to be escorted from St John's to Halifax for repairs or onward routing.[36] Murray admitted, quite correct-

---

30. COAC WD, Dec. 1941 and Jan 42, DHH, NSS 1000-5-13, v 9; NCSO Halifax, Convoy Records, DHH 77/553 v 5. For example, HX 171 sailed on 20 Jan. with *Hamilton*, *Weyburn*, and *Fredericton*. They were reinforced by *Saskatoon* and *Clayoquot* of the HLDF.

31. Adm, "Control of Shipping in West Atlantic during U-boat Campaign, Jan.-June 1942," 8, PRO, ADM 205/21

32. FONF WD, Jan. 1942, DHH, NSS 1000-5-20, v 1

33. Ibid

34. COAC WD, Jan. 1942

35. FONF WD, Jan. 1942

36. SC 63 had scattered on 13 Jan. in what the captain of *U 333* called a "heavy storm that dragged on without ceasing for over a week, during which the wind backed and veered between SW and NW, screaming and howling up to hurricane strength." NCSO, HMC Dockyard Sydney, ROP, Jan. 42, DHH, NSS 1000-5-13 (9); P. Cremer, *U-Boat Commander: A Periscope View of the Battle of the Atlantic* (New York 1984), 38; NCSO Halifax, Convoy Records, DHH 77/335 v 5

Two life boats from SS *Cyclops*, sunk by *U 123* in the opening strike of *Pauckenschlag*, as seen from HMCS *Red Deer*. The sailors in the life boat awash were all dead from exposure. (DND, PMR 87-100 and 87-101)

A fisherman from the American trawler *Foam*, sunk eighty miles off Halifax by *U 432* in May 1942, discusses his ordeal with the commanding officer of *Red Deer*. (DND, PMR 87-103)

The lifeline. Merchant navy and DEMS gunner survivors. (PA 204362 and PA 204361)

ly, that these coastal convoys were quite inadequate, but could claim from the evidence that they had "a deterrent effect."[37]

Independents and stragglers were still vulnerable, however, and they suffered grievously. In January the fourteen U-boats off Newfoundland and Nova Scotia sank twenty merchant ships, most of which were steaming alone. In addition, while on passage to their patrol areas they had sunk four more vessels in the ocean approaches to Newfoundland.[38] A chronicle of this slaughter of independents in the Canadian zone in January 1942 serves to highlight the terrible ferocity of the war at sea —and how close it could come to Canadian shores—and emphasizes, yet again, the value of convoy.

The sinking of *Cyclops* on 12 January was the first in a rapid succession of attacks. Korvettenkapitän E. Kals, commanding the type IX *U 130* of the original *Paukenschlag* group, allocated a large area between Cape Breton Island and Newfoundland, had been unaware that Sydney was closing for the winter, and he decided to position himself on the shipping lane from there to Cape Race. Two RCAF aircraft surprised him on the surface on 12 January, but he escaped damage. This encounter and subsequent air activity out of Sydney caused Kals to report "heavy air cover." He shifted south to the shipping lanes between Halifax and Cape Breton and on 12 and 13 January, sank the freighters *Frisco*, bound for Argentia, and *Friar Rock*, carrying a cargo for Britain. Just six of *Frisco's* crew of nineteen survived. One of *Friar Rock's* boats capsized soon after launching, but the second boat, with twelve frozen corpses and seven survivors, was found four days later 110 miles southwest of St Pierre by the destroyer HMS *Montgomery*.[39] Kals kept moving southward and on the 21st sank the Norwegian tanker *Alexandra Höegh*, bound for Halifax from Venezuela with crude oil, 160 miles off the southern tip of Nova Scotia.[40]

The other type IX ordered to Canadian waters, *U 109*, assigned a large area southeast of Nova Scotia but delayed by heavy weather did not reach station until 16 January. Kapitänleutnant H. Bleichrodt chose to patrol close to shore at night, moving offshore during the daylight hours. Scouting the coast from Liverpool around to Yarmouth his only success came on the 23rd when he sank the British freighter *Thirlby* twelve miles southwest of Seal Island.[41] Bleichrodt then heard several reports of sinkings in US waters and shifted further south. By 27 January both *U 109* and *U 130* had moved out of the Canadian area.

Ziethen boats were now also active off Newfoundland. With the freedom to choose his own operating area, Topp in *U 552* decided to make for St John's. During the night of 14 January he sank the medium-sized freighter *Dayrose*, which had sailed for Portland, Maine, twenty-five miles east of Cape Race. Topp then operated close off the harbour entrance, observing activity while sub-

---

37. FONF WD, Jan. 1942. See also, Adm, "Control of Shipping in West Atlantic," 8; D.J. Payton-Smith, *Oil: A Study of War-Time Policy and Administration* (London 1971), 286

38. The armed trawler HMS *Rosemonde* disappeared while crossing the Atlantic from the Azores and was posted missing on 22 Jan. The severe storm which scattered SC 63 south of Newfoundland during the second week of January damaged three destroyers escorting convoys, *Skeena*, *Saguenay*, and *Ottawa*. All three required repairs, but *Skeena* and *Saguenay* were out of service for three months, a serious reduction in strength for the NEF.

39. Sarty, *Canada and the Battle of the Atlantic*, 94

40. The entire crew survived after thirty-six hours in their boats.*U 130*, KTB; *Lloyd's War Losses* II, 338

41. All but three of her crew of forty-five survived. *Lloyd's War Losses* II, 339; *U 109*, KTB, Jan. 1942; W. Hirschfeld, *Feindfahrten* (Munich 1991), 204-5

merged during the day, and closing in on the surface at night.[42] He moved south along the coast during the night of 16 to 17 January, sighted the first small southbound convoy to sail from St John's and attacked with torpedoes before being driven off by one of the escorts. Topp next lingered off Cape Race, where on 18 January he sank the American freighter *Frances Salman*, bound for Corner Brook.[43]

More opportunities opened up for the *Ziethen* boats when they intercepted and attacked three tankers from ON 52, a convoy that had scattered in heavy weather. *U 553*, just entering the Canadian area, sighted the British motor tanker *Diala* of 8,106 tons 340 miles east-southeast of Cape Race on 15 January. Two torpedoes blew off her bow and most of the crew abandoned ship. Eight men remained on board and were rescued by another merchant vessel five days later.[44] *U 86*, which had been patrolling off the Avalon Peninsula for several days, torpedoed and damaged the British tanker *Toorak* some ten miles off St John's on 16 January.[45] Later that day *U 87*, the *Ziethen* unit in the southernmost patrol box, attacked the Norwegian tanker *Nyholt* 180 miles south of Cape Race. Because the ship was in ballast she proved difficult to finish off. *U 87* obtained a hit with the first torpedo and then fired seven more over four and a half hours in steadily rising seas at the zigzagging ship. After the final torpedo had found its mark, the U-boat closed to shell the target, which finally sank an hour later. Miraculously, twenty-four Norwegians who had taken to one of the lifeboats survived nine days in stormy, cold weather before being rescued by HMCS *St Clair* on 26 January.[46]

On 17 January *U 203*, assigned an area just south of Cape Race, sank the small Norwegian freighter *Octavian* just after the ship had rounded the cape. She went down with all hands. The following day *U 86* sank the Greek freighter *Dimitrios G. Thermiotis* some thirty miles northeast of St John's. This ship, the entire crew of which also perished, had been outbound in SC 63, a convoy dispersed in heavy weather. *U 552*, heading for home after expending all its torpedoes, sank the Greek freighter *Maro*, another westbound ship separated from her convoy by heavy weather, with gunfire 510 miles east of Cape Race.[47]

There was at least one U-boat operating off Cape Race throughout the second half of the month. During the night of 21/22 January, two of the RCN's improvised coastal convoys and a merchant ship routed independently encountered three U-boats off the Avalon Peninsula. Their experiences

42. *Dayrose's* radio report of the attack was heard and five warships searched for the U-boat and survivors. Four of the forty-two men in *Dayrose* survived and were picked up by the destroyer *USS Ericsson*. Report of Torpedoing of SS *Dayrose* and Naval Message, NAC, RG 24, 4023, NSC 1062-1-13 (6); *U 552*, KTB, Jan. 1942

43. Rohwer, *Axis U-Boat Successes*, 74

44. Survivors from another tanker, *Athelcrown*, spent 30 Jan. to 7 Feb. in the derelict, which was briefly taken in tow by two small warships on Feb 25. Efforts to salvage her were still under way on 19 March but did not meet with success and were finally abandoned. Rohwer, *Axis Submarine Successes*, 73, 87; *Lloyd's War Losses* I, 336; Interview with the Master of SS *Diala*, NAC, RG 24, 4024, NSS 1062-13-10 (7); and FONF WD, Apr. 1942

45. *Toorak* was escorted into harbour and was observed with her screening destroyers by *U 552* who considered that the water was too shallow to attack.

46. Three of the twenty-four rescued survivors subsequently died. Jon Rustung Hegland, *Notraships Flate* 11 (Oslo 1976), 25; SS *Nyholt*, Particulars of Attacks on Merchant Ships by Enemy Submarines, NAC, RG 24, 4023, NSC 1062-13-10 (6); and *St Clair* ROP, 28 Jan. 1942, DHH, Sydney file 48-2-2 (7)

47. *U 552*, KTB, Jan. 1942; Rohwer, *Axis Submarine Successes*, 74; *Lloyd's War Losses* II, 1304. *Maro* was bound for Halifax. The crew took to boats in heavy seas; none survived.

provide a glimpse of the haphazard way in which opposing forces were operating. The two small convoys passed each other off Ferryland Head, roughly a third of the distance between Cape Race and St John's. *U 754*, commanded by Kapitänleutnant J. Östermann, moving towards a patrol area immediately south of Cape Race, sighted both the southbound convoy and a northbound freighter without escort. Östermann decided to attack the freighter, the Norwegian *Belize* bound for St John's first and sank her with a single torpedo.[48] A second submarine now became involved. After midnight *U 203* under Kapitänleutnant R. Mützelberg sighted a southbound convoy of two small merchant ships bound for Halifax from St John's escorted by the corvettes *Wetaskiwin* and *Camrose*. Both vessels had been sailed for "extensive repairs" in Halifax; neither had a working radar or radio telephone, and *Wetaskiwin*'s asdic was unserviceable. *U 203* fired three torpedoes at the 888-ton US Army transport *North Gaspé*, but missed. Both the escorts and the submarine heard an explosion, and *Wetaskiwin* dropped depth charges as a scare tactic. *North Gaspé* reported that she had been "hit twice," but subsequent examination showed no damage.[49] Meanwhile, Östermann in *U 754* was trying to overtake the southbound convoy originally located when he saw a merchant ship with an escort astern. This was the northbound convoy of another small Norwegian freighter, *William Hansen*, bound from Argentia to St John's escorted by the Bangor HMCS *Georgian*. *U 754* got off a snap shot from short range and hit *William Hansen*, which eventually sank. *Georgian* was unable to gain asdic contact, but dropped six depth charges. *U 754* escaped on the surface. Ironically *U 701*, a third submarine patrolling of Cape Race, observed the torpedoing and was then shaken by the depth charge explosions.[50]

Admiral Murray in St John's reacted promptly, but further efforts to locate the U-boats were unsuccessful. Two corvettes were despatched to Cape Race and, in addition, the Bangor *Minas*, returning from escorting another coastal convoy, and the destroyer HMS *Burnham* were ordered to assist *Georgian*. Allied aircraft and a USN warship from Argentia also joined in the search. These forces failed to contact any submarines—although aircraft forced *U 754* down three times on 23 January—but *Minas* rescued five survivors from *William Hansen*, which proved to be the only ship sunk in coastal waters in January while under escort.[51]

The U-boats' January harvest of independent shipping continued unabated. On the afternoon of the 22nd, *U 333*, operating south of Newfoundland, sank the Greek freighter *Vassilios Polemis*, which had straggled from ON 53 in heavy weather, 140 miles south of Cape Race.[52] Less than two

---

48. *U 754*, KTB, Jan. 1942. *Belize* sank so quickly that she made no report. There were no survivors; a lifeboat with four bodies was found on 22 Jan. by HMCS *Spikenard*. FONF to NSHQ, 25 Jan. 1942, NAC, RG 24, 6894, NSS 8871-5527; *Lloyd's War Losses* II, 1302

49. *U 203*, KTB, Jan. 1942. The corvette captains later concluded that the two "hits" reported by *North Gaspé* had been the depth-charge explosions. The times recorded by Allied and German reports conflict and time zone differences may have been incorrectly reflected in the Allied reports. Cdr (D) Halifax to COAC, 29 Jan. 1942, Dispersal of Convoy Escorted by *Wetaskiwin* and *Camrose*, *Wetaskiwin*, and *Camrose*, Joint ROP, both in Cdr (D) ROP, Jan. 1942, DHH, Sydney file, 48-2-2 (8)

50. *U 754* and *U 701*, KTBs, Jan. 1942; *Georgian*, 30 Jan. 1942, quoted in CNMO Narrative A, "Canadian Participation in North Atlantic Convoy Operations, June 1941 to December 1943," 5

51. Nine of *William Hansen*'s crew of nineteen survived. FONF WD, Jan. 1942

52. Twelve of the crew of thirty-three got away in a boat. The U-boat approached and pumped them for information and supplied bandages, biscuits, and cigarettes. They were rescued two days later by the merchant ship *Leonidas M.Condylis*, although five died of wounds or exposure. *U 333*, KTB, Jan. 1942, Lt F.B. Watt, RCNVR, Report on Torpedo Attack SS *Vassilios A.Polemis*, nd, DHH, NSS, 4161, Casualties (Merchant Ships); SS *Vassilios A. Polemis*, Particulars of Attacks on Merchant Ships by Enemy Submarines, 23 Jan. 1942, NAC, RG 24, 4023, NSC 1062-13-10 (6); Cremer, *U-Boat Comander*, 41-2

hours later, about eighty miles southwest of Sable Island, *U 553* sank the Norwegian tanker *Inneröy* on passage from Aruba for Halifax.[53] That same evening, the large 9,600-ton Belgian freighter *Gandia*, bound for Saint John from Liverpool, was torpedoed by *U 135*, a *Ziethen* boat heading home after seven uneventful days south of Newfoundland.[54] Some ninety minutes later, 480 miles east of Cape Race, *U 82* sank the large British tanker *Athelcrown*, 11,999 tons, bound for Aruba from Britain in ballast.[55] *U 82*, one of a second wave of eight type VIIs arriving in the Canadian area, struck again on 23 January, 380 miles of Cape Race, sinking the 6,118-ton Norwegian tanker *Leiesten*, a straggler from ONS 56.[56]

The next four attacks occurred further west. On 24 January eighty-five miles southeast of Cape Race, *U 333* sank MV *Ringstad*, a Norwegian freighter from the recently storm-scattered ON 55.[57] Meanwhile, at first light on the 25th, *U 754* destroyed the Greek freighter *Mount Kitheron*, creeping along at seven knots waiting to pick up a pilot seven miles off St John's. *U 754* then moved south.[58] The next afternoon, he sighted a lone westbound ship, the Greek freighter *Icarion* bound for Halifax in ballast from Manchester after being dispersed from ON 59. After an unsuccessful first attack *U 754* sank the freighter during the night of 26 January, ninety miles southeast of Cape Race.[59]

U 582 had been operating south of Sable Island and Newfoundland for four days when the westbound British tanker *Refast*, bound for Louisiana in ballast, came into view 230 miles south of Cape Race on 26 January. During the next three hours, *U 582* manoeuvred into an attacking position. Like *Icarun*, *Refast* had been in a recently dispersed westbound convoy and was zigzagging. But when the submarine heard a U-boat warning being broadcast for an area 120 miles further north, the tanker was heard to repeat back the warning message. Lulled into a false sense of security, *Refast* then settled on a steady course, and *U 582* sank her with three torpedoes.[60] The next night, *U 582* tried unsuccessfully to sink two westbound merchant ships in the same area. In the first attack, it missed with two torpedoes, and when the U-boat then tried getting closer to the target the venerable British freighter *Mariposa*'s DEMs gunners took the submarine under fire in the moonlight with a gun

---

53. *Inneröy* was zigzagging aggressively and *U 553* fired from only 400 m. The ship immediately burst into flames when struck by the single torpedo. *U 553* circled the tanker "which is burning with continuous powerful explosions with huge torches of flame from bow to stern." Five of the thirty-six men on board managed to launch a motor boat and to escape the burning flames spreading over the water. They were rescued by SS *Empire Amethyst* fifteen hours later. *U 553*, KTB Jan. 1942, SS *Inneröy*, Particulars of Attacks on Merchant Ships by Enemy Submarines, 22 Jan. 1942, NAC, RG 24, 4023, NSC 1062-13-10 (6)

54. Only thirteen of the seventy-nine on board eventually survived. *U 135*, KTB, Jan. 1942; *Lloyd's War Losses* I, 339

55. *Athelcrown*'s distress call was heard by the Camperdown Radio Station outside Halifax. Forty-six of the fifty crew and gunners survived. FONF WD, Jan. 1942; *U 82*, KTB, Jan. 1942; *Lloyd's War Losses* I, 339

56. *Lloyd's War Losses* I, 339; *Sudbury* and HMS *Prudent* searched unsuccessfully for survivors. FONF WD, Jan. 1942

57. Thirteen of the forty-three men on board survived. *U 333* told the lifeboats their position and offered provisions. One boat was found by a US destroyer five days later. *U 333*, KTB, Jan. 1942, Cremer, *U-Boat Commander*, 42-3

58. *Mount Kitheron* was bound for Argentia but had to pick up a pilot off St John's. Twenty of the thirty-six on board survived: HMCS *Spikenard* rescued twenty men from a lifeboat on the 25th. Report of the Chief Officer of SS *Mount Kitheron*, 30 Jan. 1942, NAC, RG 24, 4023, NSC 1062-13-10 (6); *U 754*, KTB, Jan. 1942

59. Twenty survivors landed in St Mary's Bay on the south shore of Newfoundland, nine men perished. Report by the Master of SS *Icarion*, 31 Jan. 1942, NAC, RG 24, 4023, NSC 1062-13-10 (6); *U 754*, KTB, Jan. 1942; *Lloyd's War Losses* I, 341

60. Thirty-three of the forty-three men on board survived. *U 582*, KTB, Jan. 1942; *Lloyd's War Losses* I, 341; SS *Refast*, Particulars of Attacks on Merchant Vessels by Enemy Submarines, NAC, RG 24, 4024, NSC 1062-13-10 (7); *U 582*, KTB, Jan. 1942

mounted aft, while the captain manoeuvred to present a narrow stern target. *U 582* dived to escape and subsequently fired her last torpedo at another freighter but missed.[61] That was the final attack by a *Ziethen* boat. At the end of the month *U 82* of the next wave of type VIIs and operating south of Sable Island located the fast troop convoy NA 2, carrying Canadian troops, and on 31 January sank the Town class destroyer HMS *Belmont*. Little is known about the attack, as *U 82* was destroyed in the eastern Atlantic on 11 February, and the other ships in NA 2 did not realize immediately that *Belmont* had been sunk. Sadly, she went down with all hands, including six Canadians.

The heavy losses of independents and stragglers in Canadian waters helped boost sinkings by submarine in the North Atlantic from 56,957 tons in December to 290,303 in January, including 124,183 tons in the Canadian area. Seven tankers were among the ships lost off Canada. Eight tankers and seven other ships for a total of 98,718 tons went down off the United States Eastern seaboard.[62] Thus, fourteen U-boats in the Canadian area had accounted for an average of just 1.8 ships each, compared with a rate 3.75 for the four boats in American waters.[63] The discrepancy is easily explained. U-boats in American waters operated in better weather, encountered far fewer surface and air patrols and a larger number of ships proceeding independently, and benefited from shipping concentrated in focal areas. In his war diary on 19 January, just six days after his first *Paukenschlag* sinking, the commanding officer of *U 123* noted in particular the heavy density of targets encountered further south: "Our operation has been most successful: eight ships, including three tankers ... within 12 hours. It is a pity there were not a couple of large U-minelayers with me the other night off New York, or ten to twenty U-boats here last night, instead of one. I am sure all would have found ample targets. Altogether I saw about twenty merchant ships, some undarkened."[64]

The biggest reason for the discrepancy was the coastal convoys organized by Jones and Murray. They were effective because by grouping even small numbers of ships together they reduced the opportunities for U-boats to find them. Moreover, the escorts that had been scraped together in St John's and Halifax, even though underequipped and undertrained, fulfilled their primary task simply by being present. U-boat war diaries invariably record a reluctance to attack when escorts were sighted singly or in groups—and such sightings were frequent—and when they did attack it was with extreme caution.[65] The war diary of the Flag Officer Newfoundland aptly concluded at the end

---

61. *U 582*, KTB, Jan. 1942; SS *Mariposa*, Particulars of Attacks on Merchant Vessels by Enemy Submarines, NAC, RG 24, 4024, NSC 1062-13-10 (7)

62. Sinkings off the United States coast: by *U 66*: *Allan Jackson*, *Lady Hawkins*, *Olympic*, *Empire Gem*, *Venore*; by *U 106*: *Empire Wildebeest*, *Rochester*; by *U 123*: *Norness*, *Coimbra*, *Norvena*, *City of Atlanta*, *Ciltvaira*; by *U 125*: *West Ivis*; by *U 130*: *Varanger*, *Francis Powell*. In addition, 23,657 tons (two tankers, two freighters) were lost in the western Atlantic east of the US. A further four ships had been damaged and would be out of service for months: two tankers off the US and one tanker and one freighter in the Canadian area. Figures from Rohwer, *Axis Submarine Successes*

63. All but two of the submarines in Canadian areas achieved sinkings. Data derived from Rohwer, *Axis Submarine Successes*, 73-6. Total sinkings for Dec. and Jan. (also based on Rohwer) taken from Rahn, 367. Sinking rates per boat reflect that *U 123* sank one ship in the Canadian area but then operated further south, and the fact that while *U 130* and *U 109* shifted from Canadian waters during *Paukenschlag*, *U 109* did not leave until after 27 Jan. and made her first sinking off the US in Feb. Four type IXs were thus operating in US waters in Jan. The discrepancy in results per boat in the two areas are even more striking in terms of tonnages: 24,697 per boat off the US; 8,870 in the Canadian area.

64. Quoted in MOD, *U-Boat War* II, 5

65. See, e.g., *U 86*, KTB, 23 Jan. 1942; *U 87*, KTB, 12 Jan. 1942; *U 130*, KTB, 12, 14, and 18 Jan. 1942; *U 333*, KTB, 25 Jan. 1942; *U 552*, KTB, 14 and 17 Jan. 1942; *U 654*, KTB, 8 Feb. 1942; *U 701*, KTB, 19 Jan. 1942; and *U 754*, KTB, 22-3 Jan. 1942. *U 84* operated submerged off Cape Race in low visibility because the CO feared that in those conditions an aircraft would not be sighted by the lookouts. *U 84*, KTB, 20 Jan. 1942

of January: "It is realised that the escort of the coastal convoys, which is more often than not one minesweeper only, is quite inadequate, yet as far as can be seen it appears to have the requisite effect."[66]

The U-boat presence off the Avalon Peninsula, five submarines along the sixty miles of coast between Cape Race and St John's at various times between January 12 and 25, and off "Newfy John" on eight of these days, was one of the heaviest concentrations of U-boats off a comparatively short stretch of coastline during the long six years of the Atlantic campaign. Considering the large investment of resources, the results—five independents sunk and one damaged, as well as the vessel sunk in convoy—were meagre indeed in contrast to the heavy sinkings of independents further out to sea.[67] The *Paukenschlag* and *Ziethen* boats, deployed individually on likely shipping routes to intercept independents and not in scouting lines straddling suspected convoy routes, intercepted only one convoy, NA 2, of the eleven eastbound ocean convoys that sailed through the Canadian area from Sydney or Halifax between 13 and 31 January, and sank only one warship, the British four-stacker *Belmont*.[68] By the same token, the only damage inflicted on U-boats in January was by air attacks on *U 86* on the 19th and 28th, which holed tanks outside the pressure hull. *U 85*, attacked 150 miles south of Cape Race on 30 January, suffered no damage from the single "well-aimed bomb."[69] The German assessment was that "the intense cold and the heavy ground swell on the Newfoundland bank caused considerable discomfort ... the enemy took countermeasures [in the Canadian zone] ... much more speedily than off the American coast. Probably bad weather prevented stronger air patrols, without which the surface A/S forces were unable to drive the U-boats from the Newfoundland Bank."[70]

The RCN's success came at a stiff price. As we have seen, by late 1941 the Canadians had exhausted their numbers of trained officers and ratings by drafting them throughout the expanding fleet.[71] The remaining source of manpower available for the new construction ships—and ad hoc escorts, such as armed yachts—were the inexperienced officers and men of the RCNVR who, although they had received individual training, had had little or no chance to apply and hone their theoretical knowledge under the guidance of seasoned personnel in well-run ships. In November 1941 the Director of Naval Personnel stated "the Navy must still be regarded largely as a 'training' Navy for the whole of 1942." Accordingly, the naval staff put plans into place in late 1941 to con-

---

66.   FONF WD, Jan.1942

67.   *U 84, U 86, U 552, U 701, U 754,* KTBs, 12-25 Jan. 1942. Sketchy intelligence caused BdU to direct boats to a non-existent "convoy assembly area" northeast of St John's. The U-boats also suffered a large number of torpedo failures. *U 654* recorded nine torpedo misses, including seven on motionless targets. *U 553* had seven misses against a tanker, *U 701* had two pistol failures and three other undetermined misses. *U 552* suffered five inexplicable misses in good attacking conditions. *U 203* missed repeatedly firing at a motionless ship. The torpedo problems persisted in February, but were corrected in time to benefit later waves of boats sent to North America. BdU, KTB, 29 Jan. 1942; MOD, *U-Boat War* II, 4; Blair, *Hitler's U-Boat War*, 485

68.   Convoys shown in Rohwer and Hummelchen, *Chronology*, 113-14

69.   *U 582* and *U 85,* KTBs, Jan. 1942

70.   MOD, *U-Boat War* II, 4

71.   Capt C.P. Nixon, RCN, remembered manning the corvette fleet in 1941: "Here were these two destroyers [*Skeena* and probably *Restigouche*] who had been a year in operational waters and our ship's companies formed the nucleus of many of the corvettes that were just commissioned. They'd draft two hands to one corvette and two to another and so forth. We were just cleaned out of people ... We had these experienced people who were obviously useful to make the backbone of the ship's companies of the newly commissioned ships." Nixon interview, DHH, Nixon biog file

duct a two-stage training program before new escorts were handed over to the east coast commanders. These plans came to nothing, however, when *Paukenschlag* forced the navy to forego training for operational necessity. For the second time during the war, Canadian escorts had to be rushed into action with marginally prepared crews. Hence, the RCN faced a paradox at the beginning of 1942. On the one hand, operational performance could be effective in responding to the requirements of *Paukenschlag*; on the other, irreparable damage could be inflicted on personnel development.[72]

Atlantic convoy operations in 1941, particularly in heavy weather, had been gruelling for the escorts of all three allied navies involved, and discussions aimed at revising convoy and escort arrangements had been under way for some time.[73] The sudden entry of the United States into the war precipitated the Anglo-American Arcadia Conference in Washington to agree on grand strategy and provided extra impetus for considering allied strategy at all levels. Following preliminary discussions with the USN in London in the first days of the new year, the Admiralty proposed a plan for reorganization of the transatlantic convoy system that formed the basis of discussion at a conference convened in Washington on 22–3 January.[74] The reader will recall that by the end of 1941 there were three relays of escorts for an eastbound ocean convoy. The Sydney and Halifax Escort Forces provided local escort as far as the Western Ocean Meeting Point off St John's. NEF vessels out of St John's or the USN Task Force 4 escorts based at Argentia then accompanied the convoy to the Mid-Ocean Meeting Point south of Iceland, where protection was turned over to an RN local escort group from Western Approaches Command for the final leg to Britain. The Canadian and American mid-ocean escorts lay over in Iceland before joining westbound convoys at the Mid-Ocean Meeting Point and taking them to about 55° West (south of Placentia Bay) where they dispersed.

During the autumn of 1941, routing convoys north of the shortest great circle track to avoid submarine concentrations had prolonged the crossings, and had made for an uneconomical use of escorts. As U-boat operations spread ever further in what was now a global conflict, increasing demands on the already-strained pool of Allied escorts favoured a more southerly direct track, where one rather than two escort groups could take a convoy between Newfoundland and Great Britain. From mid-January 1942 the SC convoys proceeded by the shorter route, which enabled the NEF escorts to avoid turning around in Iceland. Moreover, the entry of the United States into the war in December 1941 removed the legal obstacles to American warships using their new base at Londonderry in place of Iceland. But there were serious drawbacks. The shorter route passed further from Iceland, so more of the track lay outside air coverage, and destroyers employed as escorts had no opportunity to refuel when crossing the Atlantic, meaning that it was no longer possible

---

72. DNP memo to DCNS and CNS, 19 Nov. 1941, in DHH, NHS 8440-70; Sarty, *Canada and the Battle of the Atlantic*, 92

73. King papers, DHH 91/431 mfm, series I, roll 1. See the correspondence between King and VAdm A.L. Bristol, USN, CTF 4, dated 2, 13, 17, and 20 Nov. and 20 Dec. 1941, and the report of discussions between the Admiralty and the USN representative in London (SPENAVO), dated 21 Dec. 1941. Discussion centred around the adoption of "straight through routing" from Newfoundland to Northern Ireland.

74. Copy of SPENAVO's 071146 to OPNAV, DHH, 121.003. This partial document briefly describes the recommendations of a conference on 2 Jan. Western Approaches rejected the proposals and another conference was held on 6 Jan., but no further details are provided.

to make wide diversions of convoys in response to new intelligence about the locations of U-boat concentrations. [75]

The proposals made at the January conference by British officers were designed to improve Allied posture in the Atlantic.[76] The British plan would, however, have ended the employment of RCN ships in national groups by separating the Canadian long-range destroyers of the Newfoundland Escort Force from Canadian corvettes. The RCN representatives, Captain R.E.S. Bidwell, Chief of Staff to FONF and Commander H.N. Lay, Director of Operations at NSHQ, argued that this "dislocated all the present operational and administrative arrangements for all types of convoys." They urged that the existing NEF group system should be continued, pointing out that St John's could not accommodate the large number of Western Approaches escorts that would have to be supported by the base under the British proposals. The RN representatives gave way to the Canadian view, agreeing in principle before the main conference with the USN.[77]

Experience had proved the effectiveness of teaming the slower but more numerous corvettes with faster destroyers. This could be exploited in a new system of allocating ships from a pool of Allied escorts that would provide protection across the entire ocean passage. The Canadian contribution would be substantial: for planning purposes it would provide seventy of the 131 (53 percent) corvettes and thirteen of the ninety-four (14 percent) destroyers.[78] Although its ratio of destroyers to corvettes was out of balance, the total number of ships the RCN was to provide is an indicator of the essential role being undertaken by the RCN in the protection of Atlantic shipping.

The new organization proposed by the conference underwent considerable modification in an exchange of messages in late January and early February between Admiral Sir Dudley Pound, the First Sea Lord, and Admiral Ernest J. King. The latter had moved to Washington on 20 December 1941 to take up the new appointment Commander-in-Chief US Fleet, with authority to direct fleet operations in the Pacific as well as the Atlantic; he styled the title COMINCH. The arrangements adopted for the Atlantic early in February 1942 supplanted the NEF with a new Mid-Ocean Escort Force. The initial plan was for fourteen escort groups, each of two destroyers and four corvettes. FONF was to operate four groups (C1 to C4), employing the RCN's eight long-legged destroyers and corvettes, while Western Approaches and CTF 4 would each contribute five groups (B1 to B5 and A1 to A5). The demands of the U-boat campaign off the US east coast, coupled with the war in the Pacific, progressively reduced the American contribution until, by April 1942, it came down to a single mixed group. And despite the national A, B, and C designations, there was substantial cross-pollination of escorts, with RCN, RN, and other Allied corvettes allocated to round out the American groups. Also, because of periodic maintenance requirements, eight Canadian destroyers could not

---

75. Adm, "Control of Shipping in West Atlantic," 1. American construction firms had built a new base for the USN at Londonderry using lend-lease funds. S. Morison. *History of United States Naval Operations in World War II* I: *The Battle of the Atlantic* (Boston: 1947), 53, 119

76. The British representatives were Capt C.J.L. Bittleston, Assistant Director of the Trade Division, and Capt G.D. Belben of the BAD. The USN was represented by Capt F.S. Low, USN, for COMINCH, and Capt R.B. Carney, USN, for CTF 4. DOD, memo to CNS, 25 Jan. 1942, DHH 81/520/1270, Conferences (1920-45) (2)

77. Ibid

78. The planning figures used by the conference were fifty long-legged (twenty-eight USN, fourteen RN, and eight RCN) and forty-four short-legged destroyers (twenty-four RN, fifteen USN, and five RCN), and 131 corvettes (seventy RCN, fifty-eight RN, and three Free French). In the event, USN destroyer participation was reduced.

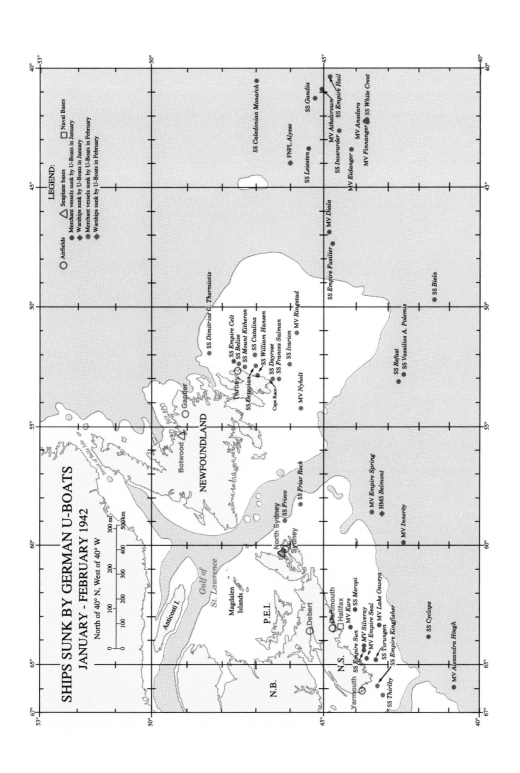

SHIPS SUNK BY GERMAN U-BOATS
JANUARY - FEBRUARY 1942

North of 40° N, West of 40° W

LEGEND:

○ Airfields   △ Seaplane bases   □ Naval Bases

● Merchant vessels sunk by U-Boats in January
◆ Warships sunk by U-Boats in January
● Merchant vessels sunk by U-Boats in February
◆ Warships sunk by U-Boats in February

Strait of Belle Isle

Gulf of St. Laurence

Anticosti I.

Magdalen Islands

P.E.I.

N.B.

N.S.

Yarmouth

Dartmouth
Halifax

Debert

Gander

Botwood

NEWFOUNDLAND

North Sydney
Sydney

SS Frisco
SS Friar Rock

SS Caledonian Monarch

FNFL Alysse

SS Leiesten

SS Gandia

MV Athelcrown
SS Empire Hail

SS Inverarder

MV Eidanger

MV Anadara

MV Finnanger

SS White Crest

MV Diala

SS Empire Fusilier

SS Dimitrios G. Thermiotis

SS Empire Celt
SS Belize

SS Mount Kitheron

SS Catalina

SS William Hansen

SS Dayrose

SS Frances Salman

SS Icarion

MV Ringstad

SS Botavon

Torbay

Cape Race

MV Nyholt

MV Ringstad

SS Refast

SS Vassilios A. Polemis

SS Biela

MV Empire Spring
HMS Belmont

MV Innerøy

MV Kars
SS Meropi

MV Silveray
MV Empire Seal

SS Empire Sun

MV Loke Osuerg

SS Torungen

SS Empire Kingfisher

SS Thirlby

SS Cyclops

SS Alexandra Hoegh

MV Alexandra Hoegh

300 mi.
500 km

0 100 200 300 400 500 km
0   100   200   300 mi.

53° 50° 45° 40°

sustain four C groups, and the shortfalls were made good by British ships.[79] The Americans would use their new base at Londonderry and agreed that it could also provide maintenance and other facilities to RCN corvettes and destroyers. The B groups would use Argentia for their western terminus instead of St John's. A shift in American commitments from the protection of trade to troop convoys was reflected in an increase of USN destroyers to this task to thirteen from four, with a simultaneous reduction in the British contribution from ten to three.[80] The USN also undertook to use five destroyers to shuttle ships bound for Iceland from transatlantic convoys.[81]

Three escort forces would provide interlocking protection for ocean convoys. A local escort force based at Halifax would escort HX and SC convoys to WESTOMP at about 45° West. This became known as the Western Local Escort Force, which would refuel at St John's and then return to Halifax with an ON or ONS convoy. These local escorts were to be operated by COAC, having at his disposal twelve RN and five RCN short-leg destroyers and twenty-seven Canadian corvettes and Bangor minesweepers. MOEF warships would take over escort of outbound convoys at WESTOMP. Finally, an Eastern Local Escort Force under the control of Western Approaches was formed using RN short-leg destroyers and corvettes. The Mid-Ocean Meeting Point was dropped, and ELEF escorts would now take convoys from a Eastern Meeting Point at 20° West (roughly 300 miles west of Ireland), freeing the MOEF ships to carry on to Londonderry at economical speed. The RN released twenty-four British antisubmarine trawlers for escort duty on the US eastern seaboard in addition to the earlier transfer to the USN of ten corvettes building in Canada. The new arrangements still freed up ten American destroyers for coastal antisubmarine duty.[82]

In the post-conference discussions, Pound also sought to have the strategic direction of all transatlantic escorts centralized under the control of the C-in-C Western Approaches. Not surprisingly, Admiral King rejected this outright, arguing that "Existing control by CTF 4 under C in C Atlantic Fleet is of some months' standing and is working satisfactorily. Therefore propose that U.S. shall continue to exercise general strategic direction of escort of convoy operations in [the] Western Atlantic Area." Pound accepted this "with considerable reluctance as [the] new scheme perpetuates a system of dual control with all its proved disadvantages and delays. We will do all we can to make [the] scheme work but I must be free to re-open question should I consider our trade is suffering. At present time with U-boats working mainly in Western Atlantic the scheme should prove less disadvantageous than it would if they were working in mid-Atlantic." NSHQ approved the new arrangements on 4 February and confirmed that COAC and FONF would maintain the Western Local and Mid-Ocean escort groups respectively.[83] Separate discussions between the Admiralty and COMINCH at this time also fixed the change of operational control position

79. The RCN MOEF destroyers were the six River class *Assiniboine, Ottawa, Restigouche, Saguenay, Skeena*, and *St Laurent*, and the two long-range Town class *St Croix* and *St Francis*. These Towns had been given extra endurance by converting one of their boiler rooms to fuel storage.

80. NSHQ, PD, "History of North Atlantic Escort Organization and Canadian Participation Therein," 3-14, DHH, 81/520/8280, Convoy Operations, 8280A (1); Morison, *Battle of the Atlantic*, 117

81. Blair, *Hitler's U-Boat War*, 459

82. Adm, "Control of Shipping in West Atlantic," 1-3. The Admiralty often claimed that the new system freed up twenty-one US destroyers (instead of ten as the USN maintained) and that the balance of eleven destroyers must have been employed elsewhere.

83. NSHQ, PD, "History of North Atlantic Escort Organization,"13-14

(CHOP) line in the North Atlantic at 26°West between 57° and 43°North. South of 43°North it proceeded along 40°West. Thus, Canadian waters were wholly within the sphere of American control. CTF4 in Argentia remained the overall operating authority west of the CHOP line, therefore Atlantic convoy operations continued to straddle two commands.[84]

British, American, and Canadian command responsibilities would be revised in the spring of 1943 to address the problem of divided control, but the operational policy developed in January 1942 based on the southerly route, the MOEF, and local escort forces would remain unchanged for the rest of the war. So too would the importance of the Canadian fleet to sustaining the Mid-Ocean and Western Local escort forces. The large and expanding Canadian contributions to these forces became a major national commitment, a touchstone of Canadian participation in the Second World War. Bidwell and Lay, who understood the national significance of the RCN's contribution, had succeeded in keeping Canadian destroyers and corvettes together in national groups. Unhappily, their argument that this would facilitate group training would not be borne out in the coming months. Pressure to meet ever increasing operational taskings resulted in the persistence of the problems so clearly identified by Rear-Admiral Murray the previous autumn. The inexperience of newly built Canadian escorts that had to be rushed to sea, the lack of manning stability within ships, and the constant shifting of ships from one group to another would continue to hinder performance. As far as the high number of sinkings on the US eastern seaboard was concerned, Admiral King and the commanders of the sea frontiers on the US coast decided that they could not spare ships to commence coastal convoys in face of the commitments to maintain the "A" groups of the MOEF and to escort troop convoys to the UK, together with the need to retain destroyer squadrons to screen the capital ships of the Atlantic Fleet. King advised Pound that there was "no prospect of providing extra protection on the [Atlantic] coast except by new construction."[85]

The decisions at and deriving from the Washington Conference on 22–3 January were based on the assumption that high-grade signals intelligence would continue to be available so that the overstretched escort forces could be deployed to best effect. Within a week, however, British intelligence lost the ability to decrypt messages to and from U-boats operating in the Atlantic. The Germans had issued a new model of the Enigma machine to the Atlantic submarines that featured four rotors as compared with three in the earlier type, and the resulting Triton cipher—known as Shark to the Allies—defeated the equipment and techniques the British code-breakers at Bletchley Park had developed against the simpler three-rotor ciphers. Although the Germans' continued use of three-rotor ciphers for U-boat movements in the Arctic, Baltic, and western European waters, together with lower grade ciphers for naval administrative traffic, allowed the Admiralty's Submarine Tracking Room to make well-informed estimates about the numbers of U-boats heading west, HF/DF and traffic analysis now had to be depended upon to shed light on U-boat dispositions. That remained the case until December 1942. This gave added importance to Canadian sources of signals intelligence, and it happened just at the moment that the RCN's Foreign Intelligence Service, an organization still in the formative stages after two years of sometimes acri-

---

84.   Milner, *North Atlantic Run*, 105

85.   R.W. Love, "The USN and Operation *Roll of Drums*, 1942", in Runyan and Copes, *To Die Gallantly*, 108. Although the best work on the subject, Love suggested—but did not stress—the central issue, which was that Adm King would not remove his destroyer squadrons from their principal task of standing by to escort the capital ships in the Atlantic Fleet.

monious dealings with the Admiralty, had won approval to promulgate HF/DF fixes to all units in the western Atlantic (see Chapter 9).[86]

Soon after Triton defeated Allied cryptographers, the Germans gained a further advantage in the intelligence war. Towards the end of January, the B-Dienst broke the British Naval Cypher No. 3, used for signals concerning the movements of convoys and stragglers, and were able to decrypt about 10 percent of this voluminous traffic in time to be of operational value. To exploit this breakthrough, BdU recalled twelve type VII boats from patrol lines west of England to their bases in western France so that they could refuel for operations in American and Canadian waters. The shipyards in the Bay of Biscay had plenty of space and the boats could be made ready to sail before the *Paukenschlag* and *Ziethen* boats returned from their patrols in the west.[87] Luckily for the Allies, Hitler was preoccupied with the possibility of an Allied assault on Norway. "The outcome of the war would be decided in Norway," he decreed, "and for its defence every available surface craft and U-boat would be needed." Even though the success in the western Atlantic gave him pause, his discussions with the naval staff resulted in the allocation of twenty type VII U-boats to the defence of Norway in a plan approved in early February.[88] This deployment provided a brief respite while the three Allied navies implemented the new operational arrangements.

Dönitz was nevertheless determined to exploit the new opportunities in North American waters and organized a second wave of boats. Eight type VII U-boats assigned to relieve Group *Ziethen* in Canadian and Newfoundland waters crossed 46°West between 25 January and 3 February.[89] U-Boat Headquarters kept the number in the Canadian area at this strength through February. An average of five submarines—four long-range type IXBs and one type VII—hunted in US waters and, by mid-month, five long-range type IXCs were operating in the Caribbean. The type VII crews proved that the endurance of this class was better than expected, and by the end of February fresh boats were passing through the Canadian area to operate further south off New York, and eventually Cape Hatteras, where the number of sinkings was far greater than in waters to the north.[90] In the Canadian area the focus of operations shifted westwards to the area between Sable Island and Nova Scotia, as the type VII crews searched better hunting grounds than in the waters around southeastern Newfoundland, where conditions were harsh and traffic limited. One or two submarines operated off Cape Race throughout February but without success.

The creation of the Western Local Escort Force had placed a heavy strain on the Halifax base by "the pressing into service of newly commissioned corvettes before fully completed and finally

---

86.   The inability to break Triton during this period, and the consequent inability to respond with precision to the latest submarine intelligence, may actually have helped preserve the Ultra secret in the long run by giving German naval authorities no reason to doubt the security of Enigma. Adm to NSHQ, Jan. 1942, NAC, RG 24, 3807, NSS 1008-75-44; Memo DDSD(Y) to DOD, 1008-75-1, 30 Nov. 1942, NAC, RG 24, 3807, NSS 1008-75-44, which refers to the Adm message OIC SI no 86, 9 Feb. 1942, PRO, ADM 223/9; Message Adm to DNI, 26 Feb. 1942, NAC, RG 24, 3805, NSS 1008-75-10; Hinsley, *British Intelligence* II, 229-33

87.   Hinsley, *British Intelligence* II, 176-7, app 1, 636. J. Rohwer, "The Wireless War," in S. Howarth and D. Law (eds), *The Battle of the Atlantic, 1939-1945: The 50th Anniversary International Naval Conference* (London 1994), 408-17; BdU, KTB, 24 Jan. 1942

88.   MOD, *U-boat War* II, 8; Adm, *The Fuhrer Conferences on Naval Affairs, 1942*, 8

89.   The second wave of type VIIs consisted of *U 82*, *U 85*, *U 98*, *U 564* (which moved further south into US waters), *U 566*, *U 575*, *U 576*, and *U 751*. Rohwer and Hummelchen. *Chronology*, 118; BdU, KTB, 22 Jan.-3 Feb. 1942

90.   MOD, *U-Boat War*, 4-5, and diagram15

worked up, and the administrative duties attached to a newly formed and increased group system escort force."[91] These teething troubles diminished in March, but they did not disappear. Despite the arrival of the allocated destroyers and corvettes by the end of that month, it still had not been possible "to form definite escort groups," on account of "overtaxed repair facilities and additional escort duties mainly to the westward, demanded by continued enemy submarine activities in these waters." It was enough at this stage that each transatlantic convoy was afforded the "initial protection of at least five escorts," which usually included two destroyers. Groups of fixed composition, with all the advantages of training and teamwork, would have to wait until the crisis had abated or sufficient escorts were in hand.[92]

In the meantime, coastal convoys continued to operate under an informal system. There were no schedules or timetables: convoys sailed when escorts were available, making sure that all merchant ships "of any value bound coastwise from St John's to the westward" sailed under escort. Eleven coastal convoys and thirty-nine merchant ships sailed to Halifax in February. Five convoys and eight merchant ships made the reverse trip to St John's in the same period, as well as several miscellaneous convoys between Argentia, St Pierre, and Louisbourg.[93] None had more than one or two warships to defend them. About half of the escorts in February came from the MOEF, the rest from minesweepers released from local patrols off Bay Bulls, patrols that were suspended for the time being by FONF. Fortunately, the arrival at St John's, in the last week of the month, of the first ten British antisubmarine trawlers on passage to the American coast temporarily relieved the shortage for westward coastal convoys. The trawlers HMS *Le Tigre* and *St Cathan* sailed from St John's on 26 February with two merchant ships for Halifax. FONF designated this convoy CL1, for Coast Local, the first named and numbered coastal convoy. Return convoys from Halifax to Sydney or St John's were dubbed LC.[94]

The story was different in American waters. Although the USN had devoted a great deal of attention to the development of antisubmarine capabilities prior to Pearl Harbor—and, of course, American naval forces had previous experience in the Battle of the Atlantic—its response to February's attacks off the US coast proved ineffective. Of the hundred or so destroyers based in the Atlantic Fleet, only those of Task Force 4, operating in the MOEF out of Argentia, routinely protected allied shipping, and only a few were detached to subordinate headquarters such as the Eastern Sea Frontier for use as convoy escorts. As Vice Admiral R.E. Ingersoll, USN, King's successor as C-in-C Atlantic Fleet, later recalled:

> Whenever there was a submarine menace inside of the Eastern Sea Frontier, which was a coastal organization, or the Caribbean Sea Frontier, I would give them ships if I had them to spare and I would let them keep them as long as I could spare them, until I needed them for escort purposes. The Sea Frontiers had their own coastal forces but they were small ships and were not really good anti-submarine vessels. The Submarine-chaser, of which the Navy had a lot, weren't very good. They were one of Mr Roosevelt's fads ... the submarine-chaser was no craft to combat submarines on

---

91. COAC WD, Feb. 1942

92. Ibid, Mar. 1942

93. FONF WD, Feb. 1942

94. Ibid, Feb. and Mar.1942

> the high seas ... I didn't have anything to do with the escort of the coastal convoys,
> up and down the coast, except that if they got into trouble, we tried to help them.[95]

The American response has vexed naval scholars ever since. Part of the answer, it is argued, lies in the context of American global interests—the need to be strong in both the Pacific and the Atlantic—but some point unforgivingly, and arguably unfairly, to an institutional "failure to learn" that produced "an unparalleled massacre of American shipping."[96] Part of the answer, too, was a late start and initially slow progress in the construction of escort vessels, like the British corvette, that could be mass-produced. To Vice-Admiral Adolphus Andrews, USN, the Commander of ESF, it was clear that his own escort vessels were "incapable of going to sea and maintaining a patrol," and that "the effectiveness of the [convoy] method depended directly upon the strength of the forces engaged in implementing it."[97] Thus, as American historian Robert Love has observed, although "no responsible [American] navy leader believed that a strategy other than escort-of-convoy would defeat the U-boat offensive ... shifting Atlantic Fleet escorts to the Eastern Sea Frontier offered the only immediate means to check [*Paukenschlag*] in February and March owing to the material condition of the Naval District's few ocean-going vessels and the slow pace of new PC patrol craft and SC sub-chaser construction." Until the numbers had been made good, "King, who believed that only greatly strengthened ocean escort groups could successfully fight their way through large, mid-ocean U-boat concentrations, was reluctant to spread his escort pool more thinly."[98] As a result, convoying was not implemented, shipping remained unescorted, and losses escalated.

Dönitz expected the Allies to introduce a North America–wide convoy system "sooner or later," but he suspected that "the length and disparity of the shipping lanes to be protected, as well as lack of suitable escort craft will not permit a really workable safeguard for some time to come."[99] The Dönitz strategy was to sink Allied shipping wherever this could be done most cost-effectively. By mid-March, he had decided that Canadian waters were of secondary importance compared with the American eastern seaboard and the Caribbean, and had firmly shifted the centre of effort for medium-range U-boats to the east coast of the United States. However, three type VIIs that reached the western Atlantic with insufficient fuel to continue south were assigned to the Newfoundland area where two, *U 656* and *U 503,* would be sunk by American patrol aircraft.[100] Boats passing through the Canadian area intercepted two convoys, but the ten sinkings during the month were either of independents or stragglers.

---

95. "The Reminiscences of Admiral Royal E. Ingersoll," Columbia University Oral History Collection, pt II, 92

96. Love stated in 1992 (and published in 1994) that "the reasons for the success of ... *Roll of Drums* ... remain one of the most controversial aspects of the US Navy's conduct of the Second World War." Love, "The USN and Operation *Roll of Drums*," 95. Love argued that the events could only be understood if placed in the context of "American global strategy, competing theatre demands or institutional history." Others have been less kind. Cohen and Gooch used the USN experience as an example of a "failure to learn" in their analysis of failures in military history. See E.A. Cohen and J. Gooch, *Military Misfortunes—The Anatomy of Failure in War* (New York 1990), 59-94. See also, Gannon, *Operation Drumbeat.*

97. VAdm A. Andrews, cited in Love, "Operation *Roll of Drums*,"112

98. Love, "Operation *Roll of Drums*," 111-13

99. BdU, KTB, 15 Mar. 1942

100. FONF WD, Mar. 1942; Cdr Patrol Squadron 82 to COMINCH, 19 Mar. 1942, Report of Engagement with Enemy Submarine on Mar. 15, DHH, 91/289 f 5; Niestlé, *German U-boat Losses* II, 79, 125

Faced with continued U-boat operations on Canada's doorstep during March, the RCN increased its efforts to protect shipping in its area of responsibility by extending operations of the WLEF further south to include westbound ocean convoys transiting the vulnerable area between Halifax and Boston. The Western Ocean Meeting Point therefore shifted westward to 50° West. ON, and ONS convoys were routed closer to Halifax so that ships bound for that port could detach safely. This westward shift, in turn, extended the coverage provided by the mid-ocean escort groups, but they had been joining eastbound convoys early for some time and improved weather could be expected to reduce wear and tear on the escorts.[101] COAC also initiated a series of improvised convoys to the Bay of Fundy and Boston. Designated XB westbound to Boston and BX eastbound, these sailed only when escorts could be cobbled together.[102] The first XB convoy sailed from Halifax on 18 March with twelve merchant ships, some of which detached for Saint John. Finally, coastal convoys continued: during March fourteen in the CL series, with a total of forty-one merchant ships under escort, were sailed westward from St John's.

By March the mounting tanker losses in the western Atlantic were causing increasing concern. Tankers were important targets not only because they were in short supply but because their cargo was the life-blood of all allied operations to come. The entry of Japan into the war had compelled the United States to transfer forty tankers to the west coast in December 1941, and Britain had had to shift forty-nine tankers of some 570,000 deadweight tons from the Atlantic to the Indian Ocean by the end of February. This alone comprised more than 12 percent of British tanker tonnage in the Atlantic.[103] Not surprisingly, Winston Churchill—and indeed the British in general—were eager to inaugurate convoys between Halifax and the Caribbean even if it came at the expense of American destroyer strength in the Pacific, and this remained a point of contention in Anglo-American relations.[104] President Roosevelt responded coolly to Churchill's scheme, noting that while tanker losses were "very disturbing," no escorts could be spared from the Pacific for this duty.[105] The shipping crisis thus fostered disagreements among the Allies, no less fundamental than those between Dönitz and the German High Command, and a source of no less friction.

In mid-March, a reorganization of the USN offered the possibility of some relief when Admiral King assumed responsibility as CNO as well as COMINCH, becoming both administrative head and operational commander of the navy. He thus wielded great power and, bureaucratically at least, there was nobody to stand in the way of coastal convoys if King wanted them. At the same time, the long-promised British antisubmarine trawlers entered USN service on 4 March, with more expected to follow.[106] Would King now bend his principles and, with these additional resources, give more emphasis to convoy protection? Certainly his Chief of Staff, Captain F.S. Low, thought it was time, observing on 7 March that "In view of the shipping losses ... and the mounting, justified criticism of our methods of combatting the submarine menace ... I do not feel we are on firm ground in continuing to counter all criticism by the simple formula that Sea Frontier forces are not avail-

---

101. Adm, "Control of Shipping in West Atlantic," 1; and FONF WD, Mar. 1942

102. FONF and COAC WDs, Mar. 1942; *Ottawa* ROP, XB 1 and BX 1, 25 Mar. 1942, DHH Sydney file, 48-2-2 (8)

103. Payton-Smith, *Oil*, 283; Memo, "Oil Flow to East Coast Tightening, 16 Jan. 1942," NAC, RG 20, 409, C-10

104. PM to H. Hopkins, 12 Mar. 1942, PRO, ADM 205/13

105. President to PM, 17 Mar. 1942, ibid

106. Love, "Operation *Roll of Drums*," 114

able."[107] The Admiralty was also pressing the issue, pointing out that "U-boats have recently shown a marked reluctance to attack escorted ships in the West Atlantic." Nevertheless, King still considered there to be too few escorts to provide adequate protection for coastal convoys. What is more, the Americans began to complain that the British destroyers allocated to US troop convoys did not have sufficient endurance for the passage. Such are the vagaries of coalition warfare.[108]

Admiral Pound was aghast, and on 19 March he reiterated his assessment:

> I know you are considering the introduction of coastal convoy on your Eastern seaboard and that lack of escort vessels due to other commitments has hitherto prevented its introduction. Shipping losses are, however, so serious, particularly in tankers, that I regard the introduction of such convoy as a matter of urgency both on the Atlantic coast and in the Caribbean ... The only way I can see of providing some additional escorts for these areas is to accept the resulting loss of imports into the United Kingdom and to open out temporarily the cycle of the Trans-Atlantic convoys from six days to seven which would release two escort groups.

He proposed "that the two groups to be released from the mid-ocean escorts for this duty should be selected from A one to five ... with the forces you have available you will only be able to provide a weak escort with each convoy in the early stages. As, however, the U-boats have recently shown a marked reluctance to attack escorted ships in the West Atlantic I am convinced that the starting of convoy should not be delayed until stronger escorts are available."[109]

Although losses continued to rise, King still would not be moved, and together with his sea frontier commanders, steadfastly resisted responding to the mounting disaster with ad hoc convoys. They again emphasized the argument, at a second Coastal Convoy Board convened at the end of March, that "effective convoying depends upon the escorts being in sufficient strength [to take] the offensive against submarines ... Any protection less than this simply results in the convoy's becoming a convenient target for submarines."[110] In accordance with this principle—as well as the implied understanding that the destroyer squadrons earmarked for capital ships would not be used on any account—the board agreed to await the arrival of corvette-like 173-foot Patrol Craft. On that basis, Admiral King and his commanders undertook to implement a partial daylight convoy system in mid-April, although full convoying would be delayed for another month. Admiral Andrews accordingly instituted what he termed a "Bucket Brigade"; ships moved only in daylight from one protected anchorage to another, and in exposed areas were moved in convoys with surface and air cover. The number of sinkings immediately fell.[111]

In mid-April Pound visited King in Washington for talks that resolved at least some of their differences. They agreed that the RN would increase its commitment of destroyers to the MOEF, and that Western Approaches would take over the two American mid-ocean escort groups, both of which had a large contingent of British corvettes. In return, with their longer-legged destroyers, the Americans would assume sole responsibility for escorting troop convoys, something they had

107. Capt F.S. Low cited in ibid, 116

108. President to PM, 17 Mar. 1942; Adm to OPNAV, CNS to CNO, 19 Mar. 1942, PRO, ADM 205/13

109. Adm to OPNAV, CNS to CNO, 19 Mar. 1942, ibid

110. King cited in Love, "Operation *Roll of Drums*," 117

111. Ibid, 117-18

wanted to do anyway. That would leave A3 as the only USN group in the MOEF, but by combining these British destroyers with the sixteen corvettes of A4 and A5, two new British groups, B6 and B7, could be formed. Of the six American destroyers from A4 and A5, three would go to troop convoys and three to reinforce the eastern seaboard.[112]

Because of the weakness of British escort groups, the Americans were initially reluctant to let Western Approaches Command take over the two A groups, but CINCLANT and CTF24 (as CTF4 at Argentia had been redesignated in March), supported the transfer provided that King was satisfied with Admiralty assurances that they would increase the numbers of destroyers in their B groups.[113] British promises eventually overcame the American reservations. Rear-Admiral R.S. Edwards, USN, Deputy Chief of Staff to COMINCH, recommended on 13 April "that the only way to get this thing started is to do so and continue to press the British if they fail in their commitments" to maintain their mid-ocean escort groups at a minimum strength of two destroyers and four corvettes.[114] These discussions paved the way for another naval staff conference, this time to be held in Ottawa.

Earlier in April COMINCH had requested that the RCN establish a regular coastal convoy between Boston, Halifax, and Sydney.[115] As a result, NSHQ convened a convoy conference in Ottawa on 15–16 April to discuss these arrangements, chaired by Commodore H.E. Reid, Vice Chief of the Naval Staff. The arrangements worked out at the end of March called for the western local escort groups to remain with ON and ONS convoys until they reached the Boston area, so the primary task of the conference was to arrange for a one-way convoy from Boston to Halifax to complement the existing system. The timing of this convoy had to link up with the cycles of the established transatlantic convoys from Halifax and Sydney.[116]

The conference recommendations would modify the operations of the Halifax-based WLEF. Boston–Halifax convoys would sail on a three-day schedule escorted by western local escort groups after they had completed a westward run with an ON or ONS convoy and a brief lay-over for refuelling and any urgent repairs in Boston. Ships of all speeds would be included. Vice-Admiral Andrews, CESF, would be responsible for routing the BX convoys and they would be diverted by him or COAC in their respective zones. Ships required at Sydney for SC convoys would sail from Halifax in coastal convoys organized by COAC. To make these arrangements work, the WLEF had to be expanded from seven to eight escort groups and WESTOMP had to be shifted slightly west again from 50° to 52°West, thereby extending the run of the Mid-Ocean groups to ease the burden on Western Local escorts. In addition, the conference recommended that, fuel permitting, two

---

112. Adm, "Control of Shipping in West Atlantic," 4; *Battle of the Atlantic: General Review Feb.-May 1942*, "Summary of Convoy and Escort Policy," ns, nd, PRO, ADM 1/12062; CTF 24 to CINCLANT, 18 Apr. 1942, Subject: British and Canadian Corvettes Allocated to Affirm Escort Groups, NARA, WNRC, RG 313 Red, CINCLANT, 1942 Secret, A 14-1, Convoys General, box 162-3

113. Adm, "Control of Shipping in West Atlantic," 4

114. Capt R.S. Edwards, memo for COMINCH, 13 Apr. 1942, DHH 91/431, series I, roll 1

115. COMINCH to VCNO, 3 Apr 42, in "Informal Board to Organize Gulf Caribbean–Halifax Convoy System to Commander in Chief, United States Fleet," 27 Mar. 1942, para 25, DHH, 91/289, f 13

116. Conference on Atlantic Coastal Convoy Section–Boston to Halifax and Sydney, 16 Apr. 1942, NARA, WNRC, RG 313 Red, LANTFLT, 1942 Secret, A 14-1 Convoys General, box 163. A brief description of the Ottawa Conference is provided by Capt R.B. Carney in a memo to CTF 24, dated 23 Apr. 1942, found in NARA, WNRC, RG 313 Red, 1942 Confidential, file A 3-2, box 8810

or three of the mid-ocean escorts with ON and ONS convoys remain with the merchant ships bound for Sydney and the Gulf of St Lawrence. These recommendations were approved by the CNS and CINCLANT. Western Approaches, however, objected that the arrangements would strain the endurance of mid-ocean escorts and "cut down their harbour time unduly," but eventually conceded the point.[117]

Thus, the famous "Triangle Run" was born, escorts sailing from Halifax to St John's with an SC or HX convoy, back to Boston with an ON or ONS convoy, then to Halifax with a BX convoy.[118] Thanks to the U-boat concentration so far to the south, the RCN was able to put the revised system into effect without serious interruption. The extension of WLEF responsibilities for ON and ONS convoys to the Boston area went smoothly, as did the turnaround of the local groups at St John's with the westward shift of WESTOMP. Bangor minesweepers and destroyers awaiting refit in Halifax escorted BX and XB convoys, and nine XB convoys sailed during April. The informal coastal convoy network between the Maritime Provinces and Newfoundland also expanded. Twenty-two CL and LC convoys with a total of fifty-nine merchant ships shuttled between Halifax and St John's. No merchant ships under western local escort or in coastal convoys were torpedoed during April.[119]

As usual, success came at a price. Keeping WLEF escort groups up to strength reduced the time available for training. Captain (D) Halifax complained that because all of the escorts of the WLEF "are suffering the effects of the North Atlantic winter weather the greater part of their harbour time has been taken up by repairing and refitting. Consequently, not as much working up and exercising has been carried out as was desired."[120] Moreover, Murray reported that although all of the C groups of the MOEF "sailed up to strength" (two destroyers and four corvettes) in April, he was concerned that the B groups "have not yet been brought up to strength, and consist on average of 1 destroyer and 4 corvettes." This may have been the result of the demands created by the transfer of the two A groups to Western Approaches, but it also suggests that the British were taking advantage of the lull in the mid-ocean battle to get their escorts in for refit, modernization, and training. The RCN, hard-pressed in the western Atlantic by its responsibility for the newly established coastal convoys, had no such opportunity. Nor, it must be said, did the Canadians appear to seek one. Rather than husband resources for training and maintenance, Murray hoped to boost the strength of the C groups to two destroyers and five or six corvettes with the coming summer weather "and fewer ships away refitting."[121] The sudden expansion of the RCN's responsibilities in early 1942 was thus continuing to compromise training and maintenance, which would have repercussions on the North Atlantic later in the year.

---

117. Conference on Atlantic Coastal Convoy ...16 Apr. 1942; CESF to Commandant First and Third Naval District, "Coastal Convoys Boston–Halifax–Sydney," 23 Apr. 1942, NARA, WNRC, RG 313 Red, LANTFLT, 1942 Secret, A 14-1 Convoys General, box 163; Adm, "Control of Shipping in West Atlantic," 5

118. For a popular history of these convoys, see J.B. Lamb, *On the Triangle Run* (Toronto 1986).

119. COAC and FONF WDs, Apr. 1942

120. COAC WD, Apr. 1942

121. FONF WD, Apr. 1942

In April BdU concentrated its effort on areas further south and there were only three sinkings in Canadian waters. On 7 April *U 84*, when 360 miles south of Cape Sable during its outbound passage for the United States eastern seaboard, encountered thick fog. The commanding officer, Kapitänleutnant H. Uphoff, dived to listen, heard a vessel, and began a sixteen-hour pursuit that took him northwards into the Canadian area. It ended with the sinking of the Yugoslav freighter *Nemanja* 180 miles south of Cape Sable on 8 April.[122] Five days later, another outbound submarine, *U 402*, sank the freighter *Empire Progress* 390 miles south of Cape Race. Another merchant ship picked up thirty-eight survivors. The corvette *Dauphin* sailed from St John's to search the area, but did not find any trace of the other twelve men on board.[123] The American freighter *West Imboden* was northbound 130 miles southeast of Cape Sable on 20 April when a fire broke out on board and the smoke attracted the attention of an outbound submarine's lookouts. *U 752* waited until after dark to attack and sink the freighter early on 21 April.[124]

Undesirable as they were, the three sinkings in Canadian coastal waters in April were the lowest for any month since the beginning of the U-boat campaign in the western Atlantic. By contrast, that same month enemy submarines destroyed twenty-four ships in the Eastern Sea Frontier and losses dropped off during the latter part of the month only because American authorities took drastic steps to deprive the enemy of targets. The USN suspended all tanker sailings along the eastern seaboard for ten days beginning on 16 April, and the commander ESF introduced small convoys, which ran only in daylight, between Chesapeake Bay and Cape Lookout, North Carolina, in order to provide increased protection to merchant ships in the vicinity of Cape Hatteras, where sinkings were heaviest. Elsewhere on the seaboard, Admiral Andrews "bucket brigade" used inland waterways where possible, and made passages along the open coast in daylight hours between defended anchorages.[125] U-Boat Command misinterpreted the reason for the decline in the number of sinkings: "This at first gave the impression that traffic conditions on the American coast had changed and that the constant stream of independently routed ships and ships in convoy had ceased ... But during the last days more frequent reports from boats, which had lain right under the coast despite bright full-moon nights, have shown this view to be false." Meterological conditions therefore seemed to be the source of the difficulties. "The U-boat's fighting superiority over the anti-S/M defenses, which has so far always been proved, cannot be exploited in moon and weather conditions such as this," concluded the BdU war diary. Indeed, the daily rate of sinkings for each U-boat at sea had risen slightly in April, in spite of increased antisubmarine activity, which indicated that U-boat operations should continue in American waters.[126]

In May U-boat Command had more boats available for operations. The number at sea during this month increased to sixty-one each day, compared with forty-two in January, and thanks to the deployment of the first purpose-built U-tanker, boats already in the western Atlantic could remain longer on station.[127] For the first time, Dönitz could send type VII submarines into the Caribbean

---

122. *U 84*, KTB, Apr. 1942; Summary of Statements by Survivors, SS *Nemanja*," NAC, RG 24, 8190, NSS 1870-173 (1)

123. *U 402*, KTB, Apr. 1942; Summary of Statements by Survivors, SS *Empire Progress*, 21 May 1942, NAC, RG 24, 8190, NSS 1870-173 (1); and FONF WD, Apr 1942

124. *U 752*, KTB, Apr. 42; Gentile, *Track of the Gray Wolf*, 155-6; COAC WD, Apr 1942

125. ESF WD, Apr. 1942, copy in DHH, 85/588 mfm, v 1; Morison, *Battle of the Atlantic*, 132-3, 254-5

126. BdU, KTB, 30 Apr. 1942

127. Ibid

Sea and extend the operations of the type IXs into the far reaches of the Gulf of Mexico. Other boats continued to operate along the eastern seaboard from Cape Cod to Florida and there was a resumption of U-boat patrols in the Canadian area. Five operated off Nova Scotia during the first three weeks of May. In his memoirs Dönitz explained why he had dispersed these greater resources:

> I ... decided to use all U-boats becoming available for operations from the end of April onwards in a simultaneous attack on a number of other, and widely separated focal points for shipping off the American coast. I would thus compel the enemy to split up and scatter his defensive forces, withdrawing considerable portions from the concentration he had just established off the east coast in order to protect other important areas which would now be equally threatened.[128]

In the Canadian area the first encounter of the month came to nothing. The homebound *U 576* sighted the American troop convoy AT 15 fifty miles southwest of Cape Sable on 1 May, reporting it on an easterly course at medium speed. The escort for the convoy was a sizable force that included a battleship, a cruiser, a British escort carrier, and fourteen USN destroyers. *U 576* had no torpedoes left and, with a defective diesel, was unable to shadow effectively. Four outbound U-boats were patrolling 600 to 1,000 miles ahead of AT 15, and although the chances of intercepting the formation were slim BdU formed them into a north–south patrol line to intercept, making the effort because of the value of the targets. Aircraft forced *U 576* down repeatedly, but the boat was able to report that the convoy's course lay close in along the coast of Nova Scotia. The patrol line moved thirty miles north towards the coast, but AT 15 escaped detection and put into Halifax on 2 May, where it combined with NA 8 and sailed the following day.[129] The only U-boat success to come out of this operation took place on 3 May, when *U 455* (one of the four outbound submarines organized into the patrol line to try to intercept AT 15) sank a straggler from ON 89, the tanker *British Workman* 155 miles south of Cape Race.[130] The next encounter in Canadian waters occurred on 6 May when *U 553*, commanded by Kapitänleutnant Karl Thurmann, who had been "given freedom of action from Nova Scotia to New York," encountered a merchant ship and a corvette eighty miles south of the Burin Peninsula on the south shore of Newfoundland. The escort attacked with a single depth charge that caused "minor periscope damage," followed by a full pattern that caused no damage of consequence. *U 553* escaped this unidentified escort but the following day, while lying submerged off Cape Breton's Atlantic coast, twenty miles southeast of Scatarie Island, heard explosions that Thurmann believed were "aircraft bombs." In search of a quieter zone to make repairs, *U 553* pushed into the Gulf of St Lawrence, where Thurmann would launch the antishipping campaign described in Chapter 8 below.[131]

BdU despatched the second boat to Canadian waters, not primarily to attack shipping but on a clandestine mission to land a German agent. *U 213* under Kapitänleutnant Ameling von Varendorff stole into the Bay of Fundy, slipping past Grand Manan Island during the night of 12 to 13 May. The U-boat lay on the bottom in sixty metres of water some two miles off the coast until

128. Dönitz, *Memoirs*, 219

129. BdU, KTB, 1-3 May 42; and COAC WD, May 1942

130. A USN aircraft attacked *U 455* later in the day, but caused only minor damage. Statement of Master of SS *British Workman*, 5 May 1942, NAC, RG 24, 4025, NSS 1062-13-10 (9); FONF WD, May 1942; and *U 455*, KTB, May 1942

131. Hadley, *U-Boats against Canada*, 84-5; BdU, KTB, 4 May 1942

the night of 13 to 14 May, when von Varendorff surfaced and cautiously approached to within 1,200 metres of the shore, thirty miles up the coast from Saint John near the village of St Martins. An inflatable boat, launched into the mist with the agent, an officer, and two sailors, took four long hours to find a place to land on the rocky shore of Melvin's Beach and then return to the U-boat. The mission accomplished, *U 213* slipped out of the Bay of Fundy the following night and on the afternoon of 15 May came under attack by the Norwegian destroyer *Lincoln,* eighty miles south-west of Yarmouth. The boat suffered no damage and radioed U-Boat Command that the mission, which ultimately proved to have been futile, had been completed.[132]

The third boat ordered to Canadian waters was *U 588*, under Kapitänleutnant Viktor Vogel, which had been part of the patrol line formed to intercept AT 15. Assigned an attack area between Halifax and Cape Sable, Vogel proceeded to the Halifax approaches, arriving in fog during the night of 9 May. Within three hours he sighted and attacked the inbound American freighter *Greylock* off the harbour entrance. Crew members observed the torpedoes passing ahead and astern of the freighter, but reached port safely. *U 588* moved south, and the next day sank the 4,031-ton freighter *Kitty's Brook* ninety miles south of Halifax.[133] Vogel then operated south of Cape Sable for two days before returning to the Halifax approaches. He pursued two ships moving up the coast for several hours, having to dive twice because of aircraft, and then waited to attack off the light vessel. On 13 May *U 588* fired at the freighter *Egba,* but missed. Vogel reported his mixed results, stating that there were "heavy ship patrols off Halifax. Air activity in clear weather heavy but inattentive." In search of better operating conditions, he slipped westward along the Nova Scotia coast past Cape Sable into the Gulf of Maine. When sixty miles southwest of Yarmouth on the afternoon of 17 May, Vogel torpedoed and sank the Norwegian freighter *Skottland*, bound for Sydney.[134] An RCAF Canso aircraft sighted twenty-three survivors and directed the Canadian fishing vessel *O.K. Service IV* to their position.[135] Later that night Vogel attacked the Free French SS *Fort Binger* on the surface. His first torpedo passed twenty yards astern, and a second failed to explode when it struck the port side of the ship. *Fort Binger* turned to ram the U-boat, which replied with the deck gun and machine-gun fire. About seven shells hit the merchant ship, which twice missed in attempts to ram. When the range opened out to about one-half mile, *Fort Binger*'s DEMs gunners fired four rounds from their 4-inch gun forcing Vogel to submerge. The French vessel suffered one killed and four wounded, but reached Yarmouth safely.[136]

That wild encounter marked the end of *U 588*'s adventures on the fringes of the Canadian zone. Frustrated by the omnipresent fog, Vogel noted ruefully that "a boat with radar would have good

---

132. The agent avoided capture in subsequent travels through Saint John, Moncton, Montréal, and finally, Ottawa. Broke and no doubt feeling isolated, he gave himself up to naval intelligence on 1 Nov. 1944. He apparently never engaged in espionage. COAC WD, May 1942; Hadley, *U-Boats against Canada,* 144-8; D. Beeby, *Cargo of Lies: The True Story of a Nazi Double Agent in Canada* (Toronto 1996), ch 7

133. Nine men were killed, but twenty-three survivors rowed into Lockport, Nova Scotia, in two lifeboats. SS *Kitty's Brook*, Particulars of Attacks on Merchant Ships by Enemy Submarines, NAC, RG 24, 4025, NSS 1062-13-10 (9); *U 588*, KTB, May 1942

134. SS *Skottland*, Summary of Statements by Survivors, 6 Jul. 1942, NAC, RG 24, 8191, NSS 1870-173 (2); *U 588*, KTB, May 1942

135. Rohwer, *Axis Submarine Successes*, 96; and SS *Skottland*, Summary of Statements by Survivors, 6 Jul. 1942

136. Rohwer, *Axis Submarine Successes*, 96; and SS *Fort Binger*, Summary of Statements by Survivors, 28 Jun. 1942, NAC, RG 24, 8191, NSS 1870-173 (2)

hunting in this operating area," and moved south.[137] In the meantime, the final U-boat assigned to operations in Canadian waters had arrived on station. *U 432*'s patrol area embraced the waters north of 41°North and west of 61°West. Eighty miles south of Halifax, Kapitänleutnant Schultze sank the 324-ton fishing trawler *Foam* with gunfire on 17 May. All twenty-one of the crew escaped, but one died later from injuries.[138] Schultze found no other traffic along the coast of Nova Scotia "except motor fishing vessels" and complained of the "high pressure weather conditions with constant fog."[139]

On the fringes of the Canadian zone, during the night of 16 to 17 May, *U 135*, proceeding to an attack area between Long Island and Cape Hatteras, torpedoed the SS *Fort Qu'Appelle* in a position just south of the Canadian limit. The survivors escaped in a lifeboat equipped with a radio transmitter. Shore stations received their distress call and an RCAF Canso aircraft from Yarmouth sighted the lifeboat on 19 May and dropped some food and flares. The pilot then directed HMCS *Melville* to the lifeboat to rescue the survivors.[140] *U 566*, operating off Cape Cod, reported "medium single ship traffic from Boston to Cape Sable." On 17 May the U-boat fired a "double miss" at a small unidentified freighter, 120 miles southwest of Cape Sable.[141]

U-boats operating in the Eastern Sea Frontier did not fare much better. They reported no traffic, and BdU speculated on 17 May that sailings had been stopped for the moment, or at least "so reorganized that so far the boats have not been able to pick it up. A complete cessation, even for a short time," reasoned Dönitz, "is unthinkable, as America could not stand the loss."[142] In fact, the hold-up of tanker sailings and the organization of small daylight convoys around Cape Hatteras in late April, together with fuller development of the "bucket brigade" arrangements for daylight sailings between protected anchorages had created this perception. In addition, plans to introduce formal convoys between Norfolk and Key West on 15 May probably resulted in many merchant ships being held in port pending the sailing of the first convoys.[143]

At the beginning of the third week in May, Dönitz created the *Pfadfinder* group "to establish whether traffic from N American ports from and to Central and S America is sailing further out to sea. Boats which have so far had little success off the coast of Nova Scotia on account of very frequent fog have been used for this." The patrol line was to operate parallel to the American coast starting 200 miles west of Bermuda and ending just south of the Canadian zone. Since it would "not be possible to cover all routes leading from Trinidad to Halifax or from Pernambuco to Chesapeake Bay," Dönitz warned that the group might have to undergo further redistribution later on.[144] Allied HF/DF had revealed the presence of the group; the RCN alone obtained forty-two fixes north of

---

137. *U 588*, KTB, May 1942

138. Rohwer, *Axis Submarine Successes*, 96; and S/T *Foam*, Summary of Statements by Survivors, 10 June 1942, NAC, RG 24, 8191, NSS 1870-173 (2)

139. BdU, KTB, 21 May 1942

140. Rohwer, *Axis Submarine Successes*, 96; and EAC, MASR, May 1942, 3, DHH 181.003 (D25)

141. BdU, KTB, 18 May 1942. The attack was made in quadrant CB-1145 (about 42°30' N, 68°W). It may have been on either SS *Skottland* or *Fort Binger*, which were attacked northeast of this position by *U 588*.

142. BdU, KTB, 17 May 1942

143. Morison, *Battle of the Atlantic*, 257

144. BdU, KTB, 21 May 1942

Bermuda between 17 and 31 May, which allowed evasive routing of shipping.[145] U-boat Command, because the group had found no "fresh information on the traffic situation," dissolved *Pfadfinder* at the end of the month. There were reports of "very heavy traffic on the coast of New Jersey," the stoppage of shipping appeared to be over, and it was important to shift the *Pfadfinder* boats quickly to positions closer to the coast. Only those low on fuel and torpedoes remained offshore.[146]

After forming part of *Pfadfinder*, *U 432* moved northward into Nova Scotia waters. On 30 May, about fifty miles off Cape Sable, the boat attacked but failed to hit a large passenger freighter escorted by a destroyer. Schultze then moved westward. Thirty miles south of Yarmouth he sank the Canadian *Liverpool Packet*, of 1,188 tons, bound from New York to Halifax to join a coastal convoy for Newfoundland. On the afternoon of 2 June he sighted smoke from convoy BX 23 about fifty miles southwest of Cape Sable and identified two tankers and two freighters, but heavy air cover forced him to crash dive three times. (See map at page 420.) On the third dive he received three depth charges "at medium range" for his troubles and lost contact. The next targets encountered were two American trawlers. He sank them with gunfire on 3 June on the fringes of the Canadian zone. Schultze, who encouraged the crews to take to their dories with bursts of machine-gun fire, caustically noted, "I hope that this has taught these fishermen a bit more respect for U-boats." The six-and eight-man crews of the two trawlers escaped in their dories and rowed to shore, landing at Mount Desert Rock, Maine.[147]

When midway between Cape Cod and Cape Sable on 9 June, Schultze heard a convoy while submerged. He closed and sighted BX 23A, and identified two destroyers, two corvettes, and airships providing cover overhead. The sea was mirror-smooth. *U 432* closed from the convoy's port quarter and fired a salvo at what appeared to be the largest freighter, and single torpedoes at two other ships. The Norwegian freighter *Kronprinsen*, proceeding to Halifax to join an ocean convoy, was hit. The U-boat was damaged slightly during attacks by the destroyer HMS *Wanderer* and the corvette HMCS *Summerside*. Another attack that evening by the submarine chaser *PC 464* did no damage. Schultze remained at 140 metres for eleven hours. The escorts took *Kronprinsen* in tow for Shelburne, but she eventually had to be beached near Seal Island where she was later refloated and salvaged.[148]

During the third week of June *U 87*, after operating in the Boston area, approached Halifax but found no targets and was so roughly handled by RCAF aircraft on 23 June that the severely damaged submarine had to abandon the patrol.[149] On 3 July *U 215*, after sinking the liberty ship SS *Alexander McComb*, a straggler from BX 27, a hundred miles south of Nova Scotia, met destruction by the destroyer HMS *Veteran* of the WLEF and the trawler HMS *Le Tigre*.[150]

---

145. "U-boat Attacks and H/F D/F Fixing," DHH, NHS 1650-U-boats, 1939-42

146. BdU, KTB, 26-7 May 1942

147. *U 432*, KTB, June 1942; and Gentile, *Track of the Gray Wolf*, 184-5

148. ESF WD, 9-14 Jun 1942; and MS *Kronprinsen*, Summary of Statements by Survivors, 1 Aug. 1942, NAC, RG 24, 8191, NSS 1870-173 (3); Rohwer, *Axis Submarine Successes*, 96-102; BdU, KTB, 11 June 1942

149. *U 87* attacked XB 25 thirty miles northeast of Cape Cod on the night of 15-16 June and sank the 8,402-ton SS *Port Nicholson* and the 5,896-ton *Cherokee*. Rohwer, *Axis Submarine Successes*, 104

150. Douglas,*Creation of a National Air Force*, 517-18; Blair, *Hitler's U-Boat War*, 605, 625. It was *Le Tigre*'s depth charges that were credited with this result. SO(O) ROP, in COAC WD, July 1942

With these actions, the offensive in Canadian waters that had begun in January 1942 petered out. Despite periods when U-Boat Command had concentrated a large effort in the Canadian area, results had been far better further south. By March operations in Canadian waters were peripheral to the overall U-boat offensive off North America. This did not happen because the area was unimportant for the Allies. "The vast majority of [North American] shipping destined for Britain passed through Halifax or Sydney. It did so in convoy and did so safely," Marc Milner has observed about this period. "The object of Admiral Karl Dönitz's strategy in the Atlantic war was sinking shipping wherever that could be done with the greatest facility. The reason that there was no disaster of global proportions off Canada's coast was not because the area was strategically insignificant, but because the ... system of convoys made finding shipping and attacking it much less profitable than operations off the US coast."[151] However, continued German efforts to probe for weakly protected areas, and the resulting demands of the expanding convoy system, would stretch the RCN's escort fleet ever more thinly in the summer of 1942. (See map at page 420.)

Canada was by no means immune to the effects of German successes as the U-boats pressed further to the south along the US seaboard and into the Caribbean. Crude oil from Venezuela and Columbia, carried in tankers along the routes that were increasingly the focus of the German assault, fed the refineries at Halifax and Montréal that, in turn, were the source of petroleum products for the eastern part of the country and Newfoundland. Oil is the lifeblood of any war effort, and protection of the precious tankers thus became a matter of urgency.

Even before the U-boat offensive on the North American coast, supplies of crude from the Caribbean were tightening. Most Canadian oil companies chartered foreign-flag tankers, and Britain, desperately short of these types of vessels, had requisitioned some of them from Canadian service in 1940 and 1941. The loss to U-boat attack off the US coast in February 1942 of two of the four large tankers that were Canadian owned increased the strain, despite the fact that the opening of a pipeline between Portland, Maine, and Montréal had shortened the run from the Caribbean for tankers servicing the Canadian city by some 2,000 miles. Heightened demand for oil to fuel wartime activities and the shortages of supply resulted in the imposition of rationing in Canada on 1 April 1942. When, later that month, the United States stopped tanker sailings from its ports in response to mushrooming losses, George M. Cottrelle, the Oil Controller at the Department of Munitions and Supply, who had full powers over the tankers in Canadian service, followed suit and refused to let these vessels leave port.[152] By the end of April naval fuel stocks at Halifax and St John's dwindled to 45,000 tons, only fifteen days' supply.[153] Dramatic utterances are rare in Canadian naval history, but faced with this situation Vice-Admiral Percy Nelles declared, "To hell with that, we'll get our own." On 28 April he ordered HMS *Burnham* and *Caldwell*, two British destroyers assigned to the RCN, to proceed to Caribbean ports to escort Canadian tankers and Norwegian flag tankers under Canadian charter.[154]

---

151. Milner, "Squaring Some of the Corners," 103

152. R. Fisher "'We'll Get Our Own': Canada and the Oil Shipping Crisis of 1942," *The Northern Mariner* 3/2 (1993), 33-7

153. Tucker, *Naval Service of Canada* II, 137, 527-8. Halifax and St John's consumed 21,000 tons of naval fuel per week. One ton of fuel oil is approximately seven barrels.

154. NSHQ to Adm and C-in-C AWI, 1908z/28 Apr. 1942; NSHQ to FONF, 1909z/28 Apr. 1942, both signals in NAC, RG 24, 11969, NW223; and M. Whitby interviews with VAdm H.G. DeWolf, RCN, 10 Dec. 1987 and 25 July 1991, DHH, DeWolf biog file; ESF WD, Apr. 1942, ch 7, "Merchantmen and Tankers," 349

As the destroyers headed south in response, events were transforming this emergency measure into more substantial arrangements. Although American authorities permitted tankers to sail again starting 29 April, Cottrelle, "refused to allow the few remaining tankers under [Canadian] charter ... to move without naval escort."[155] Captain Brand, Director of the RCN Trade Division, explained to the naval attaché in Washington that Cottrelle's "emphatic" decision forced the RCN "to make serious inroads into our escort forces."[156] The difficulty was that the 2,000-mile run from Halifax to the Caribbean was nearly the equivalent in length to a transatlantic crossing, and the two short-legged British destroyers could not complete the passage without putting into Bermuda to refuel, necessitating delays that could not be accepted for a regular service in which speed was of the essence. NSHQ proposed that in the near future four corvettes should be transferred from the mid-ocean groups to COAC to "continue escorting tankers from Halifax to Trinidad and other ports in Venezuela."[157] The British and Americans, although somewhat surprised by the independent Canadian action, concurred in this request.[158]

The Canadian initiative would benefit from the Admiralty's arrangements in response to the tanker losses. To avoid the danger along the North American seaboard, the British were sailing tankers independently from the Caribbean directly across the Atlantic to Freetown in West Africa, where they could join convoys to Great Britain in the eastern part of the ocean. The immediate challenge in this scheme was to provide protection to tankers for the run of more than 600 miles from Aruba, where large refineries processed crude from Venezuelan and other South American oilfields, through the U-boat infested southern Caribbean to Trinidad. Once there, the tankers could disperse to make the Atlantic passage to Africa in the relative safety of that vast expanse of ocean. The Americans could not supply escorts to establish convoys for the Aruba to Trinidad service, but on 4 May Admiral King agreed to the reduction of the North Atlantic mid-ocean escort groups from twelve to eleven, to free one British group for this mission. The new British convoy between Aruba and Trinidad (OT eastbound and TO westbound) began to operate before the end of the month.[159] This resolved a difficulty for the RCN. Although the Halifax refinery used crude from Caripito, Venezuela, close to Trinidad, the Montréal refineries used different grades, for aviation fuel and lubricants, from Cartagena, Colombia, over a thousand miles west of Trinidad, and the navy had to reject the Oil Controller's demand that escorts be found for this distant run.[160] Aviation-grade crude was available, however, at Puerto la Cruze, Venezuela, about 250 miles west of Trinidad, and tankers servicing Montréal could therefore proceed there and back in the Aruba convoys. This allowed the RCN to focus its efforts on a direct run from Halifax to Trinidad, where tankers designated to service Montréal could be dropped off for, or picked up from, the British convoy.[161]

---

155. NSHQ to Adm and COMINCH, 1658Z/1 May 1942, PRO, MT 59/1998

156. Capt E.S. Brand to Cmdre V.G. Brodeur, 8 May 1942, NAC, RG 24, 11969, NW223

157. NSHQ to Adm and COMINCH, 1658/1 May 1942, PRO, MT 59/1998

158. Memo from DG to W. Humphreys, 6 May 1942, ibid

159. Payton-Smith, *Oil*, 258; "Control of Shipping in West Atlantic," 5-9

160. German to Caulton, 19 May 1942, Caulton to German, 23 May 1942, NAC, RG 24, 6789, NSS 8280-800/9

161. Caulton to German, 19 May 1942, NAC, RG 24, 11014, 5-2-2A pt 1; NSHQ to COMINCH, 2223z/28 May 1942, PRO, MT 59/1998. There would, however, be shortages of certain kinds of lubricants in Canada until the summer when fuller convoy arrangements in the Caribbean gave access to sources of suitable crude in the Gulf of Mexico.

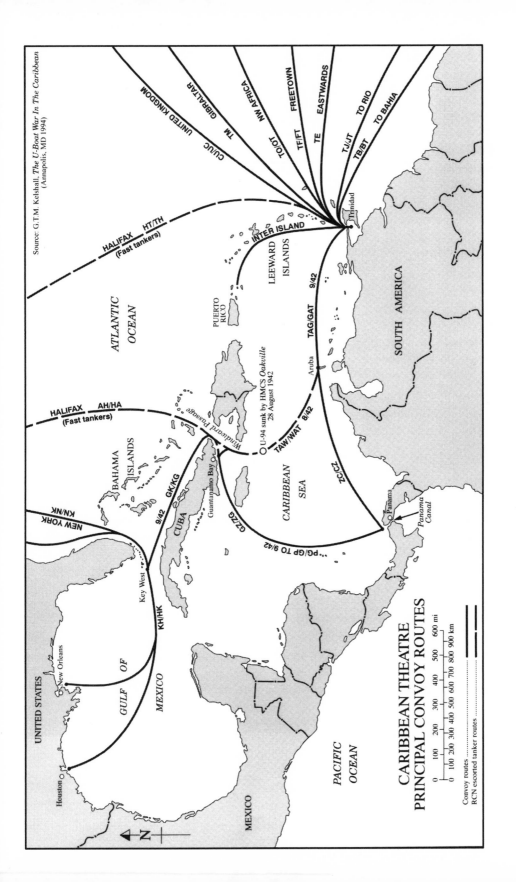

Source: G.T.M. Kelshall. *The U-Boat War In The Caribbean* (Annapolis, MD 1994)

CARIBBEAN THEATRE
PRINCIPAL CONVOY ROUTES

UNITED STATES

ATLANTIC OCEAN

PACIFIC OCEAN

GULF OF MEXICO

Houston

New Orleans

MEXICO

Key West

BAHAMA ISLANDS

CUBA

Guantanamo Bay

Windward Passage

PUERTO RICO

CARIBBEAN SEA

Panama
Panama Canal

Aruba

SOUTH AMERICA

Trinidad

LEEWARD ISLANDS

INTER ISLAND

UNITED KINGDOM

GIBRALTAR

NW AFRICA

FREETOWN

EASTWARDS

TO RIO

TO BAHIA

CU/UC

TM

TO/OT

TF/FT

TE

TJ/JT

TB/BT

HALIFAX HT/TH
(Fast tankers)

HALIFAX AH/HA
(Fast tankers)

NEW YORK KN/NK

9/42 GK/KG

KH/HK

GZ/ZG

PG/GP TO 9/42

ZC/CZ

TAW/WAT 8/42

TAG/GAT 9/42

○ U-94 sunk by HMCS Oakville
28 August 1942

N

0   100 200 300 400 500 600 mi
0 100 200 300 400 500 600 700 800 900 km

Convoy routes
RCN escorted tanker routes

The Allied commands implemented these measures against the backdrop of one of the gravest crises of the war for shipping. In view of the promising successes in the southern waters on the North American seaboard, and the availability of the U-tankers to extend the range of the submarine force, Dönitz dispatched reinforcements to the east coast of Florida and into the Caribbean. The number of boats operating in these waters grew from seven in late April to sixteen by mid-May, and for the first time boats penetrated deep into the Gulf of Mexico. The devastating results included the destruction of forty-one merchant ships in the USN's Gulf Sea Frontier (which included the Gulf of Mexico and the Atlantic coast of Florida) and thirty-eight in the Caribbean. These losses accounted for the majority of the 120 ships sunk by U-boats in May 1942, the largest number in any month to that point of the war. Among the vessels lost in the western Atlantic, Caribbean, and Gulf of Mexico were thirty tankers and another eight were damaged.[162]

During this mayhem, the British destroyers *Burnham* and *Caldwell* that were escorting the improvised convoys ordered by NSHQ each safely made a trip to the Caribbean and back. *Caldwell* brought two loaded tankers into Halifax on 17 May, and *Burnham* arrived with three more on 28 May, thereby relieving the immediate fuel crisis at the Atlantic ports. On 30 May one of the tankers that had come into Halifax on the 28th joined a Halifax–Boston convoy in order to deliver its cargo to Portland for transmission to Montréal by the pipeline, thus resolving the question as to how crude could be carried to the St Lawrence under the protection of convoy without the necessity of the week or more of additional steaming required by the Gulf of St Lawrence route. These passages without loss were no small achievement, not least because, as we have seen, BdU had established the *Pfadfinder* group near Bermuda, across the route between Halifax and Trinidad during *Burnham*'s run north in the last week of May.[163] By contrast, the Canadian-owned *Calgarolite*, which sailed independently in disregard of the Oil Controller's prohibition, was destroyed by *U 125* south of Cuba on 5 May.[164] On 25 May *U 593* sank SS *Persephone*, one of twelve American and Panamanian-flag tankers assigned by the US Wartime Shipping Administration to Canada to make up for losses and shortfall of carrying capacity, before the vessel entered Canadian service.[165]

NSHQ had meanwhile hammered out the details of the formal Halifax–Trinidad (HT and TH) convoys. The basic plan was for COAC to run a tanker shuttle at fourteen-day intervals between the two ports with an escort of two corvettes. Four corvettes, HMCS *Sudbury*, *The Pas*, *Hepatica*, and *Snowberry*, were assigned to the new Tanker Escort Force at Halifax for this service. NSHQ and the C-in-C America and West Indies Station were responsible for diversion of these convoys, to the north and south of Bermuda respectively.[166]

On 22 May HT 1, the first tanker convoy with Canadian escort, departed Halifax, even as the last of the improvised convoys escorted by the British destroyers made its way to Halifax. *Sudbury* and *The Pas* shepherded three tankers bound for ports in Venezuela, and the cable ship *John W. MacKay*, which detached south of Bermuda to make its way independently to Freetown, on pas-

162. Dönitz, *Memoirs*, 221; Robert Goralski and Russell Freeburg, *Oil and War* (New York 1987), 112; Morison, *Battle of the Atlantic*, 410-14; MOD, *U-Boat War* II, 15, and diagram 16; Rohwer, *Axis Submarine Successes*, 92-9

163. HMS *Burnham* and HMS *Caldwell*, Ships Movement Cards, DHH; HMS *Burnham* ROP, 29 May 1942, NAC, RG 24, 6789, NSS 8280-800/9; Naval Attaché, min sheet, 29 May 1942, NAC, RG 24, 11968, f S222 pt 1

164. USN, Gulf Sea Frontier, J.A. Reynolds, *History of the Gulf Sea Frontier* (Key West 1945), 84; Rohwer, *Axis Submarine Successes*, 94; Tucker, *Naval Service of Canada* II, 542; Margaret Hogan, *Esso Mariners* (Toronto 1980), 41-4

165. Gentile, *Track of the Gray Wolf*, 176-8

166. NSHQ to COAC, 1652z/14 May 1942, NAC, RG 24, 11969, NW223

sage to South Africa. Although *Pfadfinder* lay across the path of HT 1 and "a number of submarines were reported in the track" of the convoy, it reached Trinidad unscathed on 31 May.[167]

Efforts to achieve greater efficiency in the next sailing from Halifax revealed the challenges of coordinating tanker movements in accordance with a regular convoy schedule. One of the objectives of the Oil Controller and NSHQ in the early convoys was to group tankers of similar speed together so that every second sailing could proceed at thirteen knots, rather than the normal speed of ten knots; the effect would be to speed the movement of the fast ships and thus achieve much needed increased carrying capacity. On 28 May, it will be recalled, HMS *Burnham* had arrived at Halifax with three tankers, the last of the emergency group sailings; this passage received the designation TH 1, as its arrival set the schedule for the following convoys. Among the three tankers that *Burnham* escorted was the fast *Britomar*, which would have to be unloaded and turned around quickly so that the next sailing from Halifax could be a fast group. *Britomar*'s cargo, however, was destined for Montréal. Thus Rear-Admiral Jones ordered the slow tanker *Vancolite* quickly to discharge its Halifax-bound cargo, and take on *Britomar*'s load, which *Vancolite* could take to Portland while *Britomar* joined the fast group back to Trinidad.[168] None of this could be achieved quickly enough, and in the end neither *Britomar* nor *Vancolite* could be readied in time for HT 2, which sailed with only two tankers under the escort of HMCS *Hepatica* and *Snowberry* on 3 June.[169] Difficulties like these persisted, and the effort to create the fast and slow convoys had to be abandoned: the delay in having fast tankers proceed at the slow speed was less serious than having tankers miss their sailings.

On 3 June *Sudbury* and *The Pas* left Trinidad with TH 2, the first Canadian escorted northbound tanker convoy. The convoy consisted of three Canadian tankers and five British oilers. It was not routed through the Sombrero Passage as the previous groups had been but, instead, south and east of Barbados, well out into the Atlantic, so that three British tankers could detach on 6 June and proceed to Africa. This diversion was undoubtedly intended to provide some measure of protection for these Freetown-bound oilers until they were clear of coastal waters, but the eastward route of TH 2 took it "through areas south of 30 degrees North in which no less than six enemy submarines had been reported inside the preceding twenty-four hours." BdU's war diary reveals that on 9 June five submarines lurked in this vicinity; three returning to base and two bound for Caribbean waters. TH 2 made several evasive alterations of course and arrived unscathed at Halifax on 15 June after a voyage of eleven days. Still, Rear-Admiral Jones complained that the creative arrangements, which were probably made by the British authorities at Trinidad, had sent the convoy into dangerous waters.[170]

167. The tankers were *Reginolite*, *Cities Service Fuel*, and *Britamsea*. COAC to Adm (Sailing tg HT 1), 1520z/23 May 1942, DHH, NSHQ Convoy Files, Halifax–Trinidad convoys; *Sudbury* ROP, HT 1, 16 June 1942, DHH, Convoy Reports, 89/34, v 8

168. NSHQ to COAC, 1958z/28 May 1942, and NSHQ to COAC, 1428z/29 May 1942, DHH, NSHQ Convoy Files, HT-TH convoys. See also correspondence between George Caulton and Cdr P.B. German in NAC, RG 24, 6789, NSS 8280-800/9

169. *Hepatica* ROP, HT 2, 11 July 1942, Convoy Reports, DHH, 89/34, v 8; and *Hepatica*, Deck Log, 3-6 June 1942, NAC, RG 24, 7392

170. The tankers were *Clio*, *Stanvac Cape Town*, *Cities Service Fuel*, *Murena*, *British Governor*, *El Grillo*, *Tide Water*, and *Associated*. The latter two might have been one ship, *Tide Water Associated*, so TH 2 may have had only seven ships. *Sudbury* ROP, TH 2, June 1942, DHH, Sydney file 48-2-2(C), v 2; and BRO Trinidad to Adm, 0428z/5 June 1942, DHH, NSHQ Convoy Files, HT-TH convoys; BdU, KTB, 8-10 June 1942. Submarines in vicinity of TH 2 were probably *U 67*, *U 106*, *U 129*, *U 594*, and *U 753*. Having commanded the first RCN tanker escort to complete the round trip to the Caribbean, McLarnon reported to Capt (D) Halifax on naval facilities at Trinidad and tropical conditions. McLarnon found the Port Engineer Officer very attentive and noted that basic repairs could be made at the local machine shop. Fresh provisions, however, were scarce and the heat was oppressive. As a result, McLarnon recommended that improved refrigeration and ventilation be provided for corvettes on the Caribbean run.

There were two more convoys in June, one northbound and the other southbound. TH 3 (HMCS *Hepatica* and *Snowberry*) left Trinidad on 17 June, late because of delays in loading tankers, and proceeded slowly as one of the tankers had a best speed of only nine knots.[171] The convoy, which included a full complement of six tankers, reached Halifax on 28 June.[172] On 20 June HT 3 (*Sudbury* and *The Pas*), also with six tankers, had left Halifax.[173] There may at that time have been as many as twelve U-boats between Halifax and Bermuda. Nevertheless, the convoy, which made several large evasive changes in course, arrived safely at Trinidad on 29 June.[174] The final convoy in the Halifax to Trinidad service, TH 4 (*Sudbury* and *The Pas*), sailed from Trinidad on 4 July and was routed further out into the Atlantic than any of the other convoys because of HF/DF evidence of renewed U-boat activity in the vicinity of the Windward Islands.[175] All five of the tankers that sailed had cargoes destined for the Montréal refineries, and so the convoy made directly for Portland, Maine, arriving without loss on 17 July.[176]

During the safe passage of these convoys, the German offensive in southern waters had gained in intensity, destroying some forty-eight vessels in the Caribbean and twenty-one in the Gulf Sea Frontier. In July, when broader improvements to Allied defence of shipping in the region took effect, losses still included seventeen vessels in the Caribbean and sixteen in the Gulf Sea Frontier.[177] The Halifax to Trinidad convoys, for all their shortcomings in organization, rate as an unqualified success, bearing out the Canadian and British belief that convoys with light escort were far better than no convoy at all.

The RCN, in May through July, escorted thirty-seven oil tankers between Halifax and Trinidad, without the loss of a single vessel. Twenty-three tanker loads of petroleum products arrived in Halifax and Portland by TH convoy. Nineteen of these cargoes, representing over 1.8 million barrels of oil, fuelled the Canadian war economy.[178] Given the high concentration of submarines and the heavy sinkings of independents in these waters, it is obvious that without these convoys several Canadian tankers would have been lost, and losing even one, as the first official account of RCN operations remarked, might well have caused "a temporary paralysis of operations."[179]

---

171. *Polycastle* and *Fenja*, both of HT 2, failed to turn around for TH 3, *Reginolite*, which because of engine defects had missed TH 2, and *Christy Payne*, although considered too slow, went because no other tankers were ready, and *Sunoil* completed the convoy. NSHQ to FOIC Trinidad, 0515z/15 June 1942, DHH, NSHQ Convoy Files, HT–TH

172. BRO Trinidad to Adm, 0630z/18 June 1942, DHH, NSHQ Convoy Files, HT-TH. The six tankers were *FQ Barstow*, *Britamsea*, *JH Senior*, *Sunoil*, *Reginolite*, and *Christy Payne*, all for Halifax except *Britamsea*, which broke off early for Portland under an escort sent out from Halifax.

173. COAC to Adm, 1355z/20 June 1942, DHH, NSHQ Convoy Files, HT-TH. The six Canadian tankers were *Vancolite*, *Wallace E. Pratt*, *Cities Service Fuel*, *Stanvac Cape Town*, *Alar*, and *Britamer*.

174. *Sudbury* ROPs, HT 3 and TH-4, 21 July 1942, DHH, Sydney file 48-2-2(C), v 4. During this period 16-30 June, Dönitz claims that large numbers of independent ships routed south of their usual route were sunk mid-ocean in quadrants DD, DE, DO, DP by U-boats passing between the bases in France and their theatres of operations in the Caribbean. This may account for the large number of submarine reports received by TH 3 and HT 3. BdU, KTB, 30 June 1942

175. When departing from the Windward Islands on the night of 2-3 July, *U 126* signalled that the straits between Tobago and Grenada were a good hunting ground, *U 126*, KTB, 3 July 1942; Convoy TH 4, Orders for Ocean Escort, 3 July 1942, DHH, Sydney file 48-2-2(C), pt 4; BRO Trinidad to Adm, 1538q/4 July 1942, DHH, NSHQ Convoy Files, HT-TH

176. BRO Trinidad to Adm, 1538q/4 July 1942. The tankers were *Britamer*, *Wallace E. Pratt*, *Alar*, *Fenja*, and *Polycastle*. *The Pas*, Deck Log, 13-17 July 1942, NAC, RG 24, 7936; *Sudbury* ROPs, HT 3 and TH 4, 21 July 1942, DHH, Sydney file 48-2-2(C), pt 4

177. Morison, *Battle of the Atlantic*, 413

178. NHS Convoy files, TH-HT series; DHH, Convoy Reports 89/34; DHH Sydney file 48-2-2(C), pt 4

179. Schull, *Far Distant Ships*, 110

The Canadian endeavour, small as it was, did nothing to shake Admiral King's conviction that fully adequate escort forces were needed before a general system of convoys in the Caribbean, the Gulf of Mexico, and along the US seaboard could be attempted without risking an even worse disaster than the one that was taking place. King, however, proved willing to consider halfway measures, provided the British and Canadians joined in with sufficient escorts. Hard preliminary bargaining between all three navies laid the groundwork for a conference at Washington on 9 June that hammered out new arrangements that would come into effect in July. The Americans held firm that sufficient escorts were not yet available for the through, east–west Caribbean service the British especially wanted. The Americans did, however, agree to extend their only regular coastal convoy, between Key West, Florida, and Norfolk, Virginia, north to New York. The British, for their part, agreed to end their Aruba–Trinidad convoys and make available the RN escort group, B5, that had run the route, to support a new north–south route between Key West and Trinidad, which also passed close to Aruba, the "WAT–TAW" series.[180] In short, there would now be continuous coastal convoy available between Trinidad, Aruba, and New York. Both the British and Americans had expected that Canada would terminate its Halifax–Trinidad service and make these corvettes available for the new Caribbean run between Key West and Trinidad. Admiral Nelles firmly resisted because the routing through Key West and up the US seaboard would take thirteen days longer than the nine-day direct run of the HT–TH series. Such delays, given the small numbers of tankers available to Canada, would create a serious shortfall of deliveries to the Montréal and Halifax refineries.[181]

The efficient through convoys from the Caribbean to Halifax that the RCN insisted must continue to run would, in fact, also serve urgent British needs, but only if the Halifax Tanker Escort Force was considerably expanded. With only two corvettes per convoy, as we have seen, the number of tankers was limited to six which had allowed only two or three British ships in addition to the Canadian ones. The conference in Washington on 9 June, reflecting the extent to which the success of Dönitz's Caribbean offensive had overshadowed operations on the North Atlantic, agreed that the mid-ocean escort groups should be reduced to six vessels, and thereby free about ten RCN corvettes to create three tanker escort groups of four corvettes apiece. Each of these expanded groups could escort as many as sixteen tankers; the first six billets would be reserved for Canadian ships, leaving room in each convoy for ten British tankers. To further accommodate British needs, the conference concluded that the southern terminus of the convoys should be changed from Trinidad to Aruba, with the series receiving the new designation HA–AH.[182]

The British had hoped that the Canadians might go further and also supply corvettes for service within the Caribbean to help establish the much-needed through east–west convoy. The Canadian staff refused, insisting once again on national priorities. Although the RCN's coastal escort forces would be augmented by the withdrawal of the ten Canadian corvettes from the mid-ocean force, NSHQ was unwilling to deploy them away from Halifax where they would be readily available in case they had to be quickly recommitted to the mid-ocean run or to reinforce the very

180. COMINCH to Adm and NSHQ, 1610z/9 June 1942, PRO, MT 59/1998

181. CNS to Adm, 2136z/7 June 1942 and Adm to NSHQ, 1133b/6 June 1942, NAC, RG 24, 3975, NSS 1048-48-31, v 1

182. COMINCH to Adm, NSHQ, 1610z/9 June 1942, PRO, MT 59/199; Trade Division, "Annual Report of the Director of the Trade Division, 1942," DHH, Brand papers, 81/145, 7-8; NSHQ to COAC, 1914z/17 June 1942, NAC, RG 24, 3975, NSS 1048-48-31, v 1

light escorts in the Gulf of St Lawrence.[183] It was probably no coincidence that in mid-June NSHQ redesignated the Tanker Escort Force as the Halifax Force.[184]

NSHQ was taking a hard line, and it is easy to see why. The staff was at this time taking stock of the commitments that had mushroomed since early in the year. On 19 June Captains Lay and DeWolf, the directors of the operations and plans division respectively, passed a memorandum to the minister, CNS, and VCNS that warned that the navy had fewer than half of the destroyers and corvettes needed properly to meet its obligations in the Atlantic and in North American coastal waters. Even when all the ships scheduled to join the fleet during 1942 were included, the RCN would have only thirteen destroyers and seventy corvettes compared with a requirement for forty-seven and 165 vessels of these types. The service was meeting the shortfall with the help of seventeen RN destroyers and six RN corvettes assigned to Canadian control, and especially because of the submarine threat that now existed in the Gulf of St Lawrence (see Chapter 8 below) by employing as escorts—at the great risk of virtually denuding the defences in the immediate approaches to ports—Bangors, Fairmiles, and armed yachts. The yachts and Fairmiles were ill-suited for escort, and the Bangors might at any moment have to be released for their designed minesweeping function if, as seemed likely, the Germans followed through with their interest in inshore waters like the St Lawrence by laying minefields.[185] Soon after, the Canadian staff in Washington passed an assessment of Allied escort requirements prepared by the Combined Staff Planners, which, in using a lower ratio of escorts to the expected number of merchant ships in convoy, suggested that the actual Canadian deficit was considerably higher, some 130 destroyers and corvettes. By these calculations, the RCN's fleet included barely a third of the number of ocean-going escorts needed to meet a suitable standard of defence for the shipping under its charge.[186]

Something of the mood in Ottawa at this time is captured by notes the journalist Grant Dexter made of an off-the-record interview with the minister, Angus L. Macdonald.

> He is less worried about shipping losses than before. We are still losing more ships than we are building but the heavy losses off the US seaboard have been largely the result of pig-headed qualities of US navy chiefs. They refused to convoy along the seaboard on the ground that they hadn't enough escort vessels and to bundle the cargo ships, under these circumstances, would be to invite wholesale sinkings. The British and Canadian authorities argued that this was untrue. It had been proved in British and North Atlantic waters that the convoys were successful even if you could not give perfect escort protection. You might only have three escort ships instead of six, but the submarines would sheer away and seek easier prey. The US navy had been over-ruled and Canadian and British naval forces had come in to help. Convoying was being rapidly expanded ... There is no reason to believe, he says, that there are fewer U-boats loose now than previously or that

---

183. BAD to Adm, 0029z/9 June 1942, NAC, RG 24, 3975, NSS 1048-48-31 v 1

184. *NWR*, 25 June 1942, DHH, NSS 1000-5-7, v 3

185. DOD and DOP to minister, CNS and VCNS, "Canadian Naval Commitments on the Atlantic Coast and Number of Escort Vessels Required to Meet these Commitments," 19 June 1942, DHH, NHS 8200, "Construction Ships, 1939-45," pt 3

186. DOD to CNS, "Canadian Escort Vessel Requirements," 26 June 1942, ibid

Despite devastating damage from a torpedo from *U 751*, the tanker SS Corilla managed to limp into Halifax in May 1942. (NAC, PA 105758)

German output does not still exceed losses. He hasn't much faith in the capacity of air raids to knock out [German] industry.

As for our navy, he now has 37,000 men in it but says that the past rate of expansion cannot be continued. You cannot train men quickly enough and past a given point, nearly reached, you cannot spread your trained men more thinly.[187]

Canadian persistence in national priorities for assignments of the overstretched fleet caused considerable strain with the Admiralty and Navy Department during July when the arrangements for the Caribbean agreed at Washington came into effect. There were delays in the arrival of mid-ocean corvettes reassigned to the Halifax Force because most needed dockyard work, and of the ships present and ready, the RCN, as will be seen (Chapter 8), allocated two for a new Québec City to Labrador route in view of *U 553*'s incursion into the St Lawrence.[188] The result was that only three corvettes were available when the first Halifax to Aruba convoy sailed on 6 July. That, according to the scales of defence agreed among the Allies, restricted the number of tankers permitted to sail to only twelve, and several British tankers were therefore delayed at Halifax. In Washington, Admiral King, whose headquarters (as we will see) had just assumed control of all shipping outside of Canadian coastal waters, rumbled a protest at Rear-Admiral Brodeur.[189] Worse was to follow. The RCN shuffled seven additional corvettes into the Halifax Force to bring it up to a strength of fourteen—twelve for the Caribbean convoys and two for the Labrador convoys—with effect from 7 July. The day before *U 132* had sunk three ships from QS 15 in the St Lawrence River. NSHQ immediately postponed the sailing of the second Halifax to Aruba convoy, HA 2, "owing to the urgent need for corvettes in the St. Lawrence," and proposed that, once the Aruba sailings began again the escort should be limited to three corvettes, the maximum that could be supplied in view of the need for six corvettes in the St Lawrence.[190]

The British, as in their advice earlier in the year, urged NSHQ not to allocate "these valuable ocean-going vessels" to the St Lawrence, but leave its defence to aircraft, Bangors, yachts, and Fairmiles.[191] Admiral King, for his part, doubted that escort groups of only three, and possibly fewer, corvettes could provide an adequate defence for the tanker convoys, and suggested that if the Canadians could not do better, then the enterprise should be abandoned, and all tankers routed through the US coastal convoy system.[192] NSHQ was willing to concede neither a reduction in the St Lawrence defences nor the end of separate, fast convoys to Aruba. The Canadian staff reminded King's headquarters that, given Canada's shortage of tankers, reliance on the slow US coastal route would cause critical fuel shortages, most immediately to the Allied fleets operating from Halifax and St John's. Canada could thus not agree to cancel the Halifax–Aruba sailings unless the US War Shipping Administration allocated additional tankers to the Canadian trade "to offset the delays

---

187. F.W. Gibson and B. Robertson (eds), *Ottawa at War: The Grant Dexter Memoranda, 1939-1945* (Winnipeg 1994), 331

188. Milner, *North Atlantic Run*, 124, and FONF to NSHQ, 16 June 1942, NAC, RG 24, 11969, NW223

189. Adm to ON 103, 28 June 1942, DHH, NSHQ Convoy Files, HA; and COAC to NSHQ, 2105z/30 June 1942, DHH, NSHQ Convoy Files, HA-AH. The British had twelve tankers for inclusion in HA 1; "Report of Mtg Held in Navy Department, Washington, 1 July 1942," NAC, RG 24, 11969, NW223. Brodeur was promoted Rear-Admiral on 1 July 1942.

190. NSHQ to CAFAC, CESF, and others, 1401z/8 July 1942, and NSHQ to Adm and COMINCH, 1506z/11 July 1942, NAC, RG 24,11973, S264-3-3

191. Adm to NSHQ, 0010b/13 July 1942, PRO, ADM 199/2083

192. COMINCH to Adm, 1239/13 July 1942, NAC, RG 24,11973, S264-3-3

caused by coastal convoys."[193] King ruled that if the Canadians persisted in running the Aruba convoys with escort groups of only three corvettes, then a maximum of eight tankers only could be included.[194] When the second Halifax–Aruba convoy, HA 2, finally sailed on 24 July, two weeks later than scheduled because of the delay caused by the deployment of corvettes to the gulf, it included three Canadian and four British tankers, and a Dutch ocean tug.[195]

Although the convoy sailed well clear of danger, the Halifax approaches were at that time again the focus of a U-boat concentration. From the north came *U 132* after its mission in the St. Lawrence. From the south there were *U 89, U 458,* and *U 754*, part of a group Dönitz had dispatched to the Cape Hatteras area in June. The group had not succeeded in finding much shipping because of the newly introduced US coastal convoys, and it had been roughly handled by the strengthened defences, especially shore-based aircraft. On 19 July Dönitz decided to abandon the now unproductive and dangerous US Atlantic seaboard and ordered these three boats to test the waters south of Halifax, that area having been unoccupied for some two weeks. The submarines found Nova Scotia waters no more promising for locating shipping than in the spring, and the defences were no less punishing than those off Hatteras. Together, the U-boats destroyed only one merchant vessel and two fishing craft, but all were attacked at least once by Eastern Air Command aircraft. One of these attacks, by a Lockheed Hudson piloted by Squadron Leader N.E. Small, commanding officer of No. 113 Squadron based at Yarmouth, destroyed *U 754* on 31 July, the first destruction of a U-boat by the RCAF (see Chapter 9).[196]

With the growth of the U-boat offensive in the western Atlantic, the Admiralty had delegated to NSHQ, with effect from 1 February 1942, responsibility for diverting clear of danger all shipping not bound for the United Kingdom or Gibraltar in the western Atlantic north of Bermuda.[197] The C-in-C America and West Indies exercised this function in the waters to the south of Bermuda, while continuing to control British warships in the western Atlantic that had not been assigned to Canadian control. This was why, when the USN proved unable to introduce convoys to protect the Commonwealth oil tanker traffic in the Caribbean, it was Canadian naval authorities, the British commander-in-chief in Bermuda, and the British naval control of shipping staffs in the West Indies that made and controlled all arrangements.[198] In Admiral King's eyes, this was precisely the sort of British strategic direction within the US sphere that he had always been determined to avoid. His sensitivity on this point explains the initiative he took in the negotiations with the Canadians and British over the protection of the Caribbean oil trade in the spring of 1942 to ensure that when diversion authority over Commonwealth shipping in the US sphere passed to the Navy Department on 1 July, US control would be complete. King made his concerns clear when Admiral Pound suggested that a senior British officer, of vice-admiral rank, was still needed at Bermuda to adminis-

---

193. NSHQ to COMINCH, 1421z/15 July 1942, ibid

194. NSHQ to CAFAC, 1614z/25 July 1942, ibid

195. COAC to Adm, 1317z and 1323z/24 July 1942, DHH, NSHQ Convoy Files

196. Douglas, *Creation of a National Air Force*, 519-21; Blair, *Hitler's U-Boat War*, 625-8

197. Farmer, Convoy and Routeing Section, "Report on Work of Diversion Office," 10 July 1942, NARA, RG 38, 370-46-32/4, f 1-5-33 Canada General

198. NSHQ, "Outline History of Trade Division ...," DHH, 35—speaking of the success of the Halifax-based oil tanker convoys to the Caribbean in the spring and summer of 1942: "The fact that no losses were sustained by them was a tribute to the work of the Diversion Rooms in Ottawa and Bermuda."

ter British warships operating under US control, and oversee the work of RN offices and establishments "in Central and South America as well as in Bermuda and British West Indian possessions," all subject to the agreements for overall US direction. Pound suggested the neutral title Senior British Naval Officer Western Atlantic for the flag appointment in Bermuda. King minuted "OK but 'SBNOWA' should *not be operational!*"[199]

When Admiral Nelles invited US and British representatives to a conference in Ottawa on 23 July to discuss means of overcoming the RCN's shortage of escorts, King was furious. Evidently the inclusion in the agenda of arrangements for the Halifax–Aruba convoys, which now sailed under US control, was what brought King to blast at Rear-Admiral Brodeur, the Canadian attaché in Washington, that NSHQ "was not fully recognizing him as in strategic control in certain areas outside Canadian coastal zone."[200] The lack of prior consultation with King's staff, and the "personal contacts" King noted between Captain Brand at NSHQ with the British Admiralty Delegation to Washington aroused the American admiral's suspicion that the two royal navies were conspiring "to reach a common British understanding" behind the Navy Department's back.[201] "Any meetings concerning their [the US] sphere of strategic control must be held in Washington not Canada!" a shaken Brodeur warned Nelles. "Their feelings or sensitivities are offended when we consult with Admiralty or BAD first!"[202] Only a special appeal from Brodeur convinced King's staff to send a representative to the Ottawa Conference.

Nevertheless, the conference was not without result. Following from its recommendations, SC convoys began to assemble at Halifax instead of Sydney starting with SC 95, which sailed in early August. Analysis of the convoys revealed that fully 61 percent of the ships that assembled at Sydney came from ports south of Halifax, mainly in the United States, and only 30 percent from the Gulf of St Lawrence. The change therefore allowed reductions in the escort service between Halifax and Sydney, freeing warships to strengthen the "variable" escort on the critically important Boston to Halifax run. In the matter of the Gulf of St Lawrence, whose defence was causing such difficulties for the RCN, "The conference unanimously agreed that from the escort point of view it would be most desirable for the maximum number of ships ... to load in Nova Scotian or New Brunswick ports in summer as well as in winter." So far as the controversial Halifax to Aruba tanker convoys were concerned, the conference concluded "that every effort should be made to continue" them because there were too few tankers to sustain adequate fuel supplies to Canada, Newfoundland, and the United Kingdom through the slow US coastal convoys. Admiral King had already been convinced of this. The conference proceedings tactfully concluded: "The situation regarding the HA–AH Convoys will be reviewed as soon as the US Authorities feel able to institute any form of direct Convoy between the West Indies and Northern US Ports."[203]

All this did nothing to meet British needs. Admiral Pound, warning of the impending oil supply crisis in the United Kingdom, immediately brought all the pressure he could to bear on Nelles and King greatly to expand the direct service for tankers from the Caribbean to northern ports. Captain

199. BAD to COMINCH, 23 Apr. 1942, with undated minute by King, E.J. King papers

200. Brodeur to CNS, 1508z/17 July 1942, NAC, RG 24, 11969, NW223

201. Ibid

202. Brodeur to CNS, 21 July 1942, NAC, RG 24, 11969, NW223

203. SecNB to Adm and COMINCH, 25 July 1942, forwarding "Minutes of Ottawa Conference on Trade and Escort Problems, 23-24 July, 1942," DHH 89/100 folder 8A [NARA, RG 38, box 152]; Tennyson and Sarty, *Guardian of the Gulf*, 267-8

H.W. Morey, RN, Staff Officer (Trade) at the BAD, pulled together the bits of common ground between the Canadians and Americans and hammered together a sweeping proposal. In essence, he followed to a logical conclusion the recent decision of the Ottawa conference to shift the assembly port of the SC convoys southward to Halifax to allow more efficient movement of shipping from US ports. Assembly for both the HX and SC transatlantic convoys, Morey suggested, should be shifted all the way to New York, as the bulk of not just tanker, but all shipping, now originated there or at ports to the south, and there would be a saving in the voyage to the UK of the four days lost in the slow movement through coastal convoys up to Halifax. In the Caribbean, the northern terminus of the convoy from Trinidad and Aruba (TAW–WAT) should be moved south from Key West to Guantanamo, the American base in Cuba, which by greatly shortening the run to Trinidad would release British escorts used in this service. These escorts, together with the Canadian ones used on the Halifax to Aruba run would be sufficient to create a larger and more frequent direct tanker convoy on the considerably shorter Guantanamo to New York route.[204]

Admiral King accepted the British proposals, providing as they did the increased escort strength that he was convinced was essential. Indeed, King, who called a conference in Washington for 1 August, was prepared to go further because more US escorts were becoming available than had previously been projected. The USN had recently organized the east–west through Caribbean convoy from Panama to Guantanamo that the British had always wanted and was now prepared to extend convoy into the Gulf of Mexico, thus creating the complete integrated system that had long been the goal of both British and US planners.[205] Brand, who represented the RCN, later recalled the rapid pace of these developments and his elation: "On 30th [July] I had to go to New York for half a day and then on to Washington for a meeting which lasted all Saturday. This was the best I had been to and was to set up coastal convoys at last. Left them with my 'Railway' train graph system for working out Convoy schedules just as they do trains and caught the 6:00 train to NY and the 11:15 home on the Saturday night.'"[206] The Admiralty, for its part, had responded to King's initiative with visible relief: "On proposed convoys we have no comments to offer. They give everything we could ask."[207]

The nub of the new scheme was the development of New York as the main shipping entrepot. It would now be both the destination of vessels coming from the south in the US coastal convoy system and the main assembly point for transatlantic convoys. The new US coastal convoys were scheduled to start 1 September. Thereafter, the Naval Control Service would begin to hold vessels bound for the United Kingdom at New York, rather than sending them to Boston and Halifax; the first transatlantic convoys to sail from New York would be HX 208, on 17 September, and SC 102 on the 18th. The convoys would be routed close to Nova Scotia, so that fast ships loaded at Canadian ports could join in a feeder convoy, "HHX" from Halifax, and slow ships would similarly come out from Sydney in "SSC" feeder convoys. Thus, the new arrangements would in no way delay the sailing of ships that loaded in Canada, while speeding the passage of those—the majority—that originated from US ports.[208]

---

204. BAD to Adm, 2143z/28 July 1942, PRO, MT 59/1998

205. COMINCH to Adm and NSHQ, 2145/28 July 1942, NAC, RG 24, 3974, NSS 1048-48-27, v 1

206. Brand journals, ch 33, 55, DHH, Brand papers

207. Adm to COMINCH, 0101b/30 July 1942, NAC, RG 24, 11968, S221 pt 1

208. SecNB to COAC, "Rearrangement Convoys East Coast of North America," 3 Aug. 1942, DHH 81/520/8280B pt 3; ESF WD, Aug. 1942, "Chapter IV: The Convoy System Revised," DHH 85/588 mfm reel 3

The effect of the change to New York, Brand estimated, would be to reduce by as much as 65 percent the number of ships coming into Halifax for convoy. "You will realize," explained NSHQ when it promulgated the results of the conference to the commands, "that the decision to move the main assembly ports to New York was not taken without the most careful thought. It involves the partial abandonment of many facilities for ocean convoy assembly which have been labouriously built up in Halifax and Sydney during the past three years."[209] Yet, the dependence of the British Commonwealth on supplies from the United States, and the global shortage of escorts that had resulted in the RCN taking such a large share in the protection of those shipments, allowed no other choice. "It is clear ... that under the existing circumstances where we are forced to escort ships up and down the American coast that the new arrangement should very considerably speed up the movements of ships and might possibly result in a slight saving in escort forces."[210]

The scheme, like all measures for the antisubmarine escort of shipping across the Atlantic since the spring of 1941, was utterly dependent upon the Royal Canadian Navy. The Western Local Escort Force would now conduct the HX, SC, ON, and ONS series for the entire distance between New York to the waters east of Newfoundland, a distance of some 1,100 miles, fully a third of the full ocean crossing. Yet the logic was irresistible. With the savings in escort time through the reduction or elimination of the Halifax–Boston run, and those already being realized through the reduction in the Halifax–Sydney run, the WLEF could cover the additional distance to New York with its existing strength. As part of the agreement reached in Washington, the RCN also committed the six corvettes it was employing on the Halifax–Aruba convoy to the new New York–Guantanamo tanker service. Although the corvettes would be operating under US control, the Americans promised that the ships would be released "should enemy activity render their return to the Canadian coastal zone essential."[211]

During and immediately after the Washington Conference, the means for resolving Canada's oil supply crisis began to become available from the enormous resources of the United States. The Wartime Shipping Administration was finally able to respond to the repeated pleas from Ottawa for additional tankers, assigning a total of thirteen vessels to the Canadian Oil Controller, more than doubling the size of the available fleet.[212] Also, during the first part of August NSHQ and the Oil Controller were able to arrange for Canadian tankers to proceed by way of the US coastal convoy network direct from Portland, Maine, to Gulf of Mexico ports to load the crude for lubricants that were unobtainable in Venezuela. As a result of the urgent need to take advantage of these supplies, only two Canadian tankers, together with five British, were included in HA 3, which sailed from Halifax on 13 August.[213] This was to be the last RCN escorted convoy from Halifax to the Caribbean, and like all the others it arrived, at Aruba on 22 August, without loss, having been routed by the Navy Department clear of U-boats that were north of the Netherlands Antilles.[214] This safe

209. Director of Trade Division to Director of Merchant Seamen, Commissioner of Immigration, et al, 8 Aug. 1942, DHH 81/520/8280B pt 3

210. SecNB to COAC, "Rearrangement Convoys East Coast of North America"

211. Ibid

212. C.D. Howe to CNS, 31 July 1942; Capt E.S. Brand to British Routing Officers, East Coast, 10 Aug. 1942, NAC, RG 24, 6789, NSS 8280-800/9

213. NSHQ to Adm, 2010z/4 Aug. 1942, DHH, NSHQ Convoy Files, HA–AH. Access to gulf oil ports may have been granted at the Washington Conference, 1-2 Aug. to compensate for the termination of the tanker run.

214. CONNAV to *Halifax*, 1639Z/20 Aug. 1942, DHH, NSHQ Convoy Files, HA–AH; *Halifax* ROP, HA 3, DHH, Convoy Reports, 89/34, v 6

passage was only the prelude to events that would mark the high point, in terms of contact with the enemy, for the Canadian effort in the Caribbean.

Partly as a result of the introduction of the Trinidad–Aruba–Key West run early in July, losses in the Caribbean and Gulf of Mexico had fallen to thirty-three ships that month, but in August they were climbing again and would reach a total of forty-six.[215] This sharp increase was largely the work of a group of U-boats dispatched by Dönitz from Germany at the end of June, refuelled from a submarine tanker southeast of Bermuda. The recently introduced convoys in the West Indies perplexed Dönitz. Ships sailing independently would be scarce and "wolf-pack tactics could not be applied in these narrow, coastal waters, which were now under strong and constant air patrol." As a result, he decided on a compromise, and used "this new group for independent enterprises or for combined attack, as opportunity offered." Recognizing that "the geographical conformation of the islands forced the convoys to follow certain, well-defined tracks," he concentrated his force on the focal points, and in particular, the Windward Passage.[216]

This strategy bore fruit. It made "the approaches to the Windward Passage ... as dangerous for shipping as any part of the ocean."[217] In the space of seven days, submarines torpedoed twelve merchant ships, sinking eleven. *U 598* and *U 600* combined to form the first "wolf pack" in these waters and torpedoed five ships in TAW 12, while *U 162* and *U 564* teamed to sink three ships from TAW Slow.[218] The slaughter of the Trinidad–Key West convoys was clear evidence that German submarines were no longer reluctant to attempt combined attacks on convoyed vessels in Caribbean waters.

Given these disastrous developments, it is not surprising that American officials at Aruba–Curaçao searched for additional escorts. When *Halifax*, *Oakville*, and *Snowberry* arrived at Willemstad with HA 3 on 23 August, Commander Allied Forces Aruba–Curaçao, a US officer, assigned them to bolster the escort of TAW 15 between Aruba and Key West. The three corvettes and the Dutch minelayer, HNMS *Jan Van Brakel,* sailed from Curaçao on 25 August with nineteen ships from that port, and later that afternoon linked up with the Trinidad section of TAW 15, twelve merchant ships escorted by the destroyer USS *Lea* (Commander J.F. Walsh, USN, SOE), and four smaller American ships, *PC 559*, *SC 449*, *SC 506,* and *SC 522*.[219]

Two submarines lurked near the convoy's path. On 26 August Dönitz had given *U 511* freedom of action within a 300 mile radius of Kingston, Jamaica. The day before Dönitz had allocated a broad operational area centring on Cuba to *U 94*, and during the 27th this boat stalked the southern approaches to the Windward Passage.[220] *U 94* was a veteran type VIIC boat, on her tenth war cruise. She was commanded by Oberleutnant Otto Ites who, although only twenty-four years old, was an experienced and successful U-boat captain. Since taking command, Ites had torpedoed fourteen ships of almost 80,000 tons and was awarded the Knight's Cross of the Iron Cross in April 1942 for his exploits.[221]

---

215. Morison, *Battle of the Atlantic*, 410-13

216. Dönitz, *Memoirs*, 251

217. Morison, *Battle of the Atlantic*, 348

218. Adm, Trade Division Monthly Reports, Aug. 1942, PRO, ADM 199/2083, and Rohwer, *Axis Submarine Successes*, 115-17

219. *Halifax* ROP, TAW 15, 16 Jan. 1943, DHH, Sydney File 48-2-2, v 9, and USS *Lea*, Submarine Attack on TAW 15, NAC, RG 24, 6902, NSS 8910-331/71

220. BdU, KTB, 24-8 Aug. 1942

221. USND, *Post Mortems on Enemy Submarines*, V: *Report on the Interrogation of Survivors of U 94* (Washington 1942), 2-3; and Rohwer, *Axis Submarine Successes*, 58-102

The presence of flying boats during the morning of the 27th led Ites to suspect the approach of a convoy. Despite close aerial surveillance, *U 94* escaped detection. The stragglers may have given away TAW 15's position because Ites sighted the convoy at 1830z and gave chase. *U 94* shadowed TAW 15 throughout the afternoon and evening, signalling regular reports on its progress to BdU, who in turn relayed the position, course, and speed of the convoy to Kapitänleutnant F. Steinhoff, captain of *U 511*. At 0232z, on the morning of 28 August, *U 94* reported TAW 15 in quadrant EC-1614 and closed to attack.[222] Conditions were favourable, the night moonlit and bright. *U 94* crept towards the convoy's port bow trimmed down. Ites informed his executive officer that they would "wait until the last minute" before submerging if an aircraft was sighted.[223] Walsh had positioned his screen about 5,000 yards from the convoy. HNMS *Jan Van Brakel* was stationed ahead, *Halifax*, *SC 506,* and *PC 559* covered the starboard column, *SC 522* was stationed astern and, beyond her, USS *Lea* swept at long range. *Snowberry* screened ahead on the port bow and *Oakville* patrolled the port quarter. *SC 449* was between the two RCN corvettes on the port beam, but not actively patrolling her sector because of "limited fuel capacity."[224]

U 94 penetrated the screen between *Snowberry* and *Oakville*. Ites selected a target but, as he prepared to fire, a lookout sighted an aircraft. *U 94* crash-dived. The aircraft, a Catalina of Patrol Squadron 92, piloted by Lieutenant Gordon R. Fiss, USN, swept in and dropped four 650-pound depth-bombs on the swirl from an altitude of fifty feet. These exploded when the U-boat was between thirty and sixty feet beneath the surface. Unknown to the crew, the depth-bombs had blown the bow hydroplanes off *U 94*, crippling her ability to dive.[225] *Oakville* heard three explosions and saw a column of water one mile ahead. The corvette altered course and increased speed to fifteen knots. Lieutenant Fiss signalled the corvette and circled back to drop a flare along the probable course of the U-boat.[226]

Sub-Lieutenant E.G. Scott, RCNVR, the officer of the watch, summoned *Oakville*'s captain, Lieutenant-Commander Clarence A. King, RCNR, who called his crew to action stations. King knew what he was about. During the First World War he had served in the Royal Naval Reserve and rose to the rank of lieutenant. As captain of a Q-ship, King was credited with the destruction of one enemy submarine and two possible kills and was awarded the Distinguished Service Cross for his efforts—ultimately, no U-boat was confirmed destroyed on the day King claimed. During the interwar years he farmed in the Okanagan Valley in British Columbia. In 1939 King rejoined the RNR, serving ashore in Panama and Bermuda, but despite his fifty-five years he wanted to serve at sea and transferred to the RCNR in January 1942 to fulfil this ambition, and assumed command of *Oakville* in May 1942.[227]

King closed at full speed and dropped a pattern of five depth charges, set at a hundred feet, close to where Fiss had dropped his flare. He then reduced to search speed and was immediately rewarded with a firm asdic contact. Less than a minute later, the submarine surfaced about a hundred

221. USND, *Post Mortems on Enemy Submarines*, V: *Report on the Interrogation of Survivors of U 94* (Washington 1942), 2-3; and Rohwer, *Axis Submarine Successes*, 58-102

222. BdU, KTB, 27-8 Aug. 1942

223. USND, *Post Mortems* V, 15

224. USS *Lea*, Submarine Attack on TAW 15

225. USND, *Post Mortems* V, 15-16

226. *Oakville* ROP, TAW 15, 29 Aug. 1942, NAC, RG 24, 6902, NSS 8910-331/71

227. Records in C.A. King's DHH Biog file

metres ahead on the starboard bow, heading left. *Oakville* fired two white rockets to signal the U-boat's presence and altered course to ram, but the submarine, not yet fully surfaced, passed under her bow. Immediately, King went hard a-port and the U-boat grazed the corvette's port side.[228]

After this glancing blow, Ites ordered emergency speed to escape on the surface. The damaged submarine, however, could only make twelve knots.[229] *Oakville*'s 4-inch gun opened fire, and one round hit the U-boat's conning tower. German gunners tried to reach their weapons, but the corvette's Oerlikon, Lewis gun, and .5-inch machine-guns raked the deck "making it impossible for the submarine to man any gun throughout the action." The U-boat passed ahead to starboard and King again altered course to ram. A 4-inch shell blew away the enemy's 88-mm deck gun as the corvette bore down. Once again, the Canadian warship's hull struck the submarine only a glancing blow. Too close to *U 94* for *Oakville*'s guns to depress onto target, King fired depth charges and one exploded directly below the U-boat, which "rapidly decreased speed."[230]

King increased the distance between the two vessels and swung around to ram once again. Ites decided, apparently after the second ramming, to give up the fight. Despite a bullet wound in his leg, he climbed below deck and ordered his crew to abandon ship.[231] *Oakville* bore in upon the submarine and rammed it "squarely abaft the conning tower" at 0345z. The Canadian crew felt three distinct shocks as the corvette ran right over the battered U-boat.[232] King brought his ship around and pulled her port side along *U 94* and ordered away the boarding party. In fairly difficult sea conditions Sub-Lieutenant Hal Lawrence, RCNVR, and Stoker Petty Officer Art Powell, RCN, leapt from the corvette and landed on board the forward deck of the stricken submarine, a drop of eight feet.[233]

Lawrence and Powell turned for the conning tower, "riddled with bullet holes." Two Germans on the port side offered no resistance, and Lawrence ordered them over the side. Two more submariners emerged through the escape hatch. The young officer gestured to them with his hand gun to stay below but they continued to advance, and when they lunged at them, Lawrence and Powell shot them; survivors later suggested that they were trying to surrender. While Powell guarded the hatch, Lawrence found another submariner crouching behind the conning tower and forced him overboard. Lawrence led the crew out of the submarine and the petty officer herded them aft, as the boarding officer went below. He searched the compartment, but could find little of value in the darkness and descended to the lower deck. This was flooded to about four feet from the deck head and permeated by gaseous fumes. When *U 94* suddenly began settling by the stern, Powell told Lawrence he had better get up, "we're sinking," and ordered the prisoners over the side. Lawrence returned to the deck, and at approximately 0400z, the submarine sank by the stern, her bow rising high above the sea then silently settling beneath the surface.[234]

---

228. *Oakville* ROP, TAW 15

229. USND, *Post Mortems* V, 16-17

230. *Oakville* ROP, TAW 15, and H.E. Lawrence, *A Bloody War* (Toronto 1979), 98-9

231. USND, *Post Mortems* V, 15-16

232. *Oakville* ROP, TAW 15

233. Ibid, and Lawrence, *A Bloody War*, 99-100. King drilled his crew regularly at action stations, boarding party, man overboard, and abandon ship exercises. The deck log shows that boarding party drills had been practised as recently as 31 July and 19-20 Aug. 1942. *Oakville*, deck log, July-Aug. 1942, NAC, RG 24, 7703

234. SLt H.E. Lawrence, RCNVR, Report of Boarding *U 94*, 29 Aug. 1942, NAC, RG 24, 6902, NSS 8910-331/71; Lawrence, *Bloody War*, 99-103; interview with Chief Stoker Arthur Powell, DSM, in Jean E. Portugal, *We Were There: A Record for Canada* I: *The Navy* (Toronto 1998), 133-6. In his memoirs (in DHH, Biog files), John D. Henderson recalls that boarding parties were instructed to shoot the first two Germans they encountered.

After the departure of the boarding party, *Oakville* opened the range to about 100 metres. The port sea boat was lowered, under the command of Sub-Lieutenant K.D. Fenwick, RCNR, to rescue the boarders and Germans. King also requested help from the nearby *Lea*, and her boat arrived as *U 94* sank. Ultimately, *Lea* recovered twenty-one survivors from *U 94* and *Oakville* five; Ites and a mechanic, probably the first Germans forced overboard by Lawrence, swam to the corvette. Of the boarding party, Powell later recalled, "It was dark and suddenly there was a light on us and we heard a motor launch approaching ... I heard a call 'Where are those Canadians?' and finally they were close enough and they picked us up before the Germans. Then the Jerries were picked up. They were trying to get on first. They took us to the *Lea* and then back to our own ship."[235] As the rescue proceeded, *Oakville*'s crew assessed the extent of her damage, most of it to her forward section. The asdic dome and oscillator had been crushed, and water flooded the asdic compartment. More seriously, the after boiler room was flooded, and the main bulk head had to be shored-up. Despite the damage, King informed *Lea* that *Oakville* could make Guantanamo under her own power.[236]

In the midst of the excitement, another nearby U-boat threatened TAW 15. Shortly after hearing Ites's sighting report, *U 511* had altered course to intercept, finally homing on tracer fired at *U 94*. Steinhoff hoped to create a diversion but arrived too late, making contact at 0415z, fifteen minutes after *U 94* went to the bottom. As the convoy approached the southwestern tip of Haiti, *U 511* crept in on the port bow close to *Snowberry*. Exploiting the gap in the screen caused by *Oakville*'s absence, Steinhoff manoeuvered behind *Snowberry* at a range of 1,000 metres, and at 0430z fired a spread of four torpedoes at the convoy. Steinhoff then turned sharply to port, fired a stern salvo at a large tanker and crash-dived.[237]

Snowberry heard three explosions as torpedoes struck three tankers, *San Fabian* and *Rotterdam*, the first two ships in the second column, and *Esso Aruba*, the first ship in the third column. The first two sank immediately, but the latter remained afloat and managed to continue under her own power. *Snowberry* fired two white rockets and conducted a starshell search on the port side of the convoy. In the absence of *Oakville*, the corvette executed an extended antisubmarine sweep off the port quarter and closed the port column, sweeping up the side of the convoy. *Snowberry* saw nothing (defects plagued her radar) and made no asdic contacts.[238] The remaining escorts searched their stations but discovered no trace of the escaping U-boat. *SC 522* recovered fifty-nine survivors from the two sinking ships. At 0530z, the escorts gave up the hunt and TAW 15 resumed its normal course.[239] *U 511* surfaced at twenty minutes later, sighted an escort screening the damaged SS *Esso Aruba* three or four kilometres distant, and two more escorts another two to three kilometres away. Steinhoff mistakenly assumed the tanker was sinking, and retired south of Haiti to repair damage suffered during the crash-dive.[240]

235. Powell interview

236. *Oakville* ROP, TAW 15, and USS *Lea*,
     Submarine Attack on TAW 15

237. *U 511*, KTB, 28 Aug. 1942

238. *Snowberry* ROP, 31 Aug. 1942, DHH, 81/520 Snowberry 8000

239. USS *Lea*, Submarine Attack on TAW 15

240. *U 511*, KTB, 28 Aug. 1942

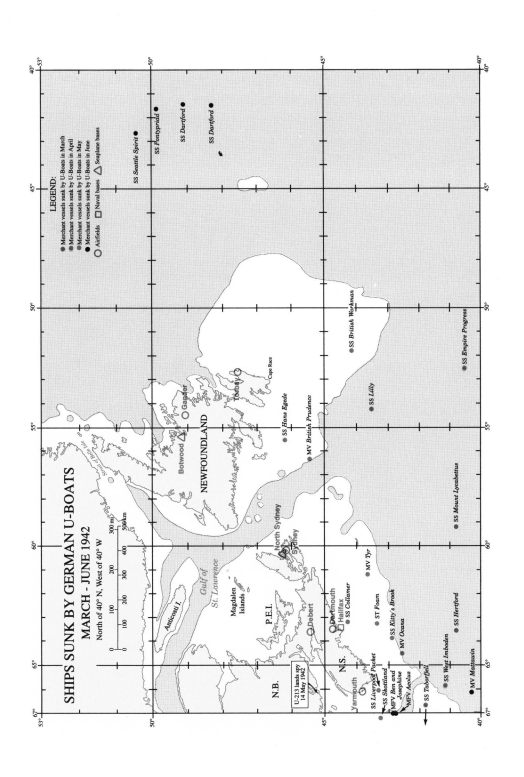

SHIPS SUNK BY GERMAN U-BOATS
MARCH - JUNE 1942
North of 40° N, West of 40° W

LEGEND:
● Merchant vessels sunk by U-Boats in March
● Merchant vessels sunk by U-Boats in April
● Merchant vessels sunk by U-Boats in May
● Merchant vessels sunk by U-Boats in June
○ Airfields   □ Naval bases   △ Seaplane bases

SS Seattle Spirit ●
SS Pontypridd ●
SS Dartford ●
SS Dartford ●

SS British Workman ●
SS Empire Progress ●
SS Lilly ●

SS Hans Egede ●
MV British Prudence ●

Cape Race
Torbay ○
Gander ○
Botwood △
NEWFOUNDLAND

SS Mount Lycabettus ●

North Sydney □
Sydney

Gulf of
St. Lawrence

Anticosti I.
Magdalen Islands
P.E.I.
Debert ○

N.B.

Strait of Belle Isle

U-213 lands spy
14 May 1942

MV Tyr ●
SS Collamer ●
ST Foam ●
SS Kitty's Brook ●
MV Ocana ●

Dartmouth ○
Halifax □

N.S.
Yarmouth ○

SS Liverpool Packet ●
SS Shottland ●
MFV Ben and
Josephine ●
MFV Aeolus ●

SS Taborfjell ●
SS West Imboden ●
SS Hertford ●
MV Mattawin ●

0   100   200   300   400   500km
0   100   200   300 mi.

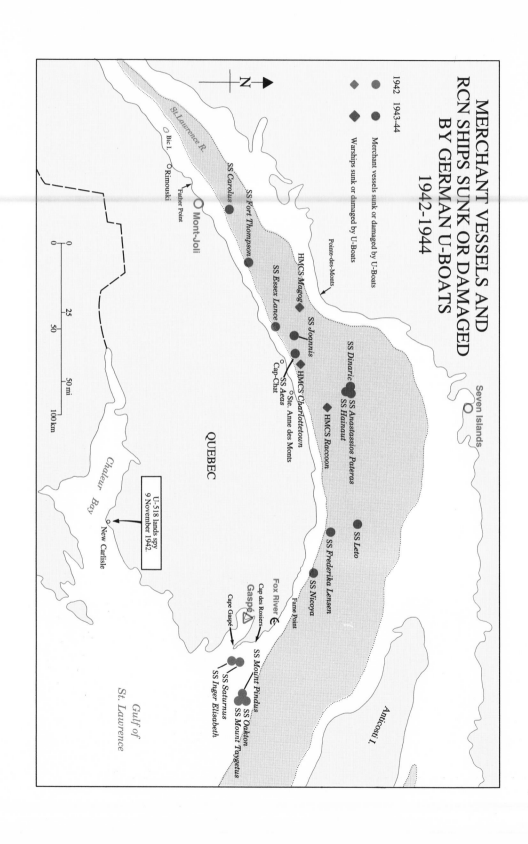

MERCHANT VESSELS AND
RCN SHIPS SUNK OR DAMAGED
BY GERMAN U-BOATS
1942-1944

1942   1943-44

Merchant vessels sunk or damaged by U-Boats

Warships sunk or damaged by U-Boats

N

St. Lawrence R.

Bic I.

Rimouski

Father Point

Mont-Joli

SS Carolus

SS Fort Thompson

Pointe-des-Monts

HMCS Magog

SS Essex Lance

SS Joannis

Cap-Chat

SS Aeas

Ste. Anne des Monts

HMCS Charlottetown

SS Dinaric

SS Anastassios Pateras

SS Hainaut

HMCS Raccoon

SS Leto

QUEBEC

U-518 lands spy
9 November 1942

New Carlisle

Chaleur Bay

SS Frederika Lensen

SS Nicoya

Fox River

Cap des Rosiers

Faine Point

Gaspé

Cape Gaspé

SS Mount Pindus

SS Oakton

SS Saturnus

SS Mount Taygetus

SS Inger Elisabeth

Seven Islands

Anticosti I.

Gulf
of
St. Lawrence

0

0

25

50

50 mi

100 km

A/S James Luke, RDF operator, HMCS *Oakville*, autumn 1942. (CFPU WO99-0131)

HMCS *Oakville* in refit,
Halifax, autumn 1942.
(CFPU WO99-0131)

Oakville limped into Guantanamo Harbour during the afternoon of 28 August, and the convoy arrived at Key West, without further incident, on 31 August. *Halifax* had sailed independently on 30 August from Guantanamo, the new southern terminus for Canadian ships on the Caribbean run, to join *Snowberry* for service with the CESF.[241] These corvettes, along with *Fredericton*, *Sudbury*, and *The Pas*, would now escort American coastal convoys from Guantanamo and Key West to New York. *Oakville* received basic repairs and was then able to sail north for refit.

The sinking of *U 94* marked the climax of the Caribbean campaign for the Royal Canadian Navy. The month of August also marked a turning point in the submarine war against shipping in the West Indies. Allied warships and aircraft destroyed three German submarines in the region. With the adoption of convoy in the Caribbean Sea and the Gulf of Mexico, "these waters became less favourable for the conduct of U-boat warfare." As a result, Dönitz decided that "it was no longer worthwhile continuing to regard them as the main theatre in U-boat operations" and shifted the main thrust of the submarine attack back to the North Atlantic convoys.[242]

This was not an abandonment of coastal waters in the Western Atlantic. With over 200 U-boats in operation—nearly double the number at the beginning of the year—Dönitz was able to continue to press in distant theatres while concentrating his main force in the central North Atlantic.[243] Such distant operations, by compelling the Allies to disperse their forces, directly supported Dönitz's renewed concentration against the main convoys between North America and the United Kingdom. As will be seen in the next chapter, these considerations would be instrumental in influencing Canada's response, both military and political, to the German submarine threat in the Gulf of St Lawrence.

---

241. *Halifax* ROP, TAW 15

242. Dönitz, *Memoirs*, 237

243. AHS, *Defeat of the Enemy Attack on Shipping*, IB, plan 7

Top: In 1942 the RCN established the Women's Royal Canadian Naval Service. These are members of the First Class at Kingsmill House, Ottawa, 24 September 1942. (NAC, PA 207683)

Bottom: Rear-Admiral H.E. Reid and Superintendent J. Carpenter inspect the graduating class, September 1942. (NAC, PA 207685)

CHAPTER EIGHT

The Battle of the St Lawrence
February 1942 to December 1943

BETWEEN FEBRUARY AND MAY 1942 improved defences in the western Atlantic first persuaded Dönitz to shift the weight of the submarine effort to less protected areas. For their part, the Canadian Naval Staff and operational authorities, besides committing Canadian escorts to their new convoy tasks between Halifax, Boston, New York, and the Caribbean, were bracing for an expected U-boat offensive in the Gulf of St Lawrence.

Like the Caribbean, the Gulf offered broad waters where heavy steamer traffic had to follow routes circumscribed by islands and shorelines, where submarines could wait to ambush shipping and then readily evade detection from the weak escort forces that Dönitz believed to be on hand. Important Canadian interests were at stake. The Gulf and the St Lawrence River—virtually an inland sea thrusting deep into the industrial and transportation heartland of the eastern part of the country, its waters surrounding the province of Prince Edward Island, and washing upon long shorelines of Newfoundland, Nova Scotia, New Brunswick, and Québec—was the main artery in summer and autumn for ocean-going shipping that carried Canadian goods overseas and for steamer traffic that sustained local populations and industries.

It was in the face of these concerns that the RCN tended to act unilaterally, and it was because commitments to the Caribbean, St Lawrence, and mid-ocean convoys competed for the same limited pool of escorts in the Royal Canadian Navy's thinly stretched inventory of hastily commissioned, new construction warships, that conflicts between Canadian and Allied priorities created some tension. Ultimately this was resolved by the closer integration of Canadian convoys into the expanding American system during the late summer of 1942. Partly as a result of that pooling of Allied resources, Canada would respond with striking readiness to British pleas that the RCN lay aside national concerns and assign precious escorts from the home defence forces to the Allied invasion of North Africa. In fact, the RCN's insistence on national priorities in response to the oil supply crisis, and the menace in the St Lawrence, proved to be only a brief departure from the unstinting support Canada had given to Allied needs since May 1940, and would continue to give until the end of the war.

The U-boat campaign in the Gulf of St Lawrence, for all its immediate significance to Canada and subsequent importance for German operations, began by happenstance. (See map at page 460.) *U 553*, as we have seen, suffered damage in an encounter with escorts south of Newfoundland in early May 1942. Additional, more serious mechanical defects, also required repairs, and Kapitänleutnant Thurmann concluded that he could not do this while continuing with his assigned mission in the well-defended approaches to Halifax. He correctly anticipated he could find a quieter area, while still remaining handy to the heavy steamer traffic in coastal waters, if he went instead into the Gulf of St Lawrence, from which the winter ice had recently cleared and where the shipping season was just getting under way. During the early hours of 12 May, arriving off the north shore of the Gaspé Peninsula, Thurmann found and sank SS *Nicoya* and then SS *Leto*. Both ships had sailed from Montréal on the 10th, and were making their way independently for Halifax and Sydney respectively to join transatlantic convoys.[1]

Nicoya, which did not sink until Thurmann fired a *coup de grace* nineteen minutes after the initial attack, went down slowly enough that her crew got away in boats and later came ashore at the Gaspé hamlets of Cloridorme and L'Anse-à-Valleau, where the local people rendered such immediate and complete assistance that the RCMP officers who arrived on the scene reported that there was nothing they need do to look after the survivors.[2] Of the eighty-seven people on board, six were lost. *Leto*, which Thurmann attacked further to the west off Cap-de-la-Madeleine, two-and-a-half hours later, went down quickly. Only a small boat and a life-raft got clear; many of her people went into the water. *Dutch Mass* and *Titus*, two independently sailed freighters, came across *Leto*'s survivors and rescued them within "about two hours," but twelve among the forty-three who had been on board were missing or known to have died.[3] The rescue ships themselves had probably been the targets of a third attack by Thurmann, which took place fifty-two minutes after his shot at *Leto* and in the same vicinity. *U 553* had been operating on the surface throughout the night, but because of the lightening sky submerged for this final attack. Thurmann reported he had hit one of the ships and claimed a sinking, but he had not been able to see the ship go down because of the "misty" conditions.[4]

The sinkings were a shock, but hardly a surprise. Only seven weeks before, on 25 March 1942, the prime minister had announced to the House of Commons that "officers of the Canadian naval service have expressed the view that within a few months submarines may well be found operating within the Gulf, and even in the St. Lawrence river."[5] King had been warning of the vulnerability of

---

1. Unless otherwise stated the information in the following paragraph is from the forms "Particulars of Attacks on Merchant Vessels by Enemy Submarines," for *Nicoya* and *Leto*, both stamped 19 May 1942, NAC, RG 24, 4025, NSS 1062-13-10, v 9, and the forms "Shipping Casualties ... Founderings ... Nicoya," and "Shipping Casualties ... Founderings ... Leto," both endorsed "Entered May 30/42," NAC, RG 12, 887. These sources correct Sarty, *Canada and the Battle of the Atlantic*, 104, which states both ships were Dutch, and under charter to the British MWT. That was true only of *Leto*. *Nicoya*'s owners were Elder and Fyffes Ltd, London, England, and the vessel had been requisitioned by the MWT.

2. *U 553*, KTB, 12 May 1942; Sarty, *Canada and the Battle of the Atlantic*, 104

3. "Ottawa Has No Reports of Sub in St Lawrence Taking Additional Toll," *Hamilton Spectator*, 14 May 1942, clipping in Canadian War Museum, HSC, reporting on an interview with two of the *Leto* survivors who were in the water. As the "two hours" included the time that would have been required to search for and recover the people clinging to flotsam, *Dutch Mass* and *Titus* were likely following *Leto* by an hour or less.

4. Sarty, *Canada and the Battle of the Atlantic*, 104

5. HofC, *Debates*, 25 Mar. 1942, 1630

the St Lawrence to just this kind of attack since the mid-1930s in an effort to find common ground between isolationists, especially those in French Canada, who believed the conflicts in Europe and the Far East were no affair of Canada's, and those, largely among English-speaking Canadians, who called for open-ended overseas military commitments and denigrated the emphasis the prime minister placed on the need for strong forces in Canada. In the spring of 1942, King was struggling to reconcile these conflicting convictions as never before, fighting for the political survival of his government. From this perspective, Thurmann's initiative could not have been better timed.

In the face of enormous pressure from English Canada, King had been forced to hold a plebiscite on 27 April 1942 asking whether the country would release the government from its pledge not to send overseas men conscripted for home defence duty in the army. That pledge had really been made to French-speaking Québeckers, and King made a last-ditch appeal to them on the eve of the vote. So great was the Axis threat, he argued, that the government had to have complete freedom of action as to where to send Canadian forces, although that did not necessarily meant that conscripts would ever be sent overseas, leaving Canada's own coasts unprotected. "The Canadian army is in Britain" King emphasised, "for exactly the same reason as the troops of the United States are now also in the British Isles, and for exactly the same reason as the troops of the United States are in Australia. They are there to help preserve freedom in this world, to keep the enemy away from this continent."[6]

In Québec this argument fell on deaf ears. The plebiscite brought an overwhelming "Yes" in all eight predominantly English-speaking provinces, but Québeckers voted "No" by an equally resounding margin. On 12 May, just as King was girding himself for the grim task of meeting the divided Liberal caucus, and to interpret the unhappy results of the plebiscite in such a way as to win himself some room for manoeuvre, he got word of Thurmann's exploits. The news from Gaspé magically revived his spirits; it was "evidence of guidance"—intervention on King's behalf from the spirit world. He revealed the sinkings to the caucus as dramatically as he could.[7] The next day, he mused that he could "imagine nothing more fortunate for the larger outlook" than the timing of *U 553*'s successes. "Several lives have been lost which would bring home the whole situation to the people as nothing else. We simply cannot believe that this war is [not] likely to reach our shores."[8] Thurmann had, or so it seemed to the prime minister, justified the government's political balancing act.

At about the time King was breaking the news to the Liberal caucus, Naval Service Headquarters issued a press release.

> The first enemy submarine attack upon shipping in the St Lawrence River took place on the [night of] the 11th of May, when a freighter was sunk. Forty-one survivors have been landed from this vessel. The situation regarding shipping in the river is being closely watched, and long prepared plans for its special protection under these circumstances are in operation.

This was to be the last early release of information that the government would make: "Any possible future sinkings in this area [concluded the press release] will not be made public, in order

---

6.   W.L. Mackenzie King, *Canada and the Fight for Freedom* (Toronto 1944), 149-52

7.   Mackenzie King diary, 12 May 1942

8.   Ibid, 13 May 1942

that information of value to the enemy may be withheld from him."[9] It was an odd statement. It suggested that although in this particular instance immediate confirmation by the government of an enemy success would not give him useful information, in future similar announcements would not be made because they would be helpful to the enemy. Yet the very next day the naval minister rose in the House of Commons to announce the loss of the second vessel, arguing that it was simply part of a single incident, that did "not come within the scope of the prohibition which I laid upon myself yesterday."[10]

There seems to have been more bluster than logic in the rationalization Macdonald continued to offer for breaking his own rules, and the navy accepted he was making the announcements "for political reasons."[11] But the speed with which the government confirmed the sinkings, naval authorities believed, stimulated more than necessary interest in the media. By putting the events in the public domain, Macdonald opened the way to publication of moving, and at times hair-raising, accounts from the survivors. They did not name the ships or identify the precise area where the sinkings took place, but they did provide some tactical detail and left no doubt that the ships had been caught by surprise in an area their crews considered to be completely safe from attack.[12]

Naval intelligence and censorship authorities may have been dismayed, but the government, and especially the prime minister, had every reason to be pleased. The Opposition never homed in on the essential reason for Macdonald's convoluted statements in the House, that the government was making a selective release of military information in order to bolster the credibility of its intention to continue conscription for home service only, despite the results of the plebiscite. Rather, the Opposition speakers, primarily R.B. Hanson, the Conservative leader, and T.L. Church, the Conservative member for Toronto-Broadview, attacked the inadequate preparations for home defence, and criticized the government's declaration that future sinkings would not immediately be confirmed as violating the public's right to know in an apparent effort to cover up the shortcomings of the home defences.[13] J-S Roy, the Independent member for Gaspé, demanded a secret session of the House so that he could divulge sensitive information he possessed about the dangers in the gulf.[14] He accepted the prime minister's invitation to pass the information in writing to the naval minister, and highlighted—quite properly as it turned out—the extent to which weaknesses in infrastructure made the waters off the undeveloped north shore of the peninsula especially vulnerable to enemy operations. But ministers recognized that he was also reiterating old arguments that had as much to do with unemployment as about defence of the region.[15]

---

9. Quoted in DOC, "Sinkings in the St Lawrence, May 11, 1942. Notes on the Publication of News Stories," 21 May 1942, DHH, NHS 1650-239/16B, v 1

10. HofC, *Debates*, 13 May 1942, 2389-90

11. Ibid, 13 May 1942, 2390; NSHQ, "Outline History of Trade Division," 35

12. The DNI itemized for the DOC the information of possible use to the enemy that had been divulged in the press accounts, and the DOC distributed the lengthy document to the media as a warning of the standards that would have to be met in the future DOC, "Sinkings in the St Lawrence, May 11, 1942." CWM, HSC, box 180, "149: War: European: 1939: Submarine Warfare St Lawrence," contains a good selection of clippings.

13. HofC, *Debates*, 13 May 1942, 2390-1, 14 May 1942, 2415-17, 2419-20. See also, "Is the Enemy Fooled?" *Globe and Mail*, 15 May 1942, copy in CWM, HSC.

14. HofC, *Debates*, 15 May 1942, 2470, 2500, 19 May 1942, 2541

15. Roy to Ralston, 15 May 1942, Queen's University Archives, C.G. Power papers, box 70, D-2032. This file also contains correspondence with the Gaspé region MPs from June 1940.

The gulf was not, in fact, so wide open to attack as the grim media reports suggested. Not surprisingly, in view of panics over the U-boat threat in the gulf during the First World War,[16] military staffs had paid a great deal of attention to the needs of the region, and beginning in 1938 made detailed plans for the deployment of ships and aircraft there in the event of attack. The main result of these efforts was the construction of naval and air force operating bases at Gaspé, beginning in 1940. Besides the naval and air bases at Sydney, the Royal Canadian Air Force squadrons that flew from Gander and Botwood in Newfoundland, and aerodromes for air training at Mont Joli, Québec, Chatham, New Brunswick, and Charlottetown and Summerside, Prince Edward Island, were all well placed for operations in the gulf. The training bases, a fortunate byproduct of the British Commonwealth Air Training Plan, were a vital resource because the navy could never provide enough ships for anything more than minimal escorts of convoys. The air force, besides covering convoys, would have to take on the major burden of hunting for U-boats.

Planning for defence of the region in 1942 had begun in March. Almost certainly, the German offensive in coastal waters would extend to the gulf and the St Lawrence after the ice cleared. "During the 1941 season of navigation 750 ocean-going vessels arrived and departed from the Port of Montréal," warned a staff paper, "and it is anticipated that approximately the same number of ocean-going vessels will arrive from and depart for overseas from this port during the forthcoming season." Nor was that all. There was a large number of coastal and "canal" steamers that carried such bulky commodities as coal and pulpwood between gulf, river, and Great Lakes ports.[17] The volume and tempo of traffic would require a convoy in each direction every three days between Sydney and Bic Island, near Rimouski. The staff selected this as a western convoy assembly area, believing it was beyond the likely limit of U-boat operations, and because it saved 130 miles of steaming by escorts to Québec City. All available ocean-going escorts being fully occupied on the east coast and transatlantic routes—unexpected demands placed on the Canadian fleet by events in the Atlantic had never permitted more than periodic patrols in the Gulf—Commander H.N. Lay, Director of the Operations Division, advised the Admiralty and the US Navy Department that it would be necessary to reduce the RCN's forces in the Atlantic in order to provide the escorts for the gulf.[18] The Admiralty responded by urging the Canadians to avoid these withdrawals if at all possible, and hoped that air patrols would be successful in suppressing any submarines that entered the gulf.[19] Since conditions there were essentially the same as those in the open ocean, light craft—Fairmiles and armed yachts—could not carry out escort in heavy weather. The Canadian staff, therefore, turned to recently built Bangor minesweepers scheduled to enter service. It would be possible to assign eleven to the gulf without withdrawing ships from the ocean forces, allowing only a minimal escort to each convoy of one or two Bangors, and accepting the fact that in heavy weather Fairmiles and armed yachts would not be available.[20]

In view of these limitations, the 1942 defence plan, like the 1940 and 1941 versions, only allowed for general escort after there had been "any confirmed attack by U-boats against shipping

16. See, e.g., Hadley and Sarty, *Tin-Pots and Pirate Ships*, 116-17, 124-5

17. SecNB to COAC, NOICs Québec, Montréal, Gaspé, Sydney, 11 Apr. 1942, NAC, RG 24, 11503, 1-14-1

18. Deputy Secretary (Staff), "Follow-up on Defence of Shipping—Gulf of St Lawrence," 7 Mar. 1942, NAC, RG 24, 6788, NSS 8280-166/16, v 1

19. Adm to NSHQ, 1312a/27 Mar. 1942, ibid

20. Min NS mtg, 30 Mar. 1942

in the Gulf." As in the earlier plans, if the forces available proved unable to prevent severe losses, the gulf would be closed to shipping. The rationale for this was straightforward; dislocations to the shipping system were more acceptable than the heavy losses that would result from the diversion of a substantial number of escorts from the Atlantic run.[21] The 1942 plan did, however, provide for new construction escorts coming down from builders on the St Lawrence River and in the Great Lakes to receive outfits of armament and ammunition at Québec, so that, during their passage to Halifax, they could serve as escorts for whatever merchant ships happened to be ready to sail from Bic Island.[22]

The first improvised convoy, QSS 1 (presumably for Québec to Sydney Special) under the escort of the newly commissioned corvette *La Malbaie* and the Bangor *Granby* on 9 May, exhausted the available escort forces.[23] No vessel could be found to protect the ill-fated *Leto* and *Nicoya* when they sailed from Montréal the next day. There were, however, other defence measures that took effect at this time. Pure accident had resulted in command authorities being alerted to the possible presence of *U 553* before *Leto* and *Nicoya* sailed. Around daybreak on 9 May a shore observer at Cape Ray reported a submarine heading into the gulf. This was a false sighting, as Thurmann had passed through the Cabot Strait some twenty hours earlier during the morning of 8 May, and bad weather prevented an air search in response to the report, but on 10 May, an RCAF Douglas Digby and a US Army Air Corps Flying Fortress swept the waters south of Anticosti on the correct assumption the U-boat would have made its way along the main steamer channel. During the early evening the American aircraft sighted *U 553* on the surface and attacked with depth charges, but the submarine dived in time to avoid serious damage.

These were fortunate coincidences. Regrettably, however, flaws in the reporting system prevented appropriate and timely actions in response. Although the US Army Air Corps quickly disseminated word of the attack, it did not follow up with the results of the detailed debriefing of the crew after the aircraft returned to base. This was critical. False U-boat sightings abounded on Canada's east coast, because of the copious flotsam and frequent fogs and rain squalls. The commander of the US Army forces in Newfoundland was unwilling, as it seemed to Canadian and US Navy commanders, to adjust procedures to include swift liaison with other services, and confirmation that the US Army air crew had indeed seen a fully surfaced submarine did not reach Canadian authorities until the next afternoon.[24] Eastern Air Command did despatch two Canso flying boats from Dartmouth—Gander was again closed by weather—to patrol the vicinity of the attack and the possible tracks of the submarine from first to last light on 11 May, but it did no good. Thurmann, not taking chances after the encounter with the American aircraft, ran submerged from well before dawn until long after nightfall that day, making his way up the north shore of the Gaspé Peninsula. It was there, on the 12th, that he found his first and only victims in these waters, *Nicoya* and *Leto*.

21. SecNB, "Defence of Shipping—Gulf of St. Lawrence—1942 (Short Title—Plan GL 2)," 1 Apr. 1942, NAC, RG 24, 11692, H1002-1-8, v 1; NSec, "Defence of Shipping—Gulf of St Lawrence," 29 Apr. 1940, NSec, "Defence of Shipping—Gulf of St. Lawrence (Short Title—Plan GL)," 25 Apr. 1941, NAC, RG 24, 6788, NSS 8280-166/16, v 1

22. SecNB, "Defence of Shipping—Gulf of St Lawrence—1942"

23. *La Malbaie* to Capt (D) Halifax, 14 May 1942, DHH, NHS 48-2-2 (C), v 1

24. W.A.B. Douglas, "'Democratic Spirit and Purpose': Problems in Canadian-American Relations, 1939-1945," in Sokolsky and Jockel, *Fifty Years of Canada-U.S. Defence Cooperation*, 42-5

As *U 553* carried out the second attack, against *Leto*, a Canso flying boat was just arriving in the northern gulf for a patrol throughout the daylight hours. This was the first of four aircraft from Dartmouth that EAC immediately assigned for duty at Mont Joli in light of the confirmed U-boat attacks.[25] There being no warships at Gaspé, the Bangor *Medicine Hat*, one of the first escorts to take up station at Sydney for the season, sailed from that port the moment word came of *Nicoya*'s submarine signal early on 12 May, but did not reach the position until late in the day.[26] Less than four hours after that attack, the navy closed the gulf to shipping. Gulf-bound groups of ships that had split off from ON convoys, to be escorted by warships of the Western Local Escort Force only as far as the Cabot Strait and then to disperse for independent passage, now came into Sydney to await the organization of Sydney-Québec convoys.[27] To clear through ships that came into Sydney from ON 90 and ON 91, the two WLEF corvettes that had brought in these groups escorted a special convoy to Bic Island, SQS 1, that sailed from Sydney on 14 May.[28] As the east coast commands scrambled to assemble a few Bangors and smaller vessels, a regular schedule began, with the sailing of SQ 1 from Sydney and QS 1 from Bic Island on 17 May.

Because several of the recently completed warships earmarked for the gulf would not be worked up and equipped for operations until well into the summer, there were by the end of May still only five Bangors, two armed yachts and three Fairmiles at Gaspé, the main gulf escort base, and one Bangor, one armed yacht and six Fairmiles at Sydney.[29] The tiny Sydney force was also responsible for another new series of gulf convoys, between Sydney and Corner Brook, Newfoundland, known as SB (northbound) and BS (southbound). These convoys, which began sailing on 19 May, usually included only two or three ships, escorted by the single-armed yacht, and depended upon the air cover the Sydney-based air force squadrons provided over the Cabot Strait. Until additional Bangors began to reach Sydney in June, the Newfoundland railway ferries between Sydney and Port-aux-Basques, whose sailings were known as 'SPAB' convoys, relied entirely upon the air cover over the Cabot Strait.[30]

These improvised defence measures proved effective. Thurmann continued to patrol along the Gaspé coast, but had no more success before he slipped out through the Cabot Strait on 22 May. He was seeking to repeat what he had done on the 12th by once again intercepting outward bound "bunches" of unprotected ships independently sailed to make Sydney and Halifax in time for the ocean convoy schedules. They never appeared: this was because the navy had immediately organized convoys. His ability to search, moreover, was hampered by the "very careful air patrol," and the appearance of naval patrol craft, that compelled him to remain submerged by day.[31]

---

25. Douglas, *Creation of a National Air Force*, 496

26. NOIC Sydney to COAC, 2 June 1942, enclosing "HMCS Medicine Hat, ROP," DHH, NHS 48-2-2 (C), v 2

27. NWR no. 139, 14 May 1942, DHH, NSS 1000-5-7, v 3; COAC to HN or MS *Lincoln, Snowberry, Chedabucto*, 0730Z/12 May 1942, DHH, 89/34 mfm, NSS 8280-ON 90; COAC to HMS *Vanquisher, St Clair, Arrowhead, Weyburn*, 0630Z/12 May 1942, DHH, 89/34 mfm, NSS 8280-ON 91

28. *Arrowhead* ROP SQS 1, 22 May 1942, DHH, 89/34 mfm, NSS 8280-ON 90

29. COAC to NOICs Sydney, Gaspé, Québec, 1836z and 1844z/13 May 1942, NAC, RG 24, 3876, NSS 1048-48-32, v 2; RCN daily states, 17-30 May 1942, DHH, 81/520/1650-DS

30. Douglas, *Creation of a National Air Force*, 496-7

31. *U 553*, KTB, 21-2 May 1942; BdU, KTB, 20 May 1942

Dönitz, who was pleased with Thurmann's results, instructed *U 132*, commanded by Kapitänleutnant E. Vogelsang, to follow up.[32] Dönitz had been impressed by the fact Thurmann had been able to strike in the gulf even after incurring damage and suffering defects, and perhaps that was why he thought the mission suitable for *U 132*, which had suffered damage while participating in an attack on the Gibraltar–United Kingdom convoy HG 84 on 13 June.[33] In accordance with Thurmann's experience, *U 132* was to make for the estuary of the St Lawrence River, where the navigable channel narrowed and steamer traffic could most readily be located. Dönitz, determined as in 1941 to ambush traffic in the narrow Strait of Belle Isle, instructed Vogelsang to reconnoitre this passage from the south to see, now that the late spring ice had cleared, if shipping was using the route. He was to remain submerged by day in view of Thurmann's experience with air cover, but BdU also relayed Thurmann's report that "surface forces are weak."[34]

U 132 came in through the Cabot Strait on the night of 30 June to 1 July, and by the 4th had worked up to the vicinity of Cap Chat, where the boat began to sweep back and forth across the shipping channel. During the evening of 5 July, Vogelsang sighted QS 15, twelve merchant vessels escorted by only the Bangor *Drummondville* under the command of Lieutenant J.P. Fraser, RCNR. A few minutes after midnight, 6 July, he attacked on the surface, closing within 1,500 metres from the south side of the convoy. At 0021, he fired four individually aimed torpedoes, which sank two steamers, one at the head of the fifth column and the other at the head of the second column, positions so widely separated that the escort commander concluded that two submarines had attacked. There was pandemonium. In Vogelsang's words, "The convoy disperses in all directions, the larger portion turns inbound. [i.e., reverses course]." None of the ships fired emergency rockets, however, leaving Fraser, ahead in *Drummondville*, mystified as to what was going on. He had heard the explosions and initially thought that the Fairmile *Q 061*, which had helped the convoy assemble the previous evening, had remained in company and was now dropping depth charges. Fraser fired starshell, dropped a depth charge, and, upon learning from the convoy commodore that as many as three ships had been hit in a torpedo attack, began to search. The confusion created by the stampeding ships had meanwhile allowed Vogelsang to stay on the surface, and fire again, at 0058 and 0101, but both torpedoes missed and apparently did not detonate. At 0145, he fired once more, at SS *Dinaric*. In Vogelsang's words, "Hit midships. I proceed around the stern. The vessel is blowing off steam and is listing to starboard, turns towards the coast. I turn to a new approach course when there is a muzzle flash on the port bow ... A starshell lights the area astern of the boat."[35] *Drummondville* had heard an explosion, and headed towards it at full speed.[36]

32. *U 553*, KTB, 23 May 1942

33. Vogelsang had rejected headquarters suggestion that he should return to port. Hadley, *U-boats against Canada*, 97-8; Blair, *Hitler's U-Boat War*, 623-4

34. *U 132*, KTB, 27 June 1942

35. Ibid, 6 July 1942; *Drummondville*, "ROP Convoy QS 15 ...," 11 July 1942, NAC, RG 24, 12009, G018-1, v 1; *Drummondville*, "Report of Attack on U-Boat ... July 6, 1942," ibid

36. *Drummondville*'s report states that the explosion was at 0207, some twenty minutes after Vogelsang's attack, at 0145. Possibly there had been an explosion in *Dinaric* as it settled, or possibly, in the confusion of that night, the Bangor's crew recorded an incorrect time. It says something of the visibility on that misty night that although *Drummondville* fired starshells ahead while advancing, *U 132* saw nothing as the Bangor approached.

A 1943 aerial shot of the Wabana anchorage on Bell Island where *U 513* sank two ore carriers in a daring daylight attack on 5 September 1942. The torpedo defences were added later. (NAC, PA 204256)

The Bangor class minesweeper, HMCS *LaMalbaie*, stationkeeping. (NAC PA 204605)

The Fairmile motor launch *Q052*, on her maiden voyage from Toronto to Halifax. (NAC PA 204681)

Shortly afterwards the SS "Dinaric" was passed, with a torpedo hole in her starboard side and the crew in a lifeboat nearby. Rounding the stern of the "Dinaric" the submarine was sighted directly ahead in the light of star shell, laying on the surface stopped—distance about 900 to 1000 yards .... The submarine was apparently blinded by the star shell, did not gather headway and dive until the "Drummondville" was almost on top of her. "Drummondville" at this time altered course sufficiently to follow the line of dive and three depth charges set at 50 feet were dropped at three-second intervals. The explosions brought up debris and the submarine surfaced astern apparently turning in a half-circle before stopping completely and starting to settle. At this time, although the hull was clearly silhouetted, the conning tower was not showing and it would appear that the sub was on its side, bottom up or the conning tower was blown off. Another attempt was made to ram, but the submarine was sinking fast. One depth charge dropped in the disturbed water covered the sea with strong-smelling oil.[37]

U 132 had in fact survived, but barely. The first three depth charges had come close and inflicted damage because Vogelsang could not get the boat to dive deeper than twenty metres, the result of the particularly pronounced water density layering in the mouth of the river and in the gulf. Relatively warm freshwater from the river flows over the colder, and therefore denser and heavier, saltwater from the gulf, chilled by the Labrador current which comes through the Strait of Belle Isle in the north. Tides caused even more mixing. As the U-boat commanders realized, this layering could provide them with nearly perfect protection in a close encounter with escorts, for asdic could not find targets below the cold water layer. The sound beams are either deflected off the top of cold layer water, or dissipated by it as they slow down in the denser medium. In this case, however, *U 132* found itself trapped close under *Drummondville*'s snap depth charge attack. The resurfacing of the boat that *Drummondville* reported was probably the result of the buoyancy problem, compounded by damage that the Bangor's depth charges did to the line that fed water to the buoyancy tanks.

In a desperate attempt to get through the cold water layer, Vogelsang flooded the forward torpedo tubes. That worked, but created an uncontrolled dive: the submarine plunged to 185 metres, and it proved impossible to keep an even keel. At 0246, therefore, Vogelsang blew his buoyancy tanks to try his luck in an escape on the surface. He only ran at half-speed, possibly because he did not want to produce a large bow wave, which would have advertised his presence given the strong phosphorescence in the water that night. At 0330 *Drummondville*'s asdic operator heard the sound of diesel engines through the water. The Bangor pursued, fired starshell, and briefly sighted the phosphorescence of the U-boat's wash, which then disappeared. Believing the submarine had dived, the Bangor dropped depth charges, but made no asdic contact. Vogelsang had actually continued on the surface, waiting until he got to the 100-metre depth line close to the south shore before diving, so that in the event he again lost control of the boat it would not plunge to a depth from which it could not recover. *U 132* stayed under for over eighteen hours, not surfacing until the night of 6 to 7 July.[38]

The air force endeavoured to respond to the sinkings as soon as word of them first reached shore authorities at about 0230, 6 July. The response was ineffective. Closest to the scene was the

37. *Drummondville*, "Report of Attack on U-Boat"

38. Ibid; *U 132*, KTB, 6-7 July 1942

training airfield at Mont Joli, Québec, but there were no antisubmarine aircraft there. The detachment that had operated from the base in May had since been withdrawn in favour of the new flying boat station at Gaspé that was just being completed, but on the morning of 6 July, Gaspé was fogged in. Four Curtiss P 40 Kittyhawks, a short-ranged, single-engined fighter unsuited to antisubmarine patrols, took off from Mont Joli before dawn. One of the machines, piloted by Squadron-Leader J.A.J. Chevrier, never returned; Chevrier probably died in a crash reported by shore-watchers in the Cap Chat area, not far from the sinkings. A little later crews from the training school at Mont Joli took off in two Fairey Battle aircraft with improvised bomb armament and radio equipment. Later that day six Lockheed Hudson antisubmarine bombers reached Mont Joli from stations on the east coast and began intense patrols.[39]

In the meantime, the navy held shipping in port, despatched two armed yachts and two Bangors from Gaspé to the scene of the sinkings, and deployed three corvettes from the summer work-ups base at Pictou, Nova Scotia, in the Northumberland Strait.[40] The last three ships, *Ville de Québec* and *Port Arthur*, both newly commissioned, and *Kamloops*, the experienced vessel that supervised work-ups, did a sweep north of the Gaspé Peninsula into the river, and on 9 July took over the escort through to Sydney of QS 16, whose sailing had been delayed until the arrival of reinforcements.[41] These were only temporary measures, while Rear-Admiral Jones, COAC, extracted six corvettes from the Halifax Force and permanently assigned them to the Gulf Escort Force. By mid-month the escort of each Sydney–Québec convoy included at least a corvette and a Bangor, and often one of the armed yachts, together with one or more Fairmiles—the latter, of which four were at each of the Sydney, Gaspé, and Québec City commands, helped screen the convoys as they formed up at each end and, weather permitting, accompanied the convoys, breaking off or joining part way to escort ships into and out of the river ports.

The sixty-six survivors of two of the vessels sunk in QS 15 came ashore in three lifeboats in the Cap Chat area and, as with the survivors of *Nicoya*, were warmly cared for by the local inhabitants. The news spread quickly "along the waterfronts of the country," but the press, in the absence of a government announcement, respected the ban on publication until 10 July when J-S Roy rose in the House: "According to information received from my constituency ... three ... ships forming part of a fourteen-ship convoy were torpedoed last Sunday night opposite Cap Chat in the St. Lawrence river."[42] Roy thus revealed the depressing news that the ships had been defended at the time of the attack and that it had taken place deep within the river. He repeated his demand that the government hold a secret session so that MPs could know "the seriousness of the situation."[43] Macdonald was not present, but on 13 July he confirmed what Roy had said and attacked him for revealing information of potential use to the enemy. When M.J. Coldwell, leader of the Cooperative Commonwealth Federation, supported Roy on the grounds of MPs' duty to protect their con-

39. Douglas, *Creation of a National Air Force*, 498-500

40. NSHQ to COPC for CNS, 1603Z/7 July 1942, DHH, 89/34 mfm, NSS 8280-QS 15; NOIC Gaspé, ROP, 6 Aug. 1942, DHH, NSS 1000-5-17

41. *Ville de Québec*, "ROP—A/S Sweep ... and Subsequent Escort of Convoy QS 16," 12 July 1942, NOIC Québec to NCSO Rimouski, *Burlington*, 1540Z/8 July 1942, DHH, 89/34 mfm, NSS 8280-QS 16

42. H.J. Roy, Customs and Immigration Officer to Commissioner of Customs, "Re SS Hainaut ... &: SS Anastassios Pateras ...," 11 July 1942, NAC, RG 12, 1425, 8117-45, v 1; HofC, *Debates*, 13 July 1942, 4124-5

43. HofC, *Debates*, 10 July 1942, 4098

stituents, Macdonald lashed back: "If [Roy] thinks for one moment that the whole Canadian navy is going to line up along his shores and defend those shores only, letting the convoy system we have and the protection we have for all the rest of Canada go to the dogs, he is making a tremendous mistake. I am not ready to change the disposition of one ship of the Canadian navy for him or all the questions he may ask from now until doomsday."[44] This was an enunciation, albeit an angry one, of the blue water policy that the King government pursued, or in some instances acceded to, during much of the war. Macdonald's vehemence, however, may have revealed a defensive attitude. At that very moment, as has been seen, the RCN was diverting corvettes from the Atlantic to the gulf in defiance, as will be recounted later in this chapter, of protests from the British and Americans that the RCN was thereby leaving undefended Atlantic shipping that was more important to the Allied cause than any vessels that might be lost in the St Lawrence.

The government again resisted the demands of the Opposition and some of its own members from Québec for a secret session, but then suddenly relented, and the session took place on 18 July.[45] Possibly the prime minister was swayed by evidence, including an impassioned letter from Adelard Godbout, the Liberal premier of Québec, of panic in the population, and of doubts about the capacity of the armed forces. Certainly the session, during which C.G. Power and Macdonald described the defending forces and their operations in the most positive light, served the prime minister's own needs.[46] On 7 July, the day after Vogelsang struck, the government carried the second reading of Bill 80, which amended the National Resources Mobilization Act to allow the despatch of army conscripts overseas, but it had done so in the face of strong opposition among the government's own Québec caucus. King was fighting all the while a rearguard action to reassure that province's voters that the government would not, in fact, send conscripts overseas anytime soon, possibly never, unless a grave military crisis made the decision inescapable.[47] The prime minister had never ceased to refer to the actual menace in the St Lawrence in his struggle to find some middle ground in what he had always perceived as the interminable conflict between English Canadian imperialists and French Canadian isolationists.[48]

While the parliamentarians debated, Vogelsang carried out BdU's orders to reconnoitre the Strait of Belle Isle. Two new convoy series had begun to use the strait. The LN–NL convoys, from Québec City to Labrador and back, carried building materials, supplies, and personnel for construction of the big new RCAF base at Goose Bay. This was yet an additional commitment that pulled resources away from the Atlantic coast, requiring the full-time commitment of two corvettes at Halifax for the duty. When the merchant ships were ready to sail from Québec, the escorts came up from Halifax, refuelling at Gaspé if necessary, and joining the convoy at Bic Island. The second new series, SG–GS, Sydney to Greenland and back, supplied US air base construction projects in the Arctic, starting in early July. This was almost entirely a US operation, Sydney serving as a convenient assembly port for the merchant ships, which mostly came from American ports via the

44.   Ibid, 13 July 1942, 4125-6

45.   Hadley, *U-Boats against Canada*, 103-4

46.   Douglas, *Creation of a National Air Force*, 500

47.   Pickersgill, *Mackenzie King Record* I, 394-6; J.L. Granatstein and J.M. Hitsman, *Broken Promises: A History of Conscription in Canada* (Toronto 1977), 179-180

48.   For example, HofC, *Debates*, 10 June 1942, 3241, reprinted in King, *Canada and the Fight for Freedom*, 190

coastal convoy system. The escorts were US Coast Guard cutters, which formed part of the Greenland Patrol, the sub-command of CTF 24 that carried out operations in the far north. Canada's only commitment, officially, was to provide the services of the Naval Control Staff at Sydney to organize the convoys and lay out routes for them, a task that proved challenging given the inexperience of the Coast Guard's seasoned Arctic voyagers with the fine points of convoy and antisubmarine operations. It was also proved necessary for the Canadian naval establishment to pitch in with a great deal of additional assistance because the tiny USN liaison staff at Sydney was overwhelmed by the mail and stores that arrived in vast quantities for the Coast Guard escorts.[49]

Vogelsang encountered shipping, including one small southbound convoy, which confirmed the strait was clear of ice, but he could not get into a position to attack because patrol aircraft kept appearing.[50] On 12 July *U 132* turned back from the southern entrance to the Strait of Belle Isle and arrived off the north shore of the Gaspé Peninsula on the 14th. He had come by way of the Jacques Cartier Passage, north of Anticosti, which, the week before, had been the focus of Canadian countermeasures. A false sighting from shore and an air attack on what had appeared to be a submarine had led command authorities to conclude that *U 132* was hiding there following the attack on QS 15. From 15 to 18 July Vogelsang patrolled in the vicinity of his earlier success in the river, but although he saw shipping, frequent air patrols over the confined waters prevented him gaining an attack position. He pulled east along the north shore of the Gaspé Peninsula to the vicinity of *U 553*'s successes, and during daylight on the morning of 19 July sighted two, apparently unescorted steamers, which may in fact have formed part of the westbound SQ 20. Because of the foggy conditions he felt safe in surfacing to pursue, but then abandoned the effort as the visibility began to clear and he saw escorts.[51]

Vogelsang remained in the same area and the next day, 20 July, sighted the eastbound QS 19 in daylight when he was in position to make a submerged approach. As the convoy, which was escorted by the corvette *Weyburn* in the van, the Bangor *Chedabucto* on the port beam, one Fairmile to starboard, and two more astern, passed over him, he fired two torpedoes, one of which hit the freighter *Frederika Lensen*. The Fairmile on the southern flank, where *Frederika Lensen* had been stationed, made asdic contact and dropped depth charges, but *Weyburn* was unable to pick up the contact. The Fairmile's attack brought a large number of dead herring to the surface, leading the escorts to conclude that the asdic had located only a school of fish, which was probably correct as none of the depth charges came close to *U 132*. *Frederika Lensen*, although severely damaged, remained afloat, and Vogelsang watched through his periscope as *Weyburn* took the hulk under tow. The submarine followed, but did not attempt to attack, possibly because air cover became intense. Despite *Weyburn*'s success in getting the hulk to the little port of Grande Vallée, the ship proved to be a total loss. Vogelsang, for his part, began to work his way further eastward so as to be clear of the gulf in the full moon period; evidently he had seen enough of the RCAF's coverage of the region that he did not want to be there when he could not manoeuvre on the surface under the protection of dark nights.[52]

49. Tennyson and Sarty, *Guardian of the Gulf*, 266-7

50. *U 132*, KTB, 8-12 July 1942

51. Ibid, 13-19 July 1942; Douglas, *Creation of a National Air Force*, 500

52. *U 132*, KTB, 20-1 July 1942; *Weyburn*, "ROP, Convoy QS 19," 23 July 1942, DHH, 89/34 mfm, NSS 8280-QS 19; *Q-074*, "Disabling of 'Fredericka Lensen' in QS 19," 22 July 1942, NAC, RG 24, 6892, NSS 8871-3769; SecNB to COAC, 17 Feb. 1943, enclosing master and chief officer *Frederika Lensen*, "... Report on the Loss of the SS Frederika Lensen," nd, NAC, RG 24, 11015, COAC 5-2-3A

These first German incursions into the St Lawrence coincided with the RCN's initiative to escort oil tankers to and from the Caribbean. The British had hoped that the Canadians might go further and also supply corvettes for service within the Caribbean to help establish the much-needed through east–west convoy. The Canadian staff refused, insisting on national priorities. Although the RCN's coastal escort forces would be augmented by the withdrawal of the ten Canadian corvettes from the mid-ocean force, NSHQ was unwilling to deploy them away from Halifax where they would be readily available in case they had to be quickly recommitted to the mid-ocean run, or to reinforce the very light escorts in the Gulf of St Lawrence.[53] As the negotiations described in Chapter 7 suggest, it was probably no coincidence that in mid June NSHQ redesignated the Tanker Escort Force as the Halifax Force.[54]

U 132's achievements in the Gulf of St Lawrence, and, especially, the boat's encouraging intelligence that shipping was moving through the evidently weakly protected Strait of Belle Isle revived Dönitz's long-standing hopes for landing a heavy blow in these far northern waters.[55] During the last week of August, three large type IXc submarines, *U 165*, *U 513*, and *U 517*, arrived off Belle Isle, the first of a dozen that would hunt along the Atlantic coast of Newfoundland and all through the St Lawrence during the autumn of 1942.[56] This scale of attack matched the offensive off southern Newfoundland and Nova Scotia in January and February 1942. Losses would not be so heavy as in the attacks at the beginning of the year, and the increasingly efficient defences would compel the Germans to abandon the effort just as it got into full stride. The U-boats, however, achieved some of the most dramatic—and tragic—sinkings that took place in Canadian waters during the war. As a result, politicians and the media voiced profound doubts about the effectiveness of Canada's maritime forces even as they were blunting and then shutting down the enemy's thrusts.

U 517 approached the Strait of Belle Isle on 26 August and pressed on through the strait that night. The boat's commanding officer Kapitänleutnant Paul Hartwig noted, with apparent relief, "proceeded roughly 3 nm off the land along the coast until reaching the southern entrance ... Since all navigation beacons are lit pilotage is no problem." After daylight on 27 August, Hartwig dived and began a submerged patrol of the southern entrance to the straits.[57] His timing was perfect.

The straits were, in fact, seldom used by ocean shipping, save for the intermittent convoys that sustained construction of the airfield at Goose Bay, and the US Army Air Forces bases in Greenland. As it happened, on the morning of 27 August no fewer than three groups of ships were approaching the straits from the south. In the lead was the US Coast Guard cutter *Mojave*, escorting the US Army Transport *Chatham*. In addition to its crew of 134, this passenger vessel was carrying 428 Canadian and US labourers destined for Goose Bay and the Greenland bases. *Mojave* and *Chatham* were the "fast section" of convoy SG 6, whose main, slow body of four merchant vessels under the escort of the US Coast Guard ships *Algonquin* and *Mohawk*, was following some hours behind.

---

53. BAD to Adm, 0029Z/9 June 1942, NAC, RG 24, 3975, NSS 1048-48-31, v 1

54. NWR, 25 June 1942, DHH, NHS NSS 1000-5-7, v 3

55. MOD, *U-Boat War in the Atlantic* II, 37-9, and diagram 18

56. BdU, KTB, 21 and 24 Aug. 1942

57. *U 517*, KTB, 26-7 Aug. 1942

Close behind the fast section of SG 6, and ahead of the slow component, was the Canadian convoy LN 6, two merchantmen under the escort of the corvette *Trail*, bound for Goose Bay from Québec City.[58] At approximately 0848 on the morning of 27 August, in clear weather, *U 517* fired two torpedoes at *Chatham*. The first missed but the second hit near the boiler room, and soon after two of the boilers exploded. Nevertheless, it took nearly half an hour for the ship to sink, allowing almost all of the 562 people on board to get away in lifeboats and on rafts.[59]

The fast section of SG 6 had been sailing without air cover. RCAF patrols focused on the main, slow body of the convoy, still well to the south of the straits. Fortunately, however, the RCAF Catalina escorting LN 6, which was at the time of the sinking perhaps twenty-five miles from the site of the attack, came across the lifeboats during one of its sweeps ahead of LN 6. The Catalina hurried back to *Trail*, and alerted the corvette to the disaster. *Trail* shepherded the two merchantmen in its charge into the safety of nearby Forteau Bay and hurried back towards the position of the lifeboats. *Trail* reached the scene just after 1300 and joined *Mojave* in the rescue work, guided by the Catalina which dropped flares to mark the position of rafts. The rescue continued until the late afternoon, when *Mojave*, crammed with survivors, turned back towards Sydney, and *Trail*, with another eighty-eight survivors, returned to Forteau Bay, the Catalina all the while flying in support.[60]

U 517 did not see the actual sinking of the *Chatham*. At the moment of firing the submarine had "inadvertently" dipped below periscope depth—possibly the result of the difficult water conditions—and Hartwig had then dived more deeply for forty minutes to avoid counter-attack. When he returned to periscope depth, he had the impression *Mojave* had continued to the north, whereas the cutter was, in fact, carrying out an antisubmarine search. Hartwig saw *Trail* arrive and was sharply aware of the Catalina's presence. Later in the day Hartwig let the strong northward current from the gulf carry his boat out through the northern entrance to the strait.[61] Neither *Mojave* nor *Trail* obtained any promising asdic contacts. *Trail*'s captain concluded that it was probably hopeless: "Whilst searching for survivors in the vicinity of the torpedoing, it was observed that Asdic conditions were bad, non-sub contacts could be obtained all around the ship on tide rips and water temperature gradients, and it was obvious that the effectiveness of an A/S screen would be greatly affected in that part of the Straits."[62]

US headquarters at Argentia was almost entirely in the dark about what was going on. There were two problems. The first arose from a failure of communication between the Canadian and US

---

58.   *Trail*, "HMCS 'Trail,' ROP, Convoy LN-6," nd, DHH, 89/34 mfm, reel 16, NSS 8280 LN 6

59.   *U 517*, KTB, 27 Aug. 1942; ns, nd, narrative "Compiled for the Interest of CTF 24 ...," NARA, RG 313, CTF 24 Red, box 8702, "SG 6"; Rohwer, *Axis Submarine Successes*, 119. The US reports for this action are three hours earlier than Greenwich Mean Time, corresponding to Atlantic Daylight Time, and the present account follows this practice. *Trail*'s ROP, cited above, uses Atlantic Standard Time, four hours earlier than GMT. The German records state that *U 517* fired against *Chatham* at 1348 Central European Time, which corresponds to 0848. Allied sources state the hit was at 0846. Morison, *Battle of the Atlantic*, I, 330, gives the time as 0915, possibly a rendering of the events in Newfoundland local time, which was two-and-a-half hours earlier than GMT, and would correspond to 0845 in the time kept by the US escorts.

60.   AOC EAC to AFHQ, 0300Z/29 Aug. 1942, DHH, 181.003 (D304); Group Capt M. Costello for AOC EAC to sec, DND for Air, "Sinkings in Belle Isle Straits 27-8-42," 29 Aug. 1942, DHH, 181.009 (D121); *Trail* ROP; ns, nd, narrative "Compiled for the Interest of CTF 24"

61.   *U 517*, KTB, 27 Aug. 1942

62.   *Trail* ROP

shore commands, which shared responsibility for the SG convoys. In the convoy sailing message for SG 6, sent on 25 August, two days before the convoy sailed, the RCN convoy authorities at Sydney had stated that *Chatham* and *Mojave* would be proceeding more quickly than the main body of the convoy.[63] This fact did not stand out from many other details in this long, pro forma signal, and the staff at Argentia had not grasped that essential detail; nor, it must be said, had the Sydney staff underscored the change in the normal sailing routine.[64] The second difficulty was that the USCG escorts, inexperienced as they were in convoy operations, failed to inform Argentia about the change in the sailing arrangements, then, at the time of the attack, the US escort commander did not pass essential information. An admonishment later sent by Admiral Brainard's staff to the Commander Greenland Patrol, who was responsible for the escorts for the SG series, describes the distorted picture that Argentia had as a result of these lapses.

> 4. When the *Chatham* was torpedoed, the *Mojave* did not communicate the fact to the Force commander or other US Naval authority. The only information received by Commander Task Force *Twenty-four* was a plain language message relayed by Belle Isle Radio Station to the effect that the *Chatham* had been torpedoed, or mined, with inference that the latter was more probable. Even this plain language despatch did not state the position. The failure to provide Commander Task Force *Twenty-four* the information, both as to splitting of convoy and later as to the nature and position of attack, prevented his taking such action as the circumstances warranted. It was naturally assumed that the *Mojave* (escort commander) was with the entire convoy and it was hoped that with the knowledge of the situation at the scene of action he would divert the convoy as necessary for its protection. However, receiving no further information, Commander Task Force *Twenty-four* directed the *Mojave* to return the convoy to Sydney, the only answer received from the *Mojave* in this matter indicated that the time of the receipt of the directive he was not with the convoy. However, subsequent information confirms that he did not issue any directive to the *Algonquin* to divert the convoy in accordance with Commander Task Force *Twenty-four*'s orders as addressed to the *Mojave*. Due to the slowness in communications and lack of necessary information, Commander Task Force *Twenty-four* did not know that the convoy had not been diverted nor turned toward Sydney.[65]

The main body of SG 6, in short, continued to sail northwards. At 2130, about an hour after moon rise, a torpedo ripped into the side of the freighter SS *Arlyn*, carrying dynamite, high test gasoline, and other cargo for Greenland; a minute or two later another torpedo hit the navy oiler USS *Laramie*.[66] The attacker was *U 165* under Korvettenkapitän E. Hoffman, who was patrolling in the same area where *U 517* had been hunting earlier in the day. *Arlyn*'s crew abandoned ship immediately after she was hit, and unknown to any Allied authority, the ship remained afloat in

---

63. NCSO Sydney to Cdr Greenland Patrol, Senior Officer Present Afloat Greenland, CTF 24, 1725Z/25 Aug. 1942, DHH, NHS, CCSC, "Coastal Convoys SG ... GS," June 1942–30 Apr. 1943

64. NCSO Sydney to NOIC Sydney, 3 Sep. 1942, NOIC Sydney to COAC, 3 Sep. 1942, DHH, 89/34 mfm, reel 30, NSS 8280-SG 6

65. Acting/CTF 24 to Cdr Greenland Patrol, "Attack on SG 6," 21 Sep. 1942, NARA, RG 313, CTF 24 Red, box 8702, file "SG 6"

66. *Lloyd's War Losses* I, 52

the darkness.[67] Hartwig, now on patrol in the northern approaches to the strait of Belle Isle, saw the starshells and rockets fired by escorts and other merchant vessels in response to *U 165*'s attack, headed back south and at 0344, 28 August, fired a *coup de grace* that sent *Arlyn*'s hulk to the bottom.[68] By that time *Laramie*'s crew, in what can only be described as a heroic action given the fact the tanker's decks were awash in explosively flammable aviation gas, had got their vessel back under way and the ship, although severely damaged, was able to make Sydney under her own power.[69]

In the early hours of 28 August shore authorities, on learning of the additional sinkings in the Strait of Belle Isle, ordered *Trail* and the two merchant ships of LN 6, which were still sheltering in Forteau Bay, to return to Gaspé. After reaching that port on 31 August, these three ships then sailed the next day to join with convoy LN 7, the corvette *Shawinigan* and a single freighter that were on their way from Québec City to Goose Bay, to provide increased defences in view of the danger on the northern route.[70]

U 517 had meanwhile left through the northern entrance to the Strait of Belle Isle on 29 August and searched along the southern Labrador coast. On the morning of 30 August Hartwig tracked what appeared to be "two steamers" and dived ahead of them for a submerged attack, but abandoned the attempt when he saw that, in fact, it was "a search group which is zigzagging vigorously and slows to listening speed in our vicinity."[71] This was probably the Bangor *Clayoquot* and the corvette *Weyburn*, completing a sweep of the Strait of Belle Isle on their run north to Goose Bay, which they reached early on 31 August. On the morning of 1 September, the two warships put to sea once more from Goose Bay, escorting the three merchant vessels of NL 6, towards Québec.[72] Some hours before, during the night of 31 August to 1 September, *U 517* and possibly *U 165* as well, re-entered the Strait of Belle Isle, having received instructions from BdU to hunt along the northern shore of the Gaspé Peninsula where *U 132* and *U 553* had had success.[73]

By the late morning of 2 September *U 517* was east of Anticosti Island, when it submerged to avoid an approaching aircraft. This was almost certainly the Gaspé-based Canso that was escorting LN 7 on its northward passage. Hartwig soon saw the convoy through his periscope, but was too far away to have any chance of catching it at his slow submerged speed. He surfaced two-and-a-half hours later and began to dash back to the east, seeking to position himself ahead of the convoy for an attack. While doing so, he radioed at least two contact reports with the intention of having *U 165* join in the attack.[74] DF stations picked up two transmissions, and the plots placed them in the general northeastern part of the gulf. By the time NSHQ passed the warning to LN 7 and

67. USCGC *Algonquin*, "Report of Escort Operations; Convoy G-S 6," 31 Aug. 1942, USCGC *Mohawk*, "Action Report 27-8 Aug., Report of Escort of Convoy," 29 Aug. 1942, NARA, RG 313, CTF 24 Red, Confidential, 1942, box 8814, "A14-1," f 3; Morison, *Battle of the Atlantic* I, 331; BdU, KTB, 27 Aug. 1942

68. *U 517*, KTB, 28 Aug. 1942; Rohwer, *Axis Submarine Successes*, 119

69. USS *Laramie*, "USS Laramie (AO16); Report of Battle Action Occurring on Aug. 27, 1942," 7 Sep.1942, NARA, RG 313 Red, CTF 24, Confidential, 1942, box 8815, file A16-3 (General), f 3

70. *Trail* ROP; NOIC Gaspé, ROP, Aug.-Sep. 1942, DHH, NSS 1000-5-17

71. *U 517*, KTB, 29-30 Aug. 1942

72. *Weyburn*, "ROP—Convoys SQ 32 & NL 6," 5 Sep. 1942, DHH,89/34, NSS 8280-SQ 32

73. BdU, KTB, 30 Aug. 1942; *U 517*, KTB, 1 Sep. 1942

74. BdU, KTB, 2 Sep. 1942; *U 517*, KTB, 2 Sep. 1942

Weyburn's NL 6 on the evening of 2 September—the two groups of ships were now approaching each other from opposite courses—the convoys were in heavy fog that had forced aircraft back from the scene. Hartwig had caught up to LN 7 at around the time NSHQ broadcast the warning, but again he could not get into a firing position and then lost the convoy in the fog. During the early hours of 3 September Hartwig made contact once more, east of Cape Whittle, where Québec's north shore bends northward towards the Strait of Belle Isle. The fog had just cleared. Unknown to *U 517*, at the moment it closed on the southern flank of *Trail*'s LN 7, NL 6 was passing immediately to the north. *Weyburn*, of NL 6, was screening well off the southern flank of its convoy, at such a distance the corvette was covering the southern flank of LN 7 as well. *Trail* was on the northern flank of LN 7 and *Shawinigan* was in the van, thus both were much further removed from *U 517*'s approach than *Weyburn*. Hartwig, not realizing a second, southbound, convoy had come into the picture, had no reason to expect the sudden appearance of a southbound escort on his flank, believing he had evaded the northbound escorts, as indeed he had.[75] Here is Hartwig's account:

> Convoy in sight. Screen on port [north] side. Convoy moving in echelon starboard [e.g., line abreast, extending southward from *Trail*, and north of *U 517*]. Placed myself astern of the convoy and prepared to attack from starboard [i.e., from the south]. Just before firing I passed along the starboard side. Guard ship [*Weyburn*] 600 m away. When he is on my beam I go into the attack at full power, firing two single torpedoes. The guard ship then turns sharply, heading towards me. The torpedo hits and a steamship [SS *Donald Stewart*] goes up in flames. I try to go around the burning steamship in order to sink the second freighter. The guard ship is now 300 m away. Crash dive ... Guard ship makes further action impossible.[76]

From *Weyburn*'s perspective,

> 10. At [0245] passed LN 7 with HMCS Trail ahead, NL 6 passing to northward. Weyburn passed to southward of both convoys. Visibility had just commenced to improve. When just abaft the beam of LN 7, Weyburn observed a submarine trimmed right down (only conning tower showing above water) ... travelling at high speed. Speed was increased to emergency Full (CERA reported later engine was running 198 revs. which gives an estimated speed of 18.65 knots), and course altered to ram. Distance was about five cables. Once on a collision bearing, submarine altered course rapidly to port. About 30 seconds after altering, a ship was torpedoed and immediately burst into flame ... Course was again altered in an effort to ram, but submarine was too fast, moving away all the time. Its ability to turn rapidly was astonishing. Gun was brought to the ready and two rounds were fired. On the firing of the first round, S/M commenced to dive, swinging first to starboard. At the second round she was almost submerged and on Weyburn's starboard bow. Only two depth charges at shallow setting were dropped, as the starboard throwers misfired.

---

75. EAC, WIR, week ending 5 Sep. 1942, para 30, DHH, 181.003(D423) lists the DF reports; *Weyburn* ROP; *Trail*, "Form for Reporting Submarine Attacks on Convoys," nd, NAC, RG 24, 4027, NSS 1062-13-19, v 1

76. *U 517*, KTB, 3 Sep. 1942

All four escorts joined in the hunt, but none made asdic contact.[77] Their efforts were not completely without effect, however. Twice more Hartwig tried to close at speed on the surface for a renewed attack, and both times found his way blocked by evidently alert escorts and had to crash-dive and abandon the attempt. Even so, Hartwig made a third attempt, surfacing and running fast to the north to try to get ahead of LN 7. Late in the morning an RCAF Douglas Digby from 10 Squadron at Gander that had come out to cover the little convoy sighted the submarine. *U 517* dived in ample time to avoid its aerial depth charges, but the aircraft then lingered over the area. Hartwig, realizing he now had no hope of continuing the fast surface pursuit, gave up the hunt. He remained south of the Strait of Belle Isle searching out quiet waters where, on the night of 4 to 5 September he surfaced to move torpedoes from their upper deck storage into the submarine, and then set out once again towards Anticosti and the north shore of the Gaspé Peninsula.[78]

Korvettenkapitän R. Rüggeberg in *U 513*, who had remained on patrol to the east of the Strait of Belle Isle, had seen no shipping, but had to make four emergency dives on 28 August as aircraft swooped overhead in response to the attacks on SG 6. BdU cleared Rüggeberg to search further afield, and recommended Conception Bay, immediately west of St John's. *U 513* reached the mouth of the bay on the night of 2 to 3 September, reconnoitred close offshore, and went in the next night to try a fast surfaced attack, but pulled back from Wabana because powerful shore-mounted searchlights lit up the northern entrance to the anchorage. In the early hours of 5 September, Rüggeberg stole into the anchorage submerged and then attacked in broad daylight when he had clear visibility through his periscope.[79] There were four ore ships at anchor and the first indication anything was amiss came shortly after 1145 when "there was a terrific explosion in *Saganaga*. Two men, ventilator, decking, ore, etc. blown into air."[80] The ship, loaded with ore, sank almost instantly, as did a second vessel, *Lord Strathcona* when it was hit a half hour later. This second attack was a tribute to Rüggeberg's determination, for shortly before, another of the steamers had got under way and unknowingly struck the submerged submarine, damaging its conning tower — "The bridge has shrunk by 3/4 metre," as *U 513*'s log laconically remarked. After the attacks, the submarine crept away, not surfacing until it was clear of Conception Bay on the night of 5 to 6 September.[81]

In retrospect, the events at Wabana had the inevitability of a Greek tragedy. As has been seen, the RCN had tried to make provision for local antisubmarine patrol forces in Newfoundland's coastal waters from the spring of 1941, only to have these warships drawn away by the ever growing demands of ocean escort. In the autumn of 1941, when the Admiralty, on the basis of decrypt intelligence, warned of Dönitz's interest in Conception Bay, the navy and shipping authorities had immediately ceased the assembly of ocean convoy joiners in the bay. Yet the hunger of the steel

---

77. *Weyburn* ROP. See also, *Trail*, "Form for Reporting Submarine Attacks on Convoys."

78. *U 517*, KTB, 3-5 Sep. 1942; Douglas, *Creation of a National Air Force*, 501-2

79. *U 513*, KTB, 28 Aug.-5 Sep. 1942

80. SO (Intelligence) *Avalon* to DNI, 9 Sep. 1942, printed in *Documents on Relations between Canada and Newfoundland* I, 642. This document indicates the first explosion was at 1130, but *U 513*'s log indicates that it fired at 1145, and the hit was three minutes later. Reports by the Canadian forces in Newfoundland, printed in Neary, *Enemy on our Doorstep*, 19 and 23, indicate that the first explosion was at 1146 and that the army's Headquarters St John's Defences received the first message about the attack at 1148.

81. *U 513*, KTB, 5-6 Sep. 1942

mills at Sydney for ore to sustain increased production that was essential to the war effort and, paradoxically, the delays in sailings of the ore ships because of the coastal convoy schedule, resulted in them regularly sitting fully loaded in the Wabana anchorage. In August Captain Mainguy, acting Flag Officer Newfoundland, noted that coastal convoy was making such a demand on his small force of Bangors that it was impossible to carry out any antisubmarine patrols off Wabana. He noted, however, that plans were in hand to run a new series of Wabana to Sydney (WB–BW) convoys especially to speed up the movement of the ore ships, and the resulting quicker turnaround would keep the anchorage clear of ships.[82] Final preparations for the new convoy were in train at the moment *U 513* struck. In the wake of the attacks, Mainguy remained optimistic. Additional warships were being assigned to his command, including Fairmiles for harbour defence, and these would be available to screen the anchorage during the brief periods when, under the new convoys arrangements, ships would be waiting at Wabana.[83] He had no choice but to be optimistic, for regional and national military authorities had long recognized the danger at Wabana and other unprotected ports on the east coast, but accepted the risk given the necessity of moving strategic materials and the paucity of warships and aircraft. The story of Wabana's defence was in this sense a microcosm of the hard choices the RCN and Canadian government economic authorities faced concerning oil supplies from the Caribbean and the protection of the Gulf of St Lawrence.

Larger events in the gulf, and still larger ones out in the Atlantic and among Allied councils, left little time and even fewer resources to dwell on the tragedy at Wabana. By the time of the attack, the U-boat plotters at NSHQ had rightly concluded that there were at least two submarines in the gulf. Early on 3 September, a few hours before the attack on LN 7, the armed yacht HMCS *Raccoon*, while escorting SQ 33 just off Matane on the south shore of the estuary of the St Lawrence River, reported that it was the apparent target of a torpedo attack, two tracks passing near the little warship. *Raccoon* searched up the tracks and dropped depth charges, but made no asdic contact.[84] Hoffmann reported attacking the convoy, and within an hour DF stations picked up his signal.[85]

The main reinforcements immediately available for the western gulf were additional EAC aircraft at Mont Joli. When, on 6 September, QS 33 formed up at Bic Island and commenced its eastbound passage along the south shore of the St Lawrence, two Lockheed Hudson bombers flew close escort, while three others swept up and down the river.[86] The help was much needed, for the eight merchant ships of QS 33 had a minimal escort that included only one seagoing, fully equipped and experienced warship, the corvette *Arrowhead*. The rest of the screen comprised *Raccoon*, two Fairmiles, and the newly commissioned Bangor *Truro*. The aircraft departed shortly

82. FONF WD, Aug. 1942, 2. See also, July 1942, 1, DHH, NHS NSS 1000-5-20, pt 2; DOD to CNS, "Conference at St John's, Nfld., 22 Aug. on Escorts for Atlantic Convoys," 26 Aug. 1942, NAC, RG 24, 3973, NS 1048-48-1, v 8

83. FONF WD, Sep. 1942, NSS 1000-5-20, pt 2, 2; "Min Mtg of the Joint Service Sub-Committee, Newfoundland," 28 Sep. 1942, printed in *Documents on Relations between Canada and Newfoundland* I, 643

84. "Director of Operations Division Report for Week Ending 10 Sep., 1942," paras 5-6, DHH; ns, "Raccoon's Report of Attack while with SQ 33," 4 Sep. 1942, DHH, 89/34 mfm, NSS 8280-SQ 33

85. EAC, WIR, week ending 5 Sep. 1942, para 30, DHH, 181.003 (D423) lists the DF reports; *U 165*, KTB, 3 Sep. 1942; BdU, KTB, 3 Sep. 1942

86. Sarty, "Eastern Air Command Anti-Submarine Operations in the Gulf of St Lawrence, 1942, RCAF History II: Narrative," Aug. 1982, DHH, 89/97, box 4, file 15

after 2100, and it soon became clear that they had not succeeded in suppressing *U 165*. At 2300, not long after the convoy had passed Cap Chat, Hoffman attacked. The Greek freighter *Aeas*, bound for the United Kingdom with Canadian lumber and steel, suffered two heavy explosions and sank in five minutes.[87] Starshell and an asdic search turned up nothing. At 0210 on 7 September the escorts heard what sounded like depth-charge explosions from the direction of *Raccoon*'s place in the screen. Since the yacht did not have radio-telephone, the only secure and convenient method of communication, *Raccoon* would have closed to flash a light signal only if something significant had turned up, and so the other escorts did not think it unusual when they heard nothing more. In fact, the explosions almost certainly marked the destruction of the yacht by torpedoes from *U 165*; none of the thirty-five men on board survived.[88]

Early in the morning of 7 September Hoffman transmitted a report of his attack. Hartwig in *U 517* had just reached the Gaspé coast. He copied the signal and realized the convoy would hug the shore as a defensive measure, so he worked his way westward along the coast. Wary after previous encounters with aircraft, he submerged at dawn, and when during the late morning he sighted the convoy, it was a Canso amphibian flying close cover with the four surface escorts that prevented him from surfacing to gain an attack position. It was only when fog came down along with rain, a few hours later, that he could surface and run back towards Gaspé Bay at speed. In the late afternoon, an aircraft, probably the Canso escorting QS 33, forced the submarine to crash dive off Cape Gaspé, but Hartwig had already seen smoke in the distance and was able to close on a sound bearing. With the help of a sudden clearing of the visibility that gave him a good periscope view, at 1801 he fired three torpedoes, each of which found and destroyed a target, the Greek steamers *Mount Pindus* and *Mount Taygetus*, both of which had loaded cargoes for Britain in Montréal and carried tanks on deck, and the British freighter *Oakton*, loaded with coal for Corner Brook.[89] Of the three escorts in position for countermeasures, *Arrowhead*, *Truro,* and *Q 083*, only *Arrowhead*'s asdic was working, but the corvette made no contacts. Both *Arrowhead* and *Truro* dropped depth charges to deter the attacker, but *U 517* had plunged deep.[90]

Ten merchant vessels and two warships had now been sunk in the gulf and the St Lawrence, and three more in the Strait of Belle Isle. These heavy losses confirmed the conclusion the Canadian Naval Staff had already reached that the St Lawrence should be closed to ocean shipping and the vulnerable Sydney–Québec convoys discontinued as soon as possible. The Naval Staff had always believed that this might be necessary if the small number of escorts available for the gulf proved unable to prevent major losses. In July staff officers were considering such a step for the 1943 season, given the difficulty of finding additional escorts in response to *U 132*'s successes, the growing strength of the U-boat offensive in areas of greater importance to the Allied cause, and the appreciation that

87. All but two of thirty-one on board survived, *Lloyd's War Losses* I, 530; *U 165*, KTB, 7 Sep., 1942

88. COAC to COMINCH, "Report of Submarine Attack on Convoy QS 33," 23 Nov. 1942, NAC, RG 24, 4027, NSS 1062-13-19, pt 1, includes ROPs of all of the escorts and analyses by staff; SO (Bases and Rents), NSHQ, "HMCS Raccoon. Movements between Sep. 3 and Sep. 7 1942," 12 Sep. 1942, DHH, DOD, "Weekly Operational Summaries," 1942; "Loss of HMCS Raccoon (Armed Yacht)," 13 Sep. 1952, DHH, 81/520/8280 QS 33; *U 165*, KTB, 7 Sep. 1942

89. *Lloyd's War Losses* I, 529-30

90. *U 517*, KTB, 6-7 Sep. 1942; ns, "Second Attack on QS 33, 7 Sep. 1942," nd; *Truro*, "ROP—Convoy QS 33,"18 Sep. 1942, both enclosures to COAC to COMINCH, "Report of Submarine Attack on Convoy QS 33," 23 Nov. 1942, NAC, RG 24, 4027, NSS 1062-13-19, pt 1

Allied escort building programs would not produce enough additional warships to overcome the shortage for some time to come.[91] The naval conference in Ottawa on 23 July, as has been seen, concluded that given the fact shipping originating from US ports now outweighed that from the St Lawrence by two to one, it made sense in terms of efficient use of both escorts and merchant vessels to redirect traffic from Sydney and the St Lawrence to Halifax and Saint John. That argument became still more compelling when, in early August, the naval conference in Washington shifted the terminus of ocean convoys to New York, one result of which would be to leave much of Halifax's capacity unused. There was further pressure in late August and early September when the Admiralty made a strong appeal for the RCN to supply as many ocean-going escorts as possible for the impending Allied invasion of North Africa. This task, as Churchill himself underscored in a personal message to Mackenzie King, was more important to Allied objectives than anything other than the defence of the SC and HX convoys. Cessation of the Sydney–Québec series would free up six corvettes and six Bangors, which could then be redeployed to the Atlantic coast forces to free another six corvettes for service in North African waters. There was, moreover, no apparent logistical impediment to closure of the gulf, quite the reverse: the transfer of the HX and SC convoys to New York would further aggravate the underutilization in summer and autumn of the facilities at Halifax and Saint John. These Atlantic ports had unused capacity to handle ships that would normally load in the gulf.[92]

On 9 September the Cabinet War Committee approved the Naval Staff's recommendation that a total of seventeen corvettes should be provided for the North African campaign, twelve by closing the gulf to ocean shipping and five from the west coast.[93] According to Mackenzie King's diary, he was the only member of the Cabinet War Committee to have doubts about the decision:

> I presented the view that the few [corvettes] we could send [to North Africa] might be relatively unimportant for the purpose for which they were needed compared to the purpose which they would be serving while here …
>
> … There have been, in the last few days, serious sinkings; much submarine activity around Newfoundland, in the Gulf of St Lawrence and in the St Lawrence itself. It is a great pity that we cannot make known what is happening. Letting corvettes go means routing freight by the river will have to stop for this season.
>
> Nelles is making it a condition that the ships must be returned not later than April [1943]. My fear and guess is that they will all either be gone or be kept by British for continental purposes for an early offensive when Spring comes.[94]

These were all telling points and they cut to the very core of the Liberal government's war policies, especially King's own public pledges that the government would give priority to the security of Canada's own shores. Yet, now that the balance between the effort at home and abroad was being posed in its starkest form, with U-boats sinking ships within sight of constituents on shore,

---

91.   Huband, Montréal representative, MWT to MWT, London, 30 July 1942, PRO, MT 59/592, extracts in DHH, 81/742

92.   Plans Division, "History of North Atlantic Convoy Escort Organization and Canadian Participation Therein, Sep.1939 to Apr., 1943," 15; SecNB to COAC, "Rearrangement Convoys East Coast of North America," 3 Aug. 1942, DHH, 81/520/8280, box 1, 8280 B, pt 3; PM, GB, to PM, Canada, 5 Sep. 1942, *Documents on Canadian External Relations* IX, 353

93.   Plans Division, "History of North Atlantic Convoy Escort Organization," 15-16; SSEA to BHC, 9 Sep. 1942, BHC to SSEA, 14 Sep. 1942, *DCER* IX, 354

94.   King diary, 9 Sep. 1942

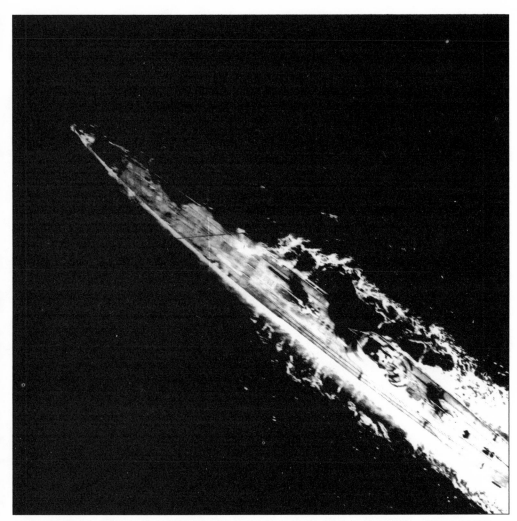

Air power played a critical role in harassing U-boats during the Battle of the St Lawrence. This is *U 165* under attack from a Hudson of 113 Squadron, south of Anticosti Island, 9 September 1942. (DND PMR83-427)

King allowed himself to be brought around by Churchill's appeal and to the fact that, according to his diary, all other members of the CWC believed the corvettes should be sent to North Africa. King was never so readily swayed in proposals for the expansion of the overseas army. His agreement to close the gulf and send a substantial naval force to join the North African operation is one of the clearest examples of the prime minister's willingness to sanction aggressive, distant employment of the navy, despite direct and immediate cost to Canadian national interests.

The instant Cabinet gave approval on 9 September, the Naval Staff signalled British and US authorities to divert cargo ships bound for the St Lawrence to Atlantic coast ports. Time was of the essence, for, the staff estimated, a schedule would have to be maintained on the Sydney–Québec route for two weeks to clear ships that could not be diverted or were already loading at St Lawrence ports.[95] As the fate of QS 33 demonstrated, it would be no small task to fight these convoys through. COAC assigned two destroyers from the WLEF, the RN Towns *Salisbury* and *Witherington* for duty with the SQ–QS convoys.

Eastern Air Command had already, on receiving word of the one-sided QS 33 battle, rushed more aircraft to the gulf, including a detachment of Lockheed Hudson bombers at Chatham, New Brunswick. From this position these fast aircraft could provide concentrated coverage in the Gaspé area and the central gulf. The detachment came from 113 Squadron at Yarmouth, which had proved itself the most successful of the RCAF units in applying effectively the latest aerial anti-submarine weapons and tactics. As will be seen in the next chapter, the squadron had accounted for the first U-boat to be sunk by the RCAF, late in July. The Chatham detachment, together with other gulf detachments, and additional operational and training aircraft that flew special missions from bases in Nova Scotia and Prince Edward Island, scoured the central gulf. These searches featured an increasing number of night missions, an endeavour in which the command's newly fitted ASV radar provided some help, although less than expected because of teething problems and the confusing returns that came from the land masses around the gulf. Meanwhile, the Gaspé naval command had responded to the attacks on QS 33 by sending out a total of at least eight Bangors and corvettes, together with several Fairmiles, to search areas where the submarines might be lurking, and, like the aircraft, to chase down every possible contact report. Most of these reports were undoubtedly false, but in mid-morning on 9 September one of the 113 Squadron Hudsons made a firm sighting of a surfaced submarine and delivered an aerial depth charge attack that was just a few seconds too late, off the southern shore of Anticosti Island.[96]

The attack may well have been on *U 165* for Hoffman later reported to BdU that it was "difficult to contact" convoys between Gaspé and Anticosti "because of air patrols." He recommended instead the waters between Cap Chat and Pointe-des-Monts, where the St Lawrence narrows and it was possible to sight and attack convoys from a submerged position.[97] Hartwig had already come to the same conclusion. On 8 September, the day following his successful attack, he attempted to patrol the waters north of the Gaspé Peninsula, but encountering only the RCN's search groups he

95. NSHQ to Adm, repeated CONNAV et al, 2223Z/9 Sep. 1942, NAC, RG 24, 6789, NSS 8280-166/16, v 3

96. Douglas, *Creation of a National Air Force*, 502; Operations Plotting Room, "The Following Is a Summary of Patrols Carried Out as a Result of Attacks on QS 33," 12 Sep. 1942, DHH, 89/34 mfm, NSS 8280-QS 33. See also, Staff Officer (Bases and Rents), NSHQ, "HMCS Raccoon, Movements between Sep. 3 and Sep. 7, 1942," 12 Sep. 1942, DHH, DOD, "Weekly Operational Summaries," 1942

97. BdU, KTB, 17 Sep. 1942

moved west into the mouth of the river that night, patrolling off Cap Chat. When he dived at dawn on 10 September Hartwig believed he saw the silhouette of *U 165*. That day SQ 35 passed to the north of the U-boats without being detected; evidently hoping to repeat their earlier successes close to the coast, the submarines were hugging the south shore.[98]

Their confidence was rewarded next morning, 11 September. The Bangor *Clayoquot* and the corvette *Charlottetown*, which had escorted SQ 35 and were now returning to base at Gaspé, steamed directly towards *U 517*'s submerged patrol. Because *Clayoquot* was short of fuel, the ships were not zigzagging. Shortly after 0800, while onlookers watched from shore, six to seven miles away, one torpedo hit the starboard quarter of the corvette and another close to the engine room. The crew calmly abandoned the rapidly sinking ship. Tragically, the explosion of the torpedo in the stern had evidently damaged the pistols of the depth charges stored there, all of which had been checked to make sure they were set to "safe" the day before. One of the charges detonated as the stern slipped below the surface, and it was this explosion that caused most of the casualties, five dead, including the commanding officer, and thirteen seriously injured.[99]

Clayoquot's counter attacks knocked its own radio out of commission, and so the Bangor was unable to signal until over three hours after the destruction of *Charlottetown*. Meanwhile, reports from people who had seen the incident from shore that reached senior commands within about an hour and a half, and EAC sent three aircraft to the scene. During the afternoon the British destroyer *Witherington* searched the Cap Chat area. The sailing of QS 34 had been delayed until *Witherington* arrived from Halifax on the morning of the 11th, and the convoy was only a few hours out of Bic Island when *Charlottetown* had been attacked. *Witherington* had dashed ahead of the convoy in response to the news of *Charlottetown*'s sinking, and through much of the rest of the convoy's passage to Sydney over the next two days operated at a distance, leading other warships from Gaspé in searches around Anticosti where sighting reports—from observers on shore and a transport aircraft, both dubious sources—suggested the U-boats might be operating.[100] *U 517* had, in fact, made its way through the passage between Anticosti and the Gaspé Peninsula, south of the areas identified by the sighting reports, hoping to locate a convoy off Gaspé. All Hartwig saw were searching escorts and, more frequently, aircraft—he described the waters close to the Gaspé shore as "heavily patrolled" —and therefore he had pushed east across the gulf towards Newfoundland and then reconnoitred towards Bird Rock, north of the Magdalene Islands. "Only heavy air cover encountered," Hartwig recorded, possibly reflecting the efforts of the air force General Reconnaissance schools at Charlottetown and Summerside in Prince Edward Island, which were routing as many as 140 training flights per day over the waters north of the island to support the shipping defences. The situation did not improve as the

---

98. *U 517*, KTB, 8-10 Sep. 1942

99. Ibid, 11 Sep. 1942; "HMCS 'Charlottetown,'" 18 Sep. 1942, DHH, DOD, "Weekly Operational Summaries," 1942; *Charlottetown* to NOIC Gaspé, "Report on Loss of HMC Ship," 13 Sep. 1942, NAC, RG 24, 12009, G018-1, pt 2; *Clayoquot* to NOIC Gaspé, "Report on Sinking of HMCS 'Charlottetown,'" 12 Sep. 1942, "Minutes" and "Findings of the Board of Inquiry Held on Board HMCS 'Fort Ramsay' at Gaspé, Québec ... 12 Sep., 1942, to Inquire into the Loss of HMCS 'Charlottetown,'" NAC, RG 24, 12009, G22-1-2

100. HMS *Witherington*, "ROP of HMS Witherington during Period 9 to 14 Sep., 1942," 17 Sep. 1942, NAC, RG 24, 12009, file G018-1, pt 2; "HMCS 'Charlottetown,'" 18 Sep. 1942, DHH, DOD, "Weekly Operational Summaries," 1942; on the sighting reports see DOD, "Report for Week Ending 17 Sep. [1942]," ibid; EAC WIRs, weeks ending 11 and 18 Sep. 1942, DHH, 181.003(D432); Sarty, "EAC Anti-Submarine Operations," 59

submarine made its way back towards Gaspé on 13 to 14 September; Hartwig sighted thirteen aircraft.[101]

Nevertheless, during the night of 14 to 15 September, *U 517* was able to reach a promising position for a submerged patrol off Cap des Rosiers, just to the north of where the submarine had previously attacked QS 33. As in the Strait of Belle Isle, Hartwig's timing was perfect. On 13 September SQ 36, which with twenty-two merchant vessels was one of the largest of the gulf convoys of the season, had sailed from Sydney. There was also the strongest escort yet assembled for a gulf convoy, including the destroyer HMS *Salisbury*, two corvettes, two Bangors, and two Fairmiles, together with close air cover. Despite these efforts, the passage of the convoy was a near repetition of the ill-fated QS 33. As SQ 36 passed Cap des Rosiers on the afternoon of 15 September, Hartwig made a submerged attack that destroyed two merchant vessels. The next morning, after daybreak, as the convoy approached Cap Chat, *U 165*, in another submerged attack, hit two merchant ships, one of which did not sink and was later salved.[102] *U 165*, having expended all its torpedoes, departed for home, only to be sunk by a mine in the Bay of Biscay.[103] *U 517* had meanwhile, during the night of 15 to 16 September, surfaced to move rapidly around the north shore of the Gaspé Peninsula, hoping to catch up with the convoy. Hartwig gave up as fog descended, but remained on the surface as he worked his way back to the east, running midway between Anticosti and the Gaspé coast. During the late morning of the 16th, a 113 Squadron Hudson sighted the boat, but it dived in time to escape damage from the aerial depth charges.[104] That night *U 517* pulled off once more towards the western coast of Newfoundland where she shifted more torpedoes into the hull on the night of 17 to 18 September. The boat then made a sojourn into the Cabot Strait but saw little in the fog and headed back towards Gaspé.[105]

At mid-day on 21 September, once more in the vicinity of Cap des Rosiers, Hartwig sighted smoke from convoy SQ 38, and tried to close, but could not do so at his slow submerged speed. At 1519, when the convoy was disappearing over the horizon, Hartwig suddenly saw an escort coming towards him from astern. This was the Bangor *Georgian*, which formed part of the escort for SQ 38, had gone into Gaspé earlier in the day, and was now coming back out to rejoin. *Georgian* had been alerted by strong asdic returns, and the crew then sighted not just *U 517*'s periscope, but "part of the conning tower." In his war diary (KTB), Hartwig noted recurring difficulties in maintaining depth because of the pronounced layers of water under different densities, and the submarine was apparently riding higher than he realized. *Georgian* raced in to ram, but the submarine crash-dived before it reached the position. *Georgian* made a snap depth charge attack over the swirl, and then swung around to deliver a deliberate attack. As the Bangor made this slow run, Hartwig prepared to fire a torpedo, but at the last moment the warship suddenly changed course. Immediately after the Bangor's deliberate attack, according to *Georgian*'s account, "the submarine surfaced astern about 900 yards. HMCS Georgian turned towards target again with the intention

101. *U 517*, KTB, 11-14 Sep. 1942

102. Ibid, 12-15 Sep. 1942; SO (AS), COAC, "Analysis of Attacks by a U-Boat on Convoy SQ 36 on 15 and 16 Sep. 1942," 3 Nov. 1942, NAC, RG 24, 11504, 21-1-14

103. BdU, KTB, 16 Sep. 1942; Niestlé, *German U-boat Losses* II, 123

104. *U 517*, KTB, 15-16 Sep. 1942; Douglas, *Creation of a National Air Force*, 503

105. *U 517*, KTB, 16-21 Sep. 1942

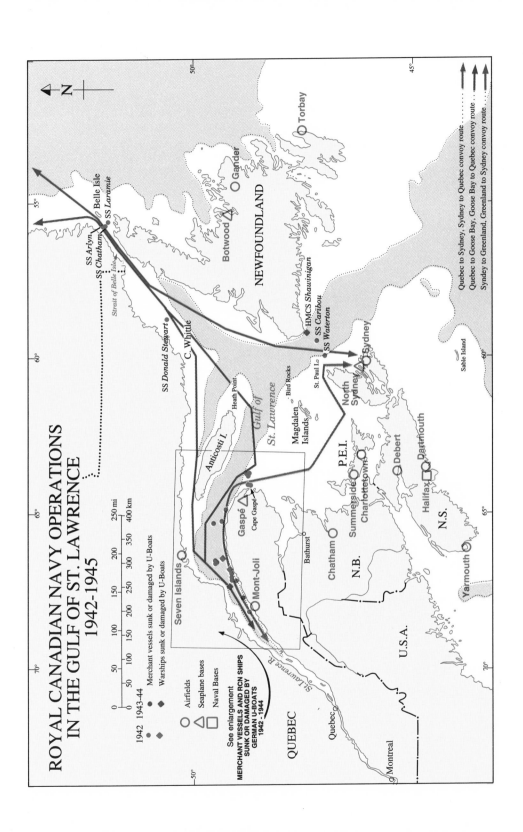

ROYAL CANADIAN NAVY OPERATIONS IN THE GULF OF ST. LAWRENCE 1942-1945

N

1942 1943-44

○ ● Airfields
△ ◆ Seaplane bases
□ ◼ Naval Bases

See enlargement
MERCHANT VESSELS AND RCN SHIPS SUNK OR DAMAGED BY GERMAN U-BOATS 1942 - 1944

Merchant vessels sunk or damaged by U-Boats
Warships sunk or damaged by U-Boats

0 50 100 150 200 250 mi
0 50 100 150 200 250 300 350 400 km

Quebec to Sydney, Sydney to Quebec convoy route ....
Quebec to Goose Bay, Goose Bay to Quebec convoy route ....
Syndey to Greenland, Greenland to Sydney convoy route ....

QUEBEC

Montreal

Quebec

St. Lawrence R.

Seven Islands

Mont-Joli

Gaspé
Cape Gaspé

Heath Point

Anticosti I.

C. Whittle

SS Donald Stewart

Gulf of St. Lawrence

Bird Rocks

Magdalen Islands

St. Paul I.

North Sydney

Sydney

Bathurst

Chatham

N.B.

U.S.A.

Summerside
Charlottetown

P.E.I.

Debert

Halifax Dartmouth

N.S.

Yarmouth

Sable Island

Strait of Belle Isle

SS Arlyn
SS Chatham
Belle Isle
SS Laramie

HMCS Shawinigan

SS Caribou
SS Waterton

NEWFOUNDLAND

Botwood
Gander

Torbay

50°

55°

45°

70° 65° 60°

70° 65° 60°

of ramming, but before reaching the position the submarine turned over on her side ... and sank ... A full pattern set at 150 feet was then dropped on the position where the submarine sank. Huge patches of oil appeared."[106] Hartwig does not mention coming to the surface, but does state that shortly after the first deliberate attack he was having difficulty controlling his depth: "The first depth charge explodes. The boat drops to depth 100 [metres] at cruising speed. When I slow to listening speed, the boat climbs to 60 [metres]. These water layers!" It seems unlikely that he could have mistaken the depth by a matter of some sixty metres, but it is striking that the German's report of loss of control coincides so closely with the timing of *Georgian*'s report that he broke surface. Whatever happened, the submarine suffered only superficial damage in *Georgian*'s attacks, although Hartwig noted that the "depth charges were close by as long as it was light." Hartwig's log explains the upwelling of oil that convinced the Bangor—and COAC staff—the enemy had probably been destroyed: "I assume we had left an oil slick, which had proved to be the case on an earlier occasion and a second one after that (presumably fuel oil test line from the inner bunker)." The Bangor remained in the area until 2000, when it went into to Gaspé to replenish its depth charges, having expended a total of thirty-four.[107] *Salisbury*, which had come from SQ 38, about ninety minutes fast steaming away, arrived at 2015 and searched the area until 2130 before setting course to rejoin the convoy.[108]

During the night of 21 to 22 September, when all was quiet once more, Hartwig made towards the north shore of the St Lawrence. He needed to repair damage and here would be clear of the heavily patrolled traffic lanes, but within reach of the next convoy. *U 517*, while lurking in the central estuary, south of Sept Iles, sighted the eastbound QS 37 late in the morning of 24 September; the escort group was the same one, under *Salisbury*, that had brought SQ 38 west a few days before.[109]

QS 37, as it turned out, had the benefit of a defence fully as effective as that provided SQ 38 by *Georgian*'s chance encounter, but one that reflected a good deal more art. The losses to the heavily escorted SQ 36 on 15 and 16 September, and the subsequent success of one of the Chatham-based Hudsons in locating the submarine while searching over areas through which the U-boat was likely to attempt to move off, had converted the air staff to offensive tactics, at least for the special conditions in the gulf. The attacks on SQ 36 by submerged U-boats had confirmed that because of water layering the escorts' asdics were nearly useless at choke points, where a submarine hovering beneath the surface had an excellent chance of remaining undetected even when in asdic range. The main purpose of an aircraft perched over a convoy was to persuade submarines to submerge, and therefore lose contact, but this open-ocean tactic had demonstrably failed. Still convinced that close air escort was necessary, the air staff took measures in providing additional machines for offensive searches. This used up the shoestring resources around the southwestern part of Nova Scotia, so EAC turned over those patrol areas to US air forces. This meant that RCAF Station Yarmouth's complement of aircraft—the rest of 113 Squadron—could be moved to the gulf.

---

106. *Georgian*, "Sinking of Enemy Submarine ... 2158/21 Sept.," 23 Sep. 1942, NAC, RG 24, 6905, NSS 8910-443/23

107. *U 517*, KTB, 21 Sep. 1942; *Georgian*, "Sinking of Enemy Submarine"

108. HMS *Salisbury*, "ROP whilst Acting as Senior Officer of Escort for Convoys SQ 38 and QS 37," 26 Sep. 1942, DHH, 81/520/SQ 38

109. *Salisbury* ROP; *U 517*, KTB, 22-4 Sep. 1942

The resulting reinforcement on 16 to 18 September had increased the total number of combat aircraft at Mont Joli, Chatham, and Gaspé, from about nine to fifteen, and the strength at Sydney, which was responsible for the eastern gulf and the Atlantic approaches to the Cabot Strait, from about sixteen to twenty.[110]

During the afternoon of 24 September one of the Hudsons carrying out sweeps sighted *U 517* just as it was submerging after running on the surface to get ahead of the convoy. The submarine was too far away for the aircraft to attack, and Hartwig appears not to have realized he had been spotted. The aircraft flew off to warn the convoy, which was about thirty miles away. The Hudson then returned to the vicinity of the earlier sighting, shortly after Hartwig had resurfaced. A lookout saw the swooping Hudson, and the submarine dived in good time; because of an equipment failure, the aircraft dropped only one of the normal stick of four depth charges.[111]

After dark, Hartwig made another surfaced run in pursuit of the convoy. EAC launched a large flying program that night. At risk, depending upon which way the U-boat known to be present hunted, was the westbound SQ 39, now in the St Lawrence estuary, as well as the eastbound QS 37. Another 113 Squadron Hudson caught *U 517* fully surfaced, south of the western end of Anticosti, about thirty-five miles eastward of the earlier attack, with a well-executed attack. "2 powerful explosions astern," Hartwig recorded, "3 bombs dropped; 3rd bomb right next to ship's side so that stern gets flooded over by impact. Presumably a dud." The submarine, in other words, had come within a hair's breadth of destruction. Later that night, Hartwig resurfaced to continue the pursuit, and again sighted the convoy after daylight on the 25th, but within twenty minutes was forced down by a Hudson, as he was again on two later occasions. Hartwig gave up the chase only in the afternoon, when, near the Magdalene Islands, another Hudson—the same aircraft and crew that had attacked him the night before—surprised the U-boat and delivered an attack that did no damage, but which Hartwig described as "well-placed." That night, early on the 26th, *U 517* pressed on to the Cabot Strait, hoping to catch the convoy as it neared port, but found only naval and air patrols and then, on the 28th, heavy fog.[112]

Hartwig, who had acquired a good sense of the convoy schedules, headed back towards Gaspé, and in the early dark hours of 29 September sighted QS 38, escorted by HMS *Witherington* and four Canadian Bangors south of the central part of Anticosti Island. The convoy had an all-night close air escort, as was becoming a common precaution, but it did not help.[113] The bright moonlight that silhouetted the ships enabled Hartwig to sight the convoy at a distance, and he was able to close on the surface from the darkness down moon from the convoy. He was pushing into a gap in the screen between the destroyer in the van, and the Bangors on the flank, but the latter swept forward at the critical moment compelling him to fire all four forward tubes early, at a range of 2,000 to 2,500 metres. Hartwig tried to swing around to fire his after tubes, but had to crash dive as the Bangors continued to patrol towards his position.[114] The torpedoes hit nothing, but at least two exploded at the end of their runs, causing one of the merchant ships in the rear to fire warn-

---

110. Douglas, *Creation of a National Air Force*, 504

111. Ibid; *U 517*, KTB, 24 Sep. 1942

112. Douglas, *Creation of a National Air Force*, 504-5; *U 517*, KTB, 25-8 Sep. 1942

113. EAC operations summary signal for 28 Sep. 1942, DHH, 181.003 (D304); *U 517*, KTB, 29 Sep. 1942

114. *U 517*, KTB, 29 Sep. 1942

ing rockets. *Witherington* realized what had happened and called for additional air support.[115] Also at risk were two other convoys, NL 8, on its way to Québec from Labrador and a "Sydney–Québec St Lawrence Group"; the latter comprising eleven gulf-bound ships that could not be diverted to Atlantic ports under the order of 9 September because they were carrying out essential services within the gulf.[116] The heavy schedule of air patrols that began before dawn on 29 September in response to *Witherington*'s alert came up empty-handed, until mid-afternoon, when a Chatham-based Hudson returning from its patrol surprised the submarine. It was still in the Gaspé Bay approaches and had come to the surface to search for shipping. Again Hartwig commented that the aircraft's near-miss attack as he crash dived was "well placed."[117]

Hartwig continued to hover in the vicinity of the main shipping channel, east of Gaspé and south of Anticosti for the next five days. Perhaps he hoped to pick up the next Sydney–Québec convoy; if so he waited in vain. SQ 39, which had sailed from Sydney on 23 September and QS 38, which had departed Bic Island on the 27th, were the last of the regularly scheduled through-gulf convoys.[118] When *Witherington* delivered QS 38 at Sydney on 30 September, *Salisbury* was waiting there, and the two destroyers headed off to Halifax the next day.[119] By that time all the corvettes and six of the Bangors had left the gulf as part of the reorganization required to provide escorts for Torch. Naval forces assigned to the gulf now included only seven Bangors (five at Sydney, two at Gaspé), two flotillas of Fairmiles (one each at Sydney and Gaspé), and the two Halifax-based corvettes earmarked for the Québec to Labrador convoys.[120]

NSHQ had to abandon its intention of entirely shutting down the through-gulf convoys after SQ 39 and QS 38. The Naval Staff may have assumed that most of the essential trade within the gulf was carried in small coasting vessels that had not been included in convoy and had never been bothered by the U-boats. If so, they were disabused by the naval control service at Québec, which warned that many of the ocean-class ships that had sailed in the Sydney–Québec series were engaged in local services that supported key mining and forest industries. There was also ocean traffic originating from or destined for the Great Lakes that could not be diverted.[121] The "Sydney–Québec St Lawrence Group" mentioned above proved to be a continuation of the SQ series, which again adopted the SQ numbering starting with SQ 43, which departed Sydney on 18 October.[122] The QS series maintained its sequential numbering, but like the continuation of the SQ series, sailed only as needed at intervals of seven to ten days. Because only one of these convoys would be on passage at a time, COAC was able to lift the dividing line between east-bound and

---

115. Ibid, 28-9 Sep. 1942; *Witherington* ROP; HMS *Witherington* to NOIC Sydney, 1130Z/29 Sep. 1942, NOIC Sydney to HMS *Witherington*, 1642Z/29 Sep. 1942, DHH, NHS CCSC, "QS" file

116. NCSO Sydney to NCSO Québec, 1317Z/29 Sep. 1942, DHH, NHS CCSC, "SQ"

117. EAC, operations summary signal for 29 Sep. 1942, DHH, 181.003 (D304); Douglas, *Creation of a National Air Force*, 505; *U 517*, KTB, 29 Sep. 1942

118. SO (Operations), COAC, ROP Sep. 1942, para 6, DHH, NHS NSS 1000-5-13, pt 4

119. *Witherington* ROP

120. RCN daily states, 30 Sep. 1942, DHH, 81/520/1650-DS

121. NCSO Québec to NOIC Québec, 28 Sep. 1942, CNS to DM, "Traffic in St Lawrence River and Gulf," 7 Oct. 1942, DHH, 89/34 mfm, NSS 8280-QS; SecNB to COAC, FONF, NOIC Sydney, "Local Shipping in St Lawrence," 6 Oct. 1942, NAC, RG 24, 11,503, 1-14-1

122. NCSO Sydney to NCSO Québec, 1807Z/17 Oct. 1942, DHH, NHS CCSC, "SQ" and "QS"

west-bound traffic, and thus allow more scope for diverse routing, an important measure because of the small surface escort forces available.[123] The "Sydney–Québec St Lawrence Group" that had departed from Sydney on 29 September was a good, if extreme example. Because of the dislocations created by the redeployment of warships away from the gulf, the only escort available was two Fairmiles. For that reason the convoy sailed close along the New Brunswick shore and, never realizing the imminent danger, slipped into Gaspé from the south at the very time *U 517* was searching out in the main shipping approaches to the east.[124] The merchant ships, now escorted by Bangors, slipped out of Gaspé on 2 October and ran close along the shore to Rimouski, again escaping Hartwig's notice.[125]

The first of the convoys to continue the Québec to Sydney series, QS 39, departed from Bic Island on 4 October. Its sailing awaited the arrival of the special group from Gaspé so that it could have a reasonably strong escort of three Bangors and three Fairmiles, together with the new construction Bangor *Westmount*.[126] There was also full air coverage, including two aircraft flying close escort. These arrangements probably reflected fresh evidence that there was still at least one submarine in the gulf. *U 517* had laid low, but Kapitänleutnant Gräf in the type VII *U 69*, the first of the five additional submarines ordered to the gulf by Dönitz on the basis of *U 517* and *U 165*'s encouraging reports, was not so circumspect.

Gräf arrived in the Cabot Strait on the night of 29/30 September, and patrolled between Cape Breton's Cape North and Newfoundland's Cape Ray, surfacing only at night because of the aircraft that frequently appeared. Early on 2 October, he sighted a small convoy, and tracked it all day but could not get into firing position because of the escorts' sweeps, air patrols, and the nearness of the Cape Breton coast, which limited his sea room. The intensity of the air patrols was partly Gräf's own doing, for he flashed off an early sighting report, rebroadcast when he did not get an acknowledgment, and then radioed a further report later in the day; the Canadians DF'd these signals, and launched air sweeps in the area.[127]

U 69 proceeded into the gulf on the night of 2/3 October. Further to the west, Hartwig, still silent, abandoned his vigil off Gaspé on the third and began to work his way towards Cap Chat to try to pick up an outbound convoy. He succeeded late on the fourth, locating QS 39 in mid-channel of the estuary. He attacked twice in the early hours of 5 October, once on the surface and once submerged, but made no hits, the result it seems of the active air and sea escort and equipment failures, caused in part at least by damage in earlier attacks on the submarine. None of the torpedoes detonated, and the escorts noticed nothing. After daybreak, only two hours after *U 517*'s second failed attack, *U 69* sighted QS 39 while running submerged north of the Gaspé Peninsula. Gräf decided not to pursue the convoy, because he would have had to run on the surface, a risk he was

123. COAC to NOICs Québec and Sydney, 1529Z/19 Sep. 1942. See also, NOIC Sydney to COAC, "New Proposal for Gulf of St Lawrence Convoys," 15 Sep. 1942, NAC, RG 24, 6789, NSS 8280-166/16, pt 3.

124. NCSO Sydney to NCSO Québec, 1317Z/29 Sep. 1942, DHH, NHS CCSC, "SQ"; RCN Daily States, 30 Sep. 1942, DHH,81/520/1650-DS, confirms that only two Fairmiles sailed with the group, *Q 080* and *Q 085*.

125. *Red Deer* to NOIC Gaspé, 4 Oct. 1942, DHH, 89/34 mfm, NSS 8280-QS 39; NOIC Gaspé to NOIC Québec, 0229Z/29 Sep. 1942, DHH, NHS CCSC, "QS"

126. NOIC Gaspé to COAC, 1916/30 Sep. 1942, DHH, NHS CCSC, "QS"; *Gananoque*, "Letter of Proceedings re QS 39 ...," 7 Oct. 1942, DHH, 89/34 mfm, NSS 8280-QS 39

127. *U 69*, KTB, 29 Sep.–2 Oct. 1942; Tennyson and Sarty, *Guardian of the Gulf*, 272

not willing to take because there was low cloud cover, perfect conditions for air patrols to catch him by surprise. While he turned to continue west, however, he broadcast a sighting report, which was immediately DF'd; the convoy made a radical diversion, and EAC laid on special sweeps. Further DFs on 6 and 7 October, probably *U 517*'s homebound signals as Hartwig made his way from Gaspé towards the Cabot Straits, tended to confirm that the main threat was in the eastern gulf rather than in the river. *U 69,* in fact, penetrated far up the river, some sixty miles west of Cap Chat, within twenty-five miles of Rimouski.[128]

U 69, like the other submarines that followed *U 517* into the gulf, carried the new German radar search receiver *Funkmessbeobachtung* (*FuMB*), popularly known as *Metox* after the French company that manufactured it, which detected long-wave radar emissions, such as those of the ASV that equipped EAC aircraft and the RCN's SW1C. The constant alarms from *Metox* helped the defence by encouraging caution on the part of Gräf and the submarine commanders who followed. But it also helped U-boats find targets; during the very dark early hours of 9 October, *Metox*, evidently set off by the radars in the escorts *Arrowhead* and *Hepatica,* alerted the submarine to the presence of NL 9, on the last leg of passage from Labrador to Québec City. By right of all previous experience, the convoy should have been well clear of danger. The manoeuvres of the escorts forced *U 69* to fire early, at a range of some 2,000 meters. At least one of the three torpedoes hit the small Canadian freighter *Carolus*: "Tall dark explosive plume with substantial flames, the target broke in two." Eleven of the crew of thirty died. The explosions of the torpedoes and the depth charges and starshells from the corvettes could be clearly heard in the resort town of Metis Beach on the south shore. The keeper of the lighthouse on Petit Metis, a point of land that was closer to the scene, warned authorities that a shore bombardment was under way, shut down the light, and headed inland with his family. Gräf, convinced by the strong *Metox* returns that the corvettes had made radar contact, was surprised when they did not pursue as he fled in the darkness. He speculated that the Canadian radar operators must have been fast asleep, but in fact the SW1C, whose effectiveness against the small profile of submarines was marginal, had not detected *U 69*. By 11 October intense air and sea searches in the river and estuary, which produced more nerve-wracking *Metox* alarms, persuaded Gräf to head back towards the Cabot Straits. He was having problems with the compressed air system, which was critical for submerged operations, and at the strait he could make for the relative safety of the open ocean in the event his ability to dive was impaired.[129]

Meanwhile, on 10 to 11 October, two more large submarines, the type IXa *U 43* under Kapitänleutnant H. Schwantke and the type IXb *U 106* under Kapitänleutnant H. Rasch, were approaching the Cabot Strait from the Atlantic. Both noticed enough of the defence, including *Metox* warnings, that they operated cautiously, not sending radio reports and surfacing only at night. Rasch in *U 106*, hoping to repeat Gräf's discovery of coastal convoys at the southwestern end of Cabot Strait, headed directly for St Paul Island, off Cape Breton's North Cape. He was in luck. Late in the morning of 11 October, amid choppy seas that obscured his periscope from view, he sighted the Sydney-bound BS 31, two steamers escorted by the armed yacht HMCS *Vison* and a low-flying Canso of 117 Squadron, coming almost directly towards him. The two torpedoes fired by Rasch at the close

128. *U 69* and *U 517*, KTB, 2-7 Oct. 1942; *Gananoque*, "Letter of Proceedings re QS 39," 7 Oct. 1942, and attached signals, DHH, 89/34 mfm, NSS 8280-QS 39; EAC WIR, week ending 9 Oct. 1942, paras 3 and 25, DHH, 181.003 (D423)

129. *U 69*, KTB, 9-11 Oct. 1942; Sarty, *Canada and the Battle of the Atlantic*, 113

range of 220 metres hit the Newfoundland-registered SS *Waterton*, bound for Cleveland. She sank within eight minutes, but her crew got away safely. *Vison*'s snap counter-attack and follow-up searches with the help of additional naval vessels and aircraft from Sydney found nothing, but were more effective than Canadian authorities realized. Rasch, who had been keenly aware of the Canso, believed the first depth charges had been dropped by the aircraft. He interpreted the sound of *Vison*'s screw, and then those of the armed yacht HMCS *Reindeer* that had come out in support, as those of destroyers. Although, as Rasch observed, the water conditions were "very poor" for the transmission of sound, he was struck by the fact that the first of the deliberate depth charge counter attacks was "fairly well placed." In sum, Rasch believed he had come up against a well coordinated air-sea hunting group, and dove to 145 metres where he hid for the next eight hours.[130]

BdU, on the basis of Hartwig's report and *U 69*'s recent success, signalled Rasch and Schwantke to push through to the mouth of the St Lawrence to take advantage of the dark nights of the new moon period. It also warned of the "suspected standing U-Boat pursuit patrols ... with continual surveillance of adjacent areas" in the vicinity of Gaspé. *U 106* began passage early on the 12th. *U 43* had had to dive so often in response to *Metox* warnings and the appearance of escorts and aircraft during its initial approach towards the strait, that its batteries were depleted. Schwantke pulled back out to the open waters south of Newfoundland on the night of 11 to 12 October so he could surface and recharge the batteries before pushing through the Cabot Strait on the following night.[131]

Gräf, in *U 69*, was coming in the opposite direction, making a submerged passage across the eastern gulf on 12 October. That night, in an exchange of positions with *U 106*, Gräf began to patrol near St Paul Island, the promising hunting ground he had identified during his inward passage. While submerged during daylight on the 13th, he identified three Swedish freighters bound for Montréal to load grain. BdU had advised that these three neutrals were expected to pass through the Cabot Strait. He surfaced after dark that evening but made no effort to track them, patrolling back and forth across the north–south route to Sydney.[132]

Shortly after midnight, 14 October, Gräf sighted the Newfoundland Railway ferry *Caribou*, making one of its thrice-weekly passages between North Sydney and Port-aux-Basques, Newfoundland, and its escort, HMCS *Grandmère*. In accordance with doctrine for escort of a single ship, the Bangor was keeping station about 2,500 yards off the starboard quarter of the ferry. So dark was the night, however, that she could not see *Caribou*, and like most of the Bangors and other patrol craft operating in Canadian waters, she had not yet been fitted with radar. *U 69* therefore had no difficulty in remaining undetected as it pulled ahead, swung around and fired a torpedo into *Caribou*'s starboard side at 0321, about forty miles off the Newfoundland coast. Tragically, the boilers blew up almost immediately and the vessel went down in minutes. *Grandmère*, closing the scene at maximum speed, only saw the surfaced U-boat at a distance of 350 yards. She altered to ram, and Rasch crash-dived, going to 140 metres depth, right under the position of the sinking, expecting that the Bangor would not drop depth charges among the many survivors on the surface. In a decision that haunted him for the rest of this life, Lieutenant James Cuthbert, RCNR, commanding offi-

---

130. *U 43* and *U 106* KTB, 10-11 Oct. 1942; Tennyson and Sarty, *Guardian of the Gulf*, 273

131. *U 106*, KTB, 12 Oct. 1942; *U 43*, KTB, 11-13 Oct. 1942

132. *U 69*, KTB, 12-13 Oct. 1942

cer of *Grandmère* did his duty and hunted the submarine—without result—for two hours, knowing all the while that people in the sea were dying.[133]

The ferry had gone down so rapidly that only one lifeboat could be launched, so survivors were clinging to wreckage, and being widely dispersed by the wind and seas, which in turn further delayed their recovery. Of the 237 people on board *Caribou*, 135 perished, including many women and children and members of the Canadian and US armed forces. Communities on both sides of the Cabot Strait were abuzz with the news. Realizing that any attempt at censorship would fail and fuel fear and speculation, the navy released all information about the disaster immediately, holding back only details about escort and antisubmarine methods.[134]

Hunts in the area of the sinking by a Bangor, two armed yachts, and a Fairmile—all that could be spared from Sydney—kept *U 69* down until after dark on 15 October.[135] Gräf, detecting blasts on his *Metox* upon surfacing—presumably the result of the round-the-clock air patrols from Sydney undertaken following the sinking of *Caribou*—crept away towards Cape Breton's Atlantic coast. He hoped to contact coastal traffic to Halifax which, the U-boat commanders incorrectly suspected, also included considerable gulf shipping that was routed through the narrow Canso Strait between Cape Breton and the Nova Scotia mainland. Continued air coverage from Sydney, however, persuaded him to move up along the south coast of Newfoundland. On the night of 19/20 October, south of Placentia Bay, he fired at the ore carrier SS *Rose Castle*, which, in the severe storm conditions, had become separated from its Sydney to Wabana convoy. There was no result, and Gräf's assessment of pistol failure is confirmed by reports from *Rose Castle*'s crew that they heard the torpedo strike the side. This was Gräf's last torpedo, and he could not close for a gun attack because of the wild seas. On 21 October, as he was shaping course for home southeast of Cape Race, he was surprised by a Hudson from 145 Squadron, which was on a sweep in response to a DF bearing on Gräf's radio report earlier that day regarding his failed attack on *Rose Castle*. Although the aircraft's depth charges exploded only after the U-boat had safely crash-dived, this parting encounter amply justified the report he had already made to BdU about the "continuous heavy air cover" in the St Lawrence.[136]

To the west, Rasch, in *U 106*, reached the river mouth, in the vicinity south of Pointe-des-Monts on 15 October. The situation was so discouraging that on the 17th he departed for the more promising waters of the Cabot Strait. When he was seaward of Cape Breton on 22 October he reported to BdU: "Have shifted from [mouth of St Lawrence River] to [Cabot Strait area] because of moon and defences. Nothing sighted in [St Lawrence River]. Strong defensive forces since 16.10. Search units using asdic in [area north of Gaspé peninsula], air surveillance cooperating with surface search forces and also operating everywhere without surface forces."[137] That same day, 22 October, he concluded, as had Gräf a week before, that the ocean approaches to Cape Breton were no safer than the gulf, so he headed south, towards Sable Island, alluding to the toll the extended sub-

---

133. Ibid, 14 Oct. 1942; D. How, *Night of the Caribou* (Hantsport 1988)

134. Tennyson and Sarty, *Guardian of the Gulf*, 274-9

135. SO (Operations), COAC WD for Oct. 1942, DHH, NHS NSS 1000-5-13, pt 15

136. Tennyson and Sarty, *Guardian of the Gulf*, 279; *U 69*, KTB, 14-16, 20 Oct. 1942; DDSD(Y), "Ottawa W/T Procedure Y Summary no. 13," 20 Jan. 1943, 11, NAC

137. *U 106*, KTB, 12-22 Oct. 1942

merged runs in the gulf and off Cape Breton was taking on his crew: "The ship's company has to get some fresh air for a change. (Too much operating submerged spoils the fighting spirit.)"[138]

Schwantke in *U 43* also arrived in the St Lawrence estuary on 15 October and proceeded to search further up the river. His log confirms Rasch's observations about the effective defences: "The following has now been observed several times: Searching escorts appear roughly one hour after radar detection by aircraft. Presumably these escorts continually have steam up so as to be ready to proceed. This good cooperation between air and naval forces is striking." An incident on 19 October, when *U 43* was just east of Baie Comeau, brought him to reflect on the protection afforded him by the water conditions: "Observed escort ... during all-round look through periscope ... Escort ... obviously searching. She turns towards me ... went to depth 110 m. The pronounced temperature layers favourably influence depth keeping for the boat as well as listening and the chances of being detected. Thus far, the boat has not once been detected by a surface vessel."[139] Placing greater stock than Rasch in the reports by previous submarines of the plentiful shipping traffic in the river, Schwantke persisted. He was rewarded at mid-day on 21 October when, off the north shore of the Gaspé Peninsula, west of Cap Chat, he made a periscope sighting of SQ 43, three steamers escorted by two Fairmiles and the Bangors *Gananoque* and *Burlington*. *U 43* manoeuvred past the escorts, so Schwantke thought, and was just about to fire into the exposed merchant ships when: "5–6 depth charges which explode almost simultaneously. The battery circuit automatic breaker is knocked off. The torpedo in Tube V is activated in the tube. Several light bulbs etc. are knocked out." Schwantke dropped to 130 metres and waited there seven hours, until after dark, making no attempt to pursue the convoy. He was especially worried about the attack because he had seen no surface escort near him, and therefore assumed that an aircraft had somehow detected his periscope.[140] In fact, this, one of the most effective counter-attacks by the Canadian forces during the St Lawrence campaign, had been delivered in almost an off-hand manner. In the words of Lieutenant B. Williams, RCNVR, the antisubmarine control officer in *Gananoque*, "The echo was at first most doubtful ... The echo then seemed to improve. It was decided that it would be advisable to carry out a counter-attack. It was necessary to make this attack quickly as the target was in the path of the convoy." A further search after the attack failed to regain the contact, *U 43* having gone deep, and Williams observed, "It is to be noted that later in the afternoon other very similar echoes were heard, all of which proved to be 'non-sub,' and it was assumed that this attack was made on a shoal of fish or tide rip."[141] The incident was so typical of many "non-sub" asdic echoes in the St Lawrence that senior authorities did not note it in their periodic intelligence compilations, which as a matter of policy included even highly unlikely contacts. On 25 October Schwantke had a similar encounter with another convoy, although this time the depth charges did no damage.[142] During the next ten days Schwantke saw no trace of traffic, although at least two convoys, QS 42 and SQ 44 would have passed through the river during the period he was searching, and little of defences. Late on 4

---

138. Ibid, 22 Oct. 1942

139. *U 43*, KTB, 15, 18-19 Oct. 1942

140. Ibid, 21-2 Oct. 1942; *Gananoque*, "Letter of Proceedings SQ 43," 24 Oct. 1942, DHH, 89/34 mfm reel 32, NSS 8280-SQ 43

141. *Gananoque*, "Report of Attack on Doubtful Target ... at 1550z 21/10/42 ...," nd, DHH, 89/34 mfm reel 32, NSS 8280-SQ 43

142. *U 43*, KTB, 25-6 Oct. 1942; RCN daily states, 24 Oct. 1942, DHH, 81/520/1650-DS

November he began to work his way east, and early on the 7th departed through the Cabot Strait.[143]

Reinforcements were already close at hand. *U 43, U 69,* and *U 106* were only part of a large new effort U-boat headquarters was mounting in Canadian and Newfoundland waters to follow up the successes of *U 517* and *U 165* in the Strait of Belle Isle and the gulf, and of *U 513* on Newfoundland's Atlantic coast. Rüggeberg in *U 513,* after his spectacular feat at Wabana early in September, had limited success, although he continued to patrol close off the Avalon Peninsula for another five weeks. He found only three opportunities to attack, claiming a sinking on 10 September when he had in fact missed the target, destroyed the steamer *Ocean Vagabond* on 29 September only eight miles off St John's, and fired a miss on 2 October. On 24 to 27 September he had tracked an ocean convoy off the coast, but was driven off by the escorts.[144] "Only limited chances for an isolated boat," he informed headquarters on 30 September.[145] His difficulty in finding targets owed a good deal to the fact virtually all shipping was now moving in coastal convoys, and he particularly noted the movement of the big ore ships under escort, the result of the introduction of the special Wabana–Sydney convoys soon after his attack in Conception Bay. He watched the great activity at RCAF Station Torbay, on the coast to the north of St John's, with fascination from a respectful distance. "There is heavy air activity during the day and the latest development is air activity along the coast by night ... Prospects for success are heavily dependent on weather conditions. During this operation there were 17 foggy days. There is a groundswell off the coast in NNE to SSW winds, steering at periscope depth therefore often not possible."[146] BdU sent *U 455,* which had carried out a mine-laying mission off Charleston, South Carolina, to replace *U 513,* but after nine days off St John's, that submarine departed on 14 October because of equipment problems, and like *U 513* it encountered very little shipping.[147]

To follow up the successful attacks by *U 513* and *U 455,* BdU sent two more large-type IXs to the entrance of the strait. *U 183* and *U 518* arrived on 18 October. They were to maintain a patrol in the northern waters until early November and then take advantage of the new moon to move into the gulf. The boats found the northern strait "completely dead." On 29 October, therefore, BdU changed the intended plan and cleared Schäffer to operate off southern Nova Scotia before moving into the gulf, and the boat patrolled down the Atlantic coast of Newfoundland. The intention was that *U 183* would support *U 522,* which was on its way towards the southern approaches to Halifax; Dönitz expected that the boats would achieve results through surprise, as they would be the first to operate in the area since early August. The situation changed quickly, for on the 30 October *U 522* made contact with the transatlantic convoy SC 107 south of eastern Newfoundland. BdU immediately diverted two other submarines, *U 520* and *U 521,* to pursue the convoy; these boats had just arrived off Newfoundland to follow up *U 513*'s successes with patrols that were to have focused on Conception Bay and St John's. Kapitänleutnant F. Wissman in *U 518,* knowing from radio traffic about the diversion of *U 520* and *U 521,* decided to penetrate Conception Bay himself.[148]

143. *U 43,* KTB, 27 Oct.–7 Nov. 1942; DHH, NHS CCSC, "SQ" and "QS"

144. *U 513,* KTB, 6 Sep.–10 Oct. 1942

145. BdU, KTB, 30 Sep. 1942

146. *U 513,* KTB, 10 Oct. 1942

147. BdU, KTB, 14 Oct. 1942; MOD, *U-Boat War in the Atlantic* II, 57

148. *U 518* and *U 183* KTB, 17 Oct.–1 Nov. 1942; BdU, KTB, 17, 24, 28-31 Oct. 1942

During the early hours of 2 November 1942 Wissmann replicated Rüggeberg's earlier feat. The defences provided since *U 513*'s attack, two Fairmiles and a corvette, had no effect at all in screening such a wide-open anchorage. The corvette *Drumheller* was sweeping off the western shore of Bell Island, and the duty Fairmile was on the northern leg of its patrol within the anchorage.[149] Wissmann was unaware of these vessels as he came in on the surface through the main body of Conception Bay past Bell Island, and then crept back up along the eastern shore to enter the anchorage from the south, opposite to Rüggeberg's approach.[150] The first the warships knew something was wrong was when they saw emergency rockets bursting over the anchorage after four torpedoes had hit. The ore carriers *Rose Castle*, less than two weeks after its fortunate escape from *U 69*, and *PLM 27*, a survivor of *U 513*'s attack of two months before and of the harrowing battle for SC 42 in the autumn of 1941, went down, both with heavy losses of life—twenty-eight in *Rose Castle* and twelve in *PLM 27*. Another torpedo that missed other ships further north in the anchorage hit the Scotia pier, doing severe, but not crippling damage to the facility. As the corvette and both Fairmiles rushed to the position of the sinkings, *U 518* had already fled on the surface, back out the wide southern approach.[151] The next day, 3 November, an RCAF Digby from 10 Squadron at Gander sighted and attacked the boat south of Cape Race. The submarine crash-dived and was at forty metres when the four depth charges exploded, only putting the gyro compass out of action for a short period.[152]

It was galling that *U 518* had so completely eluded the Wabana naval patrols, even after the submarine had revealed itself by firing. The rush of the warships to the scene of the sinking, rather than undertaking sweeps in the approaches to cut off the submarine's escape, reflected lack of experience, organization, and planning. The Board of Inquiry into the incident, on which sat two British and one Canadian officer, thought that the commanding officer of *Drumheller* should be held responsible for these failures. Captain R.E.S. Bidwell, chief of staff to FONF, refused to support a reprimand. "Whilst the Commanding Officer of HMCS Drumheller may not have done the best thing under the circumstances, at least he did something, and it is not considered that he should be censured for having tried to do something to the best of his ability."[153] This was fair as the board discovered that the east coast commands had produced no instructions for the Conception Bay patrol, nor even any general guidance as to how commanding officers should approach the task of screening exposed anchorages. In fact, searches of inshore coastal waters is one of the most difficult challenges of antisubmarine warfare, and the full scope of that difficulty had just begun to dawn on the RCN with the experience gained in the summer and autumn of 1942. The real answer for the protection of port facilities such as those at Bell Island was fixed net defences. As soon as the antitorpedo nets at Sydney were raised for the winter season at the end of November, they were rushed to Wabana, and installed around the loading piers in December. Already FONF had directed that the anchorage be "abandoned"; ships waited at St John's and came

149. "Board of Inquiry in the Circumstances Surrounding the Sinking of Two Ships at Wabana, Bell Island, on 2 Nov., 1942," 4 Nov. 1942, printed in Neary, *Enemy on Our Doorstep*, 79-86

150. *U 518*, KTB, 2 Nov. 1942

151. Neary, *Enemy on Our Doorstep*, 79-86

152. *U 518*, KTB, 3 Nov. 1942; Douglas, *Creation of a National Air Force*, 530

153. Quoted in Neary, *Enemy on Our Doorstep*, 93

round to Wabana under escort, a maximum of two at a time, the number that could simultaneously be loaded. The navy also began work to provide fixed underwater defences for the other two places on the east coast where important traffic was vulnerable to the sort of U-boat attack that had occurred at Wabana: Louisbourg, Sydney's alternate port, and the inner Canso Strait, where the railway ferry linked Cape Breton with the Nova Scotia mainland.[154]

U 518 entered through the Cabot Strait on the night of 6 November to fulfil another mission. During the early hours of 9 November, on the north shore of Chaleur Bay near the town of New Carlisle, Wissmann put ashore an *Abwehr* agent, Werner Alfred Waldemar von Janowski.[155] For an hour and a quarter, while the U-boat's dinghy carried the agent and his equipment to the beach, *U 518* lay about 700 metres offshore, partly submerged, resting on the bottom. Wissmann had one bad moment: "An automobile appears on the road ... The road curves directly ahead of us so that the car's headlights sweep across the water for a brief moment. I hold my breath. Involuntarily, I quickly order heads down before the light hits us ...The scattered houses and all small details ashore can be clearly seen in the car's headlight beams. The houses make a miserable impression."[156] *U 518* cleared Chaleur Bay before dawn on 9 November and proceeded to patrol in the waters off Gaspé.[157]

Janowski had meanwhile been arrested by the Québec Provincial Police within hours of his landing. After daybreak, the agent had made his way into New Carlisle, where the appearance at such an early hour of a stranger with a guttural accent and foreign-looking clothes that had the odd pungent smell of diesel and damp—"U-boat-stink," as submariners called it—who paid for his bath and breakfast with old-fashioned oversized dollar bills, aroused the suspicions of the family who ran the hotel. That night Janowski, an experienced agent, convinced his guards—and the navy—that he was, in fact, waiting to be picked up by a submarine. "The prisoner ... started up in bed with a cry of 'My God! My boat!' and had rushed to the window. The detectives on guard stated they had clearly heard a sound like diesel engines. They had then taken the prisoner down to the local wharf ... and had used a flashlight to signal to seaward to endeavour to get an indication if a submarine was in the vicinity. After some time they gave up the attempt, although they stated they had seen lights which may have been a reply from seaward."[158] The naval command at Gaspé arranged to have Chaleur Bay patrolled by aircraft and by the Bangors *Red Deer* and *Burlington* until the 12th, by which time Janowski, under further questioning, admitted he had just come ashore, and he claimed the submarine was heading for the Bay of Fundy.[159] This version was not an entire fabrication, for BdU had cleared *U 518*, in the event that the gulf proved as unpromising as the latest signals from *U 43*, *U 69,* and *U 106* suggested, to operate in the whole area south

---

154. FONF WD, Nov. 1942, para 4, DHH, NSS 1000-5-20, pt 2; Tennyson and Sarty, *Guardian of the Gulf*, 306-8

155. See Hadley, *U-boats against Canada*, 153-61, and Beeby, *Cargo of Lies*.

156. *U 518*, KTB, 9 Nov. 1942

157. Ibid, 10 Nov. 1942

158. *Fort Ramsay* to SecNB, "Apprehension of Suspect at New Carlisle, PQ," 7 Dec. 1942, NAC, RG 24, 11,127, MS 0011

159. NOIC Gaspé to COAC, 0125Z/12 Nov. 1942, NSHQ to COAC, 2213Z/12 Nov. 1942, NAC, RG 24, 11,127, MS 0011; *Red Deer*, "ROP, Chaleur Bay," 12 Nov. 1942, NAC, RG 24, 12,009, G 018-1, pt 2; Sarty, "Eastern Air Command Anti-Submarine Operations," 95-6. There was a report of a suspicious flashing light on the water off New Carlisle on 12 Nov., so after the Bangors had refuelled, the air and sea watch of Chaleur Bay continued until 14 Nov. COAC WD, Nov. 1942, para 28, DHH, NSS 1000-5-13, pt 16

and west of Halifax.[160] Wissmann, however, was still off Gaspé and saw the two Bangors returning from Chaleur Bay: "2 old single-funnel destroyers ... appear to be entering [Gaspé] bay. The two
destroyers make a very rattle-trap and neglected appearance." After an unsuccessful attack on a
tanker, Wissmann departed through the Cabot Strait on 17 November.[161]

U 183, which BdU had cleared to enter the gulf at the same time as U 518, did not carry out
its mission. The boat approached the Cabot Strait on 3 November, but turned away in the face of
air patrols from Sydney; defects in the submarine evidently made Kapitänleutnant H. Schäfer, the
commanding officer, unwilling to run the risk of entering such well-defended waters. He continued down the Cape Breton coast, making unsuccessful attacks on shipping in the approaches to
Canso Strait and off Canso. After patrolling south of Halifax, Schäfer returned to the waters off
Cape Breton, and fired, again wide of the mark, at a Halifax to St John's coastal convoy on 28
November, before heading out to sea. The reports of the failed single-salvo attacks that had not
been followed up led Canadian intelligence to conclude that Schäfer was on a "reconnaissance"
mission. That was not the case, and BdU criticized the commanding officer's lack of initiative.[162]

———————

Schäfer was the only commanding officer assigned to the Gulf of St Lawrence who was not aggressive and experienced, and yet BdU's reinforcement of this apparently promising theatre in the
autumn of 1942 yielded meagre results. In contrast to the eighteen merchant vessels and two
escorts destroyed by four U-boats from May through mid-September, the four that had entered thereafter sank a total of only three merchant ships, and the fifth submarine assigned, U 183, had been
entirely deterred. Indeed, nearly two-thirds of the total losses—twelve merchantmen and the two
escorts—had been suffered during the period of less than three weeks, from late August until mid-
September, when U 517 and U 165 succeeded in making coordinated attacks. Improvements in
defence measures had then brought quite dramatic results, shutting down U 517's run of success
during the last three weeks of that boat's operation in the St Lawrence. Although two to three submarines were always present from late September until early November, they never again achieved
coordinated attacks. All three victories after mid-September, and the two by U 518 at Wabana, outside the limits of the gulf, were hit-and-run attacks, a tactic to which submarines resorted in the
face of effective defences. In each case, the U-boat remained submerged much of the time to avoid
Canadian patrols and was able to strike only when it was newly arrived in an area and had not yet
been detected by Allied intelligence. It then departed the instant it had made its first attack and
thereby revealed its presence to the enemy. What was more, the Canadian forces that compelled the
U-boats to operate so cautiously were modest, including by October a half dozen Bangor
minesweepers, a dozen Fairmile launches, and fewer than three dozen maritime patrol aircraft.

Unfortunately for the public image of the Canadian armed services, the few successful enemy
attacks in the autumn of 1942 were among the most dramatic and tragic of the war. Timing, moreover, assured that the bad news had the greatest possible impact. In mid-October the government
allowed publication of reports of *Carolus*'s destruction "200 Air Miles Below Citadel of Québec" as

160. *U 518*, KTB, 31 Oct. 1942

161. Ibid, 12, 15-19 Nov. 1942

162. Tennyson and Sarty, *Guardian of the Gulf*, 280-1

Toronto's *Globe and Mail* proclaimed, just when *U 69* torpedoed *Caribou*, and the magnitude of that disaster compelled the navy immediately to release that story to the press as well.[163]

The *New York Times* observed that the news of the sinking of the *Carolus* and *Caribou* had brought the war very near to Canada.

> Such warnings as Prime Minister W.L. Mackenzie King gave last evening [16 October 1942] in Montréal during a war-loan speech, that an attack on this continent from both East and West was not impossible, are no longer considered fantastic ...
>
> Taken side by side with such a story of adventure and such tragedy as that of the Caribou, the formation by Maxime Raymond of a 'Bloc Populaire Canadien,' in which he is seeking to strengthen provincial autonomy and 'put an end at Ottawa to this humiliating regime, which holds French Canadians to the role of perpetual protesters,' has become only an academic affair.[164]

That was not the case, as the divisions over the conscription issue that had led to the formation of the bloc were by no means diminishing. The report, however, accurately reflected the government's political perspective. King's war loan speech in Montréal on 16 October contrasted "Our nationhood ... founded on the faith that two of the proudest races in the world, despite barriers of tongue and creed, could work together, in mutual tolerance and mutual respect" with the manner in which "Germany and Japan have made of nationality an evil thing." Canadians had to stand united in their war effort at home and overseas to prevent an Axis victory in Europe or Asia that could lead to full-scale invasion of Canadian territory.[165] Less subtly, Angus L. Macdonald declared that *Caribou*'s destruction "brings the war to Canada with tragic emphasis ... those for whom our hearts bleed most are the ... women and children ... If there were any Canadians who did not realize that we were up against a ruthless and remorseless enemy, there can be no such Canadians now. If anything were needed to prove the hideousness of Nazi warfare, surely this is it."[166]

Charges were already appearing in the media that the reason for the heavy losses in the St Lawrence was not so much Nazi bloodthirstiness as the Canadian government's negligence and the military's incompetence. Starting 14 October the Québec journalist Edouard Laurent published a series of articles in *L'Action Catholique* under the title "Ce qui se passe en Gaspésie":

> Une rapide randonnée à travers la Gaspésie m'a convaincu que l'habitant de la péninsule sait, beaucoup mieux que nous, le danger qui pèse sur le pays. La guerre est tout proche de lui. Un bon nombre ont vu des sous-marins enemis; d'autres ont été les témoins de torpillages de navires alliés; un plus grand nombre ont entendu dans le lointain, le bruit de la canonnade. Ceux qui sont allés dans les hôpitaux de région ont vu ou entendu parler des marins blessés qui se remettent de leurs blessures ...
>
> Ce qui augmente l'angoisse collective, c'est d'abord le silence du gouvernement sur tout ce qui se passe dans le bas du fleuve. Les gens de la Gaspésie savent bien que si le gouvernement exposait la véritable situation, l'opinion publique réagirait assez vigoureusement pour exiger une action plus efficace de la part des authorités.[167]

---

163. *Globe and Mail*, 16 Oct. 1942, 1
164. *New York Times*, 18 Oct. 1942, clipping in CWM, HSC, box 180, file 149, "... Submarine Warfare St Lawrence"
165. King, *Canada and the Fight for Freedom*, 211-12
166. Quoted in Hadley, *U-Boats against Canada*, 142
167. *L'Action Catholique*, 14 Oct. 1942, copy in Queen's University Archives, C.G. Power papers, box 70, file D-2032

Laurent's allegations that the government was covering up a thin and amateurish defence further hamstrung by "red tape" were reprinted in leading newspapers in both languages. Drawing as Laurent did on the sorts of charges that Gaspé area political representatives had been making since the spring, he gave renewed impetus to their campaign for more effective defences.[168] Especially worrying for the authorities in Ottawa was Québec premier Adelard Godbout's private endorsement of Laurent's work to King as "the most complete and objective articles I have seen." Godbout warned of the danger of full-scale panic in the coastal districts of the province, and begged for any information with which his government could reassure the population.[169]

Captain Mainguy, acting FONF, was at this same time grappling with similar alarm among the local population and shipping community following *U 513*'s attack at Bell Island. In his report to NSHQ he provided an unvarnished reaction:

4. The losses of ships in convoy and of escorts must ... be accepted as the Fortunes of War; but the loss of ships at Wabana and close to St John's, although also the Fortunes of War, are harder to explain to a population who consider that anything sunk on their doorstep is due to a dereliction of duty on the part of the Navy. It also, somewhat naturally, results in a clamour for protection from outlying ports out of all proportion to their value in the strategic plan as a whole.

5. In a word, the lack of local escorts is most keenly felt, and there is no shadow of doubt that, should the enemy make resolute attacks on coastal shipping in this Command, the trade of Newfoundland could be brought to a virtual standstill. In this connection it is interesting to note that it was necessary to re-assure the Dutch Naval Attache on the measures of protection taken at Wabana so that he, in his turn, could re-assure the crew of a Dutch ship chartered for the ore trade—although the chances of attack at Wabana with no protection at all, other than air, are probably far less than in an ON, HX or SC convoy and the chances of rescue considerably higher ...

7. It is fully realised that the number of local escorts available depends on the number of ocean escorts which are, in the long run, far more important, and the above remarks are only intended to emphasise the psychological effect of attacks which are seen by the local population, and the speed with which reports of these attacks travel. No news of the sinkings at Wabana has been published in the Press.[170]

We have seen that with the virtual repetition of the *U 513*'s feat by *U 518* in early November, the navy moved instantly to provide the most effective—and visible—protection in the form of anti-torpedo nets.

The wind-up of shipping on the St Lawrence for the winter freeze-up made such action in the gulf less urgent, but the federal ministers provided Premier Godbout detailed information that disproved most of the reports from Edouard Laurent and the Gaspé area members of Parliament about the armed services' failure to provide protection to threatened shipping and to respond to U-boat

---

168. Chouinard, "La Bataille du Saint-Laurent et la presse Québécoise," 6-9; Douglas, *Creation of a National Air Force*, 507-8

169. Godbout to King, 21 Oct. 1942, NAC, MG 26 J-1, reel C-6806, 276171; CWCM, 28 Oct. 1942

170. FONF, "Monthly Report for September 1942," 16 Oct. 1942, DHH, NSS 1000-5-20, pt 2

sightings by the local population.[171] On 24 November Macdonald gave a press conference in which he replied to reports that at least thirty and as many as forty ships had been sunk in the gulf with the precise figure of twenty, fourteen in the gulf and six in the Cabot Strait and Strait of Belle Isle. Interestingly, in view of Janowski's recent capture, the minister did not dissemble in the face of questions about the danger of enemy agents coming ashore:

> Mr. Macdonald said it was quite possible for enemy submarines to land people on Canadian coasts in remote areas. They had done that in the United States and an American party had landed from a submarine in North Africa and come away. If there were any such landings it would probably be for purposes of sabotage.
>
> There were reports of submarine crews landing [in the Gulf of St Lawrence] to purchase supplies. The submarines carried ample supplies and there was no necessity for them to take that risk.[172]

When, with the opening of the legislative session in Québec early in March 1943, Onésime Gagnon, a provincial member for Gaspé, repeated Laurent's allegations, and the federal members renewed their complaints, Macdonald replied in the federal Parliament with a full exposition that was close in tone to Mainguy's private reflections:

> The hon. Member for Gaspé [J.-S. Roy] ... said that the battle of the St Lawrence Gulf was lost through selfishness and lack of organization. I say that the battle of the St Lawrence has not been lost ... of the total tonnage which used the river and the Gulf last year, only three out of every thousand tons was sunk ... I know the general average of convoy sinkings throughout the world, and I can say that if you only lose three tons out of every thousand which you have at sea you are doing pretty well, in fact somewhat better than average. We have not lost the battle of the Gulf. Some people think the Gulf is easily defended ... Let them remember that the St Lawrence river, at the point farthest inland where an attack was made last year, is thirty miles wide. That is almost like the open sea. It is wider than the straits of Dover between England 'and France. If the great British navy with all its experience and skill and strength and devotion to duty has not succeeded in making the straits of Dover absolutely safe from submarines—indeed only a year ago it was unable to prevent certain great enemy ships from going through the straits—if that cannot be done there, is it to be wondered at that we cannot guarantee complete immunity to ships in the river St Lawrence ...?
>
> ... We shall have more ships, I hope, to guard the Gulf and river [in 1943]. But I am not here to say that even if we double or treble the number of ships we had last year we shall be able to guarantee complete safety for every ship sailing up and down that river. It cannot be done; if you had the whole Canadian navy strung out in the Gulf of St Lawrence, abandoning all the other places you have to protect, you still could not guarantee complete immunity from submarine attack. That cannot be done; it has not been done by any nation in the world. To-day off the very shores of Japan United States submarines are operating and sinking ships; Japanese submarines

---

171. Douglas, *Creation of a National Air Force*, 508

172. *Evening Citizen*, Ottawa, 24 Nov. 1942, 1

approached the west coast of America last winter and fired shells on American soil; there are sinkings on the British coast; submarines get there in spite of all they can do.[173]

Gagnon had repeated that at least thirty ships had been sunk in the gulf, to which Macdonald now responded with the names of the eighteen merchant vessels and two escorts that had been destroyed, and explained that a nineteenth merchant vessel, *Frederika Lensen*, had been successfully beached after suffering torpedo damage, but then broke up because of weather conditions.[174] Macdonald provided to the House most of the detailed information that had been given to Premier Godbout to debunk alarmist rumours, but also admitted that in one case a submarine sighting report, made by the lighthouse keeper at Pointe des Rosiers on 15 September 1942 just before the attack on SQ 36, had indeed been delayed by the poor communications on the north shore of the Gaspé Peninsula.[175]

Macdonald thus went to extraordinary lengths to set the record straight. He was right that the amount of tonnage sunk by no means signalled an important defeat, especially in light of the limited resources the Canadian forces could deploy. He was, moreover, on firmer ground than he or the military realized in insisting that Canada had not lost the battle of the St Lawrence. Because of the codebreakers' inability to read German U-boat radio traffic during much of 1942, Allied intelligence had no inkling that the final groups of U-boats had been virtually driven out of the gulf by the air force's offensive sweeps and by the more aggressive patrolling by surface escorts.

The paradoxical result was that military officers tended to agree with the conclusions of the most unfriendly journalists that the forces had been ill-organized, and therefore slow to concentrate when and where they were needed. Expert British officers, who visited the Canadian commands during 1942 to assist in organizing the defences according to the proven methods of the RN and Coastal Command, had been critical of the lack of cooperation between the Canadian services.[176] Commander C. Thompson, RN, commanding officer of the destroyer HMS *Witherington*, described such cooperation as "non-existent" during the period his ship served in the gulf in mid-September.[177]

The senior planning staffs of the three armed forces began a detailed review of the events of the 1942 season early in December as the first step in making preparations for 1943. The ministers and the chiefs of staff had ordered this review and kept close touch with the progress of the planners, a clear signal, amid the glare of unfavourable publicity, that everything possible should be done to avoid a repetition of the events of the past season. Under this pressure, there was more than a trace of interservice tension.[178] Commander Lay blamed the air force for the problems in 1942: "It appeared that, whereas the RCN contribution towards [the] defence was comparable with similar defences provided in the Atlantic, the contribution of the RCAF had been less than had been hoped for." This drew an acid minute from an air force staff officer who observed that "at the

---

173. HofC, *Debates*, 17 Mar. 1943, 1344

174. Ibid, 1338

175. Ibid, 1342-3

176. Douglas, *Creation of a National Air Force*, 523-5

177. *Witherington* ROP, 9-14 Sep. 1942, 17 Sep. 1942

178. NBM, 30 Nov. 1942; CSCM, 4 Dec. 1942, 20 Apr., 11 May 1943, DHH 193.009 (D53); Defence Council min, 5 Feb. 1943, NAC, RG 24, 4047, NS 1078-5-18, pt 6

beginning of the 1942 season the Navy had *nothing* in the Gulf despite our advice to them that U/boats were operating there."[179] He could have added that the analysts on the staff of COAC had concluded that during the run of successes by *U 517* and *U 165* against the large SQ and QS convoys in September, the naval escorts, having been hastily reinforced by ships not used to working with each other, had failed to achieve a cohesive defence. Even though both Macdonald and C.G. Power, the air minister, highlighted in Parliament the string of air attacks on the U-boats that, in fact, resulted from the adoption of Coastal Command tactics and the integration of naval intelligence into air operations, no one at the conferences in Ottawa, or among the staffs at Halifax, Sydney, and Gaspé, gave much credit for these achievements, or for the greater cohesion and aggressiveness shown by the surface escorts after mid-September.[180]

Additional intelligence that became available to planners during the winter of 1942 had the effect of underscoring German success. On 21 November 1942 British forces sank *U 517* in the eastern Atlantic, and all but one member of the crew survived, including Hartwig, the commanding officer, who provided a detailed account of the recent St Lawrence mission. He left little doubt that only pure luck had enabled the submarine to escape the repeated battering by surface escorts and aircraft; the crew counted twenty-seven air bombs and 118 depth charges and vividly recalled the occasions when attacks had been so close the boat should have been destroyed. Even the hardened British interrogators, however, were profoundly impressed that the submarine had persisted in its mission under these conditions, describing Hartwig as "cool and efficient" and remarking on the evident strength of his faith that "the gods were on his side."[181] Allied intelligence had already warned that Dönitz's recent promotion to commander-in-chief of the entire German navy meant that "daring U-boat tactics are to be expected," and senior Canadian officers believed that Hartwig's mission would provide the model:

> Especially in view of the successes last year of U-517, we must expect increased U-boat activity ... It is well known that the Germans are methodical people and somewhat bound to precedent and therefore operations this year in the Gulf will be greatly influenced by the operations last year of U-517.[182]

The planners erred on the side of caution in designing defence measures for the 1943 season. From the first meeting in December 1942, the Naval Staff ruled that the St Lawrence should remain closed to ocean shipping. The continuing shortage of ocean escorts, and the higher priority demands of Atlantic coastal waters and the transatlantic run, would more than absorb any additional corvettes or larger warships that were expected to become available, so it would be impossible to escort large convoys of ocean ships in any greater strength than those that had suffered heavy losses in 1942. Furthermore, the closure of the gulf to ocean shipping had not persuaded the U-boats to hunt elsewhere, as the loss of the *Caribou* had demonstrated. Local traffic would therefore require

179. "Minutes of St Lawrence Operations Conference Held in Ottawa, Feb. 22-4, 1943," DHH 79/179. See also, DOD to Air Member air staff, 11 Dec. 1942, "Naval Aspect of the Defence of the Gulf and River St Lawrence," 11 Dec. 1942, DHH, NHS 1650-239/16B, pt 2

180. Douglas, *Creation of a National Air Force*, 508, 512

181. Adm, *MASR,* Jan. 1943, 20-2

182. C-in-C Canadian Northwest Atlantic (CNA), "Defence of the Gulf of St Lawrence Appreciation," 14 May 1943, NAC, RG 24, 11064, f 38-2-1A. This appreciation, with amendment of details, became C-in-C, CNA, "Defence of Gulf of St Lawrence 1943 (Short Title— GL 43)," 25 May 1943, ibid

substantial defences, and that local traffic was so significant that a full convoy system would have to be maintained, from Wabana on Newfoundland's Atlantic coast through to the river, and north through the Strait of Belle Isle.[183] A study by the trade division in January 1943 concluded:

> 56. ... it is economically impossible to cut out movement of all shipping in the Gulf and River when those waters are open to navigation. The local movements ... of coal, ore, bauxite, pulp and various other commodities which are essential to the war effort, will therefore have to continue.
>
> 57. ... there [will be] a very heavy programme totalling approximately 6,000,000 tons, including bauxite, coal, fluorspar and cryolite to Port Alfred; ore and limestone from Newfoundland; large quantities of coal and civilian supplies to Newfoundland; and substantial movements from lower points in the Gulf which are not connected by rail. The livelihood of numerous small communities in the Lower St Lawrence is, absolutely dependent on water transportation.[184]

On learning of the intention to keep the gulf closed to ocean shipping, moreover, the British Ministry of War Transport protested that schedules for timber imports to the United Kingdom could only be maintained if ships in the transatlantic service loaded directly at timber ports. Raising concerns about the ability of the limited forces to provide adequate protection in the event of another U-boat offensive, the Canadian Naval Staff ultimately allowed a maximum of no more than twelve timber ships per month to enter into the river and another ten to load at ports in the gulf.[185]

The navy was able to allocate more warships to the St Lawrence than had been present in the autumn of 1942 by such measures as withdrawing additional Bangors from Pacific command. Almost all of the vessels, however, were of the lightest classes. The air force, which was receiving additional medium-and long-range aircraft, endeavoured to double the number of combat machines that had been on station in and around the gulf in 1942.[186]

The planned deployments took full account of the repeated British advice that aircraft and small warships could, if used offensively, drive U-boats out of the gulf, and thereby keep requirements for ocean-type surface escorts to a minimum.[187] Surface forces identified for escort duty were only somewhat stronger than in the autumn of 1942: five borrowed British antisubmarine trawlers for the Sydney to Québec series, and six Bangors for the ferry, ore ship, and other traffic between Cape Breton and Newfoundland. The trawlers would be based at Sydney, with refuelling facilities available at Rimouski, to save the shuttling back and forth from Gaspé that had eaten up sea time of the

---

183. DOD to Air Member air staff, 11 Dec. 1942, "Naval Aspect of the Defence of the Gulf"

184. Trade Division, NSHQ "Review of General Trade Situation in Canadian Coastal Zones 1942-1943," 23 Jan. 1943, 9-10, DHH, NHS 1650-239/16B, v 1

185. Hurcomb, MWT, London to Huband, MWT, Montréal, 10 Mar. 1943, Director of Trade Division to Huband, 24 Mar. 1943, NAC, RG 24, 6789, NSS 8280-166/16, pt 4

186. CNS to COAC and COPC, 12 Mar. 1943, NAC, RG 24, 11064, 32-1-8A; Douglas, *Creation of a National Air Force*, 509

187. See esp, Cdr P.B. Martineau [note forwarding his reports of 31 Oct. and 8 Nov. 1942], nd, PRO, AIR 15/217/4080, encls. 38G: "Once U-boats have entered the St Lawrence they are difficult to cope with, due to lack of aircraft and surface ships. I put forward the suggestion that the Fairmile motor boats, used to escort the convoys, would be better employed in 'sweeps' with aircraft. This was not accepted, probably due to the Reactions of the Politicans if convoy was attacked and had no Fairmiles. I am convinced that the only method which would prove satisfactory is continuous sweeps with surface craft and aircraft." For very similar Canadian views expressed during the planning for St Lawrence operations in 1943, see SO (AS), COAC, min, 5 Jan. 1943, NAC, RG 24, 11064, 38-2-1A.

escorts in 1942. There would only be four corvettes allocated for the Labrador convoys, and these were to be based at Québec rather than Halifax, which would save sea time for the vessels at the expense of making them less readily available for emergency service on the Atlantic coast. Gaspé was now to be the centre for offensive operations, with six Bangors and three Fairmile flotillas, each of six to eight vessels, all assigned for offensive patrols in conjunction with air sweeps, and to reinforce threatened convoys. The main gulf striking forces were thus organized for rapid response to intelligence of U-boat operations around the north shore of the Gaspé Peninsula, where, during 1942, the submarines had found sixteen of their victims. Another flotilla of Fairmiles was to be stationed at Sydney for support of air sweeps in the Cabot Strait, and four Fairmiles together with a support ship were to take up position once again at the Strait of Belle Isle.[188]

Events in late April and early May 1943 seemed to leave no doubt that the Germans would aggressively follow up their success of the previous season, and spurred rapid implementation of the gulf defence plan. On 24 April an observer on shore at New Carlisle, Québec, where Janowski had landed, reported a U-boat on the surface about a mile out in the Baie des Chaleurs. The command staffs at Halifax doubted that this was a submarine because there was still a good deal of ice in the gulf, but they took no chances and began to send aircraft to the gulf stations. On 29 April NSHQ sent a report based on high grade intelligence that "a U-boat will enter the Gulf of St Lawrence during the first week of May presumably to land or pick up enemy agents. May four is most likely date but there is no indication of place operation will take place."[189]

The phrasing of this signal suggests that the Allies had decrypted veiled messages from BdU to *U 262* concerning its mission to rescue German prisoners of war who were planning to escape from Camp 70 near Fredericton, New Brunswick.[190] *U 262* passed through the Cabot Strait on 26 to 27 April, in a bold feat of seamanship. The strait was still clogged with pack ice, and the boat suffered serious damage as it pushed through and dove under the floes. Although the gulf was generally clear, there were "fields of drifting ice." "These waters are like a morgue," commented the commanding officer, Kapitänleutnant H. Francke: "I am probably the only vessel swimming in the Gulf of St Lawrence."[191] He kept to deep water, approaching Anticosti, before heading south for the rendezvous at North Point, Prince Edward Island, where he hovered close off shore from 2 to 6 May, submerging by day. Fishermen had reported a U-boat in the vicinity on 30 April, certainly a false sighting, but there had been air searches both by combat aircraft and by training aircraft, assigned to exercise in the area, that continued until the weather closed in on 4 May.[192] Franke noted the presence of three aircraft as he made his submerged approach during daylight on 2 May, and found it "very suspicious that all 3 aircraft are flying surveillance precisely above my rendezvous position." Although he correctly surmised there were training bases in the area, this incident accounts for his great caution during his five-day wait off North

188. C-in-C CNA, "Defence of the Gulf of St Lawrence Appreciation," 14 May 1943, C-in-C CNA, "Defence of Gulf of St. Lawrence 1943"

189. NSHQ to C-in-C CNA, 2258Z/29 Apr. 1943, AFHQ to AOC EAC, signal A 2614, 1 May 1943, DHH 181.002 (D68A)

190. *U 262*, KTB, 15 Apr. 1943. See also, BdU, KTB, 16-23 Apr. 1943, which indicates that the boat signalled regularly as it approached the Canadian coaSt The fullest account of *U 262*'s mission is Hadley, *U-Boats against Canada*, 168-75.

191. *U 262*, KTB, 30 Apr.–1 May 1943

192. "EAC Anti-Submarine Report April, 1943," app A, DHH 181.003 (D25); EAC daily operations summary signals 30 Apr.– 4 May 1943, DHH 181.003 (D3254)

Point.[193] Eastern Air Command, for its part, took particular care to cover the ferry between New Brunswick and Borden, PEI—an obvious echo of the *Caribou* disaster—and repeatedly swept the main shipping channel through the gulf in anticipation of the first sailings of ships from the river.[194] Franke, having waited in vain as the prisoners of war had not in the end attempted the escape, had no intention of searching for shipping with his damaged boat. He quietly slipped out the Cabot Strait on the night of 8 May.

Escorts assigned to the gulf and shipping had meanwhile been gathering at Sydney since late April, unusually early because the pack ice in the Cabot Strait had not moved into the harbour. The first of the ore convoys departed for Wabana on 29 April, and SQ 47, the first scheduled St Lawrence convoy of the season sailed on 12 May, almost precisely a year after *U 553*'s attack in 1942. The shipping season began with considerable excitement, for submarine sighting reports had continued to come in from around the gulf, including possible detections by aircraft and warships, that, paradoxically increased in number in the days following *U 262*'s quiet departure.[195] Given the high-grade intelligence about *U 262* these reports had to be taken seriously, and for a time the submarine tracking room in Ottawa judged there must be two submarines present in the gulf.[196] By mid-June, intelligence had concluded that the "assorted collection of sightings" from the gulf had "a somewhat Munchausen-like flavour ... not much credence can be attached to any of them."[197] The gulf forces would have a quiet summer, but Dönitz's efforts to revive distant operations in the wake of the defeat of U-boat assault on mid-ocean convoys did not allow much relaxation of preparations. When, in the autumn of 1943, Canadian authorites did finally suspend convoys in the Gulf in response to British appeals for faster movements of transatlantic shipping that could most conveniently load bulk cargoes at St Lawrence ports, almost immediately there was evidence of submarines making for the St Lawrence. This would not, in fact, be the harbinger of a new offensive in the gulf, although the intelligence available was not clear.[198]

Canadian assessments that Dönitz would not forget the initial successes of *U 553*, *U 132*, *U 165,* and *U 517* ultimately proved correct, but not until 1944. Significantly, Dönitz would not attempt that return to the gulf until his forces had the advantage of new technology. In a signal of 23 September 1944 BdU admitted that in the autumn of 1942 strengthened Canadian defences, especially the offensive air sweeps, had made the gulf untenable for hunting operations by conventional submarines, and they had therefore "evacuated" the St Lawrence at the end of the 1942 season.[199]

---

193. *U 262*, KTB, 2 May 1943

194. EAC, daily operations summary signals 1-8 May 1943, DHH 181.003 (D3254)

195. NOIC Sydney, ROP, Apr.-May 1943, DHH, NSS 1000-5-21, pt 2

196. Operational Research Section, EAC, "EAC Statistics of Anti-Submarine Operations May 1943," para 6, DHH 181.002 (D379)

197. "Eastern Air Command Operational Intelligence Summary," no. 57, 13 June 1943, NAC, RG 24, v 5272, S.28-5-12, pt 1

198. Sarty, "EAC Anti-Submarine Operations in the Gulf of St Lawrence," 26-40

199. ZTPG 31873, BdU [to *U 1223*], TOO 1339/1459/1855/2005/2058, 23 Sep. 1944, PRO, DEFE 3/736

CHAPTER NINE

North Atlantic Convoy Operations I
July to September 1942

WHEN *PAUKENSCHLAG* LOST MOMENTUM during the summer of 1942, the Atlantic war came full circle. In 1941 strengthened defences in British waters had driven U-boats into the mid-ocean to seek out weakly protected convoys, and a year later improved defences in Canadian and US waters produced the same result. "The main weight of our attack in the war on shipping," Dönitz later recalled, "had now [in the late sumer of 1942] to be transferred back to Operations against convoys to and from Britain, in mid-Atlantic, where they were beyond the range of land-based air cover."[1] The analogy of the ocean as a huge chess board, with the opponents countering each others' moves, is particularly apt in describing the changing deployments of the defending and attacking forces.

The Allies could not be strong everywhere. This was especially the case in 1942, when the German submarine assault along the length of the North American seaboard and in the Caribbean followed closely on the heels of Japan's offensives in the Pacific. The effect of this sudden and dramatic widening of the maritime war was to draw off American—and British and Canadian—forces that otherwise would have been available to protect North Atlantic convoys. In February 1942, as we have seen, the Allies trimmed back the transatlantic escorts by ending the routing of convoys towards Iceland and the relief of Newfoundland-based escorts in those waters by groups based in Iceland and Britain. Now a single Newfoundland-based group, from the newly created Mid-Ocean Escort Force that pooled the British, Canadian, and the small number of US escorts available for the North Atlantic, escorted each convoy all the way between Newfoundland and Ireland. Because many of the escorts had limited endurance, convoys had to be sailed on the great circle route, the most direct path between North America and the United Kingdom.[2] In early May 1942, when spring conditions eased the strain on the North Atlantic escorts and allowed still further economies, Allied authorities had reduced the number of mid-ocean escort groups from twelve to eleven, and thereby transferred escorts to the unprotected waters of the Caribbean where the Germans were striking with devastating effect.[3]

The organization of shipping into escorted convoys on the American seaboard and then in the Caribbean did deprive Axis submarines of easy targets in these theatres. *Rudeltaktik*, or wolf pack tactics, for attacks on these convoys was not practicable. The long voyages to coastal waters in the

---

1. Dönitz, *Memoirs*, 237

2. Terraine, *Business in Great Waters*, 435

3. Milner, *North Atlantic Run*, 104. Escort group B 5 was transferred to the Trinidad–Aruba convoys.

western hemisphere left U-boats too little patrol time to concert effective group operations, and the proximity of shore-based aircraft made the extended surface searches necessary to find convoys very dangerous. In late June and the first part of July 1942, a series of aircraft attacks, and one by an escort, destroyed or seriously damaged fully a third of the submarines operating on the US coast.[4] By contrast, in the western part of the mid-ocean area, there was still a wide gap between the patrol limits of aircraft based in Iceland and Newfoundland, unchanged from the conditions that in 1941 had made this area a fruitful one for U-boat attacks on convoys. A single under-strength Coastal Command squadron of four-engine Consolidated Liberator bombers, stripped of all non-essential equipment and fitted with additional fuel tanks, was able to produce dramatic results on occasion, with patrols occasionally extending as far as 900 miles from Iceland and Northern Ireland. The Allied strategic bombing offensive against Germany, however, took first priority in the allocation of aircraft, and pleas from the maritime air forces for additional four-engine bombers suitable for "very long range" (VLR) conversion fell, for the most part, on deaf ears.[5]

In the northwest Atlantic, the Canadian, US Army and USN aircraft available in Newfoundland had a theoretical patrol range of about 600 miles, but the sudden appearance of fog often shut down bases, meaning aircraft had to retain sufficient fuel reserves for long diversions to the Maritime provinces or eastern Québec. The "air gap" therefore often began within 500 miles of the Newfoundland coast, and frequently closer still. As the Admiralty's *Monthly Anti-Submarine Report* put it, in uncharacteristically despairing tones, "there is still a black pit of excessive danger in the main traffic area northeast of Newfoundland and it seems clear that the German U-Boat Command is making strategic dispositions to intercept S.C. and H.X. convoys so near as may be to Cape Race—in some cases actually well within potential air cover from Canadian bases."[6]

The number of U-boats available for operations in the Atlantic was climbing steadily and reached ninety-nine by 1 July 1942, an increase of thirty-four since January. In addition, German shore staffs made strenuous efforts to shorten maintenance periods at the French bases. By mid-1942 more than two-thirds of the operational boats were on station, on average, as compared to slightly over half a year earlier. U-boats were also able to remain on patrol longer because of the entry into service of U-tankers, the so-called Milch-cows, which began to take up station in the air gap. Patrol lengths for type VII boats, which had been forty-one days at the beginning of the year, could be extended to sixty-two with a single replenishment, or even eighty-one with two.[7] BdU could now form two or more groups for operations in the air gap and send other boats to find shipping in focal points in the Caribbean, off Brazil, and in the waters off south and west Africa.[8] In deploying the expanded U-boat force, BdU also had the advantage in radio intelligence. The Allies still could not read the U-boat *Triton* cypher, thus depriving them of the detailed information that had been so essential to routing convoys clear of danger in 1941. The system for plotting U-boat transmissions by DF sta-

---

4.   MOD, *U-Boat War in the Atlantic* II, 20

5.   In 1943 the Allied Anti-Submarine Survey Board defined a VLR aircraft as one with a range of 600 miles with the ability to then remain over a convoy for four hours. AASSB to CNS, 19 May 1943, PRO, ADM 1/13756

6.   Adm, *MASR*, Oct. 1942, 5

7.   Rahn, *Der U-Boot Krieg* VI, 367 and 341; and Rahn, *Einsatzbereitschaft und Kampfkraft deutscher U-Boote 1942*, *Militärgeschichtliche Mitteilungen* 1 90 (Freiburg 1990), 80-1

8.   Dönitz, *Memoirs*, 238; and BdU, KTB, 2 July 1942. At the beginning of July four U-tankers were in service.

tions on shore had been much improved—not least the Canadian part of the operation—but this was no replacement for the decrypted German radio traffic.[9] B-Dienst, meanwhile, was having considerable success in reading Allied convoy signals, and as one historian has commented, Dönitz took full advantage: "from June to November [1942] virtually every order he sent to a U-boat group at sea was an attempt to exploit information he had obtained from decrypted Allied signals."[10] These revealed that mid-ocean convoys rarely deviated from the great circle route, and thereby allowed Dönitz to establish patrol lines where they had the best chance of locating shipping.[11]

Allied authorities were well aware of the danger that regular sailings on the great circle route entailed, but there was no alternative. The escort shortage that had originally dictated the use of the shortest possible passage between North American and the British Isles became even more acute in July 1942 with the establishment of the Caribbean convoy system. This had to be established to stop the slaughter of shipping in southern waters, but it could only be sustained by transferring still more mid-ocean escorts to service on the North American coast. The British initially proposed to remove yet another escort group from the MOEF, leaving the force with only ten, but instead reduced the size of each group to six escorts. This released ten RCN corvettes for coastal duty, but at a high price.[12] The 1,770 mile run between Newfoundland and Ireland already strained the fuel endurance of destroyers and corvettes, limiting their capacity for aggressive sweeps to push back submarines before they reached attacking positions (refuelling at sea was still in the early stages of development in the RN and RCN and would not be dependably achieved until later in the war).[13] In the summer of 1942 the reduction in the number of warships in each group further hindered group commanders' ability to assign escorts for sweeps against shadowers just when the U-boats' return to the central ocean and BdU's discovery that the convoys were adhering to the great circle route increased the likelihood that convoys would be located by the submarines. In sum, the Allies had been able to counter the offensive in North American waters only by weakening the defences of the transatlantic convoys, opening a fresh opportunity for the enemy. BdU, by continuing to deploy submarines to the North American coast despite the greatly reduced chances of success there, ensured that the Allies were not able readily to reconcentrate their forces at mid-ocean.

Among the many challenges the Canadian fleet faced in 1942 as it endeavoured to bridge the most critical gaps in the Allied escort forces was the unavailability for RCN warships of the latest antisubmarine equipment being fitted in British and American escorts. As mentioned in Chapter 5, the RCN had lagged in the development of centimetric radar and most of its mid-ocean escorts would not receive that equipment until early 1943. Neither British or American production could promptly meet Canadian needs, and the NRC's attempt at an independent design, the RX/C, moved

---

9. The experience of integrating information from HF/DF fixes and other sources with Enigma during the eight months ending in Jan. 1942 enabled the Admiralty's Submarine Tracking Room to project general U-boat movements with greater confidence than prior to June 1941. The general accuracy of HF/DF fixes had also improved. However, the lack of Enigma was a major setback and according to Hinsley, "the daily plot of U-boat dispositions soon ceased to be reliable." Hinsley, *British Intelligence* II, 230-2; Beesley, *Very Special Intelligence*, 111-12

10. Stephen Budiansky, *Battle of Wits: The Complete Story of Codebreaking in World War II* (New York 2000), 287

11. BdU, KTB, 19 July 1942

12. Milner, *North Atlantic Run*, 109-10; and COMINCH to Adm and NSHQ, June 1942

13. Milner, *North Atlantic Run*, 105. The great circle distance between St John's and Londonderry was roughly 1,770 miles, but routing and weather could make for much longer voyages. For example, HMS *Burnham* steamed 2,820 miles on one passage.

The "lantern" of the capable type 271 centimetric radar on HMCS *Bittersweet*, March 1942.
(NAC, PA 105753)

Left: The radar console in HMCS *Camrose*, December 1941. The operator rotated the antenna manually using the wheel, and picked up range "spikes" on the A-scan display to the right of the voice pipe. (NAC, PA 105720)

Bottom: The asdic compartment of a typical corvette. (NAC, PA 204279)

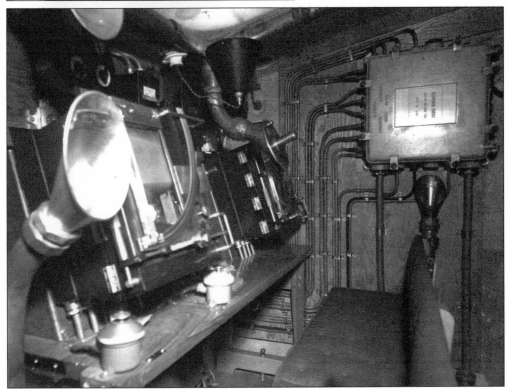

much more slowly than the SW1C project because of the vast leap to centimetric engineering. In this and other areas, the rapid pace of technical change was overwhelming the RCN, and not surprisingly so. Antisubmarine warfare posed challenges that stretched the resources of the RN and USN, with their vast array of specialists, their integral scientific services, and their well-developed relationships with industries and universities. Lacking almost all of these assets, senior Canadian officers found it increasingly difficult to grasp the torrent of new developments and their complex, interrelated implications. At the same time, the specialists required to establish close, effective liaison with the British and American equipment programs, and to provide essential, detailed guidance to the NRC and industry did not exist.[14]

For these same reasons, the RCN was also slow to acquire the compact HF/DF sets that began to be fitted in RN escorts in early 1942.[15] Modelled on the shore stations that gave bearings on U-boat's radio signals, the small ship-borne version was even more useful for escort commanders. Experienced operators could readily distinguish between distant transmissions and those on the "ground wave" within about thirty miles of the convoy. Such information was sufficient for one of the destroyers of the escort to make a fast run "down the bearing" of the transmission, forcing the U-boat to submerge and probably lose contact with the convoy. If two or more sets were available in the convoy, they could give more precise information by triangulating the approximate position of the U-boats. Ship-borne HF/DF was a complement to centimetric radar, and was in some ways more effective. High seas did not affect its performance, and it could detect U-boats at greater ranges than radar, enabling escorts to respond before the submarines were in an attack position.[16]

The failure to address the severe equipment problems of one of the major escort fleets was symptomatic of lapses in coordination among the navies and air forces of the three Allied powers that shared the bulk of the responsibility for the Atlantic war. Too often, British, American, and Canadian naval and maritime air commanders, separated one from another by geography, service background, and nationality, seemed not to grasp a common purpose. Heavy losses to wolf-pack attacks on convoys during the latter half of 1942 would highlight these difficulties and exacerbate tensions.

The U-boats' concentration in North American waters during the first half of 1942 had not entirely freed the transatlantic convoys from enemy attention. From the beginning of January to the end of April, submarines in transit to the Canadian and American seaboard sank or damaged some nineteen merchant vessels in these convoys as well as several other vessels that had straggled from them. Nearly half of the losses in convoy—nine ships including seven tankers—were suffered in late February by ONS 67, escorted by four USN destroyers and the corvette HMCS *Algoma*, which had the misfortune to be one of the only two convoys attacked by more than two boats.[17] German

---

14. Sarty, *Canada and the Battle of the Atlantic*, 120

15. Historian Ralph Erskine has calculated that by the end of Nov. 1942, sixty-four ships in WAC were fitted with FH-3 HF/DF equipment. See Erskine ms "British High Frequency Direction Finding in the Battle of the Atlantic," 3.

16. Ibid; Sarty, *Canada and the Battle of the Atlantic*, 120

17. Rohwer, *Axis Submarine Successes*, 73-92; Blair, *Hitler's U-Boat War*, 509-12; MOD, *U-Boat War in the Atlantic* II, 6; Morison, *Battle of the Atlantic*, 120-1

successes against the transatlantic convoys in early 1942 also included the destruction of four Allied escorts, among them the corvette HMCS *Spikenard*, torpedoed by *U 136* on the night of 10 February while escorting SC 67 south of Iceland; there were just eight survivors.[18]

Early in May, Dönitz organized eight submarines bound for the American coast into Group *Hecht* and gave them orders to sweep along the Atlantic convoy routes. After attacking ONS 92, *Hecht* refuelled and continued sweeping in the air gap rather than dispersing to coastal waters as had originally been planned, and intercepted two more convoys, ONS 100 and ONS 102. Overall, *Hecht* achieved considerable success during its five-week existence, sinking twelve merchant ships and a corvette. In many respects, it was a trial run for the renewed mid-ocean offensive that began in July.[19]

On 9 July 1942, BdU formed Group *Wolf*, whose seven boats were disposed on a north–south line across the great circle route for a westward sweep beginning from about half way between Ireland and Greenland. The next day BdU added two more submarines to the group, but over the next thirteen days *Wolf* had only fleeting contact with two convoys and missed four others that passed through its zone.[20] Foggy conditions largely accounted for this lack of success, an illustration of the difficulties that poor visibility caused U-boats, with their low height of eye as they attempted to sight shipping. Allied intelligence had also been able to warn convoys of danger in the area on the basis of shore-based HF/DF bearings on the German submarines' transmissions.[21] On 20 July, however, the balance began to shift when B-Dienst decrypted a message from a convoy in *Wolf*'s area, and BdU ordered the group into a new patrol line.[22]

By the late afternoon of 23 July, the fast westbound convoy ON 113 of thirty-three merchant ships was 600 miles east of Newfoundland, two-thirds of the way across the Atlantic. The mid-ocean escort was the Canadian group C 2, comprising the Town class destroyers HMS *Burnham* (Commander T. Taylor, RN, SOE) and HMCS *St Croix* (Lieutenant-Commander A.H. Dobson, RCNR), and the corvettes HMS *Polyanthus*, HMCS *Brandon*, *Dauphin*, and *Drumheller*.[23] The group had little experience together and had not trained as a unit; indeed, the two British escorts had joined C 2 solely for ON 113, and it was only *Dauphin*'s second trip with the group. The two RN ships had type 271 centimetric radar, and although none of the escorts possessed ship-borne HF/DF, they, and four of the merchant ships, were equipped with MF/DF, which could obtain bearings on U-boat

---

18. The torpedoes blew away much of *Spikenard*'s side and deck, destroyed the bridge and wireless office, and started a raging fire. She "began to settle by the head, with her whistle, set off by the explosion, blowing a continual eerie requiem. Five minutes later she went under, and as the sea closed over her another explosion, either from her boilers or from a depth charge, smashed the remaining boat and one of the Carley floats." When it became apparent after dawn that *Spikenard* was missing, HMS *Gentian* carried out a search astern of the convoy, and after six or seven hours came upon the one Carley float that had escaped destruction, with its four shocked and battered occupants. Schull, *Far Distant Ships*, 103

19. Twelve U-boats operated in *Hecht* at various times. Interestingly, only two, *U 124* and *U 94*, were responsible for all but one of the thirteen sinkings. The SOE for ONS 100 was Lt-Cdr J.S. Stubbs, RCN, in *Assiniboine* who "conducted a courageous and intelligent defence of ONS 100, helped by fog." Terraine, *Business in Great Waters*, 451. The three convoy actions are described in Blair, *Hitler's U-Boat War*, 598-602 and Milner, *North Atlantic Run*, 113-22.

20. BdU, KTB, 9-11 July 1942

21. COMINCH to CTU 24.1.14, 13 July 1942, COMINCH to CTU 24.1.14, 13 July 1942, and Adm to Escorts of HX 197, 13 July 1942, all in DHH, 88/1 mfm, v 33, SC 90; BdU, KTB, 13 July 1942; Rohwer and Hümmelchen, *Chronology of the War at Sea*, 150; and Adm, OIC, U-boat Situation Report, 20 July 1942, PRO, ADM 223/15

22. BdU, KTB 20 July 1942; MOD, *U-Boat War in the Atlantic* II, 33

23. *U 552*, KTB, 22-3 July 1942; Mowat, *Grey Seas Under*, 111-12

transmissions in the vicinity of the convoy. While no substitute for the more precise HF/DF, the MF/DF bearings were, in the absence of better intelligence, used by Canadian escorts to advantage during the battles in the summer of 1942.[24]

Fog that had persisted for several days lifted on 23 July, and visibility was excellent when Korvettenkapitän Erich Topp in *U 552* glimpsed an escort, observed smoke from the convoy and made a sighting report at 1906z, amplified almost immediately by another from *U 379*.[25] *U 90* made contact within fifteen minutes of Topp's initial sighting report and another boat, *U 597*, found ON 113 two hours later.[26] The Allies also reacted quickly. Six minutes after Topp's transmission, Canadian intercept stations obtained a DF fix and, at 2051z, the Admiralty issued a submarine warning.[27] *Burnham*, however, had already sighted a submarine fifteen minutes earlier, pursued, and at 2132z forced it under with gunfire. Taylor also ordered a large alteration of course before sunset, and a further change three hours later. It nearly worked. After dark, *U 552* and the other boats lost the convoy, but the experienced Topp divined Taylor's intentions. Ignoring orders to join a new patrol to the west, he headed south and helped by heavy smoke from ships in the convoy, was able to make a new sighting report at 0857z on 24 July, a report intercepted and fixed by the Admiralty just over ten minutes later.[28] A three-day running scrap was about to begin.

St Croix, stationed ahead of the convoy at the limit of visibility, drew first blood. At 1535z on 24 July, her masthead lookout, Able Seaman Jim Pullen, sighted two U-boats on either bow of the convoy, at five and twelve miles distant. *Burnham* hunted the submarine to starboard, but it escaped. Taylor instructed the convoy commodore to alter course to north for three hours and then back to the west, and ordered Lieutenant-Commander G.H. Griffiths, RCN in *Drumheller* to take charge of the close escort. Meanwhile, Dobson in *St Croix* chased the U-boat on the port bow for an hour until it submerged at 6,000 yards range. The destroyer obtained an asdic contact at 2,400 yards, and fired two patterns of depth charges set deep. After the second pattern erupted at 1909z, oil and splintered wood gushed to the surface. Dobson regained contact, and fired a shallow pattern at 1922z that produced a large quantity of debris and human flesh that marked the destruction of *U 90*. *Burnham* arrived to screen *St Croix* while she collected evidence of her kill.[29]

After starting back to the convoy, *Burnham* and *St Croix* encountered another submarine on the surface, which they forced under and hunted without result. Six U-boats were now in contact with ON 113, and the course alteration had not shaken them off. Smoke guided Topp back to the convoy, and at 2157z—a half hour before sunset—he reported it on a northerly course. From his conning tower, he could see five other boats in pursuit against the bright evening horizon.[30]

---

24. Cruising Order for ON 113, 17 July 1942, PRO, ADM 237/87; HMS *Burnham*, ROP, ON 113, 27 July 1942, NAC, RG 24, 11319, 8280-ON 113

25. *U 552*, KTB, 23 July 1942; and BdU, KTB, 23 July 1942

26. BdU, KTB, 23 July 1942

27. Adm to CTU 24.1.12, 2151b/23 July 1942; and Cdr J.M. de Marbois, DDSD, RCN, Memo to Director, Anti-Submarine, 8 Oct. 1942; both in DHH, 89/34, v 17, ON 113. The RCN DF fix at 1912z was probably on *U 379*'s signal which according to BdU came "almost immediately" after *U 552*'s sighting report.

28. HMS *Burnham* and *St Croix*, ROPs ON 113; BdU, KTB, 23-4 July 1942; and *U 552*, KTB, 23-4 July 1942; Adm to Escorts of ON 113, 1148b/24 July 1942, PRO, ADM 237/87. The patrol line was to be from AJ-98 to BC-35; *U 552* contacted ON 113 in BC-33.

29. *St Croix* ROP; and HMS *Burnham*, Report of Attacks ON 113, 29 July 1942, DHH, 89/34, v 17. *U 90* was on her first patrol.

30. BdU, KTB, 24 July 1942; *U 552*, KTB 24-5 July 1942

By now ON 113 had entered the American command area. The USN routing authority, CONNAV, ordered a diversion to the south for twelve hours after dusk. The convoy received this instruction, which was based on the incomplete tactical intelligence available ashore, after Taylor had already ordered a diversion to the north. Griffiths and the convoy commodore agreed the CONNAV's diversion would take them back to the vicinity of the previous U-boat sightings and decided to steer east rather than west after twilight and then, after midnight, turn south as ordered. Griffiths stationed his four corvettes on the convoy's bows and quarters.[31] These alterations of course and deteriorating weather shook off most of the pursuers, but the tenacious Topp held contact. After running blind through a rain squall, he overtook the convoy, penetrated the reduced screen, and steered between the two starboard-most columns. At 0159z on 25 July, Topp torpedoed and disabled the 8,093 ton tanker *British Merit* at the rear of the convoy. Startled merchant ships fired snowflake illumination rockets but they proved ineffective. *U 552* remained inside the rear of the convoy, and at 0212z torpedoed and damaged the 5,136 ton freighter *Broompark* before gunfire from the Norwegian tanker *Solsten*, Topp's next intended target, forced him to dive. *U 552* then lost contact.[32]

The two stricken merchant ships remained afloat astern of the convoy in the rising sea. *Broompark*'s entire crew and more than half of *British Merit*'s had abandoned ship. *Brandon* swept the rear of the convoy for survivors. The corvette's commanding officer, Lieutenant J.C. Littler, RCNR, later described the scene:

> The ocean seemed to be covered with little lights attached to life-jackets, indicating men in the water, and these were being rapidly dispersed down wind and sea. It was now or never if these merchant seamen were to be saved, so we went in, my crew lining the sides with ropes and rope nets. My orders were quite simple: I would be steaming alongside men and lifeboats without stopping or going astern and it was not long before merchant seamen were coming over the side into *Brandon* like tunny fish and being rushed off into the bowels of the ship to be warmed up or treated in some way by a backup crowd."[33]

British Merit eventually reached St John's under tow, but *Broompark* foundered when just twenty-seven miles short of harbour.[34]

Wolf lost contact, but only temporarily. At 0857z on 25 July, Kapitänleutnant Schug in *U 86* made a sighting report—both the Admiralty and Canadian D/F services obtained fixes—and over the next twelve hours the pack reformed.[35] After dark, *Wolf* closed in, but the screen kept the pur-

---

31. *Drumheller* ROP, 30 July 1942, PRO, ADM 237/87

32. BdU, KTB, 24 July 1942; *U 552*, KTB, 24-5 July 1942; Rohwer, *Axis Submarine Successes*, 111; Commodore's Report, ON 113, PRO, ADM 237/87; *Drumheller* ROP and track chart on ON 113; CONNAV to CTU 24.1.12, 1446/24 July 1942, DHH, 89/34, v 17, ON 113; SS *British Merit*, Attack on Merchant Vessel by Enemy Submarine, 24 July 1942, NAC, RG 24, 4025, NSS 1062-10-13; "Report of Interview with Chief Officer of SS *Broompark*," 17 Feb. 1943, PRO, ADM 237/87; HMS *Burnham* ROP; *Brandon* ROP, ON 113, DHH, 81/520 Brandon 8000; *Brandon* and *Polyanthus* took over rescue operations, "Monthly Report for July, 1942, St John's," NSS 1000-5-20(1), in DHH, 81/520 St Croix 8000

33. J.C. Littler, *Sea Fever* (Victoria 1995), 189

34. *Brandon*, ROP. Towing and screening the two modern and thus particularly valuable ships more than 300 miles to Newfoundland developed into a major salvage effort involving four tugs and four additional escorts.

35. BdU, KTB, 25 July 1942; *U 43*, *U 86*, and *U 454* KTB, 25 July 1942; *Burnham* ROP; Adm to Escorts of ON 113 and 112, 1723b/25 July 1942; and Cdr J.M. de Marbois, Memo to Director, Anti-Submarine, RCN, "DF fixes in Relation to ON 113," both DHH, 89/34, v 17, ON-113; Cmdre's Report; COMINCH to CTU 24.1.12, 1933/25 July 1942, DHH, 89/34, v 17, ONS 112

Top: Rear-Admiral Leonard Murray, Flag Officer Newfoundland, congratulates Able Seaman Jim Pullen on sighting *U 90*, which led to its destruction. *St Croix*'s CO, Lieutenant-Commander A.H. Dobson, RCNR, is behind Murray, while Lieutenant C.J. Smith, RCN, the First Lieutenant, is at right. (NAC, PA 204343)

Bottom: The British Town Class destroyer HMS *Lincoln* in May 1942. Her equipment is superior to most RCN escorts at the time with type 271 centimetric radar abaft the bridge and an HF/DF antenna at the head of the foremast. (NAC, PA 205171)

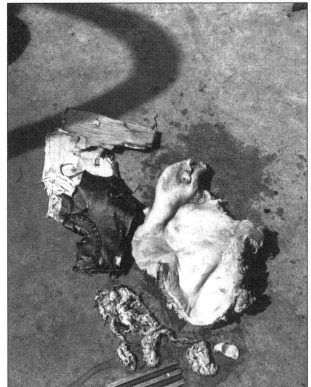

Top: The valiant warrior *St Croix* coming alongside Halifax in December 1940. (NAC, PA 104474)

Right: Evidence was collected from the sea to provide proof of U-boat kills. These are the grisly remains from *U 90*, destroyed by *St Croix* on 24 July 1942 during the defence of ON 113. (NAC, PA 204344)

suers at bay in the bright moonlight. The convoy again made an evasive alteration of course during the night, but the pack maintained contact. Despite the presence of at least six U-boats, none closed to attack until an hour before morning twilight when clouds darkened the sky and visibility dropped. The experienced Kapitänleutnant Mengersen in *U 607* seized the opportunity to move up around the starboard side of ON 113 and penetrate between *Burnham* and *Dauphin*. Mengersen glimpsed the ships in the starboard column and at 0557z on 26 July fired a spread of four torpedoes that struck the 6,942 ton freighter *Empire Rainbow* at the head of the column before slipping away in the fog. At the same time, *U 704* under Kapitänleutnant Kessler pierced the screen from ahead. At 0611z, he fired a spread of four torpedoes at a large freighter and heard detonations. Mengersen also heard these hits as he opened out to the north; both boats had apparently torpedoed the same ship. Kessler tried to escape on the surface but was forced to dive by escorts carrying out a Raspberry search—a tactic where escorts proceeded to pre-arranged sectors in hopes of illuminating an unseen attacker. Subsequently, *Burnham* and *Dauphin* (Lieutenant-Commander R.A.S. MacNeil, RCNR), while rescuing *Empire Rainbow*'s crew from the hulk, gained asdic contact on *U 704* and attacked. The U-boat, with its batteries and oxygen nearly depleted, was able to creep away after about two hours to repair damage. Despite Lieutenant-Commander MacNeil's best efforts, *Empire Rainbow*'s wreck looked unpromising for salvage, and *Dauphin* sank it with gunfire.[36]

During the daylight hours on 26 July when, for much of the time, *St Croix* and *Drumheller* were the only escorts in company as the others had detached to fuel in St John's or were engaged in rescue operations, the shadowing U-boats were unable to attack. Fog helped. In the late afternoon of 26 July, the Town class destroyer HMCS *Annapolis* and the WLEF group W 7, comprising the destroyers HMS *Walker* (Commander J.M. Rowland, RN) and HMCS *Columbia*, and the corvettes HMCS *Calgary* and *Chicoutimi*, joined the remaining escorts of C 2. *Wolf* finally lost contact that evening.[37]

W 7 safely shepherded ON 113 as far as Sable Island. The convoy was on a track towards New York, which would take it into the patrol area of Kapitänleutnant Vogelsang's *U 132*. Although the boat had only two torpedoes left after operations in the Gulf of St Lawrence, (Chapter 8 above) BdU had sent *U 132* to an area to the south of Sable Island to intercept shipping expected on the great circle between New York and Britain.[38] On 29 July, when BdU ordered Vogelsang to report on fog conditions and traffic, his transmissions resulted in two HF/DF fixes shortly after 2100z that were reported to Rowland by COMINCH. Soon afterwards, an RCAF Hudson joined, but visibility was poor, and neither the HF/DF intelligence nor the air cover provided sufficient defence against a submarine lying in wait for the convoy.

Shortly before sunset, *U 132* sighted ON 113 emerging from a rain squall and dived immediately to attack. After passing under an escort, Vogelsang fired his two remaining torpedoes at the

---

36. *U 607* and *U 597* penetrated the screen from ahead but could not attack, and the screen prevented two other boats from penetrating from astern. BdU, KTB, 25 July 1942; COMINCH to CTU 24.1.12, 0527/26 July 1942; *U 86, U 71, U 607,* and *U 704* KTBs, 26 July 1942; *Burnham* ROP; HMCS *Dauphin*, deck log, 26 July 1942, NAC, RG 24, 7253; Rohwer, *Axis Submarine Successes*, 111

37. BdU, KTB, 26 July 1942; *U 71*, KTB, 26 July 1942; HMS *Walker* ROP, ON 113, 4 Aug. 1942, NAC, RG 24, 11020, 7-2-1, pt 4; *Drumheller* ROP, ON 113

38. *U 132*, KTB, 26-8 July 1942

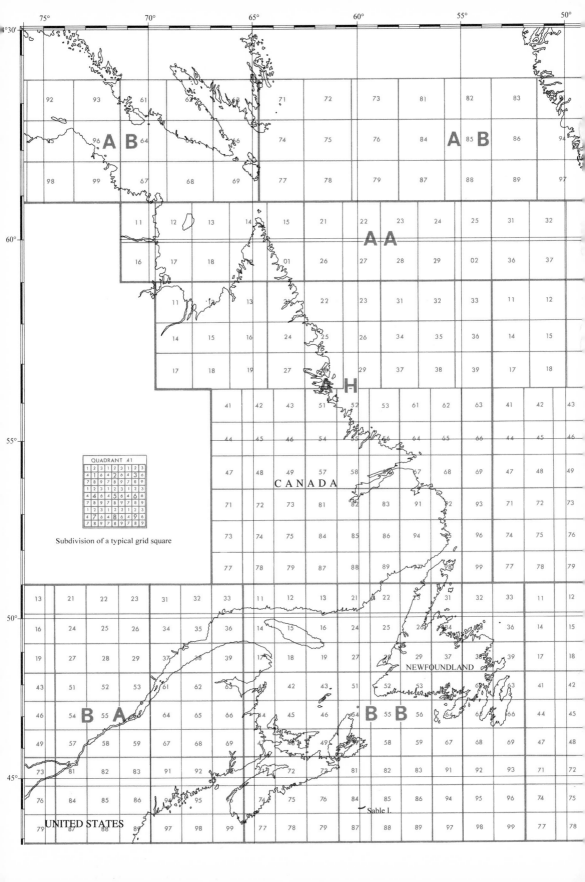

GREENLAND

45° 40° 35° 30° 25°

A D A J A K A B C B D

37 38 39 47 48 49 57 58 59 47

92 93 61 63 64 71 72 73 81 82 83 71

95 96 64 65 66 74 75 76 84 85 86 74

98 99 67 68 69 77 78 79 87 88 89 77

33 34 91 92 93 94 11 12 21 22 31 32 11 12 21

38 39 40 95 96 97 98 13 14 23 24 33 34 13 14 23

3 21 22 23 31 32 33 15 16 25 26 35 36 15 16 25

6 24 25 26 34 35 36 17 18 27 28 37 38 17 18 27

9 27 28 29 37 38 39 19 01 29 02 39 03 19 01 29

51 52 53 61 62 63 41 42 43 51 52 53 61 62 63 41 42 51

54 55 56 64 65 66 44 45 46 54 55 56 64 65 66 44 45 54

57 58 59 67 68 69 47 48 49 57 58 59 67 68 69 47 48 57

81 82 83 91 92 93 71 72 73 81 82 83 91 92 93 71 72 81

84 85 86 94 95 96 74 75 76 84 85 86 94 95 96 74 75 84

87 88 89 97 98 99 77 78 79 87 88 89 97 98 99 77 78 87

13 21 22 23 31 32 33 11 12 13 21 22 23 31 32 33 11 12

16 24 25 26 34 35 36 14 15 16 24 25 26 34 35 36 14 15

19 27 28 29 37 38 39 17 18 19 27 28 29 37 38 39 17 18

43 51 52 53 61 62 63 41 42 43 51 52 53 61 62 63 41 42

46 54 55 56 64 65 66 44 45 46 54 55 56 64 65 66 44 45

49 57 58 59 67 68 69 47 48 49 57 58 59 67 68 69 47 48

73 81 82 83 91 92 93 71 72 73 81 82 83 91 92 93 71 72

76 84 85 86 94 95 96 74 75 76 84 85 86 94 95 96 74 75

79 87 88 89 97 98 99 77 78 79 87 88 89 97 98 99 77 78

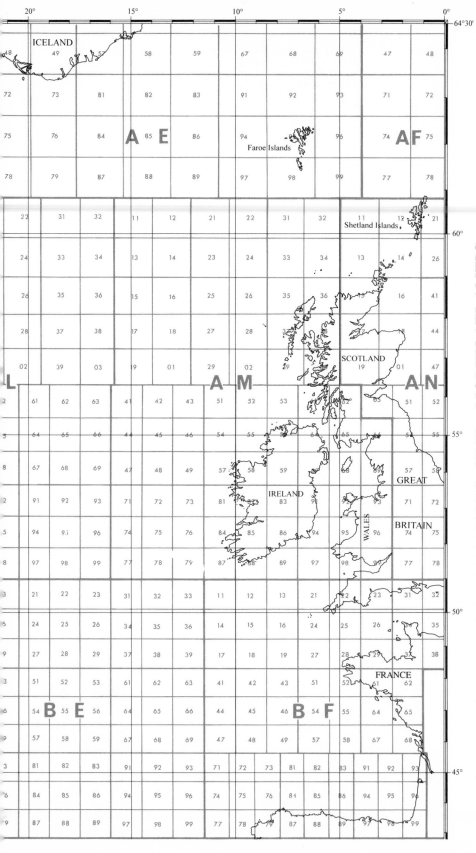

GERMAN NAVAL GRID - NORTH ATLANTIC

6,734 ton freighter *Pacific Pioneer* at the head of the fourth column. As a torpedo exploded against the ship, which sank rapidly, *U 132* dove deep to avoid an oncoming vessel, but plunged uncontrollably to the bottom in eighty metres of water and could not break free. All four escorts carried out an asdic search in which *Calgary* obtained a contact and attacked with depth charges. When *U 132* finally broke free from the bottom damage from the depth charges had reduced her maximum surface speed to twelve knots. Despite this, BdU ordered Vogelsang to relocate ON 113, and directed three other boats, *U 89*, *U 458*, and *U 754* that were operating southwest of Nova Scotia, to hunt for the convoy on the assumption that it was destined for Boston. They failed to find anything, but Canadian D/F stations intercepted a signal from *U 754* while it searched for ON 113 on 31 July, and passed the bearings to Eastern Air Command. As described earlier, Squadron Leader N.E. Small gained the RCAF's first U-boat kill when he delivered a swift depth charge attack that destroyed *U 754*. Nor was that all. Later that day, and on 2 and 5 August, 113 Squadron aircraft also attacked *U 132*, *U 458*, and *U 89*, although without inflicting damage.[39]

This outstanding performance by the Yarmouth-based squadron owed much to Small's extraordinary drive, imagination, and leadership. At a time when Eastern Air Command was consumed by the day-to-day challenges arising from excessive commitments, shortages of equipment and trained personnel, and half-developed base facilities, Small threw himself into studying and applying the latest doctrinal memoranda from the RAF's Coastal Command, at that time the world's most successful maritime air force. Its experience emphasized the need for rapid response to the latest and best intelligence about probable U-boat positions, and Small accordingly arranged to have the navy's DF bearings on U-boat signals immediately telephoned to his squadron, where aircraft took off instantly to search the vicinity of the transmission.

The prompt availability of DF triangulations that gave the approximate position of where a U-boat had broadcast in turn reflected recent and continuing improvements in the RCN's signals intelligence capabilities. In fact, the signals intelligence group at NSHQ crowed over the air force's successes: "Numerous sightings occurred in Canadian coastal waters and several NSHQ fixes were proved gratifyingly accurate by excellent co-operation from the RCAF, resulting in prompt A/S attacks by their craft. Communications between the two services in regard to H/F D/F positions of U-Boats have been really improved with splendid results."[40]

The Canadian naval signals intelligence organization had always depended upon expert advice from Britain, and in the spring of 1942, RN intelligence authorities provided the most comprehensive assistance yet in an effort to bring Canadian and, especially, US resources more closely into line with proven British methods. The impetus came from the heavy shipping losses on the US seaboard, which in part derived from the Americans' inexperience in the quick collation, analysis, and dissemination of intelligence necessary for anti-U-boat warfare. Britain had forged intelligence into a major weapon in the maritime war through the development of the Operational Intelligence Centre at the Admiralty. The centre was lavishly provided with the communications, expert personnel, and authority necessary to function as the one and only clearing house for maritime intelligence, and it was in direct touch with the operational headquarters that directed the maritime forces and movements of shipping. By contrast, the decentralized organization of the US

---

39. Hadley, *U-Boats against Canada*, 108; Douglas, *Creation of a National Air Force*, 519-20

40. DDSD (Y), "Report for July, 1942," 3. See also, "Report for December, 1942," 10-11, NAC

Navy and Army, the ferocious competition between these services and other agencies, the country's delayed entry into the war, and, until January 1942, the remoteness of enemy forces from the shores of the continental United States had prevented such a close integration of resources.

In Washington, from 6 to 16 April 1942, a tri-service British delegation led by Captain H.R. Sandwith, RN, head of the Admiralty's "Y" and D/F section, met with their American counterparts and a Canadian delegation, led by Captain J.M. deMarbois, head of the Foreign Intelligence Section at NSHQ. The Sandwith mission failed to persuade the American armed forces and other US intelligence agencies to integrate their efforts, but it did lay the groundwork for the Anglo-British-Canadian naval signals intelligence organization that would contribute mightily to the Allied to victory in the Atlantic. Much of the conference's work was technical, concerning equipment, areas for further research, and arrangements for fast, secure communications for sharing of time-sensitive material such as DF bearings among London, Ottawa, and Washington. There was also a clearer division of national responsibilities for signals intelligence tasks, which confirmed London as the main centre for material concerning Germany and Italy, and the United States for coverage of Japanese traffic. Accordingly, the discussions provided firmer guidelines for direction by US intelligence centres of Canadian intercept and direction-finding stations in the western part of the country that were assigned to Japanese communications. As had been the case since the outbreak of war, the nascent Canadian intelligence organization was developing as a subordinate part of the Allied effort.[41] This junior status was also evident in the fact that the Canadian delegation was apparently excluded from discussions in which the British representatives described in detail the activities of Bletchley Park and sought closer cooperation with the Americans.[42]

The conference agreed, however, that there should be three plotting centres for maritime intelligence in the Atlantic: London, with primary responsibility for the eastern part of the ocean, as well as Ottawa and Washington, sharing responsibility for the western ocean.[43] This decision reflected the capabilities Canada had developed since 1939, and the significant role it was already playing in the radio war because, until December 1941, Britain had no other source of essential support in the western hemisphere. At the time of the discussions in Washington, twelve stations run by either the RCN, RCAF, or the Department of Transport, were forwarding DF bearings to NSHQ. Although the organization was workable, and sometimes produced superb results—witness Hartlen Point's evident role in the hunting of the *Bismarck* (See Chapter 3)—there was nonetheless considerable room for improvement. Sandwith and members of his mission came to Canada before and after the Washington conference, visiting stations in the eastern and western part of the country, as well as Ottawa. They found, in the words of one historian, "a loosely organised system which produced uneven results because of problems with priorities, equipment, and personnel; but which only needed some adjustment and additional

41.   A.H. Bath, *Tracking the Axis Enemy: The Triumph of Anglo-American Naval Intelligence* (Lawrence 1998), 74-80; B.F. Smith, *The Ultra-Magic Deals and the Most Secret Special Relationship, 1940-1946* (Novata 1993), 119-22; U.S. Stephenson (ed), *British Security Coordination: The Secret History of British Intelligence in the Americas 1940-45* (London 1998), 480-6; Catherine E. Allan, "A Minute Bletchley Park: Building a Canadian Naval Operational Intelligence Centre, 1939-1943," in M.L. Hadley, R. Huebert, and F.W. Crickard (eds), *A Nation's Navy: In Quest of Canadian Naval Identity* (Montréal and Kingston 1996), 168; and John Bryden, *Best-Kept Secret: Canadian Secret Intelligence in the Second World* (Toronto 1993)

42.   Major C.E. Allan, "Canadian Naval Signals Intelligence in the Second World War," 95, DHH, 2000/5. See also, Bath, *Tracking the Axis Enemy*, 75, and Smith, *Ultra-Magic Deals*, 121-2.

43.   Allan, "Minute Bletchley Park," 175

resources to meet the needs of its parent organisation [the Admiralty]."[44] The time had come, Sandwith advised, for the RCN to get beyond its "clever" improvisation in using DOT and RCAF radio stations for naval tasks. The RCN should focus its effort on fewer stations with better equipment, fully under naval control and staffed by qualified naval personnel. To a large extent, the mission encouraged developments that were already under way, but they indicated the required scope of effort; the mission's recommendations looked to the expansion of the personnel committed to naval signals intelligence duties from 425 to 700. The mission also emphasized the need for centralization of analysis at NSHQ. Only in this way could the RCN make proper use of the fuller and more timely information that would be coming from London and Washington, and, similarly, ensure that material gathered by Canadian stations reached the British and American centres with sufficient speed. One of the major challenges was to improve domestic communications across the vast distances that separated Ottawa from the intercept and direction finding stations and from the operational commands on the east coast.[45] The links to Halifax and St John's especially had to be improved because those commands were doing their own analysis of the daily U-boat location signals from the Admiralty and the periodic intelligence reports from Ottawa and Washington. These analyses, as NSHQ's Foreign Intelligence Section complained, made incorrect assumptions, because the staffs on the coasts lacked the full information and expertise available in Ottawa. The challenge was to provide fuller and more timely reports from NSHQ so that the plotting done there would subsume the independent efforts on the coast.[46]

At about this time, the Foreign Intelligence Section established a U-boat tracking room, which on 2 May began to send a daily U-boat location estimate to the east coast commands, the RCAF, Washington, and London. The officer who ran what evolved into a most successful operation from its inception until the end of the war in Europe was Lieutenant John B. McDiarmid, RCNVR. As with many members of the allied naval intelligence fraternity, McDiarmid was far from the stereotypical naval officer. A classicist, he had graduated from the University of Toronto with a Bachelor of Arts in Latin and Greek before earning a Ph.D in Greek at Johns Hopkins University in Baltimore. McDiarmid had also studied Sanskrit for two years, and had good schooling in French and a rudimentary knowledge of German. By his own admission, "I had never seen an ocean, and my only experience afloat was a few months as a deckhand on a lake steamer."[47]

With the attack on Pearl Harbor, McDiarmid left his teaching position at John's Hopkins to join the RCN. In April 1942, after a month's general training in Halifax, he was appointed to NSHQ for duty with the Operational Intelligence Centre. Because of the increased signals traffic from the shift of U-boat operations into North American waters, there was a need for someone to work full time in correlating data and preparing the daily situation report. As the newest member of the OIC, that job fell to McDiarmid. A babe in the woods of naval operations and intelligence, McDiarmid

44.   Allan, "Canadian Naval Signals Intelligence," 107

45.   Capt H.R. Sandwith, "Report on RCN 'Y' Organization," 19 May 1942, NAC, RG 24, 3806, 1008-75-20; Allan, "Minute Bletchley Park," 167-8

46.   For example, SecNB to FONF, 12 May 1942, DHH, NSS 8910-166.25, pt 1

47.   J.B. McDiarmid to VAdm Peter Gretton, RN (Ret'd), 23 July 1982, 1; Notes from M. Whitby interview with J.B. McDiarmid, Jan. 1999. Both DHH, 2000/5

attacked the challenge with academic rigour, learning everything he could about the subject by analysing all available evidence:

> I set about educating myself in the nature and behaviour of U-boats, keeping constant watch on the evidence from both sides and reading everything that was known or thought about submarines past and present—particularly, of course, the Admiralty's red-bound intelligence reports and "Daily Situation Reports." I did not know that TETIS and other cyphers were being decrypted, but I surmised that the Admiralty had good intelligence from reconnaissance and informants about the boats' departures and could predict the times of return in a general way of knowledge of the U-boats' endurance. On the where-abouts of U-boats in mid-ocean and on patrol the Admiralty seemed less well-informed; for sometimes the Situation Reports were vague, changed markedly over a few days , and did not anticipate a sinking or contact. I therefore took the Situation Reports as a datum for departures, general directions to patrol, and rate of return to port. For the rest I attempted to construct a picture of the West Atlantic from contacts, D/F, and U-boat signal traffic.[48]

As McDiarmid found his way, he profited from direct advice from Commander Winn, head of the Admiralty's Submarine Tracking Room.[49] Winn had gone to Washington on the heels of the Sandwith mission to persuade the USN to establish its own U-boat tracking room, a task in which he succeeded, before continuing to Ottawa to look in on NSHQ's new endeavour.[50] According to McDiarmid, Winn "was not the remote wizard I expected, but a gentle and sympathetic man. He asked me how I kept the plot, and he gave me valuable information on the departures of U-boats from the French ports, but he did not correct my notions about the sources of the information or give any hint that the U-boat cypher had ever been decrypted."[51] For his part, Winn described the U-boat tracking group as a "highly intelligent group of keen young men."[52]

Winn also helped delineate the responsibilities of the Canadian and US plotting centres, both of which were promulgating reports for the entire western Atlantic. Following from his suggestion, NSHQ concentrated on the area west of 40°West and north of 40°North, while the US centre focused on the area to the south of 40°North.[53] As will be seen in Chapter 11 of this history, that decision would have important ramifications in the RCN's pursuit of increased autonomy.

———

The heavy and tenacious enemy attack on ON 113—especially the first phase in which ten U-boats had persisted in the hunt for three days—signalled clearly what could now be expected from the *U-bootwaffe*. Nevertheless, the final tally was in favour of the defence. The U-boats torpedoed a total of four empty merchant ships, of which one made harbour and was subsequently repaired. For these meagre results *St Croix* had sunk *U 90* and the RCAF had destroyed *U 754*, a rate of exchange that

48. McDiarmid to Gretton, 1-2

49. "Chronological History of Operational Intelligence Centre, 1942," 6, DHH, NHS NSS 1440-18

50. Beesley, *Very Special Intelligence*, 112-14; Bath, *Tracking the Axis Enemy*, 76-8

51. McDiarmid to Gretton, 2

52. Quoted in Allan, "Canadian Naval Signals Intelligence," 108

53. OIC 4, "D/F Plotting Section— NSHQ: History 1942," 2

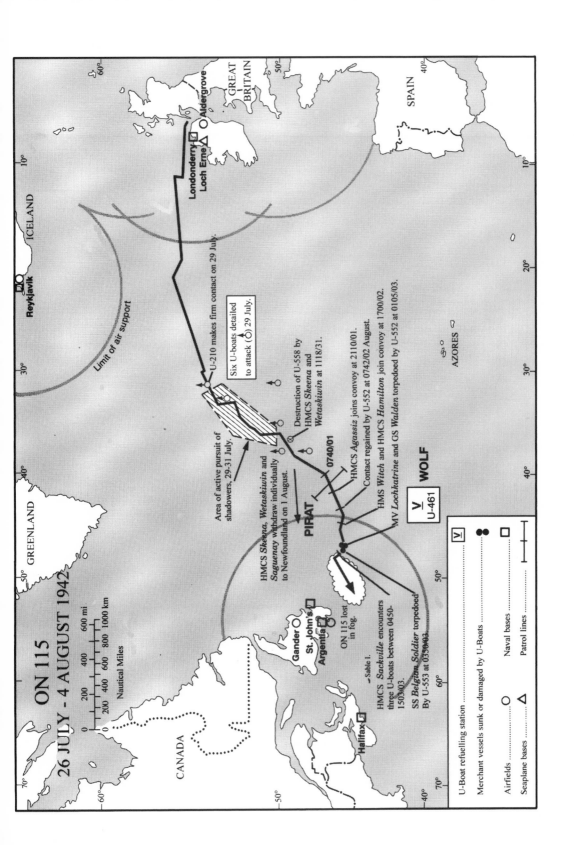

ON 115
26 JULY - 4 AUGUST 1942

Nautical Miles

0   200   400   600 mi

0   200 400 600 800 1000 km

GREENLAND

CANADA

ICELAND

Reykjavík

GREAT BRITAIN

SPAIN

Limit of air support

Londonderry
Loch Erne
Aldergrove

U-210 makes firm contact on 29 July.

Six U-boats detailed to attack (○) 29 July.

Destruction of U-558 by HMCS *Skeena* and *Wetaskiwin* at 1118/31.

Area of active pursuit of shadowers, 29-31 July.

HMCS *Skeena*, *Wetaskiwin* and *Saguenay* withdraw individually to Newfoundland on 1 August.

PIRAT

0740/01

HMCS *Agassiz* joins convoy at 2110/01.

Contact regained by U-552 at 0742/02 August.

HMS *Witch* and HMCS *Hamilton* join convoy at 1700/02.

MV *Lochkatrine* and GS *Walden* torpedoed by U-552 at 0105/03.

WOLF

U-461

Gander
St. John's
Argentia

ON 115 lost in fog.

Sable I.

HMCS *Sackville* encounters three U-boats between 0450-1503/03.

SS *Belgian Soldier* torpedoed By U-553 at 0330/03.

Halifax

AZORES

U-Boat refuelling station ....

Merchant vessels sunk or damaged by U-Boats ....

Naval bases ....

Airfields ....

Seaplane bases ....

Patrol lines ....

was utterly unacceptable in Dönitz's campaign to destroy Allied shipping. BdU blamed poor weather, inexperienced commanders, and "the [evasive] movements of the strongly escorted convoy" for the outcome.[54] On the Allied side, the lack of shipboard HF/DF was a tactical handicap for C 2; although reports of HF/DF intercepts by shore stations were valuable, they were one to four hours stale by the time they were received at sea. Also, CONNAV's intervention on the second night of battle had the bizarre effect of causing ON 113 to steam a large circle. Although this extreme course alteration may have contributed to several boats losing contact for several hours, it kept the convoy inside both *Wolf*'s area and the air gap. When Western Approaches analyzed the battle, they found that the combination of CONNAV's decision and the vigorous evasive alterations ordered by Commander Taylor during successive nights had also slowed the convoy's westward progress; Admiral Noble observed dryly that in the twenty critical hours, during which two ships were torpedoed, ON 113 "made good NIL and in fact went to the Eastward."[55]

During the battle for ON 113, CONNAV and the Admiralty, had routed SC 92, HX 199, HX 200, and ON 114 clear of *Wolf*. Four U-boats transited the Iceland–Faeroes gap in this period—three of which were attacked by Allied aircraft south of Iceland—and the Admiralty's situation report drew the conclusion that U-boat reinforcements were heading towards these convoys.[56] Two fast westbound convoys that put to sea during 25 and 26 July—ON 115 (C 3) and ON 116 (C 4)—were standing into precisely the kind of danger to which ON 113 had been exposed. ON 115 suffered the consequences.

Escort group C 3 consisted of the River class destroyers *Saguenay* (Commander D.C. Wallace, RCNR, SOE) and *Skeena* (Lieutenant K.L. Dyer, RCN), and the corvettes *Wetaskiwin* (Lieutenant-Commander G.S. Windeyer, RCN), *Sackville* (Lieutenant A.H. Easton, RCNR), *Louisbourg* (Lieutenant-Commander W.F. Campbell, RCNVR,) and *Galt* (Lieutenant A.D. Landles, RCNR). ON 115 was just Wallace's second trip as senior officer, but the group had achieved a degree of stability, *Louisbourg* being the lone newcomer. The others had sailed together on three passages, and the two destroyers had been together longer. None of the group had HF/DF or type 271, but MF/DF was to prove especially effective as the convoy commodore, Admiral A.J. Davies, RN (Ret'd), in MV *Pacific Grove*, passed MF/DF bearings obtained by two merchant ships to the escorts throughout the passage.[57] The level of effectiveness of the ships varied greatly. In May, *Galt* had been the first escort through a new work-up program in Halifax, and Commander J.C. Hibbard, the Training Commander, judged her to be "average and knows what to do in an emergency."[58] By contrast, *Skeena* and *Wetaskiwin* were veteran ships whose commanding officers had recently trained

---

54. Six of the U-boat commanders were making their first patrol in command. MOD, *U-Boat War in the Atlantic* II, 33; and Milner, *North Atlantic Run*, 127

55. C-in-C WA to Sec of the Adm, 28 Sep. 1942, Memo, "Subject: ROPs ON-113 and ON-115," NAC, RG 24, 11088, 48-2-2, v 51. See also, Convoy cover, PRO, ADM 237/87 and 237/88.

56. Adm, OIC, U-Boat Situation Report, 27 July 1942, PRO, ADM 223/15. *U 210* reported "frequent air attacks" and depth charges from 24 to 26 July as she passed south of Iceland, from "Report of the Interrogation of Survivors of *U 210*," extracts of diaries, DHH, NHS 1650-U 210. *U 164* mentions two aerial attacks during her Iceland passage on 25-6 July in her KTB on 31 July.

57. For a technical analysis of the role of MF/DF in the battle, see "U-Boat[s] Operating against Convoy ON 115 on 30, 31 July, 2 and 3 Aug. 1942," 16-17, and appendices, in DDSD (Y), "Report for July 1942," 26 Aug. 1942, NAC. Of ninety-seven DFs picked up by ships or shore stations during the convoy, thirty-nine were MF/DF bearings, and the remainder HF/DF.

58. *Galt*, Work-Up Report, NAC, RG 24, 6910, NSS 8970-331/39

together at St John's under the tutelage of Commander G.A.M.V. Harrison, RN, who ran the Mobile A/S Training Unit (MA/STU), a double-decker bus stocked with operable ASW equipments, including an attack teacher.[59] Harrison appears to have trained Dyer and Windeyer to a fine edge. In his attack report written on the events that followed, Windeyer referred to an operating procedure as "one of Commander Harrison's pet tricks at the M.A/S T.U., St. John's ... It is with much gratitude we now recall his many reiterations [*sic*]." The training clearly had a practical bent; later in the report Windeyer described the smell of U-boat diesel, and suggested that "Commander Harrison reproduces this smell for the benefit of COs." Windeyer concluded with the declaration that "success was due to a happy co-operation between two ships which have been accustomed to working together."[60] It was an old lesson, but one the rapidly expanding RCN found difficult to follow.

ON 115 consisted of forty-one merchant ships in nine columns. On 27 July the escort began to receive warnings from the Admiralty that HF/DF bearings placed submarines in the vicinity of ON 115's track; these were almost certainly the outbound *U 210* and *U 164*. MF/DF bearings by ships in the convoy on what appeared to be signals from submarines in near pursuit caused false alarms; the transmissions actually came from a German medium-frequency decoy beacon in Lorient.[61] In fact the U-boats made no contact until, at 2109z on 29 July, *U 210* sighted a "wisp of smoke," and located ON 115 in quadrant AK-59, almost exactly halfway between Ireland and Newfoundland. Within less than three hours *U 164* homed in on *U 210*'s signals. No other U-boats were in the immediate vicinity, but BdU ordered four outbound boats then 400 miles to the southwest to operate against ON 115. Bold evasive course changes by the convoy, aggressive sweeps by the two destroyers down MF/DF bearings, and *Skeena*'s sighting and pursuit of *U 164* during daylight on the 30th, kept the initial two U-boats at a safe distance for twenty-four hours.[62] During the evening of 30 July, however, there were new warnings from the Admiralty and from the convoy's own MF/DF guard of an increasing number of submarine transmissions in the vicinity of the convoy. The Admiralty estimated that two U-boats were nearby; in fact the four additional U-boats that BdU had ordered to the scene were arriving, for a total of six in close pursuit. Wallace ordered two sharp emergency turns to port, and directed *Skeena* and *Wetaskiwin*, his two well-tuned work horses, to protect the starboard flank, where MF/DF bearings indicated the U-boats were shadowing.[63]

Dyer and Windeyer's close working relationship and time on the training bus paid dividends. At 0636z on 31 July *Skeena* sighted the diesel exhaust of a submarine in the morning twilight eight miles on the convoy's starboard beam. Dyer pursued and actually came across three U-boats. Suddenly forced on the defensive, *U 588* and *U 511* dived while *U 210* escaped on the surface. Faced with a difficult tactical situation, the imaginative young Canadian resorted to tactics he had

59. *Canadian Navy List*, June-Sep. 1942, 258. For more on the MA/STU see Anti-Submarine Warfare IV: A/S Training, Technical Staff Monograph 1939-1945, 17 May 1950, 6-7, PRO, ADM 239/238

60. *Wetaskiwin*, "Attack on U-Boat—July 31, 1942," 9 Aug. 1942, PRO, ADM 237/88, pt 2

61. *Saguenay* ROP, ON 115, 3 Aug. 1942, DHH, 81/520/8280B, box 5, ON 115 ; C-in-C WA to CTU 24.1.13, 1643b/27 July 1942, PRO, ADM 237/88, pt 1; BdU, KTB, 27 July1942; *U 164*, KTB, 27 July 1942; "Notes on U-Boat Homing M/F Traffic Intercepted in Convoy ON-115," 27 Aug. 1942, PRO, ADM 223/3; R. Erskine, "U-Boats, Homing Signals and HF/DF," *Intelligence and National Security* (Apr. 1987), 325-6

62. BdU, KTB, 29 July 1942; "Extract from Diary of Masch Gefr. Monien of *U 210*," DHH, NHS 1650-U 210; *U 164*, KTB, 30 July 1942; *Saguenay* ROP; *Skeena* ROP, DHH, 3 Aug. 1942, 81/520/8280, box 5, ON 115

63. BdU, KTB, 29-30 July and 2 Aug.1942; and *U 511*, KTB, 31 Jul. 1942; Adm to Escorts of ON 115, 0215b/31 July 1942, PRO, ADM 237/88, pt 1

devised for a single escort attack on a submerged U-boat. By dropping depth charges at the furthest points of a diamond-shaped perimeter at the rough distance he calculated the enemy could
reach, he hoped to contain the submarine so that a deliberate attack could be made. It worked.
Skeena obtained a "definite submarine contact" at 0705z, and began a series of depth charge
attacks—possibly against more than one contact. *U 511* sustained damage and "took on a great
deal of water" after depth charges that were "well-aimed but higher than the boat."[64] In the meantime, Wallace ordered *Wetaskiwin* to assist, but by the time she joined at 0800z, *Skeena* had lost
contact. The two ships began a systematic search, which was rewarded when *Wetaskiwin* gained
a deep contact just under an hour later. Over the next two hours, using well-coordinated deliberate tactics where one ship held contact and directed the other over the target, *Wetaskiwin* delivered
four attacks and *Skeena* two. Finally,

> Wetaskiwin ... directed Skeena onto the submarine for the final attack at 1118. Before
> this time, oil patches were visible which were caused by Wetaskiwin's last attacks.
> Skeena only had nineteen charges left so it was decided to fire a five charge pattern,
> the settings ... were changed from 350 to 550 feet during the run in, as contact was
> lost at 600 yards. The final course to steer was given by the plot, and firing by
> Chernikoff [log], plot and dipping of J flag in Wetaskiwin. Again, all three coincided.
> Wetaskiwin's signal of "excellent attack" was further confirmed three minutes later by
> two distinct underwater explosions, thirty seconds apart ...[65]

They had destroyed *U 588*. Oil and floating debris, including human remains, boiled to the surface, giving "enormous pleasure to the assembled ship's company and, incidently, to the seag-
ulls."[66] Dyer and Windeyer lowered boats to collect the grim evidence of their kill.

Although successful, this prolonged hunt had repercussions, as it took two of C 3's most effective escorts away from the convoy. *Skeena*, now short of fuel from her extended sweeps, detached
from the convoy when it was still more than 400 miles east of St John's. To make matters worse,
Westaskiwin was unable to relocate the convoy in the heavy fog after its course alteration and also
proceeded to base.[67] The screen was thus reduced to just four escorts—*Galt* was still rejoining from
astern after being detached on the 30th to keep down a U-boat sighted on the convoy's quarter—
in the air gap with relief several steaming days away. Luckily, misty rain and fog cloaked ON 115.
Even though there had been five other U-boats in the vicinity early on 31 July all had lost contact
after ON 115 made an alteration of course to the southwest at 0740z.

BdU ordered the boats, now designated group *Pirat*, to run to the west, and establish a patrol
line across the convoy's projected track.[68] Although the German estimates of ON 115's course were
accurate, by an extraordinary stroke of luck the convoy avoided detection. As it reached the patrol
line at about 1410z on 1 August, Wallace had to detach to St John's in *Saguenay*, again because

---

64. *U 511*, KTB, 31 July 1942

65. *Skeena* ROP

66. *Skeena* ROP; *Wetaskiwin* ROP, 10 Aug. 1942, DHH, 81/520/8280, box 5, ON 115. See also, Robert Fisher, "Tactics, Training
     and Technology: The RCN's Summer of Success, July-Sep.," *Canadian Military History* 6/2 (1997), 9-12.

67. *Saguenay*, *Skeena*, and *Wetaskiwin* ROPs

68. MOD, *U-Boat War in the Atlantic* II, 33; CONNAV's signal to CTU 24.1.13, 1510/31 July 1942, instructed C 3 to alter to new
     position "Q" (47°N, 40°W) thence to "F" to shake off the shadowing U-boats.

of the fuel burned in his long distance sweeps. *U 511* sighted the destroyer as she withdrew, crash-dived to avoid detection, and so created a gap in the line through which ON 115 unwittingly steamed unscathed. Fog prevented the *Wolf* boats from joining *Pirat*, creating more gaps, so Dönitz abandoned the search, ordered several boats to the Caribbean, and directed the remainder to form Group *Steinbrink* in a patrol line northeast of Newfoundland.[69]

In the early hours of 2 August before the redeployment of the submarines away from the vicinity of ON 115's track took place, the convoy's luck finally ran out. FONF had despatched the corvette HMCS *Agassiz* and later two destroyers, HMS *Witch* and HMCS *Hamilton*, from St. John's to augment the depleted escort. *Agassiz* rendezvoused with ON 115 at 2110z on 1 August and her captain, Lieutenant-Commander B.D.L. Johnson, RCNR assumed duties as SOE.[70] Now with an escort of four corvettes and a new SOE, the convoy approached thirteen enemy submarines—the five original *Pirat* boats plus eight refuelled boats formerly in *Wolf* that were proceeding to new taskings. The fog lifted, and Topp in *U 552*, who had played such a key role against ON 113 the week before, glimpsed the convoy about 300 miles southeast of St John's. Forced to submerge when the moon emerged from behind clouds, Topp surfaced at dawn, held contact despite worsening visibility, and transmitted a sighting report at 0742z on 2 August. BdU ordered both *Pirat* and *Wolf* to close.[71]

The Admiralty intercepted Topp's sighting report and warned the escort at 0911z on 2 August that the enemy had re-established contact.[72] ON 115 was now within the range of shore-based aircraft, but poor weather prevented EAC from locating the convoy and shut down USN flight operations at Argentia.[73] As the convoy tried to close the reinforcing destroyers coming from St John's by steering directly for them, the remnants of C 3 braced for assault. During the daylight hours, five U-boats operated around the convoy. At 1320z on 2 August, *Agassiz* sighted *U 704* on the surface seven miles away, gave chase, and opened fire, forcing it to submerge. Her lookouts then sighted *U 597* on the surface, and also forced it down by gunfire. *Agassiz* and *Galt* kept both boats under with random depth charges and proceeded back to the convoy at 1606z.[74] On the port beam of ON 115, Lieutenant Alan Easton, commanding *Sackville*, climbed up to the crowsnest to get a better view and suddenly noticed an object fine on the starboard bow, seven miles distant. He ordered full speed, but did not get an asdic contact when the object disappeared. Easton had probably glimpsed *U 552*. Topp reported "contact on destroyer" at 1400z and one hour later, "positioned a bit ahead of the convoy," could not elude "a pursuing destroyer even at maximum speed." He submerged at 1501z and recorded that the escort was "conducting a depth charge pursuit a long way off."[75] *Sackville* gave up the hunt and rejoined ON 115 about an hour later.

---

69. BdU, KTB, 1 Aug. 1942; *U 511*, KTB, 31 July 1942; and *Saguenay* ROP

70. *Agassiz* ROP, nd, ON 115, DHH, 81/520/8280, box 5

71. BdU, KTB, 2 Aug. 1942; and *U 552*, KTB, 2 Aug. 1942. Topp reported convoy's course as 240 degrees and position BC-59 at 0744z/2.

72. Adm to Escorts of ON 115, 1011b/2 Aug. 1942, PRO, ADM 237/88, pt 1. The USN also DF'd this signal but was slower to relay it to the escort.

73. No. 1 Group, "Intelligence Report for Week Ending Aug. 7, 1942," 9 Aug. 1942. DHH, 181.003 (D2178)

74. *Agassiz* ROP; BdU, KTB, 2 Aug.1942; and *U 704*, KTB, 2 Aug. 1942

75. *Sackville* ROP, 10 Aug. 1942, DHH, 81/520/8280, box 5, ON 115; Easton, *50 North*, 125-7; *U 552*, KTB, 2 Aug. 1942

HMS *Witch* (Lieutenant-Commander C.H. Holmes, RN), equipped with HF/DF, and *Hamilton* joined from St John's at 1700z on 2 August. Holmes, the fourth SOE in the short life of ON 115, immediately ordered *Galt* and *Agassiz* to return from their sweeps, and then, with *Hamilton*, kept down *U 71* and *U 217* as they tried to attain attack positions. After dark—sunset was at 2235z— *U 552, U 553,* and *U 217* lost contact. Soon after midnight, just as the screen came back to full strength, Topp sighted an escort and over the next hour manoeuvred ahead of the convoy. His first torpedoes missed their target, but a second spread of three hit the freighter MV *Lochkatrine* and the tanker *G.S. Walden.* The night came alive with illuminating rockets, flares, and starshell. On firing snowflake, the Commodore's ship, *Pacific Grove,* sighted *U 552* at close range, but her DEMS gunners could not get off a shot before the U-boat escaped on the surface. As the screen executed Operation Raspberry, the Commodore ordered two emergency turns to starboard, bringing the convoy's heading to 330°, and at 0140z, after the escorts had failed to get contact, *Hamilton, Agassiz,* and *Sackville* went to the assistance of the torpedoed ships. Meanwhile, confusion set in on the convoy's starboard wing. The lead ship of the ninth column turned a further 45° to starboard, followed by the ships in the three starboard columns, which effectively split the convoy in two. *Louisbourg* realized what happened and stuck with the wayward section until daylight. Unhappily, as so often happened, the snowflake put up after the attack served as a beacon for the U-boats that had lost contact.[76]

Korvettenkapitän Karl Thurmann in *U 553* profited from the confusion by torpedoing *Belgian Soldier,* a 7,167 ton freighter that remained afloat. He had to crash-dive to avoid an escort, but asdic conditions were poor and Thurmann was able to hide beneath a thermal layer at about 120 metres. Meanwhile, at 0230z on 3 August, *Sackville,* while screening the rescue ships, got a radar contact at 2,500 yards, and when Easton turned towards, his lookouts sighted *U 43* on the surface. When Easton saw he would narrowly miss ramming he attacked with a five-charge pattern set at fifty feet. *U 43*'s crash-dive had been slowed by a faulty hatch and the depth charges blew out all lights, stopped the motors, caused the depth gauges to fail, and forced the boat to "rise out of the water at a distance of about 20 or 30 yards from the stern [of *Sackville*]." The boat rolled as another depth charge exploded beneath it, then plunged downward at maximum angle. *Sackville*'s asdic team gained a good contact and Easton fired a ten-charge pattern set to 100 and 225 feet that brought diesel oil to the surface, then fired another five-charge pattern that produced an underwater explosion. Against all odds, the submarine survived, but had to return to base for repairs.[77]

Unaware that the convoy had split into two, Holmes had *Galt* rescue survivors from *Belgian Soldier,* left *Hamilton* and *Agassiz* to salvage *G.S. Walden,* and gave the latter corvette permission to take the tanker in tow. Not until 0350z on 3 August did he discover that the ships escorted by *Louisbourg* had become separated from the main body, which was now without any escort at all. Fortunately, Topp in *U 552* was none the wiser. At 0302z, he approached under dark low rain

---

76. HMS *Witch*, ROP, ON 115 , 5 Aug. 1942, NAC, RG 24, 11088, 48-2-2 (51); *U 71, U 217, U 552,* and *U 553*, KTBs, 2-3 Aug. 1942; *Hamilton, Agassiz, Sackville,* and *Louisbourg* ROPs, ON 115; "Report of an Interview with the Master of *Lochkatrine*," PRO, ADM 237/88; and Cmdre's Report, ON 115, PRO, ADM 237/88

77. *Sackville* ROP; Easton, *50 North*, 137-142; Dönitz, *Memoirs*, 247; *U 43*, KTB, 3 Aug. 1942. *U 43* returned to France for repairs: the port diesel clutch had seized up, the gyro and magnetic compasses had failed, the servicing hatch leaked, the starboard diesel starter block was cracked, the mountings and housings of both compressors were cracked, and one man had suffered internal injuries.

A 1944 photograph of Lieutenant-Commander A.H. Easton, RCNR, CO of HMCS *Sackville*, who tangled with *U 552* during the fight for ON 115. (NAC, PA 206442)

Top: *U 552* arrives in St Nazaire in August 1942, showing some of the damage from her skirmish with *Sackville*. Korvettenkapitän Erich Topp is holding the megaphone. (Courtesy Alan Easton)

Bottom: Smoke led to the sighting of many convoys. This is a small Panamanian freighter photographed from HMCS *Pictou* in March 1942. (NAC, PA 204601)

clouds and occasional drizzle for a second attack. "As seen from the side," he noted that, "one vessel overlaps the other ... [with] hardly any space for a shot to go past." Expecting a response from escorts, he rushed the attack and failed to hit a target, even though *Pacific Grove* and SS *Dorcasia* felt heavy explosions that toppled their gyros—probably torpedoes exploding at the end of their run. These were Topp's last *Aale*—or eels, as the German submariners dubbed their torpedoes—but he continued to shadow until dense fog came down at 0400z, when he lost contact.[78]

Submarines and escorts now became caught up in a game of blindman's buff in the thick fog. On 3 August at 0452z *Sackville* obtained another SW1C radar contact at close range, swiftly followed by a visual sighting of *U 704*, 125 yards on the port beam. Too close to depress the 4-inch gun, and unable to ram because the submarine was inside his ship's turning circle, Easton fired a five-charge pattern just as the U-boat vented tanks and crash-dived to safety under the thermal layer 120 metres down. After failing to gain contact, Easton resumed screening the derelict *G.S. Walden*, plodding along at two knots under tow from *Agassiz*. *Sackville* then came upon *Belgian Soldier*, prematurely abandoned, and put away a boarding party that rescued two more survivors.[79] Then, at 1502z the same day, *Sackville*, following up on hydrophone effect and a radar contact, confronted *U 552* on the surface. In postwar memoirs, both Easton and Topp described the excitement and anxiety of their fleeting encounter in the North Atlantic mists.

First, the hunter. In his classic memoir *50 North*, Alan Easton recalled:

> I was craning my head over the dodger trying to see through the murk. My heart was beating fast.
>
> A dark smudge appeared dead ahead. In three seconds it revealed its shape—long and low, high amidships. A submarine!
>
> She was crossing our course with slight closing inclination going from starboard to port. Her bow wave made it evident she was making eight or ten knots.
>
> "Hard aport. Full ahead. Open Fire!"
>
> The submarine was on the port bow now a little more than a hundred yards off. The ship was swinging to port—but not fast enough—the U-boat was inside our turning circle; we could never reach her. Would the gun never fire! Eighty yards...seventy only...broader on the port bow now.
>
> At last!
>
> With the gun on the depression rail and the ship swinging fast, it fired at point blank range, scarcely a ship's length away, two hundred feet, the enemy broadside on to the line of fire.
>
> On that instant a gaping hole appeared at the base of the U-boat's conning tower, squarely in the centre. It was accompanied by a hail of fire from the port point-fives and the Vickers machine-guns. The high explosive shell burst, ripping the near side of the conning tower out. I saw the pieces fly and then the yellow smoke of the projectile rising within.
>
> She was visibly diving. Another round went out of the gun but went over; her bow was under water. A depth charge from the port thrower sailed through the air, fell with a splash

---

78. *Witch, Galt, Agassiz,* and *Hamilton* ROPs; Cmdre's Report, ON 115; *U 552*, KTB, 3 Aug. 1942

79. The tug *Foundation Franklin*, which responded to *Sackville*'s call, never did find *Belgian Soldier* in the fog (*U 607* sank the vessel with a *coup de grace* on 4 August).

80. Easton, *50 North*

into the water but was short of its mark. The boat went down fast and was beneath the surface before the fog closed over the place where she submerged.[80]

Erich Topp, the hunted, remembered:

> I decided to lie down for a nap while the engineer officer, after long hours of demand-
> ing work, retired to the boat's head for some private business. Suddenly a cry comes
> from the bridge: "Alarm!" The shrill sound of the alarm bell jars everyone awake. I
> jump up and run into the central control room. When I arrive there the men of the
> watch are tumbling down the conning tower from the bridge, falling all over one
> another. What's going on? The technical personnel on duty has already secured the
> vents. A look at the depth gauge shows that the boat is going down slowly. The chief
> engineer dashes by me to turn one of the valves. I see the terrified face of our chief
> navigator, the last man to slide down from the bridge into the control room. His only
> word of explanation: "Destroyer!"
>
> There is no time to ask questions now. Our bow is raised up instead of pointing
> down. "All hands to the forward compartment," howls the chief engineer. The men
> chase down the centre passageway to the forward torpedo room. Everybody acts
> according to our standard emergency procedures, practised a thousand times and tak-
> ing but a few seconds. There is nothing for me to do but to go along, especially since
> I have no idea yet of our overall situation. Our depth gauge shows 30 feet. The con-
> ning tower must be above the surface.
>
> At this moment the boat is rocked by an immense blow. It shakes and then the
> lights go out. The dim lights of the emergency back-up system reveal that the upward
> movement of the boat has been arrested and that it has begun to sink like a stone
> with a strong forward inclination. "All hands aft!" We must regain control. Depth
> charges! Water in the engine room! The chief engineer at last manages to level out at
> 586 feet.

U 552 survived, but news leaked to Germany through American newspapers that she had been
sunk at the hands of *Sackville*. As Topp recalls, tears of sorrow among friends, family and relatives
turned to relief when *U 552* and her crew turned up safe and sound.[81]

As Easton and Topp tangled, the battle for ON 115 reached its final throes. BdU concluded that
contact was now "interrupted through continued poor visibility," and because the convoy had
"reached the Newfoundland Banks, an area of constant thick fog, there was no chance of finding
it again."[82] *Galt* had also lost the convoy in the poor visibility. She reached the limit of her
endurance, set course for St John's and came upon two stragglers, *Topdalsfjord* and *Empire Ocean*.
The corvette took them under her wing, but *Empire Ocean* became separated in fog, went aground
on the coast of Newfoundland and foundered despite gallant efforts to salvage her. The final loss
to ON 115 came the following day, 5 August, when the straggler SS *Arletta* was sunk off Sable

81. E. Topp, *The Odyssey of a U-Boat Commander: Recollections of Erich Topp* (Westport 1992), 79-80

82. BdU, KTB, 2-3 Aug. 1942; and *U 552*, KTB, 3 Aug. 1942

83. Rohwer, *Axis Submarine Successes*, 113; and Cmdre's Report, ON 115. SS *Arletta* had been one of the splinter group and
     smoked badly. There were only five survivors. Another missing ship SS *Agwidale* arrived at St John's with collision damage.

Island by *U 458*.[83] Despite the presence of several German submarines, no further attacks developed and the ragged convoy finally arrived safely off Cape Cod on 8 August.

ON 115 had been attacked by two successive concentrations of U-boats. By first light on the 31st, thirty hours after it had first been sighted, six submarines had converged and were in the vicinity of the convoy. *U 588* had then been destroyed and the five other boats were shaken off. About thirty-six hours later ON 115 had been relocated and a new concentration of boats closed. Although the convoy was within flying range, fog grounded aircraft in Newfoundland. Seven U-boats had encounters with escorts during this second phase and during the night of 2 to 3 August three ships were torpedoed, and two U-boats severely damaged during counterattacks.

German failure to take full advantage of the convoy's weakness between 31 July and 2 August was the principal reason for the favourable exchange rate—three merchant ships torpedoed for one U-boat destroyed and two badly damaged. As in the case of ON 113, the German assessment of the battle for ON 115 emphasized the unfavourable weather and the inexperience of the U-boat commanders. Dönitz noted "thick fog had descended just as the main attack was about to be delivered" and limited his boats to only "modest success." In addition, he noted that successful attacks "east of the Newfoundland Bank were again mainly carried out by experienced commanders (Topp and Mengersen)."[84] Along with Thurmann, another veteran, they had accounted for all the torpedoings.

The successful U-boat commanders absorbed tactical lessons from their engagement of ON 115. Most of all, they emphasized the difficulty of establishing and maintaining contact. Thurmann argued that because "of the far outer screen, you only see the convoy itself now and then, and very little of it, even when the visibility is good." Topp stressed how funnel smoke was vital to maintaining contact. If the merchant ships were not making smoke, dead reckoning and hourly approaches to view mastheads could be used to shadow the convoy, but he felt that it was "better to have contact broken at times than to be seen." Both commanders attested to the effectiveness of course alterations after nightfall. Topp emphasized that the "greatest dangers are wide evening tacks" coupled with destroyer sweeps. Thurmann argued that "any chance of establishing the evening tack of the convoy, during the transition from day to night, is practically ruled out" because of the distant screen. The U-boat commanders both expressed the belief that Atlantic convoy defences had been strengthened, but they had confused the aggressiveness of the escort with greater strength in numbers, which was not the case.[85]

On the allied side, post-action comments noted equipment deficiencies in C 3. While conceding that *Sackville*'s radar "assisted in the sighting of 2 U-boats on the surface in low visibility," the Western Approaches RDF officer remarked that had she been equipped with the superior type 271 radar "it is difficult to see how these U-boats could have escaped destruction." He emphasized that "The urgent need for fitting all Canadian corvettes with type 271, to replace their present sets, is becoming increasingly obvious." For his part, the staff signals officer at Liverpool thought that ON 115's ordeal demonstrated "the value of HF/DF, and shows at what a disadvantage an escort group who is not so fitted finds herself." He advised that "every opportunity should be taken to progress fitting of Canadian escorts during their short stays on this side of the Atlantic."[86] The command-

---

84.   BdU, KTB, 2 Aug. 1942; Dönitz, *Memoirs*, 246

85.   *U 552* and *U 553*, KTB, 3-6 Aug. 1942

86.   WA min sheet, PRO, ADM 237/88

ing officers of both *Saguenay* and *Skeena* made similar comments. Dyer noted that "The sighting and eventual finding of a U-boat below the surface by a single ship is largely a matter of luck unless efficient R.D.F. such as type 271 is fitted." Not surprisingly, given that they were both forced to detach early, both commanding officers also emphasized the need for fuelling at sea.[87]

Staff at Western Approaches, realizing that only luck had allowed the RCN to avoid a disaster between 31 July and 2 August, also drew lessons from the battle around ON 115 for future actions involving similar forces. The British officers identified two tactical practices as being inconsistent with the doctrine of the "safe and timely arrival of the convoy." The first was the large number and size of the course alterations initiated by the convoy commodore, the SOE, and CONNAV. Drastic course changes had prolonged the passages of both ON 113 and ON 115, and in October the Admiralty suggested to the USN that shore authorities, lacking as they normally did a full and current picture of the situation of a particular convoy, should order evasive diversions only in exceptional circumstances. CTF 24 in Argentia had separately made a similar request to COMINCH. The Department of the Navy agreed that in future evasive alterations of course by CONNAV would be "confined to special cases after consultation in Submarine Tracking Room."[88]

The second issue was the number and duration of the sweeps undertaken by the destroyers, which led to their early withdrawal to refuel. Commander C.D. Howard-Johnston, RN, Staff Officer (Anti-Submarine) at Western Approaches Command and a veteran of the 1941 convoy battles, considered that C 3 failed to meet its prime objective:

> This is an example of reckless expenditure of fuel and disregard of the object which must always include "timely arrival." The "timely arrival" was ignored to an exceptional degree, resulting in Destroyers being forced to quit the convoy when their job was far from being completed; this in turn jeopardized the Object even more by reducing the protection given by the escorts. The success achieved against the enemy in destroying a U-boat should not be allowed to cover up this basic failure.
>
> Before the convoy had reached 12 degrees West the *Saguenay* was tearing off at midday to run down MF/DF bearings to a depth of 30 miles astern. I find in this story the ignorance of inexperienced officers who think they are being offensive by acting in a reckless manner and without real consideration of their obligation to protect the convoy throughout the period it is entrusted to them.[89]

Howard-Johnston did not know, as we now do, how disruptive C 3's aggressive actions had been for the U-boats converging on ON 115. German records show that Wallace's destroyer sweeps and large evasive course alterations after dark had in fact been effective in keeping *Wolf*—including bold COs like Thurmann and Topp—at bay. Whether less-drastic alterations would have achieved the same results while permitting a faster passage can only be speculated, but there is no doubt that the sweeps did eat up fuel and force destroyers to detach early. It is also clear that caus-

---

87. *Saguenay* and *Skeena* ROPs

88. Messages from Adm to BAD Washington, 20 Oct. 1942, and reply dated 29 Oct. 1942, PRO, ADM 199/1338

89. Min by Cdr C.D. Howard-Johnston, RN, 18 Sep. 1942, PRO, ADM 237/88. This minute, and others, were not meant for use outside their headquarters and the Admiralty, but instead, were to form the basis for a general written assessment made by the Admiralty.

tic comments triggered by C 3's performance betrayed doubts at Western Approaches about the RCN's proficiency.

After the operations against ON 115, BdU carried on with the redeployments of the submarines in the vicinity of the Grand Banks that had originally been ordered on 1 August. The eight type VII boats, now designated Group *Steinbrink*, were to establish a patrol line about 400 miles northeast of Newfoundland. Except for *U 607*'s Mengersen, the captains of these boats were inexperienced. They sighted several ships, but until 5 August they were unable to attack, partly because of weather, partly because of successful diversions based on HF/DF fixes by shore stations, and partly because aircraft kept them down. What changed their luck was a missed course alteration signal that caused six ships and two corvettes of the eastbound SC 94 to lose their convoy in the dense and seemingly omnipresent fog, and the timely arrival of additional submarines outbound from their bases in Europe to reinforce the group.[90]

The thirty-three merchant ships of this convoy were under the escort of C 1, with Lieutenant-Commander A. Ayre, RNR commanding the corvette HMS *Primrose* as SOE. The destroyer *Assiniboine* and the corvettes HMS *Nasturtium* and *Dianthus*, and HMCS *Battleford, Chilliwack,* and *Orillia*, made up the rest of the group. They had sailed together for two previous passages under Ayre, and a nucleus of three or four ships had been together for five convoys. The three British corvettes had type 271 radar, but none of the group were fitted with HF/DF.[91] In the afternoon of 5 August, Kapitänleutnant Kelbling of *U 593*, which had not joined the ON 115 operation and was thus the first to reach the *Steinbrink* patrol line about 300 miles north of the rest of the group's boats coming up from the Grand Banks, sighted the separated group of the convoy through a break in the fog: two columns of three ships with *Nasturtium* on the port bow and *Orillia* on the starboard. Kelbling submerged for a daylight attack, and at 1649z torpedoed and sank SS *Spar*, a 3,616 ton freighter leading the starboard column.[92]

Assiniboine arrived on the scene as the escorts were picking up thirty-six survivors, and directed the straggling group back to the main body, a task not all that difficult as SC 94 was belching so much smoke that the destroyer could see it from thirty miles away. So did Kapitänleutnant Quät-Faslem in *U 595*, one of the newly arrived boats outbound from Europe, who sighted SC 94 at 2008z and attempted an attack.[93] Although an escort depth-charged his boat and made him lose contact, *Steinbrink* was able to capitalize on the sighting. The pack's strength was growing, BdU having assigned to it *U 595* and two other outbound boats for a total strength of eleven submarines.[94] Fog patches throughout the day shielded submarines moving in for the attack, and after dawn on 6

---

90. BdU, KTB, 4 Aug. 1942; *U 704*, KTB, 4 Aug. 1942; Adm to Escorts ON 116, 1706b/4 Aug. 1942, DHH, 89/34, v 17, ONS 116; and No. 1 Group, WIR, 7 Aug. 1942, DHH, 181.003 (D2178); Naval Messages, DHH, 89/34 mfm, v 17, ONS 116; "Extract from Diary of Monien from *U 210*"

91. HMS *Primrose*, ROP, SC 94, 12 Aug. 1942, DHH, 81/520/8280B, box 9, SC 94; Adm, *MASR*, Aug. 1942, 28

92. *U 593*, KTB, 5 Aug. 1942

93. *Assiniboine*, ROP, SC 94, 10 Aug. 1942, NAC, RG 24, 11020, COAC 7-2-1, pt 4

94. Adm, *MASR*, Aug. 1942, 28-39; Radio Messages from *U 595* in *U 593*'s KTB, 6 Aug. 1942; BdU, KTB, 5 Aug. 1942. *U 595* heard thirty depth charges, but the Admiralty analysis synthesized all available ROPs without showing any attacks by C 1 at this time.

August, when the changeable visibility lifted to eight miles, smoke led *U 704* to SC 94. Fog suddenly came down again, but, almost at the same time, Quät-Faslem found the convoy from a different direction. *Assiniboine* sighted *U 595* six miles off the port bow at 1125z on 6 August and forced the boat down with gunfire. *Dianthus* (Lieutenant-Commander C.E. Bridgman, RNR) and *Assiniboine* made three coordinated depth charge attacks but *U 595* managed to escape. *U 607, U 454,* and *U660* also homed on the convoy's smoke, but as *Dianthus* and *Assiniboine* joined from astern shortly after 1700z they came across *U 454* and were able to throw it off the scent.[95]

With visibility now less than 2,000 yards and closing, *Assiniboine* obtained a doubtful type 286 radar contact at 1836z, but shortly confirmed it with a visual sighting. This was *U 210*, commanded by Kapitänleutnant Rudolf Lemcke. It was the first war patrol for *U 210*, and the boat was Lemcke's first command. He was an experienced seaman, having recently transferred from destroyers to the *U-bootwaffe*. His opponent, Lieutenant-Commander John Stubbs, was a young, respected permanent force officer, who was about to display his considerable shiphandling prowess.[96] Also on board the destroyer was the official naval historian, Dr Gilbert Tucker, who wanted to experience the war at sea at first hand.

When the two adversaries sighted each other in the swirling mist, Lemcke increased speed and disappeared into the fog, but *U 210* soon reappeared at 1,200 yards. *Assiniboine* closed at full speed and after one minute, Dr Tucker later recalled, the U-boat "suddenly appeared out of the mist ... some fifty yards away and about to cross our bow."[97] The guns of both ships erupted at point blank range. Stubbs, so close he could watch his opponent leaning over to pass helm orders, prepared to ram, and he foiled Lemcke's attempt to get inside the destroyer's turning circle by going full astern on the inside screw as he put the wheel hard over.[98] *Assiniboine*'s 4.7-inch guns could not depress enough to fire, but her .5-inch machine-guns swept *U 210*'s deck, which prevented the 88-mm deck gun from being manned. The U-boat responded with her 20-mm flak gun, which riddled the destroyer with hits. Shells hit gasoline tanks on deck, igniting a fire that raged across *Assiniboine*'s fo'c'sle and bridge. Chief Petty Officer Max Bernays, RCNR found himself alone in the threatened wheelhouse while the damage control party led by Lieutenant Ralph Hennessy, RCN, fought the blaze. With flames engulfing his only exit, Bernays remained in the compartment and, doing the job of two, calmly executed Stubbs's rapid succession of helm and telegraph orders.[99] He was subsequently awarded the Conspicuous Gallantry Medal for "valour and dauntless devotion to duty."[100]

95. *Assiniboine* ROP; BdU, KTB, 6 Aug. 1942; and *U 660, U 704,* and *U 454* KTBs, 6 Aug. 1942

96. See M. Whitby, "LCdr J.H. Stubbs, RCN," *Crowsnest* (Sep. 1991)

97. USN, DNI, *Post Mortem of U-210* (Serial no. 4), 12, DHH, 79/479; *Assiniboine* ROP; G.N. Tucker, "Short Range Was Feature of Sea Battle," DHH, PRF HMCS *Assiniboine*

98. Dr Tucker's admiring description of Stubbs's concentration, judgment, and disregard for personal safety was echoed years later by one of his ship's company, PO C.G. Vander Haegen, RCN. Interviews with VAdm R.L. Hennessy and CPO C.G. Vander Haegen, DHH, Biog files; and Tucker, "Short Range."

99. *Assiniboine* ROP; Hennessy and Vander Haegen interviews; and Schull, *Far Distant Ships*, 135-6. The CNS and the Naval Minister recommended Bernays for the Victoria Cross. Stubbs was awarded the DSO and Hennessy the DSC.

100. For Bernay's complete CGM citation, see E.R. Paquette and C.G. Bainbridge (eds), *Honours and Awards: Canadian Naval Forces, World War II* (Victoria 1986), 42.

101. Ibid; *Assiniboine* ROP; and interviews with Hennessy and Vander Haegen

Three or four times *Assiniboine* narrowly missed ramming the elusive target. Smoke and flames billowed from the destroyer; the U-boat's 20-mm shells disabled *Assiniboine*'s "A" gun, killing one and wounding three of the gun's crew. Then the destroyer's .5-inch machine-guns silenced the flak gun, and the after 4.7-inch gun scored a direct hit on the conning tower, killing Lemcke and the bridge crew.[101] Leutnant Heinz Sorber, the Engineer Officer, made one final attempt to submerge, but to do so *U 210* had to hold a steady course, and with that opportunity *Assiniboine* rammed the submarine abaft the conning tower. The U-boat descended to eighteen metres, but the electric motors failed and the screws were damaged. Water flooded in through the diesel air intake and her ruptured stern, so Sorber gave the order to blow tanks and abandon ship. After the submarine surfaced, Stubbs rammed again well abaft the conning tower and let go a shallow pattern of depth charges as another 4.7-inch shell slammed into the battered U-boat's bow. Scuttled by the crew, *U 210* sank at 1914z on 6 August. This dramatic, close-quarters action had lasted thirty minutes in the fog. With flooding below the waterline, considerable additional damage, and casualties of thirteen wounded and one killed, *Assiniboine* headed to St John's for repairs.[102]

Dianthus, with defective radar, arrived in time to see *U 210* slide beneath the surface and to recover twenty-eight survivors, and transferred several prisoners to join the ten gathered up in *Assiniboine*. Then, while trying to catch up with SC 94, *Dianthus* sighted *U 454* on the surface at 2301z and forced the U-boat to crash-dive. *U 454* escaped, but damage precluded deep dives, and the boat limped back to France for repairs. As a result of this encounter, the wayward *Dianthus* was lost to C 1 until late afternoon on 8 August. Down to five corvettes, and in receipt of a constant flow of warnings from the Admiralty, Lieutenant-Commander Ayre could do little to avoid the pack, but for the next thirty-six hours, from the evening of of 6 August until daylight on the 8th, held them off with what U-boat commanders described as a very strong defence.[103]

The pack was too large—on 8 to 9 August BdU ordered six more boats to join—and the convoy too far beyond aircraft range, for SC 94's luck to hold.[104] In a submerged attack during daylight on 8 August, *U 176*, and possibly *U 379*, rapidly fired a series of torpedo salvos that resulted in the loss of five ships.[105] Later that day, *Dianthus* finally rejoined the screen, and at 2308z sighted *U 379*, which the corvette destroyed after an hour-long chase and final ramming attack that closely resembled *Assinobine*'s action against *U 210*.[106] The destroyer HMS *Broke* had been sent out to replace *Assiniboine*, arriving just before *Dianthus* pursued *U 379*, and the British destroyer's commanding officer, Lieutenant-Commander A.F.C. Layard, RN succeeded Ayre as SOE. As the convoy emerged from the air gap on the 9th, RAF Liberators from Northern Ireland and USN Catalinas from Iceland helped to keep the U-boats at bay, and the Polish destroyer *Blyskawica* also joined.

---

102. *Post Mortem of U 210*, 18-19; and *Assiniboine* ROP. For a personal account, see Hennessy in Lynch, *Salty Dips* II, 11-12.

103. *Assiniboine*, HMS *Dianthus*, HMS *Primrose*, and HMS *Nasturtium* ROPs, SC 94, PRO, ADM 1/12271; *U 454*, *U 176*, *U-660*, and *U 607*, KTBs, 6-8 Aug. 1942; Adm, *MASR*, Aug. 1942, 31-2; "Analysis of U-Boat Operations in the Vicinity of Convoy SC 94," 15 Sep. 1942, PRO, ADM 199/2007; SS *Duchess of Bedford*, Attack on Merchant Vessel by Enemy Submarine, 9 Aug. 1942, NAC, RG 24, 4025, NSS 1062-13-10

104. *U 256*, *U 605*, *U 335*, *U 174*, *U 705*, and *U 438*. *U 335*, however, had been destroyed five days earlier by the submarine HMS *Saracen*, near the Shetland Islands. BdU, KTB, 8-9 Aug. 1942

105. Rohwer, *Axis Submarine Successes*, 114; R. Fisher, "The Fog of War: The Battle of the Atlantic, Summer 1942," 103-5, 107, 111-12, DHH, 2000/5

106. *Dianthus* ROP; Adm, *MASR*, Sep. 1942, 31-2

107. AHB, *The R.A.F. in Maritime War* III, 479–80; Adm, *MASR*, Aug. 1942), 35-8; Rohwer, *Axis Submarine Successes*, 115

Four more ships were sunk by *U 438* and *U 660* in daylight on 10 August, before BdU finally terminated operations against SC 94 the following day in the face of heavy air cover.[107]

SC 94, hounded by *Steinbrink* for five days, had suffered the worst losses on the northern transatlantic routes since the fall of 1941; eleven merchant ships—fully one-third of the convoy—in exchange for two U-boats sunk by ramming, both of which had caused debilitating damage to the escorts. Despite the additional three severely damaged and five slightly damaged boats, Dönitz considered it a good result against a stronger escort than usual and concluded that attacks were feasible on even heavily defended convoys.[108]

SC 94 had faced heavy odds—sixteen U-boats had made contact during the five-day battle. The absence of a destroyer for two critical days in the air gap was a serious handicap, as was the lack of HF/DF until *Broke* and *Blyskawica* joined on the third and fourth days. Shore-based HF/DF had not been particularly useful for Ayre; most contacts had been made before submarine warnings had reached the SOE. So although air cover relieved the pressure significantly as SC 94 emerged from the air gap, it was the inexperience of the U-boats—four separate boats fired torpedoes on 9 and 10 August despite air cover but all missed—and the ubiquitous fog more than anything else that saved the convoy from a greater disaster.

Practically no convoy at sea, especially in mid-ocean, could now help standing into danger. An average of 100 U-boats operated in the Atlantic in September. "Little can usefully be said this week about the dispositions of U-boats in the Atlantic," reported Commander Winn. "Over 80 are estimated to be at sea in this area but there is no clear indication of their objectives or operational areas."[109] Clearly, the operations of the previous two months had been no more than a prelude to Dönitz's main offensive thrust. As August came to an end, nine boats in Group *Vorwärts* stretched southwest of Iceland between quadrants AK-37 and AK-66, while another six boats in Group *Stier* lay between quadrants AL-71 and AL-78 to the south of *Vorwärts*. On 28 August, nine boats of Group *Lohs* began refuelling southeast of Newfoundland, while the other four returned to base. ON 123 and ONS 124 slipped past *Lohs* unharmed, but the eastbound convoys, HX 204 (B 4) and SC 97 (C 2), steamed directly towards *Vorwärts* and *Stier*. Dönitz received intelligence that an east-or westbound convoy would be in AK-30 or AK-60 on 29 August and ordered *Vorwärts* to search to the southwest. The fast convoy slipped through the patrol line during the night of 30 to 31 August to the safety of air cover, but SC 97 stumbled into *Vorwärts* next morning.[110]

SC 97 had sailed from Halifax on 22 August with sixty-four merchant ships. Six vessels had straggled or returned to harbour in dense fog, reducing the size of this large and cumbersome convoy to fifty-eight. C 2, which had joined from St John's on 26 August, now consisted of the RN Town class destroyers *Burnham* (Commander T. Taylor, RN, SOE) and *Broadway*, and the corvettes, HMS *Polyanthus*, HMCS *Brandon*, *Dauphin*, *Drumheller*, and *Morden*. Two US Coast Guard cutters,

108. Rahn, *Die Seekriegsführung im Atlantik und Küstenbereich*, 348

109. Adm, OIC, U-Boat Situation Report, 31 Aug. 1942, PRO, ADM 223/15; MOD, *U-Boat War in the Atlantic* II, plan 59

110. BdU, KTB, 25-31 Aug. 1942; HMS *Highlander*, ROP, HX 204, 4 Sep. 1942, DHH, ADM 199/717; and Naval Messages, DHH, 89/34, v 9, HX-204

111. HMS *Burnham*, ROP, SC 97, 5 Sep. 1942, NAC, RG 24, 11505, 220-PR/BM

U 210 tries to evade *Assiniboine* — unsuccessfully — during their duel in the fog on 6 August 1942. (DND, E-50834)

Opposite and Below: *Assiniboine* did not
emerge unscathed from the fight, suffering
damage to her superstructure and stem.
(DND, PMR 98-18 and PMR 98-20)

Assiniboine's crew side when she arrives in St John's on 9 August 1942. The elation is not just a result of the destruction of *U 210*, but also because of the refit leave to come. (NAC, PA 204349)

Ingham and *Bibb*, joined from Iceland on 29 August. All three British warships were equipped with type 271 radar, but none of the escorts had HF/DF.[111] *U 609*, commanded by Kapitänleutnant Rudloff, first sighted the convoy at 0532z on 31 August, submerged an hour later to await his prey and worked under the screen undetected. At 0804z, he fired a salvo of two torpedoes at the 5,625 ton SS *Capira* from a range of 600 metres and followed this with a stern shot at the 4,663 ton SS *Bronxville* from 800 metres. Torpedoes struck both targets and breaking-up noises were heard in the U-boat. While SS *Perth*, the rescue ship, and *Morden* recovered the entire crew of *Bronxville* and all but five of *Capira*'s crew of fifty-four, *Drumheller* and *Brandon* carried out a series of depth charge attacks that kept *U 609* down, but did no damage.[112] For the next forty-eight hours, the escort, joined late that night by the destroyer USS *Schenk* from Iceland, not only held off numerous submarine attacks but kept *Vorwärts* at a constant tactical disadvantage by sweeping far ahead of the convoy and using cooperative tactics similar to those successfully employed by *Skeena* and *Wetaskiwin* on ON 115.

At 0050z on 1 September, *Morden*'s SW2C radar detected *U 756* on the starboard quarter. Lieutenant J.J. Hodgkinson, RCNR altered to investigate and sighted the U-boat at close range. *U 756* crash-dived before Hodgkinson could ram, but the corvette dropped two depth charges set to fifty feet in the swirl. *Morden* made asdic contact, and at 0128z fired a pattern of five depth charges set to 150 feet, followed by a ten-charge pattern set between 150 and 300 feet. In Hodgkinson's opinion, it was "difficult to imagine that the U-boat could have avoided being hit by the depth charges." He was right. Although at the time the stringent Admiralty Assessment Committee ruled that there was as "Insufficient evidence of damage" after *Morden*'s attack, postwar reassessment has credited her with the destruction of *U 756*.[113]

Before dawn on 1 September, after the first day's fighting, aircraft arrived from Iceland, forcing under *U 407*, *U 409,* and *U 411*. Effective air cover continued to make the U-boats' task exceptionally difficult during the rest of SC 97's passage. Rudloff in *U 609*, who was less cautious than other submarine commanders in the presence of aircraft, shadowed on SC 97's starboard bow until 1100z on 1 September, found himself directly ahead of the convoy and, at 1140z, in full view of *Burnham* and *Broadway*, as the result of a course change. The destroyers chased and put him down. At this same time, *U 409*, while attempting a submerged attack, became the object of a depth-charge hunt by *Dauphin* and USCG *Bibb*, and suffered damage to both periscopes.[114] In the afternoon, at about 1800z, SCL 97 detached with eleven ships bound for Iceland, escorted by *Ingham*, *Bibb*, and *Schenck*.[115] The main body's reduced screen proved adequate, partly because air cover continued to be effective in the September twilight, and partly because *Vorwärts* was also reduced in strength.

112. Ibid; Adm, WIR, 11 Sep. 1942, 55; *Brandon*, Report of A/S Operations while Escorting SC 97, 9 Sep. 1942, DHH, 81/520 Brandon 8000; Adm U-Boat Assessment Committee, Precis of Attacks by HMCS *Brandon* and *Drumheller*, 31 Aug. 1942, NAC, RG 24, 6895, NSS 8910-14 (1); BdU, KTB, 31 Aug. 1942; *U 609*, KTB, 31 Aug. 1942; E.H. Chavasse ms, "Business in Great Waters," 53-6, DHH, 88/181

113. HMS *Broadway*, Narrative of A/S Operations, SC 97, 31 Aug. 1942, NAC, RG 24, 6906, NSS 8910-500/64; Adm U-Boat Assessment Committee, "Precis of Attack by HMCS *Morden*," 1 Sep. 1942, NAC, RG 24, 6895, NSS 8910-14 (1); Niestlé, *Axis U-Boat Losses*, 87. Allied authorities subsequently and mistakenly credited Catalina B/73 with this kill.

114. *U 604*, *U 407*, *U 409*, *U 609*, and *U 411*, KTBs, 31 Aug.–1 Sep. 1942; *Burnham* ROP; CTU 24.3.10 to C-in-C Atlantic Fleet, 7 Sep. 1942, NARA, WNRC, RG 313, Red CTF 24, box 8813, 44-1(2); Atlantic Fleet ASW Officer, "Analysis of Action Report, HMCS *Dauphin*," 1 Sep. 1942, NAC, RG 24, 11020, COAC 7-2-1 (4); and *Dauphin*, deck log, 1 Sep. 1942, NAC, RG 24, 7253; AHB, *RAF in Maritime War* III, B, 483

115. *Burnham* ROP

U 604, with defective equipment, and *U 409*, damaged by *Dauphin* and *Bibb*'s attack, were out of the battle. *U 609*, its weapons and fuel seriously depleted, departed for base during the night. *U 407*, with one diesel unserviceable, barely managed to keep in contact and finally lost touch in a rain squall at 0300z on 2 September. *U 91* found the convoy at 0500z and tried a long-range attack, but lost touch in rain squalls shortly after. The outbound *U 211* approached at daybreak, but two attacks by aircraft and another by *Burnham* forced the boat off.[116]

At this point, BdU decided to cut its losses. Deeply disturbed by the appearance of aircraft 800 miles from England and 450 miles from Iceland, Dönitz considered the battle for SC 97 a total failure. He made a plea for long-range aircraft to support U-boat operations, and sent *Vorwärts* off to form another patrol line further west.[117] After only one day's fighting, air support had allowed the SOE to keep his escorts close to the screen without losing the initiative, despite visibility conditions that would normally have favoured the U-boats. At the same time, it is important to point out that on the day before coming within range of aircraft from Iceland and Ireland, the screen had been most effective in keeping U-boats at a distance, and had achieved an acceptable exchange rate of one submarine for two ships in a fifty-eight ship convoy; this was an especially good result with a slow convoy. In post-action analyses, Canadian and American staff officers criticized instances of poor coordination among the ships of the escort—in particular between *Bibb* and *Dauphin* in their attack—but C 2's overall performance in this convoy battle brought well-merited satisfaction.[118]

The limitations of type VII and type IX U-boats operating against convoys, even when they had the advantage of numbers and could hunt in packs well beyond the range of aircraft, can easily be overlooked. It is remarkable that convoys ON 125 (A 3), HX 205 (B 6), SC 98 (C 3), ONS 126 (B 3), and the fast troop convoy AT 21, all sighted by patrolling submarines, avoided attack by Groups *Stier*, *Lohs,* and *Vorwärts* in the first six days of September. Indeed, only four of the fifteen Atlantic convoys that arrived in September were attacked.[119] Although B-Dienst was reading most convoy radio traffic at a time when the Admiralty's Submarine Tracking Room had only a general idea of U-boat dispositions, actually locating a convoy and then marshalling sufficient submarines for group attacks posed difficulties. North Atlantic weather often made it difficult for shadowers, which depended for the most part on visual sightings to maintain contact and home others in on a convoy.[120] Moreover, submarines at the far ends of a scouting line—which could extend 200 miles for a 12-boat group—perpendicular to the convoy track had difficulty closing in on a convoy for a group attack. Accurate navigation, critical for homing packs on to convoys, was a particular challenge for U-boats, especially as overcast skies could make celestial fixes unobtainable for days. Much depended on the experience and skill of captains, and on the strategic sense of their admiral; however reliable the latter, the former was often still wanting.[121]

---

116. Ibid; BdU, KTB, 2 Sep. 1942; *U 91, U 92, U 211, U 407,* and *U 609* KTB, 1-2 Sep. 1942; *Burnham* ROP

117. BdU, KTB, 2-3 Sep. 1942

118. Capt (D) Newfoundland to FONF, 1 Oct. 1942, DHH, 81/520 Brandon 8000; CTU 24.7, Report on SC 97, 14 Sep. 1942, cited in Narrative A, 75, DHH, 84/123; Cmdre's Report, SC-97

119. Hague, *Allied Convoy System*, app 3

120. Hinsley, *British Intelligence* II, 636

121. BdU, KTB, 1-6 Sep. 1942; CTU 24.1.3 (A 3) WD, DHH, 91/289, f 5, (box 65); CONNAV to AIG 313, 0210/3 Sep. 1942 (Position of Ocean Convoys Signal), DHH, NSHQ Convoy Files; Adm, OIC, U-Boat Situation Reports, PRO, ADM 223/15; Adm, WIR, 11 Sep.1942. The difficulties in mounting pack attacks are discussed in Blair, *Hitler's U-Boat War*, 666-7.

Dönitz had dissolved *Stier* and ordered the six boats to join *Vorwärts* in the hope of intercepting ON 126 on 4 September. When this was unsuccessful, he arranged a new patrol line, at the very eastern end of the air gap, to intercept the next westbound convoy, expected on 9 September. SC 98 got safely through the northern end of the patrol line on 8 September in low visibility, despite heavy smoke from the ships, perhaps aided by the group's preoccupation with the expected westbound convoy.[122] By the 9th, therefore, the thirteen boats of Group *Vorwärts* lay between quadrants AK-66 and AL-78 about 500 miles west of Ireland awaiting the approach of ON 127.[123] Visibility was under 1,000 metres at 1826z on 9 September when *U 584*, glimpsing the convoy through rain squalls, reported eleven to fifteen steamers on a southwesterly course in quadrant AL-74, about a third of the distance between Ireland and Newfoundland. *Vorwärts* had thus intercepted ON 127 "in exactly the position plotted by dead reckoning," at which Dönitz professed amazement that Allied convoys still persisted in sticking so close to the great circle route after previous large-scale attacks in the same area.[124]

Between *Vorwärts* and the thirty-four merchant ships of ON 127 was the mid-ocean escort group C 4. Lieutenant-Commander Dobson in *St Croix* was SOE and with him was the destroyer *Ottawa*, and the corvettes *Arvida*, *Sherbrooke*, *Amherst,* and HMS *Celandine*. None had HF/DF, and only *Celandine* had type 271 radar. Sadly, *Ottawa* had the opportunity to have 271 fitted before she sailed but her commanding officer declined. It is a particularly telling incident that demonstrates both the *ad hoc* arrangements that often governed the modernization of RCN ships as well as the negative reaction of some officers to the replacement of traditional fighting equipment by specialized ASW sensors. Lieutenant L.B. Jenson, RCN, the Gunnery and RDF Officer in *Ottawa* recalled, "The final time we were alongside in Londonderry I ... was informed by the dockyard authorities that we were to be fitted with a RDF 271 in lieu of the [main gunnery] rangefinder [atop the bridge]. The 271 arrived alongside ... and I casually so informed the Captain [Lieutenant-Commander C.A. Rutherford, RCN], whom I assumed had been informed about this. He became very upset and seemed to have the impression that I had authorized this on my own. I was to cancel it at once, which I did. I was very sorry as I was ... very aware of the limitations of the 286M RDF (Radar)."[125] Those limitations would contribute all too soon to *Ottawa*'s tragic loss.

Sporadic air cover had accompanied the convoy as it sailed from the United Kingdom on 5 to 6 September. During the morning of 9 September, five ships straggled in rough weather as the convoy steamed towards the centre of *Vorwärts*. The daylight screen placed three escorts ahead, one on either bow, and one astern.[126] BdU ordered *Vorwärts* and two outbound boats, *U 599* and *U 259*, to attack, but *U 584* lost touch after dark. Dönitz ordered the outbound boats to continue westward and join Group *Lohs*.[127] After dawn, visibility improved to ten miles, and again *Vorwärts* closed to attack. *U 584* made renewed contact with ON 127 at 0755z on 10 September, and thirty minutes later *U 594* sighted smoke plumes from the convoy. An aircraft forced *U 584* to submerge but, between 1145z

---

122. At 0800/8 SC 98 was in position 55°12' N, 27°38' W. BdU, KTB, 2-7 Sep. 1942

123. BdU, KTB, 7 Sep. 1942

124. Ibid, 9 Sep. 1942; *U 584*, KTB, 9 Sep. 1942

125. L.B. Jenson to W.A.B. Douglas, 13 Sep. 1991, cited in T.C. Pullen, "Convoy ON 127 & the Loss of HMCS *Ottawa*, 13 Sep., 1942: A Personal Reminiscence," *The Northern Mariner* 2/5 (1992), 24

126. Milner, *North Atlantic Run*, 159; Cmdre's Report, ON 127. The convoy had reached only 14°W by 7 Sep., still several hundred miles east of Group *Vorwärts*.

127. BdU, KTB, 9 Sep. 1942; and *U 584*, KTB, 9-10 Sep. 1942

and 1320z, five more submarines, *U 608*, *U 380*, *U 404*, *U 96,* and *U 659*, established contact. *Vorwärts* had its hooks well and truly into the convoy, and would not let go for four days.[128]

There was some warning. Shore authorities had intercepted two U-boat signals late on 9 September and relayed the information to C 4 next morning. The fixes placed U-boats astern of the convoy: apparently Dobson disregarded them.[129] Fixes on two more U-boat transmissions the next forenoon did not reach C 4 until about 1630z on the 10th, so Dobson was taken unawares when Kapitänleutnant Hellriegel in *U 96*, having submerged ahead of the convoy, slipped past a "two-funnel destroyer"—probably *Ottawa*—and at 1431z fired four torpedoes at four merchant ships from ranges of 400 to 2,000 metres.[130] They hit the second ships in the first three columns, the tankers *Sveve* and *F.J. Wolfe*, and the freighter *Elisabeth van Belgie*.[131] The convoy made an emergency turn to starboard, and Dobson ordered *Sherbrooke* to stand by the stricken vessels while the remaining escorts hunted *U 96*. Hellriegel had gone deep to 160 metres and released an asdic decoy. *St Croix* obtained a contact at 1525z and fired a pattern of depth charges, but these fell far from *U 96*. Escorts rescued the entire crew of SS *Sveve* and forty-nine of *Elisabeth van Belgie*'s crew of fifty, and the 12,190 ton *F.J. Wolfe*, which refused to sink, rejoined the convoy under her own power. Dobson ordered *Sherbrooke* to remain behind and sink the two derelicts with gunfire, and stationed *Ottawa* astern at the range of maximum visibility to prevent the attacker from shadowing.[132] He gave no evidence of suspecting that other boats might be in contact; there were in fact six.

The submarines had an ideal attacking position in the path of the convoy, but *U 584*, *U 404*, and *U 594*, approaching shortly after 1500z, found the screen alert. *Arvida* depth-charged *U 594*, inflicted considerable damage, and forced the boat down to 160 metres, also disrupting the attack of *U 404*. *St Croix* forced *U 584* down to 140 metres.[133] At about 1800z, *U 659* and *U 407* made similar attempts. The former, forced down to avoid collision with a merchant ship, came back to periscope depth and torpedoed the tanker SS *Empire Oil*. *St Croix* sighted its periscope in the convoy, attacked with depth charges, and did enough damage to force *U 659* out of the battle. *U 407* penetrated from ahead between *Arvida* and *Amherst*, but sudden changes of course left it out of firing position, and it withdrew silently to the south.[134]

128. BdU, KTB, 10 Sep. 1942; and *U 584* and *U 594* KTBs, 10 Sep. 1942. The aircraft sighted at 0825z/10 has not been identified. Earlier, WA had informed ON 127 that three Fortresses would be sweeping the convoy's track between 0740 and 1340a/9 but these were not seen.

129. COMINCH to Adm, 0100z/10 and 0327z/10 Sep. 1942, PRO, ADM 237/90. COMINCH estimated the DF's at 23°W and 21°30' W, when ON 127 was close to 25°W. The originators have not been identified, although *U 584* signalled BdU at 2351z/9, close to the 2353z transmission.

130. *St Croix*, ROP, ON 127, DHH, 81/520/8280, box 6, ON 127; and COMINCH to *St Croix*, 1347/10 Sep. 1942, PRO, ADM 237/90

131. *U 96*, KTB, 10 Sep. 1942; Rohwer, *Axis Submarine Successes*, 121; and Report of an Interview with the Master of SS *Empire Thackeray*, 14 Dec. 1943, PRO, ADM 237/90

132. *St Croix* ROP; Cmdre's Report, ON 127; SS *Elisabeth van Belgie*, Attack on Merchant Vessel by Enemy Submarine, 10 Sep. 1942, NAC, RG 24, 4025, NSS 1062-10-13; and *U 96*, KTB, 10 Sep. 1942. HMCS *Sherbrooke* rescued thirty-nine survivors from SS *Sveve* and one from *Elisabeth van Belgie*. HMS *Celandine* picked up the rest from the latter ship.

133. BdU, KTB, 10 Sep. 1942; *U 404*, *U 584*, and *U 594*, KTBs, 10 Sep. 1942; *Arvida*, Report of Attack on U-Boat, 10 Sep. 1942, NAC, RG 24, 6901, NSS 8910-331/6; and D.G. King, *Reminiscences*, DHH, 2000/5, 98

134. *St Croix* ROP; *St Croix*, Report of Attack on U-Boat, 10 Sep. 1942, NAC, RG 24, 6904, NSS 8910-354/23; *U 659* and *U 407*, KTB, 10 Sep. 1942; and Rohwer, *Axis Submarine Successes*, 121. The four-stackers had a large turning circle so all Dobson could do was steam down between columns five and six, but his asdic team managed to regain contact at 1918z.

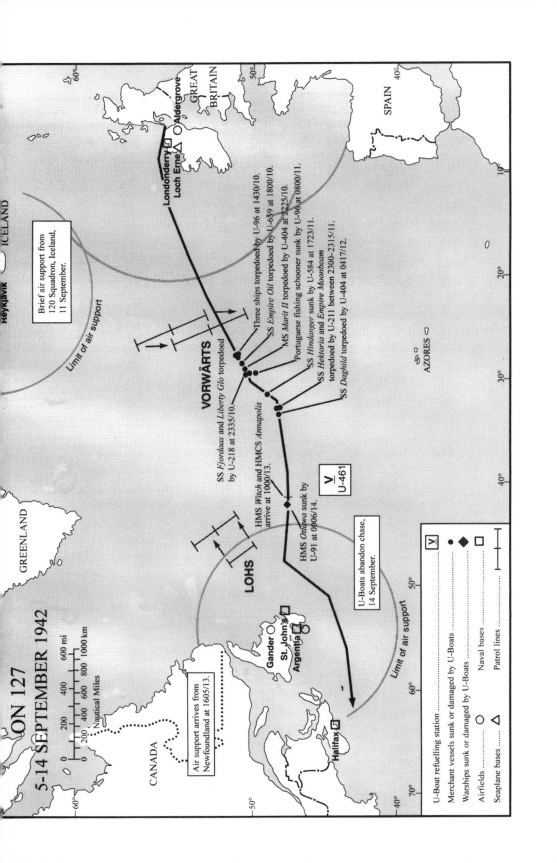

ON 127
5–14 SEPTEMBER 1942

GREENLAND

Reykjavík

ICELAND

Brief air support from
120 Squadron, Iceland,
11 September.

Limit of air support

GREAT
BRITAIN

Aldergrove

Londonderry
Loch Erne

Three ships torpedoed by U-96 at 1430/10.
SS Empire Oil torpedoed by U-659 at 1800/10.
MS Marit II torpedoed by U-404 at 2225/10.
Portuguese fishing schooner sunk by U-96 at 0800/11.
SS Hindanger sunk by U-584 at 1723/11.
SS Hektoria and Empire Moonbeam
torpedoed by U-211 between 2300–2315/11.
SS Daghild torpedoed by U-404 at 0417/12.

SPAIN

VORWÄRTS

SS Fjordaas and Liberty Glo torpedoed
by U-218 at 2335/10.

AZORES

V
U-461

HMS Witch and HMCS Annapolis
arrive at 1000/13.

HMS Ottawa sunk by
U-91 at 0006/14.

LOHS

U-Boats abandon chase,
14 September.

Gander
St. John's
Argentia

Limit of air support

CANADA

Air support arrives from
Newfoundland at 1605/13.

Halifax

0   200   400   600   800 1000 km
0   200   400   600   mi
0   200   400   600   Nautical Miles

U-Boat refuelling station ....
Merchant vessels sunk or damaged by U-Boats ....
Warships sunk or damaged by U-Boats ....

Airfields .... O
Seaplane bases ...... △

V

Naval bases ....
Patrol lines ....

Because Dobson had four escorts searching for *U 659*, rescuing survivors or disposing of dere-licts, only *Arvida* and *Amherst* remained in the screen.[135] *U 404* and *U 608* easily got among the ships after nightfall, and although both fired spreads of four torpedoes, they hit only one vessel, the MS *Marit II*, a 7,417 ton tanker, which did not sink and was able to continue under its own power. *Celandine*, joining from astern, assumed tactical command and Lieutenant P.V. Collings, RNR ordered Operation Raspberry. Snowflake and starshell lit up the night sky and forced the U-boats to move off, but the search was singularly ineffective, *Amherst* having simply steamed down the columns rather than steer the required pattern outside the convoy.[136] *U 218*, in the meantime, approached the port side of ON 127 and at 2335z fired torpedoes at three merchant ships from a range of 2,000 metres, a fourth torpedo at an escort, and a stern shot at the first steamer from 800 metres. Torpedoes struck SS *Fjordaas*, a 7,361 ton tanker, and possibly the 4,979 ton SS *Liberty Glo*, which straggled at this time and was not heard from again by the convoy. Both ships made it home safely. Collings, who attributed the firing of snowflake to "nervousness" and not to "any-thing more concrete," was evidently unaware of the attack.[137] The starshell, however, revealed ON 127 to *U 92*, which at 0024z on 11 September fired four torpedoes at four merchant ships with-out result.[138] *Arvida* sighted *U 608*, illuminated with starshell, and fired a pattern that, although "well-placed," did no damage. The corvettes continued to hunt astern, but in uncoordinated fash-ion: in the darkness, *Arvida* mistook *Amherst* for a surfaced U-boat and closed to attack until only 300 yards off.[139]

St Croix and *Ottawa* now rejoined, and it finally became what might have been described as an uneventful night, were it not for the tension and weariness of captains who had seldom been able to leave the bridge for twenty-four hours or more. *Ottawa* attacked a doubtful contact, and HF/DF fixes from shore began coming in soon after. As daylight came on 11 September, the pack closed in. *U 584* and *U 218* sighted the convoy first, and by 0800z, eight more U-boats were in contact. Smoke and fine weather favoured the U-boats, although a hapless Portuguese fishing schooner in the vicinity, the *Delaes*, threw some of them off the scent before being torpedoed by one of the submarines.[140]

U 584 and *U 404* gained attacking positions ahead of ON 127 by the afternoon of 11 September. The return of *Sherbrooke* with SS *Marit II* earlier in the afternoon had brought C 4 back to full strength, and Dobson took *St Croix* to maximum visibility distance ahead of the convoy where he

---

135. *St Croix* and *Celandine* ROPs; SS *Empire Oil*, "Attack on Merchant Vessel by Enemy Submarine," 10 Sep. 1942, NAC, RG 24, 4025, NSS 1062-10-13; *U 659* and *U 584*, KTBs, 10 Sep. 1942. All but two of *Empire Oil*'s crew of fifty-one were rescued: twenty-seven by HMCS *St Croix* and twenty-four by *Ottawa*. One of the latter died of injuries aboard *Ottawa*. Seven of the remaining twenty-three were rescued after *Ottawa* was torpedoed.

136. *U 404* and *U 608*, KTBs, 11 Sep. 1942; *Celandine* ROP; HMCS *Amherst*, ROP, ON 127, 17 Sep. 1942, PRO, ADM 237/90 mfm; Rohwer, *Axis Submarine Successes*, 121. MS *Marit II* managed to continue under her own power and later rejoined the convoy.

137. *U 218*, KTB, 11 Sep. 1942; *Celandine* ROP; Cmdre's Report, ON 127; "Report of an Interview with the Master of *Fjordaas*, ON 127," PRO, ADM 237/90 mfm; and Rohwer, *Axis Submarine Successes*, 121

138. *U 92*, KTB, 11 Sep. 1942

139. *U 608*, KTB, 11 Sep. 1942; *St Croix* and *Amherst* ROPs; and HMCS *Arvida*, "Report of Attack on U-Boat," 11 Sep. 1942, NAC, RG 24, 6901, NSS 8910-331/6; and HMCS *Arvida*, "ROP during Attacks on ON 127— HMCS *Amherst*," 26 Oct. 1942, NAC, RG 24, 11319, NSS 8280-ON 127. *Arvida* did not open fire on *Amherst*.

140. Truly an innocent victim, the hapless vessel encountered several U-boats, all of which recognized her neutrality except for *U 96*, which destroyed *Delaes* with gunfire. *U 96*, *U 404*, *U 407*, *U 594*, and *U 608*, KTBs, 11 Sep. 1942; BdU, KTB, 11 Sep. 1942; Rohwer, *Axis Submarine Successes*, 121

sighted *U 404*, forcing it to withdraw westward at high speed. In the meantime, *U 584* avoided detection and at 1723z fired two torpedoes, one of which hit the 4,884 ton SS *Hindanger*. *Arvida*, screening the port bow, obtained a doubtful echo and MacKay, deducing correctly that the U-boat had gone deep—it was at 160 metres—fired a ten-charge pattern set between 150 and 385 feet. *Ottawa* also made contact and fired a second pattern, but her depth charges exploded harmlessly above *U 584*. The convoy made an emergency turn to port while *Ottawa* and *Arvida* swept across the stern of the formation without regaining contact.[141] Because *St Croix* was scouting well ahead, and *Amherst* was detailed to rescue survivors and sink the derelict *Hindanger*, the screen was temporarily reduced to four escorts. *U 91, U 92, U 608,* and *U 380* were unable to launch successful attacks as the convoy made evasive turns, but at 2300z, just as the still absent Dobson was receiving a submarine warning from shore, *U 211*, under Kapitänleutnant Hauser and *U 218*, Kapitänleutnant Becker, so close to each other that they almost collided in the darkness, penetrated the reduced screen.[142] Hauser, firing from 2,000 metres, hit the 13,797 ton SS *Hektoria*, a whaling factory ship, and the 6,849 ton SS *Empire Moonbeam*, the rear-commodore's ship.[143] *Hektoria* was "obliterated by flames," which, with starshell ordered by *Ottawa*, forced *U 218* to crash dive. Becker's war diary records a vigorous depth charge attack on the boat, but Hauser in *U 211* refused to submerge and at 2315z tried a stern shot at a 4,000 ton freighter.[144] That missed, and he moved off on the surface to reload.[145]

Confusion reigned, especially on the devastated port side of the convoy, where nine of sixteen ships had either straggled or been torpedoed. SS *Laurits Swenson*, capable of thirteen knots, romped ahead at full speed and SS *Heranger* followed suit. SS *Empire Thackeray* collided with a submerged object, believed to be a periscope, which scraped along her bottom, other ships opened fire at imagined periscopes, and the scene was lit up with snowflake for the next thirty minutes.[146] *U 91* and *U 404* steered for the illumination, and *U 92*, also attracted by the pyrotechnics, encountered *Amherst* well astern, but missed with a four-torpedo spread.[147]

The convoy had now separated into two groups. At about 0200z on 12 September, *U 404* crept past the two escorts guarding the rear section to overtake the lead group, and *U 91*, "in very close proximity," was manoeuvring to attack the rear section from astern.[148] The night was still dark and

---

141. *U 404* and *U 584*, KTB, 11 Sep. 1942; *St Croix* and *Celandine* ROPs; *Arvida*, Report of Attack on U-Boat; Cmdre's Report, ON 127; and Rohwer, *Axis Submarine Successes*, 121

142. *U 91, U 92, U 608,* and *U 380*, KTBs, 11 Sep. 1942; BdU, KTB, 11 Sep. 1942; Cmdre's Report, ON 127; Rohwer, *Axis Submarine Successes*, 122; *St Croix* ROP; and COMINCH to *St Croix*, 1824/11 Sep. 1942 (TOR 2249/11), PRO, ADM 237/90 mfm. Sunset was at 2030z/11.

143. *U 211* and *U 218*, KTBs, 11-12 Sep. 1942; and Rohwer, *Axis Submarine Successes*, 122. The commodore believed that SS *Heranger* had also been torpedoed in this attack, but in fact she had gone on ahead.

144. *U 218*, KTB, 12 Sep.1942; and *Celandine*. This lengthy depth charge pursuit may have been the attack mentioned earlier by Struckmeier in *U 608*. He surfaced at 0000z/12 but crash dived immediately and counted three more depth charge patterns. These combined with the eighteen to twenty that he reported earlier would come close to the forty-one reported by *U 218*. *Ottawa*, because she was sunk in this convoy battle, submitted no ROP. No attacks are mentioned in the deck logs of the other escorts in C 4.

145. *U 211*, KTB, 12 Sep. 1942

146. Cmdre's Report, ON 127; and *St Croix* ROP

147. Probably *Amherst*, because although Walkerling called it a two-funnel warship he was too far astern to have encountered *Ottawa*. *U 92*, KTB, 12 Sep. 1942; Rohwer, *Axis Submarine Successes*, 122

148. *U 404*, KTB, 12 Sep. 1942

cloud-covered, but the sea was brightly phosphorescent. Screening on the starboard quarter, *Celandine* drove off *U 91* at 0305z with two depth-charge patterns that caused only slight damage.[149] *U 404* pressed on ahead of the convoy, and at 0417z fired a spread of three torpedoes from a range of 2,000 metres.[150] The freighter *Daghild*, the only vessel hit, kept under way and managed to resume station in the convoy. Dobson, who had just detached *Celandine* to sink *Hektoria* if she was still afloat, again ordered a Raspberry. *U 404* escaped, but for the moment the convoy had shaken loose from the grip of the pack. At 0435z, Brüller, the commander of *U 407*, one of the few boats still in close pursuit, reported that he was "completely exhausted" by the strain and retired from the fray to await daybreak.[151] Astern of ON 127, *Celandine* drove off *U 92* trying to overhaul the convoy.[152]

The pack was still in pursuit. Again favoured by good visibility, several boats were in contact during the daylight hours on 12 September.[153] Dobson deployed all his available forces ahead of the convoy, two corvettes in the centre—*Arvida* had rejoined at 0930z—and the two destroyers on the wings, to provide an asdic barrier against submerged daylight attacks. In addition, ON 127 altered course at 1000z because CONNAV feared that routing papers left aboard the derelicts might have fallen into enemy hands. *Amherst* and *Celandine* covered the rear when they rejoined.[154] By nightfall most of the U-boats were having difficulty shadowing, and after sunset all lost contact. *U 407* found the convoy again at 0113z on 13 September, but its attack several hours later was unsuccessful.[155]

CONNAV diverted the convoy to a westerly course during the night to bring it closer to air cover.[156] When the pack regained contact after dawn on 13 September, the convoy was still beyond aircraft range, but the U-boats, some of which were experiencing mechanical difficulties, failed to press home any attacks. At 1605z on 13 September, a Botwood-based Catalina of 116 Squadron, RCAF piloted by Flying Officer R.M. MacLennan, reached the vicinity of ON 127, operating at its maximum range 550 miles from base. MacLennan sighted a half-submerged U-boat, but the swirl had vanished before the slow-moving flying boat could attack. Nonetheless, within ten minutes the Catalina forced down *U 96*, *U 411*, and *U 380*. Another aircraft replaced MacLennan at 2050z and conducted a radar sweep around the convoy.[157] These sweeps probably prevented an early evening attack.

The arrival of the destroyers *Witch* and *Annapolis*, which had sailed ahead of their WLEF group W 2, should have complicated the U-boats' task still further. At 2314z on 13 September, Lieutenant-Commander S.R.J. Woods, RNR of *Witch* signalled that the two destroyers were 10,000 yards ahead of the convoy and requested that Dobson in *St Croix* remain SOE until morning.

149. *Celandine* ROP; *Celandine*, Report of Attack on U-Boat, 12 Sep. 1942, PRO, ADM 237/90 mfm; and *U 91*, KTB, 12 Sep. 1942

150. *U 404*, KTB, 12 Sep. 1942; and Rohwer, *Axis Submarine Successes*, 122

151. *U 407*, KTB, 12 Sep. 1942; and *St Croix* ROP

152. *U 92*, KTB, 12 Sep. 1942; and *Celandine*, "Report of Attack on U-Boat"

153. BdU, KTB, 12 Sep. 1942; *U 404*, *U 407*, *U 411*, and *U 218*, KTBs, 12 Sep. 1942; Amherst and *St Croix* ROPs

154. *Arvida* deck log, 12/13 Sep. 1942; *Arvida*, Report of Attack on U-Boat, 12 Sep. 1942, NAC RG 24, 6901, NSS 8910-331/6; routing signals, 11-12 Sep. 1942, PRO, ADM 237/90 mfm

155. *U 407*, KTB, 13 Sep. 1942; and BdU, KTB, 12 Sep. 1942

156. CONNAV to CTU 24.1.14, 1649/12 Sep. 1942, and COMINCH to *St Croix*, 1817/12 Sep. 1942, PRO, ADM 237/90 mfm

157. Douglas, *Creation of a National Air Force*, 521-2; EAC, MASR, Sep. 1942, 15, DHH, 181.003 (D25); and COMINCH to *St Croix*, 1841z/13 Sep. 1942, PRO, ADM 237/90 mfm. Sunset was at 2100z/13. ON 127 did not make an evening evasive alteration as *U 91* and *U 404* believed. The U-boat sighted by the pilot was probably *U 96*.

Dobson deployed *Witch* and *Annapolis* at the van and on the port beam of the convoy respectively, which would strengthen the protection offered by *Ottawa*, 5,000 yards ahead of the convoy's starboard column.[158] Lieutenant T.C. Pullen, RCN, *Ottawa*'s first lieutenant, later recalled, "All was tranquil. The sea lay calm beneath a starry sky and the familiar swishing sounds of our bow wave fell gently away from the shoulders of ship. We were slipping along at ten knots."[159]

At 2352z, *Ottawa*'s type 286P radar picked up contacts at 6,000 and 8,000 yards and Lieutenant-Commander Rutherford assumed they were the approaching destroyers. When the range had closed to 2,000 yards and *Ottawa*'s lookouts glimpsed an object fine on the starboard bow, Rutherford challenged, and by the time *Witch* responded she had closed to 1000 yards, forcing the Canadian ship to alter course to port.[160] Thus preoccupied, *Ottawa* became vulnerable to *U 91*, which had been manoeuvring into position for an attack against a "twin-funnel destroyer" moving "under slow speed"—something that type 271 centimetric radar would likely have detected. At 0005z on 14 September, Kapitänleutnant Heinz Walkerling fired two torpedoes from a range of 1,000 metres. After one minute and fifty seconds one struck home, and the destroyer exploded in a cloud of smoke and "bright red flames."[161] On board *Ottawa*, "The ship's forward superstructure, funnels, bridge," recalled Pullen, "all that part visible from where I stood agape, became momentarily silhouetted by an orange glow, followed by darkness and an ominous silence." Falling debris could be heard, "splashing into the sea and clattering onto the upper deck."[162]

Woods observed the explosion, and fired two white rockets while informing Dobson of the attack. *Witch* then swept across the front of the convoy to the port bow while *St Croix* increased to fifteen knots and steamed towards *Ottawa*, which did not appear to be badly damaged.[163] But Walkerling sighted the second destroyer approaching in the glare and circled around to attack. At 0015z, he fired another torpedo but, instead of striking *St Croix*, who he believed had stopped to assist his initial victim, it burst into the hapless *Ottawa*.[164] The convoy made an emergency turn to starboard while *Witch* swept back towards the stricken warship, but she failed to detect the U-boat and rejoined ON 127. The sweeps of the other escorts were also without success, although *Annapolis* dropped a pattern of six depth charges for good measure.[165]

U 91 had in fact remained on the surface heading "towards the dark horizon" at high speed, and Walkerling then cut short his follow up attack on the convoy in the face of a "rapidly closing destroyer," probably *St Croix*.[166] Ölrich in *U 92*, guided back by the illumination, fired three torpedoes that missed their targets, and withdrew to reload. *U 407*, forced down by *St Croix*, and *U 411*,

158. *St Croix* ROP; and HMS *Witch*, ROP ON-127, 18 Sep. 1942, NAC, RG 24, 11088, 48-2-2 (51)

159. Pullen, "Convoy ON 127 and the Loss of HMCS *Ottawa*," 1-27

160. Ibid, 12; *Witch* ROP; and *U 91*, KTB, 14 Sep. 1942

161. *U 91*, KTB, 14 Sep.1942. *U 91* was making her first patrol and was Walkerling's first command.

162. Pullen, "Convoy ON 127," 13

163. *Witch* and *St Croix* ROPs

164. *U 91*, KTB, 14 Sep. 1942; and Rohwer, *Axis Submarine Successes*, 123

165. *St Croix*, *Celandine*, and *Witch* ROPs; HMCS *Annapolis*, deck log, NAC, RG 24, 7033; and Pullen, "Convoy ON 127," 14-15

166. *U 91*, KTB, 14 Sep. 1942

attracted as well by the light, but interrupted by *St Croix* and *Annapolis*, failed to get in any attacks. Eventually, *St Croix* carried out an attack on *U 411* that effectively disabled that boat.[167]

Meanwhile, poignant scenes unfolded onboard *Ottawa*. The destroyer now beyond saving, Rutherford gave the order to abandon ship. "During those final moments," Pullen remembered. "some grim dramas were being played out":

> The pitiable entreaties emanating from the voice pipe to the bridge from the two young hands trapped in the asdic hut far below became unbearable to those on the bridge, who were totally helpless to do anything for them. What could, what should, one do other than offer words of encouragement that help was coming when such was manifestly out of the question? What happened at the end is hard to contemplate for the imprisoned pair, as that pitch black, watertight, soundproofed box rolled first 90 degrees to starboard and then 90 degrees onto its back before sliding into the depths and oblivion. It is an ineradicable memory.[168]

Dobson ordered *Celandine* and *Arvida* to search for survivors.[169] *Ottawa* had slipped below the surface at 0030z leaving "a bewildered collection of oil-covered swimmers and crowded carley floats." The emergency turn to starboard carried ON 127 over the position where *Ottawa* had sunk: Pullen recalled that "the convoy appeared silently out of the darkness steaming majestically through our area and just as quietly was gone. A tanker in ballast passed so close we could see a cavernous hole in her port side."[170] That ship did not slow down, but SS *Athelduchess* threw down rafts while SS *Clausina* stopped to search for survivors. Unfortunately, *Arvida*—also searching for *Ottawa*'s men—thought that *Clausina* had been torpedoed and reported this fact to Dobson to add to the general confusion. *Arvida*, *Celandine*, and *St Croix* closed the tanker to sweep the area and begin rescue work, greatly hampered by the extreme darkness and the freshening wind, which prevented use of a sea boat. *Annapolis* circled the rescue operation at a distance to offer some protection, leaving only *Witch*, *Sherbrooke,* and *Amherst* on the screen until 0336z when *Annapolis* received an urgent order from *Witch* to rejoin. By daybreak, four escorts and a patrolling Catalina shielded the remnants of the convoy.[171]

While *Ottawa*'s survivors awaited rescue in the numbing seas, an incident occurred that demonstrated the close bond that often developed between those who served in Canadian warships. When *Ottawa* had gone down, many of the survivors had sought out Carley Floats, but Lieutenant "Yogi" Jenson, the young RCN Gunnery and RDF officer from Calgary, had swum to a spar buoy, to which he clung alone:

> The hours went by, the cold became colder and now jelly fish came up against my hands
> and arms like touches of cold fire. My spar was gradually drifting in towards one of the

---

167. *St Croix* ROP, ON 127; HMCS *St Croix*, "Report of Attack on U-Boat," 13 Sep. 1942; and *U 404* and *U 407*, KTBs, 14 Sep. 1942. The counterattack must have been on *U 407* as it was too early to be against *U 411*, which did not submerge until 0330z/14. Dobson's reports, however, make no mention of an attack between 0243z and 0407z. *Celandine* observed the destroyer attacking at 0340z. At least two torpedoes were definitely fired at *St Croix*.

168. Pullen, "Convoy O.N. 127," 15. For an equally moving account, see L.B. Jenson, *Tin Hats, Oilskins and Seaboots: A Naval Journey, 1938-1945* (Toronto 2000), 136.

169. *St Croix* ROP

170. Pullen, "Convoy ON 127," 17; and Cmdre's Report, ON 127

171. *St Croix* and *Witch* ROPs; and *Annapolis*, deck log, 14 Sep. 1942; Douglas, *Creation of a National Air Force*, 522

Top: The last photograph taken of HMCS
Ottawa. (Courtesy Ken Macpherson).

Right: Lieutenant L.B. Jenson, RCN, the
young officer who struggled to survive
the sinking of *Ottawa*. (NAC, PA 204653)

floats. It had lost most of the original crowd, the centre part was empty and now the sides were crammed with men hanging on. When my spar drifted closer in, one of the men, a Petty Officer named [Maurice. M.] Locke, grabbed me and held me between him and the float. He could hardly have had much more strength than I at this stage. Years later I asked this gentlemen, who was by then a Lieutenant, why he was so kind and good to me. When I was on the Newfie Bullet [the train to St. John's] travelling to join *Ottawa*, his wife and a shipmate's wife had been on the train going to St John's to be closer to their husbands. Evidently I had taken them to dinner and been pleasant and helpful to them. I had no recollection of this other than just meeting two nice ladies, but my reward was great.[172]

Celandine recovered forty-nine survivors from *Ottawa*, and *Arvida* twenty-seven, including some previously saved from *Empire Oil*. Altogether, 137 men perished, among them Rutherford, who reportedly gave his life jacket to a young rating, and the ship's doctor, Surgeon Lieutenant George Hendry, RCNVR, who died while trying to ensure the safety of a sailor he had recently operated upon.[173]

The loss of the destroyer was the final blow in a hard stretch for the RCN. Not only was she of a type of which the navy was desperately short, but *Ottawa* was the third Canadian warship lost in just seven days—as will be recalled from Chapter 7, the armed yacht *Raccoon* and the corvette *Charlottetown* had been torpedoed in the Gulf of St Lawrence on 7 and 11 September 1942 respectively. One hundred and seventy-seven young Canadians died in the worst week of the young navy's history.

———————

With the sinking of *Ottawa*, *Vorwärts* had shot its bolt. When, on 14 September, BdU ordered the pack to continue the hunt to the limit of their endurance, the response of the boats was wary, and hampered by low visibility, so the operation was terminated that afternoon.[174] But the adventure was not over. The main convoy arrived without further mishap off Halifax on 18 September, but *Amherst* and *Sherbrooke* detached on the 15th escorting four merchant ships—three of them with torpedo damage—to St. John's.[175] Early on 16 September, this tiny convoy blundered into SC 100 in the fog off the Newfoundland coast, and one of the ON 127 tankers, *F.J. Wolfe*, collided with the eastbound SS *Empire Soldier*. The tanker remained afloat but the *Empire Soldier* sank, luckily without loss of life. *Amherst*'s captain, whose handling of the ship during U-boat attacks had already raised serious questions about his performance, was relieved of his command.[176]

Dönitz could derive great satisfaction from the battle for ON 127. A third of the thirty-four vessels in the convoy had been torpedoed: seven merchant ships and a destroyer had been sunk, and another four merchant ships had been damaged. In return, no U-boats were lost, although three

172. Jenson, *Tinhats, Oilskins and Seaboots*, 140

173. *St Croix* and *Celandine* ROPs; *Arvida*, deck log, 13-14 Sep. 1942; and Pullen, "Convoy ON 127," 18-19. Sunrise was at 0837z/14. Pullen maintained that all of the crew of *Empire Oil* perished, but *Arvida*'s deck log states that she rescued five. The master of *Empire Oil* reported that seven of the twenty-three aboard *Ottawa* were rescued.

174. BdU, KTB, 14 Sep. 1942; and *U 91*, KTB, 14 Sep. 1942

175. *Witch* ROP

176. WA min sheet, HMCS *Amherst* ROP, ON 127; CTF 24 to CINCLANT, "ROP on Convoy ON 127/HMCS *Amherst*," 17 Oct. 1942, PRO, ADM 237/90; *Arvida* ROP; Audette, "Naval Recollections," 41-6; and Johnston, *Corvettes Canada*, 272

U-boats had to terminate their patrols because of damage. Since the convoy had been intercepted soon after it entered the air gap, *Vorwärts* had been able to savage it for three days before the first patrol aircraft appeared from Newfoundland. The German analysis concluded that good visibility had favoured the U-boats. Eight of the thirteen submarines were making their first patrols but, unusually, every boat involved had closed sufficiently to fire torpedoes, and this was the only North Atlantic convoy battle in 1942–3 in which every U-boat did so.[177]

Although even a well-equipped and highly trained group like B 6 had lost four merchant vessels from ONS 122 to a pack of ten submarines that shadowed it for only twenty hours, it is not surprising that ON 127, stalked by thirteen U-boats for four to five days, sustained much heavier losses. That, however, by no means lessened the disquiet of naval staff on both sides of the Atlantic. The first challenge was to untangle the course of events at sea during the action, which proved difficult because of the low quality of the reports received, especially from *St Croix*. Rear-Admiral R.M. Brainard, CTF 24, observed that "From the material at hand it is extremely difficult to analyze the actual tactical movements and no attempt will be made herein to comment on them."[178] After reviewing the reports from C 4, Captain R.W. Ravenhill, RN, Deputy Chief of Staff (Operations) at Western Approaches, commented simply "It is a waste of time trying to go into what happened ... It seems to me to be a complete muddle."[179]

Post-action analysis on both sides of the Atlantic exposed differences among the Allied navies in tactical doctrine and reinforced British lack of confidence in the proficiency of Canadian escort groups. In his analysis, Captain Harold Grant, RCN, newly appointed Captain (D) Newfoundland, "considered that St Croix handled the situation well throughout," but criticized specific escorts. American and British officers were less satisfied with the decisions made by Dobson. Brainard criticized his reluctance to use aggressive daylight sweeps. Noting that *St Croix* made only one such effort, he commented "that a greater use of the destroyers in sweeping at visibility distance during daylight periods might have been beneficial." Brainard also considered that since six escorts were insufficient to provide an effective asdic barrier, "their loss from a daylight screen ahead of the convoy [on sweeps] would have been well justified." These comments exposed a radical difference between CTF 24 convoy defence doctrine and that of Western Approaches. A Western Approaches staff officer commented that the "escorts were active and took lively countermeasures against attacking U-boats."[180] While the British did not comment directly on C 4's destroyer sweeps, analyses of recent daylight attacks against convoys had led them to the opposite conclusion, and they had promulgated more stringent directives on the integrity of screens. On 14 September, after the battle for ON 127 had reached its climax, Western Approaches ordered "that the policy of escorts must be to maintain maximum strength around the convoy in order to deter attackers and provide a heavy scale of counter-attack. The detaching of escorts to chase off U-boats sighted on the horizon was therefore to be restricted, and the policy of leaving the convoy to keep down submarines until dark was not to be resorted to unless at least two-thirds of the available escorts were present with the convoy." In addition, "the picking up of sur-

---

177. Rohwer and Hümmelchen, *Chronology of the War At Sea*, 161

178. CTF 24 to CINCLANT, "Report of Escort Operations—Convoy ON-127", 11 Nov. 1942, NAC, RG 24, 11088, 48-2-2, v 51

179. WA min sheet, *St Croix* ROP, ON-127, PRO, ADM 237/90

180. WA min sheet, HMCS *St Croix* ROP, ON 127; CTF 24 to C-in-C Atlantic Fleet, "Report of Escort Operations—Convoy ON 127," 11 Nov. 1942

vivors was not to be allowed to delay immediate offensive action unless absolutely necessary."[181] Brainard disagreed, arguing that "It is not considered that employment of all escorts in the immediate vicinity of the convoy, because of renewal of daylight attacks, is sound procedure. Only by high-speed sweeps can trailers be driven down and concentrations be prevented. Failure to carry out high-speed sweeps permits the enemy to concentrate a relative[ly] large number of submarines without being molested, this facilitating disastrous attacks both by night and by day." Such fundamental disagreement between the allied operational commanders over tactics contributed to criticisms of Canadian escort groups.[182] And, of course, they put RCN escorts in the unfortunate position of having to please two masters, both of whom who wanted to fight the same battle differently. But until the RCN had operational control of its own forces and a say in how the battle was fought, there was little it could do but, as one historian has suggested—"muddle through."[183]

As it was, the Western Approaches analysis of ON 127 was scathing towards Dobson's tactics and on the fragmented records received from the RCN. Without the benefit of Enigma, the British based their conclusions on an assumption that only five or six U-boats rather than, as we now know, thirteen, "shadowed and intermittently attacked," still Dobson's desperate attempt to prevent submerged daylight attacks by placing four escorts ahead of the convoy had been achieved by leaving the convoy's flanks unscreened, which was contrary to Western Approaches doctrine.[184] His decision to use his escorts to sink damaged merchant ships, which had weakened the screen when U-boats were in the vicinity, also provoked harsh criticism. In regard to the poor quality of the reports, Captain Ravenhill complained that Captain (D) Newfoundland and FONF "never make any attempt to collect the reports of one convoy and forward them under one covering letter with remarks. Neither have the remotest idea of what is expected of them nor have they any conception of how to deal with reports of proceedings."[185] Coherent after action reports were essential to the effective analyses of operations. Part of the explanation for the failure of Newfoundland command to provide them may lie in the relatively small, overburdened staff at St John's; nevertheless, if the RCN, or any professional service, was to improve its effectiveness, it had to understand what was going wrong and why.

While group *Vorwärts* savaged ON 127, additional U-boats were gathering on both sides of the air gap. *Lohs*, whose seven boats had recently refuelled from a U-tanker, was still on station northeast of Newfoundland, and BdU now assigned three additional outbound boats to this patrol line. Nine other outbound boats formed group *Pfeil* in the eastern part of the air gap. On 15 September, *U 221*, a member of the new group, located ON 129, thirty-one merchant ships escorted by C 2, 300 miles west of Ireland. The convoy escaped in low visibility, and when other *Pfeil* boats approached the next day, C 2 drove them off.[186]

181. Adm, Tactical and Staff Duties Division, *Preliminary Narrative: The War at Sea, Jan.-Dec. 1942*, III, 297

182. CTF 24 to COMINCH, "Report of Escort Operations—Convoy ON-125," 26 Sep. 1942

183. D.M. McLean, "Muddling Through: Canadian Anti-Submarine Doctrine and Practice, 1942-1945," in Hadley et al, *A Nation's Navy*, 176-7

184. Adm, *MASR*, Sep. 1942, 5

185. WA min sheet, 20 Oct. 1942, *St Croix* ROP

186. BdU, *U 221*, *U 258*, *U 356*, KTBs, 15-16 Sep. 1942; HMS *Burnham*, ROP, ON 129, 20 Sep. 1942, NAC, RG 24, 11319, 8280-ON 129; naval messages, DHH 88/1, reel 10, ON 129. Rohwer and Hümmelchen, *Chronology of the War at Sea*, 164 states *Pfeil* contacted a second Canadian escorted convoy, SC 99 (C 1), but this was in fact the British escorted HX 206 (B 1).

On the other side of the ocean, SC 100 had sailed from Halifax on 12 September with twenty-five merchant ships, one of which, it will be recalled, was lost off the Newfoundland coast on 16 September after colliding with one of the ships detached from ON 127. The mid-ocean escort for SC 100, a small slow convoy, was unusually large: A 3 (Captain P.R. Heineman, USN), comprised two US Coast Guard cutters and four Canadian corvettes. Three additional corvettes bound for Operation Torch in the Mediterranean reinforced the screen. HMCS *Trillium* and HMS *Nasturtium* had type 271 radar, but none of the escorts had HF/DF. On 18 September, after B-Dienst decoded a convoy course instruction, *Lohs* was able to locate SC 100 on the great circle route, 280 miles northeast of Newfoundland. Over the next seven days, *Lohs* and *Pfiel*— a total of twenty or more U-boats—operated against the convoy, with a maximum of seven in contact at one time. A deep equinoctial depression that overtook the convoy starting on 21 September, three days into the battle, caused merchant ships to straggle and made conditions exceptionally difficult for submarines plunging through giant seas. Heineman and A 3 conducted a well-coordinated defence and air coverage was decisive in ending the battle once SC 100 cleared the air gap. By then, *Lohs* had sunk five merchant ships, two from within the convoy and three stragglers. In exchange, two U-boats were forced back to port with heavy damage, inflicted in one case by HMCS *Rosthern*.[187]

As SC 100 had moved slowly eastward trailed by U-boats, an event occurred that left some officers questioning the judgement of naval headquarters in Ottawa. On 19 September, when SC 100 was trying to shake off shadowing U-boats, NSHQ recalled to Halifax the three corvettes slated for Torch—*Nasturtium*, *Weyburn*, and *Lunenburg*—so that they could be fitted with the 20mm Oerlikon anti-aircraft guns needed for operations in the Mediterranean. The three escorts obediently if reluctantly left the convoy at their highest speed until *Nasturtium* monitored a message from the Admiralty to Ottawa offering to fit the guns on arrival in the United Kingdom. Anticipating approval, the corvettes reversed course again, and rejoined the convoy early on 20 September. But they had used up much valuable fuel, and during the nineteen hours they had been absent SC 100 had been under constant pursuit by Group *Lohs*.[188]

Such "to-ing and fro-ing" is the bane of all sailors and that this event caused some bitterness is evident from a poem that Lieutenant J.B. O'Brien, RCNVR, an officer in the corvette *Trillium*, sent to his friend John Connolly, executive assistant to the minister for naval services. Set to the popular song "Bless 'Em All," O'Brien's poem was entitled "SC 100 and HMCS Trillium":

> Bless them all, Bless them all
> The long and the short and the tall
> Bless all the Brass hats
> And the chairs where they sit,
> Planning our Westomp and the rest of that Shit.
> ...Bless them all, Bless them all
> The long and the short and the tall
> Bless old CICWA and COMINCH too

---

187. CTU 24.1.3 WD, DHH, 91/289 folder 5, box 65; CTU 24.1.3 to CTF 24, report of escort of SC 100; USCGC *Campbell*, Action Report, SC 100, 28 Sep. 1942, NAC, RG 24, 11335, NSS 8280-SC 100; BdU, KTB, 24-5 Sep. 1942; *U 221* and *U 259*, KTB, 24 Sep. 1942.The first so-called Support Group, EG 20, had been ordered to reinforce A 3, but its presence was not needed by the time the ships of the group had located the convoy. HMS *Stork*, ROP EG 20, 10 Nov. 1942, PRO, ADM 199/618

188. HMS *Nasturtium*, ROP, SC 100, NAC, RG 24, 11335, NSS 8280-SC 100; CTU 24.1.3 war diary; and Adm to NSHQ, 1154a/19 Sep. 1942, and NSHQ to Adm, 1608z/19 Sep. 1942, PRO, ADM 237/197

> Bless old COAC and N-S-H-Q.
> As we've waited all trip for this day
> To stalk these U-boats as prey
> It's then they combine, to spoil our good time
> By taking three escorts away.[189]

It is an axiom of war that those at the "sharp end" doing the fighting tend to vilify those at headquarters who are not, particularly when the latter's folly seems self-evident. In this case, however, as in others, the sharp end simply did not and could not comprehend the bigger picture. The Director of the Operations Division at NSHQ, Commander Nelson Lay wrote his friend Captain Roger Bidwell, Chief of Staff to FONF, "I am afraid you people in Newfoundland must have thought we were absolutely crazy here with the various signals about additional escorts for H.X and S.C. Convoys."

> Originally the matter [of sending RCN corvettes overseas for Torch] was very hush-hush and C.N.S. was asked not to give details to anyone. The result was we cooked up a story about additional escorts and told the Admiralty to peel them off at the other end.
>
> To make matters even more complicated, one Immediate Most Secret signal from Admiralty addressed to N.S.H.Q. was held up in Washington by B.A.D. for seven days. This signal gave the additional armament required [for Torch] and said that this could not be done in U.K. When we eventually got the signal, six corvettes were already at sea, so we asked C.T.F. 24 to haul them back to Halifax. Within a few hours of this being done, the two convoys were reported by U-boats. Fortunately Admiralty "came up" and said they would try to re-arm these six in U.K. so we sent an Immediate to the ships concerned to rejoin their convoys.[190]

The incident is not all that important in itself, except that it foreshadows important events to come; as we will see later in this history, unofficial grousing, both informed and uninformed, by seagoing officers to the executive assistant to the naval minister would have significant consequences.

––––––––––

The gale that roared across the Atlantic on 21 to 23 September scattered five or six U-boats in the wake of the eastbound SC 100. They were well positioned, as it turned out, to intercept the westbound ON 131, fifty-four merchant ships escorted by C 3 under Commander Wallace in *Saguenay*. As the convoy steamed through the area in which these U-boats were patrolling on 24 and 25 September, there were several inconclusive attacks and counterattacks—including the dramatic depth-charging of a submarine by *Skeena* that blew the U-boat to the surface, but evidently without inflicting fatal damage. For their part, the submarines sank no vessels in the convoy, only a straggler, the SS *John Winthrop*, torpedoed by *U 619*.[191]

---

189. O'Brien to Connolly, NAC, Connolly papers, MG32 C71, v 4:14. Cited in Richard Mayne, "Behind the Scenes at Naval Service Headquarters: Bureaucratic Politics and the Dismissal of Vice-Admiral Percy W. Nelles," Master's thesis, Wilfred Laurier University (Waterloo 1998), 50

190. Capt H.N. Lay to Capt R.E.S. Bidwell, 28 Sep. 1942. NAC, RG 24, 11987, 1292

191. *Skeena*'s submarine appears to have been *U 661*, which would be destroyed on 15 Oct. by HMS *Viscount*. Lt Dyer, commanding *Skeena*, was using the "MacMitch Diamond Search," which he had devised for hunting U-boats that had submerged within sight, and which he had previously used during the battle for ON 115. The tactic attracted some interest at Western Approaches, although searches considered to have more potential were under development there. WA min sheet, DHH, 88/1, v 10, ON 131

The main body of U-boats operating on the northern routes had moved steadily eastward in the sustained operations against SC 100 and also against RB 1, a "one-off" eastbound convoy of small passenger ships that was sailing to the south of SC 100. Reinforced and reorganized as Groups *Luchs* and *Letzte Ritter* between 27 and 30 September, the large concentration of U-boats south-west of Iceland posed the greatest threat to convoys outbound from the British Isles, but failed to make any firm contact.[192] One Canadian-escorted convoy at risk, ON 133, thirty-four ships escorted by C 1 under Commander J.D. Prentice, passed sixty miles north of *Luchs* on the 29th, supported by aircraft from Iceland.[193] Ironically, the one torpedoing on the northern ocean routes as September 1942 drew to a close was not achieved by a member of the large packs in the eastern Atlantic, but rather by *U 513*, the lone U-boat hovering off the Atlantic coast of Newfoundland as an outrider to the offensive in the Gulf of St Lawrence. Although the victim, SS *Ocean Vagabond*, made port, Captain Mainguy, acting FONF, remarked that this attack "within 8 miles of St John's harbour" made a suitably dismal end to an "unhappy" month: "no definite U-boat sinkings can be recorded (although promising attacks have been carried out) and the enemy have scored successes on convoys at sea [and] sunk HMCS 'Ottawa'..."[194]

The convoy battles between July and September 1942 highlighted the importance of chance—the weather, and the experience and personalities of officers on both sides to name but a few elements—to the course and outcome of these complex and fast-moving events at sea. Chance in countless forms and guises affected the hundreds of fast decisions made by overtired SOEs, COs, and watchkeepers in poor visibility on cold, wet, and inadequately equipped open bridges. More often than not, the decisions concerned sweeps during the shadowing phase. Clearly high-speed sweeps cost fuel, and convoys were left unattended during such sweeps and subsequent attacks, and possibly permanently, when too much fuel was expended. The agonizing question facing every SOE and often COs of destroyers was, "Should I sweep wide, or deep, and for how long, and if I am in contact, should I hunt to the death?" Strain and discomfort was no less pervasive in the U-boats. It was impossible then, and it remains so today, to determine why certain officers took the decisions that they did in the heat of mid-ocean battles that often lasted for days.

For the Allies, convoy operations during the summer of 1942 were a holding action. The meagre forces available had to make do as best they could pending the production of more and better war-ships and aircraft and the development of improved equipment and tactics that would make possible an offensive against the wolf packs in 1943. The RCN, even as it struggled to fill yawning gaps in the British and American escort forces, was at a greater disadvantage than these great navies. The vast majority of the Canadian warships had commissioned during the latter part of 1941 or later, and the young, underdeveloped RCN lacked the large numbers of expert personnel and the training and industrial resources needed to bring the raw ships and their equally raw reservist crews to an efficient state within the space of a few short months. The enemy's relentless and expanding

------

192. C-in-C WA to Adm, 28 Oct. 1942, DHH, ADM 199/717; BdU, KTB, 27-9 Sep. 1942; and *U 259*, KTB, 27-8 Sep. 1942

193. *Chambly* ROP, ON 133, and Naval Messages, DHH, 88/1, v 10, ON-133; and *U 118*, KTB, 29-30 Sep. 1942

194. FONF, ROP, Sep. 1942, DHH, NSS 1000-5-20, pt 2

assault, and the insistent demands of the senior allies for help allowed no respite for the Canadians to overcome the well-recognized shortcomings in equipment, maintenance, and training.

Nevertheless, German wolf-pack operations in the summer of 1942 resulted in a surprising string of RCN successes over a short period of time. In the six-weeks from mid-July through to 1 September, Canadian escorts defending convoys on the North Atlantic destroyed four U-boats, and *Oakville* had also sunk *U 94* in the Caribbean. There was no apparent pattern in the kills around convoys, except, perhaps, for the skill and experience of the individual commanding officers.[195] They were made by night and by day, by destroyers and by corvettes, and by professional and by reserve escort captains. Initial detection was by visual sighting in three cases and by radar in the other two. The means of destruction included both ramming and depth charges. The victims included both inexperienced and veteran U-boat commanders. All the U-boat killers formed part of the close escort of a convoy.

U-boats managed to attack only eight of the fifty-two convoys—15 percent—that crossed the Atlantic between the beginning of July and the end of September. However, sustained assaults on convoys in the air gap had demonstrated that Dönitz was able to attack with large numbers of submarines and saturate the escort. In early August seventeen U-boats had operated against SC 94, defended by C 1, sinking one third of its thirty-three merchant ships. In early September ON 127, escorted by C 4, had been attacked by thirteen boats, which torpedoed eleven of its thirty-four ships, sinking seven as well as HMCS *Ottawa*. Canadian escorts had defended convoys stubbornly and had achieved kills during this first phase of operations by large wolf packs. They made the best of what they had. When Commander Wallace as SOE of ON 115 used MF/DF bearings from merchant ships to keep shadowing U-boats off balance, he demonstrated tactical ingenuity and exploited the limited intelligence available. But Canadian escorts were fighting the battle with less thorough preparation than their British counterparts and without advances in electronic equipment such as type 271 and ship-borne HF/DF that were giving many RN escorts an edge. Canadian work-up training was only in an embryonic stage and use of the harbour training facilities at both ends of a crossing had to compete with other requirements at those ports. Canadian escort groups all too often lacked cohesion because their composition fluctuated from crossing to crossing, with different SOEs often in charge. If U-boats were to be chased clear of a convoy, destroyers with their speed were critical, but because the RCN had so few of that type, groups frequently sailed with just one.

The presence of VLR aircraft in Iceland and the brief appearance of a British support group—designed to reinforce the close escort of threatened convoys—foreshadowed some of the antisubmarine developments that would mark operations in the spring of 1943. These developments, however, would not provide any help to the Canadians in the fall of 1942. The escort for SC 100 was oversized because RCN corvettes were leaving the North Atlantic to prepare for the Torch landings in North Africa. In the coming months, the Torch commitment would strip the RCN groups of their winter reserve, and absorb British and US warships and aircraft that would otherwise have supported the North Atlantic convoys. The U-boats would exact a heavy toll from allied merchant shipping.

---

195. This argument is made in Fisher, "Tactics, Training, Technology: The RCN's Summer of Success, July-Sep. 1942," 19

CHAPTER TEN

North Atlantic Convoy Operations II
October to December 1942

WHEN CAPTAIN H.C. FITZ, USN, an experienced American escort group commander, visited Western Approaches Command Headquarters in October 1942, he found that "British naval officers as a class think the Canadians very ineffective. In all the time I was there I did not hear one single word in their favor. When I pointed out the expansion in their Navy and that they had always seemed to be giving their best efforts and were quite keen, they usually said that one of their main objections was that they would not take advice or would not benefit from British experience."[1]

Royal Canadian Navy ships and personnel could compare unfavorably with their counterparts in the Royal Navy, and this was recognized in Ottawa. Canadian naval authorities, however, emphasized the generosity of Canada's contribution to the defence of convoys, and this generosity in response to urgent Allied appeals for escorts that were available from no other source accounted in no small part for the shortfalls in quality. "Possibly," commented Captain Fitz, "Canadians do not desire that the British should run their Navy."[2] Admiral Ernest King, USN, had concluded as much in 1941 and that view somewhat oversimplified the close relations between the two Royal navies. Perhaps also less evident to American observers was that the US Navy's control over convoy operations in the western Atlantic, and over Canada's mid-ocean escorts, was no less responsible than British demands for the overextension of the Canadian fleet. Certainly, there were sound strategic reasons for the commitment of Canadian escorts in late 1942 to the northern seaboard of the United States, the Caribbean, and operations related to the invasion of North Africa, as well as the Mid-Ocean Escort Force. It was also true that Canada had insisted on redeploying escorts for particular national interests only for the shortlived Halifax to Caribbean tanker convoys and the organization of full convoy schedules in the St Lawrence for an equally brief period of time; both of these commitments wound down in the summer and early autumn of 1942. Thereafter, British and American needs almost entirely accounted for the strains on the RCN.

There is no question about the urgency of the needs of the RN and USN for help. They were fully stretched because of the insatiable requirements for escorts for other theatres, particularly the Pacific and the Mediterranean. Nevertheless, the Canadian contribution allowed the two major navies a sufficient margin in their North Atlantic escort pools to withdraw one ship in four—and at times one in two—for maintenance and training. From the beginning of October 1942 the

---

1.   Capt H.C. Fitz, USN, to CTG 24, 12 Oct. 1942, NARA, RG 313, Red CTF 24, box 8701

2.   Ibid

impact of the landings in North Africa, Operation Torch, would force Canadian authorities to adopt practices reminiscent of those followed in 1941. To maintain commitments in the MOEF—four Canadian groups, besides four or more corvettes allocated to the American group A 3—the RCN simply assigned ships as they became available, even if not worked up. As the Director of Plans at NSHQ, Captain H.G. DeWolf, would inform his American and British counterparts during a conference in December 1942, "We have never reached the 10 or 12 [trained escort ship] stage. It is a question of 5 or 6, and then it is a little difficult. I agree that six well-trained escorts are better than 12 untrained. But when you have only 6 untrained ones, then you hesitate to take one away ... We have even kept them at sea against our better judgement."[3]

The demands on a young navy were extraordinary, and the "bloody winter" of 1942–3 became, perhaps, the single most important, but certainly the saddest, period in the Canadian navy's history.[4] On the North Atlantic in the final months of 1942 the navy faced both its sternest test and its greatest scrutiny.

By September 1942 initiatives by the Allies had bettered the odds in the defence of shipping. Aside from completion of the convoy system on the North American seaboard and in the Caribbean that finally denied the U-boats unprotected targets in these vitally important waters, there had been improvements in the thinly stretched defences of the transatlantic convoys. These included the assignment of additional ships to the admittedly still understrength mid-ocean escort groups, and the deployment of the first Very Long Range Liberators to Iceland, which had immediate results and particularly alarmed the U-Boat Command. The formation of the first RN support group, the kind of backup for the hard-pressed close escorts that British and Canadian officers had wanted since 1940–1 but had never had the resources to create, was a promising portent for the future. Despite an additional twenty-four U-boats in Atlantic service, sinkings in the Atlantic fell to 408,440 tons in September from 526,709 tons in August.[5] In October, however, support groups went by the board because escorts, especially destroyers, were required for the invasion of North Africa. As noted in Chapter 9, the movement of RCN corvettes to the Mediterranean did temporarily increase the size of some escort groups with certain eastbound convoys, but air coverage still fell short. Until March, 1943 Coastal Command had only one Liberator squadron operating in the mid-ocean, and eight recently commissioned escort carriers—four British and four American—supported Torch rather than the Atlantic battle.[6] The African invasion also had repercussions for convoy organization. In the latter half of September the assembly port of SC and HX convoys had been shifted from Halifax to New York to link up with the new coastal convoy network in American and

---

3.   Conference Minutes, "Fuel Supplies to UK and Africa: Related Escort Problems," Day Two, 30 Dec. 1942, NAC, RG 24, 1968, 222-1, 5

4.   Weinberg, *World at Arms*, 364-8, 380; Stacey, *Arms, Men and Governments*, 397-413; Douglas, *Creation of a National Air Force*, 343-73, 520-7, 545-9; J.M. Waters, *Bloody Winter* (New York 1957)

5.   Rahn, "Die Seekriegführung im Atlantik und Küstenbereich," 367. U-Boat Command had 110 Atlantic U-boats at the beginning of Aug. 1942 and 134 at the beginning of Sep. 1942.

6.   AHB, *R.AF in Maritime War* III, 514-15, 519-21; W.A.B. Douglas and David Syrett, "Die Wende in der Schlacht im Atlantik: Die Schliessung des 'Grönland-Luftochs,' 1942-43" ("The Turning Point in the Battle of the Atlantic: Closing the Greenland Air Gap, 1942-43"), trans Jürgen Rohwer, *Marine-Rundshau* 83/I, II, III (1986), 2-11, 70-73, 147-149

Caribbean waters (see Chapter 6). The transfer of escorts for Torch, both British and Canadian, would cause the SL and OS convoys between Britain and Sierra Leone to be suspended for six months.[7] In place of this route, almost all ships going to South America and southern Africa would sail in October with alternate ON and ONS convoys steaming "as far to the southward as the endurance of the escorts would allow," be dispersed near the Azores and proceed independently to their destinations.[8]

This southern shift entailed longer passages for escort groups. To ease the strain, starting in late October convoy cycles would be opened out from seven to eight days. The British also proposed to reduce the number of mid-ocean escort groups from eleven to ten in order to use B 3 as a support group or as a source of replacements for members of existing groups that suffered weather damage. But Canadian and American operational commanders in Newfoundland, FONF and CTF 24, drawing on the punishing experiences of the previous winter, argued that an eight-day cycle could not be maintained during a North Atlantic winter with only ten groups. Their objections quashed the proposal for the time being, and although the Admiralty continued to press for this reduction in future discussions, the number of MOEF groups remained at eleven, with seventy-six escorts, or an average group strength of about seven escorts including the Torch corvettes, throughout October and November.[9]

On the "other side of the hill," the *U-Bootwaffe*'s front-line force in the Atlantic was increasing steadily. At the beginning of October 105 of the 161 Atlantic boats were at sea. In addition, because of U-tankers, individual boats could remain on task longer before returning home, meaning there were enough boats to maintain patrol lines astride the convoy tracks at both ends of the air gap.[10] Technological improvements also enhanced their capabilities. As seen in Chapter 8, the first *FuMB* or *Metox*, search receivers capable of detecting radar transmissions, had come into service in August, and by October, most of the German U-boat fleet had been fitted with the equipment. With a range of about thirty miles, depending upon environmental conditions and the sensitivies of the equipment, *Metox* could detect transmissions from metric radar sets such as type 286, SW1C, and SW2C, or the airborne ASV II, but not those produced by centimetric radar sets such as type 271 or ASV III. Since the vast majority of RCN escorts were fitted with metric search radar, this goes a long way in explaining their lack of U-boat kills and apparent subpar performance on the North Atlantic in the autumn and winter of 1942, something not fully appreciated at the time.[11]

The large U-boat force at sea, benefiting from experience gained since the spring in the coordination of massed attacks on convoys and from the information on Allied routes and practices accumulated by the regular penetration of convoy signal traffic, enjoyed marked success on the north-

7. Hague, *Allied Convoy System*, 139

8. First Lord of the Admiralty and the MWT, "Resumption of Convoys between UK and Freetown," 28 Dec. 1942, PRO, CAB 86/3; and SecNB, "Rearrangement of Convoys East Coast of North America," 3 Aug. 1942, DHH, 81/520/8280B, box 1, Convoy Organization, v 3

9. Adm to COMINCH, 10 and16 Oct. 1942; and Adm to NSHQ, 16 Oct. 1942 , all in PRO, ADM 199/2084

10. BdU, KTB, 2 Oct. 1942 ; MOD, *U-Boat War in the Atlantic* II, 50

11. R. Fisher, "The Impact of German Technology on the RCN in the Battle of the Atlantic, 1942-1943," *The Northern Mariner* 7/4, 1-13; Donald E. Graves, "German Navy Radar Detectors, Radar Foxing and IFF Equipment, 1939-1945: An Overview and Descriptive Narrative," DHH, 2000/5; AHB, *RAF in Maritime War* III, 522; MOD, *U-Boat War in the Atlantic* II, 1942 - 3; Terraine, *Business in Great Waters*, 479. Mr Bob Gurney has also shared his considerable knowledge of German naval radar detectors with the authors.

ern routes. Fourteen of the forty-eight convoys that crossed the ocean in October, November, and December would lose ships to submarine attack as compared with eight of fifty-two in July through September.[12] Two convoys under Canadian escort, attacked by large numbers of U-boats over several days, suffered particularly heavy losses: SC 107 lost fifteen of forty-two merchant ships in November and the next month ONS 154 lost fourteen of forty-seven. Other convoys under American, British, and Canadian escort—especially SC 104 (B 6), HX 212 (A 3), and SC 144 (B 6)—also suffered severe if less grievous losses, but several convoys, including some under Canadian escort, came through extreme danger with little or no loss. That said, the disasters to two convoys under Canadian escort would jolt Naval Service Headquarters and reinforce the low opinion of the RCN already held in British naval circles; severe losses merited adverse comment and demanded remedy. However, as an analysis of all the convoys transiting the North Atlantic during this period demonstrates, it is open to question whether with the equipment and training then available to them, the huge packs concentrated against them, and the loss of Ultra intelligence, the C Groups could have done much better.

The storms that had prevented the U-boats from making firm contact with convoys during the last week of September continued to frustrate their operations during the first part of October. The Admiralty's U-boat situation report for the week ending 12 October 1942 observed that there were now so many U-boats at sea in the central North Atlantic—the rough estimate possible with the limited intelligence available was between thirty-three and fifty submarines—that "it is remarkable that any convoy should pass through this area without being intercepted."[13] Even as the staff officers completed this report, Group *Wotan*, ten submarines 300 miles northeast of Newfoundland that had escaped the notice of Allied intelligence by maintaining radio silence, contacted convoy SC 104. The escort, B 6, was well equipped and experienced, but the heavy seas masked the low hulls of the submarines from the warships' type 271 radar. On the nights of the 12th and 13th the U-boats torpedoed and sank eight of the forty-eight merchant ships. Significantly, when the seas moderated on 14 October and the escorts were able to use their sensors to full effect, they regained the initiative. There were no further losses, even though BdU had sent reinforcements, designated Group *Leopard*, and the escorts destroyed two of the enemy on 15 to 16 October.[14]

Over the next ten days, the patrol lines in mid-Atlantic intercepted three successive westbound convoys as well as the eastbound HX 212. Canadian ships escorted three of these convoys, the first to encounter the enemy being ON 137 under the protection of C 4. BdU expected a westbound convoy, and when groups *Wotan* and *Leopard* broke off the operation against SC 104 they were added to Group *Panther* on a long patrol line that straddled the convoy tracks at the eastern end of the air gap.[15] ON 137, a fast convoy of thirty-eight ships, its departure delayed by foul weather, had finally cleared the North Channel and was joined by C 4 coming out of Londonderry on 11 October. The

---

12.   Interceptions from Douglas and Rohwer, "The Most Thankless Task Revisited," in Boutilier (ed), *The RCN in Retrospect*, 191; sinkings from Hague, *Allied Convoy System*, 123-37

13.   Syrett, *Battle of the Atlantic*, 89

14.   R. Fisher, "Group Wotan and the Battle for Convoy SC 104, 11-17 Oct. 1942," *The Mariner's Mirror* 84 (Feb. 1998), 64-75

15.   MOD, *U-Boat War in the Atlantic* II, 55

convoy clawed its way southwest through heavy seas, but three days later was hove to in what the master of the rescue ship described as "tremendous seas. Am being left behind, shipping much water ... Convoy making headway. I am not. The sea smashes aboard amidships and fills her up."[16]

Once clear of this gale ON 137 worked westwards. For this crossing C 4 consisted of the destroyers *St Croix* (Lieutenant-Commander Dobson, SOE) and *Restigouche*, and the corvettes *Amherst*, *Arvida*, *Sherbrooke*, and HMS *Celandine*. As usual, the British ship was the sole escort with type 271 radar, but *Restigouche* and the rescue ship *Bury* both had HF/DF, the Canadian destroyer having "scrounged" a set in Londonderry nearly a year before. Apparently, ship-borne HF/DF did not pick up the first contact report on the morning of 16 October, when *U 704* in the southern part of *Panther*, spotted flashing signal lights at 0647z. The submarine was then able to pick out the convoy in the growing daylight and transmitted a contact report. A second boat, *U 609*, sighted the convoy at 0815z. By 1016z, when the Admiralty warned Dobson that ON 137 had been reported, the two boats were shadowing.[17] Fortunately, fog closed down visibility, and Dobson made a sound tactical decision by sending the type 271-equipped *Celandine* to circle the convoy.[18] Meanwhile, the submarines had dived ahead to attack. Kapitänleutnant Rudloff in *U 609* was unable to see the convoy, but groped through the fog at periscope depth using sound bearings. *Celandine*'s radar detected his periscope three miles ahead of ON 137 and promptly attacked, heavily damaging *U 609*, which escaped by going deep. Dobson in *St Croix* and *Amherst* both gained asdic contact and dropped charges while the convoy made an emergency turn.[19] *U 609* eventually limped back to base. The other submarine, *U 704*, fired torpedoes from within the convoy, but missed and then lost contact.[20] BdU now ordered twenty-five more boats to close.[21] HF/DF bearings announced the presence of pursuers, but a massive storm was rapidly moving in and Dobson decided against running down the contacts as it would take escorts away for extended periods in the rough seas.

According to the master of the rescue ship, "From noon, October 17th the barometer fell at an alarming rate, the wind freshened ... 1700 hrs ... whole gale ... 2000 hrs wind cyclonic force."[22] Heavy pounding in high seas disabled the asdics in *Sherbrooke*, *Celandine*, and *Amherst*. The convoy began scattering badly and a good many ships suffered serious weather damage.[23] The shrieking winds, driving rain, and tremendous seas also stymied the searching U-boats. The commanding officer of *U 704* considered remaining on the surface "pointless" and dived.[24] Kapitänleutnant Baberg in *U 618*, having broken off searching because of his fuel state, recorded being "in the eye of a hurricane" at 2100z on 17 October, but remained on the surface. Four hours later, his look-

---

16. "Report of Master of Rescue Vessel 'Bury,' Voyage ON 137," NAC, RG 24, 11319, NS 3280-ON 137

17. *U 609* and *U 704*, KTBs, 16 Oct. 1942

18. *St Croix* ROP, ON-137, 24 Oct. 1942, NAC, RG 24, 11087, 48-2-2, v 50; and Convoy signals in DHH, 89/34, v 18, ON-137

19. HMS *Celandine*, "Report of Attack on U-Boat," 1057/16 Oct. 1942; *U 609*, KTB, 16 Oct. 1942; *St Croix* ROP; HMCS *Amherst*, "Report of Attack on U-Boat," 1147/16 Oct. 1942, and Cover Letter by Capt (D) Newfoundland, NAC, RG 24, 1087, 48-2-2, v 50

20. *U 609* and *U 704*, KTBs, 16 Oct. 1942

21. MOD, *U-Boat War in the Atlantic* II, 55

22. "Report by Master of Rescue Ship 'Bury'"

23. *St Croix* ROP; Audette, *Naval Recollections*, 55; *Chambly*, deck log, 17 Oct. 1942, NAC, RG 24, 7185; and BdU, KTB, 16-17 Oct. 1942

24. *U 704*, *U 71*, *U 442*, *U 356*, *U 258*, *U 662*, and *U 381*, KTBs, 17 Oct. 1942

outs sighted flashing light traffic, and then a large freighter. Baberg closed and eventually fired four torpedoes in the churning seas. His target was the American freighter *Angelina* that had romped ahead as ON 137 scattered. Also nearby was HMCS *Arvida* (Lieutenant D.G. King, RCNVR), having closed *Angelina* to order her to douse a light. Possibly it was the exchange of messages by light with the corvette that Baberg had seen and which spelled the freighter's doom. *Arvida*'s radar was "as usual out of order," and the submarine was not sighted. In fact, Baberg dived because *Arvida* was closing. After the torpedoes slammed home, *Angelina*'s crew scrambled for boats and life rafts and King circled them as the rescue ship *Bury* closed; only nine of the crew of fifty-five survived.[25] Another American cargo ship, *Steel Navigator*, straggled and two days later fell victim to *U 610*. By the time she sent her distress call at 1128z on 19 October, the number of escorts was down to four—*St Croix* had left to fuel in the Azores not having enough to reach St John's—the rescue ship was gone, and no escort could be spared to help the stricken vessel.[26] Eight days later, HMS *Decoy* picked up sixteen survivors.[27]

With the departure of *St Croix*, Lieutenant-Commander D.W. Piers in *Restigouche* became SOE, and by the evening of 19 October his ship and *Sherbrooke* were the only remaining escorts. *Arvida* and *Bury* had lost contact with the convoy; the corvette subsequently stayed with *Bury* beyond her prudent limit of endurance as they made for St John's, but lost touch on 20 October, ran out of fuel, and had to be towed in by tug.[28] *Amherst* and *Celandine*, also short of fuel, had to detach for Newfoundland. The fact that escorts ran short of oil as a result of two major storms and a route diversion once again underlined the chronic problem of getting a group across the Atlantic with a sufficient reserve of fuel to prosecute HF/DF bearings or attack submarines.[29] Fortunately, defeated by the severe weather, Dönitz had terminated the operation after dusk on 19 October.[30]

Piers was not to know any of this, of course. And whether or not the U-boats had been called off, the lightly escorted convoy, steaming through the area near a "milch cow" refuelling point, and where the last eleven *Panther* boats were forming up into Group *Veilchen*, was still in great danger. Piers acted on several HF/DF bearings astern of the convoy, some of them very strong, by making an evasive turn under the cover of rain and stationed *Sherbrooke*, her asdic still unserviceable, eight miles astern. CTF 24, Rear-Admiral Brainard, monitoring the growing number of HF/DF contacts in the vicinity, recommended scattering the convoy while the Admiralty recommended dispersing only the faster twelve-knot ships; CONNAV rejected both options. Poor visi-

25. *Arvida* ROP ON 137, NAC, RG 24, 11319, NS 3280-01-ON 137; "Report of Master of Rescue Vessel 'Bury'"; *U 618*, KTB, 17 Oct. 1942

26. Portugal had granted the Allies facilities at the Azores on 12 Oct., and *St Croix* was one of the first ships to take advantage of this agreement. Adm, Trade Division, Monthly Survey, Oct. 1942, PRO, ADM 199/2083

27. *Arvida* ROP, ON 137; *Restigouche* ROP; BdU, KTB, 18-19 Oct. 1942; "Report of Master of Rescue Vessel 'Bury'"; Rohwer, *Axis Submarine Successes*, 129; and Moore, *Careless Word*, 266

28. The master of the rescue ship accused *Arvida* of deserting his ship in the middle of the ocean, but Capt (D) Newfoundland found the charge entirely unjustified. *Arvida* ROP; Dudley G. King, *Reminiscences* V, 106-7, DHH, 2000/5

29. ON 137 had been diverted southwards on 13 Oct. to search for survivors from the torpedoed independent SS *Stornest*. *St Croix* ROP; "Report of Master of Rescue Vessel 'Bury'"; MOD, *U-Boat War in the Atlantic* II, 55

30. Ironically, Dönitz concluded from this failure that it was the edge in Allied radar that put his boats at a disadvantage. C 4 was hardly the group to single out for superior radar performance. BdU, KTB, 19 Oct. 1942

bility happily served as a shield, and on 22 October the western local escort relieved the remnants of C 4.[31]

In his after-action analysis, Brainard commented that the "counter-action ... during the daylight attack on the 16th was most effective and unquestionably saved the convoy from further damage." He questioned Dobson's use of HF/DF but thought C 4 well trained and indoctrinated, and complimented Dobson for his initiative in using the Azores to refuel. Piers received particular commendation for "aggressive action against shadowing U-boats [which] unquestionably saved the convoy from further attack." His deployment of limited escort forces and "evasive turns by the convoy under cover of low visibility and away from HF/DF bearings" showed "splendid judgement" and "excellent technique."[32]

Material defects had once again had a dismal impact on operations. Both *St Croix* and *Celandine* suffered engine breakdowns that forced them to reduce speed for several hours and prevented the destroyer from rejoining ON 137 after refuelling—such problems were occurring with increasing regularity among the RCN and RN Towns. What is more, three escorts without radar for most of the voyage and three corvettes without asdic after the second gale was unacceptable. Brainard commented pointedly that "strenuous efforts toward material upkeep methods are essential if our basic task is to be successfully accomplished."[33]

American naval officers tried to recast the RCN in their own image. Brainard had noted in September that expansion in the RCN "has necessarily been so great that in many ships there can be little if any naval technical experience other than that acquired the hard way." He tried to interest the Canadians in adopting the USN system of making captains and ships' officers of the executive branch, rather than officers of the engineering branch and, in smaller vessels, the chief engine room artificer, directly responsible for technical maintenance repairs, and offered help in setting-up arrangements, including increased engineering training for executive officers. As this would necessitate a complete change in the way the RCN manned its ships and developed its officers, the offer was politely, and rightly, turned down. Captain Mainguy, acting FONF, observed that "this is a most sincere offer of assistance ... every possible advantage of it should be taken," but opposed training executive officers in engineering. Rear-Admiral Murray, who had recently become COAC, was typically frank:

> It is fully realized that the Canadian Naval executive personnel on the whole lack knowledge of ship maintenance, but they also, to some extent, lack knowledge of the tactical handling of ships employed as escorts.
>
> With the pleas from all sides for more and more escorts, ships have been sent to sea as soon as officers could be trained to handle them, and maintenance has taken second place in the training programme of Executive Officers.

Staff officers in Ottawa agreed, although Commander (E) W.W. Porteous thought it might be useful to have an American engineer officer on the staffs of Captain (D) in Halifax and St John's. The newly appointed VCNS, Rear-Admiral G.C. Jones, who had until then served as COAC and had some

---

31. *Restigouche* ROP; BdU, KTB, 19 Oct. 1942; and Convoy cover sheet, NARA, WNRC, RG 313, Red CTF 24, Convoy Series, ON-137 file, box 8707. The convoy was in position 47°28' N, 35°35' W (quadrant BD-42) at 1400z/20. In addition to Group *Panther*, ON 137 was not far from the U-boat refuelling zone in quadrant BD-57.

32. CTF 24 to COMINCH, 24 Oct. 1942—Third Endorsement to *Restigouche* ROP, NAC, RG 24, 6901, NSS 8910; CTF 24, "Report of Escort Operations—Convoy ON 137," 19 Nov. 1942; Atlantic Fleet Anti-Submarine Warfare Officer to CINCLANT, "Escort of Convoy ON-137," 5 Dec. 1942, DHH, 89/34, v 18, ON-137

33. "Report of Escort Operations"

firsthand knowledge of problems in maintenance and repair, instructed FONF "to reply in the sense that owing to the differences between the two services it is not seen how we can avail ourselves to advantage of his generous offer."[34] What the Naval Board was really after was not this kind of help, however well intentioned, but destroyers to replace those that had been lost, damaged, or like the old four-stackers were in need of replacement. On 5 October, the members had agreed on a minimum requirement of fourteen destroyers to keep C groups in a state of operational efficiency.[35]

A B-Dienst decrypt indicated that the next westbound convoy would, like ON 137, follow a southerly track, and BdU formed the *Panther* boats that had not operated against that convoy into a new group, *Puma*.[36] On 22 October, as ON 137 was escaping *Panther* and *Wotan* further to the west, Oberleutnant von Puttkamer in *U 443*, the southernmost boat in *Puma*, contacted ON 139 about 600 miles west of Ireland. C 2, the escort, consisted during this crossing of the Town class destroyers HMS *Broadway* (Lieutenant-Commander E.H. Chavasse, RN, SOE), *Sherwood*, and *Winchelsea*, the RN corvettes *Polyanthus* and *Primrose*, and the Canadian corvettes *Drumheller*, *Morden,* and *Pictou*. All but the Canadian ships had type 271 radar, and the commodore's ship, SS *Cairnvalona*, had HF/DF. This was strong protection for a convoy that included only twenty-eight merchant ships.

Fortunately, when sighted, ON 139 was too fast and too far south to be intercepted by most of *Puma*. Realizing that the other seven boats were poorly placed to close, BdU gave von Puttkamer permission to attack immediately. *U 443* worked around the periphery of the screen and then dived ahead of ON 139 at sunset to lay in wait. Once the escorts had passed over him, von Puttkamer torpedoed the cargo liner *Winnipeg II* and the tanker *Donax*, then went deep to avoid detection.[37] The British freighter *Tucurinca* hauled out of line and received permission to engage in rescue work, while *Morden* screened the operation. When *U 443* came back to periscope depth, *Morden* drove it down with minor damage and sent *Tucurinca* back to the convoy, not realizing that *Winnipeg II* was carrying a substantial crew and a large number of passengers, including elderly people, women, and children. By a considerable feat of seamanship, *Morden*'s crew saved more than 190 people.[38] Von Puttkamer remained submerged for eight hours after being depth charged. On surfacing he had to plow directly into a strong head wind to maintain contact, and finally noted ruefully, "It would take thirty-five hours to overtake the convoy with a speed advantage of 3 knots."[39] ON 139 had escaped. By its prompt counterattack after von Puttkamer's attack, C 2 had shaken off the shadower.[40]

---

34. CTF 24 to COAC and FONF, 21 Sep. 1942 and min 1, 29, and 31 Oct; COAC to SecNB, 10 Nov. 1942, NAC, RG 24, 3844, NSS 1017-10-35

35. NBM, 5 Oct. 1942

36. H. Bonatz, *Seekrieg im Äther: die Leistungen der Marine-Funkaufklärung 1939-1945* (Herford 1981), 238; MOD, *U-Boat War in the Atlantic* II, 55

37. BdU, KTB, 21-2 Oct. 1942; and *U 443*, KTB, 22 Oct. 1942; HMS *Broadway* ROP, ON 139, PRO, ADM 199/1338; *Polyanthus* ROP, ON 139; Rohwer, *Axis Submarine Successes*, 129

38. SS *Winnipeg II*, Attack on Merchant Vessel by Enemy Submarine, 22 Oct. 1942, NAC, RG 24, 4025, NSS 1062-13-10, v 11; Adm, *Preliminary Narrative: The War at Sea, Jan.-Dec. 1942* III, 446; *U 443*, KTB, 22 Oct. 1942; and *Morden*, Report of Attack on U-Boat, 2101/22 Oct. 1942 , NAC, RG 24, 6902, NSS 8910-331/65

39. *U 443* KTB, 23 Oct. 1942

40. BdU, KTB, 22-3 Oct. 1942; MOD, *U-Boat War in the Atlantic* II, 54-55; HMS *Broadway*, ROP, ON-139. Ships bound for the South Atlantic were subsequently detached from ON 139. The CAM freighter *Primrose Hill* was sunk 200 miles northwest of the Cape Verde Islands by *UD 5* on 29 Oct.

BdU directed the other *Puma* boats to pursue, but then ordered them into a new patrol line. Meanwhile, four submarines about to be replenished northwest of the Azores were designated Group *Südwärts* and ordered to close the convoy approaching their area. At 1309z on 23 October, Kapitänleutnant von Zitzewitz in *U 706* sighted smoke plumes at extreme range "approximately 5 hours ahead of its position by plot." This was the westbound ONS 138 of forty-eight merchant ships, escorted by B 2, a powerful group of three destroyers and three corvettes.[41] The SOE was Commander D.G. Macintyre, RN, in HMS *Hesperus*. Besides considerable destroyer command experience before the war, Macintyre had been at sea almost continually since September 1939 where he had achieved fame for capturing the celebrated U-boat ace Otto Kretschmer. With ONS 138, Macintyre's experience—plus the fact that he had three destroyers to work with—enabled him to lead *Südwärts* a merry chase.[42]

ONS 138 had sailed on 11 October. Like so many convoys that autumn, it immediately encountered several days of foul weather. As the slow convoy subsequently started working laboriously southwestwards, Macintyre wrestled with the same problem of steadily decreasing fuel states in his escorts as had Dobson a week earlier. The weather fortunately improved on 21 October, and B 2 took the opportunity to top up from an oiler in the convoy. (Oilers were a relatively new innovation to the Atlantic battle, and refuelling could be a tricky undertaking in which the ships had to manoeuvre within one to two hundred yards of one another and maintain their close relative positions for an hour or more as the oiler pumped fuel through a single hose.[43]) Upon sighting ONS 138 on the horizon two days later, von Zitzewitz shadowed all afternoon. He attempted a submerged attack in the evening twilight, but waited too long and was unable to see the convoy clearly as it passed overhead. Macintyre aggressively chased down HF/DF bearings that night as *Südwärts* converged. Von Zitzewitz was forced to move off at 2343z and lost contact, but *U 260* sighted the convoy in bright moonlight three hours later and by the forenoon three other boats were in contact. During daylight on 24 October, glassy seas and excellent visibility prevented the five submarines from attacking. Macintyre used all three destroyers ahead of the convoy to pursue HF/DF bearings and visual sightings of U-boats at extreme range on the horizon. The escort put down three submarines and depth charged two of them.[44] That evening, the convoy made a large course alteration as the destroyers laid smoke to deceive the shadowers. Von Zitzewitz again planned to attack from ahead while dived, but his periscope was spotted by the corvette *Gentian*. *U 706* was depth charged and lost contact; a second submarine attempting to attack from ahead during twilight, *U 662*, fired at an approaching escort, crash-dived and was unable to make a submerged attack. *U 260* had already been forced away in the growing halflight by an escort and lost the convoy. *U 301*, the only unit in contact

---

41. BdU, KTB, 23-6 Oct. 1942; *U 706*, KTB, 23 Oct. 1942; and MOD, *U-Boat War in the Atlantic* II, 54-55. Zitzwetiz initially thought that he had relocated ON 139 because the convoy he saw was on a similar course. Within hours U-Boat Command had concluded that a new convoy was involved and energetically redirected the search by Südwärts. They thought, however, that this was one of the OS series bound for west Africa. For a long time after the war some German historians, following conclusions reached by Dönitz, continued to believe that it was an OS convoy.

42. Macintyre, *U-Boat Killer*, 75-8. Macintyre was one of the most acerbic critics of the RCN in the postwar years.

43. US Naval Historical Center, Operational Archives, Paul R. Heineman papers, box 9, "Fuelling at Sea"

44. *U 260, U 301*, and *U 620*, KTBs, 24 Oct. 1942: *U 620* recorded "truly well-aimed depth charges" at 1135z which did little damage because the boat was at 160 m; *U 301* recorded charges at 1412z which did ño damage at depth 150 m.

after dark, realized that escorts had laid smoke but lost contact in the increasing gloom at midnight. B 2 had successfully shaken off five submarines.[45]

Dönitz was disappointed with the lack of success, but considered that as the U-boat captains were all on their first patrol they would have found attacking difficult in calm seas. He also noted that the search with such a small force of submarines might easily have missed the convoy completely.[46] For the Germans, the consistent ability of convoy escorts to detect U-boats was a disquieting trend. Unaware of ship-borne HF/DF, they continued to attribute the problem to radar.[47] On the Allied side, analysts in Liverpool, London, and Argentia considered the thirty-two hour engagement a model of how to disrupt shadowing submarines by aggressive use of HF/DF and a tactical ruse. With the benefit of German records it is now clear that environmental conditions were ideal for Macintyre's aggressive use of ship-borne HF/DF. Evasive steering and long-leg zigzags also made shadowing difficult for submariners relying on periodic glimpses of smoke plumes.[48] That said, Macintyre had clearly kept the initiative and demonstrated what could be achieved by a well-equipped, well-trained, cohesive, and numerically strong escort group.

German hopes for better results under prevailing weather conditions still lay in the eastbound convoys.[49] Patrol lines again straddled the convoy routes at both ends of the air gap: the new *Veilchen* group of eleven submarines northeast of Newfoundland, and *Puma*, of ten boats, in mid-Atlantic. Radio silence had been ordered for both, which greatly reduced the probability of successful evasive routing by the Allies. SC 105, HX 212, and SC 106 passed safely through *Veilchen*, and ONS 140 got by *Puma* under cover of darkness during the night of 25 to 26 October. *U 224* and *U 627* did sight SC 105 and its Iceland section on 26 and 27 October, but air cover effectively dealt with that threat when a Flying Fortress of 206 Squadron RAF destroyed *U 627* south of Iceland.[50] On 26 October, however, HX 212 pierced the centre of *Puma*'s patrol line, where it was sighted an hour before sunset by the seasoned Kapitänleutnant Seibicke in *U 436*, 430 miles southeast of Cape Farewell.[51] Within hours, despite filthy weather conditions, *U 575* closed in using Seibicke's homing signals. At 0300z on 27 October, the prolonged squalls ceased and Kapitänleutnant Heydemann observed HX 212 plunging through high swells. An escort drove off the experienced submariner but he shadowed for two hours, in part using *FuMB*, but then lost contact. [52]

This forty-four-ship convoy was escorted by A 3, consisting of the cutter USCG *Campbell* (Captain H.C. Fitz, USN, SOE), the four-stack destroyer USS *Badger,* and five Canadian corvettes—

45. *Gentian*, Report of Attack on U-Boat, 1803/24 Oct. 1942, PRO, ADM 237/126; Convoy signals, PRO, ADM 237/126; *U 260, U 301, U 620, U 662,* and *U 706*, KTBs, 23-5 Oct. 1943; BdU, KTB, 24-5 Oct. 1942; Macintyre, *U-Boat Killer*, 79-80

46. BdU, KTB, 26 Oct. 1942. Zitzewitz carefully analysed why his two attempts at attacking in twilight failed. *U 706*, KTB, 24-5 Oct. 1942

47. "Submarine Situation on 19.10," in BdU, KTB following entry for 31 Oct. 1942

48. *U 301*, KTB, 25 Oct. 1942

49. BdU, KTB, 24-5 Oct. 1942; Adm, OIC, U-Boat Situation Report, 26 Oct. 1942, PRO, ADM 223/15

50. *U 224*, KTB, 26-7 Oct. 1942; HMS *Hurricane* ROP, SC 105; BdU, KTB, 21-6 Oct. 1942; Rohwer and Hümmelchen, *Chronology of the War at Sea*, 170

51. *U 436*, KTB, 26-7 Oct. 1942; *Puma* was working to the northeast at high speed to search for a westbound convoy reported by B-Dienst. Dönitz commented later that this lucky interception showed "how uncertain were the indications on which U-boat operations were based and how very considerable a part was played by chance in the vast areas over which the war at sea was being waged." Dönitz, *Memoirs*, 274

52. *U 575*, KTB, 27 Oct. 1942. A *FuMB* signal was heard shortly before the escort closed. In Heydemann's judgment attacks had been possible only during the first part of the night while clouds obscured the moon.

two regular members of A 3, *Rosthern* and *Trillium*, and three on passage for Torch, *Ville de Québec*, *Alberni,* and *Summerside*. *Campbell* had recently been fitted with HF/DF, and *Trillium* and *Summerside* were the only escorts with type 271 radar.[53] As HX 212 plowed through heavy seas, HF/DF warnings from shore alerted Fitz that several submarines were operating against the convoy. BdU urged the submarine commanders to strike aggressively before dark and during the coming night as the convoy would be under air cover the following day, but the increasing seas were too high for submerged attacks in daylight.[54]

Because it was a few days after a full moon, Seibicke in *U 436* planned to attack well before moon rise when it would become more difficult to remain undetected. He approached from up-sea and got through the screen on the port side. It was "pretty dark," he recorded; "in addition we are continually being washed over by the seas. The shapes of the freighters can be glimpsed only from one wave top to the next. The boat is yawing heavily." At 2308z on 27 October, *U 436* fired five torpedoes at "a cluster of overlapping freighters," and hit three tankers in the two port columns; *Frontenac*, *Sourabaya*, and *Gurney E. Newlin*. *Frontenac* dropped out of the formation but later reached port safely. *Sourabaya* remained afloat for a time before going down, and *Gurney E. Newlin* was finished off later by another U-boat.[55] *U 436* escaped illumination from starshell in the rough seas, and five other U-boats used the illumination to home in on the convoy.[56] For the rest of the night, in rough sea conditions, escorts and six U-boats jostled in the moonlight.[57] The escorts forced down two boats and two others fired torpedoes that missed. At one point, *U 563* observed the "wild firing of starshells" at close range before a "destroyer tore past ahead in the light of the full moon at maximum speed whilst zigzagging."[58] The escort then re-emerged from a rain squall surprising the boat, which crash-dived. Shortly after 0300z on 28 October, *U 606*, under Oberleutnant Döhler, closed slowly to within striking range: "I am on the port corner. The ship stationed in the corner is a very large tub. A destroyer is providing escort on the vessel's outboard side. The line abreast stretches out to starboard with ships at close intervals." Döhler worked his way down sea, slipped past *Campbell* to fire two torpedoes at 0319z that missed the "large tub." Keeping a watchful eye on the escort, he moved in closer and at 0337z fired a second salvo that struck the 16,966-ton Norwegian whale-factory ship SS *Kosmos II*, which burst into flames. Despite heroic efforts to save the ship, she later fell victim to a second attack by *U 606*.[59]

---

53. Milner, *North Atlantic Run*, 175-6; interview with Lt-Cdr F.O. Gerity, RCNR, DHH, NHS 1650-239/15

54. *U 436* and *U 621*, KTBs, 27 Oct. 1942

55. BdU, KTB, 27 Oct. 1942; *U 436*, KTB, 27 Oct. 1942; CTU 24.1.3, Report of Escort, HX 212, DHH, 89/34, v 9; Rohwer, *Axis Submarine Successes*, 130; interview with the Master of SS *Frontenac*, 3 Dec. 1942, and Questionnaires for Ships Attacked by U-Boat, PRO, ADM 199/1710. Sunset was at 1831z/27.

56. *U 436*, KTB, 27 Oct. 1942; CTU 24.1.3, Report of Escort, HX 212; and interview with the Master of SS *Sourabaya*, 12 Nov. 1942, PRO, ADM 199/1710. The two corvettes rescued eighty-two survivors out of 161 crew and passengers aboard *Sourabaya* and twelve out of sixty-nine crew aboard *Gurney E. Newlin*. SS *Bic Island* picked up survivors from both ships, but it is not known how many because she was later torpedoed and all were lost.

57. CTU 24.1.3, Report of Escort, HX 212; *U 383, U 602, U 621, U 606, U 383, U 563,* and *U 443*, KTBs, 27-8 Oct. 1942 ; Rohwer, *Axis Submarine Successes*, 130

58. *U 383, U 443, U 563, U 602, U 606,* and *U 621*, KTBs, 27-8 Oct. 1942. *U 383* decided sea conditions were too rough to attack.

59. *U 563* and *U 606*, KTBs, 28 Oct. 1942; BdU, KTB, 27 Oct. 1942; Rohwer, *Axis Submarine Successes*, 130; interview with the Master of SS *Barrwhin*, 11 Nov. 1942, PRO, ADM 199/1710; Report by Finn Wathne (Norge), Chief Officer, Merchant Navy, PRO, ADM 199/1710; and "Report by Chief Officer Sperre of the Whaler *Kosmos II*," DHH, 89/34, v 9

At daybreak on 28 October the convoy came within range of VLR Liberators from Iceland. Squadron Leader T.M. Bulloch, the most successful pilot of the RAF's 120 Squadron demonstrated the value of very long-range aircraft as he cooperated most effectively with the escort during the daylight hours, forcing most of the U-boats out of position.[60] But after twilight the pack returned. A strong gale was still blowing with steep seas, cloudy skies, and rain and hail. The moon rose at 2150z making visibility two or three miles, but it was often less in the spray. Oberleutnant Count von Soden-Fraunhofen in *U 624* had lost sight of the convoy in the twilight at 1800z, picked up hydrophone effect and sighted HX 212 at 2215z, three miles distant, waited for rain and hail showers that obscured the moon and reduced visibility and then worked down sea like the previously successful attackers. At 0105z on 29 October he fired two torpedoes at a freighter and a large tanker, from ranges of 1,000 and 2,000 metres.[61] One of the torpedoes hit the American *Pan New York*, which burst into flames when her cargo of gasoline exploded. Von Soden-Fraunhofen crash-dived after the attack; "Everything was illuminated as if by day. The entire convoy complete with escorts could be seen ... starshells are being fired all around the convoy and I am being brightly illuminated by the burning tanker." *U 624* surfaced at 0220z and again went in pursuit, unseen by the escort in the spray and high seas. "The bridge was almost continually awash and the bridge watchkeepers were frequently dashed onto the gratings by the breakers." He moved slowly up sea in what he described as tacking movements. Five other boats had also seen the flames and closed the convoy. Von Soden-Fraunhofen re-established contact with stragglers and at 0415z, with his third torpedo, hit the 4,000-ton Canadian-flag freighter *Bic Island*, lagging astern of the second column. She went down like a stone with all hands, including survivors from SS *Sourabaya* and *Gurney E. Newlin*. At 0420z, a second boat, *U 224*, penetrated the port side screen and fired three torpedoes at two merchant ships, but missed.[62] Once again the difficult visual, asdic, and radar conditions allowed the U-boats to escape undetected, but because air cover had been so effective the previous day Dönitz ordered Group *Puma* to break off operations against HX 212 after daybreak except for boats "still in favourable position for attack."[63]

A misunderstanding in communications at this point led to the needless loss of the British freighter *Barrwhin*, which was returning with survivors under the escort of *Rosthern*. The corvette had prevented *U 563* from attacking the merchant ship on the afternoon of 28 October, but on receiving instructions to "return with 14," Commander P.B. Cross of *Rosthern* took it to mean "return with a speed of 14 knots" rather than with ship number 14. *Rosthern* thus increased speed

---

60. The escort commander noted that "RT communication with the plane was excellent and the assistance rendered was intelligent, timely and most valuable." CTU 24.1.3, Report of Escort, HX 212; *U 436, U 441, U 443, U 224, U 383, U602,* and *U 621,* KTBs, 28-9 Oct. 1942. Dönitz noted that "boats were often forced to retire and submerge" because of aircraft. BdU, KTB, 28 Oct. 1942

61. Von Soden's approach in the limited visibility was made easier because the convoy was poorly darkened. *U 624,* KTB, 29 Oct. 1942

62. *U 624* and *U 224,* KTBs, 29 Oct. 1942; and Rohwer, *Axis Submarine Successes,* 130. Rohwer gives the time that *U 224* sank SS *Bic Island* as 2215z/28, six hours before she was torpedoed. The BdU KTB gives the correct time. *U 224* observed the ship sinking, whereas *U 624* did not observe her target being hit or sinking.

63. At 0458z *Ville de Québec* smelled diesel exhaust fumes to windward while screening the port beam. These may have been from *U 443,* which had a defective starboard diesel and was closing to attack. Oberleutnant von Puttkamer submerged at 0555z when he saw an escort approaching. *Ville de Québec* failed to make contact, but sense of smell had proven to be the group's most effective sensor this night. *U 443, U 606, U 624,* and *U 383,* KTBs, 29 Oct. 1942; BdU, KTB, 29 Oct. 1942; and CTU 24.1.3, Report of Escort, HX 212

to rejoin, pausing on the way to persuade the remaining thirteen men, on the after deck of the burning *Pan New York*, to jump into the flaming sea to be rescued. Cross then finished off the blazing wreck with gunfire and depth charges and, having discovered his misinterpretation of the SOE's signal, went off to search for the *Barrwhin*. Tragically, it was *U 436* that found and, after dusk, sank the merchant ship. She had on board fifty-four of her own crew and sixty survivors from *Kosmos II*. Ninety survived and were picked up on the following day by HMCS *Kenogami*, in company with *Shediac* on passage independently to Great Britain.[64]

HX 212 was now well within aircraft range from Britain and reached safety without further incidents. Twelve submarines had operated against the convoy, which with a poorly equipped ad hoc group of seven escorts had lost six merchant ships to night attacks during its four-day ordeal. Typically for convoy battles, only four of the twelve U-boats had been responsible for the torpedoings. Allied post-action reviews concluded that A 3 had done as well as could be expected in the weather conditions, while U-Boat Command was pleased by *Puma*'s successes despite the heavy seas and considered that these conditions had handicapped the escorts.[65] Not for the first time, both American and Canadian authorities, however, worried about mix-ups resulting from different USN and RCN procedures, and Rear-Admiral Jones in Ottawa recommended that "every effort be made to divorce our corvettes in A 3 Group from the US Coast Guard Cutters."[66]

Operation Torch was now imminent. This major amphibious assault, which took place on 8 November 1942, involved sea lift on a scale not previously attempted and the demands for escorts were heavy. Canada's escort force in the North Atlantic was directly affected by the deployment of seventeen of the best-equipped corvettes, as recounted in Chapter 8 and 11. The Allies were able to achieve complete surprise despite having sent large armadas across the oceans from the United States and the British Isles. Although the U-boats were poorly placed to react to Torch during the final run-up to the landings, they dealt two Atlantic trade convoys heavy blows. Both convoys, SL 125 and SC 107, had weak escorts and encountered large packs. SL 125, the last such convoy from west Africa for six months because of the drain by Torch on Allied escort forces, was mauled off northwest Africa by ten boats in favourable weather over a period of seven days, 26 October to 1 November. Defended by only four corvettes, it lost twelve of thirty-seven merchant ships. As SL 125 pushed northwards past Madeira it drew the U-boat group in the area, *Streitaxt*, with it. As a result, the convoy became what Corelli Barnett called "an unwitting sacrificial decoy," and the Torch convoys moving towards the Gibraltar approaches remained unnoticed.[67]

SC 107, the second convoy that was to suffer heavily, had sailed from New York on 24 October, and by the time feeder convoys had joined it had swelled to forty-two ships. U-boat Command, aware of the normal convoy tracks, had positioned the *Veilchen* patrol line, which now included

---

64. *U 436* and *U 441*, KTBs, 29 Oct. 1942; *Rosthern* ROP, 24 Oct.–1 Nov. 1942, PRO, ADM 199/717; "Report by Master and Chief Officer of SS *Barrwhin*," 30 Oct. 1942, PRO, ADM 199/1710; and Rohwer, *Axis Submarine Successes*, 131. HMCS *Kenogami* and *Shediac* were sailing to the UK to reinforce C 1 with ON-143.

65. BdU, KTB, 29 Oct. 1942

66. The only additional sinking on 29 Oct. was a fast independent of 11,330 tons, SS *Abosso*, torpedoed by *U 575*, Rohwer, *Axis Submarine Successes*, 131; CTF 24 to C-in-C US Atlantic Fleet, "Report of Escort Operations—Convoy HX 212"; CTU 24.1.3, Report of Escort HX 212; Memo to DOD from SO (A/S), 30 Dec. 1942, and Flag Officer, Newfoundland Force to the SecNB, 11 Dec. 1942, both in DHH, 89/34, v 9, HX-212

67. C. Barnett, *Engage the Enemy More Closely* (London 1991), 556; MOD, *U-Boat War in the Atlantic* II, 61-4; Roskill, *War At Sea* II, 212; Hinsley, *British Intelligence* II, 476-9, 556-7, and 634-40

thirteen boats, northeast of Newfoundland, where eastbound convoys entered the air gap. In addition, as seen in Chapter 8, there were five large type IX U-boats bound for Halifax and the Gulf of St Lawrence south and east of the island. BdU first received hard intelligence about SC 107 on 29 October, when B-Dienst decrypted a signal altering its route from the West Ocean Meeting Point. *Veilchen's* patrol line was accordingly rearranged to put it astride SC 107's new track.[68] The next day Kapitänleutnant H. Schneider in *U 522*, one of the type IXs south of Newfoundland, sighted a feeder convoy and then, when about to surface after being put down by an RCAF aircraft, observed SC 107 through his periscope: "Mastheads and funnels popped up on the starboard side, a convoy, range approximately 5 nautical miles, course 080." *U 522* surfaced and reported.[69] BdU was now certain that the convoy was heading for the centre of *Veilchen* and ordered three of the additional type IXs in the area to close. SC 107 would have to fight its way through, rather than around, an exceptionally strong and well-prepared force. All but four of the fifteen U-boats eventually involved in the seven-day battle were seasoned veterans with several previous patrols to their credit. During their encounters with the convoy, these experienced commanders would make extensive use of *FuMB* to evade escorts, and also glean valuable information from listening to the escorts' voice net on which escorts and aircraft exchanged tactical information, largely in the clear. For example, in a KTB entry on 3 November, *U 84*'s captain noted that "all of the enemy's defensive measures can be intercepted on the convoy voice nets immediately after successful attacks."[70]

The Operational Intelligence Centre in Ottawa had become aware of increasing U-boat activity northeast of Newfoundland, and on 30 October, two Hudsons of 145 Squadron RCAF made a sweep based on HF/DF intelligence ahead of SC 107.[71] Almost at the limit of their endurance, some 290 miles east of Torbay, the aircraft sighted and sank *U 658*, in the centre of *Veilchen*. The same day, but much closer to SC 107, a Digby of 10 Squadron destroyed *U 520*, which had been ordered to shadow the convoy. On 31 October another Hudson from 145 Squadron attacked and put down *U 521*. The Catalinas of 116 Squadron sent out from Botwood to provide cover on 1 November forced several U-boats to dive, but had difficulty maintaining contact with the convoy. Despite these successes, the activities of *Veilchen*, the existence of which still appears to have been unsuspected by convoy routing authorities, were not overly disrupted.[72]

The mid-ocean group entrusted with the protection of SC 107 was C 4, consisting of the destroyer *Restigouche*, and the corvettes *Amherst*, *Arvida*, *Algoma* and HMS *Celandine*. The stability and cohesion so necessary to an escort group simply did not exist in C 4. Although an experienced SOE,

---

68. Douglas and Rohwer, "Most Thankless Task Revisited," 210, Bonatz, *Seekrieg im Äther*, 238

69. *U 522*, KTB, 30 Oct. 1942

70. The KTBs for *U 71*, *U 84*, *U 521*, and *U 571* in particular cite tactical decisions based on information from *FuMB*. Regarding the interception of voice transmissions, *U 522*'s KTB for 3 Nov. in a summary of "lessons learned" observed "the convoy voice frequency (124.5 m) was constantly in use during attacks. During the period that there was still air cover off Newfoundland this frequency appeared to be used as a communications net with aircraft ground stations and a voice net between the aircraft and the convoy commander."

71. "Ottawa W/T Procedures," in "'Y' Summary no. 12," Nov. 1942, 2, NAC

72. Douglas, *Creation of a National Air Force*, 527-9. Group *Veilchen*, after the sinking of *U 658* on 30 Oct., consisted of twelve type VII boats. Two type IX boats, *U 521* and *U 522*, joined the pack after trailing SC 107 for two days. *U 437*, at the southern tip of the patrol line on 29 Oct., had broadcast a sighting report on ON 140. This may have suggested the presence of U-boats, but it was not enough to reveal the extent of the line. SC 107 received warnings from Ottawa of the type IX boats encountered on 30 Oct., but no routing diversions. *U 71*, *U 84*, *U 89*, *U 132*, *U 381*, *U 402*, *U 437*, *U 438*, *U 442*, *U 454*, *U 521*, *U 522*, *U 571*, and *U 704*, KTBs, 30 Oct.–.6 Nov. 1942

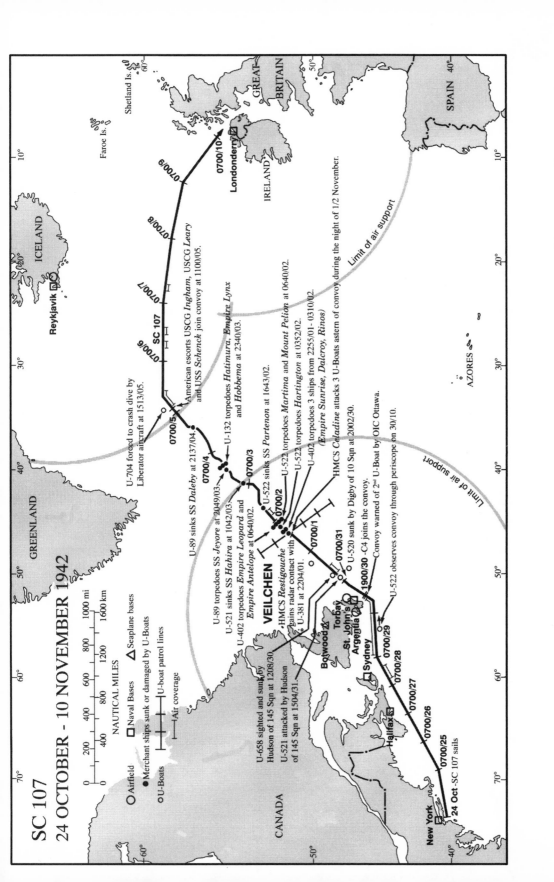

SC 107
24 OCTOBER - 10 NOVEMBER 1942

ICELAND

Reykjavík

GREENLAND

Faroe Is.

Shetland Is.

GREAT BRITAIN

IRELAND

Londonderry

0700/9

0700/8

0700/7

SC 107

0700/6

U-704 forced to crash dive by
Liberator aircraft at 1513/05.

American escorts USCG *Ingham*, USCG *Leary*
and USS *Schenck* join convoy at 1100/05.

U-132 torpedoes *Hatimura*, *Empire Lynx*
and *Hobbema* at 2340/03.

0700/5

0700/4

U-89 sinks SS *Daleby* at 2137/04.

U-522 sinks SS *Partenon* at 1643/02.

U-522 torpedoes *Martima* and *Mount Pelion* at 0640/02.

0700/3

U-522 torpedoes *Hartington* at 0352/02.

U-89 torpedoes SS *Jeypore* at 2049/03.

U-402 torpedoes 3 ships from 2255/01- 0310/02.
(*Empire Sunrise*, *Dalcroy*, *Rinos*)

U-521 sinks SS *Hahira* at 1042/03.

0700/2

U-522 sinks SS

U-402 torpedoes *Empire Leopard* and
Empire Antelope at 0640/02.

HMCS *Celadine* attacks 3 U-Boats astern of convoy during the night of 1/2 November.

0700/1

Limit of air support

0700/31

U-520 sunk by Digby of 10 Sqn at 2002/30.

VEILCHEN

HMCS *Restigouche*
gains radar contact with
U-381 at 2204/01.

1900/30 -C4 joins the convoy.

Convoy warned of 2ⁿᵈ U-Boat by OIC Ottawa.

U-522 observes convoy through periscope on 30/10.

U-658 sighted and sunk by
Hudson of 145 Sqn at 1208/30.

U-521 attacked by Hudson
of 145 Sqn at 1504/31.

Botwood

Torbay

St. John's

Argentia

Sydney

0700/29

0700/28

0700/27

0700/26

CANADA

0700/25

Halifax

New York

24 Oct -SC 107 sails

SPAIN

Limit of air support

AZORES

NAUTICAL MILES

0 200 400 600 800 1000 mi

0 400 800 1200 1600 km

○ Airfield   □ Naval Bases

☐ Seaplane bases

● Merchant ships sunk or damaged by U-Boats

○U-Boats   ⊢ U-boat patrol lines

━ Air coverage

Restigouche's captain, Lieutenant-Commander Piers, had only recently taken over C 4 when the group's other regular destroyer had gone into refit. The commanding officers of *Amherst* and *Arvida* had assumed command only five weeks earlier and had made only one crossing with C 4, while *Algoma* and a fifth corvette, *Moose Jaw*, which would join late on 2 November during the battle, were only with the group for passage to Torch. *Celandine* was the only escort with type 271, but it was unserviceable throughout the most critical days of the battle. *Restigouche* and the rescue ship *Stockport* both had HF/DF. Piers, an experienced practitioner with HF/DF, planned to pounce immediately on bearings of U-boat transmissions, but as events unfolded the relatively small C 4 would be overwhelmed.[73]

U 522's first contact report on 30 October was intercepted ashore and the convoy was warned that it was being shadowed. When Schneider subsequently reported the main convoy from astern, the signals were intercepted by *Restigouche* and *Stockport*. Piers promptly requested that *Columbia*, of the Westerm Local Escort Force group that had just turned over to C 4, investigate. She put down *U 522* and dropped depth charges as a scare tactic, while the U-boat returned fire with torpedoes. This engagement was inconclusive, but *U 522* lost the convoy and would not regain contact until late on 2 November.[74] Meanwhile, SC 107 plowed northeastwards towards *Veilchen* throughout 31 October. BdU, confident that the convoy was heading for the centre of the patrol line, disregarded other convoys in the vicinity and shortened the length of *Veilchen*'s patrol line to reduce the chances that the convoy could slip through in low visibility.[75] The strategy succeeded two hours after sunrise on 1 November, when *U 381* in the middle of the line sighted ships to the north. *Restigouche* and *Stockport* detected the transmission and, after asking the convoy commodore to make an emergency turn to port, Piers promptly chased down the bearing, obtaining a disappearing radar contact.

Convoy battles were often avoided when the shadowing U-boat was driven off and could not re-establish contact, but this occasion was different.[76] BdU immediately ordered the remainder of *Veilchen* to converge on the convoy. The two ends of the patrol line were equidistant from SC 107 and closed like a hinge with the most distant boats only eighty-one miles away. Moreover, moderate northwesterly winds and a calm sea enabled the submarines to cover the distance easily as they converged from both sides.[77] By sunset on 1 November five were in contact even though several had been put down by aircraft during the afternoon. Reports by the U-boats produced constant HF/DF bearings and Piers made "vigorous sorties in the direction of the likely threat" and sent *Celandine* to investigate a transmission from *U 704*, which kept the U-boat down until after dusk. Unhappily, *Celandine*'s type 271 now broke down. *Arvida*'s radar was also unserviceable, so when Piers ordered a night screen he knew that it would provide only limited protection.[78]

---

73. Douglas and Rohwer "Most Thankless Task," 215. Piers later wrote that he discussed his planned tactics with the corvette captains prior to sailing, but as he only met SC 107 two hours after sailing there was no opportunity to exercise his doctrine.

74. *Columbia* ROP, SC 107, 6 Nov. 1942 , RG 24, 11093, 48-2-2, v 73; *U 522*, KTB, 30 Oct. 1942

75. *U 402*, KTB, 31 Oct. 1942. In good visibility the masthead of a merchant ship would be seen at roughly thirteen miles by day. Unknown to U-Boat Command the unit directly on the convoy MLA at the centre of the *Veilchen* line, *U 658*, had been sunk on 30 Oct. By closing the distance between boats BdU also inadvertently compensated for the gap created by loss of this submarine.

76. *U 381*, KTB, 1 Nov. 1942

77. BdU, KTB, 1 Nov. 1942

78. Ibid; *Restigouche* ROP, SC-107

Lieutenant-Commanders D.W Piers and D.W. Groos in June 1943. They were CO and First Lieutenant of HMCS *Restigouche* during the battle for SC 107. (NAC, PA 204363)

Preserving the flow of supplies and war materiel to the United Kingdom was the raison d'etre of the Battle of the Atlantic:

Top: Longshoremen loading cases of TNT explosive in the hold of an unidentified merchant ship, 29 November 1941, Halifax, Nova Scotia. (NAC PA 106527)

Bottom: An aerial view of a cargo vessel, its deck laden with packing crates and aircraft. (NAC PA 204590)

The attackers took full advantage. When after dark *Restigouche* illuminated *U 71* with starshell after gaining contact with radar, this also forced *U 402*, commanded by the audacious Oberleutnant Baron von Förstner, to break away after he had moved up SC 107's starboard side. *Restigouche* and *Arvida* kept *U 402* from closing for several hours, but at 2355z on 1 November, von Förstner exploited the gap in the screen on the starboard side and torpedoed *Empire Sunrise*, the third ship in the ninth column. The escorts immediately executed Raspberry, and *U 402* dived when *Arvida* closed. *Restigouche,* astern of the convoy, gained a fleeting asdic contact and dropped ten depth charges. *U 402* recorded these as having been "poorly aimed," surfaced and worked around the rear of the convoy so as to be able to attack from the port side where ships would be silhouetted against the moon.

Meanwhile, *U 381*, having observed explosions and starshells, approached the convoy from the port quarter and at 0305z on 2 November fired a spread of four torpedoes at *Restigouche*. They missed and the submarine was forced down. Five minutes later, von Förstner attacked from the port bow, evading *Amherst*, the only escort on that side. He torpedoed the lead ships in the first and second columns, *Dalcroy* and *Rinos*. The escorts again carried out asdic and starshell sweeps around the convoy, but Schneider in *U 522* was able to penetrate from the starboard side and at 0352z torpedoed *Hartington*, the third ship in the seventh column. At about the same time, *U 402* was making another approach from the port side, but was driven under by fire from *Amherst* and a merchant ship. *U 84*, coming up from astern, fired torpedoes at a stationary damaged merchant ship, probably the abandoned *Empire Stockport*, eventually sinking her.

By chance, at 0640z, von Förstner and Schneider launched simultaneous attacks from the convoy's port and starboard sides. Von Förstner managed to evade *Amherst* on the port bow and *Celandine*, which had finally rejoined and was now on the port quarter. He torpedoed the second and third ships in the second column, *Empire Leopard* and *Empire Antelope*. Meanwhile, closing from starboard, and avoiding *Algoma* and *Arvida*, Schneider torpedoed the fourth ships in the ninth and seventh columns, *Martima* and *Mount Pelion*. C 4 again carried out a Raspberry, which revealed *U 522* who was forced under. Roughly an hour later "the first streaks of dawn arrived," Piers later reported, "to relieve a most critical situation."[79] SC 107 had lost eight ships in less than seven hours —three of the vessels hit did not sink immediately but were finished off astern by other boats. Aided by explosions, starshell, and snowflake visible for miles, five additional U-boats had made contact with the convoy during the night, augmenting the five that had already been in touch at sunset. While half of the ten submarine captains had closed and attacked, two—von Förstner, who torpedoed five ships, and Schneider, who torpedoed three—were primarily responsible for the rout. In return, *U 437* was sufficiently damaged by eight "well-aimed depth charges" to break off and turn for home.[80]

Fog and rain cloaked SC 107 during the daylight hours on 2 November. The convoy was already in the "black pit" of the air gap.[81] Piers reorganized his screen with *Moose Jaw*, which had joined before first light, on the port bow, *Algoma* to starboard, *Restigouche* in the van, and *Celandine*

---

79. *Restigouche* ROP, SC 107

80. *U 84, U 89, U 132, U 402, U 437, U 438, U 442, U 521,* and *U 522,* KTBs, 2-3 Nov. 1942; Douglas and Rohwer, "Most Thankless Task," 216-17; Rohwer, *Axis Submarine Successes,* 132-7

81. A Catalina from Botwood, flying in marginal conditions and without functioning radar, could not find SC 107. Douglas, *Creation of a National Air Force,* 529

ahead at the limit of visibility. *Amherst* and *Arvida* covered *Stockport* astern. Piers tried to take advantage of rain and fog by bold evasive turns and aggressive thrusts down HF/DF bearings. *Veilchen* achieved only sporadic contact in the patchy visibility, but *U 522* was able to work up the starboard side of the convoy, and at 1643z when it emerged from a fog bank, Schneider fired two torpedoes that sank the fifth ship in the eighth column, SS *Parthenon*.[82] *Celandine*, sent out in the fog to investigate an HF/DF bearing, spent the next twenty-four hours searching for the convoy without benefit of radar, but during the night the destroyer HMS *Vanessa*, from B 2, equipped with type 271 radar and HF/DF, reinforced the screen. BdU now received a decrypt from B-Dienst of a routing signal giving details of SC 107's planned track. Boats were instructed to move along with the convoy as the chances of regaining contact were good.[83] Unseen, the submarines on SC 107's periphery exchanged information based on sound bearings and glimpses of escorts.[84] Towards morning the visibility began improving and several boats encountered ships of the convoy. Oberleutnant R. Franzius in *U 438* had to make several violent alterations of course to avoid collision. "I cannot understand," he wrote in his war diary, "how I can remain undetected ... The freighters must have felt perfectly secure in the fog."[85]

Von Förstner in *U 402* surfaced in the morning twilight on 3 November and closed SC 107's port bow where he was spotted by *Amherst*. The corvette's commanding officer, Lieutenant L.C. Audette, climbed the mast and directed fire on the submarine with one hand crooked around the mast and his free hand grasping his binoculars, but von Förstner got away on the surface.[86] Shortly afterwards, *U 521*, closing from the starboard side submerged, observed a tanker and fired, torpedoing the second ship in the eighth column. SS *Hahira*, Piers wrote, "went up in a massive burst of flame and smoke." *Arvida* attacked the submarine, forcing it to go deep.[87] The ever-aggressive von Förstner characteristically dived to attack on sighting *Restigouche* ahead of SC 107 at 1245z. Piers subsequently attacked a "doubtful" asdic contact. The depth charges exploded "close aboard" *U 402*, putting both diesels out of action for some time. When von Förstner shook off his attacker he raised his periscope and found that he was inside the convoy. A "periscope was sighted in between the third and fourth columns," Piers wrote. "Most ships in Convoy blazed away with every gun they had." *U 402* aborted the attack and dropped astern.[88] *Hahira*'s crew were rescued by the indefatigable *Stockport*. This small converted coastal passenger ship was now seriously overcrowded with 256 survivors from seven ships, a record for the Rescue Service that would stand for

---

82. The convoy was zigzagging, but an alteration brought it towards *U 522* at the right moment. Rohwer, *Axis Submarine Successes*, 132-3; *U 522*, KTB, 2 Nov. 1942

83. Douglas and Rohwer, "Most Thankless Task," 210; *U 521*, KTB, 2 Nov. 1943

84. *U 404*'s KTB includes several such reports. *Restigouche* and *Stockport* obtained several HF/DF bearings, many of which were investigated. *Restigouche* ROP

85. *U 438*, KTB, 3 Nov. 1942; BdU, KTB, 2 Nov. 1942; *U 522*, KTB, 2 Nov. 1942; Douglas, *Creation of a National Air Force*, 529; Douglas and Rohwer, "The Most Thankless Task," 217

86. Audette, *Memoirs*; *U 402*, KTB, 3 Nov. 1942

87. *U 521*, KTB, The fires in *Hahira* were put out by her suppression system and the derelict fell astern along with *U 521* which fired a *coup de grace* at 1415z .

88. *Restigouche* ROP; *U 402*, KTB. *Restigouche* dropped astern to search without success after Piers decided that a coordinated Artichoke by all escorts would leave the van exposed with other U-boats known to be in the vicinity. The depth charging forced *U 402* from the battle. Only one diesel was repaired within a few hours and von Förstner now had insufficient speed to regain contact.

the rest of the war; therefore, Piers directed two USN harbour tugs with the convoy on passage to Iceland to assist in rescue duties.

Celandine rejoined after dark, having attacked three U-boats astern of the convoy during the day—"The enemy has become smarter after all," noted *U 522's* Schneider in his war diary as he tried to evade the corvette at 1250z, "and has stationed a destroyer [sic] as a distant escort"— and the screen was at full strength as night brought conditions that favoured surface attacks.[89] *Veilchen* was soon busy and three submarines attacked shortly after sunset at 1941z. Two boats missed, but the convoy then made an evasive turn that took it directly towards *U 89*. Korvettenkapitän Lohmann evaded *Vanessa* on the port bow and *Moose Jaw* on the starboard— two strangers to C 4 and to each other—5,000 yards from the main body. His first two salvoes missed, but a stern shot at 2049z struck SS *Jeypore*, the convoy commodore's ship at the head of the fifth column, which swung out of line wildly, barely missing the vessels astern of her in nearby columns. A Raspberry was ordered, but it was not coordinated. *Moose Jaw* and *Algoma* dropped back to hunt *U 89*, and subsequently chased off another submarine closing to attack.[90] This left a yawning gap in the van, which *U 132* exploited, torpedoing the second freighters in the seventh and ninth columns, *Hatimura* and *Empire Lynx*, as well as *Hobbema* at the head of the eighth column. Both *Hatimura* and *Hobbema* were carrying explosives and ammunition, and, at 2340z, the night erupted in a massive explosion. The shock wave bounced *Arvida's* stern out of the water, damaged *Algoma's* engine, and a sailor recording events on the bridge of *Restigouche* thought the destroyer had been torpedoed.[91] The crew of SS *Titus*, thinking their ship had been hit, abandoned ship but the master subsequently reboarded with a some of his men, rescued survivors from *Empire Lynx* and *Hatimura*, and with this new combined crew steamed the ship independently to Liverpool.[92] *U 132*, likely a victim of its own success, was never heard from again. Over the next hours of darkness four submarines launched unsuccessful attacks, while escorts thwarted two other approaches.[93]

First light brought some respite. Good visibility during the early daylight hours of 4 November kept the shadowing U-boats at arm's length as SC 107 streamed northeastwards on its third day in the air gap. That afternoon Piers despatched the rescue vessels, filled to capacity with more than three hundred survivors, to Iceland along with an oiler, all escorted by *Celandine* and *Arvida*, both

---

89. *Celandine's* skirmish with *U 522* developed into a classic illustration of how a determined escort could eliminate an aggressive submarine as a threat. *Celandine* opened fire at extreme 4-inch gun range immediately on sighting the U-boat to force it down. Because the gun layer and trainer were unable to see the target, "it was a matter of keeping the gun still and training the ship." *U 522* was seen to "crash dive at once with much splash and foam." The corvette promptly closed at "emergency full speed"and zig-zagged. *U 522* fired two torpedoes which were seen and evaded. *Celandine* eventually gained asdic contact and dropped depth charges which were recorded by *U 522* as "well-placed" and caused various problems. *U 522* withdrew from the pursuit of SC 107 to effect repairs. HMS *Celandine* ROP, SC 107; *U 522*, KTB, 3 Nov. 1942.

90. *U 89* and *U 704*, KTBs. *U 89* was put down at 2138z by an escort which dropped depth charges, probably *Moose Jaw*. *U 704* was first driven off repeatedly by starshells at 2115z and then an hour later on a new approach taken under fire and dived.

91. *Restigouche* ROP, SC 107. The KTB of six boats record a heavy underwater explosion and *U 84* heard an escort report a heavy explosion directly below on the convoy net; *Arvida* dropped two depth charges on a doubtful contact at 2337z which may have countermined the explosives in one of the sinking ammunition carriers. E. Zimmermann, "Analysis of U-Boat Attacks on Convoy SC 107"; Douglas and Rohwer, "Most Thankless Task," 218-19

92. Bezemer, K.W.L. *Geschiedenes van de Nederlandse Koopvaardij in de Tweede Wereldoorlog* II, 817

93. *U 71*, *U 381*, *U 442*, and *U 521*, KTBs

low on fuel.[94] By then rain and hail had moved in. The remaining attackers attempted to close in but were driven off by escorts.[95]

By this stage of the battle *Veilchen* was shrinking, six boats having broken off because of damage or insufficient fuel.[96] However, an hour after twilight on 4 November, Lohmann in *U 89*, with a last determined effort, battled the high swell, steep seas, and wet conditions on the bridge, to move in astern of *Moose Jaw*. Under bright northern lights he sank the port wing ship, SS *Daleby*. Easily evading detection in the lively sea state, Lohmann went off to reload and report his success, as the escorts again fired starshell over the convoy.[97] Six submarines were in contact during the night, but *U 89* made the only attack. On 5 November welcome reinforcements arrived from Iceland. Three American escorts arrived at dawn and "the long awaited Liberator" joined, seriously damaging *U 89* on the basis of *Restigouche*'s HF/DF bearing at 1222z. The same aircraft made *U 704* crash-dive on the strength of another bearing from the destroyer at 1513z, forced the boats that were left to keep a low profile, and departed at dusk "having had a good day's sport."[98] After detaching the Iceland section of the convoy with the three American escorts, SC 107 limped into British waters on 10 November with no further losses.[99]

Over the seven days since SC 107 had first been sighted by *U 522* south of Cape Race to when *Veilchen* withdrew southeast of Greenland, the convoy had covered 1,100 miles, almost two-thirds of the distance across the Atlantic. Hounded across the air gap by fifteen U-boats, it had lost fifteen of its forty-two ships.[100] Although the RCAF had destroyed two submarines in the opening phase of the battle, SC 107's thin escort had simply been overwhelmed. Large numbers of U-boats were in contact during the two nights when conditions were favourable for attack—ten during the night of 1 to 2 November and eight on the night of 3 to 4 November. Commodore H.E. Reid, who had replaced Rear-Admiral Murray as FONF, described it as "one of the most disastrous convoys we have ever had." Captain Hewlett Thebaud, USN, now commanding Task Group 24.7 at Londonderry, concluded after reading Piers's report of proceedings that "against such a scale of attack, a group of this kind cannot be expected to suffer other than heavy losses." Piers had earned a good reputation among USN observers, and if he had been in the position of a permanent group commander, in a stronger group that was not subject to so much change in composition, they clearly thought he could have done better.

---

94. *Celandine* had repaired her type 271 with a spare part from HMS *Vanessa* and after her numerous encounters with U-boats was low on depth charges. *Celandine* ROP

95. *U 71*, *U 84*, and *U 704*, KTBs, 4 Nov. 1942

96. *U 437* had broken off on 2 Nov. because of damage, *U 454* dropped out during the night of 2/3 Nov. because of insufficient fuel, *U 402* and *U 522* were unable to pursue further after depth chargings on 3 Nov., and *U 442* and *U 571* detached because of insufficient fuel on 4 Nov. Various KTBs

97. *Restigouche* ROP, SC 107; *U 89* and other boats, KTBs, 5 Nov. 1942

98. U-boats were forced to dive by aircraft at least eleven times during the daylight hours on 5 Nov. *U 84*, *U 89*, *U 438*, *U 521*, and *U 704*, KTBs

99. *U 89*, *U 521*, and *U 704*, KTBs, 5-6 Nov. 1942; BdU, K

100. The efficient work, almost all at night under harrowing conditions, by the rescue vessels, escorts, and ships in SC 107 was noteworthy in limiting the loss of life. According to *Lloyd's War Losses* I, 560-71, the fifteen ships sunk carried 767 people of which 150 were lost. By contrast, the twelve ships sunk in SL 125 carried 1191, of which 405 were lost.TB, 5-6 Nov. 1942; *Restigouche* ROP, SC 107; Douglas and Rohwer, "Most Thankless Task," 219

In the climate then prevailing in Britain, the dreadful losses suffered by a convoy under Canadian escort received no sympathy at all. The arrival on 19 November of the new C-in-C Western Approaches, Admiral Sir Max Horton (see Chapter 11), only hardened British naval opinion. "The safety of our trade," observed Horton after reading Piers's report, "is one of the most important, if not the most important, consideration [sic] in this war." A convoy's defence should be entrusted to "an experienced and seasoned leader capable of adjusting his tactics and dispositions to meet the severe threat encountered," and not, he inferred, to a twenty-six-year-old lieutenant with only five years seniority. If C 4 had been commanded by a more qualified officer, Horton argued, "the losses might well have been cut down and some casualties inflicted on the enemy." Staff officers in the Admiralty claimed incorrectly that most of the convoy's HF/DF bearings "were not of signals made by U-boats shadowing the convoy"[101] and concluded that "the Canadian escorts were insufficiently trained in the use of their equipment and the handling of their ships both in individual and group tactics."[102] There was substance in these criticisms, but they hit hard nonetheless. "I very strongly resent the whole tone of this letter," complained Captain Roger Bidwell, Chief of Staff at St John's, and Commodore Reid argued to NSHQ that Piers "has had as much convoy escort experience, it is supposed, as any other officer so employed at this time. He had been in command of 'Restigouche' since June 1941, and on several occasions has been Senior Officer of the group."[103] Such protestations, of which the RN probably remained unaware, would do nothing to quell rising discontent in England about the RCN's performance.

The principal RCN demand arising specifically out of SC 107 was for better air support from Newfoundland. "The experience of this convoy," wrote Vice-Admiral Percy Nelles to Air Vice Marshal L.S. Breadner, Chief of the Air Staff, "undoubtedly is one which again emphasizes the necessity of effective long range aircraft and it is earnestly hoped that this question is well to the forefront as regards the provision of the required type of aircraft for service on the North-western Atlantic."[104] That letter, when it was written in January 1943, served more than anything else as a formal record of discussion already in progress between two headquarters that did not often cooperate closely with each other. Conceivably, it also hastened action by the RCAF, which had established an operational research centre in August and was rapidly developing its antisubmarine capability.

Inter-service meetings in Ottawa on 1 and 3 November 1942 had resulted in recognition of the northwest Atlantic as a joint RCN/RCAF commitment and led to vigorous debate about the role of aircraft in antisubmarine warfare. Canadian modifications to Canso "A" amphibians flying out of Gander, Newfoundland, were to increase the effective range of these cumbersome but reliable aircraft to over 700 miles. Moreover, ever since early November when the British Cabinet's Anti-U-Boat Committee had formally designated the Liberator as the most suitable heavy bomber for conversion to the VLR role, RCAF delegations to Washington had been making the case for the provi-

---

101. Macintyre's ROP for HX 213 stated that HF/DF in *Hesperus* made it clear that "all the U-boats in the area were gathering around SC 107 which was some 30 miles to the north of us." HMS *Hesperus* ROP, HX 213, 9 Nov. 1942

102. C-in-C WA to Adm, 8 Dec. 1942, with attached min, PRO, ADM 199/715; *Hesperus* ROP; Interview with Lt-Cdr F.O.Gerity, RCNVR, DHH, North Atlantic Convoy Operations (prior 1943), NSS 1650-239/15

103. FONF to SecNB, 12 Jan. 1943, NAC, RG 24, 11335, NSS 8280-SC 107

104. FONF to CTF 24, 22 Dec. 1942 , NAC, RG 24, 11335, NSS 8280-SC 107; CNS to CAS, 15 Jan. 1943, NAC, RG 24, 11093, 48-2-2, v 73

sion of that type for Eastern Air Command, albeit with disappointing results. These measures aside, at the time of the convoy battle itself, the RCAF had provided better support than the RCN gave credit for, but senior Canadian naval officers were not on the whole air-minded enough to understand what the airmen were up against, while only the posting of officers with recent operational experience to Air Force Headquarters had alerted the RCAF to the full extent of the navy's need. Whatever the tangible results, SC 107 had undoubtedly brought an added sense of urgency to the deliberations and decisions of both headquarters.[105]

An even more immediate concern, because it could be remedied by the RCN with the resources to hand, was the adaptation of Atlantic Convoy Instructions to suit the limitations of C Groups. In the opinion of most Canadians, equipment and tactical doctrine, more than training, were responsible for the shortcomings of Canadian escort groups. The shortage of destroyers aggravated the equipment problem. The loss of *Ottawa*, the damage to *Assiniboine* from her battle with *U 210*, and the refits under way for *St Croix, St Francis, St Laurent,* and HMS *Burnham*, left the four C Groups with just five operational destroyers. Bitter experience demonstrated, again and again, the need for speed. More critical than the size of a force defending a convoy was the proportion of the escorts that could make high speed dashes to put down a U-boat. Destroyers alone could do this as corvettes were incapable of making offensive thrusts without creating lengthy, exploitable gaps in the screen.[106] A Canadian staff officer, most likely Captain Roger Bidwell, unburdened himself of a common feeling when he scribbled on Horton's cover letter to Piers's report for SC 107: "How about giving us a few decent destroyers in the C Groups, Maxie? Instead of the discarded sweepings you've given us now!"[107]

The procedures laid down by Western Approaches for convoy screens added to the difficulty. They called for escorts to be stationed at approximate radar range from each other, assuming the availability of type 271. Familiar with the actual state of equipment on RCN escorts, Piers knew better and argued in his report that "the distance of 5000 yards laid down for Escorts in the Night diagrams appears too great to prove effective in preventing an attack on a Convoy. A bold U-Boat commander can penetrate the screen by keeping out of the Asdic distance and still pass between Escorts ... even in ideal operating conditions." Three thousand yards would be more airtight, and Captain Thebaud supported Piers's recommendation in correspondence with the RCN. Western Approaches appears to have recognized the Canadian dilemma and issued instructions to help resolve it. But while giving a nod to the RCN's deficiencies in equipment and leadership, Horton and his staff nevertheless stuck to their belief that the lack of training was the fundamental problem of Canadian escort groups. Fairly or not, given the readiness with which Ottawa had been trying to assist with Torch, they would soon find more ammunition to support their case.[108]

---

105. Douglas, *Creation of a National Air Force*, 525, 537-8, 541-2

106. D. Macintyre, *The Battle of the Atlantic* (London 1961), 161

107. C-in-C WA to Adm, 8 Dec. 1942, NAC, RG 24, 11335, NSS 8280-SC 107

108. CTG 24.7 to C-in-C WA, 25 Nov. 1942, PRO, ADM 199/715; interview with Lt-Cdr F.O. Gerity; *Restigouche* ROP. Milner notes that at just this moment P.M.S. Blackett produced an analysis of convoy operations that supported Horton's view of Canadian escort groups, *North Atlantic Run*, 190-1

In a belated effort to staunch the flow of Allied troops and supplies headed for Torch, BdU redeployed resources from the North Atlantic. Twenty-five boats with sufficient fuel were ordered to form Group *Schlagetot*, off Morocco and *Westwall*, off the Gibraltar approaches.[109] There remained only a token group of nine submarines in the mid-Atlantic, designated *Kreuzotter,* and they were either damaged or short of fuel and torpedoes. In addition, four boats lay off the coast of North America between Newfoundland and New York. As these major changes in strategic emphasis were set in motion on 8 November, the BdU war diary observed tellingly, "Operation of U-boats against convoys has ceased."[110]

Dönitz did not like the fact that fully one-third of the Atlantic submarines at sea were now committed off northwest Africa.[111] He informed the German naval staff on 18 November that two-thirds of the U-boats in the Mediterranean had either been destroyed or put out of action in a ten-day period (for the RCN's role in these operations, see Chapter 11). U-boats west of Gibraltar and Morocco had suffered smaller losses, but had also scored fewer successes. He predicted that U-boat losses would rise and the success rate fall as Allied air superiority was asserted through newly acquired bases in the area. Using Atlantic U-boats to intercept supply convoys from the United States west of the Azores, beyond the range of air cover, would be unprofitable. Conditions in this region were "fundamentally different" than those in the North Atlantic, "where current information regarding time and course of convoy movements," through the efficiency of the B-Dienst, made successful operations possible "in spite of the expanse of the area." Dönitz related the unusually large number of recent sinkings on northern transatlantic routes to the stripping of escorts for the African invasion. Recalling how the withdrawal of U-boats for the Arctic and "first Gibraltar operation at the end of 1941 and beginning of 1942" came at the expense of U-boat strength in the happier hunting grounds off the coast of the United States (see Chapter 7), he urged that the weight of the attack should be shifted back to the North Atlantic. It still offered the best prospects for success, and his first priority was to replenish Group *Kreuzotter* so that convoy operations could be undertaken.[112] Once that was accomplished, the group, thirteen U-boats strong, would be deployed on a patrol line straddling the convoy tracks at the eastern end of the air gap.

Three Atlantic convoys—ON 143 (C 1), SC 108 (C 2), and HX 214 (B 4)—crossed the ocean undisturbed during Dönitz's reorganization of submarine deployments. United States–Gibraltar convoys—UGF, UGS, GUF, and GUS—also remained unmolested.[113] This lull came to an end at 2126z on 15 November, when the *Kreuzotter* boat *U 521* intercepted the westbound ONS 144 (B 6) about 900 miles southwest of Iceland. BdU promptly ordered the rest of the group to close, and in a running three-day battle marked by stalwart defence from the five corvettes then constitut-

---

109. BdU, KTB, 4 and 7-8 Nov. 1942.

110. Ibid, 8 Nov. 1942

111. Of the ninety-nine boats at sea, twenty-five boats were in *Schlagetot* and *Westwall* and nine in *Delphin*.

112. The pack consisted of *U 521, U 522, U 84, U 704, U 624, U 224, U 454, U 383,* and *U 606,* to which *U 753* had been added on 9 Nov. Unfavourable weather delayed the transfer of fuel and supplies, and by 13 Nov. only *U 454, U624,* and *U 606* had refuelled from *U 117.* BdU, KTB, 10-15 Nov. 1942; BdU, KTB, Estimate of U-Boat Situation, 18 Nov. 1942 (after entry for 15 Nov.)

113. BdU, KTB, 8-9 Nov. 1942 ; USND, *History of Convoy and Routing, 1939-1945,* 31-43, DHH, NSS 1650-239/15, North Atlantic Convoy Operations, 1939-1945

ing B 6, the group sank five merchant ships and the Norwegian corvette *Montbretia* at the cost of one U-boat. [114]

While *Kreuzotter* had been closing in on ONS 144 in mid-Atlantic, the eastbound SC 109 was sighted ninety miles east of St John's on 16 November by *U 43*. Oberleutnant Schwantke had been patrolling east of Newfoundland after four weeks in the Gulf of St Lawrence and observed smoke plumes at noon, just as C 3 was taking over from the WLEF group. He shadowed the convoy as it plodded northeastwards, but air cover complicated his task. Canso amphibians from 5 Squadron RCAF forced *U 43* to lose contact several times and prevented Schwantke from closing the convoy until the night of 17 to 18 November. At first light on the 18th, however, after using the dark hours to gain a good attacking position on the starboard side of the convoy, he torpedoed the tanker *Brilliant*. The vessel burst into flames, but the crew saved the ship, which returned to St John's for repairs.[115] *U 43* survived an ineffectual depth charging during the Operation Raspberry that followed the attack, but fell behind and under the persistent close air support was unable to do any further damage.[116] On the night of 18 November, CONNAV ordered a diversion to the north to avoid an encounter with *Kreuzotter* boats shadowing ONS 144.

C 3, as the only all-Canadian group in the Mid-Ocean Escort Force, had built up a good rapport between ships. They also had a distinctive appearance. The first lieutenants of *Saguenay* and *Skeena* painted red and white bands on their funnels, which led to the group being dubbed "The Barber Pole Brigade," a tradition that still continues in the Canadian navy.[117] For this convoy, Lieutenant-Commander Kenneth Dyer, RCN, was SOE in HMCS *Skeena* because *Saguenay* had collided with a merchant ship outside St John's the day before.[118] Dyer, although only twenty-seven and relatively inexperienced, had distinguished himself in sinking *U 558* in the battle over ON 115, and was an innovative tactician. Replacing *Saguenay* was the venerable four-stacker HMS *Winchelsea*. The corvettes *Agassiz*, *Galt*, *Sackville,* and *Wetaskiwin*, all regulars, completed the group. SS *Bury*, the HF/DF-equipped rescue ship, had done yeoman duty with ON 137.[119] None of the escorts had HF/DF, but *Winchelsea*, *Galt,* and *Wetaskiwin* had type 271 radar, the two corvettes having it fitted in Halifax just prior to sailing. C 3's other three members had either type 286 or SW2C radar.

At this point came another skirmish in the technological war so integral to the Atlantic battle. In September British intelligence had learned that the Germans had developed *Metox*, which they dubbed the German Search Receiver (GSR), but they realized they could gain an advantage from

---

114. Adm, *MASR,* Jan. 1943.), Analysis of ONS 144, 14-16; *U 184* and *U 264*, KTBs, 20 Nov. 1942. The Admiralty credited *Potentilla* with the destruction of this submarine, but a radio signal emanated from *U 184* two hours after the corvette's last attack. There is no detail on these attacks in *Potentilla*'s report, but Capt (D) Liverpool's comments provide the exact times. *U 264*'s account matches up extremely well if the two-hour time zone adjustment is made to her KTB. *U 184* is shown as missing on 20-1 Nov. by Niestlé, *German U-boat Losses*, 127

115. Later, when on passage to Nova Scotia for repairs not available in St John's, *Brilliant* foundered in a storm.

116. *Skeena* ROP, SC 109, 1 Dec. 1942 , NAC, RG 24, 11335, 8280-SC 109; *U 43*, KTB, 16-18 Nov. 1942; Rohwer, *Axis Submarine Successes*, 138

117. Schull, *Far Distant Ships*, 130. In 1943, the name and marking was taken up by C 5.

118. *Saguenay* had collided with SS *Azra* while on passage to St John's on 15 Nov., the day before. The merchant ship sank and the damage to the destroyer was so severe that she was consigned to training duties for the remainder of the war. DHH, "Saguenay History," 11-13

119. *Skeena* ROP; and "Saguenay History," 11-13

the fact that it could only detect metric radar transmissions.[120] Measure: countermeasure. Western Approaches promulgated an instruction describing the weakness of GSR, which Dyer incorporated into the C 3's standing orders. Considering the risk of detection by *Metox* to be greater than the chances of SW2C or type 286 radar detecting a U-boat, he ordered strict radar silence for the three escorts equipped with metric radar. This tactic soon paid dividends. The shadower, *U 43*, had *FuMB* rigged, and although the U-boat made several detections against aircraft before the convoy moved beyond the range of Newfoundland-based aircraft, it gained none from escorts.[121]

Dyer gained warning of a shadower after *U 43*'s sighting report had been intercepted by shore stations on 16 November and subsequently had received good HF/DF intelligence from *Bury*. He believed that even though many of these transmissions would have been from boats in contact with ONS 144, there could be at least two shadowers with SC 109, one on the starboard bow and one on the quarter. He disposed his screen so as to get the most benefit from 271 radar, but feared that the shadowers would wait until after moon set at 0600z on 19 November, when it got really dark, to close and attack.[122] To stave off the assault and increase the chances of catching U-boats, Dyer instructed the escorts to launch Major Hoople, an aggressive night illumination procedure conceived by Dyer to disrupt concerted pack attacks by calculating the time when the convoy was most vulnerable and then having the entire screen fire starshell simultaneously from pre-arranged positions. The sudden illumination, if timed correctly, could catch the U-boats red-handed moving into attack positions. Dyer instructed the escorts to proceed to their sectors at 0625z, and to open up with starshell twenty minutes later. Almost immediately upon executing Major Hoople, *Wetaskiwin* observed and illuminated what was thought to be a U-boat 1,500 yards on the starboard beam, and blazed away with her main and secondary armament. Contact was lost, and *Wetaskiwin*'s commanding officer believed the submarine had crash-dived, but as the corvette's asdic had been knocked out of commission by the blast from the main armament, this could not be confirmed. In reality, German documents indicate that no U-boats were subject to any such attack—*Wetaskiwin*'s type 271 also never reported a contact—but at least the tactic had been tried under realistic conditions.[123]

The risk inherent in Major Hoople was that the fireworks could reveal the convoy's position to U-boats that were not in contact, and *U 43* indeed observed the illumination from twenty-five miles to the northeast and tried to close but without success.[124] Despite several more HF/DF contacts, which the escorts pursued over the next twenty-four hours, and although BdU allocated *U 522* to take over the shadowing task on 20 November and sent three fresh boats that had been too late to operate against ONS 144 to intercept SC 109, no U-boats succeeded in attacking the convoy before fog came down on 20 November and the pursuit was broken off.[125]

120. *RAF in Maritime War* III, 491, 522; Hinsley, *British Intelligence* II, 685

121. *U 43*, KTB, 16-18 Nov. 1942

122. *Skeena* ROP

123. *Wetaskiwin*, Report of Attack on U-Boat, 0346/19 Nov. 1942, and CTG 24.7 to C-in-C WA, 8 Dec. 1942 both PRO, ADM 237/199; Easton, *50 North*, 178-82. A careful check of the German records shows that no submarines other then *U 43* made contact. *U 43*, *U 445*, *U 623*, and *U 663*, KTBs, 18-20 Nov. 1942

124. *U 43*, KTB, 19 Nov. 1942

125. The boats were *U 445*, *U 623*, *U 663*, BdU, KTBs, 20-1 Nov. 1942; *Skeena* ROP, SC-109

Western Approaches response to the reports from C 3 was full of praise. Unaware that no U-boats had actually been driven off, Commander C.D. Howard-Johnston at Western Approaches declared Major Hoople "brilliant and most encouraging, coming as it does from an RCN group. It is bold, it takes risks *and* it succeeded. In addition it probably frightened the U-boat out of its wits, and there is every chance that other U-boats when they hear of it will be alarmed and think they are up against some new means of detecting them." He put Dyer "at the top of the list for originality and skill," and proposed to Admiral Horton that the young Canadian—"Seniority under 5 years Lieut[enant]"—be "highly commended for the initiative displayed in the planning and the skill in execution" of the tactic (interestingly, Howard-Johnston's praise of the young Dyer was completely at odds with Horton's earlier criticism about Lieutenant-Commander Piers's youth and low seniority in connection to the defence of SC 107). Howard-Johnston recommended that the Western Approaches Tactical Unit pursue Major Hoople and it was later disseminated in convoy instructions as Porcupine.[126]

In the meantime, BdU was forming a new group, *Drachen*, to intercept the eastbound SC 110 (C 1), which German intelligence suggested would be approaching the patrol line about 250 miles northeast of Newfoundland on 25 November.[127] *U 518*, commanded by Kapitänleutnant Wissmann, patrolling the convoy tracks east of Sable Island after operations in Canadian waters (see Chapter 8), was ordered to *Drachen*'s area. However, within hours he sighted ON 145 in moonlight 135 miles south of the Avalon Peninsula just after midnight on 21 November. The westbound convoy was screened by local escort group W 2 consisting of the destroyer HMS *Wanderer*, the corvettes *Buctouche* and *Timmins*, and the Bangor *Minas*. Wissmann attacked from ahead as the convoy conveniently zigzagged towards him. At 0316z on 21 November he fired a spread of torpedoes that hit the freighter *Empire Sailor* and the tankers *British Renown* and *British Promise*. Both tankers later reached port but *Empire Sailor* sank the following morning; *Timmins* and *Minas* rescued sixty survivors.[128] Immediately after the attack, some of the merchant ships sighted *U 518* on the port bow, opened fire, and forced Wissmann to crash-dive ahead of the convoy where *Buctouche* picked up an asdic echo a few minutes later. Skipper-Lieutenant G.N. Downey, RCNR, fired four depth charges set to 100 feet on the target. Although not realized at the time, *Buctouche*'s prompt counterattack seriously damaged *U 518*, which reported being "scarcely able to dive" and received orders to return to base.[129] Captain J.D. Prentice, now Captain (D) Halifax, analysed the attack on ON 145 and, echoing Piers's report on SC 107, recommended that escorts fitted with SW1C and SW2C radar "should keep within 3,000 yards of the convoy instead of opening out to 5,000 yards"

---

126. As a postscript to this episode, Dyer's tactical thought made a lasting impression at Liverpool, resulting in a memo to the commodore at Londonderry instructing him to bring "matters of exceptional or immediate interest such as trials of new tactics etc" to the immediate attention of Western Approaches "so that arrangements may be made for the Commanding Officer to visit Derby House before proceeding to sea again." See C-in-C, WA to Cmdre Commanding Londonderry Escort Force, 8 Jan. 1943, and WA General Orders, both in Staff min sheet, 25 Feb. 1943, PRO, ADM 237/199

127. BdU, KTB, 22 Nov. 1942

128. Seventeen survivors later died of poisoning from the ship's cargo, which included phosgene bombs and mustard gas. *Lloyd's War Losses* I, 584; USCGC *Campbell*, Report of Escort, ON 145, 21 Nov. 1942 , NARA, WNRC, RG 313 red, CTF 24 convoys, box 8700; "Analysis of Attack by a U-Boat on Convoy ON 145," NAC, RG 24, 4027, NSS 1062-13-19; BdU, KTB, 20-1 Nov. 1942; *U 518*, KTB, 21 Nov. 1942; Rohwer, *Axis Submarine Successes*, 138

129. Despite the damage Wissmann struck again on 23 Nov. and sank the fast independent SS *Caddo*, a brand new American tanker on passage to Iceland. Rohwer, *Axis Submarine Successes*, 139; *U 518*, KTB, 23 Nov. 1942, BdU, KTB, 23 Nov. 1942

as stipulated in the Atlantic Convoy Instructions. Prentice argued that with the escorts at the greater range it was "a simple matter for a submarine to pass between them, fire his torpedoes and escape again on the surface without being picked up."

On 25 November a northwesterly gale reduced visibility and scattered ships in the eastbound SC 110 (C 1) and HX 216 (B7) as they approached *Drachen*. Alerted by HF/DF, HX 216 passed through the centre of the patrol line in the early hours of the 26th without being detected. SC 110 had similar good fortune. C 1's senior officer was Lieutenant-Commander Guy Windeyer, who had just taken command of *St Laurent*. It will be recalled that Windeyer had done well in *Wetaskiwin* when he and Dyer had developed the coordinated attacks that led to the destruction of *U 588* in July. His performance with SC 110, however, suggested that he was unequal to the greater responsibility of group command. When the convoy, like so many that winter, became scattered, he lost touch and did not report promptly to shore authorities. The British freighter *Barberrys*, carrying the convoy commodore, had turned back for harbour, which Windeyer did not report either, nor that he could not render assistance when she was sunk 300 miles northeast of St John's on 26 November by *U 663*, one of the *Drachen* boats that had been ordered to search independently for stray shipping. When the weather moderated on 27 November the SOE rounded up his convoy and completed the crossing without further loss, but his turnover to the local escort at the eastern end of the voyage was sloppy.[130] Although Windeyer had solid operational experience and professional background in the RN, it appears that he was now showing signs of what today would be called "burn out." When reviewed in Western Approaches, Windeyer's actions caused unease: "The Commanding Officer, St Laurent," wrote Admiral Horton, "does not appear fully to have realized his responsibilities as Senior Officer Escort, which is also borne out by the manner in which he has drafted his report of proceedings."[131] By the time this assessment was signed in February, Windeyer had been removed from command after a harrowing ordeal with ONS 154.

While heavy weather was affecting both shipping and U-boats northeast of Newfoundland, Dönitz was redeploying the boats still operating west of Gibraltar. As Allied antisubmarine forces, particularly aircraft, were severely limiting U-boat operations in this area, Dönitz proposed that the submarines off Gibraltar be shifted outside aircraft range to west of the Azores to search for convoys running between the United States and the Mediterranean. Intelligence about these routes was sketchy at best, but attempting to locate them was preferable to squandering resources in the deadly area closer inshore. The German naval staff approved the deployment of twelve boats in Group *Westwall* in a north–south patrol line that would probe westwards into the central Atlantic. *Westwall* eventually extended 260 miles and searched out to 800 miles beyond the Azores before working back to the east. The patrol line failed to intercept any of the American–Mediterranean

---

130. It was a misfortune that *Eyebright*, C 1's only escort with type 271, had to return to St John's with defects. Two stragglers—*Ocean Crusader* from HX 216 and *Barberrys* from SC 110—were sunk on 26 Nov. by *U 262* and *U 663* respectively. Another vessel from SC 110, SS *Blair Atholl*, was apparently damaged in a collision and foundered at 0514z on the 27th while attempting to return to St John's in heavy seas. BdU, KTB, 26-7 Nov. 1942; Rohwer, *Axis Submarine Successes*, 139; Cmdre's Report, HX 216, PRO, ADM 199/576; Positions of Ocean Convoys signal, 24-6 Nov. 1942, DHH, NSHQ Convoy Files; NSHQ to CTU 24.1.11, 1315z/25 Nov. 1942, and *St Laurent* ROP, SC 110, 5 Dec. 1942, both in DHH, 89/34 mfm, v 28, SC-110

131. C-in-C WA to CTG 24.7, 27 Dec. 1942, and C-in-C WA to Adm, 26 Feb. 1943, both in NAC, RG 24, 11335, NSS 8280-SC 110

convoys, but on 7 to 8 December four of its boats sank an equal number of merchant ships dispersed for the South Atlantic from ON 149.[132]

In parallel with the attempt to intercept convoys in the central Atlantic, Dönitz reconstituted his forces on the North Atlantic. Boats fresh from Germany or bases in France were deployed in two new groups at the eastern end of the air gap: *Panzer* with seven boats and *Draufgänger* with eight. *Panzer* moved westwards in a patrol line straddling the convoy tracks and would arrive northeast of Newfoundland, where it would be joined by the four *Drachen* boats by 5 to 6 December. [133] One of the *Panzer* boats, *U 524*, had been fitted with a special VHF receiver before sailing and had embarked a B-Dienst team to listen for Allied convoy voice traffic. On 4 December, the German eavesdroppers monitored voice transmissions and were able to identify ten different ships. The patrol line was moved northeastwards to intercept.

At 1040z on 6 December, the *Panzer* boat *U 524* sighted HX 217 about 350 miles northeast of Newfoundland in unlimited visibility.[134] The escort was B 6, the destroyers HMS *Fame* (Commander R. Heathcote, RN, SOE) and the Polish ORP *Burza,* with the Norwegian corvettes *Potentilla, Eglantine,* and *Rose*, and HMS *Vervain*. A rescue ship fitted with HF/DF, *Perth*, was included in the convoy of thirty-three ships. The ensuing six-day battle, in which U-boats sank two vessels in the convoy and a straggler, was marked by the customary fighting efficiency of B 6 as well as tactical innovations by its senior officer.

B 6 had experienced more convoy battles than any other mid-ocean escort group since August and had been fortunate in having well-equipped ships and continuity in its composition and leadership. Heathcote drew on his experience and familiarity with B 6 to make two tactical departures. The first was the increased use of asdic in the passive mode, a procedure where the operator listened for hydrophone effect (HE) from U-boats rather than transmitting active pulses, which allowed the escort to "run silent" and mask its presence. In no preceding convoy battle had escorts used it to such effect; *Eglantine* alone intercepted six U-boats closing to attack by these means. The second innovation—which echoed the ideas expressed by Prentice and Piers—was to deploy the escorts at night 2,500 yards from the convoy instead of the 5,000 yard distance then prescribed by the Atlantic Convoy Instructions.[135]

Heathcote's experience had taught him that even a group equipped with centimetric radar could not prevent U-boats from piercing a screen with the escorts stationed at 5,000 yards. Since HX 217 originally had thirty-three—later reduced in a severe storm to twenty-five ships—its perimeter was smaller than larger convoys, which helped in decreasing gaps between escorts. A U-boat captain attacking at night had two separate tasks: penetrate the escort and close the convoy itself to select a target. With the escorts stationed at 5,000 yards in the standard night screening diagram, this process could be achieved in two stages. However, with the screen stationed at 2,500 yards, the captain would have to manoeuvre between two escorts while simultaneously making the precise

132. BdU, KTB, 16-26 Nov. 1942; MOD, *U-boat War in the Atlantic* II, 65-6; Rohwer, *Axis Submarine Successes*, 136-40; Blair, *Hitler's U-Boat War*, 116; the Adm OIC was not aware of *Westwall's* search into the Central Atlantic. By 16 Dec. it was reporting "patrols north and west of the Azores," but by then the group was well to the east. "U-Boat Situation," weekly reports 51, 52, 53, "U-Boat Trend," report 54. Syrett, *Battle of the Atlantic*, 105-7

133. BdU, KTB, 30 Nov.–3 Dec. 1942

134. Ibid, 4-12 Dec. 1942 ; MOD, *U-Boat War in the Atlantic* II, 68; Bonatz, *Seekrieg im Äther*, 238

135. Adm, *MASR,* Dec. 1942, 28-9, HMS *Fame*, ROP, HX 217, 12 Dec. 1942 , PRO, ADM 199/717

calculations for his attack. The close-in screen worked: the presence of the escorts in the zone immediately around the convoy where U-boats wanted to launch their attacks thwarted many of the attempts against HX 217. As Heathcote observed, "The U-boats seemed somewhat timid and unwilling to press home their attacks in the face of opposition." His report of proceedings noted that only one intruder breached the screen, and Heathcote was "convinced that it would have been impossible to prevent the screen" from being pierced if the "escorts had been 5,000 yards or more from the convoy." In fact, three U-boats penetrated the screen, but this was still a low figure.[136]

Like SC 110 a week earlier, HX 217 had been scattered by heavy weather northeast of Newfoundland. U-Boat Command eventually operated twenty-two submarines against the convoy—nearly one-to-one odds—during what evolved into a five-day battle.[137] During the night of 7 December the screen beat off numerous attacks in heavy weather, but *U 524* sank a tanker. On 8 December three VLR Liberators from Iceland harassed the pack. That night only two U-boats attacked, but Thurmann in *U 553* sank a freighter carrying ammunition. Aircraft were unable to fly on 9 December, and B 6, using HF/DF and radar, again beat off all attacks that night. By daybreak, the convoy was closer to Iceland and several aircraft operated overhead, one of which destroyed *U 611*. BdU called off its attacks the next morning.[138]

Dönitz was hoping for substantial sinkings when packs attacked convoys and, believing that six ships had been sunk and another four damaged, was disappointed that heavier losses had not been inflicted. [139] In reality, only two ships were sunk. Normally, the best results were achieved early in a convoy battle. In this case, poor visibility during the first night had caused the pack to lose the convoy.[140] In view of B 6's demonstrated effectiveness, Dönitz considered that its tactics had been overly defensive and could not understand why the escorts had not counterattacked with more vigour with the aim of destroying the attackers.[141] This assessment was shared by one of Dönitz's most aggressive opponents, the celebrated U-boat killer Captain F.J. Walker, who as Captain (D) Liverpool, complained that no U-boats were sunk by B 6. Heathcote, perhaps with the aim of "the safe and timely arrival of the convoy" in mind, had deliberately placed less emphasis on counterattack than defence.[142]

With the termination of the operation against HX 217, BdU organized the eleven submarines left over from the pursuit into the new group *Ungestüm*, positioned about 600 miles west of Ireland. A second group, *Raufbold*, was already in position to the west. It was hoped that these two patrol lines at the eastern end of the air gap would intercept a westbound convoy expected on 15 December. Only a few boats were available at the other end of the air gap off Newfoundland. As

---

136. Ibid

137. During the dark night of 8 Dec. *U 221* (Trojer) rammed and sank *U 254*. Trojer's boat survived but *U 254* was lost with all but four of the crew. Dönitz decided that to minimize the risk of collision, no more than thirteen to fifteen boats should be in close proximity of a convoy. *Potentilla* sighted wreckage and believed that a Liberator might have sunk a submarine in daylight. BdU, KTB, 8 Dec. 1942, MOD, *U-Boat War in the Atlantic* II, 68; Blair, *Hitler's U-Boat War*, 125

138. BdU, KTB, 6-11 Dec. 1942 ; Blair, *Hitler's U-Boat War*, 125-6

139. BdU to *Panzer*, 1810/6 Dec. 1942, PRO, DEFE 3/705

140. MOD, *U-Boat War in the Atlantic* II, 68

141. BdU, KTB, 9-10 Dec. 1942

142. Adm, *MASR*, Dec. 1942, 28-9; *Fame* ROP

B-Dienst had broken a signal giving the route for HX 218, three boats, designated Group *Büffel*, were positioned astride the convoy's projected track.[143]

The Allies had also achieved success in the intelligence battle. The Admiralty's Submarine Tracking Room had gleaned more precise information about enemy dispositions on the main convoy routes during the operation against HX 217. It was "known that 2 groups of U/boats were concerned, one in establishing and maintaining the contact and the second in reinforcing in the later stages of the operation," and that about twenty U-boats were involved in the pursuit.[144] Even better intelligence would soon be available as a result of the capture by a boarding party from the destroyer HMS *Petard* of current code books for the four-rotor Enigma from *U 559*. To that point the four-rotor Enigma had defied decryption, but from 13 December until 13 March 1943, Bletchley Park broke *Shark* cypher messages with some regularity and, from then until the end of the war, the Submarine Tracking Room would increasingly have the benefit of special intelligence to shape its appreciation of enemy dispositions.[145] The fruits of the gallantry of *Petard*'s boarding party, two of whom died when the U-boat suddenly went down, were great indeed.

On the North Atlantic, the U-boat patrol lines deployed at the eastern end of the air gap were so ubiquitous that evasion became increasingly difficult over the next two weeks. On 15 December *Raufbold*, the southernmost group, now thirteen strong, intercepted ON 153 (B7); on 16 December ONS 152 (C 3), which had been forced to reverse course the day before to rendezvous with the Iceland section, and had been routed to pass well south of the U-boats near HX 217, ran into the eleven boats of Group *Ungestüm*; and finally on 23 December, ONS 154 (C 1) came into violent contact 500 miles southwest of Ireland with Group *Spitz*, eight U-boats fresh from base joined by three boats from *Raufbold*.[146]

ONS 152 suffered only one loss when a straggler was torpedoed. The convoy had been located by *Ungestüm* as the patrol line was working westwards to intercept HX 218.[147] Eleven boats operated against ONS 152 for six days, but were frustrated by severe weather. On 17 and 18 December *Ungestüm* was reporting hurricane force winds.[148] The convoy was scattered, but as conditions moderated the searching submarines caught fleeting glimpses of ships plunging in the seas. Kapitänleutnant Zetzsche in *U 591* sank the straggling British freighter *Montréal City* 550 miles

143. BdU, KTB, 7 and 11-12 Dec. 1942 ; *U 465*, KTB, 12 Dec. 1942; MOD, *U-Boat War in the Atlantic* II, 69

144. "U-Boat Situation. Week Ending 14/12/42," Syrett, *Battle of the Atlantic*, 107

145. D. Kahn, *Seizing the Enigma* (Boston 1991), 222-7; J.P. Showell, *Enigma U-Boats: Breaking the Code* (Annapolis 2000), 88-95; Hinsley, *British Intelligence* II, 50-2; Syrett (ed), *Battle of the Atlantic*, 96; Adm, OIC, Weekly U-boat Situation Report, 14 Dec. 1942, PRO, ADM 223/15

146. BdU, KTB, 14-23 Dec. 1942; *Burnham* ROP, ONS 152; HMS *Sunflower*, ROP, ON 153, 26 Dec. 1942 , NAC, RG 24, 11320, NSS 8280-ON 153; *St Laurent*, ROP, ONS 154, 3 Jan. 1943, NAC, RG 24, 11332, 8280-ONS154

147. On 15 Dec. USCG *Ingham* escorting a convoy working southwards to join ONS 152 sank *U 626*. *Ingham* had dropped a single large depth charge on a doubtful contact. Clay Blair described this as "the luckiest Allied shot of the war." Blair, *Hitler's U-Boat War*, 127

148. The storm completely disrupted BdU's attempts to control an organized search to regain contact. On 19 Dec. the pursuing U-boats could only be told that ONS 152 was believed to be within a rectangular area 180 by 120 nautical miles. BdU, KTB, 19 Dec. 1942

east of Newfoundland during the night of 20 to 21 December.[149] While severe weather had been decisive, the "Barber Pole Brigade" had performed well.[150] During the recent lay-over in the United Kingdom, new equipment had been fitted, so that this was the first C group to be completely equipped with centimetric radar, as well as the first to have two destroyers with HF/DF.

The ordeal of the west-bound ON 153 (B 7), which crossed at the same time as ON 152, has been overshadowed by the disaster that befell ONS 154 shortly afterwards. The experience of ON 153, however, provides important context to the situation that existed on the North Atlantic in December 1942. The weather, as in the case of ON 152, was a significant factor. "By God's mercy," wrote the convoy Commodore of ON 153, Commodore E. Manners, RNR, "heavy weather undoubtedly saved more losses."[151] Lieutenant-Commander J.T. Jones, RNR, in HMS *Sunflower*, who took over mid-way as SOE, described it as "the worst crossing I have ever experienced ... The difficulties in the corvettes under such weather conditions had to be experienced to be believed."[152]

B 7 consisted of two destroyers, both fitted with HF/DF—HMS *Firedrake* (Commander E. Tilden, RN, SOE) and the four-stacker HMS *Chesterfield*—plus four corvettes. Less inured to large-scale pack attacks than other Mid-Ocean Escort Force groups—during 1942 no attacks had been made on any convoy escorted by B 7—the escort was under the command of a senior officer who does not appear to have kept up with developments in antisubmarine warfare doctrine. On 15 December the thirty-nine-ship convoy ran into the middle of the *Raufbold* patrol line. It was sighted by *U 609*, and before nightfall three further boats had established contact. None of their initial sighting or contact reports appear to have been picked up by the HF/DF operators, but after dark, *Chesterfield* and two corvettes were sent down a HF/DF bearing and at about the same time *U 356* carried out an unsuccessful attack from ahead. Later in the night HF/DF and MF/DF transmissions were monitored, but there were no successful attacks until two hours before twilight when at 0742z on 16 December *U 610* manoeuvred in behind the starboard screen and torpedoed the tankers *Bello* and *Regent Lion*. The first ship went down quickly, but *Regent Lion* remained afloat. Tilden ordered Operation Raspberry, but cancelled the order at 0752z when *Chesterfield* sighted a U-boat with her casing just awash 500 yards on the starboard beam. Unable to ram in the heavy seas running, the destroyer opened fire with her secondary armament and *U 610* crash-dived only 200 metres away. In the "extremely bad" asdic conditions, *Chesterfield* gained an echo, but lost it before an attack could be made.[153]

Alisma and *Chesterfield* located and attacked *U 609*, *U 610*, and *U 623*, but inflicted no serious damage. Tilden then ordered these two escorts to stand by *Regent Lion* as long as possible, rejoin-

---

149. Another straggler from ONS 152, SS *Oropos*, never reached port. The 4,474-ton Greek freighter was bound for Halifax and reported missing from the convoy by HMS *Burnham* at 1345z/18 Dec. Rohwer gives *U 621* the credit, but the time, position, and circumstances of *U 621*'s attack do not fit the ship's likely movements. The Lloyd's Missing Ship Committee, without specifically saying that a marine accident could be responsible, subsequently ruled simply that *Oropos* was lost on 21 Dec. BdU, KTB, 19-22 Dec. 1942; Rohwer, *Axis Submarine Successes*, 142; *U 336* and *U 591*, KTBs, 20-1 Dec. 1942; *Lloyd's War Losses* II, 1314

150. *Burnham* ROP, ONS 152; C-in-C WA to Escorts of ONS-152, 0950z/15 Dec. 1942, DHH, 88/1, v 10, ONS 152

151. Cmdre's Report, ON 153, PRO, ADM 237/94

152. *Sunflower* ROP

153. BdU, KTB, 15 Dec. 1942; *U 609*, KTB, 15 Dec. 1942; *Sunflower* ROP; Rohwer, *Axis Submarine Successes*, 141; *U 610*, KTB, 16 Dec. 1942; D. Syrett, "The Sinking of HMS *Firedrake* and the Battle for Convoy ON 153," *The American Neptune* 51/2, 106

ing by dark.[154] All day the weather worsened, slowing the convoy's speed to five knots, and at least two U-boats still shadowed. *U 621* penetrated the reduced screen, but an unsuccessful attack went unnoticed by B7.[155] At about 1900z, while *Chesterfield* and *Alisma* were still some thirty miles astern, *U 664* located the convoy, manoeuvred between the screen of four escorts and torpedoed the Belgian freighter SS *Emile Francqui*. Tilden again ordered Raspberry but B 7 found no trace of the enemy in the poor radar and asdic conditions.[156]

Firedrake had now taken up station on the convoy's starboard beam, apparently in response to MF/DF bearings, while *Snowflake* was 4,000 yards ahead of the convoy's starboard bow and *Sunflower* patrolled the port quarter. In the bright moonlight *U 609* slipped past the reduced screen and at 2122z fired a spread of three torpedoes from a range of 1,200 metres at a large freighter but missed despite "perfect firing data." An hour later *Firedrake* DF'd a shadowing report to BdU but took no definite action, probably because of the small number of escorts available.[157] Towards midnight *Snowflake*'s radar broke down, leaving *Sunflower* on the port quarter as the only escort with functional centimetric radar. Meanwhile, on the starboard flank *Firedrake* had courted danger, steaming slowly at only five knots in the ever-building seas for two hours on a steady course without zigzagging. She paid the price at 0015z on 17 December when *U 221* fired two torpedoes from 1,000 metres. The destroyer broke in two, her fate unnoticed by any other ship.[158] The bow section sank about thirty minutes later, while the stern section remained afloat with about thirty-five men who fired a starshell at 0045z to alert the other escorts to their predicament. HMS *Alisma*, which was just rejoining from astern tried to report this to the senior officer, but received no reply. Lieutenant-Commander Jones in *Sunflower*, realizing something was amiss, called up all of the other escorts, including *Firedrake*, to see who had fired the starshell. When all but the senior officer replied in the negative, Jones took charge of B 7 and altered course to investigate. He first stumbled upon SS *St Bertrand*, still rejoining from astern, but eventually at 0200z made radar contact with the stern section of *Firedrake*. The "very rough sea and heavy swell" prevented immediate rescue, but at 0330z the hulk began to settle and the survivors took to the water. *Sunflower* recovered six officers and twenty men over the next two hours; unfortunately, Commander Tilden and most of his ship's company were killed outright by the torpedo or perished in the sea.[159]

From this point until nearing the Western Ocean Meeting Point on 23 December, the convoy simply struggled to survive the elements. One corvette recorded seas of forty to fifty feet. The convoy hove to on 19 December and ten ships straggled. The horrific conditions improved slightly, but then worsened. When winds reached hurricane force on 22 December, ON 153 again hove to. A

---

154. *U 609, U 623,* and *U 610,* KTBs, 16 Dec. 1942; *Sunflower* and *Chesterfield* ROPs, ON 153; "Remarks by Commodore Commanding Londonderry Escort Force," ON 153, 9 Feb. 1943, PRO, ADM 237/94. MV *Regent Lion* was abandoned, later found and towed into port. *Lloyd's War Losses* I, 792, and II, 1561

155. BdU, KTB, 16 Dec. 1942; Rohwer, *Axis Submarine Successes*, 141; *Sunflower* ROP

156. *Sunflower* ROP, ON 153; Rohwer, *Axis Submarine Successes*, 142; *U 664* and *U 609*, KTBs, 16 Dec. 1942; "Remarks by Commodore Commanding Londonderry Escort Force"

157. *U 609*, KTB, 16 Dec. 1942; BdU, KTB, 17 Dec. 1942; *Sunflower* ROP

158. Syrett, "Sinking of HMS *Firedrake*," 107-8; Lt D.J. Dampier, RN, to CTF 24, Report on the Loss of HMS *Firedrake*, 19 Dec. 1942, PRO, ADM 237/94; *U 211*, KTB, 17 Dec. 1942; Rohwer, *Axis Submarine Successes*, 142

159. Lt J.W. White, RN, the officer who had done so much to put the RCN's asdic training on a firm foundation earlier in the war (see Chapter 1) was among those who did not survive.

VLR Liberator from Iceland provided welcome cover during daylight on 18 December and forced down one U-boat; four other submarines sighted the aircraft, but were not detected in the heavy weather. Several boats still had fleeting glimpses of scattered ships on the next day. After battling heavy weather over several days, B 7's fuel began to run out reducing the group's strength even further, however, the U-boats had lost contact for good on the 21st.[160] There had been one more sinking, when *U 621* torpedoed a straggling tanker *Otina* on 20 December.

The loss of *Firedrake* and three merchant ships was testimony to the determination and fighting effectiveness of U-boats in the face of extremely difficult weather conditions.[161] Their task, however, was simplified by the kind of mistakes so often made by inexperienced escort groups. The prolonged detachment of escorts for hunting and rescue work astern after the initial sinking left large gaps in the screen, easily exploited by the submarines. There also seems indeed to have been a general HF/DF failure within ON 153. Unlike the impressive HF/DF performances turned in by some of the other B groups, a high percentage of the signals made by the pack were not intercepted or fixed by either *Chesterfield* or *Firedrake*. And by steering a steady course at slow speed for two hours *Firedrake* exposed herself unnecessarily. Finally, the group's sensors were plagued by weather damage and breakdowns at critical times.[162]

On this occasion, the loss of the SOE and the severe weather tempered criticism with compassion. Authorities on both sides of the Atlantic agreed no useful purpose would be served by a Board of Enquiry into the loss of *Firedrake*, since all bridge personnel had gone down with the forward part of the ship. At both Argentia and Western Approaches, the fatal mistake of escorts steaming a straight course at slow speed drew comment. Staff at Western Approaches also criticized the failure to investigate unexplained explosions and HF/DF or MF/DF bearings: "Had action been taken it might have influenced the U-boats from pressing home their attacks at later stages." This was precisely the criticism the Admiralty's Director of Anti-Submarine Warfare would soon level, in much less temperate terms, at C 1 about that group's defence of ON 154. [163]

When ONS 154 sailed on 18 December, seven days behind ONS 153, two U-boat patrol lines about 200 miles long—*Ungestüm* and *Spitz*—lay across the main convoy routes southwest of Ireland. The mission of the eleven boats in *Spitz* was to intercept the westbound convoy expected on 23 December.[164] Intelligence about this threat became available to the Allies late, and in a very incomplete form. On 22 December Bletchley Park was able to decrypt a signal intercepted four days earlier at 2040z on 18 December, ordering U-boats to quadrant AL 72, directly in the path of ONS 154. The cryptographers were still unable to break new Enigma settings for 19 December, leaving the

160. Syrett, "Sinking of HMS *Firedrake*," 109

161. Loss of life was heavy: thirty-three of the forty-one aboard *Bello* and forty-six of the eighty-seven in *Emile Franqui* were not rescued. *Lloyd's War Losses* I, 598

162. Syrett, "Sinking of HMS *Firedrake*," 106-11

163. Capt A.S. Russell, RN, for C-in-C WA to Adm, 17 Mar. 1943, PRO, ADM 237/94; Remarks by Commodore Commanding Londonderry Escort Force, ON 153, 9 Feb. 1943, ibid; Cdr (D) Argentia to C-in-C WA, 27 Dec.1942, ibid; CTF 24 to COMINCH, 1 Feb. 1943, NARA, WNRC, RG 313 Red, CTF 24 convoys, box 8707; Atlantic Fleet ASW Officer to CINCLANT, 19 Feb. 1943

164. In spite of changes to Naval Cypher no. 3, B-Dienst may have provided signals intelligence for this. Hinsley, *British Intelligence* II, 553

OIC in the dark about the formation of *Spitz* and relocation of *Ungestüm*. Thus, the only signals intelligence available for routing ONS 154 came from a single relatively uninformative message that had been decrypted only when the convoy had already been at sea for four days, steaming towards a new U-boat concentration.[165] On 22 December Western Approaches ordered ON 154 to divert on the basis of the newly available intelligence. The Submarine Tracking Room rightly described the information as "fragmentary"; shore authorities did not yet know the expanse of the enemy's deployment, and ONS 154's new route in fact did not clear the southern end of *Spitz*.[166]

Weather initially slowed the progress of ON 154, but the stormy conditions did not result in the the kind of protection afforded to previous convoys, especially ONS 153. Because of the delay *Spitz* failed to make its interception during daylight on 23 December, as BdU had anticipated. When ONS 154 remained hove to that night in a strong gale, the U-boats were still too far to the west to make any sightings.[167] Dönitz deduced what was happening and moved the pack southwest to pick up three reinforcements from *Raufbold* so that a patrol line of eleven boats could sweep northeast on Christmas Day.[168] Western Approaches diverted ONS 154 to the south to avoid the suspected danger.[169] Christmas Day passed without contact being made, but the U-boat patrol line grew to a length of over 300 miles when the remaining eight *Ungestüm* boats overlapped *Spitz*.[170] At 1245z on 26 December, *U 662*, one of six boats moving to form a new patrol line picked up hydrophone effect just to the south of *Spitz*. Korvettenkapitän Hermann waited until the noises had decreased slightly then surfaced to have a look. He sighted ONS 154 directly ahead but was surprised by a Liberator, which dropped three depth charges and made him lose touch. His sighting report failed to reach BdU, but he had set in train the events of the next few days.[171]

The information that a Liberator had attacked a U-boat twenty-two miles astern of the convoy reached the escort just as ONS 154 was steaming out of the range of Coastal Command aircraft.[172] In the meantime, Oberleutnant Gräf in *U 664*, who had submerged on sighting an aircraft an hour before *U 662*'s encounter, heard three explosions "at long distance." On surfacing ninety minutes later, he glimpsed smoke plumes from the convoy, sighted the merchant ships at 1635z on 26 December, made his sighting report, and began shadowing.[173] U-Boat Command ordered the seventeen other boats of *Spitz* and *Ungestüm* to close and attack.[174] During the evening of 26 December, perhaps helped by intercepts of the U-boats' sighting reports, Bletchley Park broke the Enigma settings that had eluded them since the 19th, but it was too late to divert the convoy clear of the pack. In the Submarine Tracking Room, where Lieutenant Patrick Beesley, RNVR, had taken

---

165. Ibid, 556; PRO, DEFE 3/705 and DEFE 3/706

166. Syrett (ed), *Battle of the Atlantic*, 110-13; C-in-C WA to ONS 154, 1141z/22 Dec. 1942, DHH, 89/34, v 25; and TOI 2040/18, DHH, DEFE 3/706. The time of decryption is missing from this signal, but the sequence shows it to be from 22 Dec.

167. BdU, KTB, 23 Dec. 1942; *St Laurent* ROP; CTU 24.1.11 to AIG 303, 1515z/23 Dec. and 2014z/24 Dec. 1942, C-in-C WA to ONS 154, 0926z/25 Dec. 1942, DHH, 89/34, v 25; Revely, *Convoy that Nearly Died*, 46-8

168. BdU, KTB, 24-5 Dec. 1942

169. C-in-C WA to ONS 154, 0926z/25 Dec. 1942, DHH, 89/34, v 25

170. BdU, KTB, 25 Dec. 1942

171. *U 662* and *U 664*, KTBs, 26 Dec. 1942

172. *St Laurent* ROP; and *St Laurent*, deck log, 26 Dec. 1942

173. Gräf was ordered not to attack but to shadow; *U 664*, KTB, 26 Dec. 1942

174. BdU, KTB, 26 Dec. 1942

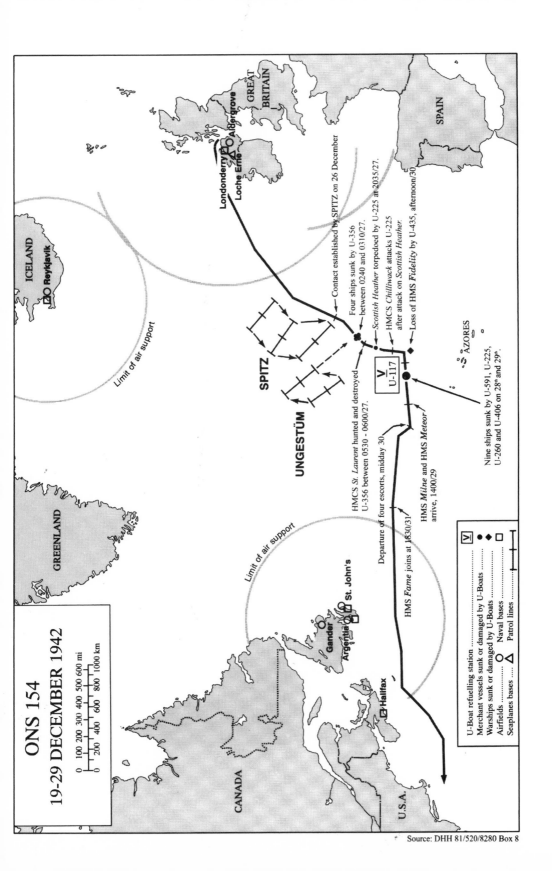

ONS 154
19-29 DECEMBER 1942

0 100 200 300 400 500 600 mi
0 200 400 600 800 1000 km

ICELAND
Reykjavik

GREENLAND

CANADA

U.S.A.

Halifax

HMS *Fame* joins at 1830/31

Departure of four escorts, midday 30

HMS *Milne* and HMS *Meteor* arrive, 1400/29

Nine ships sunk by U-591, U-225, U-260 and U-406 on 28th and 29th.

Gander
St. John's
Argentia

Limit of air support

HMCS *St. Laurent* hunted and destroyed U-356 between 0530 - 0600/27.

UNGESTÜM

SPITZ

V
U-117

AZORES

Loss of HMS *Fidelity* by U-435, afternoon/30

HMCS *Chilliwack* attacks U-225 after attack on *Scottish Heather*.

Scottish Heather torpedoed by U-225 at 2035/27.

Four ships sunk by U-356 between 0240 and 0310/27.

Contact established by SPITZ on 26 December

Limit of air support

SPAIN

GREAT BRITAIN

Londonderry
Loche Erne Aldergrove

Legend:
- V — U-Boat refuelling station
- ● — Merchant vessels sunk or damaged by U-Boats
- ◆ — Warships sunk or damaged by U-Boats
- ○ — Airfields
- △ — Seaplanes bases
- □ — Naval bases
- — Patrol lines

Source: DHH 81/520/8280 Box 8

charge after Commander Winn had collapsed from exhaustion earlier in the month, all that could be done was to monitor the growth of the pack. It was a tragedy that cracking the Enigma, such a brilliant success for British codebreakers, occurred just too late to avoid one of the worst convoy disasters of the war.[175]

ONS 154's mid-ocean escort was C 1, which for this crossing comprised the destroyer *St Laurent* and the corvettes *Battleford, Chilliwack, Napanee, Shediac,* and *Kenogami.* C 1 had had the most severe problems of equipment shortages and organizational instability of any group in the MOEF. *Chilliwack* and *Battleford* were the only regulars in the group, and since June five different senior officers had been at the helm.[176] During the layover in Britain after SC 110, the entire group had been fitted with type 271 radar, but had no opportunity to train with it before sailing. As a result, some of the ships continued to use their SW1C or SW2C metric radar enabling U-boats to make *Metox* detections against surface escorts at critical moments during the battle. There were also difficulties with HF/DF equipment. *St Laurent* had it fitted, but there had been insufficient time to calibrate the new system, rendering it virtually useless, and the destroyer's HF/DF officer missed sailing.[177] The convoy did include SS *Toward*, a rescue ship with HF/DF but, because she had no gyro compass, her bearings could not be trusted. Also in company was HMS *Fidelity*, a Special Duty ship that was equipped with HF/DF, asdic, two Grumman Kingfisher float planes, and a motor torpedo boat. On passage to the Far East, this extraordinary vessel was an old coal-burning merchant ship with a maximum speed of twelve knots. The escort commander was not, to begin with, even aware of her presence in the convoy.[178]

A second destroyer, HMS *Burwell*, was designated to join the group for ONS 154, but the four-stacker suffered mechanical defects and was unable to leave port.[179] This placed C 1 at a serious tactical disadvantage since, with only one fast escort, the group had little flexibility—*St Laurent* would have to watch her fuel consumption and could not react to U-boat shadowers with deep, high-speed sweeps. An exasperated Commodore Reid later complained to NSHQ about the failure to provide a replacement for *Burwell*, remarking that "it is felt some effort might have been made [by Western Approaches] to substitute another destroyer as it is noted that there is always another destroyer forthcoming in the case of such occurrences in B groups."[180]

It fell to Lieutenant-Commander Windeyer, SOE of C 1, to confront these challenges. As we have seen, his performance with SC 110 had not pleased C-in-C Western Approaches, and events surrounding the departure of ONS 154 also did little to instil confidence. There was no preparatory group conference, ostensibly because the escorts had been dispersed to different ports for the fitting of the radar, but the senior officer did not seize the opportunity to meet on the day of sailing. One result was that three of the corvettes did not have copies of the Atlantic Convoy Instructions

---

175. Hinsley, *British Intelligence* II, 556; Beesly, *Very Special Intelligence*, 158-63; and Decrypted German signals, PRO, DEFE 3/706

176. The five senior officers were Stubbs, Ayre, Layard, Prentice, and Windeyer.

177. *St Laurent* ROP

178. For this fascinating ship, see Revely, *Convoy That Nearly Died*, 38-41, and A. Burn, *The Fighting Commodores* (Annapolis 1999), 158

179. FONF to NSHQ, 1211z 26 Jan. 1943, DHH, 81/520 HMS Burwell 8000. In Jan. 1943, with her poor reliability in mind, FONF recommended using *Burwell* only as a spare destroyer.

180. FONF to NSHQ, 1745/29 Dec. 1942, DHH, 89/34, v 18

on which the group orders were based. *St Laurent* herself collided with the oiler at Moville and sailed late to overtake the convoy after hurried repairs to her bow. Then, upon catching the convoy two days later, her asdic coil burned out, and Windeyer had actually detached to return to base when technicians managed to make good repairs. Not until the afternoon of 20 December did he finally assume command of C 1. The fact that the membership of the group had not changed since SC 110 was doing little for the cohesion of C 1.[181]

ONS 154 proceeded in twelve columns, forming a rectangle about six miles wide and two deep. The greatest danger of attack would be from ahead and from the bows, but with six escorts Windeyer's screen would inevitably have gaps. As had been the case in the fateful battle around SC 107 in November, the submarines ranged against C 1 were a formidable force. All but one of the nineteen boats that operated against the convoy would make contact, and only three of the commanding officers were new.[182] Helping them further was the fact that, because eighteen of the convoy's forty-six merchant ships were bound for the South Atlantic and would be detached west of the Azores, ONS 154's track was roughly 500 miles south of that used by ONS 153, which meant a longer passage across the air gap.[183]

The documentary record of the battle that now took place is flawed, but U-boat war diaries, ships' logs, and copies of signal traffic—Windeyer transmitted an abnormal number of signals to Western Approaches, giving British shore authorities a unique perspective on the action—make it possible to fill some of the gaps left by the inadequate reports of proceedings. C 1 had its first encounters with U-boats within hours of the first enemy contact, by *U 664*. At 2105z on 26 December, *Shediac* (Lieutenant J.C. Clayton, RCNR), screening the port bow of the convoy, investigated a radar echo and sighted the shadowing submarine. Clayton fired starshell and drove the submarine under.[184] *U 664* lost contact with the convoy, but additional starshell from the escorts, followed by sporadic snowflake from ships in the convoy that continued for an hour after this incident served as a beacon to other boats.[185] At 0142z on 27 December, Oberleutnant Ruppelt, closing from the north in *U 356*, transmitted a new sighting report and *St Laurent*, following up an HF/DF bearing from SS *Toward*, obtained a fleeting radar contact.[186] As the convoy made prearranged course changes to the southwest, *U 356* apparently closed the starboard side of the convoy in poor visibility, and at 0240z torpedoed the freighters *Melrose Abbey* and *Empire Union*, at the head of the tenth and twelfth columns respectively. The escort performed a half-Raspberry on the starboard flank—known as Operation Hot Dog or half-Hot Dog by the group—but the starshell sweep did

---

181. *St Laurent* ROP; and *St Laurent*, deck log, 18-23 Dec. 1942

182. Rohwer and Hümmelchen, *Chronology of the War At Sea*, 183, patrol histories in Wynn, *U-Boat Operations of the Second World War*, I and II; R. Busch, *Der U-Boot Krieg 1939-1945: Die Deutschen U-Boot Kommandanten* (Hamburg 1996). Because of the steady attrition of the *U-Bootwaffe*, the experience levels of new U-boat COs were becoming an issue. Rahn, "Der U-Boot Krieg," 355

183. ON/ONS convoys generally spent longer in the air gap than eastbound convoys in any case because their routes were 200 to 400 miles further south; Grove, *Defeat of the Enemy Attack on Shipping*, 36; Syrett, "The Battle for Convoy ONS 154," *The Northern Mariner* (April 1997), 19-42

184. *U 664*, KTB, 26 Dec. 1942 ; and *Shediac*, ROP, ONS 154, 7 Jan. 1943, NAC, RG 24, 6903, NSS 8910-331/94

185. SS *Fort Lamy*, VCmdre's Report, ONS 154; *U 441*, *U435*, *U373*, and *U336*, KTB, 26 Dec. 1942; Decrypted German signal, intercepted 2002/26 Dec. 1942, DEFE 3/706; Adm to Escorts of ON 154, 2235a/26 Dec. 1942, DHH, 89/34, v 25

186. *U 356*, KTB, 29 Dec. 1942 (compiled from radio reports by BdU staff); BdU, KTB, 26 Dec. 1942

not reveal any trace of the attacker. Windeyer ordered *Napanee*, the starboard quarter escort, to screen *Toward* while she rescued survivors astern.[187]

Meanwhile, *U 441*, drawn to the convoy by the pyrotechnics, had penetrated from the starboard bow, and at 0213z fired torpedoes at three different vessels. While *Napanee* remained astern to screen the rescue vessel, *U 356* closed again and at 0310z torpedoed the freighter *Soekaboemi* at the rear of the eleventh column. Five minutes later, *King Edward* at the head of the eighth column appeared to suffer a torpedo hit on the port side, and shortly later broke in two when her boilers exploded.[188] *Soekaboemi* remained afloat down by the bow but the crew escaped in four lifeboats. Survivors from the two victims were later picked up by the *Toward*.[189] In the meantime, the captain of *U 664* noted, "Enormous fireworks above the convoy," as the escorts and merchant ships attempted to illuminate attackers. *St Laurent* picked up a radar contact at 0300z, forced *U 441* down at 0352z, and carried out several depth charge attacks.[190] There is no precise account of other action by the screen; *St Laurent* was still attacking *U 441* and, for the moment, *U 356*, having torpedoed four ships in forty-five minutes, escaped unharmed.[191]

At 0530z, about ninety minutes after her last attack, *St Laurent*—now in *Napanee*'s station on the starboard quarter—obtained another radar contact and sighted *U 356* on the surface, trimmed down, moving towards the convoy. The starboard oerlikon registered several hits before the U-boat dived directly ahead. Windeyer fired a pattern of five depth charges set to fifty feet where he saw the submarine plunge, then opened out the range to 1,300 yards to hunt. The asdic operator heard a roar, considered to be the sub blowing tanks, and made a firm contact. *St Laurent* ran in for a second attack, holding the echo until the distance had closed to 100 yards, fired a pattern of ten charges set between fifty and 140 feet and counted eleven explosions; the last was "delayed and intense, and 'threw' our 110 volt breaker." A third attack produced "a large oil slick" on the port bow, and was followed by a final attack at 0600z. The contact disappeared but there was no evidence of a kill. It is now clear, however, that *U 356*, from whom nothing more was heard, was destroyed in this action.[192]

Shortly after despatching *U 356*, *St Laurent* forced down the shadowing *U 664*. At the same time, *Toward* and *Napanee* were rescuing twenty-seven crew members from the *Melrose Abbey*,

187. *Kenogami*, deck log, 27 Dec. 1942, NAC, RG 24, 7428; *Battleford*, deck log, 27 Dec. 1942; *Battleford* ROP, ONS 154; *Napanee* ROP, ONS 154, 3 Jan. 1943, DHH, RG 24, 11332, 8280-ONS154; SS *Fort Lamy*, VCmdre's Report, ONS 154; SS *Empire Union* and *Melrose Abbey*, "Particulars of Attacks on Merchant Vessels by Enemy Submarines," 27 Dec. 1942, NAC, RG 24, 4026, NSS 1062-13-10, pt 12; CTU 24.1.11 to AIG 303, 0203z/27 Dec. 1942, DHH, 89/34, v 25; *U 441* and *U 664*, KTB, 27 Dec. 1942; Rohwer, *Axis Submarine Successes*, 142. Rohwer's evidence, based on the absence of other claims in view of the subsequent loss of *U 356* is the best available. That *U 441*, which fired at 0213, 0227, and 0301z but did not observe or hear any hits, might have fired the torpedoes responsible for these sinkings has been discounted for lack of supporting data, but the possibility remians

188. Rohwer, *Axis Submarine Successes*, 142

189. SS *King Edward* and SS *Soekaboemi*, "Particulars of Attacks on Merchant Vessels by Enemy Submarines," 27 Dec. 1942 , NAC, RG 24, 4023, NSS 1062-13-10, pt 12

190. *U 441* was not damaged by the "well-placed" depth charges but remained submerged for five hours, losing the convoy. *U 441* and *U 664*, KTBs, 27 Dec. 1942; *St Laurent*, deck log, 27 Dec. 1942

191. *U 664*, KTB, 27 Dec. 1942 ; SS *Fort Lamy*, VCmdre's Report, ONS 154

192. *St Laurent* ROP; *St Laurent*, "Report of Attack on U-Boat," 0338/27 Dec. 1942, NAC, RG 24, 11332, 8280-ONS154; Lt J. George, RCNVR, Historical Records Officer, Account of ON 154, DHH, 81/520/8280, box 8, ONS 154; Niestlé, *German U-Boat II*, 57

sixty-three from the *Empire Union*, sixty-five from the *Soekaboemi* and twenty-five from the *King Edward*. This remarkable life-saving effort, helped by moderate seas and good visibility, lasted till just before dawn. At 0914z the screw noises of rescuing ships having faded, *U 441* surfaced in the vicinity, sighted the damaged *Soekaboemi*, pursued her all day and eventually sunk her in the evening twilight.[193] Plagued by a break down in its port diesel, the U-boat could not catch up with the convoy and withdrew from the battle.[194]

The situation remained grave. ONS 154 was warned by the Admiralty that three or four boats were in contact and that six more were believed to be within 110 miles and trying to close. Western Approaches looked in vain for reinforcements, and Windeyer attempted, by radio-telephone conversations with imaginary destroyers, to deceive the U-boats into thinking additional escorts were joining, but the ruse apparently had no effect.[195] Eventually, the destroyers HMS *Milne* and *Meteor*, at sea with a Torch convoy, were ordered to assist, but they would not arrive for two days. At 1615z 27 December, Western Approaches, informed by Enigma intercepts, instructed Windeyer to alter course southward to 192° until further orders.[196] That afternoon, visibility decreased in mist as five boats of group *Spitz* overhauled ONS 154 from astern guided by shadowing reports from Oberleutnant Leimkühler in *U 225*.[197]

Two hours after dark, *U 225*, still the only boat in firm contact, observed the oiler *Scottish Heather* as she returned from refuelling *Chilliwack* astern of ON 154 and ruthlessly took up an attack position ahead of the vessel "to create a torch at the rear of the convoy"—an attempt, literally, to create "flaming datum."[198] He torpedoed the tanker at 2035z, but it struggled on, frustrating Leimkühler's plan, and eventually limped back to harbour. *Chilliwack*, commanded by Lieutenant-Commander L.L. Foxall, RCNR, counterattacked, driving the submarine under with furious oerlikon fire but inflicting no serious harm. There was the usual flurry of snowflake from the convoy, but the Commodore ordered it to cease, with the result that *U 225* lost ONS 154. The only U-boat continually in contact in the mist that night was *U 260*, commanded by Kapitänleutnant Purkhold, who kept station by using *Metox*. Purkhold, who sighted an escort at 0013z on 28 December and then started trailing, considered that he was on ONS 154's starboard quarter. He increased range whenever the signal strength of the escort's radar grew louder, and transmitted hourly homing signals and contact reports for the rest of the pack, reporting "radar signals were detected every 2-6 min. and were up to 30 sec[onds] in length."[199] *U 260* kept touch

193. *U 441*, KTB, 28 Dec. 1942; Rohwer *Axis Submarine Successes*, 142

194. *Napanee* ROP; *Napanee*, deck log, 27 Dec. 1942; SS *Toward*, ROP, ONS 154, 11 Jan. 1943, NAC, RG 24, 11989, file Rescue ships 1942-43; SS *King Edward*, *Soekaboemi*, *Melrose Abbey*, and *Empire Union*, "Particulars of Attacks on Merchant Vessels by Enemy Submarines"; *U 441*, KTB, 27 Dec. 1942

195. Although U-boats had exploited information gleaned by the convoy voice net in SC 107 and other earlier battles, the KTBs for this prolonged action contain no mention of such eavesdropping.

196. *St Laurent* ROP; SS *Fort Lamy*, VCmdre's Report, ONS 154; CTU 24.1.11 to AIG 303, 1017z/27 Dec. 1942, DHH, 89/34, v 25; C-in-C WA to HMS *Woolwich*, *Badsworth*, and *Wolverine*, 0938z/27 Dec. 1942, C-in-C WA to ONS 154, 1002z, 1318z and 1428z/27 Dec. 1942, CTU 24.1.11 to AIG 303, 1140z/27 Dec. 1942, NARA, WNRC, RG 313 Red, CTF 24, ONS 154, box 8702; *Kenogami*, deck log, 27 Dec. 1942; Revely, *Convoy that Nearly Died*, 81

197. KTB, 27 Dec. 1942

198. *U 225*, KTB, 27 Dec. 1942

199. *U 260*, KTB, 27-8 Dec. 1942; and Rohwer, *Axis Submarine Successes*, 143-4

for over seven hours during the night, all the while sending homing signals and contact reports. BdU, believing that the convoy had altered to the southwest was sceptical, but Purkhold's dogged persistence prevented ONS 154 from escaping in the fog.[200]

At 0225z on 28 December, *St Laurent* picked up *U 615* on radar. The boat had just obtained a sound bearing, but could not establish visual or asdic contact. Fifteen minutes later, while returning to the screen, the destroyer regained radar contact, made a sighting, and closed at twenty-five knots to about 700 yards as the U-boat crash-dived. Adopting the same tactics he had used against *U 356*, Windeyer dropped one depth charge pattern by eye, opened to about 1,000 yards and carried out a deliberate attack on an asdic contact that he lost at 200 yards. This time the U-boat survived without damage, but Windeyer, having sighted a large oil slick on the surface, made a triumphant signal to Western Approaches: "Got him. Dropped 10 charges counted 14 explosions one enormous. Psalms 119 Verses 97 and 98."[201] The biblical reference in this exuberant signal, beginning with "I love thy laws ..." seems to indicate that the tactics had been devised by Western Approaches.

By morning on the 29th the Admiralty estimated twelve U-boats were in pursuit and six in company. An alteration to the west failed to throw off the pack, and by early afternoon the first of the *Ungestüm* units were arriving. Several of those boats caught brief glimpses of escorts through the mist, and when the fog suddenly lifted at least eight submarines sighted the convoy itself. By 1803z, thirty minutes before sunset, eleven U-boats were in visual contact, so many that they were having difficulty getting their sighting reports through to BdU. HF/DF bearings swamped the receivers in *Fidelity* and *Toward*, the latter now impossibly crowded with survivors. *St Laurent* dropped astern while putting down a U-boat. As Windeyer started back in the approaching darkness, he came across *Fidelity*, which had also dropped astern. He urged her to hoist out one of the Grumman Kingfisher floatplanes to help cover the alteration of course but, in spite of an oil slick that *St Laurent* laid down to calm the seas, the aircraft crashed on take off, and the destroyer only rescued its two-man crew with great difficulty.[202]

An arduous night clearly lay ahead. Years later, Lieutenant F.C. Frewer, RCN, *St Laurent*'s first lieutenant, could still vividly recall the chilling effect that the sight of U-boats relentlessly stalking ONS 154 on the surface had on his sailors:

> Never have I been faced with a situation [like it] ... when I came up on deck one night [I] found nearly the whole ship's company sleeping on the upper deck ... my first reaction ... was ... what the hell are you doing up here, get down below. It wasn't all that cold but everyone had their lifebelts inflated and they were all sleeping on deck because it was a sort of a scary situation ... you could see a couple of U-boats on one side about five miles away, just outside range, in clear visibility, and there were no

---

200. *U 260*, KTB, 28 Dec. 1942

201. *St Laurent* ROP; *St Laurent*, Report of Attack on U-Boat, 0040/28 Dec. 1942, RG 24, 11332, 8280-ONS154; *Battleford* ROP; *Napanee* ROP and deck log, 27 Dec. 1942; *Chilliwack*, Report of Attack on U-Boat, 1830/27 Dec. 1942, NAC, RG 24, 11332, 8280-ONS154; SS *Fort Lamy*, VCmdre's Report, ONS 154; CTU 24.1.11 to AIG 303, 1957z/27 Dec. 1942, C-in-C WA to CTU 24.1.11, 2259z/27 Dec. 1942, NARA, WNRC, RG 313 Red, CTF 24, ONS 154, box 8702; *U 615*, *U 225*, *U 203*, *U 260*, and *U 406*, KTBs, 27-8 Dec. 1942; CTU 24.1.11 to AIG 303, 0313z/28 Dec. 1942, DHH, 89/34, v 25

202. Adm to Escorts of ON 154, 1151a/28 Dec. 1942, NAC, RG 24, 11332, 8280-ONS154; *U 123*, *U 336*, *U 664*, *U 440*, and *U 435*, KTB, 28 Dec. 1942; *St Laurent* ROP; *St Laurent*, deck log, 28 Dec. 1942; Jullian, *HMS Fidelity*, 193-5, Burn, *Fighting Commodores*, 158

less than three on the port side and they were again bearing on the convoy ... recharging batteries and reloading torpedoes ... but you couldn't leave the convoy because we only had ... four corvettes and ourselves ... even if you pinned down a submarine, you couldn't stay with him to carry on the attack ... .if you stayed with your contact for an hour, you'd be twelve miles behind and it would take a couple of hours to catch up and get back in position ... when you were going at 24 ... knots to regain position you couldn't use your Asdic ... because of the quenching ... this was a terrifying time.[203]

Certain German submariners saw the approaching darkness differently. Kapitänleutnant Zetzsche in *U 591* noted, "excellent visibility, ideal weather for a night attack!"[204] Several decided to close and fire immediately in the moderate seas prior to moonrise.

Night fell into inky blackness that obscured the horizon and at least four boats lost contact. It was not enough. *Battleford*, under Lieutenant F.A. Beck, RCNVR, closed to investigate a radar contact off the convoy's starboard bow and suddenly "was presented with a sight the like of [which] no other ship had ever seen, or was likely to see again—[four] U-boats coming towards him, travelling in line ahead on the surface, exchanging light signals."[205] Beck illuminated and opened fire. Probably with the help of *Chilliwack*, he had surprised the first concerted attempt by the pack to get among ONS 154, but *Battleford*'s radar, jarred by the gun blast, broke down.[206] *Chilliwack* attacked *U 615* on the port bow of the convoy, forcing it out of the battle.[207] At 2008z *St Laurent*, returning from rescuing *Fidelity*'s airmen, sighted a surfaced U-boat 600 yards ahead in a cloud of dense exhaust smoke. Both *St Laurent* and *Kenogami* attacked and drove it down. Neither ship gained asdic contact, but the destroyer dropped five charges by eye. A few minutes later *Napanee* obtained an asdic contact on the starboard quarter at 1,800 yards—this suggests conditions were exceptionally good for asdic—illuminated a boat on the surface and forced it under. At 2045z Windeyer signalled Western Approaches: "Attack repulsed. No ships torpedoed. Every escort has had a fight. Some promising attacks were made." The escorts had indeed driven off or forced down ten of the twelve shadowing U-boats, but the night's activities had scarcely begun.[208]

The fighting and a series of course alterations left the screen badly disorganized. *Shediac* remained astern with *Fidelity*, which was too valuable a target to abandon without escort, and *Battleford*, her radar still unserviceable and unaware of a change of course to starboard, spent a good part of the night hunting for the convoy; Windeyer knew nothing of her absence. With only four escorts remaining on the screen, and the starboard bow and probably the port beam of the

---

203. Capt F.C. Frewer, interview by Mac Lynch, 1990, 17-18, DHH, Frewer Biog file

204. *U 591*, KTB, 28 Dec. 1942

205. Burn, *Fighting Commodores*, 157

206. *U 664* crash dived and never relocated the convoy, *U 662* opened out and lost contact but subsequently sank a derelict astern. Diagram, Night of 29 Dec., NAC, RG 24, 11332, 8280-ONS154; *Battleford* ROP; *Battleford*, deck log, 28 Dec. 1942; *U 664* and *U 662*, KTBs, 28 Dec. 1942; Rohwer, *Axis Submarine Successes*, 144

207. *U 615*, KTB, 29 Dec. 1942

208. *St Laurent* and *Napanee* ROPs; CTU 24.1.11 to AIG 303, 2045z and 2050z/28 Dec. 1942, and *Chilliwack* to AIG 302, 2007z/28 Dec. 1942, all in NARA, WNRC, RG 313 Red, CTF 24, ONS 154, box 8702; *Chilliwack*, "Report of Attack on U-Boat," 1745/28 Dec. 1942; *St Laurent*, "Report of Attack on U-Boat," 1808/28 Dec. 1942; *Napanee*, "Report of Attack on U-Boat," 1808/28 Dec. 1942, NAC, RG 24, 11332, 8280-ONS 154; *Battleford*, deck log, 28-9 Dec. 1942; *U 203*, *U 225*, *U 336*, *U 435*, *U 440*, *U 591*, *U 615*, *U 628*, *U 659*, *U 662*, and *U 664*, KTBs, 28 Dec. 1942

convoy uncovered, ONS 154 was steaming into an ever larger concentration of submarines. *U 628* and *U 591* now sighted starshell and made their first visual contact, and although *U 659* received orders to break off pursuit to escort the German blockade runner *Rhakotis*, there were still thirteen U-boats within striking distance. In one of the most devastating attacks of the entire Battle of the Atlantic, six of them torpedoed nine ships in just two hours.

The first two almost simultaneous attacks at 1941z and 1944z by *U 203* and *U 435* were unsuccessful, but may have distracted the escorts.[209] An hour later *U 591*, under Kapitanleutnant Zetzsche, with one diesel unserviceable but positioned ahead, submerged to avoid an escort, then surfaced to find the convoy's course alteration had placed it in ideal firing position on the starboard bow. Zetzsche fired at 2052z, hitting the second ship in the eleventh column, *Norse King*, and then dived.[210] It was possibly another barrage of torpedoes from Zetzsche, fired at 2056z as he passed under the convoy, that *Napanee* avoided as her lookouts reported seeing two submarines; starshell revealed only a possible wake and no firm contact. At the same time, the aggressive Oberleutnant Leimkühler in *U 225* was also closing from the starboard bow. Windeyer ordered a Major Hoople and a half-Hot Dog, both without apparent result. At 2102z *U 225* fired a spread of four torpedoes, followed by a stern shot. Leimkühler then came under machine-gun fire and crash-dived, but he had torpedoed two freighters in the eleventh column, *Melmore Head* and *Ville de Rouen*. Surfacing on the other side of the convoy, *U 225* withdrew to reload.[211] While the survivors took to boats, *St Laurent* astern of the convoy and *Chilliwack* on the port bow, both attacked and thought they had sunk submarines before returning to the screen. Windeyer, now aware of *Battleford*'s absence, moved up to the starboard bow. Almost simultaneously, an alteration by the convoy to the west put Purkhold in *U 260* directly ahead, and he fired torpedoes at 2127z, hitting the only cargo ship remaining in the eleventh column, *Empire Wagtail* carrying a full cargo of coal.[212] Exploding in a mass of flames, she went down instantly with all hands.

Snowflake and starshell filled the sky, exploding high in the cloud cover. Under the glow, *U 406* manoeuvred to attack the convoy from ahead with a pattern of the newly introduced pattern-running FAT torpedoes.[213] Fired at 2217z, they caused havoc on the port side of the convoy, hitting three cargo vessels in the first and second columns, *Baron Cochrane*, *Lynton Grange,* and *Zarian*. *U 406* withdrew rapidly away from the port side of the convoy to avoid being illuminated, and about twenty minutes later crash-dived to avoid an escort close abeam to port. The expected counterattack never developed. Neither *Chilliwack* nor *Kenogami*, stationed on the port side, detected *U 406*. Both ships had defective radar, and *Chilliwack* had received serious damage from one of her own depth charges in a previous attack.[214]

---

209. *U 203* and *U 435*, KTBs, 28 Dec. 1942

210. *U 591*, KTB, 28 Dec. 1942. Zetzsche submerged because with only one diesel his ability to evade on the surface was too limited.

211. *U 225*, KTB, 28-9 Dec. 1942

212. W.H. Mitchell and L.A. Sawyer, *The Empire Ships* (London 1990), 409, *Lloyd's War Losses* I, 601

213. FAT torpedoes were just reaching Atlantic boats and raised the number of hits in convoy attacks to 75 per cent of torpedoes fired. MOD, *U-Boat War in the Atlantic* II, 84-5

214. Rohwer, *Axis Submarine Successes*, 143; *Battleford*, deck log, 28 Dec. 1942; CTU 24.1.11 to AIG 303, 2106z/28 Dec. 1942, NARA, WNRC, RG 313 Red, CTF 24, ONS 154, box 8702; Revely, *Convoy that Nearly Died*, 92-4, 108-11

The screen now lost all cohesion. Windeyer ordered the corvettes to fire starshell independently, a useless tactic that only illuminated them for the attacking U-boats.

Since his first attacks almost two hours earlier, Leimkühler in *U 225* had worked his way back to a position ahead, but had been unable to close because of "attacks by other boats and subsequent fire works." He entered the convoy for a second pass and fired five separate shots, hitting *Empire Shackleton*, the commodore's ship at the head of the sixth column, and the tanker just astern, *President Francqui*.[215] "The scene," wrote Lieutenant Stuart Henderson of *Napanee*, "suggested a holocaust. All the ships appeared to be firing snowflakes, and tracers criss-crossed in all directions, escorts firing starshell. The sea was dotted with lights from boats and rafts, and two burning wrecks which had hauled out to starboard helped the illumination, though one of them was pouring out dense black smoke." Astern of the convoy, where six crippled ships were finished off during the night, Zetzsche in *U 591* observed, "Just when one tube had been reloaded and I wanted to close for a second *coup de grace*, the freighter explodes in front of my eyes. The burning freighter is also sunk after a further 2 minutes. Such cooperation is too much!"[216]

Fortunately, the cooperation did, in fact, dissipate and the convoy itself escaped any further losses. Three U-boats remained in the vicinity of ONS 154, and two attempted unsuccessful submerged attacks in daylight on 29 December. After the long pursuit at speed to intercept the convoy and the frenzied night actions, several submarines were now low on fuel and were directed to search astern for damaged vessels. *Fidelity*, also still behind the convoy and proceeding to the Azores with engine problems, was attacked unsuccessfully after dark by *U 225* and *U 665*. *Fidelity* proved a difficult target because of her array of weapons; the remaining aircraft had forced three submarines to each crash-dive twice during the afternoon, while the MTB interfered with *U 615*'s attack. Her luck finally ran out the next day, when she was sunk by *U 435*.[217]

By dark on 29 December increasing winds were making it difficult for the U-boats to gain position on the convoy, and only Purkhold in *U 260* maintained contact by using *Metox* before losing touch at 2300z. The fleet destroyers HMS *Milne* and *Meteor* had reinforced the escort that day and during their first night fired starshells over HF/DF bearings. Five boats were still pursuing the convoy, but did not regain firm contact.[218] By the next afternoon the two destroyers and the corvettes *Battleford* and *Shediac* were all low on fuel and had to be detached for the Azores.[219] The

---

215. Leimkühler in *U 225* got among the approaching merchant vessels, receiving a furious and accurate fire from them before he dived. *Empire Shackleton* headed for the Azores, even though some of the crew had abandoned ship. About four hours later *U 123* and *U 435*, coming across the ship, sank her with four torpedoes and surface gunfire. Rohwer, *Axis Submarine Successes*, 143; SS *Lamy*, VCmdre's Report, ONS 154; *St Laurent* ROP; CTU 24.1.11 to AIG 303, 2255z/28 Dec. 1942; C-in-C WA to Capt (D) 3rd Destroyer Flotilla, 0213z/28 Dec. 1942, both in NARA, WNRC, RG 313 Red, CTF 24, ONS 154, box 8702; *U 123*, *U 435*, and *U 628*, KTBs, 28 Dec. 1942

216. *Napanee* ROP; *U 591* sank *Ville de Rouen*; *U 591*, KTB, 28 Dec. 1942

217. *Shediac* had remained with *Fidelity* until recalled in the early hours of 29 Dec. The Admiralty had ordered a tug to assist *Fidelity*. *U 225*, *U 203*, and *U 615*, KTBs, 29 Dec. 1942; *U 435*, KTB, 30 Dec. 1942; Syrett, "Battle for Convoy ONS 154," 45. MOD, *U-Boat War in the Atlantic* II, 70

218. *U 662*, *U 664*, and *U 591* observed illuminants in the distance during the night, but they never gained contact. *U 406* sighted escorts at 2250z and opened out, while *U 455* crash dived at 2345z on suddenly sighting an escort. *U 591* broke off because of lack of fuel at 2320z. *U 662*, *U 664*, and *U 591*, KTB, 29/30 Dec. 1942

219. *Shediac* had to be towed the last forty miles to port by *Battleford*, while *Milne* towed *Meteor* for the last five miles. Burn, *Fighting Commodores*, 166. The tanker *Scottish Heather* had been designated as the "escort oiler" for ONS 154, but it had been damaged by a torpedo.

convoy now was more vulnerable than ever, with only *St Laurent, Chilliwack, Kenogami,* and *Napanee* in the screen, but no attacks occurred. Windeyer concluded later that the U-boats had "had enough." In fact, BdU urged his boats to pursue the remnants of the convoy but ONS 154 proved elusive. When *U 455* eventually sighted it at 1652z on a westerly course, shadowing proved difficult in increasing westerly seas. Four other boats still in pursuit were scouting southwards and were therefore too far distant to intercept. Finally, U-Boat Command ordered boats not in contact to cease operations at nightfall on 30 December.[220] HMS *Fame* arrived on the 31st and Commander Heathcote assumed duties as SOE, but by that time the five-day ordeal of ONS 154, now more than halfway across the Atlantic, was over. Fourteen ships had been sunk and close to 500 lives lost.

It had been a disaster, and probably the worst defeat in our navy's history. Previous convoys outbound on the southerly track with ships for the South Atlantic had not been seriously mauled, but in this case not routing the convoy for maximum air cover proved a grievous misjudgment. The failures to provide a second destroyer to replace *Burwell* and to ensure that the escort had functioning HF/DF equipment were also serious oversights. The Admiralty's Operational Intelligence Centre was preparing its weekly "U-Boat Trend" report to senior commanders and officials, even while receiving information that one-third of the convoy had been lost. Its discussion of ONS 154 highlighted how in the absence of air cover large numbers of U-boats could overwhelm an escort force:

> This grave disaster was suffered in an area out of range of any available home-based aircraft and affords a grim demonstration of the relative power of a fairly typical convoy escort (consisting of one destroyer and 5 corvettes) and of a U-boat pack of a strength which may frequently be mustered in the North Atlantic. All experience of convoy engagements with U-boat packs indicates with increasing emphasis ... that heavy concerted attacks by considerable numbers of U-boats can be and usually have been prevented if aircraft are in company with convoy but that beyond a certain point of saturation a surface escort alone cannot hold its own against any force of U-boats which outnumbers the escort in a ratio of or exceeding two to one.[221]

Post-action analysis focused mainly on the tactical conduct of the battle. The defence of ONS 154 pointed up all the weaknesses of inadequately trained, poorly equipped, and badly led escort groups. Windeyer, possibly as a result of the cumulative strain caused by months of uninterrupted seatime, suffered a breakdown late in the battle and was relieved by Lieutenant Frewer on New Year's Day. In Newfoundland, Commodore Reid was inclined to give Windeyer the benefit of the doubt because the convoy had been exposed to an exceptionally strong and well-positioned submarine force, but there was no denying the poor organization and preparation of the escort group. The US Atlantic Fleet Anti-Submarine Warfare unit remarked on unreliable records, poor use of HF/DF intelligence, and excessive use of illumination.[222] Western Approaches emphasized the lack of organization and

---

220. *U 455*, BdU, KTBs, 30 Dec. 1942. *U 455* lost contact during the night.

221. "U-Boat Trend. Period 21/12/42-30/12/42," Syrett, *Battle of the Atlantic,* 114

222. Interestingly, although on occasion driven off by illumination and forced down by escorts U-boat commanders also commented on the heavy use of illuminants and a lack of robust opposition by the escorts. *U 225* and *U 260*, KTBs, 29 Dec. 1942, *U 441*, KTB, 27 Dec. 1942

control, and in the Admiralty, the Director of Anti-Submarine Warfare described Windeyer's report of proceedings as "somewhat hysterical." Pointing out the complete absence of an appreciation of the threat as the convoy was approaching a known concentration of U-boats, he drew attention to "the very real necessity of delegating the control of operations of this magnitude and importance only to officers whose experience and ability are proportionate to the task."[223]

It will be recalled that when similar observations had been made about Piers after the ordeal of SC 107, Canadian naval authorities had expressed some resentment. There was no such reaction after ONS 154. Even as the battle was being fought, arrangements were being made in Ottawa for the temporary withdrawal of Canadian groups from the MOEF (see Chapter 11). This was, as the historical records officer in Britain was to note some months later, the low point for the Royal Canadian Navy in the Battle of the Atlantic. That being said, if an additional destroyer had been found to reinforce the escort group, the defence might have been conducted in a more effective manner. And if Bletchley Park had solved Enigma a few days earlier, the convoy might have been routed clear of *Spitz* and *Ungesüm*. The battle might then never have taken place. But those are the "What if's?" of history; the reality was that all the elements of tragedy were present, and ONS 154 was a tragedy of epic proportions.[224]

The final three months of 1942 were a severe test for Canadian escort groups on the North Atlantic. They had played a key role as the *Kriegsmarine* continued its sustained effort to interdict the convoys. Over ninety U-boats—more than double the forty-two at the beginning of the year—were continually at sea in the Atlantic. Ocean crossings were made even more arduous by particularly severe winter storms, which would, in the words of an American participant, "break records of fifty years standing."[225] Full gales or storms were recorded on 116 days out of 140 between 1 October 1942 and 18 February 1943.[226] At the same time, the horrific conditions also affected the ability of the U-boats, with only limited detection horizons at best, to locate and attack convoys. Radio signals intercepted by both sides affected the struggle. The Allies were unable to read German traffic that autumn, but used HF/DF information gleaned by a network of stations ashore to route convoys clear of suspected U-boat concentrations.[227] Meanwhile, the Germans were decrypting a high percentage of Allied convoy routing signals. Helped in part by signals intelligence, BdU was able to deploy its patrol lines so effectively that fourteen of the forty-eight convoys that crossed the

223. DASW minute, 29 Mar. 1943, PRO, ADM 199/356; Notes on *St Laurent* ROP by captain (D)'s staff, FONF, 4-6 Jan. 1943; FONF to SecNB, 23 Jan. 1943; Lt-Cdr P.M. Bliss to DOD, 20 Mar. 1943, all in RG 24, 11332, 8280-ONS 154; Atlantic Fleet ASW Unit to CINCLANT, 4 Mar. 1943, NARA, WNRC, RG 313 Red, CTF 24, ONS 154, box 8702; PRO, ADM 199/222, f 382

224. "It may be found desirable to acknowledge in detail just how hard the going was at this low ebb in the Battle of the Atlantic in those days, when North African convoys were putting an added burden on our escort resources, even to the extent of admitting that the Senior Officer of a Canadian group suffered a nervous collapse while on duty and that the group became disorganised during the main series of attacks on the night of 28th /29th." Historical Records Officer (Lt James George) to CCCS, 2nd report 31 May 1943, app A

225. Waters, *Bloody Winter*, 119

226. This was a staggering increase over previous experience as during the first three winter seasons of the war there had been 79.7 days with storms and gales. Memo from First Sea Lord to Anti-U-Boat Committee, 30 Mar. 1943, PRO, CAB 86/4

227. Dr Jürgen Rohwer has calculated that between July 1942 and May 1943 the Allies successfully diverted about 60 per cent of all North Atlantic convoys around German submarine concentrations. Rohwer, *Critical Convoy Battles*, 36

North Atlantic in October, November, and December—almost one-third—came under attack. The bitter convoy battles were fought in the air gap. They involved as many as twenty-two submarines, and the most gruelling stretched out over several days, and in SC 107's case, a week. It was the Canadian escorts that bore the brunt of the assaults that autumn since eight of the fourteen convoys under attack were escorted by the four C groups and the single A group, which consisted largely of Canadian corvettes. And of the fifty-five ships sunk, thirty-seven were in those eight convoys.[228]

The fierce battles must be viewed in the context of a successful campaign by the Allies to manage resources, after all, U-boats sank only fifty-five of 1,830 merchant ships that crossed the North Atlantic in convoys in the period under review. It was the cumulative effects of sinkings of independents and ships in convoy by submarines and other causes that year, combined with the shipping resources required to sustain Torch, that were straining Allied logistics and caused a major import crisis in Britain by the end of 1942.[229] Losses on the scale of a SC 107 or ONS 154, the worst disasters on the North Atlantic that autumn—or of a SL 125—could not be sustained, and they drew close attention in Western Approaches Command and the Admiralty, which had direct responsibility for fighting the Atlantic campaign. The escorts involved were subjected to harsh scrutiny, but with the benefit of a longer perspective and access to records from both sides, it can be seen that the efficiency of the escorts was only one factor in a complex equation. Evasive routing; weather; the availability of air cover; the number of U-boats that could actually reach a given convoy; how many that could then concentrate; which groups were defending the slower convoys as they plodded across the air gap; whether individual groups had more than one destroyer to prosecute HF/DF bearings; the size of the convoy relative to the number of escorts; whether the parent navy had a margin of fresh resources when required; tactical leadership; the state of training and equipment of both escorts and submarines; and, finally, luck, were all relevant. What is more, the autumn of 1942 was still near the dawn of electronic warfare. The overwhelming majority of U-boat attacks were made on the surface at night, and submarines were largely dependent on visual information to locate and attack ships. Ambient light was an important tactical factor in the equation that determined whether an attack would succeed or was even feasible. The phase of the moon, cloud cover and light conditions at twilight, also became significant tactical considerations. The important fact is that the Allied navies fighting the Battle of the Atlantic were grappling with the myriad challenges: lessons were being absorbed and corrective action was either under way or on the horizon. By the following autumn, German submarines would rarely be able to operate on the surface in large packs and the hard-fought actions of the autumn of 1942 would be seen as just one stage in the long struggle to defeat the U-boats.

---

228. Statistics from Hague, *Allied Convoy System*, 123-64. See also, Milner, *North Atlantic Run*, 129.

229. Milner, "The Battle of the Atlantic," *Journal of Strategic Studies* 13/1 (1990), 51

CHAPTER ELEVEN

The Creation of Canadian North-West Atlantic Command

ON 15 DECEMBER 1942 A.V. Alexander, the First Lord of the Admiralty, advised Prime Minister Churchill that immediate measures should be taken to alleviate the critical shortage of oil in the United Kingdom. Britain faced a general crisis of imports in the wake of the heavy losses of shipping to enemy action during the year, but the oil situation was particularly acute because the great demands of the Torch operations in North Africa coincided with protracted delays in tanker sailings from the Caribbean resulting from the necessity for the ships to proceed up the coast of the United States in local convoys before crossing the Atlantic (see Chapter 7).[1] Alexander proposed the institution of direct tanker convoys between the Caribbean and Britain sailing every twenty days. This scheme, because of its requirement for a significant number of long-range escorts from the limited Allied pool, would have wide-ranging ramifications, not least for the Royal Canadian Navy. The transatlantic convoy cycle would have to open up from eight to ten days in order to release four groups of escort vessels. The Atlantic convoys would be operated by eight British groups, while four mid-ocean groups—the single American A group and three Canadian C groups—were to be shifted for a limited time to the United Kingdom–Gibraltar run to allow them access to Royal Navy training facilities.[2] This, in turn, would release four long-endurance groups, which would be reorganized into three, for the oil convoys between the Dutch West Indies and the United Kingdom, and direct US tanker convoys from the Caribbean to the Mediterranean.[3] Thus, RCN escorts would be under British control, for both training and operations, and this, the Admiralty hoped, would satisfy "the paramount importance of bringing the Canadian groups up to standard."[4]

Such was the gravity of the situation that Churchill sent a personal appeal to both President Roosevelt and Prime Minister Mackenzie King asking for their cooperation in carrying out these

---

1. First Lord to PM, 15 Dec. 1942, "Memo on the Measures Necessary to Improve (1) The Oil Situation in the UK; (2) Training of Canadian Manned Escort Groups," PRO, PREM 3/331/8

2. "Re-Allocation of Escort Groups to Provide Escorts for the DWI–UK Tanker Convoys and the Necessity for Giving Better Training to the Americans and Canadian Escort Groups," Ibid, para 16

3. Adm to NSHQ, 1319A/18 Dec. 1942 cited in Plans Division, "History of North Atlantic Convoy Escort Organization and Canadian Participation Therein 9/39–4/43," in Convoy Operations, DHH 81/520/8280 box 1, 8280A, v I

4. Conference Minutes, "Fuel Supplies to UK and Africa; Related Escort Problems," NAC, RG 24, 11968, 222-1, 5

recommendations. On the question of the efficiency of RCN ocean escorts, Churchill was diplomatic but frank with the Canadian leader:

4. I appreciate the grand contribution of the Royal Canadian Navy to the battle of the Atlantic but the expansion of the RCN has created a training problem which must take some time to solve.

5. An advantage of the Admiralty proposal is therefore that until your training facilities are built up it will afford the Canadian and American groups an opportunity of using the unique training facilities available on this side of the Atlantic which their employment on the shorter voyage between the United Kingdom and Gibraltar and the longer lay-over in the United Kingdom will enable them to do.

6. ... there is no question that we must put a stop to the heavy toll which U-boats are taking from our Atlantic convoys and this can only be achieved by training our escorts to the highest possible pitch of efficiency.[5]

For the Canadian navy these proposals were profoundly disturbing. Minister Angus L. Macdonald described them as "drastic" when he presented Churchill's messages to the Cabinet War Committee on 23 December: "Canadian naval forces would be divided and the majority diverted from Canadian waters, beyond Canadian control."[6] A few days later, Admiral Nelles, who according to the recollections of Captain Eric Brand was furious,[7] made much the same point as the minister but in stronger language:

This is the third, but most serious, attempt on the part of the Admiralty to get operational control of our ships.

When North Africa was in the planning stage, we were asked to give anything. We scratched as deeply as we could and were able to get seventeen [corvettes] and stated that that was the maximum we could provide. In November we were informed that a frightful shortage of minesweepers had developed and were asked to assist; we regretted that this was not possible. Now it is oil shortage.[8]

Wisely, the navy's senior leaders assigned the initial management of the issue to the Director of Plans at Naval Service Headquarters, Captain H.G. DeWolf, who took a balanced view. DeWolf, a thorough-going professional and future chief of the naval staff, advised that it was in the best interests of the navy to accept the Admiralty's proposals. He challenged some of the statistical assumptions about the Canadian record in defending convoys on which the British case was built, and like other staff officers at NSHQ observed that inadequate equipment as much as insufficient training lay behind Canadian operational shortcomings, but urged a dispassionate search for solutions. "We are equally concerned with the Admiralty," he pointed out, "in checking the heavy toll which U-Boats are taking from the Atlantic convoys ... The Admiralty propos-

---

5. DSec to SSEA, tg 264, 17 Dec. 1942, in John F. Hilliker (ed), *Documents on Canadian External Relations* XI: *1942-1943* (Ottawa 1980), 355. Churchill also enclosed two telegrams he had sent to President Roosevelt concerning the oil crisis, Ibid, 356-7.

6. CWCM, 23 Dec. 1942

7. Brand journal, XV, 64, DHH, 81/145

8. CNS, "Reference—Despatches 264 and 265 from PM of UK to PM of Canada...," nd [late Dec. 1942], NAC, RG 24, 6796, NSS 8375, pt 4

als are calculated to further this object and at the same time meet an emergency situation. The shortage of escort vessels in general, and the pooling of our resources would ensure their most economical use ... Unless we have a better solution to offer we should place no obstacle in the way of the proposal."[9]

DeWolf went to Washington on 29 to 31 December, where Commodore J.M. Mansfield, RN, Chief of Staff at Western Approaches Command, presented the Admiralty's scheme to a conference of Canadian, British, and American naval officers. A snow storm delayed DeWolf's arrival until the second day of the conference. On the first day the officers had concluded that the fourth C group should go to the eastern Atlantic in place of the United States-Canadian A 3 group, possibly as a result of the Roosevelt administration's initial belief that the British were overstating the oil supply crisis that lay behind the whole reorganization.[10] DeWolf underscored that only the government of Canada could authorize the redeployment of Canadian warships, and would not do so lightly: "The government's view is that we have sort of grown up with this North Atlantic problem and feel we have a permanent interest in it." He admitted that training fell short, and that the "equipment situation is almost as bad," but pointed out that it was Allied demands for more and more escorts that had resulted in this situation. "We are convinced that any ship is better than none. We have done that for the past two years ... We have even kept [ships] at sea against our better judgment. Any ships are better than none." In the face of this enormous and prolonged strain, DeWolf allowed "that our groups will benefit by the change [to the shorter run between the United Kingdom and Gibraltar], and I think that is the main point, that they reach the standard. They will come back to the North Atlantic run. We won't have any trouble convincing the government that is the necessary step."[11]

Prior to DeWolf's departure for Washington, Captain H.N. Lay, Director of the Operations Division at NSHQ, agreed that a temporary withdrawal of the C groups to British control might be warranted, but argued that the navy should also seize the occasion to assert Canada's right to full command authority over convoy operations in the western part of the North Atlantic.[12] Lay, a nephew of Mackenze King, was a warm sponsor of nationalist causes.[13] His advice drew on a lengthy memorandum he had prepared earlier in December in which he had urged the readjustment of command arrangements in the North Atlantic, on the principle that "operational control of the convoys themselves, the Escorting Forces, and other related matters" should go to the navy that had committed the largest number of escorts. "In the Western Atlantic," he had argued, "this is obviously the Royal Canadian Navy and not, repetition not, the United States Navy."[14] Although DeWolf did not raise the issue in Washington, the naval staff was already pressing the case for increased Canadian control, and would do so with growing tenacity in the weeks following the conference.

---

9.   Brief for the Minister, 21 Dec. 1942, ibid

10.   Milner, *North Atlantic Run*, 202-3; Roosevelt to Churchill, tg 239, 18 Dec. 1943, printed in Francis L. Loewenheim, Harold D. Langley, and Manfred Jonas, *Roosevelt and Churchill: Their Secret Wartime Correspondence* (New York 1975), 299-300

11.   [verbatim transcript of conference proceedings], "Second Day," 30 Dec. 1942, NAC, RG 24, 11968, 221-1

12.   DOD to CNS and VCNS, "Conference at Washington re Opening of Convoy Cycle and re Distribution of Escorts," 26 Dec. 1942, NAC, RG 24, 3998, NSS 1057-5-1

13.   Lay, *Memoirs of a Mariner, passim*

14.   Memo to CNS, 2 Dec. 1942, NAC, MG30, E420, Lay Papers, Correspondence

This assertiveness, of which Lay was only the most vocal exponent, grew from the RCN's efforts since the beginning of the war to ensure that, in measure with the ability of the service to contribute to the Allied cause, Canadian forces should be organized, recognized, and controlled as distinct national forces. The unheralded events of 1942—both the enterprise of the enemy and the demands of the allies—had severely tested the capacity of the Canadian service, but it had nevertheless continued to meet existing commitments while also taking up new ones.

What was more, the navy had simultaneously persuaded the government to embark on an ambitious new program of expansion. In addition to the thirty frigates and thirty-eight corvettes ordered on Canadian account for the 1942–3 fiscal year, in December 1942 the government approved a new shipbuilding program that included orders for no fewer than sixty-four additional frigates, the maximum number that industry could produce by mid-1945. Although the frigates were, in some respects, intended to fulfil the function of destroyers, the first of the new ships would not be available until the latter part of 1943, and the naval staff was in any case unwilling to have these stopgap, emergency-built vessels take the place of the service's valuable complement of destroyers, whose numbers and capabilities were dwindling as a result of losses and the severe wear of constant operations in the North Atlantic.[15]

As early as September 1942—well before the battles for SC 107 and ONS 154 had underscored the desperate need for the RCN groups of the mid-ocean force to have more destroyers—the naval staff was endeavouring to obtain additional destroyers of types comparable to the RCN's River class from the RN. The staff, in a measure of its growing confidence, responded to reluctance on the part of the Admiralty to part with such precious ships, by suggesting Canada would otherwise have to assign the four big Tribal class destroyers building for the RCN in Britain to convoy duties, a waste of the great gun-power of these ships, which the Admiralty urgently needed to combat enemy surface forces in European waters. By pairing deployment of the Tribals under Admiralty control with the request for as many as fourteen additional River class destroyers for the C groups, the naval staff also skilfully overcame the resistance of the Canadian government—which wanted to make increased provisions for the defence of Canadian waters in view of the German successes in the St Lawrence and who had even hinted at deploying the Tribals on the west coast[16]—to overseas employment of the Tribals. In short, during the autumn and winter of 1942 the staff took effective steps to ensure the acquisition of improved and more numerous ships with which the service could fully sustain the very large responsibilities that had fallen to it in the defence of shipping, while also safeguarding the means by which it had always intended to achieve a prominent role in offensive surface warfare in European waters.[17]

The new expansion program, Macdonald informed the Cabinet War Committee, "would require total naval personnel of some 90,000 men" by 1945, nearly double the service's existing strength.

---

15. NBM, 5, 12 Oct. and 24 Nov. 1942; CWCM, 2 Dec. 1942; Tucker, *Naval Service of Canada* II, 69, 71, 75-6, 80

16. See DOP, "Employment of Tribal Destroyers," 7 Dec. 1942, NAC, RG 24, 6797, NSS 8375-355.

17. Michael Whitby, "The 'Other' Navy at War: The RCN's Tribal Class Destroyers 1939-44," Master's thesis, Carleton University, 1988, 25-33; Whitby, "Instruments of Security: The RCN's Procurement of the Tribal-Class Destroyers," *The Northern Mariner* 2/3 (1992), 8-10; DOD and DOP to CNS, VCNS, Minister, 19 Sep. 1942, DHH, NHS 8200 "Construction Ships 1939-45," pt 3; CWCM, 7, 28 Oct., 2 Dec. 1942

Knowing the sentiments of his colleagues, he added that "Canada was carrying approximately 45% of the convoy work in the North Atlantic. This was a natural responsibility for Canada to undertake."[18] To compete with the need for continued large intakes of personnel (an average of 2,000 per month in 1942),[19] and the requirement, which had become fully apparent only with the German offensive in North American waters, to sustain the bulk of the fleet from Canadian bases, plans were well in hand by the autumn of 1942 greatly to augment facilities in the eastern part of the country. Notable among the projects was the creation of a vast new training base at Deep Brook on the Bay of Fundy coast of northwestern Nova Scotia, with facilities for 10,000 personnel, as the new home for HMCS *Cornwallis*, the designation for the training schools crowded into the limited accommodation at Halifax. However, this training base, a large new dockyard in Sydney, and expansion projects at other east coast ports and in Newfoundland would not be ready until the spring of 1943 at the very earliest.[20]

Reassignments among the navy's senior leaders in September and October 1942 were another step towards consolidation of the service. Rear-Admiral L.W. Murray left St John's to become Commanding Officer Atlantic Coast in Halifax, relieving Rear-Admiral G.C. Jones, who went to Ottawa as Vice Chief of the Naval Staff. In October Commodore H.E. Reid, Jones's predecessor as vice chief, went to St John's as Flag Officer Newfoundland. Jones, perhaps the navy's most "political" flag officer, thus assumed the key position at the national headquarters, and Murray, its most accomplished operational commander, took over the major national command. By contrast, Reid's appointment without promotion somewhat downgraded the Newfoundland command, which within the alliance command structure had always been subordinate, initially to the British Western Approaches Command and, since September 1941, to the US Commander Task Force 24.[21]

Jones's posting to Ottawa followed from the rapid expansion of the headquarters staff during 1942. Captain Lay, an exponent of the view that NSHQ should, in the interests of effective national control, have a firmer grip on operations at sea on the model of the direction exercised by the British Admiralty, reported proudly in December 1942 that since October his Operations Division had been assigned nine additional officers. The division now boasted seven sections, organized to provide expert analysis of such specialized operational matters as hydrography, gunnery, and antisubmarine warfare, and a fully equipped and staffed plotting room to track current operations.[22] The efficiency and cohesion of all the headquarters divisions had been enhanced by the move of the staff from seventeen buildings into a large, purpose-built naval headquarters building on Elgin Street in Ottawa in November 1942.[23]

Canadian efforts to consolidate and expand the service during the latter part of 1942 echoed the initiatives that had established the Newfoundland and western local escort forces as prominent national commitments in 1941 and the early part of 1942. In these instances Canada reacted to thrusts by the enemy, but also to forestall or modify responses by the senior allies that might have

---

18. CWCM, 28 Oct. 1942

19. J.M. Hitsman, "Manpower Problems of the Royal Canadian Navy during the Second World War" (Report no. 71, Historical Section (G.S.) Army Headquarters), 12, DHH

20. Tucker, *Naval Service of Canada* II, 178-9, 198-9, 281-2; Tennyson and Sarty, *Guardian of the Gulf*, 288-90

21. *Niobe Newsletter*, no. 6 (1 Nov. 1942), in *Salty Dips* IV: *"Well, All But One!": The Wartime Niobe Newsletters* (Ottawa 1993), 19

22. "Summary of Naval War Effort," 1 Oct.–31 Dec. 1942, p. 4, DHH, NSS 1000-5-8 pt 3

23. Tucker, *Naval Service of Canada* II, 430

ignored Canadian interests. Despite the very great expansion of the Canadian war effort, the access of the armed forces to the highest level of Anglo-American military decision-making had not improved much since the initial British and US staff meetings of January to March 1941. At that time, as seen in Chapter 4, the larger powers had deemed that the British service delegations in Washington effectively represented Canada and the rest of the Commonwealth, and the resulting ABC-1 agreement took no particular account of Canadian capabilities or interests. The awkward situation that this subordinate status created for Rear-Admiral V.G. Brodeur, who as naval attaché served as an adviser to the Canadian minister in Washington under the authority of the Department of External Affairs, has been seen in Chapter 5. Determined efforts by the Canadian government to have the US government accept the creation in Washington of a Canadian military staff that would represent the armed forces and have direct access to the US military departments, as well as to US–British planning groups—which following the American entry into the war in December 1941 took formal shape as the Combined Chiefs of Staff organization—achieved little until the summer of 1942. On 4 August Brodeur became the Naval Member of the new Canadian Joint Staff in Washington, but even then only the chairman, Major-General M.A. Pope, who was also the army representative, had access to the Combined Chiefs of Staff organization.[24] Among the early reports Pope passed to the Chiefs of Staff Committee in Ottawa, in late August and early September, was that the Combined Chiefs of Staff were examining "the definition of the western Atlantic area."[25]

As these arrangements were gradually taking shape, senior British and American naval officers were discussing changes in Allied organization for the Battle of the Atlantic that might follow from the USN's heavy engagement in escort of coastal convoys in North American waters, and the virtual removal of American escorts from the transatlantic routes.[26] In September Admiral Pound had the British Admiralty Delegation in Washington propose to Admiral King's headquarters that the change of operational control (CHOP) line from Western Approaches Command to the US Navy Department should be shifted from 26°West, near Iceland, to 50°West, nearly to Newfoundland, where Western Local Escort Force groups relieved the mid-ocean groups. "Dual control is wrong in principle," a British paper argued, "It is not difficult to envisage an attack being in progress ... when control changes resulting in a possible confliction of operational practice by the two authorities." King's staff could see the need for British control only to the limits of air coverage from Iceland, 35°West since the Royal Air Force's introduction of very long range aircraft, and this compromise agreement came into effect on 12 November 1942.[27]

Although changing the CHOP line as Pound suggested would clearly have an impact on RCN operations, Canadian naval authorities only learned of the British proposal in October through the good offices of the Americans. "The United States Navy very kindly gave me a personal copy,"

24. Stacey, *Arms, Men and Governments*, 162-6, 354-7, 530. Commander H.G. Nares, RCNVR, formerly assistant naval attaché, became naval attaché. See Naval Attaché to Minister, Canadian Legation, 30 Nov. 1942, NAC, RG 24, 3821, NSC 1012-11-48

25. JS 45 to COS, 25 Aug. 1942, DHH, 193.009 (D 10); JS 49 to COS, 4 Sep. 1942, NAC, RG 24 (acc 83-84/167), 561, S1700-193/139 v 1

26. "History of the Joint Chiefs of Staff: The War Against Germany. Chapter VI: The Battle of the Atlantic (to April 30, 1943)," by Lieutenant Abbot Smith, USNR, 3 June 1948, 95-7, NARA, RG 218, box 6. See also, "Memo for Admiral Stark from Admiral Thebaud," 9 June 1942, Stark to Knox, 2 Nov. 1942, "Extract from Private Papers of Admiral Harold R. Stark, USN Anti-Submarine Warfare," NHC, NRS 236.

27. USND, "History of Convoy and Touring, 1939-1945" (unpublished narrative), 31-43; unsigned memo, 12 Oct. 1942, enclosed with Naval Member Canadian Joint Staff to CNS, 26 Oct. 1942, DHH 81/520/1550-157/1, quoted

Brodeur advised Nelles, "which again goes to prove the willingness of the USN to keep us in the picture, when they discover we have been left out."[28] Brodeur's observation reflected his long-standing bitterness at any British slight to Canada's status. In Ottawa, by contrast, Lay and DeWolf saw in the initial British proposal that the change in operational control should take place where the Halifax-based escorts exchanged with the Newfoundland-based escorts the opportunity to push for increased Canadian command authority. The RCN might replace the USN in the direction of convoy operations to the west of 50°West, and thereby bring the North Atlantic route under shared Anglo-Canadian control. The staff officers soon put the idea to one side in the face of American resistance to British control as far west as the approaches to Newfoundland, but it was one of the first, well-developed expressions of the case for Canadian control of convoy operations in the ocean areas adjacent to Atlantic Canada and Newfoundland.[29]

Even as Lay and DeWolf concluded that the time was not right to raise the general question of national command relationships, responsibility between the RCN and the USN for signals intelligence—a critical element of the larger command issue—became the subject of controversy. On 26 October Commodore Reid, who had just the day before taken up his new appointment as Flag Officer Newfoundland (FONF), informed NSHQ, COMINCH, and the BAD that senior officers of escort groups were complaining about the "volume of signal traffic promulgated by COMINCH concerning HF/DF."[30] Despite the delineation of areas of responsibility for locating and reporting U-boat fixes arranged by Commander Winn on behalf of the Admiralty in May 1942 (see Chapter 9), ships and establishments in the Canadian Coastal area were receiving messages from both USN and RCN sources. The Americans no doubt felt justified because since 1 July the USN was the diversion authority for all convoys west of the CHOP line. Nevertheless, because each originating authority used different codes—a potentially dangerous practice that could compromise security—only after decoding a message could it be known that the information had already been received. Reid enclosed messages sent to SC 107 as examples, and asked for a reduction in traffic.[31]

On 2 November NSHQ followed up Reid's signal by asking Admiral King for exclusive authority to promulgate fixes from enemy units broadcasting from the area "North of 40°North" and "West of 40°West," the area that Winn had arranged to be assigned to the RCN earlier in the year. The USN replied through the BAD, who informed Reid and NSHQ that the Americans were unsympathetic to Canadian demands because "escorts liked everything given to them as soon as possible," and suggested that FONF sort out "sea opinion" within TF 24. Moreover, they "consider that the RCN should only originate signals to escorts within the Canadian Coastal Zone, while COMINCH will confine theirs to outside Canadian Coastal Zone."[32] That zone included only the area from the waters off the southern tip of Nova Scotia, across to the waters immediately east of St John's, and thence northward along the Atlantic coast of Newfoundland and Labrador. The USN, it seemed,

---

28. NMCJS to CNS, 26 Oct. 1942, DHH 81/520/1550-157/1

29. DOD to FONF, 26 Oct. 1942, NAC, RG 24, 11979, file 51-15

30. FONF to NSHQ, 26 Oct. 1942. NAC, RG 24, 3806, 1008-75-29, v 1

31. Ibid. Curiously, convoy reports for Sep. and Oct. 1942 include no complaints about duplication of HF/DF or about an onerous amount of signals traffic; only a couple of reports commented on the increased volume of signal traffic. One can only assume that SOEs and COs had complained in person to Reid or, more likely, to Capt E.R. Mainguy, who was acting FONF before him.

32. BAD to NSHQ, 7 Nov. 1942. NAC, RG 24, 3806, 1008-75-29, v 1

wanted to revert to the strictures of ABC-1, virtually ignoring the hard-won expansion of the RCN's capabilities and responsibilities since that time. The Canadians reacted sharply. NSHQ, without making a further bid for US concurrence, declared its intention of continuing to broadcast fixes obtained in the whole area north of 40°North and west of 40°West, but with improvements in procedure that would reduce the amount of traffic that had to be managed in escorts.[33]

This initiative, from the perspective of NSHQ, was a part of a wider effort to improve the performance of Canadian antisubmarine forces in the northwest Atlantic by strengthening the national system of command and control. As seen in Chapter 9, progress in the development of the U-Boat Tracking Room in Ottawa during the spring of 1942, and the communicating of timely naval direction-finding fixes on enemy broadcasts to Eastern Air Command, had had dramatic results in the sinking of *U 754* south of Yarmouth by 113 Squadron in July and the destruction of two U-boats in the path of SC 107 by aircraft of EAC's 1 Group in Newfoundland on 31 October to 1 November. These achievements, coupled with searing criticism by expert British officers of the failure by the RCN and the RCAF to ensure that air and sea forces consistently concentrated their efforts in the areas where the latest high-grade intelligence indicated U-boats might be present, resulted in a great deal of soul searching among senior Canadian naval and air officers.[34] The result was a new directive, entitled "The Conduct of A/S Warfare by RCN and RCAF" issued by NSHQ on 26 November 1942:

> The fact that the Western Atlantic area has become an Anti-U-Boat War Zone of great strategic importance is now recognized by all Canadian authorities ...
>
>   All RCN command and sub-Command whether in the Western Atlantic or elsewhere are to direct their utmost effort to improving the offensive action of all available Forces in the prosecution of A/S Warfare. They are also to ensure that every possible form of co-operation with the RCAF is put into effect.

"Cooperation" fell short of the full British model, in which the RN exercised operational control over the RAF's Coastal Command; the two young Canadian services were still too anxious to establish their own identities and status to accept such a measure. However, the services endeavoured to duplicate the British intelligence organization, wherein the Admiralty's Operational Intelligence Centre, with its means quickly to collate, analyse, and distribute the best current information, was the sole and authoritative source of the intelligence estimates that guided air and sea operations. Investigation of complaints about duplication in broadcasts of intelligence revealed that part of the problem was transmission by COAC of that command's estimates of enemy activity. The new directive ended that practice, ruling that all information about the enemy gathered by the air and naval commands on the east coast had immediately to be transmitted to the U-Boat Tracking Room in Ottawa: henceforth, the east coast commands of both services could broadcast only fully analysed information received from NSHQ. Direct, dedicated teletype lines were to be installed between Ottawa and Halifax and between Halifax and St John's, and a combined operations room was to be established at Halifax for the staffs of COAC and the air officer commanding EAC so that the air force and navy could coordinate their operations on the basis of the common intelligence plot fed by the U-boat Tracking Room.[35]

---

33. SecNB to COMINCH, 14 Nov. 1942, ibid

34. Douglas, *Creation of a National Air Force*, 523-5

35. SecNB, "The Conduct of A/S Warfare by RCN and RCAF" 26 Nov. 1942, NAC, RG 24, 11927, 1300-1, pt 1. See also, NSHQ to BAD, 2043z/20 Nov. 1942, NAC, RG 24, 3807, NSS 1008-75-44.

Captain H.N. Lay, Director of the Operations Division, ponders the COAC command boundaries in the days following the Atlantic Convoy Conference, which created Canadian Northwest Atlantic Command. (NAC, PA 204259)

Top: An operational planning conference at COAC HQ in Halifax. From left, Lieutenant-Commander G.M. Mitchell, RCNVR, Commander A.F. Peers, RN, Lieutenant-Commander H.S. Rayner, RCN, Captain W.B. Creery, RCN, Lieutenant-Commander M.A. Medland, RCN, Lieutenant-Commander H.J. Craig, RCNVR and Lieutenant P.F.X. Russell, RCN. (NAC, PA 93998)

Left: A Karsh portrait of Admiral Sir Max Horton, RN, Commander-in-Chief Western Approaches 1942-1945. (NAC PA 206625)

As NSHQ distributed the new directive, Admiral King's headquarters again demanded that the Canadians limit promulgation of U-boat intelligence to their own coastal zone. King continued to deal with the RCN through the BAD, which lent full support to the American view, claiming that the larger Canadian promulgation zone established by Winn earlier in the year had only been a temporary measure intended to remain in effect until the USN had time to organize its own operational intelligence. That time had arrived.[36]

Nelles wrote directly to King on 1 December. The Canadian admiral barely concealed his anger and frustration, but suggested that the source was Admiralty meddling in matters best resolved in the first instance by the North American navies. King, by channelling correspondence through the BAD, was continuing to encourage the RN in its habit of dealing with the RCN as a subsidiary part of the British service, and as a result had not got the right facts. "As you are, of course, aware, my Naval representative in Washington is Rear-Admiral V.G. Brodeur, RCN, who is the Naval Member of the Canadian Joint Staff in Washington. Apparently he was not consulted in this question by your staff." Nelles detailed how the arrangements made by Winn in May 1942 were in no sense temporary, but had built upon Admiralty requests since early in the war that the RCN assume progressively wider responsibilities for intelligence promulgation. Given the RCN's greatly increased commitment in the North Atlantic since early 1942, and the USN's near withdrawal from convoy escort, Nelles declared, Canadian responsibilities should be still larger. He wanted to revert to the arrangements of January 1942, in which the RCN promulgated intelligence to escorts operating as far as 30°West. Because British and Canadian warships formed 98 percent of the North Atlantic escort forces, and the British and Canadian navies shared communications and operating procedures that in some cases differed from those in the USN, it would be more efficient if the RCN promulgated intelligence to forces on the northern routes. The time had come, Nelles concluded, for a conference that would thoroughly reassess command relationships in the western part of the North Atlantic, and he asked for King's support for an increased Canadian role "before the matter is discussed with Admiralty."[37]

King's reply, aside from an apology for not including Brodeur in the distribution of signals, was uncompromising. Intelligence promulgation should be carried out by the headquarters that had operational control, that is, the authority to divert convoys and deploy escorts. In the area west of 35°West that was the USN for all waters other than those immediately off the coasts of Canada and Newfoundland. King allowed that he might be willing to hold a conference, but saw no need for a larger Canadian command role: "The setting up of an additional operational control authority will increase the complexity of the Atlantic shipping problem rather than to simplify it."[38]

As the RCN struggled to safeguard its position in the promulgation of signals intelligence against imperatives laid down by the larger Allied navies, the Canadian service found itself similarly pressed in the matter of escort allocation. Heavy losses, especially those incurred by SC 107, in the western part of the central ocean, beyond the limits of air cover from Iceland and Newfoundland, brought a fresh British initiative to improve defences in these vulnerable waters. On 18 November the Admiralty sent a message to the US Navy Department, copied to NSHQ, urgently requesting that the

---

36.   BAD to NSHQ, 2245z/26 Nov. 1942, NAC, RG 24, 3807, NSS 1008-75-44

37.   CNS to COMINCH, 1 Dec. 1942, ibid 1008-75-29, pt 1

38.   COMINCH to CNS, 17 Dec. 1942, NAC, RG 24, 11976, 282-1

eighteen British and Canadian destroyers in the WLEF—all of which were Town class or compara-ble old British types—should be withdrawn to form a Western Support Force based at St John's. Although these old destroyers were short-legged, the Admiralty hoped that with the techniques being developed for refuelling at sea, the endurance of the ships could be extended. The intention was that they should reinforce the escorts of eastbound SC and HX convoys as far as 35° West, and change over to westbound ON and ONS convoys for the voyage back to St John's.

The signal arrived while British, Canadian, and US naval representatives met in Ottawa on 18 to 20 November, at the request of NSHQ in order to consider the organization of Canadian coastal and transatlantic convoys and the RCN's planned allocation of escorts for 1943. Ever sensitive about discussions concerning waters under USN strategic control that the Americans did not initi-ate, Admiral King had asked that the meeting be only an exchange of views, with no formal agen-da. When Captain Lay, in the chair, noted a recent Admiralty proposal that the transatlantic con-voy cycles should be further opened, so as to release a mid-ocean escort group to act in a support role to reinforce threatened convoys, Rear-Admiral M.K. Metcalf, the senior US representative, announced that his instructions were that the conference was not to address the question. Although the conference considered the new and more modest British proposal for the Western Support Force, it did not recommend for or against the scheme, but warned that if accepted it would have to be implemented flexibly so that destroyers could be returned to the WLEF groups at the first indication that U-boats were pushing west of Cape Race.[39] It was timely advice for, as seen in Chapter 10, on 21 November *U 518* attacked ON 145 southwest of Cape Race.

Admiral King approved the creation of the Western Support Force on 23 November and dele-gated control to Admiral Brainard, CTF 24, including the authority to reassign ships back to the WLEF if conditions warranted.[40] Brainard, in turn, made Commodore Reid, FONF, his deputy to administer the ships in much the same way he administered the C groups of the Mid-Ocean Escort Force (MOEF), that is, to attend to the discipline, welfare, and efficiency of the crews and the main-tenance of the ships, and assign them for duty according to the directives of CTF 24. Brainard, in view of the recent attacks west of Cape Race, left four of the RCN Town class destroyers with the WLEF, and assigned the remaining two Canadian Towns and all thirteen British destroyers to the new support force.[41] Early in December, in the first operations, HMS *Montgomery* was able to assist B 6 in the opening phase of the battle for HX 217, while HMS *Roxborough* and HMS *Wanderer* sup-ported SC 111, which was threatened by the same concentration of U-boats; at mid-month HMS *Georgetown* and the Norwegian destroyer *Lincoln* contributed to the successful defence of ONS 152 and HX 218. It was not, however, possible to achieve the intended sustained shuttle by groups of three destroyers. In the severe conditions of that particularly harsh winter refuelling at sea proved impossible, and weather damage repeatedly sent the old destroyers into dockyard hands. During December, FONF reported, only six of the fourteen ships were available at any one time and these only with the help of "continuous repair and patching up."[42]

39. DOD, "Ottawa Conference," 20 Nov. 1942, NAC, RG 24, 11968, S221.1

40. COMINCH to CINCLANT, CTF 24, Adm, NSHQ et al, 2040/23 Nov. 1942, DHH, NHS 8440-130 "Western Support Force"

41. CTF 24 to COMINCH et al, 0005/25 Nov. 1942, FONF to CTF 24, 2132z/25 Nov. 1942, DHH, NHS 8440-130 "Western Support Force"

42. Fisher, "The RCN on Probation: The Battle of the Atlantic Nov.-Dec. 1942" (unpublished narrative, Aug. 1995), 88-92, 122, 131, 135, DHH, 2000/5; FONF WD, Dec. 1942, DHH NSS 1000-5-20, pt 2

Disappointing as the performance of the old destroyers proved to be in long-range missions from Newfoundland, their removal from Admiral Murray's command greatly weakened the groups of the WLEF. That force, moreover, had already been stripped down as a result of other Allied requests: it had been the source of most of the seventeen corvettes deployed to the Torch convoys, as well as the six allocated to the US Eastern Sea Frontier for the protection of tanker convoys from the Caribbean to New York. In those instances, it should be noted, the Allied navies had fully consulted the RCN, but Canada's only chance to comment on the Western Support Force scheme had been at the conference in Ottawa that King had limited to informal discussion. Although the American admiral had respected the advice of the conference that provisions be made for the quick return of the destroyers to Murray's control in the event of enemy operations in the Canadian area, that decision would be made by US authorities alone. On 10 December 1942 NSHQ alerted COM-INCH to the fact that the repeated Allied redeployment of ships from the WLEF had now resulted in its groups often sailing with as few as only "2 corvettes and 1 minesweeper," and requested that CESF return to Canadian control as early as possible in 1943 the six RCN corvettes that had been assigned to the tanker convoys in August.[43] This was the opening volley in an effort to consolidate Canadian naval resources under national control that paralleled efforts to assert Canadian authority in the promulgation of signals intelligence.

The Admiralty intervention that led to the creation of the Western Support Force reflected the extreme pressure on the RN in the late autumn of 1942 to reverse the increasing success of wolf-pack attacks against the principal transatlantic convoys. On 4 November Prime Minister Churchill, in the face of rising shipping losses, gloomy news about shortfalls in essential imports, and mounting political criticism, established the Cabinet Anti-U-Boat Warfare Committee. Like its model, the Battle of the Atlantic Committee of 1941, it was intended to focus the nation's best minds and most powerful administrators on the problem of trade defence.[44]

Whether or not the Admiralty intended to draw attention to the gravity of the crisis in the Atlantic, a change in senior appointments carried this message. On 17 November Admiral Sir Max Horton replaced Admiral Noble as Commander-in-Chief Western Approaches, with Noble moving to Washington as head of the BAD. The change placed Noble, who had led the British forces in the Atlantic battle since February 1941, in the key position to win essential American support,[45] and it put Western Approaches Command in the hands of an officer who could not have been a greater contrast to the courtly, patient Noble. A submariner who had commanded the RN's submarine force since 1940, Horton, in the words of one historian, "was a case of poacher turned gamekeeper."[46] He was also an irascible, single-minded professional with a reputation for getting things done. One officer remembered him as:

---

43. NSHQ to COMINCH, 1636z/10 Dec. 1942, DHH, NHS 8440-140 "Western Support Force"

44. Winston S. Churchill, *The Second World War* IV: *The Hinge of Fate* (Boston 1950), 130; S.W. Roskill, *Hankey: Man of Secrets* III: *1931-1963* (New York 1974), 568-73

45. See, e.g., Stark to Knox, 2 Nov. 1942, DHH, mfm, NHC, NRS 236, "Extract from Private Papers of Adm Stark": "Of course you know Sir Percy Noble will relieve [Admiral A.B.] Cunningham [as head of the BAD]. Fighting the submarine menace has been his particular job and you will be able to get his thoughts first hand from him ... I contact him every chance I get."

46. R. Brodhurst, *Churchill's Anchor: The Biography of Admiral of the Fleet Sir Dudley Pound* (London 2000), 256

> Quite ruthless and quite selfish .. .If you knew your job, all was well; if you didn't,
> God help you! He knew everyone's job, but provided you knew your job a little better
> than Max did, you were alright ... he had some maddening habits. He would play golf
> all the afternoon, then return, dine, play a rubber or two of bridge, and come down to
> his office (overlooking the Ops. Room) at 1130 p.m. and start sending for his staff.[47]

Change was immediate. Commander C.D. Howard-Johnston, the Staff Officer Anti-Submarine Warfare at Western Approaches, recalled that "the arrival of Max as C-in-C WA was a breath of fresh air after Percy Noble ... P.N. was not much good. He never really knew his stuff. One had the impression that he was vain and full of his importance. He returned from London usually empty-handed and we at sea suffered therefrom."[48] Under Horton professionalism in antisubmarine warfare became the watchword, and there was no tolerance for ambiguous standards. Canadians at all levels were to feel his influence quickly, sharply, and for the rest of the war.

Horton quickly grappled with three well-known requirements in his surface and maritime air forces: adequate facilities and appropriate standards for group training; fast, long-endurance escorts to provide support groups to reinforce convoys threatened or under attack, and enough VLR aircraft to eliminate the air gap.[49] Within three weeks of his takeover Horton wrote the Admiralty on antisubmarine warfare training and the principle of Escort Group cohesion.

> The Escort Group System has proved itself to be beyond all doubt the basic principle of
> successful anti-submarine operations. There are many examples of well trained and
> equipped groups, resolutely led, beating off determined U-boat attacks. There are also
> examples of convoys suffering disastrous losses when escorted by a collection of ships
> strange to one another, untrained as a team and led and manned by an officer inexperi-
> enced in convoy protection. Until each group is led and manned by competent officers, and
> until it has attained a high degree of group efficiency and is completely equipped with the
> latest devices, heavy losses will continue. The immediate object must therefore be: to raise
> the standard of the less efficient groups to the level of the most efficient ones.[50]

There can be little question that Horton's ruthless application of the "Escort Group System" influenced the Admiralty's decision in December to call for the redeployment of the C groups to the eastern Atlantic where they could avail themselves of Western Approaches training and support facilities.

Churchill's message of 17 December calling for the removal of the C groups to British control was a natural follow-on to the new emphasis on antisubmarine warfare. But it also threatened Canadian efforts to assert a national presence in the Atlantic battle. The larger Allied navies had recently joined ranks to reject a large role for Canadian signals intelligence in the northwest Atlantic, and had peremptorily removed most of the destroyers from the WLEF. Yet the initial anger

---

47. RAdm W.S. Chalmers, *Max Horton and the Western Approaches* (London, 1954), 150

48. VAdm C.D. Howard-Johnston to Roskill, 7 May 1979, Roskill Papers, ROSK 7/210, Churchill Archives Centre, Churchill College, Cambridge

49. Throughout the autumn and winter of 1942-3 Horton stressed the need for VLR aircraft. He persisted at this for months, and it was not until the following spring that Liberator aircraft would be in operation and able to close the air gap. Douglas, *Creation of a National Air Force*, 537-67

50. Chalmers, *Max Horton*, 162-3

of the navy's senior leaders about the proposal to transfer the mid-ocean groups soon dissipated. This was only partly because the staff had to acknowledge the well-known shortcomings of the fleet that cruel fate conspired to highlight as the disaster of ON 154 unfolded on 26 to 30 December, even as DeWolf travelled to Washington for the conference on escort efficiency and deployments. Perhaps more to the point, the fact that this time NSHQ was not being treated as an adjunct of BAD counted for much. Churchill's approach at the government-to-government level showed respect for the status of Canadian forces, as did the invitation of Canadian navy representatives to the conference in Washington. Furthermore, the British and American members of the conference understood DeWolf's message that the transfer of the C groups raised questions of national policy that could be addressed only by the Canadian government. Finally, Commodore Mansfield, Horton's Chief of Staff at Western Approaches who had come to explain the RN position, did so with diplomacy and skill.

Immediately after the Washington conference, Mansfield travelled to Ottawa to brief Admiral Nelles in person on 2 January. Nelles's notes of the meeting show that Mansfield succeeded in putting the proposals into the best possible context:

> It was anticipated there would be an increase in the number of German submarines operating in the Atlantic in 1943 with very little corresponding increase in the number of escorting vessels until such time as USA production comes into service ... he did not anticipate any appreciable output of escorting craft from that country until the autumn 1943.

Under the circumstances, the obvious alternative to Horton and the Admiralty was to increase the killing efficiency of escorts: British, American, and Canadian.

> Coming specifically to Canadian groups, it is recommended that they be put through this intensive training for a period of four months and then return to the North Atlantic; and further that, as and when Canadian groups are considered to be 100% efficient, they will be interchanged with other groups without waiting for termination of four months.

Nelles was completely persuaded: "By the above arrangement we not only receive the benefit of the intensive training but we also establish the fact that we consider the North Atlantic to be our operational area."[51]

Nelles and DeWolf presented the results of the Washington conference and the Mansfield briefing to the Cabinet War Committee on 7 January and recommended that the government approve the transfer of the C groups.[52] Mackenzie King sent word of Canada's agreement to Churchill on 9 January in a message that could not have been a stronger statement of the country's commitment to a national presence in the Battle of the Atlantic. The groups would have to "be returned to the North Atlantic Convoys as soon as they have reached a satisfactory state of efficiency and in any case not later than

---

51. CNS to Minister, "Re: Disposition of Escort Ships of the RCN," 5 Jan. 1943, NAC, RG 24, 6796, NSS 8375, pt 4. The Admiralty had repeated a frequent error by sending Mansfield to Washington, rather than Ottawa, first. Terraine, *Business in Great Waters*, 537. See also, Godfrey, "Notes on DNI's visit to Washington Sep.-Oct. 1942," 1 Nov. 1942, PRO, ADM 223/107. Capt E.S. Brand, who had recently transferred from the RN to the RCN, helped assure the success of the meeting by briefing Mansfield, an old shipmate, about the personalities and politics of the Canadian naval staff. Brand Journal, chap. 32, 64-5; see also chap. 21, 20-1.

52. CWCM, 7 Jan. 1943

May, 1943," and the government was attaching the further condition that the RN should not remove the destroyers it had committed to the WLEF and the Western Support Force.

2. It has been our policy to build up Canadian escort forces for the specific purpose of protecting North Atlantic trade convoys in addition to our coastal communications. Public interest in the Canadian Navy is centred on the part it has taken in this task, which is without question one of the highest and enduring priority upon which the outcome of the war depends. We are satisfied that the Canadian Navy can serve no higher purpose than to continue to share this task, which we have come to look upon as a natural responsibility for Canada and one which geographically and strategically we are well placed to undertake.

3. It is our desire, therefore, to concentrate all Canadian escort vessels for this purpose to which end the above conditions and the early return of the seventeen corvettes loaned for Torch are necessary. [53]

In the spirit of this message, NSHQ did not miss a beat in its campaign for an increased national presence in the Battle of the Atlantic. On 15 January Nelles met Admiral King's flat denial of the RCN's authority to promulgate U-boat intelligence outside of the Canadian coastal area with an equally intransigent response. The RCN had consulted with CTF 24 to trim the number of signals as King wished, but would continue to broadcast to the wider western Atlantic area; Nelles again called for a general conference on command relationships. At the same time NSHQ supported Admiral Murray in refusing to carry out orders from CTF 24, on 5 and 20 January 1943, to deploy the remaining WLEF destroyers to the Western Support Force, whose number of operating vessels had fallen to four as a result of the battering of the Atlantic winter. Nelles explained in a signal to Admirals King and Pound that the COAC and FONF were national commands subordinate to national headquarters and that they operated only those forces allocated to them by that authority: NSHQ alone could authorize the transfer of warships from one command to the other. The Canadian headquarters had never delegated authority to CTF 24 to allocate warships to the support force because NSHQ had been consulted only in the November conference that King had insisted was informal. King's staff and Noble of the BAD saw the point, but were surprised that the Canadians should suddenly raise these objections fully six weeks after the establishment of the Western Support Force about which they had been kept fully informed.[54]

It was likely that NSHQ's stand on 13 January moved Admiral Brainard, CTF 24, to appeal to Admiral Ingersoll, Commander-in-Chief of the US Atlantic Fleet, for increased authority. In the patchwork arrangements that had been pieced together in the northwest Atlantic, Brainard exer-

---

53. SSEA to DSec, tg 3, 9 Jan. 1943, *DCER* IX, 359. Nelles had already sent a copy of this message to Pound, and received his agreement: CNS to Adm, "Personal for First Sea Lord," 2214z/6 Jan. 1943, and Adm to CNS, "Personal from First Sea Lord," 1426a/8 Jan. 1943, DHH, NHS, 8440-30 "Mid-Ocean Escort Force"

54. CNS to COMINCH, repeated Adm, 1920z/12 Jan. 1943, text in "Survey of file NSS 8440-1," DHH 81/520/8280B, pt 1A; CNS to Chief of Staff, COMINCH, 22 Jan. 1943, Brodeur to Nelles, 26 Jan., 1943, NAC, RG 24, 11969, 222-4; Chief of Staff, COMINCH to CNS, 17 Jan. 1943, NAC, RG 24 (Acc 83-4/167), 4000, 740-239/3. It must be said that at least one senior officer at FONF, Capt R.E.S. Bidwell, chief of staff, was irritated and perhaps embarrassed by the fuss NSHQ was making over the Western Support Force. As Bidwell minuted on one of the Headquarters memoranda: "I am getting a little tired of H.N. Lay who fancies that he is an operational authority ... In future we'll have to pass everything to NSHQ I suppose." Bidwell to FONF, min, 8 Jan. 1943, NAC, RG 24, 11,953, file 250-4-1. Cmdre Reid had already formally complained about NSHQ's heavy-handed response to his initial call for greater efficiency in intelligence promulgation. FONF to SecNB, 9 Nov. 1942, NSS 1008-75-29

cised "coordinating supervision" over operations to protect convoys by no fewer than six US and Canadian commands: the RCAF's Eastern Air Command at Halifax and No 1 Group at St John's (which although part of EAC operated with considerable independence), the RCN's FONF and COAC, the US Army's Newfoundland Base Command (which operated maritime patrol aircraft), and the USN Commander Eastern Sea Frontier.[55]

Although Brainard could direct the movements of warships at sea and had complete command of USN aircraft based in Newfoundland, he had no authority over the aircraft of the RCAF and the US Army. Both services had stoutly refused to accept naval control; in the working compromise that had grown up Brainard issued his orders as "proposals" to the RCAF and as "requests" to the US Army. Moreover, the assignment of warships to escort groups, and the readiness and training of the warships, was the responsibility of FONF, COAC, and CESF, to whom Brainard could only offer advice. "Certain important decisions are unduly delayed by the necessity of resorting to the 'telegraphic conference' system of administration ... with resultant harmful delay." It was no way to fight "a clever, ruthless enemy whose widely scattered forces are under strong and able *central* command." Brainard noted that east of 35°West convoys had the benefit of protection by "*one* command (C-in-C WA) who has *operational control* over *all* air and surface craft ... and *direct command* [i.e., for assignment to groups and training and readiness] over a large proportion of the surface craft." He suggested it was no coincidence that "losses from ... convoys within 500 miles of the United Kingdom have been almost negligible for the past year."[56] He did not have to mention the number of attacks that convoys had endured within 400 miles or less of Newfoundland and the coast of North America.

The British had always operated the convoy system according to the principle of strongly centralized command through their system of Area Combined Headquarters (ACHQ). They had succeeded, in June 1941, in making the Canadian FONF a subcommand of Western Approaches for all purposes of transatlantic convoy protection, although the RCN had successfully resisted the further extension of Western Approaches control to Halifax. The strategic and political imperatives that had brought the USN into convoy operations in September 1941 had then created the division at mid-ocean and, as seen in Chapter 5, had severed direct British authority over the Canadian FONF because of Admiral King's rigid insistence on full American control in areas assigned to the USN. The British missions to Canada and the United States in 1942 that urged the development of central U-boat tracking rooms, whose intelligence product was quickly despatched to all air and escort forces, were attempts to help the North American forces unify their efforts, even as the Admiralty, with partial success, pressed to move Western Approaches Command's control over convoys further west. It was this British pressure, together with nationalistic pride in the RCN's achievement in largely replacing American escorts in the North Atlantic, that had brought officers at NSHQ first to conceive of the idea that the RCN might entirely replace CTF 24 in the northwest Atlantic. On 19 January 1943 Nelles informed Reid, Murray, and Brodeur that he intended immediately to aim for this solution; he cited the difficulties over the Western Support Force and intelligence promulgation.[57] A week later, on

---

55. CTF 24 to CINCLANT, "Escort of North Atlantic Trade Convoys—Command Relations," 13 Jan. 1943, NARA, RG 313 Red, CTF 24, 1943 confidential, box 8745, A14-1 "Convoying General"

56. Ibid. Emphasis in original

57. CNS to COAC, FONF, NMCJS, Washington, 19 Jan. 1943, NAC, RG 24, 11969, 222-4

26 January, Brodeur replied to Nelles in some excitement about "all the rumours that were going around the last few days about changes in Command and Convoy."

The Atlantic command issue had indeed become pressing at the highest levels. On 30 November 1942 Sir Stafford Cripps, a member of the British Anti-U-boat Warfare Committee, had urged the creation of a supreme commander for the North Atlantic. Both Winston Churchill and Admiral Pound rejected the idea as impracticable. The proposal, nevertheless, was symptomatic of the political pressure building for success by whatever means in the Battle of the Atlantic. Cripps, a senior Labour member of the government, had recently resigned from the War Cabinet because he believed the war effort suffered from lack of sufficient top-level coordination; Churchill had persuaded him to become Minister for Aircraft Production and was most anxious to keep him in the government.[58] In Washington, General George C. Marshall, Chief of Staff of the US Army, similarly urged that command in the Atlantic had to be more unified. Admiral King reacted much as Churchill and Pound reacted to the Cripps proposal, but like them felt pressure for action. At the Anglo-American summit at Casablanca in mid-January 1943, where Churchill and Roosevelt together with their chiefs of staff decided their grand strategy for the coming year, Pound and King agreed to avoid the establishment of a single Allied commander in the Atlantic. Instead, there would be a board of expert senior American and British officers who would visit all Atlantic antisubmarine commands and make detailed recommendations on reforms necessary to achieve a uniform, high standard of operations. Immediately, a subcommittee of the Anglo–US combined staff planners in Washington set to work to analyse what the best standards were and how the organization of the Allied antisubmarine commands should be changed to attain them. In a very preliminary report, completed on 28 January, just when King was returning from the conference, the combined planners exceeded their brief by recommending a three-stage reform of the command structure: First, unification of the maritime air and naval forces of each nation under a single commander on the British model; then, the appointment of two overall Allied commanders, one in the eastern Atlantic and the other in the western part of the ocean; and, finally, the development of a single supreme command.[59] As will be seen later in this chapter other important decisions dealing with antisubmarine warfare were taken at Casablanca, and it was this attention by the highest level of the Allied command structure to the Battle of the Atlantic that created the stir in Washington that Brodeur reported to Nelles.

As soon as King arrived back in Washington, he moved to implement the consolidation of national forces suggested in his discussions with Pound. On 31 January King responded to Nelles's complaints about the Western Support Force by agreeing that the arrangements had intruded upon Canada's national command structure, while chiding the Canadians for finding "it necessary to retain six destroyers in the relatively quiet coastal zone when there is such urgent need for reenforcing the ocean escorts." He virtually quoted Brainard's letter about the unworkability of "coordinating supervision," but then, in a complete *volte face* to the viewpoint he had clung to so strongly before, he came down squarely on the side of the Canadian solution.

> Personally, I have considered for some time doing away with Task Force Twenty-four, leaving to the Canadians and the British the whole matter of United States–United

---

58.   Cripps to Churchill, 30 Nov.1942, PRO, ADM 1/12198; Churchill, *Hinge of Fate*, 554-61; Roskill, *Hankey* III, 564-5

59.   "History of the Joint Chiefs of Staff: The War against Germany. Chapter VI: The Battle of the Atlantic (to April 30, 1943)," by Lt Abbot Smith, USNR, 3 June 1948, 103, 110-6, NARA, RG 218, box 6

Kingdom convoys, because I am opposed by conviction to mixed forces. Certainly to my mind, the current situation in respect of Vice-Admiral Brainard's authority is a shining example of the "evils" of mixed forces.

King noted Nelles's renewed request for a conference on command relations, and he was no longer lukewarm towards the idea: "I agree with you and will take up your proposal with the Admiralty."[60] On 1 February King ordered Brainard not to conduct transfers of Canadian forces without Canadian authorization, and on 2 February he announced a conference to be held on 1 March "at the request of the NSHQ." King advised that his intention was to discuss the "withdrawal of Task Force 24 from the trade convoy setup in order to put an end to the confusion of mixed forces in the Canadian area."[61] This was the genesis of the important Atlantic Convoy Conference held in March 1943 that British and American records, and the published literature on Allied strategy, rightly describe as having resulted from a Canadian initiative.[62]

Events at sea, and the bottlenecks in maritime logistics whose constraining effects on Allied strategy were a focal point of Anglo-American contention at the Casablanca summit, help to explain Admiral King's reversal on the Canadian navy's bid for a large role in command. As King noted, the RCN's position essentially supported Britain's long-standing argument that the north–south division of the Atlantic into American and British strategic zones dating from ABC-1 should be ignored for purposes of convoy operations whose orientation was east–west. The logic became more apparent as USN itself became responsible for regular trade convoys across the southern part of the North Atlantic as a result of the Torch operation. The US forces that landed at Casablanca on the Atlantic coast of North Africa sailed directly from US ports on 23 to 24 October, and thereafter there were large fast and slow convoys (UGF and UGS; GUS and GUF for the return passage) from New York and Hampton Roads that delivered additional troops, equipment, and supplies; as needs in the theatre grew the convoys became larger and more frequent.[63]

This horizontal division of the ocean between the British and Canadian routes in the north and American routes to the south was reinforced by the measures to ease the British oil crisis that had led Churchill to call on the Canadians and the Americans for the reorganization of the North Atlantic escort forces on 17 December. The danger of spreading escort forces too thin to create the new tanker convoys to run directly from the Caribbean to the Torch bridgeheads and the United Kingdom, as the British proposed, became apparent with the fate of the first such convoy, TM 1, which sailed from Trinidad on 28 December 1942: seven of the nine tankers were lost to U-boat attack. The escort comprised a single destroyer and three corvettes from group B 5, and on the night of the heaviest attacks, 9 to 10 January, the radar in two of the corvettes broke down. As had been shown on the northern routes, a slow convoy escorted by only four vessels, most of them corvettes, was exceedingly vulnerable. With the assignment of fast US tankers, two fast convoys under British escort, TMF 1 and TMF 2, made the passage from the Caribbean to North Africa without loss in January; in February the United States assumed responsibility to supply Torch's petroleum requirements (and

---

60.   COMINCH to CNS, 31 Jan. 1943, reproduced in CINCLANT, "Administrative History of the US Atlantic Fleet in World War II" I, 1946, 476-7, DHH mfm. There is a copy of the letter in NAC, MG 30 E420, v 1.

61.   COMINCH to Adm and NSHQ, 2 Feb. 1943, NAC, RG 24, 11968, NMS 222-3-1

62.   See, e.g., Howard, *Grand Strategy* IV, 305; Buell, *Master of Sea Power*, 292

63.   Richard M. Leighton and Robert W. Coakley, *Global Logistics and Strategy, 1940-1943* (Washington 1955), 466-80

thereby ease the drain on UK stocks) by taking over a new series of regular convoys from the Caribbean, OT. Still more important in allowing the British to replenish their domestic oil supply was the American success in using land transportation to build up stocks at New York. This saved British tankers the long passage to and from the Caribbean in the US coastal convoy system, allowing fast turnarounds of tankers sailing in the HX and SC convoys on the northern routes.[64]

Despite the achievements of the New York oil pool and the fact that the Americans ultimately provided all the assistance the British requested on the southern routes, the Admiralty was not able to detach the C groups to the Gibraltar run for the full four months anticipated in the proposal made during December. Only three of four groups would go, and for no more than ten weeks. This, nevertheless, was a substantial commitment that built on the hard service done by the seventeen RCN corvettes that had supported Torch from the beginning and would not depart until March 1943. The run to Gibraltar and into the western Mediterranean was thus a major focus of Canada's naval effort in the critical winter of 1942-3 and a significant element in the fleet's development.

The Allied landings in North Africa took place on Sunday, 8 November 1942, at Algiers, Casablanca, and Oran. The worst fears, that French troops loyal to the Vichy regime would fight hard against the Anglo-American forces, were not realized, and although there was some sporadic fighting it was evident by day's end that a good foothold had been achieved. It was not the full-blown "second front" in Europe, nevertheless, Torch could not be ignored by the Germans because it meant that the *Afrika Korps*, already engaged with the British 8th Army under General Montgomery in Libya, now had an enemy to its rear. Axis possession of North Africa was threatened, and both the *Kriegsmarine* and the *Luftwaffe* had to do what they could to slow the Allied build-up. Their response exposed the seventeen RCN corvettes assigned to Torch to a multidimensional war of a type they had not experienced in the North Atlantic campaign, having to defend themselves and the merchant ships under their control from attack by submarines, aircraft, and mines. That they measured up to the challenge is evident from the observation of one RN officer who proclaimed in the midst of the campaign, "A useful lot these Canadian ships."[65]

The main role of the Canadian corvettes in Torch was to escort assault and follow-up convoys. To start with, these were the KMF (United Kingdom–Mediterranean—Fast) and KMS (United Kingdom–Mediterranean—Slow) convoys, subdivided into sections for either Algiers or Oran, and scheduled to arrive at each port at fourteen-day intervals.[66] Because they lacked the speed to stay with the fast convoys, the RCN corvettes were chiefly assigned to the slow series, which proceeded at seven to ten knots, faster than their equivalent on the North Atlantic run. The KMS convoys were normally routed closer inshore, on about the meridian of 18°West, so as to remain within range of Coastal Command aircraft from British bases, while the thirteen-knot KMF convoys stayed at about 26°West and relied on carrier-borne air cover.[67] Both the fast and slow series remained

---

64. Payton-Smith, *Oil*, 314-22

65. "Accounts of Regina's Sinking of Italian Submarine Avorio," DHH, 81/520 HMCS Regina 8000. This sections relies heavily on S. Cafferky, "'A Useful Lot These, Canadian Ships': The RCN and Operation Torch, 1942-1943," *The Northern Mariner* 3/4 (1993), 1-17.

66. The KMF convoys were operational convoys transporting the assault troops, and then reinforcements, to the theatre. The KMS were trade convoys carrying support materiel. See Hague, *Allied Convoy System*, 168

67. Roskill, *War at Sea* II, 317; *RAF in Maritime War* III, pt B, 502, DHH 79/599

RCN OPERATIONS IN THE MEDITERRANEAN 1942-1945

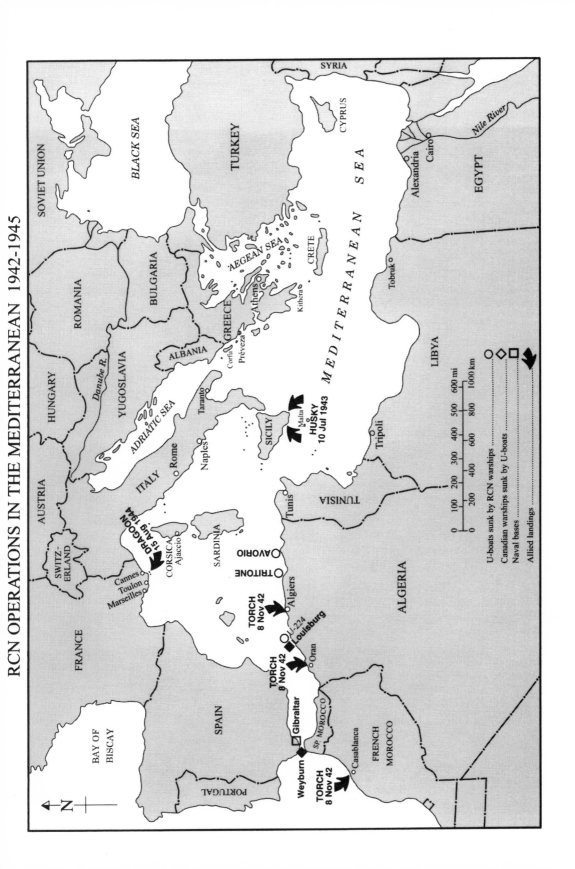

under Admiralty control until they crossed the meridian of 10°west-south of the Iberian peninsula, where they "chopped" to the Naval Commander Expeditionary Force, Admiral Sir Andrew Cunningham. Ocean escorts for KMS convoys, once having delivered their charges in southern waters, took over the escort of the ships from the previous outbound convoy for the passage back to the United Kingdom, so that the escort for, say, KMS 5, would return with MKS 4.[68]

As has been described previously in this history, the Canadian corvettes proceeding to Torch were tacked onto the close escort of eastbound North Atlantic convoys. The first group, *Woodstock, Prescott,* and *Louisburg*, departed St. John's on 15 September. *Weyburn, Lunenburg,* and HMS *Nasturtium* followed four days later. In October, after fitting Oerlikons at Halifax, *Port Arthur* and *Baddeck* sailed with SC 105, *Alberni, Ville de Québec,* and *Summerside* with HX 212; *Kitchener, Calgary,* and *Camrose* with SC 106, *Moosejaw* and *Algoma* with SC 107; and *Regina,* after returning to harbour from SC 107 for engine repairs, a little later. The first six corvettes proceeded to HMS *Western Isles*, the British work-up base at Tobermory, for an antisubmarine work-up. They also received various technical and structural improvements, including the fitting of type 123D asdic and, where necessary, Oerlikons and type 271 radar.[69] This work took time and because of congestion in British ports only *Louisburg, Prescott, Woodstock, Weyburn, Lunenburg,* and HMS *Nasturtium* were ready to sail with the first of the Mediterranean convoys.[70]

Initially based at Londonderry, under the operational control of C-in-C Western Approaches, the ships received administrative support from HMCS *Niobe,* the Canadian manning depot at Greenock. They were formed into three groups: the First Canadian Corvette Group, later known as Canadian Escort Group 25, comprising *Woodstock* (Commander G.H. Griffiths, RCN, SO), *Nasturtium, Weyburn, Louisburg, Prescott,* and *Lunenburg*; the Second Canadian Corvette Group (CEG 26), consisting of *Ville de Québec* (Commander A.R.E. Coleman, RCNR, SO), *Port Arthur, Baddeck, Alberni,* and *Summerside*; and the Third Canadian Corvette Group (CEG 27) of *Regina* (Lieutenant-Commander H. Freeland, RCNR, SO), *Calgary, Kitchener, Camrose, Moosejaw,* and *Algoma.* Some exchanges of command had taken place to ensure the presence of experienced officers in the senior ships.[71]

The first convoy to include Canadian warships, KMS 2, sailed from the Clyde area on 25 October 1942, escorted by *Louisburg, Woodstock,* and *Prescott* of CEG 25 and the RN EG's 40 and 43 (KMS 1 had sailed on 22 October and KMF 1 on 25 October). On this occasion, both the slow and fast convoys followed the more seaward route south, at about 26°West, relying on air cover from the escort carriers HMS *Avenger* and *Biter.*[72] The security measures that cloaked these sailings, together with the preoccupation of the German U-boat Group *Streitaxt* with convoy SL 125, as well as that of Group *Veilchen* in the northwest Atlantic with SC 107 (see Chapter 9), gave the assault convoys a virtually uncontested run to the Mediterranean. When KMS 2 passed through the Straits of

---

68. NCEF, "Operation Torch—Naval Operation Orders (TON SIX), Instructions for Follow-up Convoys" (Henceforth TON SIX), 2, PRO, ADM 199/852

69. Cmdre Londonderry to Adm, 12 Nov. 1942, NAC, RG 24, 11701, 7-4-48

70. C-in-C WA to NOIC Londonderry, 12 Oct. 1942, DHH, NHS Operation Torch 1650; Cmdre Londonderry to Adm, 2221/4 Nov. 1942, NAC, RG 24, 11701, 7-4-49

71. Adm to C-in-C WA, 5 Sep. 1942; C-in-C WA to Adm, 1 Oct. 1942; Adm to C-in-C WA, 8 Oct. 1942, DHH, NHS Operation Torch 1650

72. *RAF in Maritime War* III, pt B, 502-03

Gibraltar on the morning of 10 November, *Louisburg*, *Woodstock*, and *Prescott* were detached to Gibraltar, and over the next five days carried out various local escort duties before joining MKS 1 for its passage to the United Kingdom.[73]

The intervention of both German and Italian submarines came too late to endanger the initial landings, and by 11 November the Allies had secured the major ports. Nevertheless, Admiral Cunningham announced: "Our task is not finished. We must assist the Allied armies to keep up the momentum of the assault."[74] The warning was timely. Well aware of Allied intentions, Dönitz was convinced that U-boats "should be able to work effectively against the subsequent follow-up landings and against the supply line."[75] By mid-November there were about a dozen U-boats operating west of Gibraltar, as well as another twenty-five inside the Mediterranean. In addition, Italy deployed ten submarines to operate off North Africa soon after the invasion began. Moreover, Axis air forces devoted additional aircraft to anti-invasion operations.[76] Ensuring the safe and timely arrival of convoys in the face of this opposition was the main task of the RCN corvettes.

Dönitz had positioned the U-boats outside the Mediterranean on an arc between Cape St Vincent in Spain and Safi on the Moroccan coast.[77] On 19 November *U 519* sighted KMS 3, fifty-five ships protected by four escorts of EG 37 and, from CEG 25, *Weyburn* and *Lunenburg*, and HMS *Nasturtium*. Other boats were ordered to attack, and at 0914z on 20 November torpedoes from *U 263* under Korvettenkapitän Nölke struck three ships in the van of the convoy. *Prins Harald* and *Grange Park* both sank, while *Ocean Pilgrim* was saved by her net defence equipment, antitorpedo nets hung from booms projecting from the sides of the vessel. Twenty minutes after this devastating attack *Lunenburg*, carrying out an asdic search on the port flank of the convoy, sighted what appeared to be the feather of a periscope 400 yards off its starboard bow. As the corvette closed to attack the wash disappeared and a shallow depth-charge pattern was dropped on the last known position of the suspected contact. *Weyburn* joined the hunt but no further contact was made by either corvette.[78] Indeed, apart from brief attacks by two British escorts on the starboard side of the convoy, there were no more signs of U-boats and the convoy passed into the Mediterranean without further incident.

During the entire engagement, which lasted a little more than an hour, the senior officer thought just one U-boat was in contact. Indeed, he noted sarcastically after the attack, "There has been no opportunity for interrogation but in the absence of other evidence of a second U-boat, it would appear probable that *Lunenburg* attempted to ram a torpedo which had so far missed everything, and he may be congratulated on his failure." In fact, five U-boats—*U 413*, *U 519*, *U 103*, *U 185*, and *U 263*—are now known to have been in contact with KMS 3 and were well handled by the defences. Both *U 263* and *U 519* suffered damage from depth charges, while *U 103* and *U 185* had to break off attacks when they were forced to dive deep to avoid air and surface forces. Unhappily, the escort also shot down a Catalina aircraft by mistake.[79]

---

73. "Report by Cmdre of Convoy no. MKS 1(X)," PRO, ADM 199/728

74. Quoted in Roskill, *War at Sea* II, 318

75. Dönitz, *Ten Years and Twenty Days*, 279

76. NCXF, ROP Operation Torch, 14 Nov. 1942, PRO, DEFE 2/602; Roskill, *War at Sea* II, 333-4

77. MOD, *U-Boat War in the Atlantic* II, 65, plan 27, and diagram 17, point 8

78. "ROP of HMCS *Lunenburg*," 20 Nov. 1942. DHH, Narratives of Important Operations, NHS 1870-7

79. *RAF in the Maritime War* III, pt B; HMS *Black Swan* to Capt (D) WA, 23 Nov. 1942, as cited in DHH, 81/520/8280, box 4

Over the next month, convoys KMS 4 and KMS 5 sailed for the Mediterranean: the former on 26 November with *Port Arthur, Baddeck, Alberni, Ville de Québec,* and *Summerside* of CEG 26, in company with EG 30 and four ships of the RN's 15th Minesweeping Flotilla; the latter on 11 December with *Kitchener, Calgary, Regina,* and *Algoma* of CEG 27, as well as *Prescott* and *Woodstock* of CEG 25. KMS 4 had a relatively untroubled passage, reaching the Straits of Gibraltar on 8 December and steaming safely on to Oran and Algiers, but KMS 5, plagued by defects among the escorts,[80] experienced hurricane-force winds and high seas—the same storm endured by ON 153 (see Chapter 10)—that not only scattered the convoy, but damaged *Regina*'s asdic dome and oscillator so severely that she had to return to Londonderry for repairs. *Algoma,* with HMS *Lulworth* and *Landguard,* spent the better part of three days rounding up stragglers.[81] On 18 and 20 December HF/DF intercepts suggested that U-boats were in contact but the rest of the passage was uneventful, and at 0800 on Christmas Eve escorts of the Gibraltar Escort Force joined. The Canadian corvettes entered Gibraltar to refuel and await their next assignment.[82]

CEG 26, for all intents and purposes, now became part of the Gibraltar Escort Force, although Admiralty intentions for the disposition of the seventeen RCN corvettes did not become evident until reorganization of North Atlantic convoys got under way, and the Admiralty set about resuming OS/SL convoys between the United Kingdom and Sierra Leone. Every long-endurance escort available had to be found for this vast effort, and on 2 January 1943 Admiral Cunningham received a request for nine sloops under his command to be returned to Western Approaches. In exchange, *Louisburg, Prescott, Woodstock, Camrose, Calgary, Kitchener, Regina, Algoma,* and *Moosejaw* were to be placed under Cunningham.[83] This had probably been under consideration for some time in view of what CEG 26 was now doing, but British naval authorities gave the appearance of discussion with the Canadians by a message to the CCCS in London "to report on what changes, if any, are recommended in the RCN administrative authorities under which these 17 corvettes will be placed and the port or ports on which they will be based," and whether the manning arrangements would have to be changed when the ships were no longer based at Londonderry under Commander-in-Chief Western Approaches.[84]

The seventeen RCN corvettes would now be based closer to the main theatre of operations at historic Gibraltar.[85] As Captain DeWolf pointed out from NSHQ, this had some benefits; better

---

80. Defects held back *Louisburg, Moosejaw,* and HMS *Petunia. Kitchener* was without radar, which had defeated attempts to repair it in Londonderry. *Regina* did not rejoin the convoy and was not ready to rejoin the group again until its return passage. *Calgary* had to return to port for asdic repairs before rejoining the convoy. C-in-C WA to NSHQ, 27 Feb. 1943, Narrative of Important Operations, NSC 1870-7, v 1, DHH; Cmdre Commanding Londonderry Escort Force to C-in-C WA, 23 Jan. 1943, ibid; HMS *Londonderry,* ROPs—Convoy KMS 5, 24 Dec. 1942, ibid; Notes and Extracts on Convoy KMS 5, cited in Convoys 81/520/8280, box 4, DHH

81. On 17 Dec., 36 ships were in company, six were missing. *Londonderry* ROPs

82. HMS *Lulworth, Report of Attack on U-Boat,* 18 Dec. 1942; *Londonderry* ROPs

83. NSHQ to Adm, (R) NCXF (R) FOCNA, C-in-C WA and NSHQ, 2 Jan. 1943, DHH, NHS Operation Torch 1650. It was intended to sail the nine corvettes, escorting KMS 8, on 21 Jan.

84. NSHQ to Adm (R) FOCNA, C-in-C WA, CCCS, and HMCS *Niobe,* 6 Jan. 1943, DHH, NHS Operation Torch 1650

85. Adm to NSHQ and NCXF (R) CCCS, HMCS *Niobe,* C-in-C WA and FOC Gibraltar, 9 Jan. 1943; NCXF to NSHQ (R) Adm, CCCS, HMCS *Niobe,* C-in-C WA and FOC Gibraltar, 11 Jan. 1943, DHH, NHS Operation Torch 1650. Naval Weekly Report Re: RCN Ships on Loan—Jan. 1943, 22 Jan. 1943, 1000-5-7 (3), DHH, NHS Corvettes (A-Z General) 8000

weather and shorter runs, fewer repairs, and time for training that "on this side during the winter months is almost impossible."[86] Vice-Admiral Nelles, picking up DeWolf's argument that the North African campaign was probably forcing the German high command to regroup its forces, commented with some satisfaction: "The ships will have the same, or greater submarine menace, plus that from enemy air forces. Thus it may be a hotter spot."[87] Events bore him out.

CEG 26 formed part of the screen for KMS 4 on its passage from Algiers to Gibraltar, then on 28 December left with the last outward bound follow-up convoy of the year (TE 11) to Oran and on to Algiers, Bougie, Philippville, and Bône.[88] *Kitchener, Camrose, Algoma, Calgary, Woodstock,* and *Prescott*, all from the other two Canadian groups, joined the escort for MKS 4 from Gibraltar to the United Kingdom. On 29 December *Prescott* and *Woodstock* detached to search for survivors from ONS 154. Sadly, their efforts were in vain, but they continued their search until lack of fuel forced them to break off for Ponta Delgada in the Azores. They eventually returned to Londonderry on 13 January.[89] *Moosejaw* and HMS *Lulworth* went on a hunt for the blockade runner *Rhakotis*, and on 4 January *Kitchener* received orders to stand by the merchant ship *Barrister*, which had run aground on the Irish Coast. KMS 4 arrived in port—part to Londonderry and the rest to the Clyde—on 5 January 1943.[90]

With twenty-three German U-boats and twelve Italian submarines now in the Mediterranean, as well as a strong *Luftwaffe* presence, Canadian corvettes were bound to meet the enemy sooner or later. On the evening of 30 December off Algiers, *Alberni* (Lieutenant-Commander I.H. Bell, RCNVR), part of the escort of TE 11, obtained a radar contact at 4,000 yards, then at 800 yards sighted what appeared to be the conning tower of a U-boat. Bell increased speed to ram but was diverted by an asdic contact on the starboard bow. There was no further sign of a submarine and Bell confessed that with the white caps and phosphorescence in the sea, he could have been mistaken about sighting a U-boat. Nevertheless, Captain (D) Gibraltar considered that *Alberni*'s prompt action saved the convoy from attack. TE 11 arrived at Bône without further incident on 31 December.[91]

The corvettes arrived back in Gibraltar on 5 January at the same time KMS 6 was about to arrive. It had left the United Kingdom on 24 December, with the Canadian corvettes *Woodstock*, *Louisbourg, Weyburn, Prescott,* and *Lunenburg*, and HMS *Nasturtium*. The convoy entered the Mediterranean on 7 January, and in the early evening, when halfway between Algiers and Bougie,

86. DOP to CNS, 21 Dec. 1942, NAC, RG 24, 6796, 8375-4

87. Quoted in Milner, *North Atlantic Run*, 205

88. TON SIX, PRO, ADM 199/852

89. *Woodstock* was able to rescue eight survivors from *MTB-105*, launched from HMS *Fidelity* in her last desperate effort to withstand repeated U-boat attacks on 1 Jan. 1943 and now out of fuel. (See Chapter 10.) The MTB had eventually to be sunk because the corvette had to address the primary task of locating additional ONS 154 survivors. DHH 81/520/8280, box 8 ONS-154; DHH, Ships Movements Cards—HMCS *Woodstock*. For *MTB 105*, see *Jane's Fighting Ships, 1944-1945* (New York 1947), 561.

90. The cruiser HMS *Scylla,* which had been involved in the hunt from the outset, was guided to *Rhakotis* by the "unorthodox but effective method of laying flame floats along the course to be steered." *Scylla* finally sank the enemy ship about 140 miles northwest of Cape Finisterre." *Barrister* was abandoned at 1050/4 Jan. Good seamanship led to the safe removal of all her crew even though the corvette had no large-scale charts of that dangerous coast. Report of Cmdre of Convoy MKS 4, 7 Jan. 1943, DHH 81/520/8280, box 5, MKS 4; Roskill, *War at Sea* II, 276

91. This attack was provisionally assessed classification "F" (U-boat present, no damage). *Alberni*, Report of Attack on U-Boat, 3 Jan. 1943, NAC, RG 24, 6901, NSS 8910-331/2. DHH Ships Movement Cards, *Ville de Québec*

it came under attack by at least fourteen He 111 torpedo-bombers, as well as a number of JU 88s. In the twenty-five-minute engagement *Weyburn*, under Lieutenant-Commander T.R.M. Golby, RCNR, received credit for shooting down one Heinkel and shared in the probable kill of another torpedo bomber with the DEMS gunners of SS *Pacific Exporter*.[92] In return, the enemy sank two ships, *Akabara* and *Benalbanach*. The destroyer HMS *Bicester,* which had been astern of the convoy, managed to rescue everyone from *Akabara*, but only twenty-eight out of 448 in *Benalbanach* survived.[93]

A week later, on 13 January, approximately ninety miles west of Algiers, convoy TE 13—fifteen ships escorted by *Ville de Québec* (Lieutenant-Commander A.R.E. Coleman, RCNVR, SO), *Port Arthur*, *Alberni,* and *Baddeck*, and HMS *Clacton* and *Brixham*—came under attack from *U 224*. The boat, on its third patrol, had passed through the Strait of Gibraltar on the night of 10 January and, acting on intelligence from shore authorities, was lying in wait for the convoy.[94] When he sighted the ships, *U 224*'s captain, Oberleutnant-zur-See Kosbadt, singled out a 14,000-ton tanker and approached his target at periscope depth without paying adequate attention to the screen. Only when he was within 4,000 yards of the tanker did he notice *Ville de Québec*, which was in firm asdic contact, bearing down on an attack run. *U 224* crash dived to twenty metres. According to the sole survivor of the submarine, "The corvette was so close that [the crew] heard her screws directly overhead. Kosbadt gave the order 'Full speed ahead! On lifejackets!' and added that a DC [Depth Charge] attack might be expected. Several explosions were heard, with the boat keeping a steady course at full speed."[95] *Ville de Québec*'s accurate attack caused such damage that "the Engineering Officer reported that the boat was no longer capable of diving [and] Kosbadt ordered her to be brought to the surface."[96] *U 224* popped to the surface, her bow approximately twenty feet in the air, with her engines still racing at full speed, in the middle of *Ville de Québec's* depth-charge pattern. The corvette, turning to starboard, opened fire with its starboard Oerlikon guns—the main 4-inch gun could not depress low enough to train on the U-boat—and prepared to ram. As the ship heeled around and the target opened up for the port bridge Oerlikon crew, they also opened fire. Approximately 600 rounds were expended in the attack, with multiple hits—over forty peppered the conning tower alone.[97] *Ville de Québec* then rammed the submarine between the conning tower and the forward gun. "The U-boat's hatch," recalled Lieutenant-Commander Coleman, "was seen to be open and one man was thrown clear as the U-boat rolled over."[98] *U 224* disappeared beneath the sea at 1608z. Two minutes later a heavy explosion shook the area and

92. "Leading Seaman W.F. Maskill reported he followed a plane as it dived into the sea ahead of *Weyburn* and the convoy. He had been training on this aircraft through open sights." This report was substantiated later by troops aboard SS *Pacific Exporter* which had been directly astern of *Weyburn* during the attack. *Weyburn*, Report of Enemy Air Attack, 10 Mar. 1943, PRO, ADM 199/1318; Director of Gunnery and Anti-Aircraft Warfare's assessment of Report of Enemy Air Attack, 30 Mar. 1943, PRO, ADM 199/1318

93. Adm Records, Park Royal, Case 7584, C-in-C Mediterranean, WD for Jan. and Feb. 1943, DHH 81/520/8280, box 4, KMS 6

94. DNI to DA/S, DOD, DDSD, NID, and SOMC, Re: Interrogation report of the sole survivor of *U 224*, 22 May 1943, DHH, NHS *U 224* 1650. Following the completion of her four-week patrol, *U 224* was to be attached to the 29th Flotilla based on La Spezia.

95. Ibid

96. NID to DOD, DSD, DDSD, DWT, Re: Interrogation report of the sole survivor of *U 224*

97. *Ville de Québec*, Report of Attack on U-Boat, dated 19 Jan. 1943, NAC, RG 24, 6903, NSS 8910-331/112

98. Interview of Lt-Cmdr R.E. Coleman, CO of *Ville de Québec*, 26 July 1943, DHH, NHS Ville de Québec 8000

bubbles broke the surface, followed by telltale flotsam and jetsam.[99] Although the convoy had altered course as soon as *Ville de Québec* gave a submarine warning, the merchantmen had a grandstand view of the action as they slowly lumbered around on their evasive turn. "One ship was quite near to us," related Sub-Lieutenant Raymond Hatrick, RCNVR, gunnery officer in *Ville De Québec*. "I have never seen such a demonstration of joy. The sailors were hanging from the yardarms, cheering and shouting as if we had won the war."[100]

Another Canadian success followed soon after on 19 January, when MKS 6, twenty-nine merchant ships escorted by *Port Arthur*, *Baddeck*, *Alberni*, and *Summerside* of CEG 26, *Lunenburg* from CEG 25, and HMS *Brilliant*, *Antelope*, *Avondale*, *Bide*, and *Felixstowe*, encountered the Italian submarine *Tritone*, under *Capitan di Corvetta* Monechi. First of the new *Flutto* class, which had the approximate size and endurance of the type IX U-boat,[101] *Tritone* was on its first patrol, off the Tunisian coast, near Bougie. Damaged by an attack by an American aircraft, the submarine was taking on water at the rate of six tons an hour, but despite being unable to crash dive, Monechi was determined to attack MKS 6 when it came into view. It took nearly three hours to manoeuvre into a satisfactory attacking position, at which point *Port Arthur* (Lieutenant E.T. Simmons, RCNVR) stationed in the centre of the convoy's advance screen, picked it up on asdic. Continually losing trim, and having trouble maintaining periscope depth, *Tritone* was altering towards *Port Arthur* intending to pass under the corvette, but by this time the corvette was on her attack run. At 1418z, she fired a ten-charge pattern that broke or distorted the air pressure system pipes, holed fuel tanks, and put the electric motors out of action. Forced down to 250 feet, all Monechi could do was blow ballast tanks. *Tritone* surfaced 700 yards ahead of the destroyer HMS *Antelope*, which opened fire and attempted to board. Several hits with 4.7-inch, Oerlikon and pompom fire caused casualties, and Monechi surrendered after opening the sea cocks. The submarine sank by the stern at 1425, just twelve minutes after *Port Arthur* first gained contact. Although *Antelope* certainly contributed to *Tritone*'s fate, her commanding officer acknowledged it was "definitely *Port Arthur*'s bird."[102]

The destruction of the two submarines resulted in a personal message from Winston Churchill to Mackenzie King asking him to "convey to the Commanding Officer and ships' company of HMCS *Ville de Québec* and HMCS *Port Arthur* my warm congratulations on [the] success they have recently had against U-boats in the North African theatre. They have made another important addition to the many successes already achieved by the Royal Canadian Navy."[103] That message was a time-

---

100. As usual, this so damaged the ship that she was effectively out of action for two months. "Ramming ripped open two compartments, started a third, and ripped off the asdic dome. [In addition] the stem of the ship was bent 150 degrees to the port. A collision mat had to be rigged over the bow to take pressure off the bulkheads." Reports and draft narrative of *Ville de Québec's* ramming of *U 224*, DHH, NHS HMCS Ville de Québec 8000; Coleman interview

101. Flutto class: normal displacement, 945 tons surfaced, 1,113 tons submerged; dimensions (first series) 206 ft 9 in. X 22 ft 9 in. X 16 ft.; range 5,400 miles at eight knots surfaced, eighty miles at four knots submerged; maximum speed sixteen knots surfaced, seven knots submerged; torpedo tubes six 21-inch–four forward, two aft; torpedoes–twelve; guns one 3.9-inch, four 13.2-mm (2X2). E. Bagnasco, *Submarines of World War Two* (London 1977), 164-5

102. Adm, WIR, no. 168, 28 May 1943, cited in DHH, NHS HMCS Port Arthur 8000; account of destruction of Italian submarine *Tritone*, ibid; Cmdr P.M. Bliss, RN Senior Officer A/S at NSHQ concurred with *Antelope*'s assessment. He noted that this engagement was a "classic attack and *Port Arthur* deserves the greatest credit for its execution. The submarine was downed by the stern when it was forced to the surface and was undoubtedly finished. Her destruction was entirely due to *Port Arthur*." SO A/S to DOD and VCNS, 9 Mar. 1943, NAC, RG 24, 6902, NSS 8910-331/79

103. USSEA to CNS, 29 Jan. 1943, NAC, RG 24, 6902, NSS 8910-331/79

ly and useful gesture, and perhaps compensated to some extent for the rather harsh things that had lately been said about the RCN: it also may have helped vindicate the naval staff in the eyes of Ottawa politicians.[104]

Enemy air attack was a constant threat in the Mediterranean, and on 6 February a Canadian ship fell victim. At 1915z on 6 February 1943, three torpedo bombers[105] attacked KMS 8, with *Regina, Louisburg, Prescott, Algoma*, and *Woodstock* among its escort, approximately sixty miles northeast of Oran. The ship's company of *Louisburg* (Lieutenant-Commander W.F. Campbell, RCNVR) had just closed up to action stations, and the depth-charge crews were carrying out a routine practice drill. After an aerial torpedo had narrowly missed the British destroyer *Laforey* on *Louisbourg*'s starboard quarter, an aircraft coming from that direction flew low over the corvette's bow. Oerlikon gun crews opened fire until the aircraft lost so much height that they could not continue without hitting *Woodstock* beyond the aircraft. It was while in this helpless condition, at 1920z, that an aerial torpedo exploded against *Louisbourg*'s port side. She immediately took on a heavy list and seemed about to capsize. The commanding officer, Lieutenant-Commander W.F. Campbell, RCNVR gave the order to abandon ship, but as he went below decks to make sure nobody was left behind, *Louisburg* plunged beneath the surface. The time was 1924z, less than four minutes after the torpedo struck.[106]

Louisbourg has the unhappy distinction of being the only Canadian warship ever to be sunk by air attack. She suffered a heavy loss of life: forty-one of her eighty–four men, including the captain, and three British seamen taking passage in the vessel. Some depth charges, although apparently set to safe with their primers withdrawn, exploded as the ship went down. That, and the cumbersome methods of lowering boats and Carley floats in the scant minutes it took the ship to go under, helped to account for the death toll, because in the view of the senior surviving officer, Lieutenant R.A. Jarvis, RCNVR, 90 percent of the crew had successfully abandoned ship. *Lookout*, a British destroyer, picked up the survivors and took them to Algiers for hospitalization. It was some compensation for this tragedy that the naval staff ordered several necessary improvements to lifesaving equipment in Canadian warships.[107]

On the night of 6 to 7 February, as KMS 8 continued its passage to Bône, it passed through a concentration of Italian submarines. Early on the 7th the boats *Acciaio* and *Platino* attacked the convoy, the latter sinking the antisubmarine trawler *Tervani*.[108] During this action *Camrose* (Lieutenant-Commander L.R. Pavillard, RCNR) sighted one of the submarines on the surface at a range of 500 yards and attempted to ram, but the boat manoeuvred clear, crash-dived, and,

---

104. M. Milner, *The U-Boat Hunters: The RCN and the Offensive Against Germany's Submarines* (Toronto 1994), 4

105. Confusion remains as to whether the aircraft were German or Italian.

106. *Louisburg*, Report of loss from enemy air attack, 16 Feb. 1943, PRO, ADM 199/318; Loss of HMCS *Louisburg*, DHH, NHS HMCS Louisburg 8000; Lt R.A. Jarvis to Capt Flotillas Algiers, 17 Feb. 1943, NAC, RG 24, 11700, "Louisburg"; Rohwer and Hummelchen, *Chronology of the War at Sea*, 299

107. Rohwer and Hummelchen, *Chronology of the War at Sea*, 299. *Fort Babina*, also torpedoed during the attack but not sunk, went under tow by HMS *Stornoway*, to Algiers. Loss of HMCS *Louisburg*, DHH, NHS HMCS Louisburg 8000; Lt R.A. Jarvis to Capt Flotillas Algiers, 17 Feb. 1943.; Lt R.A. Jarvis to CCCS, 11 Mar. 1943, NAC, RG 24, 6889, NSS 8870-331/56; Deputy Sec, NS memo, Life-Saving Facilities in HMC Ships, 10 Apr. 1943, NAC, RG 24, 6889, NSS 8870-331/56. See also, NSM 168-3, 8 Apr. 1943.

108. Rohwer, *Axis Submarine Successes*, 243

although receiving at least one hit from the 4-inch gun, avoided destruction.[109] The next day another submarine would not be as fortunate.

The Italian submarine *Avorio* had encountered KMS 8 later in the morning of 7 February, but lost contact with the convoy when forced under by an MTB. She remained submerged all day on 8 February, but surfaced at nightfall to charge batteries. Cruising at seven knots with all hatches open and with engine noise reducing the efficiency of the hydrophone watch, the boat failed to detect the approach of *Regina*, which had parted company with the main convoy the day before in order to make good some defects in Algiers, and the Bangor minesweeper HMS *Rhyl*, escorting two stragglers from KMS 8.[110] At 2310z, *Regina* picked up a radar contact 6,200 yards ahead and closed to investigate. *Avorio* did not sight the corvette until it was upon her, crash-dived, and although this forced *Regina* to lose contact, she dropped a ten-charge pattern over the last known position, which destroyed the boat's forward torpedo tubes, put the 3.9-inch gun out of action, and jammed the rudder hard over. *Avorio* surfaced and a short, sharp engagement ensued. After several rounds from the submarine's machine-gun damaged the corvette's wheelhouse and bridge, *Regina*'s Oerlikons silenced the enemy weapon, while her pom-pom and 4-inch gun killed or wounded others on deck. Just as *Avorio*'s captain gave the order to abandon ship, a 4-inch shell burst against the conning tower, killing him and his first lieutenant. The survivors—twenty-six out of forty-two men—"swarmed up on the deck crying 'surrender' and 'help,' some of them jumping overboard."[111] Lieutenant-Commander Freeland altered course to avoid ramming, illuminated the submarine with his signal projector, and sent off a boarding party. The Italians, who the Canadians had ordered "to keep the submarine afloat or else" while the ship carried out a precautionary antisubmarine sweep, attempted to scuttle their boat anyway, but the vent controls were damaged and the compartment containing the explosives was flooded.[112] *Regina*'s boarding party, led by Lieutenant F.B. Marr, found both diesel engines, the batteries, and gyro compass fully operational. They closed all water-tight doors and hatches still in working order, and although seawater poured into the submarine through the damaged hatch connecting the conning tower and control room, they considered *Avorio* salvageable. Along with the Italian engineer officer and *Regina*'s Chief ERA, they remained on board while the rest of *Avorio's* crew transferred to the corvette.[113]

Regina signalled *Rhyl* requesting that a vessel be sent to take the prize in tow, but by the time the tug *Jaunty* arrived on the scene at 0345z, water was flooding into the main compartment. When the tug attempted to tow, "the submarine swung stern to the swell, began to take on water

---

109. Engine room personnel reported hearing a scraping noise along the ship's bottom as it passed over the submarine. Extracts on *Camrose's* attack on a U-Boat, Mediterranean 7/2/43, DHH, NHS HMCS Camrose 8000

110. Submarines of the *Acciaio* Class, displaced 715 tons surfaced, 870 tons submerged. 197 ft X 21 ft 4 in. X 14 ft 9 in, their maximum speed was 14 knots surfaced, 7.3 knots submerged. They had a range of 2,300 miles at 14 knots surfaced, 5,000 miles at 8.5 knots surfaced, 7 miles at a 7 knots submerged, 80 miles at 3 knots submerged, and carried 4 torpedo tubes forward, 2 aft, had one 3.9 (100 mm) 47 cal., and four 13.2 mm guns, and a complement of 48. Bagnasco, *Submarines of World War Two*, 137-65

111. Draft narrative on *Regina's* sinking of Italian submarine *Avorio*, DHH, NHS Regina 8000

112. The bilge pumps were turned on but the suction lines were damaged. The deck and fittings just aft of the conning tower were badly damaged over an area of approximately ten feet, and there was a five-foot-square hole on the starboard side of the conning tower. Report by Boarding Officer, *Regina,* Report of Attack on U-Boat, 8 Apr. 1943, NAC, RG 24, 6903, NSS 8910-331/83

113. Ibid

at an ever increasing rate through the shell holes at the base of the conning tower." At 0515z *Avorio* succumbed, leaving the boarding party to swim about 200 yards to the boat sent for them by *Regina*.[114] Disappointing as this was, there was much satisfaction to be derived from the third submarine destroyed by Canadian ships in as many weeks, and it earned a kind message from Admiral Cunningham: "I have now received report of your successful and spirited action with a U-boat and congratulate you on the efficiency of your ship. Well done."[115] For *Regina*, about to return to the MOEF, it was a nice send-off.[116]

On 22 February 1943 a hundred ships formed up off Gibraltar into two groups; convoy GUS 4, fifty-one ships bound for the United States and MKS 8, forty-nine ships bound for the United Kingdom. Commander F.J. Walker in *Black Swan* was senior officer of the escort. HMS *Vanoc*, *Velox*, *Zetland*, and *Wivern* were slated for GUS 4; FFS *La Malouine*, HMS *Aubretia* and *Boreas*, HMCS *Weyburn*, *Summerside*, *Port Arthur*, *Alberni*, and *Lunenburg* for MKS 8. The Canadian corvettes had arrived with the North African section of the convoy, replacing RN escorts that had been reassigned to convoy MKF 8. Walker did not like the arrangement, made to accommodate the return of four of the Canadian ships to the MOEF. "The Canadian corvettes ... were said to be excellent ships individually and had distinguished themselves against submarines during their service in the Mediterranean, but I had hoped it was realized that a collection of escort vessels hastily thrown together under a Senior Officer whom they have never met before is no substitute for an effective group and does not constitute adequate escort." It was an old complaint and Walker sent an officer by air to Algiers to make contact with the Canadian corvettes and the commodore, and although stormy conditions in Algiers harbour prevented him from boarding more than three of the corvettes, "This arrangement did ... ease the problem of co-operation and was of great value in establishing an understanding with the Commodore."[117]

Weyburn's brief period with MKS 8 was marked by the bravery and sacrifice that so often characterizes war at sea. At 1115z on 22 February, as the corvette rejoined the convoy off Cape Spartel after refuelling at Gibraltar, she hit a mine about 3,000 yards from the convoy and well within the swept channel.[118] The explosion amidships on the port side opened a large hole in *Weyburn*'s hull, buckling the deck and splitting the funnel vertically. The engine room flooded rapidly with water and oil, and flanges and steampipes burst throughout the ship. She still had way on, steaming at eight knots in a circle to port.[119] The destroyer HMS *Wivern* immediately came to her assistance,

---

114. *Regina*, Report of Attack on U-Boat

115. NCXF to *Regina* (R) NSHQ, 15 Feb. 1943, NAC, RG 24, 6903, NSS 8910-331/83

116. She resumed screening the stragglers, arrived at Bône on 9 Feb., came back to Gibraltar with convoy ET-11, arriving on 13 Feb. Her final mission, before returning to Canadian waters, was to escort a tug from Gibraltar to bring in *SS Fort Pascoyac*, which had been torpedoed while with KMS 10. DHH, Ships Movements Cards, *Regina*; Short History of HMCS Regina, DHH, NHS Regina 8000

117. Walker may have recalled that *Weyburn* and *Lunenburg* sailed under his command with KMS 3 in Nov. 1942. HMS *Black Swan*, ROP—Convoy MKS 8, 2 Mar. 1943, PRO, ADM 199/975

118. At about the same time SS *Thorsholm* suffered the same fate. *U 118* had laid a minefield here early in Feb., and after similar losses to MKS 7 the areas had been swept until 17 Feb. The Director of Torpedoes and Mining in the Admiralty thought that the mine was the new German non-contact buoyant mine known as "Emma," Draft narrative on loss of *Weyburn*, DHH, HMCS Weyburn 8000; Gunnery—C.B. Officer, *Weyburn* to Capt (D) Gibraltar, NAC, RG 24, 6889, NSS 8870-331/115; Rohwer and Hummelchen, *Chronology of the War at Sea*, 296; Adm Records, Park Royal, Case 7584, C-in-C Mediterranean WD for Jan. and Feb. 1943, DHH 81/520/8280, box 5, MKS 7; *Black Swan* ROP

119. Gunnery—C.B. Officer, *Weyburn* to Capt (D) Gibraltar; HMS *Wivern* to Capt (D) Gibraltar, 23 Feb. 1943, NAC, RG 24, 6889, NSS 8870-331/115

HMCS *Alberni* displaying some of the modifications fitted to RCN corvettes deployed on Operation Torch. She has Type 271 radar aft of the charthouse and 20mm Oerlikons on the bridge wings and in the after gun position, but retains her short fo'c'sle. (DND O-6140)

Regina's sailors celebrate their victory over the Italian submarine *Avorio*. Many Canadian corvettes decorated their ships with colourful "gunshield graffiti." (DND PMR83-1618)

and *Black Swan* detached from the convoy to provide an A/S screen.[120] Although some men were jumping over the side of the crippled vessel, and two Carley floats had cleared the ship, there were a good many still on board, some of them wounded. The commanding officer of *Wivern* therefore "placed my foc'sle on hers, bow to stern." Twenty-two of the ship's company, including wounded, came over this way. *Weyburn*'s captain, Lieutenant-Commander T.W. Golby, RCNR, and Lieutenant Wilfred Bark were struggling to lower an unconscious lookout from the bridge to *Wivern*, when Stoker Petty Officer Sydney Frank Day of *Wivern* jumped over to *Weyburn*'s foc'sle to her bridge to lend a hand. Just then the ship "took an alarming list and started to sink rapidly. In another ten seconds she had sunk, stern first."[121] The time was 1131z. She took Golby, Bark, Day, and the lookout with her.

Before *Weyburn* went down, Lieutenant P.S. Milsom and Ordinary Seaman D. Tansey had frantically tried to remove the primers from the depth charges on her stern and succeeded in getting all but two, which were inaccessible because of damage. Sadly, shortly after the corvette slipped below the surface, they exploded, probably killing some men in the water, besides seriously damaging *Wivern*.[122] Her medical officer suffered two broken ankles, and in this condition attended to one of *Weyburn*'s officers, Lieutenant W.A.B. Garrard, whose leg had been crushed between the hulls of the two ships while he was assisting wounded men across. No anaesthetic was available, and the medical officer himself "several times passed out from pain during the course of the operation."[123] At 1410z, after four hours spent rescuing survivors "under intermittent and ineffectual bombardment from the Spanish batteries," *Black Swan* took *Wivern* in tow.[124] Miraculously, only eight men lost their lives.

On the heels of the loss of *Weyburn*, the RCN corvettes wound up their service in the Mediterranean. After escorting MKS 8 safely to British waters, *Woodstock*, *Alberni*, *Summerside*, and *Port Arthur* were on their way back to Canada in mid-March accompanying ON 172. *Lunenburg* remained in the United Kingdom from April until August of 1943, undergoing a refit. *Algoma* was the last corvette to leave the Mediterranean station, escorting MKS 10 to the United Kingdom at the end of March.

The Torch corvettes had measured up in a war that featured air as well as subsurface threats, and they returned to the northwest Atlantic with much improved confidence in their capabilities. Similar results were expected of the C groups during their temporary deployment on the United Kingdom–Gibraltar run, whose main purpose was to hone the groups' fighting power for the struggle in the North Atlantic. Heavy as were the demands of the North African campaign on the supporting naval forces, the defence of shipping on the northern transatlantic routes continued to have the greatest strategic importance and continued to cause the greatest concern to the Allied high command.

---

120. *Weyburn* had reported sighting a submarine off her port side as she prepared to join the convoy.

121. HMS *Wivern* to Capt (D) Gibraltar

122. Ibid; Gunnery—C.B. Officer, *Weyburn* to Capt (D) Gibraltar

123. Draft narrative on loss of *Weyburn*

124. *Black Swan* ROP; J.C. Mossop, Military Branch to M.S. Williams, Foreign Office, 18 May 1943, ibid. The letter also states that at no time was *Black Swan* within four miles of the coast.

Even as the reorganization of the North Atlantic escorts called for by the British in late December to resolve the oil supply crisis and allow the C groups to rebuild came into effect in the latter part of January, it was being overtaken by events. Five days into the New Year, a survey by the Admiralty in close consultation with the Ministry of War Transport of requirements for shipments across the North Atlantic in 1943 had raised profound concerns. The lengthening of the convoy cycle from eight to ten days, which would only take place later in the month, would have to be reversed as soon thereafter as possible; and even that measure would produce the level of shipments needed only if means were found to reduce losses to U-boats by fully 25 percent. The only solution, the study concluded, was to ask the Americans for still further help.[125] In early January, however, the United States was reacting cautiously to Churchill's call of December for assistance with the oil supply crisis. Substantial American help with shipment of oil supplies would come, as we have seen, but not until February and March; in the meantime the disaster that befell TM 1, the experimental British escorted tanker convoy on the southern route, gave little grounds for optimism. Although the New York pool, which the Americans promoted as the real solution to British oil supply, would prove to be just that, it would take time to demonstrate its success, and the British could not assume that such a complicated scheme—dependent as it was on a thousand variables within the US domestic transport system and economy—would deliver as promised.

The overriding difficulty for both the British and the Americans in January 1943 was that follow-up supply of Operation Torch was proving to be a vastly larger enterprise than anticipated because of the determined resistance once the German and Italian forces consolidated after the Allied landings. About two-thirds of the supplies came from Britain, and the drain on British stocks—which could only be replenished by supplies delivered to the United Kingdom in the transatlantic convoys—was 50 to 100 percent greater than planners had predicted. The Americans, as has been seen, faced a similar challenge in delivering supplies to the Atlantic ports of North Africa across the long routes from the United States. There was, as a result, no scope for scaling back in the number of Torch convoys.[126]

The logistical demands of Torch, and the strain these put on the crucial North Atlantic convoys, underlay the discussion of the maritime aspect of future strategy by Churchill, Roosevelt, and their chiefs of staff at Casablanca in January 1943.[127] At issue was the fundamental question of where the western Allies should focus the offensive against the European Axis powers in the coming twelve months. The British, chary as always about a premature attempt to invade northwest Europe, wished to continue operations in the Mediterranean, striking north across that sea once Axis forces had been cleared from North Africa. The American chiefs, who were sceptical of the "Mediterranean strategy" and who had always regarded Torch as a sideshow, gave first priority to Bolero, the build-up of US and Commonwealth forces in Britain for an early assault across the English Channel. Torch, however, had not just brought Bolero to a halt, but it had also drained

---

125. War Cabinet Anti-U-Boat Warfare. "A/S Warfare in Relation to Future Strategy. Memo by the First Lord of the Admiralty," 5 Jan. 1943, PRO, ADM 1/14793

126. Behrens, *Merchant Shipping and the Demands of War*, 308-13

127. Richard M. Leighton, "US Merchant Shipping and the British Import Crisis," in Ken Roberts Greenfield (ed), *Command Decisions* (Washington 1960), 99-223; Kevin Smith, *Crisis Over Convoys: Anglo-American Logistics Diplomacy in the Second World War* (Cambridge 1996), 106-76

forces from Britain to North Africa, leaving a negative net balance. The compromise the British and American leaders reached was to attempt to do it all: the Americans agreed to an invasion of Sicily following completion of the North Africa operations, and the British agreed to the continuing priority of Bolero and planning for the invasion of France. Thus, the needs the Admiralty and Ministry of War Transport had identified for increasing capacity on the North Atlantic route became more urgent still, and the combined chiefs acknowledged as much. The first paragraph of their statement of priorities for the "Conduct of the War in 1943" declared that "the defeat of the U-boat must remain a first charge on the resources of the United Nations."[128] In considering what might be done, the conference resolved to take steps to close the air gap by assigning additional VLR aircraft to the Atlantic battle and devoting auxiliary aircraft carriers to the campaign "at the earliest practicable moment."[129] In the matter of surface escorts the prospects were not encouraging: "The minimum acceptable requirements of escort craft will not be met until about August or September 1943. We ought not to count on the destruction of U-boats at a rate in excess of the production rate before the end of the year."[130] Nonetheless, the staffs decided to "scrutinize the disposition of all existing destroyers and escort craft" and to allocate "as much new construction, or vessels released by new construction ... to convoy protection."[131]

While these decisions were being made in Morocco, the British plan of December to run the North Atlantic convoy system with fewer groups was proving difficult in the face of the ferocious winter weather. On 27 January Commodore Reid at St John's warned that convoys were arriving "up to four days" late. "Last winter every escort ship without exception arriving St John's after westbound passage had sustained weather damage, often considerable, and experience so far this winter is similar."[132] Only the most extreme example was the Town class destroyer HMS *Roxborough*, which on the night of 14 to 15 January was smashed by seas so heavy that they "left her bridge a tangled mass of metal," killing eleven, including the commanding officer and the first lieutenant.[133] Far from being able to streamline operations with the opening of the convoy cycle towards the end of January, Reid was having to pull escorts from one group to replace gaps in others resulting from weather delays and damage.[134] Nevertheless, after escorting HX 222 eastward, C 1 put into Londonderry on 22 January to begin training as laid down in the Admiralty's plan of December. Similarly C 4, after escorting HX 224, arrived at Londonderry on 6 February, C 2, after escorting HX 225, on 15 February, and C 3, after escorting HX 226, on 24 February.[135]

The Admiralty was willing to accept the strain in Newfoundland, but was anxious to close the transatlantic convoy cycle to eight days as soon as possible. Early in February, Their Lordships notified NSHQ that they now intended to employ the C groups on North Atlantic convoys, but on

---

128. Proceedings of CCS Mtg, 21 Jan. 1943, in *Foreign Relations of the United States, The Conferences at Washington, 1941-1942, and Casablanca, 1943* (Washington 1968), 668

129. Ibid, 668-9

130. Ibid, 792

131. Ibid, 668-9

132. FONF to NSHQ, 1615z/27 Jan. 1943, reproduced in "Survey of file NSS 8440-1," DHH 81/520/8280B, pt 1A

133. "Canadian Participation in North Atlantic Convoy Operations June, 1941 to December, 1943," 127; A. Haig, *The Towns* (Kendel, UK 1988), 77

134. FONF WD, Jan. 1943

135. Jurgen Rohwer, *The Critical Convoy Battles of March 1943: The Battle for HX.229/SC.122* (Annapolis 1977), 42

a reduced schedule so as to allow time for the training programs at Londonderry. [136] However, the Mediterranean situation continued to interfere with these new intentions. Determined German resistance in Tunisia created additional logistical demands for the Allied armies in February and March, making it necessary to run a number of fast troop convoys as well as Torch follow-up convoys in quick succession. Besides forty German U-boats patrolling in the Bay of Biscay–Azores–Madeira–Gibraltar area, and a further fifty-seven operating between Iceland and Newfoundland, there were still eleven submarines operating in the Mediterranean during these months, in addition to the ever-present air threat. C groups could not, therefore, all be returned to North Atlantic convoy duty until they had escorted the necessary convoys to and from the Mediterranean. [137]

Like the Torch corvettes, the C groups worked up their ships' companies before taking up their new task. Based on Admiral Horton's dictum that every hundred-day training cycle should include at least fourteen days in harbour and seven sea-training days, the ships trained for a week or so at Londonderry's shore training facilities—the depth-charge drill unit, night lookout trainer, antiaircraft dome teacher, 4-inch gun mounting, asdic and radar trainers, and a mock-up of a U-boat conning tower for boarding parties—in every case ships' teams being exercised as units. [138] They then went to sea for work-ups, mostly at Tobermory. During the first full day at HMS *Western Isles* the ships' companies went ashore for lectures and training. For the next five days they exercised in harbour and trained at sea, conducting high-and low-angle firing, depth-charge drills, and antisubmarine exercises either individually or in company, and usually with a tame submarine.

Although they had not all been able to bring their equipment up to standard, some of the ships received dockyard attention as space allowed to fit new equipment, principally type 271 radar and Oerlikon 20 mm guns. They were then allowed several days to perform routine harbour duties and prepare for sea. The other C groups arrived after the appointment of Captain A.J. Baker-Cresswell, RN, an officer with considerable antisubmarine experience, to the newly established position of Training Captain Western Approaches, and thus carried out their sea exercises off Moville with the large yacht HMS *Philante*, a vessel that served both as headquarters ship for Baker-Cresswell and as a notional convoy. Ashore, the Londonderry training facilities were particularly useful. Although the Canadian night attack teacher developed by Commander J.C. Hibbard in Halifax was at least on a par with that at Londonderry (Hibbard had trained a large proportion of personnel in the Torch corvettes on the teacher before their departure), [139] the time allotted to C groups in Londonderry was more generous than had been possible in Halifax. Because it included consecutive days at sea following shore training, and because even after completing convoying duties to Gibraltar and back the C groups repeated the Londonderry phase of their training, it also proved more useful than anything that had been available to them before. [140] Stephenson at Tobermory and Baker-Cresswell in

136. NMCS Washington to NSHQ, 1958z/2 Feb. 1943, DHH, NHS, 8440-60 "Mid-Ocean Escort Force"; "History of North Atlantic Convoy Escort Organization and Canadian Participation Therein September, 1939 to April, 1943," 18; C-in-C WA to FONF, 0931z/11 Feb. 1943, reproduced in "Survey of file NSS 8440-1," DHH 81/520/8280B, pt 1A

137. Adm, OIC, U-Boat Situation Ending 1 March 1943, PRO, ADM 223/15

138. Goldrick, "Work-Up," in Howarth and Law, *The Battle of the Atlantic, 1939-1945*, 220-40

139. "Their remarkable successes in the Mediterranean are sufficient testimony," he observed, "of the radical methods employed." Hibbard to Lt James George, Office of the Naval Historian, 18 Feb. 1944, DHH, NSHQ 1650-239/15

140. Ibid, 220-221; *Napanee* deck log, NAC, RG 24, 7673; P.M. Bliss to DOD, 24 Dec. 1942, RG 24, 6796, 8375-4

Philante were, furthermore, exceptionally good at their job, and the ships' companies entrusted to their not always tender mercies underwent a memorable experience. Just as important, the Canadian liaison officer in Londonderry, Lieutenant-Commander W.E.S. Briggs, RCNR, formerly commanding officer of HMCS *Orillia*, tried to keep Canadian naval authorities abreast of the situation with insights about Canadian operational efficiency.[141]

It was on 27 February 1943, a few days later than planned, that C 1, consisting of *St Croix* (Lieutenant-Commander A.H. Dobson, SOE), *Napanee*, *Battleford*, *Kenogami,* and *Shediac*, in company with HMS *Burwell*, and from the 16th Minesweeping Flotilla HMS *Fort York*, *Parrsboro*, *Qualicum,* and *Wedgeport*, sailed from Londonderry to escort KMS 10 to Gibraltar.[142] The group was without *St Laurent*, which had gone into dockyard in Halifax for refit, but *St Croix* now had FH3 HF/DF equipment.[143] On 4 March 1943, about 250 miles north of Cape St Vincent, two Focke-Wulf 200 *Kondor* reconnaissance aircraft attacked from the west. They achieved little in the face of the antiaircraft fire put up by both escorts and merchant ships, and when one of the aircraft attacked a Catalina patrol aircraft astern of the convoy the Catalina itself engaged the enemy and observed several hits.[144] The air attack, as regularly happened on the Gibraltar run, was the prelude to contact with U-boats. In this case, at 1240z on 4 March *Shediac*, stationed six miles astern of the convoy, detected *U 87*.[145]

The corvette carried out a total of five attacks on the U-boat, dropping thirty-eight depth charges over a three-hour period. At 1400 *St Croix* left the screen to join the corvette, which was running short of depth charges. *Shediac's* last two attacks produced underwater explosions and "globules of oil distinctively different from depth charge scum." The asdic team heard the sound of blowing tanks, and "the ship pointed toward the bubbles with engines stopped and all guns brought to bear amidst loud cheers from the crew."[146] To their disappointment the U-boat failed to surface, so at 1430 when *St Croix* got a contact close to *Shediac's* position she fired a six-charge pattern, followed this up with a stern sweep, and fired a second six-charge pattern on a dubious contact that soon faded.[147] *Shediac* and *St Croix* then carried out Operation Observant without success. At 1510 both ships broke off and returned to the convoy. Lieutenant J.E. Clayton, *Shediac*'s commanding officer, was probably right in thinking "that the U-boat had attempted to surface and was unable to do so and eventually sank."[148] Official credit for the kill was given to both ships, although it seems likely that *Shediac*'s last attack sealed the submarine's fate.

Aircraft continued to shadow KMS 10, and on 6 March three boats from the *Robbe* group turned up. They were unable to close for an attack until 1418z, when *U 410* torpedoed the *Fort Paskoyac*

---

141. Lcdr N.E.S. Briggs, RCN, "Personal Appreciation of Situation for RCN Ships in UK," 23 Apr. 1943, RG 24, 3997, 1057-3-24

142. *Napanee* deck log, NAC, RG 24, 7673; Remarks by Cmdre Commanding Londonderry Escort Force, Convoys KMS 10 and MKS 9, dated 4 Apr.1943, PRO, ADM 199/975

143. NSHQ, *Particulars of Canadian War Vessels*, Half-Yearly Return, June 1943 (Ottawa 1943)

144. *St Croix* ROP, Convoy KMS 10, 15 Mar. 1943, PRO, ADM 199/975; U-Boat and Air Attacks Beaten Off by C 1 group, PRO, ADM files A/S W 885/43 and A/S W 110/43, DHH, 81/520/8280, box 5 KMS 10; Adm, *MASR*, Apr.1943, 13

145. Ibid, 14

146. The position of this contact was given as 41 36' N, 13 31' W. Narrative and Reports on KMS 10, Mar. 1943; U-Boat and Air Attacks Beaten Off by C 1 group

147. Adm, *MASR*, Apr. 1943, 14

148. Narrative and Reports on KMS 10, Mar. 1943; U-Boat and Air Attacks Beaten Off by C 1

from the starboard side, and one minute later *Fort Battle River* from the port side. *St Croix* dropped a shallow pattern of depth charges ahead of number one column. Lieutenant-Commander Dobson ordered *Shediac* to stand by the merchant ships and requested a tug.[149] As *St Croix* and *Napanee* were carrying out Operation Artichoke, *St Croix* attacked a firm contact between the torpedoed ships without apparent result, then returned to the screen with *Napanee*, leaving *Shediac* to screen the torpedoed ships.[150] At 1714z *Shediac* again got contact and dropped a five-charge pattern set deep to 550 feet. Unfortunately, one of the torpedoed ships lay directly in *Shediac*'s path, and it was impossible to follow through with the attack. Moreover, after a further five-charge pattern had been laid, an hour later there were only eight depth charges left in the ship. "The contact was a good one," reported Clayton; breaking off his attack was "one of the most exasperating experiences of my naval career." Although Dobson sent a second escort to help *Shediac*, the submarine, which had been operating alone, now evidently withdrew owing to depth-charge damage.[151]

The Gibraltar Escort Force relieved C 1 on 7 March.[152] Dobson earned a moderate reproof from Commodore G.W.G. Simpson, Commodore (D) Londonderry, for some of his tactics on 6 March. First, when he took *Napanee* with him to investigate an HF/DF bearing, "with an aircraft in the vicinity, he should have detailed the aircraft to do the necessary search. This would have meant that a stronger close escort would have been left round the convoy. Even if no aircraft had been present, *St Croix* should not have weakened the escort by taking *Napanee* away on the information of an H/F D/F bearing only." Second, when *Shediac* was short of depth charges she should have been recalled and another escort should have been detailed to follow up her contact. Nevertheless, and in spite of the losses, C 1's defence of the convoy was effective. In particular, "*Shediac* carried out most determined attacks, and the firing of 68 depth charges without failure showed a satisfactory standard of depth charge drill."[153]

On 8 March 1943 C 1, joined by HMS *Fort York* and *Qualicum*, and the Torch corvettes HMCS *Baddeck*, *Prescott,* and *Regina*, sailed from Gibraltar with MKS 9. This convoy of fifty-six merchant ships came under air observation on 12 March, and the next evening, when the convoy was north-west of Finisterre, *U 163* made contact. *Prescott*, commanded by Lieutenant-Commander W. McIsaac, RCNVR, stationed 10,000 yards on the convoy's starboard bow, obtained a radar target at 3,400 yards, altered towards and saw the boat at 1,400 yards, just as it was diving. At 2155z, with very strong hydrophone effect at 1,200 yards, *Prescott* began her attack. Suddenly what McIsaac thought to be a second U-boat appeared 900 yards fine on the port bow, and after a few

---

149. *Fort Battle River* was sinking, but *Fort Pasoyac*, thanks to her torpedo nets, remained afloat. *St Croix* ROP, KMS 10; *Napanee* deck log, NAC, RG 24, v 7673; Adm, *MASR*, Apr. 1943; Remarks by Cmdre Commanding Londonderry Escort Force Convoys KMS 10 and MKS 9, 4 Apr. 1943, PRO, ADM 199/975

150. Narrative and Reports on KMS 10, Mar. 1943; U-Boat and Air Attacks Beaten Off by C 1; Cmdre Londonderry signal 1929/19/3/43, DHH, 81/520/8280, box 5 KMS 10

151. BdU, KTB, 6 Mar. 1943; Narrative and Reports on KMS 10, Mar.1943; U-Boat and Air Attacks Beaten Off by C 1; Remarks by Cmdre Commanding Londonderry Escort Force, Convoys KMS 10 and MKS 9

152. Before reaching its destination beyond Gibraltar the convoy again came under U-boat attack on 9 March and two ships were damaged by torpedoes. On entering Bône harbour on 11 March there was another air attack, but no more losses occurred. Narrative and Reports on KMS 10, March 1943; U-Boat and Air Attacks Beaten Off by C 1, Ref: C-in-C Mediterranean signal 1528/13 Mar. 1943, HMS *Vanoc* signal 1943/9 Mar. 1943

153. 1 *Shediac* ROP, 18 Mar. 1943, DHH, 81/520/8280, box 5 KMS 10; Remarks by Cmdre Commanding Londonderry Escort Force, Convoys KMS 10 and MKS 9

moments hesitation (since by Doppler effect and range the asdic team estimated the first boat was steering directly for him) MacIsaac turned his attention to the boat he could see, as it "began to loom very large on the bow. " It was too late to stop the firing of a five-charge pattern at the first target at 2158z, but MacIsaac observed that, although it would have been wide of the mark, it probably kept the first boat down while he engaged the second with gunfire. At approximately 700 yards this boat, apparently undamaged, also dived. *Prescott* obtained an asdic contact at 600 yards, maintained it to a range of 200 yards, and at 2204z fired a nine-charge pattern.[154] *Prescott*, *Napanee,* and *Baddeck* carried out Operation Observant until 2319z, when *Prescott* established asdic contact at 1,500 yards, and attacked with a nine-charge pattern. McIsaac stayed on the scene for about three hours with no further sign of a submarine. Commodore Simpson in Londonderry considered *Prescott* had saved the convoy from attack, but had lost the opportunity for a kill by not concentrating on one target. McIsaac believed that " had there been only one U-boat, we would have had him cold." That assessment proved correct for there actually was only one boat, and later analysis showed that *Prescott* destroyed *U 163* on 13 March 1943.[155] MKS 9 arrived safely the next day.[156]

In the meantime, on 6 February 1943, C 4 had arrived at Londonderry. The group embarked stores and ammunition, completed the required training, and on 2 March 1943 HMS *Churchill* (Commander A.M. McKillop, RN, SO), HMCS *Restigouche, Amherst, Brandon, Collingwood,* and HMS *Celandine* sailed to escort eight troopships (KMF 10B) bound for Algiers. *Restigouche* had type 271 radar, but the only other ship in C 4 to have this equipment was *Brandon,* fitted with the latest version just before sailing. The first four days allowed radar operators in *Brandon* time to acquaint themselves with the new equipment. On 8 March KMF 10B passed through the Straits of Gibraltar (*Amherst* and *Celandine* detaching long enough to refuel in Gibraltar) and arrived at Algiers on 9 March.[157] After an uncomfortable day in port when German aircraft bombed the harbour at least twice, C 4 sailed for the United Kingdom on 11 March with MKF 10B, consisting of four troopships. On 14 March four *Kondor* aircraft attacked the formation damaging the *Duchess of York,* but she was able to remain in company and the convoy arrived safely on 17 March. The group's performance in the defence of KMF 10B and MKF 10B had earned good marks from both Commodore (D) Londonderry and the Admiralty's Director of Anti-Submarine Warfare.[158]

---

154. *Prescott* to Cmdre Londonderry, "Report of Attacks on Two U-Boats," 15 Mar. 1943, PRO, ADM 199/975

155. Extracts of Cmdre Commanding Londonderry Escort Force, ROP, 4 Apr. 1943, DHH, 81/520/8280, box 5 MKS 9; HMCS *Prescott*, "Report of Attacks on Two U-Boats"; *Prescott*, "Report of Attack on U-Boat," 4 Apr. 1943, PRO, ADM 199/975; R.M. Coppock, Naval Staff Duties (Foreign Documents Section) MOD, to W.A.B. Douglas, April 1987

156. HMCS *St Croix*, ROP—Convoy MKS 9, 22 Mar. 1943, PRO, ADM 199/975; HMCS *Napanee* deck log, NAC, RG 24, 7673; Report by Cmdre of Convoy MKS 9, 18 Mar. 1943, ADM 199/728

157. During the night of 8-9 Mar., between Cape de Gata and Oran, *Brandon* and *Restigouche* pursued a radar contact picked up by the corvette, but *Brandon* lacked the speed to make optimum use of type 271 radar. *Brandon* deck log, NAC, RG 24, 7104; *Collingwood* deck log, NAC, RG 24, 7223; *Restigouche* deck log, NAC, RG 24, 7794; *Amherst* deck log, NAC, RG 24, 7023; Extracts on KMF 10B escorted by C 4 Group and Attacks by *Brandon* and *Restigouche* on U-Boats, Mar. 1943, *Amherst* and *Collingwood*, DHH, 81/520/8280, box 4 KMF 10B; *Brandon*, ROP, 9 Mar. 194

158. *Amherst* attacked an asdic contact astern of the convoy on 13 Mar., the only suspicion of submarines during this passage. Cmdre Commanding Londonderry Escort Force to C-in-C WA, 31 Mar. 1943 and Director Anti-Submarine Warfare Minute, 6 May 1943 cited in Extracts on KMF 10B escorted by C 4 Group and Attacks by *Brandon* and *Restigouche* on U-Boats, March 1943, *Amherst* Extracts on KMF 10F escorted by C 4 Group and Attacks by *Brandon* and *Restigouche* on U-Boats, March 1943, *Amherst* and *Collingwood*, DHH, 81/520/8280, box 4 KMF 10B; *Amherst* deck log; Brief History of HMCS *Amherst*, DHH, HMCS Amherst 8000; *Collingwood* deck log; *Restigouche* deck log

C 2, after its arrival at Londonderry on 15 February, spent the next four weeks undergoing the same training and maintenance routine as the previous groups. On 14 March HMS *Broadway* (Lieutenant-Commander E.H. Chavasse, RN, SO), *Sherwood*, *Lagan,* and *Primrose*, with HMCS *Drumheller*, which had been outfitted in Halifax with type 271 radar and 123D asdic, and *Morden*, sailed as escort for KMS 11. It was now policy to combine KMS with OS (United Kingdom–West Africa) convoys, and the twenty-day cycle was to be reduced by five days. OS 46 and KMS 11 were the first to be combined, seventy ships sailing to Gibraltar. Ships for Spanish and Portuguese ports were included in these combined convoys, thus making it unnecessary to resume the OG and HG convoys. There were some additional escorts. *Chambly*, for instance, joined direct from Halifax, after completing a refit. HMS *Waveney* also joined this convoy, while HMS *Polyanthus* went into refit.[159]

Except for occasional contacts nothing further of note occurred until 19 March, when a *Kondor*—one of eight operating from Bordeaux on long-range reconnaissance to the west of Portugal and apparently looking for KMS 11—was shot down north of Cape Finisterre. Another *Kondor* attacked the convoy and scored a hit on *City of Christchurch* on 21 March, about 160 miles west of Lisbon. She was damaged but managed to proceed under her own steam making about four to six knots. *Churchill* ordered *Morden* to detach and stand by the merchant vessel early on 22 March, and at approximately 1750 that day, when the engine room bulkhead finally gave way, *Morden* sent away boats to pick up the crew. A boarding party prepared to salvage three motor launches on deck but could do little else as the ship rapidly settled. At 1920z on 22 March, thirty-five miles off Lisbon, *Morden* sank the hulk with gunfire.[160]

At 2045z *Morden* and *ML-1229*, which had been salvaged from the wreck, got under way for Gibraltar. During the night the wind increased to a force eight gale and created dangerous wave conditions. The motor launch had little fuel to spare, so the vessels reduced speed to six knots, but after forty-five harrowing hours they completed the 295-mile journey safely and arrived in Gibraltar at 1530z on 24 March. The men on the launch, with no hot food or drink, had constantly been working the main bilge pumps as the vessel pounded into the sea and swell. In the end, *Morden* rescued 102 men from *City of Christchurch,* which enhanced the corvette's reputation, first established on 21 October 1942 in the rescue from SS *Winnipeg II* of 124 crew and 68 passengers during a North Atlantic storm, as the "champion survivor-carrier of her class in the United Nations Navies."[161]

On 27 March C 2, with HMS *Broadway*, *Lagan,* and *Sherwood*, and HMCS *Chambly*, *Drumheller*, and *Morden*, together with minesweepers HMS *Shippigan*, *Dornoch*, *Ilfracombe*, *Lord Hotham*, and FFS *Commandant Drogou* sailed from Gibraltar as escort to MKS 10. HMCS *Algoma* joined later on 28 March. Originally assigned to MKF 11, she had not been able to keep up with the fast convoy. Apart from an unsuccessful search by *Broadway* and *Sherwood* for a German blockade runner, the convoy had an uneventful passage, arriving at Londonderry at 2135 on 5 April. On 19 April, following the required training and maintenance routine, C 2 with HMS *Broadway* (SO), HMS *Lagan*,

159. FOIC. Northern Ireland to C-in-C WA, 24 Mar. 1943, PRO, ADM 199/631; *Morden* deck log, NAC, RG 24, 7536; Adm, *MASR*, Apr. 1943; Capt (D) Halifax to C-in-C CNA, 5 Apr. 1943, NAC, RG 24, 6910, NSS 8970-331/30

160. *Morden* deck log; Daily Summary of Naval Events, No. 1292, 20 Mar. 1943, DHH 81/520/1650 D.S. v 16; *Morden* ROP, 25 Mar. 1943, NAC, RG 24, 11304, "Morden"

161. Lt D.R. Watson, RCNR, 1st Lt, the Ship's Coxswain, CPO English, RCNR, with three seamen, one signalman from *Morden,* as well as a PO Motor Mechanic and two Stokers attached to motor launches took *ML-1229* to Gibraltar. Brief History of HMCS *Morden*, DHH, Morden 8000

and HMCS *Amherst, Drumheller, Morden*, and *Primrose*, in company with the Torch corvettes *Algoma* and *Calgary,* sailed for North America with convoy ON 179.[162]

C 2 and its consorts were the last of the Canadian naval forces committed to Torch to return to the North Atlantic. C 3, which had done three weeks of training and maintenance at Londonderry but never joined the Gibraltar run, took up the escort of ON 172 on 11 March. In company with the ships of the group, HMS *Burnham*, HMS *Jed*, and HMCS *Bittersweet, Eyebright, Mayflower,* and *La Malbaie*, were the returning Torch corvettes *Alberni, Port Arthur, Summerside,* and *Woodstock*. C 1, *St Laurent, St Croix, Napanee, Battleford, Kenogami,* and *Shediac*, in company with the Torch corvettes *Camrose, Moosejaw,* and *Ville de Québec*, had set out on 29 March as the escort of ONS 2 (the Admiralty had recently separated slow westbound transatlantic convoys into this new series, reserving the ON designation for fast convoys). C 4, with HMS *Churchill* and HMCS *Restigouche, Brandon*, and *Collingwood* (*Amherst* remained at Londonderry for repairs), formed up as the escort for ON 177 on 7 April. With the manner in which the deployments of the C groups to the eastern Atlantic had been staggered, all four were absent from the northern convoy routes only during the first half of March, but even then the RCN was not unrepresented; the mixed US–Canadian group A 3 never left, and was indeed heavily engaged.[163]

The one benefit of the horrendous weather on the northern routes in January was that the U-boats—on the average ninety-one of them at sea and forty-two in their operational areas[164]— had almost no success intercepting convoys. HX 222, escorted by C 1, had the misfortune to be intercepted about 450 miles southwest of Iceland by *U 268*, commanded by Oberleutnant E. Heydemann, in transit to its station farther west. Boats from Group *Falke* had sighted the convoy the day before, on 16 January, but in view of the proximity to air cover from Iceland, did not follow up the contact. An aircraft sighted *U 268* thirty miles ahead of the convoy on 17 January and reported it, but not directly to the convoy escort, allowing Heydemann to evade the screen and sink the Panamanian whale factory ship *Vestfold*. C 1 reacted sluggishly to this attack, partly because the group was sailing under a senior officer in HMS *Vansittart* who was new to the group (and only for this passage) and included another stranger to the group, HMS *Chesterfield*.[165]

February had seen a renewal of warfare in the so-called Greenland air gap. HX 224, escorted by C 4 with HMS *Highlander* (Commander E.C.L. Day, RN) replacing *Restigouche* as senior officer, was the first convoy to be affected. Diverted away from Group *Jaguar* in the western Atlantic, and on course to do an end run around Group *Landsknecht*, which had been waiting west of Ireland for a westbound ON convoy, HX 224 did not escape *U 456* on the northern end of *Landsknecht*, possibly because Enigma decrypts were still coming through too slowly for the Admiralty to make another timely diversion. *U 456* stayed in contact for three days in a heavy westerly gale and sank

---

162. Brief Note on MKS 10 escorted by C 2 Group, Mar. 1943, DHH, 81/520/8280, box 5 MKS 10; *Morden* deck log; Milner, *North Atlantic Run*, 228

163. Rohwer, *Critical Convoy Battles*, 39, 41-2

164. BdU, KTB, 31 Jan. 1943

165. "Canadian Participation in North Atlantic Convoy Operations June, 1941 to Dec. 1943," Canadian Naval Mission Overseas (CNMO), 27 Nov. 1945, DHH, 122.103 (D2), 125-7; MOD, *U-Boat War in the Atlantic* II, 73-4, diagram19; Rohwer, *Axis Submarine Successes*, 147

the *Jeremiah van Rensellaer* on 2 February and the *Inverilen* the day after that.[166] In the ensuing battle SC 118 (B 2) suffered much worse losses. German radio intelligence and interrogation of a survivor from HX 224 allowed group *Pfeil* to make an interception and sink eleven of sixty-three ships. Considered one of the hardest-fought convoy battles of the war, SC 118 is said to have given Admiral Horton the ammunition he needed to bring in support groups and to reinforce escort groups. As will be seen later in this history it also gave Canadian staff officers at NSHQ ammunition for their campaign to form a naval aviation branch in the RCN.[167]

The next major convoy battle was for ON 166, escorted by A 3. BdU, alerted by intelligence from aircraft and German HF/DF, had formed exceptionally strong groups, and was able to keep them on station for extended periods by refuelling them from strategically placed milch cows. Allied intelligence was aware of these developments, but delays in deciphering Enigma traffic prevented the information reaching the convoys before *U 604* made contact with ON 166. Eventually, nineteen U-boats of Groups *Ritter* and *Knappen* took part in the operation, and thirteen actually attacked targets. Of sixty-three ships initially assigned to ON 166, thirteen had already returned or had not sailed from the United Kingdom, one returned to Iceland, nine became stragglers, and fourteen, including the rescue vessel *Stockport*, fell victim to torpedoes between 20 and 25 February. Only twenty-eight ships arrived safely in convoy.[168] BdU attributed the success to the fact that the commanding officers of the boats "were for the most part experienced older men."[169] That aside, A 3, which included *Chilliwack* (returning to Canada from the Mediterranean for refit), and the established Canadian members of the group, *Dauphin*, *Rosthern*, and *Trillium* (all with type 271 radar), performed well under difficult circumstances. USCG *Campbell* sank *U 606* by ramming and had to be towed into St John's, and the Canadian escorts earned praise not only for the rescue of hundreds of survivors, but for aggressive tactics that probably prevented further losses. VLR Liberators of 120 Squadron RAF provided air cover until 21 February and on the other side of the air gap RCAF Cansos, modified to extend their effective range, prevented some attacks on 24 February. The next day, when fog grounded all aircraft, one more ship was sunk.[170]

Because of the intense pressure of Allied logistical needs to close up the cycle of the North Atlantic convoys, A3 was at sea again on 4 March to escort the eastbound SC 121. The escort group, which for this crossing included its three usual Canadian members, had had less than a week in port for rest, replenishment, and repairs after the ON 166 battle. Fearful storms again swept the northern ocean, which soon drove back the two old British destroyers of the Western Support Force that sailed in company, caused HMCS *Trillium* to lose contact with the convoy on 8 March, and grounded Iceland-based aircraft that were to have provided support at mid-ocean. Unfortunately,

---

166. Ibid, 148; MOD, *U-boat War in the Atlantic* II, 75-6, diagram 19, point 3; BdU, KTB, 3 Feb. 1942; Milner, *North Atlantic Run*, 222; Hinsley, *British Intelligence* II, 560

167. MOD, *U-boat War in the Atlantic* II, 76; David Syrett, "German U-boat Attacks on Convoy SC 118: 4 Feb. to 14 Feb. 1943," *American Neptune* 44 (Winter 1984), 48-60; Milner, *North Atlantic Run*, 222-5; Chalmers, *Max Horton*, 165

168. "Canadian Participation in North Atlantic Convoy Operations," 131-2

169. BdU, KTB, 26 Feb. 1943

170. BdU, KTB, 24-6 Feb. 1943; MOD, *U-Boat War in the Atlantic* II, 77; David Syrett, "'Situation Extremely Dangerous': Three Atlantic Convoys in February 1943," in Runyan and Copes, *To Die Gallantly: The Battle of the Atlantic*; Douglas, *Creation of a National Air Force*, 542-3. Marc Milner has observed, in his account of Canadian participation in the MOEF: "It is likely that similar efforts of co-ordination and teamwork within C groups in late 1942 would have been equally effective, at least in mitigating criticism." Milner, *North Atlantic Run*, 227

the advantage in intelligence had again shifted in favour of the enemy; B-Dienst continued to deliver timely information to BdU, while the Allies were encountering extended delays in the decryption of the four-rotor Shark cypher, and from 10 to 19 March had no success. At this same time, the Operational Intelligence Centre at the Admiralty reported that a "record number of sixty-six U-boats are estimated to be in the North Atlantic north of 50°West, most between 20°West and 35°West."[171] On 6 March *U 405* located the convoy southeast of Greenland; BdU ordered the seventeen submarines of group *Westmark* to close immediately, while positioning the ten submarines of group *Ostmark* to take up the attack further to the east. Although the weather hindered the approach of the U-boats, by daylight on 10 March, when the convoy passed south of Iceland, they had sunk twelve of the fifty-nine ships that had originally sailed. The experienced senior officer of the escort, Captain P.R. Heineman, USN, commented on the "urgent need for more air coverage" and the "impracticality of maintaining reasonable A/S screen with few escorts." He also noted the "urgent need for better material upkeep of escorts especially in detection devices. At one time two out of three HF/DF sets were inoperative. Similarly, four of eight escorts had their Radars out of commission, while the Asdic sets of three of the eight ships present were defective."[172]

Convoys that followed SC 121 into the air gap south of Greenland— HX 228, HX 229, and SC 122, all escorted by B groups—suffered a similar fate. In total, U-boats destroyed 108 Allied ships during March.[173] "A disconcerting feature," remarked the Admiralty's *Monthly Anti-Submarine Report*, "is the large proportion of tonnage sunk in convoy ... about 68 per cent. This is the highest monthly total of tonnage sunk in convoy since the war began."[174]

Against the backdrop of the continuing crisis at sea, during February and March the three Allied navies prepared for the Atlantic Convoy Conference in Washington, convened for the unusually long period of twelve days. Canada's senior naval and air officers were keenly aware at all stages of pitfalls as well as opportunities.

Rear-Admiral Brodeur's report to Admiral Nelles of 26 January about the flurry of rumours concerning command in the Atlantic highlighted the pressures on the Canadian services. Interestingly, in light of Brodeur's earlier comments about the consideration shown by the Americans in contrast to the habit of British officers in treating the RCN as a subordinate part of the RN, he went to Admiral Noble, the new head of the BAD, to find out if there was substance to the rumours: "I believe it is better for me to wait for USN to ask for me ... as I am afraid that I may have given them a wrong impression by going down to them and asking questions, i.e., that they need not tell me anything unless I specifically ask for it, that has certainly been their attitude in all these Convoy and Escort matters so far."

Yet Brodeur had by no means overcome his mistrust of the British. "Of course our taking over from CTF 24 would certainly suit the Admiralty better, but we will have to watch from that side

---

171. CTU 21.4.3 to CTF 24, "Report of Escort of Convoy SC 121," 18 Mar. 1943, NARA, RG 313, Red, CTF 24, box 8703, SC 121; Syrett, *Battle of the Atlantic*, 147, 150; Hinsley, *British Intelligence* II, 561

172. CTU 21.4.3, "Report of Escort of Convoy SC 121"; BdU, KTB, 10 Mar. 1943; Blair, *Hitler's U-Boat War* II, 250-4

173. Hinsley, *British Intelligence* II, 680; P. Gretton, *Crisis Convoy: The Story of HX 231* (London 1974); Terraine, *Business in Great Waters*, 545-76; Adm, *Defeat of the Enemy Attack on Shipping*, IB, table 13

174. Adm, *MASR,* Mar. 1943, 3. See also, Rohwer, *Critical Convoy Battles*, 186-8.

also that a RN Vice-Admiral does not arrive accidentally at Argentia, it is not beyond the bo[u]nds of possibility if I know my Admiralty as I think I do." Typically, Brodeur did not hide his views. Pleased to see Noble "worried about the whole mix-up" over the allocation of Canadian destroyers to the Western Support Force, Brodeur "asked him how he would have liked to have had a full USN Admiral being placed over him when he was C-in-C WA, which I said was exactly the same for us having a USN Vice-Admiral over our Rear-Admirals to run our navy." For good measure he informed Captain Patterson, one of the USN members of the combined staff planners subcommittee that was examining the command structure in the Atlantic, "that the RCN had *no intention whatever* to become a Dutch Navy, i.e., to be split up as they like" and reported with evident satisfaction that Patterson "is worried now and I think he believes we mean it too."[175]

Brodeur's fears were exaggerated. The Director of the Trade Division at the Admiralty, Captain B.B. Schofield, had already scouted and rejected the idea of taking the Canadians under British control, realizing that "this would be more than the Americans were prepared to accept in one bite."[176] Other studies on "the case for unified control in the North Atlantic" carried out during January in Schofield's branch of the Admiralty suggested that "COAC Halifax under NSHQ/Ottawa act as an operating authority west of Westomp in lieu of Comtask 24."[177]

Noble appears to have intimated the trend of the Admiralty's post-Casablanca thinking to Brodeur, for the latter emphatically told Nelles that the time had come to combine COAC and FONF into a single command. As seen in Chapter 3, NSHQ had in 1941 separated the newly created Newfoundland command from COAC so that the necessary direction of Canadian mid-ocean escorts by Western Approaches would not result in British control of Canadian coastal waters and the service's principal base at Halifax. Nicely as that arrangement had served Canadian purposes in the past, Brodeur warned, "our ... set up has given the impression that we are running a divided command, which is not considered as *one* for the Coast, as it splits it up in such small areas."

> Our friends here I am certain looked upon this as a weakness for flexibility of operations, and immediately seized on the occasion to place a "super-man" there. I would suggest that the whole Eastern Canadian Coast be placed under our Naval Command ... this I am sure will give us a much stronger position against all comers, and will prevent any future piece-meal absorbing by any outside naval authority as the mouthful would be just a little too much.[178]

Confirmation of much of what Brodeur said came on 2 February, when the RCAF staff in Washington signalled Air Force Headquarters in Ottawa that they had been shown a copy—apparently by the RAF delegation—of the interim report by the Atlantic subcommittee of the combined staff planners. This report, it will be recalled, recommended a three-stage unification of command in the Atlantic: "(A) centralization of all anti-submarine effort in the Atlantic under one commander within each of the Allied nations concerned. (B) Centralization of operational control of all the anti-submarine resources assigned by each nation on each side of the Atlantic to this effort—

---

175. NMCJS to CNS, 26 Jan. 1943, NAC, RG 24, 11969, 222-4

176. Capt B.B. Schofield, Director of Trade Division to DOP, VCNS, ACNS (UT) et al, 4 Feb. 1943, PRO, ADM 1/12663

177. "The Case for Unified Control in the North Atlantic," Feb. 1943, PRO, ADM 1/12663

178. NMCJS to CNS, 26 Jan. 1943, NAC, RG 24, 11969, 222-4

western Atlantic under a US commander Eastern Atlantic under a UK commander. (C) Centralization of strategic control under one commander of all the antisubmarine resources in the Atlantic ocean." The combined staff planners made it clear that the report had not been considered by any senior British or American authority, but said it would be shortly. The difficulty for the Canadian naval staff was with stage "B," which seemed to augur the appointment of a US Western Atlantic antisubmarine commander cloaked with the powers to exercise detailed local control over Canadian forces that CTF 24 lacked. At the meeting of senior RCAF and RCN officers hastily convened on 3 February to consider this news, the air force officers passed along further information, gathered by Wing Commander C.L. Annis, a member of the headquarters staff, during a recent trip to Washington:[179] "COMINCH would give favourable consideration to turning over the whole control of Trade Convoys and Escorts, in the North West Atlantic, to Canada provided 'they put their own house in order and have unified command.'"[180] This suggested that NSHQ's recent direct dealings with Admiral King, in which he stated that the Canadians should take over from CTF 24, had precedence over the draft recommendations from the combined planners. This was in fact the case, but it did not matter in terms of the issues immediately to hand. The salient point was that King and the combined planners and, as Brodeur had intimated, the Admiralty, all agreed that Canada had to pull together its east coast commands. The emergency meetings of the air and naval staffs in Ottawa concluded that "if centralization plan ... for Canadian area can be formulated before RCN staff proceeds to Washington [for the Atlantic Convoy Conference this] will greatly strengthen their hand towards regaining local strategic control."[181]

Action was nearly instantaneous. At midday on 3 February Nelles warned Admiral Murray and Commodore Reid that "it was probable a single Canadian Naval command in the Atlantic would be set up."[182] The Allied pressure abruptly ended the RCAF's long-standing resistance to naval control; a further inducement came from Wing Commander Annis's discussions in Washington with USN and US Army Air Corps officers who had said they would look more favourably on the RCAF's repeated requests for VLR Consolidated Liberator maritime patrol bombers if the Canadians unified their antisubmarine commands. The air staff quickly agreed that Eastern Air Command's antisubmarine squadrons should operate under naval direction on the model of the RAF's Coastal Command.[183] On 4 February Nelles and Air Vice-Marshal N.R. Anderson, Deputy Chief of the Air Staff, acting for Air Marshal L.S. Breadner who was out of town, briefed the Cabinet War Committee, and won the government's support to move ahead with rapid unification of the Atlantic command in order to forestall the combined planners' recommendation for an American-led Allied regional command in the western Atlantic.[184]

179. AFHQ to ROYCANAIRF London, signal C.477, 4 Feb. 1943, NAC, RG 24, 5270, S 28-1-2

180. DOD to CNS, "Washington Conference on Convoy and Escort Arrangements in the Western Atlantic," 16 Feb. 1943, DHH, NHS 8440-130 "Western Support Force"

181. AFHQ to ROYCANAIRF London, signal C.477

182. DOD, "Washington Conference on Convoy and Escort Arrangements in the Western Atlantic"

183. AFHQ to AFCS Washington, signal C.479, 5 Feb. 1943, NAC, RG 24, 5270, S. 28-1-2; formal approval awaited Breadner's return to Ottawa: CWCM, 18 Feb. 1943 and CAS to CNS, 21 Feb. 1943, Queen's Unviersity Archives, C.G. Power papers, box 71, file D-2034

184. CWCM, 4 Feb. 1943; DCAS to Minister, 4 Feb. 1943, NAC, RG 24, 5270, S 28-1-2. Angus L. Macdonald was out of town, so the air minister, C.G. Power, sponsored the submission.

The garnering of the government's support essentially repeated the tactics the naval staff had employed in managing the British request of December 1942 to remove the C groups from the North Atlantic. Nelles passed a personal message to Admiral King that "the Canadian Chiefs of Staff are now discussing the appointment of a Canadian Commander-in-Chief for the North-western Atlantic, who will have under his control all Canadian forces which are engaged in anti-submarine warfare."[185] At the same time, the naval and air staffs sent word to the liaison officers in Washington that they should say this much and no more to the members of the Atlantic subcommittee of the combined planners who were asking probing questions about precisely how the Canadian forces achieved coordination. As in the case of the proposal to transfer the C groups, the Canadian staffs were making clear that the ultimate decision concerning unification of command was a Canadian, not an Allied one. The documents also suggest that the rapidly moving events of January had driven home to the Canadian staffs how inadequate were the existing arrangements. In this light the NSHQ directive of 26 November 1942, which called for increased cooperation between the naval and air forces, looked very preliminary. The Canadian staffs did not want the combined planners to gather information about shortcomings that could influence the conference proceedings.[186]

On 20 February, King signalled to Nelles that he expected large results from the Atlantic Convoy Conference, and so it was to prove.[187] At the opening of the first session, at the Navy Department in Washington on Monday 1 March 1943, Admiral King noted that the Canadians had unleashed profound questions: "While this conference was originally called at the suggestion of Vice-Admiral Nelles, for the purpose of exploring two questions—the operational control of the north-west Atlantic escorts, and the promulgation of radio-direction-finder fixes in the western North Atlantic—it has, as was said of Topsy, 'Just growed' until we now have the opportunity of give much needed consideration to anti-submarine warfare throughout the Atlantic."[188] The RCN delegates initially present were Brodeur, Lay, and DeWolf, Captain W.B. Creery, chief of staff to COAC, and Commander J.G. Mackinlay, the convoy and routing specialist who was now serving as liaison officer to the COMINCH staff, but partway through the first day the participation of Captain Brand, Director of the Trade Division at NSHQ, was requested. Still later arrivals were Commander J.M.B.P. DeMarbois and Lieutenant-Commander D.R.H. Macdonald, RCNVR, of the Foreign Intelligence Section. Like Brand, they were summoned by the Canadian delegation because, as warned, King intended to include trade and signals intelligence in the revised command arrangements for the Battle of the Atlantic.[189]

Admiral King's opening address was characteristically blunt. It was also sombre, emphasizing the need to use existing antisubmarine forces more efficiently so that ocean shipping could deliver the resources upon which Allied offensives against the enemy depended.

> The Combined Chiefs of Staff ... have laid down the principle "that the defeat of the U-boat must remain the first charge on the resources of the United Nations." Thus we see that the High Command recognizes that the anti-submarine war is a matter of first

---

185. Reproduced in Tucker, *Naval Service of Canada* II, 409

186. CNS to NMCS, 1441/4 Feb. 1943, Cdr J.G. Mackinlay to NMCS, 8 Feb. 1943, NAC, RG 24, 11968, 222-3-2. See also, DOD to VCNS and CNS, 5 Mar. 1943, NAC, RG 24, 8080, NSS 1271-24 pt 1, and correspondence from Jan. 1943 on this file

187. Tucker, *Naval Service of Canada* II, 409. See also, "Correspondence between Nelles and King," DHH, "National Defence Policy 1939-1945 (Navy)

188. Atlantic Convoy Conference Minutes, DHH, 181.009 (D268), (henceforth ACCM), 2

189. Brand Journal, DHH, 81/145, v 15, 67; Allan, "Canadian Naval Signals Intelligence," 144

importance; but we must also see that the defeat of the U-boat is not of itself the goal we seek however much it is an essential step in reaching the goal ... We have got to devote our somewhat limited overall resources only in part to fighting submarines. That makes it necessary that we use what we have to the very best advantage. The aim we seek is unification of effort.[190]

King's views on unity of command were distinct, most notably in the great importance he attached to "areas of national responsibility which have been established for good and sufficient reason."[191] This was a reference to the division of the oceans into American and British strategic zones in the ABC-1 agreement of 1941 that, in King's view especially, served to safeguard the USN's proper place in the Allied direction of the war. "Unity of command is [not] a panacea for all military difficulties," King explained, "nor is [it] the *sine qua non* of unity of effort ... A point upon which I have very strong personal opinions is the avoidance of mixed forces ... When we are faced with the necessity for stretching our fighting resources ... it is not always feasible to avoid mixing ships and units. But insofar as it is possible we should give each nation an area of responsibility in which the operating forces are all that of one nation."[192] The assumption behind this argument—the sanctity of the western Atlantic as an American strategic zone—had clashed with the British, and more recently, Canadian experience of the need to adjust operational control on an east–west axis in response to enemy thrusts all along the transatlantic route. However, the USN's recent relief of British escorts on southern routes, and King's willingness to define the whole northern route as a Canadian and British national area for purposes of convoy operations, augured well for what the British and Canadians wanted.

The senior British representative at the conference, Admiral Noble, spoke after King, and made no direct comment on the question of unity of effort. Rather, he addressed practical issues on which his old command, Western Approaches, had long been pressing: the need for additional aircraft suitably employed under naval control and the overriding importance of training for surface escorts, especially higher-level training for groups. He particularly emphasized the proven necessity for stability in the membership of groups: "Just taking a team picked at random and sending them out has sometimes led to disaster." Noble also warmly endorsed the newly formed Allied Anti-Submarine Survey Board, "the beginning of a very great advance towards a common policy in all these matters."[193] Admirals Pound and King had intended the board as an alternative to an Atlantic supreme commander, and Noble had every reason to be pleased with the development of the project. The antisubmarine subcommittee of the combined planners was now well advanced in its detailed investigations of all aspects of the war against the U-boats in order to establish the standards that the survey board would apply, and these investigations were confirming policies and practices developed in Western Approaches, notably including the escort group system.[194]

---

190. ACCM, 2-3

191. Ibid, 2

192. Ibid, 4

193. Ibid, 4

194. "Report of Subcommittee on Measures to Combat the Submarine Menace," esp App "D," "Proposed Plan for Improving Training of A/S Forces," 14 Feb. 1943, Naval Historical Center, Operational Archives, 10th Fleet A/S Measures Division, box 40. See Smith, "Battle of the Atlantic," 119: "The Convoy Conference ... freely used the collected papers and preliminary reports of the Combined sub-committee ... In fact it had very largely stolen the thunder of this committee."

Brodeur followed King and Noble with a long, passionate statement that reflected his suspicions of "the two big boys," both the Royal and US navies.[195] Regrettably, he had not been provided with an up-to-date agenda for the meeting and complained mistakenly that the question of operational control in the North and Northwest Atlantic, "the main reason why Canadian representatives are here today," was not up for discussion. The oversight, unfortunate as it was—Brand recalled that there was talk in the USN of demanding Brodeur's recall until Admiral Henry Moore, the Admiralty representative, smoothed things over[196]—did result in putting the Canadian position on record in strong terms. Canada was proposing:

1. A NW Area to be established and defined as the area north of 40 N. In this area control of convoys and A/S warfare be exercised solely by British and Canadian authorities.

2. The present COAC to become C-in-C NW Atlantic and to have general direction of all surface and Air Forces deployed in A/S warfare in NW Atlantic.

3. Control of convoys, U-boat information, diversion of convoys to be exercised in NW A. by NSHQ and control exercised by NSHQ and C-in-C NW A to be similar to that by Admiralty and C-in-C WA.[197]

The arguments then presented were a reprise of Lay's appreciations submitted in 1942, and, perhaps somewhat more forcefully than DeWolf had pointed out during the December conference over the oil crisis, Brodeur reminded the meeting that Canada was a sovereign nation, in which approval by the government of the day was always necessary for the deployment of Canadian armed forces.[198]

The plenary session of the conference continued with statements by Admiral R.S. Edwards, USN, who corrected Brodeur's misapprehension about the agenda, by Air Vice-Marshal Anderson, who in a brief and clear statement urged that VLR aircraft be allocated to the RCAF in Newfoundland, and by General C.P. Gross of the US Army explaining the logistical needs of both building up forces in Britain and continuing offensive operations in the Mediterranean. Admiral Moore concluded with an assessment of the global operational problems that had to be taken into consideration. Like Noble, Moore emphasiszd the vital role of air forces and the need for combined air–navy headquarters. "We feel it is not enough being in different rooms or buildings, they should be side by side, working the common cause."[199]

During the next eleven days the conference, which broke into specialized subcommittees and periodically reconvened to consider their reports, arrived at principles that would govern the defence of shipping in the North Atlantic for the remainder of the war. The key subcommittee on command relations, on which Brodeur represented the RCN, reported on 6 March and received the conference's approval on the 8th. The report recommended detailed measures for implementation of east–west transoceanic control of convoys by Britain and Canada in the north and the United

195. Brodeur to Murray, 5 Feb. 1943, NAC, RG 24, 11928, NSS 8740-102/1, pt 1

196. Brand journal, XV, 67, DHH, 81/145

197. Ibid, 6

198. Ibid

199. Ibid, 9; Douglas *Creation of a National Air Force*, 549-50. See also, Richard M. Leighton, "Merchant Shipping and the British Import Crisis," in Kent Roberts Greenfield (ed), *Command Decisions* (New York 1959), 199-224.

States to the south as the Admiralty, then NSHQ, and finally COMINCH had urged, each for differing national reasons. This effectively buried the scheme for a supreme command in the Atlantic recommended by the subcommittee of the combined planners, who in the following weeks revised the studies for the Allied Anti-Submarine Survey Board to prescribe unified national commands as the standard for antisubmarine warfare.[200]

In the words of Lay, who together with his friend DeWolf, had rightly read the direction of Admiralty thinking in the autumn of 1942 in order to define a larger role for Canada, the "RCN got practically everything which they asked for ... It was extremely satisfactory." CTF 24 would withdraw from trade convoy operations (save for the SG series that supplied US bases in Greenland and the Arctic), and the CHOP line would move west to 47°West, the changeover point between the western local and mid-ocean escort forces, as the Admiralty had long urged. The Admiralty, through Western Approaches, would now control trade convoy operations through the whole passage of the mid-ocean escort between the United Kingdom and the seaward approaches of Newfoundland, and NSHQ, through the Halifax command, would control operations to the west, while the western local groups were in company. Because of the increased status and responsibility of the Halifax command as an Allied theatre headquarters, its designation would change from Commanding Officer Atlantic Coast to Commander-in-Chief, Canadian North-west Atlantic (C-in-C CNA). In deference to the fact that the northwest Atlantic was a US strategic zone, in which the USN continued to control all operations other than those for the protection of trade convoys, the geographical boundaries of the Canadian North-west Atlantic area were the same as those for the former Canadian Coastal Zone. However, Canadian control extended over a much wider area— south to New York, with the exception of US coastal waters under Commander Eastern Sea Frontier, in the case of the transatlantic convoys. Under the direction of the C-in-C CNA, moreover, Eastern Air Command would control all antisubmarine aircraft flying from bases in Canada and Newfoundland to the limits of aircraft range; with the promised allocation of VLR types, this would extend far out into the central ocean, 40°West or further east still.[201] The USN also largely withdrew from the promulgation of signals intelligence to convoy escort forces in the northern part of the western ocean, and NSHQ received the authority it had sought to carry out this role.

The success of the RCN in defending its bid to win recognition of NSHQ as an operational headquarters was in no small measure due to the credibility of its resources for naval control of shipping and for signals intelligence. The delegation was wise to have called in Brand, who had helped mentor the Navy Department's convoy and routing organization, and who had supervised routing of shipping in the western Atlantic by NSHQ until COMINCH was able to take over the job in July 1942. The need to convince British and American authorities of Canadian capabilities in signals intelligence, and particularly the capacity to develop the Foreign Intelligence Section into a full-fledged Operational Intelligence Centre, had brought the despatch from Ottawa on 2 March of Commander de Marbois and Lieutenant-Commander Macdonald. They joined in the work of the communications and operational intelligence subcommittee, which reported its recommendations to the conference on 5 March. These largely concerned the communications necessary to make the

200. Tucker, *Naval Service of Canada* II, 414; Smith, "The Battle of the Atlantic," 119

201. Lay to Bidwell, 19 Mar. 1943, NAC, MG 30 E420, v 1; ACC Mar 43, App "A" to ACC 1, "Report of Sub-Committee on Command Relations, Control of the UK–North west North Atlantic Convoy System." See also, Tucker, *Naval Service of Canada* II, 414-16, and "History of North Atlantic Convoy and Escort Organization and Canadian Participation Therein," 19-20.

new Canadian centre effective, and to increase the speed and capacity of communications between London, Washington, and Ottawa.[202] On 6 March, in a closed meeting, de Marbois and senior representatives of the operational intelligence centres at the Admiralty and COMINCH, delineated the areas of responsibility among the three centres.[203] Canada was to promulgate U-boat warnings and estimates as far east as 30° West and south to 35° North.[204]

At the heart of the conference was the need to increase the shipping capacity of the North Atlantic convoys in the face of a continuing shortage of escorts, and as always had been the case since 1940, Canada's fleet was a critical part of the solution. The British proposed to increase the average size of the transatlantic convoys to sixty merchant ships from the forty to fifty that frequently sailed, and further tighten the sailing schedules. At the time of the conference, the HX-ON series was beginning to sail on an eight-rather than a ten-day schedule, and the Admiralty wanted to achieve sailings every five days, while closing the SC–ONS cycle from ten to eight days. This would require fourteen mid-ocean escort groups, each with a strength of nine warships, with the objective of having at least six operational at all times, and eleven western local groups, each of five escorts to maintain a running strength of four. To meet these commitments, the Canadian delegates asked for the early return of the Torch corvettes, for the reassignment to the WLEF of the old British destroyers then assigned to the Western Support Force, and that eight large Western Isles class antisubmarine trawlers that had been built in Canada on British account be left for coastal defence and local escort duties with the RCN to free larger escorts for ocean-going service. As has been seen, the Torch corvettes would shortly return with the C groups; the British reversed their earlier refusal to leave the trawlers in Canadian waters and readily agreed that the old destroyers should remain. The USN had previously agreed to the RCN's request that the six corvettes serving under CESF should come back to Canadian service, and these would shortly return. Consolidation of the fleet, which had seemed a distant hope in the autumn and winter of 1942, was now being achieved in a matter of weeks.

The Americans, for their part, agreed to take up a large share of responsibility for supplying the Mediterranean theatre. They would continue to run the Caribbean–West Africa tanker convoys (OT), and close the cycle of the UGS convoys from twenty-five to fifteen days. The direct tanker service from the Caribbean to the United Kingdom that Churchill had urged Roosevelt to undertake in December had just begun in early March, with the sailing of tankers from Britain as UC 1 under a combined British–US escort; henceforth, the USN would run this service. Britain accepted the responsibility for escorting supply ships to Iceland, which had been shepherded to and from the main northern convoys by an Iceland-based US destroyer division now needed in southern waters, and also to replace the US Coast Guard cutters in the US–Canadian A 3 mid-ocean group.[205] The Admiralty arranged with NSHQ that this would become a fifth RCN mid-ocean group, C 5, with the transfer of the first two additional River type destroyers that the Canadians had demanded in

---

202. The Signals Division at NSHQ, in cooperation with the other services' communications staffs and civilian carriers, had already identified these requirements. Work had started in the Atlantic area.

203. DDSD(Y) to DSD and VCNS, "Report on Sub Committee Mtgs re Communications and Promulgation of Operational Intelligence, Washington 6 March," 11 Mar.1943, NAC, RG 24, 3807, NSS 1008-75-44, pt 2. For security reasons these recommendations were not included in the ACC 5 "Communication and Operational Intelligence" section of the final report.

204. DDSD(Y), "Report on Sub Committee Mtgs"

205. ACCM, 17-18, and ACC 2, App "A"

exchange for the overseas deployment of the new RCN Tribal class destroyers. HMS *Decoy* entered the RCN as HMCS *Kootenay* on 12 April, and HMS *Griffin* shortly after its transfer on 20 March, became HMCS *Ottawa II*.[206]

Canada was uniquely placed to offer further help. The vast movements of US military personnel and equipment to the Mediterranean and Britain were straining the capacity of even the great US Atlantic ports—New York, Boston, and Hampton Roads. As a result there were delays in the turnaround of all types of shipping, which could not be accepted given the extreme strain on the Allied pool of merchant ships. The problem had been discussed at the informal Ottawa conference in November 1942, and now the three navies accepted what Lay had suggested at that time, increased use of Canadian ports. The slow transatlantic convoys, starting with SC 125 on 31 March, sailed from Halifax, and ONS 1, the first of the reorganized slow westbound series, arrived there on 4 April.[207]

In contrast to the elation among the Canadians at the results of the conference—the normally acerbic Brodeur expressed "sincere appreciation for the full cooperation and understanding of the Canadian problems"[208]—Admiral King was cautious. As he reported to his former chief, Admiral Stark, in London:

> The Anti-U-Boat Conference has labored—and brought forth some reallocations of forces which are gradually being put into effect—but it is going to be difficult to implement it fully for some time to come "in escort vessels and in aircraft." Perhaps the most important change is turning over of the US–UK convoys wholly to British–Canadian operations which is, to my mind, a move toward simplification. However, the Canadians appear to wish to rush in and take over on the western end, without realizing the scope and magnitude of their undertaking. It may be that we shall have to "demur" and keep them under "tutelage" until we are satisfied that they are competent to handle matters— this because we have a decided stake in the safety of the convoys "in the general sense and in the special sense of our own US shipping."[209]

Although the formation of the Canadian North-west Atlantic theatre was retroactive to the beginning of the Atlantic Convoy Conference on 1 March, Admiral King suggested that Rear-Admiral Murray understudy Vice-Admiral Brainard before assuming the responsibilities of the command. This prompted a heated reaction from Murray. In 1941, as commander of the Newfoundland force, Murray had gracefully accepted American direction and had worked well with his USN colleagues since then. He had accepted the very principal of unity of command among Allied navies that King was now rejecting. In his view—and there was some justification for it—it was the Canadians who had shown the USN how to conduct defence of shipping operations in the hostile and unfamiliar environment of the northwest Atlantic. Murray considered he had nothing to learn from Brainard. He suggested to Nelles that "King had been very blunt in his statement that they

---

206. Lay to Bidwell, 19 Mar. 1943, NAC, MG 30 E420, v 1

207. DOD, "Ottawa Conference," 20 Nov. 1942, NAC, RG 24, 11968, S221.1. Capt Brand, in Nov. 1942, had tempered Lay's enthusiasm by noting the serious shipping delays caused by the coastal convoy system that had brought the original decision to shift the transatlantic convoys to New York, and quite properly counselled a "wait and see" approach. ACCM, 1-2 and ACC 2, App "A"; Hague, *Allied Convoy System*, 135, 163

208. ACCM, 27

209. King to Stark, 18 Mar. 1943, "Extracts from Private Papers of Admiral Stark"

do not think we are capable of handling the job and it may be necessary to be blunt in return."[210] Nelles, after consulting the First Sea Lord, who thought the Americans were simply trying to be helpful, agreed to leave Brainard in command until 30 April, although Murray assumed the title of commander-in-chief on 1 April.[211] Murray's subsequent signal to Brainard was temperate, but it had a certain edge:

> I accept the torch as from 1200z April 30th and hope to carry it as successfully as it has been carried since Admiral Bristol received it from my hand in September 1941. It has been a pleasure to serve under your direction and in co-operation with your staff whose excellent understanding of our problems has made our task a simple one.[212]

The RCN thus officially took over responsibility for trade convoys in the northwest Atlantic on 30 April 1943. Murray's resentment at the suggestion the east coast command needed continued help from CTF 24 in carrying out daily operations that the RCN had been competently managing for nearly two years was in no sense hubris. As has been seen frequently in this history, Murray was well aware of, and brutally frank about the shortcomings of training, and ship maintenance, and the flaws in organization that so often seemed to put NSHQ and the east coast command at cross-purposes in overcoming these problems. Even Lay, perhaps the most nationalistic of the service's senior officers, reflected on the myriad long-standing and unresolved shortcomings that confronted the RCN as it took up its new responsibilities. When writing to Captain Roger Bidwell and Captain Wallace Creery on the coast to announce the good results of the Washington conference, he admitted he was "extremely worried" about the "refitting situation." He continued to confess that the challenge of turning NSHQ into an operational headquarters was much larger than he had realized a few short months before, and the obstacles to be overcome more daunting.[213]

The Royal Canadian Navy, nevertheless, had achieved control over Allied trade convoys from the waters off New York to the ocean approaches of Newfoundland and Labrador, and partnership with the RN in the protection of shipping across the entire breadth of the Atlantic. In January 1943 the government had declared that the "Canadian Navy can serve no higher purpose .... We have come to look upon [this task] as a national responsibility for Canada and one which geographically and strategically we are well placed to undertake," and now, in matters of real substance, the great Allied powers had recognized Canada's special place in the Atlantic war. There was still well-founded scepticism in British and American circles about the ability of the RCN to carry the full weight of its new command responsibilities, and still much work to do before the fleet acquired the ships and materiel that would put Canadian escort groups on a par with the RN and USN. The fact remained that the RCN, already indispensable to Allied strategy, had acquired sufficient competence to control operations in the northwest Atlantic. By firm insistence on the capability to exercise command and control over escort forces, the RCN (not without a measure of opportunism) had come of age in a real and practical, as well as an institutional sense.

---

210. C-in-C CNA to CNS, undated, probably part of a teletype conversation with CNS, with both dictating to the operator, DHH, Murray Papers

211. Tucker, *Naval Service of Canada* II, 147

212. C-in-C CNA to CTF 24, 18 Apr. 1943, cited in Lund, "The RCN's Quest for Autonomy"

213. DOD to COS, FONF, cc to COS, COAC, 19 Mar. 1943, NAC, MG 30 E420, v 1. See also, DOD to VCNS and CNS, "Organization of A/S Warfare Group at NSHQ," 22 Mar. 1943, DHH 81/520/1000-973 "TAS 1940-50," pt 4.

Appendices

Royal Canadian Navy Personnel Casualties - 1939-1945

The word "casualty" is frequently misunderstood in tables of naval wartime statistics. Often enough it is assumed to mean those killed by enemy action in battle, but war takes its toll in many ways beyond the most obvious one. Besides the usual perils of the sea, deaths occurred in the normal course of military duty, and still others had entirely natural causes: disease and accident are not affected by declarations of war and peace. During the Second World War fatalities were categorised as "killed in action," "missing, presumed dead," "died from wounds," or "killed while on active service." Not all casualties were fatal, however, and those who were wounded (sometimes permanently) and those taken prisoner by the enemy are also included in the statistical record.[1] This appendix is concerned with members of the RCN, RCNR and RCNVR who were killed, wounded, taken prisoner or died from accidents and natural causes in the RCN and RN during the period 3 September 1939 to 30 September 1945. It is not only meant as a commemoration of sacrifice and a tribute to service, but also to demonstrate the experience of Canadian sailors who fought in a wide variety of service on oceans far from Canada's shores. Although only a few individuals are named herein, their names and the descriptions of the circumstances of their deaths serve as representative of all those who paid the ultimate sacrifice.

Naval casualties were lower than those of the Canadian Army and Royal Canadian Air Force in both absolute and proportional terms. The army suffered just over 69,000 total casualties, 20,843 of them fatal, while the RCAF experienced 14,838 fatalities out of a total of just over 20,000 casualties. In the RCN, total casualties number 2,407, of which 1,990 were fatal. Proportionally, the death rate in the RCAF was just under 25 per thousand of those who served per year, just under 12 per thousand per year of those who served in the Army, and almost 8 per thousand per year of those who served in the navy. However, if deaths as a proportion of total casualties are calculated, the rankings change: 30 per cent of all army casualties were fatal, 75 per cent of all air force casualties, and a staggering 82 per cent of all naval casualties.

Both the comparatively low number of naval casualties and the high proportion of deaths to total casualties experienced by the RCN reflect the nature of naval warfare and the type of operations in which the navy was engaged during the war. Beyond enemy action, "perils of the sea" such as storms and collisions also accounted for significant casualties. In 1940, for example, 13 officers and 275 men were listed as fatal casualties, of whom some 217 officers and men were lost when three Canadian ships sank—two as a result of collisions at sea when there was no enemy presence and the third foundering in a violent storm. In addition, two Canadians serving in a British corvette died when their ship collided with a merchantman and sank while another man was washed overboard from his ship at sea and never found. During the entire year only one Canadian ship suffered casualties as a result of enemy action; one officer and one seaman died as a result of direct action with the enemy while they were serving with the RN in European waters; and one Canadian officer was killed when a German mine sank the British ship in which he was serving.

Table One RCN Fatalities by year of the war 1939–1945

CATEGORY	1939 OFFICERS -RATINGS	1940 OFFICERS -RATINGS	1941 OFFICERS -RATINGS	1942 OFFICERS -RATINGS	1943 OFFICERS -RATINGS	1944 OFFICERS -RATINGS	1945 OFFICERS -RATINGS	TOTAL OFFICERS -RATINGS	COMBINED TOTAL OFFICERS -RATINGS
1. KILLED IN ACTION		0–66	6–38	11–165	6–39	1–48	2–25	26–381	407
2. DIED FROM WOUNDS		0–2	0–1	0–6	0–5			0–15	15
3. MISSING PRESUMED DEAD		9–174	5–24	5–45	10–139	37–386	9–91	75–859	934
TOTAL FATALITIES (1,2,3)		9–242	11–63	16–216	16–183	38–435	11–116	101–1,255	1,356
4. DUE TO ENEMY ACTION OTHER THAN (1)		3–12	11–22	21–43	7–4	8–31	10–6	60–118	178
5. ACCIDENTS		1–12	0–22	5–59	2–43	7–64	16–67	31–267	298
6. NATURAL CAUSES	0–1	0–9	1–21	5–17	5–23	8–37	5–26	24–134	158
TOTAL FATALITIES (4,5,6)	0–1	4–33	12–65	31–119	14–70	23–132	31–99	115–519	634
COMBINED TOTALS	0–1	13–275	23–128	47–335	30–253	61–567	42–215	216–1,774	1,990

The Fatalities

It is now accepted that 1,990 officers, men and members of the RCN and WRCNS were "fatal casualties" during the Second World War. Naval historian E.C. Russell put forward that number in a hand-written memorandum dated 8 June 1954, clearing up previously conflicting statistics that had appeared even in official documents and were widely reproduced in the press. The explanation that seems to have been accepted in generating this final number was that some deaths that had occurred after the shooting ceased in August 1945 could in fact be attributed to war service and thus should be included in the overall amount.[2] The total can be further subdivided as follows:

a) 408 killed in action in HMC ships at sea comprising twenty-six officers, 381 men, one Nursing Sister, and one man who remained unidentified.

b) fifteen men died as a result of wounds.

c) seventy-five officers and 859 men classed as missing and presumed dead.

d) sixty officers and 118 men killed by enemy causes other than in HMC ships (such as while on loan to the RN or in merchant ships as DEMS Gunners).

e) thirty-one officers, 263 men, and four members of the WRCNS, for a total of 298, were killed in accidents.

f) 158 others—twenty-four officers, 133 men, and one member of the WRCNS—died from natural causes.

When these statistics are broken down by type of enlistment—RCN, RCNR and RCNVR—as shown in Table 2 below, it is not surprising that the volunteer reserve bore the brunt of the casualties since they quickly became the navy's largest component during the war.

Table Two. Naval Fatalities by Service Component 1939–1945

COMPONENT	OFFICERS INCLUDING NURSING SISTER	RATINGS INCLUDING WRCNS	TOTALS
RCN	25	314	339
RCNR	35	180	216
RCNVR	155	1,280	1,435
TOTALS	216	1,774	1,990

The terms "missing, believed killed" and "missing, presumed dead" were used when there was no doubting the time and place of a death but it was not witnessed directly and no body was recovered—when, for example a ship was lost but the total number of survivors and bodies recovered did not match the known number of crew aboard. Those not found would initially be classed as missing and then, after an appropriate interval, be presumed dead. Of course, bodies were often recovered at sea long after the incident causing death, but that simplified the issue and merely confirmed the death. Compared to the army, and for obvious reasons, few naval personnel escaped or evaded capture, and few were taken prisoner. Those who died at sea and whose bodies were never recovered are named in perpetual remembrance on the panels of the Sailors' Memorial at Point Pleasant Park in Halifax, NS.

Wounded

A total of 319 —thirty-three officers and 286 men—were wounded and survived their wounds.

Prisoners of War

All told, fourteen officers and eighty-one men became prisoners of war—all but two in the hands of the German Forces and the bulk of them survivors from the sinking of HMCS *Athabaskan* in the English Channel in 1944. Others were taken prisoner following operations such as the raids on St Nazaire and Dieppe, while three, a Sub-Lieutenant and two Midshipmen, were interned in Algeria after they were rescued from the sinking of HMS *Manchester* in the Mediterranean in August 1942. Two officers, survivors of the loss of the cruiser HMS *Exeter* in the Java Sea on 1 March 1942, were held in Japanese prison camps.

Losses in HMC Ships

The first officially recorded casualty in naval service during the war was twenty-nine-year-old Acting Leading Seaman James Westcott from Victoria, BC, who was serving in *Fraser*. Westcott was regular navy, having enlisted in May 1928 and signed on again for seven years in 1935. He collapsed in a forward mess deck while the ship was alongside in Halifax, NS on the morning of Monday, 6 November 1939. A subsequent Board of Enquiry established cardiac arrest as the cause of death and thus "natural causes."

Fraser was the first ship loss for the RCN and recorded the first large casualty list. As recounted in Chapter 2, on the night of 25 June 1940 she was cut in two by the cruiser HMS *Calcutta*. Forty-five members of her ship's company, including twelve Chief and Petty Officers, were killed. Two others, a Stoker Petty Officer and an Able Seaman, later succumbed to their injuries. During rescue operations, a young Able Seaman from *Restigouche* drowned after being thrown from a survivor-filled whaler by the unexpected movement of the destroyer's stern, which tipped the boat over as it tried to secure alongside. Of those from *Fraser* who died, forty-one were permanent force RCN and mostly fully trained in their rank and trade. The others were RCNVR, "Hostilities Only" ratings.

Most of *Fraser*'s survivors went to HMCS *Margaree* but, tragically, the sea was not finished with them. In an eerie replay of the earlier incident, *Margaree* collided with a merchant ship in the convoy she was escorting in the early morning hours of 22 October 1940. The destroyer was cut into two just aft of the bridge and the forward section, where the bulk of the off-watch crew were located, sank quickly, taking nearly everyone there with it. Four officers and 136 men were lost, as were three RN ratings serving in the ship. Eighty-six of them had survived the loss of *Fraser* only to succumb in *Margaree*. All but 20 of the men were regular force RCN.

In an ironic twist of fate, two Ordinary Seamen who had the same last name and the sequential service numbers of 3421 and 3422 (but who were not related) were among those lost. Ackland Jones and Alfred Jones joined the RCN as Boy Seamen on 31 July 1939, together with Donald Mitchell who was given the service number 3424. The Jones boys were from the Vancouver region and Mitchell was from Edmonton. On 6 March 1940 the trio joined their first ship, *Fraser*, in Halifax. Mitchell, who had been promoted Ordinary Seaman at the end of May 1940, died when *Fraser* was lost. The other two were made Ordinary Seamen in August 1940. Alfred Jones performed some heroic work during the rescue of *Fraser's* survivors but did not earn official recognition in the form of a decoration or citation.

Three days before the loss of *Margaree* the RCN lost another ship, but this one went down in Canadian waters. HMCS *Bras D'Or* was a small trawler requisitioned from duties with the Canadian Government to serve as an auxiliary minesweeper. She was accompanying a merchantman from Baie Comeau to Sydney, NS in foul and cold weather on the night of 18/19 October. It is believed that *Bras D'Or* foundered in the Gulf of St Lawrence about 0350 on 19 October when the watch on the merchant ship saw her navigation lights disappear. Five officers and twenty-five ratings went with her—all but three of whom were RCNR or RCNVR.

The final blow of 1940 came on 1 December when HMCS *Saguenay* was damaged by a torpedo from an Italian submarine. Twenty-one members of her ship's company were killed, eight RCN and thirteen reserves—all of them in the forward part of the ship where the torpedo struck and where the sailors' mess decks were located.

The first full year of the war was hard on the RCN—nine officers and 242 sailors were lost at sea, effectively the ship's company of a destroyer. Only in 1944 would this number of casualties in ships be exceeded and by then there was much more interaction with the enemy.

All told the RCN lost 101 officers and 1,255 sailors at sea who were either killed, died from their injuries and wounds or were posted as missing and presumed dead (i.e. their bodies were never recovered). Included in this total is the RCN nursing sister Agnes Wilkie, killed when the ferry SS *Caribou* was torpedoed in the Cabot Strait during the night of 13/14 October 1942. In many cases they died because they were in the vicinity of a torpedo hit: engine room crews on watch or hands off watch asleep in forward mess decks were particularly vulnerable here. Some ships that sank quickly had relatively low loss of life simply because the attack occurred at a change of watch and most hands were up and moving about the ship. Of all, however, engine room crews in corvettes and minesweepers faced the greatest risk. These small ships sank rapidly after taking a hit in the engineering spaces, and little time was available for those below decks to escape. Some were trapped because jammed doors and hatches blocked escape routes; more died after they survived the initial explosion and sinking. Too often, depth charges could not be set to "safe" before the ship sank and the shock and pressure from exploding charges killed many in the water. The late-war introduction of the RCN pattern life jacket, which was designed to help protect the wearer from fatal injury from such underwater explosions, is considered to have saved some lives. More still died from cold and exposure before they could be rescued.

Losses while serving with the RN and in Merchant Ships

As related in the body of this volume, throughout the Second World War Canada sent officers and men to the RN for training and for service in British ships. This was a long established practice as the RN provided much of the advanced training and seagoing experience for Canadian officers and sailors in the pre-war years. Between 1922 and 1942, the years when no Canadian naval college existed, it was the practice to send young Canadian cadets of the RCN to train at the Britannia Naval College, Dartmouth. Subsequently they served as Midshipmen and Sub-Lieutenants in ships of the British fleet before returning to the RCN. Some were still in that training pipeline when war came. Moreover, at the outset of the war the Admiralty needed technically educated officers on an urgent basis to train and serve at sea in British ships as radar officers. In May 1940, nineteen new RCNVR officers arrived in Britain for radar training and by early July all but five were serving in major warships of the RN. By the end of the war, more than 120 RCNVR officers served as radar officers in RN ships.

Many other Canadians were also sent to the RN over the course of the war. A group of Acting Sub-Lieutenants RCNVR, who were among the skilled yachtsmen loaned to the RN (see Chapter 1), had arrived at Plymouth in mid June 1940 prior to undertaking basic training at HMS *King Alfred*. By early July all had been assigned to ships. Two joined HMS *Godetia*, a Flower class corvette based in Plymouth, on 3 July. Sub-Lieutenant Peter Hincks, aged twenty-one, from Victoria BC, had been a member of the Royal Victoria Yacht Club and was experienced in small craft, both sail and power. Sub-Lieutenant Ker was the son of the Vice President and Managing Director of the Hamilton *Spectator*, and both his grandfather and great grandfather were members of the Southam family of newspaper owners.

Convoy OA 207 departed Methil Roads on 31 August 1940 and proceeded northward through the Irish Sea into the Atlantic. HMS *Godetia* escorted this convoy until 6 September when she then turned about and proceeded back toward the Irish Sea for another convoy job. Later that night, *Godetia* collided with the merchant ship SS *Marsa* in foggy weather, three miles off Altacarry Head lighthouse on the north eastern tip of Rathlin Island, Northern Ireland. The corvette went down quickly and both Canadians died. They became the first Canadian officers to die overseas. Ker's body was later recovered and buried in a cemetery in Ayrshire, Scotland but Hincks was never found and he is therefore commemorated on the memorial in Halifax.

Sub-Lieutenant Auston Proctor RCNVR from Toronto was twenty-one years of age when he volunteered for the navy. He was part of the group that included Ker and Hincks, but was sent on anti-submarine training prior to joining his first ship. On 20 July 1940 Proctor was appointed to HMS *Recoil*, an anti-submarine trawler. During the night of 27/28 September while on patrol off Portland Bill in the English Channel, she apparently struck or activated a German mine and sank with all hands. Neither the ship nor any bodies were found. Thus, Sub-Lieutenant Proctor became the first Canadian officer to die as a result of enemy action while serving with the RN. His name is also inscribed on the memorial in Halifax.

The initial group of officers sent for radar training completed their course on 6 July 1940 and 14 went to major British warships. Sub-Lieutenant George "Pat" Strathy RCNVR, from Toronto and twenty-two years of age, was appointed to HMS *Ajax*, one of the cruisers that forced the scuttling of the *Graf Spee* after the Battle of the River Plate in December 1939, and for which the town of Ajax, Ontario is named. She was completing a refit to repair her battle damage when Strathy joined as her first radar officer. On the night of 11/12 October, while serving with the Mediterranean Fleet, *Ajax* sank three Italian destroyers in a confused action, but took hits that caused damage to the bridge and put her radar out of action. Two officers and twenty sailors were killed, among them Strathy. Five and a half months later another Canadian radar officer, Sub-Lieutenant D. H. Robb, RCNVR from Toronto, was killed when the cruiser HMS *Bonaventure* was sunk south of Crete on 31 March 1941. Four other Canadians also died in the ship; Paymaster Sub Lieutenant Donald Eden, RCN aged twenty-three, from New Westminster, BC, Ordinary Telegraphist Charles McGuire, twenty-one, from London, ON, Ordinary Signalman Conn Templeton, twenty-one, from North Vancouver, and Ordinary Seaman Theodore Rising from Saint John, NB. Another rating, Ordinary Seaman Sidney Watson, twenty-one, from Port Credit, ON, was badly wounded in the action and died in hospital in Alexandria on 2 April 1941.

Other Canadian naval ratings also trained and became casualties in RN service. Able Seaman Rodney Trevor Woodward, RCN, aged twenty from Moose Jaw, Saskatchewan, had been taking submarine detector courses in England since November 1939, and had then extended his stay by undergoing motor boat coxswain courses with two other Canadian volunteers. On 19 July 1940 two German Me-110 aircraft attacked a British anti-submarine motor boat in the North Sea. In the subsequent exchange of gunfire Woodward was killed, and thus became the first RCN battle casualty and the first from his hometown killed in the war.

Many ratings, and some officers, went to sea as gunners in merchant ships known as DEMS—Defensively Equipped Merchant Ships. Able Seaman Nelson Conrad, RCNR, from Lower East Chezzetcook, NS, joined the Norwegian tanker *Davanger* in HX 77 leaving Halifax on 30 September 1940 bound for Liverpool. In mid-Atlantic on 11 October, the tanker was torpedoed with the loss of seventeen men including Able Seaman Conrad. He was the first Canadian DEMS gunner to be killed in action.

Canadians also served with distinction in the RN submarine service and two lost their lives. Lieutenant Hugh Russel RCNVR of Montreal undertook submarine training in England in June 1942 and joined HMS *Traveller* in the eastern Mediterranean that September. The submarine was on patrol off the Italian port of Taranto when it is believed she struck a mine and sank with all hands—six officers and fifty-nine sailors including Russel. The second officer was Lieutenant Charles Bonnell, DSC, RCNVR from Toronto who had also arrived in England in mid-1940 and at age thirty was considered an "elder." Bonnell eventually went to MTBs and won the DSC for sinking an enemy supply ship in the North Sea. As if this was not hazardous enough, he then volunteered for "Chariot" service—human torpedoes. In late December 1941, he embarked with eight other "charioteers" in the British submarine *P311* for an attack on enemy shipping in a port in northern Sardinia. The submarine never returned and it has been established that she likely hit a mine in the Strait of Bonifacio and sank with all aboard sometime on 2 January 1943.

One other select group of Canadians trained and served with the RN. One hundred and fifty volunteers from naval reserve divisions across Canada were despatched to HMS *Raleigh* near Plymouth as Ordinary Seamen RCNVR, arriving in November 1940. They are now known as the Canadian Raleighites and those who passed their training were subsequently commissioned. Their most famous member was Lieutenant R. H. "Hammy" Gray, VC, DSC, RCNVR, a naval aviator killed in action against Japanese naval forces on 9 August 1945—just five days before the end of the war. Seventeen other Raleighites were killed on active service including the four sailors mentioned above from HMS *Bonaventure* and Lieutenant Bain the DEMS gunnery officer. The first Raleighite to die on duty was Ordinary Seaman Robert Sinclair, twenty-six, from Red Cliff, Alberta. He was a DEMS gunner and was posted as missing, believed killed from his ship the SS *Medoc* on 26 November 1940.

Losses in the Far East and Pacific Theatres

There were Canadian officers in the British ships in Singapore when the Japanese invaded South East Asia in 1941. Two survived the loss of the battleship HMS *Prince of Wales* on 10 December 1941 but Lieutenant Ralph Ripley RCNVR, twenty-six, from Hamilton, Ontario subsequently failed to return from a mission in HMS *Fanling*, a yacht requisitioned for war service, early in 1942, and was posted missing presumed killed on 16 February 1942. Two Canadians, a radar officer and a Midshipman, served in HMS *Exeter*, a British cruiser sunk in the Java Sea on 1 March 1942. Both were posted as missing, believed killed, but in fact survived and became prisoners of war until their release after the end of hostilities.

As the fighting in Europe wound down, the British contribution to the fight against Japan increased with deployment of the British Pacific Fleet (BPF) in early 1945. Eventually, there were over 200 Canadian pilots and observers serving in the aircraft carriers of the BPF. The first fatality among this group of aircrew was Lieutenant (P) Arthur "Bud" Sutton RCNVR from Saskatoon. He was part of a strike group from HMS *Illustrious* that attacked targets at Palembang on the island of Sumatra on 24 January 1945. His aircraft was last seen in flames from flak hits as it crashed into a hangar full of enemy aircraft. Two more pilots would be killed in action in April 1945 in the bitter fighting for Okinawa. One, Lieutenant (P) Charles Thurston, RCNVR, from Toronto was accidentally shot down and killed by so-called "friendly fire." On 18 July another Canadian pilot, Lieutenant (P) William Asbridge, RCNVR, from Edmonton, was killed in action when he was shot down attacking a target east of Tokyo. Then, on 30 July 1945 Lieutenant (P) James Ross, RCNVR from Truro, Nova Scotia died in a freak accident when a wing of his Corsair aircraft folded during take-off from HMS *Formidable*.

As noted earlier, Lieutenant Gray died in action on 9 August 1945 and his valour and sacrifice were recognized with the award of the Victoria Cross. He was the last to die from enemy action but he was not the last naval casualty. Lieutenant (P) Gerald "Andy" Anderson, RCNVR from Trenton, Ontario was in the second wave of aircraft to attack Onagawa Bay where Gray had died earlier that same day. With his aircraft leaking fuel from flak hits Anderson opted to attempt a landing on the carrier rather than ditch in the sea. His engine quit just as he approached the stern of the ship and the aircraft struck the rear edge of the flight deck, killing Anderson. A little more than twenty-four hours later, the Japanese government would announce acceptance of the Allies' surrender terms.

Closure

Many names had been added to the honour rolls by the time hostilities ceased in 1945. For surviving next of kin of those listed as missing, closure would be difficult, as there was no grave to give evidence of the passing of a loved one. Those mentioned by name above are representative of the many. But those who live on pay homage to those who served in the RCN and who made the ultimate sacrifice in its service. Each May, Battle of the Atlantic ceremonies are conducted across the country in tribute to the RCN of the Second World War with the modern navy leading the parade at the national Sailor's Monument on the shore overlooking the Atlantic in Halifax. This appendix is also a tribute to those who passed before.

---

1. Notes on Sources.

   All statistical data related to personnel casualties is drawn from files in the National Archives in the Records Group 24 (DND) file series 4160-3 to 4160-7 and their counterparts in DHH. These were cross referenced with Records Group 38 (Department of Veterans Affairs) Volumes 424 and 425 with further reference to the listings in the Veterans Affairs Virtual Memorial website: (http://www.vac-cc.gc.ca/general/sub.cfm?source'collections/virtualmem). In some cases individual Service Records were verified.

Secondary Sources used were:

Hague, Arnold. *The Allied Convoy System 1939-1945, Its Organization, Defence and Operation* (St Catharines, Ont., Vanwell Publishing, 2000)

Lynch, Mack. *Orion Mighty Warrior* (Toronto, Lugus Publications, 1992)

MacFarlane, John, and Robbie Hughes. *Canada's Naval Aviators* (Victoria, BC, Maritime Museum of British Columbia, 1994)

McKee, F.M. and R. Darlington, eds. *The Canadian Naval Chronicle 1939-1945.* (St Catharines, Ont., Vanwell Publishing, 1996)

O'Neill, E.C., ed.. *The Canadian Raleighites.* (Waterloo Ont., The Canadian Raleighite Publishing Project, 1988)

Soward, Stuart E. *A Formidable Hero, Lt R.H. Gray, VC, DSC, RCNVR* (Toronto, CANAV Books, 1987)

Information on the RCN Special Entries, Book of Remembrance is drawn from *Soundings*, the Newsletter of the Ottawa Branch of the Naval Officer's Association of Canada, (November 1997), 20.

2. This explanation is substantiated by examination of the machine generated list of fatal casualties (as opposed to the 'official casualty lists' released to the Press) which shows some fatalities later in 1945 that are clearly counted as part of the World War II totals. It is further substantiated by the appearance of the names of such individuals on the Veterans Affairs commemorative lists and the Book of Remembrance.

3. There were Canadians serving in the Fleet Air Arm as members of the RN or RNVR but data on these personnel has not been included in any of the statistics, as they were not part of the RCN or its components.

APPENDIX II
Senior Appointments within the Royal Canadian Navy, September 1939 to April 1943

NAVAL SERVICE HEADQUARTERS (NSHQ) OTTAWA

Minister of National Defence for Naval Services

A.L. Macdonald   12 July 1940 – *

Prior to Macdonald's appointment, the Navy was under the direct authority of the Minister of National Defence.

Deputy Minister of National Defence for Naval Services (DM)

W. G. Mills

Chief of the Naval Staff (CNS)

Vice-Admiral P.W. Nelles   1 Jan 1934 –

Deputy Chief of the Naval Staff (DCNS)/Vice Chief of the Naval Staff (VCNS) *

Captain L.W. Murray   30 Aug 1939 – 15 Oct 1940
Commodore H.E. Reid   15 Oct 1940 – 9 Oct 1942
Rear-Admiral G.C. Jones   9 Oct 1942 –

Title changes from DCNS to VCNS Jan 1942

Chief of Naval Personnel (CNP)

Captain C.R.H. Taylor   15 Dec 1938 – 2 Sep 1940
Captain H.T.W. Grant   2 Sep 1940 – 23 Sep 1942
Captain E.R. Mainguy   15 Nov 1942 –

Director Technical Division (DTD)/Chief of Naval Equipment and Supply (CNES)*

Engineer Commander J.F. Bell   15 July 1940 – 18 Feb 1941
Captain G.M. Hibbard   18 Feb 1941 –

* Title changes from DTD to CNES during Jan 1942

Engineer in Chief (Naval Engineering Branch)/
Chief of Naval Engineering and Construction (CNEC)*

Engineer Captain A.D.M. Curry   1 May 1935 – 10 Feb 1941
Engineer Rear-Admiral G.L. Stephens   10 Feb 1941 –

* Title Engineer in Chief was replaced by CNEC on 24 Oct 1942

Naval Secretary/Secretary Naval Board (Sec. N.B.)

Paymaster Captain M.J.R. Cossette   1 May 1934 – 9 Feb 1942
Paymaster Captain R.A. Pennington   9 Feb 1942 –

Director of the Operations Division (DOD)

Commander J.W.R. Roy   20 Dec 1937 – 10 June 1940
Captain R.E.S. Bidwell   10 June 1940 – 1 June 1941
Captain H.N. Lay   30 June 1941 – 24 Apr 1943

Director of Trade Division (DTD)

Captain E.S. Brand	29 July 1939 –

Director of Naval Intelligence (DNI) *

Captain E.S. Brand	29 July 1939 – 1 July 1942
Commander C.H. Little	1 July 1942 –

* Prior to 7 Jan 1942 Intelligence was incorporated with Trade

Director of Plans Division (DPD)

Captain F.L Houghton	8 July 1939 – 25 May 1942
Captain H.G. DeWolf	25 May 1942 –

Director of the Signals Division (DSD) *

Captain G.A. Worth	16 Feb 1942 –

* Prior to the Jan 1942 reorganization Signals was incorporated with Plans (Plans and Signals Division)

HALIFAX

Commanding Officer Atlantic Coast (COAC)

Commodore H.E. Reid	1 Oct 1938 – 28 Sep 1940
Rear-Admiral G.C. Jones	28 Sep 1940 – 18 Sep 1942
Rear-Admiral L.W. Murray	18 Sep 1942 – 1 Apr 43

Chief of Staff to COAC

Lieutenant-Commander H.N. Lay	27 Aug 1939 – 1 Dec 1939
Captain H.T.W. Grant	2 Dec 1939 – 26 Aug 1940
Commander H.G. DeWolf	1 Oct 1941 – 28 Apr 1942
Captain Wallace B. Creery	28 Apr 1942 – 24 Apr 1943

Commander-in-Chief Canadian Northwest Atlantic (C-in-C CNA) *

Rear-Admiral L.W. Murray	1 Apr 1943 –

* C-in-C CNA replaced COAC effective date 1 Apr 1943, but Murray did not relieve CTF 24 until 30 Apr 1943

Chief of Staff to C-in-C CNA

Captain R.E.S. Bidwell	24 Apr 1943 –

Commodore/ Captain Halifax Force (CCHF)

Commodore G.C. Jones	7 June 1940 – 24 Sep 1940
Commodore L.W. Murray	24 Oct 1940 – 12 Feb 1941

Captain (D) Halifax

Captain E.R. Mainguy	27 Aug 1941 – 1 Nov 1941
Captain G.R. Miles	1 Nov 1941 – 7 Dec 1942
Captain J.D. Prentice	7 Dec 1942 –

ESQUIMALT/VANCOUVER

Commanding Officer Pacific Coast (COPC)

Captain V.G. Brodeur	14 Oct 1938 – 4 Sep 1940
Commodore W.J.R. Beech	4 Sep 1940 –

ST. JOHN'S NEWFOUNDLAND

Commodore Commanding Newfoundland Force (CCNF)/Flag Officer Newfoundland (FONF) *

Commodore L.W. Murray	10 June 1941 – 28 Aug 1942
Captain E.R. Mainguy	28 Aug 1942 – 24 Oct 1942
Commodore Howard E. Reid	24 Oct 1942 –

* The appointment of CCNF was replaced by FONF in Sep. 1941

Chief of Staff

Captain R.E.S. Bidwell	3 July 1941 – 22 Mar 1943
Captain F.L. Houghton	22 Mar 1943 –

Captain (D)

Captain E.B.K. Stevens, RN	June 1941 – 8 Nov 1941
Captain E.R. Mainguy	8 Nov 1941 – 23 Sep 1942
Captain H.T.W. Grant	23 Sep 1942 – 10 Mar 1943
Captain J. Rowland, RN	10 Mar 1943 –

OVERSEAS REPRESENTATIVES

LONDON

Commodore/Captain Commanding Canadian Ships (CCCS)

Captain C.R.H. Taylor	Jan 1941 – 12 Feb 1941
Commodore L.W. Murray	12 Feb 1941 – 1 June 1941
Captain C. R. H. Taylor	1 June 1941 – 1 Feb 1942
Captain R.I. Agnew	1 Feb 1942 – 20 Apr 1943

Senior Canadian Naval Officer (London)

Commander F.L. Price	20 Apr 1943 –

WASHINGTON, DC

The Naval Member of the Canadian Joint Staff Washington (NMCJS)*

Rear-Admiral V.G. Brodeur	1 July 1942 -

Canadian Naval Attaché*

Commodore V.G. Brodeur	4 Sep 1940 – 4 Aug 1942
Commander H.G. Nares	4 Aug. 1942 – 1 Feb 1943
Captain E. C. Sherwood	1 Feb 1943 –

* Position remained but was subordinate to NMCJS after its creation in July 1942

APPENDIX III

Canadian Navy Warship Losses, September 1939–April 1943

DATE	HMCS	CAUSE	TASK	AREA	POSITION
1940					
25 JUNE	*FRASER* (DESTROYER)	COLLISION WITH HMS *CALCUTTA*	EVACUATION	BAY OF BISCAY	45°44N 01°31W
19 OCT	*BRAS D'OR* (AUXILIARY)	UNKNOWN	PATROL	GULF OF ST. LAWRENCE	UNKNOWN
22 OCT	*MARGAREE*	COLLISION WITH SS *PORT FAIRY*	ESCORT OL 8	NORTH ATLANTIC	53°24N 22°50W
1941					
26 MAR	*OTTER* (ARMED YACHT)	EXPLOSION AND FIRE	PATROL	OFF HALIFAX	44°23N 63°26W
19 SEP	*LEVIS* (CORVETTE)	TORPEDOED BY *U 74*	ESCORT SC 44	NORTH ATLANTIC	60°07N 38°37W
7 DEC	*WINDFLOWER* (CORVETTE)	COLLISION WITH SS *ZYPENBERG*	ESCORT SC 58	OFF GRAND BANKS	46°19N 49°30W
1942					
10 FEB	*SPIKENARD* (CORVETTE)	TORPEDOED BY *U 136*	ESCORT SC 67	NORTH ATLANTIC	56°10N 21°07W
7 SEP	*RACCOON* (ARMED YACHT)	TORPEDOED BY *U 165*	ESCORT QS 33	ST. LAWRENCE RIVER	49°01N 67°17W
11 SEP	*CHARLOTTETOWN* (CORVETTE)	TORPEDOED BY *U 517*	ESCORT SQ 30	ST. LAWRENCE RIVER	49°12N 66°48W
14 SEP	*OTTAWA* (DESTROYER)	TORPEDOED BY *U 91*	ESCORT ON 127	NORTH ATLANTIC	47°55N 43°27W
1943					
6 FEB	*LOUISBURG* (CORVETTE)	TORPEDOED BY GERMAN AIRCRAFT	ESCORT KMS 8	MEDITERRANEAN SEA	36°15N 00°15E
22 FEB	*WEYBURN* (CORVETTE)	MINED	ESCORT MKS 8	OFF GIBRALTAR	35°46N 06°02W

APPENDIX IV
Axis Submarine Losses to Canadian Forces, September 1939–April 1943

DATE	SUBMARINE	KILLER	TASK	AREA	POSITION
1940					
16 NOV	FAA DI BRUNO	HMCS OTTAWA, HMS HARVESTER	PATROL	NORTH ATLANTIC	51°05N 17°32W
1941					
10 SEP	U 501	HMCS CHAMBLY, MOOSE JAW	ESCORT SC 42	NORTH ATLANTIC	62°50N 37°50W
1942					
24 JUL	U 90	HMCS ST CROIX	ESCORT ON 113	NORTH ATLANTIC	48°12N 40°56W
31 JUL	U 588	HMCS SKEENA, WETASKIWIN	ESCORT ON 115	NORTH ATLANTIC	49°59N 36°36W
31 JUL	U 754	RCAF SQUADRON 113	AIR PATROL	OFF NOVA SCOTIA	43°02N 64°52W
6 AUG	U 210	HMCS ASSINIBOINE	ESCORT SC 94	NORTH ATLANTIC	54°25N 39°37W
28 AUG	U 94	HMCS OAKVILLE, USN SQUADRON 92	SEA/AIR ESCORT TAW 15	CARIBBEAN SEA	17°40N 74°30W
1 SEP	U 756	HMCS MORDEN	ESCORT SC 97	NORTH ATLANTIC	57°41N 31°30W
30 OCT	U 658	RCAF SQUADRON 145	AIR PATROL	OFF NEWFOUNDLAND	50°32N 46°32W
30 OCT	U 520	RCAF SQUADRON 10	AIR ESCORT	OFF NEWFOUNDLAND	47°47N 49°50W
27 DEC	U 356	HMCS ST LAURENT, CHILLIWACK, BATTLEFORD, NAPANEE	ESCORT ONS 154	NORTH ATLANTIC	45°30N 25°40W
1943					
13 JAN	U 224	HMCS VILLE DE QUÉBEC	ESCORT TE 13	MEDITERRANEAN SEA	36°28N 00°49E
19 JAN	TRITONE	HMCS PORT ARTHUR	ESCORT MKS 6	MEDITERRANEAN SEA	37°06N 05°22E
8 FEB	AVORIO	HMCS REGINA	ESCORT KMS 8	MEDITERRANEAN SEA	37°10N 06°42E
4 MAR	U 87	HMCS SHEDIAC, ST CROIX	ESCORT KMS 10	NORTH ATLANTIC	41°36N 13°31W
13 MAR	U 163	HMCS PRESCOTT	ESCORT MKS 9	NORTH ATLANTIC	45°05N 15°00W

German Officer Ranks and RCN/RN Equivalents

Grossadmiral	Admiral of the Fleet
Generaladmiral	No equivalent
Admiral	Admiral
Vizeadmiral	Vice-Admiral
Konteradmiral	Rear-Admiral
Kommodore	Commodore
Kapitän zur See	Captain
Fregattenkapitän	No equivalent
Korvettenkapitän	Commander
Kapitänleutnant	Lieutenant-Commander
Oberleutnant zur See	Lieutenant
Leutnant zur See	Sub-Lieutenant
Oberfähnrich zur See	No equivalent
Fähnrich zur See	Midshipman

Index of Ships

HMC Ships

Agassiz 161, 195, 200, 260-261, 497-498, 501, 556

Alberni 161, 195, 200, 236, 242-243, 248-249, 256, 541, 600, 602-605, 608-609, 611, 619

Algoma 482, 544, 546, 549, 551, 600, 602-603, 606, 611, 618-619

Amherst 515-516, 518-520, 522, 524, 535-536, 544, 546, 549-550, 617, 619

Annapolis 140, 199, 208-209, 228, 270, 488, 520-522

Arrowhead 154, 262, 450-451, 461

Arvida 515-516, 518-520, 522, 524, 535-536, 544, 546, 549-551

Assiniboine 65, 70-71, 142-143, 152-153, 159, 196, 220, 222, 272, 505-507, 509, 511-512, 554

Aurora 29-30

Baddeck 272-273, 275-276, 279, 283

Barrie 304-305

Battleford 505, 568, 573-575, 615, 619

Bayfield 352

Bittersweet 154, 480, 619

Brandon 617, 619

Buctouche 288, 291, 558

Burlington 380, 464, 467

Calgary 488-489, 522, 600, 602-603, 619

Camrose 272, 275, 280, 283, 387, 481, 600, 602-603, 606, 619

Canso 352

Caradoc 91, 134

Caraquet 352

Chambly 154, 161, 190-192, 195, 199-200, 203, 239-240, 245-249, 255-256, 306, 618

Champlain 31, 37

Charlottetown 455, 524

Chedabucto 443

Chicoutimi 488

Chignecto 348-349, 368

Chilliwack 220, 505, 568, 571, 573-574, 576, 620

Clayoquot 447, 455

Cobalt 288

Collingwood 195, 199-200, 202-203, 229, 298, 617, 619

Columbia 140, 152, 166, 198, 250, 270, 272, 275, 277-280, 283, 286, 488, 546

Cornwallis 583

Cougar 342, 352

Dauphin 402, 483, 488, 508, 513-514, 620

Dawson 348, 358-359, 361-362, 367-368

Drumheller 305, 312, 323, 326, 466, 538, 618-619

Drummondville 436, 440

Dundas 352

Edmundston 348, 353-354, 358

Eyebright 154, 262, 619

Fraser 31, 33, 38, 52, 55-57, 62, 65, 68, 71, 91, 96-101, 108, 117, 126, 436

Fredericton 427

Galt 556

Gananoque 464

Georgian 387, 456-457

Givenchy III 366

Granby 434

Grandmère 462-463

Guysborough 352

Halifax 96, 421-422, 427

Hamilton 208, 270, 497-498

Hepatica 154, 163-165, 167, 410-412, 461

Ingonish 352

Kelowna 352

Kenogami 543, 568, 573-574, 576, 615, 619

Kitchener 600, 602-603

Kootenay 629

La Malbaie 619

Lévis 227, 260-261

Lockeport 352, 356-357

Louisbourg 396, 467, 494, 498, 603, 606

Louisburg 600-602, 606

Lunenburg 527, 600-601, 603, 605, 608, 611

Mayflower 154, 260-261, 295, 619

Medicine Hat 435

Melville 405

Minas 387, 558

ML 1229 618

Moosejaw 600, 602-603, 619

Morden 305, 508, 513, 538, 618-619, 646

Napanee 85, 568, 570, 573-576, 615-617, 619, 646

New Westminster 352

Niagara 140, 151-152, 166, 168, 196, 198, 270

Niobe 28, 167, 600

Oakville 265, 421-427, 530, 646

Orillia 190, 193, 195, 199-200, 236, 242-244, 256, 258, 297, 505, 615

Ottawa 31, 52, 56, 65, 68, 105, 108, 110-111, 115-116, 118-122, 162, 168, 195, 197, 199-200, 202-205, 272, 515-516, 518-519, 521-524, 530, 554

Ottawa II 629

Outarde 349, 368

Patriot 29-31

Patrician 29-31

Pictou 113, 226, 278, 281-283, 286, 441, 500, 538

Port Arthur 441, 600, 602, 604-605, 608, 611, 619, 646

Prescott 600-603, 606, 616-617, 646

Prince David 331, 333, 335, 337, 343, 347, 351-353, 359, 362, 365

Prince Henry 84, 311, 331, 333-335, 337, 347, 351, 359, 363

Prince of Wales 194, 220-222

Prince Robert 278, 331-333, 337, 343, 347, 350-353, 359, 362-363, 365

Q 061 436

Q 083 451

Quatsino 349, 357

Quesnel 342, 354

Raccoon 450-451, 524, 645

Rainbow 28, 350

Red Deer 380, 382-383, 467

Regina 600, 602, 606-608, 610, 616, 646

Reindeer 83, 462

Restigouche 31, 52, 56, 65, 68, 91-92, 96-101, 108, 152-153, 195-198, 220, 272, 535-536, 544, 546-547, 549-553, 617, 619, 637

Rosthern 272, 275, 527, 541-542, 620

Royal Roads 147, 149, 363

Sackville 494, 497-499, 501-503, 556

Saguenay 31, 37-38, 52, 57, 62, 65, 68-69, 71, 116, 118, 120-125, 127, 152, 195, 220, 253-254, 272, 294, 372, 377, 494, 496, 504, 528, 556, 638

St Clair 140, 151-152, 164, 166, 196, 270, 386

St Croix 138, 140, 142, 151, 153, 199, 209, 224, 250, 255, 326, 483-484, 486-488, 492, 515-516, 518-522, 525, 535-537, 554, 615-616, 619

St Laurent 31, 38, 52, 55-57, 62, 65, 68, 91, 96-98, 101-104, 109-110, 120-122, 127-128, 175-176, 298-299, 554, 559, 568-570, 572-574, 576, 615, 619

Sans Peur 55, 348, 352-353, 356-357

Shawinigan 447-448

Shediac 272-273, 275, 543, 568-569, 573, 575, 615-616, 619

Sherbrooke 515-516, 518, 522, 524, 535-536

Skeena 31, 52, 62, 65, 69, 71, 96, 98, 101, 110, 116, 118, 120-122, 125, 175-176, 236, 240-243, 245, 247-250, 256-257, 259, 272, 372, 494-496, 504, 513, 528, 556

Snowberry 154, 298, 410-412, 421-422, 424, 427

Sorel 143, 305

Spikenard 154, 645

Sudbury 410-412, 427

Summerside 61, 406, 433, 455, 541, 600, 602, 605, 608, 611, 619

The Pas 410-412, 427

Timmins 352, 356-357, 558

Trail 220, 356, 445, 447-448

Trillium 153-154, 163-167, 527, 541, 620

Truro 450-451, 641

Vancouver 31, 37, 352, 358-359, 361-362

Ville de Québec 441, 541, 600, 602, 604-605, 619, 646

Westmount 460

Wetaskiwin 161, 195, 200, 202, 250, 257, 272-273, 275, 277-278, 280, 282-283, 387, 494-496, 513, 556-557, 559, 646

Weyburn 443, 447-448, 527, 600-601, 603-604, 608, 611, 645

Windflower 153-154, 156, 163-165, 167, 288, 291, 645

Wolf 342, 352, 483, 485, 488, 494, 497, 504

Woodstock 600-603, 606, 611, 619

Fishermen's Reserve Vessels

BC Lady 342

Ehkoli 338, 342

Kuitan 345

Leelos 342, 345

Macdonald 55, 342, 345

Marauder 342

Merry Chase 356

Moolock 342, 356

PLM 27 466

PML 8 342

Queen Bee 342

San Tomas 338, 356

Signal 197, 342

Takla 342

Talapus 342, 350

Van Isle 342

HM Ships

Abelia 278, 280, 283

Acasta 31

Alisma 563-564

Antelope 120, 549, 605

Aubretia 608

Audacity 375

Avenger 600

Avondale 605

Bicester 604

Bide 605
Biter 600
Black Swan 73-75, 608, 611
Boreas 608
Brilliant 556, 605
Brixham 604
Broadwater 278, 280, 282, 284
Broadway 166, 288, 290-291,
    508, 513, 538, 618
Broke 507-508
Bulldog 278, 283
Burnham 298, 387, 407, 410-
    411, 483-484, 488, 508, 513-
    514, 554
Burwell 288, 292, 568, 576, 615
Caldwell 407, 410
Celandine 202, 205, 515, 518,
    520, 522, 524, 535-537, 544,
    546, 549-551, 617
Chesterfield 260-261, 563-565,
    619
Churchill 617-619
Clacton 604
Decoy 536, 629
Dianthus 505-507
Diomede 333
Dornoch 618
Fame 560, 576
Felixstowe 605
Fidelity 568, 572-573, 575
Firedrake 70, 563-565
Fort York 615-616
Gentian 129, 539
Georgetown 194, 283, 590
Gladiolus 200, 202, 205-206,
    250, 272, 277-278, 283
Griffin 226, 281, 286, 629
Harvester 118-119
Hesperus 539
Highlander 122-124, 278, 280,
    282-283, 285, 619
Honeysuckle 260
Ilfracombe 618
Jaunty 607
Jed 619
Jervis Bay 350
Laforey 606

Lagan 618
Landguard 602
Le Tigre 396, 406
Lookout 606
Lord Hotham 618
Lulworth 602-603
Meteor 571, 575
Milne 571, 575
Montgomery 385, 590, 598
Nasturtium 202, 205, 288, 290-
    291, 505, 527, 600-601, 603
Norfolk 35, 405, 413
Parrsboro 615
Petard 562
Philante 614-615
Polyanthus 200, 298, 483, 508,
    538, 618
Primrose 298, 505
Qualicum 615-616
Rhyl 607
Richmond 283
Roxborough 590, 613
St Cathan 396
Salisbury 164, 454, 456-457,
    459
Scottish Heather 571
Sherwood 538, 618, 644
Shippigan 618
Sunflower 563-564
Torbay 465, 544
Vanessa 550-551
Vanoc 608
Velox 608
Veronica 278, 280, 283-284
Vervain 560
Veteran 237, 250, 256, 406
Walker 488
Wanderer 109-110, 406, 558,
    590
Waveney 618
Wedgeport 615
Western Isles 163, 600, 614, 628
Winchelsea 538, 556
Witch 109-110, 497-498, 520-
    522
Witherington 454-455, 458-459,
    472

Wivern 608, 611
Zetland 608

Free French Ships
Aconit 288, 290
Commandant Drogou 618
La Malouine 608
Mimosa 250, 272, 278-279, 283

United States Ships
Algonquin 444, 446
Augusta 220, 269
Badger 540
Bibb 513-514
Campbell 540-541, 620
Casco 362
Charleston 368
Decatur 278
Eagle 348
Gilmer 348
Greer 278-279
Hatfield 368
Ingham 513
Kearny 278, 281
Laramie 446-447
Livermore 278
Mohawk 444
Mojave 444-446
Morris 348
Onandaga 348
Oracle 368
PC 464 406
PC 559 421-422
Plunkett 278, 280
Reid 362
SC 449 421-422
SC 506 421-422
SC 522 421-422, 424
Schenck 513

Norwegian Warships
Eglantine 560
Lincoln 404, 486, 590
Potentilla 560
Rose 560

Polish Warships
Blyskawica 507-508

Dutch Warships

Jan Van Brakel 421-422

Merchant and Troop Ships

Aeas 451
Akabara 604
Alexander McComb 406
Alexandra Höegh 385
Angelina 536
Arctic 349, 443
Arletta 502
Arlyn 446-447
Athelcrown 388
Athelduchess 522
Athenia 337
Awatea 337
Barberrys 559
Barfann 282-283
Baron Cochrane 574
Barrister 603
Barrwhin 542-543
Belgian Soldier 498, 501
Belize 387
Bello 563
Benalbanach 604
Bic Island 433-435, 442, 450, 455, 459-460, 542
British Merit 485
British Promise 558
British Renown 558
British Workman 403
Britomar 411
Broompark 485
Bury 535-536, 556-557
Burza 560
Calgarolite 410
Capira 513
Caribou 462-463, 469, 473, 476, 638
Carolus 461, 468-469
Chatham 444-446, 454
City of Christchurch 618
Clausina 522
Coast Trader 353, 355
Cyclops 380-381, 385
Cynthia Olson 337
Daghild 520

Dalcroy 549
Diala 386
Dimitrios G. Thermiotis 386
Dinaric 436, 440
Donald Stewart 448
Donax 538
Duchess of York 617
Dutch Mass 430
Egba 404
Elias Howe 362
Elisabeth van Belgie 516
Empire Antelope 549
Empire Gemsbuck 291
Empire Heron 278
Empire Leopard 549
Empire Lynx 551
Empire Moonbeam 519
Empire Ocean 502
Empire Oil 516, 524
Empire Progress 402
Empire Rainbow 488
Empire Sailor 558
Empire Shackleton 575
Empire Soldier 524
Empire Stockport 549
Empire Thackeray 519
Empire Union 569, 571
Empire Wagtail 574
Erriken 280
Esso Aruba 424
Everoja 291
F.J. Wolfe 516, 524
Fennel 154
Fjordaas 518
Flynderborg 290
Foam 405
Fort Battle River 616
Fort Binger 404
Fort Camosun 353-355, 358
Fort Paskoyac 615
Fort Qu'Appelle 405
Fort Ville Marie 309
Foundation Franklin 298
Frances Salman 386
Frederika Lensen 443, 472
Friar Rock 385
Frisco 385

Frontenac 541
G.S. Walden 498, 501
Gandia 388
Grange Park 601
Gretavale 290
Greylock 404
Gurney E. Newlin 541-542
Hahira 550
Hatimura 551
Hektoria 519-520
Heranger 519
Hindanger 519
Hobbema 551
Icarion 388
Inneröy 388
Jeypore 551
John W. MacKay 410
John Winthrop 528
King Edward 570-571
King Malcolm 288
Kitty's Brook 404
Kosmos II 541, 543
Kronprinsen 406
Laurits Swenson 519
Leiesten 388
Leto 430, 434-435
Liberty Glo 518
Liverpool Packet 406
Lochkatrine 498
Lord Strathcona 449
Lynton Grange 574
Mariposa 388
Marit II 518
Maro 386
Martima 549
Melmore Head 574
Melrose Abbey 118, 569-570
Montréal City 562
Mount Kitheron 388
Mount Pelion 549
Mount Pindus 451
Mount Taygetus 451
N.B. McLean 154
Nicoya 430, 434-435, 441
North Gaspé 387
Nyholt 386
O.K. Service IV 404

Oakton 451
Ocean Pilgrim 601
Ocean Vagabond 465, 529
Octavian 386
Pacific Exporter 604
Pacific Grove 494, 498, 501
Pacific Pioneer 489
Pan New York 542-543
Parthenon 550
Pasteur 272
Persephone 410
Perth 65, 513, 560
Pirat 496-497
President Francqui 575
Prins Harald 601
Refast 388
Regent Lion 563
Rhakotis 574, 603
Rinos 549
Rotterdam 424
Rym 280
Saganaga 449
San Fabian 424
Satartia 362
Sea Breeze 355
Skottland 404
Soekaboemi 570-571
Solsten 485
Sourabaya 541-542
Spar 505
Steel Navigator 536
Stockport 546, 549-550, 620
Sveve 516
Thirlby 385
Titus 430, 551
Toorak 386
Topdalsfjord 502
Toward 537, 568-570, 572
Tucurinca 538
Tuscaloosa 220
Vancolite 411
Vancouver Island 278, 333
Vassilios Polemis 387
Ville de Rouen 574
Virginia I 353
W.C. Teagle 280

Waterton 462
West Imboden 402
West Neris 299
William Hansen 387
Winnipeg II 538, 618
Zarian 574

U-boats

U 43 111, 461-462, 464-465,
   467, 498, 556-557
U 66 379
U 69 261-262, 460-463, 465-
   467, 469
U 71 202, 205-206, 498, 549
U 73 278
U 74 260-262, 287, 645
U 77 196
U 82 242-245, 247, 249, 388-
   389
U 84 244-245, 249, 402, 544,
   549
U 85 239-241, 243-244, 255-
   257, 390
U 86 386, 390, 485
U 87 386, 406, 615
U 89 417, 489, 551-552
U 90 484, 486-487, 492
U 91 514, 519-521, 645
U 92 518-521
U 94 129, 261, 421-424, 427,
   530, 646
U 96 516, 520
U 101 96, 127, 278, 284
U 103 601
U 106 299, 461-463, 465, 467
U 109 379, 385
U 123 287-288, 290-291, 379-
   380, 382, 389
U 125 379-380, 410
U 130 379, 385
U 132 416-417, 436, 440, 443-
   444, 447, 451, 476, 488-489,
   551
U 135 388, 405
U 136 483, 645
U 162 421
U 163 616-617, 646

U 164 495
U 165 444, 446-447, 451, 453-
   456, 460, 465, 468, 473, 476
U 176 507
U 183 465, 468
U 185 601
U 202 244, 247-249, 290-291
U 203 199-200, 202, 206, 291-
   292, 386-387, 574
U 210 495, 506-507, 509, 512,
   554, 646
U 211 514, 519
U 213 403-404
U 215 406
U 217 498
U 218 518-519
U 221 526, 564
U 224 540, 542, 604, 646
U 225 571, 574-575
U 259 515
U 260 539, 571, 574-575
U 262 475-476
U 263 601
U 268 619
U 301 539
U 333 387-388
U 356 563, 569-570, 572, 646
U 374 288, 290, 299
U 379 484, 507
U 380 516, 519-520
U 381 546, 549
U 402 402, 549-550
U 404 516, 518-520
U 405 621
U 406 574
U 407 513-514, 516, 520-521
U 409 513-514
U 410 615
U 411 513, 520-522
U 413 601
U 432 240, 242, 244, 247-249,
   278, 280-283, 383, 405-406
U 435 574-575
U 436 540-541, 543
U 437 549
U 438 508, 550
U 441 570-571

U 443 538
U 454 506-507
U 455 403, 465, 576
U 456 619
U 458 417, 489, 503
U 502 278-279, 284
U 503 397
U 511 421-422, 424, 495-497
U 513 437, 444, 449-450, 465-466, 470, 529
U 517 444-449, 451, 455-458, 460-461, 465, 468, 473, 476, 645
U 518 465-468, 470, 558, 590
U 519 601
U 520 465, 544, 646
U 521 465, 544, 550, 555
U 522 465, 544, 546, 549-552, 557
U 524 560-561
U 552 261-262, 379, 385-386, 484-485, 497-502
U 553 276-279, 282, 286, 379, 386, 388, 403, 416, 430-431, 434-435, 443, 447, 476, 498, 561
U 556 204-205
U 558 278-283, 556
U 559 562
U 563 541-542
U 564 203-204, 421
U 566 405
U 568 277-279, 281-282
U 569 290
U 575 261, 540

U 576 403
U 582 388-389
U 584 515-516, 518-519
U 588 404, 495-496, 503, 559, 646
U 591 562, 573-575
U 593 410, 505
U 594 515-516
U 595 505-506
U 597 484, 497
U 598 421
U 599 515
U 600 421
U 604 514, 620
U 606 541, 620
U 607 488, 505-506
U 608 516, 518-519
U 609 513-514, 535, 563-564
U 610 536, 563
U 611 561
U 615 572-573, 575
U 618 535
U 619 528
U 621 564-565
U 623 563
U 624 542
U 627 540
U 628 574
U 654 379
U 656 397
U 658 544, 646
U 659 516, 518, 574
U 660 508
U 662 539, 566
U 663 559

U 664 564, 566, 569-570
U 665 575
U 701 387
U 704 488, 497, 501, 506, 535, 546, 552
U 706 539
U 751 278, 283, 415
U 752 402
U 754 387-388, 417, 489, 492, 586, 646
U 756 513, 646

German Ships

Bismarck 190, 194-195, 198, 490
Hermonthis 334-335
Leipzig 334
Monserrate 334
Muenchen 334-335
Orion 333
Weser 278, 332-333, 343

Japanese Submarines

I 25 353-354, 357, 370
I 26 337, 353, 355-357
RO 61 362

Italian Warships

Acciaio 606
Avorio 646
Platino 606
Tervani 606
Tritone 646

Peruvian Warships

Almirante Grau 335

Index

5 Squadron RCAF 556
10 Squadron RCAF 449, 466, 544
36 Squadron 436, 456-457, 472
113 Squadron RCAF 417, 453-454, 456-458
116 Squadron RCAF 544
117 Squadron RCAF 461
120 Squadron RCAF 542
145 Squadron RCAF 463, 544

ABC-1 agreement 211, 217
ABC-22 347, 360
36 340
Abwehr agent. *See* von Janowski
Africa 207, 211, 429, 452, 454, 533, 555
Agnew, Capt R.I. (CCCS) 37, 304-305, 333-335
Aircraft, VLR 478, 530, 542, 553, 561, 565
Air gap 533, 540, 544, 549, 551, 555, 560, 569, 578
Alaska 331, 333, 335, 337, 339, 341, 343, 345, 347, 349, 351, 353, 357, 361, 365, 367
Aleutian Islands 337
Alexander A.V., First Lord of the Admiralty 98
Alexander, Maj-Gen R.O. (Chairman, JSC) 364
Algerine class minesweepers 310, 316
American-Mediterranean convoys 579

Andrews, VAdm Adolphus, USN 397, 399-400, 402
Anticosti 443, 456, 459, 475
Arcadia Conference (Wash., Jan 1942) 391
Argentia 172, 264, 291, 301, 319, 385, 387, 391, 393, 396, 400, 445, 540, 565
Armed merchant cruisers 40, 46, 64, 74, 78, 140, 152, 167, 172, 229, 331, 333, 350, 360
Armed yachts 83, 140, 208, 337, 352, 390, 414, 433, 435, 441, 463
Arnold, Gen H.H. USAAF 220
Aruba 71, 375, 378, 388, 408, 413, 416, 424
Asdic 37, 38, 57, 69, 103, 107, 124, 143, 387, 424, 457, 563
American Troop convoys
AT 15 403, 404
Atka Island 362
Atlantic Convoy Conference 587
Atlantic Fleet (USN) 172, 174, 212, 215, 217, 219, 224, 231, 233-235, 270, 301, 393, 396, 576
Attu 359, 360, 368
Audette, Lt L.C. 123, 168, 550
Australia 148, 431
Avalon Peninsula 287, 300, 301, 379, 386, 390, 465, 558
Aviation, shore-based. *See* Air gap; aircraft, VLR; Coastal Command; Eastern Air Command, RCAF

Aviation, carrier-based. *See* escort carriers.
Azores 533, 537, 614

Baberg, Kapitänleutnant 535-536
Bahia del Callao, Peru 334
Baker-Cresswell, Capt A.J, RN 285
Bamfield 342, 344, 349
Bangor class minesweepers 145, 270, 307, 309, 317, 337, 348, 363, 381, 401, 433, 438- 443, 447, 450, 455, 460, 468, 558
engines in 82
operational roles 41, 75
Barber Pole Brigade 556, 563
Barclay Sound 349
Barnett, Corelli 543
Barrett, Lt R.D. 348, 354
Battle class trawler 54-55, 337
Battle of the Atlantic Committee 271
Bay of Biscay 103, 375, 395, 456, 614
Bay of Fundy 48
B-Dienst (German signals intelligence) 107, 395, 479, 483, 514, 527, 538, 544, 550, 555, 560, 562
BdU (*Befehlshaber der U-booten*) 101, 111, 195, 255, 279, 374, 379, 402, 405, 411, 422, 442, 476, 514, 534, 541, 546, 555, 576, 620
Beard, Cdr C.T. 332-333
Beck, Lt F.A. 573

Beech, Cmdre W.J.R. 337-341, 346, 348, 350-353, 357, 359, 363, 367

Beesley, Lt Patrick, RNVR 566

Belfast 116, 304

Bell, LCdr I.H. 603

Bell, Eng Cdr J.F. 300, 338, 437, 466, 470

Bell Island 300, 437, 466, 470

Bella Bella 345

Bermuda 41, 49, 69, 96, 104, 130, 137, 167, 187, 195, 199, 209, 333, 335, 375, 405, 408, 410, 412, 417, 421

Bic Island 433-435, 442, 450, 455, 459-460, 542

Bidwell, Capt R.E.S. 145, 392, 394, 466, 553-554

Black Sea 374

Bletchley Park. *See also* Enigma 195, 206, 236, 260, 273, 278, 287, 299, 394, 562, 565, 577

Bloc Populaire Canadien 469

Bloody winter of 1942-43 532

Blue water policy 442

Bombers, very long range (VLR) 35, 175, 441, 450, 454

Bonham-Carter, RAdm, RN (FO North Atlantic Escort Sqdn) 67, 69, 188, 271

Borden, PEI 476

Boston-Halifax convoys. *See also* 'Triangle Run" 398, 400, 401
    BX 398, 400, 401, 406
    XB 398, 401

Boston 83, 301, 379, 381, 398, 400-401, 405-406, 410, 418-420, 429

Boucher, Cdr S., RN 280, 285

Brainard, RAdm R.M., USN (CTF 24) 446, 536-537

Brand, Capt E.S. 32-33, 47-49, 228, 242, 369, 408, 418-420

Breadner, AM L.S. CAS 553

Bremerton, Wash. 350

Briggs, LCdr W.E.S. 236, 242-244, 258-259, 297

Bristol, Adm A.L., USN 174, 233-234, 264, 301-302

British Admiralty Delegation (BAD) 213, 217, 223, 268, 419, 565, 589

British Cabinet Anti-U-boat Committee 591

British Commonwealth Air Training Plan (BCATP) 469

Brodeur, RAdm Victor G. 213-215, 218, 225, 228, 370, 416, 418

Brooke, Lt W.S. 366

Brüller (CO of *U 413*) 520

BS convoys
    BS 31 461

Bucket Brigade coastal convoys 399, 402, 405

Burin Peninsula 403

BX convoys
    BX 23 406
    BX 23A 406
    BX 27 406

C-Force 337

C-Groups. *See* Escort groups

Cabinet (Canadian Federal) 47, 49-50, 56-57, 74-75, 80, 108, 148, 150, 309

Cabinet War Committee (Canadian) 92, 95, 108, 134, 145, 147-150, 187, 316, 318, 353, 360, 368, 452

Cabot Strait 48, 188, 208, 379, 434, 456, 458, 460, 465, 467, 471, 475

Camp 70 (POW) 475

Campbell, LCdr W.F. 99, 136, 540-541

Canadian Coastal Zone 377, 418, 420

Canadian Escort Groups (CEG) 554, 577

Canadian National Railways (CNR) 368

Canadian Naval Attaché, Washington. *See also* Brodeur, RAdm Victor, G. 218

Canadian Vickers Ltd 64, 143

Canadian-American hemispheric defence plan 347

Canso, Nova Scotia 32, 467-468

Canso (aircraft). *See also* Catalina 352, 404-405, 434-435, 447, 451, 461-463, 553, 556, 620

Cap Chat 436, 441, 451, 454-456, 460, 464

Cape Breton 104, 127, 133, 173, 385, 463, 467

Cape Cod 379, 403, 405

Cape Farewell 183, 199, 237, 239, 260, 299, 540

Cape Flattery 353-354

Cape Hatteras 379, 395, 402, 405, 417

Cape Lookout 402

Cape Race 32, 182, 194, 196, 199, 207, 286, 299, 379, 385-388, 390, 395, 402, 463, 466, 552

Cape Sable 379, 402-406

Cape Whittle 448

Captain (D) Halifax. *See also* Capt E.R. Mainguy; Capt J.D. Prentice. St. John's Newfoundland. *See also* Capt E.B.K. Stevens, RN; Capt E.R. Mainguy; Capt Harold T.W. Grant; Capt J. Rowland, RN 157, 167, 169, 210, 293, 303, 319, 401, 537, 558, 561

Cassidy, Ch Skipper G. F. 342

Catalina (aircraft). *See also* Canso 168, 243-245, 248, 283, 380, 422, 445

CESF (Commander Eastern Sea Frontier US) 400, 427

Chaleur Bay 467-468

Charlottetown 433, 455

Chavasse, LCdr E.H., RN 538

Chernofski Harbor 361

Chesapeake Bay 104, 402, 405

Chief of Naval Personnel (CNP). *See* Capt C.R.H. Taylor; Capt H.T.W. Grant; Capt E.R. Mainguy

Chief of the Naval Staff (CNS). *See also* VAdm P.W. Nelles 28, 33, 53, 77, 108, 145, 230, 317, 359, 401, 414

China 161, 331, 347

CHOP Line 394

Church, T.L. 148, 432

Churchill, Rt Hon Winston S. 57, 95, 130, 134, 170, 175, 181, 212, 220, 222, 308, 319, 398, 452, 454

messages to King re Canadian ships 580, 605

CINCLANT (Commander in Chief US Atlantic Fleet). *See also* Atlantic Fleet 212, 271, 400-401

Clarke, Desmond A. 113, 316, 349

Clayton, Lt J. 569

Coast Guard, US 207, 301, 348, 370, 443-444, 543

Coastal Command (RAF) 102, 106-107, 115-116, 121, 129, 188, 256, 472-473, 532, 566

Coastal Convoy Board (CCB) 399

Colombia 408

Collingwood Shipyards Ltd 138

Combined Operations, RN 172, 364, 366

Combined Operations Training Centre, Courtney, BC 364

COMINCH (Commander in Chief US Fleet) 392-393, 398, 400

Commander Greenland Patrol 446

Commander in Chief, America and West Indies Squadron (C-in-C AWI) RN 54, 97, 134, 187, 229, 332, 335, 410, 417

Commander in Chief Canadian North West Atlantic (C-in-C CNA). *See also* RAdm L.W. Murray 627

Commanding Officer Atlantic Coast (COAC). *See also* Commander in Chief North West Atlantic: Cmdre H.E.

Reid; RAdm G.C. Jones; RAdm L.W. Murray 55, 66, 69, 87, 140, 173, 187, 209, 230, 272, 393, 398, 400, 408, 410, 441, 454, 457, 459, 473, 537, 587

Commanding Officer Pacific Coast (COPC). *See also* RAdm V.G. Brodeur; Cmdre W.J.R. Beech 67, 87

Commodore Commanding Newfoundland Force (CCNF). *See also* Flag Officer Newfoundland (FONF); Radm L.W. Murray; Cmdre H.E. Reid; Capt E.R. Mainguy 198, 234, 263-264

Communications, to and from Ottawa 151

Comox 55, 83, 364, 366

Compasses, gyro vs magnetic 160, 190, 244, 355, 466, 568

Conception Bay 236, 300

CONNAV (US routing Authority) 536, 556

Conscription plebiscite 74, 141, 147, 318, 432, 469

Convoy. *See also* by convoy number; "Bucket Brigade" coastal convoys 381-387, 389 safety relative to independent sailings 97, 389, 406 Adm E.J. King and US coast 394-398, 399 through convoys across Atlantic 393

Corvette British orders 72 building programs 72 Canadian construction 72, 307 design 72, 74 modifications (long forecastle) 135 upgrading 303

Costa Rica 332

Creery, Capt W.B. 68, 97, 99-100, 318-319, 588

Cross, Cdr P.B. 542, 543

Crude Oil 385, 407

Cryptographers. *See also* Bletchley Park, Enigma, B-Dienst 287, 395, 565

CTF 24 (Commander Task Force 24, US) 443, 533, 536

Cuba 410, 419, 421

Curry, Eng Capt A.D.M. 33, 72

Cuthbert Lt James 462

Cypher. *See also* Enigma 42, 48, 107, 115, 195, 197, 297, 300, 348, 395, 562

Davie Shipbuilding (Sorel) 85, 143, 156, 308

Davis LCdr S.W. 277, 279, 286

DeFreitas, Lt P.F.M. 362, 367

DEMS (defensively equipped merchant ship) gunners 256, 384, 388, 404

Department of Transport (Canadian) 32, 154, 313-314

Deputy Chief of the Naval Staff (DCNS). *See also* RAdm L.W. Murray; Cmdre H.E. Reid; RAdm G.C. Jones 158-159, 228

Destroyers. *See also* individual ships by name A (Acasta) class 31, 531 Town class 141, 145, 151, 157, 163, 166, 176, 198, 206, 208, 210, 224, 227, 270, 296, 486, 538 River class 32, 77, 135, 140, 152, 157, 160, 175, 195, 210, 236, 256, 272, 318 Tribal class 57, 73, 75, 144, 147, 259, 308, 317, 320

Destroyers-for-bases deal 159, 171-172

DeWitt, LtGen J.L. 359

DeWolf, Capt H.G. 93, 97-98, 102, 157, 318-319, 414, 532

Dexter, Grant 414

DF (direction finding). *See also* HF/DF; MF/DF; RDF 32, 111, 115-116, 190, 194, 236, 269, 285, 288, 313-314, 394, 405,

412, 447, 450, 460, 463, 486, 535-541, 544, 546, 550, 552, 556, 559, 563, 568, 572, 575
Diesel engines 317, 440, 467
Digby Island 368
Director of Anti-Submarine Warfare (Admiralty) 101, 182, 565, 577
Director of Naval Intelligence (DNI). *See also* Director of Trade; Capt E.S. Brand; Cdr C.H. Little 43, 47
Director of Trade (DTD). *See also* Capt E.S. Brand 369
Divided control 394
Dobson, LCdr A.H. 486, 535, 537, 539
Döhler, Oberleutnant 541
Donald LCdr C.D. 448
Dönitz, Grossadmiral K. 57, 101, 103, 105, 106, 111, 115, 120, 124, 128, 180, 183, 195, 198-3, 206, 207, 210, 233, 250, 259, 261, 273, 278-3, 284, 286-288, 291, 299, 301, 373-375, 378-380, 395, 397, 402, 405, 407, 413, 417, 421, 427, 429, 436, 444, 449, 460, 465, 473, 476, 477, 479, 483, 494, 497, 503, 508, 514, 515, 524, 542, 544, 557, 561-563, 568, 603
Downey, Skipper Lt G.N. 558
Dufferin and Haldimand Rifles, 1st Bn 363
Dunbar-Nasmith, Adm D.A., RN 101
Dyer, Lt K.L. 556-559

Eastern Air Command (EAC). *See also* Royal Canadian Air Force 66, 67, 194, 417, 434, 435, 450, 454, 455, 457, 461, 476, 497, 554
Eastern Local Escort Force (ELEF) 393
Eastern Sea Frontier (ESF) 396-397, 402, 405

Easton, LCdr Alan 153, 272-273, 276, 283, 499-500
Eddy, Lt F.N. 370
Ediz Hook 347-348
Edwards, RAdm R.S., USN 400
Eggleston, Capt T.F. 354
electrical engineering in Canadian shipbuilding 143
Engineering 33, 72, 82, 89, 143, 279, 303-305, 307-308, 315, 537
English Channel 92, 96, 102, 135
Enigma 195-196, 198-199, 206, 236, 288, 394, 562, 565-566, 568, 571, 577
Escort carriers 532
Escort Groups 114, 129, 214, 220, 231, 263, 292, 298, 301-302, 392, 396, 408, 532, 554, 565, 576
3rd 278, 283, 285
4th 168
36 275, 302, 375, 381 538
A3 353, 532, 534, 540-541, 543, 622
B3 533
B4 555
B6 534, 555-556, 560-561
B7 563-565
C1 555, 558-559, 562, 565, 568-569
C2 538, 555
C3 556-558, 562
C4 534, 537, 544, 546, 549, 551, 553
W2 558
Esquimalt 28, 30, 32, 40, 50, 52, 55, 62, 65, 67, 83, 87, 96, 148, 161, 316, 333, 335, 337, 339, 342, 347, 355, 357, 363, 368
Estevan Point, wireless station 355-357
External Affairs, Department of 41, 43, 46, 92, 213, 340

Fairmile (motor launch) 316, 352, 363, 414, 416, 433, 435, 436, 439, 441, 443, 450, 454, 456, 459, 463, 466, 468, 475
Feeder convoys; HHX and SSC 73, 419, 543
Fenwick, SLt K.D. 424
Ferryland Head 387
Finance, Department of 74, 78-79, 149-150, 309
First Lord, British Admiralty. *See also* A.V. Alexander 57, 98
First Sea Lord, British Admiralty. *See also* Adm Sir Dudley Pound 29, 66-67, 76-77, 140, 145, 184, 215, 268, 270, 392
Fishermen's Reserve 337-339, 342, 344, 350, 356, 358, 363, 366
and internment of Japanese-Canadians 341
recruitment 338
Fitz, Capt H.C., USN 531, 540-541
Flag Officer Newfoundland (FONF). *See also* Commodore Commanding Newfoundland Force (CCNF); RAdm L.W. Murray 272, 380, 389, 392, 396, 466, 470, 533, 537, 552
Flemish Cap 300
Fletcher, VAdm F.J., USN 367
Fog 190, 194, 198-200, 208, 250, 258, 286, 291, 298, 361, 402, 404, 448, 451, 456, 458, 509, 535, 549, 557, 572
Force D 360
Forcible evacuation 339
Foreign Intelligence Service (RCN) 394
Fort Stevens 357
Forteau Bay 445, 447
Francke, Kapitänleutnant H. 475
Fraser, Lt J.P. 31, 33, 38, 52, 55-57, 62, 65, 68, 71, 91, 96-101, 108, 117, 126, 345, 436
Free French 260, 279, 288, 293, 404

Freetown 210, 214, 408, 410-411

Frewer, Lt F.C. 572, 576

Frigate (twin-screw corvette) 310, 315-317
British orders 310
production of 310
RCN orders 310

Funkmessbeobachtung (FuMB) *See also Metox* 461, 533, 540, 544, 557

Gagnon, Onésime 471-472

Galveston 375

Gardner, Lt W.C. 366

German *Abwehr* agent von Janowski. *See* von Janowski

German High Command (OKW) 300, 398

German Search Receiver (GSR). *See also Metox* 556, 557

Gaspé 430-435, 441-443, 447, 449, 451, 454, 455-464, 467, 468, 470-475

Gibraltar 118, 182, 268, 375, 378, 417, 436, 555, 559

Gibraltar Escort Force 602, 616

Godbout, Adélard 442, 470, 472

Godfrey, Cdr V.S. 351, 362-363, 365

Goose Bay 442, 444-445, 447

Gordon Channel 347, 349

Gräf, Kapitänleutnant 460-463, 566

Graf Spee 63

Grand Manan Island 403

Grant, Capt H.E.T. 27, 112, 147, 363, 414

Great circle route 64, 181, 185, 208, 264, 287, 379

Greenland 131, 240, 243, 273, 275, 286, 299, 442, 446, 552, 619

Greenock 98, 108, 119, 159, 167, 169

Greger, Oberleutnant-zur-See 239-241, 243-244

Griffin, Lt A.G.S. 226, 281, 286

Grubb, Lt F.E. 239, 246, 250, 257

Guantanamo, Cuba 419-420, 424, 427

Gulf of Maine 49, 404

Gulf of Mexico 403, 410, 413, 419-421, 427

Gulf of St Lawrence 73, 76, 83, 188, 291, 401, 403, 410, 414, 418, 427, 429, 444, 450, 452, 468, 471, 475, 544, 556

Gulf Sea Frontier (USN) 410, 412

Gumboot Navy 338

HA (Halifax-Aruba) convoys
HA 2 416-417
HA 3 420-421

Halifax-Boston convoys. *See* Boston-Halifax convoys

Halifax Escort Force 64, 381

Halifax Local Defence Force 381

Halifax Shipyards 152, 227, 308, 317, 320

Halifax Tanker Escort Force 413
redesignation as Halifax Force 142, 157, 159, 162, 172, 414, 416, 441, 444

Hanson, R.B. 432

Hardegen, Kapitänleutnant Reinhard 380

Harland and Wolff Shipbuilders, Belfast 304

Harris, LCdr R.F. 152

Hart, Cdr 350-352

Hartlen Point Radio Station 194-195, 313-314
and sinking of Bismark 195

Hartwig, Kapitänleutnant Paul 444-445, 447-449, 451, 454-462, 473

Hatrick, SLt Raymond 260-261

Heathcote, Cdr R., RN 560-561, 576

Hecate Strait 342, 347

Henderson, Lt Stuart 575

Hermann, Korvettenkapitän 566

Hesquiat Harbour 355-356

Heydemann, Kapitänleutnant 540

HF/DF (high frequency direction finding). *See also* DF 115, 236, 285, 394, 405, 412, 486, 535-541, 544, 546, 550, 552, 556, 559-561, 563, 565, 568, 572, 575-578

HG (Gibraltar-United Kingdom convoys)
HG 76 375
HG 84 436

Hibbard, Cdr J.C. 93, 237, 243, 247, 249, 255-256, 258-259, 372

Hitler, Adolf 48, 63-64, 99, 136, 175, 198, 286, 373-374, 395

Hoffman, Korvettenkapitän E. 446, 451, 454

Hong Kong 337, 350

Honolulu 337

Hope, Cdr A.M. 39

Horton, Adm Sir Max, RN 553, 558, 588
dictum on training cycle 592

Hose, Cmdre Walter 30, 34, 148, 335, 539

Hot Dog, Operation 569, 574

Houghton, Capt F.L. 33, 228, 230, 269, 320, 350, 352, 362, 365

House of Commons 44, 68, 91, 134, 309, 430, 432

Howard-Johnston, Cdr C.D., RN 205, 558

Howe, Hon C.D. 80, 142, 144, 309, 317, 362

HT (Halifax-Trinidad) convoys
HT 1 410-411
HT 2 411
HT 3 412
shortcomings and success 411, 412

HX convoys
HX 62, 64, 68, 77, 83, 102-105, 111, 114-116, 118, 127-129
HX 144 224, 269

HX 145 269
HX 208 419
HX 212 534, 540-543
HX 214 555
HX 216 559
HX 217 560-562
HX 218 562
Hyde Park Agreement (Apr 1941)
   310
Hydrophone effect (HE) 281,
   291, 348, 542, 560, 566

Iceland 116, 129, 132, 177, 180,
   181, 183, 185, 196, 208, 211,
   217, 220, 237, 243, 262, 264,
   278, 279, 301, 302, 478, 529,
   532
Imperial Japanese Navy 347
Indian Ocean 398
Ingersoll, Adm R.E., USN,
   CINCLANT 396
Intelligence Division 340
   Submarine Tracking Room
      237, 380, 394, 476, 492,
      504, 514, 562, 566
Ireland 57, 62, 101, 110, 116,
   129, 168, 262, 283, 393, 538,
   561, 565
Isolationists 43, 134, 211, 431,
   442
Italy 91, 104, 130, 378
Ites, Oberleutnant Otto 421-424
Japan 331, 337, 339, 346, 357,
   361, 366, 368, 373, 398, 469,
   471
Japan Current 361
Japanese Combined Fleet 353
Japanese submarines 353, 355,
   361, 471
Japanese-Canadians 339, 341,
   345
   fishermen 337
   forcible evacuation of 341-346
Jellicoe, Adm of the Fleet Earl,
   RN 29, 148
   visit to Canada and
      recommendation re RCN 29

Jenson, Lt L.B. ("Yogi") 523
Joint Chiefs of Staff 368
Joint Services Committee-Pacific
   Coast (JSC) 363, 369
Jones, RAdm G.C. 39 265, 286,
   318, 319, 380, 381, 389, 411,
   441, 537, 543, 583
Jones, LCdr J.T., RNR 563

Kaien Island 368
Kals, Korvettenkapitän E. 385
Keenleyside Hugh 92, 95, 130,
   340-341
Key West, Florida 405, 413, 419,
   421, 427
King, Adm Ernest J., USN. *See
   also* COMINCH 172, 174-176,
   183-184, 187, 212-213, 215,
   217-218, 220-221, 224-226,
   231-235, 263, 268-271, 288,
   296, 301-302 346, 392-394,
   396-400, 408, 413, 416-419,
   531
   and convoys along US coast
      394, 398, 399
King, LCdr Clarence A. 422-424
King, Rt Hon William Lyon
   Mackenzie 30, 41, 44, 49, 52,
   56, 74-75, 80, 91, 95, 130-
   137, 147, 150, 161, 170, 318,
   430, 442, 452, 454, 469
   message from Churchill re
      Canadian ships Jan 1943
      580, 605
Kingston, Jamaica 49, 71, 85,
   88, 91, 134, 141, 421
Kiska 359, 362, 368, 370
Kodiak 359, 362, 365
Krech, Kapitänleutnant 280
Kretschmer, Korvettenkapitän
   Otto 127, 177, 539
Kriegsmarine (German Navy) 57,
   65, 378, 577

Labrador Current 440
L'Action Catholique 469
Lally, R.M. 355-356
Landing craft LCI(L) 364, 366

Landing Ships (Infantry) (LSI)
   360, 367
Landymore, Lt W.M. 109, 117
Lawrence, Lt Harold (Hal) 423
Lay, Capt Horatio Nelson 92, 93,
   96, 98, 100, 157, 197, 392,
   394, 414, 433, 472, 528, 581-
   583, 585, 587, 590, 624, 626-
   630
Leimkühler, Oberleutnant 571,
   574, 575
Lend-Lease 170, 310
Little, Adm Sir Charles, RN 214,
   215, 225
Little, Cdr C.H. 268
Liverpool (UK) 196, 200
Liverpool, Nova Scotia 101, 108,
   159, 184, 189, 385, 388, 406,
   540, 551, 561
LN-NL convoys
   LN 6 445, 447
   LN 7 447-450
   NL 6 447-448
   NL 8 459
Londonderry 116, 119, 160, 166,
   174, 271, 391, 393, 535, 552
Long Island 405
Louisbourg, Nova Scotia 396,
   467
Love, Lt A.B. 169, 366, 397, 572
Low Point 577
Luftwaffe (German Air Force)
   129, 177

Macdonald, Hon Angus L. 55,
   112, 133, 137, 144, 147-150,
   158, 184, 186, 188, 213, 215,
   308, 316-318, 342, 345, 360,
   414, 432, 441, 469, 471-473
MacDonald, LCdr D.R.H 624, 628
Macdonald Lt J.H.S. 152, 154,
   164
MacDuff, LCdr T. 356-357
Macintyre, Cdr D.G., RN 539-540
Mackinlay, Cdr J.G. 216
MacLachlan, Col 133, 315
MacMillan, H.R. 309, 315-316
Madeira 543

Mainguy, Capt E.R. 70, 110-112, 118, 162, 183, 189, 197, 202-205, 450, 470, 537

"Major Hoople" (later "Porcupine" in WACI) 557-558, 574

Manners, Cmdre E. 563

Marshall, Gen George C., Chief of Staff, US Army 221

McCulloch, Cdr J. 340, 350, 354

McNaughton, Gen A.G.L. 331, 364

McQuarrie, Lt L.F. 349

Mediterranean Sea 27, 81, 104, 171, 211, 273, 300, 317, 374, 378, 531, 555, 559

Melvin's Beach 404

Merchant marine, Canadian 44, 319

Merchant shipbuilding. *See also* shipbuilding; merchant ships 307, 319

Merchant ships (North Sands type) 307

Metox 461-463, 533, 556, 568, 571, 575

Mexico 332, 403, 410, 413, 419-421, 427

MF/DF. *See also* DF, HF/DF, radar 563-565

Mid-Ocean Escort Force (MOEF) 367, 392-394, 396, 399-401, 531-533, 556, 563, 568, 577

Mid-Ocean Meeting Point (MOMP) 271, 299, 301, 391, 393

Midway, Battle of 353, 357, 406, 456

milch cow. *See also* U-tanker 478, 536, 620

Millbanke Sound 345, 357

Mills, W.G. 450

Milner, Marc 407

Minefields 102, 122, 414

Minesweeping Flotilla
15th (RN) 607
16th (RN) 622

Minister of National Defence for Naval Services. *See also* Hon Angus L. Macdonald 133

Ministry of War Transport (UK) 310, 474

Monthly Anti-Submarine Report (Admiralty) 205-206, 210, 478

Moore, Adm H.R., RN 271

Morey, Capt H.W., RN 419

Morocco 555

Munitions and Supply, Department of 142, 145, 154, 307, 315, 407

Murray, RAdm L.W. 33, 37, 48, 52, 76, 132-134, 157-160, 172, 183, 186, 188, 197, 210, 218, 224, 229-232, 234, 239, 255, 260, 263, 267, 269, 285, 293, 296, 300-302, 304, 380, 387, 389, 394, 401, 486, 537, 552

Mützelberg, Kapitänleutnant R. 200, 202, 387

NA convoys
NA 2 389-390
NA 8 403

Naden 346

Nagumo, Adm, IJN 337

Nakagawa, Sasuke 342, 345

Nanaimo 348, 364

Nass River 342

National Research Council of Canada (NRC) 72, 144, 305, 306, 479, 482

National Resources Mobilization Act. *See also* conscription 442

Naval Control Service 44, 48, 54, 62, 66, 256, 369, 419, 459

Naval Secretary/Secretary Naval Board 33, 149

Naval Service Headquarters (NSHQ), Ottawa *See also* VAdm P.W. Nelles; Hon A.L. Macdonald 28, 32, 41, 45-54, 56, 63, 66-71, 78, 83, 87, 105, 107, 109, 124, 141, 143, 151, 157, 160-161, 167, 173, 183, 186-189, 194, 197, 213, 224, 228-230, 232, 235, 263, 269, 293, 300, 303-305, 307,

310, 315, 331, 332, 335, 339-341, 366, 369, 380, 392, 400, 408, 410, 413, 416-418, 420, 431, 444, 447, 450, 459, 470, 475, 489-492, 527, 532, 534, 553, 568

Nazan Bay 362

Nelles, VAdm Percy W. 28, 33, 38, 41, 46, 49-54, 56, 66-68, 71, 73-79, 81, 86-92, 108, 112, 119, 135-137, 140, 142-145, 148, 152, 157-159, 173, 175, 183, 188, 213, 215, 218, 228, 231, 263, 267, 270, 317, 332, 359, 367, 407, 413, 418, 452, 553

Netherlands Antilles 420

New Brunswick 32, 418, 429, 433, 454, 460, 475-476

New Carlisle 467, 475

New Jersey 406

New York 83, 105, 135, 170, 307, 375, 378, 389, 395, 403, 406, 413, 419, 427, 429, 452, 469, 488, 533, 542, 555

Newfoundland Escort Force (NEF) 112, 187, 191, 195, 199, 207, 210, 212, 214, 217, 224, 228, 234, 236, 257, 263, 296, 267, 270, 273, 288, 293, 297, 302, 304, 391

Nimitz, Adm Chester W., USN 360

Nisei. See also Japanese Canadians 339

Nixon, Lt C.P. 39

Noble, Adm Sir Percy, RN. *See also* Western Approaches Command 158-, 169, 256, 264, 285, 494

Nölke, Korvettenkapitän 601

Nootka Sound 349, 357

Norfolk, Virginia 35, 405, 413

North Africa, invasion of 104, 300, 429, 452, 454, 471, 530-532

Northern routing scheme 267

Northwest Sea Frontier (US) 367, 369

Norway 92, 97, 273, 395
NRC . *See* National Research
    Council
NSHQ. *See* Naval Service
    Headquarters

O'Brien, Lt J. 165, 527
Ocean Falls 351
Oerlikon (20mm anti-aircraft
    gun) 423, 527, 570-571
Oil
    Aruba 408
    importance of 407
    pipeline Portland to Montreal
        407, 410
    supply crisis in UK 579
    Venezuela 385, 407, 410, 420
Oil Controller, Dept of Munitions
    and Supply 407-408, 410-411,
    420
Oland, Capt R.H. 54, 59, 63, 65,
    104
ON convoys
    ON 33 298-299
    ON 34 299
    ON 52 386
    ON 53 387
    ON 55 388
    ON 59 388
    ON 89 403
    ON 113 483, 487, 492, 494,
        497, 503
    ON 114 494
    ON 115 494-499, 502, 513,
        530, 556
    ON 116 494, 577
    ON 125 514
    ON 126 515
    ON 127 515, 518, 520, 524-
        527, 530
    ON 137 534-538, 556
    ON 139 538
    ON 143 555
    ON 145 558
    ON 149 560
    ON 153 562-565

ONS convoys
    ONS 56 388
    ONS 67 482
    ONS 92 483
    ONS 100 483
    ONS 102 483
    ONS 122 525
    ONS 124 508
    ONS 126 514
    ONS 138 539
    ONS 140 540
    ONS 144 555-557
    ONS 152 562
    ONS 154 534, 559, 562, 565,
        568, 571-578
Operational Intelligence Centre
    (Admiralty) 115, 273, 380,
    576
Operational Intelligence Centre
    (NSHQ) 489, 491, 544
Operations Division (NSHQ) 83,
    145, 433, 528, 587
OPNAV 292
Östermann, Kapitänleutnant J.
    387
Ottawa
    as distant from operational
        commands 151
    need for improved
        communications 151
Pacific Coast Command 346, 349-
    350, 363, 367, 368, 371
Pacific Fleet, USN 337, 360
Pacific war 41, 337-339, 341,
    351, 353, 370-371
Pan-American Safety Zone 374
Panama 65, 332-333, 419, 422
Panama Canal 65, 332-333
Park Steamship 310
Parkwold 342
Parliament. *See also* House of
    Commons 41, 45, 47, 49, 52,
    54, 73, 95, 148, 470, 473
Patrol Squadron 92, USN 422
Paukenschlag, Operation 373,
    375, 377-381, 383, 385, 387,
    389-391, 393, 395, 397, 399,

401, 403, 405, 407, 411, 413,
    415, 417, 419, 421, 423, 425,
    427
Pearl Harbor 341, 348, 352, 369,
    373-374, 396, 491
Peck, Cox D.W. 356
Pernambuco 405
Petroleum products 407, 412
Piers, Lt D.W. 97-98, 466, 536-
    537, 546-547, 549-554, 558,
    560, 577
Pillar Point 353-354
Pine Island 349
Placentia Bay 379, 391, 463
Plan 4 218, 263
Plan Orange (USN) 171
Pope, Maj-Gen M.A. 47, 54
"Porcupine" 558
Port Alberni 357, 364
Port Angeles 353
Port-aux-Basques 435, 462
Porteous, Cdr(E) W.W. 537
Portland, Maine 119, 380, 385,
    407, 410-412, 420
Pound, Adm Sir Dudley, RN (First
    Sea Lord) 66, 77, 135, 152,
    158, 180, 184, 188, 221, 229,
    231, 263, 267-271, 392-394,
    399, 417, 422
Powell, Stoker PO Art 423-424
Power, C.G. (Air Minister) 132-
    133, 149
Prentice, Capt J.D. 160-163, 189-
    191, 194, 236, 239, 245-247,
    256, 296, 529, 558-560
Prien, Gunter 101, 111, 127,
    173, 177
Prince Edward Island 429, 433,
    454, 475
Prince Rupert 55, 148, 337, 342,
    345-347, 350-352, 364, 368-
    370
Prisoners of war 475-476
Pullen, AB Jim 484, 486
Pullen, Lt T.C. 88, 142, 169, 521-
    522
Purkhold, Kapitänleutnant 571-
    572, 574-575

QS convoys
  QS 15 436, 441, 443
  QS 19 443
  QS 33 450-451, 454, 456
  QS 34 455
  QS 37 457-458
  QS 38 458-459
  QS 39 460
  QS 42 464
QSS convoys (Québec-Sydney
  special)
  QSS 1 434
Quät-Faslem, Kapitänleutnant
  505, 506
Quatsino Sound 349
Québec City 45, 73, 316, 416,
  433, 441, 442, 445, 447, 461
Québec Provincial Police 467
Queen Charlotte Islands 339, 369
Queen Charlotte Strait 347, 349-
  350

Race Rocks 347-348
radar. See also RDF, National
  Research Council of Canada;
  radar detectors; Metox;
  German Search Receiver
  centimetric 284, 479, 482,
    486, 521, 533, 560, 563
  RX/C 306, 479
  short wave 285, 306-307
  SW1C 61, 306, 312, 361, 461,
    482, 501, 533, 558, 568
  SW2C 306, 361, 513, 533,
    556-558, 568
  type 271 305-307, 480, 483,
    486, 494, 503-505, 513,
    515, 521, 527, 530, 533-
    535, 538, 541, 546, 550,
    554, 556-557, 568, 609
  type 286 115, 125, 305-306,
    506, 533, 556-557
Radio-telephone (R/T) 168, 197,
  204, 258, 285, 298, 305, 451,
  571
RAF 106, 115, 168, 256, 305,
  489, 507

Raiders, German armed
  merchant 332
Rasch, Kapitänleutnant H. 461-
  464
Raspberry, Operation 488, 498,
  518, 520, 549, 551, 556, 563-
  564, 569
Rationing in Canada 129, 407
Ravenhill, Capt R.W., RN (DCOS
  WA) 525-526
Raymond, Maxime 469
RDF. See also radar 125, 305,
  425
Redford, Ed T. 356
Reed, Wm, ship designer 72
Reed, Cdr A. 342
Reid, Cmdre H.E. 48, 51, 55, 63,
  66, 83, 112, 173, 225, 228-
  233, 270, 320, 359, 362, 400,
  428, 552, 568, 576
Reykjavik 283
Rimouski 433, 460-461, 474
Robertson, Seaman Donald 165-
  166
Robertson, Norman 213, 340-
  341
Rohwer Jürgen 278, 283
Roosevelt, Franklin D. 92, 95,
  130, 134, 170, 175, 187, 211,
  219, 319, 396, 398
Rowland, Capt J.M., RN 488
Roy, J-S 432, 441-442, 471
Roy, Capt J.W.R. 83, 109, 117
Royal Canadian Air Force (RCAF)
  See also Eastern Air
  Command; Western Air
  Command 31, 51, 55, 62, 74,
  300, 337, 343, 347, 349, 351-
  353, 356, 360, 369, 385, 404-
  406, 417, 434, 442, 445, 449,
  454, 457, 465, 472, 488-492,
  520, 544, 552-554, 556
  1 Group 300
Royal Canadian Mounted Police
  (RCMP) 54-55, 87, 339, 341,
  345, 430
Royal Canadian Naval Reserve
  30

Royal Canadian Naval Volunteer
  Reserve 30
Royal Canadian Navy (RCN) 27-
  29, 31-34, 37, 40, 46, 55, 63,
  71, 75, 77, 90, 148
  as branch of Royal Navy 27,
    28
  "Can-do" ethos 34
  difficulties dealing with
    Admiralty 34
  equipment problems of RCN
    ships 533, 554
  insistence on national
    priorities 145
  lack of staff tradition 33, 34
  long-term goals 142-145
  national control 540, 541
  prewar history 373-380
  planning for postwar navy 75
Royal Military College 286
Royal Navy 27, 30, 32, 37, 40,
  49, 63, 71, 86, 90, 94, 108,
  129, 137, 145, 148, 158, 207,
  293, 310, 531
Royal Rifles of Canada 337
Rudeltaktik. See also wolf pack
  106, 115, 477
Rudloff, Kapitänleutnant 513,
  535
Rüggeberg, Korvettenkapitän R.
  449, 465-466
Ruppelt, Oberleutnant 569
Russia 198, 286, 331, 347
Russian vessels 351
Rutherford, Cdr C.A. 515, 521-
  522, 524
Ryan, LCdr T.P. 368

Sable Island 190, 379, 388, 395,
  463, 488, 502, 558
Saint John, New Brunswick 29,
  32, 45, 48, 54, 197, 381, 388,
  398, 404, 452
San Francisco 353, 359
Sandwith, Capt H.R., RN 490-492
SC convoys 105, 122, 208, 223,
  228, 231, 235, 263, 267, 269,
  300, 391, 393, 400, 418, 452

SC 40 224, 269

SC 42 235, 239, 244, 250, 255, 259, 262, 268, 284, 291, 304, 466

SC 45 263, 271

SC 46 263, 270, 287

SC 48 267, 270, 272, 275, 278, 280, 282, 284, 291, 293, 374

SC 52 288, 291-293, 296, 298-301, 374

SC 63 381, 386

SC 67 483

SC 92 494

SC 94 505-508, 530

SC 95 418

SC 97 508, 513

SC 104 514

SC 100 524, 527-530

SC 102 419

SC 104 534

SC 105 540

SC 106 540

SC 107 465, 534, 543, 546, 549-554, 558, 569, 577

SC 108 555

SC 109 556

SC 110 558, 561, 568

SC 144 534

Schäfer, Kapitänleutnant H. 468

Schneider, Kapitänleutnant H. 544, 546, 549-551

Schug, Kapitänleutnant 485

Schull, Joseph 34

Schultze, Kapitänleutnant 240, 242, 247-248, 405-406

Schwantke, Kapitänleutnant H. 461-462, 464, 556

Scott, SLt E.G. 349, 351, 357, 422

Seal Island 385, 406

Seattle 353

Seekriegsleitung (SKL) German naval staff 374

Seibicke, Kapitänleutnant 540-541

SG-GS convoys

SG 6 444-446, 449

Shadowers 116, 194, 285, 479, 514, 539, 557, 568

Shark cypher. *See also* Triton 562

Shelburne 142, 406

Sheringham Point 347, 349, 353-354

Sherman, Capt F. 220

Sherwood, Capt E.C. 538

Ship design, improvement in. *See also* Corvettes; Frigates 303

Shipbuilding

Canada vs UK 72, 75

Halifax paper on 318, 319

RCN orders 72

Shipyards

Canadian 85, 154, 307, 315

Great Lakes vs coastal 310

Sierra Leone convoy 182, 533

Signals intelligence. *See* B-Dienst; Bletchley Park; Enigma; Submarine Tracking Room

Signals personnel, shortage of 303

Simmons, Lt E.T. 246, 257

Simpson, LCdr(E) G.L. 305

SL 125 543, 578

Small, S/Ldr N.E. RCAF 417, 489

Sombrero Passage 411

Sooke Inlet 348

Sorber, Leutnant Heinz 507

South America 95, 211, 332-333, 418, 533

South Atlantic 168, 273, 332, 560, 569, 576

Spain 44

SQ convoys

SQ 20 443

SQ 33 450

SQ 36 456-457, 472

SQ 38 456-457

SQ 39 458-459

SQ 43 459, 464

SQ 44 464

SQ 47 476

St John's 112, 151, 153, 172, 174, 178, 183, 188, 194-199, 207, 218, 230, 232, 236, 239, 263, 270, 272, 287, 293, 296, 298, 304, 318, 335, 379-381, 385-393, 396, 398, 401, 407, 416, 449, 465, 468, 470, 485, 488, 491, 495, 502, 507, 512, 524, 526, 529, 536, 553, 556, 559

St Lawrence River 104, 154, 157, 176, 416, 418, 427, 431, 433-437, 439, 441-445, 447, 449-455, 457-465, 467-476, 529, 531

St Paul Island 461-462

St Pierre 385, 396

Stark, Adm Harold, USN 134, 171, 211-212, 215, 217-218, 221, 231-233, 235, 268, 271

Stephens, Eng RAdm G.L. 112, 316

Stephenson, Cmdre G.O. (VAdm RN ret) 158, 163, 167

Stevens, Capt E.B.K., RN Capt(D) (at St John's) 189, 210, 239, 255-256, 296, 357

Steveston 341, 345-346

Strait of Belle Isle 173, 182, 208, 239, 260, 272, 286, 290-293, 436, 440, 442, 447, 451, 456, 465, 471, 474

Strait of Georgia 368

Strait of Gibraltar 378

Strait of Juan de Fuca 347-348, 350

Strategy 137, 170-171, 188, 211, 233, 363, 378, 391, 397, 407, 421, 546

Stubbs, LCdr John 222, 506-507

Submarine chasers (US) deficiencies of 397

Submarine Tracking Room. *See* Intelligence Division

Summerside 61, 406, 433, 455, 541

Support groups
  first RN 527
  as improvement to convoy
    defences 530, 532
Sydney 29, 45, 48, 54, 60-61,
  73, 76, 83, 104, 114, 148,
  160, 190, 196, 199, 208, 224,
  235, 260, 263, 267, 270, 272,
  288, 291, 298, 300, 375, 379,
  381, 385, 390, 396, 400, 404,
  407, 418, 430, 433, 441, 445,
  450, 454, 458, 465, 473

Tanaga Island 359
Tanker
  escort force at Halifax 410,
    413
  redesignation as Halifax Force
    444
Task Force 4 (USN) 300, 391,
  396
TAW-WAT. See WAT-TAW
TAW 15 421, 424
Taylor, Capt C.R.H. 33, 87, 141-
  142, 151-152, 157, 167-168,
Taylor, Cdr T., RN 288, 290-292,
  483-485, 494, 508
TC (troop) convoys 98, 118, 120,
  230, 264, 272, 278, 389, 403
TC 14 267, 272, 278, 280
TH (Trinidad-Halifax) convoys
  TH 1 411
  TH 2 411
  TH 3 412
  TH 4 412
Thebaud, Capt Hewlett, USN
  279, 284, 285, 552
Theobald, RAdm R.A., USN 360,
  363
Thompson, Cdr C., RN 472
Thompson, R.C. (shipbuilder)
  307
Thurmann, Kapitänleutnant Karl
  276-279, 282, 284, 286, 403,
  430, 434-436, 498, 503, 561
Tilden, Cdr E., RN 563-564
Tobermory 163, 167, 228-230,
  267, 304

Topp, Korvettenkapitän Erich
  379, 385-386, 484-485, 497-
  498, 500-504
Torch, Operation 260, 363, 367,
  459, 527, 530, 532, 541, 543,
  546, 554, 571, 578, 609
Trail, Lt D. 220, 286, 445, 447
Trawler 30, 54, 70, 73, 119, 195,
  337, 383, 405
Triangle Run 401
Tribal class destroyers
  as basis for postwar RCN 307
  difficulties of building in
    Canada 74, 75
  employment overseas 582
Trident Conference (May 1943)
  368
Trinidad 375, 378, 405, 408,
  410-413, 419, 421
Triton
Triton cypher (German; known
  as Shark to Allies) 394, 478
Tucker, Dr. Gilbert 32, 338, 340,
  506
Turbines, steam 72

U-boat
  cyphers. See Bletchley Park,
    Enigma, Triton
  grid squares 288
  patrol lines 198, 206, 210,
    235, 237, 395, 479, 533,
    540, 561, 565, 577
  type VII 375, 379, 395, 402,
    460, 478, 505, 514
  type VIIC 421
  type IX 375, 378, 380, 385,
    514, 544
  type IXB 461
  type IXC 444
U-boat Command. See also BdU
  120, 211, 250, 260, 262, 287,
  300, 378, 402, 404, 406, 478,
  532, 543, 561, 566, 576
U-boat groups
  Büffel 562
  Brandenburg 262
  Drachen 558-560

Draufgänger 560
Hecht 483
Kreuzotter 555-556
Leopard 534, 549
Letzte Ritter 529
Lohs 508, 514, 526
Luchs 529
Markgraf 241
Mordbrenner 286-288
Panther 534-536, 538
Pfadfinder 405, 410
Pfeil 527, 620, 622
Pirat 496-497
Puma 538-540, 542
Raubritter 288, 299
Raufbold 561-563, 566
Reissewolf 286-287
Ritter 529
Schlagetot 555
Seeräuber 375
Seydlitz 379
Spitz 562, 565-566, 571, 577
Steinbrink 497, 505, 508
Steuben 299-301
Stier 508, 514-515
Streitaxt 543
Strosstrupp 287
Südwärts 539
Ungestüm 561, 565, 572
Veilchen 536, 540, 543, 546,
  550-552
Vorwärts 508, 513-516, 524-
  526
Westwall 555, 559
Wolf 264, 317, 421, 477, 483,
  485, 488, 497, 529-530
Wotan 534, 538
Zeithen 346
U-bootewaffe (German submarine
  foce) 374
U-tanker. See also milch cow
  402, 526
Ucluelet Inlet, amphibious
  exercises 363
Ultra 198, 200, 206, 275, 288,
  380, 534
United States Army 369

United States-Gibraltar convoys
UGF 555
UGS 555
GUF 555
GUS 555
United States Marine corps 366
training at San Diego 346
United States Navy (USN) 77,
133, 207, 374
Uphoff, Kapitänleutnant H. 402

Vancouver 31, 37, 52, 54, 333,
337, 340, 342, 347, 349, 351,
354, 357, 361, 367, 371
Vesca signals 369
Vice Chief of the Naval Staff
(VCNS) 271, 320, 359, 400,
414, 537
Vladivostok 351
Vogel, Viktor 404
Vogelsang, Kapitänleutnant E.
436, 440, 442-443, 488-489
Von Förstner, Oberleutnant Baron
549-550
Von Janowski, Werne Alfred
Waldemar (German *Abwehr*
agent) 467
Von Puttkamer, (CO *U 43*) 538
Von Soden-Fraunhofen,
Oberleutnant Graf 542
Von Varendorff, Kapitänleutnant
Ameling 403-404
Von Zitzewitz, 539

Wabana, Newfoundland 437,
449-450, 463, 465-468, 470,
474, 476
Walker, Capt F.J., RN 488, 561,
608
Walkerling, Kapitänleutnant
Heinz 521
Wallace, Cdr D.C. 494-496, 504,
528, 530, 630
Walsh, Cdr J.F., USN 421-422
Wartime Shipping
Administration 410, 420
Washington, DC 92, 95, 131,
134, 171, 212-214, 217, 225,
228, 230, 268, 271, 292, 391,
399, 408, 413, 416, 418, 452,
490-492, 528, 553, 581, 584,
589, 591, 596, 621, 628
Washington Conference (April
1942) 394, 420, 490, 593,
630
Weather, Oct 1942-1943.
See also Bloody winter of
1942-43 590, 613, 619, 621
Welland. Lt R.P. 350
West Ocean Meeting Point
(WOMP) 381, 544
Western Air Command (RCAF)
368-369, 371
Western Approaches Command.
See also Adm D.A. Dunbar-
Nasmith; Adm Sir Max
Horton; Adm Sir Percy Noble
108, 119, 130, 137, 145, 159,
188, 232, 269, 296, 391, 400,
504, 531, 578, 581, 583, 591,
595

Western Approaches Convoy
Instructions (WACI) 273
Western Local Escort Force
(WLEF) 393, 395, 398, 400,
406, 420, 435, 454, 488, 520,
556, 584, 590-592, 594, 628
Western Patrol 349
Williams, Lt V. 140, 464
Williams Head 364, 366
Windeyer, LCdr G.S. 366, 494-
496, 559, 568-577
Windward Islands 412
Windward Passage 421
Winn, Cdr Roger, RNVR 380,
492, 508, 568, 585, 589
Wissler, LCdr F. 342
Wissmann, Kapitänleutnant F.
466-468, 558
Wolf pack. *See also Rudeltaktik*
421, 477
Woods, LCdr S.R.J., RNR 491,
520-521
Worth, Capt G.A. 42, 92, 100,
205, 234

Yarmouth 385, 404-406, 417,
454, 457, 489, 586
Yarrows (shipbuilder, Victoria)
316
Yokata, Cdr, IJN 353, 355, 357

Zetzsche, Kapitänleutnant 562,
573-575

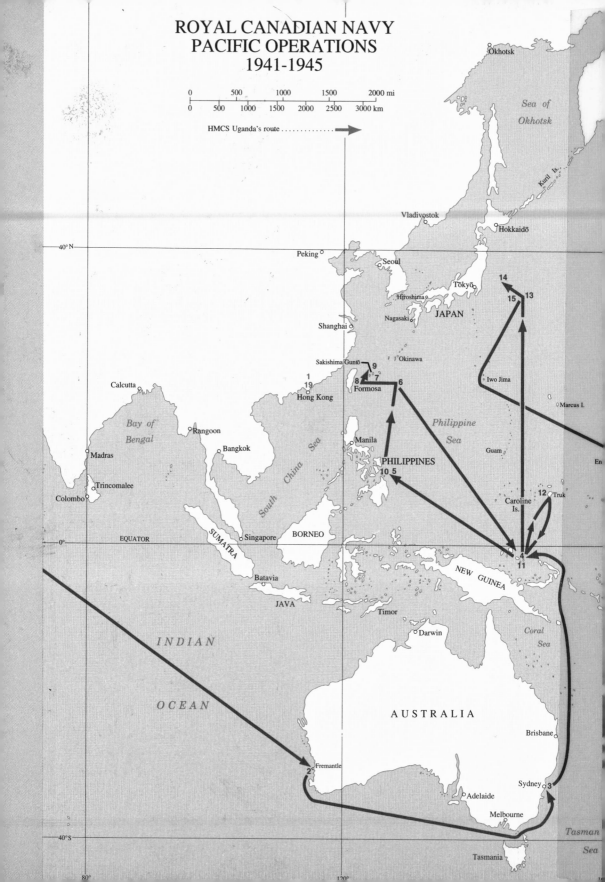

ROYAL CANADIAN NAVY
PACIFIC OPERATIONS
1941-1945

0   500   1000   1500   2000 mi
0   500 1000 1500 2000 2500 3000 km

HMCS Uganda's route . . . . →

Okhotsk

Sea of
Okhotsk

Kuril Is.

Vladivostok

Hokkaidō

40° N

Peking

Seoul

Tōkyō

14

15   13

Hiroshima

JAPAN

Nagasaki

Shanghai

Okinawa

Iwo Jima

Sakishima Guntō   9

1   8   7
19   Formosa   6

Marcus I.

Calcutta

Hong Kong

Philippine
Sea

Rangoon

Bay of
Bengal

Bangkok

Manila

Guam

En

Madras

PHILIPPINES

Trincomalee

10 5

Caroline   12   Truk
Is.

Colombo

EQUATOR   0°

Singapore   BORNEO

4

11

Sumatra   South China Sea

NEW GUINEA

Batavia

JAVA

Timor

Coral
Sea

Darwin

INDIAN

OCEAN

AUSTRALIA

Brisbane

2 Fremantle

Sydney 3

Adelaide

Melbourne

Tasman

40° S

Tasmania   Sea

80°   120°